The IEBM Handbook of Economics

Titles from the International Encyclopedia of Business and Management Library

International Encyclopedia of Business and Management, 2nd edition
Edited by Malcolm Warner
8 volume set, hardback, 1-86152-161-8
IEBM Online, 1-86152-656-3

Concise International Encyclopedia of Business and Management
Edited by Malcolm Warner
1 volume edition, hardback, 1-86152-114-6

Pocket International Encyclopedia of Business and Management
Edited by Malcolm Warner
Paperback, 1-86152-113-8

The IEBM Dictionary of Business and Management
Edited by Morgen Witzel
Paperback, 1-86152-218-5

The IEBM Encyclopedia of Marketing
Edited by Michael J. Baker
Hardback, 1-86152-304-1
Paperback, 1-86152-635-0

Regional Encyclopedia of Business and Management
Edited by Malcolm Warner
4 volume set, hardback, 1-86152-403-X

IEBM Handbook Series

The IEBM Handbook of Economics
Edited by William Lazonick
Hardback, 1-86152-545-1

The IEBM Handbook of Human Resource Management
Edited by Michael Poole and Malcolm Warner
Hardback, 1-86152-166-9
Paperback, 1-86152-633-4

The IEBM Handbook of Information Technology in Business
Edited by Milan Zeleny
Hardback, 1-86152-308-4
Paperback, 1-86152-636-9

The IEBM Handbook of International Business
Edited by Rosalie L. Tung
Hardback, 1-86152-216-9
Paperback, 1-86152-631-8

The IEBM Handbook of Management Thinking
Edited by Malcolm Warner
Hardback, 1-86152-162-6
Paperback, 1-86152-632-6

The IEBM Handbook of Organizational Behaviour
Edited by Arndt Sorge and Malcolm Warner
Hardback, 1-86152-157-X
Paperback, 1-86152-634-2

http://www.iebm.com

The IEBM Handbook of Economics

Edited by William Lazonick

THOMSON

Australia • Canada • Mexico • Singapore • Spain • United Kingdom • United States

THOMSON

The IEBM Handbook of Economics

Copyright © 2002 Thomson

The Thomson logo is a registered trademark used herein under licence.

For more information, contact Thomson, High Holborn House, 50/51 Bedford Row, London, WC1R 4LR or visit us on the World Wide Web at: http://www.thomsonlearning.co.uk

---

All rights reserved by Thomson 2002. The text of this publication, or any part thereof, may not be reproduced or transmitted in any form or by any means, electronic or mechanical, including photocopying, recording, storage in an information retrieval system, or otherwise, without prior permission of the publisher.

While the publisher has taken all reasonable care in the preparation of this book the publisher makes no representation, express or implied, with regard to the accuracy of the information contained in this book and cannot accept any legal responsibility or liability for any errors or omissions from the book or the consequences thereof.

Products and services that are referred to in this book may be either trademarks and/or registered trademarks of their respective owners. The publisher and author/s make no claim to these trademarks.

British Library Cataloguing-in-Publication Data
A catalogue record for this book is available from the British Library

---

ISBN 1-86152-545-1

Typeset by HWA Text and Data Management, Tunbridge Wells

Printed in Great Britain by TJ International, Padstow, Cornwall

Contents

List of contributors ix
Introduction xv

Labour, technological change, and income distribution
Employment relations, *Robert Buchele and Jens Christiansen* 3
Labour markets, *Alan Williams* 16
Industrial and labour relations, *Michael Poole* 33
Skill formation systems, *Colin Crouch* 52
Workfare, *Lars Magnusson* 60
Gender and ethnic divisions in the US labour force, *Jean L. Pyle and Meg A. Bond* 66
Intellectual property rights, *Dominique Foray* 75
Cleaner production, *Kenneth Geiser* 84
Development and diffusion of technology, *Nick Von Tunzelmann* 90
Innovation, *Keith Smith* 98
Pension systems, *Gordon L. Clark* 106
Comparative income and wealth distribution, *Edward N. Wolff* 117

Business and industrial organization
Corporate control, *Mary O'Sullivan* 129
Dynamic capabilities, *David J. Teece* 156
Business economics, *John Kay* 172
Transfer pricing, *Timothy J. Goodspeed* 180
Industrial dynamics, *Jackie Krafft* 187
Cooperation and competition, *Jacques-Laurent Ravix* 195
Privatization and regulation, *Jonathan Michie* 203
Small and medium sized enterprises, *David B. Audretsch* 213
Built environment, *David Gann* 231
Growth of the firm and networking, *Edith Penrose* 239
Industrial agglomeration, *David Jacobson, Kevin Heanue and Chris van Egeraat* 248
Securities and exchange regulation, *Jonathan Sokobin and Jon A. Garfinkel* 259

Industrial sectors
Aerospace industry, *Beth Ann Almeida* 269
Chemical industry, *Ashish Arora and Ralph Landau* 278
Global machine tool industry, *Bob Forrant* 286
Telecommunications industry, *Martin J. Fransman and Jackie Krafft* 294
Biotechnology, *Maureen McKelvey* 304
Steel industry, *Peter Warrian* 311
Electronics industry, *Dieter Ernst* 319
Automobile industry, *Mari Sako* 340
Service economy, *Johan Hauknes* 346

National economies and the international system
East Asian economies, *Ha-Joon Chang* 359
Economies of central and eastern Europe, transition of, *Andrzej K. Kozminski* 368
Capitalism, varieties of, *Ronald Dore, William Lazonick and Mary O'Sullivan* 376

Contents

Banking systems, *Marcello de Cecco* 397
Economy of Japan, *Takatoshi Ito* 403
Economic growth and convergence, *Jan Fagerberg* 413
Exchange rate economics, *Ronald MacDonald* 421
Multinational corporations, *Nagesh Kumar* 429
Globalization, *Bruce Kogut and Michelle Gittelman* 435
International financial stability, *Christian Weller* 452
Money and capital markets, international, *Wilbur Monroe* 460
Economic integration, international, *Dennis Swann* 470
World Bank, *Franck Amalric and Francesco Martone* 483
European Central Bank, *Roger Henderson* 490
International Monetary Fund (IMF), *Sanjay Reddy* 499
World Trade Organization (WTO), *Christoph Scherrer* 505

Theories and tools
Evolutionary theories of the firm, *Geoffrey M. Hodgson* 515
Institutional economics, *Geoffrey M. Hodgson* 522
Neo-classical economics, *Francis Fishwick* 538
Managerial theories of the firm, *R.L. Marris* 550
Enterprise ownership, types of, *David Ellerman* 561
Rationality in economics, *Richard N. Langlois* 568
Trust, *Edward Lorenz* 578
Monetarism, *Kent Matthews* 586
Growth theory, *Mark Setterfield* 600
Modelling and forecasting, *Lawrence A. Boland* 608
Transaction cost economics, *Christos Pitelis* 622
Innovative enterprise, theory of, *William Lazonick* 638

Biographies
Smith, Adam (1723–90), *Donald Rutherford* 663
Mill, John Stuart (1806–73), *Morgen Witzel* 669
Marx, Karl Heinrich (1818–83), *G.C. Harcourt and Prue M. Kerr* 674
Marshall, Alfred (1842–1924), *John K. Whitaker* 681
Veblen, Thorstein Bunde (1857–1929), *Geoffrey M. Hodgson* 686
Weber, Max (1864–1920), *George Ritzer* 692
Keynes, John Maynard (1883–1946), *Victoria Chick* 697
Schumpeter, Joseph (1883–1950), *John Cunningham Wood* 707
Means, Gardiner Coit (1896–1988), *Frederic S. Lee* 711
Galbraith, John Kenneth (1908–), *Donald Rutherford* 716
Coase, Ronald (1910–), *Martin Ricketts* 721
Schumacher, Ernst Friedrich (1911–77), *James Curran* 726
Friedman, Milton (1912–), *John Cunningham Wood* 731
Penrose, Edith Tilton (1914–96), *Michael Best and Jane Humphries* . . 734
Samuelson, Paul Anthony (1915–), *Roger E. Backhouse* 740
Simon, Herbert Alexander (1916–2001), *Richard Butler* 746
Williamson, Oliver E. (1932–), *Geoffrey M. Hodgson* 750

Index 755

List of contributors

Beth Ann Almeida
Research Economist
Strategic Resources Group
International Association of Machinists and Aerospace Workers (IAMAW)
Maryland
USA

Franck Amalric
Society for International Development
Rome
Italy

Ashish Arora
Associate Professor of Economics and Public Policy
H. John Heinz III School of Public Policy and Management
Carnegie Mellon University
USA

David B. Audretsch
Director
Institute for Development Strategies
Indiana University
USA

Roger E. Backhouse
Professor of the History and Philosophy of Economics
Department of Economics
University of Birmingham
UK

Michael Best
University Professor and Co-Director of the Center for Industrial Competitiveness
University of Massachusetts at Lowell
USA

Lawrence A. Boland
Department of Economics
Simon Fraser University
British Columbia
Canada

Meg A. Bond
Professor and Co-Director, Center for Women and Work
Department of Psychology
University of Massachusetts at Lowell
USA

Robert Buchele
Professor of Economics
Smith College
Northampton
Massachusetts
USA

Richard Butler
Professor of Organizational Analysis and Chair of Graduate School of Social Sciences and Humanities
The Management Centre
University of Bradford
UK

Ha-Joon Chang
Assistant Director of Development Studies
Faculty of Economics and Politics
University of Cambridge
UK

Victoria Chick
Professor of Economics
Department of Economics
University College London
UK

Jens Christiansen
Associate Professor of Economics
Economics Department
Mount Holyoake College
South Hadley
USA

Gordon L. Clark
Halford Mackinder Professor of Geography
School of Geography
University of Oxford
UK

List of contributors

Colin Crouch
Professor
European University Institute
Florence
Italy
and Fellow
Trinity College
University of Oxford
UK

James Curran
Emeritus Professor of Small Business Studies
Small Business Research Centre
Kingston University
UK

Marcello de Cecco
Professor of Monetary Economics
Faculty of Economics
University of Rome
Italy

Ronald Dore
Centre for Economic Performance
London School of Economics (LSE)
UK
and The European Institute of Business Administration
INSEAD
France

David Ellerman
Economic Advisor to the Chief Economist
World Bank
Washington, DC
USA

Dieter Ernst
Senior Economist, East-West Center
Hawaii
and Centre for Technology (TIK)
University of Oslo
Norway

Jan Fagerberg
Professor of Economics
Centre for Technology, Innovation and Culture
University of Oslo
Norway

Francis Fishwick
Cranfield School of Management
Cranfield University
Bedford
UK

Dominique Foray
Directeur de Recherche, CNRS
IMRI
Université-Dauphine
Paris
France

Robert Forrant
Associate Professor
Department of Regional Economic and Social Development
University of Massachusetts at Lowell
USA

Martin J. Fransman
Professor of Economics; Founder-Director of the Institute for Japanese-European Technology Studies
University of Edinburgh
Scotland

David Gann
IMI/RAEng Chair in Innovative Manufacturing
SPRU
University of Sussex
UK

Jon A. Garfinkel
Assistant Professor of Finance
Department of Finance
University of Iowa
USA

Kenneth Geiser
Professor of Work Environment
University of Massachusetts at Lowell
USA

Michelle Gittelman
The Wharton School
University of Pennsylvania
USA

List of contributors

Timothy J. Goodspeed
Professor of Economics
Department of Economics
Hunter College – CUNY
New York
USA

G.C. Harcourt
Jesus College
Cambridge
UK

Johan Hauknes
Director of Research
STEP Group
Oslo
Norway

Kevin Heanue
Research Associate
Dublin City University Business School
Dublin
Ireland

Roger Henderson
Reader in International Finance
Leeds Busines School
Leeds Metropolitan University
UK

Geoffrey M. Hodgson
University Lecturer in Economics
The Business School
University of Hertfordshire
UK

Jane Humphries
Reader in Economic History
All Souls College
University of Oxford
UK

Takatoshi Ito
Professor of Economics
Institute of Economic Research
Hitotsubashi University
Tokyo
Japan

David Jacobson
Senior Lecturer in Economics
Dublin City University Business School
Dublin
Ireland

John Kay
London Economics
UK

Prue M. Kerr
Australia
(Formerly University of Leicester)

Bruce Kogut
Professor
The Wharton School
University of Pennsylvania
USA

Andrzej K. Kozminski
Professor
Leon Kozminski Acadamy of Entrepreneurship and Management
University of Warsaw
Poland

Jackie Krafft
CNRS Researcher, Dr in Economics
CNRS- LATAPSES – IDEFI
Université de Nice Sophia Antipolis
France

Nagesh Kumar
Professor
United Nations University
INTECH
Maastricht
The Netherlands

Ralph Landau
Stanford University
USA

Richard N. Langlois
Professor of Economics and Professor of Management
University of Connecticut
USA

List of contributors

William Lazonick
University Professor
University of Massachusetts at
Lowell
USA
and
Co-director of the project on Corporate
Governance, Innovation and Economic
Performance
INSEAD
France

Frederic S. Lee
Department of Economics
University of Missouri at Kansas City
USA

Edward Lorenz
Professor of Economics
Centre d'Etudes de l'Emploi
Noisy-le-Grand
France

Ronald MacDonald
Professor of Economics
Department of Economics
University of Strathclyde
Glasgow
Scotland

Lars Magnusson
Professor of Economic History and
Research Director at National Institute for
Working Life
Ekonomisk-historiska Institutionen
Uppsala Universitet
Sweden

R.L. Marris
Emeritus Professor of Economics
Birkbeck College
University of London
UK

Francesco Martone
Coordinator
Society for International Development
Roma
Italy

Kent Matthews
Sir Julian Hodge Professor of Banking and
Finance and Head of Economics Section
Cardiff Business School
Cardiff University
UK

Maureen McKelvey
Associate Professor
Industrial Dynamics
Chalmers University of Technology
Sweden

Jonathan Michie
Sainsbury Professor of Management,
Department Chair and Head of School
Department of Management
Birkbeck College
London
UK

Wilbur Monroe
US Department of Treasury
Washington, DC
USA

Mary O'Sullivan
Associate Professor of Strategy
INSEAD
France

Edith Penrose
Before her death, Professor Emeritus
University of London
UK
and INSEAD
France

Christos Pitelis
Director, Centre for International Business
and Management
University Senior Lecturer in International
Business and Industrial Strategy, The Judge
Institute of Management
Director of Studies in Management and
Fellow in Economics, Queens' College
University of Cambridge
Cambridge
UK

List of contributors

Michael Poole
Professor of Human Resource Management
Cardiff Business School
University of Wales, Cardiff
UK

Jean L. Pyle
Professor; and Co-Director, Center for Women and Work
Department of Regional Economic and Social Development
University of Massachusetts at Lowell
USA

Jacques-Laurent Ravix
Professor of Economics
IDEFI-CNRS
Université de Nice Sophia Antipolis
Valbonne
France

Sanjay Reddy
Assistant Professor of Economics
Department of Economics
Barnard College
Columbia University
New York
USA

Martin Ricketts
Professor of Economic Organization
School of Business
University of Buckingham
UK

George Ritzer
Professor of Sociology
Department of Sociology
University of Maryland at College Park
USA

Donald Rutherford
Lecturer in Economics
Department of Economics
University of Edinburgh
Scotland
UK

Mari Sako
Professor of International Business
Said Business School
University of Oxford
UK

Christoph Scherrer
Professor
University of Kassel
Kassel
Germany

Mark Setterfield
Professor of Economics
Department of Economics
Trinity College, Connecticut
USA

Keith Smith
Professor
United Nations University
INTECH
Maastricht
The Netherlands

Jonathan Sokobin
Professor of Finance
Southern Methodist University
Texas
and Senior Research Scholar
Office of Economic Analysis
US Securities and Exchange Commission
Washington, DC
USA

Dennis Swann
Professor of Economics
Department of Economics
Loughborough University
UK

David J. Teece
Mitsubishi Bank Professor of International Business and Finance
and Director of the Institute for Management
Haas School of Business
University of California at Berkeley
USA

List of contributors

Chris van Egeraat
Research Associate
Dublin City University Business School
Dublin
Ireland

Nick Von Tunzelmann
Professor
SPRU
University of Sussex
UK

Peter Warrian
Adjunct Professor of Political Science and Industrial Relations
University of Toronto
Canada

Christian Weller
Research Economist
Economic Policy Institute
Washington DC
USA

John K. Whitaker
Georgia Bankard Professor of Economics
Department of Economics
University of Virginia
USA

Alan Williams
Professor of Management
College of Business
The Institute for Executive Development
Massey University
New Zealand

Morgen Witzel
London Business School
UK

Edward N. Wolff
Professor of Economics
Department of Economics
New York University
USA

John Cunningham Wood
Pro Vice-Chancellor (Research and Advancement)
Edith Cowan University
Australia

Introduction

Economics is about the allocation of resources to alternative uses to improve economic performance. Given their professional training, the vast majority of economists think of the market as the social institution that does, or at least should, accomplish this task. In conventional theory, the role of "the firm" is, or, normatively, should be, to respond to the dictates of market forces in making its allocative decisions. Although for some firms, and for some activities, the firm may play such a passive role in the allocation of resources, such a perspective does not accord a significant role to management in the allocation of resources, and renders business activity in general derivative of market forces in the economy as a whole.

In assuming the position of economics editor for the second edition of the International Encyclopedia of Business and Management (IEBM) and for the first edition of the IEBM Handbook of Economics, I have sought to draw upon the expertise of economists (and some people in related social sciences with expertise on economic subjects) who do not share this conventional point of view. In particular, I have solicited entries from people who concur that in one way or another, for better or for worse, business enterprises, through their allocative decisions, play a role in determining the development of productive capabilities in the economy, and, hence over time, the alternative productive uses to which resources can be allocated. Some entries have taken up this theme directly, while other entries have sought to explain the economic and social environments in which such economic activity on the part of business enterprises takes place. In all the entries, the goal has been to present clear and logical economic analysis on major economic issues, with an explicit recognition of the centrality of business activity and its management to the operation and performance of a modern economy.

In putting together the collection of entries that appear in this Handbook, I did not have to start from scratch. My predecessor as IEBM economics editor, Francis Fishwick, with input from general IEBM editor, Malcolm Warner, had already gathered together a large number of entries for the first edition of IEBM. All of the biographical essays, save that of Edith Penrose, had been produced for the first edition of the IEBM, and I was in general agreement with the list of economists for whom my predecessor had secured biographies. As the new editor, I selected those analytical entries from the first edition of the IEBM that best fit my vision of the Handbook, and provided the authors with comments for revision and updating. About one-third of the analytical essays included in this Handbook were revised from the first edition of the IEBM. In soliciting new entries, I placed particular emphasis on ensuring that issues of innovation, industrial dynamics (generally and with reference to particular industrial sectors), income distribution, and international institutions would be well represented. Although a few entries that I had wanted to be produced for the Handbook failed to materialize, in general, as an editor, I had remarkable cooperation from authors, old and new. I would also like to acknowledge the considerable time and energy that So-Shan Au at Thomson Learning put into this project, as well as valuable secretarial assistance provided by Michèle Plu and Wendy Burwood at INSEAD.

William Lazonick
INSEAD
Fontainebleau, France
September, 2001

Labour, technological change, and income distribution

Employment relations

1. The employment relationship
2. Forms of worker representation
3. Major current issues: globalization, flexibility, and training
4. Employment relations and economic performance

Overview

Employment relations are characterized by both inherent conflicts and shared interests between employers and workers. At the level of the workplace, employment relations refer to the interactions of labour and management trying to negotiate both their convergent and their divergent interests. At the societal level, these negotiations are carried out within an institutional structure of laws, rules, social norms and policies that comprise the industrial relations system.

While conventional economic theory would predict a convergence of employment relations – as competition among firms drives out all but the most efficient – what is remarkable is the diversity of practices and structures that survive over time. Even within the same institutional environment and industry, union and non-union companies, 'high performance workplaces' and 'sweatshops', employee-owned firms and firms without any employees (in which workers are either 'independent contractors' or the employees of temp agencies or subcontractors) co-exist. Indeed, it is this variation in employment systems and management practices that gives rise to employment relations as a scholarly discipline.

This article is organized into four parts: First we consider the nature of the employment relationship, its undercurrents of conflict and cooperation, and how they are addressed in theory and practice. Second, we discuss the major institutions of worker representation found in the advanced capitalist countries (labour unions and works councils) and their respective roles in negotiating the terms and conditions of employment and the workplace concerns of labour and management. Third, we address some of the major issues and challenges in the study of contemporary labour-management relations: the impact of globalization, the push (on the part of employers) for greater 'flexibility', and the institutional logic and economic implications of alternative national training systems. Finally, we briefly review current debates concerning the impact of a country's industrial relations system on key aspects of economic performance: employment, productivity growth and income distribution.

1 The employment relationship

Neo-classical economics does not accord any special status to the relationship between employers and employees; labour is simply another input in the production process (see INDUSTRIAL AND LABOUR RELATIONS). As Paul Samuelson has observed, 'In the competitive model, it makes no difference whether capital hires labour or the other way round' (Samuelson 1957: 894) (see SAMUELSON, P.). In fact, of course, capital almost always hires labour. And for a good reason: employers' control over capital insures that labour will be working for capital and not the other way around. Indeed, the boundary between the firm and the labour market is drawn, in theory, where the allocation of human resources by command is perceived to be more efficient than its allocation by voluntary exchange. As Ronald Coase noted in his classic article, 'The nature of the firm,' market relations stop at the factory gate, where hierarchical command replaces voluntary exchange: 'If a workman moves from department X to department Y, he does not go because of a change in relative prices, but because he is ordered to do so' (Coase 1937: 333) (see COASE, R.).

In the employment contract, the employee freely agrees to the employer's disposition over his or her work activities for a specified time period in return for a specified wage. This contract completes the market exchange but does not resolve the issue of how much work actually gets done. Unlike a private contractor, the employee has not entered into a legally enforceable agreement to produce a specific good or service. Thus, the employer still has the problem of extracting work from the employee, getting him or her to work diligently at the assigned tasks. The problem is that the employment contract cannot possibly fully specify all of the duties involved in a job, because it cannot anticipate every possible contingency that may arise. (Indeed a common 'job action' to pressure employers to yield to worker demands is to 'work to rule', whereby workers undermine the production process by performing their duties exactly as specified by their job description.)

What the employer needs from his or her employees is for them to energetically and conscientiously apply themselves to the goal of long-run profit maximization. Profits are a residual which legally accrues to owners but which depends on the activities and efforts of employees (both workers and managers). The key actors, employees whose efforts affect the size of the residual, have no direct claim on it. This is described in economic theory as an agency problem in which the objectives of the principals (owners or residual claimants) are affected by the actions of the agents (employees, who may have little incentive to work any harder than they have to hold on to their jobs). The more difficult or costly it is to monitor the activities of the agents, the more serious this problem may be. The increase in monitoring costs and decrease in labour productivity resulting from such incentive incompatibilities represent an efficiency loss that is directly attributable to the employment relations of the conventional firm (Bowles and Gintis 1995). It is management's challenge to minimize this loss, ideally by creating incentive systems that recognize the legitimate claims of employees to a share of the residual. (We note also that this characterization of the problem constitutes an efficiency argument for transferring residual claimancy from the principal to the agent, i.e. for worker ownership.)

Management is presumed to represent the interests of owners at the workplace and, in fact, may be motivated to do so by a sufficiently large ownership stake. Assuming that managers are so motivated, the problem for management is to get workers to work as diligently and effectively as they can. One way to do so is by some combination of piece-rate pay and intensive supervision. But payment by the piece is rarely feasible in today's highly integrated work systems, and close supervision is costly and creates adversarial relationships in which workers often resist management's efforts to raise productivity (see, e.g. Whyte 1955).

Another strategy to induce employees to work diligently is to pay what labour economists call 'efficiency wages'. The term derives from the idea that worker effort depends positively on the wage rate, so that raising wages raises labour productivity (or efficiency). There are two versions of the efficiency wage model – the 'cost of job loss' version and the 'gift–exchange' version (see Akerlof and Yellen 1986, for a review of this literature). In the first, raising wages raises the 'cost of job loss', thus motivating workers to work harder (raising productivity) and reducing the need for close supervision (reducing monitoring cost). Workers are motivated by both the 'carrot' (the efficiency wage premium which raises their stake in their job) and the 'stick' (the threat of dismissal and consequent loss of the wage premium if caught 'shirking'). In the more benign 'gift–exchange' version, workers are motivated by an ethos of fairness and reciprocity. They respond to the 'gift' of the wage premium with the gift of 'extra' effort. In this vein, the employment relations of large Japanese firms are often characterized as eliciting the loyalty and discipline of appreciative workers. But practices such as seniority wages and promotion from within also 'lock in' employees by raising the cost of leaving their job for an entry-level position elsewhere.

In the abstract, firms make 'strategic choices' concerning the employment relationship (see Kochan *et al.* 1987). At one extreme, they may adopt an adversarial approach that seeks to minimize labour costs and relies on close supervision and the threat of dismissal to motivate workers. At the other, they may seek a more cooperative relationship with greater emphasis on teamwork, participation and long-term employment relations. In practice, however, most firms will follow the practices of other firms (Marsden 1999). Technology and product market characteristics will shape prevailing norms within specific industries. More broadly, so will the aspirations of workers, their representational strength and public policy regulating employment relations.

These strategic alternatives concerning employment relations have their counterparts in recent debates over 'shareholder' vs. 'stakeholder' models of corporate governance, which in turn have antecedents in earlier debates about the separation of ownership and control of the corporation and the rise of managerial capitalism (Blair 1995; O'Sullivan 2000). In the shareholder model, the outside owners (shareholders) are the 'principals' in whose interests the corporation should be run. The agency problem arises because the corporation's employees (the 'agents') have no direct incentive to pursue the goal of 'maximizing shareholder value.' In the alternative stakeholder model, managers and production workers with long-term employment prospects and significant investments in firm-specific skills also have a legitimate claim on the residual or surplus generated by the firm's operations. These competing visions have quite different implications about the management of corporate resources. Lazonick and O'Sullivan (2000) characterize them as 'downsize and distribute' (i.e. downsize the workforce and distribute the earnings to shareholders) in the name of maximizing shareholder value vs. 'retain and reinvest' in the spirit of growing the business and rewarding all of its stakeholders.

2 Forms of worker representation

While neo-classical economics sustains the pretence of a balanced and equal relationship between employee and employer, large numbers of workers in the real world feel the necessity to organize collectively to protect their interests and increase their bargaining power. Workers have sought collective representation through labour unions since the beginning of the Industrial Revolution and unions have pushed for public policies protecting their right to organize workers without interference from employers. The US labour movement, at least in the form of the AFL-CIO, is characterized as business oriented (non-ideological and non-political). Collective bargaining is highly decentralized, with local unions negotiating separate contracts (though the national union is typically heavily involved and will attempt to impose a uniform pattern on contracts with employers in any particular industry).

Union membership in the US has fallen from a peak of 35 per cent of the workforce in the mid-1950s to 15 per cent of all employees, and only 10 per cent of private sector employees, in the late 1990s. Unions seem to have a substantial effect on wages, however, with unionized workers earning 15–20 per cent more than their non-union counterparts. (This is much larger than the union wage differential in Europe and Japan, but this is more likely due to the greater influence that unions there have on non-union wages than to their lack of influence on union wages.) Differences in benefits (including health care, pensions, paid vacations) are even greater, with unionized workers receiving nearly double the benefits of non-union workers. US unions therefore raise labour costs and reduce profits substantially, and this is probably one of the reasons for US employers' general antipathy for unions and typically fierce resistance to union organizing efforts (Freeman and Medoff 1984).

A national Worker Representation and Participation Survey, conducted in 1994 by Richard Freeman and Joel Rogers (1999), found that a large majority of US workers want both more cooperative relations with management and more say in decisions affecting their jobs. However, only a third of non-union workers say they would vote for the union if an election were held at their workplace today. Many American workers' misgivings about union representation stem from their belief (expressed by 73 per cent of those surveyed) that 'employee organizations' (read unions) cannot be effective without management's cooperation. This suggests that employers' strong opposition to dealing with unions suppresses unionization both directly (by successfully resisting attempts to unionize) and indirectly (because their employees believe that union representation will not benefit them as long as it is opposed by management).

Unions are much more influential, both politically and economically, in Western Europe than they are in the USA. In Germany, for example, sectoral or regional negotiations between unions and employers' associations are extended by government mandate to other employers (whether or not they are unionized or members of the employers' association). Thus, while union density in Germany is only around 30 per cent, collective bargaining coverage is probably around 90 per cent (Freeman 1994).

Workers in all Western European countries, except Ireland and the UK, are also represented by legally mandated works councils (Rogers and Streeck 1994). This 'second channel' of worker representation is intended to give workers a voice in shop floor governance and to facilitate labour–management cooperation on production-related matters. Works councils have a legal obligation to seek cooperation with the employer and are prohibited from striking. Council members are democratically elected by the workers they represent. Although they function independently of any union that might also represent employees at the workplace, union activists are usually well represented in works councils. All European works councils have information and consultation rights regarding workplace and personnel issues, such as health and safety, work reorganization, changes in technology, additions or reductions in the workforce, and overtime. In some countries, most notably in Germany, works councils have more substantive rights to 'codetermination' in these matters, requiring the employer to obtain council approval for decisions (or to withstand a legal challenge by the council where differences cannot be resolved).

Works councils attempt to accommodate the concerns of both labour and management and to reconcile their conflicting interests. While workers seek in works councils a collective voice in the workplace, employers seek productivity gains that derive from gaining employees' trust – a trust based in varying degrees on legal obligations, moral commitments and, ultimately, the knowledge that workers have the power to retaliate if that trust is broken. This presents a problem for advocates of works councils in the USA. While they might seem to have great appeal to American workers who wish for more say and greater cooperation, such councils in the absence of an independent union, run the risk of becoming little more than company dominated employee associations. And indeed, labour law prohibiting such 'company unions' stands as a legal obstacle to the formation of works council-type bodies in US workplaces.

Union density in Japan has followed a similar trajectory as in the USA, falling from over one-third in the mid-1950s to around 20 per cent in the late 1990s. As in the USA, unions are concentrated in the public sector and in large firms in transportation, communications, utilities and heavy industry. Unlike the USA (but like Germany), the finance and insurance industries are also relatively highly unionized.

Japanese unions are highly decentralized and strongly employer-identified – characteristics which have led them to be referred to as 'enterprise unions' (Shirai 1983; Hart and Kawasaki 1999; Hashimoto 1990). Labour's wage demands, however, are coordinated through regional and industrial federations that bargain with employer associations in *shunto*, the annual spring wage offensive which sets the pattern for wage increases throughout the economy. Japanese enterprise unions combine, in important respects, the roles of US-style local unions (engaging in collective bargaining and contract enforcement) and German-style works councils (engaging in joint consultation over a wide range of production and business-related issues). However, unlike German works councils, Japanese enterprise unions are voluntary associations (not mandated by law), and they are financially independent and have the right to strike. In theory, the strength of the enterprise union is that it is in a position both to cooperate with management in promoting the shared interests of employees and the employer and to confront management when their interests conflict. The challenge to the enterprise union is that these contradictory functions can lead it in opposite directions, acting both in concert with and in opposition to management.

3 Major current issues: globalization, flexibility, and training

Globalization

Globalization affects domestic employment relations through both trade and direct foreign investment (see GLOBALIZATION). And by either of these measures international economic integration has greatly advanced over the last several decades. Here we consider what impact this has had on the industrial relations systems of the advanced economies.

Both increased trade and capital mobility threaten the domestic status quo in employment relations. They do so by increasing competitive pressures on labour costs and labour productivity and shifting the balance of power in favour of the more mobile factor – capital. Trade throws workers who produce traded goods into competition with one another, and capital mobility enhances employers' bargaining power where there is a credible threat to subcontract work or to relocate production to areas with lower labour standards. Globalization has also changed public perceptions about the role and effects of unions and collective bargaining, especially in the USA. In the post-World War II period, labour's push for higher wages was compatible with the new Keynesian macroeconomic model in which economic growth is led by the expanding purchasing power of workers. Increased emphasis on competition in global markets has cast rising wages in an entirely different light. Rather than a hallmark of growing prosperity, rising wages are perceived as a threat to prosperity, driving up costs and making a nation's goods less competitive in world markets. A change in perceptions about the compatibility of labour's goals (more for workers) and the nation's prosperity has weakened labour politically and undermined public support for unions.

Globalization threatens the very survival of the labour market and social institutions that brought prosperity and stability to the advanced industrial nations (see LABOUR MARKETS). Globalization is portrayed as an irresistible, world-historic force that compels nations to adopt the neo-liberal agenda of free trade, privatization, and deregulation or to be left behind by those nations who do. Everywhere, governments have come under pressure to 'deregulate' labour markets and shrink social spending. In the USA (which was relatively regulation-free to start with) and in the UK, conservative governments have pushed deregulation the farthest, and in these countries there has been declining unemployment and growing wage and income inequality.

Elsewhere in Europe, where labour market institutions and social protections have remained largely intact, there have been a variety of outcomes. Some countries have achieved low unemployment without the sharp rise in inequality that has taken place in the USA and the UK. But in most of Western Europe unemployment has remained stubbornly high. Whether this is due to these countries' reluctance to reform the labour market institutions and social programmes that prevent sharp increases in inequality or to other causes is intensely debated by European and American economists and policy analysts (Freeman 1994; Nickell 1997).

Flexibility

Flexibility has been at the centre of policy debates in the 1980s and 1990s over the relative performance of alternative industrial relations systems. In the broadest sense, it refers to the adaptability or responsiveness of firms to changes in product markets and production technologies. The obvious advantages of flexibility (at this level of generality) have been espoused both at the level of firm performance and at the level of macroeconomic performance. In the USA, discussion has focused on *internal* or *functional flexibility* and the constraints upon it imposed by detailed job descriptions and bureaucratic work rules that govern job assignments. In Europe, the focus has been on *numerical* or *employment flexibility* and the constraints imposed by employment protection legislation that raises the costs of individual dismissals and mass layoffs (Piore 1986).

Internal flexibility
Internal flexibility refers to the ease with which firms are able to redeploy workers among jobs. The hallmarks of internal flexibility are job enlargement, broadly trained workers capable of performing a variety of jobs, and an emphasis on teamwork, in which work groups have some decision-making power over how to carry out their work. In Piore and Sabel's (1984) flexible specialization thesis internal flexibility is a competitive, market driven adaptation to the demands of more rapidly evolving and fragmented 'niche' product markets.

In the USA, the push for greater internal flexibility is associated with rising global competition and the recessions of the early 1980s. In the unionized sector it took the form of a direct attack on rigid work rules (with detailed job descriptions and criteria for assigning workers to jobs). Employers also sought greater 'wage flexibility' by eliminating automatic cost-of-living adjustments and instituting 'two-tier' wage scales, in which a lower scale applied to new hires. Thus, employers' push for greater internal flexibility challenged the principle of 'job control unionism' that was at the very heart of job security in the union sector (Kochan *et al*. 1987). Under job control unionism, the job security of long-term employees rests on detailed job definitions and rules (favouring senior workers) governing job assignments, promotions, layoffs and recalls. As a result, the drive for greater internal flexibility in US manufacturing has usually been resisted by unions, which have viewed it as an attack on their ability to protect the jobs and wages of their members.

The success of large Japanese firms in such industries as autos and consumer electronics has been attributed to a work organization that allows for great flexibility in allocating workers to jobs. Japanese workers and unions do not seek job security by establishing a worker's contractual 'right' to a specific job. Rather, they rely on employers' (demonstrated) commitment to permanent employment. This commitment removes a major source of worker and union resistance to increased internal flexibility. It also encourages employee loyalty and identification with the goals of the enterprise and reduces turnover and (thus) the cost of training a more broadly skilled, flexible workforce. In effect, Japanese employers have been willing to forgo employment flexibility, at least with respect to their core workforce, in return for a high degree of internal flexibility (Dore 1986). However, the Japanese system of lifetime employment does not cover all Japanese workers. For example, workers in small firms outside of manufacturing and temporary workers in large firms are not covered. These temporary workers give Japanese firms some flexibility in adjusting employment levels in response to business conditions. In addition, while Japanese employers may avoid direct layoffs, they may transfer workers to less desirable jobs at subsidiaries or suppliers, and when employees reach 'retirement' age in their mid-fifties, demote them to lower paying positions.

Numerical flexibility
Numerical flexibility refers to employers' ability to vary employment levels in response to changes in demand for output. Among the advanced capitalist countries, US employers are generally thought to enjoy the greatest degree of numerical flexibility and European – particularly southern European – employers the least. As mentioned above, numerical flexibility in Europe is inhibited by employment protection legislation that limits employers' freedom to lay off workers. Such legislation may take the form of advance notice and severance pay requirements or procedural requirements (e.g. requiring firms to demonstrate 'just cause' in the case of individual dismissals or economic necessity in the case of layoffs, or to negotiate the terms of a layoff with employee representatives) (see Buechtemann 1993; Mosley 1994; OECD 1994, 1999).

Among the major OECD economies of North America and Europe, the USA stands out for its near-absence of employment protection legislation. The UK and Canada are next in terms of imposing relatively few constraints on employers' ability to lay off workers (although this varies across provinces in Canada). At the other end of the spectrum,

France, Germany, and Italy are judged to have relatively onerous restrictions on layoffs and dismissals. In France, these primarily take the form of securing the approval of public authorities. In Germany, they principally involve requirements that a 'social plan' for minimizing the economic impact on affected workers and communities be developed in consultation with the plant's works council. And in Italy, they involve relatively large severance payments to affected workers.

It is possible of course, at least in principle, to achieve a given degree of numerical flexibility by adjusting hours rather than employment levels. And this appears to occur in practice as well. In a comparative study of labour adjustment in selected manufacturing industries, Abraham and Houseman (1993) find that German employers adjust employment levels less to short-run changes in demand than do US employers. But they make proportionately larger adjustments in average hours per worker, with the result that total labour hours are similarly flexible in the two countries.

Flexibility and labour market performance
There are important potential benefits to both firms and workers of limiting firms' freedom to adjust employment levels quickly to current levels of demand. Stable, long-term employment relations foster trust and cooperation and serve to unify the goals of employers and employees. Employers will invest more in training long-term employees, and employees who are 'in it for the long run' will be more willing to invest in firm-specific training, more accepting of technical change, and more involved in efforts to raise productivity and improve quality. As suggested above, there is probably an inverse relationship between the degree of internal flexibility a firm enjoys and the amount of numerical flexibility it exercises. That is, the *quid pro quo* for a flexible, broadly skilled, 'involved' workforce is a willingness to forgo the short-run benefits of freedom to adjust employment levels to current levels of production.

Of course, employers may attempt to 'have it both ways' by offering permanent jobs to their core workforce and hiring other workers on a temporary or contract basis to absorb fluctuations in labour demand. (As discussed previously, this seems to be a feature of Japanese employment practices.) But the argument here is that *for a given group of workers* numerical flexibility is incompatible with internal flexibility. Effective internal flexibility requires a high degree of cooperation and trust, which, in turn, is based on the presumption of permanent employment.

Empirical studies of the impact of employee involvement and participation (two important correlates of internal flexibility) on labour productivity in US firms have generally shown positive, though often statistically insignificant, effects (see surveys in Levine and Tyson 1990 and Levine 1995). More recent studies reinforce these earlier findings. Ichniowski *et al.* (1997), for example, find that steel finishing lines that use 'innovative work practices' (including profit sharing, teamwork, flexible job assignments and more extensive training) have higher levels of productivity than do lines with more traditional practices.

Training

It is commonplace to observe that worker training (and retraining) have become increasingly important in a world of rapidly changing technology and work organization. But despite general agreement on the importance of training, there are wide differences among countries in both the kind and the amount of training that workers receive.

US vocational training is highly decentralized (taking place in local high schools and community colleges, as well as proprietary schools and the military), reflecting the high degree of local autonomy and decentralization of the US school system itself. There is no national training strategy or structure to coordinate vocational training or system for certifying vocational skills. Formal employer-provided training in the USA is restricted almost exclusively to professional and managerial employees. Only 4 per cent of young workers who are not college graduates receive formal training at work (Lynch 1994). It has been argued that a focus on formal schooling or employer training ignores the importance of informal on-the-job training. And it may be the case that US employers rely more heavily on informal, learning-by-doing than do employers elsewhere.

With relatively high turnover, less employer-based training – especially general training – takes place. Lack of nationally recognized accreditation for training reduces its value to future employers and thus to workers and makes workers reluctant to pay for company training by accepting lower pay than they could get in a similar job which did not offer any training. As Lynch (1994) observes, the institutional structure of training in the USA tends to lock the country into a 'lower training equilibrium' (i.e. an underprovision of training), because firms are unable to capture the benefits of their training investments. Other countries have developed public policies, training systems and social norms that overcome this public good problem and achieve a higher level of training for their workers.

Germany lies at the opposite end of the spectrum from the USA in terms of the emphasis given to vocational training. Almost all young people who do not pursue university degrees (and even some who do) participate in apprenticeships that combine on-the-job training with off-site classroom study. Training standards are high, and there is a significant general education component aimed at developing learning skills that enable workers to adapt to changing job requirements. Completion of apprenticeship training in Germany (usually taking about three years) confers nationally recognized certification of a worker's skills and the prospect of a high-paid job, often at the company in which the apprenticeship was served.

Japanese employers invest heavily in formal workplace training. For example, a late 1980s study of Japanese and US auto plants found that new hires in Japan and in Japanese-owned US plants receive six times more formal training than their US counterparts (approximately 300 hours vs. 48 hours according to Lynch 1994: 74). Training emphasizes general decision-making and communication skills required for team-based production systems. In addition, job rotation is used to broaden workers' skills and understanding of how their jobs fit into overall operations.

Workers are encouraged to become broadly trained by pay-for-knowledge systems in which earnings depend on the number of jobs a worker is trained to do, rather than the particular job to which he or she is currently assigned. The prevailing system of entry-level hiring, promotion from within, and steeply rising seniority wages limits interfirm mobility and reduces turnover, enabling employers to recoup their investments in worker training.

The great variation in approaches to training across countries reflects corresponding differences in labour market institutions. For example, Japanese enterprise unions, lifetime employment norms and seniority wages limit labour mobility and encourage more company-based training than occurs in higher-turnover US labour markets. The German apprenticeship system is supported by the involvement of the school system, local chambers of commerce, and trade unions and works councils, which codetermine, along with employers, the content of apprenticeship training. Three main factors motivate German employers to provide general, as well as firm-specific, training. They know that even though many of their apprentices may leave for jobs elsewhere, they will benefit from the training that the workers they hire have received from other employers. Apprentices bear part of their own training cost by working for significantly lower wages than they could otherwise earn in an unskilled job with no training. And there is a widely shared moral commitment on the part of employers to contribute to the nation's youth apprenticeship system.

4 Employment relations and economic performance

Employment relations affect macroeconomic performance through their impact on individual firm performance. Here we consider the effect of employment relations (and the broader industrial relations system) on three crucial determinants of economic well-being: labour productivity, unemployment and income distribution (Buchele and Christiansen 1999).

First and foremost among measures of a nation's ability to improve the economic welfare of its population is long-run productivity growth. Periods of rapid productivity growth are fuelled not just by technical innovation but also by new forms of work organization that elicit the involvement and cooperation of workers in raising productivity (Lazonick 1990). Long-term employment relations featuring seniority wages, ongoing training aimed at broadening skills, and worker participation in efforts to raise productivity and improve quality can create the basis for a high trust, high involvement, highly flexible, and often high pressure, workplace. This view attributes both Japan's and Germany's strong productivity growth and global competitiveness (at least up through the 1980s) to the human resource management practices of their corporations. These practices have been held up to the rest of the world as a model for raising productivity, improving quality and competing more successfully in world markets. (For a critical assessment of the impact of Japanese production systems and management practices on workers' work lives see Parker and Slaughter 1988.)

In Japan, this system remained compatible with very low unemployment rates through the early 1990s. Provisions against layoffs were no obstacle to employment growth during decades of rapid economic growth and slow population growth. Although a decade of economic stagnation has put considerable strain on the employment and pay policies of Japanese firms, it appears that most major companies remain committed to the principle of avoiding layoffs of permanent employees. Firms have cut employment primarily through reduced hiring, early retirement and transfers among *keiretsu* (firms related by interlocking ownership of shares). Western diagnoses of Japan's difficulties in recovering from its protracted recession have focused primarily on the failure of its banking system to deal with its bad debt burden. Employers' reluctance to lay off workers (and thereby reduce labour costs and improve profit margins) has come in for surprisingly little criticism, even in the mainstream US business press. While Japanese employment practices could not prevent recession and a rise in unemployment (to over 4 per cent by the end of the decade), it is difficult to imagine that the Japanese economy (or the average Japanese) would be better off if employers had resorted to mass layoffs as demand fell.

Unemployment in many European countries, on the other hand, has been at unacceptably high levels since the early 1980s. In the neo-classical view, the unemployment rate fluctuates around the long-run 'natural' rate of unemployment, which is determined by the effect of labour market institutions on labour supply and demand (rather than by the effect of aggregate demand on the labour demand curve). From this perspective, the key policy issue is to what extent this long-term increase in unemployment is due to labour market frictions and distortions created by union wage setting power, employment protection laws, payroll taxes and overly generous unemployment benefits and social welfare systems (Layard *et al.* 1991; OECD 1994; Nickell 1997). While evidence on this question is mixed, two important observations suggest scepticism: one is that many 'European-style' labour market rigidities were in place in the 1960s and 1970s when unemployment rates in Europe were typically far below the US rate. The other is that a great deal of variation exists in employment performance among European countries with similar kinds of labour market 'rigidities' (Buchele and Christiansen 1998).

Analysts have noted that differences in overall unemployment rates among OECD countries are primarily due to differences in their long-term unemployment rates (percentage of labour force unemployed for more than one year). It is not surprising, therefore, that unemployment insurance replacement rates and (especially) benefit duration are often found to have statistically significant positive effects on unemployment rates. The general recommendation here is to reduce the duration of benefits and increase spending on retraining, job placement services, and subsidies to employers for hiring the long-term unemployed (see, for example, Nickell 1997).

Higher unemployment rates are also associated with high union density and collective bargaining coverage. The theoretical connection here is that the long-term unemployed (the 'outsiders') are so removed from the active labour market that their presence does little to hold down wages. At the same time, strong union representation of employed workers ('insiders') keeps wages above market-clearing levels. But in countries where collective bargaining is important, research has found that a high degree of union coordination and (separately) employer coordination in the bargaining process offsets the tendency of collective bargaining to set wages 'too high' (because each side is more likely to take the macroeconomic consequences of the settlement into account). Finally, there is little evidence that employment protection legislation that raises the cost of layoffs and dismissals (and thus potentially discourages hiring) has contributed significantly to the rise in European unemployment. Reducing employment security seems unlikely to reduce unemployment.

The almost exclusive focus of this research on the effects of labour market institutions and policies is predicated on the neo-classical view that the long-run 'natural' rate of unemployment is determined in the labour market. Fluctuations in aggregate demand cause only transitory departures from the natural rate. This sharp distinction between structural (long-run equilibrium, 'natural') unemployment vs. cyclical (temporary) unemployment has been challenged by the 'hysteresis' hypothesis. In the hysteresis model, a sustained increase in the unemployment rate due to insufficient demand gets built into the natural rate as unemployed workers' skills, self-confidence, and reputations erode with prolonged joblessness. A cyclical rise in unemployment that is allowed (by passive macroeconomic policy) to persist eventually becomes structural and ratchets up the natural rate of unemployment (see Blanchard and Summers 1986; Ball 1999). In this scenario, high unemployment that originates in cyclical downturns and the failure of macro-policy to respond aggressively is eventually transformed into long-term unemployment that is associated with relatively generous, long-duration unemployment benefits – and the true causes and appropriate remedies for persistent high unemployment in Europe are not so clear.

Income distribution in advanced capitalist countries depends largely on the distribution of earnings and the size of transfer payments to jobless, low-income and retired persons. The earnings distribution itself depends on (1) the distribution of skills (education and training) in the labour force and the relative demand for workers with different levels of skills and (2) the pay policies of employers (including institutional constraints on those policies).

Increasing earnings inequality in the USA since the early 1970s has been attributed by most mainstream economists to 'skill-biased technical change' that has increased the demand for more skilled (educated) labour relative to less-skilled labour. Other economists have argued that growing imports and increased immigration from low-wage countries and increased capital mobility have depressed US wages by throwing less-skilled US workers into competition with very low-paid workers around the world. Of course, more than one of these explanations for rising wage inequality can be true. Moreover, it is possible that increased trade with low-wage countries has induced low-wage labour-saving innovation in the advanced countries. Freeman has argued (1995 and elsewhere) that the rise in earnings inequality in the USA should be viewed as the 'flip side' of the rise in unemployment in Europe with both being the result of a relative decline in demand for less-skilled workers. In Europe, where wage-setting institutions prevent wages at the bottom from falling, unemployment rose; in the USA, where wages are more flexible, the earnings of low-wage workers took the hit.

Of course, employers' responses to such market forces are mediated by their pay policies, by organized labour's objectives and bargaining power, and by public policy (e.g. minimum wage laws and income support levels for jobless workers). The importance of employer-specific pay policies is highlighted by Levy and Murnane's (1992) survey of recent research on growing earnings inequality in the USA, which reports that earnings inequality among workers of the same age, education and gender has increased steadily since the 1970s and that much of this within-group variation in earnings involves plant-specific differentials within industries. These wage differentials suggest that there is significant latitude for discretion in setting pay and significant differences across firms in the extent to which workers are treated as stakeholders with a legitimate claim on residual earnings vs. a factor cost to be minimized in the drive to maximize shareholder value.

ROBERT BUCHELE
SMITH COLLEGE

JENS CHRISTIANSEN
MOUNT HOLYOAKE COLLEGE

Further reading

(References cited in the text marked *)

* Abraham, K. and S. Houseman (1993) *Job Security in America: Lessons from Germany*, The Brookings Institution. (Comparative assessment of employment security in the USA and Germany.)
* Ackerlof, G. and J. Yellen (1986) *Efficiency Wage Models of the Labour Market*, Cambridge: Cambridge University Press. (Explores labour market equilibria wherein employers prefer to pay wages in excess of the market clearing wage.)
  Ackerman, F. *et al.* (eds) (1998) *The Changing Nature of Work*, Island Press. (Summarizes 86 seminal articles on the causes and effects of the rapid transformation of the world of work.)
* Ball, L. (1999) 'Aggregate demand and long-run unemployment', *Brookings Papers on Economic Activity* 2. (Points to tight monetary policies as the principal source of the chronically high unemployment in many European economies.)
* Blair, M. (1995) *Ownership and Control: Rethinking Corporate Governance for the Twenty-first Century*, The Brookings Institution. (Examines the governance structure of the modern corporation.)
* Blanchard, O. and L. Summers. (1986) 'Hysteresis and the European unemployment problem', in Stanley Fischer (ed.) *NBER Macroeconomics Annual* 1. (Develops the idea that cyclical unemployment can become long-term and thus ratchet up the 'natural' rate of unemployment.)
* Bowles, S. and H. Gintis (1995) 'Productivity-enhancing egalitarian policies', *International Labour Review* 134 (45). (Argues for productivity-enhancing asset redistribution that avoids the negative incentive consequences of income redistribution schemes.)
* Buchele, R. and J. Christiansen (1999) 'Employment and productivity growth in Europe and North America: the impact of labour market institutions', *International Review of Applied Economics* 13 (3). (Argues that employment and income security regulations interacting with aggregate demand give rise to a tradeoff between employment and productivity growth.)
* Buchele, R. and J. Christiansen (1998) 'Do employment and income security cause unemployment? A comparative study of the US and the E-4', *Cambridge Journal of Economics* 22 (1). (A detailed analysis of unemployment in the USA and the four largest European countries from 1969 to 1995.)
* Buechtemann, C. (ed.) (1993) *Employment Security and Labour Market Behavior: Interdisciplinary Approaches and International Evidence*, ILR Press. (An edited volume of studies of the impacts of employment protection in the USA, UK, West Germany, France and Italy.)
* Coase, R. (1937) 'The nature of the firm', *Economica* 4, November, reprinted in *Readings in Price Theory*, Irwin, 1952. (A classic article on the neo-classical theory of the firm.)
* Dore, R. (1986) *Flexible Rigidities*, Athlone. (A study of Japanese employment relations that emphasizes the internal flexibility that derives from the Japanese system of lifetime employment.)
* Freeman, R. (1995) 'Are your wages set in Beijing?' *Journal of Economic Perspectives* 9 (3). (Review of the debates over the impact of globalization on the wages for low-skilled workers in the advanced countries.)
* Freeman, R. (1994) 'How labour fares in advanced economies', in R. Freeman (ed.) *Working Under Different Rules*, Russell Sage. (Comparative assessment of employment, productivity, and pay in the USA vs. Europe.)
* Freeman, R. and J. Medoff (1984) *What Do Unions Do?* Basic Books. (An analytical and empirical study of US labour unions and their role in the economy.)
* Freeman, R. and J. Rogers (1999) *What Workers Want*, Cornell University Press. (A comprehensive survey of employees' attitudes towards participation and representation in the workplace.)
* Hart, R. and S. Kawasaki (1999) *Work and Pay in Japan*, Cambridge University Press. (A detailed discussion of all aspects of employment relations and pay systems in the Japanese labour market.)
* Hashimoto, M. (1990) 'Employment and wage systems in Japan and their implications for

productivity', in A. Blinder (ed.) *Paying for Productivity*, The Brookings Institution. (Emphasizes the importance of joint consultation and consensus-based decision making in the Japanese firm.)

* Ichniowski, C., K. Shaw and G. Prennushi (1997) 'The effects of human resource management practices on productivity: a study of steel finishing lines', *The American Economic Review* (June).

* Kochan, T., H. Katz and R. McKersie (1987) *The Transformation of American Industrial Relations*, Basic Books. (An account of the significant transformation in US industrial relations in the 1980s.)

* Layard, R., S. Nickell and R. Jackman (1991) *Unemployment: Macroeconomic Performance and the Labour Market*, Oxford University Press. (A comprehensive theoretical and empirical treatment of the problem of high unemployment in Europe.)

* Lazonick, W. (1990) *Competitive Advantage on the Shop Floor*, Harvard University Press. (A historical and theoretical treatise on work organization and technology and their impact on value-creation.)

* Lazonick, W. and M. O'Sullivan (2000) 'Maximising shareholder value: a new ideology for corporate governance', *Economy and Society* 29 (1). (A critique of the view that the recent US economic boom results from managing US corporate assets to maximize 'shareholder value'.)

* Levine, D. (1995) *Reinventing the Workplace: How Business and Employees Can Both Win*, The Brookings Institution. (Argues that greater employee involvement in the workplace can significantly increase both productivity and worker satisfaction.)

* Levine, D. and L. Tyson (1990) 'Participation, productivity and the firm's environment', in Alan S. Blinder (ed.) *Paying for Productivity*, The Brookings Institution. (A comprehensive survey of theories and empirical studies of worker participation and its effects on productivity.)

* Levy, F. and R. Murnane (1992) 'U.S. earnings levels and earnings inequality: a review of recent trends and proposed explanations', *Journal of Economic Literature* XXX (3). (An extensive review article of the causes of increasing inequality in earnings in the USA.)

* Lynch, L. (1994) 'Payoffs to alternative training strategies at work', in R. Freeman (ed.) *Working Under Different Rules*, Russell Sage. (A comparison of training systems in various countries.)

* Marsden, D. (1999) *A Theory of Employment Systems: Micro-foundations of Societal Diversity*, Oxford University Press. (An in-depth theoretical exploration of the employment relationship and its international diversity.)

* Mosley, H. (1994). 'Employment protection and labour force adjustment in EC countries', in G. Schmid, (ed.) *Labour Market Institutions in Europe*, M. E. Sharpe. (A detailed account of employment protection regulations and their effects on labour force adjustments in Western Europe.)

* Nickell, S. (1997) 'Unemployment and labour market rigidities: Europe vs. North America', *Journal of Economic Perspectives* 11 (3). (A summary analysis of the impact of labour market institutions and regulations on employment growth and unemployment.)

* OECD (1999) *Employment Outlook*. (Annual publication that provides assessments of recent labour market developments as well as detailed chapters on various labour market topics.)

* OECD *Jobs Study* (1994). (A comprehensive multi-volume study of labour market regulations in OECD countries, aimed at developing policies for reducing unemployment in Europe.)

* O'Sullivan, M. (2000) *Contests for Corporate Control: Corporate Governance and Economic Performance in the United States and Germany*, Oxford University Press. (An historical analysis of the debate over whether corporations should be run to solely in the interests of shareholders or in the interests of a broader group of 'stakeholders'.)

* Parker, M. and J. Slaughter (1988) 'Management by stress,' *Technology Review* October. (A critical view of the impact of Japanese-style production systems and management practices.)

* Piore, M. (1986) 'Perspectives on labour market flexibility', *Industrial Relations* 25 (2). (An exploration of the different aspects of labour market flexibility and the relationship among them.)

* Piore, M. and C. Sabel (1984) *The Second Industrial Divide*, Basic Books. (Describes the change in the organization of work based on principles of mass production to those of 'flexible specialization'.)

* Rogers, J. and W. Streeck (1994) 'Workplace representation overseas: the works councils story', in R. Freeman (ed.) *Working Under Different Rules*, Russell Sage. (A detailed account of the functions and performance of works councils in a number of European countries.)

* Samuelson, P. (1957) 'Wage and interest', *American Economic Review* 42 (6).

* Shirai, T. (1983) 'A theory of enterprise unions', in *Contemporary Industrial Relations in Japan*, University of Wisconsin Press. (A description

and appraisal of the role of enterprise unions in Japan.)
* Whyte, William F. (1955) *Money and Motivation*, Harper and Row. (A classic sociological study of incentives and motivation in the American workplace.)

See also: COASE, R.; COMPARATIVE INCOME AND WEALTH DISTRIBUTION; EMPLOYMENT RELATIONS; INNOVATION; LABOUR MARKETS; SAMUELSON, P.; SKILL FORMATION SYSTEMS; WORKFARE

Labour markets

1. Theories of the labour market: an evolutionary overview
2. Issues and controversies in labour market theory and analysis
3. Some new agendas for labour market analysis
4. Conclusion

Overview

The conventional textbook notion of the labour market treats the relationship between the employer and worker as a process whereby the various attributes and skills of the employee are transformed into the output requirements of the employer. But despite the conventional notion that labour is a commodity market, the process of exchange that creates the wage–price nexus has a social as well as an economic dynamic. For the existence of wage-based work provides a number of important social functions quite apart from the provision of the means of economic survival. By its existence over time, it actively shapes the lives of families as the primary social unit in society. This is specifically true in the developed economies because it is the discretionary income created by an appropriate level of wages or salary that decides the quality of life of most of a nation's population.

Like so many other fields of economic theory, labour market analysis consistently refuses to yield an order of precise laws with attendant substantive rules and universal applications that may be held to be the final word on the subject. As a result those scholarly investigations that seek to reveal the origins of some major controversy or some seminal theory continue to rediscover a range of evolutionary links with the quite distant theoretical past. These add fuel to the arguments and speculations that seem to consistently inform the research agendas for successive generations of scholars.

It also means that in order to evaluate our current state of understanding with regard to the modern labour market, the contributions made by earlier theorists must be undertaken as an initial task. This in turn involves the location of labour market theories within an evolutionary context.

Discussion will therefore begin with a consideration of the evolution of labour market analysis, in which some selected concerns that have shaped the emergence of various contemporary theories are examined. This will be followed by a further evaluation of the salient claims that inform current controversies in labour market analysis. The entire process will be set against the structural shift that has taken place within the dominant macroeconomic paradigm, by which is meant the theoretical dominance of new classical (neo-liberal) thought, over the former Keynesian hegemony.

Attention will be directed for the balance of the entry towards some of the emergent matters that are now calling for investigative attention from labour economists. They include such dominant questions as the persistence of unemployment, changes in the nature of capitalism as a market order, the theory of dual and segmented labour markets and the changes taking place in the international division of labour. They also include the serious problems associated with the growth of informal labour market sectors in both the less-developed and the transitional economies.

Their growth has a symbolic meaning as an indicator of manifest and rising inequalities in the matter of economic and occupational life chances for an increasingly large proportion of the world's population. Finally, the focus of discussion be directed toward the new themes requiring labour market analysis that appear to be created by the rapid growth of the information-based industries which produce 'weightless' products and services defined as knowledge goods.

1 Theories of the labour market: an evolutionary overview

The shaping influences of medieval scholasticism

References to industrial labour as a purposeful activity can be found in the writings of antiquity. But it is safe to say that the beginnings of our understanding of labour markets coincided with the growing attention given by medieval scholars to the ethical and moral nature of commerce as a human activity. Faced with a growing and increasingly international world of trade they developed the notion of the 'just price', which proposed that nothing should be sold for more than its value. This led Albertus Magnus to introduce the notion that the ultimate value of a given product depended upon the amount of labour by its producer that had shaped its final form.

He went on to assert that any product has two essential ingredients: labour and expenses. In effect he was adding the concept of the cost of production to the assumption of value in exchange. His pupils later added the idea that labour should be measured in terms of the time required for the completion of a given task. Nearly 600 years later, these concepts were to emerge as the labour theory of value, first in the seminal work of Ricardo and then later as the cornerstone of Marxist analysis.

Magnus' most brilliant pupil, St Thomas Aquinas, built on these original principles by proposing that there was a difference between what he called 'natural' valuation and 'economic' valuation. For him human wants and needs were the key measures of value since they had a direct affect on variances in price levels. An incremental assumption was then added later by Geraldus Odonis, who identified an essential variation in the value of labour; the fact that skill could command a premium, when measured against unskilled labour.

The emergence of mercantilism and the national economy

The emergence of a national self-consciousness in which the nation-state is both the epitome and the focus of national feeling marked the end of the medieval age. A burgeoning theory of political economy during the seventeenth century gave rise to *mercantilism* in which a central tenet was the need, expressed in 1664 by Sir Thomas Mun, in his magnum opus *England's Treasure by Forriagn Trade,* to always export more to other countries than was imported by return. The value of labour was placed at parity with land by important mercantilists like Sir William Petty, whose concept of the division of labour both pre-dated and strongly influenced the later work of Adam Smith (see SMITH, A.). Much that was contained in Petty's *Political Arithmetick,* was to anticipate classical economic theory, and included in its contents, social issues that were echoed by Thomas Malthus. It is also clear that amongst the earlier mercantilists a concept such as the subsistence wage signalled a gap between those who owned property and those who worked for the owners.

In his *Essai sur la nature du commerce en general* (1755), Richard Cantillon, a successful banker, money market player and founding father of price theory, argued that the value of labour should be equal to the level of a subsistence wage. In anticipation of Malthus, Cantillon noted that 'men multiply like mice in a barn if they have unlimited means of subsistence'. The idea that too much income for peasants inevitably resulted in increased copulation and a rise in the number of sturdy beggars was also to inform the arguments for a managed economy put forward by Sir James Steuart, an Edinburgh contemporary of Adam Smith.

Meanwhile, in France the Physiocratic School identified Jean Baptiste Colbert, the chief minister of Louis XIV, as a leading advocate of European mercantilism, who was to become the focus of an intellectual counter-revolution. Led by François Quesnay, it advocated a primary role for agriculture as a source of value larger than manufactures. While it began to decline as an intellectual force in the 1770s, Physiocracy, was to leave a significant intellectual legacy. Its model of the circular flow of goods was given a practical expression in the *Tableau Economique*. But it is its classic dictum 'laissez faire – laissez passer' that has been passed down to the present, where it lies embedded in the contemporary and dominant professional value system of new classical or neo-liberal economic thought.

The emergence of classical economic thought

It was one of Adam Smith's avowed intentions in writing his *Enquiry into the Nature and Causes of the Wealth of Nations* (1776) to advance beyond the theoretical limitations of mercantilism and to put in its place some set of principles upon which a totally comprehensive measure of economic value could be built. The reality over 200 years later is a long history of controversy, presentation of contradictory hypotheses, and the adoption by free market theorists and think tanks of Adam Smith as their patron saint.

From a labour market perspective his key contribution was to take the notion of labour as 'the ultimate and real standard of value' and move it to centre stage in the emergent theoretical world of classical economics. For Smith, the long-term wages of labour were not to be treated simply as the means of subsistence, but as the recognizable rewards to be paid to specific occupational classes in a society where the common law principles of master and servant prevailed. More importantly, suggest Loveridge and Mok (1979), Smith clearly understood the role of social power and its material influence in the labour market.

The advent of classical economics also saw the emergence of a theorist who has been described as the first modern economist, David Ricardo. Like Smith he sought some theoretical basis for the notion that land would allow some hypothetical commodity to hold its value constant, even if the distribution of income changed. The result was Ricardo's labour theory of value, which treated as axiomatic the idea that both the value of commodities held, and the balance of those with which they might be exchanged, should be pegged against 'the relative quantity of labour that is necessary for its production'. The outcome was both controversial and, during the classical age, theoretically inconclusive. In fact debate remained inconclusive until 1960, when Piero Sraffa introduced the concept of the standard commodity.

It is an irony of history, that Marx (see MARX, K.H.) was to make Ricardo's model the basis of his own theoretical output, to which he was later to add the concept of surplus value, which was morally the property of labour. But the most telling immediate critique came from Jean-Baptiste Say, who turned the whole notion of demand and supply on its head. Commodities were desired he suggested because they yielded utility, and for no other reason. Value on the other hand could be categorized as a duality, in the sense that the riches endowed by nature were different from social riches, which were the product of capital and labour.

Only the latter needed to be paid for since in the act of creating an exchange value, they also created a price. The central principle argued that supply creates its own demand. In the event Say made little progress in advancing his argument, until his theoretical reincarnation as a dominant influence on supply-side theory in the latter half of the twentieth century.

Ricardian theory was also limited in another sense. Its explanatory value in the case of wage rates was limited to the short run and through the wage fund theory, which implied a finite return available to the factor labour. With the loss of the Malthusian argument that a subsistence wage ensured social as well as economic stability, the time was ripe for theoretical challenge. Of note in this regard was Nassau Senior's assertion that scarcity might well have an effect on the value of given factors of production. But the most damaging effects to Ricardian theory were felt with John Stuart Mill's theoretical apostasy (see MILL, J.S.). His initial acceptance and later rejection of the wage fund argument came from the growing empirical awareness that employers were covering their wage costs from the earnings of current production.

It was an essential article of faith for Ricardo that the factor labour be treated as homogeneous. Mill did irreparable damage with his inference that while competition existed within firms; it did not exist between firms.

The central notion of free mobility of labour which was implicit in Ricardo's labour theory of value, thus had to be abandoned and with it the primacy of Ricardo's model as a formal explanation.

By the 1870s the classical view of political economy was in decline, and with it the centrality of political economy as a modus operandi for political decision making. The balance of the nineteenth century also signalled the emergence of the professional economist, and the end of the search for some universal natural law governing human behaviour in the marketplace. The philosophical as well as the practical issues that emerged with the onset of a modern industrial capitalism had fascinated all manners of educated men, bankers, public servants, lawyers and successful businessmen. They were now to be replaced. Those whose lives and interests heralded the emergence of economic studies in which the search for a scientific basis of a discipline, grounded in the same principles that informed the physical and biological sciences and described in the language of pure mathematics, were to establish a new primacy.

From the perspective of labour market analysis, there remained a tradition of institutional research in which Thorsten Veblen, Richard Ely and John R. Commons (see VEBLEN, T.B.) in the USA, and Sydney and Beatrice Webb in the UK, played leading roles (see INDUSTRIAL AND LABOUR RELATIONS). But the *'marginal revolution'* now dominated the theoretical high ground and the first age of *neo-classicism* was born.

The marginal revolution and the emergence of neo-classicism

The concept of marginality emerged from a period of considerable intellectual ferment, which in turn produced a number of path-breaking studies. In 1867, Marx's *Das Kapital* appeared, which was followed at the end of the decade by William Stanley Jevons' *Theory of Political Economy*. Coincident with Jevons' book, Carl Menger's *Principles of Economics* was published in France, while in 1874, Leon Walras' initially neglected *Elements of Pure Economics* appeared in Vienna. With the advent of Alfred Marshall's *Principles of Economics* in 1890 (see MARSHALL, A.), neo-classical economics was replete with both a microeconomic framework which contained both marginality and equilibrium at its core and the mathematical tools with which to develop its axiomatic principles. With Cambridge exercising a hegemonic authority through Marshall, the direction of labour market analysis was set on a course that did not really deviate until the appearance of Keynes' *General Theory of Employment, Interest and Money* in 1936.

The competitive neo-classical model of the labour market relegated labour to the role of a factor of production, in which demand for its use was derived, in turn, from the secondary demand for its product, which itself derived from a further secondary demand as a contribution to the final goods market. The wage level also derived from the price or revenue product, which was in turn derived from the final price obtained at the point of sale. Labour's contribution was no longer seen as an instrument of final value in the Ricardian sense, but as a factor to be measured purely in terms of its actual contribution to the costs of production. In turn the notion of the unit cost of labour which was to dominate notions of efficiency in mass production was in turn imputed to be determined by the market price at which each worker was willing to sell his/her services to the employer.

Furthermore, in estimating an offer price, an employer would be both aware of and try to estimate the employee's own evaluation of the 'disutilities' of work. In other words, the model assumes that each employee would evaluate the utility of income from working against the loss of income incurred, where the utility or value of leisure was greater than the income foregone by not working. If the utility for work is greater than the utility for leisure then the employer will base his/her offer on the estimate of the balance of the two utilities against the fact that other employers are seeking labour and other workers are seeking work.

The shaping influence of marginal theory can be seen when the concepts of perfect competition and diminishing returns are added to the theoretical mix. For the first assumption requires that all markets clear at equilibrium, while the second, to be found in the work of John Bates Clark, noted that marginal productivity has a negative convexity, which makes it diminish over time. This takes into consideration the fact that each new entrant to the firm creates a successively smaller additional increment to its aggregate labour productivity, resulting in effect in the law of diminishing returns. The employer in making a wage offer will realize that it should not exceed the value added to output of the last person offered a job.

Given the fact that capital stock is fixed, the correct strategy would be to hire labour to the point where wage paid to the 'nth' employee would be just equal to his/her marginal product. In other words the marginal cost of employing the 'nth' person should be just equal to, or greater than, the marginal revenue that person produces. It must also be remembered that this is a perfect market, which means that labour is homogeneous. This means that the labour market will clear at a point where the aggregate marginal cost of employing the final person in all firms in the market would be either equal to, or less than, the sum of each final employee's marginal productivity. At this point full employment equilibrium is reached.

Unfortunately, the emergence of mass unemployment in the inter-war period revealed that labour markets do not clear in the way the perfect competition model prescribes. Neo-classical orthodoxy called for real wages to follow falling demand downward, so that workers could continue being employed at a lower wage. This in turn would have the further effect of exerting a downward pressure on unemployment.

Orthodox opinion then suggested that one way of forcing real wages down would be to simply cut them. The argument gained support from the emergence of the theory of imperfect or monopolistic competition associated with the work of Edward Chamberlin and Joan Robinson whose books, *Theory of Monopolistic Competition* and *Essays in Monopolistic Competition,* were both published in the early 1930s. The emergence of the concept of market imperfections removed from labour market analysis, the restrictions of perfect competition. Unfortunately, the prevailing orthodoxy of the times led by the Bank of England for example, was profoundly non-interventionist, and was to remain so until the appearance of Keynes and the General Theory.

Trade unions and collective bargaining were perceived as inhibiting the natural processes of adjustment, since they held wages above the level that would prevail in their absence. There remains even today amongst advocates of market de-regulation a central assumption that there is a strong correlation between persistent unemployment and trade union intransigence in the matter of the need for real wages to fall.

By the middle of the 1930s, the failure of neo-classical theory to offer adequate policy prescriptions that might combat mass unemployment had turned into a call for fresh and alternative approaches to the problem. In 1936, these were delivered with the publication of John Maynard Keynes' *General Theory of Employment, Interest and Money* (see KEYNES, J.M.)

Keynes and the macroeconomics of labour markets

Despite popular claims as to the innovative originality of the *General Theory*, the massive posthumous literature on Keynes as an economist now acknowledges the major roles in terms of analysis, form and content played at Cambridge by Cecil Pigou, Richard Kahn, Joan and Austin Robinson and Ralph Hawtrey. In turn the work of the Stockholm School led by Bertil Ohlin and Gunnar Myrdal has been identified as moving in the same direction. It is also very significant that the work of Michal Kalecki, which was admired by Keynes, is now recognized as the intellectual equivalent of the *General Theory,* but without its obscurities and ambiguities.

Apart from the fact that its publication in 1936 was politically opportune, the relative eclipse of the Marshallian tradition placed the *General Theory* at the forefront of academic discussion. Highly complex, often ambiguous and sometimes contradictory, the attraction of professional attention to Keynes magnum opus was well served in the UK outside Cambridge, by John Hicks, James Meade and Roy

Harrod, and in the USA by Alvin Hansen and Paul Samuelson (see SAMUELSON, P.A.). The resultant neo-classical model which was built on Hick's *IS–LM analysis* made Keynesian macroeconomics not only the major source of influence on the minds of several generations of students, but also the policy basis of post-war reconstruction.

In his approach to the labour market Keynes accepted the orthodox conclusion that the demand for labour was equated with its marginal production function. His prime target for criticism was the supply side, and he made the important distinction between the nominal or money wage and the real wage. He went on to argue that it was actually the money wage to which workers reacted in the face of unemployment at a given real wage level. He also went on to suggest that workers would accept a reduction in the real wage if it were attained through increases in the price level and not through actual wage cuts.

In taking up this line of argument, Keynes introduced the notion of the money illusion, the idea that people would not in the short run connect a rise in the price level with a decline in their economic well-being. His real target in following this line of argument was the classical notion that the labour market would clear at some point of full employment equilibrium.

In Keynes' view the notion of an automatic clearing mechanism at some point when equilibrium was reached was severely limited. Even assuming the willingness of trade unions to concede lower money wages, prices would fall in the same proportion. Unfortunately, this would leave both the real wage and the equilibrium level of unemployment quite unaffected. The real problem was on the demand side, since a fall in private spending would create a deficiency in demand. From a labour market perspective this would mean that at the existing level of real wages, aggregate demand would be insufficient to employ all workers willing to supply labour at that wage rate.

The result would be an increase in involuntary employment, because it would be beyond the ability of trade unions, employers and governments to remedy the situation. This created a need for government to intervene on the demand side with policies that would stimulate demand. The consequences of demand deficiency reflected in sticky wages and prices could last for a medium to long term, with social as well as economic consequences that would be unacceptable. The prescriptive remedy, which informed the larger policy contexts to which the *General Theory* was deliberately addressed, was a series of fiscal remedies, which would 'pump prime' or 'kick start' the economy in the direction of a full employment equilibrium

The debate generated by the *General Theory* has gone on ever since. But during the 1960s, both its direction and purpose changed. Countervailing theories began to emerge, and Keynesian labour market theory in particular came under heavy challenge. An initial and highly technical debate led to the conclusion that a full employment equilibrium could exist, and that what Keynes had really discovered was the economics of disequilibrium, where the market forces pushing toward equilibrium were actually too weak to restore full employment.

What had become Keynesian orthodoxy came under attack at this time from two major sources. The first critiques were made by scholars wishing to peel back the synthesized overlays that had built up since 1936, in quest of deeper and more original meanings in the text. The more profound attack however came from the supporters of a counterfactual macroeconomics, which was based initially on a comprehensive re-statement of an earlier doctrine, *The Quantity Theory of Money*, identified with the University of Chicago and the foundation studies of Frank Knight. Inflation and unemployment were becoming identified as key issues that required more effective tools for analysis than those supplied by mainstream Keynesian orthodoxy and *monetary theory* was more than ready to replace Keynesianism.

The time was therefore ripe to mount a challenge to demand management, and it came initially in the form of a new approach to inflation driven by Milton Friedman (see FRIEDMAN, M.).

The re-emergence of a refurbished supply-side approach was to become the first step in a new formulation of neo-classicism, in which Chicago was to supplant

Cambridge, both theoretically and ideologically. It involved a paradigm shift that was to have a profound impact on labour market analysis with on-going influences that remains with us today.

Monetarism and the labour market: a return to the supply side

It is one of the ironies of theoretical evolution that the major controversy that finally saw the end of Keynesian demand management as the received orthodoxy, had little to do with Keynesian theory *per se*.

By the late 1960s and early 1970s, those charged with the task of making labour market policies saw the causal influences that created inflation as stemming from two distinct trigger mechanisms – those caused by demand-pull, and cost-push influences.

In the first category, demand-pull was attributed to rigid market prices, which did not allow the price of good A to fall when that of good B rose. This meant that inflation was boosted by the fact that the price of good A would simply stay at the level it had attained before price B began to rise. On the cost-push side the cause was perceived to be market power. In effect firms would adjust the cost of unionized demands for wage increases by passing on the increase in unit labour cost through higher prices to the consumer.

The intention in so doing was to protect profit margins. The ultimate result of this pattern of union demands and employer responses was presumed in the aggregate; to create a spiral in which an increase in wages would translate into higher consumer prices, which would then trigger a further wage demand based on an increase in the cost of living. The result, notably in the British case, saw the 1960s and 1970s become a period of policy interchanges between incomes policies and wage freezes.

The elements of a unified wage policy model can be found in a single paper, which in the tradition of seminal studies created a vast literature of its own. In testing his model, Alban Phillips utilized a considerable mass of longitudinal data on historical wage trends, which had been assembled by his LSE colleague, Henry Phelps-Brown. The time-series based on the British building industry ran from 1861 to 1956, and he was able to identify an empirically stable relationship between the rate of change of money wages and the rate of unemployment; the result was the Phillips Curve. In his original analysis Phillips concluded that the lower the rate of unemployment, the higher the rate of change in wage rates. What he was saying is that any policy that sought a low rate of inflation as well as a low rate of unemployment was theoretically inconsistent.

The Phillips Curve went on to imply that governments had to choose what proportions of unemployment and inflation, expressed as percentages of each, it was to target as a policy goal. Substantial work was then undertaken to convert this to an inflation policy model. This led to the presumption that a trade-off could be obtained in which a reduction in unemployment could only be achieved through wage increases. What this boiled down to in policy terms was a basic question: What level of inflation would policy makers be willing to trade for a fall in unemployment?

The monetarist critique

The fact that the empirical basis of the Phillips Curve was predicated on a fifty-two year time-series raised serious doubts in the mind of Milton Friedman, who was preparing a theoretical counter-attack on Keynesian orthodoxy. The result from a Chicago perspective was the notion of the natural rate of unemployment in which a stable-price employment rate signalled the labour market was at equilibrium, under market conditions that specified: all imperfections, stochastic variability in demand and supply, information costs, mobility costs and all other variables. When this state had been obtained, unemployment would be consistent with a constant rate of inflation. Any attempt to push unemployment below this equilibrating state would only be effective in the very short run.

Armed with what was to become the non-accelerating inflation rate of unemployment Friedman went on to criticize the Phillips curve on the ground that Keynes had missed the point of real concern: that it was the rate of growth of real and not nominal wages that actually mattered, since everybody was concerned with them. At this point the monetarists raised a new and important issue: that when labour and management enter into negotiations, what matters is not the current and actual wage-price situation, but what it is anticipated to be in the future. There is some empirical evidence from US studies of collective bargaining dynamics that contingency issues do influence wage fixing behaviours, as the following example reveals.

In the USA, unionized collective bargaining agreements are traditionally set for a multi-year period. They typically preset terms of employment, which are based upon forecasts of future economic conditions. They have also included a contingent wage provision, which automatically adjusted wages to changes in the general index of consumer prices. Known as cost-of-living adjustments (COLAs), they provide only partial cover for increases in the CPI (Consumer Price Index). Studies made during the 1980s suggest that the degree of protection found in COLA arrangements reveals that employers as well as workers are risk-averse. This is reflected in the fact that the variety of COLA arrangements only partially insures the parties for the risk of costs incurred during a contractual term.

The monetarists also obtained support from independent studies led by Edmund Phelps. Following to some extent John Stuart Mill's theory of non-competing groups, they investigated the important question as to how labour markets operate when information is both incomplete and costly? The outcome was supportive of the original view that expectations are central to the entire process and inflation-adjusted expectations became the Friedman–Phelps hypothesis.

The incorporation of inflationary expectations saw the traditional Phillips Curve placed in intellectual jeopardy. The identification of *stagflation* in Europe, with its coterminous rise in both unemployment and inflation, together with a growing economic depression, simply made demand management theories irrelevant. It was to be rejuvenated with the emergence of a new neo-classicism, grounded in the theory of *rational* expectation, which heralded the emergence of a *new neo-classicism*. For in order to fit these new and axiomatic prescriptions, it was necessary for the Phillips Curve to be vertical in the long run.

These changes also fit within the larger structural shifts that have occurred within what is somewhat erroneously called the Keynesian orthodoxy. With aggregate supply-demand curves displacing the IS–LM model, the Phillips Curve has also been extensively modified. In its modern formulation, the short run variant argues that the rate of unemployment is inversely or negatively related to the rate of inflation where the expected rate of inflation is held constant. In the long-run version the fact that the curve is vertical signals that after short run adjustments in expectations have occurred, it turns into an aggregate supply curve at the natural rate of both employment and unemployment.

It remains to note somewhat ironically that monetarism's central tenet, which proposed a stable monetary regime based on an annual growth rate of the money supply set at 3 per cent, has in turn been found seriously wanting, in the press of events during the 1990s. The brutal fact is that no one in today's chaotic world of privatized money markets and increasingly volatile central banking systems can actually agree as to what the money supply is? From a labour market perspective, the policy device of the non-accelerating inflation rate of unemployment (NAIRU) has also been found both conceptually and empirically wanting.

2 Issues and controversies in labour market theory and analysis

Rational expectations and the labour market

During the 1970s, the demise of demand-side macroeconomics was filled by a new generation of Chicago theorists, led by Robert Lucas who created a thought experiment that was to earn him the Nobel Prize and become the basis of a new neo-classical Chicago School. The work of a non-economist, John Muth, supplied the foundation of rational expectations, since it was he who introduced the stylized fact that people are constantly learning and using the information they have gained to maximize personal utility. It follows that the notions of profitability and efficiency inform this process, which is very complex.

The stylized facts of this model seek some equilibrium point in the learning process, which is most logically that location where learning has come to an end. By this is meant that there is no longer a profit or efficiency incentive which might alter the way that expectations are formed. The key link is the further assumption that people have learned everything there is to learn, such that anything that is capable of prediction will be predicted correctly. Errors in prediction can in turn be explained as the results of random events not subject to prediction.

In the labour market context, it was rational expectations that really killed the Phillips Curve, since it is axiomatic that if expectations are in fact rational, they must be correct on the average and in the long run. Any alternative view would be unsustainable since people would have to ignore information that is easily available to them, which by definition would be irrational.

From the point of view of government policy the model is grounded in the axiom that there is little point in any administration trying to apply stabilization policies to an economy unless it is in possession of information that is not know to the citizens. Otherwise individuals will simply read the implications of a given strategy and then adjust their expectations accordingly, if they see that the effect of government action on their personal expectations will be dysfunctional.

From a labour market perspective, any attempt to employ a strategy aimed at stabilizing unemployment levels could only work if there were errors in expectations, which would be, using by the definition already employed above, random, and therefore not subject to control. In sum, there is no trade-off as proposed by the Philips Curve, even in the short run.

This line of argument, which has engendered lengthy controversy especially over persistent and high levels of unemployment, is limited by its axiomatic framework to the defence of the notion that all unemployment is voluntary, because spot markets for labour would always exist irrespective of general economic conditions. It also took the selective expectations assumption a stage further by drawing on the pioneering work on search developed by George Stigler to introduce the concept of intertemporal substitution.

In essence this concept reinforced the concept of unemployment as a voluntary phenomenon by suggesting that workers may substitute leisure for income in a given time period (t), because the current wage level offered in the job market does not meet their reservation wage. They do this on the assumption that in the period $(t + 1)$, the wage rate for their occupational class will be above its prevailing level. This line of argument has become increasingly difficult to sustain given the identification of lagged hysteresis effects found in the causal mechanisms of long-term unemployment.

The G7 economies in particular, suggests Eatwell (1995), are now faced with persistent high unemployment which place them under severe pressure from technological change, structural changes taking place in world trade, export competition from the developing countries, coupled to reduced levels of world trade growth and low commodity prices. Increased levels of market mediation in which contingency plays a key role (Ackerman *et al.* 1998) is also being driven by the growth of information and knowledge-based production.

Duality, internalization and segmentation in labour markets

Institutional analysis of labour markets dates back to the nineteenth century and was carried forward into modern times by modern institutionalists such as Clark Kerr, Jack Barbash and John Dunlop. Building on their work, Peter Doeringer and Michael Piore, Ray Loveridge and Albert Mok and Frank Wilkinson went on to define the firm as an internal labour market, characterized by dual employment conditions. The existence of duality assumed a primary labour market housing workers who enjoyed a substantial career-based relationship with the employer, and a secondary labour market external to the firm from which through ports of entry, short run and contingent workers were drawn.

While such a model gave expression to manifest inequalities within the labour market, this was not its main intention. It initial purpose was to critique the conventional textbook treatment of labour as a factor of production. At the same time the development of institutional analysis along these lines did not extend to an attack on the neo-classical assumptions of market efficiency. The result of one major theoretical approach that spun off the concept of dual labour markets was a restated institutionalism in which non-conforming behaviours are perceived as incurring costs through inefficiencies. These are translated into informational and transactional costs, and informed the works of Costa Azariadis and Joseph Stiglitz on risk, Oliver Williamson on transactional costs and Arthur Okun on the implications of implicit and informal contract arrangements (see WILLIAMSON, O.E.).

At the core of the dual labour market lies the structural concept of segmentation. According to Peck (1996), segmentation theory has progressively moved through three generations of development. In its original form the concepts of internalization rested on primary and secondary forms of internalization.

Moving into a second generation of analysis, a radical theory of the labour market emerged from the work of Michael Reich, David Gordon and Richard Edwards, which formally linked labour market structures to the evolution of control imperatives. A third generation of scholarship, represented by the work of Jill Rubery, seeks multi-causal explanations based on contingency, the nature of regulative governance and institutional variability.

The theoretical agenda in the third generation, suggests Esping-Anderson (1998), is to perceive labour as a socially produced and supply-based phenomenon, which embraces the family, labour union strategies and marginalized groups in the labour market. It is also informed by serious concern that the basis of segmentation is now between core and contingent workers. In effect, where skills are generic, the pattern of demand is increasingly likely to be contingent. By contrast, workers with highly firm-specific skills tend to form the core work group.

Contemporary labour market dualism thus implies that there exists alongside the small primary core, a secondary contingent labour market which exhibits four principal forms of employment: seasonal part-time; permanent part-time; temporary; and independent individual contracting. It is important to note here that the key concern does not lie in the distinction between core firm-specific employment and high skill contingent employment. Rather, it is found in their relationship to a third group, those in low skilled contingent employment.

Underlying the rise of low skilled contingent employment is the empirical evidence that labour market de-regulation does not, despite neo-classical expectations, result in a consequential rise in competitive efficiencies. In other words segmentation does not go away; rather, the terms of reference for employer–employee interaction are simply shifted in the employer's favour.

Implicit contracts

The emergence of the new institutional microeconomics allowed scholars to address some important issues, such as the significant costs of attempts to reduce real wages, despite the fact that there are unemployed persons in the labour market willing to work at a lower wage. This issue has considerable significance in core internal labour markets, especially where there has been investment in human resource development.

A second example can be found where an employee's propensity to quit is clearly influenced by the level of real wages. Both Gary Becker (1965) and Arthur Okun (1981) saw the answer to the problem as finding a means whereby the wage rate is linked to tenure and an attendant incremental value for seniority.

A second approach to the issues presumes on the basis of antecedent theories on search and expectation that employers are actually risk-neutral, while employees are risk-averse. This assumes that where employment is stable over time, employees will always prefer a less volatile stream of income to higher wages which are often aimed at off-setting a shortterm engagement. In this situation, the longer term of employment ensures a lower but longer income stream.

Such a contract has to be implicit by definition, and must exist within the interstices of formal arrangements. This is because trade unions will challenge any attempt by an employer with an excess supply of labour to reduce real wages, treating such an action as a breach of the labour contract. The model runs into empirical difficulties, largely because where skill requirements are low, employers will tend to ignore the question of replacement costs and simply lay off workers. This limits the explanatory power of implicit contract theory to large firms with highly skilled labour forces.

Efficiency wage models

Identified closely with the new Keynesian schools, the basic premise that informs the efficiency wage argument seeks to find the answer to an important question. How may firms succeed in pushing down wages to market clearing levels, in the presence of high levels of involuntary employment? The efficiency wage approach also seems to possess theoretical linkages with both Lester Thurow's model of job competition and the segmented labour market arguments rehearsed above. These are found in the somewhat idiosyncratic question as to why workers with equivalent skill endowments face systematic differences in job outcomes when they seek employment?

The answer proposed initially by Akerlof and Yellen (1986) is that wages are set high as a substitute form of employee monitoring. The behavioural supposition is that workers work harder when higher wages are offered as an incentive, with a further translation of effort into higher productivity.

On the presumption that workers will shirk if they are not supervised, a two-fold role for higher wages is assumed. First, the notion of a premium for effort is perceived to be a lesser cost than supervisory monitoring. On the other hand, a high wage imposed a higher cost for shirking since the normative penalty is dismissal when caught.

Empirical work has yet to obtain the degree of comprehensiveness that would give credence to the central tenets of the efficiency wage model. The problem is that labour market rules and institutions tend to be highly country-specific. The result is a current war of the models in which the labour market has moved from the periphery to centre stage.

The insider–outsider relationship

An element of dualism returns to the discussion at this point following pioneering work by Linbeck and Snower (1988). The assumption is made that certain key workers in a given firm can extract an additional rent during contract negotiations through a collusive relationship with the employer. This takes the conventional form of a demand for a premium or differential in pay that will effectively discriminate against new entrants to the firm.

In pressing such a claim, the union ignores the fact that its end result will be involuntary unemployment in the external labour market. The ability of trade unions to impose such a relationship is empirically no longer viable. This is particularly true in labour markets such as the USA and the UK, where trade unions as collective organizations have seen their power bases weakened during the 1980s and 1990s.

3 Some new agendas for labour market analysis

There is a growing consensus that the transition into the new millenium marks a profound historical turning point in the history of capitalism, in which the processes of globalization, exemplified by the increasing volume of cross-border interactions and resource flows, provide some common yardstick. The term globalization has proven very difficult to fit within some universally acceptable definition, which has tended in turn to put pressure on economic and business analysis as a possible general source of understanding.

As a result economic actors such as transnational corporations (TNCs) and international financial institutions have become a form of organizational key intended to unlock the processes, future direction and impact of the globalization phenomenon. These are joined by a number of other significant developments, including the emergence of new information technologies, the presence of which has reshaped the geographical nature of international economic activities.

The collapse and demise of central planning in eastern Europe has also been hailed as a major success for the political economy of the minimalist market, with an attendant and strong convergence around a universal notion of the de-regulated or at most a weakly regulated national economy. This became prevalent in the 1980s when a number of both the developed and developing countries signalled a return to a re-vitalised neo-liberal agenda for organizational change.

Some further claims for labour market flexibility

As reported by the OECD, globalization has an increasingly complex effect on the labour market, with adaptation and displacement present as constant variables. What distinguishes the contemporary period as described above, is the fact that firms are now able to conduct their major strategic activities both in real time and on a planetary scale. As a result, a degree of increasing interdependence makes it possible for patterns of labour market segmentation to also develop across boundaries.

This means, critics suggest, that the labour force can be treated as a disposable element in the total organizational inventory. It can be hired, fired and automated offshore depending upon market demand and labour costs. The result according to specific circumstances can mean the elimination of both job security and career paths within national economies

But it can, especially in developing countries, supplement primary employment and adjust the work-sharing process within households. It can also be a positive force for gender equality, providing that the strategy employed attempts to harness increasing labour market flexibility with least social costs.

The theory of the flexible firm

During the 1980s the recurring theme of primary and secondary labour markets within the organization gave rise to the notion of the flexible firm. The primary unit consisted of key workers, contingent specialists and sub-contractors together with trainees on subsidized work experience programmes. The exact proportions between the functionally flexible labour force and its numerically flexible adjunct then becomes a matter of managerial choice. It also became a focus of subsequent technical criticism, not least the claim that the flexible firm was really a model for a totally de-regulated labour market in which management held all the power.

The controversies that arose over this particular model of organizational flexibility raised a number of related questions with regard to flexible work systems, especially in markets for value-added products, such as services, where the process can be the product. Again, the division of labour, which has always been based on the close linkage between skill and control, may also shift under the pressures to create a new organizational architecture. This in turn could lead to the point where there is no rational connection between the specialist employee and the processes of work coordination.

The view of labour market flexibility, according to Siebert (1997), emerges as a counterfactual notion based on the common professional assumption that institutional rigidities in the labour market stem from practices and regulations that are largely aimed to protect workers, but which actually inhibit market clearing. This gives rise in turn to the presumption that in the absence of such inhibitors, the labour market would clear at equilibrium as prescribed in the neo-classical model. A more neo-liberal view would argue that market rigidities are really measures that inhibit employer prerogatives.

This view is countered by Nickell (1997), who suggests that there is a detrimental effect caused by such factors as indefinite terms for unemployment benefits and high rates of unionization with no rules for employer–union coordination. He goes on to add to the list, high taxation through payroll and minimum wage legislation and low educational skills at the bottom end of the labour market. On the other hand, he suggests that employee protection in law, high labour standards and high levels of union coverage do not create rigidities.

In his Keynes Lecture for 1998, Robert Solow also strongly criticized the lack of precision that has been involved to date in the use of the term labour market rigidities. He suggested that it owes more to symptomatic description than hard definition. He also notes that the concept of a wage gap first introduced by Bruno and Sachs in 1985, which presumes that unemployment is a function of economy-wide real wages being too high does not stand up empirically. The basis of the wage gap assumption as an explanation suggests that, in Europe, real wages outran labour productivity, with high unemployment emerging as a function of low profitability joined to low investment.

By contrast, suggests Solow, the 1980s saw a shift towards profits in Europe, which also signalled a fall in the general wage share. The wage share he, goes on to assert, continues to decline into the late 1990s. He went on to suggest that there are two major reasons why a more systematic approach to the notion of labour market rigidities needs scholarly attention. First there is a need for at least a roughly quantifiable and standard set of measures which should be joined to a further task. The need to build the concept of rigidities into normative macroeconomic model building when wage determination is the focus of attention. In the latter case, Solow argues for the use of the Beveridge Curve as an initial summary indicator, while further work is developed around these issues.

Flexibility and the network organization

The implications of Solow's findings in the case of Europe are also reflected in the fundamental changes that have been taking place in the USA since the early 1970s, in the matter of the growth of real wages. This has been demonstrated by the decline in the rate of growth in real wages coupled to the fact that earnings have become manifestly more unequal over time. There is now empirical evidence that not only have relative inequalities in income occurred between occupations with different skills. A similar pattern of inequality has tended to emerge within homogeneous skill groups, from work that has identified a distinct tendency for salary differentials to emerge between older workers and younger workers, with youth in the ascendant.

The managerial labour market in particular, as described in Robert Reich's *The Work of Nations,* has increasingly taken on the appearance of a network, in which common law contracts for service, or the employment of executives rented for fixed terms, often through the services of an agency, have become reasonably commonplace. The result for the USA is a major paradigm clash between the shift toward fixed-term individual contracts of employment and a historical labour market culture in which loss of permanent employment incurs further losses of future pensionable security, career progression, organizational identity and personal status (Gordon 1996). The empirical argument is further served by the fact that the top *Fortune 500* companies noted in the past for their sheer size and market reach have seriously dropped off the pace as employers. Where in the early 1970s one in five workers were employed within this group of firms, by the early 1970s it was down to one in ten.

Given the increasing prevalence of individual contractual relationships in the future, on-going work by scholars at MIT led by Thomas Malone suggests that the twenty-first century could well herald the return of some modified form of a guild system. This would see employment, skill upgrading, social benefits and the range of normative advantages that are assumed to be the product of conventional career activities, actively mediated for a fee, by a specialized agency where membership based on a defined and accredited professional skill is the requirement for entry. The alternatives they suggest involve a massive dislocation between the traditional and the new in labour market terms.

Labour markets in the information society

The popular notion of a global economy based upon information and knowledge raises some interesting problematics for labour market analysis, not least in the predictive imagination: as already noted above we find the idea of the worker as an individual contractor located in a network, rather than in a more traditional collective environment. On the other hand, as Shapiro and Varian (1999) have pointed out, the changes predicted do not drift too far away from more conventional economic analysis, though there are new and specific problems to address.

They note, for example, the existence of what has come to be called the zero price problem. In essence, information goods are infinitely expansible, a property that has very important implications for market competition. At the research and development stage the cost of an initial prototype, say a CD disk, is extremely high. But immediately production commences, costs and prices follow each other down to zero.

In terms of market competition, the timing of entry is vital since it allows the first firm to enter total market dominance, especially where demand is in the short run. The question has been well put by Quah (1999), when he asks, what incentives then remain for those firms who lose out consistently in the struggle to be first, to even try to enter the market? It is a view that gains strength from the fact that the research designs and launch of new products is now costed in billions of dollars.

These are really matters which lies outside the terms of reference for this discussion. However, a leading question can be asked from a labour market perspective. What are labour market conditions going to be like if the dominant organizational entity in a given market is a single monopolistic firm or at least a small oligopolistic market of mega-firms? The question can be asked from a variety of perspectives, including that of the virtual firm, whose purported work environment will comprise an electronically driven network peopled by individuals somewhat akin to Reich's 'symbolic analysts'.

International labour market liberalization and the migrant worker

Neo-classical theory has always perceived of labour mobility as a simple process of exchange mediated through various institutional controls in which the state is an active party. The German '*gastarbeiter*' system is perhaps the most useful example of such arrangements. As general rule guest workers tend to occupy those locations in the labour market where occupational shortages are manifest and where domestic supply cannot meet demand.

But outside the western experience of the guest worker, the pattern of demand for migrant labour becomes much more subject to a new order of complexity. In the Asian case it is reported (Rosewarne 1999) that labour market liberalization has shifted the weight of control over migrant labour towards private agencies.

This has resulted from the end of the 1980s in the growth of unofficial or clandestine movements of migrant workers, with the regulatory authority of the state diminishing as a consequence. In fact, the state in some countries is now often bypassed. Given the fact that the mass of migrants are recruited for what is called three-D work (dirty, difficult and dangerous), and that they are also mainly representative of the rural poor, their presence in increasing numbers in the larger metropolitan centres poses serious welfare and social services issues for the already overburdened cities of Asia. Many of the Asian economies are dealing with some proportion of a population that according to work done by the Harvard Institute for Development Studies is somewhere between seven hundred million and a billion people.

The increasing volatility and extent of labour migration is further exemplified by the fact that China is currently experiencing a rural-urban drift in what has been described by Kenneth Roberts (1997) as the largest labour flow in history. The result is still uncertain but there indications that the central government is aware of the political ramifications of a division between the modern and the developing sector with increasing attention being paid to the need to develop the rural provinces of the west.

In another variation on this version of dualism, exploratory econometric work by Danny Quah and others on the major issues of convergence as a developing function of economic growth, runs counter to the popular assumption that the processes of economic globalization signal a general rise in the levels of economic well-being, in which presumably all people would benefit. In sharp contrast they point to an emerging model of growth which does not aim towards integration. In labour market terms their early results predict a world in which income bipolarity and the division is between the rich and the poor is the norm. The middle class is notable in the model by its integration upward or downward.

4 Conclusion

If there is single and growing perception that links all of the themes of this entry, it points to the current inability of conventional labour market analysis, as personified in neo-classical mainstream theory, to explain current complexities and structural changes. These are of a substantive order that require a shift from axiomatic to behavioural assumptions, and a move away from the search for putative laws based upon nineteenth-century physics. Such a shift would be timely, given the fact that labour market issues now occupy a significant role in the agendas of global agencies such as the G8, the World Bank and the IMF.

At the same time it is necessary to repeat the injunction given in the first edition of the *IEBM*. That attempts to develop conclusive arguments about labour markets at this stage of the twenty-first century would be previous in the extreme. What is most important is the growing fact that labour market analysis is now perceived as an essential tool for understanding our increasingly complex socioeconomic world. How well these tasks are carried out might well inform the third edition.

ALAN WILLIAMS
MASSEY UNIVERSITY

Further reading

(References cited in the text marked *)

* Ackerman F., Goodwin, N., Dougherty, L. and Gallegher, K. (1998) (eds) *The Changing Nature of Work*, New York: Island Press. (A useful compendium of readings based about a range of labour market issues.)
* Akerlof, G.A. and Yellen, J.A. (1986) (eds) *Efficiency Wage Models and the Labour Market*, Cambridge: Cambridge University Press. (Remains an important introduction to efficiency wage theory and contains some seminal papers.)

Azariadis, C. and Stiglitz, J.E. (1982) 'Implicit contracts and fixed price equilibria', *Quarterly Journal of Economics*, special supplement. (Presents a seminal collection of papers on implicit labour contracts; requires a grasp of basic econometrics to obtain full value.)
* Becker, G. (1965) *Human Capital: A Theoretical and Empirical Analysis with Special Reference to Education*, Chicago: University of Chicago Press. (Recognized as the standard neo-classical work on returns to schooling and the intellectual basis of human capital investment theory.)

Card, D. and Kreuger, A.B. (1995) *Myth and Measurement: The New Economics of the Minimum Wage*, Princeton: Princeton University Press. (A strong counterfactual approach to the neo-classical view that minimum wage initiatives actually raise unemployment.)

Carnoy, M. and Castells, M. (1997) *Sustainable Flexibility: A Prospective Study of Work, Family and Society in the Information Age*, Paris, OECD Working Papers, Series 5, Number 29. (An initial study of a very important issue, the impact of the knowledge economy on social as well as economic institutions.)

Castro, A., Mehaut, P. and Rubery, J. (1992) (eds) *International Integration and Labour Market Organization*, London: Academic Press. (Representative of the third generation approach to labour market duality.)

Doeringer, P.B. and Piore, M.J. (1975 and 1985) *The Internal Labour Market: Internal Labour Markets and Manpower Analysis*, Lexington, MA: D.C. Heath and Company. (Provides the basic location from which to examine internal labour market theory.)
* Eatwell, J. (1995) (ed.) *Global Unemployment: Loss of Jobs in the 1990s*, New York: M.E. Sharpe. (Represents the modern institutional approach to labour market analysis as exemplified in the work of the New School of Social Research.)
* Epsing-Anderson, G. (1998) *Social Foundations of Post-industrial Economics*, Oxford: Oxford University Press.
* Friedman, M. (1977) *Inflation and Unemployment: The New Dimension of Politics*, Institute of Economic Affairs, Occasional Paper Number 51. (A more extended version of his Nobel acceptance speech which traces the rise in the theoretical importance of the NAIRU.)
* Gordon, D. (1996) *Fat and Mean: The Corporate Squeeze of Working Americans and the Myth of Managerial Downsizing*, New York: Martin Kessler Books and The Free Press. (Explores the dimensions of change in the US labour

market in terms of the quality of employment and the social implications of a rising inequality.)

* Keynes, J.M. (1936) *The General Theory of Employment, Interest and Money,* London: Macmillan. (Remains a focus of controversy to this day, and the source of conflicting interpretations.)

* Linbeck, A. and Snower, D. (1988) *The Insider–Outsider Theory of Employment and Unemployment,* Cambridge, MA: MIT Press. (An important survey of the theories of collusive behaviour between employers and permanent employees.)

* Loveridge, R. and Mok, A. (1979) (eds) *Theories of Labour Market Segmentation,* The Hague: Martinus Nijhoff. (A useful review and critique of the early stages of the segmentation debate.)

Marglin, S. and Schor, J. (1991) *The Golden Age of Capitalism; Reinterpreting the Post-War Experience,* Oxford: Clarendon Press. (An important series of radical critiques.)

McNulty, P.J. (1980) *The Origin and Development of Labour Economics,* Cambridge, MA: MIT Press. (Somewhat dated but very user-friendly introduction to the field.)

Michie, J. and Smith, J.G. (1998) *Unemployment in Europe,* London: Academic Press. (An important review of contemporary approaches to the causes of unemployment, especially in the long term.)

Muth, J. (1961) 'Rational expectations and the theory of price movements', *Econometrica* 29 (3): 315–35. (The seminal paper on which Lucas, Sargent and Wallace constructed the economic theory of rational expectations.)

* Nickell, S. (1997), 'Unemployment and labour market rigidities in Europe and North America', *Journal of Economic Perspectives* 11 (3): 55–74.

* Okun, A. (1981) *Prices and Quantities,* Oxford: Blackwell. (Introduced an early form of the notion of collusive behaviour in bargaining, with his immortal concept of the 'invisible handshake'.)

* Peck, J. (1996) *Work Place: The Social Regulation of Labour Markets,* New York: The Guildford Press. (A valuable contribution to the analysis of labour markets as social institutions as well as markets for the exchange of factor services.)

Phelps, E.S. (ed.) (1970) *Microeconomic Foundations of Employment and Inflation Theory,* New York: Norton and Co. (A very important book for its time, which paralleled the work of Friedman and created a strong associative identity for both scholars.)

* Phillips, A.W. (1958) 'The relationship between unemployment and the rate of change in money wages in the UK, 1861–1957', *Economica* 25 (100): 283–99. (Like Muth and Coase, in their respective fields, this seminal work made Phillips a major figure in labour economics.)

Piore, M.J. and Sabel, C. (1984) *The Second Industrial Divide,* New York: Basic Books. (A major contribution to the debate on organizational change. Michael Porter has taken up its notion of industrial clusters amongst others.)

* Quah, D. (1999) 'The weightless economy in growth', *The Business Economist* 30 (1) March: 40–53.

* Roberts, K. (1997) 'China's tidal wave of migrant labour', *International Migration Review* 31 (2): 249–53.

* Rosewarne, S. (1999) 'The globalization and liberalization of Asian labour markets', *The World Economy,* 21 (7): 963–80)

* Reich, R.B. (1991) *The Work of Nations,* New York: Vantage Books. (Presents a highly futuristic view of the world of work that will emerge as a consequence of globalization.)

Sapsford, D. and Tzannnatos, M. (1993) *The Economics of the Labour Market,* 2nd edn, London: Macmillan. (Designed as a text for advanced undergraduate study but useful as a technical overview of some of the major labour market issues of the 1990s.)

* Shapiro, C and Varian, H.R. (1999) *Information Rules: a Strategic Guide to the Network Economy*, Boston: Harvard Business School Press.

* Siebert, H. (1997) 'Labour market rigidities at the root of unemployment in Europe', *Journal of Economic Perspectives* 11 (3): 37–54.

* Solow, R.M. (1998) 'What is labour market flexibility? What is it good for?', The Keynes Lecture for 1998, London, *Proceedings of the British Academy,* 98: 189–211.

Stigler, G. (1972) 'Information in the labour market', *Journal of Political Economy* 70 (5): 94–105. (A seminal paper on search in employment theory. The paper models a marginal outcome from search in which the final wage offer is equal to the marginal returns from search.)

Ward, A. (1994) *North–South Trade, Employment and Inequality: Changing Fortunes in a Skill Drive World,* Oxford: Clarendon Press. (A useful introduction to the increasing problems of global inequality in which the basis of differentiation is the presence or lack of industrial skills.)

Williamson, O.E. (1985) *The Economic Institutions of Capitalism: Firms, Markets and Relational Contracting,* New York: The Free Press. (Represents the new institutionalism in

Labour markets

economics being led by the Nobel Laureates, Ronald Coase and Douglas North.)

See also: FRIEDMAN, M.; INDUSTRIAL AND LABOUR RELATIONS; KEYNES, J.M.; MARX, K.; MARSHALL, A.; MILL, J.S.; SAMUELSON, P.; SMITH. A.; VEBLEN, T.; WILLIAMSON, O.E.

Industrial and labour relations

1 Historical context
2 The main actors in the industrial relations system
3 Major themes in industrial relations
4 Emergent issues in industrial relations

Overview

Industrial (or labour) relations encompasses the study of the employment relationship. Ultimately the rationale for the discipline is the continued significance of work for the maintenance and advance of human societies. This necessitates the existence of a vitally consequential labour or employee group, which is involved in a fundamental economic, social and political relationship with employers and management. Moreover, the outcomes of this relationship are so crucial to the long-term survival, let alone continued prosperity of any given country, that it inevitably includes the state or government as well.

To define the subject in these terms is not necessarily contentious but it is an approach which is not universally accepted. Thus US scholars have typically adopted an even broader understanding of the subject, viewing it as an interdisciplinary field which covers all aspects of people at work. For scholars in the Third World, the saliency of the state for employment relationships has been underscored and, hence, the independent role of labour and management is generally considered to be of limited consequence. By contrast, many British definitions have been much more narrow, focusing either on different patterns of job regulation associated with the institutions of collective bargaining or, in more radical accounts, on the 'processes of control over work relations'. But to centre on the employment relationship is sufficiently general to be applicable to all types of industrial and industrializing society; and yet it is sufficiently circumscribed to differentiate the disciplinary boundaries of industrial relations from other cognate social science and management disciplines.

In more detail, industrial relations scholars tend to assume that in every industrial and industrializing country, there are three main 'actors' or parties with partly common and partly divergent interests: employers and managers, employees and labour (and often trade unions), and the state. A degree of conflict between these groups is regarded as inevitable, but there are typically mechanisms to ensure that it is channelled or accommodated, notably: (1) individual resolution (supported by freedom of contract and by the lack of any substantial restrictions to the operation of the labour market); (2) unilateral determination (by employers, managers, the state, trade unions or workers); and (3) plural modes of regulation (typically under collective bargaining and in which differences are 'expressed, articulated and defended' through independent associations of employers and working people and in which joint determination and responsibility for the terms and conditions of employment has been instituted).

It is further assumed that interests may be shared or conflicting in both so-called production and distribution spheres (the first encompasses the actual work process, the second economic rewards which accrue from employment). On the one hand, then, a series of creative or productive activities are defined by the functions of all organizations. But while their performance may be free of conflict (for example, when managerial decision-making is legitimated), equally there are often fundamental struggles along the so-called 'frontier of control', between working people who seek 'freedom on the job' and managers and supervisors who endeavour to plan the overall organization and conduct of work. On the other hand, the allocation of rewards from work may also occasion consensus or conflict. The former depends on fairness or justice governing the principles of distribution. However, in its absence, antagonism is likely and is reflected in familiar disputes over pay and income.

1 Historical context

The earliest writings on industrial relations were linked with an analysis of the Labour Movement and with the various assessments of the potential of trade unions for the radical transformation of capitalist societies. As it happens neither Marx nor Engels left behind a systematic or coherent analysis of the limits and possibilities of trade union action; but they are broadly linked with the so-called 'optimistic tradition' in which a radical character for trade unions was identified. Essentially, on this view, trade unions were viewed as 'schools of solidarity' and 'schools of socialism' which would play a fundamental role in societal transformation. Nevertheless, even Marx and Engels were aware of the limitations of trade union action and clearly came to view economic crises as having at best the potential for the radicalization of the labour movement. For Lenin, Luxemburg and Trotsky the obstacles to revolutionary consciousness emerging from within trade unions were more strongly crystallized. Lenin in particular articulated the case of the so-called 'pessimistic tradition' which suggests that revolutionary consciousness can never stem from the spontaneous economic struggles of working people; but rather (if it is to occur at all) has to be brought in from 'outside the sphere of production' by intellectuals.

Amongst other of the earliest analysts of industrial relations were Perlman and Commons in the USA and the Webbs in the UK. Perlman was one of the earliest of the critics of Marxist approaches to the study of industrial relations. In a *Theory of the Labor Movement* (1928) he argued against not only the 'orthodox Marxians' but also 'ethical' intellectuals (such as Christian Socialists) and 'social efficiency' intellectuals (the Webbs and the Fabians) on the ground that they viewed 'labour' as an 'abstract mass in the grip of an abstract force' that existed only in the intellectual imagination and was not based at all on the mentality of manual workers. Perlman went on to emphasize that the home grown ideology of labour is based on 'scarcity consciousness' (namely the perception of limited opportunity). This, in turn, leads to so-called 'communism of opportunity' whereby labour seeks to establish job control, ration the opportunities amongst the group and practice solidarity through trade unionism (the ownership of the production and distribution systems being largely irrelevant from this perspective).

No less pre-eminent amongst the earliest US writers on industrial relations and the founder (along with Perlman) of the Wisconsin School was John R. Commons. Against the view of classical economists that behaviour in the workplace may be explained in terms of individual choices, Commons along with other institutionalists focused on the history, origins and behaviour of trade unions. Moreover, the practical emphasis on protective labour legislation and union organization recognized a clash of interests between employers and workers, but one which was not necessarily the product of capitalism itself. Indeed this assumption was later developed by Barbash who viewed the central labour problem as the conflict between the job security of workers and the organizational efficiency or effectiveness needs of employers (for a review see Kochan 1980).

Earlier, in the UK, the Webbs had laid a further foundation of an analysis of trade unionism and industrial relations in *The History of Trade Unionism* and in *Industrial Democracy*. Above all the most influential definition of a trade union in the entire industrial relations literature as 'a continuous association of wage-earners for the purpose of maintaining or improving the conditions of their employment' is encompassed in the very first sentence of '*The History*'. But the main emphasis of the Webbs' writings was empirical, historical and descriptive. However, they were to contribute monumentally to the study of industrial relations in a number of respects. First of all, they not only classified a series of trade union methods but they were the forerunners of the notion of the 'theory of a labour aristocracy' arguing that the organizing abilities of skilled workers within craft-type trade unions were fundamental in establishing sound principles of organization within other types of trade unions. And, above all, they argued forcefully the merits of collective bargaining (by means of which unions negotiate for improvements in pay and conditions with employers), viewing industrial democracy itself as being ultimately founded on this process.

Moreover, in the evolving discipline of industrial relations the writings of Hoxie and Tannenbaum from the USA were also influential. Hoxie identified a number of labour union types (business, uplift, revolutionary, predatory and dependent). In particular, business unionism was seen as a bargaining institution and as being essentially trade rather than class conscious. He was also a major critic of Taylor and the 'scientific management movement' on the grounds that this approach viewed the worker as 'a mere instrument of production' and that it occasioned 'mutual suspicion and controversy' as a result of its inherently anti-democratic assumptions about the management of work. As such, his writings to some extent mirrored those of Mayo and of other contributors to the human relations movement. However, there was a subtle but fundamental difference in that Hoxie emphasized the desirability of labour union organizations (rather than the reform of management) as the main checkweight to the advance of Taylorism.

Of all the early to mid-nineteenth century US scholars of industrial relations it was, however, Tannenbaum who came closest to embracing the class-based notions of European theorists. Indeed, he viewed the ultimate goal of labour to be the displacement of the capitalist system by a participative democratic model. And, analytically, his work was important in its understanding of labour unions as a defence against competition (occasioned, not least, by the technology of machine-based production) and their provision for greater security for the individual worker.

Modern systematic analysis

Modern systematic analysis of industrial relations, however, largely began with *systems theory*. The most influential of the attempts to define the field of industrial relations in these terms was by John Dunlop (1956). In *Industrial Relations Systems* he argued that, in any given society (or social system), it was possible to identify three interlocking systems (the industrial relations system, the economic system and the political system) which were on the same logical plane and were interrelated. That is to say, developments in the political and economic systems influenced the industrial relations system and vice versa. Within the industrial relations system itself, three groups of actors were identified (workers and their organizations, managers and their organizations and governmental agencies concerned with the workplace and work community).

Furthermore, in Dunlop's view, every industrial relations system creates a complex set of rules to govern the workplace and work community. These rules may take a variety of forms in different systems: agreements, statutes, orders, decrees, regulations, awards, policies, and practices and customs. And these 'actors' in the industrial relations system are regarded as confronting an environmental context at any one time. This is composed of three interrelated contexts:

- technology
- market or budgetary constraints
- the power relations and status of the actors

The function of the industrial relations system was seen to be to establish rules which could encompass substantive rules (for example, remuneration in all its forms) and procedures used for setting and administering the substantive rules. Finally, in Dunlop's view, the system is bound together by an ideology of understandings shared by all the actors.

A variety of refinements of the system model were later to be developed but the systems model itself has not been without its critics. It has been viewed as static and not dynamic or historical in its compass. It has been seen as focusing more on structure than on process. Its emphasis on stability rather than conflict has been a principal source of controversy. And other criticisms include its stress on formal rather than informal relationships, its abstract rather than concrete form, its identification of common rather than diverse or pluralist ideologies and its environmental bias so far as explanations for differences in industrial relations systems are concerned.

The *social action perspective* which is based on Weberian sociology has also emerged as a major strand of modern industrial relations thinking. The fundamental assumption is that the actors' own definitions of the situations in which they are engaged is the fundamental basis of explanation of their behaviour and relationships. Rather than viewing behaviour in industrial relations as a function of the systems in which the actors (labour, managers and the state) are enmeshed, the social action perspective stresses the fundamental importance of freedom of action, the ability of actors to influence events based on distinctive orientations, and the importance of choice. Moreover, given that choices are in practice varied and often in conflict, the importance of power in explaining outcomes is constantly stressed. The social action perspective has thus provided a radically different approach to systems theory. However, it is deficient in respect of the limited emphasis placed on economic, technological and political conditions in shaping rather than determining orientations and choices and an appropriate synthesis does combine the notions of action, power and structure to provide a more encompassing explanation.

This desideratum was partly accomplished by the notion of 'frames of reference' (unitary, pluralist and radical). A frame of reference embodies 'the main selective influences at work as the perceiver supplements, omits and structures' what is noticed. A unitary frame of reference emphasizes common values, the notion of the team and a unitary form of authority in the enterprise. A pluralistic frame of reference emphasizes that the workplace is composed of actors with a variety of different interests, aims and aspirations within diverse and often conflicting organizations and groupings (for example trade unions and management), and with diverse foci of loyalty and allegiance. Finally, a radical perspective entails a focus not only on conflict between industrial relations actors but is based on the assumption that there is structured social inequality and substantial imbalances of power amongst the various parties. Nevertheless, frames of reference are best understood as analytical devices rather than as fully developed explanations for different industrial relations phenomena (Fox 1974).

Comparative and international perspectives

Indeed, the evolving discipline of industrial relations has gradually become more international in its compass. Rather than analysing single countries (or being based on debates in specific national contexts), there have been many attempts to analyse patterns of global uniformity and difference. Comparative industrial relations involves the isolation of environmental and other variables to explain patterns of similarity and diversity in more than one country. International studies are more typically referred to as the focus on supranational phenomena (such as European Community (EC) institutions, international trade union organizations and multinational enterprises (MNEs)), while so-called foreign studies encompass the examination of phenomena in a foreign environment and, for theoretical purposes, do not differ substantially from like cases in a home environment.

There are inevitably very many methodological problems involved in comparative industrial relations. First, there is the level of analysis (for example country or industry) to be selected. There are also problems with actual data, for even when there are reasonable sources of international statistics (as for strikes), there are many pitfalls involved in their use stemming not least from different modes of compilation. There is, then, the choice of countries to compare. Is it better to take matched pairs, groups of countries or to assess phenomena globally? Moreover, phenomena which are superficially common to many countries (for example industrial conflict) may not only have very many different forms from one country to the next but also may be understood and interpreted in radically different ways. And finally there is the problem of the dynamic development of industrial relations and of building models which contain elements of a long-term pattern of movement rather than involving only so-called comparative statics (namely where countries or phenomena are compared at a single point in time) (see Whitfield and Strauss

2000). None the less, the richness of insights, the explanatory importance and the practical significance of comparative industrial relations substantially outweigh these disadvantages.

Convergence revisited

The first attempt to formulate a general theory of comparative industrial relations is usually traced to Clark Kerr and his colleagues' (1960) seminal work, *Industrialism and Industrial Man*, though in subsequent discussions, its central arguments have been frequently misinterpreted. Certainly Kerr *et al.* envisaged a convergence to a greater degree of uniformity in the world's industrial relations systems in the future. Moreover, the central logic of industrialism or 'common denominator' was seen to stem from the homogenizing forces of new technology. And a wide variety of sources of uniformity were identified that included history and homogeneity, technology and society, the push of progress, education and equality, government and enterprise, and the 'compulsion of comparisons'. But various potent 'threads of diversity' were also isolated that included the persistence of strategies, the imprint of culture, the hour clock of evolution, the culture of industry, and people and performance. This position was further developed by Kerr in the *Future of Industrial Societies* (1983) where the idea of a relatively wide range of possible industrial relations patterns within pluralistic industrialization was reaffirmed and extended. Indeed, although various elements of 'current comparability' and 'increasing similarity' were noted an extensive range of areas of 'continuing substantial dissimilarity' between the world's economic and industrial relations systems was also observed. This applied not least in the areas of ideology and patterns of belief.

In the early 1990s, however, there may well have been a new pattern of convergence in industrial relations systems. There is thus a significant dependence on markets and free enterprise, coupled with trade unions and employers relatively free from government intervention, and still extensive (if declining) collective bargaining and tripartite consultation. This is occurring not only in the former communist nations but also in the dynamic Asian economies (such as Korea) and in Africa and South America. There remain substantial differences between the democratic market countries, but globally there have been some far reaching convergent trends in industrial relations systems. The forces behind this movement include: (1) markets and global competition; (2) the internationalization of knowledge; (3) the internationalization of production; and (4) new technology.

Diversity in industrial relations systems

There are, then, several modern forces for convergence in industrial relations systems. But, the forces for dissimilarity are no less insistent. These include cultural values and ideologies, political and economic conditions, the institutional framework for industrial relations, the power of the actors, and various temporal movements. In particular, new nations of the Third World may evolve along different trajectories of development from the West and hence emerge with different industrial relations systems (for instance, in respect to the role of the state and legislature and types of trade union). And this may partly override some other homogenizing forces.

How, then, do we explain diversity in industrial relations systems? The most obvious starting point is a social action perspective and an emphasis on the importance of choice. In most industrial relations systems the three main actors (employers and managers, labour, and the state) thus have some measure of determination over institutional arrangements; and this builds a high degree of potential diversity into industrial relations systems given the differences in objectives and power balances which are in practice feasible. Moreover, strategic choices have a potential significance as potent forces for both stability and change (see Kochan *et al.* 1986).

But if we are to build a satisfactory spatial model of diversity in industrial relations systems, the forces which help to shape strategic choices also require identification. After all, the choices of the actors are focused by orientations which are, in turn, affected by cultural conditions and ideologies (see Figure 1).

Industrial and labour relations

```
Cultural          Orientations      Strategic choices     Selection of particular
conditions                          of the actors         institutional
                                                          arrangements for
                                                          industrial relations
```

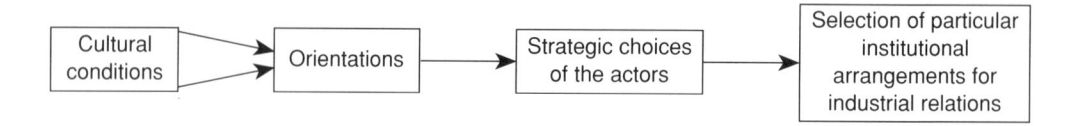

Figure 1 Strategies of choice of the actors
Source: Adams and Meltz (1993)

It is also vital to note the importance of the distribution of power in the shaping of actual industrial relations outcomes. Whether or not given actors are able to achieve their objectives depends on a process of interaction and struggle and the marshalling of different power resources. These, in turn, are linked with, but not determined by, wider political, economic and technological conditions (see Figure 2).

A temporal model focuses particularly on processes of institutionalization. This implies that industrial relations institutions (for instance, for collective bargaining) can develop in a functionally separate way from wider environmental conditions. Institutions thus modify the effects of major changes in the environment and ensure a degree of continuity in industrial relations practices over time. They help us to explain the distinctive character of particular industrial relations systems which can continue to differ despite the effects of internationalization.

The way in which diversity continues over time is developed in Figure 3, where the functional separation and autonomy for institutions is shown.

At the point when industrial relations institutions become established (or a major development departs from existing arrangements), the pattern may be understood in terms of the outcome of distinctive strategies of the 'actors' – in specific cultural, ideological, and politico-economic conditions and with a given distribution of power. However, and of great importance, once institutional structures take root they can continue without major change for prolonged periods, despite marked alterations in, say, political and economic conditions. This is partly because of the efforts of those in dominant roles in the institutions concerned who have a clear interest in organizational survival, but also because of processes of socialization (at induction and in committee proceedings and so on) which ensure that new recruits continue to sustain the established machinery. Certainly institutions do change, partly through adaptation to new environmental circumstances, partly through a gradual decline as new arrangements supersede them, and partly through radical transformation in crisis periods. But, over time, they can develop a degree of autonomy from the environmental conditions in which they are situated. Thus, for a long period, the institutions of collective bargaining in the UK appeared to have largely survived the 'Thatcher years', even though the Workplace Industrial Relations Survey (WIRS 3; Millward *et al.* 1992) does suggest a more substantial decline.

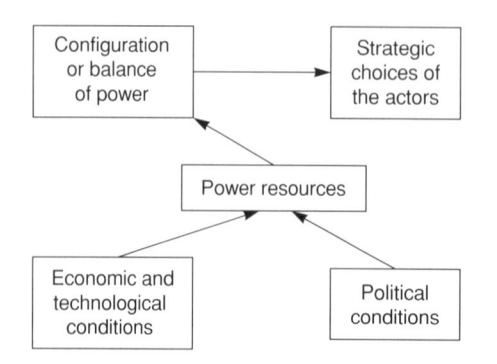

```
Configuration           Strategic
or balance    ──────►   choices of
of power                the actors
    ▲                       │
    │                       ▼
            Power resources
    ▲                       ▲
    │                       │
Economic and            Political
technological           conditions
conditions
```

Figure 2 Action, power and structure
Source: Adams and Meltz (1993)

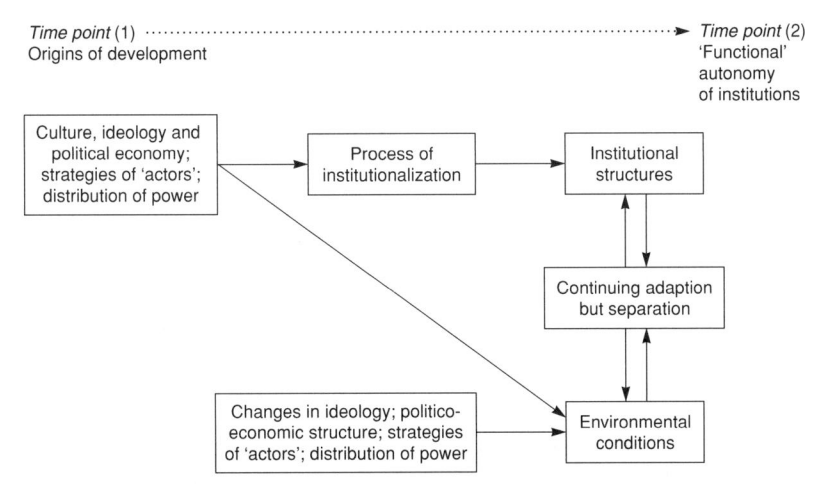

Figure 3 Functional separation

2 The main actors in the industrial relations system

Labour, trade unions and collective bargaining

Turning more specifically, then, to an analysis of the actors in the industrial relations system, in many respects the discipline of industrial relations commenced as we have seen with the study of labour movements. The original impetus was an intellectual concern with their radical potential and based on the recognition that labour forms the largest single group in industrial society, the foundation upon which the wealth of nations ultimately rests. More latterly (and linked with the rise of human resource management) has been an understanding of the importance of the motivation and commitment of the workforce for organizational effectiveness and for national competitive advantage.

However, the special focus of industrial relations has been in labour organizations and particularly with trade unions. It was once reasonable to classify trade unions from a comparative perspective into:

1. *trade unionism under collective bargaining* (where unions have predominantly instrumental purposes, a high degree of independence from state and management, and largely oppositional functions);
2. *oppositional-type trade unions, with political, religious or nationalist objectives* (political and legislative means predominate in the accomplishment of labour objectives and alignment with political parties is close);
3. *trade unionism under socialism* (predominantly integrative functions and relatively limited independence from the state and management. Given the radical transformation of eastern Europe, however, the last category is no longer so significant).

Trade unionism under collective bargaining tends to occur in countries with a high degree of industrialization, a strong market economy, a democratic political system and with pluralist rather than corporatist institutions. Collective bargaining involves negotiations between labour organizations (normally trade unions) and either managements or employers' associations and, although a wide range of issues may be encompassed, the typical discussions focus around pay and working conditions.

The more specific aspects of the analysis of trade unions under collective bargaining cover *density* (namely the percentage of the workforce in trade unions), *structure* and *government*. Clegg (1976) viewed the extent and depth of collective bargaining and support for union density either from employers or from collective bargaining agreements as basic to high levels of union density. In particular, a characteristic of countries with high levels of union density (typically evident in Scandinavian countries) has been the functional separation of political and industrial objectives of labour and the use of Social Democratic parties to ensure a favourable context for trade union recognition. Nevertheless, in the 1990s, the Scandinavian model of industrial relations has been in a process of radical change. Indeed, most (but not all) countries experienced a loss in union membership in the 1980s and early 1990s, a situation which is often attributed to the fulfilment of many labour objectives, as well as to managerial strategies, unfavourable legislation and economic and industrial change (Baglioni and Crouch 1991).

When trade unions use collective bargaining as the foremost means of influencing the terms and conditions of employment, union structure is likely to reflect industrial and occupational divisions and not political or ideological principles. The most common classification of union structures encompasses: craft unions (closed to groups of skilled workers); general unions (open unions prepared in principle to recruit any worker); and industrial unions (linked with specific industries). Later, white-collar and public sector unions emerged and formed independent categories of trade union in countries such as the UK.

How are these variations to be explained? The most detailed and influential thesis is that of Clegg (1976), who focused to begin with on the state of technology and industrial organization at the time of birth and growth of a trade union movement. Although, on his testimony, the new skills of the industrial revolution led to craft unions; mass production favoured industrial and general unions. Furthermore, as white-collar employees have multiplied, so: 'their unions have grown with the large-scale organizations of the present century' (Clegg 1976: 39). But the methods of trade union regulation are also relevant. Before the advance of collective bargaining unilateral regulation required organization by occupation. But as collective bargaining proliferated, general unions expanded around the previously established crafts which had once relied on unilateral controls. Similarly, if there are no strong occupational unions, industrial unions become pre-eminent. This type of union structure is also strongly favoured on ideological grounds and hence, where unions have been destroyed and when a subsequent reconstruction on a pre-determined pattern is feasible, industrial unionism typically emerges. Finally, white-collar employees: 'tend to perceive their interests as different from those of manual workers and to prefer their own separate occupational unions' (Clegg 1976: 39). Over time, craft unions have tended to decline and a broad evolutionary logic tends to favour either white-collar or general unions. Public sector unions have been affected adversely by trends towards privatization and although industrial unions are preferred on grounds of rationalization, and succeed if they are effectively promoted, they are vulnerable to the fortunes of particular industries.

Trade union *government* involves the internal administrative structures within trade unions and the foremost debates have centred on their democratic potential. The role of the legislature in affecting governmental processes within unions has also been profound. Essentially, environmentalists view the forces affecting democracy or oligarchy in labour unions in terms of external constraints. The political culture (and whether or not it favours pluralism or corporatism) is viewed as of importance here as is the ideological commitment of leaders to democratic principles, environmental uncertainty (which favours oligarchy) or legal provisions. Organizational theorists have examined democratic potential such as participation in elections, divisions of powers and constitutional checks as being salient. In particular, ballots within unions (for the selection of officials) have been seen as fundamental in avoiding oligarchy and these have been supported by the legislature in a variety of countries (for example the USA and the UK).

But trade unions with predominantly instrumental purposes relying on the method of collective bargaining are only one of the main types of labour organization. Indeed, in many instances, a variety of political, religious or nationalist objectives are uppermost and this has pronounced consequences not just for trade union character but also for density, structure and government. Even in the West, many countries in which trade unionism under collective bargaining now predominates once had far more radical labour movements (for example Germany) and important examples remain in which trade unions are dominated by political parties and wider religious affiliations (for example France, Italy). For the bulk of trade unions in the Third World, too, political and legislative channels, rather than collective bargaining, are the foremost means for securing improvements in pay and working conditions.

Globally, then, a second principal type of trade unionism is characterized by: (1) a dominance of political over instrumental purposes; (2) a focus on political or legislative means; (3) a formally oppositional role; and (4) a varied extent of interdependence from state and management.

Most countries with labour organizations of this type have not insignificant private sectors. Above all, however, the strategic choice to establish and to persist with such arrangements rests on: (1) a favourable cultural or ideological background; (2) the stage of industrialism; and (3) a significant state role in industrial and economic activities.

Finally, trade unionism under socialism is characterized by predominantly integrative functions and by a relatively close organic link with state and management. The origins of the main model may be traced to the Leninist conception of democratic centralism which allowed unions some independence but within the strict confines of broader party and government policies. The main break with this model occurred with the rise of Solidarity in Poland that encompassed demands not just for free trade unionism, but also the right to strike, the appointment of managerial staff on the basis of competence, and a range of political demands. Further radical changes in various eastern European countries include: a redefinition of functions including 'pluralization' and 'restructuring' of trade unions; traditional unions having the representation of workers' interests to be their exclusive function, renouncing that of being a 'transmission belt' of party ideology to the workforce; the rise of works collective councils which conflict with traditional trade unions; and a greater independence of trade unions from management and the state generally (Szell 1992; Martin and Cristesco-Martin 1999).

Managers

Managers are a ubiquitous and expanding group within modern societies and increasingly it has been recognized that their ability to determine many aspects of the employment relationship is of far reaching importance to industry and society. To understand the managerial role in industrial relations, the concepts of strategy, style and frame of reference have been fundamental. Strategies are consistent patterns in streams of decisions and actions and are inter-temporal, involving a series of choices taken over a period of time for a given objective. To some extent strategies are linked with market conditions and with the firm's financial performance for, in unfavourable demand conditions, managements are likely to seek greater control over the employment relationship (and not least over pay settlements), whereas organizational slack and local autonomy are more likely where competition in the product market is relatively weak.

Strategies are also linked with preferred styles of industrial relations management. The main styles are authoritarian (directive), paternal (directive but welfare orientated), constitutional (negotiated and based on reaching agreements with organized labour and governments) and participative (involving employees in decisions). The first pair are typically linked with unitary frames of reference and the second pair with more pluralistic notions. Variations of these styles include traditionalism (based on forceful opposition to trade unions), sophisticated paternalism, sophisticated modern and standard modern approaches.

The analysis of the role of manager in industrial relations has also been linked with strategic human resource management (SHRM). Even though many firms still do not practice SHRM, the recognition of the key role of human resources for competitive advantage has occasioned a rich seam of analyses of the importance of employee involvement, human resource flow policies, high commitment work systems and appropriate incentives and rewards of which all managers (and not only those directly involved in personnel or industrial relations) need to have cognizance.

Governments and the role of the state

Despite considerable problems in identifying the personnel, locating its various segments and reaching an acceptable definition, the state is indisputably the third force in the industrial relations system. The state is not easy to define unambiguously, but it is a shorthand expression for a series of institutions encompassing the legislature, the executive, central administration (the civil service), the judiciary, the police and local government. Moreover, all these institutional agents may be involved in industrial relations depending on context and country.

In the West, the main types of state intervention are:

1 *pluralism* (a circumscribed state influence in a fragmented and decentralized political economy such as the USA and the UK);
2 *societal corporatism* of the so-called corporatist democracies (in which centralized or moderately centralized governments reach agreements with strongly organized and usually centralized interest groups such as Austria and Sweden);
3 *state corporatism* (where strongly interventionist governments are unchecked by independent organizations of labour, for example in Franco's Spain).

The establishment and maintenance of pluralist industrial relations institutions is fostered by: (1) a wider culture in which there is an enduring commitment to 'freedom of association' and a 'moral duty' to seek compromises and concessions; (2) broad ideologies which are in opposition to monist forms of government and in which consensus is seen to rest on deeply rooted political beliefs and not on the performance or output of the system; (3) an economic structure which has evolved from a pronounced *laissez-faire* stage; (4) a democratic political structure comprised of a two- or multi-party system; (5) countervailing powers amongst the other actors in the industrial relations system (the independent strength of labour being vital); and (6) at an institutional level, the durability of collective bargaining institutions and willingness, by managements in particular, to recognize and to bargain in good faith with representatives of labour.

Corporatism in industrial relations is a common form of state role in countries in which governments have always been active in economic planning. It is also nurtured by a commitment to harmony and identity of interests at a cultural or ideological level, reflected in a range of ethical and political philosophies that include Catholicism, Conservatism and Social Democracy. Societal corporatism is the logical outcome of powerful, centrally organized interest groups and of open competitive political systems. By contrast, state corporatism is facilitated by the concentration of powers in government, monopoly forms of capital, the absence of independent association of labour, and political systems with a single party.

In the erstwhile eastern bloc there were once pronounced variations in the state's role in industrial relations, encapsulated in the divergent experiences of command systems and market systems. But in all cases, the patterns of industrial relations were affected by single-party government and by the public ownership of the means of production, ensuring the absence of an independent body of employers and a largely integrative function for trade unions.

In developing societies the role of the state in industrial relations is almost invariably substantial, suggesting that the divergencies amongst nations stem in part from the timing of industrialism. Thus, in the predominantly corporatist countries of the Third World, *laissez-faire* policies in the economy and in industrial relations were seldom considered (as in Latin America). Moreover, in the developing socialist nations (for example China), planning ensures that the state's impact is more substantial than at a comparable stage of industrialism in the west.

It was once assumed that the state would not wither away but would become more important globally as governments intervened both in the economy and in the resolution of labour disputes. But if anything, what appears now to be the case is a trend towards an increasingly legalized form of industrial relations but a diminishing coordinating state role overall. Moreover, privatization has curtailed the state role and diminished the saliency of national-level collective bargaining.

3 Major themes in industrial relations

Industrial conflict

Turning now to examine some of the ascendent themes of industrial relations, conflict in the employment relationship (and attempts to explain its incidence and variations and to develop channels to accommodate it) are basic to the rationale of industrial relations. The systems analyst views conflict as ubiquitous, but ultimately as a form of deviant behaviour, and hence focuses upon rule-making processes for tension management and grievance resolution. Pluralists and Marxists see it as endemic in industrial societies with substantial private sectors (the former stress interest-group divisions and the latter the cleavages based on social class).

Conflict, however, is multidimensional and includes *qualitative* dimensions (for example expressions of hostility) as well as *quantitative* dimensions (for example strike activity). Moreover, strikes themselves are not homogeneous events. They involve a cessation of work, a breakdown in the flow of consent and an open expression of aggression, and remain a social phenomenon of enormous complexity. Indeed, leaving aside problems of validity and reliability of data the experience of particular countries is by no means consistent on every measure of strike activity. The disparate measures of strikes used in comparative analysis yield four main dimensions:

1 *frequency* (the number of work stoppages in a given unit of analysis over a specified time period);
2 *breadth* (the number of workers who participate in work stoppages);
3 *duration* (the length of stoppages, usually in man-days work lost);
4 *impact* (the number of working days lost through stoppages).

Internationally, the following profiles of strikes have been typically identified.

Type 1: Long duration of stoppages is dominant: characteristic of the USA, Canada and Ireland.
Type 2: Considerable breadth of disputes largely determines overall shape, as exemplified by Italy and to a lesser extent Finland, Spain and Israel.
Type 3: The structure of strikes is determined principally by the relatively high frequency figures: the case for Australia and New Zealand and, to a lesser extent, France and Portugal.
Type 4: A similar ranking in terms of frequency, duration and membership involvement produces the characteristic strike 'shape' of the UK and Japan.
Type 5: A typically low incidence of strike activity, but the duration of the few stoppages is not insignificant: characteristic of Belgium, Denmark, The Netherlands, Norway and Sweden.

Explanations for variations in conflict include culture, political and economic conditions, the strategies of management and industrial relations institutions. Culture, for instance, has been used to explain varied conflict patterns in the Third World with the commitment to harmony in neo-Confucian countries in part accounting for a low incidence of strike activity. Political conditions have usually been linked with the low levels of conflict in the Social Democracies of northern Europe where historical compromises between employers, labour and the state have been isolated as central to relative industrial democracy.

Economic variables such as inflation are seen as enhancing conflict, while high levels of unemployment tend to reduce it. Authoritarian management styles are also seen as likely to enhance conflict. Finally, institutionalists see the level of collective bargaining as crucial with national collective bargaining tending to be associated with low levels of conflict and highly fragmented, decentralized labour–management agreements being viewed as conducive to it. Moreover, for the most part the 1980s and early 1990s witnessed a reduction in the incidence of conflict in most countries of the West (because of changes in legislation, higher levels of unemployment, weakened labour movements and better procedures for resolving disputes).

In the erstwhile eastern bloc, however, strikes were once relatively rare (conflict typically was expressed in terms of protests and high rates of absenteeism and poor workmanship), though this situation has now changed considerably (Martin and Cristesco-Martin 1999). The Third World revealed (and still reveals) a varied incidence of strike activity (relatively high in India and the Caribbean; very low in east Asia amongst the 'little dragons' such as Taiwan and South Korea), the explanations being linked with culture, the degree of radicalization of labour movements and divergent management styles.

Industrial democracy

During the twentieth century few issues have been more consequential in debates on industrial relations than industrial democracy. The term usually encapsulates the notion of the exercise of power by workers and their representatives over decisions within their place of employment, coupled with a modification of the distribution of authority within the workplaces. For the Webbs, it will be recalled, it was to be rooted in the institutions and processes of collective bargaining. Increasingly it has proved to be conceptually valuable to distinguish economic and industrial democracy and to attempt a synthesis of the two terms in an inclusive theory of organizational democracy. Economic democracy denotes a variety of forms of employee participation in the ownership enterprises in which they are employed and in the distribution of economic rewards. Conditions which favour the growth of industrial democracy may also facilitate economic democracy but the two developments are not invariably co-terminous.

A classification of the main types of industrial democracy encompasses:

1 workers' self-management (as in the old Yugoslavia);
2 producer cooperatives (as at Mondragón);
3 co-determination (as in Germany);
4 works councils and similar institutions (as in Germany and The Netherlands);
5 trade union initiatives (as in the UK);
6 shop-floor programmes (as in Sweden and the USA).

Globally, each of these main types has distinctive defining characteristics, internal structural properties and range of incidence.

With respect to the explanations for the development of industrial democracy, however, three main approaches have been dominant based on the notions listed below:

- favourable conjunctures
- evolutionary forces
- cycles.

The favourable conjunctures approach involves the isolation of underlying factors which account for the rise of industrial democracy; but it does not assume the inevitability of either so-called evolutionary or cyclical movements in its development. By contrast, evolutionary thinkers have argued that the state and the legislature have increasingly influenced moves towards organizational democracy. In their view, this has arisen in part because of a determination to regulate industrial relations, but also because of the electoral consequences of governments failing to secure labour peace by means of the active participation of the workforce in ownership and control of the enterprise. It is also argued that modern managers are likely to be well versed in human resourcing techniques that promote employee influence and involvement. However, in the early 1980s, a cyclical interpretation of organizational democracy gained increasing currency. Under this view, the idea that there are long-term movements in modern societies which consistently favour the advance of industrial democracy is disputed. Developments in industrial democracy are viewed as neither radical nor irreversible; and a high failure rate can be explained by the search for consensus coming up against the reality of conflict between the industrial relations parties. Increasingly, there has been the focus on the analysis of micro-situations to highlight the complex patterns which occur in reality and, in the advanced European researches of the Industrial Democracy in Europe International Research Group, on the patterns of influence and power distribution from one country to the next.

The case for industrial democracy (organizational participation) has been supported by three broad arguments (humanistic, power sharing and organizational efficiency) (Heller et al. 1998). The last mentioned argument has been deployed, from the mid-1990s onwards, in a series of studies on the links between employee participation and high performance work organizations. Above all, the growth of work teams, financial participation and decision-making involvement has been seen to be linked with both the industrial relations and the financial performance of firms.

The distribution of economic rewards

The distribution of economic rewards has always been a major source of conflict within industrial relations and a key theme within the literature itself. Much of *labour* economics has been associated with labour markets and their imperfections and this strand within industrial relations thinking has seen a resurgence associated with the decline of institutional machinery for collective bargaining for reaching agreements on pay and associated issues occurring in many countries in the 1980s and early 1990s (see LABOUR MARKETS).

The theory of human capital has been particularly influential within debates on labour economics and in its contribution to the analysis of industrial relations issues. The basic concept of human capital implies that those who have been trained have incurred a foregone earnings loss. However, their productivity will have increased also which enables them to be paid more assuming that earnings equal marginal product. Moreover, human capital theory implies that rates of return on human and physical capital will be broadly comparable, an argument which is used not only to support increasing investment in education and skills acquisition within industry, but also to persuade governments to invest in their people in this way. There is a convergence between human capital theory and modern versions of human resource development in these respects.

Furthermore, there is a long tradition of economic analysis of trade unions viewing these organizations as attempting to maximize a 'utility function', with a focus on wages and employment. However, it should be said that union behaviour is in actuality shaped by a complicated pattern of interdependent relations and unions are clearly not just market bargainers but have a range of political and social objectives.

Typically trade union members do have an income advantage over non-union members and low dispersal of income is generally correlated with trade union density (as in the Scandinavian countries). Furthermore, the power of the state is important. If incomes policies are in operation, typically dispersal of incomes is reduced as a consequence of the narrowing of differentials. But the late 1980s and 1990s have typically seen a spread of differentials in the advanced economies associated with the substantially greater role for markets and the declining power of trade union movements (Baglioni and Crouch 1991).

In so far as comparative analyses of the distribution of economic rewards is concerned a range of cultural, political and economic conditions affect the varying patterns which occur. Broadly speaking, accompanying economic development, income inequality tends first to increase and then substantially to diminish over time. In many Third World countries income dispersal is affected by the penetration of multinational companies and by dualism in labour markets (as in Kenya and Brazil).

Increasingly, there has been a focus on the so-called 'new pay'. This is based on the notion of the 'fit' between rewards and the strategy of the firm, flexibility and variability of pay systems and unitarism in the decision-making processes whereby rewards are determined. Performance related pay, pay for skill and competencies, and for innovation and creativity are also emphasized as firms have had to become increasingly competitive in open markets where the trend towards globalization is ever more pervasive.

4 Emergent issues in industrial relations

So far we have examined various theories of industrial relations (and particularly those focused on comparative analysis) together with the historical origins of the discipline and the main areas of coverage of the subject. At this point some emergent themes are assessed, with the focus on seven areas:

- new technology
- Japanization
- 'new' realism
- human resource management strategies
- privatization and the transformation of eastern Europe
- internationalization
- flexibility

New technology

Technology has been viewed as a key determinant of industrial relations but for much of the time it has been analysed in a deterministic and ahistorical framework. But the rise of new technologies (associated with the microelectronics revolution) has in part been the stimulus for new debates on the impact of technology. These have increasingly encompassed the notion of choice and the ways in which technology offers options from which management, trade unions and governments can select. Moreover, technology has been seen to link with broader product and market strategies and not as a force independent of social institutions.

The early debates on new technology have also been enriched by labour process theory. The origins can be traced to Braverman's *Labor and Monopoly Capital* (1974) in which new technologies were seen to be associated with the relentless tightening of managerial control and the consequent 'de-skilling' and 'degradation of work'. However, opponents of this view have focused on its deterministic character, the under-emphasis of worker resistance and the ways in which new skills are constantly thrown up by radical changes in technology. However, from this analysis has arisen a variety of attempts, in both the USA and Europe, to link technology with the organization and control of the labour process that has added an important dimension to earlier analyses.

The effects of new technology have been increasingly analysed and research suggests that upskilling is more common than downskilling, that work with advanced technology entails higher skill demands, that skill is related to gender and that a polarization of skill has occurred. Evolving patterns of flexible working, such as homeworking, have been facilitated by new technologies. Moreover, trade unions have sought new technology agreements but have only occasionally been successful in achieving this end.

Japanization

The emergence of Japan as a leading world power in the latter part of the twentieth century has also been accompanied by an increasing focus on the phenomenon of 'Japanization'. Originally, the analysis tended to focus on industrial relations in Japan itself and typically involved the identification of three main pillars (lifetime employment, enterprise trade unionism and seniority-based payment systems) as crucial. Gradually, however, the tendency not only for Japanese firms operating outside Japan but also for other firms to emulate Japanese practices has stimulated fresh analyses and debates.

The first of these has been associated with the notion of the strategic management of the 'human resource' informed by company and country culture. This, in turn, has been seen to link with a range of more specific practices such as total quality management, quality circles, just-in-time, flexibility, direct employee communications, single status facilities, single union deals and team briefing. Critics of Japanization have argued that these practices are not all easily traceable to Japanese conditions (and that some practices indeed were imported from the USA); that many practices do not easily take root in different cultural and institutional conditions; and that practices in Japan are not static and immutable but are subject to considerable change over time. Indeed, debates have increasingly shifted to encompass east Asian countries (the little dragons) more generally as a consequence of the economic expansion of the whole of this geopolitical region.

Moreover, the downturn in the Japanese economy in the 1990s did suggest some evidence of a reverse pattern of convergence. The lifetime employment system was seen as increasingly subject to erosion (it had, in any case, only applied to a minority of Japan's working population). Internal labour markets were seen as being replaced by the enlargement of related internal labour markets and flexible job categories and a variety of employment contracts appear to have been emerging.

'New' realism

In part associated with the phenomenon of Japanization has been the focus on new realism and new strategies for labour movements. Accompanying a significant decline in trade union membership in most advanced western economies there has been a major rethink of labour strategies in many countries. Even so-called traditional unions have turned away from a reliance on voluntarism and collective bargaining and have increasingly sought legal protection. Moreover, unions operating on the basis of a new realism in countries such as the UK have, in return for recognition, accepted 'no strike clauses', single union agreements and compulsory arbitration.

These debates are familiar in North America where the issue of union membership decline has been a preoccupation for a longer period than in western Europe. Here the case has been articulated for 'associational unionism' including a focus on principles (to advance employee rights generally), the support of increased internal education and participation, multiple forms of representation and service, a wider choice of tactics and extended alliances. Certainly a range of contrasting theoretical and empirical issues have emerged as a consequence of debates on the notion of a long-term decline in labour movements, the reduced importance of collective bargaining and collectivism generally and a far less influential role for trade unions in governmental policy at a national level and in the joint regulation of the employment relationship.

'New' realism is also linked with the notion of 'new' unionism. In order to attempt to redress the decline in membership, unions in a number of countries have moved from a servicing to an organizing concept. For instance, in the UK, the 'Organising Academy' has been formed by the Trade Union Congress (TUC). The organizing model also encourages members to own the campaign to unionize their workplaces.

Human resource management strategies

The enhanced power of managers at enterprise level has led to a range of industrial relations issues being increasingly subsumed under human resource management. Rather than the joint regulation of the employment relationship by unions and management under collective bargaining, increasingly a resurgent management has sought to determine many aspects of pay and working conditions at enterprise level on a unilateral and unitaristic basis, linked with the overall business strategy of the firm and the striving for competitive advantage in the market place.

Human resource management, which involved more strategic approaches to personnel and was the responsibility of all management (particularly general), originated in the USA and arrived in the mid-1980s in the UK and much of Europe. It was associated with changes in the political climate and a reduced power of labour. Its focus on employee involvement and total quality management, on strategic human resource flow policies (including the maintenance of core labour forces), on different reward systems (including performance and profit-related pay, and profit sharing), and new work systems (multi-skilling, multiple roles and job enrichment) represented a radical challenge to many aspects of decision making on the employment relationship.

There have been many controversies on the meaning and compass of human resource management, and above all, on whether it is merely a relabelling of practices rather than the harbinger of fundamental changes in the workplace. Moreover, empirically it is often the case that firms with the greatest evidence of having at least traces of human resource management practices are also more likely to have trade unions (albeit with far less influence over decision making in the employment relationship than was once the case). But in most European countries, and in other countries as well, no issue has been of greater importance to debates in the 1980s and 1990s on the changing nature of industrial relations than the rise of human resource management and the resurgence of managerial power on which this is ultimately based (see Dowling, Welch and Schuler 1999).

Privatization and the transformation of eastern Europe

The global ascendance of markets as a means of resource allocation in the 1980s and 1990s also has had profound consequences for industrial relations. In the West and in many Third World countries there has been extensive privatization and restructuring; a process which has been gaining momentum in a far more fundamental way in eastern Europe.

The advent of privatization (on a large scale) within western Europe has of course ideological roots in political and economic as well as industrial relations assumptions. But in industrial relations terms, in countries such as the UK, the main arguments have been based on the perceived deleterious consequences of the power of unions in the public sector (founded on favourable recognition policies and national collective bargaining agreements), the lack of streamlining of industrial relations, the provision for unilateral arbitration in some procedural agreements, and the lack of responsiveness of pay settlements in the public sector to local, regional and occupational labour markets. Moreover, although the evidence suggests that there have been substantial differences between industries so far as the effects of privatization are concerned, greater flexibility, extensive subcontracting, decentralization of management structures and policies on industrial relations, performance-related pay and profit sharing and employee share ownership have typically emerged from this radical process of change in the ownership of key industries and services (for example in the UK, France and Greece).

But these changes (however dramatic and consequential they may have been) have been dwarfed to some extent by the events in eastern Europe in the 1990s. The upshot of these events is likely to be diverse (although almost inevitably privatization will feature as a major issue). To take some examples: the former German Democratic Republic is likely to witness the extension of West German institutions more or less intact. In that sense, the West German capital labour settlement is likely to be exported and to include works councils, co-determination and a strong legal and institutional basis for trade unionism and collective agreements. On the other hand, the stresses of unification are unlikely to overcome the wider problem of the friction between national modes of regulation and industrial relations and the increasingly internationalized economy which is affecting all European countries. In the various republics which have replaced the old Soviet Union again diversity is to be expected, albeit with greater autonomy for managers at factory level, more independence for trade unions and plant-based organs of worker representation being typical and consequential developments. In Hungary there has been the emergence of independent trade unionism as part of the wider reform process. But, unlike Solidarity in Poland, these are not mass trade union organizations; reform of the existing trade unions has been more typical in countries like Bulgaria and Russia rather than the emergence of radically different trade union movements.

The situation in eastern Europe is volatile and far from static. The speed of institutional change slackened from the late 1990s. Industrial conflict increased and overall economic performance differed between the central and eastern European countries. It is clear that collective bargaining has only partially developed and overall trade unionism has declined. In firms with unions, managers have continued to recognize them, but increasingly foreign and private firms are not recognizing trade unions (Martin and Cristesco-Martin 1999).

Internationalization

A further dominant tendency in industrial relations in the latter part of the twentieth and into the twenty-first century is the internationalization of markets, production, knowledge and institutions. In respect of industrial relations there have been in any event a series of International Labour Organization (ILO) standards, and indeed its conventions and recommendations are a major source of labour law. Employers' organizations (such as the Union of Industrial and Employers' Confederations of Europe (UNICE)) have developed internationally. And there are three main international federations of trade unions – the International Confederation of Free Trade Unions (ICFTU), the World Federation of Trade Unions (WFTU) and the World Confederation of Labour (WCL). But the modern development of internationalization has not only been enhanced by the spread of knowledge that enables, say, managements to introduce practices developed originally in a different national context (the spread of Japanese practices being an obvious example), but by the growth of geopolitical groupings such as the EC.

In particular, the single European market is likely to impact on industrial relations in member states in a variety of different ways. The development of a single market is linked with the social dimension which covers diverse aspects of the employment relationship such as safety and health, working hours and remuneration. Its effects are likely to be considerable on both institutions and outcomes in member states though harmonization is in practice likely to be uneven. Furthermore, there are the models for the European company and the European works council proposals, even though uneven patterns of development are probable in practice. Centralized pay bargaining is however unlikely and given that the current gender pay differentials appear to depend on the degree of fragmentation of bargaining (being narrower in more centralized bargaining systems) any trend towards decentralization of bargaining (and the erosion of national institutions) may lead to greater convergence but bring about greater rather than lesser inequality.

The rise of the MNE is also of signal importance to industrial relations. Part of this stems from the deployment of common human resource management philosophies and policies in some companies (for example IBM, McDonald's). But, in any event, in their search for productivity and quality improvements, MNEs increasingly seek to win agreements in local bargaining. These operations tend thus to undermine national and regional collective agreements and, in the Third World, to occasion as well as to reinforce segmentation in labour markets. Moreover, and not surprisingly, international union organizations such as the ICFTU have the activities of MNEs high on the agenda of their emerging action strategies.

Theoretically, too, multinational enterprises have been seen to dilute the very notion of national systems of industrial relations. In regard to unions, they have so-called 'industrial relations scale economies' that give them a variety of production and location options. Moreover the lack of hard financial information relating to multinational subsidiaries makes effective trade union bargaining extremely difficult. In response, a variety of trade union federations have formed globally and a series of international labour standards have become increasingly important issues for industrial relations.

Flexibility

The ascendance of market over planned systems is intimately linked with the further issue of flexibility. This encompasses a number of arrangements such as numerical flexibility (where the peripheral rather than the core labour force adapts to the varying labour requirements of the enterprise); functional flexibility (where the core labour force becomes more flexible, multi-skilled and eschews traditional demarcation) and financial flexibility (where the reward and pay systems are flexible, for example by means of profit-related pay or profit sharing). None the less comparative research on these issues suggests a major rethinking of these categories is necessary. Employers in practice develop strategies in an ad hoc and incremental fashion and there are configurations rather than either/or choices that are informed by business objectives but which also integrate specific social and national factors.

But the flexibility debate is important in the further respect of highlighting potential future scenarios for industrial relations. First of all, the changing sociopolitical environment which fosters flexibility clearly impacts critically on industrial relations elements such as the influence and role of trade unions and the extent and scope of collective bargaining. Above all, however, it is associated with new (or arguably very old) employment patterns with legislature based on radically overturning bargained job or employment security and protection. The outcomes include short-term contracts, radical alterations to patterns of working time, pay flexibility and job content flexibility. The outcome of this is that in modern discussions, the future often is viewed no longer in terms of an alternative industrial relations system built around human resource management and a heightened managerial prerogative. Rather, what may increasingly emerge are non-union enterprises with very little organized industrial conflict; high labour turnover and industrial injuries; more performance-related and merit pay; little interest in job evaluation; high pay differentials; extensive use of freelance and transitory labour; the resort to compulsory redundancy as a means of reducing a labour force; limited use of formal grievance procedures; limited use of consultative committees or employee health and safety representatives; and limited information for employees (Cully *et al.* 1999).

Indeed, the issue of flexible labour has gradually assumed greater prominence. Rather than being confined to part-time and temporary workers and selfemployment, it is now envisaged as encompassing such activities as freelancing, outsourcing, homeworking, teleworking and many other types of non-standard employment. These have arisen for a variety of reasons but the most important forces appear to be globalization, the opening of markets, the focus on consumer rather than producer interests and the rise of new technologies. Conceptually too, this has been associated with a move from Fordist to post-Fordist organizations on an international basis (see Felstead and Jewson 1999). Moreover, from an industrial relations standpoint, the concerns about insecurity at work have been articulated in a range of studies (see Heery and Salmon 2000).

In short, one scenario for the future is the flexible non-union firm, the insecure workforce and the end of institutional industrial relations as it emerged in the West over a century of struggle. Moreover, although globally the outcomes are unlikely to be quite so stark, it remains a likely outcome of the modern trend towards globalization of production and markets. Nevertheless, divergent as well as convergent forces are unmistakeable in a cross-national context and, for this reason, major transformations in political and economic systems are unlikely to produce an identity of outcomes and will ensure that the considerable variations in industrial relations systems which still characterize global experience are likely to continue well into the twenty-first century.

MICHAEL POOLE
CARDIFF BUSINESS SCHOOL

Further reading

(References cited in the text marked *)

* Adams, R.J. and Meltz, N.H. (eds) (1993) *Industrial Relations Theory: Its Nature, Scope and Pedagogy*, Metuchen, NJ: IMLR Press/Rutgers University and the Scarecrow Press Inc. (An assessment of various approaches to a range of theories of industrial relations. Covers the teaching of industrial relations theory, the nature and scope of the subject.)
* Baglioni, G. and Crouch, C. (eds) (1991) *European Industrial Relations*, London: Sage Publications. (Covers some of the major changes in European industrial relations occasioned by the new political and economic conditions of the 1980s; an important source of analysis and debate.)
* Braverman, H. (1974) *Labor and Monopoly Capital*, New York: Monthly Review Press. (This is a formative work arguing for a de-skilling of work as a result of technological changes and the developments within capitalist society.)
* Clegg, H.A. (1976) *Trade Unionism under Collective Bargaining*, Oxford: Blackwell. (An important comparative work analysing the factors explaining variations in trade unionism and collective bargaining in selected Western industrial societies.)
* Cully, M., Woodland, S., O'Reilly, A. and Dix, G. (1999) *Britain at Work*, London: Routledge. (Present the latest data from the 1998 Workplace Employee Relations Survey.)
* Dowling, P.J., Welch, D.E. and Schuler, R.S. (1999) *International Human Resource*

Management, Cincinatti, OH: South Western College Publishing ITP. (Examines industrial relations and human resource management in multinational enterprises.)

* Dunlop, J.T. (1956) *Industrial Relations Systems*, New York: Henry Holt & Co. Inc. (A classic theoretical work outlining the systems approach to industrial relations and establishing the 'content' of the discipline.)

Edwards, P.K. (ed.) (1990) *Industrial Relations: Theory and Practice in Britain*, Oxford: Blackwell. (A valuable, critical and informed overview of the British experience.)

* Felstead, A. and Jewson, N. (1999) *Global Trends in Flexible Labour*, Basingstoke: Macmillan Business. (A good international collection on developments in flexibility and flexible work practices.)

* Fox, A. (1974) *Beyond Contract: Work, Power and Trust Relations*, London: Faber & Faber. (An important and influential work on the evolution of industrial relations thinking in which the notion of 'frames of reference' (unitary, pluralist and radical) are developed.)

* Heery, E. and Salmon, J. (eds) (2000) *The Insecure Workforce*, London: Routledge. (Examines a variety of industrial relations issues associated with the debates on the increasing insecurity of the workforce.)

* Heller, F., Pucik, E., Strauss, G. and Wilpert, B. (1998) *Organisation Participation: Myth or Reality*, Oxford: Oxford University Press. (An excellent book on industrial democracy with a broad international appeal.)

* Kerr, C. (1983) *Future of Industrial Societies*, Cambridge, MA: Harvard University Press. (An update of the classic study, *Industrialism and Industrial Man*. Even more diversity in the world's industrial relations systems are identified.)

* Kerr, C., Dunlop, J.T., Harbison, F. and Myers, C.A. (1960) *Industrialism and Industrial Man*, Cambridge, MA: Harvard University Press. (The foundation work for comparative industrial relations outlining the notions of pluralistic industrialism, convergence and the importance of new technology.)

* Kochan, T.A. (1980) *Collective Bargaining and Industrial Relations*, Homewood, IL: Irwin. (An influential study of industrial relations and collective bargaining in the USA. Broadly defined, it sets the historical background within the development of industrial societies.)

* Kochan, T.A., Katz, H.C. and McKersie, R.B. (1986) *The Transformation of American Industrial Relations*, New York: Basic Books. (After a prolonged period of stability, the US's industrial relations underwent a major transformation which is detailed in this major book.)

* Martin, R. and Cristesco-Martin, A. (1999) 'Industrial relations in transformation: central and eastern Europe in 1998', *Industrial Relations Journal* 30: 387–404. (A good review of developments in industrial relations in Central and Eastern Europe focusing on the varied experiences of the countries involved.)

* Perlman, S. (1928) *Theory of the Labor Movement*, New York: Macmillan. (This is a classic of management studies in which the author argues against the Marxist analysis of trade unionism.)

* Millward, N., Sevens, M., smart, D. and Hawes, W. (1992) *Workplace Industrial Relations in Transition*, Aldershot: Dartmouth Press. (The third of the influential WIRS in the UK; led to major debates on 'end of the institutinal industrial relations' and on the re-emergence of flexible labour markets and employment systems.)

Poole, M. (1986) *Industrial Relations: Origins and Patterns of National Diversity*, London: Routledge. (Attempts to uncover some of the underlying forces (and patterns) of national diversity in industrial relations systems; examples both from the Third World and developed nations.)

Southall, R. (ed.) (1988) *Trade Unions and the New Industrialisation of the Third World*, London: Zed Books. (This is an informed reader covering a variety of aspects of industrial relations in the Third World.)

* Szell, G. (ed.) (1992) *Labour Relations in Transition in Eastern Europe*, Berlin: Walter de Gruyter. (Industrial relations in eastern Europe have been in a state of 'flux' and this is a bold attempt to bring together papers highlighting developments in eastern Europe.)

* Webb, S. and Webb, B. (1902) *The History of Trade Unionism*, London: Longmans Green. (This is a monumental treatise on trade unionism in the UK which is immensely painstaking in its details of the analysis.)

* Webb, S. and Webb, B. (1920) *Industrial Democracy*, London: Longmans Green. (In this classic study the Webbs argue that collective bargaining is the key to industrial democracy.)

* Whitfield, K. and Strauss, G. (2000) 'Methods matter: changes in industrial relations research and their complications'*, British Journal of Industrial Relations* 38: 141–51. (Focuses on industrial relations research methods in this millennium number of the journal.)

See also: LABOUR MARKETS

Skill formation systems

1 The governance of skill formation systems
2 Conclusion: systems and cases

Overview

The formation of vocationally relevant skills is problematic: although skills are used within the market, there are frequently difficulties in producing them through pure market means. A diversity of mechanisms for resolving this problem have been devised, producing a diversity of skill formation systems.

Individuals must make many decisions about acquiring skills when very young, and often neither the individuals nor their parents have the knowledge about the future required to make decisions in an economically rational manner. There are major time lags and risks. Education is expensive and can take many years to complete before there is any return; it is an investment decision. Then, chances of entry into the chosen occupation can be difficult to predict. The skill requirements of occupations also change, further increasing risk. The situation is also problematic for employers. Skills have something of the character of public goods. A firm which trains its employees may find that other firms which do not do so simply recruit the workers it has trained – in the worst case attracting them with higher salaries made possible by the fact that the 'poaching' firms have not borne training costs. Interest therefore focuses on mechanisms which might resolve these information, investment and public goods problems. Research has here been able to draw on a more general literature concerning different forms of governance of economies (Crouch *et al.* 1999).

1 The governance of skill formation systems

According to governance theory, economic transactions are nested in a wider institutional context which provides sanctions to encourage certain kinds of behaviour rather than others. The main types of governance have been identified as a) market, b) hierarchy, c) state, d) association, and e) community. We shall here examine each of these governance institutions, but only in so far as they relate to the question of skill formation.

Market

Within a pure market, decisions over and expenditure on the acquisition of all education would be left entirely in the hands of young people and their parents. In practice this is rarely done; in all but the poorest countries we find state education systems which are both free of charge and compulsory up to a certain age level. Parents might lack the incentive to pay for the education of their children, and might prefer to send them to work to supplement the family income. They could also experience difficulties in assessing the quality of the education their children were receiving. However, in some countries (e.g. the United Kingdom) the market governs general education for the children of wealthy families. The parents of these children are not only rich enough to pay the high costs and to discount the long time horizons of financing their children's education, but also themselves usually come from educated backgrounds and understand in some detail the uses of education.

An alternative mode of relying on the market for the provision of education would be for potential employers to provide and/or fund education for children from a very early age, in the expectation that the children would later work for them. However, firms would have no guarantee that the children, once educated, would in fact supply their future labour to them. As investors in education, employers would also have to accept the risk of supporting a child's education long before they had knowledge of his or her capabilities. There are again some exceptions that show that the model of pure market provision is not absurd.

Some large Swedish firms have recently taken an interest in the development of company schools, which would provide normal secondary education as well as specific skill formation (Crouch et al. 1999: 123). These are usually firms in a labour monopoly position and therefore at less risk from poaching than others; and under the Swedish scheme the state subsidizes the project.

The market becomes really important at later stages, when vocational skill formation takes over from general education. The role of parents becomes smaller, time horizons become shorter, and it becomes easier to determine the aptitudes of the young people concerned. The factors that handicapped the market as a provider of general education diminish, and it becomes easier to envisage it as a major influence on the provision of education.

In a classic contribution, Becker (1962, 1975) argued that in fact the market was all that was necessary for skill formation, because skills consisted of two components: a general one and a firm-specific one. If public provision deals with the former, firms have adequate incentive to provide the latter. The poaching argument does not apply, since by definition a firm-specific skill cannot be transferred to another employer. Therefore, provided firms can pay trainees low enough wages to make the cost of the training worth while, there is no problem of vocational skill formation that the market, building on a public general system, cannot solve.

According to Stevens (1995), Becker's argument ignored the existence of an intermediate kind of skill: those that were too specific to particular work contexts to be provided through general education, but which, even if provided within the framework of an individual firm's working procedures, could be transferred from one firm to another. She called these skills 'transferable', and identified them as a case of market failure. Further, Becker oversimplified the question by focussing on it as the poaching issue alone. There are also problems in inducing young people to bear or share the costs of their skill formation, whether by directly paying fees or by accepting low wages during the training period. The issue is not absolute: many examples can be found of training markets operating in this way, but these are usually explicable in terms of some factor which reduces either the transferable cost problem or the problems of ignorance and uncertainty facing the individuals.

For example, in many countries young people (mainly young women) pay fees to commercial institutions that equip them with office skills. The skills concerned are highly transferable, reducing the willingness of employers to provide them, but the job opportunities that they make available are sufficiently widespread and predictable to give young women the incentive to pay for the courses.

A very different example is provided by certain new high-technology sectors, primarily computing software. Here individuals are regularly responsible for providing their own training, which, in contrast to the acquisition of office skills, can be very expensive. These are well-informed investors, with strong expectations that their investment will pay off after a short time lag. They are already knowledgeable in the field and therefore accurately understand their training needs. The firms for which they work are usually grouped geographically close to each other – as in the Silicon Valley case which has become paradigmatic for this kind of activity – so there is high interaction among both firms and individuals (Saxenian 1994). Knowledge of the labour market, firms' requirements and individuals' capacities are therefore high on all sides. Knowledge of this kind reduces risk, especially in a sector which to date has known only constant expansion. It has even been argued that in this field the usual theories about poaching are reversed, and that the movement of personnel from one firm to another helps advance technical creativity.

Whether the market can operate in this way in sectors lacking these distinctive characteristics is more doubtful. As we shall also see in the later discussion of community governance, it may in fact be argued that the Silicon Valley phenomenon is so underwritten by specific institutional characteristics that it does not constitute a pure market.

Lazonick and O'Sullivan (2000) have criticised Becker's model more profoundly, by questioning the very existence of many 'firm-specific' skills. Their review of the literature on firm-specific human capital found that those characteristics that make skills 'firm specific' have still not been identified, almost four decades after Becker wrote his seminal work. They point out that in Japan skilled manual workers are usually described as 'multiskilled', which is very different from training in distinct 'craft skills' (as has historically been the case for example with British workers). In recent years, German training schemes too have stressed 'polyvalent' skills and adaptability. More generally, argue Lazonick and O'Sullivan, given extensive in-house training and long-term employment relations, it may well be the social tie between employer and employee rather than skill per se which is 'specific'. The Beckerian model assumes that, whether skill is 'general' or 'specific', the only tie between employer and employee is an economic one. At the same time, the social tie may have positive productivity consequences if workers are engaged in a cumulative and collective learning process. This, they point out, is also excluded from the Becker model: there is no theory of why skills, be they 'general' or 'specific', are productive; the Beckerian theory, like neo-classical theory more generally, is about who pays for investment in skills, and even then is inconclusive, both theoretically and empirically.

Hierarchy

As has long been recognized by the theory of the firm, corporations, especially large ones, do not operate by market transactions alone, but also through internal relations of authority, or hierarchy. Sometimes a hierarchy can extend beyond the boundary of the firm itself. Inter-firm hierarchy occurs where large firms develop long-running relations with sub-contractors that are not liable to be disrupted by market fluctuations. Customer firms, for example, may sustain long-term relations with suppliers, or a manufacturing firm with distributors. It is a pattern particularly associated with the Japanese economy.

The hierarchy model is very important for skills provision (Crouch *et al.* 1999: chapter 7). Large corporations are frequently labour monopsonists. Such firms are however unlikely to pay lower wages than those in competitive labour markets, as conventional monopsony theory would suggest. Indeed, their cumulated competitive advantages enable them to pay wages to workers in local labour markets that are *above* the competitive market wages. These high wages can in turn elicit greater productivity from employees that can sustain the higher wages of these employees over time. In that case they have little fear of poaching and may well provide extensive training services. The skills transmitted may in principle be transferable, but the firm's position makes them equivalent to specific skills. Sometimes there will be small firms in the area, which will depend parasitically on recruiting persons trained by the large firm. However, provided these other firms are small enough and few enough, it is of little concern to the large firm, constituting merely a trickle of waste and not a challenge to its dominance. Sometimes these small firms may be suppliers to the large one, in which case the latter positively gains from the fact that the former are using staff which it had trained. In the case of the large firm with stable relationships with suppliers or distributors, it may even organize such training as part of its means of sustaining quality within its value chain.

This model solves most of the normal problems of vocational training. The collective goods aspects which cause problems for market provision either become private goods within the enterprise or club goods within the supplier or distributor chain. As such, it is a model found very widely wherever there are large firms. The Japanese case is exceptional, in that so much industrial production is based on firms of this type. It is notable that the Japanese formal education system has virtually no vocational component at all. Young people leave either high school or higher education with an entirely general formation. Firms recruit them on the basis of their examination achievements (as well as some informal personal criteria), and then train them, and subsequently retrain them over the years, for vocational tasks. But these Japanese employees are usually deemed to be 'multiskilled' rather than trained for specific vocational or craft functions. However, this does not make these firms vulnerable to the loss of workers to whom they have imparted transferable skills, as identified by Stevens (1995), because there is almost no transfer among the large Japanese firms; skilled individuals at all levels rarely leave the firm with whom they started their careers. Similar examples may be found, though less frequently than in Japan, among large firms in virtually all countries which cultivate long-term identities and corporate cultures linked to long-service employment. Although Becker's model seems to follow the rationale of pure markets, it in fact seems more applicable within the hierarchy model.

Hierarchy is of course of little help in sectors dominated by small firms, unless these work for customer firms which integrate suppliers. It therefore flourishes in situations of imperfect competition. While neo-classical economic theory has difficulty in accounting for dynamism and efficiency in firms having these characteristics, studies of business management in the Schumpeterian tradition have identified many ways in which such firms do in fact pursue growth paths that establish new standards of efficiency – their capacity to invest strongly in skill formation being an important aspect of this (Lazonick 1991; Lazonick and O'Sullivan 2000). (See DYNAMIC CAPABILITIES, PENROSE, E.T., SCHUMPETER, J.)

State

The most straightforward answer found in advanced societies to the problem of collective goods is provision by the state, which can use its authority either to provide them directly (funding them by taxation or other levies) or to require their provision by other entities. Not surprisingly, the state has played a major role in the provision of skill formation. In the purest cases (found, for example, in France and Sweden), vocationally relevant courses are provided as branches of the state education system (Crouch *et al.* 1999: chapter 4). Most state education systems provide general education for the majority of children until the end of the compulsory stage (nowadays around 15 or 16), with continuing general (or academic) education for those likely to proceed to higher education or enter occupations requiring advanced literacy and numerical skills. Under a system of state-provided vocational skill formation a far higher proportion of the age range continues within the school system until about age 18, but taking a diversity of vocationally related courses rather than general ones. More generally, state provision also exists for certain occupations in systems that are not generally dominated by the model: for example, the training of medical practitioners.

Direct state provision is in some respects the mirror image of market provision: they have opposite advantages and defects. If public provision scores over the market in its unproblematic solution of collective goods problems, it loses in often being remote from firms' needs. There is a constant need to bridge the gap between teachers in the training schools and employers. One solution, found very generally but particularly evident in the case of Sweden, is to have representatives of the industry concerned on the bodies which amend curriculum, set standards and regulate examinations. A second possibility is to have young people spend part of their training time working in firms (a French system known as *alternance*). Such solutions still have defects. One is the problem of deciding with which firms the public system should cooperate, to put representatives on boards or to provide placements; errors in selection based on lack of knowledge of the leading firms could lead to training being based on inadequate models.

A further issue concerns the difference between initial and further training. This distinction was not a problem in the pure hierarchy case, where, once one can assume stable long-term employment and supplier relations, it is in the large firm's interests to sustain levels of competence in the long run. Within the market form it presents the same problems as does initial training. The state can provide some good solutions to initial training, but has particular problems with further training. Further training needs are often firm-specific, but even if they are not it is difficult for public authorities to provide courses for skills upgrading for people already with careers.

The state has certain means for tackling the problem. Institutions such as distance-learning universities have been extremely useful for people seeking a change of career. Another device, again pioneered in France, is to provide a system of training levies (Aventur and Brochier 1996). Firms pay a compulsory charge which finances a state system of adult courses but can avoid the levy by providing courses themselves. Clearly they have an incentive to do the latter, since in that way they can provide courses devised by themselves. The French government has found this mechanism useful in securing an upgrading of the skills of the existing work force. There are however disadvantages: how does a government agency know which skills it is worth developing? How does it evaluate the quality of internal training provided primarily to avoid paying a levy?

Association

A mechanism that has one foot in the collective-good capacity of public authority and the other close to firm's needs is a skill formation system based on associations of firms. If an association has authority over its members it acquires something of the stature of the state. If it remains close to its members it solves the problem of remoteness common to public agencies. Associational systems can function alongside state provision: for example, one solution to the problem of recruiting employer representatives to assist public agencies is to delegate the task to associations.

Associational governance is particularly suited to the management of apprenticeships, one of the most prominent forms of skill formation (Crouch *et al.* 1999: ch. 5). Emerging out of medieval systems of craft training, it has adapted to the growth of large-scale industry and a growing diversity of services. It requires detailed co-operation between the public education system and associations which manage the contribution of firms without simply seeking advantages for individual companies, for instance the case where the state seeks direct partnerships with corporations rather than representative bodies.

Apprenticeship systems exist for various occupations in many countries, especially for highly skilled manual crafts. In Germany, Austria, and a small number of other countries it is more extensive and has become the main system of skill formation. In Germany and Austria these associations are not straightforward private organizations of employers but official chambers. These are representative bodies, democratically accountable to their member firms, but having public status. Membership in these associations is compulsory and they are financed through compulsory levies. They therefore exist in a space between the state and private associations. As such, they can have public tasks delegated to them. Many of the successes in German industry have been attributed to its apprenticeship system, though in recent years it has come under some strain (Backes-Gellner 1996; Büchtmann and Verdier 1998; Wagner 1998). It is a high-cost system, and German employers complain that they are suffering from a burden not carried by their competitors in countries which neglect skills provision and that the officers of some chambers are not close enough linked to industry at a time of rapid change. Finally, although the system has demonstrated its capacity to move into many services sectors, it can be slow to adopt new activities.

To date, these problems have not undermined the apprenticeship system as such, but they have been important at a different point. Like the state skill formation systems with which they are in fact integrated, apprenticeship schemes operate at the initial training stage. In principle they could be extended into partnerships between chambers and the formal education system at further training levels, but in practice this has never been the case (Sauter 1996). Now that further training has become so important, firms have taken the opportunity to stress their determination to place it outside the framework of apprenticeship. Instead it operates through corporate hierarchies, mainly therefore among large firms only. This could have the consequence of leaving the apprenticeship model to deal only with a static initial training, while all innovation is dealt with within firms at a higher training level.

Community

Claims that formal associations might lose touch with firms have directed attention to a final possible form of governance, the informal local community. Under the community model informal relations of reciprocity and the possibilities for behaviour control afforded by a local community enforces a production of collective goods on small and medium-sized enterprises (SMEs) (Crouch *et al.* 1999: chapter 6).

Within an advanced economy, relations of this kind are found only in specialized areas and sectors. Localities may have pre-existing traditions of cooperation and solidarity. These in turn will have made possible local production systems, where many SMEs sharing similar specializations are concentrated. These thrive in an advanced economy in sectors where there are competitive gains from interaction, mainly because of a capacity to advance knowledge ahead of its codification (so-called tacit knowledge). These include those where innovative design is required to stay abreast of fashion (clothing, footwear, jewellery), those which benefit from close relations between customers and suppliers (both supplier chains and specialized machinery producers), and those dependent on scientific advance (computer software, high-tech science industries), or other forms of knowledge (financial sector, publishing).

The most closely studied cases of this phenomenon are the local production systems of central and north-east Italy (Becattini 2000). A similar outcome can however be generated by other means. For example, in Germany, and parts of the UK and the USA, research oriented universities and research centres, rather than traditional communities, can provide the focus for concentration on specialisms. Interfirm interaction will develop from this, though it is unlikely that a community as such will emerge; the research centre or university remains the focal point for collective goods provision.

Skill formation can be among the collective goods provided in such an environment, since the required control mechanisms exist. However, with the exception of university-based systems, the training provided is often highly informal, uncertified, possibly even unnoticed. There will also be little recognizable distinction between initial and subsequent training. Indeed, in all knowledge- and innovation-based industries, including those based on university research, it becomes impossible to distinguish between further training and simply doing the job. A dress designer or applied scientist is constantly expanding her knowledge base, simply by working.

The creative community therefore represents a skill formation system where most of the distinctions that are normally crucial to the discussion of this topic break down: if the community is strong enough, the distinction between collective and private goods breaks down; distinctions between levels of training disappear; even that between training and the job itself, and therefore that between the school and the market. This has the advantages of extreme flexibility. However, as with the other systems, the strengths of the form are also its weaknesses. The Italian districts mentioned have difficulty in progressing to more advanced kinds of skill and applications of technology. Levels of formal education among Italian entrepreneurs are low. Indeed, measured by formal qualifications the prosperous districts of central Italy are considerably 'behind' the economically backward south of the country. Small enterprises employ young people who leave the education system without completing courses, and train them in vocationally relevant skills. This provides a disincentive to young people in these regions to remain in education, limiting the country's ability to excel in high-tech industries.

But this case raises a fundamental issue. Central and north-eastern Italy continue to do well in those sectors where the flexible, informal knowledge they have brings advantages. Is this a defect? From the point of view of the methodology of skill formation research, the answer is 'yes'. The starting point of this research is always formal educational qualifications. Informally acquired knowledge, however rich, counts for nothing. In terms of the value of knowledge for economic innovation, this is clearly false. This is true, not only for a Tuscan entrepreneur successfully designing shoes, but also for a Silicon Valley software specialist whose PhD tells us little about his most recent achievements in knowledge and skill acquisition. Meanwhile, many young people are today extending their formal education but finding that this does not necessarily help them find work (Béduwé and Espinasse 1995).

2 Conclusion: systems and cases

The five forms of skill formation system outlined above should not be regarded as a series of empty boxes to which individual national or other examples can be assigned. 'Does Germany count as statist or associationist?' is not a sensible question. Empirical examples, certainly if these are examined at national levels, will almost always comprise mixes. We can see that this is likely to be true when we consider that each theoretical form has weaknesses that are the obverse of its strengths. It is through the balancing of characteristics from a mix of types that it is possible to avoid the consequences of this. This should not be interpreted in a functionalist way: there is no necessary reason why actors in a particular system will have produced an optimal mix; and in any case the strengths and weaknesses of particular forms and mixes of forms will vary with time and circumstance.

But the fact of empirical mixing remains important. Very few of the cases which have been referred to above are absolute, even though they are cited because they provide clear examples of specific forms. High-tech districts such as Silicon Valley are a combination of market- and community-driven forms. The Swedish state system draws on both large-firm hierarchy and associations. Although the German system makes particularly strong use of associations, they are associations of a statist kind. The Italian industrial districts are increasingly using the hierarchy of the large firm's supplier chain to keep abreast of product innovation and marketing.

The fact that the various types of system appear in varied combinations produces considerable diversity at national and other levels. These differences in turn are likely to be associated with different performance capabilities at the level of products, markets, sizes of firm and forms of organization (Lazonick and O'Sullivan 2000; Juergens 2000; Freyssenet et al. 1998).

COLIN CROUCH
EUROPEAN UNIVERSITY INSTITUTE

Further reading

(References cited in the text marked *)

* Aventur, F. and Brochier, D. (1996), 'Continuing vocational training in France' in J. Brandsma et al. (eds), *Continuing Vocational Training: Europe, Japan and the US*, Utrecht: Uitgeverij Lemma. (Discussion of French approaches to the issue of further training.)
* Becattini, G. (2000) *Il Distretto Industriale*, Turin: Rosenberg and Sellier. (A state of the art account of the Italian industrial district model by one of its leading analysts.)
* Backes-Gellner, U. (1996) *Betriebliche Bildungs- und Wettbewerbungsstrategien im deutsch-britischen Vergleich*, Munich: Rainer Ham. (Comparison of British, German and some other skill-formation systems from an institutional economics perspective.)
* Becker, G. S. (1962, 1975) *Human Capital: A Theoretical and Empirical Analysis, with Special Reference to Education*, 1st edn 1962, 2nd edn 1975, New York: Columbia University Press. (A locus classicus for a neo-classical account of skills.)
* Béduwé, C. and Espinasse, J.-M. (1995), 'France: politique éducative, amélioration des competences et absorption des diplômés par l'économie', *Sociologie du Travail* 37 (4): 527–54. (Account of problems faced by young French people following a major expansion of education.)
  Brandsma, J., Kessler, F. and Münch, J. (eds) (1996) *Continuing Vocational Training: Europe, Japan and the US*, Utrecht: Uitgeverij Lemma. (A country-by-country survey of further training in major industrial economies.)
* Büchtemann, C.F. and Verdier, E. (1998) 'Education and training regimes', *Revue de l'économie politique* 108 (3): 291–320. (A major analysis of contrasts between French and German skill formation systems.)
* Crouch, C., Finegold, D. and Sako, M. (1999) *Are Skills the Answer? The Political Economy of Skill Creation in Advanced Industrial Countries*, Oxford: Oxford University Press. (An analysis of forms of governance of skill creation systems in seven industrial countries.)
* Freyssenet, M., Mair, A., Shimizu, K. and Volpato, G. (eds) (1998) *One Best Way?: Trajectories and Industrial Models of the World's*

Automobile Producers, Oxford: Oxford University Press. (An important study of comparative work organization.)
* Juergens, U. (ed.) (2000) *New Product Development and Production Networks*, Frankfurt-am-Main: Springer. (An important study of comparative work organization.)
* Lazonick, W. (1991) *Business Organization and the Myth of the Market Economy*, Cambridge: Cambridge University Press. (A critique of the deficiencies of neo-classical theory in the analysis of empirical business organizations.)
* Lazonick, W. and O'Sullivan, M. (2000) *Perspectives on Corporate Governance, Innovation, and Economic Performance*, Report to the European Commission, DGXII, Fontainebleau: INSEAD. (A critical survey of existing models of relations between forms of economic organization and performance, including analyses of skill formation systems.)
  Prais, S.J. (1991) 'Vocational qualifications in Britain and Europe: theory and practice', *National Institute Economic Review* 136. (A comparative study by one of the pioneers of research on skills and training.)
  Regini, M. (ed.) (1996) *La Produzione Sociale delle Risorse Humane*, Bologna: Il Mulino. (Study of skill formation in SMEs in four key European regional economies.)
* Sauter, E. (1996) 'Continuing vocational training in Germany' in J. Brandsma *et al.* (eds), *Continuing Vocational Training: Europe, Japan and the US*, Utrecht: Uitgeverij Lemma. (Discussion of French approaches to the issue of further training.)
* Saxenian, A. (1994) *Regional Advantage: Culture and Competition in Silicon Valley and Route 128*, Cambridge, MA: Harvard University Press. (A study of advanced technology districts in the US economy.)
  Shavit, Y. and Müller, W. (eds) (1997) *From School to Work*, Oxford: Clarendon Press. (A country-by-country statistical analysis of transitions from education to employment in a number of advanced economies.)
* Stevens, M. (1995) 'Transferable training and poaching externalities' in *Acquiring Skills: Market Failures, Their Symptoms and Policy Responses*, Cambridge: The Centre for Economic Policy Research. (A critique of the neo-classical model of skill formation.)
* Wagner, K. (1998) 'Costs and other challenges to the dual system' in D. Finegold and P. Culpeper (eds), *The German Skills Machine in Comparative Perspective*, Oxford: Berghahn Books. (An account of recent problems of the German training system.)

See also: AEROSPACE INDUSTRY; AUTOMOBILES INDUSTRY; CORPORATE CONTROL; DEVELOPMENT AND DIFFUSION OF TECHNOLOGY; DYNAMIC CAPABILITIES; EAST ASIAN ECONOMIES; ECONOMIC GROWTH AND CONVERGENCE; ECONOMY OF JAPAN; EMPLOYMENT RELATIONS; GLOBAL MACHINE TOOL INDUSTRY; GROWTH OF THE FIRM AND NETWORKING; GROWTH THEORY; INDUSTRAL RELATIONS SYSTEMS; INNOVATION; LABOUR MARKETS; MARSHALL, A.; MARX, K.; SMITH, A.; TRUST; VEBLEN, T.; WORKFARE

Workfare

1 History
2 Different policies
3 Neo-classical search theory
4 A gospel for today?
5 The problems of workfare

Overview

The concept 'workfare' is commonly used today by labour market researchers to designate welfare schemes that seek to encourage or even compel people to search for a job rather than to rely on welfare transfers (Heikkilä 1999: 29). Although such schemes have a long history, they have been especially emphasized during the 1990s and have eventually become the leading ideology proposed by the European Commission in its current employment policy programme. According to Robert Solow workfare can generally be regarded as a set of policy 'efforts to … eliminate as far as possible the passive receipt of transfer payments and replace it by a requirement to work, either as conditions for receiving benefits or as total substitute for receiving benefits' (Solow 1998: 6). More specifically, workfare most often refers to policies that introduce work requirements for claimants of public support: that is, claimants will have their benefits reduced or withdrawn if they are not willing to participate in work or training programmes (Heikkilä 1999: 29).

As we will see, workfare schemes are of many different kinds. Moreover, they also have widely different targets. Generally, we can trace two aims of using workfare which have different implications both for the individual and society. First, workfare can be aimed at decreasing the taxpayer's bill for the cost of unemployment relief. In order to achieve this goal the main method proposed is to create incentives for the individual to seek a job by, for example, withdrawing welfare payments or making them less generous. Secondly, workfare schemes can also be aimed at increasing the 'employability' of the individual by means of vocational training, education, on-the-job training, etc. In this case the aim is rather to empower the unemployed person and make him or her more self-sufficient. In the short run, such schemes are costly and may not at all imply lower public spending on unemployment. However, in the longer run they may cut welfare payments by making the welfare recipients less reliant on transfers and more active in searching for a new job.

1 History

Systems for subsidising workers during periods of unemployment are as old as industrial society itself. In the early period, unemployment benefits were most often voluntarily provided by trade unions or other working class organizations. However, gradually during the twentieth century unemployment relief became part of a wide range of welfare programmes pursued by an ever more ambitious welfare state. The first unemployment insurance system was introduced in Great Britain in 1911 and was followed by many others. Perhaps the most influential architect of the modern welfare state – which developed in particular after the Second World War – was William Beveridge. He regarded full employment as the main political objective for the modern welfare state and unemployment benefits as a means to protect workers from income loss during cyclical and frictional periods of unemployment.

It was among northern European nations especially that the state became involved early on in unemployment insurance systems. In most countries today the state is at least involved to some extent in subsidising schemes of unemployment protection. In present day Europe Luxembourg is the only country where unemployment insurance is fully financed by the state, while in a majority of countries employers, employees and the state share the costs in different combinations.

However, unemployment insurance benefits are only one scheme to protect workers from unemployment. More active measures to keep people employed also have a long history in the industrial countries. Hence different forms of public involvement have often been utilized during the nineteenth and twentieth centuries, especially during periods of depression and unemployment crises. During the inter-war period John Maynard Keynes was a keen supporter of state-subsidized public work schemes (see KEYNES, J.M.). However, after the Second World War active measures have been part and parcel of many countries' labour market policies to protect workers from unemployment and make them more employable. Hence, during periods of unemployment, instead of receiving welfare people have been encouraged to acquire vocational training, etc. In this context the active labour market policy of Sweden and other Nordic countries has been of special significance.

2 Different policies

We may distinguish between three types of schemes utilized by modern states to protect workers from the hardships of unemployment: unemployment insurance benefit, additional social assistance and, lastly, active policies (workfare) to make the individual more employable and protect him or her from long-term unemployment or exclusion from the labour market.

Unemployment insurance benefits

Unemployment insurance benefits vary considerably from country to country, especially with regard to how generous they are. Generally, they are intended to compensate for the loss of income which unemployment causes. However, in principle it is possible to distinguish between a system which is based on the principle of income compensation and another which consists of a flat rate. In Europe only Britain and Ireland maintain a flat-rate system, most countries preferring to use a mixture of both systems. Moreover, the duration of benefit payments vary among countries. In certain countries the length of time that benefit will be paid is affected by the length of the previous employment period.

Social assistance

In many countries social assistance is used as a protective measure, especially in cases where unemployment benefits are too small or not available. Hence, social assistance is often used in cases where the limit on the duration time for receiving unemployment relief has been reached or where the individual is an atypical worker and as such has no right to claim unemployment relief. As a consequence of the increase of part-time work and job insecurity during the 1990s, it is generally assumed that the number of the unemployed living on social assistance has increased. A problem for the individual in this context is that social assistance in general is less generous than unemployment benefit. In most countries assistance schemes are financed by the state. Generally they are flat rate and means tested.

Activating measures

Activating measures differ from place to place. Historically these measures have included extensive job training, counselling services, mobility bonuses, public sector relief work, youth programmes, measures for the disabled, vocational training, etc. during which the individual is subsidised. Perhaps the 'ideal type' in this context – as already mentioned – is the active labour market policy pursued in Sweden and other Nordic countries after the Second World War. In 1990 as much as 3 per cent of GDP was spent on government labour market programmes, and this level even increased during the following years when unemployment increased drastically. Certainly, the Nordic active labour market policies served several purposes. In Sweden in particular, its most important function was to bolster the political goal of full employment. Hence, active measures served as means to speed up structural change in the economy, to increase the flexibility of the labour market and create favourable conditions for individuals to find jobs that best suited to them. Another underlying argument was certainly the fact that passive measures such as unemployment benefits and social assistance create lock-in effects and increase the possibility of long-term unemployment and exclusion.

3 Neo-classical search theory

In a general sense, modern labour market economics – as formulated in current job search theory dominated by scholars such as Snower, Layard, Jackman, etc. – favours workfare instead of welfare. Hence, modern labour market search theory emphasizes the 'search effectiveness' of the individual in finding a new job (Layard *et al.* 1991: 216). Moreover, it is often assumed that such 'search effectiveness' has declined during the last decades because job vacancies have not fallen in proportion to the rise of unemployment: 'with more unemployed chasing fewer jobs the number of vacancies would be expected to fall' (Layard *et al.* 1991: 217). The blame for this decline in 'search effectivneness' is mainly put on 'the unemployment benefit regime', that is unemployment benefits and unemployment protection legislation. According to such a view, generous welfare payments – which include employment benefits and social assistance – make the individual less interested in finding a new job. As his or her 'reservation wage' is conditioned by the level of unemployment benefits (plus additional search costs), the availability of unemployment benefits will determine the willingness of the individual to accept a job. Most certainly, a high reservation wage will be an important disincentive to search for work, and will create a rigid labour market characterized by wages that are downward. It is important to note that the reservation wage is not only influenced by the level of unemployment benefit and assistance but also by the possibility that when an individual accepts a new job other social benefits may perhaps be withdrawn. Moreover, if the length of time for which one can remain eligible for unemployment benefits is longer, the reservation wage will be higher. According to the logic of search theory, therefore, we should expect to find that various forms of unemployment benefits serve as disincentives to take a new job. In such cases individuals will be reluctant to take a low paid or less secure job.

The policy implications that follow from this theory are quite straightforward. In order to lower the level of unemployment a better incentive structure must be created which favours an active job search on the part of the unemployed. Among the most important distortions working against such market clearing, Layard *et al.* list the 'benefit system' as well as 'the system of wage determination, where decentralized unions and employers have incentives to set wages in a way that generates involuntary unemployment' (1991: 471). Their main conclusion with regard to increasing the effectiveness of the unemployed is twofold: 'the first is to take a tougher line on benefits, and the second is to offer active help in training and the provision of jobs' (Layard *et al.* 1991: 472).

In many respects, the job search theory model is a useful tool for understanding the realities of the labour market. However, it does not always provide strong empirical proof for its predictions. It is, for example, not self-evident that a steady number of vacancies when unemployment is rising can be explained by the benefit system. Instead this might be a consequence of an increased mismatch on the labour market (lock in) and/or it may be that many individuals in a period of mass unemployment believe it is hopeless trying to find a new job. Moreover, it is also difficult to find strong evidence for the existence of a casual relationship between different unemployment benefit regimes and the level and/or the duration of unemployment. Indeed, Layard *et al.* (1991) have presented data that show that in a number of countries there is a positive correlation between the length of individual unemployment periods and the benefit duration variable. Investigations carried out by the ILO and the European Commission, however, raise doubts about the extent to which the duration of benefit influences unemployment and job search activities. Moreover, when we try to measure the impact of the level of unemployment benefits on unemployment in different countries, it is difficult to find a positive correlation (European Commisson 1995; ILO 1995). As one critical observer, Anthony Atkinson, has pointed out, it is extremely difficult to assess the impact of different unemployment benefit schemes on job search, mainly because of the existence of 'important institutional features of real-world unemployment programs, features that may mitigate the disincentive effects of benefits' (Atkinson 1998: 15f). Hence, an individual may feel that going on to unemployment benefits – although they might be quite generous – is degrading and worse than taking a job with a wage that is lower than his or her implied reservation wage. Moreover, there might be stipulations in the unemployment schemes that are easy to overlook but that mean that in practice it is difficult to refuse a job offer that pays less than the reservation wage (Atkinson 1998: 10).

Moreover, there might be benefits with (generous) unemployment regimes that are less easy to detect and even more difficult to measure. For example, a generous system of remuneration increases the welfare of the individual. However, a regime that does not force an individual to take any job that is available might lead to higher search effectiveness in the sense that it increases the likelihood of an individual finding a 'good job' (for example, in the modern high productivity sector). As Layard and others have shown, one of the most important causes behind the present high unemployment figures in Europe is an apparent mismatch between supply and demand on the labour market (Layard 1999). Hence, in order to obtain a job in the fast growing sector where demand is high, the individual must be prepared to move or to upgrade his or her skills. It is less likely that he or she will take such action if he or she feels that continuing training is prohibitively expensive or that the new job position will not be secure.

Lastly, as argued, to 'take a tougher line on benefits' might not help in a situation where mass unemployment occurs – a situation with which Western Europe has lived since the 1970s. In a situation where the unemployed feel it is more or less hopeless to get a new job (especially relevant for old, low skilled and perhaps also immigrant workers), less welfare will not make them more effective in their job search but rather may lead them to withdraw from the labour market altogether. In such cases the main result might be that the participation rate in the economy is lowered (Freyssinet 1997).

4 A gospel for today?

Although there might be positive effects from generous unemployment benefit transfers and it is difficult to find robust evidence for search theory, the neo-classical perspective on unemployment has won overwhelming political support during the 1990s. For example, in the very influential OECD Job Study report of 1994 – which certainly sought to bolster the credibility of this theory – it is stated:

> Unemployment insurance and related benefit systems were originally designed to provide temporary income support to the unemployed during the process of finding a new job. With the growth of long-term, and repeated unemployment, these systems have drifted towards quasi-permanent income support in many countries, lowering work incentives. To limit disincentive effects – while facilitating labour market adjustments and providing a necessary minimum level of protection – countries should legislate for only moderate levels of benefits, maintain effective checks on eligibility, and guarantee places on active programmes as substitutes for paying passive income support indefinitely. Possibilities should be explored for making the transition from income support to work more financially attractive.
> (OECD 1994: 263f)

In a growing number of countries this view has become accepted as a undoubted truth. In America the welfare policy reform put forward by Bill Clinton in 1997 demonstrated a strong bias for workfare in its emphasis on putting pressure on passive welfare recipients in order that they should be stimulated to search for a job (Solow 1998). Moreover, among European welfare states during the 1990s a *de facto* policy shift can be detected from an emphasis on equity, freedom of choice and security of income towards various combinations of measures to increase the work incentive and to keep people in gainful employment. Hence, in a majority of countries we can detect a strategy to increase the participation rate in the labour market by means of activation measures. For example the Swedish government – with long experience of using measures in the name of an active labour market policy – has launched a plan to increase the labour force participation rate from 75 per cent to 80 per cent (in the 20–64 year age range) up until 2002. Other countries have presented plans of the same kind. In addition, an increase in labour force participation has become a major policy goal of the European Commission. Its common employment strategy, formulated at the Luxembourg summit in 1997, sets a target of increasing the participation rate in the European Union over the next five year period from 70 per cent to 75 per cent.

The main policies proposed to achieve this goal were also presented in the Luxembourg employment policy plan in the form of four pillars. Many of them touch upon the relationship between welfare and work, especially the policy suggestions in the 'employability pillar' section (Foden and Magnusson 1999). Moreover in 1997 a communication, 'Modernizing and improving social protection in the European Union' set forth the general strategy of making social protection more 'employment friendly'. This objective can only be achieved by two means: first, by increasing economic incentives through changes in the tax and social security system in order to increase the taking up of new jobs. Secondly, by activation measures and an active labour market policy. Therefore, the overall concern is to combat unemployment by emphasizing workfare rather than welfare. It is generally assumed that welfare schemes, including unemployment benefits and social assistance, create welfare entrapments and thus disincentives to job search effectiveness (Heikkilä 1999).

5 The problems of workfare

Workfare certainly introduces greater pressure on the welfare recipient, including the claimant of unemployment benefits, and thus also diminishes his/her freedom of choice. However, such measures are largely considered in order to avoid long-term unemployment and even the individual's exit from the long-term market. Hence, as Solow has pointed out there are many arguments that speak in favour of workfare. For one thing, a great deal of a person's identity, dignity and self-respect derives from having a job. Thus to earn one's own living is a sign of independence and as such is greatly heralded in Western culture. Secondly, taxpayers will probably be more willing to give money to welfare recipients if they feel that the unemployed are actively involved in job search and therefore that their 'altruism is not exploited' (Solow 1998: 5)

However, at the same time, there are a number of problems when moving from welfare to workfare. First, if the aim is to radically decrease unemployment and even increase the participation rate by means of workfare schemes, there will be an increased supply of labour on the labour market. If appropriate vacancies are not available, new jobs will have to be created. If this job creation is not possible in the private sector – which will be difficult in the short run – these new jobs must be provided by the public sector. Such public job creation in turn may entail public spending on a level that might cancel out the gains achieved by the decreasing number of welfare recipients.

Secondly, there is a danger that a stark increase in the supply of labour created by the shift from welfare to workfare will mean that, to quote Solow, 'ex-welfare recipients and their successors will drive down the wage for unqualified workers' (Solow 1998: 28). In cases where the purpose of workfare is only or mainly to drive down the level of unemployment benefits or withdraw social assistance, such downward pressure on wages at the low end of the labour market is certainly a most realistic scenario. However, this threat might be mitigated to the extent that workfare includes schemes to upgrade the skills of the individual. There are strong doubts, however, that most workfare schemes thus far suggested really will have such an effect. Moreover, there is a danger that such skills may not be rewarded by a labour market that must absorb a steady increase in the supply of more highly qualified workers.

Thirdly, and most importantly, it is possible that workfare may not be the right method for all unemployed and present recipients of welfare. For a number of people who are disabled, socially or in other ways, from finding and holding employment, cuts in welfare may not serve as an incentive to activate job search. Rather the opposite might happen: namely they may drop out altogether from the labour force. Hence for many persons the present policy of shifting from welfare to workfare may be a real threat, not only to their freedom of choice but also to their general welfare.

LARS MAGNUSSON
UPPSALA UNIVERSITY

Further reading

(References cited in the text marked *)

* Atkinson, A.B. (1998) *The Economic Consequenses of Rolling Back the Welfare State*, Cambridge, MA: MIT Press.
* European Commission (1995) *Social Protection in Europe*, Luxembourg: Office for Official Publications of the European Communities.
* Foden, D. and L. Magnusson (eds) (1999) *Entrepreneurship in the European Employment Strategy*, Brussels: ETUI.
* Freyssinet, J. (1997) 'Unemployment compensation and labour markets: a disincentive to work?', in A. Bosco and M. Hutsebaut (eds) *Social Protection in Europe*, Brussels: ETUI.
* Heikkilä, M. (1999) 'Brief introduction to the topic', Dublin: European Foundation for the Improvement of Living and Working Conditions, Linking Welfare and Work.
* ILO (1995) *World Employment*, Geneva: ILO.
* Layard, R. (1999) *Tackling Unemployment*, Basingstoke: Macmillan.
* Layard, R., S. Nickel and R. Jackman (1991) *Unemployment*, Oxford: Oxford University Press.
* OECD (1994) *Jobs Study: Facts, Analysis, Strategies*, Paris: OECD.
* Solow, R.M. (1998) 'Lecture I and II', in A. Gutman (ed.) *Work and Welfare*, Princeton: Princeton University Press.

See also: KEYNES, J.M.; LABOUR MARKETS

Gender and ethnic divisions in the US labour force

1 Introduction
2 Historical context
3 Current ethnic and gender divisions in the US labour force
4 Challenges for organizations in the future

Overview

Ethnic and gender divisions still exist in the US labour force in ways that cannot be simply explained by differences in education, experience or people's interests. Women and ethnic groups are in very different and unequal places in the labour force (whether assessed by occupation, earnings or employment and unemployment rates) even though there has been some reduction of disparities in the past few decades. The nature of interactions in the workplace and the prevailing organizational culture often perpetuate these divisions in spite of social legislation and organizational policies designed to alleviate them. These inequalities can have adverse effects on the workers, the organizations and the society as a whole. There are continual feedback loops between workplace and societal inequities that maintain both. What can be done to diminish these differences is highly dependent upon how the issues are conceptualized and what factors are considered.

1 Introduction

In this article, we discuss the ethnic and gender divisions that exist in the United States (US) labour force and their importance to business and management. Women and people of all ethnic/racial backgrounds are not distributed across occupations and industrial or service sectors in a pattern similar to that of white men. Considerable disparities continue to exist – inequities that cannot be explained by differences in educational levels, experience or people's interests (Blau *et al*. 1998).

These divisions in the labour force are of increasing importance for business and management for several reasons. First, the US labour force is becoming more diverse – more female and less white. Organizations must therefore address the challenges that a diversifying pool of workers presents. Second, to remain competitive domestically and/or internationally, businesses are recognizing that they must draw on wider sources of creative ideas and be positioned to serve the needs of populations who vary by gender and race. Both require organizations to surmount divisions that exist by gender or race/ethnicity. This is particularly the case in tight labour markets. Further, organizations face increased pressure to avoid legal actions alleging discrimination or harassment. The number of sex- or race-based cases settled 'with reasonable cause' have risen at the Equal Employment Opportunity Commission (EEOC). High profile lawsuits have been costly financially and have generated negative public relations.

The problems surrounding divisions of labour transcend demographic shifts and organizational inequities. There is a broader social context within which these issues must be considered because societal and workplace inequalities tend to be mutually reinforcing. Social inequalities (division of labour within the family, accumulation of wealth, and access to high-quality education) shape people's opportunities in the labour force, which, in turn, reinforce social inequality. Divisions among people, such as by gender and race/ethnicity, become self-perpetuating.

In the next sections, we present some historical background useful for understanding the origins of current approaches to ethnic and gender divisions of labour. We then assess the current situation, examining representational, interpersonal, and organizational factors that contribute to gender and ethnic inequalities. We conclude by outlining challenges that organizations face as they address increased workforce diversity and work toward reducing inequity across gender and ethnic divides. While our primary focus is the US workforce, the analysis may provide insights or lessons for other countries experiencing increased workforce diversity.

2 Historical context

Workers have been divided by gender and race/ethnicity throughout US industrial history. Employers have benefited from these divisions by obtaining a low wage workforce that is not positioned to organize for better wages or working conditions. As one group of workers resisted conditions, they were typically replaced. Some racial and ethnic groups were ghettoized. For example, the labour supply for the first integrated textile factories in the USA – the 'mill girls' of Lowell, Massachusetts of the 1820–1840s – was replaced by immigrants when the women resisted speed-ups and long working hours. Over time, each new wave of immigrants became the lowest status ethnic, replacing the previous groups in some of the most dangerous and low paid jobs in the country. Native Americans were consigned to isolated reservations. Blacks – once slaves, then segregated – were relegated to a relatively limited set of occupations until the mid-1900s. This segregation of workers persisted even as the notion emerged that the USA was a 'melting pot' and as business adopted managerial approaches in the early 1900s that implied there were relatively homogeneous workers who could be scientifically managed.

Several approaches to the issue of ethnic and gender divisions in the labour force have been taken since the middle of the twentieth century, forming the context in which current divisions can be examined. Anti-discrimination legislation was initiated in the 1960s by politicians who recognized that the unrest generated by the civil rights movement had to be addressed in order to maintain social stability and the current power structure. Landmark policies required non-discrimination – first by race, then by gender. Equal employment opportunity (EEO) policies were developed to prohibit discrimination while affirmative action (AA) policies required employers to *actively* make efforts to balance their labour forces. AA consists of policies, laws, executive orders, court-ordered practices and voluntary efforts designed to promote equity and equal access to schools, jobs and business opportunities and to rectify past discrimination. It has been widely misunderstood as requiring quotas or the hiring of unqualified individuals. In the early 1980s, President Reagan weakened AA via cuts in enforcement budgets, changes in procedures and the general strategy of deregulating the economy.

The 'managing diversity' movement developed in the business community in the mid-1980s as management recognized three things: much of the *net* growth in their workforces would not be white males, the women and minorities they were hiring did not assimilate to what was essentially a white male model, and incorporation of diverse peoples could widen the pool of ideas, leading to better decision making. Many organizations considered managing diversity a strategic necessity with a sound economic rationale. It would help them effectively mobilize available human resources to increase productivity and lower costs.

It may appear contradictory that managing diversity became popular while AA was under attack, since both ostensibly focus on increasing diversity in the workplace. However, corporate policies regarding managing diversity are focused on improving corporate efficiency, competitiveness, and profitability whereas governmental EEO/AA policies are concerned with equity and fairness. It is the former rationale that is compatible with the overall ideological changes that reshaped the political economy of the USA in the 1980s – 'liberalization' or the shift toward more market control of economic activity and less government intervention.

Currently, both EEO/AA and managing diversity are very visible parts of the current institutional environment in the USA. There is also a third trend relevant to divisions among groups. Since the 1980s, corporations have shifted to increased use of contingent workers (contract workers, consultants and part-time workers) to maintain 'flexibility' (i.e. to terminate workers more easily and eliminate payment of benefits) in an increasingly competitive business environment. Women tend to be the largest proportion of part-time workers. In addition, there is widespread use of sweatshops and trafficking of workers into the USA from other countries. These typically involve non-caucasian women and children. The liberalized domestic and international trade environment pits workers in one state against those of another and labourers in the USA against workers abroad.

It is within this broad, historical context that the current ethnic and gender divisions of labour can be analysed and the problems they present for business and management evaluated.

3 Current ethnic and gender divisions in the US labour force

Current divisions within the labour force can be more fully understood by considering them in terms of: (1) the positions ethnic groups and women hold in the labour force (i.e. their representation in various sectors and occupations and at different hierarchical levels); (2) the quality of interactions among members of diverse groups; and (3) the nature of organizational cultures (Pyle and Bond 1997). This conceptualization facilitates an evaluation of the challenges the ethnic and gender divisions of labour present for business and management.

Representation in the labour force

Ethnic and gender divisions in the labour force are indicated (and perpetuated) by differences in several interrelated measures of women's and ethnic groups' positions in the workforce vis-à-vis those of males or whites – labour force participation rates, unemployment rates, occupational segregation, average earnings and promotions to higher organizational levels. There have been improvements in some of these indicators in the last few decades, but substantial disparities persist even as the US labour force is becoming more diverse. The proportion of the labour force that is female increased from 1978 to 1998 (from 41.7 to 46.3 per cent). At the same time, the percentage of the total labour force that is white decreased (from 87.7 to 83.8 per cent), while the shares of both Blacks and Asians grew (from 10.2 to 11.6 per cent and 2.1 to 4.6 per cent respectively). These trends are projected to continue through the next decade (Fullerton 1999). Perhaps more strikingly, it is estimated that white men will constitute only 27.4 per cent of the *net* change in the labour force from 1998 to 2008.

Male and female labour force participation rates (the percentage of men or women aged 16 and older who are in the labour force) differ, as do those of different racial and ethnic groups. For example, although women's participation rates have risen since the 1950s and men's have fallen, women's participation (60.2 per cent) in 2000 was still substantially less than males (74.6 per cent) (Bureau of Labor Statistics 2000). Women's lower participation reflects two factors that perpetuate gender divisions in the labour force – women's more limited access to certain occupations and higher level jobs and the fact that females still largely bear the most responsibility for the household and childcare.

Labour force participation differs by race/ethnicity and gender in more complicated ways. White males participate at higher rates than black males, partly reflecting that many black males have been discouraged from seeking jobs by high unemployment rates and discrimination. Unemployment rates differ widely among racial groups. Such differences in the difficulty of obtaining employment further perpetuate divisions of labour. For example, in early 2000, the white unemployment rate was estimated to be 3.4 per cent. This contrasts sharply with black and Hispanic rates of 8.2 and 5.6 per cent, respectively. The disparities are more pronounced for teens aged 16–19: 24 per cent of blacks seeking employment are unable to find work versus 9.1 per cent of whites (Bureau of Labor Statistics 2000).

Occupational segregation is a central factor that contributes to gender and ethnic divisions of labour in a variety of ways. For example, measures of occupational segregation show that, although occupational segregation by sex fell in the period 1972–95, over one-third of male (or female) workers in 1995 would have to change jobs for the distribution of the two sexes among nine major occupational groups to be the same. Major occupations are also still segregated by race – in 1995 one-fifth of male workers needed to change jobs to make the occupational distribution of white, black and Hispanic male workers equal. Further, within these major occupational categories, women and people of colour are predominately in the lower levels. Analyses conducted using more detailed occupational categories therefore reveal even greater occupational segregation (Blau *et al.* 1998).

Many occupational differences are socially constructed, rather than based on objective factors. This can be illustrated in several ways. Occupational segregation by sex often has a different pattern in other countries (e.g. physicians in Russia have largely been women). Further, occupations that experience an influx of women (referred to as the 'feminization' of work) and people of colour typically lose status. Relative wages fall because work done by women and minorities has been considered of less value.

Occupational segregation tends to be self-reinforcing. Many women and ethnic groups who observe occupational segregation in the labour force will not aspire to, train for, and enter otherwise desirable occupations, thus perpetuating occupational segregation. In addition, having women and ethnic groups concentrated in some occupations facilitates treating them differently. In turn, the fact that they are in different groups can legitimize the differential treatment (Reskin and Padavic 1999).

Occupational segregation is linked to earnings disparities which cause further gender and ethnic divisions between people – as workers and as members of society. Women's annual earnings were 73.2 per cent of men's in 1998 (United States Department of Labor 2000) having fluctuated around this level for several years. The ratio actually worsened from 1955 to 1975, only rising back to its 1955 level in the early 1980s. The increase since the 1980s, however, has been largely due to *decreases* in men's earnings rather than real gains in women's earnings. Earnings gaps are more pronounced when both race and gender are considered. For example, in 2000, in comparison to white males, white females' weekly earnings were 75.4 per cent, black males' were 74.9 per cent, black females 66.1 per cent, Hispanic males 61.1 per cent, and Hispanic females 54.6 per cent (Bureau of Labor Statistics 2000).

In addition, there have been significant barriers to the movement of women and minorities into top managerial levels, a phenomenon referred to as the glass ceiling. In 1995, women were less than 5 per cent of the senior managers of the Fortune 1000 industrial and 500 service companies. Minorities were less than 3 per cent (Federal Glass Ceiling Commission 1995). Zweigenhaft and Domhoff's analysis (1998) shows that this small diversification has ironically strengthened and legitimated the power elite because the new women and minorities tend to be from the same class and educational background as the largely white male majority and therefore share similar perspectives. Women's and minorities' lack of access to higher organizational levels further perpetuates gender and ethnic income disparities because earnings gaps have widened dramatically within organizations. The average CEO of a major corporation made over 400 times more than the average blue-collar worker in 1999.

Many of these indicators of gender and ethnic divisions in the labour force are shaped by both societal and labour force discrimination (particularly occupational segregation). First, there are a variety of social factors that discriminate against women and minorities in ways that affect their abilities to be equal participants with white men in the labour force. For example, minorities may have unequal access to quality education; women may not be tracked into particular fields, most notably maths and science. In addition, there are often stereotypic views of what appropriate activities in the labour force are for women and people of different ethnicities. Women are often constrained because families and society have seen them as primarily responsible for the household and childcare. Second, labour force discrimination can in turn have an adverse feedback effect on women and minorities. Seeing barriers to opportunities, they may not acquire the training for or seek many occupations. All these ethnic and gender divisions of labour also negatively impact families, since families are increasingly dependent upon multiple salaries to meet basic needs.

Interactional dynamics

These gender and ethnic/racial inequities are mediated by informal processes and institutional arrangements as well as by the cultures of organizations. There is evidence that diverse work groups can produce more creative outcomes than homogeneous groups, yet there are also indicators that such groups experience lower cohesiveness, increased turnover, and lower morale. Everyday interactions and interpersonal dynamics – such as gender and race-based preferences and biases as well as the more behavioural manifestations of discrimination and harassment – can be powerful dividing forces for women and people of colour within the workplace. Thus in order to understand the divisions, it is critical to look at the interpersonal and organizational dynamics that work against diversity within organizations.

Informal dynamics can create a press for homogeneity. Hiring practices, and even self-selection into careers, are shaped by perceptions of and preferences for similarity between new entrants and current employees. This preference for sameness affects who is invited into an organization and who is considered successful. People who have not previously experienced diversity typically prefer to work with others who are most like them. In addition, a wide range of studies show that evaluators tend to rate people of their same race higher than members of other races. Presumably due to a general increase in awareness of race and gender, such biases are not typically expressed as direct prejudices. The more recent manifestation of bias is a tendency to adopt pro-white, pro-male attitudes and policies rather than to actively ascribe negative qualities to people of colour or women. Given the current predominance of whites and men in the workplace (especially in positions with decision-making authority), interpersonal preferences for sameness often translate into organizational processes that disadvantage women and people of colour. When such hidden biases and judgements are left unchallenged, managers can honestly believe they are hiring or promoting the 'best person' while the process actually perpetuates differential and biased selection, evaluation and promotion.

There are other forms of subtle sexism and racism that also influence divisions of labour. For example, recruitment practices that rely on the informal networks of current organization members can be highly biased to favour white men given that personal networks tend to be race and gender segregated. In a related manner, people in positions to serve as mentors often select proteges who are similar to them in terms of gender, race and ethnicity. Research has clearly documented the importance of mentoring for individual career advancement and access to power and influence, yet there are numerous barriers to cross-gender and cross-race mentoring.

More direct forms of discrimination also still exist. Over the last 10 years, the number of race-based and sex-based EEOC cases settled with reasonable cause has increased as have the monetary awards (United States Equal Employment Opportunity Commission 2001). Harassment is a particularly insidious form of discrimination that divides workers by creating differential working conditions. Sexual harassment is broadly understood to include both direct threats or promises hinged on sexual cooperation (*quid pro quo* harassment) and work environments that are considered unwelcoming of women (hostile work environment harassment). Researchers estimate that about half of all working women experience some form of sexual harassment during their working lives. The legal definition of racial/ethnic harassment has not as clearly included hostile work environments, none the less there is evidence that racial jokes, dismissal of contributions made by people of colour, and treatment based on racial or ethnic stereotypes are common. While incidents of sexual harassment of men and reverse discrimination against whites are reported, they are much more rare. The harassment of men that does occur is typically perpetrated by other men.

Harassment can have serious negative personal and work-related effects on people. The more aggressive forms of harassment seem to have more adverse outcomes for the individual than hostile work environment harassment. However, relatively low level but frequent types of harassment can also chip away at people's physical health, psychological well-being and work relationships. There are other broader consequences of harassment in the workplace. In some organizations, women who observe the harassment of a coworker experience negative psychological and physical consequences similar to the victim herself. Both sexual and racial harassment are distinct sources of occupational stress and can have profound negative effects on work roles by fostering greater levels of distraction, loss of motivation, higher absenteeism and increased turnover. Harassment can also function to limit the power and influence of women and people of colour in the workplace by undermining their access to both the formal/concrete and informal/interpersonal resources needed to advance.

Organizational culture

The informal practices that foster divisions are embedded in diverse organizational cultures. The culture of an organization typically refers to the shared assumptions about what the appropriate ways of being and relating within the organization are. It embodies the taken-for-granted values and beliefs about the conduct of all aspects of organizational life that have been developed through shared experiences over time. Even though an organizational culture is essentially invisible, it can affect ethnic and gender divisions in several profound ways. First, organizational culture defines what is considered normative both within the organization as a whole and within different levels or departments of the organization. Second, it provides the basis for how an organization deals with people who do not fit organizational norms. Third, the culture of an organization is critical to the interpretation and implementation of policies that might be adopted to promote equity within an organization.

First, when organizations adopt particular assumptions and values for how things should be done, they are in essence establishing a normative model of a 'good' employee. For example, what may begin as a simple preference for homogeneous work groups and a higher comfort with people like one's self can easily evolve into strong organizational norms for behaviour consistent with the preferences of the dominant group. Since this is most often white men, some traditions adopted by organizations define women and people of colour as marginal within their work settings. By virtue of establishing normative ways of operating, the organizational culture also influences what types of people have access to power, influence and resources. Organizational values become institutionalized as the invisible biases are integrated into the design of work and criteria for advancement. For example, many workplaces value jobs that require physical strength (male dominated) over those that require precision (typically more female dominated) when both can be considered equally critical for producing a quality product. Similarly, valued employment patterns are often gendered (e.g. the value for full-time work and uninterrupted careers is rooted in traditional family roles for men).

Second, organizations vary with respect to how 'strong' or flexible their culture is (i.e. how much room there is for variation). Reactions to 'difference' are related both to the content and the strength of organizational culture. The culture or subculture shapes how much pressure there will be on new participants to conform, and how people who do not fit the dominant practices are evaluated and/or excluded. A lack of perceived fit with the dominant practices can also reduce people's inclination to join a particular group (i.e. the whole organization or particular departments/divisions or ranks within the organization). This can discourage people from seeking positions where they would be in the minority thereby perpetuating the types of gender and ethnic divisions we have been outlining. There is some evidence that increased diversity of membership pushes for changes (e.g. there is less sexual harassment in settings where women are in significant leadership positions), but the deeper transformation of the organizational culture is typically slow.

A third aspect of organizational culture that influences divisions within the workforce is the congruence between policies that might be adopted to support integration and equity and other organizational traditions rooted in shared assumptions and beliefs about what is valued within the organization. The relationship between policies and organizational culture is reciprocal. On the one hand, policies can help to shape the organizational culture by codifying organizational values. On the other hand, the effectiveness of policies is determined by the extent that they are congruent with the culture of the organization. When the informal values come into conflict with the formal policies, the impact of policies can be limited. For example, traditions that measure commitment or ambition in terms of long hours discourage people from actually utilizing any family friendly policies that might be made available. In fact, people are often informally sanctioned (i.e. taken less seriously) if they decide to make use of such options as maternity leave, part-time schedules or leave to care for an ailing elder.

4 Challenges for organizations in the future

The preceding discussion of factors affecting ethnic and gender divisions within the workforce illustrates that the substantial challenges facing business and management range from the interpersonal to the policy levels of analysis. Forces that shape these challenges exist within work groups, within organizations, within sectors of the economy, and within society at large. They encompass issues of representation, interactional dynamics and organizational culture.

One of the most basic challenges facing US businesses is in hiring and promoting diverse people, two actions that are necessary for the reasons stated in the introduction. As shown, occupational segregation can be self-perpetuating both within organizations and as women and minorities plan viable careers in light of the occupational segregation they observe in the labour force. Management must challenge stereotypic views of where women and ethnic groups best 'fit in' – in terms of type of occupation and levels within the hierarchy. Other institutionalized biases about performance criteria and preferred ways of approaching work and careers need to be reexamined. Barriers to career advancement for women and people of colour need to be addressed – because there is evidence that many women and members of minority ethnic/racial groups leave corporations to establish their own businesses because of frustration with the glass ceiling. Earnings disparities further discourage women and ethnic groups.

Therefore, organizations that provide a broader model of how women and minorities can be incorporated will not only attract diverse workers now but will also encourage future generations to aspire to and seek a wider range of occupations. To avoid loss of valuable human resources in the present and to ensure the largest possible flow of employees in the future, organizations must develop strategies to avoid perpetuating occupational segregation and glass ceilings. Accomplishing this and successfully integrating women and ethnic groups into a wider range of occupations and levels of management requires attention to interpersonal and group dynamics as well as proactive attempts to foster supportive organizational cultures and sub-cultures. It involves challenging the notion that fostering equality is best achieved by treating everyone 'exactly the same' and dealing with the backlash reactions that can occur when there is increased support for alleviating ethnic and gender divisions through diversity management programmes and EEO/AA policies (Bond and Pyle 1998). The path toward more equitable incorporation of diverse people requires organizational creativity, flexibility and commitment to respectful and productive relationships among people from different groups.

This article has examined ethnic and gender divisions of labour in the context of the USA, with its particular institutional structure and historical antecedents. Institutional and historical forces differ in other countries and, therefore, the issues or concerns for business and management vary. Much can be learned about strategies useful for alleviating ethnic and gender divisions in the labour force by developing comparisons between countries. Across other countries there is great variation in all the measures of gender divisions in the labour force investigated in this entry. For example, although it is always lower than men's, women's labour force participation varies from very low in the Middle East to high in Scandinavian countries. Occupational segregation occurs across all countries and extends over time in ways that cannot be explained by differences in educational attainment between women and men. However, the pattern it takes (i.e. what is considered female work or male work) differs across countries, highlighting that it is socially constructed. Women earn less than men worldwide, although the extent of this wage gap varies considerably. These variations are due to considerable differences in political and economic institutions as well as social, cultural and religious practices that shape the division of labour in the household, men's and women's relative access to education and, thereby, their positions in the labour force (Blau *et al.* 1998, United Nations 2000). Cross-national comparisons highlight the importance of institutional practices in establishing patterns of workplace divisions and shed light on a wider perspective on strategies needed to alleviate such divisions in the labour force.

JEAN L. PYLE

MEG A. BOND
UNIVERSITY OF MASSACHUSETTS LOWELL

Further reading

(References cited in the text marked *)

Arredondo, P. (1996) *Successful Diversity Management Initiatives*, Thousand Oaks, CA: Sage Publications. (Provides practical and strategic advice for organizations facing diversity-related change.)

* Blau, F.D., Ferber, M.A. and Winkler, A.E. (1998) *The Economics of Women, Men, and Work*, 3rd edn, Upper Saddle River, NJ: Prentice Hall. (Provides data on women, men and work in the labour market and household and examines the main explanations for differences.)

* Bond, M.A. and Pyle, J.L. (1998) 'Diversity dilemmas at work', *Journal of Management Inquiry*, 7 (3): 262–79. (Outlines some critical dilemmas that have made the incorporation and retention of diverse groups in the US workforce complicated and difficult.)

Browne, I. (ed) (1999) *Latinas and African American Women and Work: Race, Gender, and Economic Inequality*, New York: Russell Sage Foundation. (Examines how race and gender have increasingly disadvantaged black and Latina women at work over the past three decades from the point of view of sociologists and economists.)

* Bureau of Labor Statistics (2000) http://www.bls.gov United States Department of Labor. (Provides labour statistics, regional information, surveys and programmes, and current news on the Bureau of Labor Statistics.)

Chemers, M.M., Oskamp, S. and Costanzo, M.A. (eds) (1995) *Diversity in Organizations*, Thousand Oaks, CA: Sage. (Provides an edited collection of chapters that summarize theoretical and research perspectives on workplace diversity from multiple levels of analysis.)

Cox, T. (1993) *Cultural Diversity in Organizations: Theory, Research, & Practice*, San Francisco: Berrett-Koehler Publishers. (Outlines then develops a multidimensional conceptual model of cultural diversity in organizations.)

* Federal Glass Ceiling Commission (1995) *A Solid Investment: Making Full Use of the Nation's Human Capital*, Washington, DC. (Provides report and recommendations of the Federal Glass Ceiling Commission.)

* Fullerton, H.N. (1999) 'Labor force projections to 2008: steady growth and changing composition', *Monthly Labor Review* 122 (11): 19–32. (Details projected changes in the US labour force 1998–2008, with particular attention to changes by age, sex, race/ethnicity, and combinations of these attributes.)

Jackson, S. (ed) (1992) *Diversity in the Workplace: Human Resource Initiatives*, New York: Guilford Press. (Summarizes nine case studies that illustrate a wide range of diversity issues faced by US organizations.)

Powell, G.N. (ed) (1999) *Handbook of Gender and Work*, Thousand Oaks, CA: Sage Publications. (Provides a collection of review pieces on a wide variety of topics related to gender and work.)

* Pyle, J.L. and Bond, M.A. (1997) 'Workforce diversity: emerging interdisciplinary challenges', *New Solutions*, 7 (2): 415–7. (Examines the importance of workplace diversity issues and develops an interdisciplinary approach to evaluating the extent to which diversity is achieved in the US workforce.)

* Reskin, B.F. and Padavic, I. (1999) 'Sex, race, and ethnic inequality in United States workplaces', in J.S. Chafetz, *Handbook of the Sociology of Gender*, New York: Kluwer: 343–74. (Examines data and explanations for sex, race and ethnic differences in job segregation and earnings

in the USA in the second half of the twentieth century.)
* United Nations (2000) *The World's Women: Trends and Statistics*, New York: United Nations. (Provides data and analyses to examine the economic, political and social differences between men's and women's lives worldwide.)
* United States Department of Labor (2000) *http://www.dol.gov* (Provides overview of the Department of Labor along with statistics and data, laws and regulations, and news releases of the DOL.)
* United States Equal Employment Opportunity Commission (2001) *http://www.eeoc.gov* (Provides overview of the EEOC, comprehensive listing of laws, regulations and policy guidance for employers and the federal sector, statistics on cases filed, and latest rulings and news releases.)
* Zweigenhaft, R.L. and G.W. Domhoff (1998) *Diversity in the Power Elite*, New Haven: Yale University Press. (Examines the extent to which women and minority groups have attained high level positions in corporations or government and whether their presence changes the perspectives of this power elite.)

See also: EMPLOYMENT RELATIONS; LABOUR MARKETS; SKILL FORMATION SYSTEMS; WORKFARE

Intellectual property rights

1. Patents, copyrights and secrecy
2. The patent: between exclusion and diffusion of knowledge
3. Intellectual property institutions and national diversity
4. Is the privatization of knowledge excessive?
5. The challenge of ICTs

Overview

Intellectual property rights are the rights to the productive utilization and the appropriation of returns granted to the creators of intellectual products. Ideas – work of the intellect – are recognized as being part of humanity's common knowledge base, and therefore are not appropriable by a private person. In this respect they are outside the law of private property. A literary subject, an artistic principle, a political idea and a scientific vision, for example, cannot be monopolized. What can, however, have a claim to be considered as private property is the concretization of the idea, theme or principle. Only then may it be the object of a private right.

Intellectual property rights are institutional tools that allow for the creation of markets to stimulate private initiatives in intellectual creation. Basically, this amounts to restricting access to knowledge by granting temporary exclusive rights to new knowledge and thus enabling the inventor to set a price for its use. Patents and copyrights are the main intellectual property rights used to guarantee a degree of exclusivity to knowledge. Creating monopolies on knowledge lead, however, to serious problems in the allocation of economic resources. Patents and copyrights create static distortions in resource allocation due to monopoly pricing and may encourage socially wasteful expenditures by urging innovators on to inventing around the patent.

In the following section, we will present an overview of the economic and policy issues surrounding intellectual property rights, with a particular focus on patents and copyrights. Then we will discuss the main economic problem raised by the patent system, which is to keep a balance between the social objective of ensuring efficient use of knowledge, once it has been produced, and the objective of providing ideal motivation to the private producer. Then, we will briefly discuss national differences in intellectual property institutions. In the last section, we will address two issues of particular relevance for the current policy debate: the first one deals with the current trend of privatization of knowledge and the second one with the impact of the new information and communication technologies on the effectiveness of the patent and copyright system.

1 Patents, copyrights and secrecy

Traditionally, industrial property rights have been distinguished from literary and artistic rights. The former rights include patents, plant variety protection, industrial design and integrated circuit design. They also encompass other sets of items which, strictly speaking, do not fall under industrial property, such as trademarks and all contractual clauses granting exclusivity.

In this vast domain, two categories of property rights have become predominant as regards scientific and technological knowledge: copyright and patents. Surprisingly, these two categories have moved closer together over time. Initially they were far apart, with copyrights covering literary and artistic property rights and patents covering industrial property rights. The boundary was then somewhere between the beautiful and the useful. But with the development of scientific and technological knowledge these different rights have often been applied to useful knowledge that enters the industrial sphere. The merging of patents and copyrights is due essentially to the fact that copyright has conquered new ground.

By becoming the right most frequently used by the information technology and culture and multimedia industries, copyright has 'entered the corporate world' (see GLOBALIZATION).

The patent, an instrument designed to protect innovators, ensures them the right to a temporary monopoly on the commercial exploitation of a device or method. It is a property title that is valid in time (duration), in geographic space (range) and in the world of objects (scope or extent of the patent). Filing a patent application means defining a set of claims concerning the concretization or application of an idea. After an investigation into anteriority and in some cases a study of patentability, the patent authority may or may not grant property rights for a particular geographical area specified in the application. In exchange for patent rights the inventor has publicly to divulge the technical details on the new knowledge. Certain legal limits ensure that not all the knowledge produced by an economic agent is patented.

Patentability of knowledge depends on conditions of absolute innovativeness of the invention, of non-obviousness for an expert and of the possibility of industrial application. Theoretically, the condition of non-obviousness (or inventive activity) is intended to distinguish between that which is essentially the product of creative human work and that which is primarily the work of nature. One can patent a new machine but one cannot patent a fresh water spring even if one has 'discovered' it. As a result, recurrent debate on the nature of innovation in certain disciplines such as mathematics – is it an invention or a discovery? – has extensive economic implications. The interpretation of this criterion is of course at the heart of discussions on the patentability of genetic creations.

The only condition governing copyright is 'originality'. Copyright protects the expression of an idea and not the idea itself. This protection acts with regard to patrimonial rights (protection against reproduction or representation) and moral rights (protection of the integrity of expression). But with copyright parts of a protected work can be extracted and recombined to produce an original work. Copyright, unlike patents, gives the creator immediate, free protection without involving a lot of red tape.

Commercial secrecy is a different way for a company to appropriate the benefit of an innovation. As long as the secret is kept, profits from the new knowledge can be reserved. But the secret does not create a property right; by definition a secret cannot be revealed and therefore cannot be described sufficiently to make it possible to identify its nature or determine its owner. It therefore offers no protection against the risk of concurrent inventions. Moreover, if the fact of keeping a process or formula secret is a strategy that can pay, the secret has little sense since it concerns the design of a product destined to be exposed to everyone.

The mechanism of the patent seems ideal as an intellectual property right since it enables the innovator to cover the innovation costs and make a profit by means of a monopoly right. It facilitates the market test, for it allows disclosure of information while protecting against imitation. Finally, it creates a transferable right.

Yet the patent is a mechanism that is by no means always used. In Europe only 44 per cent of product innovations (52 per cent in the USA) and 26 per cent of process innovations (44 per cent in the USA) are patented (Arundel and Kabla 1998). Firms often prefer to keep their new knowledge secret or 'simply' ensure that they are always one step ahead. We can suggest four reasons for the weak propensity to patent.

First, the system provides a uniform right for very different industrial sectors. Since it is not possible to create a level of variety of intellectual property right mechanisms equivalent to the variety of sectors, inconsistencies and inappropriateness inevitably emerge. It is very difficult to imagine a system adapted to all situations. In fact, the system is ill-suited to many industries, despite the creation of particular mechanisms and ad hoc procedures. This is the case, for example, of industries characterized with a very rapid innovation cycle (like the sport industry). In such an industry, the duration of patent examination and decision is far too long as compared with the very short imitation time of rivals. And this is a problem which is not going to be solved through the new 'accelerated procedures' for examination and decision which are still too long! Thus, the patent system is simply not appropriate for cases of very rapid innovation cycles.

Secondly, the protection afforded by a property right is neither automatic nor free. The onus is on the patent owner to identify the counterfeiter and take the matter to court, where it will be assessed and interpreted. The effectiveness of property rights is therefore inseparable from the creators' capacity to watch over them. These capacities depend, in turn, on legal facilities (can someone be sued for counterfeit?), technical capacities (microscopic analysis) and organizational capacities (information networks). Moreover, globalization of markets clearly affects these surveillance capacities negatively. Yet there are systems, especially for copyright, in which these functions are fulfilled by an intermediary agency to which the owners of rights delegate a part of their management. That is typically the case of composer's societies which control the use of rights, collect subscriptions and redistribute profits. In the case of universities, licence offices have the same function.

The third reason is directly derived from the previous one: the management of intellectual property is not a simple task for a company. The issue is not only the protection of innovations by means of patents, even though this is a key element that in itself poses many problems (what should be patented? On what territory? At what time? etc.). It is also a matter of preventive management, that is, the need constantly to check that the areas of research and innovation one is aiming at are free of prior conflicting property rights. Moreover, as mentioned, the implementation of rights depends on the abilities of the holders of those rights to develop capacities for watching the relevant markets in order to identify counterfeits. Intellectual property furthermore concerns protected commercial secrets and codified know-how (often called proprietary information), such as technical drawings or training, maintenance and operating manuals. Managing this part of intellectual property is difficult and often this information has not been collected or combined and remains ill-identified in the firm. We thus see that an effective intellectual property strategy requires the codification and organization of the firm's knowledge, involving far more than just the patented products and processes which are merely the tip of the iceberg.

Fourthly, the effectiveness of the system depends strongly on the quality of the legal environment, which varies widely from one country to the next. This quality increased in the USA after the Court of Appeals for the Federal Circuit was set up for the purpose of unifying the basis of interpretation and enhancing firms' confidence by reducing legal uncertainty (Jaffe 1999). In Europe, however, although procedures for applying for and granting patents are the same all over the continent, these rights have to be defended in each individual country. As a result there are no truly European patents yet. We should note, however, that recent decisions of the European Commission make the creation of a real European patent quite likely.

2 The patent: between exclusion and diffusion of knowledge

The patent provides an obvious and recognized solution to the economic problem of the intellectual creator (see EVOLUTIONARY THEORIES OF THE FIRM; SCHUMPETER, E.F.). By increasing the expected private returns from an innovation, it acts as an incentive mechanism to private investments in knowledge production. The problem is that by imposing exclusive rights the patent restricts *de facto* the use of knowledge and its exploitation by those who might have benefited from it had it been free.

Many historical examples illustrate situations of blockage caused by measures relating to intellectual property rights that leaned too far in favour of the inventor. These situations of blockage occur because the person who has the knowledge is not necessarily in the best position to use it efficiently. The more distributed knowledge is, passing 'from hand to hand', the greater the probability of it being exploited effectively. It is therefore important to find some balance between the right to exclusivity and the distribution of knowledge.

From this point of view, whereas the duration of a monopoly is now fixed (20 years from the date of application), the scope of a patent remains a variable which can be the object of strategic choices by private agents and will be assessed very differently by the legal authorities concerned. It is at the heart of the dilemma between the protection of the first innovator and the encouragement of subsequent innovations (a classic form of public good dilemma). If the boundary is set right around the territory of the innovation, subsequent innovations that others might have been able to realize, based on the first one, are blocked. Moreover, legal uncertainty is increased, for risks of dispute are greater. If closure is too restrictive, however, the pioneer's effort may not be fully rewarded.

Different devices exist for deliberately organizing the circulation of knowledge in a patent system. First, the granting of a property right is accompanied by public disclosure concerning the protected technique. There is therefore dissemination of knowledge owing to the patent. Albeit partial (only the codified and explicit dimensions of the new knowledge are described), this dissemination is particularly important in certain industries. If it is carried out 'in time', and in so far as the information thus constituted is available at a low cost, it allows for a better allocation of resources, reduces the risk of duplication and favours the trading of information. The case of pharmaceuticals clearly illustrates the use of patents as a means of information and coordination. Patent databases are a unique medium for knowledge externalities. Each firm uses them to evaluate its own strategies and identify opportunities for cooperation or transactions concerning knowledge.

Secondly, patents create transferable rights. By granting a license, the owner of the knowledge allows it to be exploited by other agents and, in return, receives income. There are various levels of licences: exclusive licences limit diffusion to a single additional agent and may even be combined with territorial clauses, while non-exclusive licences allow for a far wider diffusion. In some sectors (computing, telecommunications) where it is important for a technology to spread so that it becomes the industry 'standard', non-exclusive licence policies are granted on a large scale. Yet the granting of licences transfers knowledge only partially. It is often essential to draw up contracts in which sale of the technology is accompanied by the assistance and expertise needed to develop practical know-how (Arora 1995). Thus, the patent is often useful for structuring a complex transaction that also concerns unpatented knowledge (tacit knowledge) (Bessy and Brousseau 1999).

Intellectual property rights seem to be reinforced everywhere, from both a microeconomic point of view (they are more and more essential to firms' strategies; their use is increasingly intense; they are entering areas formerly prohibited) and a macroeconomic one (TRIPS agreements oblige all members of the WTO to establish a minimum level of legislation in favour of intellectual property rights). Moreover, the patent system that was assumed to be devoted solely to the protection of innovation is now fulfilling other functions of increasing importance in knowledge-based economies. As patents are used to draw attention to resources and establish a reputation, patent portfolios are becoming an essential element in the evaluation of intangible assets by financial markets. The paradox is that intellectual property rights are simultaneously threatened more and more by current technological changes leading to massive reductions in the costs of formatting and transmitting knowledge. Around this paradox, the issue is indeed one of a test of strength of the institutions of intellectual property rights confronted by the knowledge-based economy.

3 Intellectual property institutions and national diversity

Two basic functions must be fulfilled by intellectual property institutions. The first function is to draw up a precise definition of rights and the objects to which exclusivity is guaranteed. The second is to make these rights enforceable, and effectively to exclude all unauthorized agents from use of the relevant resources. These functions must be fulfilled in such a way that legal uncertainty is reduced. An intellectual property system that qualifies as 'strong' is one which reduces legal uncertainty and increases the level of agents' confidence in its ability to defend their rights. Considerable differences in application procedures and modes of attribution of intellectual property rights can be observed in different countries:

National legal systems are grounded either in the principle of the first inventor (USA) or in that of the first applicant (Europe and Japan). The latter principle forces the creator to go to the patents office as quickly as possible, even before initiating cooperation and trading knowledge, for example. The first applicant principle, although unfair in a sense, has the advantage of providing an unambiguous criterion for the attribution of property rights. The US principle, on the other hand, creates a degree of legal uncertainty in so far as conflicts between inventors are always possible and often lead to court action.

Certain systems provide for the possibility of opposing the application before the rights have been granted. This is possible on condition that information concerning the application is published early enough (within 18 months of the application). These mechanisms can avoid potential conflict, a source of high legal costs. In the USA, where publication occurred at a later stage, once the property rights have been granted, this possibility of pre-empting conflict was not used. The USA are currently changing their system towards earlier publication. Late publication of information creates legal uncertainty.

Finally, the 'patent-granting culture' matters. The fact of being indulgent with inventors by granting them everything they apply for (e.g. a patent that includes subsequent developments which are not yet defined) creates fragile areas in the protection of rights and increases the likelihood of conflict. A patent more strictly limited to innovation reduces the probability of future conflict.

Intellectual creation is increasingly produced by dependent creators (we all know the current importance of collective invention and knowledge networks). There is, thus, a challenging tension between the tendency of intellectual property rights to 'individualize' invention activities through the attribution of reward to individuals and the collective nature of innovation. This tension can be mitigated through a certain mode of usage of intellectual property right. Patent systems are more or less effective as a signalling mechanism supporting collective invention (Ordover 1991).

In the US system, for instance, information was disclosed only after a property right has been granted; so that there was a long delay (the average pendency period is 18–20 months) with a lack of information. Such a long period without any information increased the risk of efficiency losses (duplication, missed opportunities). And since only 60 per cent of applications were approved, the remaining 40 per cent of the applications were never published. In Europe, the disclosure of information is realized in the 18th month after the patent application; which considerably improves the system. (There is a legal protection after the patent is disclosed such that an applicant has the right to demand compensation if someone uses the disclosed patent before the patent grant.) It is, however, in Japan that the information disclosure principle is implemented in the most fascinating way. As in Europe, the Japanese Patent Office discloses all patent applications 18 months after the applications are filed. But the most striking feature is that in Japan, only 17 per cent of the patent applications are approved, so that the preponderance of patent applications are disclosed with no ultimate benefit of intellectual property protection. Quite paradoxically, the patent system becomes a mechanism for generating public information! Moreover, patents tend to be applied for earlier in the innovation process in Japan due to the 'first-to-file' rule of priority, as opposed to the 'first-to-invent' rule of priority that applies in the USA. Both the automatic publication after 18 months and the first-to-file rule of priority could contribute to Japanese respondents' earlier awareness of what major R&D projects their rivals are working on. The Japanese system is effective for sending signals and placing a large amount of information in the public domain, and thus contributing to the essential objective of 'collective invention'. While the European system tends also to have an effective signalling function (though less powerful), the US system was not effective in terms of signalling.

Our conclusion is that 'minor' institutional differences matter to explain the disparities of the value of patents as a source of information and, thus, as a mechanism for efficient coordination. When information is properly disseminated (as in the Japanese system) and when the nature of the protection granted is specified in ways that encourage patentees to make their innovations available for use by others at reasonably modest costs (narrow patent as well as weak degree of novelty are crucial in this way), the patent system becomes a vehicle for coordination in expanding informational spillovers, rather than for the capture of monopoly rents.

4 Is the privatization of knowledge excessive?

Intellectual property rights systems have never before been so important and so threatened. There are many signs that suggest that use of intellectual property is becoming increasingly important and that within this general domain use of the patent is growing rapidly. The greater the intensity of innovation, characteristic of the knowledge-based economy, and the increase in the propensity to patent (that is, the elevation of the ratio of the number of patents to the number of innovations) related to the emergence of new research and innovation management techniques, are the main factors of this quantitative evolution (Kortum and Lerner 1997). A recent article in the *Wall Street Journal* cites startling figures for the USA: 151,024 patents were granted in 1998, corresponding to an increase of 38 per cent compared to 1997. But the evolution is also qualitative. Patents are being registered on new types of objects such as software (17,000 patents last year, compared to 1,600 in 1992), genetic creations and devices for electronic trade over the Internet, and by new actors (universities, researchers in the public sector). This general trend is also reflected in the increase in exclusivity rights over instruments, research materials and databases. The now classic example is that of exclusive rights to medical, genetic and genealogical data on Iceland's population, granted to a US company. All this contributes to the unprecedented expansion of the knowledge market and the proliferation of exclusive rights on whole areas of intellectual creation.

Many factors explain this trend. They relate to a powerful commitment to basic research by private firms in certain sectors, and to changes in the behaviour of open science institutions which are increasingly oriented towards the promotion of their commercial interests.

This trend does not necessarily lead to an excess of privatization of knowledge. Far from it. In many cases the establishment of intellectual property rights strengthens private incentives, allows the commitment of substantial private resources and thereby improves the conditions for the commercialization of inventions. Moreover, the establishment of private rights does not totally prevent the diffusion of knowledge, even if it does limit it. Finally, a large proportion of private knowledge is disseminated outside the market system, either within consortiums or by means of networks of trading and sharing of knowledge, the foundation of the unintentional spillovers discussed earlier on. But economists have identified some situations in which there is an excess of private rights. These situations are typical of a way in which the US system is developing.

There is an excess of privatization when the way in which private property rights are used blocks the exploitation of the knowledge that these rights are in fact meant to improve. We can identify two such situations. First, initial patents that are too broad and reward the pioneer inventor too generously, block possibilities for subsequent research by others and thus reduce the diversity of innovators in a field and the probability of cumulative developments (Scotchmer 1991). Secondly, an excess of privatization relates to excessive fragmentation of the knowledge base, linked to intellectual property rights on parcels and fragments of knowledge which do not correspond to an industrial application. This situation is described by the concept of an anticommons regime and can be illustrated by a case from biotechnology: when private rights are granted to fragments of a gene, before the corresponding product is identified, nobody is in a position to group the rights (i.e. to have all the licences) and the product is not developed (Heller and Eisenberg 1998).

Open science is caught between the constraints of public budgets (to be related to the increase in scientific research costs) and growing demands from firms for research services (following the restructuring of these firms and the consequent outsourcing of their R&D activities). In this context we witness an increasing commercialization of open science activities (Foray 1999).

All studies show that this represents a real risk of irremediable alteration of modes of co-operation and sharing of knowledge. Restricted access to knowledge and the retention of knowledge produced by universities comes in several forms, for example delayed or partial publication and communication, secrecy and patents. A significant form is the exclusive licence (new knowledge is sold exclusively to one firm). When there is nothing left but exclusive bilateral contracts between university laboratories and firms, we have forms of quasi-integration which undermine the domain of open knowledge.

Mowery *et al.* (1998) note that in the USA new laws authorizing universities to grant exclusive licences on the results of research financed by public funds (especially the Bayh-Dole Act) are based on a narrow view of the channels through which public research interacts with industry. In reality these channels are multiple (publication, conferences, consultancy, training, expertise) and all contribute to the transfer of knowledge, while the incentives created by such laws promote only one channel (patenting and licences), with the risk of blocking the others. The authors' conclusion is unambiguous 'The Bayh-Dole Act and its consequences on the activities of universities substantially increase the degree of "excludability" of research results and thus reduce the dissemination of knowledge in the research system'.

Of course this model of a strong domination of the market generates its own regulations which can bring about a certain equilibrium in some instances. Intense debate today on the compulsory licence mechanism (i.e. the compulsory diffusion of private knowledge for the general interest) illustrates a possible type of regulation (although its principle seriously undermines the very idea of property), as does the idea of the state or international foundations buying patents to 'put them back' in the public domain (Kremer 1997). We can also count on academic researchers who are learning to negotiate their industrial contracts more and more advantageously in order to preserve areas of public knowledge (provided that the researchers themselves are not caught up in a sort of money-making frenzy). Finally, industrial firms are often aware of the advantages of not completely undermining open and independent academic research, and try to establish 'good practice' so that universities work with and not for industry.

Probably the most promising regulatory mechanism is provided by collective invention in the form of the research consortium. The consortium creates areas for the sharing of knowledge in which technological secrecy and the retention of private knowledge are temporarily and locally disregarded. The consortium organizes and formalizes modes of sharing research tools and circulating knowledge between multiple partners. By establishing multilateral rather than bilateral relations, it forces firms to break away from models of exclusivity and to create areas for collective production. This is a valuable mechanism when the tendency to privatize knowledge becomes a real obstacle to diffusion, including in the public research domain.

The fact remains that economic studies on the US model reveal a degree of concern. We note one of the conclusions of Cockburn and Henderson (1997): 'policies that help to undermine the institutions of open science, that make academic research more directly oriented towards market needs or that allow the redistribution of rents through mechanisms aimed at increasing the exclusivity of knowledge, may prove to be counter-productive in the long run'. This is a strong conclusion that prompts us to carefully examine this new model without being blinded by the brilliance of its undeniable short-term performance.

In light of the above arguments, it is difficult to imagine that this privatization model can be reconciled with the goal of the UNESCO World Conference on Science in June 1999, that is 'the identification of new principles for safeguarding the status of scientific knowledge as a public good'. The scientific revolution under way has unequalled potential to produce tools for development in the fields of agriculture, agri-food and health. But this scientific revolution is historically the first to be essentially private, a situation that generates problems of access to and acquisition of knowledge, as well as problems of priorities as regards research programmes.

5 The challenge of ICTs

Current technological developments pose problems concerning the exercise of property rights and especially control over the use of works. The new ICTs create favourable conditions for knowledge externalities. Not only are the costs of reproduction and transmission of digital works collapsing, but reproduction and transmission are carried out without any loss of quality. The idea of an original work thus disappears. The most recent developments in the multimedia domain reveal the full intensity of the problem. The Internet offers free access to cultural and musical programmes that can be downloaded and copied onto any medium. Problems concern not only patrimonial rights but also moral rights: the integrity of the work is threatened when, to use Roger Chartier's expression, the reader writes not in the margins but in the text itself – which is exactly what the electronic book allows (*Le Monde* 19 March 1999).

Faced with these threats, there are classic solutions that the major multimedia product distributors are trying to adopt, such as the creation of new property rights to protect numeric intellectual creation. New rights on databases, as well as on the protection of digital information, push the pendulum very far towards private protection. It is as if the intellectual property system were swinging from a logic aimed at protecting invention (and the author) towards one aimed at encouraging investment and commercialization of information products and services on a global scale. Similar mechanisms include sales tax on blank disks, electronic marking and coding devices to prevent copying of programmes, and access rates to the sites that present those programmes. But this type of solution reflects the powerlessness of copyright faced with these new situations. A 'more intelligent' answer would probably be a change of behaviour in order to provide free access to programmes and draw revenue from derived products. This is a strategy familiar to firms wanting to impose their standard in the network industry.

Hence, there are two alternatives: either derived products are totally foreign to the basic trade and are essentially a form of advertising for revenue, as in the case of the *Encyclopaedia Britannica*, or they are specific charged services, complementary to the information delivered free-of-charge. That is notably the case of many statistics organizations that allow free access to information but charge for knowledge (specific work on a particular type of data).

DOMINIQUE FORAY
UNIVERSITÉ DE PARIS IX-DAUPHINE

Further reading

(References cited in the text marked *)

* Arora, A. (1995) 'Licensing tacit knowledge : intellectual property rights and the market for know-how', *Economics of Innovation and New Technology*, 4 (1). (Explains how patents can structure complex market transactions on knowledge.)
* Arundel, A. and I. Kabla (1998) 'What percentage of innovations are patented? Empirical estimates for European firms', *Research Policy* 27. (Provides up-to-date data and information on patents behaviours at the firm level.)
* Bessy, C. and E. Brousseau (1999) 'Technology licensing contracts: features and diversity', *International Review of Law and Economics*, January. (Describes the diversity of knowledge transaction mechanisms.)
* Cockburn, I. and R. Henderson (1997) 'Public–private interaction and the productivity of pharmaceutical research', Working Paper Series, WP 6018, National Bureau of Economic Research. (Analyses the complex interactions between the public and the private sectors.)
* Foray, D. (1999) 'Science, technology and the market', *World Social Science Report*, London: UNESCO Publishing/Elsevier. (Raises the policy issues related to the increasing commercial involvement of scientists.)
* Heller, M. and R. Eisenberg (1998) 'Can patents deter innovation? The anticommons in biomedical research', *Science* 280. (Describes and

discusses the phenomenon of anticommons in genomics.)
* Jaffe, A. (1999) 'The U.S. patent system in transition: policy innovation and the innovation process', NBER Working paper No. 7280. (Describes and assesses the numerous institutional changes of the US patent system.)
* Kortum, S. and J. Lerner (1997) 'Stronger protection or technological revolution: what is behind the recent surge in patenting?' Working Paper, 98-012, Harvard Business School. (Reviews the various explanations of the current patent explosion in the USA.)
* Kremer, M. (1997) 'Patent buy-outs: a mechanism for encouraging innovation', NBER Working paper No. 6304. (Analyses a mechanism for regulating the privatization of fundamental knowledge.)
* Mowery D.C., R.R. Nelson, B. Sampat and A.A. Ziedonis (1998) 'The effects of the Bayh-Dole Act on US University Research and Technology transfer: an analysis of data from Columbia University, the University of California, and Stanford University', Kennedy School of Government, Harvard University. (Describes and assesses the impact of the Bay-Dole Act.)
* Ordover, J. (1991) 'A patent system for both diffusion and exclusion', *Journal of Economic Perspectives* 5 (1). (Analyses the key institutional differences between the US and the Japanese patent systems.)
* Scotchmer, S. (1991) 'Standing on the shoulders of giants', *Journal of Economic Perspectives* 5 (1). (Raises the issue of patent scope in the case of cumulative technological change.)

See also: DEVELOPMENT AND DIFFUSION OF TECHNOLOGY; DYNAMIC CAPABILITIES; ECONOMIC GROWTH AND CONVERGENCE; EVOLUTIONARY THEORIES OF THE FIRM; EXCHANGE RATE ECONOMICS; FRIEDMAN, M.; GALBRAITH, J.K.; GLOBALIZATION; GROWTH OF THE FIRM AND NETWORKING; GROWTH THEORY; INDUSTRIAL DYNAMICS; INNOVATION; INTELLECTUAL PROPERTY RIGHTS; SCHUMPETER, J.

Cleaner production

1. The concept of cleaner production
2. Cleaner production programmes
3. The effects of cleaner production programmes

Overview

During the 1970s and 1980s, the primary approach to managing environmental pollution in countries throughout the world focused on installing pollution control technologies at the end of pollution discharge pipes. These so-called 'end of pipe' technologies were mandated by various laws and regulations to bring pollution releases into compliance with government-issued pollution permits. The permits were typically based on the best available control technology at the time and the capacity of the receiving environmental medium to dilute and assimilate the pollution at levels that science demonstrated to be below levels of concern to human health or ecological systems. Beginning in the late 1980s, a new approach called cleaner production began to appear that was more in keeping with the rapidly emerging concept of sustainable development.

1 The concept of cleaner production

The initial concepts of cleaner production were assembled during the mid-1980s, but the establishment of cleaner production within the United Nations Environment Programme provides a commonly recognized historical mark for the formal launch of the concept. In 1989, the Industry and Environment Office of the United Nations Environment Programme (UNEP) established a 'Cleaner Production Programme' to promote cleaner production in industrialized countries and to assist currently industrializing countries in adopting cleaner industrial practices. For UNEP:

> Cleaner production means the continuous application of an integrated preventive environmental strategy to processes and products to reduce risks to humans and the environment. For production processes cleaner production includes conserving raw materials and energy, eliminating toxic raw materials, and reducing the quantity and toxicity of all emissions and wastes before they leave a process. For products the strategy focuses on reducing impacts along the entire life cycle of the product, from raw material extraction to ultimate disposal of the product. Cleaner production is achieved by applying know-how, by improving technologies, and by changing attitudes.
> (United Nations Environment Programme 1992)

Cleaner production applies to both products and processes. Cleaner products are those designed to reduce impacts throughout their entire life cycle, from raw material extraction to the ultimate disposal of the product and its packaging. Cleaner production processes conserve raw materials and energy, eliminate toxic materials, and modify or upgrade processes so as to reduce the generation of wastes and emissions. Table 1 describes various cleaner production techniques by industrial sector.

In contrast to pollution control technologies that add equipment on to the production processes in order to better manage pollution, cleaner production technologies replace or retool existing production equipment in order to improve the materials' efficiencies of production and to reduce the environmental and health risks associated with the production processes themselves. In many cases the conversion to cleaner production technologies reduces or eliminates the need for pollution control technologies. Indeed, cleaner production is about much more than technologies. Cleaner production involves management practices, process modification and product design as well as new equipment and new materials.

Table 1 Examples of cleaner production by industry sector

Metal products	Forming or moulding metal to desired shape reduces wastes involved in cutting and drilling.
	Using gases to cool and vegetable oils to lubricate during drilling and cutting reduces hazardous oil wastes and the need for parts cleaning.
Coatings and paints	High solids and radiation-cured coatings improve efficiencies and reduce volatile organic emissions.
Foundries	Reclaiming and reusing green sand and chemically bonded sand reduces waste generation.
Pulp and paper	Extended pulp cooking and washing and oxygen delignification reduces bleaching requirements and dioxin emissions.
Printing	Soy-based inks and inks cured by electron beam or ultraviolet radiation improve quality, reduce volatile organic emissions, and reduce solvent use in press cleaning.
Photoprocessing	Improving chemical inventory control and recovering silver from fixers, baths and scrap papers and films conserves materials and reduces wastes.
Garment dry cleaning	Installing dry-to-dry wash and dry machines reduces solvent volatilization.
	Converting to multi-process wet cleaning with microwave drying reduces the use of solvents.
Textile manufacture	Reconstituting and reuse of dyebaths and recycling of rinse baths and metals in rinse waters conserves materials and reduces waste water.
	Converting to pad-batch or low liquor dyeing improves dye fixation and reduces energy and water consumption.

Cleaner production programmes involve a reconsideration of products as well as production processes. New techniques for considering the environmental impacts of products over their lifetime have emerged in the form of 'life cycle assessment'. Life cycle assessments conducted by firms on their products have proven useful in identifying priority points of environmental impact and in comparing the environmental attributes of various products or product components. The use of life cycle assessments has spurred an increase in firms adopting 'extended producer responsibility' programmes that commit the firm to assist in the management of their products throughout their useful life and at the point of final disposal.

When cleaner production techniques are implemented at industrial facilities, they have often produced significant results that reduce both environmental burdens and operating costs. The cost reductions have resulted from reduced expenditures for raw materials or energy, reduced costs for government compliance and the purchase of pollution control technologies, avoided costs for waste treatment services, reduced liability costs, and improved efficiencies in operating systems.

In 1979, the Commission of the European Economic Community developed the concept of 'clean technology' as 'any technical measure ... to reduce or even eliminate at source the production of any nuisance, pollution or waste, and to help save raw materials and other natural resources and energy' (Commission of the European Economic Community 1985). Such clean technologies are one of the elements of cleaner production. The production of these technologies forms the fastest-growing sector of new technologies designed for protecting the environment. The range of technologies and their application is broad and expanding. Table 2 presents examples of

Table 2 Examples of cleaner production materials, equipment and services

Materials	Biodegradable polymers
	Water-based paints and coatings
	Aqueous and semi-aqueous cleaning solutions
	Vegetable oil-based inks, dyes and machining fluids
	Recyclable and reusable materials
Equipment	Closed-loop and counter-current rinse tanks
	Conventional strippers, reactors, membranes, filters and condensers
	Ultrafiltration, microfiltration, reverse osmosis and ion exchange equipment sensors, recorders and process control equipment
	Aqueous, ultrasonic and super-critical cleaning equipment
	Photovoltaics, superconductors and new energy storage cells
Services	Process design services
	Measuring, monitoring and analytical services
	Inventory management and control services
	Facility auditing and planning services

cleaner production materials, technologies and services.

Because of the increasing costs of managing pollution from industrial processes, there are many market incentives for firms that encourage cleaner forms of production. But there are also barriers to overcome as enterprises attempt to convert. These include:

- lack of awareness of the true costs of environmentally unsound production;
- lack of knowledge of alternative, cleaner production technologies;
- lack of appropriate materials or technologies;
- conflicting government regulations;
- high initial costs of some cleaner production technologies;
- lack of investment capital and unfamiliarity of lending institutions; and
- social or cultural resistance to change.

In order to overcome such barriers, governments and non-governmental institutions throughout the world have launched programmes to encourage and assist in the conversion to cleaner production.

2 Cleaner production programmes

The ten years since UNEP established its Cleaner Production Programme have generated scores of national government programmes, over 20 national technical assistance centres, several academic research and teaching programmes, many non-government advocacy programmes and a host of manuals, books and journals focused on cleaner production. In addition, cleaner production initiatives have supported or spawned a collection of new tools, including facility assessments, full cost accounting, technology assessments, eco-balances and life cycle assessments.

In Europe, much of the promotion began in the early 1980s with the publication of a large compendium of 'low- and non-waste technologies'. Sweden, Denmark and the Netherlands set up specific technical and financial assistance programmes during the 1980s for the promotion of clean technologies. By the close of the decade there appeared a series of demonstration projects, typically regionally based, that sought to link government, academic and private resources together to identify and encourage the adoption of new cleaner production technologies and processes. Among the first was the Landskrona project in Southern Sweden, which linked researchers at the University of Lund with twelve firms in the Malmo industrial district in identifying and implementing new cleaner technologies.

In the Netherlands, a programme called the PRISMA (Project, Industrial Successes with Waste Prevention) project was launched in 1988 to promote pollution prevention experiment within ten firms. The programme combined experimentation, study and the active communication of results of projects adopted by participating firms. The success of the PRISMA project was followed by similar projects in other industrial regions in the Netherlands. By the mid-1990s, similar demonstration projects had begun in Norway, Denmark, Spain, Austria, Poland and the United Kingdom.

In the United States much of this promotion has appeared under the concept of preventing pollution at the source or, as it is variously called, 'source reduction' or 'pollution prevention'. The Federal government has recognized pollution prevention throughout many of its far-flung branches. In 1990, Congress enacted an enabling law called the Pollution Prevention Act and the EPA established a special Office of Pollution Prevention. In 1992, an internal agency reorganization resulted in the Office of Pollution Prevention and Toxics and a special policy office in the EPA Administrator's office. The agency has initiated projects to promote voluntary reductions in industrial pollutants, established a special project to integrate pollution prevention into environmental regulations, launched a series of 'design for the environment' projects for specific business sectors, initiated a 'green lights' programme to promote energy efficiency, and established a special state grants programme to assist states in catalyzing innovations in pollution prevention.

Since 1990, over two-thirds of the US states have enacted some form of pollution prevention programme. While the state programmes differ markedly in requirements and government aggressiveness, most include similar definitions, similar lists of techniques, and some kind of state technical assistance. In general, these programmes encourage firms to reduce the generation of hazardous wastes and the release of air and water pollutants through a set of techniques that include the substitution of feedstock chemicals, the reformation of products, modification of the production processes, improvements in operations and maintenance, and the installation of closed loop, in-process recycling and reuse of materials. Several states have reorganized their regulatory compliance system to integrate pollution prevention into permitting and inspections.

By encouraging firms to examine production processes and change materials, processes or management practices, pollution prevention programmes have moved beyond pollution control technologies directly into a reconsideration of the central technologies of production. These laws have extended public assistance directly into traditional engineering design and production management decisions. Central to many of these state pollution prevention programmes is the production and maintenance of a waste reduction or pollution prevention plan that inventories chemical use, sets priorities among chemicals, reviews the technical options and sets goals and schedules for implementation of the selected techniques.

Cleaner production is not merely the luxury of advanced industrial countries. The United Nations has gathered reports of cleaner production projects from developing countries and countries currently in transition to market-based economies. Drip pans are used to collect and recycle fruit juice in a pineapple processing plant in the Philippines. Substituting a surfactant for a high phosphate detergent has prolonged coolant life in Mexican automobile component manufacturing and improved the treatment of oily wastes. Recycling of cooking chemicals, water and fibre in Indonesian pulp and paper plants has reduced waste and improved efficiencies in the making of paper.

These various projects from around the world reveal that environmental issues can be integrated directly into the design and operations of industrial production processes. Where environmental effects are not seen as residuals of production, but, rather, as central design parameters in the development of cleaner production technologies and the selection of production materials, the environment can be protected and productivity can be enhanced.

3 The effects of cleaner production programmes

Cleaner production can be achieved by simple changes in management procedures, by the redesign of products, by changes in operations and maintenance, or by alterations to the production process. Often the changes in production processes require changes in the production technologies – the equipment and materials used to manufacture products. These changes can involve process innovation and the adoption of new equipment and new production practices.

The diffusion and adoption of cleaner production innovations can be quite complex. Innovations in cleaner production technologies can arise from different functional actors. Production engineers, materials suppliers, equipment manufacturers, or technical assistance programmes can develop and promote cleaner production technologies. Cleaner production innovations face competition from well-entrenched end-of-pipe technology. End-of-pipe technology tends to be mature and therefore far down its learning curve. And unlike many cleaner production innovations, these conventional technologies tend to fit the existing competencies, culture and organizational systems of potential adopters.

Certain characteristics of cleaner production innovation, such as relative cost advantage, compatibility, complexity, potential for piloting and the establishment of demonstrations, are thought to affect the adoption rate of such innovation. Still, few firms want to be among the first adopters. Only the most trustworthy firms take innovator-derived test data at face value. Many potential adopters prefer to take their technology signals from competitors – figuring that if their competitor has adopted the technology, it must have proven itself.

Government programmes can encourage cleaner production innovations. Historically, environmental regulations spurred the development of end-of-pipe pollution control technologies. Environmental regulations often play a role in technology innovation and diffusion processes (chiefly by affecting the relative advantage of one technology over another), but many of the factors that speed or inhibit the adoption of cleaner production technologies are exogenous to such regulation. Thus, many governments have turned to financial aid, training programmes, technology demonstrations and technical assistance programmes as the principal means of support.

The effects of these programmes have been significant. First, cleaner production programmes have advanced the adoption of many more resource-intensive and less hazardous production technologies. Aqueous cleaning, powder coatings, solvent recycling, non-cyanide plating, counter-current rinsing, lead-free soldering, water-based paints, vegetable-based dyes and bead-blasting strippers are all physical ramifications of many cleaner production initiatives.

Second, cleaner production has helped to expand the role of environmental values in business management by integrating environmental considerations into product design and process management decisions. Environmental performance is increasingly considered as an important management system that needs to be optimized along with management systems for quality and financial return.

Third, cleaner production has stimulated a reconsideration of environmental protection investments, which were conventionally recorded as a business overhead cost. By promoting materials and energy efficiencies, waste reduction, full cost accounting and green marketing, cleaner production has demonstrated how environmental considerations can lead to productivity benefits and market advantage. Environmental values have proven to add to, not subtract from, the economic performance of a firm.

Finally, cleaner production has provided a conceptual bridge connecting industrialization and sustainability. Since the 1992 United Nations Conference on Environment and Development, the concept of sustainability has been enshrined as the global vision for a healthy future. Cleaner production has allowed industrial production to find a place in this vision by recasting negative images of polluting industrial processes into positive images of materials conserving, energy efficient, non-polluting and low-waste technologies generating ecologically friendly products that are responsibly managed throughout their life cycle.

KENNETH GEISER
UNIVERSITY OF MASSACHUSETTS AT LOWELL

Further reading

(References cited in the text marked *)

* Commission of the European Economic Community (1985) *Official Journal of the European Communities*, No. C100/2-20.4, Brussels, Belgium. (Lists many early examples on low- and no-waste technologies.)
Gottlieb, R. (ed.) (1995) *Reducing Toxics: A New Approach to Policy and Industrial Decisionmaking*, Washington: Island Press. (Provides a good history of the pollution prevention efforts in the United States.)
Jackson, T. (ed.) (1993) *Clean Production Strategies: Developing Preventive Environmental Management in the Industrial Economy*, Boco Raton, Florida: Lewis. (Provides a valuable introduction to the intellectual ideas that lie at the core of the cleaner production concept.)
* United Nations Environment Programme, Industry and Environment Programme (1992) *Cleaner Production Program*, unpublished brochure, Paris, France. (A general public relations brochure.)
United Nations Environment Programme, Industry and Environment Programme (1994) *Cleaner Production in the Asia Pacific Economic Cooperation Region*, Paris, France. (Provides short case studies of over twenty examples of cleaner production in the Asia-Pacific region.)
US Environmental Protection Agency, Office of Pollution Prevention and Toxics (1994) *EPA Pollution Prevention Accomplishments: 1993*, EPA-100-R-94-002, Washington, DC. (Identifies many of the early pollution prevention programmes of the U.S. Environmental Protection Agency.)
World Commission on Environment and Development (1987) *Our Common Future*, New York: Oxford University Press. (A seminal statement on the need for sustainable development by the United Nations-sponsored World Commission on Environment and Development chaired by the Norwegian Prime Minister, Gro Brundtland.)

See also: DEVELOPMENT AND DIFFUSION OF TECHNOLOGY

Development and diffusion of technology

1 The nature of technology
2 The development of technology
3 The diffusion of technology
4 Conclusion

Overview

Technology has been a field whose importance in business and management has long been accepted, but a subject often lying beyond the competence of managers and social scientists unless they also happen to have engineering training. Many social sciences have tried to contribute to understanding the evolution of technology, but all have their limitations. This discussion aims to integrate social science frameworks, especially those drawn from economics, with empirical examples taken from actual cases of technologies. It is shown that the literature pertaining to the 'development' of technology has tended to take a supply-oriented focus; in particular, that the commercialization of a successful innovation is the outcome of a long process stretching back to earlier breakthroughs in upstream science. Though continuing to be taken seriously by governments as a justification for subsidizing science, this so-called 'linear model' has been much discredited in recent academic debates. Conversely the literature on 'diffusion' has tended to take a demand-oriented focus, envisaging the main problem as one of communicating the benefits obtainable from the new technology to prospective adopters. In practice, there are important issues arising on the side of *both* demand and supply in *both* 'development' and 'diffusion'. In the chain-linked, interactive model outlined below, innovation and diffusion are interconnected, as diffusion to new kinds of users encourages further improvements or adaptations in the new technology. Although the issues can be separated in the formal literature, in practical management it is the interconnections that matter.

1 The nature of technology

'Technology' is used in a variety of meanings in the economics and business literature. The first point of clarification is that technology differs from both product (goods *and* services) and from production process; though economists often equate a product with a technology as if there were a one-to-one interrelationship, and sociologists often equate a production process with a technology. It is more useful to divide technologies into product-oriented technologies and process-oriented technologies, so that innovations can take the forms of product innovations and process innovations (see INNOVATION). That is, technologies enter into both products and processes, but they are not the same thing as those products and processes (this point is elaborated further below).

The second point is that knowledge and know-how are involved, alongside the artifacts. As just noted, economists commonly confuse technologies and products, partly by identifying the former solely as artifacts (e.g. particular machines or items of equipment). Instead, the '-ology' part of the word 'technology' indicates that there is a knowledge as well as an artifactual dimension to technological change. That is, one can think of both a 'hardware' and a 'software' component of a technology. Attempts to classify technologies solely on their artifactual properties, as tend to be found in the literature on anthropology (e.g. Basalla 1988), unduly simplify the nature of technological development and diffusion.

This distinction has some practical importance, because the hardware aspect of technological change is usually assessed by indicators such as patents, which are required to be artifacts, while the software side is sometimes measured by indicators such as publications in periodicals. An implication is that ways of grouping technologies as artifacts, which rest upon the organization of patent systems, can differ markedly from ways of grouping technologies as knowledge, which are drawn from the structure of scientific and engineering disciplines. The knowledge bases implied are however to be distinguished from discoveries or 'ideas', which is how economists sometimes like to characterize them (e.g. Romer 1993), because they are actually bundled into the production or use of the artifacts.

A major implication of these definitional points is that one should distinguish between the *production* of technologies and the *use* of technologies. This underlies the distinction between the 'development' and the 'diffusion' of technologies. The use of technologies through diffusion is often regarded as an essentially passive process of adopting (purchasing) artifacts. Since there is practical knowledge and know-how involved in the application as well as in the production of technologies, the usual situation in practice is far different from such passive adoption. We will come back later to the key point that the development of technologies normally comes about through a chain-linked interaction between producers and users of technologies. This sequence may take a very long time to evolve.

Finally, it is common to draw a distinction between 'radical' and 'incremental' technological changes. Radical changes have naturally been the subject of far greater study, though it has long been established that the sum total of incremental changes may contribute at least as much to overall economic improvement (as in Hollander's 1965 study of Du Pont's development of synthetic fibres). The distinction is however a difficult one to draw in practice, primarily because of the complex sequence of produceruser interactions just mentioned. A few radical innovations spring in more or less useable form from the work of creative geniuses (one example being the steam engine of Thomas Newcomen, who designed and assembled virtually all of the components of the steam engine within a short span of years at the start of the eighteenth century, with practically no predecessor to guide his work). Most, though, are the outcome of a long period of failure and partial success, joining together the work of many contributors (think, for instance, of the evolution of the aeroplane from the Montgolfier balloon to the Wright brothers at Kittyhawk, and beyond). In this evolution, it is often difficult to point the finger at exactly where the radical breakthrough comes, because so many of the stages rely on previous advances (and setbacks). Moreover, and in contrast to the standard 'Schumpeterian' model which supposes a radical breakthrough to be followed by a string of incremental improvements, it is often the case that the radical breakthrough represents the culmination of a long sequence of apparently minor earlier advances (for example, the internet might be seen in this way). What then makes the final step 'radical' is the integration of these scattered preceding advances into a workable new entity, often coupled with a new way of thinking of what that new entity can achieve (i.e. a new 'idea' about its purpose). In contrast also to economic models drawn from game theory which depict a 'patent race' to develop a new technology, this cognitive leap regarding the purpose of the radical breakthrough often comes *after* the new artifact has come into existence, and not necessarily before. Again, it is important to consider both the artifact and the knowledge, the hardware and the 'software'.

2 The development of technology

The classic formulation of the development of technology is the so-called 'linear model', which proposes a linear sequence, starting from a scientific discovery, that becomes embedded in an invention and then commercialized as an innovation. Once the point of commercialization has been reached, at which the new technology achieves its initial impact on the market, diffusion processes take over to pursue the take-up of the technology. The diffusion processes will be dealt with separately below, but even that is an undue simplification of many actual technological sequences. One implication of what has been said above is that actual sequences are frequently much messier than this. A classic example is the development of thermodynamics as a field of engineering science out of practical work on steam engines, where the science emerged because existing steam engines were performing more efficiently than existing theories of heat allowed. In other words, technology led to science rather than science to technology.

The linear model has nevertheless had a major impact on both theories of technological change and – even more – on government policies. An early exposition by an economist of what is nowadays termed the linear model is contained in Say (1821). Say favoured supply-driven models of economic and technological change, and is best known today for 'Say's Law', that supply creates its own demand. While more nuanced than that, his exposition of the development of technology falls into much the same line of thinking. Governments have been less concerned about nuances, and for many years have tended to adopt the linear model as a justification for them to fund basic scientific research.

The case for governments to subsidize basic research was given economic blessing by the work of Nelson (1959) and Arrow (1962), who set out the view that research was subject to 'market failure'. Nelson emphasized the lack of appropriability of the returns from basic research, that is the inability to recapture all the profits from innovation as rival firms copied the new ideas, so firms and individuals under-invested in basic research. Arrow emphasized that ideally there would be zero returns to basic research, since the community or country as a whole gained from maximum diffusion of the ideas generated by research, which would be optimized by setting the price of those ideas at zero. He pointed out that the nature of information in any case drove the system in that direction, because the 'paradox of information' in an economic context meant that there was no way of establishing a viable positive price for information. This was because the buyers had no reasonable way of valuing the information they were planning to purchase *a priori*. Only when buyers actually acquired the information would they be able to establish its value, but once they learnt what it was, it had no further value to them – in this sense, information differed from most tangible commodities. Arrow therefore argued that the community should price the outputs of its basic research at zero, but reward its researchers by granting them 'prizes' out of public funds.

These ideas have been carried forwards in more recent times into the 'new economics of science'. Such writers argue that science and technology differ fundamentally in their economic motivation. Science favours the first to publish and consequent openness of the results, and thus is rewarded by 'prizes' of differing kinds, ranging from publication in refereed journals up to international prestige awards. Technology, by contrast, favours the first to profit, and aims to conceal its results as much as possible through secrecy or the like, in order to maximize the amount of appropriability from technological innovation. Such differences in underlying incentives pose tensions of communication between science and technology, without ruling out linkages altogether. Meanwhile, Arrow's paradox has evolved into the 'economics of information', in which the sources of market failure in information (moral hazard and adverse selection) and of maldistribution of information (asymmetric information) are further clarified; though this work has been applied more to financial markets than to those in science and technology.

These arguments however involve some strong assumptions. Arrow's paradox assumes for these purposes that technology flows are essentially flows of information, whereas later research has put greater emphasis on knowledge as distinct from information. Nelson has also reconsidered his position, and shown how the benefits of research can be over- as well as under-appropriated through patents, for instance in some areas of genomics. The case for government support is wider than the market failure perspective would define.

A more thoroughgoing attack on the 'linear model' and the notion of 'market failure' comes from scholars who contend that technological change is driven by demand factors rather than supply factors. This view was popularized in the 1960s at a time when Keynesianism, or at least the neo-Keynesian synthesis, had become orthodoxy in macroeconomics. The work of Jacob Schmookler (1966), in particular, used patents evidence to contend that fluctuations in patenting in some major areas of industry such as railroads and petroleum refining followed – rather than preceded – fluctuations in investment in those same fields. Thus Schmookler argued forcibly that causation ran from investment (seen in

Keynesian fashion as 'demand') to innovation (measured by patents), rather than vice versa. Such views were picked up by scholars from other backgrounds, who used case studies to argue that 'need' drove innovation; as in the popular saying, 'necessity is the mother of invention'.

Subsequent investigations have undermined parts of these lines of argument. Rosenberg (1974) noted that science and basic research would often be required before any practical innovation could meet the required demands. Needs for innovations had long gone unsatisfied in human history because of the lack of requisite scientific research (for instance, we still lack efficacious cures for many forms of cancer, for which the demand seems unquestionable). However, it must be said that, in the later chapters of his 1966 book, Schmookler (who had died prematurely by the time Rosenberg was writing) had allowed a positive role for science.

A more damaging critique by Mowery and Rosenberg (1979) challenged the notion of 'need' as an exclusive driving force. They pointed out, first, that few entrepreneurs would be willing to commercialize an innovation for which no market was foreseen; secondly, that 'need' did not equate to 'demand' in the economist's sense, and that we continue to lack studies derived from the economic theory of changes in demand of the causation of technological change. The empirical work of Schmookler also came under attack. Some were worried that its message, based on figures mainly for the late nineteenth and early twentieth centuries, would not stand up a century later, in view of the rising role of science-based industries. Indeed, Schmookler's own figures, when presented as levels rather than as fluctuations, strongly support a case for a bunching of patents at an early stage in the innovation process, well ahead of the main bunching of investments, and still further ahead of the main growth of demand as measured by product outputs.

What the above findings imply is that both supply and demand can be enlisted as causes of innovation. More strongly, the prevailing view nowadays is that the two interact with each other. This is often best seen through a historical sequence of shifts in both supply curves (from scientific research, etc.) and demand curves (from changing tastes, investment, etc.), which duly respond to the other. A more elaborate version of this interactivity is given by the so-called 'chain-linked' model of innovation, in which multiple sources of learning and multiple 'feedbacks' to other sources are envisaged as co-evolving through time. A somewhat similar view, but stemming from the area of management rather than the economics of innovation, is put forward in the model of knowledge 'spirals' advanced by Nonaka and Takeuchi (1995), which traces the generation and absorption of technological advances inside large companies.

Such approaches have joined with work coming from innovation studies and other disciplines such as psychology to place the main emphasis on 'learning', being the process of accumulation of knowledge (as before, seen as distinct from information). The structures here are far from new, even in economics. A classic exposition of the division of labour by Adam Smith (1776) (see SMITH, A.) sets out the sources of innovation as follows:

> All the improvements in machinery, however, have by no means been the invention of those who had the occasion to use the machines. Many improvements have been made by the ingenuity of the makers of the machines, when to make them became the business of a peculiar trade; and some by that of those who are called philosophers [scientists] or men of speculation, whose trade it is, not to do any thing, but to observe every thing; and who, upon that account, are often capable of combining together the powers of the most distant and dissimilar objects.
> (Smith 1776/1976: 21).

Smith's three categories amount in modern parlance to the three main types of learning: learning by using (in the process of using technological artifacts); learning by doing (in the process of producing technology); and formal learning through scientific and engineering inquiry. Modern interpretations place especially strong emphasis on the interaction between these sources of learning ('learning by interaction'). Malerba (1992) contains a fuller catalogue of modes of learning, built on these bases; in addition to learning by doing and using, which are shown to stimulate improvements in the 'yields' of production processes, he includes learning by searching (mainly from R&D, which is shown to raise quality), learning from spillovers, and learning from advances in science and technology. Learning by interacting is shown to have different effects on technical trajectories depending on whether the interaction is with equipment suppliers (which also raises 'yields'), input suppliers (which tends to save on material inputs), or users (which is linked to development of new products). Malerba's study puts high emphasis on the multiple external linkages involved in the innovation process.

3 The diffusion of technology

The same concerns have shaped some current views about the diffusion as well as the development of technology. In the chain-linked view, the knowledge-spiral view and the learning-by-interaction view, the distinction between development and diffusion is indeed often an arbitrary one, and sometimes pointless. Knowledge expands as a consequence of diffusion, especially the diffusion into new areas of application. Diffusion is therefore actively rather than passively involved in the longer-term development process.

The evolution of diffusion theory has however taken some time to come to this view. Parallel schools of thinking to those encountered in the technology development literature in fact can be observed in the diffusion literature. In the latter case, it was instead the 'demand' view which long dominated orthodox thought; indeed, the conjunction of a supply-led or science-led model of technology production and a demand-led model of technology diffusion amplified the distinction drawn between the two phenomena. The demand view originated not so much in economics as in disciplines like rural sociology, which took to examining the process of rural electrification in the US midwest in the 1930s. Such a view, which spilled over into economics and other approaches, rested on an 'adoption perspective'. The implicit assumption was that the artifact in question, such as electricity supply, was tailor-made for adoption by a hitherto untapped group of potential adopters and would vastly improve their modes of production or ways of life. What held this back was ignorance on their part, that is a lack of information communicated to them. Concomitant with the adoption perspective was therefore the notion of the key role of communicating information.

The initially crude assumptions about adopters were relaxed as the sociological literature developed, leading to a greatly expanded set of determinants of the behaviour of adopters (Rogers 1995). Economists approaching this issue were generally more specific in relating demand to its underlying economic determinants, especially relative prices and relative incomes. From a political economy perspective, it was also noted that governments might have a role to play on the demand side, especially in the early stages of adoption when private customers might be tempted to 'wait and see'. In the case of integrated circuits, the US government accounted for nearly all the initial demand (Tilton 1971), and its need for miniaturization in satellites shaped the main technological trajectory of the 'chip' (see also Hughes 1998). Alternatively, the government could subsidize the demands of private consumers, who without such subsidy might risk failure while the technology remained uncertain, as Clarke (1994) showed for US agricultural machinery.

From an economics perspective, there were unusually large profits to be earned as a consequence of a disequilibrium arising because of asymmetrically distributed information. Consistently in all the early studies of diffusion by econometricians, profitability came out as the key variable dictating adoption. Griliches (1957) analysed the case of hybrid corn, an important precursor of modern biotechnology, in the US midwest from the 1930s. He demonstrated how the adoption of hybrid corn moved from state to state depending on climatic and soil conditions determining relative profitability, but also stressed that hybrid corn was not a single product – rather it needed adaptation as its use extended to new ecological conditions, and in this sense would nowadays be better represented by a chain-linked innovation–diffusion process. He and Mansfield (1968) proceeded in two stages, first showing the generality of the pattern of diffusion (a sigmoid curve, i.e. leaning S-shape), and then correlating the parameters defining this pattern with a number of other variables such as profitability and firm size.

The basic problem, which neither of these early studies entirely overcame, is that profitability itself is endogenous within a chain-linked innovation–diffusion process, rather than being the kind of exogenous determinant the studies appeared to suggest at first blush. Profits rise and fall during the innovation–diffusion process, as outcomes as well as incentives. What is required of diffusion studies is a more careful modelling of the underlying demand and supply shifts, just as for studies of technological development. The econometric studies were nevertheless a dramatic improvement on the preceding rural sociology analyses, which assumed that the innovation would benefit all adopters and that all potential adopters would be in a position to adopt once they heard the good news.

Subsequent developments took several forms. On the one side, economic historians led the way in arguing that demand was far from homogeneous. Indirectly taking up the point made by Griliches about the differentiation of ecological conditions suiting the adoption of hybrid corn, they called attention to differentiation among potential adopters in terms of the benefits they could obtain from the innovation. David (1966) studied the case of mechanical reapers in the late nineteenth-century US midwest (a profitable region for conducting diffusion studies!), and argued for a 'threshold' of farm size. The farm had to be large enough to earn sufficient profits from its wheat output to offset the capital cost of the mechanical reaper; below this threshold the older hand reaper remained more profitable. The diffusion of the mechanical reaper was the outcome of three forces – in the short term, the price of wheat; in the medium term, the technical adequacy of the machine (though this was made exogenous); and in the longer term, shifts in the distribution of farm sizes. This however supposed that the purchase of the mechanical reaper was a matter for the individual farmer – if sharing was practised, as happened later with the combine-harvesters, small farmers could pool their resources to acquire one.

The size of the unit – the farm or the firm – thus became the main focus of attention in such threshold studies. Others, however, pointed to a variety of ways in which cost thresholds that differentiated potential adopters could arise. Variations in the cost of fuel across a country could dictate whether it was profitable or not to adopt machinery requiring that fuel. More generally, the economic circumstances of adopters could differ, for example because of differences in their incomes and access to resources required to purchase the new piece of equipment. In the absence of perfect capital markets, potential adopters could be inhibited by a lack of capital funds, even where the potential profitability from adoption seemed remunerative.

Such arguments led on to the view that the supply side also needed careful consideration. 'Vintage capital' models rested on the proposition of technologies as being embodied in successive generations of capital. One side of the vintage capital approach was the decision to scrap older generations of equipment. Salter (1966) argued that older equipment would not be scrapped until the working costs associated with using it exceeded the total costs (fixed plus working costs) of the new generation, so there was an inbuilt but quite rational 'bias' against adoption of new equipment. This, however, assumed that there was no second-hand value for the older equipment, whereas in practice the availability of second-hand markets could justify earlier disposal (by sale rather than by scrapping). Moreover, older equipment could be 'revamped' by partial reconstruction instead of total scrapping.

The other side of the vintage capital approach was a common presumption that learning-by-doing arose in the production of the equipment, so that costs of new generations would fall incrementally but persistently through time. This factor drew attention back to the innovation process underlying diffusion. Davies (1979) focused on different specifications of the learning process, contrasting the slow but sustained learning from large, indivisible investments with the fast but shorter learning from small-scale acquisitions. In his fuller specification, Davies amalgamates varieties of learning process with differentiations of consumers based on a threshold perspective (differences in sizes of firm), to set up a double integration process of diffusion, that is across firms and across consumers.

In evolutionary models of diffusion, the chain linkages are made more explicit. These models take disequilibrium to be normal rather than abnormal. Diffusion processes arise as the outcome of successive shifts in both supply and demand. In some forms of evolutionary models, it is falling rather than rising profits which attract innovation and diffusion – firms change their practices only when things are going badly. Any increase in profitability is then more a result of adoption rather than its direct cause. These models also usually distinguish more carefully between products, processes and technologies, as outlined. The same technology can enter many different products or processes (e.g. the semiconductor); conversely the one product can combine many different technologies (e.g. in a motor car). The demand for technologies is thus only indirectly derived from markets. The key to diffusion as well as the development of technologies is seen in learning processes; above all, it is the ability of the firm to create and absorb knowledge (the 'software' side of technologies) which dictates its likelihood of success. This learning stems partly from its own accumulation of knowledge and partly through learning by interaction with other firms and research institutions.

4 Conclusion

For about a quarter-millennium, innovation and diffusion have been interactive processes, embodied in a succession of 'Industrial Revolutions'. Social scientists from economics and other disciplines have however tended to see them as separate aspects of a linear process. Additionally, simplistic models which explain innovation by supply factors (the science base) and diffusion by demand factors (adoption) have prevailed. Recent theoretical developments have discarded these oversimplifying assumptions, and in doing so are very, very belatedly beginning to catch up with the real world.

NICK VON TUNZELMANN
SPRU, SUSSEX UNIVERSITY

Further reading

(References cited in the text marked *)

* Arrow, K.J. (1962) 'Economic welfare and the allocation of resources of invention', in R.R. Nelson (ed.) *The Rate and Direction of Inventive Activity: Economic and Social Factors*, Princeton NJ: NBER/Princeton University Press, 609–25. (Classic formulation of the 'paradox of information' and need to subsidize invention.)
* Basalla, G. (1988) *The Evolution of Technology*, Cambridge: Cambridge University Press. (Anthropological approach to technological evolution.)
* Clarke, S. (1994) *Regulation and the Revolution in United States Farm Productivity*, New York, Cambridge University Press. (Shows the importance of government policy for regulating product prices and credit arrangements for the diffusion of technology in US agriculture in the mid-twentieth century.)
* David, P.A. (1966) 'The mechanization of reaping in the ante-bellum Midwest', in H. Rosovsky (ed.) *Industrialization in Two Systems: Essays in Honor of Alexander Gerschenkron*, New York: Wiley, 3–39. (First extensive presentation of the 'threshold model' of diffusion.)
* Davies, S. (1979) *The Diffusion of Process Innovations*, Cambridge: Cambridge University Press. (Studies learning processes for embodied technical change from an economics viewpoint.)
* Griliches, Z. (1957) 'Hybrid corn: an exploration in the economics of technical change, *Econometrica* 25: 501–22. (First major study of diffusion by an econometrician.)
* Hollander, S. (1965) *The Sources of Increased Efficiency: A Study of Du Pont Rayon Plants*, Cambridge MA: MIT Press. (Early study calling attention to incremental innovation.)
* Hughes, T.P. (1998) *Rescuing Prometheus*, New York: Vintage Books. (Studies the development of several complex technological systems.)
* Malerba, F. (1992) 'Learning by firms and incremental technical change', *Economic Journal* 102(413): 845–59. (Combines clarification of learning concepts with empirical evidence.)
* Mansfield, E. (1968) *Industrial Research and Technological Innovation: An Econometric Analysis*, London: Longman. (Pioneering study of diffusion in an economic context.)
* Mowery, D. and Rosenberg, N. (1979) 'The influence of market demand upon innovation: a critical review of some recent empirical studies', *Research Policy* 8: 103–53. (Careful dissection of excessive claims about innovation and 'need'.)

* Nelson, R.R. (1959) 'The simple economics of basic scientific research', *Journal of Political Economy* 47: 297–306. (Early justification for subsidizing research on grounds of 'market failure'.)
* Nonaka, I. and H. Takeuchi (1995), *The Knowledge-Creating Company: How Japanese Companies Create the Dynamics of Innovation*, New York: Oxford University Press. (Explains knowledge production in large companies.)
* Rogers, E.M. (1995) *Diffusion of Innovations*, 4th edn, New York: Free Press. (Surveys diffusion models from a range of disciplinary standpoints.)
* Romer, P. (1993) 'Idea gaps and object gaps', *Journal of Monetary Economics* 32: 543–73. (Emphasis on 'ideas' by a founder of the 'new growth theory'.)
* Rosenberg, N. (1974) 'Science, invention and economic growth', *Economic Journal* 84: 90–108. (Reasserting the role of science in innovation.)
* Salter, W.E.G. (1966) *Productivity and Technical Change*, 2nd edn, Cambridge: Cambridge University Press (DAE Cambridge Monographs). (Formulates and tests theories of 'vintage capital'.)
* Say, J.B. (1821) *A Treatise on Political Economy*, London: Longman (1st French edn, 1803). (Presents 'Say's Law' of markets and the 'linear model' of science leading technology and growth.)
* Schmookler, J. (1966) *Invention and Economic Growth*, Cambridge MA: Harvard University Press. (Argues that investment leads invention.)
* Smith, A. (1776) *An Inquiry into the Nature and Causes of the Wealth of Nations*, London: W. Strahan and T. Cadell (bicentennial edn., Oxford: Clarendon Press, 1976). (Classic foundation text in economics, noting 'learning' in the division of labour.)
* Tilton, J.E. (1971) *International Diffusion of Technology: The Case of Semiconductors*, Washington, DC: Brookings Institution. (Early study of the semiconductor industry and role of government in diffusion.)

See also: INNOVATION; INTELLECTUAL PROPERTY RIGHTS; SMITH, A.

Innovation

1 The innovating enterprise: debates and issues
2 The innovation process
3 Core results of innovation research

Overview

Innovation is novelty – it involves doing new things in new ways. So new products, new processes, new organizational methods, new services, and so on, are all part of innovation. Technological innovation transforms and improves the technical attributes and performance characteristics of products and processes, and through this introduces dynamic change and productivity growth into the economic system. For this reason, all theories of economic growth rest in one way or another on ideas concerning innovation and technological change. In studying innovation, most modern research has focused on the sources, nature and characteristics of knowledge and learning. If innovation is novelty, then it must also involve learning (after all, if we already knew how to do something, it would not be an innovation). If we think of technology as forms of knowledge related to productive transformations, then innovative learning is the process that expands the existing knowledge base.

Innovation research is a relatively new field (for book-length overviews see Dodgson and Rothwell, 1994 and Sundbo, 1998; for review articles see Kline and Rosenberg, 1986, Dosi, 1988, and Freeman, 1994). Although much of the classical economics of the nineteenth century rests implicitly on ideas about technological change, it is perhaps only in the work of Marx that a sustained reflection on innovation can be found. His ideas had a profound influence on the work of Joseph Schumpeter in the first half of the twentieth century and, in turn, Schumpeter heavily influenced the revival of research on innovation from the 1960s (in particular, Schumpeter, 1943 and 1964). The dramatic growth of the field dates, however, from the early 1980s, since when researchers have explored many aspects of knowledge creation, primarily from disciplinary backgrounds in economics, management and sociology. It should be noted that much recent research has been empirical in character – it has consisted of quite basic investigations of the real characteristics of innovation, using case studies and statistical analyses. Case studies have usually been carried out at company level, and have focused on describing and analysing the complexities of knowledge-creation and competence building. Quantitative analyses have tended to focus on sectoral or national levels, and have been aided, especially in the 1990s, by new data resources (especially economy-wide surveys on innovation activity and outputs), as well as enhanced and disaggregated R&D data, much-improved patent data, and databases on scientific publications (for an overview of statistical developments with respect to innovation, see OECD, 1996).

1 The innovating enterprise: debates and issues

From an economic perspective, virtually all recent research has challenged the basic underpinnings of mainstream neo-classical economics – the idea of the representative firm, the idea of optimizing agents, the idea of well-defined choice sets, and so on. Researchers have tended to substitute either evolutionary frameworks drawing on Schumpeter's ideas, or more historically informed frameworks drawing on lessons from business and economic history (see SCHUMPETER, J.). These non-neo-classical approaches typically emphasize various empirically founded phenomena related to decision making. These include the bounded and restricted character of enterprise decision making, the role of organizational capability within enterprises, the development of technological competence within the enterprise, the impacts of extreme uncertainty associated with innovation (and hence the unpredictability of economic dynamics, even in general terms), the presence of inter-firm and inter-institutional collaboration (and hence the collective character of knowledge production and knowledge flows), and so on. All of these phenomena undercut not only the mainstream economic theory of the firm, but also the basic assumptions that are necessary for neo-classical approaches to the economic process as a whole.

However, this does not imply that a good alternative theory of the innovating enterprise exists at this time. The underlying weakness in the neo-classical theory of the firm is the assumption that the firm is a single, unitary economic agent – not fundamentally different from an individual person (see EVOLUTIONARY THEORIES OF THE FIRM). Such an approach, combined with the idea of well-defined technological choices, of course rules out most if not all issues of management and strategy in innovation. Unfortunately, many evolutionary or otherwise heterodox approaches to innovation, while emphasizing such phenomena as uncertainty and competence building, nevertheless continue to see enterprises as unified decision-making bodies. This leads to a neglect of such issues as the real nature of corporate control, strategy formation, the allocation of resources to innovation, and the management of innovation as an integrated part of the operations of the enterprise. Although economists such as Edith Penrose, and historians such as Alfred Chandler, have explored the internal organizational characteristics of the growth of enterprises (see PENROSE, E.T.), it is probably only in the work of Lazonick and O'Sullivan that the internal capabilities of enterprises are related to the wider process of economic development (see, e.g. Penrose, 1995; Chandler, 1990; Lazonick and O'Sullivan, 2000; O'Sullivan, 2000). These works, from somewhat different perspectives, see enterprises as complex social organizations: heterogeneous assemblies or coalitions of people fulfilling different functions (marketing, distribution, product development, production and so on) with different arrays of resources. The key internal capabilities that have been studied are the abilities first to organize and integrate such groups and functions, and secondly, to allocate, direct and exploit resources for investment in the tangible and intangible assets that renew and develop the products and processes of the enterprise. It is the latter process that generates enterprise growth, and that connects what happens inside the enterprise to wider processes of economic change and development.

2 The innovation process

A central theme in modern innovation research is rejection of the idea that innovation simply flows from some earlier process of scientific or technological discovery – the so-called 'linear model' of innovation. The key element of linear approaches was that technological change was seen as a *sequence of stages*, with new knowledge (usually founded in scientific research) leading to processes of invention, followed by engineering development resulting in innovation (or the commercial introduction of new products and processes). Underlying this was a technocratic view of innovation as a purely technical act: the production of a new technical device. In this framework, technology development and engineering were usually seen as forms of applied science. The linear view of innovation had two basic forms: a 'basic science' model of innovation, and a 'firm-level linear model'.

As the label suggests, the core of the 'basic science' model was that innovation sprang from discoveries in basic science, and that basic science provided a flow of results that were then transformed by firms into industrial innovations. This idea was most explicitly formulated by Vannevar Bush at the end of the World War II, and can be rather widely found in the ideologies (though not necessarily the practice) of research policy in most advanced countries. In his famous 1945 report to President Roosevelt, which led to the establishment of the National Science Foundation, Bush claimed that:

> Basic research leads to new knowledge. It provides scientific capital. It creates the fund from which the practical applications of knowledge must be drawn. New

products and processes do not appear full-grown. They are founded on new principles and new conceptions, which in turn are painstakingly developed by research in the purest realms of science. ... *A nation which depends upon others for its new basic scientific knowledge will be slow in its industrial progress and weak in its competitive position in world trade, regardless of its mechanical skill.*

Bush (1980: 19; italics in original)

This kind of thinking came under increasing challenge from the 1970s. On the one hand, countries with very substantial scientific establishments, such as Britain in the developed world, India in the developing world, and the USSR in the socialist bloc, were exhibiting relatively weak growth and/or trade performance. On the other hand, Japan was achieving strong growth and major increases in trade shares on the basis of innovations that emphasized incremental change in mature industries, and that clearly owed little to scientific research (see EAST ASIAN ECONOMIES). Rather, they rested on organizational capabilities, government-industry cooperation, new approaches to workforce skill development and participation, and so on.

The primary source for the 'firm-level' linear model was the work of Schumpeter, who adopted a micro version of this 'stages' approach to innovation. On the one hand, Schumpeter has a theory of the individual or corporate entrepreneurship which is in sharp contrast to the neo-classical theory of the firm, in the sense that the firm is seen as actively shaping its environment, rather than simply responding to a set of exogenously given prices. Linked with this is a quite distinct view of the competitive process, in which the neo-classical focus on price competition in perfect-knowledge markets for homogenous products was replaced by competition in terms of technical attributes (and hence permanent imperfect competition), radical uncertainty, and disequilibrium dynamics. In Schumpeter's approach, firms compete in terms of innovative capability, and this may involve innovations in technology (products or processes) but equally in organization, finance, and markets. This notion of competitive innovation in disequilibrium environments leads directly to the notion of generalized endogenous innovation, and it is the aspect of Schumpeter's work which underpins modern heterodox and evolutionary economics, as well as neo-classical 'new growth theory'. It should be noted, though, that Schumpeter – especially in his later work – had a particular view about the kinds of innovation that mattered for growth. These were what he called 'big' innovations, radical innovations such as railways or electricity, that changed the entire technological basis of the economy, and that Schumpeter held were central to the growth process.

On the other hand, within this view of firm behaviour, the competitive process and growth, Schumpeter also has a model of technological change itself, and this is distinctly linear: it saw innovation as a well-defined sequence of stages. Schumpeter characterizes innovation via three processes, namely *invention* (the discovery of a new technical principle and demonstration of its feasibility), *innovation* (the first development of the invention in its commercial form), and *diffusion* (the process of adoption by users). These are seen as distinct phases of innovation, and in this Schumpeter was followed by the analytical literature for many years. For example, the economic analysis of innovation diffusion has often taken the form of asking why a completed, finalized innovation – which is superior to existing technologies – takes a more or less long time to spread into use. The underlying idea here is that the innovation must be essentially complete before the diffusion process begins. However, post-Schumpeterian research has tended to agree that diffusion processes are characterized by a great deal of post-innovation improvement, and that the innovation is usually far from complete before diffusion begins – an approach that, of course, dissolves any stages approach to innovation.

Modern research can be seen, from one perspective, as a rejection of these stages ideas. It tends to see R&D as but one component of a complex mix of activities in enterprises. Innovation in an enterprise emerges out of an interaction between marketing strategies, design processes, the development of skills in employees, the acquisition of new capital and intermediate goods (along with learning how to use them), and so on.

However, even where his specific ideas have been rejected, Schumpeter has been a powerful influence to modern innovation studies. Broadly speaking, we can distinguish two main themes deriving from his influence:

- a theme which attempts to develop the theory of the innovation process itself – to explore how enterprises innovate, to develop a more subtle understanding of the processes involved;
- a theme which explores how innovation at enterprise levels affects the evolution and dynamics of industrial structures, and general economic performance.

Underlying much modern research is a more nuanced concept of technology itself, in which technology is no longer seen in a technocratic engineering sense, but in its social and economic context.

The point of departure for much modern research has been a concept of technology that sees the 'hardware' aspects of technology in a dynamic social and economic context. What is technology? Firstly, technology involves *knowledge* related to production: it implies understanding and competence relevant to material transformations. This knowledge can range from abstract scientific knowledge – codified and widely available – concerning the properties of nature, through to engineering 'know-how' or operative skills. The latter are often tacit, unwritten. Secondly, technology involves *organization*: at the most direct level this means the management and coordination systems which integrate individual activities and through which production takes place, or through which public-sector activity is organized. Thirdly, technology involves *techniques*: that is, machines, tools or other equipment with their rules and procedures of operation, and their ancillary activities such as maintenance, repair, training and so on. Technology can therefore be thought of as *the integration of knowledge, organization and technique*. However, there is a further essential aspect: technology is produced by and exists within a *social framework*. The social system makes economic and political choices which influence the development and spread of technologies, and which – through education and general culture – develop the skills needed to operate technologies. Social values and decisions thus shape the path of technological development. It seems apparent that differences in technological performance between societies have at least some of their roots in social structure and cultural forms, although how these differences operate is as yet far from clear.

Against this background, technology can be seen as generic or specific. A key element in modern innovation analysis has been the distinction between the technological knowledge base of the enterprise – which is focused on particular products and therefore highly specific – and the wider set of 'generic' knowledges which provide the framework within which the enterprise operates. Closely related to this notion of generic knowledge is the concept of 'technological paradigm'. This concept, a key development in modern theory, sees technologies not as individual technical solutions, but rather refers to the whole complex of scientific knowledge, engineering practices, process technologies, infrastructure, product characteristics, skills and procedures which make up the totality of a technology. Technology can be thought of, therefore, at enterprise level as a highly specific set of skills and competences focused tightly on specific niches and products. But these exist within a wider technological framework, which is evolving over time, and which structures activities inside the enterprise. In considering the innovation performance of enterprises, we should therefore think of technology as consisting of both internal and external components; innovation always involves an interaction between the two.

In understanding the process of technological change, modern theory begins from Schumpeter's view that competition is primarily a technological phenomenon. The basis of competition is the quality, design characteristics and performance attributes of products. Enterprises seek competitive advantage on the one hand by development of technologically differentiated products, and on the other by changing processes so as to generate these products with competitive cost structures. Usually, innovation takes the form of incremental change within fields in which enterprises have specialized skills and experience; that is to say, enterprises seek to establish a technically differentiated product range within an established technological paradigm. Alternatively, enterprises can seek to innovate by changing the paradigm itself; this is less frequent, but it does happen.

What is involved in the innovation process itself? Recent research sees innovation:

- first, as an interactive social process which integrates market opportunities with the design, development, financial and engineering capabilities of enterprises;
- second, as a process characterized by continuous feedbacks between the above activities, rather than by linear transitions;
- third, as a process characterized by complex interactions between enterprises and their external environments; and
- fourth, as a process which is cumulative, a process over time, in the sense that it depends in part on past achievements and the experience derived from them, but also on the ability to modify and develop qualitatively on the basis of the past.

The primary problem for the innovating enterprise is to build a set of technological competences and capabilities that will enable it to create distinctive areas of competitive advantage. Through marketing exploration, and general relationships with customers or product users, enterprises attempt to identify opportunities for innovation; but this is usually done within the context of an existing set of technical skills, and an existing knowledge base. Research – in the sense of a search for novel technological solutions – is usually undertaken only when enterprises face problems that they cannot solve within their existing knowledge bases. In other words, *research is not necessarily the primary process generating innovative ideas: it is better seen as problem-solving activity within the context of ongoing innovation activity.* A key point is that enterprises can combine these various components of the innovation process in many ways. Enterprises not only produce differentiated products; they generate innovations in different ways. This has two important implications.

First, the process of differentiation generates a high level of variety and diversity among enterprises. There is no single model of the innovation process: enterprises can differ very significantly in their approaches to innovation.

Second, the fact that enterprises attempt to specialize around existing areas of competence means that there are limits to their technological capabilities and awareness. This means that when enterprises seek to solve innovation-related problems, they must frequently look outside the boundaries of the enterprise for solutions: they draw in outside information, expertise, and advice. External sources of knowledge are most often other enterprises – particularly customers or suppliers. But there can of course be inputs directly or indirectly from the public sector – from universities, from libraries and databases, from research institutes, and so on. So innovation is seen as an outcome of a general search and learning process which is heavily shaped by competitive strategies, and which interacts with wider knowledge-creating processes in other enterprises and organizations. The point here is that understanding innovation means understanding the internal capabilities of enterprises, of the types described above, at the same time as understanding their relationships with their external environments.

This change from a linear to an 'interactive' approach to innovation can be summed up by perhaps the most systematic programme of theoretical and empirical research into the character of innovation. This has been the Minnesota Innovation Research Programme, which after a ten-year longitudinal research effort into fourteen innovations contrasted its findings with the conventional wisdom as shown in Table 1.

3 Core results of innovation research

In summing up innovation research, there are at least six core results that are 'robust' in the sense that they are strongly confirmed by

Table 1 Contrast between MIRP findings and conventional wisdom

	Literature implicitly assumes	*MIRP conclusions*
Ideas	One invention, operationalized	Reinvention, proliferation, reimplementation, discarding, and termination
People	An entrepreneur with fixed set of people over time	Many entrepreneurs, fluidly engaging and disengaging over time in a variety of roles
Transactions	Fixed network of people/firms working out details of an idea	Expanding, contracting network of partisan stakeholders who converge and diverge on ideas
Context	Environment provides opportunities and constraints on innovation process	Innovation process creates and constrained by multiple enacted environments
Outcomes	Final result orientation; a stable new order comes into being	Final result indeterminate; many in-process assessments and spinoffs; integration of new orders with old
Process	Simple, cumulative sequence of stages or phases	From simple to many divergent, parallel and convergent paths; some related, others not

Source: Van der Ven, 1999: 8

widely applicable data and empirical research across countries and industries. These results are as follows:

Innovation outcomes rest on complexity and variety in investment patterns that transform the capabilities of enterprises. Within the mainstream of economics, the operation of firms is in general not seen as problematic. Firms make optimal decisions (concerning both what to produce and how to produce) in the face of more or less well defined decision environments, and the capabilities that are needed for this are usually neither in question nor in focus. Innovation, however, rests on quite specific and differentiated areas of competence and capability that must be constructed. This in turn requires investment in tangible and intangible assets, the latter including a wide range of skills and knowledges that make up the intellectual capital of the enterprise. The process through which this happens is complex and highly problematic. There are difficult issues concerning strategic decision making, and managers face a constant tension between the demands of current production and the requirements of current profitability, on the one hand, and the need to create assets for the future on the other. The difficulty here is partly that the commitment of resources reduces current profitability (in the context of competing claims for these resources), and partly that the innovation process is unpredictable and uncontrollable, and outcomes are often radically uncertain. At the same time, there is no general path towards innovative success, and this introduces considerable diversity and variety in approaches to innovation, even among enterprises in similar lines of business, let alone across industries and sectors. From the perspective of enterprises, the implication is that innovation rests on the ability of managements to engage in knowledge creation and asset building in experimental circumstances where no methodological guidelines exist. From a theoretical perspective, there must be doubts about whether any general theory of innovation is possible (Van der Ven, 1999: Part 1).

Innovation is pervasive. Innovation is not something that happens only in a relatively small group of high-technology industries, nor something that is driven by a small set of industries or technologies. The new innovation data, particularly from the EU, show clearly that innovation in the sense of development and sales of new products is distributed right across the system in all advanced countries. Industries that are regarded as 'traditional' or mature or 'low-tech' often generate substantial amounts of sales from technologically new products and processes. Likewise, the service sector is also strongly innovative, across almost all of its component activities, and this is particularly important since the service sector is the largest sector in all advanced economies (see European Commission, 1997: 238–9).

Innovation relies on collaboration and interactive learning. Enterprises very rarely innovate without technological cooperation or collaboration. Knowledge creation happens through an interactive process with other enterprises, organizations, the science and technology infrastructure, and so on. Empirical research in a number of countries under the auspices of the OECD has shown that innovating enterprises are invariably collaborating enterprises, that collaboration persists over long periods, and that the publicly supported infrastructure (such as universities and research institutes) is an important collaboration partner. This is strong empirical confirmation of the idea that innovation should be seen as a collective phenomenon (see Howells, 2000, for an overview of research on this topic).

Innovation is highly uncertain. Innovation involves serious uncertainty, both in technological and in economic terms. It has very rarely been possible to predict the path of innovation, even in general terms. It is rarely possible to predict the economic outcomes for new products and processes. Enterprises very often make major forecasting mistakes, even when they are very well informed, and managed by highly competent and knowledgeable people. This leads to major problems for enterprises in making investment decisions involving innovation activity (Rosenberg, 1996).

Clusters are important, and reflect national and regional patterns of industrial and technological specialization. Geographic clustering appears central to competitive advantage, a result that has emerged from a wide variety of studies. 'Horizontal' clusters – meaning groups of enterprises in the same line of business – are widely found, and seem to be associated with better economic performance of enterprises in the clusters. Vertical clusters, meaning sustained relationships between enterprises in different activities, can be identified using input–output techniques, and reflect country specializations that often differ widely. There is some evidence that cross-border clusters may be becoming more important. These patterns of specialization are cumulative, built up over long periods, and appear to be hard to change (OECD, 1999).

Innovation is systemic. One of the most persistent themes in modern innovation studies is the idea that innovation by enterprises cannot be understood purely in terms of independent decision making at the level of the enterprise. Apart from collaboration, discussed above, there are broader factors shaping the behaviour of enterprises: the social and cultural context, the institutional and organizational framework, regulatory systems, infrastructures, the processes which create and distribute scientific knowledge, and so on. Taken together these factors make up a system, and system conditions can have a decisive impact on the extent to which enterprises can make innovation decisions, and on the modes of innovation which are undertaken. These characteristics suggest important differences between economies, and between the ways in which innovation occurs across economies, that persist over time (Edquist, 1999).

There is strong science-technology interaction in innovation. The science system is important for innovation, and there is a strong interaction between technology and science. Many inventions draw on science – for example, analyses of patents show that there have been dramatic increases in citations from patents to scientific research, and that a very high proportion of the papers cited are produced within public sector scientific research organizations. Other studies have shown strong but indirect interactions, through which industries both affect the process of scientific research and use its results; many traditional industries, from this perspective, draw intensively on scientific results in industry-level knowledge bases. Although science does not provide the raw material for innovation in any simple way, it remains a key element of industry knowledge bases across the economy, and therefore a key element of innovation capability (Martin and Nightingale, 2000).

KEITH SMITH
UNITED NATIONS UNIVERSITY/INTECH
MAASTRICHT
THE NETHERLANDS

Further reading

(References cited in the text marked *)

* Bush, V. (1980) 'Science – the endless frontier. A report to the President on a program for postwar scientific research.' New York: Amo Press. (A facsimile reprint of National Science Foundation Edition), p.19.
* Chandler, A. (1990) *Scale and Scope: the Dynamics of Industrial Enterprise*. Cambridge: Harvard University Press.
* Dodgson, M. and Rothwell, R. (1994) *The Handbook of Industrial Innovation*. Cheltenham: Edward Elgar.
* Dosi, G. (1988) 'Sources, procedures and microeconomic effects of innovation', *Journal of Economic Literature* 26: 1120–71.
* Edquist, C. (ed.)(1999) *Innovation Systems: Institutions, Organizations and Dynamics*. London: Pinter.
* European Commission (1997) *Second European Report on Science and Technology Indicators*. Luxembourg: Office for Official Publications of the European Communities.
* Freeman, C. (1994) 'The economics of technical change', *Cambridge Journal of Economics* 18: 463–514.
* Howells, J. (2000) 'Innovation collaboration and networking: a European perspective', in Science Policy Support Group, *European Research, Technology and Development. Issues for a Competitive Future*. London.
* Kline, S. and Rosenberg, N. (1986) 'An overview of innovation', in R. Landau (ed.), *The Positive Sum Strategy. Harnessing Technology for Economic Growth*, pp. 275–306.
* Lazonick, W. and O'Sullivan, M. (2000) Perspectives on Corporate Governance, Innovation and Economic Performance (Report to European Commission), TSER Project, SOE1-CT98-1114; Project no: 053.
* Martin, B. and Nightingale, P. (eds) (2000) *The Political Economic of Science, Technology and Innovation*. Cheltenham: Elgar.
* OECD (1996) *Innovation, Patents and Technological Strategies*. Paris: OECD.
* OECD (1999) *Boosting Innovation: The Cluster Approach*. Paris: OECD.
* O'Sullivan, M. (2000) *Contests for Corporate Control*. Oxford: Oxford University Press.
* Penrose, E. (1995) *The Theory of the Growth of the Firm*, 3rd edn. Oxford: Oxford University Press.
* Rosenberg, N. (1996) 'Uncertainty and technological change', in R. Landau, T. Taylor and G. Wright (eds), *The Mosaic of Economic Growth*. Stanford: Stanford University Press.
* Schumpeter, J. (1943) *Capitalism, Socialism and Democracy*. London.
* Schumpeter, J. (1964) *Business Cycles*. New York.
* Sundbo, J. (1998) *The Theory of Innovation. Entrepreneurs, Technology and Strategy*. Cheltenham: Elgar.
* Van der Ven, A (1999) *The Innovation Journey*. Oxford: Oxford University Press.

See also: AEROSPACE INDUSTRY; AUTOMOBILE INDUSTRY; BIOTECHNOLOGY; CHEMICAL INDUSTRY; CLEANER PRODUCTION; COOPERATION AND COMPETITION; CORPORATE CONTROL; DEVELOPMENT AND DIFFUSION OF TECHNOLOGY; DYNAMICS CAPABILITIES; EAST ASIAN ECONOMIES; ECONOMIC GROWTH AND CONVERGENCE; ELECTRONICS INDUSTRY; EMPLOYMENT RELATIONS; EVOLUTIONARY THEORIES OF THE FIRM; EXCHANGE RATE ECONOMICS; GLOBAL MACHINE TOOL INDUSTRY; GROWTH OF THE FIRM AND NETWORKING; GROWTH THEORY; INDUSTRIAL AGGLOMERATIONS; INDUSTRIAL DYNAMICS; INDUSTRIAL AND LABOUR RELATIONS; INTELLECTUAL PROPERTY RIGHTS; MARSHALL, A.; MARX, K.; PENROSE, E.; SCHUMPETER, J.; SERVICE ECONOMY; SKILL FORMATION SYSTEMS; SMALL AND MEDIUM-SIZE ENTERPRISES; SMITH, A.; STEEL INDUSTRY; TELECOMMUNICATIONS INDUSTRY; VEBLEN, T.

Pension systems

1 Introduction
2 Pillars of retirement income
3 Design, structure and management
4 Investment management and financial markets
5 Issues – open and unresolved

Overview

With the retirement of the baby boom generation beginning in the first decade of the twenty-first century and increased global competition between rival systems of economic governance, pension systems are an important and growing area of research in economics and management. The relationships between social security (pillar I), sponsored pension and retirement plans (pillar II), and individual retirement income accounts (pillar III) are essential to any understanding of pension systems. There are significant differences between the Anglo-American world, much of continental Europe, and Latin America with respect to the structure of relationships between the three pillars of retirement income. Moreover, there are significant differences between whole sets of nations with respect to the current funding of future pension liabilities. While the Anglo-American countries do not all fully fund social security entitlements they do rely upon the full funding of pension fund (pillar II) obligations whereas continental European countries tend to rely upon unfunded social security (pillar I). These funding arrangements have had significant consequences for the financial management of large corporations, and for the structure of the related institutional investment industry. Anglo-American pension funds and the financial services industry have accelerated the process of financial disintermediation, in part contributing to the growth of the global market for corporate control. Even in countries not contemplating changing over to funded retirement income plans, the transformation of Anglo-American economies through the actions and investment strategies of pension funds has been noted. In particular, this transformation has not been lost on continental Europe and the transition economies of eastern Europe as they redefine their social security and pension systems in the light of the looming demographic crisis.

1 Introduction

In large part, the literature on social security is about the historical roots and evolution of the twentieth century welfare state (Esping-Anderson 1989). Many studies stress the class bargain and intergenerational social contract under-pinning welfare states, mediated by nationspecific customs and traditions. Few countries fully fund expected social security pension obligations, most contributions are less than expected benefits, and progressive redistribution towards low income earners is a common albeit often-times implicit policy. Governments carry the ultimate liability for social security pensions, operating on a pay-as-yougo (PAYG) basis (see Gruber and Wise 1997 for a survey). Even so, there is considerable debate about the future of social security in relation to other forms of pension and retirement income. Indeed, there have been proposals in the US and elsewhere to partially convert social security to funded individual retirement accounts (Feldstein 1998).

The role and significance of pension provision in relation to social security has gained increasing attention for two sets of related reasons. Encouraged by the Organisation of Economic Cooperation and Development (OECD) (see Leibfritz *et al.* 1995; OECD 1998) and the World Bank (1995), policy makers in advanced industrialized economies have focused on the looming 'demographic crisis'. This crisis combines the coming retirement of the baby boom generation with projected longer average life expectancies, and lower fertility rates with much higher dependent to working age population ratios. For countries

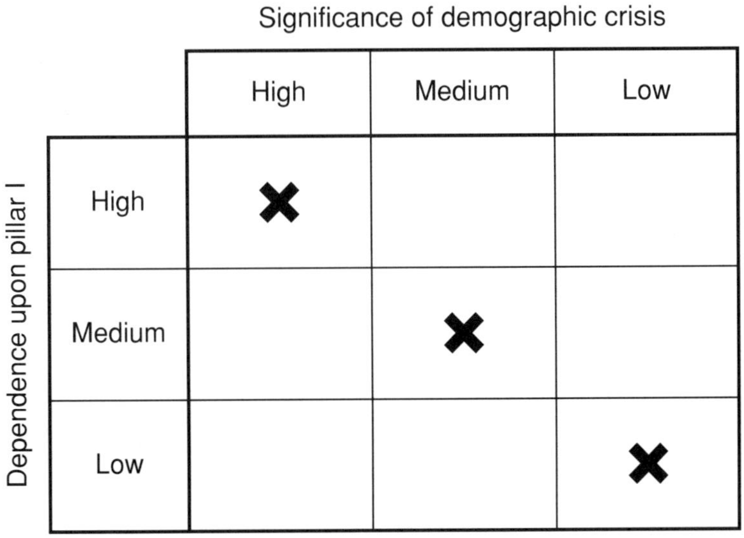

Significance of demographic crisis

	High	Medium	Low
High (Dependence upon pillar I)	✗		
Medium		✗	
Low			✗

Figure 1 Interaction between European demography and social security programmes

such as France, Germany and Italy the demographic trends will be more significant than for Ireland and the UK, the US and Canada. Reinforcing the demographic crisis is the fact that countries like France, Germany and Italy rely upon under-funded or unfunded social security systems for the provision of future retirement income (Figure 1). Even German employer-sponsored pension plans are often significantly under-funded (Prigge 1998). By contrast, in the Anglo-American countries the majority of workers rely upon funded supplementary pensions for a significant portion of their retirement income (Davis 1995).

Not surprisingly, there is considerable interest in many European countries in discounting long-term social security obligations while promoting those pension systems that might shift the financial burden of retirement to employers (and other plan sponsors) and individuals. This is especially apparent in the transition economies of eastern Europe. Having privatized large state enterprises and having introduced policies aimed at enhancing the role of small and medium enterprises, these nations have also sought to introduce pensions systems designed to circumvent the inherited problems of the welfare state. Furthermore, for advocates of supplementary pensions the robust Anglo-American financial services industry is reason enough to shift retirement income obligations from the state sector to public and private pension plan sponsors. Apparent differences in the financial structures of developed economies can be explained by reference to quite profound differences in legal structures (see La Porta *et al.* 1997, 1998). But it is also true that the astonishing growth of pension fund assets over the past thirty years in the Anglo-American economies can help explain the vitality of Anglo-American financial markets (Clark 2000). Venture capital, initial public offerings (IPOs) and the liquidity of Anglo-American securities markets are indicative of the power of pension funds and their closely related partners–institutional investors (Davis and Steil 2000).

In this entry, we begin with the relationships between different forms of retirement income, making the connection between social security (pillar I), sponsored pension plans (pillar II), and individual retirement accounts (pillar III). From that model structure, we will concentrate on pillar II and pillar III pension systems including reference to common types of defined benefit (DB) and defined contribution (DC) pension plans. The structure and management of pension fund investment is the focus of the third section while the connection between pension fund investment and financial markets is the topic of the

	Social forms of retirement income provision							
	Social Contract		Solidarity		Occupation		Individual	
	SS	Tax	Collective	Corporate	Employer	Affinity	Insurance	Fund
Pillar I	✗	✗	✗					
Pillar II			✗	✗	✗	✗		
Pillar III						✗	✗	✗

Type of retirement income

Figure 2 Interaction between pillars of retirement income and the social organization of pension provision

fourth section. We conclude with reference to some of the unresolved or most problematic issues of supplementary pension systems: the problem of low coverage rates of groups of poor workers, the appropriate degree of paternalism, and the proper allocation of risk between individuals and institutions. Recognizing the virtues of supplementary pension systems, there are limits to their scope and significance in replacing state-sponsored social security schemes (Disney 1996).

2 Pillars of retirement income

Notwithstanding the significance of the welfare state for much of the twentieth century, pillar II and pillar III pension systems have had a long history. The British government first introduced supplementary pensions for selected employees at the turn of the nineteenth century. The structure and organization of these schemes were the forerunners of twentieth century corporate and public sector sponsored pension plans across the English-speaking world (see Blake 1995; Hannah 1986; Sass 1997). At much the same time, the British government also promoted mutual insurance schemes, encouraging worker associations to pool health and retirement risks across their membership (Clark 2000). Even in Germany, believed by many to be the bastion of state-sponsored social security, a number of employer-sponsored pension plans had been established by the end of nineteenth century. Many of these plans persist to the current day, despite the turmoil of the twentieth century.

Thus provision of retirement income can take a variety of forms (see Figure 2). For example, pillar I retirement income can be provided by social security systems that are framed by a social contract between the classes and between generations; benefit levels are typically set according to accepted entitlement criteria and need, not necessarily earned income. In some countries like Germany, however, this system is augmented by preferential tax-related schemes that reflect worker incomes, being a form of income replacement upon retirement. In the Netherlands and Switzerland, there is an intimate relationship between pillar I and II pension systems. As a matter of public policy, at retirement income replacement is set through a combination of state-funded social security and compulsory membership of sponsored pension plans. At one level, solidarity may be enforced by government policy. At another level, workers and employers may both desire solidarity. In effect, membership of pillar II schemes may be a means of sustaining loyalty and collective commitment (to a union, a corporation etc.) through the pooling of risks (death, disability, retirement etc.) across different age groups within and/or between firms.

Pillar II pensions are also offered because other employers (competitors) offer plans. Likewise, professional (affinity) groups often offer plan participation as a membership benefit. In this context, pension plan contributions are treated (in law and in practice) as a deferred part of workers' current earnings whose value is enhanced by preferred tax benefits on contributions. In Anglo-American countries, there is a clear distinction between pillar II and III pension systems. Workers may be required to choose between the two forms of retirement income provision. Furthermore, different kinds of financial service firms are involved in the provision of pillar II and pillar III pension systems. For many larger employers, pension funds draw upon actuaries, custodians, investment consultants, and investment managers whereas smaller employers often rely upon insurance companies to provide pillar III insurance and pension schemes. But this is changing in the US as increasing numbers of pillar II pension funds have evolved to become more like pillar III schemes, offering individual participants the option of investing in mutual funds and related defined contribution (DC) accumulated value retirement products. There is demand amongst beneficiaries for DC plans and related investment products, going beyond the historical boundaries of DB plans and entitlements (compare with the UK, Blake 1995).

In many countries, pillar II schemes began as targeted employee benefit schemes, providing professional and related clerical staff defined benefits based upon years of service and final salary (Clark 2000; Sass 1997). Modest tax benefits encouraged shared contributions, with benefits supplementing pillar I or pillar III arrangements. In the Anglo-American world, however, after 1950 pension benefits were directly related to wages and working conditions. This dramatically increased coverage rates through to the late 1960s as the actual numbers of covered workers exploded through the entry of the baby boom generation into the workforce. Coverage rates peaked at about 50 per cent (and have marginally declined) in the Anglo-American world, excepting countries like Australia that have introduced mandatory pillar II schemes (Edey and Simon 1998). And, as noted above, in the US DB schemes have been undercut by defined contribution (DC) schemes; few new DB schemes have been established over the past ten years whereas many DB schemes have been terminated and DC and 401(K) schemes introduced in their place (Logue and Rader 1998).

Many attempts have been made to explain the US shift towards DC schemes, focusing upon the diminished supply of DB schemes (see below). With the ownership of plan surpluses highly contested in US federal courts, and the escalating costs of administrating DB plans in the light of the increasing complexity of the Employee Retirement Income Security Act (ERISA) of 1974, DB plans are relatively expensive propositions (Mitchell 1998). Elsewhere, though, DB schemes dominate the Anglo-American world and much of continental Europe including the Netherlands, Germany, Sweden and Switzerland. In Latin America and eastern Europe, however, it is apparent that the transition from welfare state dependence has been accompanied by a shift towards individual retirement accounts based upon the principle of accumulated value rather than towards sponsored pension plans (DB or DC) (Queisser 1999). Not surprisingly in the UK, the introduction of minimum funding requirements and the statutory reforms of 1995 in the wake of the Maxwell scandal separating plan sponsorship from its administration, may well have prompted the beginning of a slow shift towards DC plans.

3 Design, structure and management

Pillar II pension systems are complex institutions. Where workers are covered by collective bargaining agreements, pensions and related insurance and health care benefits are important items of negotiation between management and labour. This was especially true in the US and the UK, for example, and is also important in the Netherlands, Germany, Sweden and Switzerland. For employers, concerned to manage their human resources in the most efficient ways, pension benefits have been a means of locking-in older skilled workers while stabilizing labour turnover in competitive labour markets. For many years, long vesting periods for pension entitlements combined with age and working-life service requirements for maximum benefits conspired to limit the burden of pension liabilities and the actual value of workers' pension payments. The benefits to employers were perceived to outweigh costs. During the 1970s and early 1980s it was not unusual in US industry for initial vesting periods of 10 years and age and service requirements of 75 years (e.g. 50 years of age and 25 years of service).

During the 1970s and 1980s, however, the progressive extension of civil-rights-inspired anti-discrimination legislation to pension and related benefit entitlements broadened coverage within firms, encouraged the reduction of vesting periods, and allowed for the interruption of service (even, in some cases, for the portability of entitlements). Furthermore, sustained corporate and industrial restructuring in American industry over the past thirty years brought pension benefits into the process of labour-management bargaining over distributing the costs of 'downsizing'. In effect, early retirement pension and related insurance benefits were used to encourage older workers to retire early thereby sheltering younger workers from the immediate threat of unemployment. For DB pension systems, the combination of entitlement liberalization and corporate restructuring added enormous expected liabilities to plan sponsors. Celebrated bankruptcies, the threatened collapse of the US Pension Benefit Guaranty Corporation (PBGC), and subversion of collective bargaining encouraged the introduction of DC plans but also brought to the fore the structure and management of pillar II pension systems (see Nussbaum 1999).

In the Anglo-American world, sponsored pension plans are organized around three institutional imperatives. These can be summarized as: (1) the formal separation between sponsors' interests and plan beneficiaries' interests; (2) a legal regime of trusteeship designed to protect the interests of beneficiaries, and (3) the delegation of expertise (internal or external to the fund) in the management and investment of fund assets (Langbein 1997). In conjunction with legal requirements that DB plans are to be currently funded with respect to future expected liabilities, these kinds of plans tend to be semi-autonomous financial institutions. With DC plans, by necessity fully funded and by design managed in order to maximize the accumulated value of plan participant's separate and joint contributions, the formal separation between sponsors and beneficiaries is virtually complete. In both cases, trustees are individually liable for their decisions although liability is best understood in relation to malfeasance rather than well-intended mistakes or failures of investment strategy. For many fund trustees, delegation is the operative strategy. Hence, the growth and importance of the Anglo-American financial services industry over the past thirty years.

This organizational structure carries with it various problems, including monitoring and assessing the value of agency relationships (Ambachtsheer and Ezra 1998). Just as trustees are the agents of plan participants, so too are financial service providers the agents of trustees. Various strategies have evolved over the years to manage these agency problems. One response has been to employ consultants, acting between trustees and service providers to constantly evaluate the value and performance of agency relationships in accordance with industry benchmarks. Another response has been to use competing financial service providers for the same functions, thereby using competition to discipline costs and service quality. Yet another response has been to build trust relationships between privileged service providers, thereby sharing knowledge about the demand and supply of services. In effect, there is a hierarchy of trust and distrust between pension funds and different types of service providers (summarized in Clark 2000 and Figure 3).

During the 1990s, it became increasingly difficult for even the largest plans to maintain internal funds management functions. The salaries, bonuses, options, and career prospects for internal managers have not kept pace with those offered by leading companies like Goldman Sachs and J P Morgan. Moreover, given the increasing importance of recurrent investments in computer systems, the scale economies of the largest service providers

Trust in service providers

	High	Medium	Low
Long	Asset consultants		
Medium		Custodians	
Short			Investment companies

Length of contract

Figure 3 Interaction between trust and contract in the financial services industry

have driven many funds to outsource the provision of needed financial services.

In continental Europe, however, the market for pension-related financial services is quite different, country to country. The Dutch, for example, have developed hybrid financial service conglomerates, intimately linked to pension fund sponsors. Boards of directors overlap one-another, with many of the largest funds acting both as the consumers and suppliers of financial services. Custodial services, insurance, and investment management services can be found in Dutch pension fund related companies. Nevertheless, perhaps more than any other continental country, the Dutch have sought to purchase expert advice and advanced financial products from London and Wall Street firms. For the German and Swiss funds, by contrast, long-term relationships with banks and related actuarial firms have dominated the provision of pension fund management services. Thus, until very recently, the market for financial services in many European countries is an internal market either between directly related 'firms' or between long-term partners with substantial cross-representation on boards of management. This stands in contrast with the disintermediated market for services that characterizes the Anglo-American world (see Dufey 1998; Edwards and Fischer 1994).

In law, pension fund trustees act to maximize beneficiaries' interests. Those interests may vary considerably according to the type of plan, its relative maturity and the preferences of beneficiaries. For instance, a relatively mature DB plan with many retirees compared to active contributors would have a very different investment strategy than a DC plan open to beneficiaries' age-related preferences regarding asset allocation, investment products and retirement account accumulated value. In the first example, the plan sponsor bears the risk of the whole plan whereas in the second example, the plan participant bears the risk of his/her final accumulated retirement income value. Inevitably, these kinds of differences are often reflected in the nature and structure of financial services demanded by pension plans. At the same time, however, there is considerable evidence that pension plans tend to under-perform against the relevant standards of excellence (see Blake, Lehmann, and Timmermann 1999; Ellis 1998). Accounting for suboptimal performance is an important field of research, implicating trustee and board decision making, principal-agent relationships, market–non-market relationships and the cost structures of service providers (Clark 2000).

4 Investment management and financial markets

By this account, financial service providers and financial markets are deeply inter-related with pension fund systems (at least, in the Anglo-American world). Indeed, it can be reasonably argued that the performance of global financial markets is closely related to the investment decisions of institutional investors (pension funds and their agents). In this respect, the investment management process can be perceived as guided by theories of financial markets (for instance, the efficient markets hypothesis) as well as the observed patterns and practices of market agents. For a standard treatment see Sharpe and Alexander (1995). Here, I will not deal directly with the theory of efficient financial markets; there are many useful treatments including Houthakker and Williamson (1996). Rather, I will consider the investment management process relevant to pension funds.

For pension funds, three principles tend to drive investment decision making: (1) matching assets and liabilities, year-to-year and over the long term; (2) risk management through portfolio diversification; and (3) cost management through the market for financial services. By statute and customary practice, Anglo-American DB pension funds are required to match the current value of fund assets against expected liabilities (as indicated by the UK minimum funding requirement). For relatively immature funds, with large numbers of active participants compared to retired beneficiaries, the time horizon of expected liabilities is often very long. Therefore, such funds often pursue aggressive investment strategies aimed at maximizing returns biased towards equities and high-risk asset classes (Blake 1998). On the other hand, mature funds concerned with meeting immediate obligations tend to manage expected liabilities, allocating assets to fixed income products like bonds backed by guarantees. Likewise, younger DC plan participants often assume higher levels of risk in their early years while focusing upon less risky more reliable investments in their latter years (before retirement). Inevitably, there is a vibrant market for pension related investment products differentiated by risk and return profiles.

Given the demand for investment products, risk management is at the core of the investment management process (Ambachtsheer and Ezra 1998). Here, modern portfolio theory (MPT) has become an essential principle guiding investment decision making. From its earliest versions to its latest incarnations, MPT has significant implications for asset allocation, the demand for investment products, and the selection of investment managers. In this respect, risk is more about the profile of a fund's whole investment portfolio in relation to its asset-liability model (ALM). This theoretical point is sometimes lost in debate about the virtues or otherwise of specific investments. Likewise, it may be discounted by investment managers and pension funds alike when participating in bull markets and speculative bubbles. There appears to be a natural temptation to shift assets towards currently high performing assets and investment products and against a 'balanced' portfolio approach when it seems that markets are accelerating upwards unsullied by the risks of a 'correction'. Indeed, accounting for this kind of herd behavior and mentality is an important aspect of financial research (in general) and investment management (in particular) (Thaler 1992).

A common observation made about the performance of investment managers is that future performance according to accepted benchmarks is difficult to predict. Although investment managers routinely declare that 'past performance is not a guarantee of future performance', their advertised reputations and claimed peer-status tend to imply the opposite. Empirical evidence suggests that future performance is more akin to a lottery than a predictable management process notwithstanding claims made to the contrary. It also appears that, on average, active investment managers under-perform market indices like the DJIA and the FTSE 100. Thus, pension funds face considerable uncertainty about expected returns on invested assets compared to the relative stability of expected liabilities. Over time, as institutional consumers of investment products have come to distrust claims made by investment managers, various defensive policies have evolved. Whereas one option may be to focus upon the selection of investment managers so as to reduce the risk of under-performance, another option is to focus upon minimizing the costs of investment management eschewing active management for passive management or some combination of both. It appears that larger funds are especially concerned about cost-management protocols, recognizing the uncertainties of predicting returns.

In this environment, the investment management industry has responded in two, rather different ways. Given client concerns about cost-management, there have been mergers and acquisitions in the industry so as to reap the economies of scale. At the same time, the largest managers have also become more selective about taking on smaller clients unless those clients are willing to pool their assets into common management systems and investment products. In this context, passive index-based equity products became more popular over the 1990s because of the transparency of management costs and the apparent increasing rates of returns in the Wall Street bull market. On the other hand, notwithstanding the growth of extremely large investment houses, there remains an important market for niche players; investment managers who, by virtue of their expertise, experience, and information sources, are able to generate higher than average rates of return at a competitive price. In the Anglo-American economies there seems to be less room for medium-size investment managers who have neither the advantages of scale nor the expertise necessary to justify higher per unit costs of production (Clark 2000).

Most importantly, it is argued that the close links between Anglo-American pension funds and financial markets has prompted the development of new financial products and new financial institutions (Berlinski and Western 1998). By contrast, it is argued that those countries dependent upon banking institutions and internalized lending practices between overlapping networks of representation are now less innovative than the Anglo-American financial world. Evidence for this argument can be found in the remarkable growth of US-based technology and Internet stocks (the 'new' economy), based upon venture capital investment groups and the unmediated market for initial public offerings (IPOs). Clearly, the growth of venture capital markets allied with the increasing role of pension fund institutions in this field of financial development has distinguished the Anglo-American economies from continental Europe. But this argument remains contentious, suggesting a causeand-effect relationship that may be less robust than a simple correlation between related overlapping processes. Nevertheless, the apparent differences in developed economies' financial and economic structures may be closely related to the 'astronomical growth' of pension fund assets in the Anglo-American countries since the early 1970s (Langbein 1997).

5 Issues – open and unresolved

With the collapse of eastern European and Soviet communism, there have been opportunities to re-think the provision of retirement income and the balance between social security and supplementary pension systems. For some, the solution is clear: the discounting of welfare-state pensions in favour of the introduction of defined contribution plans and individual retirement accounts. In doing so, comparatively little attention has been paid to the limits of Anglo-American pension systems and the persistent diversity of western European pension systems (but see Disney 2000).

For all the financial benefits of DB and DC funded pension systems for the Anglo-American world, coverage rates have remained stagnant at about 50 per cent of the eligible working population for the last thirty years. Historically, coverage rates have been highest amongst older male unionized workers and lowest amongst younger female non-unionized workers. More importantly, coverage rates are currently very vulnerable to firm size, the nature of job tenure, wage levels and industry affiliation. In effect, there is a large segment of the working population that is unlikely to garner sufficient contributions over their working lives to have an adequate retirement income separate from social security. As a consequence, significant numbers of people will be very poor through their retirement years. Proffered solutions to this problem vary. For instance, Australia and Switzerland (amongst a number of countries) have introduced mandatory participation in supplementary pensions, while the UK government has introduced a low-cost 'stakeholder' option. Neither solution will solve the low-wage and variable income problem (hence the low retirement income problem).

At the same time, the shift towards DC plans amongst those participating in employer-sponsored pension plans has introduced a measure of individual risk previously thought the proper burden of employers and related institutions (Smallhout 1999). Some industry commentators believe that this risk will be rewarded with higher than expected retirement incomes. But the reliance of many DC participants on the performance of domestic and global equity markets suggests that there is a real risk of lower than expected retirement income. Here there remains an unresolved practical and theoretical issue: the proper allocation of risk between plan sponsors and participants. This problem can be re-expressed as the extent to which paternalism ought to play a role in insuring individual participants from the costs of their actions. One important distinguishing characteristic of many European supplementary pension systems is the continuing link between pension benefits and insurance. There is a presumption that individuals are properly more risk adverse than their employers.

Finally, it should also be noted that the design and structure of many European countries' pension systems owes a great deal to the immediate post-war (1945) era. For many countries, but largely excluding the Anglo-American economies, promised pension benefits were explicitly linked to current wages. But in countries like Germany, the Netherlands and Switzerland pension arrangements were also directly integrated with jointly administered collective bargaining institutions. Works councils, joint boards of representation, and boards of pension management are all closely interrelated. For many, such pension arrangements reflect the proper role of the social market as opposed to the Anglo-Saxon market society; that is, pension plan participants are equally employees with democratic rights of representation throughout the firm and its related institutions. Much has been written about this model of corporate capitalism, its virtues and vices (see Hutton 1995; Prigge 1998). Whether it will survive through the next few decades of this century remains an open question, given the corrosive processes of globalization and European integration. If it does, the structure of European supplementary pensions will remain at odds with Anglo-American pension systems. In this respect, there is a profound theoretical issue hidden just behind the imperatives driving plan sponsors and participants towards DC plans: who should bear the risks and rewards of corporate and economic restructuring?

GORDON L CLARK
UNIVERSITY OF OXFORD

Note

The author would like to record his appreciation for the support of the Economic and Social Research Council (ESRC) of the UK, AIG Financial Products (London), and the University of Oxford. Those who helped the author learn more about European pensions include Werner Nussbaum, Ulrich Jurgens, and Karel Lannoo. Officials from the European Commission (DG Internal Market) also contributed to understanding the tensions between competing EU financial service industries. William Lazonick helped structure the paper, David Blake, E. Phillip Davis, Werner Nussbaum, and Darius Wojcik provided comments on a previous draft. The author remains responsible for any errors or omissions.

Further reading

(References cited in the text marked *)

* Ambachtsheer, K.P. and Ezra, D. (1998) *Pension Fund Excellence*, New York: J. Wiley. (An informed view of the theory and practice of pension fund management.)
* Berlinski, M.R. and Western, S.R.A. (1998) 'Perspectives on the US asset management business', in H. Blommenstein and N. Funke (eds) *Institutional Investors in the New Financial Landscape*, Paris: OECD. (Explains and

documents the growth of the Anglo-American institutional investment industry.)
* Blake, D. (1995) *Pension Schemes and Pension Funds in the United Kingdom*, Oxford: Oxford University Press. (An economic account of the structure and performance of UK pension funds.)
* Blake, D. (1998) 'Pension schemes as options on pension fund assets: implications for pension fund management', *Insurance: Mathematics and Economics* 23: 263–86. (An options-based theoretical treatment of the theory of pension fund investment management.)
* Blake, D., Lehmann, B.N. and Timmermann, A. (1999) 'Asset allocation and pension fund performance', *Journal of Business* 72: 429–69. (A systematic empirical analysis of UK pension fund performance.)
Clark, G.L. (1993) *Pensions and Corporate Restructuring in American Industry*, Baltimore: Johns Hopkins Press. (A case-by-case assessment of US bankruptcy and pension policies in corporate restructuring.)
* Clark, G.L. (2000) *Pension Fund Capitalism*, Oxford: Oxford University Press. (Focuses upon the nature of Anglo-American pension fund investment decision making.)
* Davis, E.P. (1995) *Pension Funds: Retirement Income Security and Capital Markets. An International Perspective*, Oxford: Oxford University Press. (A comparative perspective on the structure and performance of pension fund systems.)
* Davis, E.P. and Steil, H. (2000) *Institutional Investors*, Cambridge, MA: MIT Press. (An economic account of the structure and organization of the institutional investment industry.)
* Disney, R. (1996) *Can We afford to Grow Older?* Cambridge, MA: MIT Press. (A review and assessment of the economic issues regarding social security and pensions.)
* Disney, R. (2000) 'Crises in public pension programmes in the OECD: what are the reform options?', *Economic Journal* 110: F12–27. (A look at the 'reform' options, assuming there is a role for government.)
* Dufey, G. (1998) 'The changing role of financial intermediation in Europe', *International Journal of Business* 3 (1): 49–67. (A contemporary account of the role of intermediation in Europe.)
* Edey, M. and Simon, J. (1998) 'Australia's retirement income system', in M. Feldstein (ed.) *Privatizing Social Security*, Chicago, IL: University of Chicago Press. (A comprehensive overview of the relationship between pillar I and pillar II pensions in Australia.)
* Edwards, J. and Fischer, K. (1994) *Banks, Finance and Investment in Germany*, Cambridge: Cambridge University Press. (The seminal economic account of German corporate finance.)
* Ellis, C. (1998) *Winning the Loser's Game*, 3rd edn. New York: J. Wiley. (A practitioner's guide to the complex world of investment management.)
* Esping-Anderson, G. (1989) *The Three Worlds of Welfare Capitalism*, Oxford: Polity Press. (A sociological analysis of various continental European welfare systems, circa 1980s.)
* Feldstein, M. (1998) 'Introduction', in M. Feldstein (ed.) *Privatizing Social Security*, Chicago, IL: University of Chicago Press. (A summary of the issues involved in privatizing social security systems, using examples from around the world.)
* Gruber, J. and Wise, D. (1997) 'Social security programs and retirement around the world', *Working Paper 6134* Cambridge, MA: National Bureau of Economic Research. (A comparative economic approach to social security systems.)
* Hannah, L. (1986) *Inventing Retirement: The Development of Occupational Pensions in Britain*, Cambridge: Cambridge University Press. (An economic history of UK occupational pensions.)
* Houthakker, H. and Williamson, P.J. (1996) *The Economics of Financial Markets*, Oxford: Oxford University Press. (An economic account of the structure and performance of financial markets.)
* Hutton, W. (1995) *The State We're In*, London: Jonathan Cape. (Argues German co-determination is a better system of corporate governance.)
* Langbein, J. (1997) 'The secret life of the trust: the trust as an instrument of commerce', *Yale Law Journal* 107: 165–89. (Provides an historical legal account of the significance of trust institutions in pension fund governance.)
* La Porta, R., Lopez-de-Silanes, F., Shleifer, A. and Vishny, R.W. (1997) 'The legal determinants of external finance', *Journal of Finance* 52: 1131–50. (Cross-country analysis of the legal and economic institutions of finance.)
* La Porta, R., Lopez-de-Silanes, F., Shleifer, A. and Vishny, R.W. (1998) 'Law and finance', *Journal of Political Economy* 106: 1113–55. (Cross-country analysis of the legal and economic institutions of finance.)
* Leibfritz, W., Roseveare, D., Fore, D. and Wurzel, E. (1995) 'Ageing populations, pension systems and government budgets: how do they affect saving?', *Working Paper 156* Paris: Economics Department, OECD. (Documents trends in savings and ageing across the OECD.)
* Logue, D.E. and Rader, J.S. (1998) *Managing Pension Plans*, Boston, MA: Harvard Business

School Press. (An administrative account of the issues in pension fund management.)
* Mitchell, O. (1998) 'Administrative costs in public and private retirement systems', in M. Feldstein (ed.) *Privatizing Social Security*, Chicago, IL: University of Chicago Press. (A rare empirical analysis of the costs of different types of pensions).
* Nussbaum, W. (1999) *Das System der beruflichen Vorsorge in den USA*, Berne: Haupt. (An analysis of the US pension and insurance system relevant to continental Europe.)
* OECD (1998*) Maintaining Prosperity in an Ageing Society*, Paris: OECD. (Sketches the dimensions and policy implications of the 'demographic bomb'.)
* Prigge, S. (1998) 'A survey of German corporate governance', in K.J. Hopt, H. Handa, M.J. Roe, E. Wymeersch and S. Prigge (eds) *Comparative Corporate Governance: The State of the Art and Emerging Research*, Oxford: Oxford University Press. (An exhaustive account of German corporate governance.)
* Queisser, M. (1998) 'Pension reform: lessons from Latin America', *Policy Brief 15* Paris: OECD Development Centre. (A policy assessment of Latin American pension reforms.)
Rein, M. and Wadensjo, E. (eds) (1997) *Enterprise and the Welfare State*, Cheltenham: Edward Elgar. (A set of studies making the connection between welfare and employers across advanced economies.)
Roe, M.J. (1994) *Strong Managers, Weak Owners: The Political Roots of American Corporate Finance*, Princeton, NJ: Princeton University Press. (A legal and economic account of US corporate governance.)
* Sass, S. (1997) *The Promise of Private Pensions*, Cambridge, MA: Harvard University Press. (Provides an economic history of US pensions.)
* Sharpe, W. and Alexander, G.J. (1995) *Investments*, 5th edn, Englewood Cliffs, NJ: Prentice-Hall. (A treatise on investments and modern portfolio theory.)
* Smallhout, J.H. (1999) *The Uncertain Future: Securing Pension Promises in a World of Risk*, Chicago, IL: Irwin. (Raises concern about the risks of current pension arrangements.)
* Thaler, R. (1992) *The Winner's Curse: Paradoxes and Anomalies in Economic Life*, New York: Free Press. (A collection of essays on behavioral lacunae in financial markets.)
Valdes-Prieto, S. (ed.) (1997) *The Economics of Pensions*, Cambridge: Cambridge University Press. (A collection of essays on the economics of supplementary pension systems.)
* World Bank (1995) *Averting the Old Age Crisis*, Washington, DC: World Bank. (A comparative assessment of the global demographic trends and the relevant policy issues.)

Further resources

http://www.pionline.com (Databases, news and information on the Anglo-American pension fund investment management industry.)
http://www.pensions-research.org (Academic electronic forum for pension and insurance research based at the Department of Economics, Birkbeck College, London.)
http://www.ssrn.com (The largest on-line source of academic literature on financial markets, economics and regulation related to pensions and insurance.)

See also: COMPARATIVE INCOME AND WEALTH DISTRIBUTION; LABOUR MARKETS

Comparative income and wealth distribution

1 Methodological problems in international comparisons of income
2 International comparisons of income
3 Methodological problems in international comparisons of wealth
4 International comparisons of wealth

Overview

International comparisons of income and wealth distributions are important because they indicate which types of political and economic systems are likely to lead to greater or lesser inequality. This article begins with a discussion of the methodological issues involved in comparative income distribution among countries of the world. This is followed by a presentation of some results for both advanced industrial countries and for a broader set of countries (section 2). Comparability problems are more formidable for wealth, and data sources are more varied. As a result, section 3 presents a more extended discussion of methodological issues involved in international comparisons of wealth distribution. Selected results are found in section 4.

1 Methodological problems in international comparisons of income

There are now official estimates of the size distribution of household income in the United States as well as most other industrialized countries in the world (see ECONOMIC GROWTH AND CONVERGENCE). The United States Census Bureau conducts an annual survey in March, called the Current Population Survey, which provides detailed information on individual and household earnings and income. On the basis of these data, the US Bureau of the Census constructs its estimates of both family and household income inequality. Moreover, the Current Population Surveys have been conducted in the United States since 1947. As a result, there exists a consistent time-series on household income distribution for the US that spans more than five decades.

There is now a very extensive set of countries for which data on personal income are available. Many countries, such as the United States, provide official estimates of personal income distribution. In others, such as Germany and the United Kingdom, research institutes carry on annual income surveys of their population. For some countries, tax and other administrative records serve as the basis for deriving distributions of personal income. The earliest data on American income inequality, compiled by Kuznets (1953), was based on personal income tax data. For some less developed ones, such as India, the only microdata available are based on surveys of household consumption.

There are also a few international data sets available. The Luxembourg Income Study has compiled microdata (mainly survey data) from about a dozen OECD counties, as well as Israel and several Eastern European countries (see Atkinson, Rainwater and Smeeding 1995, for a description). Deininger and Squire (1996) have compiled summary data on quintile shares and other inequality indices for 108 countries and, in many cases, several years, covering the period from the 1960s to the 1990s. The underlying sources include both income and consumption-based estimates.

In order to make useful international comparisons of personal income, it is necessary to have consistent information among countries. There are several methodological problems that must be solved, including:

1 the definition of income
2 the unit of observation, and
3 sampling problems and underreporting biases.

Income concept

The typical definition of income includes wage and salary earnings; proprietor (that is, self-employed) income; various forms of property income, such as interest, dividends, rent, and royalties; pension income; net alimony received; and social (or government) transfer payments, such as unemployment insurance, workers' compensation, social security income, disability payments, welfare transfers, and other government provided benefits. The basic concept is a 'cash' or 'money' concept.

There are several problematic elements in making international comparisons. For example, some data sources, such as those derived from income tax data, will also include capital gains, the appreciation in the value of assets held by households. In some cases, this will be limited to only capital gains realized from the actual sale of an asset (such as a home). Others may include a valuation of owner-occupied rent for homeowners – that is, the rental equivalent value of the amount of rent a household would have to pay in order to rent their home.

The treatment of 'fringe benefits' and 'in-kind' government transfers also presents difficult problems. For example, in most countries, employers provide not only wages and salaries but also other ('fringe') benefits such as life insurance, health insurance, and pension contributions. This may be a substantial amount of employee compensation. Countries differ in how these benefits are reported in household surveys. Moreover, in most OECD countries, the government provides many non-cash benefits such as health insurance, housing subsidies, day care, and the like. A failure to include these benefits in family income may result in a distorted comparison of personal income among nations. Tax systems also differ widely among countries. As a result, the use of pre-tax income may produce a different rank ordering among countries in terms of income inequality than the use of post-tax income.

Unit of observation

Another definitional issue revolves around the proper unit of observation. There are three basic units of observation in primary income data: the family (or household), the individual, and the taxpaying unit. However, the proper unit for either welfare or behavioural analysis may not directly correspond to the observational unit. In regard to welfare, family income, per capita family income, or some combination of the two have each been used as a measure of welfare in the literature. Family income is employed most frequently, since families are the primary unit of consumption. However, smaller families are probably better off than larger families who have the same level of family income. This recommends a family per capita income measure. Yet, there are economies of consumption, so that family per capita income may actually understate the welfare level of large families. An alternative approach is to divide household income by an 'equivalence scale' which adjusts family size for actual consumption needs. Many studies use the US poverty line levels as an equivalence scale to obtain a household income welfare measure. Others scale family income by a more general form, such as N^a, where N is family size and a is a number between zero and one (typically one half).

From a behavioural point of view, the family is used most often as the unit of analysis, since families tend to make income decisions jointly and accumulate income over time for future consumption needs. Yet, over time, the family is not a stable unit. Children leave families to set up independent family units. Moreover, it is quite common for married couples to separate or divorce, and, as a result, for family income to be split. From this standpoint, it may also be appropriate to base behavioural models on individual income decisions.

Sampling problems and under-reporting biases

Another comparability problem involves sample design. Income is generally skewed to the right, which means that there are usually a small number of families with very high incomes. If a sample does not adequately capture the 'upper tail' of the distribution, the degree of income inequality in a country may be seriously understated. Most official datasets, such as the Current Population Survey in the United States, will 'top code' income entries – that is, provide a maximum figure of, say, $100,000. This will also bias downward estimates of income inequality.

Table 1 The ratio of the ninetieth to the tenth percentile of income (P90/P10 Ratio). Based on the Luxembourg Income Study Data, 1979–87

Country	Year	P90/P10 Ratio	Year	P90/P10 Ratio
Australia	1981	4.05	1985	4.01
Belgium	1985	2.74	1988	2.79
Canada	1981	4.07	1987	4.02
Finland	1987	2.59	1990	2.74
France	1979	3.48	1984	3.48
The Netherlands	1979	2.72	1984	2.85
New Zealand	1983–4	3.56	1987–8	3.48
Norway	1979	2.77	1986	2.93
Sweden	1981	2.45	1987	2.72
United Kingdom	1979	3.53	1986	3.79
United States	1979	4.93	1986	5.94

Source: Atkinson, Rainwater and Smeeding (1995)

Most surveys provide good coverage of wage and salary and pension income. However, property income, which is heavily concentrated among the rich, is notoriously under-reported in most surveys, as are welfare payments and other social transfers to the poor. This will have the result of understating the share of income received by the bottom and top parts of the income distribution.

2 International comparisons of income

The most systematic study of international income comparisons is based on the Luxembourg Income Study. Some recent results are reported below, where considerable effort has been made to make the income concepts and sampling frame as comparable as possible. The inequality index used is the P90/P10 ratio, the ratio of income between the ninetieth and the tenth percentile of the income distribution. The P90/P10 ratio avoids many of the problems associated with the upper and lower tails.

The results of Table 1 show a wide range of inequality among countries, from 2.7 in Sweden to 5.9 in the United States in the late 1980s. Moreover, among this group of eleven countries, the United States experienced by far the highest increase of inequality over this period. In five other countries, inequality also increased over this period, four experienced no appreciable change in inequality, and one showed a decline.

Table 2 presents a broader set of comparisons. The World Bank divides countries into income groups (see WORLD BANK). The figures are based on raw data compiled by the authors and do not make adjustments for comparability in income concept or data sources. Despite this limitation, the results are very suggestive. The most equal countries in the world in terms of having the lowest concentration share of income among the top quintile (20 per cent) are the high income ones, including the US and other OECD countries. The low-income economies, including India, Pakistan, and Indonesia, are the second most equal group in this dimension. The most unequal countries are the lower-middle income group, which includes Colombia, Peru, Poland, and Brazil. For Brazil, which appears to be the most unequal country in the world, the share of the top quintile was 63 per cent.

The pattern of inequality shown in this table follows a well-known pattern referred to as the Kuznets curve. Kuznets (1955) argued that inequality would tend to be low in a country at its early stages of development, rise as the country developed from a low income to a middle income status, and then decline as the country became a high-income, industrialized economy. He predicted an inverted 'U-shaped' relation between income inequality and per

Comparative income and wealth distribution

Table 2 Percentage income shares of the bottom and top quintiles for selected countries at various levels of development, 1978–87

Country	Year	Bottom quintile	Top quintile
Low income countries			
Bangladesh	1981–2	9.3	39.0
India	1983	8.1	41.4
Indonesia	1987	8.8	41.3
Pakistan	1984–5	7.8	45.6
Average		7.6	44.7
Lower-middle income countries			
Brazil	1983	2.4	62.6
Colombia	1988	4.0	53.0
Malaysia	1987	4.6	51.2
Morocco	1984–5	9.8	39.4
Peru	1985	4.4	51.9
Philippines	1985	5.5	48.0
Poland	1987	9.7	35.2
Average		5.2	51.0
Upper-middle income countries			
Hungary	1983	10.9	32.4
Venezuela	1987	4.7	50.6
Yugoslavia	1987	6.1	42.8
Average		7.2	41.9
High income economies			
France	1979	6.3	40.8
Germany, West	1984	6.8	38.7
Israel	1979	6.0	39.6
Italy	1986	6.8	41.0
Japan	1979	8.7	37.5
Spain	1980–1	6.9	40.0
Sweden	1981	8.0	36.9
Switzerland	1982	5.2	44.6
United Kingsom	1979	5.8	39.5
United States	1985	4.7	41.9
Average		6.2	40.5

Source: Deininger and Squire (1996). Averages are for all countries in the group

capita income, a result that is consistent with the data in Table 2.

3 Methodological problems in international comparisons of wealth

While, as noted above, many countries now have official estimates of family or household income distribution, unfortunately comparable data on the size distribution of household wealth for the US or, for that matter, for any other country in the world do not exist. There are no official household surveys conducted on an annual basis for this purpose. As a result, researchers in this field have had to make estimates of household wealth inequality from a variety of sources, which are sometimes inconsistent. Compounding this problem is the fact that household wealth is much more heavily concentrated in the upper percentiles of the distribution than income. Thus, unless surveys or data sources are especially designed to cover the top wealth groups in a country, it is quite easy to produce biased estimates of the size distribution of wealth which understate the true level of inequality.

The net result is that estimates of household wealth distribution are more problematic than estimates of income distribution, and international comparisons are more difficult. The methodological problems associated with household wealth include:

1 the definition of wealth;
2 the unit of observation;
3 under-reporting biases;
4 sampling problems;
5 asset coverage; and
6 institutional differences.

I shall discuss the first issue in the following section. The other problems one encounters depends very much on the type of data one is using, and, as a result, I shall organize the discussion of these methodological issues by data source.

Definition of wealth

The conventional definition of household wealth includes assets and liabilities that have a current market value and that are directly or indirectly marketable (fungible). A typical list of assets includes owner-occupied housing and other real estate; consumer durables such as automobiles; cash, checking and savings accounts, money market funds, and certificates of deposit; bonds and other financial instruments; corporate stock shares and mutual funds; the equity in unincorporated businesses; trust funds; the cash surrender value of life insurance policies; and the cash surrender value of pension plans, such as Individual Retirement Accounts (IRAs) and 401(k) plans in the United States (see PENSION SYSTEMS). I refer to this measure as 'marketable wealth', since it represents those assets over which the family or individual has control. This notion corresponds to wealth as a store of value and is used in the standard national accounting framework.

A wider definition of household wealth will often add some valuation of pension rights, from both public and private sources, to marketable wealth. Such a measure provides a better gauge of potential future consumption. Pension wealth is defined as the discounted present value of future private pension benefits. Technically, this component refers to so-called 'Defined Benefit' pension plans only, in which future benefits are determined by a formula based on years of work at a company and earnings received. The other type, 'Defined Contribution' pension plans, are actual accumulations made by or for an individual in various financial instruments and accounts that have a current cash surrender value. This form is already included in marketable wealth. In similar fashion, social security wealth is defined as the discounted present value of the future stream of social security benefits (as they are called in the United States). All OECD countries have a similar type of public pension plan.

There are several methodological issues associated with the inclusion of both pension and social security wealth in the household portfolio. Since such items are not directly marketable (neither future pension nor social security benefits can be transferred or used as collateral for a loan) nor under the direct control of the household or individual, it is questionable whether they should be considered household wealth. In addition, future entitlements for depend on many factors, such as the health (and survival) of a company, productivity growth and other macroeconomic variables, and future legislation. Thus, estimating the value of these two forms of wealth may be problematic, particularly for younger age groups.

Some authors have also used definitions that are narrower than marketable wealth. One is liquid wealth, defined as financial assets less unsecured debt. This form of wealth can be almost immediately converted into cash (which is what is meant by 'liquidity') and thus has the most direct relevance for consumption behaviour. This measure of wealth is used quite often in analyses of the consumption behaviour of young and poor families.

Data sources

There have been four principal sources of data for developing household wealth estimates: (1) estate tax data; (2) household survey data; (3) wealth tax data; and (4) income capitalization techniques. Each has its characteristic advantages and disadvantages.

Estate tax data was the first major source of data used for wealth analysis. When someone dies, the person's assets are said to comprise his or her estate, and estate tax records are actual tax returns filed for probate. Such data have a great degree of reliability, since they are subject to scrutiny and audit by the state. Their main limitation, (in the US at least), is that the threshold for filing is relatively high, so that only a small proportion of estates (typically, 1 per cent or so) are required to file returns. In Great Britain the threshold is considerably lower, so that the majority of estates file tax returns.

Another difficulty is that the sample consists of decedents. Since most researchers are interested in distribution of wealth among the living population, a technique based on 'mortality multipliers' is used to infer the distribution of wealth among the actual population. If mortality rates were the same for each group, then the wealth of decedents would constitute a representative sample of the living population, and researchers could use the estate data directly. However, mortality rates are much greater for older people than younger ones, so that different 'weights' must be given to the estates filed by decedents of different ages. Mortality rates are also higher for men than for women (that is, women, on average, live longer than men), and also higher for black individuals than whites. As a result, estates are assigned a weight based on the inverse of the group's mortality rate (one divided by the mortality rate), and these are then used to generate the size distribution of wealth in the living population.

Estimates of wealth inequality based on this technique are, as might be expected, quite sensitive to the precision of the mortality multipliers. The estimates can have a very large standard error, particularly for the young, since there are very few of them in the sample. This means that the results are very sensitive to who happens to die in a given year and may therefore not be very reliable for young adults. There are two other problems associated with this technique. First, insofar as mortality rates are inversely correlated with wealth (that is, the rich tend to live longer), the resulting multipliers can be biased. Most studies do try to correct for this problem by using mortality rates for the wealthy that are lower than for the population as a whole.

Second, the distribution of wealth estimated by this technique is for individuals, rather than for families. Changing ownership patterns within families (for example, joint ownership of the family's house) can affect estimated wealth concentration. For example, as noted by Atkinson (1975), marital customs and relations have changed over the century. Married women now inherit more wealth and have higher wealth levels than they did in 1900 or 1930. This reduces individual concentration even if household wealth inequality does not change. For example, between 1929 and 1953, Robert Lampman (1962) reported that the percentage of married women among top-wealth holders increased from 9 to 18 per cent. As a result, additional imputations must be performed to infer family wealth from estimates of individual wealth holdings. These typically involve making assumptions about marriage patterns – in particular, the correlation between the wealth holdings of spouses (whether, for example, rich husbands tend to be married to rich wives or poor wives).

Another problem with this data source is under-reporting and non-filing for tax avoidance. Though the returns are subject to audit, the value of cash on hand, jewellery, housewares, and business assets are difficult to ascertain. Their value is typically understated in order to reduce the tax liability of the estate. Moreover, inter vivos transfers (that is, transfers of wealth between living individuals), particularly in anticipation of death, can bias estimates of household wealth among the living. If older people pass on wealth to their children just before they die, then their estates would tend to under-represent the wealth of comparably aged individuals still living. Estate tax data have been extensively used by Atkinson and Harrison (1978) for the UK, and Robert Lampman (1962), for the US. The long-term time-series on wealth concentration for Britain is based on estate tax data (see section 4 below).

The second source is household surveys, which are questionnaires that are given to a sample of households in a population. Their primary advantage is to provide considerable discretion to the interviewer about the information requested of respondents. Their major drawback is that information provided by the respondent is often inaccurate (response error), and, in many cases, the information requested is not provided at all (non-response problems). Another problem is that because household wealth is extremely skewed, the very rich (the so-called 'upper tail' of the distribution) are often considerably under-represented in random samples. An alternative is to use stratified samples, based typically on income tax returns, which over sample the rich. However, studies indicate that response error and non-response rates are considerably higher among the wealthy than among the middle-class. Moreover, there are problems in 'weighting' the sample in order to reflect the actual population distribution.

The third source of wealth data is based on the 'income capitalization' technique, which is usually applied to a sample of income tax returns. The earliest use of this technique on US data was Stewart (1939). In this procedure, certain income flows, such as dividends, rents, and interest, are converted into corresponding asset values based on the average asset yield. For example, dividends are capitalized into corporate stock holdings by dividing dividends reported in an income tax return by the average ratio of dividends to corporate stock in the economy as a whole. This technique when applied to a large sample of tax returns can provide an estimate of the size distribution of wealth.

This source also suffers from a number of problems. First, only assets with a corresponding income flow are covered in this procedure. Thus, owner-occupied housing and idle land can not be directly captured. Second, the estimation procedure rests heavily on the assumption that asset yields are uncorrelated with asset levels (that is, for example, that large stock holders will receive the same average return on their stock holdings as small stock holders). Any actual correlation between asset holdings and yields can produce biased estimates. Third, the observational unit is based on the tax return. Various assumptions must be made in order to construct family wealth estimates from tax unit wealth.

A fourth source is wealth tax return data, which are available in a number of European countries such as Germany, Sweden and Switzerland. These countries assess taxes not only on current income but also on the stock of household wealth. Though there is typically a threshold for paying wealth taxes, population coverage can be considerably greater than that of estate tax returns. However, the measurement problems are similar to that of estate tax data. First, the filer has an incentive to understate the value of assets, or even not to report them at all, for tax avoidance. Second, the assets subject to tax do not cover the full range of household assets (for example, consumer durables, pensions, and life insurance policies are often tax exempt and not reported). Third, the observational unit is the tax return unit, which does not directly correspond to the family unit. Wealth tax data have been used extensively by Roland Spant (1987) for an analysis of wealth trends in Sweden (see the next section).

Comparative income and wealth distribution

Table 3 Percentage share of household wealth held by the richest 1 per cent of wealth holders in Sweden, the United Kingdom and the United States, 1962–92

Year	Sweden	United Kingdom	United States
1920–23	40.5	60.9	36.7
1929–30	38.0	55.5	44.2
1933–36	34.0	54.2	33.3
1938–39		55.0	36.4
1945	30.8		29.8
1949–51	26.7	47.2	27.1
1953		43.5	28.4
1958		40.9	27.7
1962		31.9	31.8
1965–66	19.4	33.3	34.4
1969–70	18.6	31.3	31.1
1972		32.0	29.1
1975–76	17.0	23.1	19.9
1978–79	16.6	22.0	20.5
1981		22.5	24.8
1983	17.7	25.0	30.9
1985–86	16.5	22.5	31.9
1988–89	18.4	21.3	35.7
1990–92	20.7	21.3	34.0

Source: Wolff (1996a)

4 International comparisons of wealth

The availability of household wealth data is quite limited. Needed data to calculate measures of household wealth inequality are readily available only for Canada, France, Germany, Great Britain, Japan, Sweden, and the United States.

There are only three countries for which long-term time-series are available on household wealth inequality: Sweden, the United Kingdom and the United States. The most comprehensive data exist for the United Kingdom. The data are based on estate duty (tax) returns. Estimates are for adult persons. Figures are available on an almost annual basis since 1923. The Swedish data are available on a rather intermittent basis from 1920 onward. The data, as indicated above, are based on actual wealth tax returns. A long-term time-series for the United States was complied by Wolff (1996a). This was based on joining together estimates of the share of wealth owned by the richest wealth holders on the basis of estate tax data for the period 1922–1981 with survey data for the period from 1962 to 1995.

Comparative trends for the three countries for overlapping years are shown in Table 3. In Sweden, there was a dramatic reduction in wealth inequality between 1920 and 1975, with the share of the top percentile declining from 40 to 17 per cent of total household wealth. From 1975 to 1985, there was virtually no change in the concentration of wealth, but between 1985 and 1990, the share of the top percentile increased from 17 to 21 per cent. For the United Kingdom, there was a substantial decline in the share of wealth held by the richest 1 per cent of wealth holders, from 61 per cent in 1923 to 20 per cent in 1974 but little change thereafter. In the United States, wealth inequality declined substantially between 1929 and 1976, with the share of the top 1 per cent falling in half. However, from 1976

Table 4 The inequality of household wealth in selected countries, mid-1980s, derived from similar data sources

Country	Gini coefficient	Percentage of total wealth held by: Top 1%	Top 5%
A. Conformable databases, gross assets			
1. France, 1986	0.71	26	43
2. United States, 1983	0.77	33	54
B. Conformable databases, net worth			
1. Germany, 1988	0.69		
2. United States, 1988	0.76		
C. Net worth, comparable household surveys			
1. United States, 1983	0.79	35	56
2. Canada, 1984	0.69	17	38
3. Japan, 1981	0.58		
4. Japan, 1984	0.52		25
5. Sweden, 1985–86		16	31

Source: Wolff (1996b). See the paper for details on sources and methods

to 1992, the US showed an extremely sharp increase in wealth inequality, with the top percentile's share increasing from 20 to 34 per cent. In fact, the United States was the most equal of the three countries in the early 1920s but the least equal by the early 1990s.

Figures on the size distribution of household wealth for seven OECD countries in the mid-1980s are shown in Table 4. The comparisons are grouped by relatively comparable sources. Panel A shows comparative figures for France and the US, which are based on a special study to create conformable databases between the two countries. The study shows higher Gini coefficient and concentration shares in the US. (The Gini coefficient is an index ranging from zero for perfect equality to one for maximal inequality.) Panel B shows comparative statistics for Germany and the US derived from another conformable database – the German Socio-Economic Panel and the US Panel Study of Income Dynamics Equivalent Data File for 1988 – which attempts to make the wealth concept used in the two databases consistent by including the same set of assets and liabilities. Also, the sampling frames are relatively similar, since they are both panel datasets based on representative samples. The results also show that the US is the more unequal of the two countries, with a Gini coefficient of 0.76 compared to 0.69 for Germany.

Panel C shows wealth statistics derived from several comparable household surveys. The first of these is the United States' 1983 Survey of Consumer Finances and the second is the 1984 Statistics Canada Survey of Consumer Finances. Wealth inequality is clearly greater in the US, with a share of the top percentile almost double that of Canada's. Estimates for Japan are shown for 1981 and 1984, on the basis of 1981 Family Saving Survey and the 1984 National Survey of Family Income and Expenditure, and for Sweden from the 1985–86 survey, 'Household market and non-market activities'. The results suggest that wealth inequality is considerably lower in Japan and Sweden than in the United States.

EDWARD N. WOLFF
NEW YORK UNIVERSITY

Further reading

* Atkinson, A.B. (1975) 'The distribution of wealth in Britain in the 1960's – the estate duty method reexamined', in J.D. Smith, (ed.) *The Personal Distribution of Income and Wealth*. (Presents an evaluation of the estate duty method of estimating wealth distribution.)

* Atkinson, A.B. and Harrison, A.J. (1978) *Distribution of Personal Wealth in Britain*, Cambridge: Cambridge University Press. (Presents early time-series data on United Kingdom wealth concentration.)

* Atkinson, A.B., Rainwater, L. and Smeeding, T. (1995) *Income Distribution in Advanced Economies: The Evidence from the Luxembourg Income Study (LIS)*, Paris: OECD. (The most comprehensive study on comparative income inequality among advanced industrial countries.)

* Deininger, K. and Squire, L. (1996) 'A new data set measuring income inequality', *The World Bank Economic Review* 10 (3): 565–91. (Provides the most comprehensive international data available on personal income distribution.)

Feldstein, M. (1974) 'Social security, induced retirement, and aggregate capital accumulation', *Journal of Political Economy* 82 (5): 905–26. (Seminal article on social security wealth.)

* Kuznets, S. (1953) *Shares of Upper Income Groups in Income and Savings*, New York: National Bureau of Economic Research. (Presents some of the earliest data on income inequality in the United States.)

* Kuznets, S. (1955) 'Economic growth and income inequality', *American Economic Review* 45 (1): 1–28. (Develops a statistical relation between country income inequality and per capita income.)

* Lampman, R. (1962) *The Share of Top Wealth-Holders in National Wealth, 1922–56*, Princeton, NJ: Princeton University Press. (Presents early time-series data on United States wealth concentration.)

Lipsey, R.E. and Tice, H. (eds) (1989) *The Measurement of Saving, Investment, and Wealth, Studies of Income and Wealth*, vol. 52, Chicago: Chicago University Press. (Collection of methodological articles on estimating wealth distribution.)

Modigliani, F. and Brumberg, R. (1954) 'Utility analysis and the consumption function: an interpretation of cross-section data', in K.K. Kurihara (ed.) *Post-Keynesian Economics*, New Brunswick, NJ: Rutgers University Press. (Seminal article on the life-cycle model of wealth accumulation.)

O'Higgins, M., Schmaus, G. and Stephenson, G. (1989) 'Income distribution and redistribution: a microdata analysis for seven countries', *Review of Income and Wealth* 35 (2): 107–32. (One of the first studies of comparative pre-tax and post-tax income distribution.)

Sawyer, M. (1976) 'Income distribution in OECD countries', *OECD Economic Outlook: Occasional Studies*, July. (One of the earliest comparative studies of income distribution among OECD countries).

Shorrocks, A.F. (1975) 'The age-wealth relationship: a cross-section and cohort analysis', *Review of Economics and Statistics* 57: 155–63. (Analyses biases in estimating wealth distributions.)

Smith, J.D. (ed.) (1975) *The Personal Distribution of Income and Wealth*, New York: Columbia University Press. (Collection of methodological articles on income and wealth distribution.)

* Spant, R. (1987) 'Wealth distribution in Sweden: 1920–1983', in E.N. Wolff (ed.) *International Comparisons of Household Wealth*. (Demonstrates use of wealth tax data for estimating wealth inequality.)

* Stewart, C. (1939) 'Income capitalization as a method of estimating the distribution of wealth by size group', *Studies in Income and Wealth* vol. 3. New York: National Bureau of Economic Research. (Demonstrates use of income capitalization technique.)

* Wolff, E.N. (1996a), *Top Heavy: A Study of Increasing Inequality of Wealth in America*, updated and expanded edition, New York: Free Press. (Develops long-term time-series on American wealth inequality.)

* Wolff, E.N. (1996b) 'International comparisons of wealth inequality,' *Review of Income and Wealth* 42 (4): 433–51. (Presents international comparisons of wealth distributions.)

Wolff, E.N. (1997) *Economics of Poverty, Inequality, and Discrimination*, Cincinnati, Ohio: South-Western College Publishing. (Contains a comprehensive treatment of methodological issues in estimating income and wealth distributions.)

Wolff, E.N. (ed.) (1987) *International Comparisons of the Distribution of Household Wealth*, Oxford: Oxford University Press. (Contains articles of wealth distribution for a number of countries.)

See also: ECONOMIC GROWTH AND CONVERGENCE; EMPLOYMENT RELATIONS; INDUSTRIAL AND LABOUR RELATIONS; PENROSE, E.; PENSION SYSTEMS; WORKFARE

Business and industrial organization

Corporate control

1 Shareholder theory
2 Stakeholder theory
3 Managerial theory
4 Conclusion: innovation, development, and corporate control

Overview

Corporations are important to the operation and performance of a national economy because they exercise substantial control over the allocation of the economy's resources. Specifically, business corporations control the allocation of *people* to engage in productive activities and the allocation of *money* to finance these activities by investing in physical and human capital. Hence business corporations exercise considerable control over the *allocation of resources* in the economy in the forms of both labour and capital – the two generic factors of production. Moreover, as ongoing entities that must generate returns on these investments to survive, successful business corporations can exercise considerable control over the *allocation of returns* from productive activities. Corporate governance is concerned with the institutions that influence how business corporations allocate resources and returns. Specifically, *a system of corporate governance shapes who makes investment decisions in corporations, what types of investments they make, and how returns from investments are distributed* (O'Sullivan 2000b).

Given this definition that links corporate governance, and hence corporate control, to the economy's system of allocation of resources and returns, a perspective on corporate control and economic performance should be prepared to pose the following three types of 'who, what, and how' questions[1]:

- Who controls the corporate allocation of resources? Put differently, what are the incentives and abilities with respect to the allocation of resources and returns of the types of people who exercise strategic decision-making power in corporations?
- What types of investments in productive resources do they make? In particular, what types of productive capabilities, embodied especially in human resources, do these strategic decision-makers seek to put in place?
- How do they distribute the returns that are generated from these investments? Specifically, to what extent do they reinvest in productive capabilities and to what extent do they distribute returns to various types of 'stakeholders' such as shareholders, different groups of employees, suppliers, distributors, governments, and communities?

Contemporary debates on corporate control and economic performance are heavily influenced by arguments developed in discussions of the role of business corporations in the economies of the United States and Britain in the 1980s and 1990s. They have been dominated by (1) a shareholder theory of governance – one that argues that shareholders are the principals for whom the corporation should be run. The main challenges to shareholder theory have come thus far from (2) stakeholder theorists who contend that the corporation should be run for the benefit of other interest groups besides shareholders; and (3) management scholars who argue that managers need some autonomy from financial interests to commit resources to 'long-term' investments.

I am interested in these perspectives as arguments about how to govern corporations to improve the performance of the economy as a whole rather than as arguments for increasing the returns flowing to any particular group, be they managers, workers or shareholders. In other words, I look to these perspectives for theoretically logical and empirically supportable arguments about economic performance in an economy in which corporations play a major role in the allocation of resources and returns. I am *not* interested in these perspectives insofar as they *simply* argue that, on normative (social, ethical or moral) grounds, managers, shareholders or stakeholders should be rewarded in the economy. Nevertheless, normative arguments concerning who gains and who loses under a particular system of corporate governance have an important role to play in motivating and stimulating the corporate governance debates, and in helping to arrive at policy solutions that promote economic growth that is both equitable and stable.

I Shareholder theory

The basic argument underlying the shareholder perspective on corporate governance is that, as equity investors, shareholders are the only participants in the business corporation whose returns to their productive contributions are 'residual'. All other groups besides shareholders, such as workers, external suppliers and creditors, who provide resources to the firm, do so on the basis of contracts that specify the relation between their contributions to the productive process and the returns that they receive for those contributions. It is assumed that market forces determine the resources provided and the returns received by these other groups, and that the possessors of these resources will use the market to allocate the resources that they control to their best alternative uses. The returns to shareholders, then, depend upon what, if any, revenues are left over after all other contractual claims have been paid.

As 'residual claimants', shareholders bear the risk of the corporation's making a profit or loss. They thus have an interest in allocating corporate resources to their 'best alternative uses' to make the residual as large as possible. Since all other 'stakeholders' in the corporation will receive the returns for which they have contracted, the 'maximization of shareholder value' will result in superior economic performance not only for the particular corporation but also for the economy as a whole. Advocates of shareholder theory therefore contend that shareholders are the 'principals' in whose interests the corporation should be run even though they rely on others for the actual running of the corporation. To contribute to the optimal allocation of resources in the economy, managers should seek to maximize shareholder value, either by making corporate investments in projects that can yield at least the same risk-adjusted rate of return that shareholders could receive elsewhere in the economy, or by distributing revenues to shareholders who can then reallocate these resources themselves in search of the highest available returns (Jensen 1989).

It is regarded as economically efficacious for shareholders to bear the risk of the corporation's generating a residual. As a class, they are deemed to be better equipped to bear risk than managers and workers because they are not tied to the firms in which they hold shares. Consequently, shareholders can diversify their investment portfolios to take advantage of the risk-minimization possibilities of grouping or consolidating different types of risk. As Fama and Jensen put it: 'the least restricted residual claims in common use are the common stocks of large corporations. Stockholders are not required to have any other role in the organization; their residual claims are alienable without restriction; and, because of these provisions, the residual claims allow unrestricted risk sharing among stockholders' (Fama and Jensen 1983: 303). The financial theory of risk bearing thus hinges on 'a separation of decision management and residual risk bearing' in the corporation. That separation permits optimal risk allocation in the corporate economy; indeed, that the corporate form facilitates this allocation is financial economists' key explanation for the growth and persistence of the corporate enterprise with diffuse shareholding.

The risk allocation advantage comes, however, at a cost in terms of incentives within the corporation: '[s]eparation and specialization of decision management and residual risk bearing leads to agency problems between decision agents and residual claimants. This is the problem of the separation of ownership and control that has long troubled students of the corporation' (Fama and Jensen 1983: 312). The governance challenge of the modern corporation, as financial economists conceptualize it, is that those who bear the residual risk – the shareholders or 'principals' – have no assurance that the corporate managers or 'agents' who make decisions that affect shareholder wealth will act in shareholder interests. The costs that result from the exercise of managers' discretion to act other than in the best interests of their principals, as well as the expenses of monitoring and disciplining them to prevent the exercise of that discretion, are described as 'agency costs'. For financial economists, therefore, the central problem in corporate governance is an 'agency problem' that must somehow be resolved if the economy is to achieve an optimal allocation of its productive resources.

In the long run, given the assumptions underlying the shareholder perspective, the governance problem may well be corrected through the forces of competition. In particular, corporations that do not seek to maximize shareholder value, it is argued, will be unable to attract risk capital to fund their investment projects, whereas those corporations that do seek to maximize shareholder value will receive investment finance. Meanwhile, however, in the shorter term, managers of corporations that are generating substantial residual revenues may use their control over the allocation of these corporate revenues to pursue their own goals (ranging from lining their own pockets with corporate cash to building their egos by favouring the growth of 'their' enterprises). The result will be a misallocation of resources in not only the enterprise but also the economy as a whole unless there are effective mechanisms by which shareholders can discipline managerial behaviour.

The central preoccupation of financial economists who work on corporate governance has been the analysis of mechanisms that increase the control of financial markets over corporate resource allocation and that, as a result, limit the discretion of corporate managers to act other than in the interests of shareholders. One way to resolve the problem is through a reintegration of share ownership and managerial control. A 'big owner', for example a financial institution or a very wealthy individual, can amass sufficient shares to exercise managerial control. Or managers themselves can become the major shareholders, for example through a leveraged buyout that substitutes corporate debt for corporate equity. In either case, it is assumed that the owner-managers will have an interest in maximizing shareholder value.

Such integration of ownership and management has the disadvantage, however, of eliminating a social division of labour that proponents of the shareholder perspective view as central to the operation of a market economy; namely, the division of labour between a financier who diversifies his portfolio across many different investment opportunities and a producer who possesses specialized decision-making skills. To deal with the agency problem in a way that permits this division of labour between the financier and producer to be maintained, shareholders can use either the carrot or the stick. The carrot is to grant stock options to managers so that they will align their own incentives with that of shareholders, even though their stakes in the company *as shareholders* will typically be too small to result in the actual integration of ownership and management (Murphy 1985; Baker *et al.* 1988; Jensen and Murphy 1990). The stick is to use 'the market for corporate control' – that is, the takeover of effective control of a company by a group of shareholders – to change the behaviour of opportunistic managers by threatening their removal, or, if such discipline fails to do the job, by replacing them with new managers who will align their interests with shareholders (Jensen and Ruback 1983; Jensen 1986; Scharfstein 1988; Jensen 1988; Grossman and Hart 1988).

During the 1980s and 1990s in the United States, the widespread use of these mechanisms to align the interests of corporate managers with those of public shareholders helped to transform the rhetoric of shareholder value into a dominant ideology of corporate governance. This period also witnessed the longest stock market boom in history, with the yields on corporate stock recovering significantly from their depressed state in the 1970s (Lazonick and O'Sullivan 2000a). The critical issues for the debate on corporate governance are whether the claims of the shareholder perspective that maximizing shareholder value results in the highest common good are justified in theory and in practice.

The claims of proponents of shareholder value can be called into question on three different levels. Firstly, notwithstanding the fervour with which the efficacy of the control mechanisms proposed by shareholder advocates is propounded, unambiguous empirical evidence to support these assertions has not been forthcoming. Secondly, the two key assumptions that shareholder theory makes about the role of corporate shareholders – that they supply capital for productive investment and that they bear risk to a degree that entitles them to corporate residuals – can be challenged on the grounds that they ignore some basic facts concerning the twentieth-century operation of a corporate economy, including that of the United States. Finally, and most fundamental of all, the concept of economic efficiency on which the shareholder theory is premised precludes an understanding, not to mention an analysis, of the dynamic process through which productive resources are developed and utilized to generate higher quality, lower cost products, or what is often called innovation (see INNOVATION; SCHUMPETER, J.).

Mechanisms of control

There is a striking dearth of unambiguous empirical evidence to support the claims by proponents of shareholder theory of the effectiveness of the governance mechanisms that they propose for improving economic performance. The empirical studies that financial economists have undertaken to bolster their arguments for enhanced shareholder control over corporate resource allocation generally rely on stock market valuations of corporate equities as proxies for corporate performance. With regard to the market for corporate control, for example, most of this research consists of 'event studies' in which the 'abnormal' changes in stock prices of bidder and target companies around the time of the public announcement of these transactions are used as a proxy for their economic effects; abnormal returns represent the difference between actual and expected stock returns as calculated using an asset pricing model such as CAPM (Capital Asset Pricing Model). Yet, even if we accept the questionable assumption that corporate performance can be adequately proxied by abnormal returns to shareholders, the empirical findings based on the event-study methodology fall short of providing clear-cut support for the alleged benefits of the market for corporate control for disciplining corporate resource allocation.

Advocates of the economic merits of the market for corporate control rely heavily on one empirical finding that is unambiguous: that shareholders in target firms earn sizeable positive returns around takeover announcements. In merger and acquisition transactions during the period from 1976 to 1990, the shareholders of target companies received an average premium over market value of 41 per cent (Jensen 1993). Estimates of the total abnormal returns from the announcement of a bid through to its conclusion vary from 15.5 per cent to 33.9 per cent (Dodd 1980; Asquith 1983; see also Asquith et al. 1983; Malatesta 1983; Dodd and Ruback 1977).

In contrast to the gains of target company shareholders, however, the wealth of acquiring company shareholders showed little change or even decreased around the time of the transaction (Bhagat et al. 1990). Since the bidder firms were, on average, much larger than the targets, the enormous premia paid to target firms did not always imply a positive change in the wealth of the target and acquirer shareholders combined. Moreover, the abnormal positive returns to target shareholders are not robust over the longer term. Most event studies focus only on the weeks surrounding the takeover bid but if we extend the period of analysis the returns to bidder shareholders become negative. Michael Jensen and Richard Ruback reviewed six studies that calculated these returns one year after the takeover was concluded. These studies found abnormal negative returns, averaging –6.56 per cent, with the exception of one study which showed a slightly positive abnormal return of 0.6 per cent. As Jensen and Ruback concluded: '[t]hese post-outcome negative abnormal returns are unsettling because they are inconsistent with market efficiency and suggest that changes in stock price during takeovers overestimate the future efficiency gains from mergers' (Jensen and Ruback 1983: 21). Magenheim and Mueller (1988) and Agrawal et al. (1992) claim that abnormal returns to bidders were negative over a three-year period

(–16 per cent) and a five-year period (–10 per cent) respectively.

The unimpressive returns to acquirer shareholders, as well as concerns about the time consistency of shareholder returns on takeovers, cast doubt on the contention by proponents of shareholder theory that the market for corporate control is a mechanism for disciplining corporate management. To question the reliance on changes in shareholder wealth as proxies for corporate performance is to raise even more concerns about the empirical basis of the shareholder theory of corporate governance. With regard to the market for corporate control, for example, studies based on accounting data suggest that the returns to target shareholders overestimate the economic gains that occur through disciplinary action.

To the extent that takeovers act as antidotes to managerial deficiencies in the allocation of corporate resources, one would expect the returns to target shareholders to be abnormally low prior to the bid and to improve once the bid is completed. Some studies have found that targets of hostile bids do exhibit abnormally poor performance (Ravenscraft and Scherer 1987; Morck et al. 1988) but others find no significant difference in the pre-bid performance of the targets of hostile and friendly transactions (Franks and Mayer 1996). Nor is there persuasive evidence from empirical analyses of post-acquisition performance that the market for corporate control enhances corporate performance. Ravenscraft and Scherer (1987) found that profitability declined after acquisitions. Herman and Lowenstein (1988) concluded that during the 1980s there was a noticeable decrease in the post-acquisition return relative to the pre-acquisition period. With a few exceptions, most empirical studies of post-acquisition performance have failed to provide strong evidence of the disciplinary role of takeovers and some have even suggested that the market for corporate control reduces economic performance.

Although the merits of the market for corporate control for promoting economic efficiency have been widely touted by proponents of shareholder theory, the balance of empirical evidence can hardly be interpreted as unequivocal support for their claims.

Nor is the ambiguity of evidence confined to empirical analyses of the effects of the market for corporate control. It is also found with respect to other mechanisms of corporate governance advocated by proponents of shareholder value (for a review of the evidence on institutional investor activism, for example, see Black 1998). Scepticism about the claims of financial economists is therefore warranted *even on the basis of evidence assembled according to their own preferred empirical methodology* of event studies.

Clearly, if one challenges the central assumption behind that methodology – that shareholder wealth is an adequate proxy for corporate performance – the empirical evidence is even less persuasive. And there are good reasons to raise questions about the wisdom of interpreting stock valuations as indicators of improvements in corporate performance. One direct challenge to that assumption has come from financial economists who have attempted to analyse the source of the enormous abnormal gains to target-company shareholders in the market for corporate control. They have suggested that these gains are evidence not of efficiency improvements but of transfers of value away from other claimants on enterprises' cash flows. One argument that has been made is that shareholders gain at the expense of lower wages and pensions for employees and fewer employment opportunities. A frequently invoked example of this phenomenon is Carl Icahn's takeover of TWA in 1985 when the post-takeover reduction of $200 million in total wages was larger than the entire takeover premium (Shleifer and Summers 1988). Based on their analysis of a sample of 62 hostile takeover bids launched between 1984 and 1986, Bhagat et al. (1990) concluded that layoffs after takeovers are common and can explain 10–20 per cent of the premium. Other studies have suggested that decreased tax liabilities of target firms can in part account for takeover premia; in these cases there is a transfer of value from the government to the shareholders (Kaplan 1989; Bhagat et al. 1990). It has, however, proven difficult to account for most of the shareholder gains on takeover activity in terms of transfers from other stakeholders.

The quest for the sources of shareholder gains only makes sense, however, to those who believe that they can be accounted for predominantly in terms of changes in the real economy, be those changes associated with the creation or the redistribution of value. Conventional financial economists have traditionally attempted to rule out the alternative hypothesis of the possibility of significant dislocations between financial market valuations and corporate performance by invoking the assumption that financial markets are informationally efficient. That assumption, the efficient markets hypothesis (EMH), holds that a capital market is efficient if, as Burton Malkiel (1987: 120) put it, 'it fully and correctly reflects all relevant information in determining security prices. Formally, the market is said to be efficient with respect to some information set, Φ, if security prices would be unaffected by revealing that information.'[2] When financial economists use the concept of market efficiency in the sense of the EMH, therefore, what they are referring to is the capacity of a market to impound information.

Despite the centrality of the EMH to financial economics, the hypothesis cannot, in fact, be empirically tested in isolation from assumptions about the way in which economic actors price securities. One cannot assess whether a financial market 'fully and correctly reflects all relevant information in determining security prices' without knowing what 'correctly' and 'relevant' mean. In other words, one must rely on some assumptions about the 'appropriate' or 'rational' way to price securities. As a result, as Fama (1970: 384) put it, '[m]arket efficiency per se is not testable. It must be tested jointly with some model of equilibrium, an asset pricing model.' Basically the problem is 'that we can only test whether information is properly reflected in prices in the context of a pricing model that defines the meaning of "properly". As a result, when we find anomalous evidence on the behavior of returns, the way it should be split between market efficiency or a bad model of market equilibrium is ambiguous' (Fama 1991: 1576).

'Anomalous' evidence on the behaviour of returns is in fact rife. All of the leading models of asset pricing on which financial economists rely posit some relationship between risk and return. When these theories have been empirically tested, however, the risk-bearing explanation has proven problematic. The total real return – capital gain plus dividends – on American equities exceeded that on short-term US treasury bills by an average of 6.1 percentage points per annum between 1926 and 1992 (Siegel 1994). The difference between the return on stocks and 'risk-free' assets like t-bills is often called the 'equity risk premium' because it is thought to reflect equity holders' compensation for additional risk associated with stocks. The equity premium has been declared a 'puzzle' because the measured risk of equity returns is not high enough to justify premia of the order of 6 per cent without resorting to unreasonable assumptions about risk aversion among portfolio investors (Mehra and Prescott 1985; Kocherlakota 1996; Siegel and Thaler 1997). When mean reversion – a characteristic of the real returns on stocks but not of fixed income assets – is considered, the puzzle deepens. Although the annual standard deviation of real t-bill rates of returns is approximately 6.14 per cent compared with 18.15 per cent for real equity returns, the standard deviation of annual rates of return on t-bills over 20-year periods is 2.86 per cent which is greater than the comparable figure of 2.76 per cent for stocks. As Siegel and Thaler (1997: 195) observe in their recent review of the equity premium literature:

> This analysis suggests that the equity premium is even a bigger puzzle than has previously been thought. It is not that the risk of equities is not great enough to explain their high rate of return; rather, for long-term investors, fixed income securities have been riskier in real terms. By this reasoning, the equity premium should be negative!

Financial economists have encountered similar puzzles and anomalies in their attempts to use their risk calculus to account for differential returns among stocks. Expected returns are estimated using an asset-pricing model. The CAPM, for example, is based on the proposition that asset prices are determined by risk that cannot be reduced by holding a diversified portfolio of stocks. In other words, the model estimates the expected returns on securities as a positive linear function of risk as measured by their market ß (the slope in the regression of a security's return on the return from the market portfolio) (Sharpe 1964; Lintner 1965a, 1965b). There is, however, little empirical support for the CAPM. Market betas have been found to have little explanatory power in analyses of cross-sections of realized average returns on US common stocks (Banz 1981; Reinganum 1981; Breeden *et al*. 1989; Fama and French 1992).

The response to this 'anomaly' by some financial economists has been to search for other factors that have more power in these regressions. The list of identified variables is now extensive, and includes size, book-to-market equity, earnings/price, cash flow/price, and previous sales growth (see, for example, Fama and French 1996). Mining the data for correlations has generated these factors. As a result, the 'multifactor' models of asset pricing based upon the relationships that have emerged from this analysis have been criticized, even within financial economics, as essentially atheoretical, because none of the identified factors are linked to economic explanations of asset pricing. The relationship between risk and return that financial economists commonly assume does have a theoretical foundation but its lack of empirical support means that financial economists rely on it as an article of faith rather than a proven fact. As Richard Roll (1994: 7), a leading financial economist, put it recently:

> Perhaps the most important unresolved problem in finance, because it influences so many other problems, is the relation between risk and return. Almost everyone agrees that there should be some relation, but its precise quantification has proven to be a conundrum that has haunted us for years, embarrassed us in print, and caused business practitioners to look askance at our scientific squabbling and question our relevance. Without a risk/return model that allows one to quantify the required rate of return for an investment project, how can it be valued?

The limitations of asset pricing research means that the EMH cannot be properly tested. What then is the basis for the widespread reliance of financial economists on the EMH? The methodological difficulties of performing empirical tests of the EMH mean, as Brenda Spotton and Robin Rowley (1998: 671) put it, that:

> the commitment to EMH often stems from a prior conviction that efficiency is clearly desirable and must emerge from some evolutionary process which removes inefficient market participants, rather than from a clear evidential basis. Data, from this perspective, merely confirms the obvious presence (apart from some irritating, hopefully ephemeral, anomalies) and convenience of market efficiency.

Malkiel (1987: 122) has argued that 'the empirical evidence in favour of EMH is extremely strong. Probably no other hypothesis in either economics or finance has been more extensively tested.' Yet the empirical basis for such claims by financial economists is indirect evidence that is *consistent* with the EMH. The leading examples of empirical analysis of this type are studies that suggest that stock prices follow a random walk and those that suggest that the stock market responds quickly to announcements that convey new information about fundamentals. All of these analyses suffer from serious methodological limitations but perhaps their most important deficiency is that their findings are also consistent with theories of the behaviour of stock markets that compete with the EMH, most notably with a variety of theories that contend that stock markets are subject to fads (see, for example, Summers 1986; Davidson 1978; Glickman 1994; Raines and Leathers 1996).

Moreover, more and more evidence has accumulated of what look like 'anomalies' from the perspective of the EMH. Of particular importance has been empirical research on market volatility that suggests that price changes occur even in the absence of new information. Robert Shiller's (1981) analysis of the relationship between dividends and stock prices is the classic paper on the subject. It is generally assumed in financial economics that stock prices represent an estimate of the present value of future dividends. Shiller pointed out, however, that variations in the present value of actual dividends paid out over the century are too small to explain volatility in stock valuations. In his more recent work, Shiller (1990) contends that stock markets are, as a general rule, influenced by fads and fashions and invoked evidence on popular models used by investors to analyse the US 1987 stock market crash. Indeed, given the apparent absence of any major news that might justify it, the crash raised serious questions in the minds of a number of leading economists about the validity of their assumption of a rational connection between stock valuations and the economic fundamentals. In a paper entitled 'What moves stock prices?' David Cutler, James Poterba and Lawrence Summers (1989), for example, highlighted 'the difficulty of explaining as much as half of the variance in aggregate stock prices on the basis of publicly available news bearing on fundamental values'. Various other lines of empirical research have also fostered critiques of the EMH. For example, considerable evidence for recent decades suggests that information on the size of firms, their price-earnings ratios and their market-to-book ratios predict future returns, facts that are inconsistent with the hypothesis that stock prices reflect all publicly available information.

A number of financial theorists who describe themselves as behavioural financial economists have argued that to understand the anomalies that have already been uncovered, and stock market behaviour more generally, there is a need to overhaul the theoretical foundations of financial economics. Whereas conventional finance theorists assume that only 'rational' behaviour affects equity prices,[3] behavioural finance theorists argue that how people actually behave makes a difference to stock prices. Specifically, behavioural finance is based on the observation (from cognitive psychology and decision theory) that in some circumstances humans make systematic 'errors' in judgement and that these behavioural biases affect equity prices.

Behavioural theorists have focused on various different types of non-rational behaviour. They have argued, for example, that under certain circumstances individuals may be prone to non-wealth-maximizing behaviour such as excessive trading of stocks due to overconfidence. Individuals may also make cognitive errors usually due to their reliance on heuristics, rules adopted by economic actors to simplify their decision-making processes, which may lead to biases in certain situations. Notwithstanding its relatively recent vintage, behavioural finance has already generated a considerable body of empirical evidence to support its various claims with respect to the manner in which behavioural biases influence stock prices (for reviews of the behavioural finance literature, see Thaler 1993; Heisler 1994; see also Daniel et al. 1998).

There has been, however, far from a general acceptance within financial economics of the implications for the credibility of the EMH of the empirical findings on anomalies or, more generally, the theoretical and empirical research in behavioural finance. Orthodox financial economists have tended to respond in a defensive way. Although in his 1991 update of his original article on the EMH, Fama recognized that 'the task is thornier than it was 20 years ago', he remains firmly committed to the hypothesis on the rather dubious grounds that:

> ... the alternative hypothesis is vague, market inefficiency. This is unacceptable. Like all models, market efficiency (the hypothesis that prices fully reflect available information) is a faulty description of price formation. Following the standard scientific rule, however, market efficiency can only be replaced by a better specific model of price formation, itself potentially rejectable by empirical tests.
> (Fama 1998: 284)

Fama is by no means alone among financial economists in this view that the only possible alternative hypothesis to 'market efficiency' must be 'market inefficiency'. Indeed, there seems to be quite a consensus around the merits of, to paraphrase Keynes, being precisely wrong rather than vaguely right as revealed by the following sympathetic explanation of the resistance to behavioural finance among most financial economists:

A general criticism often raised by economists against psychological theories is that, in a given economic setting, the universe of conceivable irrational behavior patterns is essentially unrestricted. Thus, it is sometimes claimed that allowing for irrationality opens a Pandora's box of *ad hoc* stories which will have little out-of-sample predictive power.

(Daniel *et al*. 1998: 1840–1)

That the proponents of the shareholder theory of corporate governance include among their party some of the most orthodox of all financial economists in part explains their unwillingness to countenance the critiques of the EMH. Michael Jensen once famously stated, for example, that he believed 'that there is no other proposition in economics which has more solid empirical evidence supporting it than the Efficient Market Hypothesis' (Jensen 1978: 95). But their reticence is also explicable by the devastating consequences that any concession on their part would have for their arguments about corporate governance. The importance of the EMH to financial economics, and especially to the shareholder theory of corporate governance, can hardly be overstated. In the words of Terry Marsh and Robert Merton (1986), '[t]o reject the Efficient Market Hypothesis for the whole stock market ... implies broadly that production decisions based on stock prices will lead to inefficient capital allocations'.

Productive role of the corporate shareholder

Questions about the empirical bases for the claims made about the efficacy of the governance mechanisms by proponents of shareholder theory certainly cast doubt on the validity of their overall argument. There are, moreover, more direct routes to scepticism of these claims. In theory, the shareholder perspective makes two key assumptions about the role of corporate shareholders, one having to do with the allocation of resources in the economy and the other with the allocation of returns. Shareholder theory assumes that, for the allocation of resources, *productive investments* in the economy depend on *financial investments* by corporate shareholders. The theory also assumes that, for the allocation of returns, it is only shareholders among participants in the corporate enterprise who have *residual claimant status*, and hence incur *non-contractual risk* in participating in the economy. Both of these assumptions can be challenged on empirical grounds.

The assumption concerning the allocation of resources that underpins the shareholder perspective is that the stock market allocates capital to productive investments. Yet data on the sources of corporate funds flatly contradicts this assumption. Retained earnings – undistributed profits and capital consumption allowances – have always provided, and continue to provide, the financial resources that are the foundations of investments in productive capabilities that made innovation and economic development possible (Lazonick and O'Sullivan 1997a, 1997b).[4] Even, or perhaps especially in the so-called equity based system of the United States, corporate retentions and corporate debt, not equity issues, have been the main sources of funds for business investment throughout the twentieth century (Ciccolo and Baum 1985; Corbett and Jenkinson 1996). Indeed, during most years since the mid-1980s the net contribution of stock issues to corporate funds has been negative, primarily because of the increased importance of corporate stock-repurchase programmes. That is, contrary to conventional wisdom, corporate financial resources have on balance been a source of funds for the booming stock market rather than vice versa.

Even when equity has been issued, it has not necessarily played a role in funding investment in new productive assets. New corporate equity issues have often been used, not to finance investment, but to transfer financial claims over existing assets or to restructure corporate balance sheets. The ownership transfer may be an initial public offering (IPO), in which case share ownership is transferred from the original owner-entrepreneurs and their venture-capital partners to public stockholders. High levels of IPO activity, therefore, do not necessarily indicate that households and institutional investors are funding a wave of innovative investment. Rather, in absorbing IPOs, these entrepreneurs are paying the entrepreneurs who built the businesses for a claim on the enterprise's future earnings, based on investments in productive capabilities that have already been made. Whether any of the money realized from an IPO ends up committed to new innovative investment strategies, either in the issuing company or some other new venture, is at the discretion of those who control corporate resource allocation in the newly public enterprise and the original owner-entrepreneurs whose shares have been liquidated in part or full. It is not necessarily inherent in the IPO itself.

The ownership transfer may also occur for the purpose of one company acquiring another company. Typically, the acquiring company issues new stock of its corporation to exchange for the existing stock of the acquired company, the stock of which is then retired. In the aftermath of the acquisition, the acquiring company may make substantial investments in the acquired company, but once again the equity issue does not provide the source of such investment financing. Funds raised through equity issues may also be used to restructure the corporate balance sheet but here again the new equity issue does not necessarily lead to an increase in direct investment.

The assumption that an active stock market necessarily allocates capital to productive investments confuses the roles of direct investment and portfolio investment in the operation of a modern economy. When a person invests her own money in productive resources – plant, equipment and personnel – to start a new venture, she engages in direct investment. The expectation is that this investment will generate returns when the productive resources have been transformed into products that buyers want at prices that they can afford. The realization of such returns is uncertain. The technological transformation of the invested resources into outputs of sufficiently high quality and low cost to be competitive on product markets may not succeed – what Chris Freeman (1982: 148–50) calls 'technological uncertainty'. Moreover, even if the technological transformation does succeed in terms of the market conditions that prevailed when the investment in productive resources was made, by the time of the completion of the technological transformation those market conditions may have changed – what Freeman calls 'market uncertainty'.

For the direct investment in productive resources to succeed in generating returns – that is, for the initial conditions of technological and market uncertainty to be overcome and for the new venture to be transformed into a going concern – the technological and market conditions that will determine success or failure have to be *managed*, which is what a *direct* investor in a new venture must do. That is, there is an integration of asset ownership and managerial control. At some point, however, the direct investor, having successfully managed the development and utilization of the productive resources in which she has invested, may want to realize the (now enhanced) monetary value of her invested capital. To do so, she can either find a private buyer for these productive assets – that is, she can sell the business enterprise to someone else who is willing and able to take over as a direct investor who integrates ownership and control. Alternatively, she can list the company on a stock market, and sell shares in the company to portfolio investors.

In contrast to a direct investor who manages the investment in productive investment that she owns, a portfolio investor is willing to hold shares in the company precisely because his expectation of reaping returns of these shares does not require that he manage the underlying productive assets. Once the shares are listed on a stock market, if the portfolio investor is not satisfied with the returns that he is getting by holding the shares, he can readily find a buyer to whom to sell the shares. That is, in allocating their financial resources to *tradable*, and hence liquid, shares (especially ones that limit the liability of the shareholder to the purchase price of the share), portfolio investors do not have to participate in the management of the company whose shares they own.

Indeed, it is the liquidity of publicly traded shares that makes them an attractive investment for portfolio investors. They can own shares, but they do not have to manage them. In contrast to the portfolio investors' interest in financial liquidity, direct investors must be prepared to supply the corporation with financial commitment (Lazonick and O'Sullivan 1996) – a willingness to eschew the mobility of their financial resources in search of returns elsewhere in the economy for the sake of sustaining the development and utilization of productive resources in the particular business enterprise until such time that these resources can generate products of sufficiently high quality and low cost to be sold on the market.

If the assumption that the stock market plays a central role in the allocation of resources to productive investment lacks empirical support, so too does the assumption that shareholders are the only participants in the corporation whose returns are not contractually determined and who hence have an interest in generating 'residual' – or more accurately, surplus – earnings. Even when financial economists have attempted to evaluate their own theories with reference to empirical evidence, as we have already observed, the risk-bearing explanation has proven problematic. Moreover, the assumption that all other participants possess contracts that specify the relation between resources supplied and returns received derives more from the ideology of the market economy than from a study of the organizational process through which the people who participate in the corporation develop and utilize the resources that they supply to the corporation's productive processes. Corporate employees may have the expectation that the corporation will allocate some of its future returns not only to reinvestment in plant and equipment, but also to keep them productively employed and well remunerated. In keeping these people employed, those who allocate resources and returns in the corporation may expect a dynamic interaction between productive contributions of long-term employees and the long-term rewards that these employees can expect to receive; that is, the ways in which the corporation allocates resources and returns may be key to mobilizing the skills and efforts of its employees to generate the productivity that in fact makes long-term employment viable.

The expectation of sharing in a future stream of surpluses may give a variety of 'stakeholders' the incentive to devote their skills and efforts to developing and utilizing the resources of the enterprise, including their own labour services. These expectations are generally not contractual. Stakeholder thus bear the risk that, for reasons external and/or internal to the enterprise, such surpluses will not be generated – or that even if they are generated there will be shifts in the power of different participants in the corporation that allow them to lay claim to a larger share of the 'residual' than was previously expected. If workers and other stakeholders besides shareholders bear non-contractual risk, one could argue, as Margaret Blair (1995) has, that they should be included in a process that influences the corporate allocation of resources and returns.

The sources of 'residual' earnings

The obvious question raised by the shortcomings of shareholder theory in explaining the productive contribution of corporate shareholders is why the returns to corporate shareholders are so high and have been so for such an extended period of time. There are ongoing attempts within financial economics to deal with some of the empirical anomalies highlighted above. Yet it is difficult to see how such a theory could ever explain the high returns to shareholders that have been sustained for almost a century. More than half of the real returns on equities were realized by shareholders in the form of dividends,[5] paid out by corporations during a period in which wages continually increased and output prices fell. Any explanation of these returns would therefore seem to require an understanding of how the pie was being expanded in the real economy.

Innovation – the process through which productive resources are developed and utilized to generate higher quality and/or lower cost products – is central to the dynamic through which successful enterprises and economies improve their performance relative to each other as well as over time. As it provides a foundation on which wealth can be accumulated by more and more people, innovation can mitigate conflicts among different interest groups over the allocation of resources and returns: an increase in the living standards of one interest group does not have to come at the expense of another. A relevant theory of resource allocation must, therefore, incorporate an understanding of the central characteristics of the innovation process.

In studying the economics of the process through which resources are developed and utilized, the enterprise is the central unit of analysis. Indeed, historical research on innovation in all of the advanced industrial nations has highlighted the importance, as loci of innovation, of corporate enterprises that compete for markets to survive. An economy's capacity to develop is thus importantly related to the process through which corporate revenues are allocated. However, the concept of resource allocation on which the shareholder theory of corporate governance is based precludes any understanding of the dynamic process of innovation through which productive resources are developed and utilized to generate higher quality, lower cost products.

The basic foundation for the treatment of resource allocation in financial economics is Irving Fisher's theory of interest, articulated in its most complete form in his 1930 book, *The Theory of Interest*. In Fisher's (1930: 61–2) own words:

> The theory of interest bears a close resemblance to the theory of prices, of which, in fact, it is a special aspect. The rate of interest expresses a price in the exchange between present and future goods. Just as, in the ordinary theory of prices, the ratio of exchange of any two articles is based, in part, on a psychological or subjective element — their comparative marginal desirability — so, in the theory of interest, the rate of interest, or the premium on the exchange between present and future goods, is based, in part, on a subjective element, a derivative of marginal desirability; namely, the marginal preference for present over future goods. This preference has been called time preference, or *human impatience*. The chief other part is an objective element, *investment opportunity*.

For Fisher it was the interaction of these two conditions, human impatience and investment opportunity, that determined the rate of interest.

In developing Fisher's theory of the market determination of interest rates, economists in the 1950s and 1960s extended it to include an equilibrium analysis of risk. Many economists, including Fisher himself, had long attributed differences in the returns on securities to the differential risk of their income streams. In extending the Fisherian model, the objective was to develop an explanation of these differences by analysing how the market 'priced' risk. Drawing on the Arrow–Debreu theory of general equilibrium, and the concept of expected utility on which it is based, as well as a host of additional heroic assumptions about preferences and probabilities, it was argued that a linear relationship — the 'market line' — should be observed between the return on a financial asset and its risk, as measured by its contribution to the total risk of the return on an efficient market portfolio. From this perspective, the expected return on a risky security was considered to be a combination of a risk-free rate of interest and a risk margin linked to the covariance between the security's returns and the return on the market portfolio (Debreu 1959; Markowitz 1959; Arrow 1964; Hirshleifer 1965; Sharpe 1964; Lintner 1965a, 1965b; Mossin 1966). Accordingly, in the words of Jan Mossin (1966: 774), one of the key contributors to the extension of the Fisherian model, 'we may think of the rate of return of any asset as separated into two parts: the pure rate of interest representing the "price for waiting," and a remainder, a risk margin, representing the "price of risk".' It is this logic that is at the heart of modern finance theory and, as a result, the shareholder theory of governance; shareholders' returns are compensation for both waiting and risk bearing.

'Waiting' was a key element in Fisher's explanation of interest as a return to capital; in responding to socialists who think of 'interest as extortion' (Fisher 1930: 51) he claimed that:

> ... capitalists are not ... robbers of labor, but are labor-brokers who buy work at one time and sell its products at another. Their profit or gain on the transaction, if risk be disregarded, is interest, a compensation for waiting during the time elapsing between the payment to labor and the income received by the capitalist from the sale of the product of labor.
>
> (Fisher 1930: 52)

For Fisher, that the act of waiting brought forth a return to capital was inherent in the technique or the 'objective facts' of production. In *The Theory of Interest*, he repeatedly emphasized the importance of productivity in the determination of interest to correct a widespread interpretation of his theory, as one in which impatience was considered as the sole determinant of the rate of interest. In a review of Fisher's earlier work in the *American Economic Review*, for example, one critic had contended that:

> [t]he most striking fact about this method of presenting his factors is that he [Fisher] dissociates his discussion completely from any account of the production of wealth. From a perusal of his *Rate of Interest* and all but the very last chapters of his *Elementary Principles* (chapters which come after his discussion of the interest problem), the reader might easily get the impression that becoming rich is a purely psychological process. It seems to be assumed that income streams, like mountain brooks, gush spontaneously from nature's hillsides and that the determination of the rate of interest depends entirely upon the mental reactions of those who are so fortunate as to receive them ... The whole productive process, without which men would have no income streams to manipulate, is ignored, or, as the author would probably say, taken for granted.
>
> (Seager 1912: 835–7)

Fisher (1913: 610) railed against this criticism on the grounds that he was not only cognizant of the fact that the 'technique of production' entered into the determination of the rate of interest but that it was a central element in his analysis. He took pains to distinguish himself from economists who 'still seem to cling to the idea that there can be no *objective* determinant of the rate of interest. If subjective impatience, or time preference, is a true principle, they conclude that because of that fact all productivity principles must be false' (Fisher 1930: 181–2). Fisher argued that in ignoring the influence of the technique of production on the interest rate their proposed solutions were indeterminate. He considered that the rate of interest was determined by an interaction between time preference and investment opportunity. When asked to which school of interest theory he belonged – 'subjective or objective, time preference or productivity' – Fisher (1930: 182) thus replied: 'To both.' In fact, he claimed that '[s]o far as I have anything new to offer, in substance or manner of presentation, it is chiefly on the objective side'.

Fisher's conceptualization of the determination of interest owed much to that of Eugen Böhm-Bawerk, who preceded Fisher in arguing that it was the interaction between time preference and the productivity of investment that gave rise to interest. The former he took to be a general characteristic of the average man. To explain the latter, he introduced the concept of the 'roundabout process of production'. Böhm-Bawerk argued that a given quantity of goods yielded a larger physical product when those goods passed through more stages of production; that is, when they were used first to make intermediate products and then to produce consumer goods. The generation of higher productivity was, from his perspective, inextricably tied to the extension of the time during which an investment was tied up in the production process.[6]

Notwithstanding the problems with Böhm-Bawerk's theory, especially his roundaboutness theory of production, a watered-down version of it – a concept of interest as the result of the interaction of time preference with the productivity of investment – became the most widely accepted theory of interest among neoclassical economists, with Fisher as its most influential exponent. Although Fisher took issue with certain elements of Böhm-Bawerk's theory, Schumpeter (1951: 232) nevertheless observed that 'whatever may be said about Böhm-Bawerk's technique, there was no real difference between him and Fisher in fundamentals'.[7] What is certainly true is that Fisher provided no alternative theory of production to replace that of Böhm-Bawerk. Indeed, he regarded such a theory as unnecessary for his purposes: 'it does not seem to me that the theory of interest is called upon to launch itself upon a lengthy discussion of the productive process, division of labor, utilization of land, capital, and scientific management. The problem is confined to discover how production is related to the rate of interest' (Fisher 1930: 473). But lacking a theory of production, that might expose the principles of the process through which productive resources are developed and utilized, Fisher did not add anything to Böhm-Bawerk's controversial analysis of the relationship between production and interest. Consequently, his work did not provide an adequate explanation of the return to capital.[8]

One economist who did attempt to go beyond the limitations of Böhm-Bawerk's theory of interest, as well as other economists' attempts to explain interest within a theoretical framework in which technological and market conditions were taken as given, was Joseph Schumpeter. The central foundation of his theory of interest was an analysis of innovation, the process through which resources are developed as well as utilized, and its implications for resource allocation (Schumpeter 1996). The mainstream of the economics profession, and especially Fisher's followers in financial economics, did not, however, follow Schumpeter's lead.

At best, they disregarded the productive sphere as anything more than an extension of neoclassical price theory. At worst, they attempted to further colonize production by asserting that investment decisions in the productive sphere should be made according to the dictates of financial markets (Fama and Miller 1972: 108–43). In both cases their analytical frameworks were based on a concept of economic activity as the allocation of scarce resources to alternative uses where the productive capability of these resources and the alternative uses to which they can be allocated are given. By imposing this static concept of resource allocation on their analysis of interest and capital, they have thus lost even the limited appreciation in Böhm-Bawerk's work, and to a lesser extent in Fisher's analysis, of the developmental nature of the resource allocation process.

Modern financial economists are, as a result, truly guilty of that of which Fisher was accused: of providing 'an explanation of distribution as completely divorced from the explanation of production, as though incomes "just growed"' (Seager 1912: 837). They analyse why it is that portfolio investors would demand a return on the securities that they hold without ever posing the question of why such a return might be forthcoming in the economy. Without a theory of why investment can be expected to generate a return to capital in the form of interest, they give the impression 'that the determination of the rate of interest depends entirely upon the mental reactions of those who are so fortunate as to receive them' (Seager 1912: 835–7). And they compound Fisher's problem by adding another stream of capital income to interest – a risk premium – without ever explaining why a return to risk bearing might be forthcoming in the real economy. There are, of course, risks inherent in the process of production, but to say that the process is one that is risky does not imply that bearing risk is the key activity involved in generating a return.

How returns to investment are generated within the economy cannot be understood without analysing the process through which the economy develops and utilizes productive resources. Financial economists make no attempt to deal with innovation and its implications for resource allocation. Instead, following Fisher, they take investment opportunities as given. Then, as proponents of shareholder theory, they try to justify why shareholders are entitled to lay claim to the rewards that these investments generate. The subordination of the process of innovation, and of production more generally, is not exclusive to financial economics. The general tendency in neoclassical economics has been to favour the sanctity of exchange over production.

Whatever the virtues of the neoclassical characterization of resource allocation as the foundation for an analysis of exchange, the characterization is extremely confining for those who are interested in the economics of production, primarily because it is inimical to any concept of productive investment. The analytical limitations of neoclassical economics for dealing with production and investment are especially problematic for students of the corporate allocation of resources. Given its overwhelming concern with developing a theory of value, and thus with the analysis of the economics of market equilibrium, neoclassical theory has failed to develop a dynamic theory of the firm that could provide the microfoundations for a rigourous and relevant theory of corporate governance. Since it has lacks a theory of how a business enterprise might generate returns that are not market determined as well as a theory of how a business enterprise might distribute these returns, neoclassical theory provides no direct guidance on the production or distribution of the persistent profits of dominant enterprises with which the contemporary discussion of corporate governance is centrally concerned.

Rather than confronting the challenge of providing plausible explanations of how corporate residuals are generated, proponents of shareholder theory have concentrated their energies on analysing institutional mechanisms that would allow the corporate economy to mimic as closely as possible the perfect market ideal of neoclassical economics. Of course, precisely because the neoclassical framework is so badly suited to their field of inquiry, proponents of shareholder governance have had to improvise substantially within the neoclassical framework to develop their theory of corporate governance. They have focused, in particular, on developing 'explanations' for the claims of shareholders to the residual, despite their lack of plausible explanations of how these residuals are generated.

They have not questioned whether the mobility of resources is an appropriate benchmark for the corporate economy, notwithstanding the fact that since the 1920s, if not before, the very existence of the corporation as a central and enduring entity in the advanced economies has prompted a number of economists to question the relevance of neoclassical theory to an understanding of the most successful economies of the twentieth century (Veblen 1923; Berle and Means 1932; Schumpeter 1975; Galbraith 1967; see GALBRAITH, J.K.; MEANS, G.C.; SCHUMPETER, J.; VEBLEN, T.B.). Instead, the proponents of shareholder theory remain uncritically wedded to the tenets of neoclassical theory and, in particular, have failed to go beyond the confines of the neoclassical analysis of resource allocation in which individual preferences and technological opportunities are taken as given.

2 Stakeholder theory

Notwithstanding the fundamental problems with the theoretical framework that financial economists bring to the analysis of corporate governance, shareholder theory remains dominant in the governance debates. Yet, as shareholders have flexed their muscles to demand greater control over the allocation of corporate resources, there have been various attempts to develop an intellectual response by arguing that there are other 'stakeholders', besides shareholders, who have a claim to corporate residual returns. Stakeholder theories of corporate governance, like their managerial and shareholder counterparts, have important historical antecedents. For example, for more than a century, scholars and practitioners have been writing about the importance of employee involvement in enterprise governance.

Stakeholder theories of governance often have a strong political component. One important strand of the literature on worker control of enterprises, for example, justifies its position on humanistic grounds, arguing that employee involvement in enterprise governance is a necessary precondition for individual and social development. Another strand contends that traditional hierarchical relationships between employers and employees are inherently undemocratic and unjust, and must be countered by worker involvement in the governance of enterprises (for a review of the extensive literature on organizational participation, see Heller et al. 1998).

In the contemporary debates on corporate governance, the stakeholder perspective continues to be exposited more often as a political position than as an economic theory of governance. Indeed, many of its proponents rely on rather sweeping assumptions about the foundations of economic success. For example, in their recent edited volume of essays on 'stakeholder capitalism', Gavin Kelly, Dominic Kelly and Andrew Gamble identify the key challenge for proponents of stakeholder governance as reconciling in practice the competing claims of economic efficiency and social justice; they take it as given that '[i]ndividuals well endowed with economic and social capabilities will be more productive; companies which draw on the experience of all of their stakeholders will be more efficient; while social cohesion within a nation is increasingly seen as a requirement for international competitiveness' (Kelly et al. 1997: 244).

It is rare in this literature to find someone who has gone beyond such (rather hopeful) statements to analyse how the allocation of returns to different stakeholders affects economic performance. An important exception is the recent work by Margaret Blair (1995). I focus on her arguments in my analysis of stakeholder theories of governance because she has attempted to embed them in a framework of economic analysis. To do so is not to devalue the importance of the politics of corporate governance but to emphasize the importance of a cogent economic theory of governance as a foundation for an understanding of its politics.

In her book, *Ownership and Control: Rethinking Corporate Governance for the Twenty-First Century*, Blair emphasizes the need for an analysis of corporate governance that is based on 'a broader range of assumptions [than in the shareholder theory] about how wealth is created, captured, and distributed in a business enterprise' (Blair 1995: 15). She does not challenge the claims of the shareholder perspective that shareholders are 'principals'; she accepts that shareholders have 'residual claimant' status because she believes that they invest in the productive assets of the enterprise and bear some of the risk of its success. But she argues that the physical assets in which shareholders allegedly invest are not the only assets that create value in the corporation. A critical dimension of the economic process that generates wealth, Blair argues, is that individuals invest in their own 'human capital'. To some extent the assets that are developed through these investments are 'firm-specific' and, as a result, those who make these investments bear some of the risk of the corporation doing well or poorly.

> ... in most corporations, some of the residual risk is borne by long-tenured employees, who, over the years, build up firm-specific skills that are an important part of the firm's valuable assets, but which the employees cannot market elsewhere, precisely because they are specific to the firm. These employees have contributed capital to the firm, and that capital is at risk to the extent that the employees' productivity and the wages they could command at other firms are significantly lower than what they earn in that specific firm.
>
> (Blair 1995: 15)

Because employees with firm-specific skills have a 'stake' that is at risk in the company, Blair argues that they should be accorded 'residual claimant' status alongside shareholders (Blair 1995: 238). In other words, in allocating corporate returns, the governance of corporations should recognize the central importance of individuals' investments in human assets to the success of the enterprise and the prosperity of the economy.

Blair's analysis of firm-specific skills owes much to Gary Becker's theory of investments in on-the-job training. Becker contended that many workers increase their productivity by learning new skills and perfecting old ones on the job, that on-the-job training is costly, and that the nature of training – and, in particular, its relationship with the activities of the firm that undertakes it – has an important influence on the process through which resources are allocated to training (Becker 1975). Specifically, he argued that the costs of 'general training' – training useful in many firms besides those providing it – and the profit from its return will be borne, not by the firms providing it, but by the trainees themselves. In contrast, Becker contended that it is plausible, at least as a first approximation, that the costs of 'specific training' – training that increases productivity more in the firms providing it – and the returns that it generates will be borne by employers because 'no rational employee would pay for training that did not benefit him' (Becker 1975: 28). The analysis of specific training is complicated, however, by the potential for a 'hold-up problem' between employer and employee. Becker reasoned that:

> [i]f a firm had paid for the specific training of a worker who quit to take another job, its capital expenditure would be partly wasted, for no further return could be collected. Likewise, a worker fired after he had paid for specific training would be

unable to collect any further return and would also suffer a capital loss.

(Becker 1975: 29)

To overcome this problem, Becker considered that the costs of, and returns to, specific training would be shared between employer and employee, the balance being largely determined by the likelihood of labour turnover. Based on his analysis of workers' incentives to quit and firms' incentives to lay off, Becker concluded that 'rational firms pay generally trained employees the same wage and specifically trained employees a higher wage than they could get elsewhere' because '[f]irms are concerned about the turnover of employees with specific training, and a premium is offered to reduce their turnover because firms pay part of their training costs' (Becker 1975: 31). To the extent that employees pay a share of the costs of specific training, he argued, the wage effects would be similar to those for general training: employees would pay for this training by receiving wages below their current (opportunity) productivity during the training period and higher wages at later ages when the return was collected (Becker 1975: 31–2).

In Becker's human capital theory, as in neoclassical theory more generally, optimal resource allocation takes place through the market. Specifically, he argues that the appropriate incentives for investments in training, whether it is general or specific, will be provided through wage adjustments in competitive labour markets. Thus, from Becker's standpoint, market control represents the ideal system of economic governance even when firm-specific investments are taken into consideration.

By assuming that training can be firm-specific – that is, that it can increase productivity by more in the firm providing the training than in other firms – Becker implicitly recognized that firms in the same industry can differ in terms of the investments that they make and the productive resources that they control. However, Becker did not provide any explanation of the sources of these differences nor, as a result, any analysis of the source of returns to firm-specific skills. Becker argues that investments in training will be undertaken when investors, be they firms or employees, expect them to generate a return. But he treats the characteristics of different training options – the degree to which they are general or specific – as factors exogenous to the economic process with which he is concerned (for a critique, see Eckaus 1963). The returns to all participants (productive factors) in the enterprise – in such forms as wages, rent and interest – remain strictly determined, as they are in the pure neoclassical model, by technological and market forces that are external to the operation of the enterprise and human control more generally. All economic agents are assumed to optimize their objectives subject to market and technological constraints that shape the specificity of investments and the returns that they generate.

Becker's work on training has had a profound influence on labour economists. In particular, the concept of firm-specific human capital is widely employed in analyses of labour market behaviour by those supportive and critical of Becker's conclusions. Yet, to an extraordinary degree, given its centrality to their work, labour economists have failed to open the black box of firm-specificity to analyse where it comes from and, relatedly, why it makes sense to assume that it might be an important phenomenon in the economy. A review of the extensive literature in labour economics that relies on the concept of firm-specificity revealed that most scholars took as their starting point some version of Becker's definition of firm-specific human capital, and proceeded to build their models of labour market behaviour without going beyond Becker in providing a theory of who allocates resources to this type of productive investment, what kinds of investments they make, or how the returns to these investments are distributed (see Lazonick and O'Sullivan 2000b). David Donaldson and B. Curtis Eaton, for example, merely state that '[c]ertain skills or knowledge which an employee may acquire while working for a particular firm are of no value to other firms, even though such skills contribute to the productivity of the employee in that particular firm' (Donaldson and Eaton 1976: 463). The most detailed 'analysis' of the concept that we could find was in a paper by Candice Prendergast (1993: 523) who made the following statement:

Workers routinely carry out activities that increase their productivity with their current employer for which they are not directly compensated. For example, a worker may be asked to develop relationships with clients or shop floor staff, or he may develop a better understanding of how his firm operates. Firm-specific human capital of this type is difficult to quantify so that it is likely to be difficult to directly compensate the worker for its acquisition.

Blair, at least, recognizes the need for an analysis of what she calls 'wealth creation' (Blair 1995: 232–4, 240ff, 327–8) in order to make the case for a corporate governance process that allocates returns to 'firm-specific' human assets. For her, as for Becker, the role of economic governance is to get factor returns 'right' so that the individual actors are induced to make the 'firm-specific' investments that the enterprise requires. But she provides no theory of the process that enables such human capital to contribute to the generation of higher quality and/or lower cost products. She merely asserts that investment in 'firm-specific' assets can generate 'residuals' without specifying under what conditions (market, technological or organizational) such increased returns are generated. Without such a theory of wealth creation, it is impossible to determine the 'right' returns to factors of production. If one wishes to base a theory of corporate governance on investments in 'firm-specific human capital', then one needs a theory of the 'who, what and how' of such investments.

There are economists who have argued that the characteristic of firm-specificity is an outcome of organizational learning processes through which resources are developed and utilized in the economy (see, for example, Penrose 1995; Best 1990; Lazonick 1991). Yet, given the change inherent in the process of innovation, the organizational requirements of innovative investment strategies differ over time as learning within and outside the enterprise develops. Thus the firm-specific skills that result from continued innovation are constantly evolving. Firm-specific skills that were at one time part of a process that enhanced economic performance may fail to do so in another era, and may even retard it.

To focus on firm-specific skills as the critical dimension of the process of wealth creation is to ignore the dynamics of the innovation process. Linked to a theory of governance, such a perspective may well encourage the entrenchment of the claims of economic actors who have participated in and benefited from wealth creation in the past, even when the integration of their skills is no longer a viable basis on which the enterprise or the economy can generate the returns to meet these claims. That is, the stakeholder theory risks becoming a *de facto* theory of corporate welfare.

Besides the theoretical shortcomings of Blair's stakeholder theory for dealing with the process of wealth creation there is also a lack of clear-cut empirical evidence to back up Blair's central assumption that employees make significant, value-creating investments in their own human capital. To support this claim, Blair points to evidence from the US labour market that shows 'that employees accumulate valuable firm-specific skills if they stay with the same employer for an extended period' (Blair 1995: 263).

That higher returns can be attributed to firm-specific capital is, to use Blair's (1995: 263–4) term, 'construed' from the fact that high returns seem to be positively correlated with employment tenure. That employees make the investments that allegedly generate these returns requires an even greater leap of faith; we must rely on the belief that because employees were rewarded, they must have made the investments that generated these rewards. In fact, the evidence is just as consistent with the view that firms made these investments: Becker's model predicted that rational employers would pay workers a premium over the market wage precisely to reduce their turnover. He also argued that firms would be reluctant to lay off workers with specific skills unless there was a permanent decline in demand, which would be consistent with workers with long-tenure incurring high costs of layoff.

Blair's argument seems particularly implausible as applied to US blue-collar workers. The notion that they reaped supernormal returns on the basis of investments that they made in their own firm-specific human capital confronts much of what we know about the jobs that these workers did in the companies in which they were employed. Labour historians have provided extensive documentation of the process, which evolved over more than a century, through which the US blue-collar workforce was systematically excluded from any meaningful role in the productive process in all of the leading sectors of American industry (Montgomery 1987; Brody 1993). Increasingly, as the century unfolded, and certainly in the post-war period, blue-collar workers were denied the opportunities to participate in organizational learning processes through which they could develop firm-specific skills; that privilege was reserved for the managerial class (Chandler 1977; Lazonick 1990).

The managers of US corporate enterprises proved themselves vehemently hostile to initiatives taken by some union leaders after World War II to allow workers to participate in the allocation of corporate resources. Once these attempts were rebuffed, American unions did not, in general, challenge the principle of management's 'right' to control the development and utilization of productive capabilities (Harris 1982). In practice, however, the *quid pro quo* for union cooperation was that seniority be a prime criterion for promotion along well-defined job structures, thus giving older workers best access to a succession of jobs paying gradually higher hourly wage rates (Lazonick 1990, chs 8–9; O'Sullivan 2000a, ch. 3). It seems more plausible, in light of US business history, that it was this labour–management accord, rather than shop-floor workers' firm-specific skills, that provided the institutional basis on which the dominant industrial corporations were compelled to share the gains of post-Second World War prosperity.

3 Managerial theory

During the 1990s the debate on corporate governance, both within academic and policy circles, has focused on whether corporations should be run in the interests of shareholders or, alternatively, in the interests of a broader array of 'stakeholders' (see MANAGERIAL THEORIES OF THE FIRM). Until the late 1990s, this debate was primarily an Anglo-American affair, and as the debate began to be exported to continental Europe and Japan the shareholder perspective held a dominant and seemingly impregnable position. Yet even in the United States, where the principle of maximizing shareholder value has been put forth most vigorously, the argument is of relatively recent origin, with the theory and practice of maximizing shareholder value only coming into its own in the 1980s and 1990s.

Indeed, until the 1980s in the United States it was widely accepted that managers exercised control over the allocation of corporate resources and returns (see MEANS, G.C.). In the post-war decades, social scientists and legal scholars put forth a number of variants of a managerial perspective on corporate governance that sought to identify the motivations and abilities of managers that would yield superior economic outcomes. Common to most of these arguments was a view of corporate managers as trustees or stewards of corporate assets for society. The view of corporate management as trustees for society was by no means confined to the self-descriptions of corporate managers. 'Managerialism' was found among journalists, writers and many leading scholars of the corporation in the post-war period. The broad acceptance of the managerial ideology of trusteeship seemed to be rooted in the technocratic consensus that prevailed in elite circles of US society after the war, and in the faith in professionalism that it spawned (O'Sullivan 2000a, ch. 3).

Proponents of the 'managerialist' thesis of the corporation seemed content to let professionalism do the job of ensuring that the broader objectives that corporate managers espoused would be achieved. These social responsibilities were certainly not enshrined in corporate law. Although the burst of US federal regulation in the 1930s, as well as later regulatory initiatives such as industrial safety and accident laws, created new legal requirements of which corporate managers had to take account in their allocation of corporate resources, the law did not attempt to interfere with the internal governance of the corporation in a way that would directly challenge managerial control. And, with the development of the 'business judgement rule', the courts became more and more reluctant to challenge corporate management on decisions that were deemed to be part of the normal process of running a business (Kaufman *et al*. 1995: 51). But although the *de facto* legal treatment of the corporation ensured that corporate control remained firmly in the hands of managers, the acquiescence of corporation law and the courts to unilateral managerial control remained implicit. As Willard Hurst noted, with the exception of laws authorizing the use of corporate funds for philanthropic purposes, 'the law added no definition of standards or rules to spell out for what purposes or by what means management might properly make decisions other than in the interests of shareholders' (Hurst 1970: 107).

The lack of formal legal recognition of the widely accepted legal and economic obsolescence of the shareholder-designate concept of corporate management stemmed in part from the powerful emotional attachment in the United States to the idea that the shareholder 'owned' the corporation. But the failure to recognize at law the reality of corporate control stemmed not only from an emotional commitment to the ideology of private property. It also reflected the vagueness of the most widely accepted alternative, the view of the manager as trustee for society, for justifying that control. Edward Mason effectively highlighted its nebulosity in 1958 in an attack on what he called 'The Apologetics of Managerialism'. Mason contended that 'the institutional stability and opportunity for growth of an economic system are heavily dependent on the existence of a philosophy or ideology justifying the system in a manner generally acceptable to the leaders of thought in the community'. The power of classical economics, he argued, was that it had provided not only an analytical framework that could be used to explain economic behaviour, 'but also a defense – and a carefully reasoned defense – of the proposition that the economic behavior promoted and constrained by the institutions of a free-enterprise system is, in the main, in the public interest' (Mason 1958: 118). Mason recognized that, towards the end of the nineteenth century, 'the growth of large firms and other institutional changes began to call into question the assumptions on which the system was built' to the extent that 'the attempted resuscitation by the National Association of Manufacturers, in 1946, of the "philosophy of natural liberty" is inevitably a somewhat moth-eaten patchwork' (Mason 1958: 199). The problem was, from his point of view, that the managerial literature, though it undermined the intellectual presuppositions of classical economics, did not provide 'an equally satisfying apologetic for big business' because it failed to provide answers to some critical questions:

> Assume an economy composed of a few hundred large corporations, each enjoying substantial market power and all directed by managements with a 'conscience'. Each management wants to do the best it can for society consistent, of course, with doing the best it can for labor, customers, suppliers, and owners. How do prices get determined in such an economy? How are factors remunerated, and what relation is there between remuneration and performance? What is the mechanism, if any, that assures effective resource use, and how can corporate managements 'do right by' labor, suppliers, customers, and owners while simultaneously serving the public interests? The 'philosophy of natural liberty' had a reasoned answer to these questions, but I can find no reasoned answer in the managerial literature.
>
> (Mason 1958: 120)

Essentially Mason challenged proponents of managerialism to develop a persuasive theory of the relationship between the governance of corporations and economic performance. To answer his questions would have required an economic analysis of the process through which corporate organizations allocated resources and returns as well as the manner in which social institutions shaped that process. The post-war bias among US economists toward neoclassical theory, however, at best diverted them from the task and, at worst, persuaded them to treat corporate activities as reducible to market forces.

While the US economy was doing well, there was no concerted effort to challenge the legitimacy of managerial control of the nation's leading corporations. In the post-war decades the leading corporations in the US tended to retain both the money that they earned and the people whom they employed. Retentions in the forms of earnings and capital consumption allowances provided the financial foundations for corporate growth, while the building of managerial organizations to develop and utilize productive resources enabled investments in plant, equipment and personnel to succeed (O'Sullivan 2000a, chs 3 and 4). Corporate managers largely controlled the allocation of these resources without interference in strategic decisions from shareholders or workers.

In the 1960s and 1970s, however, the principle of 'retain and reinvest' common to US corporations at the time began running into problems for two reasons, one having to do with the growth of the corporation and the other having to do with the rise of new competitors. Through internal growth and mergers and acquisitions, corporations grew too big with too many divisions in too many different types of businesses. The central offices of these corporations were too far from the actual processes that developed and utilized productive resources to make informed investment decisions about how corporate resources and returns should be allocated to enable strategies based on retain and reinvest to succeed. The massive expansion of corporations that had occurred during the 1960s resulted in poor performance in the 1970s, an outcome that was exacerbated by an unstable macroeconomic environment and by the rise of new international competition, especially from Japan (Lazonick and O'Sullivan 1997b; O'Sullivan 2000a, ch. 4).

The overextension of US corporate enterprises helped to foster the strategic segmentation of top managers from their organizations. At the same time, the innovative capabilities of international competitors made it harder to sustain the employment of corporate labour forces, unless the productive capabilities of many if not most of these employees could be radically transformed. Under these conditions, US corporate managers faced a strategic crossroads: they could find new ways to generate productivity gains on the basis of retain and reinvest, or they could capitulate to the new competitive environment through corporate downsizing.

It was in this context that the shareholder perspective emerged to challenge managerial control over corporate resources and returns in the United States. When it came, however, an uprising of small shareholders did not fuel the shareholder attack. Rather, it was powered by the growing importance of institutional investors in the US economy, a phenomenon that was in turn the result of a veritable revolution in the financial sector of the economy driven by the accumulation of financial assets by older Americans and the search for higher returns on these assets. Within the new financial environment that stressed higher financial returns on corporate securities, many top corporate managers aligned their own interests with those of financial interests more generally, with an explosion in CEO pay as one very visible result. In the process, the shareholder perspective increasingly replaced the managerial perspective as the dominant corporate-governance ideology in the United States, even though top managers maintained and even enhanced their control over the allocation of resources and returns in established US corporations.

Perhaps because of the continued centrality of managerial control in practice, the managerial perspective still has its proponents in the United States. In the contemporary debates on corporate governance it has been put forward by a number of business school academics, most notably Michael Porter (Porter 1992; see also Thurow 1988; Chandler 1990; Jacobs 1991). The proponents of managerial control recognize that the competitive success of the corporate enterprise depends on investments in innovation that entail specialized in-house knowledge, and that require time, and hence financial commitment, to achieve their developmental potential. Thus they argue that, to allocate corporate resources, managers need discretion, which they are only assured if they have access to 'patient capital' that will enable them to see their investments in productive resources through to competitive success.

The managerial perspective often uses words such as 'capabilities', 'knowledge', 'skills', 'learning', 'factor creation', and 'innovation' as sources of 'sustained competitive advantage' for the enterprise. But the enduring and fundamental problem with the managerial perspective, which has made it vulnerable to critiques from shareholder advocates, is that it is not underpinned by a theory of innovation that can show how and under what conditions managerial resource allocation can yield competitive success. The proponents of managerial control are unable, therefore, to provide a systematic explanation of the conditions under which managers will make investments that promote innovation and generate returns and those under which such investments will not be made. From the managerial perspective, what determines whether or not an enterprise invests in innovation is the 'mindset' of the strategic manager, but what determines the mindset of the manager is rarely addressed. Lacking such an analysis, the managerial perspective provides little basis on which to understand how the incentives and abilities of those who exercise corporate control enhance or impede the process through which resources are allocated to generate returns in the corporate economy. Thus they provide no response to allegations from shareholder proponents that corporate managers have grown, to use the words of Michael Jensen, 'fat and lazy' (quoted in Farrell 1995).

4 Conclusion: innovation, development and corporate control

The shareholder, stakeholder and managerial perspectives all provide different answers to the 'who, what and how' of corporate governance. In doing so, all three perspectives raise the issue of how an economy not only allocates resources and returns at a point in time but also develops and utilizes resources over time. Yet, what continues to be missing from the corporate governance debates is a theory of economic development that can help to explain why resources that are allocated today may yield more or less returns to be shared tomorrow. Central to such a theory of economic development is a theory of innovation: the transformation of productive resources into saleable products that are higher quality and/or lower cost than those that had previously been available (see Lazonick and O'Sullivan 2000b).

A theory of innovation is most clearly absent in the shareholder perspective, with its foundation in the neoclassical theory of resource allocation, which takes existing investment opportunities as given. In assuming that these investment opportunities are risky, the shareholder perspective recognizes that the returns to resources that are allocated occur over time rather than instantaneously. But, as the allocator of resources to such risky investments, the role of the shareholder is to diversify his financial portfolio over large numbers of such investments rather than devote his time and effort to the development and utilization of the productive resources committed to a particular investment, as a direct investor must do. Even then, however, the shareholder perspective assumes that in general investments in productive resources will generate a residual to which the shareholder as risk-bearer can lay claim without asking how risk bearing *per se* can generate returns and hence why the average return to risk bearing may be more or less. In my view, the explanation of the residual – or surplus – as a general phenomenon requires a theory of innovation.

The stakeholder theory of governance put forward by Blair provides no theoretical basis for dealing with this reality. In particular, her willingness to accept the neoclassical assumption that resource allocation is the result of investments by optimizing individuals, and that the firm is, as a result, nothing more than a combination of physical and human assets that for some reason – labelled 'firm-specificity' – happen to be gathered together, precludes an understanding of the economic foundations of strategic control by one group of people over the learning opportunities of others and the governance institutions that shape the abilities and incentives of strategic decision makers in corporate enterprises.

The managerial perspective comes closer than the shareholder and stakeholder perspectives to locating the potential sources of innovation by recognizing that the role of managers is to allocate resources to, and returns from, a value-generating process. Porter

(1985), for example, emphasizes that managers have to oversee the 'value chain' that transforms purchased inputs into saleable outputs. Yet Porter's conceptual framework does not contain a theory of what makes the value chain more or less productive, except perhaps to argue that, as strategic decision makers who allocate resources and returns, there are 'good' managers and 'bad' managers. But what determines whether managers are 'good' or 'bad'? Specifically, what determines whether or not managers oversee an innovation process that develops and utilizes resources to generate higher quality, lower cost products? To go beyond an answer that focuses on the 'mindset' of the manager, what are the organizational and institutional conditions that enable some managers in certain corporations and epochs to be 'good' while condemning others to be 'bad'?

Moreover, who are the managers who exercise control over the allocation of resources and returns? Are they the top managers or are they members of a managerial organization? And what is the relation of these managers to the institutions of corporate governance that supports or proscribes their decisions and actions? Once one recognizes that control over the corporate allocation of resources and returns may be exercised by an organization that exists within an institutional environment rather than by an individual whose 'mindset' is disembodied from society, one must ask what makes an organization, and a set of institutions, good or bad at generating innovation.

In probing the relation between the allocation of resources by and the allocation of returns to many different types of people who participate in the corporate enterprise, the stakeholder perspective on corporate governance lends itself much more than the managerial perspective to an organizational conception of the corporate allocation process. Hence it opens the door to a theory of corporate innovation that is not confined to exploring the mindsets of top managers but delves into the allocation of resources and returns as an organizational phenomenon. As we have seen, the stakeholder perspective, in its recent re-emergence as a counter to the shareholder perspective, contends that other stakeholders besides shareholders should have rights to participate in the allocation of resources and returns. But what is the relation between the allocation of resources by and the allocation of return to particular types of stakeholders that renders the exercise of such rights sustainable?

It is also clear that to focus on the allocation of 'labour', as the stakeholder perspective does, rather than the allocation of 'capital', as the shareholder perspective does, renders the distinction between portfolio investment and direct investment untenable. Unlike 'capital', 'labour' cannot diversify its portfolio in search of a return. Even if over her career the worker moves from job to job and from firm to firm, she must be a 'direct investor' – she must work in a particular job at any point in time – in order to generate a higher return on her labour. Thus, as we have seen in the arguments put forth by Blair, the stakeholder perspective confronts the need for a theory of value creation. Indeed, a key question raised by the stakeholder perspective is whether corporate governance is about the ability of different types of stakeholders to augment their returns by reslicing a given economic pie or about how the interaction among different types of stakeholders supports the generation of bigger pies that can potentially yield bigger slices for all.

MARY O'SULLIVAN
INSEAD

Notes

1 These questions are in fact the same fundamental questions that most economists pose in considering the operation and performance of the economy, with the differences that most economists begin with the belief that the allocation of resources and returns by 'markets' rather than 'organizations' (be they states or enterprises) will generally be the preferred mode of allocation in the economy.

2 A distinction is often drawn between three different types of informational efficiency. Markets are said to be weak-form efficient when security prices reflect all information available in past prices. Semi-strong-form efficiency implies that security prices reflect all publicly available information. Finally, the strong form of the EMH means that security

prices reflect all information available, be it publicly or privately held.

3 Even if some, indeed most, traders are irrational, rational traders will ultimately drive the irrational traders out of the market by trading to drive stock prices back to fundamental values.

4 The contribution of internal funds to net sources of finance of non-financial enterprises during the period 1970–89 has recently been estimated as 80.6 per cent for Germany, 69.3 per cent for Japan, 97.3 per cent for the UK, and 91.3 per cent for the USA (Corbett and Jenkinson 1996).

5 For the period 1921–95 US stocks earned a real compound return of 8.22 per cent of which 4.84 per cent can be attributed to dividend payments (Goetzmann and Jorion 1997: 23).

6 For an introduction to the writings of Böhm-Bawerk, see 'Eugen von Böhm-Bawerk,' in Schumpeter (1951: 143–90).

7 In a discussion of Fisher (1930) Joseph Schumpeter noted that most of it was 'splendid wheat ... with very little chaff in between'. However, he went on to say that '[t]he criticism of Böhm-Bawerk's teaching on the 'technical superiority of present goods' in § 6 of chapter XX must, I fear, be classed with the chaff. By that time it should have been clear that, whatever may be said about Böhm-Bawerk's technique, there was no real difference between him and Fisher in fundamentals': see 'Irving Fisher's Econometrics', in Schumpeter (1951: 232).

8 It is surely for this reason, and notwithstanding his distaste for 'naïve productivity theories' that consider interest to express the physical productivity of land, or nature, or of man, that Fisher ended up relying to a great extent on examples of natural production to illustrate his theory.

Further reading

(References cited in the text marked *)

* Agrawal, A., Jaffe, J. and Mandelker, D. (1992) 'The post-merger performance of acquiring firms: a re-examination of an anomaly', *Journal of Finance* 47: 1605–21.

* Arrow, K. (1964) 'The role of securities in the optimal allocation of risk bearing', *Review of Economic Studies* 91: 91–6.

* Asquith, P. (1983) 'Merger bids, uncertainty and shareholder returns', *Journal of Financial Economics* 11: 51–83.

* Asquith, P., Bruner, R. and Mullens, D. (1983) 'The gains to bidding firms from merger', *Journal of Financial Economics* 11: 121–40.

* Baker, G., Jensen, M. and Murphy, K. (1988) 'Compensation and incentives: practice vs. theory', *Journal of Finance* 43: 593–616.

* Banz, R. (1981) 'The relationship between return and market value of common stocks', *Journal of Financial Economics* 9: 3–18.

* Becker, G. (1975) *Human Capital: A Theoretical and Empirical Analysis, with special references in education*, New York: National Bureau of Economic Research.

* Berle, A.A. and Means, G.C. (1932) *Private Property and the Modern Corporation*, Macmillan.

* Best, M. (1990) *The New Competition: Institutions of Industrial Restructuring*, Harvard University Press.

* Bhagat, S., Shleifer, A. and Vishny, R. (1990) 'Hostile takeovers in the 1980s: the return to corporate specialization', Brookings Papers on Economic Activity: *Microeconomics*, Special Issue: 1–84.

* Black, B. (1998) 'Shareholder activism and corporate governance in the United States', in P. Newman (ed.), *The New Palgrave Dictionary of Economics and Law*, Stockton Press, pp. 459–65.

* Blair, M. (1995) *Ownership and Control: Rethinking Corporate Governance for the Twenty-First Century*, Brookings Institution.

* Breeden, D., Gibbons, M. and Litzenberger, R. (1989) 'Empirical tests of the consumption-oriented CAPM', *Journal of Finance* 44: 231–62.

* Brody, D. (1993) *Workers in Industrial America: Essays on the Twentieth Century Struggle*, Oxford University Press.

* Chandler, A. (1977) *The Visible Hand: The Managerial Revolution in American Business*, Harvard University Press.

* Chandler, A. (1990) *Scale and Scope: The Dynamics of Industrial Enterprise*, Harvard University Press.

* Ciccolo, J.H. and Baum, C.F. (1985) 'Changes in the balance sheet of the US manufacturing sector, 1926–1977', in B. Friedman (ed.), *Corporate Capital Structure in the United States*, University of Chicago Press, pp. 81–109.

* Corbett, J. and Jenkinson, T. (1996) 'The financing of industry, 1979–1989: an international

comparison', *Journal of the Japanese and International Economies* 10 (1): 71–96.
* Cutler, D., Poterba, J. and Summers, L. (1989) 'What moves stock prices?' *Journal of Portfolio Management* Spring: 4–12.
* Daniel, K., Hirshleifer, D. and Subrahmanyam, A (1998) 'Investor psychology and security market under- and overreaction', *Journal of Finance* 53: 1839–85.
* Davidson, P. (1978) 'Why money matters: lessons from the half century of monetary thought', *Journal of Post-Keynesian Economics* 1 (1): 46–70.
* Debreu, G. (1959) *The Theory of Value*, Wiley.
* Dodd, P. (1980) 'Merger proposals, managerial discretion and stockholder wealth', *Journal of Financial Economics* 8: 105–37.
* Dodd, P. and Ruback, R. (1977) 'Tender offers and stockholder returns: an empirical analysis', *Journal of Financial Economics* 5: 351–73.
* Donaldson, D. and Eaton, C. (1976) 'Firm-specific human capital: a shared investment or optimal entrapment?' *Canadian Journal of Economics* 9 (3): 46–72.
* Eckaus, R.S. (1963) 'Investment in human capital: a comment', *Journal of Political Economy* 71: 501–5.
* Fama, E. (1970) 'Efficient capital markets: a review of theory and empirical work', *Journal of Finance* 25: 383–417.
* Fama, E. (1991) 'Efficient capital markets: II', *Journal of Finance* 46: 1575–617.
* Fama, E. (1998) 'Market efficiency, long-term returns, and behavioural finance', *Journal of Financial Economics* 49: 283–306.
* Fama, E. and French, K. (1992) 'The cross-section of expected stock returns', *Journal of Finance* 47: 427–65.
* Fama, E. and French, K. (1996) 'Multifactor explanations of asset pricing anomalies', *Journal of Finance* 51: 55–84.
* Fama, E. and Jensen, M. (1983) 'Separation of ownership and control', *Journal of Law and Economics* 26: 301–25.
* Fama, E. and Miller, M. (1972) *The Theory of Finance*, Dryden Press.
* Farrell, C. (1995) 'An old fashioned feeding frenzy', *Business Week*, 1 May: 34–6.
* Fisher, I. (1913) 'The impatience theory of interest', *American Economic Review* 3: 610–8.
* Fisher, I. (1930) *The Theory of Interest*, Macmillan.
* Franks, J. and Mayer, C. (1996) 'Hostile takeovers and the correction of managerial failure', *Journal of Financial Economics* January: 163–81.
* Freeman, C. (1982) *The Economics of Industrial Innovation*, 2nd edn, MIT Press.
* Galbraith, J.K. (1967) *The New Industrial State*, Houghton Mifflin.
* Glickman, M. (1994) 'The concept of information, intractable uncertainty, and the current state of the "efficient market" theory: a post-Keynesian view', *Journal of Post-Keynesian Economics* 16: 325–49.
* Goetzmann, W, and Jorion, P. (1997) 'A Century of Global Stock Markets', NBER Working Paper Series no. 5901.
* Grossman, S. and Hart, O. (1988) 'One share, one vote, and the market for corporate control', *Journal of Financial Economics* 20: 175–202.
* Harris, H. (1982) *The Right to Manage: Industrial Relations Policies of American Business in the 1940s*, University of Wisconsin Press.
* Heisler, J. (1994) 'Recent research in behavioural finance', *Financial Markets, Institutions and Instruments* 3 (5): 76–105.
* Heller, F., Pusic, E., Stauss, G. And Wilpert, B. (1988) *Organizational Participation: Myth and Reality*, Oxford/New York: Oxford University Press.
* Herman, E. and Lowenstein, L. (eds) (1988) *The Efficiency Effects of Hostile Takeovers. Knights, Raiders, and Targets: The Impact of Hostile Takeovers*, Oxford University Press.
* Hirshleifer, J. (1965) 'Investment decision under uncertainty: choice-theoretic approaches', *Quarterly Journal of Economics* 79: 509–36.
* Hurst, J.W. (1970) *The Legitimacy of the Business Corporation in the Law of the United States: 1780–1970*, University Press of Virginia.
* Jacobs, M. (1991) *Short-term America: the Causes and Consequences of our Business Myopia*, Harvard Business School Press.
* Jensen, M.C. (1978) 'Some anomalous evidence regarding market efficiency', *Journal of Financial Economics* 6: 95–102.
* Jensen, M.C. (1986) 'Agency costs of free cash flow, corporate finance, and takeovers', *American Economic Review* 76 (May): 323–9.
* Jensen, M.C. (1988) 'Takeovers: their causes and consequences', *Journal of Economic Perspectives* 2 (1): 21–48.
* Jensen, M.C. (1989) 'Eclipse of the public corporation', *Harvard Business Review* 67 (5): 61–74.
* Jensen, M.C. (1993) 'The modern industrial revolution. exit, and the failure of internal control systems', *Journal of Finance* 48 (3): 831–80.
* Jensen, M.C. and Ruback, R. (1983) 'The market for corporate control: the scientific evidence', *Journal of Financial Economics* 11: 5–50.
* Jensen, M.C. and Murphy, K. (1990) 'Performance pay and top management incentives', *Journal of Political Economy* 98 (2): 225–64.

* Kaplan, S. (1989) 'Management buyouts: evidence of taxes as a source of value', *Journal of Finance* 44: 611–32.
* Kaufman, A., Zacharias, L. and Carson, M. (1995) *Managers vs. Owners: The Struggle in Corporate Control in American Democracy*, Oxford University Press.
* Kelly, G., Kelly, D. and Gamble, A. (eds) (1997) *Stakeholder Capitalism*, Macmillan.
* Kocherlakota, N. (1996) 'The equity premium: it's still a puzzle', *Journal of Economic Literature* 34: 42–71.
* Lazonick, W. (1990) *Competitive Advantage on the Shop Floor*, Harvard University Press.
* Lazonick, W. (1991) *Business Organization and the Myth of the Market Economy*, Cambridge University Press.
* Lazonick, W. and O'Sullivan, M. (1996) 'Organization, finance, and international competition', *Industrial and Corporate Change* 5 (1): 1–49.
* Lazonick, W. and O'Sullivan, M. (1997a) 'Finance and industrial development, Part I: the United States and the United Kingdom', *Financial History Review* 4 (1): 7–29.
* Lazonick, W. and O'Sullivan, M. (1997b) 'Finance and industrial development, Part II: Japan and Germany', *Financial History Review* 4 (2): 117–38.
* Lazonick, W. and O'Sullivan, M. (2000a) 'Maximizing shareholder value: a new ideology for corporate governance', *Economy and Society* 29 (1): 13–35.
* Lazonick, W. and O'Sullivan, M. (2000b) 'Perspectives on Corporate Governance, Innovation, and Economic Performance', Report to the European Commission, DGXII of the INSEAD CGEP Project (*http://www.insead.fr/projects/cgep*).
* Lintner, J. (1965a) 'Security prices, risk, and maximal gains from diversification', *Journal of Finance* 20: 587–615.
* Lintner, J. (1965b) 'The valuation of risky assets and the selection of risky investments in stock portfolios and capital budgets', *Review of Economics and Statistics* 47: 13–37.
* Magenheim, E. and Mueller, D. (1988) 'Are acquiring shareholders better off after an acquisition?' in J. Coffee, L. Lowenstein and S. Ackerman (eds), *Knights, Raider, and Targets: The Impact of Hostile Takeovers*, Oxford University Press.
* Malatesta, P. (1983) 'The wealth effects of merger activity and objective functions of merging firms', *Journal of Financial Economics* 11: 151–81.
* Malkiel, B. (1987) 'Efficient market hypothesis', in J. Eatwell, M. Milgate and P. Newman (eds), *The New Palgrave: A Dictionary of Economics*, London, Macmillan, pp. 120–3.
* Markowitz, H. (1959) *Portfolio Selection: Efficient Diversification of Investments*, Wiley.
* Marsh, T. and Merton, R. (1986) 'Dividend variability and variance bounds test for the rationality of stock prices', *American Economic Review* 76: 483–98.
* Mason, E. (1958) 'The apologetics of "managerialism"', *Journal of Business* 31 (1): 1–11.
* Mehra, R. and Prescott, E. (1985) 'The equity premium: a puzzle', *Journal of Monetary Economics* 15: 145–62.
* Montgomery, D. (1987) *The Fall of the House of Labor*, Cambridge University Press.
* Morck, R., Shleifer, A. and Vishny, R. (1988) 'Characteristics of targets of hostile and friendly takeovers' in A. Auerbach (ed.), *Corporate Takeovers: Cases and Consequences*, National Bureau of Economic Research.
* Mossin, J. (1966) 'Equilibrium in a capital asset market', *Econometrica* 34: 768–83.
* Murphy, K. (1985) 'Corporate performance and managerial remuneration: an empirical analysis', *Journal of Accounting and Economics* 7: 11–42.
* O'Sullivan, M. (2000a) *Contests for Corporate Control: Corporate Governance and Economic Performance in the United States and Germany*, Oxford University Press.
* O'Sullivan, M. (2000b) 'The innovative enterprise and corporate governance', *Cambridge Journal of Economics* 24 (4): 393–416.
* Penrose, E. (1995) *The Theory of the Growth of the Firm*, 3rd edn, Oxford University Press.
* Porter, M.E. (1985) *Competitive Advantage: Creating and Sustaining Superior Performance*, Free Press.
* Porter, M. E. (1992) *Capital Choices: Changing the Way America Invests in Industry*, Council on Competitiveness.
* Prendergast, C. (1993) 'The role of promotion in inducing specific human-capital acquisition', *Quarterly Journal of Economics* 108 (2): 523–34.
* Raines, J.P. and Leathers, C. (1996) 'Veblenian stock markets and the efficient markets hypothesis', *Journal of Post-Keynesian Economics* 19: 137–52.
* Ravenscraft, D. and Scherer, F. (1987) *Mergers, Sell-offs and Economic Efficiency*, Brookings Institution.
* Reinganum, M. (1981) 'A new empirical perspective on the CAPM', *Journal of Financial and Qualitative Analysis* 16: 439–62.
* Roll, R. (1994) 'What every CFO should know about scientific progress in financial

economics: what is known and what remains to be resolved', *Financial Management Summer*: 69–75.
* Scharfstein, D. (1988) 'The disciplinary role of takeovers', *Review of Economic Studies*, 55: 185–99.
* Schumpeter, J. (1951) *Ten Great Economists: From Marx to Keynes*, Oxford University Press.
* Schumpeter, J. (1975) *Capitalism, Socialism and Democracy*, Transaction Publishers.
* Schumpeter, J. (1996) *The Theory of Economic Development*, Transaction Publishers.
* Seager, H. (1912) 'The impatience theory of interest', *American Economic Review* 2: 835–7.
* Sharpe, W. (1964) 'Capital asset prices: a theory of market equilibrium under conditions of risk', *Journal of Finance* 19: 425–42.
* Shiller, R. (1981) 'Do stock market prices move too much to be justified by subsequent changes in dividends', *American Economic Review* 71: 421–36.
* Shiller, R. (1990) 'Speculative prices and popular models', *Journal of Economic Perspectives* 4: 55–65.
* Shleifer, A. and Summers, L. (1988) 'Breach of trust in hostile takeovers', in A. Auerbach (ed.), *Corporate Takeovers: Causes and Consequences*, National Bureau of Economic Research: 33–56.
Shleifer, A. and Vishny, R. (1991) 'Takeovers in the '60s and the '80s: evidence and implications', *Strategic Management Journal* 12: 51–9.

* Siegel, J. (1994) *Stocks for the Long Run: A Guide to Selecting Markets for Long-Term Growth*, Irwin Professional Publishing.
* Siegel, J. and Thaler, R. (1997) 'The equity premium puzzle', *Journal of Economic Perspectives* 191–200.
* Spotton, B. and Rowley, R. (1998) 'Efficient markets, fundamentals, and crashes: American theories of financial crises and market volatility', *American Journal of Economics and Sociology* 57: 663–90.
* Summers, L. (1986) 'Does the stock market rationally reflect fundamental values', *Journal of Finance* 41: 591–601.
* Thaler, R. (1993) *Advances in Behavioural Finance*, Russell Sage Foundation.
* Thurow, L. (1988) 'Let's put capitalists back into capitalism', *Sloan Management Review*, Fall: 67–71.
* Veblen, T. (1923) *Absentee Ownership and the Business Enterprise in Recent Times: The Case of America*, B.W. Huebsch.

See also: BANKING SYSTEMS; DYNAMIC CAPABILITIES; EMPLOYMENT RELATIONS; GALBRAITH, J.K.; GROWTH OF THE FIRM AND NETWORKING; INDUSTRAL AND LABOUR RELATIONS; INNOVATION; MANAGERIAL THEORIES OF THE FIRM; MARX, K.; MEANS, G.; NEO-CLASSICAL ECONOMICS; PENROSE, E.; PENSION SYSTEMS; PRIVATIZATION AND REGULATION; SCHUMACHER, E.; SCHUMPETER, J.; SECURITIES AND EXCHANGE REGULATION; SKILL FORMATION SYSTEMS; VEBLEN, T.

Dynamic capabilities

1 Terminology
2 Markets and strategic capabilities
3 Processes, positions and paths
4 Dynamic capabilities and the orchestration process
5 Implications for the theory of the firm
6 Conclusion

Overview

The global competitive battles in high technology industries such as semiconductors, information services and software have demonstrated the need for an expanded paradigm to understand how competitive advantage is achieved. Well-known companies like IBM, Texas Instruments, Philips and others appear to have followed a 'resource-based strategy' of accumulating valuable technology assets, often guarded by an aggressive intellectual property stance. However, this strategy is often not enough to support a significant competitive advantage. Winners in the global marketplace have been firms that can demonstrate timely responsiveness and rapid and flexible product innovation, coupled with the management capability to effectively coordinate and redeploy internal and external competences. Not surprisingly, industry observers have remarked that companies can accumulate a large stock of valuable technology assets and still not have many useful capabilities.

We refer to this ability to sense opportunities and then seize them as 'dynamic capabilities' to emphasize two key aspects that were not the main focus of attention in previous strategy perspectives. The term 'dynamic' refers to the capacity to renew competences so as to achieve congruence with the changing business environment; certain innovative responses are required when time-to-market and timing are critical, the rate of technological change is rapid and the nature of future competition and markets difficult to determine. The term 'capabilities' emphasizes the key role of strategic management in appropriately adapting, integrating and reconfiguring internal and external organizational skills, resources and functional competences to match the requirements of a changing environment.

The notion that competitive advantage requires both the exploitation of existing internal and external firm-specific capabilities and developing new ones is partially developed in Penrose (1959), Teece (1982) and Wernerfelt (1984). However, only recently have researchers begun to focus on the specifics of how some organizations first develop firm-specific capabilities and how they renew competences to respond to shifts in the business environment (see for example, Iansiti and Clark 1994; Henderson 1994). These issues are intimately tied to the firm's business processes, market positions and expansion paths. Several writers have recently offered insights and evidence on how firms can develop their capability to adapt and even capitalize on rapidly changing environments (see Hayes *et al.* 1988; Prahalad and Hamel 1990; Dierickx and Cool 1989; Chandler 1990; Teece 1993). The dynamic capabilities approach seeks to provide a coherent framework which can both integrate existing conceptual and empirical knowledge and facilitate prescription. In doing so, it builds upon the theoretical foundations provided by Schumpeter (1934), Penrose (1959), Williamson (1975, 1985), Barney (1986), Nelson and Winter (1982), Teece (1988) and Teece *et al.* (1994).

1 Terminology

In order to facilitate theory development and intellectual dialogue, some workable definitions are desirable. We propose the following:

Factors of production. These are 'undifferentiated' inputs available in disaggregate form in factor markets. By undifferentiated we mean that they lack a firm-specific component. Land, unskilled labour and capital are typical examples. Some factors may be available for the taking, such as public knowledge. In the language of Arrow, who defines fugitive resources as ones that can move cheaply amongst individuals and firms, such resources must be 'non-fugitive'. Property rights are usually well defined for factors of production.

Resources. (Note first, the authors feel the term 'resource' is misleading, and prefer to use the term firm-specific asset. 'Resource' is used here to try and maintain links to the literature on the resource-based approach, which we believe is important.) Resources are firm-specific assets that are difficult if not impossible to imitate. Trade secrets and certain specialized production facilities and engineering experience are examples. Such assets are difficult to transfer among firms because of transactions costs and transfer costs, and because the assets may contain tacit knowledge.

Organizational routines/competences. When firm-specific assets are assembled in integrated clusters spanning individuals and groups so that they enable distinctive activities to be performed, these activities constitute organizational routines and processes. Examples include quality, miniaturization and systems integration. Such competences are typically viable across multiple product lines, and may extend outside the firm to embrace alliance partners.

Core competences. We define those competences that define a firm's fundamental business as core. Core competences must accordingly be derived by looking across the range of a firm's (and its competitors) products and services: thus, Eastman Kodak's core competence could be considering image, IBM's integrated data processing and service, and Motorola's untethered communications. The value of core competences can be enhanced by combination with the appropriate complementary assets. The degree to which a core competence is distinctive depends on how well endowed the firm is relative to its competitors, and on how difficult it is for competitors to replicate its competences.

Products. End products are the final goods and services produced by the firm based on utilizing the competences that it possesses. The performance (price, quality, etc.) of a firm's products relative to its competitors at any point in time will depend upon its competences (which over time depend on its capabilities).

Dynamic capabilities. We define dynamic capabilities as the firm's ability to learn to sense the need for change and then reconfigure internal and external competences to seize the opportunity created by rapidly changing environments. Dynamic capabilities thus reflect an organization's ability to adapt so as to achieve new and innovative forms of competitive advantage, given path dependencies and market positions.

2 Markets and strategic capabilities

A key step in building a conceptual framework related to dynamic capabilities is to identify the foundations upon which distinctive and difficult to replicate advantages can be built, maintained and enhanced. A useful way to vector in on the strategic elements of the business enterprise is to first identify what is not strategic. To be strategic, a capability must be honed to a user need (so there is a source of revenues), unique (so that the products/services produced can be priced without too much regard to competition) and difficult to replicate (so profits won't be competed away). Accordingly, any assets or entity which are homogeneous and can be bought and sold at an established price cannot be all that strategic (Barney 1986). What is it, then, about firms which undergirds (static) competitive advantage?

To answer this, one must first make some fundamental distinctions between markets and internal organization (firms). The essence of the firm, as Coase (1937) pointed out, is that it displaces market organization (see COASE, R.). It does so in the main because inside the firms one can organize certain types of economic activity in ways one cannot using markets. This is not only because of transaction costs, as Williamson (1975, 1985) emphasized, but also because there are many types of arrangements where injecting high-powered (market-like) incentives might well be quite destructive of the cooperative activity and learning (see WILLIAMSON, O.). Indeed, the essence of internal organizations is that it is a domain of unleveraged or low-powered financial incentives. By unleveraged, we mean that financial rewards are determined at the group or organizational level, not primarily at the individual level, in an effort to encourage team, not individual, behaviour. It is recognized that internal organization allows one to recognize the contributions of individuals (Lazonick 1991). However, large business units, at least in old economy firms, tend to rely less on stock options and more on traditional salary bonus compensation models. Inside an organization, exchange cannot take place in the same manner that it can outside an organization, not just because it might be destructive to provide high-powered individual incentives, but because it is difficult if not impossible to tightly calibrate individual contribution to a joint effort. Hence, contrary to Arrow's (1969) view of firms as quasi markets, and the task of management to inject markets into firms, we recognize the inherent limits and possible counterproductive results of attempting to fashion firms into simply clusters of internal markets. In particular, learning and internal technology transfer may well be jeopardized.

Indeed, what is distinctive about firms is that they are domains for organizing activity in a non-market-like fashion. Accordingly, as we discuss what is distinctive about firms, we stress competences/capabilities which are ways of organizing and getting things done which cannot be accomplished merely by using the price system to coordinate activity. The very essence of most capabilities/competences is that they cannot be readily assembled through markets (Lazonick 1991; Teece 1982, 1986a; Kogut and Zander 1992). If the ability to assemble competences using markets is what is meant by the firm as a nexus of contracts (Fama 1980), then we unequivocally state that the firm about which we theorize cannot be usefully modelled as a nexus of contracts. By 'contract' we are referring to a transaction undergirded by a legal agreement, or some other arrangement which clearly spells out rights, rewards and responsibilities. Moreover, the firm as a nexus of contracts suggests a series of bilateral contracts orchestrated by a coordinator. Our view of the firm is that the organization takes place in a more multilateral fashion, with patterns of behaviour and learning being orchestrated in a much more decentralized fashion, but with a viable headquarters operation.

The key point, however, is that the properties of internal organization cannot be replicated by a portfolio of business units amalgamated just through formal contracts as many distinctive elements of internal organization simply cannot be replicated in the market (as noted in Teece et al. 1994, the conglomerate offers few, if any, efficiencies because there is little provided by the conglomerate form that shareholders cannot obtain for themselves simply by holding a diversified portfolio of stocks). That is, entrepreneurial activity cannot lead to the immediate replication of unique organizational skills through simply entering a market and piecing the parts together overnight. Replication takes time, and the replication of best practice may be illusive. Indeed, firm capabilities need to be understood not in terms of balance sheet items, but mainly in terms of the organizational structures and managerial processes that support productive activity. By construction, the firm's balance sheet contains items that can be valued, at least at original market prices (cost). It is necessarily the case, therefore, that the balance sheet is a poor shadow of a firm's distinctive competence, such that recently scholars have begun to attempt to measure capability using financial statement data (see Baldwin and Clark 1991; Lev and Sougiannis 1992). That which is distinctive cannot be bought and sold short of buying the firm itself, or one or more of its subunits.

There are many dimensions to the business firm that must be understood if one is to grasp firm-level distinctive competences/capabilities. In this paper we merely identify several classes of factors that will help determine a firm's distinctive competence and dynamic capabilities. We organize these in three categories: processes, positions, and paths. The essence of competences and capabilities is embedded in organizational processes of one kind or another. But the content of these processes and the opportunities they afford for developing competitive advantage at any point in time are shaped significantly by the assets the firm possesses (internal and market) and by the evolutionary path it has adopted/inherited. Hence organizational processes, shaped by the firm's asset positions and moulded by its evolutionary and co-evolutionary paths, explain the essence of the firm's dynamic capabilities and its competitive advantage.

3 Processes, positions and paths

We thus advance the argument that the competitive advantage of firms lies in part with its managerial and organizational processes, shaped by its (specific) asset position, and the paths available to it. Note here also that fixed assets, like plant and equipment which can be purchased off-the-shelf by all industry participants, cannot be the source of a firm's competitive advantage. In as much as financial balance sheets typically reflect such assets, the assets that matter for competitive advantage are rarely reflected in the balance sheet, while those that do not are. By managerial and organizational processes, we refer to the way things are done in the firm, or what might be referred to as its routines or patterns of current practice. By position we refer to its current specific endowment of technology, intellectual property, complementary assets, customer base and its external relations with suppliers and complementors. By paths we refer to the strategic alternatives available to the firm and the presence or absence of increasing returns and attendant path dependencies.

Our focus throughout is on asset structures for which no ready market exits, as these are the only assets of strategic interest. A final section focuses on replication and imitation, as it is these phenomena which determine how readily a competence or capability can be cloned by competitors, and therefore the distinctiveness of its competences and the durability of its advantage.

The firm's processes and positions collectively encompass its competences. A hierarchy of competences/capabilities ought to be recognized, as some competences may be on the factory floor, some in the R&D labs and some in the way everything is integrated. A difficult to replicate or difficult to imitate competence was defined earlier as a distinctive competence. As indicated, the key feature of distinctive competences is that there is not a market for it, except possibly through the market for business units. Hence competences and capabilities are intriguing assets as they typically must be built because they cannot be bought.

Organizational and managerial processes

Static organizational processes enable coordination and integration. While the price system supposedly coordinates the economy (the coordinative properties of markets depend on prices being 'sufficient' upon which to base resource allocation decisions), managers coordinate or integrate activity inside the firm. How efficiently and effectively internal coordination or integration is achieved is very important (Aoki 1990). Indeed, Ronald Coase, author of the pathbreaking 1937 article 'The Nature of the Firm', which focused on the costs of organizational coordination inside the firm as compared to across the market, half a century later has identified as critical the understanding of 'why the costs of organizing particular activities differs among firms' (Coase 1988: 47). We argue that a firm's distinctive ability needs to be understood as a reflection of distinctive organizational or coordinative capabilities. This form of integration (i.e., inside business units) is different from the integration between business units; they could be viable on a stand-alone basis (external integration) (for a useful taxonomy, see Iansiti and Clark 1994). Likewise for external coordination (see Shuen 1994 for an examination of the gains and hazards of the technology make-vs.-buy decision and supplier co-development). Increasingly, strategic advantage requires the integration of external activities and technologies. The growing literature on strategic alliances, the virtual corporation and buyer–supplier relations and technology collaboration evidences the importance of external integration and sourcing.

There is some field-based empirical research that provides support for the notion that the way production is organized by management inside the firm is the source of differences in firms' competence in various domains. For example, Garvin's (1988) study of 18 room air conditioning plants reveals that quality performance was not related to either capital investment or to the degree of automation of the facilities. Instead, quality performance was driven by special organizational routines. These included routines for gathering and processing information, for linking customer experiences with engineering design choices and for coordinating factories and component suppliers (see Garvin 1994 for a typology of organizational processes). The work of Clark and Fujimoto (1991) on project development in the automobile industry also illustrates the role played by coordinative routines. Their study reveals a significant degree of variation in how different firms coordinate the various activities required to bring a new model from concept to market. These differences in coordinative routines and capabilities seem to have a significant impact on such performance variables as development cost, development lead times and quality. Furthermore, Clark and Fujimoto tended to find significant firm-level differences in coordination routines and these differences seemed to have persisted for a long time. This suggests that routines related to coordination are firm-specific in nature.

Also, the notion that competence/capability is embedded in distinct ways of coordinating and combining helps to explain how and why seemingly minor technological changes can have devastating impacts on incumbent firms' abilities to compete in a market. Henderson and Clark (1990), for example, have shown that incumbents in the photolithographic equipment industry were sequentially devastated by seemingly minor innovations that, nevertheless, had major impacts on how systems had to be configured. They attribute these difficulties to the fact that systems level or 'architectural' innovations often require new routines to integrate and coordinate engineering tasks. These findings and others suggest that productive systems display high interdependency, and that it may not be possible to change one level without changing others. This appears to be true with respect to the 'lean production' model (Womack et al. 1991) which has now transformed the Taylor or Ford model of manufacturing organization in the automobile industry (see Fujimoto 1994: 18–20 for an in-depth analysis of the Japanese automobile industry). Lean production requires distinctive shopfloor practices and processes as well as distinctive higher order managerial processes. Put differently, organizational processes often display high levels of coherence, and when they do, replication may be difficult because it requires systemic changes throughout the organization and also among interorganizational linkages, which might be very hard to effectuate. Put differently, partial imitation or replication of a successful model may yield zero benefits. (For a theoretical argument along these lines, see Milgrom and Robert 1990.)

The notion that there is a certain rationality or coherence to processes and systems is not quite the same concept as corporate culture, as we understand the latter. Corporate culture refers to the values and beliefs that employees hold; culture can be a de facto governance system as it mediates the behaviour of individuals and economizes on more formal administrative methods. Rationality or coherence notions are more akin to the Nelson and Winter (1982) notion of organizational routines. However, the routines concept is a little too amorphous to properly capture the congruence amongst processes and between processes and incentives that we have in mind. Consider a professional service organization like an accounting firm. If it is to have relatively high-powered incentives that reward individual performance, then it must build organizational processes that channel individual behaviour; if it has weak or low-powered incentives, it must find symbolic ways to recognize the high performers, and it must use alternative methods to build effort and enthusiasm. What one may think of as styles of organization in fact contain necessary, not discretionary, elements to achieve performance.

Recognizing the congruencies and complementarities among processes, and between processes and incentives, is critical to the understanding of organizational capabilities. In particular, they can help us explain why architectural and radical innovations are so often introduced into an industry by new entrants. The incumbents develop distinctive organizational processes that cannot support the new technology, despite certain overt similarities between the old and the new. The frequent failure of incumbents to introduce new technologies can thus be seen as a consequence of the mismatch that so often exists between the set of organizational processes needed to support the conventional product/service and the requirements of the new. Radical organizational re-engineering will usually be required to support the new product, which may well do better embedded in a separate subsidiary where a new set of coherent organizational processes can be fashioned (see Abernathy and Clark 1985).

Positions

The strategic posture of a firm is determined not only by its learning processes and by the coherence of its internal and external processes and incentives, but also by its specific assets. By business assets we do not mean for example its specialized plant and equipment. These include its difficult-to-trade knowledge assets and assets complementary to them, as well as its reputational and relational assets. Such assets determine its competitive advantage at any point in time. We identify several illustrative classes.

Technological assets. While there is an emerging market for know-how (Teece 1981), much technology does not enter it. This is either because the firm is unwilling to sell it (the 'crown jewels' metaphor is often used in such instances) or because of difficulties in transacting in the market for know-how (Teece 1980). A firm's technological assets may or may not be protected by the standard instruments of intellectual property law. Either way, the ownership protection and utilization of technological and knowledge assets are clearly key differentiators among firms. Likewise for complementary assets.

Complementary assets. Technological innovations require the use of certain related assets to produce and deliver new products and services. Prior commercialization activities require and enable firms to build such complementarities (Teece 1986b). Such capabilities and assets, while necessary for the firm's established activities, may have other uses as well. These assets typically lie downstream. New products and processes either can enhance or destroy the value of such assets (Tushman et al. 1986). Thus the development of computers enhanced the value of IBM's direct sales force in office products, while disc brakes rendered useless much of the auto industries' investment in drum brakes.

Financial assets. In the short run, a firm's cash position and degree of leverage may have strategic implications. While there is nothing more fungible than cash, it cannot always be raised from external markets without the dissemination of considerable information to potential investors. Accordingly, what a firm can do in short order is often a function of its balance sheet. In the longer run, that ought not be so, as cash flow ought be more determinative.

Reputational assets. Firms, like individuals, have reputations. Reputations often summarize a good deal of information about firms and shape the responses of customers, suppliers and competitors. It is sometimes difficult to disentangle reputation from the firm's current asset and market position. However, in our view, reputational assets are best viewed as an intangible asset that enables firms to achieve various goals in the market. Its main value is external, since what is critical about reputation is that it is a kind of summary statistic about the firm's current assets and position, and its likely future behaviour. Because there is generally a strong asymmetry between what is known inside the firm and what is know externally, reputations may sometimes be more salient than the true state of affairs, in the sense that external actors must respond to what they know rather than what is knowable.

Structural assets. The formal and informal structure of organizations and their external linkages have an important bearing on the rate and direction of innovation, and how competences and capabilities co-evolve (Argyres 1995; Teece 1996). The degree of hierarchy and the level of vertical and lateral integration are elements of firm-specific structure. Distinctive governance modes can be recognized (e.g. multiproduct, integrated firms; high 'flex' firms; virtual corporations; conglomerates), and these modes support different types of innovation to a greater or lesser degree. For instance, virtual structures work well when innovation is autonomous; integrated structures work better for systemic innovations.

Institutional assets. Environments cannot be defined in terms of markets alone. While public policies are usually recognized as important in constraining what firms can do, there is a tendency, particularly by economists, to see these as acting through markets or through incentives. However, institutions themselves are a critical element of the business environment. Regulatory systems, as well as intellectual property regimes, tort laws and antitrust laws, are also part of the environment. So is the system of higher education and national culture. There are significant national differences here, which is just one of the reasons geographic location matters (Nelson 1994). Such assets may not be entirely firm specific; firms of different national and regional origin may have quite different institutional assets to call upon because their institutional/policy settings are so different.

Market (structure) assets. Product market position matters, but it is often not all determinative of the fundamental position of the enterprise in its external environment. Part of the problem lies in defining the market in which a firm competes in a way that gives economic meaning. More importantly, market position in regimes of rapid technological change is often extremely fragile. This is in part because time moves on a different clock in such environments – an Internet year can be viewed as equivalent to 10 years in, for instance, the automobile industry, due to the rapid pace of technological change. Moreover, the link between market share and innovation has long been broken, if it ever existed (Teece 1996). All of this is to suggest that product market position, while important, is too often overplayed. Strategy should be formulated with regard to the more fundamental aspects of firm performance, which we believe are rooted in competences and capabilities and shaped by positions and paths.

Organizational boundaries. An important dimension of 'position' is the location of a firm's boundaries. Put differently, the degree of integration (vertical, lateral and horizontal) is of quite some significance. Boundaries are not only significant with respect to the technological and complementary assets contained within, but also with respect to the nature of the coordination that can be achieved internally as compared to through markets. When specific assets or poorly protected intellectual capital are at issue, pure market arrangements expose the parties to recontracting hazards or appropriability hazards. In such circumstances, hierarchical control structures may work better than pure arm-length contracts (see Williamson 1996: 102–3).

Paths

Path dependencies. Where a firm can go is a function of its current position and the paths ahead. Its current position is often shaped by the path it has travelled. In standard economics textbooks, firms have an infinite range of technologies from which they can choose and markets they can occupy. Changes in product or factor prices will be responded to instantaneously, with technologies moving in and out according to value maximization criterion. Only in the short run are irreversibilities recognized. Fixed costs – such as equipment and overhead – cause firms to price below fully amortized costs but never constrain future investment choices. 'Bygones are bygones'. Path dependencies are simply not recognized. This is a major limitation of microeconomic theory.

The notion of path dependencies recognizes that 'history matters'. Bygones are rarely bygones, despite the predictions of rational actor theory. Thus a firm's previous investments and its repertoire of routines (its 'history') constrain its future behaviour (for further development, see Bercowitz *et al.* 1996). This follows because learning tends to be local. That is, opportunities for learning will be 'close in' to previous activities and thus will be transaction and production specific (Teece 1988). This is because learning is often a process of trial, feedback and evaluation. If too many parameters are changed simultaneously, the ability of firms to conduct meaningful natural quasi experiments is attenuated. If many aspects of a firm's learning environment change simultaneously, the ability to ascertain cause–effect relationships is confounded because cognitive structures will not be formed and rates of learning diminish as a result. One implication is that many investments are much longer term than is commonly thought.

The importance of path dependencies is amplified where conditions of increasing returns to adoption exist. This is a demand-side phenomenon, and it tends to make technologies and products embodying those technologies more attractive the more they are adopted. Attractiveness flows from the greater adoption of the product amongst users, which in turn enables them to become more developed and hence more useful. Increasing returns to adoption has many sources including network externalities, the presence of complementary assets (Teece 1986b) and supporting infrastructure (Nelson 1996), learning by using (Rosenberg 1982) and scale economies in production and distribution. Competition between and amongst technologies is shaped by increasing returns. Early leads won by good luck or special circumstances (Arthur 1988) can become amplified by increasing returns. This is not to suggest that first movers necessarily win. Because increasing returns have multiple sources, the prior positioning of firms can affect their capacity to exploit increasing returns. Thus, in Mitchell's (1989) study of medical diagnostic imaging, firms already controlling the relevant complementary assets could in theory start last and finish first.

In the presence of increasing returns, firms can compete passively, or they may compete strategically through technology-sponsoring activities. Because of huge uncertainties, it may be extremely difficult to determine viable strategies early on. Since the rules of the game and the identity of the players will be revealed only after the market has begun to evolve, the pay-off is likely to lie with building and maintaining organizational capabilities that support flexibility. For example, Microsoft's recent about-face and vigorous pursuit of Internet business once the Netscape phenomenon became apparent is impressive, not so much because it perceived the need to change strategy, but because of its organizational capacity to effectuate a strategic shift.

The first type of competition, passive competition, is not unlike biological competition amongst species, although it can be sharpened by managerial activities that enhance the performance of products and processes. The reality is that companies with the best products will not always win, as chance events may cause 'lock-in' on inferior technologies (Arthur 1988) and may even in special cases generate switching costs for consumers. However, while switching costs may favour the incumbent, in regimes of rapid technological change switching costs can become quickly swamped by switching benefits. Put differently, new products employing different standards often appear with alacrity in market environments experiencing rapid technological change, and incumbents can be readily challenged by superior products and services that yield switching benefits. Thus the degree to which switching costs cause 'lock-in' is a function of factors such as user learning, rapidity of technological change and the amount of ferment in the competitive environment.

Technological opportunities. The concept of path dependencies can be given forward meaning through the consideration of an industry's technological opportunities. It is well recognized that how far and how fast a particular area of industrial activity can proceed is in part due to the technological opportunities that lie before it. Such opportunities are usually a lagged function of foment and diversity in basic science and the rapidity with which new scientific breakthroughs are being made.

However, technological opportunities may not be completely exogenous to industry, not only because some firms have the capacity to engage in or at least support basic research, but also because technological opportunities are often fed by innovative activity itself. Moreover, the recognition of such opportunities is affected by the organizational structures that link the institutions engaging in basic research (primarily the university) to the business enterprise. Hence, the existence of technological opportunities can be quite firm specific.

Important for our purposes is the rate and direction in which relevant scientific frontiers are being rolled back. Firms engaging in R&D may find the path dead ahead closed off, though breakthroughs in related areas may be sufficiently close to be attractive. Likewise, if the path dead ahead is extremely attractive, there may be no incentive for firms to shift the allocation of resources away from traditional pursuits. The depth and width of technological opportunities in the neighbourhood of a firm's prior research activities thus are likely to impact a firm's options with respect to both the amount and level of R&D activity that it can justify. In addition, a firm's past experience conditions the alternatives that management is able to perceive. Thus, not only do firms in the same industry face 'menus' with different costs associated with particular technological choices, they also are looking at menus containing different choices.

4 Dynamic capabilities and the orchestration process

A firm's dynamic capabilities are resident in its organizational process. These are in turn shaped by the firm's assets (its positioning) and the evolutionary paths available to it. Not all is predetermined. Managers do select and adapt their organizational processes; there are at least limited choices amongst going forward paths. The ability of the firm and its management to sense opportunities and then seize them is key. This activity is itself more entrepreneurial than it is administrative, and it is key to the firm's marketplace success. Because of its importance, it is now explored in a little more detail.

Learning is a process by which repetition and experimentation enable tasks to be performed better and quicker. It also enables new production opportunities to be identified (for a useful review and contribution, see Levitt and March 1988). In the context of the firm, if not more generally, learning has several key characteristics. First, learning involves organizational as well as individual skills (Levinthal and March 1993). Mahoney (1995) and Mahoney and Pandian (1992) suggest that both resources and mental models are intertwined in firm-level learning. While individual skills are of relevance, their value depends upon their employment in particular organizational settings. Learning processes are intrinsically social and collective and occur not only through the imitation and emulation of individuals, as with teacher–student or master–apprentice, but also because of joint contributions to the understanding of complex problems. Learning requires common codes of communication and coordinated search procedures. Second, the organizational knowledge generated by such activity resides in new patterns of activity, in 'routines', or a new logic of organization. As indicated earlier, routines are patterns of interactions that represent successful solutions to particular problems. These patterns of interaction are resident in group behaviour, though certain sub-routines may be resident in individual behaviour. The concept of dynamic capabilities as a coordinative management process opens the door to the potential for interorganizational learning. Researchers (Doz and Shuen 1990; Mody 1993) have pointed out that collaborations and partnerships can be a vehicle for new organizational learning, helping firms to recognize dysfunctional routines and preventing strategic blindspots. (There is a large literature on learning, although only a small fraction of it deals with organizational learning. Relevant contributors include Levitt and March 1988, Argyris and Schon 1978, Levinthal and March 1981, Nelson and Winter 1982 and Leonard-Barton 1995.)

External sensing

In order for an organization to exhibit dynamic capabilities, it must not only learn, it must sense the opportunity and the need for change, properly calibrate responsive actions and investments and move to implement a new regime with skill and efficiency. During 'sensemaking', the organization receives and interprets messages about new markets, new technologies and competitive threats. This information is necessarily evaluated in the light of the individuals' and the organization's experience and knowledge. In formulating an action plan, the organization is necessarily guided to some extent by rules and routines, which structure inquiries and responses.

Sensemaking, or interpretation, is a critical function. Well performed, it can enable the organization to connect with its environment and invest its resources wisely, thereby generating superior returns. The fundamental challenge to sensemaking is bounded rationality; one cannot learn all there is to learn about a situation or an opportunity, and action must proceed based on hunches and informed guesses about the true state of the world. In essence, business organizations and their management must interpret the world about them. Interpretative activity is basically a form of theorizing about market and firm behaviour.

Sensemaking can be assisted by sensemaking tools, like scenario planning, as well as the insights of brilliant outsiders – like a Peter Drucker or Gordon Moore. Scenario planning can help managers develop mental maps of possible complex future realities. Such mental maps assist in the interpretation of new data and information from the market and help chart courses of action. Shell Oil is well known for its effective use of scenario planning, and its investment in this activity is widely recognized inside and outside the company to have enabled planners and managers to have extended conversations resulting in shared visions of possible futures. The object of the exercise has never been to predict the future, but to understand the fundamental drivers of change and to quickly chart action plans once key uncertainties are resolved.

When the organization has figured out what is going on and calibrated the opportunity, it must choose among available action plans. These are not infinite in number, but may be restricted to one or two or maybe a handful of viable alternatives that are satisfactory. Actions are likely to be similar to those used in the past. Organizational processes and routines – distinct ways of doing things – come into play. Actions and decision routines are part of the organization's procedural memory. Procedures and policies enable internal competition to be fair, objective and legitimate.

The openness of markets, stronger intellectual property protection, increasing returns, the unbundling of artifacts and information and the possibilities for 'integration' using new information technology are necessarily a part of the sensemaking milieu. Information receipt and interpretation is by no means restricted in its importance to the understanding of business, market and technological trends. There is also the need to identify relevant external technology and bring it into the firm. An organization's absorptive capacity with respect to external technology is a function of 'the technical and managerial competence of the transferee' (Teece 1976). Absorptive capacity is greater when what is to be learned is related to what is already known (Cohen and Levinthal 1990). As Mowery (1984) has explained, a firm is far better equipped to absorb the output of external R&D if one is performing some amount of R&D internally. In short, internal and external R&D are complements, not substitutes.

Organizational action

Once an opportunity is sensed, it must then be seized. This is where the firm's starting position and its ability to quickly contract up the requisite external resources and direct the relevant internal resources comes into play. Competences, complementary assets, timing and competition must all be assessed (Figure 1). Schumpeter (1934) referred to the importance of effectuating 'new combinations'. This is precisely what management must do. A careful assessment of positions, processes and paths is required. Outsourcing from alliance partners is frequently needed to achieve rapid response. The alliance structure is favoured because markets simply don't exist for much of what must be accessed, and the alliance is a (hybrid) way to do so that shares risks and rewards but achieves a coalignment of strategy.

However, it also requires organizational structures and processes where decision making is immediate and action is swift. This typically implies high-powered incentives and decision making that is anything but bureaucratic. Smaller entrepreneurial companies appear to excel in many such environments, although dynamic capabilities are certainly not restricted to small companies. Larger enterprises can also deliver much of what is required if they are attuned to changes in their external environments and if they have adopted decision-making processes that both enable and require quick response.

5 Implications for the theory of the firm

In this approach, the firm is an incubator and repository for difficult to replicate tangible

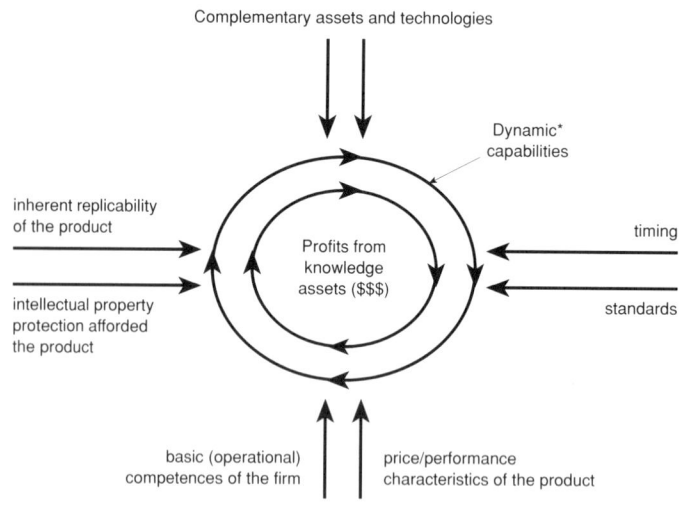

Figure 1 Using dynamic capabilities to capture value from technological (knowledge) assets
Note: * Dynamic capabilities are the capacity to sense opportunities, and to reconfigure knowledge assets, competences and complementary assets and technologies to achieve sustainable competitive advantage.

and intangible assets. Technological and knowledge assets are frequently central. Distinctive processes support the creation, protection and augmentation of firm-specific assets and competences (defined as integrated clusters of firm-specific assets). These assets and competences reflect both individual skills and experiences as well as distinctive ways of doing things inside firms. To the extent that such assets and competences are difficult to imitate and are effectively deployed and redeployed in the marketplace (reflecting dynamic capabilities), they can provide the foundations for competitive advantage.

The essence of the firm is its ability to create, transfer, assemble, integrate and exploit difficult to imitate assets, of which knowledge assets are key. Knowledge assets underpin competences and competences in turn underpin the firm's product and service offerings to the market. The firm's capacity to sense and seize opportunities, to reconfigure its (knowledge) assets, competences and complementary assets, to select appropriate organization forms and to allocate resources astutely and price strategically all constitute its dynamic capabilities.

The perspective presented here requires us to stress the entrepreneurial rather than the administrative side of management. In high-technology industries, successful firms are not so much organizations designed to minimize transactions costs – although this they do – but organizations capable of shaping and reshaping clusters of assets in the distinct and unique combinations needed to serve ever-changing customer needs. Accordingly, boundary issues (such as vertical integration) are not determined by transactions cost considerations alone. Rather, they are strongly influenced by tacit knowledge and imitability/replicability considerations. Even setting aside strategic and transaction cost issues, the tacit component of knowledge cannot frequently be transferred absent the transfer of personnel and organizational systems/routines. Tacit knowledge and its transfer properties help determine the boundaries of the firm and may well swamp transaction costs considerations.

Organizational capital, not human capital per se, lies at the core of firm-distinctive competences. Human capital cannot be owned. Firms may invest in assisting individuals to augment their human capital; but absent mechanisms to tie such assets to the firm, the individual is able to appropriate the returns, thereby denying the firm any competitive advantage. Competitive advantage is established only if the firm is able to leverage individual competences into organizational competences worth more than the sum of the parts. Dynamic capabilities, which are typically layered on top, are clearly organizational in nature, even though they may rely on the keen insights and complementation skills of key executives. Put differently, competitive advantage is not built just on 'people', human capital, or 'labour'; it is built primarily upon organizational competences and capabilities.

Competitive advantage can be attributed not only to the ownership of technological, reputational and structural assets and other assets complementary to them, but also to the ability to combine knowledge assets with other assets needed to create value. Knowing what assets to develop, and what to abandon, is a critical element in the success equation. Dynamic capabilities are critical if the firm's assets base is to support sustainable competitive advantage. The astute management of the value in a firm's competence/knowledge base is a central issue in strategic management (see Teece 1986b). The firm must therefore be understood not just in terms of its competences, but also in terms of its dynamic capabilities and the ability to orchestrate internal and external assets so as to capture value. Dynamic capabilities reflect the entrepreneurial side of management. Incentives as well as the formal and informal structure of the firm are all elements of governance affecting dynamic capabilities. These elements together help define the firm as we know it. Accordingly, competitive advantage flows from both management and structure.

Thus, the dynamic/capabilities view of the firm sees the property boundaries of the firm and governance structure being determined not only with reference to transactions costs, but also with reference to the ownership and creation of difficult to replicate assets. The boundaries of the firm, and future integration and outsourcing opportunities, must clearly be made with reference to learning and knowledge issues as well as to transaction cost economics.

The emphasis on the development and exploitation of difficult to replicate assets shifts the focus of attention from cost minimization to value maximization. Governance decisions involve both questions of what assets to build inside the firm versus accessing externally, as well as how to organize internally. This perspective thus complements transaction cost economics.

6 Conclusion

Knowledge, competence and related intangibles have emerged as the key drivers of competitive advantage in business firms operating in developed nations. This is not just because of the importance of knowledge itself, but because of the rapid expansion of goods and factor markets, leaving intangible assets as the main basis of competitive differentiation in many sectors. There is implicit recognition of this with the growing emphasis being placed on the importance of intangible assets, reputation, customer loyalty and technological know-how. While there is some recognition of these changes, there is perhaps a failure to recognize just how deep these issues go. These developments require a more robust understanding of firms – and the dynamic capabilities approach is offered as the platform upon which a theory of the firm appropriate for our times can be erected.

The value-enhancing challenges facing management are gravitating away from the administrative and towards the entrepreneurial. This is not to denigrate the importance of administration, but merely to indicate that better administration is unlikely to be where the economic 'rents' (superior profits) reside. Indeed, if one looks at the sources of wealth creation today, they are markedly different from what they were in the 1980s. The key sources of wealth creation at the dawn of the new millennium lie with new enterprise formation; the renewal of incumbents; the exploitation of technological know-how, intellectual property and brands; and the successful development and commercialization of new products and services. This is what the dynamic capabilities approach endeavours to highlight.

DAVID TEECE
UNIVERSITY OF CALIFORNIA AT BERKELEY

Note

This chapter draws in part from Teece, Pisano and Shuen (1997), 'Dynamic capabilities and strategic management', *Strategic Management Journal* 18:7: 509–33, and Teece (1998), 'Capturing value from knowledge assets: the new economy, markets for know-how, and intangible assets', *California Management Review* 40 (3) (Spring). The author wishes to thank the editor, William Lazonick, for many helpful comments.

Further reading

(References cited in the text marked *)

* Abernathy, W.J. and Clark. K. (1985) 'Innovation: mapping the winds of creative destruction', *Research Policy* 14: 3–22. (A paper containing a framework for analysing the competitive implications of an innovation through its effect on established systems of production and marketing.)
* Aoki, M. (1990) 'The participatory generation of information rents and the theory of the firm', in M. Aoki et al. (eds) *The Firm as a Nexus of Treaties*, London: Sage. (A chapter arguing that observed low-level information within firms constitutes a unique participatory mode of firm structure.)
  Argyres, N. (1995) 'Technology, strategy, governance structure and interdivisional coordination', *Journal of Economic Behavior and Organization* 28: 337–58. (A paper examining how various organizational forms compare in their capacities to solve coordination problems created by technological interdependence between firms' divisions.)
* Argyris, C. and Schon, D. (1978) *Organizational Learning*, Reading, MA: Addison-Wesley. (Argues that organizations, while able to detect and correct organizational errors, encounter extreme difficulty in attempting to alter norms, policies or objectives.)
* Arrow, K. (1969) 'The organization of economic activity: issues pertinent to the choice of market vs. nonmarket allocation', in *The Analysis and Evaluation of Public Expenditures: The PPB System*, 1, US Joint Economic Committee, 91st Session, Washington, DC: US Government Printing Office, pp. 59–73. (Argues that externalities are subsumed under market failures, which are in turn subsumed under the more general concept of transaction costs.)
  Arrow, K. (1996) 'Technical information and industrial structure', *Industrial and Corporate Change* 5 (2): 645–52. (A discussion of the interrelation between the role of information in production and the organization of industry.)
* Arthur, W.B. (1988) 'Competing technologies: an overview', in G. Dosi et al. (eds) *Technical Change and Economic Theory*. London: Pinter, chap. 5, pp. 115–35. (An evolutionary discussion of competing technologies and technological adoption suggesting theoretical and practical limits to the prediction of the economic future.)
* Baldwin, C. and Clark, K. (1991) 'Capabilities and capital investment: new perspectives on capital budgeting', Harvard Business School Working Paper #92–004. (Attempts to measure organizational capability using financial statement data.)
* Barney, J.B. (1986) 'Strategic factor markets: expectations, luck, and business strategy', *Management Science* 32 (10) (October 1986): 1231–41. (A paper on what characteristics determine the strategic nature of assets.)
* Bercowitz, J.E.L., de Figueiredo, J.M. and Teece, D.J. (1996) 'Firm capabilities and managerial decision-making: a theory of innovative biases', in R. Garud, P. Nayyar and Z. Shapira (eds) *Innovation: Oversights and Foresights*, Cambridge: Cambridge University Press, pp. 233–59. (A chapter examining how decision biases influence innovative activity in firms, drawing on the core concepts of behavioural decision theory and the resource-based, strategic management theory of the firm.)
* Chandler, A.D. Jr (1990) *Scale and Scope: The Dynamics of Industrial Competition*, Cambridge, MA: Harvard University Press. (A historical epic on the role of firms and management in comparative national economic development.)
* Clark, K. and Fujimoto, T. (1991) *Product Development Performance: Strategy, Organization and Management in the World Auto Industries*, Cambridge, MA: Harvard Business School Press. (Illustrates the role played by coordinative routines in development cost, lead time and quality during project development.)
* Coase, R. (1937) 'The nature of the firm', *Economica* 4: 386–405. (A foundational work on the nature and limits of the firm.)
* Coase, R. (1988) 'Lecture on the nature of the firm, III', *Journal of Law, Economics and Organization* 4: 33–47. (A lecture commemorating the 50th anniversary of 'The nature of the firm'.)
* Cohen, W.M. and Levinthal, D.A. (1990) 'Absorption capacity: a new perspective on learning and innovation', *Administrative Sciences Quarterly* 35: 128–52. (A theory on the importance of R&D in the integration of external knowledge.)
* Dierickx, I. and Cool, K. (1989) 'Asset stock accumulation and sustainability of competitive advantage', *Management Science* 35 (12)

(December): 1504–11. (A paper on the importance of inimitability of assets in sustainable competitive advantage.)
* Doz, Y. and Shuen, A. (1990) 'From intent to outcome: a process framework for partnerships', INSEAD Working Paper. (Shows the importance of collaborations and partnerships in interorganizational learning and the recognition of existing dysfunctional routines and strategic deficiencies.)
* Fama, E.F. (1980) 'Agency problems and the theory of the firm', *Journal of Political Economy* 88 (April): 288–307. (The separation of security ownership and control is presented as an efficient form of economic organization.)
* Fujimoto, T. (1994) 'Reinterpreting the resource-capability view of the firm: a case of the development-production systems of the japanese automakers', draft working paper, Faculty of Economics, University of Tokyo (May). (Places the resource-based and capabilities views of the firm in the context of Japanese automobile manufacturing processes.)
* Garvin, D. (1988) *Managing Quality*, New York: Free Press. (Evidence of successful quality management in the USA and Japan.)
* Garvin, D. (1994) 'The processes of organization and management', Harvard Business School Working Paper #94–084. (Provides a framework for thinking about processes and their impacts.)
* Hayes, R., Wheelwright, S. and Clark, K. (1988) *Dynamic Manufacturing: Creating the Learning Organization,* New York: Free Press. (Argues that current American disadvantages in manufacturing capability threaten the competitive advantage of American firms.)
* Henderson, R.M. (1994) 'The evolution of integrative capability: innovation in cardiovascular drug discovery', *Industrial and Corporate Change*, special issue, 3 (3): 607–30. (Using a field study of drug development in ten major European and US firms, this study explores why capabilities do not easily diffuse across an industry.)
* Henderson, R.M. and Clark, K. B. (1990) 'Architectural innovation: the reconfiguration of existing product technologies and the failure of established firms', *Administrative Science Quarterly* 35 (March): 9–30. (The theoretical introduction and industry evidence of architectural innovation.)
* Iansiti, M. and Clark, K. B. (1994) 'Integration and dynamic capability: evidence from product development in automobiles and mainframe computers', *Industrial and Corporate Change*, special issue, 3 (3): 557–606. (A discussion of knowledge and knowledge-creation as the foundations of capabilities and dynamic performance.)
* Kogut, B. and Zander. U. (1992) 'Knowledge of the firm, combinative capabilities, and the replication of technology', *Organizational Science* 3: 283–97. (A model of firms as social communities creating and transferring knowledge.)
* Lazonick, W. (1991) *Business Organization and the Myth of the Market Economy*, New York: Cambridge University Press. (Argues that the most important research question in economics is not the allocation of resources by the market, but rather the nature and sources of economic capabilities.)
* Leonard-Barton, D. (1995) *Wellsprings of Knowledge*, Boston, MA: Harvard Business School Press. (Investigates the processes and strategies central to organizations seeking to manage innovation and build knowledge.)
* Lev, B. and Sougiannis, T. (1992) 'The capitalization, amortization and value-relevance of R&D', unpublished manuscript, University of California, Berkeley, and University of Illinois, Urbana-Champaign (November). (Describes a methodology for estimating the value of intangible assets from financial statements.)
* Levinthal, D.A. and March, J.G. (1981) 'A model of adaptive organizational search', *Journal of Economic Behavior and Organization* 2: 307–33. (A model of organizational change through adaptive search for new technologies.)
* Levinthal, D.A. and March, J.G. (1993) 'The myopia of learning', *Strategic Management Journal*, Winter special issue, 14: 95–112. (A paper examining how firms approach problems of organizational learning, and how these solutions ultimately contribute to learning myopia.)
* Levitt, B. and March, J. (1988) 'Organizational learning', *Annual Review of Sociology* 14: 319–40. (A literature review on organizational learning, where learning is viewed as routine-based, history-dependent and target-orientated.)
* Mahoney, J. (1995) 'The management of resources and the resources of management', *Journal of Business Research* 33 (2): 91–101. (A paper arguing for the importance of a synthesis of resource-based theory and learning theory in understanding the relationship between firm resources and mental models.)
* Mahoney, J.T. and Pandian, J.R. (1992) 'The resource-based view within the conversation of strategic management', *Strategic Management Journal* 13 (5): 363–80. (An article illustrating the resource-based theory of the firm and its implications for firm strategy.)

* Milgrom, P. and Roberts, J. (1990) 'The economics of modern manufacturing: technology, strategy, and organization', *American Economic Review* 80 (3): 551–28. (A mathematical model of firm complementarities.)
* Mitchell, W. (1989) 'Whether and when? Probability and timing of incumbents' entry into emerging industrial subfields', *Administrative Science Quarterly* 34: 208–30. (An empirical examination of the probability and timing of entry by industry incumbents into emerging technical subfields.)
* Mody, A. (1993) 'Learning through alliances', *Journal of Economic Behavior and Organization* 20 (2): 151–70. (A view of alliances as vehicles for the pooling of complementary assets.)
* Mowery, D. (1984) 'Firm structure, government policy, and the organization of industrial research', *Business History Review* 58: 504–31. (Establishes the complementary relationship of internal and external R&D.)
* Nelson, R.R. (1994) 'Why do firms differ, and how does it matter?', *Strategic Management Journal*, Winter special issue, 12: 61–74. (A reaffirmation of the importance of firm diversity in the evolutionary theory and dynamic capabilities views of the firm.)
* Nelson, R.R. (1996) 'The evolution of competitive or comparative advantage: a preliminary report on a study', WP-96-21, International Institute for Applied Systems Analysis, Laxemberg, Austria. (Illustrates the importance of supporting infrastructure in achieving increasing returns to technological adoption.)
* Nelson, R. and Winter, S. (1982) *An Evolutionary Theory of Economic Change*, Cambridge, MA: Harvard University Press. (A theory of firm behaviour in the context of an evolutionary theory of economics.)
* Penrose, E. (1959) *The Theory of the Growth of the Firm*, London: Basil Blackwell. (A foundational work of the capabilities and resource-based literature.)
* Prahalad, C.K. and Hamel, G. (1990) 'The core competence of the corporation', *Harvard Business Review* (May–June): 79–91. (A discussion of the importance to firms of dynamic core competencies.)
* Richardson, G.B.H. (1960) *Information and Investment*, New York: Oxford University Press; 2nd edn 1990. (Identifies the market structures and arrangements that make it possible for businessmen to have enough information to make the investment decisions upon which the allocation of resources depends.)
* Rosenberg, N. (1982) *Inside the Black Box: Technology and Economics*, Cambridge, MA: Cambridge University Press. (A history and analysis of technological progress in advanced nations.)
* Schumpeter, J.A. (1934) *Theory of Economic Development*, Cambridge, MA: Harvard University Press. (A foundational work in evolutionary theories of economics.)
* Shuen, A. (1994) 'Technology sourcing and learning strategies in the semiconductor industry', unpublished Ph.D. dissertation, University of California, Berkeley. (Describes how strategic alliances assist learning.)
* Teece, D.J. (1976) *The Multinational Corporation and the Resource Cost of International Technology Transfer*, Cambridge, MA: Ballinger. (Examines the mechanics of international corporate technology transfer and provides evidence on the level and determinants of technology transfer costs.)
* Teece, D.J. (1980) 'Economics of scope and the scope of an enterprise', *Journal of Economic Behavior and Organization* 1: 223–47. (A theory of firm diversification based on the transaction cost framework of Oliver Williamson.)
* Teece, D.J. (1981) 'The market for know-how and the efficient international transfer of technology', *The Annals of the Academy of Political and Social Science* November: 81–96. (A paper defining the unique characteristics of the market for knowledge assets.)
* Teece, D.J. (1982) 'Towards an economic theory of the multiproduct firm', *Journal of Economic Behavior and Organization* 3: 39–63. (A explanation of multiproduct firms using transaction cost and organizational knowledge properties.)
* Teece, D.J. (1986a) 'Transactions cost economics and the multinational enterprise', *Journal of Economic Behavior and Organization* 7: 21–45. (A transaction cost economics explanation of multinational firms.)
* Teece, D.J. (1986b) 'Profiting from technological innovation', *Research Policy* 15 (6) (December): 285–305. (A paper explaining the importance of complementary assets, appropriability regime and dominant design in determining gains from innovation.)
* Teece, D.J. (1988) 'Technological change and the nature of the firm', in G. Dosi, *et al.* (eds) *Technical Change and Economic Theory*. (An explanation of the reluctance of innovative firms to rely on external research facilities to procure new products and processes via the market.)
* Teece, D.J. (1993) 'The dynamics of industrial capitalism: perspectives on Alfred Chandler's Scale and Scope (1990)', *Journal of Economic Literature* 31 (March): 199–225. (A focus on the organizational aspects in Chandler's work and its relevance to students of the firm.)

* Teece, D.J. (1996) 'Firm organization, industrial structure, and technological innovation', *Journal of Economic Behavior and Organization* 31: 193–224. (A paper exploring the relationship between organizational structure and the generation of new technology.)
* Teece, D.J., Rumelt, R., Dosi, G. and Winter, S. (1994) 'Understanding corporate coherence: theory and evidence', *Journal of Economic Behavior and Organization* 23: 1–30. (A paper showing that as manufacturing firms grow more diverse, they maintain a constant level of coherence between neighbouring activities.)
* Tushman, M.L., Newman, W.H. and Romanelli, E. (1986) 'Convergence and upheaval: managing the unsteady pace of organizational evolution', *California Management Review* 29 (1) (Fall): 29–44. (A discussion of the importance and nature of discontinuous changes in firm strategy.)
* Wernerfelt, B. (1984) 'A resource-based view of the firm', *Strategic Management Journal* 5: 171–80. (A primary work of the resource-based theory of the firm.)
* Williamson, O.E. (1975) *Markets and Hierarchies*, New York: Free Press. (A foundational work of transaction cost economics and new institutional economics.)
* Williamson, O.E. (1985) *The Economic Institutions of Capitalism*, New York: Free Press. (Williamson's further development of transaction cost economics.)
* Williamson, O.E. (1996) *The Mechanics of Governance*, New York: Oxford University Press. (A broad review of the discriminating alignment approach of transaction cost economics.)
* Womack, J., Jones, D. and Roos, D. (1991) *The Machine That Changed the World*, New York: Harper-Perennial. (An in-depth study of Toyota's lean production model.)

See also: AUTOMOBILE INDUSTRY; CHEMICAL INDUSTRY; COASE, R.; COOPERATION AND COMPETITION; CORPORATE CONTROL; DEVELOPMENT AND DIFFUSION OF TECHNOLOGY; ELECTRONICS INDUSTRY; GLOBAL MACHINE TOOL INDUSTRY; GROWTH OF THE FIRM AND NETWORKING; INDUSTRIAL AGGLOMERATION; INDUSTRIAL DYNAMICS; INDUSTRIAL AND LABOUR RELATIONS; INNOVATION; INSTITUTIONAL ECONOMICS; INTELLECTUAL PROPERTY RIGHTS; MARSHALL, A.; PENROSE, E.; SKILL FORMATION SYSTEMS; STEEL INDUSTRY; TELECOMMUNICATIONS INDUSTRY; WILLIAMSON, O.

Business economics

1 The evolution of business economics
2 The structure–conduct–performance paradigm
3 Government regulation of industry
4 Economics and business strategy
5 Developments in business economics since the 1970s
6 The future of business economics

Overview

Business economics is concerned with the analysis of the behaviour of firms in markets and industries and with the determination of costs and prices. It therefore differs from the ways in which economics is most commonly used in business, which are concerned with descriptions and forecasts of behaviour in a macroeconomic environment.

The economics of industry, as the term suggests, has generally focused on the industry as its unit of analysis. Firms within the same industry do not differ from each other, or do so only in essentially trivial ways. The structure–conduct–performance paradigm, which is the dominant empirical tradition, describes how the structure of the industry determines the behaviour of individual firms. Since all firms in the same industry face the same external conditions, all can be expected to perform similarly. Differences in the performance of different firms in the same market – the principal concern of senior managers – are not accounted for.

The field of business strategy, quite distinct from business economics, was developed to account for differences in the performance of firms. Since the late 1970s, however, business economics has also begun to bridge this gap. These developments include game-theoretic models of small-number interactions, the analysis of principal-agent relationships and activity-based costing systems. The resource-based theory of business strategy, which is concerned with the ability of a firm to add value – to create rents or quasi-rents – brings many of these elements of analysis together.

1 The evolution of business economics

Most business executives believe that the subject matter of economics is macroeconomics and particularly macroeconomic forecasting. The role of economists is to tell them what is likely to happen to growth, inflation, exchange rates and interest rates. Generally, managers do not have a great deal of faith in the economists who tell them these things, but they ask their opinion in any case. A majority of executives regard prices as a matter for their sales department, costs as something measured by their accountants and the analysis of their markets as a question to be dealt with by their corporate planners. They rarely know that economists also study microeconomic issues of prices, costs and markets, and the results of that work have very little influence on their behaviour. Yet these questions are the essence of business economics. The purpose of this entry is to describe the subject of business economics and its historical evolution, and to ask why its practical impact is so small.

The economics of industry

When Alfred Marshall – the great nineteenth-century economist who combined intellectual distinction with an awareness of the day-to-day operations of business that few modern industrial economists could emulate – described the relationship between firms and industries, he employed the metaphor of trees in a forest (Marshall 1890) (see MARSHALL, A). In doing so, he emphasized the essential unimportance and transitory nature of the individual firm, thereby focusing attention on the environment within which it operated.

Marshall's metaphor contains the general equilibrium perspective, one of the most important insights of business economics.

According to this theory, the relationship between prices and costs is not a technological relationship, nor is it fundamentally the product of the rules of thumb which govern day-to-day pricing behaviour; it is the product of the interplay of the demands and supplies of independent firms and independent consumers; economic equilibrium is achieved through the operation of these market forces. What happens to an industry, therefore, is not necessarily measured accurately by the sum of the experiences of individual firms. Unfortunately, many managers have little understanding of this idea, which involves the ability 'to distinguish the wood from the trees'. Thus, when a company make plans which are in aggregate inconsistent, the difference between expectation and outcome is not, as decision makers often suppose, an unforeseeable consequence of an adverse economic environment, but a predictable result of the achievement of equilibrium through the operation of market forces (see NEO-CLASSICAL ECONOMICS).

Yet the focus on the industry and the market as the units of analysis and the corresponding relative neglect of the differentiating characteristics of individual business units is a principal cause of the gulf between the theory of industrial organization and the practice of strategic management. The economist's picture of perfect competition, in which firms have no individual influence on prices and in which all firms are essentially identical in behaviour and in cost structure, appears to lack relevance to managers. They see themselves engaged in competition with a relatively small number of rivals, and it is the factors which differentiate them from these rivals that seem to be of critical importance.

The development in the twentieth century of early models of imperfect and monopolistic competition did little to reduce the gulf in perspective between the business executive, who only sees the differences between firms, and the economist, who does not see them at all. In the generalizations and elaborations of the perfect competitive model put forward by Chamberlain (1933) and Robinson (1933), firms still differed from each other only in essentially trivial ways.

Some models of oligopolistic behaviour were developed. These included the Cournot model which was developed in the nineteenth century, one of the oldest descriptions of small number competition, in which each firm makes its output decision on the assumption that the output decisions of all other firms remain unchanged. The kinked demand curve presupposes that a price cut will be matched by other firms while a price increase will elicit no response from them. The assumptions made by these models about competitive behaviour are naive and arbitrary, and it was not until game-theoretic concepts were introduced to economic thinking that a more systematic analysis of responses and interactions became possible.

Prices, costs and markets

As the twentieth century progressed, the discipline of industrial organization became increasingly concerned with describing the structure of industrial costs; it elaborated the relationship between average and marginal costs, between the short run and the long run, and between fixed and variable costs; it also provided insight into the nature of costs that were fixed in the short run but variable in the long run. With that analysis came the beginnings of an appreciation of the implications of different types of cost behaviour for industrial structure.

Here, too, the language of economics was very different from the language of business. Hall and Hitch (1939) attempted a survey of business behaviour in the light of these economic concepts. They discovered that concepts such as marginal revenue and marginal costs, which were central to the economic models described above, were simply unknown to the business people to whom they talked. They reported that decisions were in fact made by reference to rules of thumb, such as mark-up pricing, which appeared inconsistent with the behaviour and predictions that emerged from models of profit-maximizing firms in competitive markets. Thus, the approach to the analysis of costing systems and structures emphasized by economists, which stresses the importance of identifying incremental products and activities and measuring marginal costs, contrasts sharply with the approach adopted by cost and management accountants in business, for whom the allocation and attribution of aggregate expenditures is the key issue. In the analysis of costs, therefore, as well as in descriptions of markets, the perspectives of managers differ radically from those of the theorists of industrial organization. It was not until the 1980s, when accounting theories of activity-based costing were constructed, that bridges were formed between economic and accounting approaches to cost analysis.

Hall and Hitch believed that their research, and their identification of an apparent gulf between theory and practice, raised major questions with regard to industrial organization. Not all economists accepted that argument, however. A divergence of opinion continues to this day between those who argue that business economics should be more firmly rooted in an appreciation of what businessmen actually do and how they think, and those who believe that economic models do not have to be understood by those whose behaviour they explain.

Milton Friedman, a leading exponent of the latter position, has claimed that testing economic theories by asking business people what they think is like testing theories of longevity by asking nonagenarians to account for their long lives (see FRIEDMAN, M.). For those who share Friedman's methodological stance, successful prediction is the object of science. The process of natural selection and essential human greed lead to profit-maximizing behaviour, even if those who are led to behave in these ways profess different objectives and fail to understand the mathematical description of first- and second-order conditions for profit maximization. Others have found the difference between the languages of economics and business more troubling. Many influential, if rarely mainstream, commentators on economics and business, such as Baumol and Galbraith, have based their arguments on interpretations of what business people have told them about what they do (see GALBRAITH, J.K.).

2 The structure–conduct–performance paradigm

Hall and Hitch's article was published in 1939. After the Second World War, the economic study of business behaviour became centred around what was known as the structure–conduct–performance paradigm, founded by such authors as Joe Bain (1956) and Edward Mason (1939, 1949). This strongly empirical approach began with the proposition that market structure was the main determinant of behaviour and profitability. Market structure was defined by the number of firms in the industry, their market shares and the degree of concentration of the market share of the largest firms. It was therefore considered appropriate to appraise the performance of an industry by making reference to its economic structure.

The structure–conduct–performance approach dominated economists' analyses of business behaviour until the 1970s. Theorists who deviated from this tradition were principally those who proposed alternatives to the general model of (possibly imperfectly) competitive profit-maximizing behaviour. In particular, they recognized that profit maximization was not necessarily the primary goal of business and proposed instead the view that firms maximize their size (Baumol 1959; Galbraith 1986) or rate of growth (Marris 1966). Another closely related view emphasized the complex nature of the corporation as an organism and stressed that its actions were the product of both multiple objectives and the interaction of these with external constraints (Cyert and March 1963; Simon 1961). All these theories described facets of business behaviour which were ignored by conventional models. If their impact on mainstream business economics was modest, this was because they failed to generate the clear-cut predictions and prescriptions associated with the assumptions of profit maximization and perfect competition (MANAGERIAL THEORIES OF THE FIRM).

Although the structure–conduct–performance paradigm has powerful implications for *public* policy, it is limited in its application to issues of business policy. If the main determinant of performance is market structure, then firms in the same industry, which by definition face the same market structure, cannot be expected to differ substantially in performance. Many of the principal concerns of the structure–conduct–performance tradition, such as the relationship between concentration, entry barriers and profitability, are consistent with this public policy focus of research. This consistency led to some of the major developments in business economics, particularly in its application to issues of antitrust policy and regulation. This approach to business economics is inclined to view departures from a perfectly competitive model as imperfections and behaviour such as product differentiation or advertising with suspicion.

3 Government regulation of industry

Antitrust policy, designed to prevent monopolies and the restraint of trade, has always drawn on economic arguments. In the USA, courts were presented with, and took an increasingly serious view of, economic evidence. Similar developments occurred in the administrative tribunals established to operate antitrust policies in the UK and Germany and in the increasingly influential Competition Directorate of the European Union (EU).

Business economists were also concerned with prescriptions for the management of nationalized industries and public enterprises – marginal cost pricing was the general prescription. Indeed, the opportunity to introduce marginal cost prices into industries commonly characterized by joint production and natural monopoly was seen as an important advantage of nationalization. The possible existence of economies of scale and scope implied that firms could not necessarily expect to cover costs of production or use profitability as an investment criterion. This implied a need for social cost–benefit analysis, DCF (discounted cash flow) methods of investment appraisal and a concern with the determinants of social discount rates. Here, too, the opportunity to make decision-making more rational was seen as an advantage of public ownership, and the new techniques were considered to have exemplary value for private business.

Occasional critics of the new literature of business economics emphasized the difficulties of reconciling its theories with effectiveness in the day-to-day management of the business (Graaff 1957; Little 1957). The same issue was approached in a rather different manner by Liebenstein (1966), who argued that what he called 'X inefficiency' – the distance between the actual output of firms and the theoretical production frontier – was a problem of far more practical significance than possible losses of allocative efficiency due to deviations from marginal cost pricing. Although Liebenstein and other critics were to remain outside the orthodoxy of business economics, concern with the quality of management of public firms in practice became an increasingly important political concern. This trend was first reflected in the imposition of the commercial disciplines of the private sector on nationalized industries. It led subsequently to programmes of privatizing state industry, which began in the UK in the 1980s and were subsequently imitated in many countries around the world. The collapse of the centrally planned regimes of eastern Europe gave new impetus to privatization.

With utilities and other national monopolies increasingly in the hands of private-sector firms, regulation became an increasingly important area of business economics. The principal issue was how to control the prices of utilities that enjoyed local monopolies in industries such as electricity supply and telecommunications. Regulatory economics became a central theme in business economics as the scope of regulated industries increased through privatization, new styles of regulation were devised and new theories were developed to cover regulation in new areas. Such areas included the environment and industries (for example, financial services) characterized by information asymmetry between buyers and sellers. The emphasis on the relationship between government and industry was instrumental in the development of the economic analysis of rent-seeking behaviour. Firms are able to influence the structure of the market in which they operate by responding to regulatory and other government policies and, as in the structure–conduct–performance paradigm, this has consequences for their efficiency and for the overall economic perform- ance of their activities (Alchian and Demsetz 1972; Posner 1975).

4 Economics and business strategy

This entry has described the development of mainstream business economics up until 1970. A student of the subject at that date would have been introduced to a variety of models of markets, such as perfect and imperfect competition, and simple oligopolistic structures, which shared the common characteristic that the differences between firms were either given or unimportant. He or she would have learnt an approach to cost analysis and price determination quite distinct from that used by management accountants. The empirical material taught on such a course would have focused largely on the relative characteristics and performance of different industries. Its prescriptive content would have been concerned with public policy issues – that is, how government should influence or seek to influence the structure of industry. The failure of these methods of analysis to address what business people perceived as the central problems of firms led to the development in the 1960s of the distinct discipline of business strategy, seen as essentially distinct from mainstream industrial economics. The founders of business strategy were explicit on this point:

> Study of the firm has been the long time concern of the economics profession. Unfortunately for our present purpose, the so-called *microeconomic theory* of the firm which occupies much of the economist's thought and attention, sheds relatively little light on decision-making pro- cesses in a real world firm.
>
> (Ansoff 1965: 16)

Furthermore, business strategy was taught largely by means of the practically orientated technique of discussing specific problems which had confronted individual firms historically. At first, business strategy was concerned mostly with the formal planning systems of firms. It focused on the formulation of objectives for the firm, on the devising of strategies to fulfil these objectives and on the process of implementing strategy. It emphasized the preparation of quantified plans and reflected a certain naivety about the role of computers and information management in the operations of firms; this was paralleled by a faith in the efficiency of similar systems of economic planning at a national level.

As the subject of strategy developed, greater emphasis was put on competitor analysis and the market environment within which the firm operated. Techniques used in these approaches to business strategy – such as the experience curve or growth/market-share portfolio planning – had affinities with tools used by economists, although these relationships were rarely explored.

The most ambitious attempt to bring business economics into business strategy was made by Porter, whose five forces – rivalry, threat of substitution, supplier or buyer bargaining and new entry – mirrored closely the structure–conduct–performance paradigm. In the 1990s, Porter's work continues to represent the most broad-ranging attempt to make economics useful for everyday business decisions, but it is noticeably more successful when applied to the industry (1980), than when applied to the firm (1985).

5 Developments in business economics since the 1970s

The 1980s and 1990s saw major changes in both the style and content of the economist's study of industrial organization. Style has changed with the application of more sophisticated models which involve an increased use of mathematics – a tendency that had already become widespread in other branches of economics. With regard to changes in content, this entry will emphasize developments in three areas: the economics of information, transaction cost economics and game theory.

The economics of information

Akerlof (1970) made a pioneering contribution to the study of the economics of information, showing how markets might operate imperfectly or fail to exist entirely when the seller knows more about the characteristics of the product than the buyer. Such asymmetry of information became recognized as a central cause of market failure. Of greater significance for business economics, however, was the variety of devices that were developed to respond to these problems. Theories of signalling by producers, search by consumers, commitment and reputation formed the basis of an economic analysis which began to facilitate a greater understanding of phenomena such as branding and advertising and the development of supplier and customer relations. Although those issues played a major role in everyday business life, in earlier phases of business economics they were either not recognized or viewed only as market imperfections.

Transaction cost economics

In the mainstream of business economics, it was not only that the firm played no central role; it was difficult to account for the existence of firms at all. Such questions had been addressed by a more institutional tradition. Coase (1937) argued that the boundaries of the firm were determined by the balance of advantage between internal and external transactions. Williamson (1975) elaborated this distinction between markets and hierarchies, suggesting that the relative merits of the two reflected the size of transaction costs – in effect, the price of market organization – and the degree of asset specificity – the extent to which equipment or skills are customized to the needs of particular firms (see COASE, R.; WILLIAMSON, O.E.).

Williamson's system, known as transaction cost economics, was the precursor of a variety of methods of analysis. One important question is the design of relationships between parties with distinct objectives (principal–agent problems). Another is nature of contracts, including both classical contracts (where actions in many contingencies are specified precisely) and implicit contracts, which are enforced not by the courts but by the continuing need of parties to do business with each other.

Game theory

Cooperative and non-cooperative game theory was developed as a technique for understanding the interactions between small numbers of players. Pioneered by von Neumann and Morgenstern (1944), game theory seemed at first to promise more than it delivered, but its applications were gradually extended and it became apparent that many issues such as pricing behaviour, entry barriers and vertical relationships could be illuminated by being studied in a game-theoretic context. Most neo-classical economic models had assumed the existence of perfect or near perfect information, and with it equality of information between buyers and sellers in markets.

Analysis such as that carried out by Akerlof (1970) illuminated the ways in which real symmetries of information could lead to market failure. Following Akerlof, business economists developed models of reputation – often utilizing a game-theoretic framework – to explain how these market weaknesses were overcome. In this context, improved theories of the role of advertising became available (these had always fitted rather uncomfortably into a classical microeconomic framework). Various concepts of non-cooperative equilibria – the probable outcomes of processes in which players make independent decisions but the outcome for each depends on the totality of the strategies of all – are central to the use of game theory. A Nash equilibrium is one in which each player chooses the strategy most suited to him or her, given that all other players select their strategies in similar fashion. The Cournot model of oligopoly, developed around the middle of the nineteenth century, won new regard as the Nash outcome of a market in which each firm determines the quantity of a homogeneous product it will supply.

The Nash–Cournot solution is an outcome of a one-shot game, in which the various players confront each other only once. The essence of most business contexts is repeated confrontation, and game theory provides for the analysis of repeated games in which a variety of strategies can be supported as solutions that would not be appropriate for the player in a game that was played only once. Such strategies include the adoption of cooperative behaviour. Thus, learning behaviour becomes an important element in game theory, and biological analogies have indeed become important applications of these techniques.

Activity-based costing

Activity-based costing was developed in the 1980s by management accountants. Traditional analysis of industrial costs was concerned to allocate common or joint costs to products, generally in proportion to direct costs, revenues or some physical measures of output. The methods used for doing this were generally arbitrary and mechanistic, based on proportionality to direct costs, to revenues or to physical output measures. There was little, if any, relationship between average costs computed in this way and the marginal or incremental costs which economists measured.

Activity-based costing attempts to introduce direct causality as the driver of cost allocation systems. By identifying the combination of purposes for which costs are incurred, common costs can be attributed directly to specific purposes and ultimately to specific outputs. Moreover, game-theoretic approaches to the allocation of joint costs, which are associated with the development of contestable market theory, mean that the allocation of joint costs to products ceases to be wholly arbitrary. For the first time, economists and cost accountants are beginning to speak the same language.

6 The future of business economics

With an increased emphasis on issues such as styles of contracting, non-cooperative games and the role of information in markets, the industrial economics of the 1980s was far more orientated towards issues facing individual firms than the public policy concerns of previous decades. Yet, the relatively abstract style in which most business economics literature is written continues to limit its everyday relevance to business issues. One of the primary tasks for the next generation of business economists is to translate the discipline's theoretical insights into practical tools for business people.

The key element in improving the practical application of business economics, and in creating needed links between the subject of business strategy and business economics, is the resource-based view of the firm, which has become one of the most important strands of thinking within business strategy itself (Lippman and Rumelt 1982; Teece 1986; Grant 1991; Kay 1993). The resource-based theory emphasizes the degree to which the success of firms depends on their distinctive capabilities – that is, characteristics of their operations which cannot be readily replicated or imitated by their competitors.

Thus, the object of business becomes the creation, maximization and defence of economic rent. While some rents result from the establishment or exploitation of monopoly, many rents and quasi-rents result from influences that are entirely benign – for example, the development of reputation, the construction of trading relationships that facilitate trust and flows of information or early adoption of innovation. The concern of business economics is no longer only with the map of the forest, but with the defining characteristics of the individual tree. That new emphasis is one that gives the subject an exciting future.

JOHN KAY
JOHNKAY.COM

Further reading

(References cited in the text marked *)

* Akerlof, G.A. (1970) 'The market for "lemons": quality, uncertainty and the market mechanism', *Quarterly Journal of Economics* 85 (3): 488–500. (A landmark in the analysis of the problem of assymetric information.)
* Alchian, A. and Demsetz, H. (1972) 'Production, information costs, and economic organization', *American Economic Review* 62 (4): 777–95. (An important contribution to the theory of the firm.)
* Ansoff, H.I. (1965) *Corporate Strategy*, New York: McGraw-Hill. (An early text outlining the field of corporate strategy.)
* Bain, J.S. (1956) *Barriers to New Competition*, Cambridge: Cambridge University Press. (A leading explanation of the structure–conduct–performance paradigm.)
* Baumol, W.J. (1959) *Business Behaviour, Value and Growth*, London: Macmillan. (A challenge to the profit-maximizing theory of the firm.)
* Chamberlain, E.H. (1933) *The Theory of Monopolistic Competition*, Cambridge, MA: Harvard University Press. (A seminal analysis of imperfectly competitive markets.)

* Coase, R.H. (1937) 'The nature of the firm', *Economica* 4 (3): 386–405, reprinted in G.J. Stigler and K.E. Boulding (eds) (1952) *Readings in Price Theory*, Homewood, IL: Irwin (Despite its age, still one of the best explanations of why firms exist.)
* Cyert, R. and March, J. (1963) *A Behavioural Theory of the Firm*, Englewood Cliffs, NJ: Prentice Hall. (A challenge to the view that firms maximize.)
* Galbraith, J.K. (1986) *The Anatomy of Power*, London: Hamish Hamilton. (An elegantly written challenge to neo-classical economic theory.)
* Graaff, J.V. de (1957) *Welfare Economics*, Cambridge: Cambridge University Press. (A standard text on this subject.)
* Grant, R.M. (1991), *Contemporary Strategy Analysis*, Oxford: Blackwell. (A good exposition of the resource-based approach to strategy.)
* Hall, R.L. and Hitch, C.J. (1939) 'Price theory and business behaviour', *Oxford Economic Papers* 2 (1): 12–45. (Analysis of price theory.)
* Kay, J.A. (1993) *Foundations of Corporate Success*, Oxford: Oxford University Press. (A book that sets out the resource-based theory of strategy in economic terms.)
* Liebenstein, H. (1966) 'Allocative efficiency vs. "X-efficiency"', *American Economic Review* 56 (2): 392–415. (Emphasizes the importance of the internal efficiency of firms (X-efficiency) in contrast to traditional concerns of welfare economies.)
* Lippman, S.A. and Rumelt, R.P. (1982) 'Uncertain imitability: an analysis of inter-firm differences in efficiency under competition', *Bell Journal of Economics* 3 (3): 418–38. (An instructive exposition of how competitive advantage is achieved.)
* Little, I.M.D. (1957) *A Critique of Welfare Economics*, Oxford: Clarendon Press. (A theoretical critique of the earlier arguments of Lange and Lerner.)
* Marris, R. (1966) *The Economic Theory of Managerial Capitalism*, London: Macmillan. (An exposition of the implications of growth objectives for firms.)
* Marshall, A. (1890; 8th edn 1920) *Principles of Economics*, London: Macmillan. (The foundation of modern microeconomics.)
* Mason, E. (1939) 'Price and production policies of large-scale enterprise', *American Economic Review* 29 (1): 61–74. (Early description of the structure–conduct–performance approach.)
* Mason, E. (1949) 'The current state of the monopoly problem in the United States', *Harvard Law Review* 62: 1265–85. (Early description of the structure–conduct–performance approach.)
  Milgrom, P. and Roberts, J. (1992) *Economics, Organization and Management*, Englewood Cliffs, NJ: Prentice Hall. (A work which demonstrates the application of modern industrial economics to business issues.)
* Neumann, J. von and Morgernstern, O. (1944) *Theory of Games and Economic Behaviour*, Princeton, NJ: Princeton University Press. (Important work by the inventors of game theory.)
* Porter, M. (1980) *Competitive Strategy: Techniques for Analyzing Industries and Competitors*, New York: The Free Press. (A broad-ranging attempt to make economics useful for everyday business decisions which mirrors the structure–conduct–performance paradigm.)
* Porter, M. (1985) *Competitive Advantage: Creating and Sustaining Superior Performance*, New York: The Free Press. (The application of Porter's paradigm to decision making in the firm.)
* Posner, R.A. (1975) 'The social costs of monopoly and regulation', *Journal of Political Economy* 83 (3): 807–27. (Explains how rent seeking by firms undermines regulation.)
* Robinson, J. (1933) *The Economics of Imperfect Competition*, London: Macmillan. (With Chamberlain, defined the theory of imperfect competition.)
  Scherer, F.M. and Ross, D. (1990) *Industrial Market Structure and Economic Performance*, 3rd edn, Boston, MA: Houghton Mifflin. (The bible of the structure-conduct-performance tradition.)
* Simon, H.A. (1961) *Administrative Behaviour*, 2nd edn, London: Macmillan. (A contrast to the neo-classical account of firm behaviour.)
* Teece, D.J. (1986) 'Profiting from technological innovation: implications for integration, collaboration, licensing and public policy', *Research Policy* 15: 285–305. (An important contribution to resource-based theories of strategy.)
* Williamson, O.E. (1975) *Markets and Hierarchies: Analysis and Antitrust Implications*, New York: The Free Press. (The best account of transaction cost economics.)

See also: MANAGERIAL THEORIES OF THE FIRM; MARSHALL, A.; NEO-CLASSICAL ECONOMICS; TRANSACTION COST ECONOMICS

Transfer pricing

1 Introduction
2 Theoretical context
3 Empirical evidence
4 Tax competition and transfer pricing
5 Practical solutions to the transfer pricing problem
6 Conclusion

Overview

Many intra-firm transactions are non-market transactions and therefore lack a market determined price. A transfer price is the price assigned to such non-market intra-firm transfers. Transfer prices are especially important for multinational corporations since a parent company typically has subsidiaries or branches in other countries and transfers are often made between the component parts of the multinational.

As the world has become more internationally dependent, these transactions and the associated transfer prices have come under increased scrutiny. The fear often expressed by governments is that a multinational corporation may manipulate transfer prices in order to transfer profits from one country to another and thereby affect various government policies. Most notably, transfer prices can affect the tax revenues of both the home and host country.

After a brief description of international tax systems that is necessary to understand transfer pricing incentives, transfer price manipulation is discussed with respect to three broad areas: the taxation of outbound investment, the taxation of inbound investment, and non-tax factors. The empirical evidence relating to the extent of transfer price manipulation for these three broad areas is summarized. The inter-relationship between transfer pricing and tax competition is then discussed.

A general international consensus is that the appropriate transfer price is the 'arm's length' price. This is the price that would be charged by two unrelated parties. However, it is often difficult to find such a comparable transaction. Practical solutions to this problem are offered at the end of the article.

1 Introduction

Modern corporations are often organized as a set of separate entities (see MULTINATIONAL CORPORATIONS). A typical organization might involve a parent corporation and a set of subsidiaries. The parent is typically the major stockholder in its subsidiaries, often controlling 100 per cent of a subsidiary's stock. Various transactions may occur between the parent and its subsidiaries. For instance, a subsidiary may provide an input that is used in the parent's production process or the parent may provide a trademark or technical advice to a subsidiary. The price attached to these intra-firm transactions is referred to as the transfer price.

While transfer pricing occurs (implicitly or explicitly) with any intra-firm transfer, the feature that has made transfer pricing so important and controversial is its use in a multinational corporation. The transactions between a multinational corporation's parent and its foreign subsidiaries cross international boundaries and this raises a host of important issues. For instance, suppose that the parent is located in a high-tax country while the subsidiary is located in a low-tax country. Assuming that the multinational is trying to minimize its total tax payments, the multinational will try to price transfers so that most of its profits appear in the low-tax country. For example, if the subsidiary is providing the parent with an input, there is an incentive to charge a very high price for the input. Since this will result in high revenue in the low-tax country and high costs in the high-tax country, the effect will be to transfer profits from the high-tax to the low-tax country. The multinational's taxes will be lower and its after-tax profits higher than would otherwise be the case. This example illustrates the central role that transfer pricing plays both for governments and for multinational firms.

2 Theoretical context

International tax systems

The primary reason that governments have been interested in the transfer pricing practices of multinationals has been in relation to taxes. To understand the role that transfer pricing plays in minimizing worldwide taxes, one must have at least a rudimentary understanding of the taxation of multinational corporations (see GLOBALIZATION). All countries claim the right to tax income generated within their borders. Since the income of a multinational is generated in more than one country, there is the further question of whether income generated outside of the home country's borders is considered taxable. In principle, two systems have been developed: the territorial (source) system of taxation and the worldwide (residence) system. The former exempts income earned outside of a country's borders while the latter taxes it. Since the worldwide system taxes income earned abroad twice (once by the foreign country and again by the home country), a credit is usually given for taxes paid to foreign countries. To avoid giving refunds for high foreign taxes, the credit is limited to tax that would have been paid had the income been earned in the home country.

While countries generally do not adhere strictly to one system or the other, it is useful to list the system used by some major countries, since this will influence the transfer pricing incentives. Foreign source dividend income is treated on a worldwide basis by the USA, the UK, Turkey, Spain, Portugal, Norway, New Zealand, Japan, Italy, Ireland, Iceland and Greece. These countries use one of two methods to determine credit for foreign taxes. One method treats income in each foreign country separately in determining the credit. The second method determines the credit on a worldwide basis; that is, tax paid to all foreign countries is added together and credit is given as long as the weighted average is less than the home country tax. Of the countries listed, the USA, Japan, and Iceland provide credit on a worldwide basis; the others use a per country limit in determining the foreign tax credit. Other countries of the OECD treat foreign source dividend income on a territorial basis; that is, it is exempted from home country tax. Foreign source interest income is generally treated on a residence basis.

Transfer pricing and the taxation of outbound investment

Transfer pricing can be used to reduce taxes for either the territorial or the worldwide tax system. The simplest cases can be illustrated for a multinational that has foreign profits generated in a single foreign country as well as profits generated at home. Abuses under the territorial system are perhaps the most obvious: taxes can be reduced by transferring profits out of the high-tax country and into the low-tax country.

A purported advantage of the worldwide system is that this incentive disappears for a multinational that invests in a single foreign country with a tax rate lower than the home country. In this case, income derived from the foreign investment will be taxed at the home country tax rate and the incentive to shift income is eliminated. This is called capital-export neutrality.

However, several complications of the tax systems of countries that purport to use the worldwide system of taxation make it so that multinationals can use transfer pricing to reduce taxes. First, consider a multinational that invests in a single high-tax country. (In the tax jargon, such a firm would be in 'excess credits'.) Some of the foreign tax will not be credited since the credit for foreign taxes is limited; hence, taxes can again be reduced by using transfer prices to shift profits to the home country. Second, since multinationals typically have investments in a variety of foreign countries, the way in which the credit is computed is important. As mentioned above, the USA, Japan and Iceland aggregate income over all foreign countries in determining the limit. Hence, for these countries, a multinational with a large proportion of income coming from investments in high-tax countries and a small proportion of income coming from investments in low-tax foreign countries will not obtain full credit for foreign taxes paid. This firm would then have an incentive to use transfer prices to shift income from high-tax to low-tax foreign countries and thereby obtain credit for all foreign taxes paid. Third, the USA defers home country tax on income earned by multinationals in foreign countries until that income is repatriated. This is called 'deferral' and effectively converts a worldwide tax system into a territorial system. Although Subpart F provisions in the USA have limited deferral, the transfer pricing problems associated with territorial tax systems become relevant when a worldwide system incorporates deferral.

Transfer pricing and the taxation of inbound investment

Transfer pricing incentives as discussed thus far have centred on home country corporations that invest abroad (i.e. outbound investment). However transfer pricing may also be used by foreign corporations operating in the home country (i.e. inbound investment) to transfer profits out and so avoid home country taxes. This second issue has become important, especially in the USA, because the aggregate rate of return for foreign-controlled companies in the USA is observed to be much lower than the rate of return of domestically controlled companies. A concern expressed by the US Congress is that foreign-controlled US corporations are not paying US tax; the suggested culprit is transfer pricing.

There are, however, several reasons other than transfer pricing that might explain low rates of return of foreign-controlled companies operating in a home country. First, foreign companies may at first experience a lower than average rate of return because of the revaluation of the value of existing assets for tax purposes for new acquisitions or because of the start-up costs of a new business. Second, a low average rate of return in any one year may not be indicative of a long-run trend. That is, although foreign companies may have difficulty in adjusting to the nuances of a foreign market at first, one would expect this to change over time as the firms mature. Moreover, unexpected changes in exchange rates can have a large effect on profits. An unexpected fall in the dollar, for instance, would increase the cost of components imported into the USA and therefore temporarily decrease the profits of a foreign-controlled company in the USA. This effect also would be expected to diminish over time.

Non-tax factors

The tax related effects of transfer pricing are important and have received a great deal of attention. However, several non-tax factors deserve mention as well. The most important non-tax factors include a parent company's perceived need to exert control over the operations of its subsidiaries, money laundering, and diversification of political and foreign exchange risks. Consider first the need of a multinational to exert central control over the firm's operations. Much of the accounting literature emphasizes the need for central control in order to maximize profits for the entire firm. The idea is that an intra-firm transfer by definition entails some monopoly or monopsony power. In such an environment, an uncontrolled transfer price will be set to maximize the profit of a division of a corporation, but this will hurt the overall profit of the corporation.

A second non-tax factor involves political and foreign exchange risk. To the extent that such risks vary over time and can be predicted, transfer pricing can be used to transfer profits out of politically unstable regions or out of currencies that are expected to fall in value relative to the home currency. Finally, profits from illegal activities can be transferred in a covert way by inflating the profits of a legitimate business transaction.

3 Empirical evidence

The evidence on the extent of transfer pricing suggests that transfer pricing is quantitatively important. Outbound investment by US multinationals has been investigated by Harris *et al.* (1993), who use Compustat data to investigate whether taxes paid to the USA are influenced by the location of the multinational's profits overseas. Since the USA taxes multinationals based on a worldwide system and computes the foreign tax credit by aggregating on a worldwide basis, the multinational can get credit for income tax paid in a country with a tax rate higher than the US rate. Further, judicious use of transfer pricing can shift income from a high-tax to a low-tax location so as to avoid hitting the limit. Harris *et al.* find that a multinational that has a subsidiary in a low(high)-tax country has a lower (higher) than average ratio of US tax to US assets. This is consistent with the use of transfer pricing to minimize worldwide taxes, although they find that the aggregate effect on US tax revenues is moderate.

Hines and Rice (1994) investigate transfer pricing of outbound investment by concentrating on the use of 'tax havens' (a set of very low-tax foreign countries) by US multinationals. They find that reported profit rates are sensitive to local tax rates, although they note that this may not be bad for US revenue. A US multinational whose foreign source income comes primarily from a high-tax country will not be subject to additional US tax. If, however, the multinational is able to shift income so that its foreign source income appears to come primarily from a low-tax country, the US will gain tax revenue equal to the difference between taxes paid and what would be paid in the USA.

Inbound investment in the USA is investigated by Grubert *et al.* (1993). They use data from the tax returns of US corporations to investigate the difference in taxes paid by foreign-controlled as opposed to US-controlled corporations. The aggregate data suggest a much lower ratio of taxable income to assets for foreign-controlled corporations. However, the authors find that the revaluation of assets after merger or acquisition, exchange rate changes, and a maturation effect account for about half of the difference. The remaining difference could be due to transfer pricing, and the authors present some evidence that indicates that foreign-controlled companies tend to be more concentrated and persist longer at zero taxable income. This indicates that transfer pricing is used to some extent to reduce taxes, although less than might at first be feared.

Pak and Zdanowicz (1994) compare the implied prices of products from international transactions using data from the US Commerce Department. The data set is very disaggregated in terms of individual transactions and the implied prices offer some striking examples of prices that deviate from the norm. The implied prices are probably best interpreted as resulting from all forms of illegal pricing activity, including money laundering.

4 Tax competition and transfer pricing

Transfer pricing presents a problem for tax authorities when the taxes paid by a corporation differ according to the country from which it derives revenue. It is the difference in taxes that gives rise to incentives to shift income from a high-tax to a low-tax country. Why do taxes differ between countries and what impact do these differences have on transfer pricing incentives?

Certainly there are many reasons for taxes to differ between countries. One country may simply prefer to provide more public services and hence will need to collect more in taxes. A country may also use its tax system to stimulate investment by, for instance, lowering corporate tax rates. This topic has generated much debate of late. The OECD is compiling a list of countries that engage in 'harmful' tax competition (Weiner and Ault 1998). Ireland has for many years created much controversy in the EU with its low 10 per cent tax rate for certain manufacturing firms that invest in Ireland. Although Ireland has agreed to repeal this special tax break, it is being replaced by a low 12.5 per cent corporate tax rate.

A long literature that studies fiscal structure in a federation addresses many of the conceptual issues since it inherently involves the taxation of resources that are mobile (Goodspeed 1998). Part of this literature discusses tax competition, which is usually thought to occur when the tax system of one government affects the tax system of a second government, usually through an effect on the second government's tax revenues. This literature shows that tax competition can be efficient or inefficient, depending on whether taxes paid reflect the benefits of public services received.

There is little empirical work that attempts to assess the impact of tax competition, possibly because of empirical difficulties. (For an exception, see Goodspeed 2000.) For instance, although there are many aspects to the controversy involving Ireland and other EU countries, one difficulty in assessing the various arguments is that many governmental policies are at work simultaneously. For instance, although the EU complains about a low Irish tax rate, they also attempt to stimulate investment in Ireland through the EU grant system. In addition, any investment incentive created by a low Irish tax rate would be offset if the parent multinational were from a worldwide taxation country and that country taxed the residual. Yet many Irish tax treaties with EU countries contain tax sparing agreements which exempt the difference between the standard and tax holiday rates. Exemption countries also implicitly allow the incentive to stand since they exempt foreign source income from tax. In either case, the possible avenue for transfer pricing abuse is created, though it is not clear whether the fault lies with Ireland or with the other countries that implicitly allow tax differences through their own tax system.

In addition, the interconnection of transfer pricing and tax competition are rarely discussed. One exception is the work of Elitzur and Mintz (1996), who study a model of a multinational that is present in two countries. They find that a country that raises its tax rate will lower revenues in each country as the multinational lowers production in both countries. The model does not consider capital flows between countries, however.

5 Practical solutions to the transfer pricing problem

Transfer pricing may theoretically be used to evade taxes. Some rules must therefore be set by governments to control tax evasion. A generally accepted international standard is 'arm's length pricing'. The basic notion is that a transaction between a parent and its subsidiary should be priced as if it had occurred between two unrelated parties in a competitive market. Transfer prices that correspond to this are not always easy to calculate, however, since there may not exist comparable transactions by unrelated parties. Indeed, many legitimate reasons for transfer pricing such as royalties from a brand name result because of the inherent existence of monopoly power that generates economic rents. The correct transfer price in this case would not be that of a competitive market. Still, governments must provide some guidance as to what is acceptable.

Specific international standards for transfer pricing rules that try to approximate arm's length transfer prices have recently been proposed by the OECD (1995). Specific rules that are acceptable to a country's taxing authority generally vary from country to country. While directly comparable transactions by unrelated parties are often preferred, no comparable transactions between unrelated parties are observable for many transactions that involve transfer prices. The rules therefore try to set some bounds on transfer prices. Generally, an attempt is made to approximate unrelated party transactions by reference to some industry average such as a rate of return on assets or a margin on sales. The methodology used to determine the proper transfer price has become increasingly sophisticated. Frisch (1989) and Witte and Chipty (1990) suggest the use of the capital asset pricing model to determine a proper return for a project. Horst (1993) suggests using regression analysis to determine an appropriate rate of return.

Some new issues emerged in the 1990s. Two of these are the taxation of global trading of financial instruments and certain cost-sharing agreements known as 'buy-ins'.

Many of the issues involved in the taxation of global trading of financial instruments have been discussed by the OECD (1998) and Alworth (1998). Technological change and the use of derivatives have resulted in financial firms organizing their activities on a global 24-hour basis. Questions arise as to the source country for income and expenses related to these activities. The OECD suggests that these activities can be dealt with using current arm's length rules or other currently used methods such as a profit split, or perhaps sourcing based on bonuses paid to employees. Alworth (1998) is less sanguine, and suggests that it would be desirable for large businesses to be taxed on accrual of gains and losses, although the record keeping necessary for this approach makes it difficult for individual taxpayers. In any case, exchange of information is likely to prove to be important in enforcing residence tax systems in this area as in others in the information age.

A technical issue that emerged in the 1990s involves 'buy-ins'. A buy-in is a payment for pre-existing intangible assets. New technology-related companies have used buy-ins to allocate the development costs of an intangible asset in a joint development project involving a parent and a subsidiary (usually located in a low-tax country). Costs are normally allocated according to anticipated benefits of the project, but it is the fact that anticipated benefits are unknown that creates the controversy. Morgan (1999) argues that the arm's length price for the buy-in can be approximated by the subsidiary's cost of capital, while corporations argue that the buy-in payment should be much lower, effectively increasing the amount of income in the low-tax subsidiary.

6 Conclusion

Intra-firm transactions are common in large corporations. The price attached to such non-market transactions is called the transfer price. Transfer prices are particularly important for a multinational corporation since such a firm's transactions typically cross international borders. As the world has become increasingly interdependent, such transactions have become more commonplace, and have come under a great deal of scrutiny. Of primary concern to governments has been the tax consequences of transfer prices. A multinational corporation may be able to use transfer prices to transfer revenue to low-tax subsidiaries and costs to high-tax subsidiaries and thereby transfer profits from high- to low-tax countries. The empirical evidence indicates that multinationals are able to successfully reduce their worldwide taxes to some extent. To control these possible abuses, a generally accepted international practice is to use the arm's length method, which attempts to price a transaction as if it had occurred between two unrelated parties.

TIMOTHY J. GOODSPEED
HUNTER COLLEGE

Further reading

(References cited in the text marked *)

* Alworth, Julian S. (1998) 'Taxation and integrated financial markets: the challenges of derivatives and other financial innovations', *International Tax and Public Finance* 5: 507–34. (Contains a detailed discussion of the consequences of taxing various types of financial instruments.)

Dunning, John H. (1993) *Multinational Enterprises and the Global Economy*, New York: Addison-Wesley. (Chapter 18 provides a comprehensive and non-technical review of (especially non-tax) factors affecting a firm's transfer pricing decision.)

* Elitzur, Ramy and Jack Mintz (1996) 'Transfer pricing rules and corporate tax competition', *Journal of Public Economics* 60 (3): 401–22. (Develops a model that illustrates certain sorts of interactions between transfer pricing and tax competition.)

* Frisch, Daniel J. (1989) 'The BALRM approach to transfer pricing', *National Tax Journal* 261–71. (A discussion of how BALRM (the basic arm's length return method) can be interpreted in terms of the capital asset pricing model, a foundation of modern finance.)

Giovannini, Alberto, R. Glenn Hubbard and Joel Slemrod. (eds) (1993) *Studies in International Taxation*, Chicago: University of Chicago Press. (Provides several empirical studies on the effect of transfer pricing including the chapters by Harris, Morck, Slemrod, and Yeung and Grubert, Goodspeed, and Swenson mentioned in the text.)

* Goodspeed, Timothy J. (1998) 'Tax competition, benefit taxes, and fiscal federalism', *National Tax Journal* 60 (3): 579–86. (Discusses the issues involved in tax competition from the perspective of the fiscal federalism literature and the difficulties in empirically estimating the effect of tax competition.)

* Goodspeed, Timothy J. (2000) 'Tax structure in a federation', *Journal of Public Economics* 75 (3): 493–506. (An empirical examination of tax competition in a federation.)

* Grubert, Harry, Timothy J. Goodspeed and Deborah Swenson. (1993) 'Explaining the low taxable income of foreign-controlled companies in the United States', in Alberto Giovannini, R. Glenn Hubbard and Joel Slemrod (eds) *Studies in International Taxation*, University of Chicago Press, ch. 7: 237–70. (Empirical study of inbound transfer pricing for the USA; explains about half of the difference in returns between US and foreign

controlled companies by reasons other than transfer pricing.)

Grubert, Harry and John Mutti (1991) 'Taxes, tariffs, and transfer pricing in multinational corporate decision making', *Review of Economics and Statistics* 68: 285–93. (An empirical study of transfer pricing on outbound transactions that finds support for the tax minimizing hypothesis.)

* Harris, David, Randall Morck, Joel Slemrod and Bernard Yeung (1993) 'Income shifting in U.S. multinational corporations', in Alberto Giovannini, R. Glenn Hubbard and Joel Slemrod (eds) *Studies in International Taxation*, University of Chicago Press, ch. 8: 277–302. (Empirical study of transfer pricing for outbound investment that finds support for tax minimizing behaviour, although the magnitude is not large.)

* Hines, James R., Jr. and Eric M. Rice (1994) 'Fiscal paradise: foreign tax havens and American business', *Quarterly Journal of Economics* 149–82. (An empirical study of transfer pricing activities of US multinationals in very low-tax countries (tax havens).)

* Horst, Thomas (1993) 'The comparable profits method', *Tax Notes International* 14 June: 1443–58. (A discussion of the rules suggested by the Internal Revenue Service of the USA for dealing with transfer pricing and some practical problems with those rules.)

Lowell, C.H., M. Burge and P.L. Briger (1994) *US International Transfer Pricing*, Boston, MA: Warren, Gorham and Lamont. (A complete guide for the practitioner, including regulations, methodology, penalties, treaties and rules for several foreign countries.)

* Morgan, R. William (1999) 'Buy-in payments and market valuations', *Tax Management Transfer Pricing Report* 8 (10): 449–54. (Discussion of the issues and controversy surrounding buy-in payments.)

OECD (1991) *Taxing Profits in a Global Economy*, Paris: OECD. (A large study that calculates effective tax rates for the OECD countries; of interest here is the description of the international tax systems of member countries.)

* OECD (1995) *Transfer Pricing Guidelines for Multinational Enterprises and Tax Administrations*, Paris: OECD. (Guidelines that confirm the commitment of the OECD to arm's length pricing.)

* OECD (1998) *The Taxation of Global Trading of Financial Instruments*, Paris: OECD. (Description and discussion of the issues raised by global trading of financial instruments.)

* Pak, Simon and John Zdanowicz (1994) 'A statistical analysis of the U.S. merchandise trade data base and its uses in transfer pricing compliance and enforcement', in *Tax Management Transfer Pricing Report*, 11 May: 50–7. (Empirical tabulations using reported data of actual transactions that show some large discrepancies between certain products and their normal price.)

Rugman, A.M. and L. Eden (eds) (1985) *Multinationals and Transfer Pricing*, London: Croom Helm. (A discussion of many of the non-tax issues in transfer pricing.)

* Weiner, Joann M. and Hugh J. Ault (1998) 'The OECD's report on harmful tax competition', *National Tax Journal* 60 (3): 601–8. (A discussion of the OECD's report on harmful tax competition.)

* Witte, Ann and Tasneem Chipty (1990) 'Some thoughts on transfer pricing', *Tax Notes* 26 November: 1009–24. (Develops some issues in transfer pricing, including use of the capital asset pricing model employed in finance.)

See also: ECONOMIC INTEGRATION, INTERNATIONAL; GLOBALIZATION; GROWTH OF THE FIRM AND NETWORKING; INTERNATIONAL MONETARY FUND; MULTINATIONAL CORPORATIONS; WORLD BANK; WORLD TRADE ORGANIZATION

Industrial dynamics

1. Introduction
2. Emergence, decline and rebirth of industrial dynamics
3. Understanding paradoxical stylized facts
4. Understanding the industry life cycle
5. Understanding the evolution of industry
6. Research agenda
7. Conclusion

Overview

Industrial dynamics is basically dedicated to the study of the drivers of the evolution of industries. In this sense, the analysis of the dynamics of the industry seeks to capture major variables driving the processes of entry/exit, innovation and growth, and to understand their evolution over time. At a more aggregate level, industrial dynamics also seeks to analyse how the emergence, the development or the decline of various industries may influence the economic growth of modern economies. Whatever the chosen level of analysis, the study of industrial dynamics requires the collection of empirical evidence, firstly, to define major stylized facts and regularities of evolution, and secondly, to build a consistent analysis of why and how industries evolve and contribute to economic change. An increasing number of publications are available on this theme, but a full understanding of the dynamics and evolution of industries remains underdeveloped.

1 Introduction

Industrial dynamics focuses on the way in which the activities undertaken within the economic system are divided up among firms: some firms embrace many different activities while, for others, the range is narrowly circumscribed; some firms are large and others are small; some are vertically integrated but others are not. Industrial dynamics not only describes and analyses how the industry is organized now, but also how it differs from what it was in earlier periods: what forces were operative in bringing about this reorganization of the industry and how these forces have been changing over time. The study of industrial dynamics demands a permanent and sound connection between facts and theory. The stimulus provided by the patterns, puzzles and anomalies revealed by systematic data gathering and careful collection of detailed information is essential to make progress in the understanding of the forces which determine the dynamics of the industry.

Industrial dynamics is crucial for understanding the coherence that exists within a specific industry – for instance, what determines its boundaries, who does what and why within the industry, and what forces are central to its functioning – as well as the diversity which may be observed among different industries. Industrial dynamics requires a sound knowledge of the firms composing the industry and is intended to provide some guidelines for industrial and macroeconomic policies.

The object of this entry is to show that major advances have been made in the analysis of industrial dynamics since the 1980s. Nevertheless, much remains to be done. Three main elements will be considered here. First, the study of industrial dynamics has not been constant over time. Despite early work that underlined the importance of industrial dynamics studies, work on this topic was sparse from the 1950s to the 1980s, a period in which mainstream industrial organization held centre stage in the economics literature. Second, knowledge concerning industrial dynamics is still partial. The renewed interest in the literature focuses on specific dimensions of industrial dynamics that are examined in depth. But other important dimensions are still emerging domains of research. The difficulty lies in the fact that industrial dynamics is closely linked to notions such as the processes of innovation and economic growth, the analysis of which generally requires the economist to go beyond the conventional teachings of mainstream industrial organization. Third, in the age of globalization, the concept of a 'national system of innovation', which has been used to study how the coevolution of technologies and institutions favours economic growth, is now being questioned.

2 Emergence, decline and rebirth of industrial dynamics

Even if some authors such as Alfred Marshall (1890) and Joseph Schumpeter (1939) stressed the importance of studies in industrial dynamics, the economic literature from the 1950s to the 1980s turned essentially to the static analysis of structure, behaviour and performance (see MARSHALL, A.; SCHUMPETER, J.). Marshall, however, proposed many lines of inquiry which could have been developed: the fact that the economy is composed of different sectors, the growth and decline of which is unequal and intrinsically dependent on the organization of knowledge; the fact that the growth of knowledge is linked to the ability of firms to ensure a coherence between internal economies (organization and direction of the resources of the firm) and external economies (general development of the economy). Schumpeter also made significant work emphasizing the different forms of innovation and the role of the entrepreneur in this process. He made some crucial contributions to the analysis of the evolution of industry in a context of radical change and innovation. He stressed that specific forms of organization were useful to ensure the development through time of the industry.

These contributions, which provided first steps towards the elaboration of an industrial dynamics approach, were neglected, presumably because what was lacking in such a literature was a comprehensive theory that could analyse the determinants of the dynamics of the industry. Despite the willingness to deal with industrial dynamics in all its richness and complexity, these contributions were generally taken as descriptive, disparate, and not sufficient to analyse how the structures and forms of organization of industries changed over time. The need for a unified theoretical framework appeared a priority and emerged rapidly within mainstream industrial organization, with different and successive refinements. The post-Second World War decades were characterized by the development of analyses of industrial organization that focused on optimality properties and on comparative efficiency studies of different equilibrium situations, while ignoring the conditions under which an industry could emerge and evolve over time – the core conditions of industrial dynamics. This mainstream economic thinking prevailed in a period in which major changes were taking place in industry structure, economic growth and changes in industrial leadership on an international level, and despite the prior existence of the preliminary dynamic theories of economic development to be found especially in Marshall and Schumpeter. Within the mainstream perspective, from the late 1950s to the 1960s, the structure–conduct–performance paradigm, at the core of the Harvard tradition, focused essentially on the determinants of features of market structure and performance, such as concentration, firms' size and profitability. In the 1970s and the 1980s, this vision was challenged by the Chicago School and by the theory of 'contestable markets'. At the same time, the transaction cost approach reintroduced the important question of integration versus specialization (see COASE, R.; TRANSACTION COST ECONOMICS). Finally, the New Industrial Organization, using the apparatus of game theory, analysed the characteristics of different market behaviour where strategic interactions prevailed. These different analyses were major advances in the development of conventional industrial organization. But, in retrospect, they made meagre contributions to the specific problem of industrial dynamics; they were not based on a dynamic framework but on a static one (as in the Harvard tradition where production functions were left unexplained), or their unit of analysis was not the industry but transactions (as in the transaction cost approach) or rational behaviour (as in the New Industrial Organization) (see Krafft 2000).

A rebirth of industrial dynamics as an attractive field of investigation occurred in the 1980s through two lines of inquiry: the assessment of paradoxical stylized facts and the understanding of the life cycle of the industry. In the 1990s, a third line of inquiry emerged, spurred by empirical research that revealed in a systematic manner a significant gap between stylized facts about industrial dynamics and theories. This third dimension focuses especially on the understanding of the evolution of industry, and can be viewed as a new departure in the study of industrial organization that builds on the neglected work of Marshall and Schumpeter.

3 Understanding paradoxical stylized facts

Empirical research during the 1980s exhibited the following paradoxical stylized facts. At the microeconomic level, there are persistent diversity and high turbulence in the industrial dynamics within and across industrial sectors, while at more aggregate levels there are significant regularities characterizing industrial dynamics. Industrial dynamics is analysed through specific features such as the persistence of the asymmetric performance of firms, turbulence and industrial demography, firm growth and size distribution (see Geroski 1995, for a general presentation). Firms are intrinsically different in their cost and productivity, profitability, output and innovative strategies. These asymmetries in performance are generally persistent over time. In most industries, however, turbulence in demography is observed through birth and mortality rates. Birth rates are high, entrants are generally new, small and below the efficient minimum scale, but they can also be existing firms operating in other industries or countries. The probability of survival increases with age and depends on the initial size and on growth rates. Mortality rates also tend to be high and turbulence is primarily a characteristic of the fringe of the industry. Concerning growth rates of firms, Gibrat's law states that they are random variables independent of size: the growth rate of a new entrant, being initially large or small, will be driven by a purely stochastic process.

Industry-specific dimensions may complement the preceding firm-specific variables and may be used to assess the regularities observed at more aggregate levels. For instance, asymmetry in performance is in fact a more persistent phenomenon in highly concentrated industries where demand growth is rapid, economies of scale are important, sunk costs are large and advertising expenditures are high. Turbulence also differs drastically across sectors. The general result is that there is a decreasing probability of survival for new and small firms in capital intensive, highly innovative and high economies of scale industries. Finer results appear moreover when the timing of survival is considered. Concentration, economies of scale and capital intensity at the level of the industry increase survival of firms in the short run, but not in the long run. Conversely, innovation does not affect survival in the short run, but only in the long run, except in industries where small firms are important drivers of innovation. Growth of firms is favoured in innovative industries, especially in early periods after entry.

These empirical findings are paradoxical compared with mainstream industrial organization results (see EVOLUTIONARY THEORIES OF THE FIRM). These empirical observations tend to be inconsistent with the main characteristics of industrial organization models – such as entry positively correlated to supranormal profits, entry rates explained by specific indicators such as profitability or barriers to entry, average margins of firms linked with entry at the industry level. In this first group of models, the purpose is then, through empirical studies at the industry level or at the national level, to show that conventional theories of industrial organization do not necessarily provide a reliable framework for understanding industrial dynamics. However, the tools used in mainstream industrial organization, namely the definition of optimal properties and the comparative analysis of different equilibrium situations (see *Handbook of Industrial Organization*, edited by R. Schmalensee and T. Willig (1989)), remain at the core of the models. As a consequence, industrial dynamics is generally considered in this case to be a subdomain (counter-intuitive, in most cases) of conventional industrial organization, but the empirical data gathering revealing the puzzles and anomalies do not imply major changes to the analytical framework.

4 Understanding the industry life cycle

This second family of models derives from a hybrid analytical framework: some notions are inspired by mainstream industrial organization, but the global analytical framework is evolutionary-based. As a consequence, the conclusions of this kind of model can be interpreted in different ways. Evolutionary-minded economists, for example, will focus on industry life-cycle studies of the historical path-dependency of firms progressing on a new technological trajectory. Mainstream-minded economists will use this family of models to provide evidence on the industry structure (especially on the interactions between incumbents and new entrants) according to the different phases of the life cycle.

Industry life-cycle models, however, can be considered as an important attempt, not only to define major stylized facts and regularities in the evolution of industries, but also to build a consistent analysis of why and how industries evolve and contribute to economic change.

Different major stylized facts and regularities are observed. Production increases in the initial phases of the development of the industry, and then declines; entries are numerous in the beginning and tend to be exceeded by exits over time, especially when a shakeout occurs; market shares are highly volatile in the first steps and become more precisely defined later; product innovation is replaced by process innovation; first movers generally enjoy a long-term leadership; a dominant design and a process of standardization tend to appear over time.

The analytical explanation of industrial change is the following. Industries, like bio-organisms, face different stages during their lifetime, and these stages imply modifications in their characteristics. The first stage begins with the introduction of a new product on the market, either by the inventor or the first producer, and this period corresponds to the emergence of a new industry. At that time, the size of the market is narrowly defined, and there is a high uncertainty on the future growth of this market. The product is like a prototype without any clear definition of applications and, further, of potential demand. This first stage ends with the emergence of new producers (new entrants). The length of this period depends on the size of the market just after the introduction of the product, on the number of potential entrants and on their ability to copy the product innovation. The second stage is characterized by an increase in the number of incumbent producers. Output growth is high and the final design of the product is now available. In the third stage, net entry is around zero. Product innovation is decreasing and is replaced by process innovation. This stage ends with the decline of gross entry rate. The fourth stage involves a negative net entry. The fifth stage reflects the maturity of the market in which a number of incumbent firms exit from the industry: the shakeout occurs.

In this former model (which is based on two initial papers: one by Abernathy and Utterback (1978) that observes some regularities in the evolution of the automobile industry in the USA, and one by Gort and Klepper (1982) that derives empirical observations from forty-six industries), industrial dynamics depends on the changing nature of innovation. From stage to stage, both access to information and profit opportunities condition the innovative behaviour of firms. In the early stages of the cycle, information is freely accessible, opportunities for profits are high, and product innovation is favoured by the entry of new entrants. In later stages of the cycle, incumbents keep the technological information for themselves and enjoy opportunities for profit essentially through process innovation. Entries are decreasing, exits are numerous and a shakeout occurs. The whole sequence of events (entry, innovation, learning and growth) determines industrial dynamics all through the life cycle.

In the late 1980s and 1990s, the analytical content was refined by a series of complementary contributions (see Klepper 1997, for a general presentation) which have either an evolutionary or a mainstream flavour. On the mainstream side, authors focused essentially on the reasons and causes of the shakeout that corresponds to a phase of firms' concentration, and more generally to the emergence of oligopolies. Some of them stress that the shakeout is directly linked to the dominant design, which is itself a consequence of a rational choice under uncertainty. For others, survival in the phase of shakeout is driven by a stochastic process generated by exogenous technological change. On the evolutionary side, learning and adaptation capacities of firms developed in life-cycle models are used to analyse the process of competition, seen as a selection in a context of endogenous technological change. Moreover, industrial life-cycle models are useful to analyse the link between 'Schumpeter Mark 1' evolutionary models – in which entry is easy from a technological point of view, new small firms are the main engines of innovation, technological and competitive advantage of incumbents are progressively eroded – and 'Schumpeter Mark 2' evolutionary models – in which entry barriers are high for new small innovators, big incumbent firms are the main engines of innovation, a small number of incumbent firms are leaders in technology and competition. Recent research has been dedicated then to the definition of different cohorts of entrants, developing different innovation capabilities according to their specific dates of entry, and implying different evolutionary models for industrial dynamics.

Empirical studies have improved upon the analytical explanations. For instance, new entrants and latecomers generally survive better than others because the timing of their entry coincides with low exit rates (on stages 1, 2 and 5). However, if new entrants are generally the leaders of the industry, the survival of latecomers is linked with their specialization on specific segments of the industry. The process of competition in which new entrants and latecomers are engaged is primarily driven by technological innovation that necessitates a suitable accumulation of learning and competences over time. Finally and more generally, an industry is deemed not to have experienced a shakeout if the number of firms never declines below 70 per cent of the peak number, or if it does but subsequently recovers to over 90 per cent of the peak. These refinements and empirical investigations reveal an important underlying question: does the life cycle provide a general model that captures the way many industries evolve? If, for some authors, the answer is positive, others are more cautious about the potential of extension of the model to any industry. Klepper (1997) considers the life-cycle model to apply to only six industries, namely, typewriters, automobile tyres, commercial aircraft for trunk carriers, televisions, television picture tubes and penicillin).

Life-cycle models also have some connections with the national systems of innovation approach. A country can be characterized by a life cycle or, at least, by the age of its leading industries. Inter-country comparisons are then possible regarding the link between innovation and economic growth, according to the respective phases of the life cycle of these countries. Freeman (1989) notices, however, that economic growth cannot be considered as a pure product of the capacity to produce innovations in a country, as is implicitly assumed in life-cycle models. Moreover, unlike the life-cycle models in which a new cycle begins as soon as the new product is launched on the market, technological opportunities cannot be considered as given, but can be constructed in coherence with institutions at the national level. On this point, the work by the various authors in Lundvall (1992) suggests that innovation is dependent on the articulation between different institutional levels (namely, the firm, the industry and the nation), and that this articulation is crucial for innovation to involve economic growth.

The specificity of this second group of analysis is that, at the outset, empirical studies at the industry or national level are not dedicated to illustrating a pre-existing model. The problem is rather to elaborate a new analytical framework of the evolution of industries in which innovation and growth phenomena prevail. This analytical framework in terms of life cycle is based on a biological–evolutionary analogy, and is considered as different – though, for some commentators, possibly complementary – to conventional analysis of industrial organization. This approach confronts the notion that the life cycle can be considered a universal model in which the complex analysis of an evolving economy is then confined to the main regularities presented in life cycle models. If this vision were to be generalized, industrial dynamics will then be reduced to the study of one specific model and, as such, will tend to neglect the wide variety of industrial evolutions observed in the real world.

5 Understanding the evolution of industry

Within the third group of literature, which is more heterogeneous than the two preceding ones, a wider range of questions is analysed (Malerba and Orsenigo 1996). How do products and processes change throughout the evolution of an industry? Who are the new entrants? Are they new firms or are they established firms coming from other industries? How were they able to enter the market? What are their main strategies concerning production, innovation and finance? How do firms develop and modify their capabilities and activities to provide different products and process innovations? How do the boundaries of firms evolve in terms of specialization, vertical integration and long-term relations with suppliers and users? How do these different changes modify the boundaries of the industry? How can these boundaries be defined? How do specific institutions, such as universities, and financial or public institutions contribute to the evolution of industries? Different complementary work – based on different methodologies – is proposed to address these questions, generally with an intellectual background in the study of innovation and economic growth that is different from mainstream economics. In this context, patterns, puzzles and anomalies revealed by empirical work are used to make progress in the analysis of the forces that drive the dynamics of industry: they are dedicated to opening up the research agenda through a systematic process of validation/refutation of assumptions.

The first type of work intends to determine regular patterns of evolution for industries that do not conform closely to the life cycle. Three different elements can be identified as sources of alternative patterns of evolution: the presence of vertical relationships between suppliers and consumers; the elaboration of horizontal cooperation; and the diversity of demand. If these elements are present (either in isolation or in combination), the main conclusions of life-cycle models are no longer valid. For instance, product innovation can persist over time, entry can be spurred even in later stages of the life cycle and dominant design may never exist (Nelson 1998; Langlois and Robertson 1995).

The second type of work provides a detailed historical account of different industries, and elaborates and uses large longitudinal micro-databases. The purpose is to understand the impact of internal organization of the enterprise on inter-enterprise cooperation and competition, as well as on national performance. Connections between different disciplines, especially industrial organization and business history, are necessary. The work is not reduced to a simple reading of economic textbooks in the light of history. It offers a more fruitful perspective, which consists of elaborating empirical economic research programmes in relation to business history. By focusing on the conditions that guide the choices of firms, and not only on the result of these choices, an opportunity is given to get a picture of the competitive dynamics and of the drivers of secular changes in the industry in a way that is different from and very much richer than what comes naturally from the industry-level and even more aggregated data of the conventional statistical sources. Some authors, such as Lazonick (1991), develop then a history-based analysis of the dynamics of firms and industries, especially in an innovative context. Others, such as Lamoreaux, Raff and Temin (1998), make business history accessible to economists in order to improve economic models in terms of information coordination. Detailed case studies on specific industries make more precise the connection between industrial organization and business history: see, for instance, Dosi (1984) on semiconductors; Gambardella (1995) on biotechnology; Fransman (1995) on computers and telecommunications. Malerba *et al.* (1999) suggest that formalizations of the key historical features of industrial dynamics are possible. The basic framework of their 'history friendly modelling' is the development of an appreciative theory which is dedicated to reflecting what the analysts and the empirical researchers believe is really going on, their arguments presenting causal explanations of observed patterns of economic phenomena. The aim then is to build formal models to capture the gist of the appreciative theory put forth by analysts of the history of an industry or a technology. Within this perspective, formal modelling is used to identify gaps in the logic of more informal accounts and to lead to the consideration of mechanisms and factors that initially are missing or muted. The computer industry provides a first example of application of the history-friendly models, but extensions are of course needed to see how formalization can contribute to the extension of the research agenda on industrial dynamics.

Finally, a third type of work investigates the relationship between the evolution of industry and systems of innovations. Nelson (1996) notes that even if globalization stands out as a dominant system, a debate on 'technological-national' specificities still exists. The question is then: how can we characterize systems of innovation in the age of globalization? The answer is not obvious because industrial dynamics may be independent of national institutions. Firms' strategies have a coherence that goes generally beyond the limits of the nation. More generally, globalization involves a conception of firms' strategies in which nations are not the best units of analysis. Systems of innovation and industrial dynamics are based then intrinsically on an economic coherence that has to be investigated in depth. Localization is just an element of this economic coherence, and national systems of innovation are increasingly questioned.

6 Research agenda

Despite the richness and variety of the literature on industrial dynamics, most parts of the research on this theme are still in progress. Innovation and economic growth, which are fundamental notions for understanding industrial dynamics, require the development of new analytical frameworks that are still only emerging, as we have seen in the preceding sections. Three specific issues (at least) can be considered as patterns or regularities of industrial dynamics that researchers have to investigate within the next few years. First, innovation is a complex process that may be either major or incremental, and that generates recurrent and diverse changes on the evolution of industry. Second, entry tends to occur in specific periods of evolution, but not necessarily after the introduction of a major innovation. Third, the evolution of the industry is characterized by different processes of specialization, integration and diversification, which are emerging at specific periods.

7 Conclusion

The challenge of industrial dynamics is to make compatible, on the one hand, detailed and rich empirical knowledge of the evolution of industries and, on the other hand, a sound theoretical framework adapted to this richness and complexity. To proceed along the path opened up by early authors such as Marshall and Schumpeter, the following tasks are necessary.

- The collection of more accurate empirical evidence on industries, and especially on the homogeneity of the procedure, for the collection of data in order to favour the comparison and confrontation of results.
- The elaboration of taxonomies of industrial evolution in order to define some groups of industries that evolve in a similar way.
- The identification of the main relationships between firms and suppliers, customers, competitors, and more generally governmental, scientific or financial institutions.
- The necessity to propose new definitions of industries, not exclusively related to products or markets, and to infer new propositions to analyse the process of competition in a dynamic setting.
- The understanding of the link between the evolution of industries, innovation and economic growth, and their implications at the local, national or international level.

JACKIE KRAFFT
UNIVERSITÉ DE NICE – SOPHIA ANTIPOLIS

Further reading

(References cited in the text marked *)

* Abernathy, W. and Utterback, J. (1978) 'Patterns of industrial innovation', *Technology Review* 80: 41–7. (A basic paper on life-cycle models.)
* Dosi, G. (1984) *Technical Change and Industrial Transformation: The Theory and an Application to the Semiconductor Industry*, London:

Macmillan. (Describes and analyses the evolution of the semiconductor industry.)
* Fransman, M. (1995) *Japan's Computer and Communications Industry*, Oxford: Oxford University Press. (Describes and analyses the evolution of the computer industry.)
* Freeman, C. (1989) *Technology Policy and Economic Performance: Lessons from Japan*, London and New York: Pinter Publishers. (Analyses the coevolution of technologies and institutions with reference to national systems of innovation.)
* Gambardella, A. (1995) *Science and Innovation*, Cambridge: Cambridge University Press. (Describes and analyses the biotechnology industry.)
* Geroski, P. (1995) 'What do we know about entry?', *International Journal of Industrial Organization* 13: 421–40. (A prescriptive survey of recent empirical work on entry.)
* Gort, M. and Klepper, S. (1982) 'Time paths in the diffusion of product innovations', *Economic Journal* 92 (67): 630–53. (A basic paper on the life-cycle model.)
* Klepper, S. (1997) 'Industry life cycles', *Industrial and Corporate Change* 6 (1): 145–81. (Explains both the refinements and the limits of industry life-cycle models.)
* Krafft, J. (ed.) (2000) *The Process of Competition*, Cheltenham: Edward Elgar. (Analyses and compares the different notions of competition in a dynamic setting.)
* Lamoreaux, N., Raff, D. and Temin, P. (eds) (1998) *Learning by Doing in Firms, Markets and Nations*, Chicago: University of Chicago Press. (Analyses industrial dynamics through the specific problem of information coordination.)
* Langlois, R. and Robertson, P. (1995) *Firms, Markets and Economic Change*, London and New York: Routledge. (Provides an analysis of the organization of industry in terms of integration/specialization; includes case studies.)
* Lazonick, W. (1991) *Business Organization and the Myth of the Economy*, Cambridge: Cambridge University Press. (Argues that changing modes in business organization is central to economic development, and that this relation is systematically ignored by economists who place the market mechanism and equilibrium at the centre of their analyses.)
* Lundvall, B. (ed.) (1992) *National Systems of Innovation: Towards a Theory of Innovation and Interactive Learning*, London and New York: Pinter Publishers. (Analyses the coevolution of technologies and institutions with reference to national systems of innovation.)
* Malerba, F. and Orsenigo, L. (1996) 'The dynamics of evolution of industries', *Industrial and Corporate Change* 5 (1): 51–87. (A prescriptive survey on industrial dynamics.)
* Malerba, F., Nelson, R., Orsenigo, L. and Winter, S. (1999) 'History friendly models of industry evolution: the computer industry', *Industrial and Corporate Change* 8 (1): 3–40. (An attempt to provide formal economic models based on historical evolution of industries.)
* Marshall, A. (1890) *The Principles of Economics*, London: Macmillan. (A basic reference for the origins of the industrial dynamics issue.)
* Nelson, R. (1996) *The Sources of Economic Growth*, Cambridge and London: Harvard University Press. (Questions the validity of the concept of a national system of innovation.)
* Nelson, R. (1998) 'The coevolution of technology, industrial structure and supporting institutions', in G. Dosi, D. Teece and J. Chytry (eds) *Technology, Organisation and Competitiveness: Perspective on Industrial and Corporate Change*, Oxford: Oxford University Press. (Stresses the major limits of life-cycle models.)
* Schmalensee, R. and Willig, T. (1989) *Handbook of Industrial Organization*, Amsterdam: North Holland. (A basic book for mainstream industrial organization.)
* Schumpeter, J.A. (1939) *Business Cycles*, New York: McGraw-Hill. (A basic reference for the origins of the industrial dynamics issue.)

See also: AEROSPACE INDUSTRY; AUTOMOBILE INDUSTRY; BIOTECHNOLOGY; CHEMICAL INDUSTRY; COASE, R.; COOPERATION AND COMPETITION; CORPORATE CONTROL; DEVELOPMENT AND DIFFUSION OF TECHNOLOGY; ECONOMIC GROWTH AND CONVERGENCE; ELECTRONICS INDUSTRY; EVOLUTIONARY THEORIES OF THE FIRM; GLOBAL MACHINE TOOL INDUSTRY; GROWTH OF THE FIRM AND NETWORKING; INDUSTRIAL AGGLOMERATIONS; INSTITUTIONAL ECONOMICS; MARSHALL, A.; MARX, K.; SCHUMPETER, J.; SMALL AND MEDIUM SIZED ENTERPRISES; SMITH, A.; STEEL INDUSTRY; TELECOMMUNICATIONS INDUSTRY; TRANSACTION COST ECONOMICS; WILLIAMSON, O.E.

Cooperation and competition

1. Introduction
2. Industrial organization: market power and market failures
3. Knowledge and competence
4. Conclusion: key questions for the future

Overview

The notion of cooperation covers inter-firm cooperation or alliances; that is, the network of affiliations and agreements by which firms are interrelated. The firm can be defined as a unit of financial control that engages in three types of relations: (1) reversible contracts with other firms, i.e. single spot market relations, (2) cooperative agreements with other firms, (3) financial control over other firms through acquisition or, alternatively, the creation of a new unit of financial control through merger. The economic analysis of cooperation amounts to outlining the implications of cooperative agreements for economic performance and social welfare, given the alternative possibilities of market relations, on one side, and acquisition or merger on the other side.

The economic problem about cooperation is to study how firms' cooperative agreements interfere with competition. Since Adam Smith, economists have seen competition as the way in which economic performance and social welfare are enhanced, and cooperation as inimical to competition. Cooperation among competitors, particularly, is considered as highly suspect from an antitrust point of view. For example, in standard industrial organization textbooks, horizontal cooperation, that is agreements among rivals, is regarded as a collusion, whereas vertical cooperation like buyer–supplier relationships are viewed as enhancing efficiency. The last three decades of the twentieth century experienced a significant increase of joint ventures and agreements among firms, mainly due to industrial restructuring made necessary because of technological change and globalization. Since the 1980s, the academic literature has tended to integrate cooperation more fully into the analysis of the organization of industry and business institutions. Two main perspectives on the relation between cooperation and competition can be defined in the literature: one basically opposing cooperation to a static notion of competition as the benchmark of economic orthodoxy, and the other more opened to a dynamic conception of the relation between cooperation and competition where firms' internal organization can help to explain inter-firm relations.

1 Introduction

Inter-firm cooperation has been considered as an important phenomenon since the early 1980s. The role played by institutional arrangements among firms sometimes proved to be noteworthy in earlier days (e.g. cartels before the Second World War); however, empirical studies have shown that the number of cooperative agreements has substantially increased during the 1980s. Evidence from detailed sector studies indicates that most of these agreements take place in the fields of research and technology and 'high-tech' industries. Cooperative strategies are also important in international business. International alliances struck by US companies have increased in number since the 1970s; oil companies initiated the process, followed by carmakers and, in the late 1990s, information and telecommunication firms. In Europe, international alliances and R&D partnerships have been encouraged to meet the creation of the European single market and innovation policies of the European Community. The international corporate strategy of Japanese companies often entailed entering into beneficial joint-ventures and strategic alliances with Western firms. The NUMMI joint venture between Toyota and General Motors, formed to produce subcompact cars in California, was a step along the way as the giant Japanese carmaker expanded abroad. This celebrated case has been diversely analysed by economists. On one hand, it was considered to be a collusive mechanism and drew much attention to the highly concentrated aspect of the international automobile industry (Bresnahan and Salop 1986). On the other hand, it was analysed as a means for the stronger entry of Toyota into the American market, and thus as an increase in competition (see Sachwald 1998).

The above examples show that the relation between cooperation and competition has raised different issues and debates in the academic literature dedicated to industrial organization. The problem also concerns the domains of the theory of the firm, and organizational and business strategy theories (see GROWTH OF THE FIRM AND NETWORKING). Two main economic perspectives on cooperative agreements can be identified, depending on the way authors envision competition, either as a product market structure or as a market process. The first perspective is that of standard industrial organization where analyses focus on explanations based on market power or market failures. Each of these two explanations is more or less conducive to the acceptance of firms' cooperative as opposed to competitive behaviours, which remain the basic reference. The second perspective focuses on knowledge and competence implemented by business firms. In this case, the static definition of competition as a state of affairs is replaced by a more dynamic notion of competition as an ongoing process. This approach gives a greater hospitality to the existence of inter-firm as well as intra-firm cooperation within the theory of the firm and business management studies.

2 Industrial organization: market power and market failures

In a market power framework, markets are basically supposed to be efficient. The standard analysis of cooperation among competing firms considers that cooperation reduces competition, unless it is used to deal with externalities. Thus, collusion and externalities are the two main interpretative topics used to evaluate inter-firm agreements and alliances.

Recent economic analysis of collusive practices and mergers witnessed considerable changes with the development of game-theory. However, this led to a diversity of models and results which cannot help to find general conclusions about an appropriate policy dealing with industrial concentration (Jacquemin and Slade 1989). Horizontal collusion covers both explicit and tacit agreements. The principal forms of explicit agreements are cartels, joint ventures and horizontal mergers. Such agreements are generally considered as bringing restraint of trade: making price higher and output lower than it would otherwise have been inflicts a welfare loss on consumers. Because of antitrust, if explicit collusion is not allowed, firms can also have recourse to tacit collusion which replicates the effects of overt collusion, e.g. firms making identical price changes. Successful collusion requires communication between the firms about subjects such as prices, outputs and costs. In that case, agreements to exchange information are disapproved by most policy jurisdictions (Hay 1993). However, these conclusions can be questioned because agreements involving exchange of information may be needed to facilitate the establishment of successful cooperation which could promote economic efficiency by the sharing of market or technical information, and make prices more responsive to changes in demand and costs (see section 3).

Other aspects of the relation between cooperation and competition are accounted for in terms of welfare analysis. Cooperative agreements are generally considered as efficient where externalities are concerned: for instance, competitive advertising by oligopolists generates welfare losses, and agreements to limit such practice would therefore be beneficial. Similarly, agreements on R&D avoid wasteful duplication of research and allow risk sharing and the pooling of complementary skills. Cooperation among competitors may sometimes be essential for innovating firms, especially in a context of global markets. However, R&D joint ventures are not deemed as completely benign because research cooperation can be used by incumbents to deter entry of new competitors into their market.

In the framework of a market economy with perfect factor mobility and divisibility, and perfect reversibility of transactions, cooperation and alliances are generally supposed to appear because market competition may fail to achieve efficiency and optimality. The two main elements that lead to inefficient resource allocation are the existence of public goods and externalities. Institutional and informational solutions involving cooperative actions are designed to capture potential benefits that are not induced by market relations. For instance, public goods are provided collectively, so that no one can be excluded from their benefit. This principle of non-excludability leads to the 'free rider' problem, meaning that an individual, contrary to other users, can benefit from the public good without bearing any costs. The institutional solution of the problem is obtained by the intervention of the state in charge of the supplying of public goods. Other kinds of enforcement mechanisms are based on accurate dissemination of information concerning the actions of firms involved in cooperative agreements. Reputation, brand names or, more generally, long-term business relations and social norms have been described as enforcing cooperation. Mutual trust and codes of behaviour are the main characteristics for the long-run viability of formal or informal networking relationships that are at the centre of inter-firm cooperation. The main idea is that trust and cooperation can co-exist even in the case of self-seeking behaviour. This idea is the basis of the so-called 'new institutional economics' perspective that suggests a framework for the analysis of institutional relations in terms of transaction costs and contract theories.

In the realm of market failures, transaction cost and contract theories are the main analytical references for organizational theories. The first approach argues that agents can economize on transaction costs by organizing activities within the firm. Therefore a choice may be made between firms, within which coordination is by conscious planning, and markets, within which coordination is by spontaneous competition. Unlike standard industrial organization, transaction cost analysis focuses, not on market power or externalities, but on the efficient institutional response to market failures. This theory assumes that agents are only endowed with bounded rationality and that market relations are subject to *ex post facto* opportunistic behaviour, especially when transactions involve asset specificity, i.e. a situation where assets are not easily redeployable without costs. Given these hypotheses, a 'comparative institutional analysis' can be worked out: depending on the comparative efficiency of business institutions, transactions tend to be internalized into governance structures in case of market imperfections, and, alternatively, given back to the market in case of organizational failure.

Transaction cost theory has been mainly used to explain vertical integration and the multiproduct firm (see COASE, R.; TRANSACTION COST ECONOMICS). Vertical integration means that activities are organized in a single firm under hierarchical governance. However, hierarchy cannot exhaust the entire economies of scale or economies of scope, so that there may appear 'hybrid' modes of governance occupying an intermediate position between market and hierarchy (Williamson 1985). Cooperative agreements between firms are such hybrid modes, interpreted in terms of 'quasi-vertical' integration. For instance, Monteverde and Teece (1982) study the ownership by a downstream firm of specialized tools and patterns used in the fabrication of components for larger systems. In this form of subcontracting agreement, parties are engaged in transaction-specific investments creating an asymmetry in bargaining power. Consequently, an opportunistic subcontractor may appropriate 'short-term quasi-rent' by violating the terms of trade. This problem can be overcome by integrating the component supplier. In more general terms, firms resort to cooperation because the market is too vulnerable to post-contractual opportunism and because full vertical integration tends to diminish efficiency incentives. Different modes of interfirm cooperation have been studied in the transaction cost literature, among which international joint ventures, as well as subcontracting and franchising are special cases of quasi-integration and backward integration.

This approach is based on the necessity of enforcing contracts *ex ante* by credible commitments to avoid opportunism *ex post facto*.

That enforcement tends to transform the bounded rationality hypothesis into a stronger rationality hypothesis, and posit contracts as the basic unit of the analysis of industrial organization. Business institutions (firms, markets and inter-firm cooperation) are described as alternative bundles of contracts, understood as efficiency mechanisms designed to create incentives or to reduce incentive conflicts in situations of imperfect or asymmetric information.

The analyses of inter-firm cooperation described above argue within a framework dominated by market problems where productive and innovative considerations are almost completely left aside. In fact, the theory of the market economy fails to develop any theory of innovation, that is of knowledge creation, where cooperation could play a central role mainly through the developing of firms' competence. An alternative perspective on cooperation and competition can be presented, focusing more directly on production and innovation problems and the use of knowledge and competence resources by firms.

3 Knowledge and competence

Organizational theories develop another perspective appeals to activities, capabilities and competence implemented by business firms in the productive process. The so-called competence perspective argues that the process of competition is basically a process of knowledge creation and knowledge dissemination. In fact, the development and utilization of new knowledge is central to a theory of how a modern economy actually works.

The role of knowledge was first put forward by Hayek (1949) to explain the tendency towards equilibrium which secures the coordination of individual plans. The standard hypothesis of competition as a given state of affairs is replaced by the notion of competition as a genuine rivalry process. Market process is described as a 'discovery procedure' of the different kinds of private and local knowledge dispersed among individuals, leading to market 'order'. Disequilibrium creates profit opportunities for entrepreneurs endowed with superior 'alertness' to exert arbitrage based on information about price discrepancies, innovations possibilities and various exogenous shocks (Kirzner 1973). In this approach, the market process is in fact a device that creates market order or restores market equilibrium. The role of the market process or the entrepreneur is to discover *existing* knowledge and thereby move the economy closer to equilibrium.

In the knowledge and competence perspective, the notion of competition as a process focuses more precisely on the *creation* of new knowledge, that is the capacity of the economy to innovate. In such a process, cooperative efforts within and across firms are used to transform or escape from the conditions of equilibrium. Thus competition is a recurrent process where equilibrium is never achieved. This perspective refers more directly to the productive characteristics of the organization of industry (Langlois and Foss 1999), and asserts the importance of industrial activities carried out by firms, that is what firms actually do. Activities can be similar or complementary, depending on the firms' internal capabilities or competencies used to implement these activities (Richardson 1972). There is a multiplicity of ways in which complementary investments come to be coordinated – this coordination occurring either spontaneously within the market, or by means of different kinds of more specific inter-firm agreements, or else requiring deliberate planning under unified control.

The formal theory of the firm, expressed in terms of choice formulated into a given set of productive possibilities, abstracts totally from important elements that play a role in the organization of productive activities, such as knowledge, experience and skills. The productive rationale differs from a pure exchange one in that inter-firm cooperation is first of all opposed to pure market transactions. Market transactions become a limiting case in the *continuum* of cooperation and affiliations that are considered as constituting the essential institutional means to organize industry. The productive coordination of such business institutions is then analysed from a qualitative perspective, referring to an indefinite number of activities which denote not only manufacturing processes but relate to research, development and marketing activities carried out by organizations endowed with appropriate capabilities. The production process is viewed as a temporal process in which human resources and produced means of production are obtained during a construction period that precedes their utilization period. Because of the temporal articulation of the different phases of the production process, firms experience sunk costs due to irreversible commitments to specific assets and specific human resources.

In a period of economic change, in which new production processes and new products replace the old ones, production planning faces an uncertain future. An investment programme consisting of a set of planned activities is to be analysed as a tradeoff between specialization and flexibility, based on reciprocal and more or less fixed commitments, depending on the length of the investment period and the nature of uncertainty, as well as available market and technical information (Richardson 1990). In fact, uncertainty and unequal distribution of knowledge among individuals are supposed to facilitate the working of the whole system. It is so for the process of manufacturing which is not to be considered as a 'chemical reaction', but more properly as a process of 'trial and error', or search and discovery, the coordination of complementary investments being largely subject to dispersed information. In this context, transaction costs become 'knowledge costs' (Loasby 1994). Thus, vertical integration and cooperation appear to be more useful ways to cope with uncertainty than long-term contracts, for gaining control of complementary investments. Vertical integration is obtained in place of a detailed long-term contract, owing to the difficulty of forecasting. Cooperative agreements among firms are not simply hybrid modes taking place between market and hierarchy, but a specific mode of coordinating knowledge and activities which is alternative to both the market and the firm in the institutional division of labour that shapes the dynamics of the structure of industry.

Strategic and organizational considerations are also necessary to understand cooperation implemented to coordinate industrial activities and firms' competence in an innovative way. From a strategic management perspective, a fundamental issue is that cooperative agreements become a way for a firm to match its productive competence to its ever-changing environment. Strategic management thus aims at establishing coherent relationships between the competitive environment and the set of technological skills and organizational capabilities that provides the basis of the firm's competitive capacities on different markets. This approach leads to the analysis of firms' resources and their evolution, as well as the analysis of the evolution of cooperation. The distinction between 'codifiable' and 'tacit' knowledge, i.e. between easily transferable and less easily transferable – or idiosyncratic – knowledge, is at the root of the 'evolutionary theory' of the firm. In this literature, the firm is viewed as a pool of competences that conditions innovative activity (Nelson and Winter 1982). The internal structure of firms, as well as their network of external linkages, have an important bearing on the innovative activities conducted in the modern competitive economy (Teece 1996). The firm's ability to organize its growth (Penrose 1959) is also related to the analysis of competition as an ongoing innovative process. The 'economics of innovation' focuses on the idea that the point of arrival of the innovative process cannot be known in advance. Because of macroeconomic conditions, an enterprise that attempts to innovate faces two types of uncertainty: 'productive uncertainty' expressing the time lag between the resources invested and the returns generated, and 'competitive uncertainty' occasioned by the actions or reactions of competitors (Lazonick 1991). The successful innovative firm creates new knowledge through a process of collective and cumulative learning by developing integrated structures of abilities and incentives among its participants that helps to build and sustain a competitive advantage, and cannot be replicated through market coordination (O'Sullivan 2000).

The *ex ante* coordination highlighted in these approaches by no means takes the view that where there is cooperation competition disappears. In fact, competition is still at work even if it has changed its mode of operation. Monopoly should not emerge in any case simply because firms choose to come together.

There exists a force which compensates this tendency. This force is competition, but competition as a process. In this dynamic vision, market power and monopoly are in the main temporary states of affairs. Even if a sustainable competitive advantage has been obtained, this position is systematically attacked by new competitors disposing of new information and willing to take advantage of it.

4 Conclusion: key questions for the future

Further understanding of the relationship between cooperation and competition is mainly related to competition policy and the role of cooperation in the globalization of economic activities. Mainstream industrial organization argues that the purpose of competition policy is to promote economic efficiency, but remains ambiguous about the efficiency effects of various institutional arrangements implemented by firms. Given the ambiguity of welfare analysis, policy needs to identify rules and guidelines to trace the presumable boundaries between acceptable or unacceptable cooperative behaviours. Competition authorities have also to allow the parties involved some latitude to argue the efficiency benefits of their agreements. Besides, international harmonization of competition policies is recommended, as well as the setting up of some supranational competition authority (Hay 1993). The themes of competition as a process have permeated into standard industrial organization. Authors are becoming more conscious of the necessity to take into consideration the dynamic aspects of competition and to oppose productive efficiency to market efficiency (Vickers 1995). These aspects can justify not only a greater scope for the existence of inter-firm cooperation, but also their welfare effects to be accounted for in competition policies.

The vision of competition as a process suggests alternative rules for competition policy, and new criteria to antitrust exemptions to cooperation. For instance, United Kingdom competition policy does not focus essentially on economic efficiency. It also makes reference to long-run competition favoring new products and processes and furthering entry to the market (Fair Trading Act 1973, Section 84). On the other hand, competition law in the European Community, like in the USA, is much more focused on market competition and economic efficiency. Thus the Treaty of Rome, in Articles 85 and 86 dedicated to competition (Articles 81 and 82 of the New EC Treaty), prohibits restrictive agreements between firms and the abuse of dominant position. But there exist in Article 85, paragraph 3 of the Treaty of Rome (Article 81, paragraph 3 of the New EC Treaty), exemptions for agreements between firms that can be shown to be beneficial for the society. This is the case for R&D agreements aimed at promoting technical progress or improving economic progress, or agreements seeking to reduce production and distribution costs. The European competition authority is credited for having recognized very early that cooperation between large firms can be economically beneficial and politically desirable (Glais 2000).

Further studies on inter-firm cooperative agreements should focus on joint ventures and firms alliances as an important factor of globalization (Sachwald 1998). Because of R&D costs and products obsolescence, the coordination of international activities is more and more established on cooperative agreements rather than traditional direct foreign investments. The analysis of multinational enterprises, first focused on the analysis of competitive advantage and the decision to locate abroad, tends to parallel the evolution of the economic analysis of cooperation. Market failures at the international level have been analysed first as a problem of cultural differences leading to different perceptions of trust, inter-firm cooperative agreements being justified as a means to warrant 'mutual abstention' and to get acquainted with business practices abroad (Buckley and Casson 1988). Another explanation for the development of international agreements among firms must be found in the existence of 'imperfect' international markets, due to the tacit nature of knowledge involved and the relative differences between government rules and protectionist pressures. In fact, a knowledge and competence approach to the multinational enterprise can be advocated, focusing on the study of knowledge transfers and progressive changes in technology and competence. These different matters may help us to understand firm's competitiveness and their choice between regional and global cooperative strategies in the international competitive system.

JACQUES-LAURENT RAVIX
UNIVERSITY OF NICE – SOPHIA ANTIPOLIS

Further reading

* Bresnahan, T. and Salop, S. (1986) 'Quantifying the competitive effects of joint-ventures', *International Journal of Economic Organization* 4 (12): 155–75. (Proposes a measure of the influence of joint-venture on market power.)
* Buckley, P. and Casson, M. (1988) 'A theory of cooperation in international business', in F. Contractor and P. Lorange (eds) *Cooperative Strategies in International Business*, New York: Lexington Books. (An often-quoted paper on the analysis of international business.)
* Glais, M. (2000) 'Merger control law in the European Union', in J. Krafft (ed.) *The Process of Competition*, Cheltenham: Edward Elgar. (Examines competition policy in the light of different economic theories and case studies.)
* Hay, D. (1993) 'The assessment: competition policy', *Oxford Review of Economic Policy* 9 (2): 1–26. (Suggests propositions about the purpose, scope and implementation of competition policy.)
* Hayek, F.A. (1949) *Individualism and Economic Order*, London: Routledge & Kegan Paul. (A collection of Hayek's celebrated papers on knowledge and the process of competition.)
* Jacquemin, A. and Slade, M.E. (1989) 'Cartels, collusion, and horizontal merger', in R. Schmalensee and R.D. Willig (eds) *Handbook of Industrial Organization*, vol. I, Amsterdam, New York, Oxford, Tokyo: North-Holland. (The still basic reference of the game-theoretic approach to collusion and horizontal merger.)
* Kirzner, I. (1973) *Competition and entrepreneurship*, Chicago, IL: University of Chicago Press. (A pioneering book on the role of the entrepreneur in the market process.)
* Langlois, R.N. and Foss, N.J. (1999) 'Capabilities and governance: the rebirth of production in the theory of economic organization', *Kyklos* 52 (2): 201–18. (Shows that the capability perspective is conscious of the production side of the firm.)
* Lazonick, W. (1991) *Business Organization and the Myth of the Market Economy*, Cambridge University Press: Cambridge. (Analytical and historical perspectives on the innovative enterprise.)
* Loasby, B.J. (1994) 'Organizational capabilities and inter-firm relations', *Metroeconomica* 45 (3): 248–65. (Explains the coordination problem of industry as a consequence of the division of labour and the division of knowledge.)
* Monteverde, K. and Teece, D.J. (1982) 'Appropriable rents and quasi-vertical integration', *Journal of Law and Economics* 25 (2): 321–28. (An empirical analysis of subcontracting in the light of transaction cost economics.)
* Nelson, R. and Winter, S. (1982) *An Evolutionary Theory of Economic Change*, Cambridge MA: Harvard University Press. (The founding book of evolutionary economics.)
* O'Sullivan, M. (2000) 'The Innovative Enterprise and Corporate Governance', *Cambridge Journal of Economics* 24 (4): 393–416. (An operational presentation of the economics of innovation.)
* Penrose, E. (1959) *The Theory of the Growth of the Firm*, Oxford: Basil Blackwell. (Still a vivid theory of the firm and its competitive environment.)
* Richardson, G.B. (1972) 'The organization of industry', *Economic Journal* 82 (327): 883–96. (A path-breaking analysis of the organization of industry in the light of firms' activities and capabilities.)
* Richardson, G.B. (1990) *Information and Investment*, 2nd edn, Oxford: Oxford University Press. (One of the most authoritative books in the domain of knowledge and competence.)
* Sachwald, F. (1998) 'Cooperative agreements and the theory of the firm: focusing on barriers to change', *Journal of Economic Behaviour and Organization* 35 (2): 203–25. (Identifies the phenomenon of inter-firm cooperation and relates it to explanations in terms of the different available theories of the firm.)
* Teece, D.J. (1996) 'Firm organization, industrial structure, and technological innovation', *Journal of Economic Behaviour and Organization* 31 (2): 193–224. (Analyses the relations between the organizational structure of the firm and its innovative environment.)
* Vickers, J. (1995) 'Concepts of competition', *Oxford Economic Papers* 47 (1): 1–23. (Explains the links between market efficiency and productive efficiency leading to static and dynamic competition.)
* Williamson, O.E. (1985) *The Economic Institutions of Capitalism: Firms, Market, Relational Contracting*, New York: Free Press. (The basic book for an analysis of business institutions from a transaction cost perspective.)

See also: COASE, R.; CORPORATE CONTROL; DYNAMICS CAPABILITIES; EVOLUTIONARY THEORIES OF THE FIRM; EXCHANGE RATE ECONOMICS; GROWTH OF THE FIRM AND NETWORKING; INDUSTRIAL AGGLOMERATION; INDUSTRIAL DYNAMICS; INNOVATION; INSTITUTIONAL ECONOMICS; MANAGERIAL THEORIES OF THE FIRM; PENROSE, E.; SMALL AND MEDIUM SIZED ENTERPRISES; TRANSACTION COST ECONOMICS; WILLIAMSON, O.E.

Privatization and regulation

1. Institutional aspects of regulating the private sector
2. Economic theory
3. Privatization and regulation in the UK
4. The new research agenda
5. Regulating the regulators
6. The international telecommunications market
7. International developments
8. Conclusion

Overview

A feature of the global economy through the 1980s and 1990s, which appears set to continue into the next century, is the sweep of privatization. From the UK to Latin America, from the previously centrally planned economies to the emerging post-apartheid South Africa, industries previously in state ownership have been and continue to be sold off in one form or another to the private sector.

The trend toward privatization has inevitably found its reflection in economic theory. The previous era, which witnessed significant degrees of nationalization and state ownership through most of the Organization for Economic Cooperation and Development (OECD) economies, was generally interpreted in mainstream economics in terms of various forms of 'market failure' requiring state intervention. The mainstream response to privatization has therefore been to interpret the changing industrial ownership structure in terms of 'government failure' or 'public failure', which in turn must have come to outweigh the original market failure. (The balance can also be interpreted as having shifted through reductions in the degree of market failure with, for example, technological developments reducing the degree to which certain industries displayed natural monopoly characteristics.)

The economic and political factors behind the various types of privatization which have been pursued, and continue to be pursued, vary hugely between the very different country settings. Furthermore, developments such as the globalization of financial and capital markets, the growing activities of multinational corporations and the switch to a more free market orientation by international institutions, including the World Bank, all need to be analysed not only as the economic, political and institutional backdrop to the swing to private ownership but also as being fuelled by the very process of privatization itself across the globe.

In the case of the World Bank, its 1993 report *The East Asian Miracle* interprets the economic success of the high-performing southeast Asian economies as being 'primarily due to the application of a set of common, market-friendly economic policies' (World Bank 1993: vi). This is in marked contrast to the account given by Chang (1994) of South Korea's success, where an interventionist industrial policy, including the use of nationalization, is shown to have played a key role. Of course, the World Bank acknowledges that such policies were pursued, but makes a distinction between these, on the one hand, and market-friendly policies on the other, and chooses to recommend only the latter: 'The market-oriented aspects of southeast Asia's policies can be recommended with few reservations, but the more institutionally demanding aspects ... have not been successfully used in other settings' (World Bank 1993: vi–vii). However, this article argues that, to the extent that 'market-friendly' policies now embrace privatization, these have themselves become 'institutionally demanding' policies as new regulatory structures become required.

1 Institutional aspects of regulating the private sector

Privatization has become a global phenomenon with far-reaching implications, not only for those sectors of the economy transferred into the private sector, but also for firms already in the private sector. First, such private businesses may for the first time be able to tender for work previously reserved for public sector firms. Second, firms which dealt previously with public sector customers, suppliers or collaborators may now find that these have been transferred to the private sector. Third, private sector firms may find themselves faced with new competitors, as firms which were previously in the public sector have their former operating restrictions lifted. In addition, privatization has led to a significant increase in the state's regulatory activities over private business. While the new regulatory bodies are designed primarily to oversee the operation of enterprises formerly in the public sector, their regulatory activities necessarily impinge on private sector businesses. Affected businesses may be private sector firms operating in regulated areas where they previously could not – such as the newly licensed telecommunications operators in the UK – or simply private sector customers whose dealings with, say, British Telecom become subject to various forms of regulation, including price regulation.

In the economy of the future, business will therefore have to be conducted increasingly within regulated sectors, doing business with (and against) firms whose operations – and profit levels – are tightly regulated. The outputs of regulated industries may be traded internationally or at least have an impact on international trade; air travel, airports, financial services as well as gas and electricity are examples. As a result, regulation in one country may interact with that in others, and this will create in turn the possibility of cooperation and/or conflict between national regulatory authorities, and the opportunity or need for contractual relations between them.

The growing institutional use of contracts, made necessary to regulate the newly privatized sectors of the economy, raises the question of how state regulators can best influence those decisions where the outcome would otherwise be considered harmful (have negative externalities) when the wider effects on the economy and society are considered.

2 Economic theory

Economic theory would suggest a number of reasons for the private business sector having to be regulated, quite apart from the standard arguments concerning problems of monopoly power or unfair trading. The competitive advantage of any given company, for example, will depend crucially on long-term 'relational contracts' between the firm and its suppliers, customers, financiers, employees and others, which tend to reduce the uncertainty involved in market transactions. Relational contracts are restricted to some extent in the UK by the financial structure of the City of London, which is highly market-orientated, in contrast to the more institutional approach adopted in countries such as Germany and Japan. In addition to preventing the newly privatized companies from exercising their market power unduly, one aim of the regulatory bodies in the UK is to foster confidence among those who should be establishing 'relational contracts' with such enterprises. Therefore, regulators should show that regulated enterprises will indeed continue to operate in the future, neither having their markets swamped by new licensees nor having their future profits 'taxed' away by punitive price regulations.

There is a rather separate literature on globalization (see GLOBALIZATION), much of which would imply that, in the economy of the future, international business, far from having to face up to national regulatory regimes, will sweep such regulation aside as global operations bypass national governments, making any attempts at regulation futile. During the golden age of capitalism (1948–73), a fairly stable degree of state ownership was accepted as natural in economic theory and policy debates, and was considered appropriate within an efficiently functioning economy. State ownership had its own international institutional framework involving the Bretton Woods agreement, the International Monetary Fund (IMF), the World Bank and, most crucially, the dominant economic power of the USA. In the 1990s, most of these institutions have been eclipsed to a greater or lesser extent. One feature of the move to increasingly globalized financial markets – itself fuelled by the privatizations – is the idea that the decline in influence of the international framework itself limits the feasibility of new institutional arrangements, particularly the feasibility of these being able to change the behaviour of private firms or alter the functioning of markets. Such claims regarding globalization tend to be over-generalized, however, and increased international trade and investment can actually magnify the impact of national policies – whether regulatory or industrial – rather than negate them.

3 Privatization and regulation in the UK

During the 1980s and 1990s, the privatization process in the UK created a number of regulatory bodies – such as Oftel, for telecommunications, Ofgas, for the gas industry, Offer, for electricity, and Ofwat, for water – as vital areas of the economy came into the private regulated sector. The regulators are empowered to make rulings on the type of commercial contracts to be agreed between enterprises. Where competitive forces do not deliver the desired outcome, that outcome can be decreed through what is effectively a regulatory contract between the regulator and regulated enterprises. There has thus been a significant increase in the number, scope and complexity of contractual relations, as relations which were previously internal to publicly-owned industries are now the subject of market contracts between private firms or of 'contracts' between regulator and provider. Vertical relationships – for example, between electricity supply and distribution companies – have also become more complex, and contracts are required to be far more specific than those used under previous arrangements.

There was an expectation, held by some, that the new regulatory agencies would have a relatively short life, their task being to oversee the transfer of the industry from the public to the private sector, after which free market competition could be allowed to govern (see, for example, Littlechild 1983). However, the experience has been quite different, with 'free market competition' proving in many cases to be a rather difficult state to engineer. The importance of regulation has not diminished in practice; the existing regulators seem set to continue in operation for the foreseeable future, to be joined possibly by new bodies for the rail and other industries.

While the companies being regulated have, under UK company law, a legal obligation to maximize the financial interests of their shareholders, the regulator may be seen as offering some guarantee that the interests of wider stakeholders are taken into account. Regulators have therefore been charged with a mixture of the following tasks: introducing competition into the industry concerned, regulating the industry, and regulating the competition. These tasks are inextricably linked. The degree to which they are compliments of, or substitutes for, each other is not always clear.

Lack of clarity has led to disputes between the regulators and regulated over many issues, including relations between the regulated and 'unregulated'. The relationship between the rival telecommunications operators BT and Mercury is a case in point, and there are questions concerning the sort of contracts BT should be obliged to agree with Mercury for carrying Mercury calls on its local networks. Such difficulties reflect a limited understanding, among some practitioners and academics, of the processes involved – even the nature of the regulatory contract has not yet been established clearly.

Insofar as the established private sector has to do business with the newly privatized sectors – as customers, suppliers, collaborators, competitors and investors – a common understanding of the nature (and indeed the precise terms) of the regulatory contract may prove rather important for the economy of the future. Indeed, the extent to which the private sector is able to do business successfully with the newly privatized sector will depend partly on the extent to which such an understanding is achieved. One part, perhaps one-half, of the regulatory contract requires the regulator to guarantee the conditions for a sufficiently profitable operation of the regulated sector in the future to justify current investment. Thus, regulation is required to prevent the enterprises concerned from abusing their monopolistic (or monopsonistic or oligopolistic) power, and to ensure that some necessary level of service or output provision is made at an acceptable price, if necessary at a quality which also has to be regulated. The *quid pro quo* is that the regulator guarantees not to 'tax' away future profits, which derive from current investments being made on precisely this understanding.

As the regulated enterprises become increasingly involved in the functioning of international business, they will come to play an increasingly important role in the operation of private sector firms that were never in the public sector. While enterprises of the latter kind are not subject to regulation, they may yet have a keen interest in the likely operation, behaviour, performance and profitability of the regulated firms as these firms come to be suppliers, customers, partners, competitors and possible investment outlets. Investment may occur through joint ventures or simply through the regulated firm being seen as a potential home for arm's-length investments of reserve funds seeking a profitable return.

As an example, the UK's gas regulator in 1993 put forward proposals to 'ring-fence' British Gas's profits arising from the supply of gas to household customers, in order to protect this profit from any costs associated with high-risk overseas projects. British Gas had invested £1.5 billion in other countries since its privatization in 1986 and had plans to spend a similar amount before the end of the decade. Following the Monopolies and Mergers Commission report, published in 1993, which recommended that British Gas sell off its trading arm by 1997 and lose its monopoly over household supply by 2002, the company stated that this would force it to put greater emphasis on its overseas interests. However, the regulator's plan to split British Gas's profits in this way was reported as being likely to curtail its overseas expansion programme, as such 'non-ring-fenced' business would need to be funded to a greater degree on a project finance basis, which could involve having to take on more debt.

There have been several studies of the behaviour of privatized and regulated sectors to determine how privatization affects such factors as service/output levels, pricing and profitability (see, for example, Yarrow 1992, who finds a high increase in prices). However, there is also a need for research that will assist in the drawing up of accounting frameworks capable of delineating the effects of different accounting measures and for studies that will enable specialists to develop appropriate mechanisms for deriving justifiable rates of return for what are, in many cases, still fairly dominant enterprises within industries. This requires some agreement (or at least decision) on such matters as the valuation of the assets on which the rate of return is to be calculated, the assessment of the riskiness of the return from investment in regulated utilities, and hence the level at which this rate of return needs to be set.

While the above discussion has focused on the regulation of what might be thought of as the business or market sector of the economy, there has also been an increasing use of business-style regulation of welfare state functions such as in the National Health Service, education and other local and national government activities. These developments have a broader relevance throughout the economy. The role played by professionalism and managerialism in the British private and public sectors has also undergone policy-induced change as the government introduces increasing degrees of privatization and commercialization into the public sector.

The response of the professions to these developments has varied according to the structure of the sector. In the case of education, in schools that have opted out of state funding arrangements in order to manage their own budgets, it has been the head teachers who have shifted their efforts away from teaching and teaching-related duties toward management functions. In health care, the general practitioner (GP) contracts, which allow doctors to manage their own budgets, have resulted in management duties being passed 'down' by GPs to clerical staff.

The effects of privatization on the quality of professional service will depend on the impact it has on factors such as trust: for example, will the fact that service delivery is specified in contracts increase the trust which customers/patients/parents have that such services will be well provided, or will the formalization of previously unwritten rules of behaviour lead to a 'bottom line' approach, where only what is contracted for is delivered? Previously, there may have been relations of trust between professionals – as well as between professionals and service consumers – which ensured that certain professional standards would be maintained regardless of contractual obligations.

The evidence suggests that public sector quasi-markets – such as those created by the National Health Service reforms which have split hospitals as 'providers' from health authorities as 'purchasers' of services – depend on continual government intervention for their survival.

> Monitoring and regulation become major resource-consuming activities, as well as generating difficult problems of accountability and philosophical coherence. The market may survive, but at this stage its much vaunted efficiency advantages over the welfare bureaucracy will have all but disappeared.
> (Hughes 1993: 120)

There is also the danger that the introduction of accounting-dominated regulatory law can go beyond acceptable levels, creating 'juridification' ('legal pollution' or over-regulation):

> Juridification does not merely mean proliferation of law; it signifies a process in which the interventionist social state produces a new type of law, regulatory law. Only when both elements – materialization and the intention of the social state – are taken together can we understand the precise nature of the contemporary phenomenon of juridification.
> (Teubner 1987: 18)

Faced with juridification, the need would be to reverse the spread of such regulation rather than develop it further. It may be, however, that the only feasible way of escaping this new generation of regulatory activity is by avoiding – or reversing – the very privatization that spawned it; yet this option would appear to be ruled out on political grounds for the foreseeable future, regardless of the possible balance of economic or political advantages of such a course. Rather, the present level of regulatory activity seems set to continue, with all the potential problems that are associated with the public regulation of private sector business.

Since 1979, successive Conservative governments have expressed their intention to cut back the number of unelected regulatory bodies in the UK. However, as a result of privatization, these governments have done the exact opposite, overseeing a huge increase in resources devoted to regulatory activities of such entities as quasi-autonomous non-governmental organizations (quangos). (Quangos are administrative bodies that are not controlled by the government, but which nevertheless receive financial support from it; the government also makes senior appointments to these bodies.) Sir Gordon Borrie, QC, who was Director General of Fair Trading in the UK from 1976 to 1992, made the following observation in this regard:

> It may seem strange that, thirteen years after the election of a government in this country pledged to get government off the backs of British industry, we seem to have more government regulation or self-regulation within a governmental and statutory framework than ever.
> (Borrie 1992: 5)

4 The new research agenda

The regulatory contract between the regulator and the enterprises operating within that regulator's jurisdiction includes the key price cap formula (RPI-x), which is tied to certain performance measures. The price cap is preferred to a cost plus pricing formula or a rate of return rule because of the incentive effects involved (as well as the difficulty of determining true efficient costs). However, the distinction between these rules is not clear cut analytically. The more often the price cap is revised, the closer the regulatory regime moves to a rate of return concept, with all the potential incentive problems (such as the regulated enterprise boosting the capital intensity of their operations in order to translate a given rate of return into higher absolute profit levels). Fundamentally, the regulator is trying to guess what costs would be if the enterprise were operating efficiently, so as to allow a cost plus operating profit.

In practice, then, the regulatory practices pursued represent ever-changing combinations of the above three approaches rather than a choice of one and a rejection of the other two. Thus, there is a need for research into how the balance of incentive mechanisms alters as new mixes are considered.

In regulating individual enterprises (such as Oftel over BT), there are complex theoretical as well as practical problems in defining and discovering costs. These problems include how to allocate overheads between different operations, problems of joint and common costs and so on. The decision made on these issues can in turn have incentive effects. For example, if one part of an operator can only charge a competitor the same for the use of some facility as the operator would charge another part of itself, then there will be an incentive to shift overhead costs onto this part of the operation in order to be able to increase charges. Two further key issues for regulators are therefore how to define and gather data.

There is also a wider regulatory control problem: both economists and management researchers recognize increasingly that control within and between firms does not rely wholly on price mechanisms. Social and political relations of trust also exert control functions to some degree. For example, the mix of price and non-price factors in the relations between suppliers and their customers has become a focus of research in the management field as European producers seek to emulate the closer supplier–producer linkages commonly found in Japan. Thus, the social and political dimensions of regulators' relations with their industries are also important, as are the functions these dimensions have in compensating for the control dilemma posed by a reliance on cost and price performance indicators.

5 Regulating the regulators

The question of who should regulate the regulators has been the subject of considerable dispute. In general, the criteria for good regulation are considered to include the following: does the regulation achieve a satisfactory balance between the interests of consumers and shareholders and between those of domestic consumers and large corporate customers; does it ensure that investment will be sufficient to meet future demand and replace old capacity; and is it consistent with wider national objectives, such as environmental policy and longer term supply security?

In addition to the national regulatory systems that are being developed and which will have to interact in the economy of the future, there are also international regulatory agencies such as those of the European Union (EU) (see ECONOMIC INTEGRATION, INTERNATIONAL). In the 1990s, these are limited to specific functions such as competition policy, the responsibilities of the Commission of the European Community (CEC) regarding mergers, and CEC activities in pursuing the 1992 programme. This programme includes action on particular industries such as telecommunications, with the EU introducing the *Green Paper* (CEC 1987) and subsequent proposals for implementing regulatory reforms across the community.

EU regulation, although weaker than that pursued by regulatory bodies such as Oftel, is nevertheless more extensive in the sense that it includes issues of standardization – an area that had not been considered by the UK's regulatory bodies by the mid-1990s. Standardization, compatibility and so on are crucial issues for the economy of the future. How these are to be pursued is, of course, an open question.

6 The international telecommunications market

Regulatory institutions for telecommunications are not coping well with the technical changes occurring in telematics services such as electronic data interchange (EDI) (see TELECOMMUNICATIONS INDUSTRY). Radical ways of regulating the supply of public telecommunications services are needed urgently, both to overcome this failing and to ensure continued universal access in an era when private operators will be seeking profitable business openings rather than undertaking public service obligations. In telecommunications, competition has been chosen by the government as the method of achieving equity and efficiency goals.

However, cooperation is essential too, and this requires agreement on the rules of the market.

> Cooperation is essential to competition in the new telematics environment. But as we have learned from studies of innovation, firms have a history, and this affects their willingness to cooperate. In telecommunications, this is particularly important because of the weight of older institutions. Even if BT's domestic market share were to slip to 70 per cent by the year 2000, this company will have a strong base upon which to protect its market. Regulation, imperfect as it is, will continue to play a crucial role in monitoring, guiding and sometimes controlling, decisions by the main players in the market. But it is here, I suggest, that we see very few signs of radical regulatory innovation.
> (Mansell 1993: 10)

The need to force public service obligations (basically, obligations of universal access) on telecommunications operators requires public ownership or public regulation. Private operators may choose not to subsidize connection and access charges to the degree desirable (or even at all), even though such subsidies may make economic sense for society. The benefits to society come from the positive network externalities, whereby existing network subscribers benefit from additional subscribers joining the network; in the jargon of neo-classical economics, utilities are interdependent – the utility of having a telephone is non-existent if no one else has one. Encouraging people to join and then to stay on the network is one of the reasons why governments want to subsidize connection charges and line rental charges, and why Oftel has so far refused to allow BT to phase out these cross-subsidies.

It may even be in the operator's own interests to subsidize connection and rental charges if the resulting traffic is profitable. However, if there is a potential for that traffic to be lost to rival operators, then the expectation of a private gain in profits may not be certain enough to justify the investment. For example, the French Télétel service (often referred to as Minitel after the name of its terminals) proved profitable to France Télécom, despite the fact that terminals had been distributed free of charge, because it attracted additional telephone traffic. However, this commercial success was only possible on the basis of a monopoly of telecommunications by France Télécom (see Costello *et al.* 1991). In the absence of monopoly, such outcomes would have to be engineered by regulatory means.

While the pressure from international business will be for lower call charges and greater investment in the telecommunications routes used most often by the firms concerned, it is not necessarily in the best interests of international business for communications networks to shrink as market solutions impose themselves. This phenomenon may take one or more of the following forms: rising connection and rental charges; allowing investment to go disproportionately into those sections of the network most immediately useful to international business, to the detriment of the network as a whole; or failing to keep regulatory developments in line with technological advances. On the subject of technical change, Mansell makes the following comment:

> In summary, regulatory institutions are not coping with technical change, at least not very well. Some telematics services do need to be all-pervasive. The supercarriers are becoming less and less interested in public or universal service goals as they turn their strategic vision to the global market. To cope with disparities in access to the public network, there must be regulatory innovation. Structural changes in domestic markets are needed to control supplier power. A radical reorientation of regulation is also needed to ensure access to a planned set of 'universal' telematics services. This is one way of averting a tragedy – namely, the demise of the common public network.
> (Mansell 1993: 14)

7 International developments

As indicated above, the causes and effects of privatization vary across the globe: there are the industrialized economies on which the foregoing analysis has concentrated; there are what are sometimes termed 'the economies in transition' of eastern and central Europe and the former Soviet Union; and there are a wide range of economies, from the high performing southeast Asian economies, to those in Latin America and elsewhere, that are subject to outside pressure for privatization. This last point, regarding outside pressure to privatize, applies not only to those countries under explicit pressure from, say, the IMF, which have privatized as part of a structural adjustment programme, but to all countries, since the drive toward privatization is a worldwide phenomenon (see, for example, Michie and Grieve Smith's 1995 analysis).

Heath (1993) discusses privatization in the economies in transition, and also analyses the economies of such countries as China, Cuba, North Korea and Vietnam. These countries have not resorted to large-scale privatization, despite seeking to restructure their economies to allow for the development of a private sector. In the former Soviet Union, privatization is proceeding, but with many problems, including a lack of the necessary regulatory mechanisms, the creation of many private sector monopolies, no concept of corporate governance and no requirement for external auditors (see Heath 1993). Poland was the first of the former socialist states to attempt a 'big bang' approach to introducing free market capitalism, although their 'voucher system' proposed for mass privatization was abandoned by the government of Prime Minister Jan Olszewski in a bid to slow down the hectic pace of change.

The experience of privatization in developing countries is surveyed for the socialist countries (as listed above) by Heath (1993), and for the Commonwealth countries by Adam *et al.* (1992); Bhaskar (1993) focuses on Bangladesh, and two of the chapters in Clarke and Pitelis (1993) analyse privatization in Malaysia and Tanzania. All these works give useful further references. Although the message from this literature is one of diversity, a common theme is the use of privatization as a solution to inefficiency and other problems in public enterprises. This 'market failure versus public failure' analysis is finding policy expression in the move between public and private ownership.

A similar move has been witnessed in France in the 1980s and 1990s with, first, an attempt to use nationalization to force through industrial modernization, followed by repeated moves to privatize at least some of the enterprises nationalized in the early 1980s. The enlarged public sector protected France's manufacturing base in a way that privatization in the UK did not, and allowed it generally to perform well at the cutting edge of industry, transport and communications. Thus, although spending on investment, research and development in electronics fell short of the original plan, it still represented an increase over the 1970s, permitting the French electronics industry to reach a rate of growth of output of 8 per cent in 1983. However, following the Mitterrand Government's U-turn in economic policy, these achievements were limited by political and economic choices which led the new public sector to mimic the strategies of privately-owned multinationals. Such strategies involved investing heavily overseas while cutting jobs at home, rather than providing the originally intended motor of domestic industrial and social reconstruction. After 1982, the nationalized sector represented 24 per cent of industrial employment, 32 per cent of all turnover and 60 per cent of investment. Half the production of companies of more than 2000 employees was in the public sector. Most of the private industrial giants brought into the public sector were losing money on a huge scale and were highly vulnerable to foreign competition. In the context of the collapse of the government's macroeconomic expansion policies, the prospects for using the new public enterprises as the motor of growth evaporated (see Halimi *et al.* 1994).

In the 1986–8 period of 'cohabitation' between a right-wing government and President Mitterrand, three companies that had been nationalized in 1982 were privatized. With the electoral victory of the Right in 1993, a major privatization programme was launched. The share of employment within the public sector was set to fall from 11.5 per cent to 7 per cent of the non-agricultural workforce; in the financial institutions, the public sector will have its share of the workforce fall from around 33 per cent to less than 5 per cent. The case for privatization has been made almost entirely on the basis of the need to raise cash, rather than on any suggestion that the private sector is inherently more dynamic or efficient. There is no doubt that state capitalist enterprise worked effectively in France (although, of course, that was not all that was intended originally in 1981–2). Indeed, when the conservative Balladur government unveiled its privatization programme in the summer of 1993, the nationalized firms put up for sale – including those brought into the public sector in 1982 – were described as 'some of the world's finest blue-chip companies' (*Guardian*, 17 May 1993) and 'robust industrial concerns' (*Financial Times*, 27 May 1993).

8 Conclusion

In the economy of the future, it is going to be necessary to deal with increasing contractual complexities as new managerial methods and business structures emerge, with firms concentrating on their core activities and contracting out activities previously conducted within the firm. As business becomes more international, increasing numbers of international suppliers, customers and collaborators will have to be dealt with. One particular aspect of privatization is the need to deal with newly regulated enterprises – previously in public ownership and later transferred to the private sector, but unable to operate (for whatever reason) without state regulation.

It is argued in this entry that one lesson to be learned from experience in the UK is that the regulation of private sector activities is not a temporary operation involving the transfer of assets from the private sector to the public sector prior to government withdrawal, as some had originally envisaged. On the contrary, state regulation seems likely to be an important feature of the economy of the future.

JONATHAN MICHIE
SCHOOL OF MANAGEMENT AND
ORGANIZATIONAL PSYCHOLOGY, BIRKBECK,
UNIVERSITY OF LONDON

Further reading

(References cited in the text marked *)

* Adam, C., Cavendish, W. and Mistry, P.S. (1992) *Adjusting Privatization: Case Studies from Developing Countries*, London: James Currey. (This text examines why privatization has not been as easy to put into practice as was originally expected, and argues that the structure of developing economies can mitigate against the benefits of privatization.)
* Bhaskar, V. (1993) 'Privatization in developing countries: theoretical issues and the experience of Bangladesh', *UNCTAD Review*. (A survey of privatization in the developing countries which focuses on Bangladesh.)
* Borrie, G. (1992) 'Regulators, self-regulators and their accountability', TSB forum paper, London: TSB Group plc. (Sir Gordon Borrie, QC, was director general of Fair Trading in the UK from 1976 to 1992 and so is well qualified to give an inside view of public regulatory processes.)
* Chang, H.J. (1994) *The Political Economy of Industrial Policy*, Basingstoke: Macmillan. (A work which demonstrates that South Korea's economic success has been due to an active industrial policy involving, among other things, the use of public ownership.)
* Clarke, T. and Pitelis, C. (eds) (1993) *The Political Economy of Privatization*, London: Routledge. (This work draws together substantial evidence and analysis of the experience of privatization programmes in practice during the 1980s.)
* Commission of the European Communities (CEC) (1987) 'Towards a dynamic European economy', Green Paper on the development of the Common Market for telecommunications services and equipment, COM(87) 290 final, Brussels: CEC. (The CEC's views on how a common market for new telecommunications services could be developed from an integrated European basic network.)
* Costello, N., Michie, J. and Milne, S. (1991) 'Industrial restructuring and public intervention: planning the digital economy', in J. Michie (ed.) *The Economics of Restructuring and Intervention*, Aldershot: Edward Elgar. (This article argues that information technology increasingly demands the integration and compatibility of systems and networks, and that such compatibility can best be ensured by public intervention.)
* Halimi, S., Michie, J. and Milne, S. (1994) 'The Mitterrand experience', in J. Michie and J. Grieve Smith *Unemployment in Europe*, London: Academic Press. (An analysis of the Mitterrand government's industrial policies which argues that these did achieve some partial successes.)
* Heath, J. (1993) *Revitalizing Socialist Enterprise*, London: Routledge. (An analysis of

privatization in the former socialist economies of eastern Europe and the Soviet Union which also examines the situation in China, Cuba, North Korea and Vietnam.)

* Hughes, D. (1993) 'Health policy: letting the market work?', *Social Policy Review* 5 1992–3. (An article which suggests that public sector quasi-markets, such as those created by the National Health Service reforms in the UK, depend on continual government intervention for their survival.)

Laughlin, R. and Broadbent, J. (1992) 'Accounting and law: partners in the juridification of the public sector in the UK?', Sheffield University Management School discussion paper 92.2. (The case against accounting-dominated regulatory law and its potential to create unacceptable levels of juridification.)

* Littlechild, S.C. (1983) *Regulation of British Telecommunications Profitability*, London: HMSO. (A work which argues – incorrectly as it has turned out – that the regulation spawned by privatization is likely to be relatively short-lived.)

* Mansell, R. (1993) 'From telephony to telematics services: equity, efficiency and regulatory innovation', Economic and Social Research Council (ESRC) Programme in Information and Communication Technologies (PICT) annual lecture. (A text which favours the introduction of radical ways of regulating the supply of public telecommunication services.)

* Michie, J. and Grieve Smith, J. (1995) *Managing the Global Economy*, Oxford: Oxford University Press. (An analysis of the breakdown of the Bretton Woods system of international monetary arrangements which examines the reasons why repeated attempts to reintroduce some order into global economic relations have failed.)

* Teubner, G. (ed.) (1987) *Juridification of Social Sciences*, Berlin: Walter de Gruyter. (Includes Teubner's argument that juridification signifies a process in which the interventionist social state produces a new type of law, namely, regulatory law.)

* World Bank (1993) *The East Asian Miracle: Economic Growth and Public Policy*, New York: Oxford University Press. (A policy research report which attempts to rationalize the World Bank's application of a broadly Keynesian perspective to southeast Asian countries that have pursued active economic policies.)

* Yarrow, G. (1992) *British Electricity Prices Since Privatisation*, Regulatory Policy Institute Studies in Regulation 1, Oxford: Regulatory Policy Institute. (A study of the behaviour of privatized and regulated sectors which finds a high increase in prices following privatization.)

See also: ECONOMIC INTEGRATION, INTERNATIONAL; GLOBALIZATION; INSTITUTIONAL ECONOMICS

Small and medium sized enterprises

1 Introduction
2 The static view
3 The dynamic view
4 The empirical evidence
5 The public policy response
6 Conclusions

Overview

Small business has been classified by the United States Small Business Administration as enterprises with 500 or fewer employees. While this definition is arbitrary, it has generally been accepted as the definition for small- and medium-sized firms in the USA and most other developed countries.

The role that small firms play in economics has evolved considerably since the Second World War. This article seeks to document how and why small business plays a very different role in industrial organization research today than they did some three decades ago.

The most important development in the field of small business economics has been a shift in the framework for analysing small business. While there were always a few studies around analysing small business through a dynamic lens, a much more profound and comprehensive shift in the literature began in the later 1980s and early 1990s. The most salient characteristic feature of this literature was the introduction of a dynamic or evolutionary framework.

In the second section of this entry, the view of small business emerging from the static framework of the post-war analysis is described. This view identifies small business as being sub-optimal in terms of scale of production. The resulting impact on performance is negative, in terms of productivity and wages. The policy implication is that, at least in terms of economic efficiency, small business exerts a drag on economic welfare.

In the third section, the view of small business emerging from the dynamic framework of the last decade is introduced. This view provides a striking contrast to the role and contribution of small business. When viewed through the lens of a dynamic framework, small businesses are seen as *agents of change*. The empirical evidence supporting this dynamic view of small business is presented in the fourth section. The implications for public policy towards business are presented in the fifth section. In particular, we find that the role of public policy towards business has shifted from constraining the power of large corporations to enabling the creation and commercialization of knowledge, particularly by small business.

1 Introduction

As recently as a decade ago, there were serious concerns about the ability of the USA to withstand competition in the global economy, create jobs and continue to develop. Lester Thurow (1984) bemoaned that the USA was 'losing the economic race,' because:

> Today it's very hard to find an industrial corporation in America that isn't in really serious trouble basically because of trade problems. ... The systematic erosion of our competitiveness comes from having lower rates of growth of manufacturing productivity year after year, as compared with the rest of the world.
> (Thurow 1984: 23)

W.W. Restow (1987) predicted a revolution in economic policy, concluding that, 'The United States is entering a new political era, one in which it will be preoccupied by increased economic competition from abroad and will need better cooperation at home to deal with this challenge.'

In the influential study, *Made in America*, directed by the leaders of the MIT Commission on Industrial Productivity, Michael L. Dertouzos, Richard K. Lester and Robert M. Solow, a team of 23 scholars, spanning a broad range of disciplines and backgrounds, reached the conclusion that for the USA to restore its international competitiveness, it had to adapt the types of policies targeting the leading corporations prevalent in Japan and Germany.

The last decade has seen a re-emergence of competitiveness, innovative activity and job generation in the United States. Not only was this economic turnaround largely unanticipated by many scholars and members of the policy community, but what was even more surprising than the resurgence itself was the primary source – small firms. As scholars began the arduous task of documenting the crucial role played by small and medium sized enterprises (SMEs) in the United States as a driving engine of growth, job creation and competitiveness in global markets (Audretsch, 1995), policy makers responded with a bipartisan emphasis on policies to promote SMEs (see *U.S. News and World Report* 1993). For example, in his 1993 State of the Union Address to the country, President Bill Clinton proposed, 'Because small business has created such a high percentage of all the new jobs in our nation over the last 10 or 15 years, our plan includes the boldest targeted incentives for small business in history. We propose a permanent investment tax credit for the small firms in this country (quoted in Davis et al. 1996: 298). The Republican response to Clinton was, 'We agree with the President that we have to put more people to work, but remember this: 80 to 85 percent of the new jobs in this country are created by small business. So the climate for starting and expanding businesses must be enhanced with tax incentives and deregulation, rather than imposing higher taxes and more governmental mandates' (Representative Robert Michel, House Minority Leader, in the Republican Response to the 1993 State of the Union Address, quoted in Davis et al. 1996: 298).

One of the puzzles posed by the important contribution of small firms to the resurgence of the American economy is that their share of economic activity, measured in terms of share of total establishments, employment, or output, has not dramatically increased over the last 20 years (Acs and Audretsch 1993). In fact, a meticulous comparison documenting the role of SMEs across a broad spectrum of countries revealed that the share of economic activity accounted for by SMEs is considerably less than in Japan, Germany, the UK, Italy, the Netherlands and other European countries.

If SMEs are so important to the US economy, how come they account for such a small share of economic activity, at least relative to other economies? The answer to this question lies in a crucial distinction between the static role of SMEs and the dynamic role. In the second section of this entry we contrast the static and dynamic role of SMEs.

2 The static view

The starting point for the analysis of SMEs is the theory of the firm (see GROWTH OF THE FIRM AND NETWORKING). The field of economics that focuses the most on links between the organization of firms in industries and the resulting economic performance has been industrial organization. The ascendancy of industrial organization in the post-war period as an important and valued field of economics came from the recognition not only by scholars but also by policy makers that industrial organization matters. The widespread fear *vis-à-vis* the Soviet Union pervasive throughout the United States at the end of the 1950s and early 1960s was not just that the Soviets might bury the Americans because they were the first into space with the launching of the *Sputnik*, but that the superior organization of industry facilitated by centralized planning was generating greater rates of growth in the Soviet Union. After all, the nations of Eastern Europe, and the Soviet Union in particular, had a 'luxury' inherent in their systems of centralized planning – a concentration of economic assets on a scale beyond anything imaginable in the West, where the commitment to democracy seemingly imposed a concomitant commitment to economic decentralization.

Although there may have been considerable debate about what to do about the perceived Soviet threat some three decades ago, there was little doubt at that time that the manner in which enterprises and entire industries were organized mattered. And even more striking, when one reviews the literature of the day, there seemed to be near unanimity about the way in which industrial organization mattered. It is no doubt an irony of history that a remarkably similar version of the giantism embedded in Soviet doctrine, fuelled by the writings of Marx and ultimately implemented by the iron fist of Stalin, was also prevalent throughout the West (see MARX, K.). This was the era of mass production when economies of scale seemed to be the decisive factor in dictating efficiency. This was the world so colourfully described by John Kenneth Galbraith (1956) in his theory of countervailing power, in which the power of big business was held in check by big labour and by big government (see GALBRAITH, J.K.).

It became the task of the industrial organization scholars to sort out the issues involving this perceived tradeoff between economic efficiency on the one hand and political and economic decentralization on the other. The scholars of industrial organization responded by producing a massive literature focusing on essentially three issues:

1 What are the economic gains to size and large-scale production?
2 What are the economic welfare implications of having an oligopolistic market structure, i.e. is economic performance promoted or reduced in an industry with just a handful of large-scale firms?
3 Given the overwhelming evidence from (2) that large-scale production resulting in economic concentration is associated with increased efficiency, what are the public policy implications?

A fundamental characteristic of the industrial organization literature was not only that it was obsessed with the oligopoly question but that it was essentially static in nature. There was considerable concern about what to do about the existing firms and industrial structure, but little attention was paid to where they came from and where they were going. Oliver Williamson's classic 1968 article in the *American Economic Review*, 'Economies as an antitrust defense: the welfare tradeoffs', became something of a final statement demonstrating this seemingly inevitable tradeoff between the gains in productive efficiency that could be obtained through increased concentration and gains in terms of competition that could be achieved through decentralizing economic policies, such as antitrust. But it did not seem possible to have both, certainly not in Williamson's completely static model (see WILLIAMSON, O.E.).

One of the most striking findings emerging in this static view of industrial organization is that small firms generally operate at a level of output that is too small to sufficiently exhaust scale economies, even when the standard definition of a small firm employing fewer than 500 employees is applied. A large number of studies found that because the minimum efficient scale (MES) of output, or the lowest level of output where the minimum average cost is attained, large-scale production is typically required to exhaust scale economies in manufacturing. Any enterprise or establishment that was smaller than required by the MES was branded as being *sub-optimal* or inefficient, in that it produced, at average, costs in excess of more efficient larger firms. Weiss (in Audretsch and Yamawaki 1991: 403) assumed that 'The term "suboptimal" capacity describes a condition in which some plants are too small to be efficient'.

The importance of scale economies in the typical manufacturing industry relegated most small firms to being classified as sub-optimal. For example, Weiss (1979) found that sub-optimal plants accounted for about 52.8 percent of industry value-of shipments, Scherer (1976) found that 58.2 per cent of value-of-shipments emanated from the sub-optimal plants in 12 industries, and Pratten (1971) identified the sub-optimal scale establishments accounting for 47.9 per cent of industry shipments. After reviewing the literature on the extent of sub-optimal firms, Weiss (in Audretsch and Yamawaki 1991: xiv) concluded that, 'In most industries the great majority of firms is suboptimal. In a typical industry there are, let's say, one hundred firms. Typically only about five to ten of them will be operating at the MES level of output, or anything like it.'

What are the economic welfare implications? Weiss (1979: 1137) argued that the existence of small firms which are sub-optimal represented a loss in economic efficiency and therefore advocated any public policy which 'creates social gains in the form of sub-optimal capacity.' Empirical evidence suggested that the price umbrella provided by monopoly power encouraged the existence of sub-optimal capacity firms. Weiss (1979) went so far as to argue that the largest inefficiency associated with market power was not the higher prices charged to consumers but rather that it facilitated the existence of sub-optimal scale small firms.

Wages and productivity would be expected to reflect the degree to which small firms are less efficient than their larger counterparts. There is a large body of empirical evidence spanning a broad range of samples, time periods and even countries that has consistently found wages (and non-wage compensation as well) to be positively related to firm size. Probably the most cited study is that of Brown *et al.* (1990: 88–9), who conclude that 'Workers in large firms earn higher wages, and this fact cannot be explained completely by differences in labor quality industry, working conditions, or union status. Workers in large firms enjoy better benefits and greater security than their counterparts in small firms. When these factors are added together, it appears that workers in large firms do have a superior employment package'.

Seen through the static lens provided by traditional industrial organization and labour economics, the economic welfare implications of the recent shift in economic activity away from large firms and towards small enterprises is unequivocal – overall economic welfare is decreased since productivity and wages will be lower in small than in large firms. As Weiss (1979) argued in terms of efficiency and Brown *et al.* (1990) in terms of employee compensation, the implication for public policy is to implement policies to shift economic activity away from small firms and towards larger enterprises. However, the view that small firms are sub-optimal was the result of an analytical framework that is static in nature, a framework in which innovation and growth play no role (Sylos-Labini 1992). As the next section shows, incorporating the role that innovation and growth play in SMEs leads to a radically different view of SMEs that challenges the inference that they are somehow sub-optimal.

3 The dynamic view

Coase (1937) was awarded a Nobel Prize for explaining why a firm should exist (see COASE, R.). But why should more than one firm exist in an industry? One answer is provided by the traditional economics literature focusing on industrial organization. An excess level of profitability induces entry into the industry. And this is why the entry of new firms is interesting and important – because the new firms provide an equilibrating function in the market, in that the levels of price and profit are restored to the competitive levels. The new firms are about business as usual – they simply equilibrate the market by providing more of it.

An alternative explanation for the entry of new firms was provided by Audretsch (1995), who suggests that new firms are not founded to be smaller clones of the larger incumbents but rather to serve as *agents of change* through innovative activity.

The starting point for most theories of innovation is the firm. In such theories the firms are exogenous and their performance in generating technological change is endogenous. For example, in the most prevalent model found in the literature of technological change, the model of the *knowledge production function*, formalized by Zvi Griliches (1979), firms exist exogenously and then engage in the pursuit of new economic knowledge as an input into the process of generating innovative activity.

The most decisive input in the knowledge production function is new economic knowledge. And as Cohen and Klepper (1991 and 1992) conclude, the greatest source generating new economic knowledge is generally considered to be R&D. Certainly a large body of empirical work has found a strong and positive relationship between knowledge inputs, such as R&D, on the one hand, and innovative outputs on the other hand.

The knowledge production function has been found to hold most strongly at broader levels of aggregation. The most innovative countries are those with the greatest investments in R&D. Little innovative output is associated with less developed countries, which are characterized by a paucity of production of new economic knowledge. Similarly, the most innovative industries also tend to be characterized by considerable investments in R&D and new economic knowledge. Not only are industries such as computers, pharmaceuticals and instruments high in R&D inputs that generate new economic knowledge, but also in terms of innovative outputs (Audretsch 1995). By contrast, industries with little R&D, such as wood products, textiles and paper, also tend to produce only a negligible amount of innovative output. Thus, the knowledge production model linking knowledge generating inputs to outputs certainly holds at the more aggregated levels of economic activity.

Where the relationship becomes less compelling is at the disaggregated microeconomic level of the enterprise, establishment or even line of business. For example, while Acs and Audretsch (1990) found that the simple correlation between R&D inputs and innovative output was 0.84 for four-digit standard industrial classification (SIC) manufacturing industries in the USA, it was only about half, 0.40, among the largest US corporations.

The model of the knowledge production function becomes even less compelling in view of the recent wave of studies revealing that small enterprises serve as the engine of innovative activity in certain industries. These results are startling, because as Scherer (1991) observes, the bulk of industrial R&D is undertaken in the largest corporations; small enterprises account only for a minor share of R&D inputs. Thus the knowledge production function seemingly implies that, as the *Schumpeterian Hypothesis* predicts, innovative activity favours those organizations with access to knowledge-producing inputs – the large incumbent organization. The more recent evidence identifying the strong innovative activity raises the question, 'Where do new and small firms get the innovation producing inputs, that is, the knowledge?' (see SCHUMPTER, J.)

One answer, proposed by Audretsch (1995), is that, although the model of the knowledge production function may still be valid, the implicitly assumed unit of observation – at the level of the firm – may be less valid. The reason why the knowledge production function holds more closely for more aggregated degrees of observation may be that investment in R&D and other sources of new knowledge spills over for economic exploitation by third-party firms.

A large literature has emerged focusing on what has become known as the *appropriability problem*. The underlying issue revolves around how firms which invest in the creation of new economic knowledge can best appropriate the economic returns from that knowledge (Arrow 1962). Audretsch (1995) proposes shifting the unit of observation away from exogenously assumed firms to individuals – agents with endowments of new economic knowledge. But when the lens is shifted away from focusing upon the firm as the relevant unit of observation to individuals, the relevant question becomes 'How can economic agents with a given endowment of new knowledge best appropriate the returns from that knowledge?'

The appropriability problem confronting the individual may converge with that confronting the firm. Economic agents can and do work for firms, and even if they do not, they can potentially be employed by an incumbent firm. In fact, in a model of perfect information with no agency costs, any positive economies of scale or scope will ensure that the appropriability problems of the firm and individual converge. If an agent has an idea for doing something different than is currently being practised by the incumbent enterprises – both in terms of a new product or process and in terms of organization – the idea, which can be termed as an innovation, will be presented to the incumbent enterprise. Because of the assumption of perfect knowledge, both the firm and the agent would agree upon the expected value of the innovation. But to the degree that any economies of scale or scope exist, the expected value of implementing the innovation within the incumbent enterprise will exceed that of taking the innovation outside of the incumbent firm to start a new enterprise. Thus, the incumbent firm and the inventor of the idea would be expected to reach a bargain, splitting the value added to the firm contributed by the innovation. The payment to the inventor – either in terms of a higher wage or some other means of remuneration – would be bounded between the expected value of the innovation if it were implemented by the incumbent enterprise on the upper end, and by the return that the agent could expect to earn if he used it to launch a new enterprise on the lower end.

Penrose (1959) argued that the distinguishing characteristic of an enterprise is the knowledge embedded in the firm (see PENROSE, E.). Because, 'The productive activities of a firm are governed by what we shall call its "productive opportunity," which comprises all of the productive possibilities that its entrepreneurs see and can take advantage of. ... It is clear that this opportunity will be restricted to the extent to which a firm does not see opportunities for expansion, is unwilling to act upon them, or is unable to respond to them.'

Thus, each economic agent would choose how to best appropriate the value of his endowment of economic knowledge by comparing the wage he would earn if he remains employed by an incumbent enterprise, w, to the expected net present discounted value of the profits accruing from starting a new firm, π. If these two values are relatively close, the probability that he would choose to appropriate the value of his knowledge through an external mechanism such as starting a new firm, $\Pr(e)$, would be relatively low. On the other hand, as the gap between w and π becomes larger, the likelihood of an agent choosing to appropriate the value of his knowledge externally through starting a new enterprise becomes greater, or

$\Pr(e) = f(\pi - w)$

Shifting the unit of observation to the individual, and the model of entrepreneurial choice depicted in the equation does not imply that the innovation process is solely individual rather than collective. The history of industrial enterprise lends considerable support to the argument that the innovation process is collective both in terms of interactive learning and the expectations of participants in sharing in the gains from enterprise (Chandler 1990; Teece 1993; and Teece et al.1994). Rather, it does suggest that individuals will make decisions about which contexts of their endowments of knowledge and experience are the most valuable. In most cases, this means remaining with an incumbent firm. In some cases, it will mean creating a new context, either by moving to a different firm or creating a new enterprise. However, even when an individual decides to start a new firm it is almost never in an isolated context cut off from the collective process. More typically, entrepreneurs starting new firms are 'standing on the shoulders of giants' by applying knowledge they learned in one context to a different one. In any case, new-firm startups typically belong to collective networks and groups of firms. Thus, the model of entrepreneurial choice suggests that while each individual makes a choice about how best to apply his or her endowment of knowledge and experience, that choice is crucially shaped by and dependent upon other individuals, teams and groups, other firms, and a whole range of social, political and economic institutions.

The model proposed by Audretsch (1995) refocuses the unit of observation away from firms deciding whether to increase their output from a level of zero to some positive amount in a new industry, to individual agents in possession of new knowledge that, due to uncertainty, may or may not have some positive economic value. It is the uncertainty inherent in new economic knowledge, combined with asymmetries between the agent possessing that knowledge and the decision-making vertical hierarchy of the incumbent organization with respect to its expected value that potentially leads to a gap in the valuation of that knowledge between the agent and the decision-making hierarchy.

How the economic agent chooses to appropriate the value of his or her knowledge, that is either within an incumbent firm or by starting or joining a new enterprise, will be shaped by the knowledge conditions underlying the industry. Under the routinized technological regime the agent will tend to appropriate the value of his or her new ideas within the boundaries of incumbent firms. Thus, the propensity for new firms to be started should be relatively low in industries characterized by the routinized technological regime.

By contrast, under the entrepreneurial regime the agent will tend to appropriate the value of his or her new ideas outside of the boundaries of incumbent firms by starting a new enterprise. Thus, the propensity for new firms to enter should be relatively high in industries characterized by the entrepreneurial regime.

Audretsch (1995) suggests that divergences in the expected value regarding new knowledge will, under certain conditions, lead an agent to exercise what Albert O. Hirschman (1970) has termed as *exit* rather than *voice*, and depart from an incumbent enterprise to launch a new firm. But who is right, the departing agents or those agents remaining in the organizational decision-making hierarchy who, by assigning the new idea a relatively low value, have effectively driven the agent with the potential innovation away? *Ex post* the answer may not be too difficult. But given the uncertainty inherent in new knowledge, the answer is anything but trivial *a priori*.

Thus, when a new firm is launched, its prospects are shrouded in uncertainty. If the new firm is built around a new idea, i.e. potential innovation, it is uncertain whether there is sufficient demand for the new idea or if some competitor will have the same or even a superior idea. Even if the new firm is formed to be an exact replica of a successful incumbent enterprise, it is uncertain whether sufficient demand for a new clone, or even for the existing incumbent, will prevail in the future. Tastes can change, and new ideas emerging from other firms will certainly influence those tastes.

Finally, an additional layer of uncertainty pervades a new enterprise. It is not known how competent the new firm really is, in terms of management, organization and workforce. At least incumbent enterprises know something about their underlying competencies from past experience. Which is to say that a new enterprise is burdened with uncertainty as to whether it can produce and market the intended product as well as sell it. In both cases the degree of uncertainty will typically exceed that confronting incumbent enterprises.

This initial condition of not just uncertainty, but a greater degree of uncertainty vis-à-vis incumbent enterprises in the industry is captured in the theory of firm selection and industry evolution proposed by Boyan Jovanovic (1982). Jovanovic presents a model in which the new firms, which he terms *entrepreneurs*, face costs that are not only random but also differ across firms. A central feature of the model is that a new firm does not know what its cost function is, that is its relative efficiency, but rather discovers this through the process of learning from its actual post-entry performance. In particular, Jovanovic (1982) assumes that entrepreneurs are unsure about their ability to manage a new firm start-up and therefore their prospects for success. Although entrepreneurs may launch a new firm based on a vague sense of expected post-entry performance, they only discover their true ability – in terms of managerial competence and of having based the firm on an idea that is viable on the market – once their business is established. Those entrepreneurs who discover that their ability exceeds their expectations expand the scale of their business, whereas those discovering that their post-entry performance is less than commensurate with their expectations will contact the scale of output and possibly exit from the industry. Thus, Jovanovic's model is a theory of *noisy selection*, where efficient firms grow and survive and inefficient firms decline and fail.

The role of learning in the selection process has been the subject of considerable debate. On the one hand, the argument can be made that those new firms that are the most flexible and adaptable will be the most successful in adjusting to whatever the demands of the market are. As Nelson and Winter (1982: 11) point out, 'Many kinds of organizations commit resources to learning; organizations seek to copy the forms of their most successful competitors'.

On the other hand, one can argue that the role of learning is restricted to discovering if the firm has the *right stuff* in terms of the goods it is producing as well as the way they are being produced. Under this interpretation the new enterprise is not necessarily able to adapt or adjust to market conditions, but receives information based on its market performance with respect to its *fitness* in terms of meeting demand most efficiently *vis-à-vis* rivals. The theory of organizational ecology proposed by Michael T. Hannan and John Freeman (1989) most pointedly adheres to the notion that, 'We assume that individual organizations are characterized by relative inertia in structure'. That is, firms learn not in the sense that they adjust their actions as reflected by their fundamental identity and purpose, but in the sense of their perception. What is then learned is whether or not the firm has the right stuff, but not how to change that stuff.

The theory of firm selection is particularly appealing in view of the rather startling size of most new firms. For example, the mean size of more than 11,000 new-firm start-ups in the manufacturing sector in the USA was found to be fewer than eight workers per firm (Audretsch, 1995). While the MES varies substantially across industries, and even to some degree across various product classes within any given industry, the observed size of most new firms is sufficiently small to ensure that the bulk of new firms will be operating at a sub-optimal scale of output. Why would an entrepreneur start a new firm that would immediately be confronted by scale disadvantages?

An implication of the theory of firm selection is that new firms may begin at a small, even sub-optimal, scale of output, and then if merited by subsequent performance expand. Those new firms that are successful will grow, whereas those that are not successful will remain small and may ultimately be forced to exit from the industry if they are operating at a sub-optimal scale of output.

Subsequent to entering an industry, an entrepreneur must decide whether to maintain expand, or contract its output, or exit. Two different strands of literature have identified several major influences shaping the decision to exit an industry. The first, and most obvious strand of literature suggests that the probability of a business exiting will tend to increase as the gap between its level of output and the MES level of output increases. The second strand of literature points to the role that the technological environment plays in shaping the decision to exit. As Dosi (1988) and Arrow (1962) argue, an environment characterized by more frequent innovation may also be associated with a greater amount of uncertainty regarding not only the technical nature of the product but also the demand for that product. As technological uncertainty increases, particularly under the entrepreneurial regime, the likelihood that the business will be able to produce a viable product and ultimately be able to survive decreases.

An important implication of the dynamic process of firm selection and industry evolution is that new firms are more likely to be operating at a sub-optimal scale of output if the underlying technological conditions are such that there is a greater chance of making an innovation, that is under the entrepreneurial regime. If new firms successfully learn and adapt, or are just plain lucky, they grow into viably sized enterprises. If not, they stagnate and may ultimately exit from the industry. This dynamic perspective suggests, that entry and the start-up of new firms may not be greatly deterred in the presence of scale economies. As long as entrepreneurs perceive that there is some prospect for growth and ultimately survival, such entry will occur. Thus, in industries where the MES is high, it follows from the observed general small size of new-firm start-ups that the growth rate of the surviving firms would presumably be relatively high.

At the same time, those new firms not able to grow and attain the MES level of output would presumably be forced to exit from the industry, resulting in a relatively low likelihood of survival. In industries characterized by a low MES, neither the need for growth, nor the consequences of its absence are as severe, so that relatively lower growth rates but higher survival rates would be expected. Similarly, in industries where the probability of innovating is greater, more entrepreneurs may actually take a chance that they will succeed by growing into a viably sized enterprise. In such industries, one would expect that the growth of successful enterprises would be greater, but that the likelihood of survival would be correspondingly lower.

4 The empirical evidence

Not only was the large corporation thought to have superior productive efficiency, but conventional wisdom also held the large corporation to serve as the engine of technological change and innovative activity. After all, Schumpeter (1942: 106) concluded that:

'What we have got to accept is that the large-scale establishment has come to be the most powerful engine of progress'. A few years later, John Kenneth Galbraith (1956: 86) echoed Schumpeter's sentiment when he lamented: 'There is no more pleasant fiction than that technological change is the product of the matchless ingenuity of the small man forced by competition to employ his wits to better his neighbor. Unhappily, it is a fiction'.

Knowledge regarding both the determinants and the impact of technological change has been largely shaped by measurement. Measures of technological change have typically involved one of the three major aspects of the innovative process: (1) a measure of inputs into the process, such as R&D expenditures, or the share of the labour force accounted for by employees involved in R&D activities; (2) an intermediate output, such as the number of inventions that have been patented; or (3) a direct measure of innovative output.

The earliest sources of data, R&D measured, indicated that virtually all of the innovative activity was undertaken by large corporations. As patent measures became available, the general qualitative conclusions did not change, although it became clear that small firms were more involved with patent activity than with R&D. The development of direct measures of innovative activity, such as databases measuring new product and process introductions in the market, indicated something quite different. In a series of studies, Acs and Audretsch (1988, 1990) found that while large firms in manufacturing introduced a slightly greater number of significant new innovations than small firms, small-firm employment was only about half as great as large-firm employment, yielding an average small-firm innovation rate in manufacturing of 0.309, compared to a large-firm innovation rate of 0.202. The relative innovative advantage of small and large firms was found to vary considerably across industries. In some industries, such as computers and process control instruments, small firms provide the engine of innovative activity. In other industries, such as pharmaceutical products and aircraft, large firms generate most of the innovative activity. Knowledge regarding both the determinants and the impact of technological change has largely been shaped by measurement.

Acs and Audretsch (1988, 1990) concluded that some industries are more conducive to small-firm innovation while others foster the innovative activity of large corporations, corresponding to the notion of distinct technological regimes – the routinized and entrepreneurial technological regimes.

Empirical evidence in support of the traditional model of entry, which focuses on the role of excess profits as the major incentive to enter, has been ambiguous at best, leading Geroski (1991: 282) to conclude, 'Right from the start, scholars have had some trouble in reconciling the stories told about entry in standard textbooks with the substance of what they have found in their data. Very few have emerged from their work feeling that they have answered half as many questions as they have raised, much less that they have answered most of the interesting ones'.

Perhaps one reason for this trouble is the inherently static model used to capture an inherently dynamic process. Manfred Neumann (1993) has criticized this traditional model of entry, as found in the individual country studies contained in Geroski and Schwalbach (1991), because they

> are predicated on the adoption of a basically static framework. It is assumed that startups enter a given market where they are facing incumbents which naturally try to fend off entry. Since the impact of entry on the performance of incumbents seems to be only slight, the question arises whether the costs of entry are worthwhile, given the high rate of exit associated with entry. Geroski appears to be rather skeptical about that. I submit that adopting a static framework is misleading. ... In fact, generally, an entrant can only hope to succeed if he employs either a new technology or offers a new product, or both. Just imitating incumbents is almost certainly doomed to failure. If the process of entry is looked upon from this perspective the high correlation between gross entry and exit reflects the inherent risks of innovating activities. ... Obviously it is rather difficult to break loose from the inherited mode of

reasoning within the static framework. It is not without merit, to be sure, but it needs to be enlarged by putting it into a dynamic setting.

(Manfred Neumann 1993: 593–4)

Still, one of the most startling results that has emerged in empirical studies is that entry by firms into an industry is apparently not substantially deterred or even deterred at all in capital-intensive industries in which scale economies play an important role (Audretsch 1995). While studies have generally produced considerable ambiguity concerning the impact of scale economies and other measures traditionally thought to represent a *barrier to entry*, Audretsch (1995) found conclusive evidence linking the technological regime to start-up activity. New firm start-up activity tends to be substantially more prevalent under the entrepreneurial regime, or where small enterprises account for the bulk of the innovative activity, than under the routinized regime, or where the large incumbent enterprises account for most of the innovative activity. These findings are consistent with the view that differences in beliefs about the expected value of new ideas are not constant across industries but rather depend on the knowledge conditions inherent in the underlying technological regime. They also correspond to the conditions described by Christensen (2000) where large incumbent corporations experience an innovative disadvantage in some, but not all, industries, depending upon the underlying knowledge conditions.

Geroski (1995) and Audretsch (1995) point out that one of the major conclusions from studies about entry is that the process of entry does not end with entry itself. Rather, it is what happens to new firms subsequent to entering that sheds considerable light on industry dynamics. The early studies (Mansfield 1962; Hall 1987; Dunne *et al.* 1989; and Audretsch 1991) established not only that the likelihood of a new entrant surviving is quite low, but that the likelihood of survival is positively related to firm size and age. More recently, a wave of studies have confirmed these findings for diverse countries, including Portugal (Mata *et al.* 1995; Mata 1994), Germany (Wagner 1994) and Canada (Baldwin and Gorecki 1991; Baldwin 1995; Baldwin and Rafiquzzaman 1995).

Audretsch (1991) and Audretsch and Mahmood (1995) shifted the relevant question away from 'Why does the likelihood of survival vary systematically across firms?' to 'Why does the propensity for firms to survive vary systematically across industries?' The answer to this question suggests that what had previously been considered to pose a barrier to entry may, in fact, constitute not an entry barrier but rather a barrier to survival.

What has become known as *Gibrat's Law*, or the assumption that growth rates are invariant to firm size, has been subject to numerous empirical tests. Studies linking firm size and age to growth have also produced a number of stylized facts (Wagner 1992). For small and new firms there is substantial evidence suggesting that growth is negatively related to firm size and age (Hall 1987; Wagner 1992, 1994; Mata 1994; Audretsch 1995). However, for larger firms, particularly those having attained the minimum efficient scale (MES) level of output, the evidence suggests that firm growth is unrelated to size and age.

An important finding of Audretsch (1991, 1995) and Audretsch and Mahmood (1995) is that although entry may still occur in industries characterized by a high degree of scale economies, the likelihood of survival is considerably less. People will start new firms in an attempt to appropriate the expected value of their new ideas, or potential innovations, particularly under the entrepreneurial regime. As entrepreneurs gain experience in the market they learn in at least two ways. First, they discover whether they possess the *right stuff*, in terms of producing goods and offering services for which sufficient demand exists, as well as whether they can produce that good more efficiently than their rivals. Second, they learn whether they can adapt to market conditions as well as to strategies engaged in by rival firms. In terms of the first type of learning, entrepreneurs who discover that they have a viable firm will tend to expand and ultimately survive. But what about those entrepreneurs who discover that they are either not efficient or not offering a product for which there is a viable demand? The answer is that it depends – on the extent of scale economies as well as on conditions of demand. The consequences of not being able to grow will depend, to a large degree, on the extent of scale economies. Thus, in markets with only negligible scale economies, firms have a considerably greater likelihood of survival. However, where scale economies play an important role the consequences of not growing are substantially more severe, as evidenced by a lower likelihood of survival.

What emerges from the new evolutionary theories and empirical evidence on the economic role of new and small firms is that markets are in motion, with a lot of new firms entering the industry and a lot of firms exiting out of the industry. But is this motion horizontal, in that the bulk of firms exiting are comprised of firms that had entered relatively recently, or vertical, in that a significant share of the exiting firms had been established incumbents that were displaced by younger firms? In trying to shed some light on this question, Audretsch (1995) proposes two different models of the evolutionary process of industries over time. Some industries can be best characterized by the model of the revolving door, where new businesses enter, but where there is a high propensity to subsequently exit from the market. Other industries may be better characterized by the metaphor of the forest, where incumbent establishments are displaced by new entrants. Which view is more applicable apparently depends on three major factors – the underlying technological conditions, scale economies, and demand. Where scale economies play an important role, the model of the revolving door seems to be more applicable. While the rather startling result discussed above that the start-up and entry of new businesses is apparently not deterred by the presence of high scale economies, a process of firm selection analogous to a revolving door ensures that only those establishments successful enough to grow will be able to survive beyond more than a few years. Thus the bulk of new entrants that are not so successful ultimately exit within a few years subsequent to entry.

There is at least some evidence also suggesting that the underlying technological regime influences the process of firm selection and therefore the type of firm with a higher propensity to exit (Malerba and Orsenigo 1993; Dosi et al. 1995). Under the entrepreneurial regime new entrants have a greater likelihood of making an innovation. Thus, they are less likely to decide to exit from the industry, even in the face of negative profits. By contrast, under the routinized regime the incumbent businesses tend to have the innovative advantage, so that a higher portion of exiting businesses tend to be new entrants. Thus, the model of the revolving door is more applicable under technological conditions consistent with the routinized regime, and the metaphor of the forest, where the new entrants displace the incumbents, is more applicable to the entrepreneurial regime.

The general shape of the firm-size distribution is not only strikingly similar across virtually every industry – that is, skewed with only a few large enterprises and numerous small ones – but has persisted with tenacity across developed countries over a long period of time. The evolutionary view of the process of industry evolution is that new firms typically start at a very small scale of output. They are motivated by the desire to appropriate the expected value of new economic knowledge. But, depending upon the extent of scale economies in the industry, the firm may not be able to remain viable indefinitely at its start-up size. Rather, if scale economies are anything other than negligible, the new firm is likely to have to grow to survive. The temporary survival of new firms is presumably supported through the deployment of a strategy of compensating factor differentials that enables the firm to discover whether or not it has a viable product.

The empirical evidence supports such an evolutionary view of the role of new firms in manufacturing, because the post-entry growth of firms that survive tends to be spurred by the extent to which there is a gap between the MES level of output and the size of the firm. However, the likelihood of any particular new firm surviving tends to decrease as this gap increases. Such new sub-optimal scale firms are apparently engaged in the selection process. Only those firms offering a viable product that can be produced efficiently will grow and ultimately approach or attain the MES level of output. The remainder will stagnate, and depending upon the severity of the other selection mechanism – the extent of scale economies – may ultimately be forced to exit out of the industry. Thus, the persistence of an asymmetric firm-size distribution biased towards small-scale enterprise reflects the continuing process of the entry of new firms into industries and not necessarily the permanence of such small and sub-optimal enterprises over the long run. Although the skewed size distribution of firms persists with remarkable stability over long periods of time, a constant set of small and sub-optimal scale firms does not appear to be responsible for this skewed distribution. Rather, by serving as agents of change, new firms provide an essential source of new ideas and experimentation that otherwise would remain untapped in the economy.

5 The public policy response

The policy response to this new view of the knowledge production function has been to shift away from targeting outputs to inputs. In particular, this involves the creation and commercialization of knowledge. Examples include the promotion of joint R&D programmes, education and training programmes, and policies to encourage people to start new firms. As Saxenian (1995: 102) points out, 'Attracting high-tech has become the only development game of the 1980s.' Justman (1995) and Justman and Teubal (1986) show how investment in infrastructure provide an important source of growth.

The provision of venture and informal capital to facilitate the creation and growth of new firms has replaced concern about the market power of existing ones in policy debates (Hughes 1997; Mason and Harrison 1997). The lack of finance capital for new ventures has been blamed for the inability of Germany and France to shift economic activity into new industries that generate high-wage employment. One of the most repeated phrases on the pages of the business news over the last few years has been 'Put Bill Gates in Europe and it just wouldn't have worked out' (see *Newsweek* 1994).

Policy efforts to address the most pressing contemporary economic problems have focused on enablement rather than constraint. Emphasis on enabling firms and individuals to create and commercialize new knowledge is not restricted to any single country or set of countries. Laura Tyson (Tyson *et al.* 1994), former chair of the Council of Economic Advisers in the Clinton Administration, recently emphasized the importance of government policies to promote entrepreneurship and new firm start-ups in the former Soviet Union. Similarly, as unemployment in Germany surpassed four million, and stood at nearly 11 per cent of the labour force, it is not surprising that Chancellor Helmut Kohl should undertake action to spur the creation of new jobs. What is more surprising is the main emphasis announced by the Chancellor in the *Initiatives for Investment and Employment* in 1996 on new and small firms (this was announced as the Aktionsprogramm für Investitionen und Arbeitsplätze ('Soziale Einschnitte und Steuerreform sollen Wirtschaftswachstum anregen: Bundesregierung beschliesst Aktionsprogramm für Investitionen und Arbeitsplätze') *Der Tagesspiegel* 31 January: 1). The first and main point of the Chancellor's Programme consists of a commitment to the 'creation of new innovative firms'. (The original text of the *Aktionsprogramm* states, 'Offensive für unternehmerische Selbständigkeit und Innovationsfähigkeit' ('Ein Kraftakt zu Rettung des Standorts Deutschland') *Frankfurter Allgemeine* 31 January 1996: 11). The rationale underlying this policy approach by the Chancellor is stated in the Program: 'New jobs are created mainly in new firms and in small- and medium-sized enterprises' (the original text reads: 'Neue Arbeitsplätze entstehen zumeist in neugegründeten Unternehmen und im Mittelstand', see 'Ein Kraftakt zu Rettung des Standorts Deutschland', *Frankfurter Allgemeine* 31 January 1996: 11).

Audretsch and Feldman (1996) argue that industrial policies targeting the production and commercialization of new economic knowledge will have a greater impact on particular regions and not diffuse rapidly across geographic space. They point out that knowledge spillovers are a key source of new knowledge generating innovative activity, but due to the tacit nature of that knowledge, knowledge flows tend to be geographically bounded. Although the cost of transmitting information has become invariant to distance, the cost of transmitting knowledge, and especially tacit knowledge, rises with distance. By creating regions of knowledge-based economic activities, government policies can generate highly concentrated innovative clusters.

As long as the major policy issue was restricting large, oligopolistic firms in command of considerable market power, a federal or national locus of control was appropriate. This is because the benefits and costs derived from that market power are asymmetric between the local region where the firm is located and the national market, where the firm sells its product. Not only was production concentrated in one or just several regions, but the workers along with the ancillary suppliers also tended to be located in the same regions. These workers as well as the community at large share the fruits accruing from monopoly power. Systematic empirical evidence shows that wages are positively related to the degree of market power held by a firm, even after controlling for the degree of unionization. Higher profits resulting from market power are shared by labour. Workers and firms in the region have the same interest.

As Olson (1982) shows, relatively small coalitions of economic agents benefiting from some collective action tend to prevail over a large group of dispersed economic agents each incurring a small cost from that action. The costs of organizing and influencing policy are relatively low for the small coalition enjoying the benefits but large for the group of dispersed economic agents. Government policies to control large oligopolistic firms with substantial market power are not likely to be successful if implemented on the local level. Rather, as Olson (1982) predicts, a regional locus of policy towards business tends to result in the capture of policy by the coalition of local interests benefiting from that policy. Only by shifting the locus of policy away from the region to the national level can the capture of policy by special interest groups be minimized. The negative effects of market power in the form of higher prices are spread throughout the national market while the benefits accruing from that power are locally concentrated. Lazonick (1991) argues that historically encompassing organizations are often more important and enduring than Olson considered, and distributional coalitions appear in context where the key players do not have sufficient collective organization. Ferleger and Lazonick (1993) provide the compelling example of the role of the state in developing US agriculture.

Starting in the Carter administration in the late 1970s and continuing into the administrations of presidents Reagan, Bush and Clinton, antitrust has been de-emphasized and a twenty-year wave of deregulation has led to a downsizing and even closure of a number of the former regulatory agencies.

Many economists interpret the downsizing of the federal agencies charged with the regulation of business as the eclipse of government intervention. But to interpret the retreat of the federal government as the end of public intervention is to confuse the downsizing of government with a shifting of the locus of government policy away from the federal to the local level. The last decade has seen the emergence of a set of enabling policy initiatives at the local level. This new type of industrial policy is decentralized and regional in nature. As Sternberg (1996) emphasizes in his review of successful technology policies in the four leading technological countries, the most important industrial policies in the last decades have been local, not national. They have occurred in locations such as Research Triangle (Link 1995), Austin, Texas and Cambridge (UK). Sternberg (1996) shows how the success of a number of different high-technology clusters spanning the four most technologically advanced countries is the direct result of enabling policies undertaken at the regional level.

Eisinger (1990) asks the question, 'Do the American States do industrial policy?' in a 1990 article published in the *British Journal of Political Science*. Lowery and Gray (1990) confirm Eisinger's affirmative answer by analysing the impact of state industrial policy in the USA. They develop a new data set on gross state product and a new measure of state industrial policy activism. Their results suggest that the implementation of industrial policy at the state level tends to promote growth. For example, Feller (1997: 289) points out that 'in theory and implementation, state technology development programs – as in Texas, Ohio, New York, New Jersey, and Pennsylvania – may be viewed as bands on a wide spectrum from basic research to product development, with the ends reflecting quite divergent state strategies'. The Advanced Research Program in Texas has provided support for basic research and the strengthening of the university infrastructure, which played a central role in recruiting MCC and Sematech and developing a high-tech cluster around Austin. The Thomas Edison Centers in Ohio, the Advanced Technology Centers in New Jersey and the Centers for Advanced Technology at Case Western Reserve University, Rutgers University and the University of Rochester have supported generic, precompetitive research. This support has generally provided diversified technology development involving a mix of activities encompassing generic research, applied research and manufacturing modernization through a broad spectrum of industrial collaborators spanning technology-intensive multinational corporations, regional manufactures and new firm start-ups.

This shift in the locus of policy is the result of two factors. First, because the source of comparative advantage is knowledge, which tends to be localized in regional clusters, public policy requires an understanding of region-specific characteristics and idiosyncrasies. As Sternberg (1996) concludes, regional strengths provide the major source of innovative clusters. The second factor is that the motivation underlying government policy is now growth and the creation of (highpaying) jobs, largely through the creation of new firms. These new firms are typically small and pose no oligopolistic threat in national or international markets. There are no external costs imposed on consumers in the national economy in the form of higher prices as in the case of a large oligopolistic corporation in possession of market power. There is no reason that the promotion of local economies imposes a cost on consumers in the national economy, so that localized industrial policy is justified and does not result in any particular loss incurred by agents outside of the region.

6 Conclusions

While traditional theories suggest that entrepreneurship will retard economic growth, new theories suggest exactly the opposite – that entrepreneurship will stimulate and generate growth. The reason for these theoretical discrepancies lies in the context of the underlying theory. In the traditional theory, new knowledge plays no role; rather, static efficiency, determined largely by the ability to exhaust scale economies, dictates growth. By contrast, the new theories are dynamic in nature and emphasize the role that knowledge plays. Because knowledge is inherently uncertain, asymmetric and associated with high costs of transactions, divergences emerge concerning the expected value of new ideas. Economic agents therefore have an incentive to leave an incumbent firm and start a new firm in an attempt to commercialize the perceived value of their knowledge. Entrepreneurship is the vehicle by which (the most radical) new ideas are sometimes implemented.

While this policy emphasis on small and new firms as engines of dynamic efficiency may seem startling after decades of looking at the corporate giants to bestow efficiency, it is anything but new. Before the United States was even half a century old, Alexis de Tocqueville, in 1835, reported, 'What astonishes me in the United States is not so much the marvellous grandeur of some undertakings as the innumerable multitude of small ones'.

DAVID AUDRETSCH
INDIANA UNIVERSITY

Further reading

(References cited in the text marked *)

* Acs, Z.J. and Audretsch, D.B. (1988) 'Innovation in large and small firms: an empirical analysis', *American Economic Review* 78 (4): 678–90. (Documents the innovative strengths and weaknesses of small firms.)
* Acs, Z.J. and Audretsch, D.B. (1990) *Innovation and Small Firms*, Cambridge: MIT Press. (Analyses the determinants of small-firm innovative activity.)
* Acs, Z.J. and Audretsch, D.B. (1993) *Small Firms and Entrepreneurship: An East–West Perspective,* Cambridge: Cambridge University Press.

* Arrow, K.J. (1962) 'Economic welfare and the allocation of resources for invention', in R.R. Nelson (ed.) *The Rate and Direction of Inventive Activity*, Princeton: Princeton University Press. (Develops a theoretical framework for knowledge-based economic activity.)
* Audretsch, D.B. (1991) 'New firm survival and the technological regime', *Review of Economics and Statistics* 73 (3): 441–50. (Shows how the likelihood of small-firm survival is lower in innovative industries than in non-innovative industries.)
* Audretsch, D.B. (1995) *Innovation and Industry Evolution*, Cambridge: MIT Press. (Develops theory and empirical analyses of the impact of entrepreneurship on industry evolution.)
* Audretsch, D.B. and Feldman, M.P. (1996) 'R&D spillovers and the geography of innovation and production', *American Economic Review* 86 (3): 630–40. (Links geographic clustering of innovation and production to the importance of knowlegde.)
* Audretsch, D.B. and Mahmood, T. (1995) 'New-firm survival: new results using a hazard function', *Review of Economics and Statistics* 77 (1): 97–103. (Shows how the survival of start-ups are shaped by the industry environment.)
  Audretsch, D.B. and Stephan, P.E. (1996) 'Company-scientist locational links: the case of biotechnology', *American Economic Review* 86 (3): 641–52. (Shows how the geographic links between scientists and biotechnology companies are shaped by the role the scientist plays in bringing knowledge to the firm.)
  Audretsch, D.B. and Thruik, R. (1999) *Innovation, Industry Evolution, and Employment*, Cambridge: Cambridge University Press. (Links job creation and wage performance to industry evolution and entrepreneurial activity.)
* Audretsch, D.B. and Yamawaki, H. (1991) 'Suboptimal scale plants and compensating factor differentials in U.S. And Japanese manufacturing', in D.B. Audretsch and J.J. Siegfried (eds) *Empriical Studies in Industrial Organization*, Boston: Kluwer Academic Publishers, pp. 161–86.
* Baldwin, J.R. (1995) *The Dynamics of Industrial Competition*, Cambridge: Cambridge University Press. (Analysis of industry dynamics, such as entry, growth and turbulence.)
* Baldwin, J.R. and Rafiquzzaman, M. (1995) 'Selection versus evolutionary adaptation: learning and post-entry performance', *International Journal of Industrial Organization* 13 (4): 501–23. (Tests whether selection or adaptation drives industry evolution.)
* Baldwin, J.R. and Gorecki, P.K. (1991) 'Entry, exit, and production growth', in P. Geroski and J. Schwalbach, (eds) *Entry and Market Contestability: An International Comparison*, Oxford: Basil Blackwell. (Provides links between entry, exit and firm growth.)
  Best, M. (1990) *The New Competition: Institutions of Industrial Restructuring*, Cambridge: Harvard University Press. (Shows how globalization is triggering industrial restructuring.)
* Brown, C., Hamilton, J. and Medoff, J. (1990) *Employers Large and Small*, Cambridge: Cambridge University Press. (Documents that wages are systematically and positively related to firm size.)
  Carrol, P. (1993) *Big Blues: The Unmaking of IBM*, New York: Crown Publishers. (Documents the difficulties IBM had in innovating in the 1980s.)
  Caves, R.E. (1998) 'Industrial organization and new findings on the turnover and mobility of firms', *Journal of Economic Literature* 36 (4): 1947–82. (Literature synthesis and review of firm and industry dynamics.)
  Chandler, A.D. (1977) *The Visible Hand: The Managerial Revolution in American Business*, Cambridge: Harvard University Press. (Documents the emergence of the modern corporation.)
* Chandler, A.D. (1990) *Scale and Scope: The Dynamics of Industrial Capitalism*, Cambridge: Harvard University Press. (Documents the role of scale and scope in shaping the modern corporation.)
* Christensen, C.M. (2000) *The Inventor's Dilemma: When New Technologies Cause Great Firms to Fail*, New York: HarperCollins. (Documents the difficulties large corporations have in inventing.)
* Coase, R.H. (1937) 'The nature of the firm', *Economica* 4 (4): 386–405. (Basis for transactions cost economics.)
* Cohen, W.M. and Klepper, S. (1991) 'The tradeoff between firm size and diversity for technological progress', *Journal of Small Business Economics*, December.
* Cohen, W.M. and Klepper, S. (1992) 'The anatomy of R&D intensity distributions', *American Economic Review* 82(4): 773–9. (This, and the above article consider the economics of technological change.)
  Cringley, R.X. (1993) *Accidental Empires*, New York: Harper Business. (Provides anecdotal description of Silicon Valley.)
* Davis, S.J., Haltiwanger, J.C. and Schuh, S. (1996) *Job Creation and Destruction*, Cambridge,

MA: MIT Press. (Research on employment flows in US manufacturing.)

* Dertouzos, M.L., Lester, R.K. and Solow, R.M. (1989) *Made in America: Regaining the Productive Edge*, Cambridge, MA: MIT Press. (Seen as the 'definitive' account of how America works.)

Dosi, G. (1982) 'Technological paradigms and technological trajectories: a suggested interpretation of the determinants and directions of technical change', *Research Policy* 13 (1): 3–20. (Introduces the concept of technological trajectories.)

* Dosi, G. (1988) 'Sources, procedures, and microeconomic effects of innovation', *Journal of Economic Literature* 26 (3): 1120–71. (Literature review of microfoundations of innovation.)

* Dosi, G., Marsili, O., Orsenigo, L. and Salvatore, R. (1995) 'Learning, market selection and the evolution of industrial structures', *Small Business Economics* 7 (6): 411–36. (Simulation models linking small business to industry evolution.)

* Dunne, T., Roberts, M.J. and Samuelson, L. (1989) 'The growth and failure of U.S. manufacturing plants', *Quarterly Journal of Economics* 104: 671–98. (Empirical documentation of entry, growth and failure.)

* Eisinger, P. (1990) 'Do the American States do industrial policy?' *British Journal of Political Science* 20: 509–35. (Examines state policy to promote small business and economic development.)

* Feller, I. (1997) 'Federal and State Government roles in science and technology,' *Economic Development Quarterly* 11 (4): 283–96. (Shows how states play a crucial role in science and technology policy.)

* Ferleger, L. and Lazonick, W. (1993) 'The managerial revolution and the developmental state: the case of US agriculture', *Business and Economic History* 22 (2): 67–98. (Shows how the government engaged in policies to develop US agriculture.)

* Galbraith, J.K. (1956) *American Capitalism*, Boston: Houghton Mifflin. (Describes major US economic and social institutions and their functioning.)

* Geroski, P.A. (1991) 'Some data-driven reflections on the entry process', in P. Georski and J. Schwalbach (eds) *Entry and Market Contestability: An International Comparison*, Oxford: Basil Blackwell. (Reviews and interprets entry literature.)

* Geroski, P.A. (1995) 'What do we know about entry', *International Journal of Industrial Organization* (Special Issue on *The Post Entry Performance of Firms*, D.B. Audretsch and J. Mata, eds) 13 (4). (Reviews and interprets literature on the post-entry performance of firms.)

* Geroski, P.A. and Schwalbach, J. (eds) (1991) *Entry and Market Contestability: An International Comparison* Oxford: Basil Blackwell. (Contains a collection of empirical studies identifying determinants of entry in different countries.)

* Griliches, Z. (1979) 'Issues in assessing the contribution of R&D to productivity growth', *Bell Journal of Economics* 10 (Spring): 92–116. (Introduces the knowledge production function model.)

* Hall, B.H. (1987) 'The relationship between firm size and firm growth in the US manufacturing sector', *Journal of Industrial Economics* 35 (June): 583–605. (Links firm growth to firm size and age.)

* Hannan, M.T. and Freeman, J. (1989) *Organizational Ecology*, Cambridge, MA: Harvard University Press. (Treats firm demography as an ecological phenomenon.)

* Hirschman, A.O. (1970) *Exit, Voice, and Loyalty*, Cambridge: Harvard University Press. (Provides the theoretical framework for decisions to remain in a situation or change.)

Holtz-Eakin, Rosen, H.S. and Weathers, R. (2000) 'Horatio Alger meets the mobility tables', *Small Business Economics* 14 (4): 243–74. (Links entrepreneurship to income mobility.)

* Hughes, A. (1997) 'Finance for SMEs: A U.K. perspective', *Small Business Economics* 9 (2): 151–66. (Documents financing sources of SMEs in the United Kingdom.)

Ijiri, Y. and Simon, H.A. (1977) *Skew Distributions and Sizes of Business Firms*, Amsterdam: North Holland. (Documents that the firm-size distribution is skewed and consists mostly of SMEs.)

* Jovanovic, B. (1982) 'Selection and evolution of industry,' *Econometrica* 50 (2): 649–70. (Introduces a theory of selection based on entrepreneurial learning.)

* Justman, M. (1995) 'Infrastructure, growth and the two dimensions of industrial policy', *Review of Economic Studies* 62 (1): 131–57. (Links industrial policy to growth.)

* Justman, M. and Teubal, M. (1986) 'Innovation policy in an open economy: a normative framework to strategic and tactical issues', *Research Policy* 15: 121–38. (Analyses innovation policies.)

Knight, F.H. (1921) *Risk, Uncertainty and Profit*, New York: Houghton Mifflin. (Analyses role of uncertainty in decision making.)

* Lazonick, W. (1991) *Business Organization and the Myth of the Market Economy*, Cambridge: Cambridge University Press. (Shows how

- business organization preempts the market economy.)
* Link, A. (1995) *A Generosity of Spirit*, Durham, NC: Duke University Press. (Documents the formation of Research Triangle.)
* Lowery, D. And Gray, V. (1990) 'The corporatist foundation of state industrial policy', *Social Science Quarterly* 71 (March): 3–24. (Analyses the impact of state industrial poilicy in the USA.)
* Malerba, F. and Orsenigo, L. (1993) 'Technological regimes and firm behaviour', *Industrial and Corporate Change* 2 (1): 74–89. (Links technological regimes to firm behaviour.)
* Mansfield, E. (1962) 'Entry, Gibrat's Law, innovation, and the growth of firms', *American Economic Review* 52 (5): 1023–51. (Analyses the entry and growth of firms.)
- Mason, C.M. and Harrison, T. (1997) 'Business angel networks and the development of the informal venture captial market in the UK: is there still a role for the public sector?', *Small Business Economics*, 9(2), April: 111–23.
* Mata, J. (1994) 'Firm growth during infancy', *Small Business Economics* 6 (1): 27–40. (Analyses the growth patterns of start-ups.)
- Mata, J. and Portugal, P. (1994) 'Life duration of new firms', *Journal of Industrial Economics* 27 (3): 227–46. (Analyses survival patterns of start-ups.)
* Mata, J., Portugal, P. and Guimaraes, P. (1995) 'The survival of new plants: start-up conditions and post-entry evolution', *International Journal of Industrial Organization* 13 (4): 459–82. (Analyses the post-entry performance of start-ups in Portugal.)
- Moore, J.H. (1992) 'Measuring Soviet economic growth: old problems and new complications', *Journal of Institutional and Theoretical Economics* 148 (1): 72–92.
* Nelson, R.R. and Winter, S.G. (1982) *An Evolutionary Theory of Economic Change*, Cambridge: Harvard University Press. (Revisits the Soviet growth controversy.)
* Neumann, M. (1993) 'Review of entry and market contestability: an international comparison', *International Journal of Industrial Organization* 11 (4): 593–4. (Reviews a book on entry and provides critical comments on the static framework.)
* *Newsweek* (1994) 'Where's the venture capital?' 31 October: 44. (A similar sentiment was expressed by Joschka Fischer, parliamentary leader of the Green Party in Germany, who lamented: 'A company like Microsoft would never have a chance in Germany' ('Those German banks and their industrial treasures', *The Economist*, 21 January 1994: 778).)
- Olson, M. (1982) *The Rise and Decline of Nations*, New Haven, CT: Yale University Press.
- O'Sullivan (2000) *Contests for Corporate Control: Corporate Governance and Economic Performance in the United States and Germany*, Oxford: Oxford University Press. (Links corporate governance to firm performance in Germany and the USA.)
- Palfreman, J. and Swade, D. (1991) *The Dream Machine: Exploring the Computer Age*, London: BBC Books. (Documents the development of the computer industry.)
* Penrose, E.T. (1959) *The Theory of the Growth of the Firm*, Oxford: Basil Blackwell. (Provides a framework for analysing firm growth.)
* Pratten, C.F. (1971) *Economies of Scale in Manufacturing Industry*, Cambridge: Cambridge University Press. (Provides estimates of the importance of scale economies.)
* Restow, W.W. (1987) 'Here comes a new political chapter in America', *International Herald Tribune*, 2 January.
- Saxenian, A. (1990) 'Regional networks and the resurgence of Silicon Valley', *California Management Review* 33 (1): 89–111. (Documents the role of networks in Silicon Valley.)
* Saxenian, A. (1995) *Regional Advantage*, Cambridge, MA: Harvard University Press.
- Scherer, F.M. (1976) 'Industrial structure, scale economies, and worker alienation', in R.T. Masson and P.D. Qualls (eds) *Essays on Industrial Organization in Honor of Joe S. Bain*, Cambridge: Ballinger, pp. 105–22. (Links worker alienation to large corporations.)
* Scherer, F.M. (1991) 'Changing perspectives on the firm size problem', in Z.J. Acs and D.B. Audretsch (eds), *Innovation and Technological Change. An International Comparison*, Ann Arbor: University of Michigan Press. (Describes how the conventional wisdom about small firms has evolved over time.)
- Schumpeter, J.A. (1911) *Theorie der wirtschaftlichen Entwicklung. Eine Untersuchung über Unternehmergewinn, Kapital, Kredit, Zins und den Konjunkturzyklus*, Berlin: Duncker und Humblot. (Provides theory of creative destruction.)
* Schumpeter, J.A. (1942) *Capitalism, Socialism and Democracy*, New York: Harper and Row. (Suggests large corporations are more innovative than small firms.)
- Simon, H.A. and Bonini, C.P. (1958) 'The size distribution of business firms', *American Economic Review* 48 (4): 607–17. (Documents a skewed size distribution.)

* Sternberg, R. (1996) 'Technology policies and the growth of regions', *Small Business Economics* 8 (2): 75–86. (Analyses technology policies in a number of countries and links them to regional growth.)
  Sutton, J. (1997) 'Gibrat's Legacy', *Journal of Economic Literature* 35 (1): 40–59. (Reviews literature testing Gibrat's Law, which posits that firm growth is invariant to firm size.)
* Sylos-Labini, P. (1992) 'Capitalism, socialism, and democracy and large-scale firms', in F.M. Scherer and M. Perlman (eds) *Entrepreneurship, Technological Innovation, and Economic Growth*, Ann Arbor: University of Michigan, 55–64. (Notes that firms are getting larger over time and small business is disappearing.)
* Teece, D.J. (1993) 'The dynamics of industrial capitalism: perspectives on Alfred Chandler's scale and scope', *Journal of Economic Literature* 31: 199–225. (Provides an interpretation of Chandler's work.)
* Teece, D., Rumult, R., Dosi, G. and Winter, S. (1994) 'Understanding corporate coherence: theory and evidence', *Journal of Economic Behavior and Organization* 23 (1): 1–30. (Explains why large corporations may have difficulties innovating.)
* Thurow, Lester (1984) 'Losing the economic race', *New York Review of Books* September: 29–31.
* Tyson, L. d'A., Petrin, T. and Rogers, H. (1994) 'Promoting entrepreneurship in Eastern Europe', *Small Business Economics* 6 (3): 165–84. (Suggests that entrepreneurship is key to reviving Eastern Europe.)
* *U.S. News and World Report* (1993) 'What do Bill Clinton, George Bush and Bob Dole have in common? All have uttered one of the most enduring homilies in American political discourse: That small businesses create most of the nation's jobs', *U.S. News and World Report* 16 August.
* Wagner, J. (1992) 'Firm size, firm growth, and persistence of chance: testing Gibrat's law with establishment data from Lower Saxony. 1978–1989', *Small Business Economics* 4 (2): 125–31. (Tests Gibrat's Law for Germany.)
* Wagner, J. (1994) 'Small firm entry in manufacturing industries: Lower Saxony, 1979–1989', *Small Business Economics* 6 (3): 211–24. (Analyses the entry on Germany.)
* Weiss, L.W. (1979) 'The structure–performance paradigm and antitrust', *University of Pennsylvania Law Review* 127 (April): 1104–40. (Suggests that a cost of allowing oligopoly is that it enables inefficient sub-optimal scale SMEs to survive.)
* Williamson, O.E. (1968) 'Economies as an antitrust defense: the welfare tradeoffs', *American Economic Review* 58 (1): 18–36. (Argues that a tradeoff exists between corporate size and efficiency, on the one hand, and less efficiency with decentralization on the other hand.)
  Williamson, O.E. (1975) *Markets and Hierarchies: Antitrust Analysis and Implications*, New York: The Free Press. (Transactions cost analysis.)
  Winter, S.G. (1984) 'Schumpeterian competition in alternative technological regimes', *Journal of Economic Behavior and Organization*, 5 (September–December): 287–320. (Argues for the existence of two distinct technological regimes, one dominated by SMEs, the other by large corporations.)

See also: COOPERATION AND COMPETITION; DYNAMIC CAPABILITIES; ENTERPRISE OWNERSHIP, TYPES OF; GALBRAITH, J.K.; GROWTH OF THE FIRM AND NETWORKING; INDUSTRIAL AGGLOMERATIONS; INDUSTRIAL DYNAMICS; INNOVATION; MARSHALL, A.; MARX, K.; MEANS, G.; PENROSE, E.T.; SCHUMACHER, E.; SCHUMPETER, J.; SMITH, A.; WILLIAMSON, O.E.

Built environment

1 Introduction
2 Context
3 Analysis
4 Evaluation
5 Conclusions and future trends

Overview

This article focuses on the economics of the production and use of the built environment. Buildings and structures account for a significant, but declining proportion of fixed capital investment in most OECD countries. Their use underpins all other productive and social activities. Moreover, they tend to be long-lived and have to accommodate changes in use as well as the introduction of different vintages of technology.

The entry explains how broad-sweeping technical, economic, social and political changes relate to innovation in design, construction and renewal of the built environment. Such changes are important from an economic perspective within construction and its supply industries, as well as for wider issues of economic prosperity.

Three issues are considered. First, the implications of changes in demand on the market for new types of buildings and structures. Second, the impact of new technologies on the performance of the construction sector. Third, the implications of changing governance structures and the role of the state in the production and use of the built environment.

It is argued that rather than being seen solely as a mature sector, innovative approaches to the production and use of the built environment offer examples of new practices in the management of project-based enterprises. Competencies to design, integrate, install and operate complex technological systems are of particular importance for the efficient and effective production of modern urban environments and infrastructures.

1 Introduction

The production and use of the built environment is one of the oldest and most important economic activities. Buildings provide shelter from the external environment and facilities to support daily life at home, in the work place and for education, health, travel and leisure. Two elements are needed to provide these facilities: passive components, derived from the architecture and engineering of structures, envelopes and fabric of buildings; and active elements including mechanical, electrical and electronic systems which are fitted inside them. These provide the means for conditioning and controlling internal environments and the infrastructure for moving people, goods and services. Other constructed products such as transport and utilities infrastructures can also be defined in terms of their passive or structural elements and active servicing systems.

For the purposes of economic analysis, the built environment is classified into different sub-sectors: housing (public and private), commercial, industrial, civil engineering and repair and maintenance. The boundaries between these market segments are becoming increasingly blurred with changes in public and private ownership and financial structures, new forms of economic activity based on information processing and the growth of the service sector, and the need to upgrade existing facilities leading to new types of work to existing buildings.

Historically, production and use of buildings and structures has been a local and regional activity in which local materials and labour have been brought together to meet particular market needs. The local nature of production also reflects particular geological and climatic conditions. Local peculiarities of construction markets, cultural and socio-institutional contexts have been important. This remains the case to some extent in OECD countries and to a larger extent in developing economies. For example, research on earthquakes is a high priority in the USA – particularly California – and Japan; whilst coldweather construction facilities are important in the Nordic Countries and Canada. In all countries, most construction activities are carried out by local firms that compete on initial bid price, rather than on quality of technical competence. In consequence these organizations tend to have an over-developed sense of cost and an under-developed sense of value associated with the potential benefits arising from the use of the built environment.

2 Context

Production of the built environment

In OECD countries, construction activities contribute between 5 and 7 per cent of the total value of goods and services (GDP): the figure is higher if the value of construction-related materials and components is included. In some fast growing, newly industrializing regions, for example, until recently, in Japan and Korea, construction accounted for around 12 to 14 per cent of GDP. These are large industries, often employing millions of people, accounting for 8 to 9 per cent of economy-wide employment in 1994 (OECD 1997). About half of construction output is in markets for residential buildings. The proportion of work carried out as repair and maintenance varies from nearly 50 per cent in the UK to probably no more than 25 per cent in Japan (although accurate data are unavailable in Japan). Construction value added declined as a proportion of GDP between 1977 and 1997 across most OECD countries and labour productivity growth has also been slow (Gann 2000: 37).

Construction is a *process* rather than an *industry*: it includes designing, constructing, maintaining and adapting the built environment. These activities involve a multitude of organizations from a range of different industrial sectors, working together in temporary coalitions on project-specific tasks. These functions include design, engineering, supply and integration, erection and installation of a diverse array of materials, components and increasingly complex technical systems. The project-based nature of these activities is important, because this immediately creates discontinuities in the development of technical knowledge and its transfer within and between firms, from one project to the next.

In most countries, the work of designing, engineering and integrating materials, components and systems to make buildings and structures is the domain of project-based construction organizations. The structure of industry is such that the majority of firms are very small. In the EU countries, 97 per cent of the 1.8 million construction firms employ less than 20 people (WS Atkins 1994). Markets are segmented according to different product types: housing, commercial and industrial buildings, civil engineering structures and infrastructures, public works, repair maintenance and improvement work. The smallest firms are usually active in local markets where much of their work can be described as using 'traditional' technologies. Some small and medium sized enterprises specialize in particular technical areas. A proportion of these are innovative, making use of – and sometimes developing – new technologies. Medium sized firms usually work in regional and national markets. Large firms work nationally and internationally. Efficiency, responsiveness and capability to innovate depend to a large extent on the structure of the firm, the types of skills employed and relationships with other firms embodying technical expertise.

The project-based nature of production results in organizational complexity and discontinuities in which transaction costs can be high. Adversarial relations often result from attempts by different participants to pass on risk to others and blaming each other when problems arise. These problems are particularly acute in Anglo-Saxon forms of construction organization. North European and Japanese forms offer different approaches in which longer-term partnerships between suppliers and between suppliers and customers exist. There have been successive attempts to improve the organization of production through the development of new relationships. Attempts to meet customers' needs and improve productivity and quality have resulted in efforts to implement 'lean construction' principles in countries like the USA and the UK.

Use of the built environment

Construction's significance to wealth creation and quality of life extends far beyond its direct economic contributions. The products and services provided by construction create an infrastructure that supports existing and newly emerging social and economic activities. For this reason, modern, well provided, high-quality buildings and structures help to underpin performance in other branches of the economy and improve living standards. Prospects for improved social and economic conditions are compromised when inadequate, inappropriate, out-of-date buildings and structures are produced and when maintenance is poorly carried out.

Buildings and structures are usually long-lived and they often have to be adapted in-use to meet different and changing needs. Constructed products that are designed and built to cope with change are therefore likely to offer greater utility. Furthermore, construction processes and constructed products often damage the environment and disrupt older forms of social cohesion. Issues concerning the built environment often attract public interest. Its development and use therefore often raise international, regional and local issues concerning the governance of technology, and this governance process shapes the conditions within which development takes place.

3 Analysis

Changing patterns of demand

Construction output is cyclical. In many market segments, construction activities are demand-led, particularly where large facilities and infrastructures are concerned. Demand for buildings and structures, therefore, tends to fluctuate with business and investment cycles. Over the longer term, the demand for new types of buildings and structures stimulates radical innovation in both construction technologies and processes. For example, the switch from steam to electric power in factories led to demand for new types of factory buildings at the beginning of the twentieth century. Similar shifts are evident with the growth of the information economy since around 1980. The built environment had previously been designed to accommodate physical, energy-intensive production activities. Increasing use of information systems resulted in demands for new types of flexible spaces as well as specialized facilities such as silicon chip fabrication plants. Moreover, there is a close relationship between sectors of the economy which act as prime movers in the development of new productive capabilities or underpinning technologies and their first use of new types of buildings and structures. For example, the iron and steel industries were among the first to deploy iron and steel in their own buildings and facilities; similarly the telecommunications and electronics industries have been the first to develop 'intelligent buildings' (Gann 2000).

In many construction markets, the demand has increased for flexible, lightweight, multi-function spaces that can be reconfigured for different uses quickly and cheaply. Users increasingly prefer engineered solutions that offer greater choice of layout, finish and aesthetic quality. A direct relationship exists between performance in design and construction and efficient and effective operation of these facilities. Comprehension of user–producer relations has never been easy, particularly because of the involvement of so many organizations and interests in convoluted demand and supply chains. Yet rapid shifts in patterns of demand emphasize the need for closer links between producers and users than has hitherto been the case. This is particularly so if user needs are to be properly articulated and fulfilled. In addition, knowledge required for design and construction is expanding because the operation of new facilities often involves their management as part of larger and older technical systems and infrastructures. Thus individual projects must be designed and built within constraints defined by existing systems and the legacies of the technologies they embody. Products whose operating requirements and long-term costs are considered in the design process and that are planned and built to cope with change, may therefore offer greater utility.

Technological change

The development and use of new technologies is having implications for productivity, and competitiveness in construction activities and for the quality of constructed products – the built environment. Innovation is driven by the need to improve customer satisfaction, construct new types of buildings and structures, improve competitiveness and adopt materials and component innovations made upstream in supply chains by manufacturers. Current major areas of technological innovation include:

- information technology in design, engineering and construction processes – including simulation and prototyping tools, virtual reality, CAD and project management systems;
- information technology in constructed products, relating to new types of 'intelligent buildings' – including sensing, communication and control systems;
- on-site plant and equipment – including automation and robotics, programmable machines and hand-held power tools;
- new materials – including ceramics, composites, plastics, glazing products, and bio-chemical materials used in bio-remediation and cleaning processes;
- new fixing technologies – including adhesives, mastics and universal joints;
- new types of components, including modular, standardized and pre-assembled units and systems.

Many types of buildings and structures are becoming more complex as new vintages of technologies are added to older generations. There are two dimensions to this issue. First, new, cheaper or better performing materials do not necessarily replace existing ones. Rather, they enlarge the range and capabilities of the industry. Second, demands for higher performance buildings and structures (increased safety, energy efficiency and better productivity derived from use – such as better lighting, faster lifts, etc.) often result in more complex systems.

Technological innovation is closely associated with organizational and skill changes. Demand for both specialist and generalist skills has increased in the last two years. For example a range of new specialist skills has emerged from vertical transportation engineers, through fire and acoustical engineering to façade engineering. The need to coordinate a plethora of specialists in design and production, or to manage facilities throughout their life-cycles has given rise to demand for new generalists – typically those capable of systems integration (Gann and Salter 1999).

Governance and the role of the state

Production and use of the built environment raises many issues of public interest. The state plays multiple roles in its development, ranging from procurement of public buildings and infrastructure (accounting for between 30 – 45 per cent of construction work in OECD countries), sponsorship of research and development, to regulation across a spectrum of activities. The latter includes: national and local planning guidance (what is built and where); building regulations and building controls (the quality of construction and its safety and energy efficiency in use); regulations governing building materials and components; regulations governing production processes and employment (health and safety of workers, etc.).

Governments seeking to comply with the Kyoto Agreement on reduction of noxious emissions are focusing attention on the built environment sector, which is one of the largest contributors to greenhouse gases. This concern is resulting in tighter legislation regarding energy efficiency and emissions control. It is also focusing attention away from initial capital cost of buildings to whole-life costs.

Innovation creates the need for new technical competencies and R&D within construction organizations. It also raises issues concerning public safety. A dynamic environment exists with implications for a number of public policy issues in which governments continue to have a role to play in protecting the public interest, including regulation and support for R&D. In construction, public policy increasingly involves work on international regulations and standards. It is increasingly being recognized by OECD governments that performance-based regulatory regimes are more beneficial than traditional prescriptive regulations if innovative potential is not to be constrained.

4 Evaluation

Much of the conventional wisdom in industrial economics is closely linked to the production paradigm of mass-market commodity goods in which firms and markets tend to be clearly defined, recognizable entities. But in the production of the built environment, the single firm, the normal unit of analysis for prescriptive management and innovation theory, is seldom properly understood in relation to the overall process and technical change. Here, groups of firms collaborate together in temporary coalitions on projects. They have to manage networks of highly complex innovation interfaces. Competitiveness rarely depends on the single firm, but rather on the efficient functioning of the entire innovation network. The products of project-based industries rarely conform to the 'normal' concept of the market, based on mass-production commodity goods where anonymous buyers purchase goods at arm's-length. Markets for project-based industries are often highly institutionalized, frequently politicized and selection mechanisms are usually far more complex than in the markets associated with mass consumption goods, upon which much of conventional wisdom is based. In some construction markets, investments are extremely large and intermittent and may take several years. In large projects, buyers are rarely anonymous; they feed the innovation process and often fund and drive new developments.

A central requirement for improving performance in the production and use of the built environment is to provide better information for senior managers about the effects of technological and organizational innovation on the structure of firms, their strategies, competencies, knowledge bases and links with other firms. Such analysis has so far escaped the attention of most policy advisers and researchers in the mainstreams of management science, industrial economics and technology policy who have tended to focus their attention on mass-production, commodity goods and single product industries.

5 Conclusions and future trends

The production and use of the built environment is likely to continue to be of economic significance, particularly if users' demands for higher performance buildings coupled with environmental protection are to be met. Achieving increased performance is likely to result in both organizational and technological innovation. The dominant trend is likely to be away from a labour-intensive craft industry which hones and adapts materials on-site to meet barely articulated requirements, towards an engineering and assembly process, which integrates the types of systems needed for modern economic activities and lifestyles. The key issues are likely to include the following:

- *Little change in overall construction output.* It is unlikely that construction output will increase in most developed OECD countries. However, the need to modernize poor quality housing and infrastructure, particularly in Eastern European countries, together with demand for new types of buildings for the information age, could stimulate new types of construction activity. It is also possible that additional investment will be made in buildings and structures for environmental protection reasons and if significant cost reductions can be achieved through technical and organizational change.
- *Improvements in the production process as a whole.* Current levels of inefficiency and wasted materials, labour and time, together with pollution could be reduced by at least 50 per cent by streamlining supply-chains and by the introduction of better management practices. Increased use of standardized and pre-assembled components, harnessed to new IT management systems, could improve performance further. Moreover, IT systems could be used to help integration of briefing and design decision making in order to improve flexibility to meet customers' needs. They could also be

used to improve the quality of facilities management.
- *Construction employment.* Technological and organizational innovation aimed at improving performance is likely to have consequences for employment, training and recruitment. The level of productivity improvements required to bring construction up to expectations based upon modern manufacturing processes is unlikely to be achieved without a reduction of traditional on-site construction work. This will mean a reduction of employment, creating tensions in countries where construction is still viewed as a domestic industry to be used by governments to stimulate employment growth. It is unlikely that construction markets can expand sufficiently quickly in most OECD countries to ameliorate the employment lost through productivity-improving technical change. However, there could be potential to substitute new employment opportunities in construction services relating to waste management and environmental control for that lost because of more productive construction processes.
- *Productivity.* Various benchmarking studies in the UK, North America and Japan suggest that many on-site construction processes are only 30–40 per cent productive. When the total process is considered from initial client discussions to final completion and operation of facilities, there is room for large productivity improvements. This issue is directly related to technical and managerial competence and concerns skills and training as well as R&D. Immediate performance improvements could be achieved through organizational changes without changing technologies, simply by removing waste in the process. Evidence from successful demonstration projects illustrates major performance benefits when new IT systems have been implemented for coordination and control, together with new component-based approaches to construction.
- *International competitiveness.* An international construction market exists in large construction projects, and specialist development projects. Moreover, there is a well-developed international market for construction materials and components. The manufacturing firms in this segment tend to be much larger than contractors and design organizations. Firms supplying international construction markets tend to be more professional and focus more on issues of international competitiveness than their domestic counterparts. The development of further technical capabilities in international construction and consulting design and engineering firms could increase export markets in countries outside the OECD.

  Local and regional construction organizations in many countries are increasingly being influenced by issues of international competitiveness, whether through the sourcing of materials, components, plant or equipment from large multinational producers, or through the supply of technical services such as consulting engineering, design and project management. The integration of European markets and the gradual harmonization of codes, together with privatization has been accompanied by a number of mergers, acquisitions and takeovers. Cross-border trade in construction services has increased in Europe in recent years. This trade is changing the nature of competition and creating an environment where there is a need to improve performance through technical and organizational innovation in the domestic sector.
- *Quality of products.* Constructed products generally do not enjoy a high reputation for quality in comparison with goods and services produced by other industries. Clients are beginning to demand more value from construction and this is driving changes in quality. Construction activities are a long way from producing zero defect buildings and structures, and there is much room for improvement in this respect. Furthermore, technical change in materials, components and systems integration could improve physical and aesthetic durability as well as reduce embodied energy and life-cycle costs. It could also lead to greater initial flexibility in design choice, together with adaptability in use and the potential to

recycle parts during demolition, improving environmental performance.

- *Costs and prices*. The current approach to construction costs and prices is that *production costs + profits = selling price*. By contrast, manufacturing industries use the equation: *selling price – production costs = profit* (Miles 1996). In manufacturing, this equation tends to focus attention on innovation for cost reduction in production, whereas in construction a desire to improve profitability leads to high prices. Nevertheless, new ways of financing and owning constructed products may improve a general understanding of life-cycle costs as opposed to initial installed costs, thus highlighting new areas in which technical change can improve overall cost performance. More data collection and sophisticated analysis methods are required to achieve this result. Unless prices are reduced and costs kept under control, construction is likely to lose orders through substitution for other investment goods.

- *Changing industrial structure*. The structure of construction sectors in all OECD countries indicates a small number of large organizations capable of operating internationally and developing and using new technologies. In many countries a proportion of medium-sized enterprises are also able to innovate and improve performance. However, in every case there is a large number of very small firms. The majority of these operate using antiquated practices, and it is extremely difficult to raise their performance. Nevertheless, some specialist small firms are innovative and mechanisms need to be found to support the development of new technologies and organizational processes in this part of the sector. In general there are signs that industrial structure could be shifting with detailed design moving up-stream into component manufacturing firms and specialist technical subcontractors. Materials and component supply is particularly concentrated. New project management or systems integrator firms are emerging for procurement and coordination of site-based activities. In some sectors, financial institutions and clients are becoming more involved in the total process. Construction firms are partnering with clients, suppliers and finance organizations in order to spread the risks and rewards of implementing new technologies. New alliances to enable collaboration for technical development are also emerging.

- *Management of project-based firms*. Design, engineering and construction firms are developing new approaches to managing portfolios of projects. These approaches involve developing business processes which relate to specific project activities. Leading players recognize that they can play a key role in improving their use of existing technologies, thereby laying the foundations for further technological innovation. Many larger organisations have formal technical support functions with responsibilities for technical troubleshooting, problem-solving and R&D. Firms which develop these capabilities generally find that they can recognize and exploit benefits of technical and organizational change, and that they are therefore in a better position to invest in R&D and new skills which will be required to guarantee future success.

- *Education, training and skills*. It will be necessary to encourage the erosion of rigidities between professions and craft trades which now span a wide range of specialist interests from planning and development to design, engineering and management. Practices have ossified within increasingly irrelevant discipline-based value systems that hinder the development and transfer of new knowledge. A culture of innovation is needed in which people from different professional backgrounds work together in new ways, motivated by the aim of meeting emerging needs of users and thereby improving performance in the built environment as a whole.

- *Government procurement, research and regulatory policies*. Governments have a central role to play in the promotion and support of performance improvement in the built environment. A number of instruments are available, including procurement policies. Governments remain major customers for construction goods and services, and these projects can be used to stimulate performance improvements through technical and organizational change. Governments also have a duty to protect public interests and the use of appropriate regulations concerning the governance of technology can stimulate further performance improvements, for example in areas such as health and safety, environmental protection and energy use. Moreover, there is a need for a strong, coherent and cooperative research base for construction. It is unlikely that this research base can be fostered solely within the private sector in most countries (with the possible exception of Japan) because of the structure and competitive nature of the industry. Governments need to consider the sponsorship of more fundamental research within the built environment and building sciences. Few firms are likely to be able to appropriate the results of upstream science (e.g. materials and computational sciences) and the developmental work required to underpin knowledge for innovation in the built environment. Moreover, if this were to occur, appropriation by a small number of very large firms would almost certainly reinforce weaknesses in technical competence of the vast majority of small and medium-sized enterprises (Gann 1997).

DAVID GANN
SPRU, UNIVERSITY OF SUSSEX

Further reading

(References cited in the text marked *)

Duffy, F. (1997) *The New Office*, London: Conran Octopus Ltd. (Describes changing patterns of use in modern office buildings associated with information intensive patterns of work.)
* Gann, D.M. (1997) 'Should governments fund construction research?', *Building Research and Information* 25 (5): 25767. (Analysis of the role of the state in sponsoring research on the production and use of the built environment.)
* Gann, D.M. (2000) *Building Innovation – Complex Constructs in a Changing World*, London: Thomas Telford Publications. (Explains the history of innovation in the built environment through the Machine Age to the present Digital Age, explaining the relationship between changes in demand and development of new management approaches and technologies.)
Gann, D.M. and Salter, A. (1998) 'Learning and innovation management in project-based, service-enhanced firms', *International Journal of Innovation Management* 2 (4): 43154. (Develops a conceptual framework for understanding the management of project-based firms, focusing on the links between business and project processes.)
* Gann, D.M. and Salter, A. (1999) *Interdisciplinary Skills for Built Environment Professionals*, London: The Ove Arup Foundation. (Analyses changes in the nature of skills of built environment professionals and requirements for new education and training systems.)
Gann, D.M., Wang, Y. and Hawkins, R. (1998) 'Do regulations encourage innovation? – the case of energy efficiency in housing', *Building Research and Information* 26 (5): 28096. (Analysis of the relationship between regulation and innovation in the built environment.)
Groák, S. (1992) *The Idea of Building*, London: E&F.N. Spon (Explores the main ideas embodied in the process of building.)
* Miles, J. (1996) *Where is the Henry Ford of Future Housing Systems*, London: Royal Academy of Engineering.
Mitchell, W.J. (1995) *City of Bits: Space, Place and the Infobahn*, Cambridge, MA: The MIT Press. (Explores the changing nature and possible dematerialization of the built environment associated with the growth of the information economy.)
* OECD (1997) *Main Industrial Indicators Database*, Paris: OECD. (Industrial performance indicators.)
Russell, B. (1981) *Building Systems, Industrialisation and Architecture*, London: John Wiley & Sons. (Presents a history of the industrialization of building production processes.)
* WS Atkins (1994) *Strategies for the European Construction Sector*, Brussels: Office for Official Publications of the European Communities. (Provides an analysis of the structure and strategies of the European construction sector in the 1990s.)

Growth of the firm and networking

1. The significance of the growth of firms
2. Transaction costs and the growth of the firm
3. A resource- or knowledge-based theory of the growth of the firm
4. Global expansion
5. The limits to the growth of the firm
6. Networks

Overview

The firm is as an economic organization in a market economy, acquiring tangible and intangible productive assets for the purpose of producing goods and services for the market at prices that yield a profit. Innovation is an important part of its activity. This concept of the firm is the concept used in business and managerial economics and in such works of economic history as the superb analyses of Alfred Chandler, where he relates the strategy and performance of firms to their structure and where the 'visible hand' of firms becomes as important as the 'invisible hand' of the market.

This approach to the firm differs from the definition of the firm in the theoretical branch of microeconomics which is often called the 'neo-classical', or 'marginalist', theory of the firm, where it is defined almost exclusively with reference to the determination of price and output of a given commodity under given and unchanging conditions. In that theory, the firm is not an organization but an abstract entity; its equilibrium output (size) is determined by the intersection of cost and demand curves under carefully specified competitive circumstances. The theory does not deal with the operations of the firm as such, for it is designed to deal primarily with the logical implications of profit-maximizing behaviour for prices and output, for which it has proved indispensable in the analysis of market systems. Nevertheless, it is already being seriously challenged by a more institutional and sociological approach.

However, even in the neo-classical theory of the firm, the concept of disequilibrium points to considerations that promote expansion of output and which also apply when the firm is defined differently. For example, indivisibilities of plant and equipment which make economies of scale available where plant can be used more fully show up in falling costs and greater equilibrium output. But this concept can only be applied to a given product or an unchanged collection of products because it is impossible to establish the cost curve of a firm if the composition of output to which the costs refer continually changes. Joint costs arising from indivisibilities of output are also important – as, for example, in the production of wool and mutton at the same time. For the same reason, however, they cannot be used in the neo-classical theory of the firm to explain diversification of output.

If the firm is treated as an organization, its growth can in some respects be looked at in terms of the nature and development of organizations. An organization has boundaries, but in the case of firms the effective boundaries are often fuzzy and ill-defined. In a general way, however, the firm can in principle be distinguished from its environment, and its boundaries for all practical purposes reflect the extent to which its administration governs its activities. It is the administrative, bureaucratic, hierarchical or managerial characteristics of decision making with respect to transactions within the firm that distinguish these transactions from those made between independent participants in the market. Unlike market transactions, the activities within the firm are linked to each other within an administrative and managerial framework, although the characteristics of both administration and management vary widely among firms. Partly for this reason, this entry does not distinguish the administrative from the managerial characteristics of firms, although, in general, the term 'manager' implies more flexibility than the term 'administrator'. This entry will distinguish between the two terms where appropriate.

1 The significance of the growth of firms

The economic, and indeed the political, significance of the growth and size of firms as organizations often derives from the very nature of firms as independent organizational entities involved in planning and administration. The activities of firms can be contrasted with the unplanned activities of the marketplace. For this reason, the growth and size of firms is of great significance for the nature, scope, functioning and general operation of a market economy, as contrasted to an administered or 'planned' economy.

Firms and markets are both, in their different ways, networks of activity, but the difference between them is crucial to an understanding of the nature of the economy as a whole. A great deal of economic analysis and much of the economic policy of governments – for example, the theory and policy of monopoly and competition, of international trade and investment, of the role of consumer choice – derives from the assumed existence of the dichotomy between firms and markets.

As firms grow, their organizational boundaries expand as they administer their increased activity. The size of the market may or may not expand, depending on which markets are referred to, but to the extent that some individual firms in any given lines of business grow faster than the market for the relevant goods or services (or, in general, some firms grow faster than the relevant economy as a whole), administrative decision making will tend to displace market decision making in the economy.

In different economies, firms have developed at different rates and through different stages of development in response to their different environments. The relevant environmental considerations are well known, and have been analysed in considerable detail in specialized works and case studies. These considerations include the following: the state of technology, the extent of the market, the industrial, agricultural and miscellaneous composition of national output, the level of national income, the availability of natural resources, the culture of the people with and for whom they operate and the extent to which operations are extended internationally as the firms' horizons grow. All of these considerations differ from country to country and from firm to firm.

Broadly speaking, there are two major types of explanation for the growth of firms in a market economy. Each assumes that firms are in search of profit, but the two approaches ask different kinds of questions, thus emphasizing different considerations regarding the behaviour and nature of the firm. One explanation rests on an analysis of the role of market transaction costs and is concerned primarily with the factors influencing the specific economics of the specific decisions made by firms which bring about their growth. The other explanation starts with an analysis of the nature of the resources available to the firm, in particular the growth of knowledge, entrepreneurship and capabilities generally embodied in its personnel. The two approaches are not mutually exclusive.

2 Transaction costs and the growth of the firm

Any kind of economic activity that involves more than one person entails economic transactions of some kind. This is as true of activities carried on within firms as of those between firms. All such transactions have costs of one kind or another, whether they be financial outlays, costs of the time involved in negotiations, the examination of facts, the making of contracts, other direct and indirect management costs, and so on (see TRANSACTION COST ECONOMICS).

In addition, especially when the transaction involves contracts of one kind or another which relate to a transfer of ownership of or control over tangible or intangible assets, there are a wide range of costs arising from uncertainty. Under such circumstances, the possibility arises that one or more of the parties to the transaction may attempt to manipulate or interpret the terms of the transaction arrangements in their own interest, to the detriment of other parties. These are referred to as the costs arising from opportunistic behaviour or moral hazard. Measures to protect against opportunism between contractual parties can be analysed as part of the cost of ensuring the desired performance of contracts, whether explicit or implicit. There is a very large body of literature that presents a detailed analytical description of the different forms that costs arising from opportunism may take, along with suggestions as to how these can be dealt with or minimized (Williamson 1975).

A firm faced with new opportunities that offer strong prospects for growth, including the prospect of merging with or taking over another firm, must choose one of the following courses of action: to undertake the new activities itself; to leave others to take advantage of the new activities and to buy from the market those goods and services it might otherwise have itself produced; or to embark on expanding its ownership connections with another firm. If the firm is attempting to maximize profits, it will make this choice with specific reference to the relative costs, and in particular the transaction costs, of the different types of action in so far as they can be evaluated reasonably objectively. The decision will be determined in part by the extent to which the firm can make use of some of its owned assets, especially those the value of which is closely related to the fact that they are associated with the firm.

Many so-called 'firm-specific' assets will have been created within the firm itself, such as some of its technology and research facilities, and certain intangible advantages which arise from the experience and knowledge of existing personnel and from the culture of the firm and its operating procedures, especially those unique to the firm. Firms own – that is, have property rights in, or contracts respecting – such assets and thus gain economic rents from their use. To lose part of these rents to outsiders is a clear cost.

Transaction costs have a major effect on the internal administrative organization of firms. For example, such costs may determine whether the firm adopts the unitary or multidivisional form of organization and dictate the extent to which it engages in extensive devolution of control. One of the most important aspects of the role of transaction costs in the growth of firms relates to the question of vertical integration, which occurs when firms themselves undertake, directly or through the acquisition of other firms, the production of intermediate products or services.

The analysis of transaction costs presents a reasonably operational way of identifying and evaluating opportunities. Although many of the important costs are not observable, for example, costs due to the risk of opportunism or uncertainty, much work has gone into ways of developing observable proxies in individual cases which seem to be sufficiently associated with the importance of the costs concerned to permit analysis. However, from the point of view of an analytical explanation of the growth of firms, among its chief limitations is the fact that it cannot be of much practical help in dealing with the willingness of a given firm to accept different degrees of uncertainty, with all the attendant risks that affect its perception of the magnitude of costs.

3 A resource- or knowledge-based theory of the growth of the firm

The foregoing discussion brings us back to the role of the resource- or knowledge-based theory of growth and especially to the intangible services inherent in the people who are at the core of the operations of a firm. A firm consists of a collection of tangible productive resources and intangible productive services, the most important of which are the services of people. Of course, not all firms grow significantly and a great many go out of business: they may fail, get taken over by other firms, stagnate for long periods or grow very unevenly. In the life of any individual firm, anything might happen; but if one is interested in a general theory of the growth of the firm, it is essential first to enquire what are the necessary conditions for the continued growth of the firm and if there is anything in its very nature that will limit that growth. In the first place, let us assume for analytical purposes the existence of a firm for which there are no obstacles either to acquiring or to selling goods and services at market prices. In other words, if there are opportunities in an economy, the firm can take advantage of these and be unhindered by problems of market availability. However, there is necessarily one resource that is unavailable in the market: experienced people who are already in the firm and fully acquainted with it. Such people are only to be found within the firm, and the services available from them will be required even to absorb new people. Here is the starting point for a resource- or knowledge-based theory of the firm.

In the very process of working together in the firm and with the resources available to them, a firm's existing personnel develop new ideas about production technology, product improvement, new markets and new methods of market entry. The possibilities of creating new demand for new products are explored, as are new ways of using or improving the existing use of available resources. Here is to be found the font of knowledge, of new ideas for expansion, the judgements with respect to the comparison of transaction costs, the source of a firm's 'dynamism', and a major consideration in the appraisal by those consultants brought in to advise individual firms. In other words, history matters in the development of the propensities within a firm to grow. The major characteristic of competition among firms in a modern economy is competition in innovation. Innovation may be the introduction of something new from the point of view of the firm only, or from the point of view of the economy as a whole.

Knowledge is of two kinds. One kind arises from the experience and activity of individuals, a 'know-how' that is not always easily transmitted to others and which may give those having it an advantage *vis-à-vis* others. The second type, transmissible knowledge, is in principle available to all, but may be protected through secrecy or by creating specific legal or other obstacles to its use by others and therefore may become an intangible firm-specific asset.

Both types of knowledge grow as a firm conducts its business, and in the process both create further incentives for growth, not least because able and energetic men and women not only see opportunities to perhaps increase their salaries and incomes but also to extend their responsibilities, and possibly their power, if they can take advantage of the opportunities they perceive. (This aspect of entrepreneurship can be called a kind of positive opportunism within the firm.) People, and therefore firms, are not motivated by money alone. In addition, firms deliberately foster research with a view to enlarging the scope of their activities through actively increasing their knowledge. This may take the form of research and development (R&D) laboratories of many kinds, managerial experimentation and marketing surveys (see INNOVATION).

All of this creates powerful internal pressures on the firm to undertake new activities since, by definition, the increased knowledge and experience of existing personnel creates an increased, often 'firm-specific', capacity to do more than they are in fact doing. They know more about the human and physical resources they are working with, more about markets, more about technology in the widest sense. They also learn more about what is going on in the outside world, what other firms are doing and what additional opportunities for their own activities may exist. Among these are acquisitions of other firms or parts of firms; firms frequently acquire other firms as the cheapest and quickest way of acquiring the firm-specific assets these possess. Whether a particular amalgamation of one or more firms should be regarded as the growth of a single firm or as the creation of a new firm depends in part on the relative sizes of the firms; from the point of view of the economy as a whole it makes little difference which view is taken and one can simply note that the size distribution of firms has changed.

The personnel who take advantage of these developments within a firm are the entrepreneurs. These people have three main attributes: first, vision and imagination (perhaps two aspects of the same quality); second, willingness to take risks; and, third, ambition. By definition, growth decisions refer to the future. The future is not known, and judgements need to be made, some of which may be expected to introduce innovations affecting the firm or the external world in significant ways. Dynamic and enterprising firms tend frequently to act on long-run and highly uncertain entrepreneurial judgements, vague and 'non-operational' as these may often seem.

Some entrepreneurs are more averse to risk than others, but it is not always possible to come to any reasonable quantification of different types of risks in different situations. Here, a 'rational' comparison of transaction costs may be impossible and excessively costly to try to carry very far. The decision may have to turn on the 'animal spirits' (to borrow Keynes' term) of the relevant entrepreneurs in boards of directors.

Decisions with respect to increments of investment, whether through acquisitions or significant internal expansion, are often strongly influenced by the strength of the desire on the part of individual entrepreneurs and managers to do the job themselves. There is no way of judging this except by discussions with people in the firm. As already noted, each firm is unique in certain very important respects and this is one of them. In the last analysis, the so-called 'dynamic firm' is one whose decision makers are willing to take considerable risks.

It follows that quantifiable, reasonably objective transaction costs are not necessarily a decisive consideration in the overall appraisal of the likelihood of any particular expansion. This, together with the fact that 'history matters', gives rise to the uniqueness of individual firms and severely limits the validity of generalizations about the behaviour of firms.

4 Global expansion

The largest firms in the world are international (see GLOBALIZATION). In general, however, the firm that expands internationally does so for much the same reasons as the firm that expands nationally. The relevant considerations in both cases are as follows:

1 the cumulative growth of knowledge combined with the perceived advantages of expansion for both the firm and the individuals concerned with decision making;
2 the internalization of activities;
3 the fact that size, scope, market position and existing integration give rise to firm-specific assets of which better use can be made internationally than nationally;
4 the subsequent cumulatively increasing production of knowledge with respect to international possibilities.

Reams have been written about the multinational firm (or enterprise), the transnational corporation and the global enterprise, with the distinctions in terminology only reflecting the emphasis people choose to give to words. However, all these terms indicate that national borders make enough difference to justify separate treatment of international firms.

The differences arise from the additional obstacles (or advantages) relating to culture, language and similar considerations (which may apply nationally within ethnically diverse countries), to different currencies, border controls or other types of physical or financial regulations, political attitudes of foreign or home governments, size of protected markets, the configurations of firm cultures or associations, the type of technology involved, and so on. All of these factors have been analysed in considerable detail along with extensive empirical studies of individual firms.

In one respect at least, the growth of firms on an international scale does make a special difference. In discussing the significance of the growth of firms in the second section of this entry, it was pointed out, without further analysis, that the extension of the administrative control of transactions within the firm at the expense of market transactions has, if widespread, an important effect on the operation of the economy as a whole. Similarly, the expansion of firms across national boundaries has implications for the different countries within which they operate.

Many economists fear that a progressive expansion of international investment and trade will operate to an unacceptable extent to increase the economic power of the international firm *vis-à-vis* the interests of national governments and individual economies. This perceived threat of international expansion applies especially to the smaller economies which are attempting to increase their economic activities in the face of competition from the more powerful international institutions. Others take the opposite view and see the multinational corporations as one of the most important means of promoting the transfer of technology among countries, increasing access to world markets, promoting investment and generally improving the conditions of all of the economies in which they operate. These issues are beyond the scope of this entry, but they do raise the question of the limits to the growth of individual firms. How far can corporate governance displace markets on a large scale in large countries or even on an international scale?

5 The limits to the growth of the firm

The firm has been defined as an organization with boundaries. In principle, this organization contains within itself the capacity and incentives for continuous growth. When growth occurs, those entrepreneurial, managerial and administrative services that were required to plan and administer a significant expansion are less likely to be needed for subsequent operations as they become more or less routine. The 'unused services' then become available for further expansion (Penrose 1959). However, as the firm grows larger and larger, more or less routine operations will absorb larger amounts of managerial services (not necessarily proportionately) and further expansion may not find important services as easily available as before; increased size may, after a point, impose administrative strains.

While much attention has been paid to the 'diseconomies of size', a distinction must be made between economies of size and economies of growth. Economies of growth can exist for all sizes of firm when the use of unused productive services in the firm appears profitable, but the resulting increase in size of the firm need not necessarily lead to economies of size; administrative efficiency in the operation of the firm could become adversely affected. While the growth of the firm might be considered an efficient development, the resultant increase in size could easily turn out to be inefficient. Moreover, diseconomies may also arise as a result of too rapid an attempted rate of growth.

Large-scale manufacturing industry had been becoming increasingly important since at least the late nineteenth century, especially in the USA, and by the 1920s 'big business' was a dominant feature of the industrial landscape (see CORPORATE CONTROL). As the size of firms increased, new administrative structures were introduced and highly centralized forms began to give way to less centralized ones; with increasing diversification, the so-called multidivisional, or 'M', form of organization was widely adopted. The technology used in administration also changed rapidly, moving from manual typewriters and filing procedures to highly developed and sophisticated electronic equipment for communications, data processing, control and so on, in addition to changes in transportation and financial technology. Thus, developments in technology facilitated rapid increases in administrative efficiency, calling for considerable managerial flexibility to take full advantage of new developments. Even the very large firms continued to grow rapidly at both national and international levels.

Such conditions could not continue indefinitely, let alone at increasing rates. By the third quarter of the twentieth century, there were signs that the size of the firm was approaching its limits and the management of large firms was becoming strained. Many of the problems were accentuated as economic boom and recession became increasingly important considerations for management generally, affecting all sizes of firms.

6 Networks

By the 1980s and 1990s, two concepts were coming increasingly into widespread use: the concept of a 'core' and that of a 'network'. The former usually referred to what a firm considered to be its primary business or businesses and was commonly used when it decided it had overextended itself from the point of view of efficient and profitable management. The network concept first appeared in nineteenth-century literature in the form of 'industrial clusters' (Marshall 1890) and later as 'industrial districts', as described by Best (1990). Both these concepts describe numerous small and medium-sized firms which operate together closely, depending on each other for all sorts of services, including technology.

Perhaps a kind of intermediate stage between the hierarchical firm and what we shall call the business alliance is exemplified by what Bartlett and Ghoshal (1993) have called a 'context model of the managerial firm'. This model draws heavily on sociology and on organization theory, and on the role of trust and responsibility in the motivation of people. It is designed to remove as far as possible any tight hierarchical administrative controls, to reduce substantially the numerous layers of management in the firm and to create a large number of decentralized small-business 'units' consisting of 'front-line' managers with small teams directly in touch with customers, suppliers and financial providers. A layer of middle management fulfils what is essentially a 'supportive' role.

In one case described, such a large number of so-called 'front-line' manager-entrepreneurs were created, on whom was devolved such a high degree of power and authority to make independent decisions, including investment decisions, that what might be called a collection of small 'quasi'-firms seemed to have been created, the personnel of which had been successfully socialized to the values of the firm, accepting strong personal incentives to excel in meeting targets. Thus, strong network relationships throughout the firm could be relied on more than normally to maintain the administrative cohesion of the firm. This type of operational structure based on strongly manipulative guiding and advisory management adumbrates a different firm context as the growth of the firm exceeds the older types of administrative hierarchical control.

The formal contractual manifestation of associations between firms became increasingly common in the 1980s and 1990s. Although firms continued to grow through vertical and horizontal takeovers of one kind or another, there arose a growing tendency for a number of them to join together in corporate alliances or cooperative arrangements, not necessarily with monopolistic intent but as a means of gaining mutual access to such resources as technology, regional markets and information services. Sometimes, long-term associations were formed; in cases where specific operations needed to be carried out, shorter-term associations were formed.

A large variety of terms have been applied to the various ways of organizing such types of economic activity which do not fall easily into 'market' or 'firm' categories, such as 'quasi-firms', 'relationship-enterprises', 'value-added partnerships', 'virtual corporations' or 'global webs'. The term 'networking' was applied to a wide variety of relationships between firms, including cooperative agreements, alliances, associations, licensing, relational contracts, franchising and R&D arrangements. It is difficult to be more precise, since the question of whether any given arrangement should be regarded as part of an existing network or alliance or as part of the firm is essentially the problem of defining with any precision the fuzzy boundaries of the firm. The crucial point is the extent to which the administrative structure or 'managerial reach' of the firm in question is believed to be significantly involved.

Even in developing countries it had been noted in the 1980s that multinational corporations had been changing their strategy and moving increasingly towards less highly integrated operations, and away from 100 per cent equity and control towards active participation in complex types of association with local companies. Such associations include joint ventures on a minority basis, offsetting trading arrangements and licensing.

The literature on the subject at the time of writing is at an early stage and is growing rapidly. D'Cruz and Rugman (1994) apply a very interesting theory of formal networks to the Canadian telecommunications industry, seeing the network as a way of reducing costs in markets and hierarchies. They define formal networks as a: 'governance structure for organizing exchange through cooperative, non-equity relationships among firms and non-business institutions' (1994: 276). Gomez-Casseres defines a network simply as groups of companies 'joined together in a larger overarching relationship ... each company fulfilling a specific role within the group' (1994: 4).

The spread of inter-firm networking has been stimulated by the growth of global businesses, the scale of operation of which is largely independent of national boundaries, especially in technological fields. The rapid and intricate evolution of modern technology often makes it necessary for firms in related areas around the world to be closely in touch with developments in the research and innovations of firms in many centres. Formal relations among such firms may advance the competitive power of each of them; to make alliances may be not only a rational response but even at times a necessary one. Gomez-Casseres (1996) argues in a forthcoming book that what he calls the 'collective competition' including sets of allied firms can promote intense rivalry and competition in industry as a whole.

The individual companies do not lose their 'independent' identity; but the administrative boundaries of each of the linked firms may become increasingly amorphous and the effective extent to which any individual firm exercises control is often not at all clear. Although formal contracts form the legal basis of such groups, their cooperative operations may be based not so much on the exercise of control as on consensus emerging from shared goals and mutual dependence among the participants. There are advantages for individual firms that join an alliance and there are also costs – the balance between costs and benefits can shift as activities develop. As the individual firms within an alliance continue growing, difficulties often arise in their relationships, even leading at times to the disintegration of the alliance.

The business network is very different from a cartel of independent firms in its structure, organization and purpose. It is clear that this type of organization is likely to continue to spread for some time and is very different from that of the traditional textbook analysis of competition between firms in so-called free markets.

EDITH PENROSE (DECD)

Further reading

(References cited in the text marked *)

* Bartlett, C.A. and Ghoshal, S. (1993) 'Beyond the M-form: towards a managerial theory of the firm', *Strategic Management Journal*, special edition, winter (4): 24–46. (A discussion of what the authors term 'the context model of the managerial firm', which encourages the creation of decentralized small-business 'units' within a single organization.)
* Best, M.H. (1990) *The New Competition*, Cambridge: Polity Press. (A comparison of the older and newer forms of competition in selected countries; written in non-technical language with a good bibliography.)

Chandler, A.D., Jr (1962) *Strategy and Structure: Chapters in the History of the Industrial Enterprise*, Cambridge, MA: MIT Press. (Required reading about the history of US firms.)

Coase, R.H. (1937) 'The nature of the firm', *Economica* 4 (4): 386–405. (A classic early article about the origin of the firm.)

Cyert, R. and March, J. (1963) *A Behavioral Theory of the Firm*, New York: Prentice Hall. (One of the early introductions to a new theory of the firm in economics – easy reading.)

* D'Cruz, J.R. and Rugman, A. (1994) 'Business network theory and the Canadian telecommunications industry', *International Business Review* 3 (3). (An article that introduces and illustrates an original theory of business networking.)
* Gomez-Casseres, B. (1994) 'Group versus group: how alliance networks compete', *Harvard Business Review* reprint 94402. (An excellent analysis of 'alliance competition' with case studies.)
* Gomez-Casseres, B. (1996) *The Alliance Revolution: The New Shape of Business Rivalry*, Cambridge, MA: Harvard University Press. (An excellent analysis with case studies of the emergence of constellations of firms producing new units of competition in the marketplace.)

Hodgson, G.M. (1988) *Economics and Institutions*, Cambridge: Polity Press. (Includes a chapter on firms and markets and an extensive bibliography.)

* Marshall, A. (1890; 9th edn 1961) *Principles of Economics*, London: Macmillan. (A standard treatise which introduces the network concept in the form of 'industrial clusters'.)
* Penrose, E.T. (1959; 3rd edn 1995) *The Theory of the Growth of the Firm*, Oxford: Oxford University Press. (Contains a new foreword by the author suggesting a somewhat different development and future from that of the original text.)

Richardson, G.B. (1972) 'The organisation of industry', *The Economic Journal* 82 (327): 883–96. (An important and early forerunner of the development of the organization of the firm and of industry; long relatively neglected by business economists, but now regarded as a classic.)

Schumpeter, J. (1942; 6th edn 1987) *Capitalism, Socialism and Democracy*, New York: HarperCollins. (A classic work of social theory which includes a chapter entitled 'The process of creative destruction', which is particularly recommended for further reading.)

Spender, J.C. (1994) 'Organizational knowledge, collective practice and Penrose rents', *International Business Review* 3 (4). (An analysis of 'rents' obtained from organizations; includes a good bibliography.)

Thompson, G., Frances, J., Levacic, R. and Mitchell, J. (eds) (1991) *Markets, Hierarchies and Networks: The Coordination of Social Life*, London: Sage Publications. (A collection of twenty-four articles by different authors which presents an excellent overview of markets, hierarchies and networks.)

* Williamson, O.E. (1975) *Markets and Hierarchies*, New York: The Free Press. (A standard work by the economist famed for his transactions cost analysis of the firm.)

Williamson, O.E. (1985) *The Economic Institutions of Capitalism*, New York: The Free Press. (Another standard work by Williamson.)

See also: COOPERATION AND COMPETITION; DYNAMIC CAPABILITIES; INDUSTRIAL DYNAMICS; MANAGERIAL THEORIES OF THE FIRM; MARSHALL, A.; WILLIAMSON, O.E.

Industrial agglomeration

1. Origins of the idea
2. Definitions
3. Theory
4. Revival of interest in industrial agglomeration
5. Industrial districts
6. Industrial clusters
7. Core-periphery tendencies
8. Models of agglomeration

Overview

Industrial agglomeration is a process whereby firms cluster together in order to derive certain benefits. These benefits are external economies – they arise from activities, relationships or developments outside the firm. For example, when a number of firms, all producing similar products, set up close together in a place there may be interaction among people in these firms such that the diffusion of technological change and innovation is more rapid than it would have been if these firms were spatially distributed. The benefit from the more rapid diffusion of technological change and innovation is an external economy, in this case an agglomeration economy. The initial reason why firms locate in a particular place may be something other than the economies of agglomeration; the grouping of firms may still be called an industrial agglomeration if such external economies arise as a result of the firms being grouped in that place.

Industrial agglomerations encompass industrial districts or clusters. The firms in industrial districts usually produce either all or part of very similar products, they are usually very closely agglomerated (e.g. in a small village), and they are usually all small or medium-sized enterprises (SMEs). The firms in clusters are usually both small and large, they are usually not as close together as those in industrial districts, and they can be from a range of different, though related, industries.

An industrial district can be considered to be a type of cluster. Industrial districts, in addition, sometimes form part of a larger cluster.

1 Origins of the idea

Industrial agglomeration is a topic studied in the context of a number of disciplines, including economics, economic geography and industrial sociology. Marshall (1890) is referred to by most as the originator of the idea (see MARSHALL, A.). Since then, an increasing number of formal, deductive models of the kind prevalent in neo-classical economics have been developed to examine industrial agglomerations. Beginning with Weber (1929, first published in German in 1909), Lösch (1954, first published in German in 1940) and Isard (1949), economists working in this tradition have attempted to formulate a:

> general theory of location and space-economy ... conceived as embracing the total spatial array of economic activities, with attention paid to the geographic distribution of inputs and outputs and the geographic variations in prices and costs.
> (Isard 1949)

No satisfactory general theory of this kind has yet emerged. Among the reasons for this are the crucial roles played in agglomeration by a number of imprecise and dynamic processes which could not be incorporated into the model-building efforts of those attempting to formulate such theories. We will concentrate here on definition and empirical examples of industrial agglomerations, which are to varying extents relevant in all theoretical contexts. In the examination below of industrial agglomerations in practice and in theory in the 1980s and 1990s we will briefly address advances in modelling that have attempted to solve some of these problems in theory-building.

2 Definitions

At its simplest, industrial agglomeration refers to the process whereby an increasing number of production facilities are located in the same place. The noun, an industrial agglomeration, is a place in which there are a number of facilities or establishments in which production occurs. It is necessary to elaborate further, for other concepts could be adequately described by these definitions. Related concepts include, for example, cluster, industrial complex, industrial district and spatial concentration. Together with industrial agglomeration, these terms are often used interchangeably. What distinguishes an industrial agglomeration from a spatial concentration is the presence of agglomeration economies. These are benefits that a firm derives from the fact that there are other firms located in the same place. They are a subset of what Alfred Marshall (1890) described as external economies. An industrial agglomeration is a spatial concentration of firms where the motivations for and/or results of being spatially concentrated are that the individual firms are in some economic sense better off than they would have been if they were located in an industrially more isolated setting. Even if agglomeration economies were not the initial driver of the spatial concentration, that concentration may still lead to what Alfred Weber called 'accidental agglomeration economies'. On the other hand, such spatial concentration may not lead to agglomeration economies, in which case it should not be called an agglomeration. For example, where a number of firms concentrate in a particular place because of a government incentive to do so, if there is no additional gain from the fact that there are other firms in that place, such spatial grouping constitutes a concentration but not an agglomeration.

Marshall is generally credited as the main originator of the theory underlying the idea of industrial agglomeration (though he used the terms 'localisation' and 'industrial district' rather than agglomeration). He distinguished between internal and external economies of scale. The former are economies arising from an increase in a firm's scale of production; the latter economies are, in Marshall's words 'dependent on the general development of the industry' (1898: 345). In Chapter X of Book IV of his *Principles of Economics* he illustrates external economies through a discussion of 'The Concentration of Specialized Industries in Particular Places'. The importance of this chapter, even in current discussions of industrial agglomeration, is difficult to overestimate. It has been fundamental to the identification since the 1970s of industrial districts in the towns and villages of what has become know as the 'third Italy' (mainly EmiliaRomagna). These areas have been widely accepted as prototypical of modern industrial districts in many locations in both industrialized and less-developed countries. In addition, among prominent economists, Krugman (1993), for example, explicitly rests much of his discussion on localization on this chapter. Among economic geographers, Hayter (1997), in his text book on industrial location, equates agglomeration economies with external economies of scale, and echoes Marshall (implicitly) when he writes:

> Localization economies of scale in the manufacturing sector evolve over time and are most obviously revealed in so-called 'industrial districts'.
>
> (Hayter 1997: 92)

Localization economies are, for Marshall, however, merely an example of external economies. In his own summary of that section of his book, Marshall is clear about this, writing that they may arise where industries are 'concentrated in the same localities'. Whether or not industries are spatially concentrated, he continues, different firms sharing communication services like transport, telegraph and printing are deriving the benefits of external economies of scale. Thus, to be consistent with the Marshallian origins, agglomeration economies should be confined to those that arise from localization only, and should exclude external economies that arise from the sharing of services by spatially distributed firms.

If industrial agglomerations are associated with economies of agglomeration, it should be noted that the reason why such agglomerations do not grow further – or, in some cases why they do not come into existence in the first place – may be because of diseconomies of agglomeration. The economic and social costs arising from increased agglomeration, including congestion and pollution, are the localized external diseconomies of scale.

Why and how do industrial agglomerations come into existence? Marshall distinguished *causes* of localization and *advantages* of localization. His causes are basically the initial trigger or reason for the development of an industry at a particular locality, such as physical conditions, local markets and political/cultural influences. His advantages are what we can interpret as the actual agglomeration economies that lead to the further expansion of the concentration, such as 'hereditary' skills/knowledge, the growth of 'subsidiary trades' and the emergence of a local market for special skills required by the industry. We will discuss each of these briefly, updating Marshall's views as appropriate.

By physical conditions is meant raw materials, climate, energy sources and topography. Shipbuilders locate in harbours or estuaries, for example. The more expensive it is to transport the raw materials required by an industry, the more likely is that industry to be located close to the production or extraction of that raw material, all other things being equal.

Local market conditions include size, wealth and sophistication of the market. The high-income, high-quality Japanese market for consumer electronics, for example, might attract consumer electronics firms to that location.

Political/cultural influences are among the most difficult to quantify. Most practically, they include policy, of all kinds and at all levels of the state, that has an impact on the location of business activity. More widely, we can refer here to the character and values of people, the nature and consistency of rules governing economic and other behaviours, and political, social and economic institutions. These, too, can be differentiated in terms of their level or spatial extent, e.g. national or local. Rules, particularly tacit rules, culture and institutions are particularly emphasized by institutional economists.

Once an industry has located, from whatever combination of natural, political, social, cultural and accidental factors, in a particular place, there may be cumulative advantages to its continued location in that place.

Hereditary skills should not be interpreted as referring to skills inherited in the genetic sense. The reference, rather, is to a situation in which a large number of people, with similar skills and working with similar technologies, live in close proximity. After a generation or two the skills in the use of these technologies – usually employed in the production of closely related products – become almost common knowledge in that place. Inventions or innovations in products, processes and/or organization are very rapidly diffused. There is a milieu that encourages this diffusion. People meet and, through both business and social interaction, share their knowledge. The externality is the technological spillover among the agglomerated firms.

The growth of subsidiary trades in the locality results from the increase in the number of firms in the original industry to the point where their demand for various manufactured and service inputs makes the local provision of these inputs economically viable. Agglomeration facilitates specialization in the sense that if enough firms focus their production on the product itself – or retract into their core capabilities – then other firms will focus on subsidiary activities that the original firms had in the past undertaken themselves. Firms will spin off from other firms and specialize in different parts of the production process. In other words there will be vertical corporate disintegration. In a furniture agglomeration, for example, a specialist firm in the turning of table legs may become viable as a result of the growth in the number of firms manufacturing tables in the district. The table firms themselves may increasingly focus their activity on assembly. In certain circumstances, such as where the level of technology is high and the technological spillovers are particularly strong, even the production of machinery used in the furniture industry may emerge in the locality. Different externalities are mutually reinforcing. There are localized external economies of scale that result in an increase in the number of table assemblers; there are localized external economies of scope that result in an increase in the number of 'trades'. Economies of scope are the gains derived from the fact that a number of different products are produced together.

The advantages of a 'main' industry and its subsidiary trades being close together may vary between different production systems and between the production of goods at different points in the product life-cycle. This variation depends on the extent to which the main industry depends on reliability of supply of inputs (the outputs of the subsidiary trades). Where there are just-in-time (JIT) production systems, for example, the timing of delivery of raw materials and other inputs is crucial. For such systems, production must be located close to raw material or other important input sources and/or the transport system must be rapid and reliable and/or the raw materials/inputs must be capable of being warehoused close to the site of production.

The emergence of a local market for special skills required by an industry (or labour market pooling), and the localization of that industry, are mutually reinforcing processes. People with those skills will tend to want to live near the firms in that industry and the potential employers who believe that they will require people with those skills will be attracted to that place by their availability there. The skilled workers are better off because their job-search costs are minimized by the fact that there is a large number of potential employers in the place. If there is any diversity at all in the nature of the firms – such that some experience downturns in their demand when others experience upswings – then, in comparison with the situation where there is only one firm employing those skills in that place, there is also a greater likelihood of remaining in employment. For the firms the labour market pooling increases the likelihood that their peak demand for skilled workers can be met locally.

Where there is in a place only one firm requiring workers with particular skills then this reduces the attractiveness of that place for the workers. The monopsony power of the employer will be perceived by the workers as a means of bargaining wages down and it will be less likely that labour market pooling will emerge. At least in the short run this requires that those workers have jobs available in other places where there is more than one employer. In periods of sustained unemployment, workers may not have this choice. In addition, very high internal increasing returns to scale may result in high enough wages to attract labour market pooling despite the presence of monopsony power in the employer.

Just as labour market pooling both results from and causes localization, so may other advantages of agglomeration mutually reinforce one another (see LABOUR MARKETS). Local technological and other knowledge spillovers, for example, can be enhanced by political/cultural conditions. The emergence of various political, economic/industrial and social organizations at the local level increases the interactions among workers and owners of firms, enhances trust and intensifies spillovers.

3 Theory

Although Marshall is often referred to as the originator of the theory underlying the idea of industrial agglomeration, he did not really provide a theory. His brief comments on the issue list a number of advantages that firms might derive from being located in close proximity. His main theoretical insight was to see this in terms of external economies. It was Weber (1929) who provided the first substantial attempt to explain the process of agglomeration as part of a broader theory of the location of industries (see WEBER, M.). In his view, the location of production is fundamentally determined by the place of consumption and the most advantageously located material deposits. Transportation costs ultimately determine the optimal location. Like advantageous labour cost locations, agglomeration economies are presented as a deviating force in this 'basic transportational network'. The advantages of locating in the agglomeration – the development of technical equipment and 'auxiliary industries' (Marshall's 'subsidiary trades'), labour organization, marketing factors and general overhead costs – basically rest on the existence of economies of scale. An agglomeration exists for him where the auxiliary industries are, with the plants with which they work, part of a single technical whole; this functions best if all its parts are locally concentrated because this enables them to remain in touch. Agglomeration is the result of 'special' factors, that is ones that are not transport cost related. In Weber's theory auxiliary industries can also be closer to their customers because of transport costs but the implications of this for the dynamics of the agglomerative process are not addressed.

Krugman (1993), among others, has addressed this issue, at least on a theoretical level. He developed a formal model in which the interaction of demand (both final and intermediate), increasing returns and transportation costs drives a cumulative process of regional divergence and localization. Krugman incorporates explicitly the interaction between increasing returns and transport costs (or other distance related transaction costs). He assumes that firms have economies of scale in production, and that there are transport costs; agglomeration is a consequence of the interaction between these two. Places where there is substantial demand for the firms' product and/or where firms can conveniently obtain inputs, are the places where these firms will tend to locate. Once some firms have located in such places, others will do so, too. This suggests a positive path dependency. However, historically some agglomerations – though at first successful – have failed. There is no place for such failure in Krugman's model.

Accepting that there is interaction between increasing returns and distance-related transaction costs has implications for how we think about agglomerations – in particular in terms of their physical extent. Both Marshall and Weber reserved the terms localization and agglomeration for groupings of firms or industries that were concentrated in relatively small spatial areas. In Weber's model, the auxiliary industries that transmit the (external) economies of scale are always located in close proximity to the 'main' industries, for example for reasons of communication. However, this is not a requirement in Krugman's model. Here, economies of scale can be attained over larger distances. The only downside of larger distances is that firms will incur higher transport costs. Theoretically, this condition means that agglomeration economies can work at different spatial scales from the very small to the very large, an issue that has led to confusion and debate as to the interpretation of the concept agglomeration. How small does the area within which firms concentrate have to be for it to be an agglomeration?

Different agglomerative forces operate at different geographical scales. Externalities related to the scale of intermediate demand can arise over great distances; they are not necessarily regionally bounded. Other externalities, such as Marshall's 'hereditary skills' and 'local market for special skills' are necessarily more regionally bounded and will lead to agglomeration of a more restricted geographical scale.

Industrial agglomeration involves a range of different locational dynamics. Thus, as regards the advantages related to the scale of intermediate demand, spatial agglomeration can come about due to the re-location of plants from one region to the other or due to the local externalization of auxiliary activities or, in modern terms, vertical corporate disintegration. As regards the skilled labour market, this may evolve over time, where a group of plants might initially concentrate in a particular area due to the advantages of cheap labour and only subsequently avail of the advantages brought about by this 'accidental agglomeration'. In yet other cases, the dynamics are mainly related to a distance bias in information flow; a particular area might see a disproportionate rate of new firm formation in a particular industry because local entrepreneurs have the required knowledge and information. The concept of agglomeration encompasses different processes, involving different factors or forces, working at different geographical scales.

4 Revival of interest in industrial agglomeration

The renewed theoretical and empirical interest since the late 1970s in the concept of industrial agglomeration was stimulated by three main factors. First, competitive industrial agglomerations were identified, such as the Third Italy in Europe and Silicon Valley in the USA, which had prospered in spite of the global economic crises in the 1970s and 1980s. Second, notwithstanding some evidence of a long-term convergence of growth rates and technology between countries and regions with comparable economic and social structures, dissimilar industrial structures or sectoral specialization patterns between these countries and regions persisted (see ECONOMIC GROWTH AND CONVERGENCE). Third, advances in the mathematical modelling of imperfect competition and multi-equilibrium processes facilitated the incorporation of increasing returns into formal economic models of industrial agglomeration, trade and economic growth.

New evidence on industrial agglomerations was presented to a wide audience in the research on industrial districts by Piore and Sabel (1984) and industrial clusters by Porter (1990). Although an industrial district may be considered to be a cluster or part of a cluster, there are distinct differences between these two concepts. An industrial district is a more tightly agglomerated (often in a town or village) group of predominantly small, artisanal firms with extensive vertical and horizontal inter-firm linkages, often of a cooperative nature. Incorporating ideas on the social embeddedness of economic actions (Polanyi 1944 and Granovetter 1985), contemporary industrial district theory, in addition to economic factors, particularly emphasizes the specific cultural 'institutional thickness' or 'milieu' of a locality as a critical factor in industrial agglomerations. The term neo-Marshallian is often attached to these more consciously cooperative, institutionally embedded contemporary industrial districts to differentiate them from Marshall's original description. This distinction underlines the fact that there are differences over time in the nature of industrial districts. There are also differences between industrial districts at any one time, based among other things on where they are and on the industry on which they specialize.

5 Industrial districts

Among the special characteristics of the neo-Marshallian district (or what Brusco (1982) called 'the Emilian model') is a local set of rules, originating in civil society, that on one hand reduces transaction costs and on the other prevents inappropriate opportunism. Being ostracized for contravening local rules, customs or norms of economic behaviour would have serious social and economic consequences and such contravention is therefore rare. The roots of these rules go back in some cases hundreds of years, evolving into an economy of agglomeration that has been an important element in the success of the industrial districts of that part of Italy (Brusco 1982).

Marshall's original idea of industrial districts was based on patterns of nineteenth-century industrialization in England. His prime example was the Lancashire cotton textile industry. This district may well have illustrated his conviction that external economies were more important in the process of industrialization than internal economies, but in other industries – for example the automobile industry in the USA – internal economies were probably more important. In such industries, rather than the relationships between firms – and the agglomeration economies that brought them together – driving the industrialization process, it was the growth of individual firms that was most important. One consequence of Marshall's over-emphasis on external economies, as Lazonick (1991:150–6) suggests, is that the real possibility of sustained competitive advantage by an individual firm is not incorporated into his theory. This is not to say that industrial agglomeration is not also a factor in industries dominated by large firms, as the concentration of the American car industry in Detroit illustrates. External economies (and economies of agglomeration in particular) arise in widely differing production systems, in some cases as an early determinant of small-firm based industrialization in a place, and in others as a consequence of the development of a large firm (or firms) in a place.

The neo-Marshallian industrial districts that emerged in Italy in the 1960s and the Marshallian industrial districts such as the cotton textile industry in Lancashire in the late nineteenth and early twentieth centuries have a number of common characteristics. These include relatively small firms, industrial structures characterized by vertical specialization and horizontal competition, and economies of agglomeration providing incentives for high levels of spatial concentration. These similarities may explain – in different ways –

why these districts emerged when they did. It is the differences between them, however, that explain why the Italian districts continued to thrive through periods of both general economic downturn and technological change, while such factors led to the decline of the Lancashire cotton textile industry.

In the case of the Lancashire cotton textile industry, success was based in the first instance on factors similar to those underlying British industrialization in general. British domination of world markets provided a secure and growing demand to which capitalists responded. The relatively simple and cheap technology led to ease of entry. With spinning, weaving and marketing separate but related through the market, the industry was a 'neoclassical economist's dream of a hierarchy of extremely well developed markets' (Lazonick 1981). In Emilia-Romagna, Brusco (1982) suggests, initial success was based on the greater ability of small firms to resist the growing power of the unions, and on a growing demand for more differentiated products, produced in shorter series. In Lancashire cotton textiles began as – and continued predominantly to be – a small firm industry. In Emilia-Romagna the industrial districts are small-firm production systems achieving success in industries dominated elsewhere by large firms. In both places (Lancashire and Emilia-Romagna) and in both periods (late nineteenth-century in the case of Lancashire and post-1960s in the case of EmiliaRomagna), economies of agglomeration were a significant factor in their success.

There are substantial differences between the nineteenth-century British industrial district and the modern industrial districts of Emilia-Romagna. Changing technology, adopted by large and growing firms in America, was avoided in Britain. It involved vertical integration which was contrary to the vertically specialized structure that had evolved, for example, in Lancashire. No individual firm was in any case capable of introducing the changes. The separation of distribution and production left manufacturers insecure about the nature and scale of their markets. Institutional impediments included the unions, which defended workers whose skills, developed over generations, would become redundant. There was no coordinated attempt to plan for change in the structure of the industry, to introduce the new technologies or face the new competition from America. Firms' short-term response to market was to attempt to reduce costs. In Emilia-Romagna there is a wide range of ways in which firms collectively coordinate activities. These include financing, purchasing of inputs and distribution, all of which may have relevance to the short or long run. There is also co-ordinated 'real service' provision which is clearly long run, such as planning for additional factories, training and the introduction of new technologies. Economies of agglomeration in Britain were insufficient to offset the 'matrix of rigid institutional structures' that 'obstructed individualistic as well as collective efforts at economic renovation' (Elbaum and Lazonick 1986: 2). The industrial districts of EmiliaRomagna – and similar more recently emerging production systems in districts in many other parts of the world (Pyke and Sengenberger 1992) – are characterized by high levels of both competition and cooperation; those in Britain with their origins in the nineteenth century had high levels of the former, but very little of the latter.

The different paths of the Lancashire and Emilian industrial districts cannot be understood without close consideration of the institutional contexts. The presence in Emilia-Romagna (and the absence in Lancashire) of industry and municipal or commune based organizations, which have acted in the common interest of their small-firm members to coordinate important aspects of their activities, have been a fundamental part of the difference between the two stories.

The term 'Emilian model' may seem inappropriate given that first, even in Emilia-Romagna there are so many different types of production system, and second, individual industrial districts are changing, in some cases substantially. They vary in terms of technology and product, from furniture, ceramic tiles, clothing and textiles, to sophisticated machine tools, in terms of size, from 60 firms to hundreds of firms, and in terms of the importance of large firms in the district. Nevertheless, they all have high levels of both competition and cooperation and all are predominantly small-firm production systems with high external economies. Among the changes are that in some cases, larger firms are becoming increasingly important. There is evidence for example that 'the larger firms of the districts – albeit small by most standards – often orchestrate subcontracting relations, explore commercial avenues, and invest in R&D' (Lazerson and Lorenzoni 1999).

Some geographers now use the term 'industrial district' more generically to include both Marshallian and neo-Marshallian industrial districts on the one hand, and various other forms of spatial concentration of firms on the other. Markusen (1996), for example, identifies, in addition to 'Marshallian and Italianate industrial districts', 'hub-and-spoke', 'satellite platform' and 'state-anchored' industrial districts. In the hub-and-spoke district there is at least one dominant, externally oriented, vertically integrated firm surrounded by a number of smaller suppliers. In the satellite platform district there are a number of unconnected branch plants of foreign owned firms. In the state-anchored district the key tenant (or tenants) in the district is (are) government owned or sponsored, surrounded by customers and suppliers. Such key state tenants include military bases, plants for manufacturing (or researching) military equipment, universities and state administration centres. Different types of district generate different levels of economies of agglomeration. To illustrate, because the firms in the satellite platform are unrelated to one another, there are greater economies of agglomeration in the hub-and-spoke district than in the satellite platform. The only agglomeration effects in the satellite platform are through a shared, generally unskilled, labour market. There are examples of all the different types of district in many parts of the world, in both industrialized and less-developed countries.

6 Industrial clusters

An industrial cluster, like an industrial district, also refers to industries connected through vertical and horizontal relationships but is a broader concept. Geographical proximity is considered important, but the contemporary analysis of industrial clusters encompasses agglomerations at local, regional, national or even international levels. In contrast to the predominantly hierarchical network relationships among Marshallian and neo-Marshallian industrial district firms, interactions among firms in an industrial cluster are considered to be primarily marketbased; indeed rivalry among firms is viewed as a key determinant in the formation of industrial clusters. Correspondingly, there is less emphasis in cluster research on the role of milieu or non-economic institutions.

Porter's (1990) definition of clusters as based primarily on domestic competition among firms came under heavy criticism. Lazonick (1993), for example, uses extensive quotes from Porter's own work, particularly on the ceramic tile industrial district in Emilia-Romagna, to show that what Porter sees as 'domestic rivalry' is actually cooperation. Perhaps in response, in a revision of some of his ideas on clusters, Porter (1998) describes them in terms which make it more difficult to distinguish them from industrial districts. He accords substantial weight to cooperation and trust, for example. Nevertheless, he still emphasizes the non-networked nature of the relationships in clusters. The firms in industrial districts are networked. Also, whereas there is both vertical and horizontal cooperation in industrial districts, the cooperation in Porter's clusters is primarily vertical.

Examples of clusters include the computer and related industries in Silicon Valley, medical devices and related industries in Massachusetts, wine and related industries in France, similarly in Spain and Portugal, and chemicals and related industries in Germany (crossing the border into German-speaking Switzerland). They develop, according to Porter, as a result of four interrelated influences: factor conditions, demand conditions, strategy and rivalry of firms, and related and supporting industries. Alluding to agglomeration, he writes that 'Proximity – the colocation of companies, customers, and suppliers – amplifies all of the pressures to innovate and upgrade' (Porter, 1998: fn.1).

The research on industrial districts and clusters, while containing many theoretical elements, has been far more empirical than that of the formal modellers. As a result, many examples of industrial agglomerations, all over the world, have been described in some detail. Related research on urban agglomerations has arrived at similar conclusions, namely that economic activity tends to be 'lumpy' rather than smoothly spread over space.

Piore and Sabel's (1984) research on industrial agglomerations and their identification of flexibly specialized or post-Fordist systems of organization, has, in addition, contributed to a longer running economic debate. This is over whether disintegrated SMEs or large vertically integrated corporations provide the most adaptive and responsive organizational forms for changing market and technological conditions. From the examples of Lancashire and Emilia-Romagna discussed above, it follows that the answer depends on the institutional context, the industry and the type of innovation.

7 Core-periphery tendencies

The industrial agglomeration literature is also central to the analysis of agglomeration on a broader scale including core-periphery patterns of growth and the persistence of regional specialization patterns, particularly in the context of increasing economic integration in areas such as the European Union and North American Free Trade Association. For instance, although formal contributions on industrial agglomeration originating from 'new geographical economics' view the forces of agglomeration at a local scale to be essentially Marshall's 'localisation externalities', on a larger scale, pecuniary externalities or market size effects are considered important in influencing core-periphery patterns of economic development. Irrespective of the geographical scale of analysis, the forces contributing to industrial deglomeration or dispersion stem from congestion in product and factor markets, resulting for example, in increased local land and labour costs. Transport costs and labour mobility are the other factors considered central to spatial dispersion: the lower transport costs are, the more likely it is that agglomeration will occur; the more immobile labour is, the more dispersed industrial activity will become.

In contrast, perspectives based on modern innovation theory (originating from new institutional economics) consider the ability of firms and other public and private institutions in a region to create new knowledge, learn, continuously innovate and network, as the critical factor in understanding the durability of regional industrial specialization patterns (e.g. Best 1990; Lundvall 1992; Nelson 1993). As learning is an interactive process, geographical proximity or agglomeration together with an innovative regional institutional infrastructure are key factors in promoting international competitiveness based on continuous innovation. This convergence between innovation studies and economic geography is considered by Morgan (1997) through an examination of the 'learning region'; Hudson (1999) is sympathetically critical of the literature on learning regions, arguing for example that there are limits to learning, among them that learning *per se* does not solve the problems of social division.

8 Models of agglomeration

Criticisms of contemporary models of industrial agglomeration fall into two categories. First, formal models of industrial agglomeration have been criticized as being too general because they neglect the critical localized social, cultural and institutional factors which can play a key role in the geographical distribution of industry. Martin (1999) provides an excellent review of these issues. These lacunae might be revealed if there was empirical testing of the models. On the other hand, the development of new models like that of Krugman discussed above, do fit the real-world tendencies for economic development to be spatially uneven. Second, examinations of industrial districts do not facilitate development of theory because, focusing on a few regions, they are considered too specific; they are unable to provide a general perspective on the processes of industrial agglomeration. They have, nevertheless provided examples of different types of situation in which industrial agglomeration arises.

A common feature of agglomeration models is the notion of path dependence. In other words, it is acknowledged that the forces that gave a location its original advantage might not necessarily be those that contribute to the subsequent growth of the agglomeration: an initial event can have long-run cumulative consequences. The historical and institutional examinations of the origins, development and, in some cases, decline of industrial agglomerations show in greater detail what circumstances give rise to success, and how social and institutional factors can differentiate between continued success and failure.

DAVID JACOBSON

KEVIN HEANUE

CHRIS VAN EGERAAT
DUBLIN CITY UNIVERSITY

Further reading

(References cited in the text marked *)

* Best, M. (1990) *The New Competition: Institutions of Industrial Restructuring*, Cambridge, MA: Harvard University Press. (A critique of standard theories and development of new ways of understanding the successes of Japanese firms and Italian industrial districts, building on the work of Schumpeter and Penrose.)
* Brusco, S. (1982) 'The Emilian model: productive decentralisation and social integration', *Cambridge Journal of Economics* 6: 167–84. (One of the first examinations in English of Italian industrial districts, emphasizing inter-firm relations, the local labour market and local political institutions as factors in their success.)
  Dicken, P. and P.E. Lloyd (1990) *Location in Space: Theoretical Perspectives in Economic Geography*, 3rd edn, New York: Harper and Row. (This is an excellent text on the economic geography of location.)
* Elbaum, B. and Lazonick, W. (eds) (1986) *The Decline of the British Economy*, Oxford: Clarendon Press. (In their introductory chapter, the editors argue that, fragmented by horizontal competition and vertical specialization, British industry was unable to make the transition to mass production because of institutional rigidity.)
* Granovetter, M. (1985) 'Economic action and social structure: the problem of embeddedness', *American Journal of Sociology* 91: 481–510. (A seminal article reviving and building on Polanyi's work; Granovetter argues that all economic action is 'embedded' in social practices and institutional arrangements.)
* Hayter, R. (1997) *The Dynamics of Industrial Location: The Factory, the Firm and the Production System*, Chichester: Wiley. (Intermediate economic geography textbook on industrial location.)
* Hudson, R. (1999) 'The learning economy, the learning firm and the learning region: a sympathetic critique of the limits to learning', *European Urban and Regional Economics*, 6 (1): 59–72. (While sympathetic to the evolutionary approach to learning and knowledge, argues that there is a danger of fetishization of these concepts, which can result in the ignoring of social and political inequalities.)
* Isard, W. (1949) 'The general theory of location and space economy', *Quarterly Journal of Economics* 63: 476–506. (A review of neo-classical approaches up to that time, emphasizing the importance of transport costs.)
* Krugman, P. (1993) *Geography and Trade*, Boston, MA: MIT Press. (This series of lectures provides a clear presentation of Krugman's approach.)
* Lazerson, M.H. and G. Lorenzoni (1999) 'The firms that feed industrial districts: a return to the Italian source', *Industrial and Corporate Change* 8 (2): 235–66. (Argues that there is a greater organizational heterogeneity in industrial districts than is generally accepted, with some larger firms acting as leaders both in relation to internal and external inter-firm relationships.)
* Lazonick, W. (1981) 'Competition, specialization, and industrial decline', *Journal of Economic History*, 41 (1): 31–8. (An examination of the institutional circumstances leading to the decline of the cotton textile industry in Lancashire in the late nineteenth and early twentieth centuries.)
* Lazonick, W. (1991) *Business Organization and the Myth of the Market Economy*, Cambridge: Cambridge University Press. (In this book Lazonick shows, on the basis of historical evidence, that managerial coordination of firms – as opposed to market coordination – has been increasingly important for successful capitalist development.)
* Lazonick, W. (1993) 'Industry clusters versus global webs: organizational capabilities in the American economy', *Industrial and Corporate Change* 2 (1): 1–24. (Review of the work of Porter and Reich, arguing that cooperation is more important than Porter allows for, and that the national 'home' is more important to the corporation than Reich allows for.)

* Lösch, A. (1954) *The Economics of Location*, New Haven: Yale University Press. (Like Weber, this book was a translation from the German. German economists were in the first half of the twentieth century more concerned with space than Anglo-Saxon economists.)
* Lundvall, B.-Å. (ed.) (1992) *National Systems of Innovation: Towards a Theory of Innovation and Interactive Learning*, London: Pinter Publishers. (A collection of papers in which various aspects of the institutional approach to understanding national differences in systems of innovation are developed.)

  Malmberg, A. and Maskell, P. (1997) 'Towards an explanation of regional specialization and industry agglomeration', *European Planning Studies* 5: 25–42. (An approach to the topic by scholars working in the evolutionary/institutional tradition.)
* Markusen, A. (1996) 'Sticky places in slippery space: a typology of industrial districts', *Economic Geography* 73: 293–313. (Extends the term industrial district to types different from either Marshallian or neo-Marshallian versions.)
* Marshall, A. (1898, first edition 1890) *Principles of Economics*, London: Macmillan. (Although one of the early giants of neo-classical economics, Marshall also contributed, through this book and others, to the more discursive economic sociology and economic geography disciplines.)
* Martin, R. (1999) 'The new "geographical turn" in economics: some critical reflections', *Cambridge Journal of Economics* 23: 65–91. (A critical survey of the contribution of new geographical economics to spatial issues.)
* Morgan, K. (1997) 'The learning region: institutions, innovation and regional renewal', *Regional Studies*, 31 (5): 491–503. (Drawing on evolutionary economics, examines the convergence between innovation studies and economic geography using the learning region as a focus.)
* Nelson, R.R. (ed.) (1993) *National Innovation Systems: A Comparative Analysis*, Oxford: Oxford University Press. (A description of the systems of innovation of each of a number of small, medium and large countries.)
* Piore, M. J. and Sabel, C. F. (1984) *The Second Industrial Divide: Possibilities for Prosperity*, New York: Basic Books. (Research which developed and applied the concepts of industrial districts and flexible specialization.)
* Polanyi, K. (1944) *The Great Transformation*, New York: Rinehart and Co. (A critique of the market economy based on the argument that it has a negative impact on society.)
* Porter, M. (1990) *The Competitive Advantage of Nations*, London: Macmillan. (Descriptive research focusing on the role of industrial clustering in international competitiveness.)
* Porter, M.E. (1998) 'Clusters and the new economics of competition', *Harvard Business Review* November–December: 77–90. (Updates Porter's argument about the importance of the local for global competitiveness.)
* Pyke, F. and Sengenberger, W. (eds) (1992) *Industrial Districts and Local Economic Regeneration*, Geneva: International Institute for Labour Studies. (A collection of papers outlining the conclusions of an ILO research programme on small firm industrial agglomerations in Italy, elsewhere in Europe, Canada and the USA.)
* Weber, A. (1929) *Alfred Weber's Theory of the Location of Industries* (translated by C.J. Friedrich), Chicago: University of Chicago Press. (Seminal study, establishing the basis for neo-classical research on this topic.)

See also: COOPERATION AND COMPETITION; DYNAMIC CAPABILITIES; ECONOMIC GROWTH AND CONVERGENCE; GROWTH OF THE FIRM AND NETWORKING; MARSHALL, A.; SMALL AND MEDIUM SIZED ENTERPRISES; WEBER, M.

Securities and exchange regulation

1 Introduction
2 Regulation of securities transactions and ongoing disclosure
3 Regulation of securities markets
4 Regulation of investment advisors and companies

Overview

In the aftermath of the stock market crash of 1929, public confidence in financial markets in the United States was low. Not only did investors lose much, if not all, of their wealth invested in securities, but the ensuing panic caused bank failures as many investors tried to withdraw their savings simultaneously. In order to facilitate an economic recovery and restore public confidence in American financial markets, the Congress of the United States created the United States Securities and Exchange Commission (SEC) in 1933. Its purpose was, and still is, to protect investors and maintain the stability of the securities markets.

The basis that underlies all SEC rules governing securities, securities markets and its participants is to ensure the integrity of the markets. In particular, the Commission requires that all investors have equal access to both adequate and accurate information about claims and their issuers. However, the scope of the Commission's goal is also limited. It does not presume to say anything about the value or merit of any individual investment opportunity, nor does the Commission bar the sale of securities of questionable value. Individual investors are ultimately responsible for their investment decisions if they have access to truthful information.

The SEC's authority over financial markets and its participants derive directly from Acts of Congress. The Commission's primary responsibilities derive from four Acts: The Securities Act of 1933, The Securities Exchange Act of 1934, The Investment Company Act of 1940 and the Investment Advisors Act of 1940. Any rule proposed and adopted by the SEC in response to evolving markets and technologies is an implementation of and an amendment to these legislative acts.

1 Introduction

An overview of each of the Acts follows:

- The Securities Act of 1933 is the basis for SEC requirements covering the registration of security *transactions*. The Commission does not register securities, simply their sale. The Act also allows for certain exemptions, such as the sale of securities between private parties and private offerings made to a limited number of sophisticated investors.
- The Securities Exchange Act of 1934 extends the reporting requirements to include annual and periodic reports to update the information in the original securities registration. It also prohibits insider trading, thereby disallowing individuals with access to material non-public information to profit from that information. The 1934 Act governs sales and trading practices, defines and prohibits manipulative and deceitful practices; and requires registration with the Commission of securities exchanges and broker-dealers.
- The Investment Company and the Investment Advisor Acts of 1940 cover those entities (either companies or individuals) that engage in investing, reinvesting and trading in securities. The most common example of an investment company is a mutual fund. The rules protect investors by requiring investment advisors to work in the best interest of their clients and requiring pertinent information about the investment company's objectives and managerial compensation to be given to investors. As with securities themselves, the Commission does not imply the safety of the investment strategy or company. Rather the SEC

mandates a fair level of disclosure so that investors can make sound choices.

While the above Acts provide the SEC with the jurisdiction to oversee markets, they do not define the limits of the SEC's ability to affect market participants' behaviour. In particular, the (SEC) Chairman's visibility as a public figure lends a certain amount of weight to his expressed policy opinions. Thus, the SEC may implicitly encourage 'fair' behaviour by market participants simply through the Chairman's public speeches.

The above points merely provide a broad outline of the jurisdiction of the Securities and Exchange Commission. Nevertheless, even this broad outline provides a picture of the extent to which SEC regulation impacts financial transactions in the United States. Issuers are required to provide high quality information about themselves and their activities both prior to a securities sale and on a continuing basis. Exchanges must provide equal access to the best possible transaction price for all registered securities. Broker-dealers must act in the best interest of their clients and provide sufficient records to indicate that they uphold those standards. Mutual funds must abide by similarly high standards of disclosure and investor protection.

Critical to the Commission's mission is its enforcement authority. The Commission is in fact charged with enforcing federal securities laws, rules and regulations. SEC actions in the areas of insider trading, accounting misrepresentation and collusion by market makers, to name just a few areas, have had a profound impact on the integrity of financial markets in the United States.

2 Regulation of securities transactions and ongoing disclosure

Securities transactions

The earliest responsibilities of the SEC related to registration of securities for sale to the public. The purpose of the registration provisions of the Securities Act of 1933 is to protect investors in public offerings and reduce information costs through the disclosure of company- and transaction-specific information. Information includes such items as description of the business, recent operating performance, description of risks, and intended use of proceeds. The Act requires that all public offers and sales of securities be registered with the SEC unless they are exempt from registration. The Securities Act provides two broad transaction exemptions. The first exemption, under Section 4(1) of the Securities Act, exempts sellers if they are not issuers, underwriters or dealers. The second, based on Section 4(2) of the Securities Act, exempts issuers who sell securities to investors who do not need the protection of the registration requirements under federal securities law.

By the 1980s several factors had led to the need for modernization in the securities offering process. Technology increased the availability and timeliness of information. The rise of large, sophisticated institutional investors such as mutual and pension funds reduced the need to provide protection to certain investors. The Commission responded to these changes, and others, by deregulating the public offering process for large public companies and facilitating the sale of private securities. Key components of this process included:

- *Rule 415, or shelf registration.* Issuers can effectively pre-register securities to be sold at any time over the life of the registration statement. The initial registration includes issuer information, but does not provide all information about the issue to be sold. The Commission then requires the issuer to submit the 'pricing supplement' with all additional required information within two days following pricing or first use (whichever is first). Issuers can sell securities 'off the shelf' without SEC staff review prior to the sale. Shelf registration is primarily available to larger issuers with a significant filing history.

- *Regulation D.* Defines individuals with an annual income of more than $200,000 or net worth in excess of $1 million as 'accredited investors'. Companies can sell unregistered securities to an unlimited number of accredited investors and to a limited number of non-accredited investors.

- *Regulation S.* This regulation allows for the sale of unregistered securities as long as they are sold outside of the United States with no intention of selling the securities to investors within the United States.
- *Rule 144A.* Another rule to develop the private placement market, Rule 144A allowed large, sophisticated investors, designated as 'qualified institutional buyers', to trade certain unregistered securities between themselves. Previously, purchasers of privately placed (unregistered) securities could not resell their securities for two to three years unless the seller registered the resale with the SEC.

The cumulative impact of these changes was to facilitate growth in American capital markets. Rules 415 and 144A benefited primarily larger issuers by increasing flexibility with regards to the timing of sale and terms of the security sold. For instance, bond issuers could determine the coupon rate and other terms of the debt at sale rather than at the time of registration, typically weeks prior to the sale. Both methods also reduced issuers' direct costs by promoting competition between underwriters. The passage of Regulations D and S primarily benefited smaller companies. Regulation D increased the pool of investors for those companies wishing to sell securities but unwilling to incur the expense and time necessary to register with the Commission. Regulation S helped to develop overseas markets by reducing regulatory uncertainty.

The net impact of these rule changes on capital formation has been significant. In 1981, the aggregate value of private placements of corporate securities was almost $18 billion. By 1998, that amount had increased to $561 billion. Shelf registration, which did not exist in 1981, accounted for over $1,560 billion by 1998. Over the same period, 1981 to 1998, the value of public and private corporate securities issued in the United States increased over forty-fold from $81 billion to $3,412 billion (source: Securities Data Corporation).

Required disclosures

Companies become subject to the ongoing disclosure requirements once they register their securities with the Commission. These requirements include annual and other periodic reports intended to update the information in the original registration. This requirement includes annual and periodic financial statements, report of important events (such as the resignation of a board member or a change in the primary business of the company), share repurchase plans, and proxy and tender offer solicitations. Since May 1996 virtually all corporate filings are available electronically through the EDGAR database (*www.sec.gov*). The SEC's primary concern with regard to these reports is the fair and full disclosure of information to all investors.

The Commission has a responsibility to ensure that accounting and auditing practices provide fair and consistent information to investors. The primary Commission activities designed to achieve compliance with the accounting and financial disclosure requirements of federal securities law include: rulemaking and interpretation that supplement private sector accounting standards; enforcement actions that impose sanctions and serve to deter improper financial reporting; and oversight of, and participation in, private sector initiatives by domestic and international private sector standard setters such as the Financial Accounting Standards Board (FASB) and the International Accounting Standards Committee (IASC).

3 Regulation of securities markets

The Securities and Exchange (1934) Act provides for the regulation of brokers (individuals who buy or sell securities for the accounts of others), dealers (individuals who buy or sell for their own accounts), investment advisors (those who provide investment advice for compensation) and the overall markets where securities are traded. Under the Act, no person may engage in business related to registered securities as a broker, dealer or investment advisor without registering with the SEC. The SEC has responsibility to ensure that individuals in the securities industry treat their clients fairly. These provisions include prohibitions against overcharging clients, excessively trading on client accounts to maximize commission revenues, recommending inappropriate securities given the risk profile of the client, and 'front-running' (the practice of broker-dealers trading on their own account at the expense of their clients).

This regulatory scheme is somewhat complicated by the fact that Congress has delegated some authority to 'self-regulatory organizations' or SROs, which are private associations of broker-dealers such as the NYSE or NASD. SROs are charged with adopting and enforcing rules for the conduct of their members and ensuring compliance with those rules and the federal securities laws. What has evolved is a relationship wherein the SEC works with the exchanges (and other SROs) to adopt, implement and enforce rules ensuring fair and liquid markets.

An important development in the financial landscape of the late 1990s was the advent of the Electronic Communications Networks (ECNs). ECNs operate electronic trading markets in which customers trade directly with one another. They are typically registered as broker-dealers, but unlike traditional broker-dealers, ECNs allow customers to view the entire range of buy and sell orders and market depth prior to placing an order. ECNs have increased competition in the equity markets by providing alternative trading venues and lowering costs. It has been estimated that by the end of 1999, 25 per cent to 30 per cent of NASDAQ trading arose from ECN transactions.

Below, we discuss the SEC's role as a regulator of markets in the context of its relationship with exchanges and SROs, broker-dealers and ECNs. We also present evidence from academic studies of the efficiency of markets, and studies of the reforms suggested by either the SEC or SROs.

The SEC's relationship with exchanges and SROs

As noted earlier, the Commission shares responsibilities for exchange oversight with private self-regulatory organizations associated with the exchanges. Self-regulation begins with the broker-dealers who make markets in NYSE stocks. Focus is on adherence to rules of conduct and effective supervision of personnel. The NYSE also is the Designated Examining Authority for most of its member firms (firms that own seats). Thus, it maintains a system for both monitoring and regulating member firm activities.

The NYSE uses a variety of methods to monitor broker-dealers and members including: computer analysis of activity in individual stocks, visits by exchange staff, and formal investigation of exchange (and 1934 Act) rules violators. The widely recognized Stock Watch computer system is a critical component of this supervisory structure.

Stock Watch automatically flags unusual volume or price changes in any NYSE listed stock. While most unusual activity can be explained via company specific, industry, or national news, this is not always the case. If no legitimate explanation of the activity is evident, the NYSE begins an investigation. They will contact the firm to determine if any news is forthcoming, they will construct an audit trail of every trade during the day in question, and they will match traders' names to a list of individuals likely to have inside information about company prospects.

If the NYSE uncovers suspicious trading activities by member firms and/or their employees, the NYSE itself can take disciplinary action. In fact, the 1934 Act *mandates* the NYSE to discipline violations of the Act and Exchange rules by NYSE member firms and associated persons. The NYSE's Division of Enforcement is the prosecutorial arm of the exchange and can decide to take no action, informally discipline, or initiate formal charges. If a potential violation is perpetrated by someone outside of exchange jurisdiction, the exchange can turn over its information to the SEC for further consideration.

Regulation of broker-dealers

Broker-dealers play an integral role in the movement of securities between investors. If the broker-dealer acts as a market maker (posting a firm bid and offer price at which it is ready to transact), it can fill an order from its own inventory, match the order against another customer's (termed 'crossing the order') or forward the order to the trading venue. If the broker-dealer is not a market maker, it will simply forward the order to the trading venue. Given the various roles that broker-dealers play in the security trading process, it is important to ensure their safety and soundness, as well as their appropriate behaviour.

Much of the regulation of broker-dealers is done by SROs (see above). However, the procedures are similar, regardless of monitor identity, as the goals of such regulation are the same. Broker-dealers are required to keep detailed books and records, which are subject to either SEC or SRO review. These reviews address the broker-dealer's financial, operational, customer protection and sales practices, as well as a host of other regulatory rules. In addition broker-dealers that are member firms of the NYSE, and who do business with the public, are required to have an annual audit conducted by independent public accountants and file a report with the NYSE.

The SEC's relationship with ECNs

At their most basic, ECNs are venues where buyers and sellers can come together for electronic execution of trades. ECN subscribers post offers to buy or sell a fixed number of shares at a fixed price (limit orders) on the system. The ECN will then post these limit orders to the system for other subscribers to view. The ECN system will also match the order against the order of another subscriber if the other side of the limit order (buy from a seller or sell to a buyer at the same price) is already on the system. When a trade is executed, the buyer and the seller typically remain anonymous to each other. ECNs maintain subscriber anonymity by standing in the middle of every trade. ECNs have subscribers who are market makers, broker-dealers, institutional investors and retail investors.

There are several potential benefits to trading on an ECN instead of relying on the traditional exchanges. Until the full phase in of Regulation ATS in April 2000, an order on the ECN system may reflect a better price than that available on the exchanges. ECNs also provide subscribers with access to all the outstanding orders on the system and not just the best bid/offer available from the traditional exchanges. This information allows users to gauge the depth of the market.

ECNs must be registered with the Commission as a broker-dealer. Alternatively, they may apply to the SEC for exchange status, which requires them to undertake self-regulatory functions – to act as their own self-regulatory organizations – and comply with other applicable regulatory requirements. As of January 2000 three ECNs (Archipelago, Island and NexTrade) have applied for exchange status.

Assessing the impact of market regulation

As ECNs grew in prominence in the 1990s, a key feature may have led to unequal access to the best price available. ECNs have exchange-like features, but have been regulated essentially as broker-dealers. They are privately owned, do not regulate the activities of subscribers, and are not required to provide access to all investors. As such, market makers, brokers, institutions or any other subscriber could submit a price that was better than that available on a traditional exchange and that information would be invisible to the market.

In order to ensure the Commission's goal of fairness in financial markets, two major regulations of ECNs were adopted since 1997. The first are the Order Handling Rules, adopted in January 1997, which require market makers to update their quotes in the National Market System (NMS) to reflect their own best price. Thus, an order posted to the NMS may reflect a better bid or offer than available on an ECN, but market makers cannot post a better priced order on an ECN than they are willing to make available on the NMS. In December 1998, the Commission adopted Regulation ATS, which requires ECNs to display their best order to the NMS and other alternative trading systems regardless of who submitted the order. In the past, orders from institutions and non-market maker broker-dealers were not required to be reported to the NMS even if they represented an improvement over the outstanding best order displayed in the NMS. Regulation ATS does not apply to ECNs with a trivial market presence in a given security.

Significant academic work in the past several years addresses the efficacy of market regulation in both direct and indirect tests. Taken together, the evidence suggests that market regulation has positively affected market quality. The question of whether market liquidity improved in response to the Order Handling Rules is addressed in Barclay et al. (1999). They conclude that spreads fell dramatically in response to the changes, leading to better prices available for investors. This is direct evidence in support of the notion that market regulation can have a positive outcome for investors.

Indirect evidence on the usefulness of market regulation is more varied. Perhaps most compelling is the evidence that countries with less developed regulatory structures also have less developed (and less efficient) financial markets (see LaPorta et al.1997). This suggests that investors are aware of the benefits of regulation in ensuring the fairness of markets and are more willing to trade in markets overseen by more formalized regulators. Moreover, capital acquisition appears to be easier/cheaper in more developed markets. Miller (1999) notes that stock prices of foreign firms that announce cross listing on the NYSE rise significantly.

The plethora of academic papers conducting 'event-studies' provides evidence consistent with the efficacy of regulation. These papers generally document that stock prices of firms making news announcements, move significantly on the announcement (and following) day. The fact that markets are surprised by the news suggests that rampant trading on the information before it is released (in violation of rule 10b-5) is not a problem. Of course, exceptions do occur (for example, Billett, Garfinkel and O'Neal (1998) document significant stock price movements two days before announcements of bank debt downgrades, consistent with leakage), and regulations must sometimes be rewritten to encourage stronger adherence to law.

For example, insider trading laws have periodically been strengthened in response to popular press accounts of rule 10b-5 violations. The exploits of Ivan Boesky are mentioned in Congressional hearings associated with the legislation known as The Insider Trading Sanctions Act (ITSA), while similar abuses led to the Insider Trading and Securities Fraud Enforcement Act (ITSFEA) just four years later. While ITSFEA was designed to provide stronger discouragement of insider trading than ITSA, Garfinkel (1997) shows that the discouragement took an unusual form. In particular, insiders appeared to follow the letter of the law, avoiding trading prior to significant news releases (earnings announcements), while increasing their relative emphasis on trading after these events, without any significant decline in their profits on such trades. Thus, while regulations appear to affect the behaviour of market participants, the result occasionally differs from intentions.

4 Regulation of investment advisors and companies

Mutual funds and other investment companies are typically structured such that the company hires an outside advisor to manage the investments. Representatives of the advisory company typically sit on the board of directors for the fund. To ensure that the fund's investors are provided with access to high quality information and protection under the law, Congress has given the Commission oversight responsibilities for investment advisors and investment companies.

To ensure that investment companies provide critical information to investors, the SEC requires an initial registration including a detailed description of the investing style of the fund and how managers will be compensated. Once registered, the companies must distribute, at least half yearly, a detailed report to shareholders, much like the annual report security issuers must provide.

Investment companies are also required by law to establish procedures for independent review of managers. All shares must have voting rights and the investment advisor's contract must be voted on by all shareholders. Further, at least 40 per cent of the company's directors must be independent of the investment advisor.

In the late 1990s the Commission sought ways to improve investment company governance and limit misleading advertising. SEC initiatives have promoted increased director independence, better disclosure of fees charged and truth in fund performance advertising. The Mutual Fund Cost Calculator (*http://www.sec.gov/mfcc/mfcc-int.htm*) enables investors to easily estimate and compare the costs of owning mutual funds.

JONATHAN SOKOBIN
OFFICE OF ECONOMIC ANALYSIS,
US SECURITIES AND EXCHANGE COMMISSION,
WASHINGTON, DC

JON A. GARFINKEL
UNIVERSITY OF IOWA

Further reading

(References cited in the text marked *)

Aggarwal, R., Gray, I. and Singer, H. (1999) 'Capital raising in the offshore market', *Journal of Banking and Finance* 23: 1181–94. (Security sales under Regulation S were used to generate positive returns to foreign investors at the expense of domestic investors.)

* Barclay, M., Christie, W., Harris, J., Kandel, E. and Schultz, P. (1999) 'The effects of market reform on the trading costs and depths of NASDAQ stocks', *Journal of Finance* 54: 1–34. (Reforms were associated with a significant drop in trading costs – approximately 30 per cent – with apparently minimal impact on market quality.)

Baumol, W.J., Goldenfeld, S.M., Gordon, L.A. and Koehn, M.F. (1990) *The Economics of Mutual Fund Markets: Competition Versus Regulation*, Boston, MA: Kluwer Academic Publishers. (A detailed account of the regulatory, legal and economic histories of the mutual fund industry.)

Bethel, J.E. and Sirri, E.R. (1998) 'Express lane or tollbooth in the desert? The SEC's framework for security issuance', *Journal of Applied Corporate Finance* 11: 25–38. (SEC regulation has adapted to the rapid growth and change in securities markets.)

* Billett, M.T., Garfinkel, J.A. and O'Neal, E.S. (1998) 'The cost of market versus regulatory discipline in banking', *Journal of Financial Economics* 48: 333–58. (Banks face different costs of risk taking imposed by regulators versus the market.)

* Garfinkel, J.A. (1997) 'New evidence on the effects of federal regulations on insider trading: The Insider Trading and Securities Fraud Enforcement Act (ITSFEA)', *Journal of Corporate Finance* 3: 89–111. (Regulations affect insiders' trading behaviour around earnings announcements.)

* LaPorta, R., Lopez-de-Silanes, F., Shleifer, A. and Vishny, R. (1997) 'Legal determinants of external finance', *Journal of Finance* 52: 1131–50. (Countries with weaker investor protections have smaller and narrower capital markets.)

* Miller, D.P. (1999) 'The market reaction to international cross-listing: evidence from depositary receipts', *Journal of Financial Economics* 51: 103–23. (Positive stock price reactions to cross-listing announcements are largest for firms that are listed on major US exchanges.)

Protecting Investors: A Half-Century of Investment Company Regulation. SEC Staff Report (1992) Chicago, IL: Commerce Clearing House. (The historical basis of investment company regulation and recommendations for modernization.)

Securities Regulation in a Nutshell (1998) 6th edn. St. Paul, MN: West Group. (Framework for understanding of the basic content and organization of federal and state securities law.)

The Work of the SEC. A Quick Reference Guide (1997) Washington, DC: US Securities and Exchange Commission Office of Public Affairs, Policy Evaluation and Research. (The mission, history, organization and responsibilities of the Securities and Exchange Commission.)

Further resources

SEC
  http://www.sec.gov
Mutual Fund Cost Calculator
  http://www.sec.gov/mfcc/mfcc-int.htm

Industrial sectors

Aerospace industry

1 Introduction
2 Origins of the industry and competitive context
3 Analysis and evaluation – policy debates and management issues
4 Managing an increasingly global division of labour

Overview

The aerospace industry is made up of manufacturers of aircraft, aircraft engines, guided missiles and space vehicles, their propulsion units, and the parts and components these pieces of equipment are made up of. In addition, in those countries that are home to the firms that build aerospace equipment, there exists a well-developed tier of sophisticated firms providing 'after-market' support services, such as maintenance, repair and overhaul of aircraft and engines. These firms are also considered as part of the aerospace industry. Historically, the most important buyers of aerospace products were governments; both via their armed forces and often through government-owned airlines. Given the identity of the industry's primary customers, purchases of aerospace equipment have been and continue to be highly politicized events. Especially during the years of the Cold War, aircraft procurement decisions were not made on strict economic considerations, with purchase price considered secondary to issues of national security and the support of 'national champions'.

But since the Cold War has drawn to a close and as airlines across the globe have become privatized and the airline industry deregulated, the competitive dynamics of the aerospace industry have changed. In 1998, for the first time since 1934, the US aerospace industry sales to commercial and foreign customers exceeded the value of sales to the US government. And as smaller shares of national budgets are dedicated to procuring new aerospace equipment and as brand new commercial demand emerges in satellite and space markets, there is a greater emphasis than ever on reducing the costs of developing new products and bringing them to market. These new competitive realities have forced changes in the way aerospace firms do business, encouraging more cooperation between firms that were formerly competitors, an increased emphasis on outsourcing to lower cost suppliers, as well as widespread industry consolidation. These changes, in turn, have created new issues for policy makers to grapple with in the areas of national security, technology transfer and industry competitiveness.

1 Introduction

An historian of the early pioneers of the aircraft industry laments, 'How darksome it is, ... to consider the extent to which the most fertile fields of ... engineering have been shaped by wartime values' (Biddle 1991: 13). Nowhere was this comment truer than in the aerospace industry. For most of the twentieth century, government and military customers have dominated demand for aerospace products. And as governments funded the development of new fighter aircraft, transports, reconnaissance planes and a whole range of rotorcraft, the pace and direction of technological development in the industry was set by military imperatives. Given the strong national security advantage that arises from having a strong domestic aerospace industrial infrastructure, it is no wonder that being home to world-class aerospace firms has been a point of national prestige for the developed economies of the world.

But the aerospace industry is considered a 'strategic' industry in more than simply the military sense. Because aircraft are 'big ticket' items and because there are only a handful of countries in which they are produced, a competitive domestic aerospace industry greatly benefits the export position of a nation. For the USA, the world's largest producer of aerospace goods, 7.3 per cent of total merchandise exports in 1997 were exports of aerospace equipment. (In the EU, the comparable figure was about 3 per cent in 1997.) But the aerospace industry is viewed as paying dividends to the domestic economy beyond just strengthening its balance of payments. As they 'spin-off' military designs to develop new commercial jets and apply process innovations developed on military aerospace projects to commercial products in both the aircraft industry and beyond, aerospace firms produce positive technological externalities that can benefit an economy more broadly. The economic and technological impacts of military–civilian 'spin-off' are not undisputed. Indeed for every scholar who touts the benefits of spin-off there is another whose attempts to quantify the impact have demonstrated that the costs associated with maintaining a large military–industrial complex far outweigh any measurable benefit. For a discussion of these issues, see Samuels (1994: ch. 1).

Because of the high economic stakes and potential technological pay-offs of the aerospace industry, not to mention the close ties between the military and commercial sides of the aerospace business, perhaps no other industry attracts the attention of national and international policy makers in quite the way the aerospace industry does. But the special managerial challenges of an industry characterized by high costs, long learning curves and extremely long product cycles, makes the aerospace industry particularly interesting to students and practitioners of economics and management as well.

2 Origins of the industry and competitive context

While in the pre-Second World War era, the global aerospace industry was dominated by European firms, the onset of the war provided US producers with long production runs that allowed them to achieve economies of scale in this extremely high fixed cost industry and a simultaneous opportunity for technological catch-up with their competitors abroad. Decades of high levels of Cold War military expenditures continued that advantage for US firms with the result that today, the world's largest three aerospace companies, Boeing, Lockheed Martin and Raytheon, are all US-based. And despite a resurgence of the European aerospace industry, led by the rapid market ascent of the European aircraft consortium, Airbus, the industry today remains dominated by US producers. According to the European Association of Aerospace Industries, US firms accounted for 56.4 per cent of industry turnover in 1998, European producers had a 33.5 per cent share while Canadian and Japanese enterprises had about 5 per cent each. The distribution of aerospace industry employment follows a similar pattern; 53.9 per cent of the 1.14 million aerospace employees worldwide are in the USA, 37.1 per cent are in the EU, 5.9 per cent are in Canada and 3.1 per cent are in Japan.

Aircraft: airplanes, helicopters

The largest and most familiar segment of the aerospace industry is the market for large civil transports, those airplanes that airlines use to carry 70 or more passengers. Since the 1960s, US manufacturers have been the market leaders in this segment of the industry. Through the 1970s, Boeing and McDonnell-Douglas were the top two firms while fellow US producer Lockheed took third place. Lockheed exited the commercial jet business in 1981, though it remains a major player in designing and building planes for military customers. More recently, the emergence and rise of Airbus put increasing pressure on the two remaining American competitors. Founded in 1970, Airbus was able to survive its early years only because of the subsidies it received from European governments in the nations that hosted production facilities. But by the early 1990s, Airbus reached its 'survival threshold' of 30 per cent market share, pushing US rival McDonnell-Douglas into third place in the market. Just a few years later, Airbus effectively elbowed McDonnell-Douglas out of the game entirely; McDonnell-Douglas was acquired by its former US rival, Boeing, in 1997. Airbus has proved to be a strong competitor even for giant Boeing; new orders for civil transports at the close of the decade were split almost evenly between the two firms, though Boeing's deliveries still outweighed those of its rival.

On the military side of the industry, there are a larger number of firms competing in the market for fighters, military transport and other aircraft. The leaders include Boeing and Lockheed Martin of the USA, British Aerospace, French Aerospatiale Matra and Dassault, German Daimler-Chrysler Aerospace (DASA) and in Japan, Mitsubishi Heavy Industries. But again, in this segment, US producers clearly lead the pack. The European Commission estimates that in the area of fighter aircraft, for example, US producers took 80 per cent of contracts awarded, in terms of value.

The 'general aviation' sector encompasses the manufacture of regional aircraft which carry anywhere from 1070 passengers as well as business jets and recreational aircraft. European producers such as British Aerospace, Saab and Fokker as well as US-based Fairchild had a strong position in this market through the 1980s, but new competitors such as Bombardier of Canada and Embraer of Brazil have been able to capture market share away from these incumbents. In the business jet segment, five firms shared about 90 per cent of the worldwide market for business jets, estimated to be about US$5.5 billion, in 1999: Bombardier of Canada, Gulfstream, Cessna, and Raytheon of the USA, and Dassault of France.

The fourth sector of the aircraft industry is the market for rotorcraft. US producers Sikorsky, Boeing and Bell Helicopter Textron are strong leaders in this market whose primary customers are the armed forces. Important civil customers include corporations, emergency medical services and law enforcement. Orders for rotorcraft are particularly sensitive to changes in defence spending. Orders hit a low in 1993 and have been on a slow, gradual recovery since then. World production of both military and civil helicopters is projected to total $26 billion for the period 1999–2003.

Missile systems and space vehicles

The companies that put the 'space' in the 'aerospace' industry are manufacturers of missile systems and space vehicles. Traditionally, government orders accounted for the entire output of this segment of the industry. But the market for space vehicles, once the sole preserve of governments and their space administrations, has in recent years witnessed new growth thanks to a new demand for commercial launch services. The revolution in satellite communications technologies is responsible for this trend and this market is split roughly evenly between US and European companies. European Arianespace has a market share of about 40 per cent of launches for the commercial satellite market, while Boeing and Lockheed are the leading providers of launch services in the USA. US-based Loral and Hughes are two of the leading builders of satellites. The market for commercial satellite launches, unlike the rest of the aerospace industry, is one where European and American firms could face potentially stiff competition from less industrialized nations, in particular from Russia, the Ukraine and China.

The market for guided missiles remains the province of military customers and is led by US-based Raytheon-Hughes, the world's largest producer of guided missiles and their propulsion units. Other US producers include Boeing and Lockheed Martin while the leading European manufacturers of missiles are Matra and British Aerospace (BAe). These and other defence-dependent producers have seen their markets shrink substantially in the post-Cold War era and have turned toward mergers and acquisitions as a strategy for survival.

3 Analysis and evaluation – policy debates and management issues

The dynamics of cooperation and competition

While the number of 'integrated' aerospace manufacturers, those with the capabilities to design, build and market complete aircraft, missiles or spacecraft, is counted only in the dozens worldwide, of course none of these firms build their sophisticated products entirely on their own. Each of the 'systems integrators' relies on a broad and deep tier of suppliers whose number can reach into the hundreds or even thousands. Increasingly, though, as cost controls become more important than ever on both the military and commercial sides of the market, the systems integrators are also cooperating with each other, especially in Europe. Of course, the most successful and enduring example of cooperation has been the consortium that builds the Airbus jetliners.

The concept of creating a consortium to build commercial jetliners grew out of the realization that no single European nation had a domestic market large enough for a domestic producer to hope it would remain competitive, given the high fixed cost structure of the industry. While European aircraft firms could get enough business to survive thanks to military contracts none would be able to enjoy the long production runs needed to actually be profitable in a commercial sense. Moreover, the rapid pace of technological change during the 1960s (when the idea of Airbus was being conceived) meant that even on military projects, firms might have to collaborate to keep up. As it was, the foundations for cooperation in the commercial arena were laid with collaborative projects on the military side. Based on the successful track record of cross-border cooperative military projects like the Transall C-160 troop transport and the Breguet 1150 antisubmarine warfare patrol aircraft, the political thinking in Europe came around to the idea that the same model could be successfully applied to the commercial arena. Airbus Industrie was born in 1970, conceived as a private cooperative venture that would benefit from both direct subsidies and other more indirect forms of market protection. Airbus was established as a French 'Groupement d'Interet Economique' (GIE), a type of unlimited partnership comprised of corporate partners Aerospatiale of France, Daimler-Chrysler Aerospace (DASA) of Germany, British Aerospace (BAe) and Construcciones Aeronauticas (CASA) of Spain. Throughout its existence, Airbus GIE has never had any capital of its own, with all revenues flowing to and costs being paid by its partner firms.

Thanks to Airbus' unique corporate structure, the company has perennially attracted keen interest from management researchers. Those in business schools have been engaged with the question of how it is that these firms have been able to sustain cooperation in the manufacture of commercial jets, even while they are direct competitors in other aerospace market segments. Throughout its existence, the consortium has faced inherent conflicts within its ranks with respect to the degree to which Airbus partners would share detailed information on their costs and the extent to which they should share innovations.

The Airbus partners' success in managing these conflicts is reflected in the fact that at the dawn of the new century, the cooperative model has been firmly established on both the military side of the business as well as the commercial. Moreover new aircraft programmes like the Eurofighter and Eurocopter in Europe as well as the F-22 fighter in the USA demonstrate that the practice spans both sides of the Atlantic. Cooperation on military projects has been encouraged as a way for companies and nations to share the costs (and jobs and export benefits) of new product development, while on the commercial side, risk and revenue-sharing agreements are becoming more and more common in many segments of the aerospace industry (aircraft engines in particular). For the systems integrators, such agreements allow them to share the high up-front development costs of designing and building equipment with their major suppliers, costs which during the Cold War were often picked up by the government and are less likely to be so now. While for the suppliers of major subsystems, taking on an up-front commitment to finance a share of new product development (risk) is a way to lock in a fixed work share (revenue) once the production phase is entered.

It may be that in the new, post-Cold War competitive environment, these sorts of arrangements put a company in a better position to maintain a broader product line than it would otherwise be able to independently. But it also raises new issues for firms regarding which 'core competences' they should develop and maintain and which capabilities they rely on suppliers or partners to deliver. In dealing with a 'complex product' like aircraft, these issues are confounded by the technological cross-linkages involved with the integration of multiple systems. Could vertically disintegrating, abandoning certain competencies; threaten the future viability of the enterprise's position as a systems integrator? How do firms deal with the threat that by sharing technologies with key suppliers, they could be nurturing a future competitor? These issues are just beginning to be investigated but represent real concerns for firms in the aerospace industry and are potentially fertile fields for future research efforts.

Strategic trade and industrial policy: the debate over subsidies

'Notoriously nationalistic and independent', the European governments that supported the launch of the first Airbus aircraft maintained that in a high cost, high tech industry like aerospace, barriers to entry are so high that allowing and encouraging cooperation among competitors might not be enough. These nations held the unapologetic position that in the commercial aircraft market, subsidies and other market protection were in order to ensure that, in the long-term, free competition would reign. Airbus is the great success story that proponents of 'strategic trade policy' point to as proof that subsidies and other forms of market protection can help an enterprise in building competitive advantage, while preventing an industry from becoming dominated by a single, global monopolist.

But the 'success story' of the subsidization of Airbus was not without costs. First and foremost were the financial costs: estimated to have been in the range of $10 billion by an MIT study on the commercial aircraft industry published in 1989. But the subsidies had other, harder to measure costs in the collateral damage they caused to trade relations between the USA and the EU. While the American market incumbents against which Airbus sought to compete vigorously argued that the subsidies that flowed to the consortium represented a form of unfair trade competition, the Europeans countered that the high levels of defence spending in the USA served to 'subsidize' American aerospace firms in a more indirect way than the Europeans' subsidies, but with the same effects. Eventually, after years of accusations, hearings and negotiations an agreement was reached between the USA and the EU in 1992 that set limits on the size and nature of subsidies that governments could give to commercial aircraft programmes. But even after the bilateral agreement was reached, charges that Airbus reaps benefits from 'unfair' practices linger as US producers scratch their heads at Airbus' low prices wondering how their competitor can produce at such low costs.

Part of the problem all along was Airbus' structure. As previously stated, any profits or losses arising from production of Airbus aircraft flow through to its partners and become incorporated in consolidated financial statements. This lack of 'transparency' has contributed to a continued suspicion on the part of some that Airbus continues to receive subsidies indirectly. Since the 'company' for years never reported profit and loss statements, it was difficult for those on the US side to believe any figures on subsidies the consortium did report. Hopefully, this issue is on its way to becoming a moot point as the Airbus consortium makes the transition to becoming a 'regular' company. As of the summer of 2000, Airbus was a private company 20 per cent owned by British Aerospace plc and 80 per cent owned by EADS, or the European Aeronautic, Defense and Space Company, which is in turn, owned by Daimler Chrysler Aerospace AG, Aerospatiale Matra and CASA. EADS began selling shares to the public in July 2000. The Airbus partners plan for Airbus to become a stand-alone company, with shares possibly being sold to the public.

But even if the 'transparency' issues of Airbus are on their way to being resolved, the flap over aerospace subsidies is likely to continue. Indeed, a dispute over cut-rate export loans has been simmering for years between regional jet makers Embraer of Brazil and Canada's Bombardier. Each nation has alternately complained to the World Trade Organization (WTO) over the course of the late 1990s that the other's subsidized loan programmes violated WTO rules. At the time of writing, the dispute continues. But it is clear is that as long as nations around the world seek to become players in the global aerospace game, there will be a natural tendency for governments to nurture their 'homegrowns'. And as long as firms in the industry sell to both civil and military customers, there is sure to be continued disagreement between competitors about 'fair play' in the markets.

Industry consolidation: where are the economies of scale?

In 1993, then-US Deputy Defense Secretary William Perry gathered together defence industry executives at a dinner, an event which, in industry parlance, has come to be called 'the last supper'. At that meeting, Mr Perry explained that due to Pentagon budget cuts, at least half of the military contractors represented at the table would cease to exist and he encouraged them to combine into a few, larger companies that would be able to make more profit from the much smaller pie thanks to rationalization and consolidation. In the years that followed, the number of leading US defence firms collapsed from around a dozen to about four. The 1990s witnessed previously unthinkable takeovers in the aerospace industry; defence giant McDonnell-Douglas was acquired by Boeing, Lockheed merged with Martin-Marietta, while Raytheon and Hughes joined forces to become the world's largest maker of missiles. These high-profile 'mega-mergers' were only part of the story, as hundreds of smaller aerospace suppliers joined in on the game, alternately acquiring and spinning off aerospace businesses. When the proposed Lockheed Martin merger with Northrop-Grumman was turned down on antitrust grounds in 1998, the signal was sent that the consolidation of the US aerospace industry had gone far enough.

Albeit in a far less dramatic fashion, the European aerospace industry also went through its share of merger activity and restructuring during the 1990s, witnessing the merger of Aerospatiale and Matra Haute Technologies and Fairchild Aerospace's acquisition of Dornier. Fokker, the Dutch maker of regional jets, closed its doors under financial distress, unable to attract a buyer; Saab got out of the turboprop business; and BAe ended production of the Jetstream. Budget problems also encouraged European consolidation in the area of missile systems. And last, the decision by Airbus' partners to make the 'Groupement d'Interet Economique' into a 'Single Corporate Entity' via the creation of EADS has involved a restructuring of ownership among all of the group's partners, with the exception of British Aerospace.

Mergers and acquisitions have not been confined only to the equipment manufacturing side of the aerospace industry. The maintenance, repair and overhaul sector has also seen significant consolidation. The number of aftermarket support companies in the USA fell from 24 in 1993 to just 13 in 1998. Some analysts project the number to shrink even further. The forces at work in this sector come from both the supply and demand side of the aerospace equipment market. On the supply side, original equipment manufacturers (OEMs) of aircraft and engines have aggressively expanded their presence in the high-margin servicing business with an eye to smoothing out the peaks and troughs, which can wreak havoc on their bottom lines. On the demand side, airlines, under more competition than ever as deregulation and cross-border 'open skies' agreements between countries proliferate, are looking to reduce costs by outsourcing maintenance and repair activities. Even the US Armed Forces have been getting into the act, contracting with private MRO providers in order to reduce the number of personnel engaged in maintaining non-combat aircraft.

But while the pace and scale of the restructuring of the global aerospace industry far surpassed what anyone could have imagined two decades ago, what is perhaps more surprising is how elusive profits have been for these firms, despite the scale of rationalization in the industry. (Although others might say that the lack of profitability should not be surprising given the rapid pace of consolidation, which took place in something just short of a panic mode.) Certainly, the aerospace industry is not the first group of manufacturers to face the need for radical restructuring, forced by a sharp change in demand conditions.

However, given the strategic nature of the industry, aerospace manufacturers' troubles receive perhaps more attention than those suffered by others. Indeed in late 1999, the value of US defence industry stocks had sunk so low that the US Department of Defense convened a special task force to examine what, if anything, could or should be done to reverse the downward course. The ability of these firms to work through their merger-related difficulties and finally make their way back to financial strength remains to be seen as the new millennium begins. To be sure, an assessment of the long-term impact of these mergers on aerospace firms' shareholders, workforces and customers will be a line of research well worth pursuing.

4 Managing an increasingly global division of labour

While at one time it was possible to speak of an 'American aircraft' or a 'European aircraft', today's aerospace industry is truly global in character. Joining the ranks of the more established aerospace firms in North America, Europe and Japan, emerging suppliers in countries such as South Korea, Singapore, Taiwan and China are currently inserting themselves as key links in the worldwide aerospace value chain. For example, South Korea's Samsung Aerospace produces wing frameworks for Boeing, engine parts for Pratt and Whitney, and is jointly developing a Korean fighter with Lockheed Martin. Thanks to its locational advantage as a major airline hub, Singapore Technologies Aerospace, a state-owned firm, is an emerging supplier of aviation maintenance services. The company also makes components for several European aircraft programmes. The list goes on. But as the systems integrators increasingly turn to suppliers beyond their national borders, seeking out costs savings and hoping that doing business with firms abroad will increase sales abroad, a new set of issues arises as they seek to manage an increasingly global division of labour.

First, firms face the problem of coordinating an increasingly complex value chain – certainly a problem not unique to the aerospace industry, but faced by many other industries in this new global era. But the special, strategic character of the aerospace industry presents additional complexities. Foremost among these is the tricky balance between the sometimes-competing interests of private profits and national security. Since many aerospace technologies (of both product and process variety) have historically been and continue to be 'dual-use' in nature, the new competitive environment has thrust to the fore new concerns and increased tensions over technology transfer. The 1980s' row between the USA and Japan over the latter's ambitions to leverage American technology to develop an indigenous fighter jet, a conflict dubbed the 'FSX Wars', seems tame in comparison with more recent clashes between the USA and China. Hungry for business in the wake of defence cutbacks, firms like McDonnell-Douglas and Loral transferred sensitive aerospace technologies to Chinese firms with which they had engaged in production agreements, prompting the wrath of their US workforces, who called upon their employers to 'export planes, not our jobs'. But soon it was the wrath of the law these firms faced, as allegations surfaced that the Chinese firms had improperly used commercial technology in developing military projects in the areas of both aircraft and launch vehicles, allegations which led to Congressional inquiries and criminal indictments in the USA and set off a new debate around the politics of countertrade and 'offsets'.

The term 'offsets' refers to the practice, common in the aerospace industry (both on the defence and commercial sides of the business), by systems integrators of strategically placing work with foreign suppliers in the hope of securing a greater level of sales in that country. Countries purchasing aerospace equipment (either for their armed forces, or for what are often state-owned or state-subsidized airlines) negotiate with the systems integrators to have a share of the work involved in building an aircraft performed by firms in their home country to 'offset' the large, negative balance of payments effect that purchase would have. But offsets have also been used to leverage access to advanced technologies, helping fledgling aerospace producers make greater leaps forward than they would otherwise be able to. Of course, the dilemma for the systems integrator is being pressured to give away more technology or work than it would like to (or than its government or workforce would like it to) in order to close a sale.

Some observers liken offsets to the classic 'prisoner's dilemma' of game theory. That is, a buyer of aerospace equipment, considering the products of two, competing companies, seeks to leverage that purchase to gain the highest possible offset, either in dollar or technological terms. Both sellers have an incentive to grant the purchasing country larger shares of work than they would otherwise, were they able to cooperate or collude. Thus, although one firm ultimately wins the contract, it loses more jobs and output through offsets than it would ideally prefer. Given that there are clear 'externalities' in the area of national security and technology transfer, there are some who propose that the only way to 'fix' the offset 'problem' would be via international agreements to restrict firms and countries from engaging in this practice. Indeed, offsets are, at least on paper, forbidden in commercial aircraft sales according to the WTO. However, there are clear enforcement problems inherent in sales agreements and not all nations are WTO signatories. Moreover, there is no agreement at all which prohibits offsets in military sales, indicating that a public policy resolution will not be soon in coming.

While the issue of offsets at first pass would seem to be one for national policy makers, in fact, it is one that absorbs business managers in the industry. In this, the industry where the 'learning curve' was first documented, 'learning by doing' is an important determinant of competitive advantage. Outsourcing, whether driven by the desire to hold down costs or by the politics of the aircraft procurement game, could negatively impact the skill bases central to maintaining and building competitive advantage in this increasingly competitive, albeit rapidly consolidating, industry. The long product runs characteristic of aerospace manufacturing traditionally meant that once established, a competitive lead was something that a firm could count on retaining for years to come. In the new competitive environment, with firms in more countries than ever intent on establishing themselves as players in the world aerospace game, an incumbent's lead is no longer a guarantee of future success. Indeed, managing their ever-more global division of labour, remains one of the primary challenges for aerospace systems integrators and it is one which will undoubtedly keep them occupied for many years into the future.

BETH ANN ALMEIDA
INTERNATIONAL ASSOCIATION OF
MACHINISTS AND AEROSPACE WORKERS
MARYLAND

Acknowledgements

Funding for this research was provided by the President's Office, University of Massachusetts, INSEAD (the European Institute of Business Administration) Research Association, and the Targeted Socio-Economic Research (TSER) Programme of the European Commission (DGXII) under the Fourth Framework Programme, European Commission (Contract no: SOE1-CT98-1114; Project no: 053).

Further reading

(References cited in the text marked *)

Aerospace Industries Association of America (1999) *Aerospace Facts and Figures 1999/2000*, Washington, DC: Aerospace Industries Association of America. (Report detailing key statistics on the US aerospace industry, including sales, production, R&D, employment, and foreign trade.)

AECMA (1999) *The European Aerospace Industry 1998 Statistical Survey*, Brussels: European Association of Aerospace Industries (AECMA). (Report detailing key statistics on the European aerospace industry, including turnover, R&D, employment, and foreign trade.)

* Biddle, W. (1991) *Barons of the Sky*, New York: Simon and Schuster. (A detailed history of the early entrepreneurs who built the aircraft industry.)

Bilstein, R. (1996) The *American Aerospace Industry: From Workshop to Global Enterprise*, New York: Twayne Publishers. (A comprehensive study of the growth of the aerospace industry from its beginnings through to the present day, with particular focus on technological advancement and the relations between industry and government.)

European Commission (1997) *The European Aerospace Industry Meeting the Global Challenge*, COM(97) 466 Final. (A report detailing the state of the European aerospace industry and future challenges.)

Krugman, P. (1986) *Strategic Trade Policy and the New International Economics*, Cambridge MA: MIT Press. (Theoretical analysis of 'strategic trade' policy and its applications to the aerospace industry.)

March, A. (1989) 'The US commercial aerospace industry and its foreign competitors.' *MIT Commission on Industrial Productivity Working Papers*, Vol. 1. Cambridge, MA: MIT Press. (Landmark study on the changing competitive environment faced by US aircraft manufacturers as a result of Airbus' successes.)

Olienyk, J. and Carbaugh, R. (1999) 'Competition in the world jetliner industry,' *Challenge* 42 (4): 60–81. (Discusses the decline of US competitiveness in jetliner production in the context of the free trade versus managed trade debate.)

Prencipe, A. (1997) 'Technological competencies and product's evolutionary dynamics: a case study from the aero-engine industry,' *Research Policy*, 25: 1261–76. (Argues that in complex-product systems simple notions of core competencies and vertical disintegration may damage the competitiveness of the firm. Case study of Rolls-Royce's technology management strategy in its aircraft engine business.)

* Samuels, R.J. (1994) *Rich Nation, Strong Army: National Security and the Technological Transformation of Japan*, Ithaca, NY: Cornell University Press. (Analyses the links between technology, economic interests and national security objectives in Japan via a detailed historical account of the Japanese defence industrial base with particular focus on the development of the aerospace industry.)

Thornton, D.W. (1995) *Airbus Industrie: The Politics of an International Industrial Collaboration*, New York: St. Martin's Press. (Discusses the Airbus Industrie consortium's roots, structure and competitive strategy.)

Wessner, C.W. and Wolff, A.W. (eds) (1997) *Policy Issues in Aerospace Offsets*, Washington, DC: National Academy Press. (Report of a National Research Council Workshop on the economic, political, and strategic issues involved in the offsets debate.)

See also: COOPERATION AND COMPETITION; DEVELOPMENT AND DIFFUSION OF TECHNOLOGY; GENDER AND ETHNIC DIVISIONS IN THE US LABOUR FORCE; GLOBALIZATION

Chemical industry

1 Introduction
2 A brief history
3 Key issues and themes

Overview

The modern chemical industry is among the largest manufacturing industries of the USA and Western Europe, producing products that range from basic chemicals such as acids, to intermediate chemicals such as synthetic fibres and plastics, to final products such as soaps, cosmetics, paints and fertilizers. It is also one of the earliest science based industries, tracing its origins to the development of synthetic dyes in Britain in the 1850s. In the 1870s, German chemical firms overtook their British competitors by mastering the science and engineering of producing new synthetic drugs on a large scale, and Germany became the leading chemical producing nation by the turn of the century. The US chemical industry grew initially by exploiting the rich natural resource endowments in the USA and began its transformation from technology importer to innovator in the 1920s and 1930s, by developing new chemical processes and new products like nylon and synthetic rubber. Many of the well-known US chemical firms grew to prominence during this period.

The Second World War marked a watershed. The chemical industry became closely linked with the oil industry, as many chemicals were produced out of petroleum based inputs instead of the coal by-products that had earlier been the main inputs to the industry. Although the US chemical industry enjoyed an early advantage in petrochemicals, this advantage was eroded as technologies diffused widely, enabling Europe and Japan to narrow the gap and other countries to enter the industry. The increased competition, compounded by the oil shock of the 1970s, and slowing possibilities for significant product innovation culminated in a deep seated and continuing process of restructuring. The restructuring has resulted in more product focused firms and more globalized firms. It has also seen a reduction in R&D intensity in virtually all the sub-sectors except life sciences, traditionally a part of the chemical industry but now, for all intents and purposes, a separate industry.

The long historical record of the chemical industry provides a mirror for understanding the evolution of other science-based industries. It offers a rich historical case study for understanding the factors that determine commercial success in a science-based industry, and insights for managers and policy makers in managing in a technology-based economy.

1 Introduction

If the twenty-first century is going to be the information century, then the twentieth might well have been the chemical century. The chemical industry is one the largest manufacturing industries in the world. Chemicals and allied products account for 1.5–1.9 per cent of the US GDP and about 10.4 per cent of US manufacturing value added, the largest manufacturing sector in the USA and second only to the food and drink sector in Europe.

Not only is the chemical industry very large, it is also very complex. The chemicals and allied products group (SIC 28) can be divided into three major sub-groups: (1) basic chemicals such as acids, alkalis, salts and organic chemicals; (2) intermediate chemical products such as synthetic fibres, plastic materials, and colours and pigments; (3) consumer chemical products such as drugs, cosmetics, soaps, as well as paint, fertilizers and explosives. Even if one excludes closely related sectors such as refining, and paper and pulp, the chemical industry produces 50,000–70,000 products. The growth and development of chemicals has had a substantial impact on virtually every sector in the economy, from agriculture to electronics. The modern chemical industry is arguably the first 'high tech' industry, and has historically funded the vast bulk of its R&D investments privately. As the industry has matured, its R&D intensity (excluding drugs and medicines) has decreased somewhat but, even so, chemicals remains among the more R&D intensive sectors of modern economies.

Since its origins as a science-based industry with the discovery of synthetic dyes in Britain in the 1850s, the chemical industry has provided a fascinating backdrop against which to study how innovation, state policy, and factor endowments interact in the process of economic growth and industrial evolution. Chemical firms provided some of the early exemplars for Chandler's (1990) magisterial historical analyses of changing firm scale and scope and for Hounshell and Smith's (1988) insightful investigation of how science and research was made to bear commercial profit at Du Pont. Studies of productivity improvements in chemical processing industries, in oil refining (Enos 1962) and in synthetic fibres (Hollander 1965) highlighted the importance of a sequence of small process innovations in increasing productivity. Despite this, and despite the obvious importance of chemicals, the sector has received relatively little attention on the whole from economists and management scholars. This essay will discuss the insights that the 150-year history of this science-based industry provides for a variety of important and widely debated questions of policy and management.

2 A brief history

In the 1830s and 1840s, the British had the world's dominant chemical industry, which was focused on the production of inorganic chemicals. Inorganic compounds are those taken from the earth, such as salt and minerals, and which are then processed into useful products employed directly or used in further processing. One leading set of products were the alkalis, such as lime, soda ash and caustic soda, used extensively in textiles, glass and fertilizers; another includes acids such as sulfuric and nitric, which are often used in tanning, textiles, dyeing and a myriad other applications. Alkalis and sulfuric acid produced in large quantities are commonly referred to as heavy chemicals. Currently, organic chemicals such as ethylene, benzene and propylene, which are produced in large quantities, are more typical examples of heavy chemicals.

Thus, the early version of the inorganic chemical industry was in some sense closer to mining than the science-based chemistry of today. Perkin's discovery in 1856 launched the modern organic chemical industry. Since then, organic compounds have proved the most important class of chemicals because they are more varied and pervasive than the inorganic compounds. Organic chemistry begins with inputs that contain hydrocarbons (composed of hydrogen and carbon) – for instance coal, oil and natural gas – which form the backbone of final organic chemical outputs. In the first stage of processing, these raw materials are refined to produce primary outputs such as benzene and ethylene. In subsequent processing, chemicals such as chlorine and oxygen are added to the hydrocarbon backbones to give the compounds their desired characteristics. The final output may, for example, be nylon or polyester fibre, a plastic or a pharmaceutical product. The hydrocarbon backbone for British dyestuffs, and for organic chemistry throughout almost all of the nineteenth century, was provided by coal.

Britain dominated the dyestuff industry also until the 1870s. These were glory times for England. Its organic chemical industry making dyestuffs had the technical know-how, the largest supply of basic raw material (coal), and the largest customer base (textiles). But those advantages slipped and were not enough to prevent German firms forging ahead. By 1913, German companies produced about 140,000 tons of dyes, Switzerland produced 10,000 tons, and Britain only 4400 tons. The American industry was a large producer of basic inorganic chemicals, but for its organic chemicals it depended mainly on German dyestuffs and other imports, except for the domestic production of explosives.

The First World War changed the relative positions of nations in the chemical industry, at least for a few years. The USA was cut off from German dyestuffs and built its own organic chemical industry. The German industry, shattered by war, and hurt by the appropriation of its intellectual property in the

USA, Britain and France, fell on hard times. Both Britain and Germany sought to create chemical companies that could be national standard bearers. In 1925, Germany formed the I.G. Farben company, merging all dye firms into one company. Britain created Imperial Chemical Industries (ICI) through a merger of smaller entities in 1926. In the USA a number of consolidations took place among private companies, forming such large and competitive entities as Du Pont, Union Carbide, Allied Chemical and American Cyanamid. I.G. Farben soon regained Germany's former dominance over the European chemical industry and formed numerous cartels to prop up prices, and limit competition. At the same time, the US chemical industry was gaining strength through the development of a large petroleum refining base, and also building its skill in designing large-scale continuous processing plants through the use of expert chemical engineering tools. This was also a time for innovative polymer-based products such as synthetic rubber, plastics (like polyethylene) and synthetic fibres (like nylon and polyester), although the full commercial impact of these innovations would only be realized after the Second World War.

The Second World War resulted in the physical destruction of a significant portion of the German chemical industry. The US industry was now using petrochemicals to produce fibres, plastics and many other products, while dyestuffs shrank in importance. America's chemical industry grew enormously and dominated the market at least until the 1970s. However, as world prosperity returned in the decades after the Second World War, so did a successful chemical industry in Germany, and elsewhere in Europe. The chemical industry in Germany and Britain rebuilt and grew rapidly, shifting organic chemical production from coal to petrochemicals nearly as quickly as had the USA. During the 1950s and 1960s, Japan made an astonishingly rapid entry into petrochemicals, leading to a rapid growth of the chemical industry. Apart from the three main *keiretsu* – Mitsui, Mitsubishi and Sumitomo – several other companies, such as Asahi Chemical, Maruzen Oil and Idemitsu, made considerable investments in petrochemical plants. Although the Japanese chemical industry grew to become the second largest in the world, it has not yet achieved the same success in terms of major products and process innovations.

By the end of the 1960s, European countries and Japan had succeeded in closing much of the gap with the USA. Since then, relative shares in world output have largely remained constant. During the late 1980s a cheaper dollar and declining growth opportunities in their home markets prompted European firms and, to a lesser extent, Japanese firms to expand heavily into the US market. The expansion, accomplished through direct investments, as well as acquisitions and alliances, underlined the globalization of the industry.

A major story of the post-Second World War development is the tremendous growth of the chemical industry in other parts of the world, in Eastern Europe, the Middle East and South Asia. In 1959 the USA, Japan, and Western Europe accounted for virtually all chemical exports. By the 1990s their combined share had fallen to two-thirds, with the rest coming from Asia, particularly South Korea and Taiwan, Eastern Europe and the Middle East. Much of the capacity addition took place during the 1970s and especially the 1980s. The development during the 1940s and 1950s of a group of independent developers and sellers of process technology, known as specialized engineering firms (SEFs), accelerated the international transfer of technologies. The rapid diffusion of technology and the spread of the industry increased competitive pressures, so that the US chemical industry began to experience its competitive 'crisis' in the late 1960s, well before most other US industries encountered growing competitive pressure from foreign sources and well before the onset of the 'oil shocks' of the 1970s. Table 1 gives an indication of the realtive positions of the major chemical exporting countries from the end of the nineteenth century through the twentieth century.

For an industry whose growth was closely tied to manufacturing growth, the oil shock meant a decline in demand precisely at a time when its costs were rising and when opportunities to innovate were becoming rarer. The combination of increasing entry, slower demand growth and diminishing opportunities

Table 1 Percentage shares in world exports of chemicals, 1899–1993, by country of origin (selected countries and years)

Year	USA	Britain	Germany[1]	Other W. Europe[2]	Japan	Other	World exports (US$ billion)
1899	14.2	19.6	35.0	13.1	0.4	4.2	0.26
1913	11.2	20.0	40.2	13.1	1.0	0.3	0.59
1929	18.1	17.5	30.9	15.3	1.8	0.4	1.04
1937	16.9	16.0	31.6	19.4	3.0	0.3	0.98
1950[1]	34.6	17.9	10.4	20.5	0.8	0.5	2.17
1959	27.4	15.0	20.2	21.1	3.1	0.2	5.48
1993	13.0	5.2	12.7	13.1	13.0	33.4	309.20

Notes: 1 West German figures for 1950, 1959, 1993
2 Comprises of Italy, Belgium-Luxembourg, Netherlands (except in 1899 and 1913), Sweden, and Switzerland
Source: Table 2 in Eichengreen (1998) which in turn is based on Maizel (1963: 302), and *Chemical Manufacturing Statistical Handbook*

for major product innovations on the scale of nylon or polyester forced a consolidation of industrial structure. Commercialization became more expensive and required ever more sophisticated knowledge of customers and the market. Faced with overcapacity, the industry restructured. The drive to reduce costs dominated the initial restructuring phase, driven in part by the relentless pressure from shareholders and their representatives. Major realignments of the product portfolios of many firms followed, with many mergers, divestitures, acquisitions and the rise of entirely new firms in the industry (Bower 1986).

During this phase, many firms cut down on R&D and refocused R&D expenditures on shorter-term projects and away from more fundamental research. In the late 1990s, there were some indications that the industry may be entering a new phase of technological change and R&D spending appeared to be picking up as did activity in domestic and cross-border acquisitions. However, outside of the life sciences, firms are unlikely to continue to invest in basic research at the same rate as before, requiring greater government support for R&D in an industry that has traditionally financed most of its research privately.

The process of restructuring has been most marked in the basic and intermediate petrochemicals, the sectors with the strongest competition. Several traditional chemical companies in the USA and Europe are exiting from some of their commodity chemical businesses and moving downstream, focusing on businesses where product differentiation based on quality and performance allows for higher margins. In their place, oil companies such as Shell, BP, Exxon, Arco and Amoco (now BP-Amoco soon to absorb Arco) and other firms such as Vista, Quantum, Cain, Sterling and Huntsman have stepped in. Many of the latter are new firms that have taken over the existing commodity chemicals businesses of firms such as Conoco, Texaco, Monsanto and USX. In Europe as well, new, focused firms such as Borealis, Clariant and Montell have been formed by merging businesses of existing companies. The new companies seem to be separating into those that produce high value added, speciality chemicals and those that manufacture larger-volume commodity chemicals. Thus many of the synergies and economies of scope that were characteristic of the industry are seen as less important, most markedly in the apparent separation between chemicals and life sciences.

This restructuring process began earlier and has proceeded further in the US chemical industry than in those of continental Europe. Restructuring of the Japanese chemical industry remained incomplete even by the late

1990s (see Arora and Gambardella (1998) for more details).

3 Key issues and themes

The chemical industry provides a fascinating context for the study of the relationship between innovation, firm performance, industry evolution and national economic growth. Science and technology have played a key role in the development of this industry. In the 1870s, German chemical firms managed to overtake their better established British competitors due in large measure to the ability to apply the newly emerging science of organic chemistry. These firms, Bayer, BASF and Hoechst, are also thought to have pioneered the industrial R&D laboratory. Why they were able to do this and why British firms could not is part of a larger debate on the relative decline of British industry. Many explanations have been offered. The economic ones include the nature of the British financial system that promoted short-term, low-risk projects, the dominance of inorganic chemicals in the British chemical industry, and the non-technical backgrounds of British managers that prevented them from understanding the revolutionary potential of the new technologies. Other prominent explanations have stressed the 'gentlemanly' aspirations of British entrepreneurs and the elitist nature of English universities in contrast to the stronger links between German universities and industry and the greater responsiveness of university research to industry needs (see Murmann and Landau (1998) for more details).

On the other side of the coin, the German chemical companies have also been singled out as examples of the importance of coordinated complementary investments in research and development, manufacturing, marketing and management that Alfred Chandler has emphasized in his work on the sources of commercial success of firms.

But whereas German and Swiss chemical firms managed to exploit the economies of scope between chemicals and pharmaceuticals, most others failed. ICI is perhaps the only other significant chemical company to have developed a substantial pharmaceutical business (spun-off as a separate firm, Zeneca, in the early 1990s). Many others, including Dow Chemicals, tried but failed. In the 1990s, the synergy between life sciences and chemicals appears to have declined greatly and most firms have established these as separate companies. However, it is the failure of well-run, well-funded firms to enter new sectors that holds a great deal of promise for further research to shed new light on issues such as what distinctive capabilities firms have and how those capabilities condition their ability to successfully innovate and enter new markets.

The confiscation of German patents and industrial property in Britain, France and the USA provides another natural experiment to study the impact of patents on innovation. The confiscated patents were made available through a variety of means, themselves interesting topics in political economy. The difficulties Du Pont faced in entering the synthetics dyestuffs market despite the removal of patent barriers indicates that the firms that enter a technology area early may be able to build up a variety of advantages that entrants cannot easily overcome. Despite this, the loss of patents was a substantial blow to the German chemical companies and further research cannot only lay out how the gains and losses were distributed, but also shed light on the working of the patent system, an issue of great importance for the twenty-first century.

The inter-war period was an era of national and international cartels, which have been studied in some detail, particularly in the context of the development of antitrust regimes in the USA. The inter-war period was also marked by rapid product innovation, including the discovery of nylon. These new products, synthetic fibres, plastics, resins, adhesives, paints and coatings, which virtually define 'modern' materials, were based on polymer science. But many, if not most, would have remained technological curiosities but for the development of the science of chemical engineering, which made it possible to produce these materials at costs low enough to ensure their success. Both polymer science and chemical engineering flowered in the decades after the Second World War, and have been among the principal forces driving the growth of the industry over the last half of the twentieth century.

The development of polymer science and chemical engineering owed a great deal to university-based research. The role of universities, and university–industry linkages, is widely seen as being critical in the process of modern economic growth. The development of chemical engineering provides a valuable case study. German firms were renowned for their prowess in designing large-scale chemical processes using catalysts – they had pioneered, early in the twentieth century, the processes for 'fixing' atmospheric nitrogen to produce ammonia, vital for relieving the shortage of naturally occurring nitrogenous fertilizers. Furthermore, the close ties between German universities and chemical firms had played a key role in the rise of the German organic chemical industry. Yet, the discipline of chemical engineering was institutionalized in the USA during the 1940s and 1950s, not in Germany. What features of the German universities lead to their apparent failure to respond to the needs of the industry? Given the importance of universities to the growth of new high technology industries, understanding the features that enable a university to respond to the needs of industry and at the same time produce high quality research and education is critical for policy making for a technology-based economy.

Chemical engineering was critical to the development of the modern petrochemical sector, which in many ways, defines the modern chemical industry. Petrochemicals are used as starting materials for polymer products. The USA, which has abundant oil and natural gas reserves, was the first country to develop a petrochemicals industry, beginning early in the twentieth century. The Second World War had a major impact on technology and the industry's structure. As part of the war effort, the US government funded large programmes for research and the production of synthetic rubber and created a massive demand for oil for aviation fuel. Given the strong interests in various types of government-led science and technology efforts, a systematic analysis of these Second World War programmes remains an important research topic.

Petrochemicals provided the opportunity for several oil companies, most notably Shell, Exxon, Amoco, BP and Arco, to become major producers of basic and intermediate chemicals derived from petroleum feedstocks. This convergence, between oil and chemicals, provides an intriguing opportunity for distilling insights about the likely shape of the industries of the future, including the much talked about convergence between communications and computers (see Arora and Gambardella (1998) for more details).

By 1950, half of the total US production of organic chemicals was based on natural gas and oil, and this figure reached 88 per cent by 1960. Perhaps even more astonishing is the rapidity with which the European chemical industry made the transition, despite the absence of major oil and natural gas deposits, and despite their very substantial investments in coal-based technologies. In the UK, for instance, only 9 per cent of the total organic chemical production was based on oil and natural gas, and the proportion rose to 63 per cent by 1960. Similarly, the first petrochemical plant in Germany was set up in the mid-1950s, and yet by 1973, German chemical companies derived 90 per cent of their chemical feedstocks from oil. This great transformation points to the tremendous power of the development of new markets for both technology and oil in limiting path dependency and shaking loose an entire industry from its historical development trajectory (Stokes 1994; Arora and Gambardella 1998).

Although the USA led in petrochemical technology, the technological lead of US chemical producers in petrochemicals was eroded over time as oil companies and engineering design firms diffused the technology internationally. Technology for producing a variety of imported products became more widely available. Moreover, the development of a world market in oil meant that the oil and natural gas endowments of the USA did not prove to be an overwhelming source of comparative advantage. The impact that the development of new markets had on the competitive advantage of firms, a point often ignored in discussions of managerial strategy, was also dramatic. The division of labour that gave rise to the engineering design firms (SEFs) also reduced the strategic value of process technology. Not only did this affect individual firms, a critical source of advantage for the US chemical industry was removed as the SEFs diffused technology, first to Europe and Japan, and then to the developing world (Freeman 1968). The SEFs helped develop what can be justly called a market for chemical technology. The implications of having such a market, for corporate strategy, for technology management and for a variety of issues such as national policies on research and development are yet to be fully explored. However, it is quite clear that one of the implications was a marked increase in the extent to which even large and well-established chemical firms were inclined to license their technology, led by Union Carbide which became a leading licensor of polyethylene and polypropylene technology (see Arora (1997) for more details).

Slower growth for its dominant products, including polymers, along with the growth of production capacity offshore, led many leading US chemical firms to pursue diversification programmes during the 1970s, with little success. The increases in competition (due in part to the widespread diffusion of technology) and slower demand growth lowered the pay-offs to traditional types of innovations. The oil shocks of the 1970s perhaps only hastened the inevitable consolidation in the industry. The 1980s saw a far-reaching restructuring in the industry to focus firms on a narrower line of products and processes.

The timing and pattern of restructuring points to the role of capital markets. Restructuring began in the USA and has taken place far more slowly in Europe, but its pace has been even slower in Japan. The increasing importance of mutual funds and pension funds and the greater attention to 'shareholder value' have pressured managements to improve financial performance. The social welfare implications of the restructuring are unclear, and the debate has been closely tied up with the broader debate on the virtues and vices of the Anglo-Saxon system of finance versus the bank-based systems of Germany and Japan (Da Rin 1998). Stock markets appear to disfavour diversified firms with portfolios that include both commodities and specialities. The reasons perhaps lie in the greater difficulties of managing such firms as well as the greater difficulties in evaluating the performance of the management of a diversified company, particularly when the company has a mix of research intensive and less research intensive businesses. Similarly, the restructuring of the chemical industry in the 1980s and 1990s has resulted in a growing separation between chemical and life science companies. Once again, this poses an intriguing challenge for organization theorists to explain whether the separation was to prevent diversion of cash flow, as agency theorists might argue, or because chemicals and life sciences require different types of managerial regimes and cultures.

Perhaps the most important and obvious insight from studying the long history of the chemical industry is that science and technology are not enough. It is the commercialization that creates wealth and this requires a constellation of policies and institutions in order to achieve best results. This constellation includes legal and intellectual property systems, the regulatory environment and the regulatory and antitrust regime. It also includes the education and university system, which has played a crucial role in creating the modern chemical industry.

The inexorable trend toward globalization only underscores the ability of firms to escape domestic restraints, but the home markets continue to have a profound influence on firms, their culture, and their ability to compete. Even though some firms find it difficult to escape from their historical trajectories, the growth of new markets and entry and exit give much greater flexibility to the industry as a whole.

The evolution of the chemical industry has been driven by advances in technology and by the institutions that have facilitated the growth of new markets. In addition to the conventional market growth in the form of demand from developing countries, the evolution of the chemical industry has also been profoundly affected by the growth of a market for technology and a market for capital. When technology becomes widely available, albeit at a price, it can cease to be a decisive source of competitive advantage, be it for firms or for countries. Instead, competitive advantage must be sought elsewhere, in cheaper inputs or in closeness to markets.

ASHISH ARORA
CARNEGIE-MELLON UNIVERSITY

RALPH LANDAU
STANFORD UNIVERSITY

Further reading

(References cited in the text marked *)

* Arora, A. (1997) 'Patent, licensing and market structure in the chemical industry', *Research Policy* 26: 391–403. (Argues that technology licensing by chemical companies is pervasive and important.)
* Arora, A and Gambardella, A. (1998) 'Evolution of industry structure in the chemical industry', in A. Arora, R. Landau and N. Rosenberg (eds) *Chemicals and Long Term Economic Growth: Insights from the Chemical Industry*, New York: John Wiley and Sons. (Role of specialised engineering firms; industrial restructuring in chemicals.)
  Arora, A., Landau, R. and Rosenberg, N. (eds) (1998) *Chemicals and Long Term Economic Growth: Insights from the Chemical Industry*, New York: John Wiley and Sons. (Comprehensive study of what determined the growth of the chemical industry in four countries.)
* Bower, J.L. (1986) *When Markets Quake: The Management Challenge of Restructuring Industry*, Boston, MA: Harvard Business School Press. (Restructuring in the chemical industry in the 1980s.)
* Chandler, A. (1990) *Scale and Scope*, CambridgeH: arvard University Press. (Economies of scope and scale require appropriate corporate management structures for processing information and allocating capital.)
* Da Rin, M. (1998) 'Finance and the chemical industry', in A. Arora, R. Landau and N. Rosenberg (eds) *Chemicals and Long Term Economic Growth: Insights from the Chemical Industry*, New York: John Wiley and Sons. (How differences in financial institutions have shaped the evolution of the chemical industry in the USA, West Europe and Japan.)
* Enos, J. (1962) *Petroleum, Progress and Profits*, Cambridge, MA: MIT Press. (Decomposes productivity growth in oil refining into discrete process innovations and small cumulative improvements following the innovations.)
* Freeman, C. (1968) 'Chemical process plant: innovation and the world market', *National Institute Economic Review* 45 (August): 29–51. (Documents the role of engineering contractors in the post-second World War chemical industry.)
  Haber, L. (1958) *The Chemical Industry During the Nineteenth Century*, Oxford: Oxford University Press.
  Haber, L. (1971) *The Chemical Industry, 1900–1930*, Oxford: Oxford University Press. (Authoritative overview of the world chemical industry before the Second World War.)
  Haynes, W. (1945–54) *American Chemical Industry*, vols 16, New York: Van Nostrand. (Journalistic but comprehensive account; before the Second World War.)
* Hollander, S. (1965) *The Sources of Increased Efficiency: A study of Du Pont Rayon Plant*, Cambridge, MA: Harvard University Press. (Productivity growth mostly due to cumulative small improvements in the production process.)
* Hounshell, D.A. and Smith, J.K. (1988) *Science and Strategy: Du Pont R&D, 1902–1980*, Cambridge: Cambridge University Press. (Authoritative Study of the Evolving R&D strategy at Du Pont.)
  Morris, P.J.T. (1994) 'Synthetic rubber: autarky and war', in S.T.I. Mossman and P.J.T. Morris (eds) *The Development of Plastics*, Cambridge: Royal Society of Chemistry. (Case of very successful cooperative research organized by the US government.)
* Murmann, P. and Landau, R. (1998) 'On the making of comparative advantage: The development of the chemical industries in Britain and Germany since 1850', in A. Arora, R. Landau and N. Rosenberg (eds) *Chemicals and Long Term Economic Growth: Insights from the Chemical Industry*, New York: John Wiley and Sons. (How and why Germany overtook Britain in synthetic dyestuffs despite Britain's head start and many advantages.)
  Spitz, P. (1988) *Petrochemicals, The Rise of an Industry*, New York: John Wiley &Sons. (Detailed introduction to petrochemicals and some of the main players).
* Stokes, R.G. (1994) *Opting for Oil*, Cambridge: Cambridge University Press. (Argues that the dominance of petroleum feedstocks was not pre-ordained but was socially constructed.)
  Travis, A. (1992) *The Rainbow Makers: The Origins of Synthetic Dyestuffs Industry in Western Europe*, Bethlehem, PA: Lehigh University Press. (Detailed history of the discovery and commercialization of synthetic dyestuffs.)

See also: DEVELOPMENT AND DIFFUSION OF TECHNOLOGY; DYNAMIC CAPABILITIES

Global machine tool industry

1 Brief history
2 Industry data
3 Post Second World War developments
4 Approaches to innovation
5 Why the industry matters
6 The future

Overview

The machine tool industry is a small but essential sector of manufacturing. It accounts for approximately 2 per cent of manufacturing employment in the developed countries. A machine tool is power-driven, not hand-held, and cuts or forms metal. Machine tools are used to manufacture products or to produce other machines upon which goods are produced. In his history of the Burgmaster Company, Holland (1989) describes machine tools as the *mother* or *master* machines that make all other machines. He adds that 'Every manufactured product is made by a machine tool or by a machine that was made by a machine tool'. Working relationships between final goods producers and machinery builders often lead to process innovations that enhance productivity and support industry and national competitiveness. Thus, the industry has a greater impact on industrial growth and competitiveness than its size might suggest.

Metal cutting machines – including grinding machines, drilling machines, millers, and lathes – account for approximately two-thirds of world output. Forming machines include presses to stamp metal into various shapes, metal shears, and saws. It is estimad that there are 3,000 different types and sizes of machine tools. The easiest way to distinguish between the two categories of metal-working equipment is to remember that cutting machines remove material in the form of metal chips, while forming machines alter the shape of material. On a repeatable basis, machine tools can cut or form parts to required tolerances of plus or minus one ten-thousandth of an inch.

There is an important, related equipment sector that designs and builds specialized dies, moulds, tooling, and fixtures for machine tool builders and other manufacturers, usually on a contract basis (Rolt 1965).

1 Brief history

The basis for mass production came from the development of machine tools in the nineteenth century in Britain, the US, and other European countries. Machine tools made it possible to produce parts in large quantities with precise, repeatable dimensions. By the end of the nineteenth century, machine tools were employed in the production of arms, clocks, textile machinery, sewing machines, locomotive engines, farm equipment, and bicycles (Brown 1995; Hounshell 1984; Roe 1926). The ratcheting upward of machine tool performance, followed by the dispersal of the new equipment on factory floors, was a cornerstone of manufacturing growth. Advances in machine tool capabilities at the start of the twentieth century were instrumental in the development of the automobile assembly line, and led to the rapid growth of that industry in the first two decades of the century. Important customers now include the defence, aerospace, automotive, appliance, agricultural equipment, medical, and telecommunications industries.

There are several market segments, including basic machine tools, highly engineered machine tools and transfer lines, and complex computer-controlled machining centres. For example, heavily capitalized and highly skilled builders produce customized multimillion dollar transfer lines for automobile manufacturers or steel mills, while small, family-owned enterprises typically build general-purpose machines such as lathes and milling machines that may cost US$20,000. On the whole, firms are not diversified and concentrate on a particular product or market segment (Critical Technologies Institute

1994). Japanese firms dominate global sales of Computer Numerical Control (CNC) machining centres, and Japan-based FANUC is easily the world's largest producer of computer control systems, the brains of state-of-the-art machine tools.

Distinctions exist among machines depending on how they are controlled. *Conventional* machine tools – generally lower cost machines – are controlled by a skilled worker who places a part in the machine and guides that machine through its various functions. The greater the skill of the worker, the greater the capability of the machine. Newer types of machines are controlled by computers which are guided by a software program most often designed by an engineer. With the introduction of *Numerical Control* (NC) machine tools in the 1950s, movements of a machine tool could be instigated independent of the machinist. Simply stated, a basic NC system tells the machine what to do. The earliest NC tools featured a computer which was connected to the tool's control mechanisms. As computer technologies – hardware and software – improved throughout the 1950s and 1960s, so too did machine tool programming.

Modern programmable automation allows equipment operators, parts designers, and engineers to enter dimensions and details of highly intricate parts directly onto a computer which today is an integral part of the machine tool. A *Computer Numerical Control* (CNC) machine may have numerous programs stored in memory and a simple command can instruct the machine to perform work on parts of varying shapes and sizes. A machine tool programmer or machine operator can enter coded data which will tell the machine such things as what sequence of cutting or drilling operations to perform, depths and angles to cut, feed rates of the cutting tools, etc. Since the mid-1980s computer-controlled machine tools have rapidly replaced conventional equipment. The share of CNC grinding machines was only one per cent in the major tool producing countries in 1976; this rose to 11 per cent in 1984 and is well over 60 per cent today.

Direct or *Distributed Numerical Control* (DNC) is the most recent stage in the evolution of computer-controlled machine tools. With DNC, programs are stored on a central computer and sent electronically to a machine tool which is capable of performing the required task. This makes it possible for a manufacturer to make the same part in more than one location, often providing improved response to customers' requirements.

Today's technology permits separate machines to be linked through a central computer network into a system of *Computer-Aided Manufacturing* (CAM). CAM makes it possible for a manufacturer to plan, control, and manage production operations from raw material through finished and assembled parts. Through *Computer-Aided Design* (CAD), parts designs and blueprints can be stored in a computer data base and in turn generate the instructions to the machine tool to manufacture the object. This greatly limits the need for manual programming. Taken together, CAD and CAM can exponentially increase the flexibility of machine tools and dramatically enhance the diversity of work a firm may perform. For example, with sophisticated computer control, a single flexible machining centre is able to perform what were once discrete functions like milling, drilling, and lathe work. Finally, since the equipment can be programmed to work on a succession of different parts and can also be programmed to change its own tools, there can be a dramatic decrease in the costly loss of production time needed for conventional machine setups. When CAD and CAM systems are connected with a firm's manufacturing control system – most likely an MRP or MRP II systems – the result is *Computer Integrated Manufacturing* (CIM).

2 Industry data

At the beginning of the twenty-first century the industry is suffering through contraction among the leading producer nations – Japan, Germany, and the United States. Total world output in 1999 was US$34.5 billion, down from US$36.9 billion in 1998, and US$37.6 billion in 1997. The top-producing country in 1999 by production value (US$7.7 billion, US$9.16 billion in 1998) was Japan. Japan has been the top producer since 1982. Germany was a close second (US$7.5 billion, US$7.7 billion in 1998). Together, Japan and

Germany account for 44 per cent of world output. The other 1999 top producers were: United States (US$4.35 billion); Italy (US$3.76 billion); Switzerland (US$2.03 billion); Taiwan (US$1.68 billion); People's Republic of China (US$1.09 billion); Spain (US$969 million); United Kingdom (US$952 million); and France (US$800.1 million).

In 1998, sales by global region were Western Europe – US$16.34 billion; Asia/Pacific Rim – US$14.33 billion; Americas – US$5.66 billion; Eastern Europe – US$730 million. On the basis of 1998 sales, 56 of the top 200 machine tool firms in the world are in Italy, 49 are in Germany, and 25 in the US. Among the twenty largest builders by sales volume, 12 are Japanese, four are German, and two are US, with the top four – Yamazaki Mazak, Amada, FANUC and Fuji Machine – based in Japan. In 1990 seven of the top ten firms were based in Japan, as was the case in 1998 (see Table 1).

There were 625 machine tool firms in the US in 1997 according to the US Department of Commerce Manufacturing census: only 40 to 50 of these firms employed more than 100 people, while over half employed fewer than 20 people. States in the industrial midwest – Michigan, Ohio, Illinois, Wisconsin – held the largest numbers of firms, a legacy of the automobile industry located there. In Germany and Japan proportionally more builders tend to employ over 100 people (see Table 2).

Japan's sales are strong due to export strength. Foreign demand has led the market share recovery even in the face of economic recession and a sharp drop in domestic consumption; exports are 72 per cent of production. Japan had an international trade balance for most of the 1990s, and a 1999 net surplus of US$4.9 billion. Germany had a US$1.6 billion surplus, followed by Switzerland (US$1.42 billion), Italy (US$692 million), and Taiwan (US$508 million). Switzerland exported 89 per cent of its 1999 output. The US is the biggest global consumer of machine tools with purchases of US$7.1 billion in 1999 – 20.5 per cent of world output. It had the world's largest trade deficit – US$2.8 billion in 1999. By comparison, the next highest trade deficit was China's (US$1.12 billion).

3 Post-Second World War developments

From 1945 to 1975 American pre-eminence in machine tool construction and the productivity advantages that accrued to manufacturers who purchased these machines, enabled builders

Table 1 Global market share by percentage among the top three producers

	1964	1970	1975	1980	1985	1990	1996	1999
United States	25.1	18.5	17.3	18.1	12.6	6.7	12.6	12.8
Japan	6.4	14.2	7.8	14.4	24.8	23.2	23.6	23.0
Germany	15.9	18.9	18.9	17.8	14.8	18.9	20.1	21.0

Table 2 Employment trends among the top four producing countries

	1980	1985	1990	1995	1998
Japan	33,767	34,644	36,849	28,351	28,354
Germany	99,000	88,000	103,000	68,000	66,700
United States	71,700	73,000	65,700	57,000	47,500
Italy	37,200	28,200	32,000	27,900	26,850

Source: Association for Manufacturing Technology, *Economic Handbook of the Machine Tool Industry, 1996, 1998*; Japan Machine Tool Builders Association, *Machine Tool Statistics Handbook*, 1998.
Note that for Japan the figure includes only firms with more than fifty employees, thus total employment in the industry is in fact higher.

and capital goods producers to prosper. There was little competition for sales to US producers in the expanding automobile, aircraft, and other durable goods sectors. Several builders received lucrative contracts from the US military to design and build a variety of machine tools. The US was by far more advanced than its rivals in the development and application of computer numerically controlled machine tools which added to the strength of the industry. Large firms in the US – including Cincinnati Milacron, Litton Industries, Ingersoll-Rand, Monarch Machine Tool, and Giddings and Lewis – accounted for close to 70 per cent of total US output (see GLOBALIZATION; MULTINATIONAL CORPORATIONS).

Firms achieved market share during merger waves in the late 1960s and the 1980s, but not as a consequence of steady sales growth and the development of new products. The mergers resulted in the acquisition of machine tool firms by large, diversified companies with little experience in the industry. When sales were high the new owners invested their profits in other businesses, while during downturns they failed to make the necessary investments in training and technology that were required to keep the industry competitive. Instead, assets of the machine tool firms were sold off, thus further debilitating the industry.

There was a distinct focus among the majority of US firms on two large domestic markets, defence and automobiles. There was little organizational transfer of engineering and production knowledge among tool builders towards the development of machines for other markets. This would not have been a significant problem had three things remained constant: first, had the defence and automobile industries continued to grow; second, there were little or no international competition in the production of more general purpose machine tools; and third, had the pace of machine tool innovation remained slow. However, none of this held true and by the late 1960s this global pre-eminence was challenged by builders in Japan and Germany.

In the early 1970s Japanese firms had become far more adept than their US counterparts at fusing computer technologies with machine tools to design and build affordable computer-controlled machines for the many small and medium size companies in Japan and the US. Japan, in the early 1980s, wrested global leadership from the US as a result of its successful application of computer-based technologies to a broad-based pool of customers worldwide. The US went from being a net exporter to being the world's largest importer of machine tools. US firms never captured even the domestic growth potential for computer-controlled machine tools and lost their home market to Japanese imports. US machine tool employment declined almost 20 per cent, to 57,000 in 1995, from 70,000 in 1983. By comparison. total employment in 1967 was close to 120,000. By 1984 NC turning machines and machining centres comprised 25 per cent of the value of machine tools built in the US, but 42 per cent of the value of imported machine tools.

In attempts to compensate for the cyclical nature of the industry, as well as industry over-capacity, there were numerous mergers at the end of the twentieth century, several involving German and US firms. There were mergers among US firms, the largest being the consolidation of several firms into Unova, Inc. in 1998. With its acquisition of the machine tool business of Cincinnati Milacron and other purchases it became the largest machine tool producer in the US, with revenues exceeding US$1.7 billion. Unova specializes in the production of automobile manufacturing machinery. Projected 2000 sales of the company would make it the third largest machine tool builder in the world, just behind a merged German company, Thyssen. Thyssen jumped in sales and capacity with its acquisition of US-based Giddings & Lewis.

At the end of the century the merger of several venerable US firms (all in operation for nearly 100 years) into the Goldman Industrial Group took place. Firms in the holding company include long-time US leaders Bridgeport Machines, Fellows Gear Shapers, Bryant Grinders, and Jones & Lamson.

4 Approaches to innovation

Two significant differences in industry approach emerge from a comparison of machine tool builders in Japan and the United

States. Japanese firms worked together, with the encouragement and financial support of their government, to invest in NC technologies. One enterprise – FANUC – focused exclusively on the development of controls and software, while the builders perfected the design and construction of the machines to be operated with these new controls. Here, builders were assisted by Japan's Ministry of International Trade and Industry (MITI). MITI's intention was to support the development of a simple, standard set of computer controls for basic lathe, milling and grinding machines. Because the fusion of the traditional machine tool with new technologies was complex, a strategic decision was made by Japanese firms to initially perfect the technology on a series of basic milling, drilling and cutting operations. When these tasks were mastered, and organizational learning increased, more complex operations were added. The design and build path employed by Japanese firms carried with it extensive market volume possibilities among the thousands of small and medium-sized companies in Japan, the US, Germany, and elsewhere around the world.

Germany lost market share in the new technology in the late 1970s and early 1980s because it did not focus on the development of affordable controls linked to low-cost machine tools. In 1980 Japan built 22,000 computer-controlled machines, while German firms built only 4,800. In 1983 almost three-quarters of the German demand for computer numerically controlled machines was met through imports, with 43 per cent of imports arriving from Japan. Germany's Federal Ministry for Research and Technology, the machine tool builders trade association, and IGMetall, the trade union representing metalworkers in machine tool firms, responded collaboratively to this crisis in the industry, and in 1984 German firms built 10,600 computer-controlled machines. This total exceeded the number of such machines produced in the United States, Great Britain, and France combined.

During these years more than a dozen US builders constructed highly engineered and very specialized machines and controls for their defence and automotive customers with the support of the US Department of Defense, and they did so without a strenuous effort to advance an industry standard for the computer controls. The Pentagon's insistence on customized machines and controls raised design and build costs without affecting overall performance and deterred small firms from obtaining the very expensive equipment. MITI's offer of low interest loans to Japanese machine tool and other metalworking firms to purchase the computer-controlled equipment helped establish a domestic market there, which became the platform for later export to the US and European markets.

5 Why the industry matters

The machine tool industry can play a critical role as countries develop basic manufacturing sectors. An iterative, cumulative process – the ratcheting upward of machine tool performance followed by the dispersal of new more productive equipment to factory floors – is the cornerstone of prolonged manufacturing success. This relationship is symbiotic, for to ensure continuous sales gains manufacturers must push machine tool builders harder to innovate so that they can maintain their market advantage. Carlsson (1989) characterizes the industry in the recent period as a 'node' for supplying hardware and software to industry, and helping to determine the performance of large sectors of manufacturing in terms of productivity and international competitiveness.

The machine tool industry is a significant forecaster for what is taking place in national economies and in the global economy. Goods producers need machine tools, therefore an increase or decrease in orders for new equipment is an indicator of the long-term confidence that final goods producers have in their markets. Increased orders may also indicate that tool builders have developed a new, more effective technology application which will boost productivity. Heightened orders of a new type of equipment are an expression of overall business confidence. Finally, when the major purchasers of complex, specialized, and costly machine tools – for example, the automotive industry, the aerospace sector, computer chip fabrication plants – make large purchases of equipment this is a signal of the long-term health of the economy since delivery of such equipment usually takes at least one year.

6 The future

Technology

There are several trends in technology linked to the integration of personal computers and computer-controlled machinery. The technology allows the rapid and direct networking of parts designers with the factory floor. Enterprises are also developing equipment which will allow information to flow the other way — that is, engineers will be able to perform remote diagnostic checks on machine tools. Japanese builder Mazak is designing machine tools that permit remote monitoring of such things as machining cycles completed, cutting tool utilization rates and power consumption. Builders are also placing vision sensors on machinery to assist in the inspection process as well as repair.

Early twenty-first century trends are for greater speed in machining, enhanced precision and accuracy, and environmentally-friendly machining. Experimentation with cutting tool technology and machinery motors is critical for enhanced speed. The ability to manipulate clusters of molecules and atoms and even individual atoms has opened new frontiers in manufacturing and the US-based National Institute of Standards and Technology is engaged in the development of micromachines, laser measuring devices, and other so-called *nanotechnologies*. These capabilities will enable the manufacture of precise machinery for semiconductor producers and manufacturers of non-invasive surgical equipment.

Cutting fluids, oils and solvents have been a staple of the industry because they enhance tool performance. However, increased concern for the environment, government regulation, and the high cost of disposing of contaminated cutting fluids, has stimulated global research on safer cutting fluids and dry machining – machining without the use of any cutting lubricants. Japan and Germany lead the way in this research. Machine tools are historically defined as cutting or forming metal. However, major trends at the start of a new century make the definition obsolete. Equipment that works on materials including plastics, composites, and ceramics and that employs cutting techniques such as lasers needs to be considered part of the industry.

A global industry

There are numerous examples of the globalization of the machine tool industry (see GLOBALIZATION). Small firms in Italy – of the 450 firms building machine tools there, more than 70 per cent employ fewer than 50 people – have steadily increased exports to the US and to the rest of Europe. Overall, 60 per cent of machine tool production is exported, and the Italian industry is ranked fourth in the world in output. By contrast Germany, the world's second largest producer, has approximately 350 companies with an average of 200 employees each. The German industry is concentrated in two regions, Baden-Wurttemberg and North Rhine-Westphalia and employs approximately 100,000 people. Italy's success is built on significant investments in research and development and superb technical support to customers. Italian firms are geographically concentrated in the north, in and around Milan, and take full advantage of their proximity to partner on everything from design, to marketing, to service. An important strength of German firms is the attention paid to formal training to insure a flexible and highly skilled workforce. By comparison, in the US there is little focus on machinist training, and at the end of the 1990s there was a severe shortage of skilled machinists.

Machine tool builders in China, the Czech Republic and India have made significant advances since the early 1990s. As these nations continue their overall development, their machine tool sectors will most likely grow and offer challenges to the better-established firms in the US, Germany, and Japan. Already firms from the Czech Republic export several hundred machines annually to the US and firms there have entered into joint ventures with Japanese builders to produce low cost machines for global export.

Japanese machine tool builders are aggressive in developing sales and service centres in

Europe, the US, and Asia, which helps account for their lead in global exports. For example, in the late 1990s Okuma established an engineering and sales centre in Germany to assemble machine tools. Japanese firms have developed numerous production sites outside their country: Japanese firms have made large investments in India linked to the growth of the Japanese automobile industry there. Technology centres, service centres, and joint ventures with independent Indian machine tool companies were started by Yamazaki Mazac and Okuma. The Japanese textile machinery builder Murata Machinery has opened a facility in Shanghai to service equipment and will eventually start a production unit there. In parallel trend, Japan has partnered with machine tool firms in the Czech Republic and has builders there producing basic lathes and other standardized machines for export to the US market. There are many Japanese branch plants in the US building machine tools for global export. By comparison, while three of the largest US builders – Giddings and Lewis, Ingersoll Milling Machine, and Cincinnati Milacron – operate plants in Germany, none has established a vigorous presence in China or Southeast Asia.

ROBERT FORRANT
UNIVERSITY OF MASSACHUSETTS, LOWELL

Further reading

(References cited in the text marked *)

* Association for Manufacturing Technology (1996) *The Economic Handbook of the Machine Tool Industry 1996–1997*, McLean, VA: Association of Manufacturing Technology. (Handbook of data published every two years.)

Association for Manufacturing Technology (1999) *1999 Machine-Tool Scorecard*, McLean, VA: Association of Manufacturing Technology. (Data base that ranks leading international firms by sales information.)

Broehl, W. (1959) *Precision Valley: The Machine Tool Companies of Springfield, Vermont*, Englewood Cliffs, NJ: Prentice-Hall. (Historical study of firms involved in design and manufacture of machine tools used in the early US automobile industry.)

* Brown, J. (1995) *The Baldwin Locomotive Works 1831–1915*, Baltimore: Johns Hopkins University Press. (Historical study of a leading nineteenth century US builder of railroad engines and the role of machine tools and skilled machinists in the company's growth.)

* Carlsson, B. (1989) 'Small-scale industry at a crossroads: U.S. machine tools in historical perspective', *Small Business Economics* 1: 245–61.

Chokki, T. (1986) 'A history of the machine tool industry in Japan', in M. Fransman (ed.) *Machinery and Economic Development*, New York: St. Martin's Press, 124–52. (Important study of the growth of Japan's machine tool industry and the role of government agencies in stimulating research and development.)

* Critical Technologies Institute (1994) *Decline of the US Machine Tool Industry and Prospects for its Sustainable Recovery*, Santa Monica, CA: Rand. (Two-volume study of the decline of the US industry.)

Friedman, D. (1988) *The Misunderstood Miracle: Industrial Development and Political Change in Japan*, Ithaca: Cornell University Press. (Study of the role of government involvement in industry development of new technologies.)

* Holland, M. (1989) *When the Machine Stopped: A Cautionary Tale from Industrial America*, Boston: Harvard Business School Press. (Study of the impact of industry mergers on an important US firm.)

* Hounshell, D. (1984) *From the American System to Mass Production, 1800–1932: The Development of Manufacturing Technology in the United States*, Baltimore: Johns Hopkins University Press. (Historical study that traces the links between several industries and developments in machine tool technology.)

* Roe, J. (1926) *English and American Tool Builders*, New Haven: Yale University Press. (Classic study of the development of the industry, with a particular focus on the importance of skill.)

* Rolt, L.T. (1965) *A Short History of Machine Tools*, Cambridge: MIT Press. (Studies of the evolution of several types of machine tools.)

Woodbury, R. (1972) *Studies in the History of Machine Tools*, Cambridge: MIT Press. (Overview of the industry.)

Websites

www.americanprecision.org – American Precision Museum, Windsor, VT. Explore the machinery and tools that changed the world in a museum housed in a nineteenth century machine tool company. Museum holds the largest collection of historically significant machine tools in the US.

www.imfmetal.org – International Metalworkers Federation site for data, reports, industry news and links to labour relations issues. The organization is a federation of national metalworking unions from 96 countries and is headquartered in Geneva, Switzerland.

www.imts.otg – US machine tool builders site.

www.jil.go.jp – Japan Institute of Labour site. Contains up-to-date statistics on industry employment and trends, and a monthly bulletin on the economy.

www.mfgtech.org/USMTC – US machine tool consumption database.

www.mmsonline.com – Best North American online source for information about the global machine tool and metalworking industries. Contains reports by country.

www.nikkohan.or.jp – Japan machine tool distributors network. Contains data on industry there.

www.ntma.org – National Tooling and Machining Association. Started in 1943, and today has over 2,700 precision manufacturing firms as members. Site contains industry news and information.

www.smts.org – Switzerland Machine Tool Society site for data, news, and technical information.

www.ucimu.it/emg – Italian machine tool industry site for data, news, and technical information.

See also: GLOBALIZATION; WORLD TRADE ORGANIZATION

Telecommunications industry

1 Introduction: mapping the industry with a layer model
2 Characterizing the telecommunications industry layer by layer
3 The evolution of downstream layers
4 The evolution of upstream layers
5 Conclusion

Overview

What is the telecommunications industry? How does it relate to other activities in areas such as computing, software, semiconductors, the internet and electronic commerce, and the media? Where are its boundaries? What products and services should be included within it? What are its major markets? Which companies should be included in the industry?

In this paper, we tackle these important questions by developing a layer model in order to map the industry. Layer models generally have a long and distinguished history in the telecommunications and computing fields. In the area of engineering and software design, they allow engineers to reduce and render tractable the awesome complexity of complex systems. They help to achieve this purpose essentially by decomposing the system into relatively autonomous subsystems that interact with each other through an interface that is often standardized in order to facilitate coordination. But, in this paper, the layer model does more than merely decompose a complex system into component subsystems. While each layer may be thought of as a subsystem (usually further subdivided into sub-sub-systems, and even further subdivided), the layer model also, by its nature, draws attention to the interdependence of each layer on the layers below and above it.

By decomposing the telecommunications industry into different layers, and further by analysing the interdependence between the major layers that compose the industry, we will provide a detailed assessment of an industry, characterized by recurrent technological innovation and faced with an increasing diversification of demand. The reader should note that this article draws heavily on our telecoms website: *http://www.TelecomVisions.com*.

1 Introduction: mapping the industry with a layer model

In this article, the layer model is used to map the telecommunications industry and to understand its connection with 'connected' industries and activities such as computing, software, semiconductors, the internet and electronic commerce, and the media. In that perspective, the layers will refer here to different domains of economic activities which are considered as separable though related, and evolving. Depending on their technological background, their structure, their date of entry, and their ability to capture market opportunities, firms can develop some of these activities either internally or through mergers and acquisitions, and outsource others through market or cooperation agreements. In any case, it is of crucial importance to understand the process by which firms are able to enter or exit activities in the different layers. This specific issue will be omnipresent in this article.

The basic layer model is described in Table 1 which provides a mapping of the telecommunications industry in the 2000s (see http://www.TelecomVisions.com).

2 Characterizing the telecommunications industry layer by layer

Layer I: The equipment and software layer

In Layer I telecommunications equipment and software is produced. This includes not only the 'network elements' that are the building

Telecommunications industry

Table 1 The basic layer model

Layer	Activity	Example companies
VI	**Consuming/customers**	
V	**Applications layer, including contents and packaging** (web design, on-line services, broadcasting services, etc.)	Bloomsberg, Reuters, AOL/Time Warner, MSN, News Corp, etc.
IV	**Navigation and middleware** (browsers, portals, search engines, directory assistance, security, electronic payments, etc.)	Yahoo, Netscape, etc.
III	**End-to-end connectivity** (Internet access, web hosting) **TCP/IP**	IAPs and ISPs (e.g. Freeserve, etc.)
II	**Network** (optical fibre network, DSL, local network, radio access network, ethernet, frame relay, ISDN, ATM)	AT&T, BT, NTT, MCI, Worldcom, Qwest, COLT, Energis, etc.
I	**Equipment and software** (switches, transmission equipment, routers, servers, CPE, billing software)	Nortel, Lucent, Cisco, Nokia, etc.

blocks for networks of various kinds, but also customer equipment such as mobile phones, PCs and information appliances of different sorts, as well as software for billing, IT and management applications. Three types of companies are present in Layer I: (1) traditional telecommunications equipment companies (most with a long history, like Siemens and NEC, and some with recently acquired younger data networking equipment companies, like Lucent with Ascend, Nortel with BayNetworks); (2) relatively new data networking companies (Cisco); and (3) computer hardware and software companies (Oracle, Sun, EMC). Firms within that layer are extremely specialized: the penetration of equipment suppliers in other layers is indeed a very rare, punctual and transitory phenomenon.

Layer II: The network layer

Layer II contains the networks that carry the bits (binary digits) that are the lifeblood of the infocommunications industry. Examples are local, long-distance and international networks based on technologies and standards such as optical fibre, radio access (including cellular and fixed radio), cable, DSL, satellite and Ethernet. The services provided in this layer include telephone, fax, ISDN, frame relay, ATM and leased circuits. Services sold on the carrier's carrier market are also included here. All these services are closely associated technically with the networks over which they run and it is for this reason that it is usually the network operators that run the networks that also provide these services. The network operators that populate the network layer can be divided into three groups: (1) incumbents, such as the global 'Big Five' – AT&T, BT, France Telecom, Deutsche Telekom and NTT; (2) original new entrants, that is the companies that were first allowed to compete with the incumbents when liberalization was introduced into the USA, UK and Japan in the mid-1980s, namely MCI and Sprint in the USA, Mercury/Cable & Wireless in the UK, and DDI, Japan Telecom and Teleway Japan in Japan; and (3) new new entrants, including WorldCom, Qwest, Level 3, Global Crossing, Global Telesystems, COLT, Energis, Vivendi, Mannesmann, etc. The reason for distinguishing between the original new entrants and the new new entrants is that their strategies and behaviours

295

are significantly different and, in fact, the former companies have tended over time to be acquired by the latter.

The TCP/IP interface

An event of great significance for the industry emerged with the evolution of the Transmission Control Protocol/Internet Protocol (TCP/IP) which came to play an important role in facilitating networking between computers and networks. Likewise, within the network layer (Layer II) TCP/IP has facilitated the transfer of bits across the different networks, many of which use significantly different technologies. Furthermore, TCP/IP has also enabled a technical separation of the network layer (Layer II) from the service layers above it (Layers III to V). This has meant that service providers need not own nor control their own networks, but can depend on network services bought on the market from network operators. In this way, TCP/IP has allowed the possibility of vertical specialization between the different layers, enhancing the potential for specialist facilities-less service providers to emerge and prosper. It has facilitated new forms of industrial organization while creating the possibility of new layers in the industry with new products and services, and new company players.

Layer III: The end-to-end connectivity layer

The companies active in this layer provide services such as e-mail, internet access, voice over the internet (Voice IP), web hosting, intranet and extranet-related services, virtual private network services and mobile services. Many players in Layer III are network operators, active in Layer II, who have vertically integrated 'forwards' into the end-to-end connectivity layer. However, specialist facilities-less service providers also compete in Layer III and some specialize only in this layer. These include, for example, internet access providers (IAPs) and internet service providers (ISPs) that offer connectivity-related services but, apart from a few switches, may have very little of their own networks, preferring to buy network services from network operators in Layer II. Also included are resellers who sell connectivity in retail markets having bought it from others wholesale. These resellers are essentially involved in arbitrage and do not own nor control their own networks.

Layer IV: Navigation and middleware layer

The services provided in Layer IV figuratively 'sit on top' of the connectivity that has been provided in Layer III. These include navigation-related services that allow users to find their way around the connected networks of the internet and locate further services. Navigation-related services include browsers, search engines and portals, made possible by the advent in 1990 of the World Wide Web. They also include more conventional services like directory assistance and yellow pages. 'Middleware' is also located in Layer IV. This is primarily software-related services that 'sit' between the connectivity layer (Layer III) and the applications layer (Layer V). Examples of middleware products include security systems, such as firewalls used to protect websites, and electronic payment systems. Firms in Layer IV include Netscape, Yahoo, Lycos, Excite and a host of software companies that provide specialist middleware products. Many of these companies, internet-related in the minds of investors, have achieved extremely high market capitalizations as a result of rapidly appreciating share prices. It seems then that it is the new entrants who have performed best in the navigation part of Layer IV, rather than the larger established computer hardware and software companies, and the telecommunications equipment companies.

Layer V: The applications layer

With networks, connectivity, navigation and middleware being provided, it is possible for applications to be developed and distributed. These applications include the creation and packaging of content. Examples of services provided in this layer include: video-on-demand; electronic-commerce services such as online shopping, banking and auctions;

social services such as online health and educational services; web design; mobile phone services such as stock market prices, news and weather; premium services such as racing results; databases; broadcast. Examples of companies and services that have a notable presence in Layer V include AOL/Time Warner, Microsoft's MSN, NTT DoCoMo's i-mode internet mobile service, Bloomberg, Reuters and broadcasters such as News Corp.

Layer VI: The customers

At the top of the five layers are the customers. We think it is important to envision the customers as constituting a discrete layer, although this is not the usual practice in layer models. It should be noted that customers include not only those purchasing the final telecommunications goods and services, but also 'intermediate customers' who purchase intermediate products and services. These include, for example, the specialist facilities-less service providers who are customers buying network services from the network operators.

In this section, each layer was considered as an isolated system. In the next two parts, we will focus on the interdependence between layers, by choosing two specific entry keys, namely on the one hand the downstream layers (Layer I and II), and on the other hand upstream layers (Layers III to V).

3 The evolution of downstream layers

According to the analyses of some economists (Laffont and Tirole (2000) are a recent example) the structure of the Telecoms Industry changed fundamentally in the mid-1980s in Japan, the UK and the USA as a result of deregulation. It was deregulation that created the rules for new entrants to enter the telecoms services market and compete with the incumbents. This ushered in a new era of competition.

According to these analyses it was both necessary and sufficient to 'get the prices right'. More specifically, incumbents had large existing networks and low marginal costs and benefited from network externalities. This meant that it was necessary, in order for new entry to be viable, to introduce new rules requiring incumbents to allow new entrants to interconnect their networks with the networks of the incumbents at the right price. The analytical trick was to determine the 'right price' which would provide appropriate incentives for both incumbents and new entrants to compete. The fact that marginal cost pricing, the optimal practice in competitive industries, was inappropriate in the Telecoms Industry characterized by high fixed and sunk costs and low marginal costs made the trick even more demanding. Nevertheless, the conclusion was that the 'right price', together with the interconnection rules, provided both the necessary and the sufficient condition for a competitive Telecoms Industry to emerge.

However, an understanding of the interaction between Layers I and II in our layer model – namely the interaction between network operators and specialist technology suppliers – shows that the matter was far more complicated than these economists have implied. In short, entry required not only an appropriate regulatory regime and the 'right' interconnection price – though entry certainly did require this – it also required access to new technology. And this new technology was supplied by a group of specialist technology suppliers without whom entry would have been far slower and new entrants would have been significantly fewer in number. As a result the speed in introducing competition, as well as the intensity of competition, would have been much lower without the specialist technology suppliers.

The new entrants

In most analyses of the Telecoms Industry by conventional economists technology tends to be treated as an exogenous force, falling like manna from heaven and then providing the impulse for the growth of the industry. The empirical study of the most important new entrants into the telecoms services market, however, shows that technology has played a key role in the process of successful entry.

While it certainly is true that the incumbent, a former monopoly network operator and supplier of telecoms services, benefits significantly from sunk costs and low marginal costs to the detriment of the new entrant, new technology has provided a countervailing opportunity for the new entrant. Counterbalancing the importance of sunk costs and low marginal costs is the power of new technology that is capable of providing the new entrant with competitive weapons that include superior reliability, provisioning flexibility, bandwidth and security. In some areas and for some time the incumbent's strengths (sunk costs and low marginal costs) become its weakness (legacy systems that are not worth scrapping immediately but which are not capable of providing the same characteristics as the new technologies). A close reading of the company studies undertaken by financial analysts of new entrant firms such as WorldCom, Qwest, Level 3, Global Crossing, GTS, and Viatel in the USA and COLT, Energis and Atlantic Telecom in the UK reveal the extent to which superior technology has driven the valuation of shares in these companies. High market values, in turn, have facilitated both successful entry and growth by giving new entrants such as these the 'currency' with which to make mergers and acquisitions and access to loan markets on relatively attractive terms. As a result, almost without exception, the successful new entrants have performed better than the incumbents in terms of stock market indicators, an outcome that cannot be explained by the 'getting the prices right' paradigm.

Access to superior technology also explains the apparent paradox of firms that have had nothing to do with telecoms, and to begin with have little telecoms knowledge and competence, becoming some of the most successful new entrants. Examples include Mannesmann in Germany (recently taken over by the British mobile operator, Vodafone) which was an engineering company; Olivetti that was involved in computers and business machines (and acquired the Italian incumbent, Telecom Italia); COLT, the most successful rival of BT in the UK, that was established by Fidelity, the largest US mutual fund; WorldCom, a major rival to AT&T that was started by Bernard Evans, a motel owner, and his colleagues; and Qwest, begun by Philip Anschutz, who started as an oil-made billionaire. Entrants such as these were able to enter and prosper largely as a result of their access to the latest technologies. In short, technological barriers to entry were low. Again, the 'right prices' paradigm has little to say about this phenomenon.

Specialist technology suppliers

If technology has played the important role indicated in this section, where has it come from? The answer is from a group of specialist technology suppliers who have come to specialize only in Layer I of the industry (see the layer model above). The biggest and best known of these specialists include Lucent, Nortel, Ericsson, Nokia, Alcatel, Siemens, NEC, Fujitsu and Motorola. Their specialization in Layer I is the best example of vertical specialization in the Telecoms Industry (a form of industrial organization that is similar to that found in the computer industry – see TelecomVisions.com for a more detailed comparison of these two industries).

Here too, history matters. These specialist technology suppliers did not fall like manna from heaven, ready to supply the latest technologies to all new entrants who could pay for it, smoothing the latter's entry. Indeed, all but one of the firms mentioned in the last paragraph are old firms; the origins of Lucent, Ericsson and NEC, for example, go back to the late nineteenth century. Most of them began as telecoms equipment manufacturers, supplying equipment to the national telecoms monopolist – the so-called PTTs – who took the lead in researching and designing the equipment and other technologies that their networks required in their laboratories that quickly became the major source of technical change in the industry. These laboratories included AT&T's Bell Laboratories (whose researchers won more Nobel prizes than any other industrial laboratory), BT's Martlesham Laboratories, NTT's Electrical Communications Laboratories and France Telecoms's CNET laboratories. The relatively simple task of mass manufacture was left to the specialist equipment suppliers.

Over time, however, these specialist equipment suppliers, through complex processes of learning and knowledge creation, began to do more of their own R&D and gradually became powerhouses of technical change in their own right. By the 1980s they were challenging, and in some areas even surpassing, their erstwhile network operator masters at their own game. Astoundingly, by the turn of the century the main specialist equipment suppliers were some four times more R&D-intensive than the five major former monopolist incumbents, AT&T, BT, Deutsche Telecom, France Telecom and NTT (see Fransman (2000b) for a detailed analysis).

Conclusion

The discussion in this section of the interaction between Layers I and II throws further light on the dynamics of the Telecoms Industry by analysing the intricate relationship between both incumbent and new entrant service providers, on the one hand, and specialist equipment suppliers on the other. In this way the layer model assists in the task of analytically endogenizing the role of technical change as a major driver of the Telecoms Industry (see Fransman (2000b) for further details).

4 The evolution of upstream layers

The great revolution involving the TCP/IP interface is that, in the upstream layers, many different firms could appear and operate without controlling their own proprietary network and especially without bearing the prohibitive costs of constructing such a network. In fact, the technical separation between the network and the services potentially offered implied that firms could simply lease the infrastructure from network operators, or develop on it some switches and points of presence to connect their customers end-to-end. Because the access to technological infrastructures was greatly facilitated by the TCP/IP revolution, their main efforts to create competitive advantage were focused on the provision of an extended set of applications, and more generally on their ability to capture market opportunities faster than other firms. At the origins, a small flexible structure seemed to be better adapted to react to the new challenges imposed by the increasing diversity of demand, and was an important element in gaining a competitive advantage. At the moment, however, consolidation seems to increase significantly the average size of firms in the upstream layers. These features reveal that drastic changes are occurring within and between upstream layers. A deeper understanding of who does what within these layers and why is then absolutely needed.

In this section we will focus in particular on the following questions: How did Layer 3, which contains Internet Access Providers (IAPs) and Internet Service Providers (ISPs), originate and what is its relationship with the other layers? How can we explain the diversity of strategies followed by firms in upstream layers, namely the fact that moves of consolidation/integration by big players coexist with the specialization of a large number of smaller IAPs and ISPs? Taking into account this diversity, how will the upstream layers evolve in future?

The emergence of Layer III and its relationship with the other layers

In the 1980s, the Internet was primarily used to connect universities and research groups. Within this period, 'packet switched' technologies, together with the generalization of URL addresses and Hypertext links, led to concrete applications, especially the real-time transfer of documents and e-mail between dispersed groups of scientific users. New fixed operators such as MCI and Sprint – firms that were competing primarily in the network layer of the telecommunications industry (Layer II) – constructed long distance and international backbone networks to carry Internet traffic. This allowed them to move into Layer III (the layer that provides connectivity) as Internet backbone providers. At this stage, however, Internet applications were not yet market driven. Even though these private firms provided Internet backbones, the global operation and management of the Internet was still undertaken by the National Science Foundation (NSF) in the United States. With the administrative and technical assistance of ANS (a joint venture of IBM and MCI), the NSF created NSFNet, a network connecting research groups in the USA at a local, regional and national level.

It may be concluded, therefore, that Layer III in the 1980s was essentially composed of a public ISP (the NSF) which delegated some limited activities (like the operation of some parts of the network) to private firms. The scope of services offered by the NSF was relatively restricted, and only later would be enlarged with the 'privatization' of the Internet.

In the 1990s, new challenges appeared both from a technological and a market point of view and had a significant impact on Layer III. The development of the World Wide Web allowed a multiplicity of new services such as data transmission, e-commerce and the development of websites which are now profitable commercial opportunities. With the viability of the Internet having been established, and with the traffic increasing, the NSF decided in 1995 to leave the management and operation of the Internet to private firms. This allowed Internet backbone providers such as MCI and Sprint to expand their markets. This also favoured the entry of a large number of new firms in Layer III in order to provide both Internet access to firms and residential customers and Internet services such as e-mail. These new firms are often referred to as Internet Access Providers (IAPs) and Internet Service Providers (ISPs), although the same firm might provide both sets of functionality. The most successful of these included UUNet (later acquired by Worldcom) and AOL in the USA, Freeserve in the UK (that was the first firm in Europe to offer free Internet access, though the customer still had to pay the time-based cost of the local call). As a matter of fact, Layer III is then composed of two distinct categories of firms: (1) the IAPs which carry the Internet packets and are generally affiliated to firms from Layer II looking for diversification into a value-added activity to recover the sunk costs involved by the development of their backbone network, and (2) the facilities-less ISPs which offer value-added services to customers and are increasingly linked with firms operating in 'middleware' or 'content' activities (Layer IV and V).

For the 2000s, the trend is difficult to anticipate. Some events from the late 1990s, however, can possibly provide us with a vision of what will happen over the next few years. The use of the Internet is now widespread, with constant technological innovation (e.g. high capacity and intelligent networks) and open-ended applications (e.g. video-conferencing, e-commerce, IP telephony, web design, broadcasting services). In this context, different types of strategies are followed by firms in Layer III. The first strategy, generally followed by firms present also in Layer II, is to extend and upgrade the networks to meet the demand for high speed Internet and associated applications. Those following the second strategy focus on content activities and progressively leave Layer III to become one of the leaders in Layers IV and V. Finally a third strategy consists of an exclusive specialization in Layer III. Indeed, consolidation/integration moves coexists with specialization processes in Layer III.

The coexistence of consolidation and specialization within and between upstream layers

Gradually consolidation and integration occur within and between the different layers of the telecommunications industry. These strategies generally allow big players to move from one layer to another, and to gain a competitive leadership or to extend it on related activities. Different cases are observable.

First, big players in Layer II tend to integrate players in Layer III. For example, WorldCom, a firm that began as a reseller in 1983 and went on, helped by a rapidly rising share price, to develop its own long-distance and local networks in Layer II (the network layer), acquired MCI and tried to acquire Sprint (though it was thwarted by the US regulator). This allowed WorldCom to move from Layer II into Layer III and become one of the major Internet Backbone providers. Consolidation also occurs among the IAPs and ISPs. One example was UUNet that became one of the largest independent IAPs/ISPs in the USA, before being acquired by WorldCom. Another example was PSINet who acquired in 1999 about twenty other ISPs generally through stock-for-stock transactions.

Second, big players in Layer III tend to leave this layer to focus especially on other layers. For example, AOL, a firm that began before the Internet era as a network supplier of value-added information services, quickly adapted to the rapidly diffusing Internet. Though some predicted that AOL would be undermined by the Internet, this did not happen. Indeed, by the turn of the century an astounding 40 per cent of the total amount of time spent by Americans on the Internet was spent within AOL's 'walled garden'. At first AOL began to develop its own network. However, it soon decided that it should leave the transport of its traffic to specialists and accordingly sold its network (and that of Compuserve which it had acquired) to WorldCom. In January 2000, AOL further transformed itself. Having abandoned its networks, it acquired Time Warner with two purposes in mind. The first was to acquire the content that would distinguish itself from other IAPs and ISPs (and allow it to continue charging its customers a monthly fee). The second was to guarantee access to both residential and business customers by acquiring Time Warner's cable network, the second largest after AT&T's. In terms of our layer model, therefore, by early 2000 AOL had integrated downstream, from Layer III into the network layer (Layer II) and upstream into the applications and content layer (Layer V). Indeed, it also integrated into Layer IV (the navigation and middleware layer) by acquiring the browser, Netscape.

However, despite these moves of consolidation and integration by the big players, there still are large numbers of smaller IAPs and ISPs who specialize in Layer III, even though there is a good deal of debate regarding their longer term viability. Part of the problem is that Internet access and many Internet services (such as e-mail and web hosting) are becoming a commodity business driven by economies of scale and scope. The advent of free Internet access is robbing IAPs and ISPs of much of their revenue and making it increasingly difficult to differentiate themselves. While content may be a key differentiator (as AOL has recognized), the cost of differentiated high-demand content is prohibitively high for many smaller IAPs/ISPs. The end result, very likely, is a significant shakeout through exit, merger and acquisition, and falling new entry.

We may conclude, therefore, that connectivity per se, as a functionality, has become a commodity, capable of being provided by a large number of players. For those who have specialized in the layer providing connectivity – Layer III – to survive and prosper it seems that a diversification in the upstream and/or downstream directions is becoming increasingly necessary.

Conjectures about the future evolution of upstream layers

Three main conjectures were generally formulated by experts in telecommunications. First, network operators would massively integrate firms in the end-to-end connectivity layer, the navigation and middleware layer and applications, and the content packaging layer. Secondly, service providers would integrate backward into the network layer. Thirdly, facilities-less service providers would decide to stay in the services layer. We should not consider that one of these conjectures will dominate others. Rather, we should think that the complex reality will provide examples of each of these scenarios, and that the crucial issue is the understanding of why these different scenarios may occur. To date, network operators integrate firms in upstream layers, generally in order to increase their margins, sometimes to differentiate themselves, considering that from the supply (equipment) side they all rely on the same type of technology. Service providers integrating backward are less documented, but cannot be neglected if we consider market capitalizations of facilities-less service providers in regard to network operators. Specialized service providers will certainly remain in Layer III, but will not play the dominant role that they used to.

5 Conclusion

Within the telecommunications industry, some crucial issues will deserve further research in the next few years. The following list only stresses some of them that were not especially developed in this article:

- The equipment suppliers tend to be characterized by an increasing concentration. How can we explain this phenomenon? Is it a transitory or a more permanent feature? Can we consider this phenomenon as a simple implication of the currently observed concentration at the level of the telecommunications carriers? Is it possible to elaborate further developments on that point?
- The new challenges of Internet access are about to drastically change the organization of the telecommunications industry. What will be the role of equipment suppliers in this context? Will they continue to favour the entry of new firms in the high speed Internet area? What will be the economic determinant of this new process of entry?
- Financial conditions, namely the achievement of high performance on stock markets, significantly contributed to the emergence and growth (through merger) of the main competitors in telecommunications industry. How will these specific financial conditions tend to evolve over time? What will be the impact on the key dimensions of the innovation and competition processes?

MARTIN FRANSMAN
EDINBURGH UNIVERSITY

JACKIE KRAFFT
UNIVERSITÉ DE NICE – SOPHIA ANTIPOLIS

Further reading

(References cited in the text marked *)

Abbate, J. (1999) *Inventing the Internet*, Cambridge, MA: MIT Press. (A prescriptive survey on the emergence, development and generalization of the Internet.)

Antonelli, C. (1999) *The Microdynamics of Technological Change*, London: Routledge. (Develops a useful analysis in terms of technological knowledge, with applications to telecommunications.)

Armstrong, M. (1997) 'Competition in telecommunications', *Oxford Review of Economic Policy* 13 (1): 64–83. (Describes and analyses liberalization and price competition in the telecommunications area.)

Armstrong, M., Cowan, S. and Vickers, J. (1994) *Regulatory Reform, Economic Analysis and British Experience*, Cambridge, MA: MIT Press. (Focuses on the part-liberalization in telecommunications in the UK.)

Bohlin, E. and Levin, S. (eds) (1998) *Telecommunications Transformation, Technology, Strategy and Policy*, Amsterdam: IOS Press. (Valuable collective volume on major changes in telecommunications.)

Brock, G. (1994) *Telecommunication Policy for the Information Age: From Monopoly to Competition*, Cambridge, MA: Harvard University Press. (Describes and analyses basic problems involved in deregulation in telecommunications.)

David, P. and Steinmuller, E. (1999) *Information Technology and the Productivity Paradox*, Harwood Academic. (Stresses problems of compatibility standards and their influences on productivity.)

Fransman, M. (2000a) 'Analysing the evolution of the telecommunications industry', *Economics of Innovation and New Technologies* no. 3–4: **forthcoming**. (Stresses the challenges that the study of the telecommunications industry implies for economic analysis.)

* Fransman, M. (2000b) 'Evolution of the telecommunications industry into the Internet age', *Handbook on Telecommunications*, Cheltenham: Edward Elgar. (Characterizes the main drivers of the evolution of the telecommunications at the age of the Internet.)

Gong, J. and Srinagesh, P.(1996) 'Network competition and industry structure', *Industrial and Corporate Change*, 5 (4): 1231–41. (Analyses mergers and acquisitions between ISPs by focusing on costs structures.)

Katz, M. (1996) 'Remarks on the economic implications of convergence', *Industrial and Corporate Change*, 5 (4): 1079–95. (Characterizes some of the new challenges of the technological and industrial convergence in telecommunications.)

Kavassalis, P., Salomon, R. and Benghosi, J.P. (1996) 'The Internet: a paradigmatic rupture in cumulative telecom evolution', *Industrial and Corporate Change* 5 (4): 1097–126. (Stresses the important rupture that the Internet represents for the traditional telecom paradigm.)

* Laffont, J.J. and Tirole, J. (2000) *Competition in Telecommunications*, Cambridge, MA: MIT Press. (A basic survey of pricing in a context of network competition.)

McKnight, L. and Bailey, J. (eds) (1997) *Internet Economics*, Cambridge, MA: MIT Press.

(Valuable collection focusing on the new paradigm of the Internet.)

Noam, E. (1994) 'Beyond liberalization: from the network of networks to the system of systems', *Telecommunications Policy* 18: 286–94. (Stresses major changes that occurred within the telecommunications industry.)

Shapiro, C. and Varian, H. (2000) *Information Rules: a Strategic Guide to the Network Economy*, Boston, MA: Harvard Business School Press. (Presents insights from economics research to understand the real-world information economy.)

Srinagesh, P. (1997) 'Internet cost structures and interconnection agreements', in L. McKnight and J. Bailey (eds) *Internet Economics*, Cambridge, MA: MIT Press. (Analyses mergers and acquisitions between ISPs by focusing on the peering system.)

* *www.TelecomVisions.com* (Analyses what will happen to the telecommunications industry over the next five years, with specific contents on industry mapping, key questions, guest visionaries, current events, workshops, key resources and site bibliography.)

See also: COOPERATION AND COMPETITION; DEVELOPMENT AND DIFFUSION OF TECHNOLOGY; GROWTH OF THE FIRM AND NETWORKING; INDUSTRIAL DYNAMICS

Biotechnology

1. Introduction
2. New sector or new techniques?
3. Influence on firms in existing sectors
4. Networks, clusters and alliances
5. National institutions and policy

Overview

The economics of biotechnology is an area of research that attempts to explain how and why the new techniques and knowledge of modern biotechnology can have economic impacts. In addressing these questions, researchers often come from different research fields and traditions, which are interested in innovation and economic change. They analyse which organizations contribute to the development of new techniques and knowledge, and they also analyse and compare the pattern of development and use in firms, sectors, regions, and national economies. Thus, on the one hand, the research field covers a broad range of issues about knowledge-intensive goods and services while on the other hand, it addresses specific issues in relation to modern biotechnology.

1 Introduction

Modern biotechnology techniques are usually distinguished from traditional ones. 'Modern' tends to become synonymous with various techniques for genetic engineering, such as recombinant DNA techniques, monoclonal antibodies, transgenic plants and animals, enzyme engineering, etc. By so doing, the distinction is made with 'traditional' biological techniques, in that human beings have used biological techniques for transformation during a long history. Traditional examples range from making bread to brewing beer to carefully controlled animal and plant breeding programmes. Despite similarities in the logic of intervention, there is an important dividing line between 'traditional' and 'modern' biotechnology. The more recent genetic engineering techniques enable humans to add new information to the genome (DNA), which was not there initially (Aharonowitz and Cohen 1981). Adding information enables the potential to create and control mutations across species in a way that was never previously possible, although there are limits.

Although valuable and essential, genetic engineering techniques alone are not enough to explain the economic importance of modern biotechnology. The new techniques go hand-in-hand with increasingly detailed knowledge about cells, the body, plants, soil dynamics, and other areas of application. Better, more accurate, and more detailed knowledge has meant that the techniques can be further improved and that the results become more predictable and more controllable than previously. In short, the firm has the possibility to better understand what they are doing, and why it works, as well as how to improve the search process for further improvements. Search, or research and development (R&D) in firms, is a costly part of business, particularly in sectors such as pharmaceuticals. Businesses are always interested in finding useful innovations, where they can appropriate the economic benefits. In other words, the firm wants to develop new products and new ways of doing business in a timely fashion in order to make profits. Modern biotechnology can be very useful as a research tool in its own right and/or as a way to focus R&D activities.

The economic history of modern biotechnology is not, however, so clear cut about whether, nor how fast, these potential economic returns will be realized from new knowledge. Initially in the late 1970s and the early 1980s, there was great optimism about the future, both in terms of speed of knowledge development and practical applications and in terms of economic impacts. The rate and impact has been much slower than predicted and slower, than in other new areas of knowledge like information technology (IT). IT has pervasively influenced all other sectors of the economy, to the extent of stimulating a revision of American productivity data. Nothing comparable can be seen for modern biotechnology. At least not yet, proponents argue. Some of the differences between these two areas of knowledge seem to be related to the type and relative specialization of the knowledge and resulting goods and services. IT appears to be a pervasive body of knowledge, goods and services, which can affect every other sector. In contrast, modern biotechnology has so far been more narrowly specialized towards different areas of application. While some aspects of techniques, equipment, and knowledge of modern biotechnology are common to all areas of application, others seem more specific to pharmaceuticals, agriculture, environmental clean-up, and so forth (Senker 1998). This specialization of knowledge presents a challenge for managers who are trying to distinguish which aspects of modern biotechnology will be most valuable to their firm and sector and economists who are asking which might affect economic growth.

Section 2 of this article addresses whether or not modern biotechnology can be considered a new sector, in relation to implications for managers and economists. Section 3 then examines the effects such as productivity increases in existing sectors, while section 4 examines the relationships between different types of organizations. The final section examines issues about science, regulation and national policy.

2 New sector or new techniques?

One issue that has attracted much attention is whether or not modern biotechnology constitutes a new sector. Defining a new sector is often related to the start-up of new firms, in a new area of technology, knowledge, or product group, which replace existing firms in related fields. The alternative is that modern biotechnology is just a collection of new techniques, which affect many different sectors. This distinction may seem like a definitional question of no importance. However, there are at least three reasons why the rise of many new and/or small firms matters, each with implications for managers and economists.

First, if biotechnology constitutes a new sector, then we would expect to see many start-up firms. These small research firms, sometimes called new biotechnology firms or dedicated biotechnology firms, may develop new lines of inquiry before the large firms (Sharp 1990; Walsh 1993). This fits the empirical evidence from USA in terms of large numbers of small and/or start-up firms, but with more mixed evidence from the rest of the world. Large firms in industries like pharmaceuticals, chemicals, and seeds are also important for explaining the commercialization of biotechnology.

The empirical question of whether, and how much, small or large established firms are involved in order to economically develop a new knowledge area is thought to matter, theoretically. Innovation researchers would argue that small firms would tend to develop more radical innovations whereas large firms would tend to develop more incremental ones. Thus, having small and/or new dedicated biotechnology firms has been argued to matter because they can more quickly commercialize radical innovations. While this appears to fit the American evidence and the pattern of international firms having collaboration with American biotechnology firms (Dibner and Bulluck 1992), data from other countries suggest that government policy can encourage and consolidate incremental innovations and applications even in these smaller firms.

Second, if there are many new and/or small firms, then their problems and opportunities for development and innovation may differ quite considerably from those of larger and/or established firms. There is a large literature on the problems of small and medium enterprises (SME), which cannot be reviewed here. This literature is, however, relevant to the study of biotech firms and leads to interesting historical comparisons with IT start-up firms. Crucial issues include how to encourage and stimulate entrepreneurship as well as how to solve the financial requirements of financing a small firm, especially when the research and development projects involve long time horizons with much uncertainty. Issues about financial markets and corporate governance in different countries are also important to these types of firms. The American and various

European stock markets have varied over time in their estimation of the value of this type of knowledge, which is evident in fluctuations of stock offerings, of available capital, and of market ratings.

Third, if dedicated biotechnology firms constitute a new sector, then their relationships with universities, other small firms, and large firms in existing sectors becomes important to understand (see section 3 below.) One main theoretical proposition for why biotechnology firms exist, and how they survive, is that they allow an intermediary form of knowledge production. By being small, these firms may recreate some of the working practices, rewards, and organizational structures found in research institutes and universities. This organizational structure is thought to allow them to try to bridge the requirements of both basic science and applied technology, and to retain good researchers (Ryan et al. 1995). An important issue then becomes, however, how such firms can balance the demands of the market for speed in delivering a working product with the demands of basic science.

3 Influence on firms in existing sectors

Rather than seeing biotechnology as a completely new sector, with specific and specialized problems, a different approach is to analyse the effects of modern biotechnology on existing sectors. The existing sectors generally mean areas where the techniques and knowledge are being used, such as pharmaceuticals, agro-food, seeds, environmental engineering, and so forth. This line of research then argues that there is no biotechnology sector. There are, instead, biotechnology techniques, which are in turn used in various applications (Walsh 1993).

An important economic issue is then what type, and how much, potential that modern biotechnology has to influence such existing sectors. This influence implies that modern biotechnology can lead to new final products and/or change the ways of organizing production or R&D, each of which can influence profit margins and productivity. Even firms with little or no specialized knowledge of modern biotechnology may have to learn about it in order to analyse how and why it might influence their future business plans and products.

In fact, it becomes increasingly obvious that modern biotechnology can affect final consumer products, and so the firm may have to consider rather unexpected reactions from consumers. Rather than only being a completely new product (such as Internet use), modern biotechnology can change some of our familiar products. It already has changed the production of some widespread pharmaceuticals (like insulin, human growth hormone) and has allowed the development and design of some completely new pharmaceuticals. There were initially heated debates in the late 1970s and early 1980s about related medical research, but its use in pharmaceutical production and R&D has largely become accepted. In the late 1990s, the consumer products that have caught public attention and debate are in agriculture and food, with the debate over genetically modified food. There seem to be different national responses. Some purchased genetically modified foods without too much debate (Americans in the 1990s); some debated without having much of the new products available in stores or much new farming (Europe and Asia in the late 1990s). Other consumers say they want labelling of genetically modified foods in order to make conscious choices between old and new.

Although there are numerous studies of consumer opinions and of how much consumers really understand genetic engineering, many companies have had difficulties with their strategies to innovate in these areas. Agriculture and food is an interesting example of the benefits, and pitfalls, of using new knowledge in the economy. The large, and increasingly merging, multinational chemical and seed companies felt that these initial improvements were done at a level of production that should not really affect the resulting consumer product. In other words, some firms felt the initial genetically modified seeds would basically benefit the farmer, by increasing productivity with better plants and decreasing use of chemicals and other pesticides. Although aware of potential consumer reaction, most of the companies seemed to feel they could educate the public to understand the benefits of genetic engineering, so that the new products would be seen as substitutes for the old ones. A tomato is a tomato, isn't it? The companies have since argued that later consumer products will be easier to introduce, because they will demonstrate benefits (often medical or health related) to the final consumer. This change in consumer acceptance is anticipated in a situation of expected market growth (Ballantine and Thomas 1997).

Another impact of modern biotechnology on firms in existing sectors relates to the actual and potential productivity increases. Productivity is an economic measure that relates output to input. It appears that modern biotechnology has the potential to increase productivity in existing sectors, through the possibilities to develop new products and/or to increase the effectiveness of how existing and new products are made. For example, in pharmaceuticals, modern biotechnology has mainly contributed to an increase in research productivity related to discovery of new and more effective drugs whereas in agro-food, contributions have so far been centred on increasing the amount produced. Both lead to benefits for the firm through decreasing costs and/or higher returns. In both areas, however, an increasing emphasis has been put on using modern biotechnology to develop completely new products. These changes seem to come at a time of large structural changes in these sectors, where companies increasingly merge to become larger and also focus on core business activities. Some researchers have argued that modern biotechnology will be on par with IT in its potential to stimulate widespread productivity increases and institutional change across the economy (Freeman and Perez 1988).

In developing these new products and new ways of producing based on modern biotechnology, some of the theoretical literature leads us to expect that large and/or more established firms make choices about whether to develop genetic engineering competences in-house or whether to contract out through strategic alliances. Researchers using the competence-based theory of the firm in business economics argue that firms will develop that new knowledge in-house which can be made of value in relation to existing assets. An example is where a large firm contracts with a small biotech firm to obtain valuable knowledge and techniques (often protected by a patent), so that the small firm supplies the new knowledge and the large firm supplies all the surrounding assets like marketing and regulatory experience (Rothaermel 1999). Other economic and technological histories show, however, that the firm will need a variety of complementary technical knowledge areas, in addition to the economic assets (McKelvey 1996/2000). In other words, the firm that decides to outsource for new knowledge may anyway be forced to develop its own technical competences in-house, both for the core area and for complementary knowledge, or technological, areas. Doing so requires more than just purchasing knowledge, as demonstrated by studies on organizational inertia. The firm may have to change many internal organizational structures.

4 Networks, clusters and alliances

A third important area of research within the economics of biotechnology is the focus on networks, clusters and alliances. This is an important topic for researchers interested in how innovations occur as well as the implications for firms and economic change. In one way or another, all these concepts address the somewhat paradoxical fact that both small biotechnology firms and large firms in existing sectors co-exist. The specific firms may come and go, and there are certainly mergers, alliances, and bankruptcies, but all in all, the two types of firms seem mutually dependent on each other to some extent (Ryan et al. 1995). Universities are also recognized to play a key role.

There are at least two issues within this research area. The first is the unexpected result that extensive collaboration takes place and the second is to explain how and why it occurs. That extensive collaboration occurs in R&D intensive sectors like IT and biotechnology was a somewhat unexpected empirical result (Hagedoorn and Schakenraad 1992; Dibner and Bulluck 1992) because economists have long assumed that market transactions are the norm, while hierarchical control (e.g. in-house) is considered an alternative. Empirical results about collaboration identified a third option. Researchers argue that collaborative agreements are important windows to follow scientific development and a way to quickly obtain new knowledge, but that this pattern might be fairly unique to biotechnology (Arora and Gambardella 1990). It seems to be important to combine such alliances with in-house R&D and competences, because otherwise the firm has difficulties in evaluating the potential of new ideas and techniques that are developed outside the firm.

The second issue relates to explanations of why collaboration occurs. Explanations differ, but many relate either to knowledge and/or property rights. Some argue that the intrinsic characteristics of the knowledge in terms of codification and appropriability involved influence how easily knowledge may – or may not – be transferred without extended interaction (Saviotti 1998). Related, but somewhat different, explanations are that there exists a division of labour and institutions, so that organizations can choose to develop knowledge for different selection environments (McKelvey 1997) or that collaboration represents a new interorganizational form to allow the development of knowledge (Powell *et al.* 1996). Finally, the role, and importance of ownership and control rights to understanding who has alliances with whom has been emphasized (Lerner and Merges 1998). Generally, though, all these researchers agree that network, clusters and alliances matter, and increasingly, researchers are arguing that the large firms retain control over the networks.

A related, but somewhat different issue which economic geographers have addressed is where and why regional agglomeration occurs (Swann *et al.* 1998). Others have argued that rather than regional spill-overs of knowledge, regional concentration of universities and biotech firms is closely related to market transactions (Zucker *et al.* 1995). This latter research suggests that the 'star scientists' are more likely both to write scientific papers and to take out patents, thereby suggesting a link between high quality basic science and the economic value of the result.

Thus, some of the important managerial and economic issues that arise from this set of issues include:

1. How to decide when, and with whom, to enter an alliance
2. The role of internal R&D compared to external relationships with universities and other firms for stimulating innovation
3. How to understand which regions are most dynamic and offer locational benefits to different types of firms
4. Whether regional and national spillovers of knowledge occur through relationships and informal networks versus whether interaction to obtain new knowledge mainly occurs through market transactions (like patents, licensing, etc.).

5 National institutions and policy

Fourth, research on the economics of biotechnology has emphasized the importance of national institutions and public policy for the historical development. This research covers a range of issues, from science policy to the legal system to national institutions more generally.

Long-term support of basic science by governments has been identified as one of the important explanations for the development of genetic engineering (Bud 1994). Longer-term, basic scientific research is necessary in order to stimulate the development of economically important results, but the difficulty from the financing side is how much, and which types, of science to support because the results are not determined in advance. Similarly, firms are interested in knowing whether they need to be located close to universities or whether they can develop more informal networks with specific researchers in order to better understand, and access, potentially valuable basic scientific results.

A related, but different, type of issue looks at the changes in the national institutional structures. Using comparative analysis, researchers argue that these institutions may support or hinder the development of firms and innovations based on modern biotechnology. Comparative and one-country studies often analyse relationships among actors in a national context, or national system of innovation (Bartholomew 1997; McKelvey 1996). The interactions among different groups of firms, research organizations, and medical practitioners has also been used to try to identify the incentives and disincentives for national actors to develop modern biotechnology (Henderson et al. 1999). Moreover, ownership of research, through patents and other means, is considered particularly important, and historical comparisons of the USA and Europe have noted cultural as well as legal differences. These differences influence the firm's decisions and strategies about when to patent and license, compared to when and why to participate in the basic scientific dialogue. Researchers have also tried to analyse the role of government policy in influencing the development of biotechnology sectors, relative to changes in firms, national institutions, and forms of corporate governance (Casper et al. 1999; Jolly and Ramani 1996).

Taken together, this group of research suggests that it can be important for the firm to systematically compare nations in terms of quality of basic science, ownership rights, government policy, institutions, and so forth. These factors can influence the future value of any investment related to modern biotechnology, depending on whether it is in production, research alliances, etc.

MAUREEN MCKELVEY
CHALMERS UNIVERSITY OF TECHNOLOGY

Further reading

* Aharonowitz, Y. and Cohen, G. (1981) 'The microbiological production of pharmaceuticals', *Scientific American* 245 (3): 106–18. (Explains the differences among traditional and new biotechnology techniques, from a scientist's perspective.)
* Arora, A. and Gambardella, A. (1990) 'Complementary and external linkages: the strategies of the large firms in biotechnology', *The Journal of Industrial Economics* XXXVIII (4): 361–79. (Analyses collaboration and strategies among small and large firms in biotechnology, finding an unexpectedly large number of collaborations with each other.)
* Ballantine, B. and Thomas, S. (1997) *Benchmarking the Competitiveness of Biotechnology in Europe*. An independent report for EuropaBio by Business Decisions Limited and the Science Policy Research Unit. EuropaBio. (Presents an overview of European developments in modern biotechnology.)
* Bartholomew, S (1997) 'National systems of biotechnology innovation: complex interdependence in the global system', *Journal of International Business Studies* 17 (4): 365–84. Reprinted in Edquist, Charles and McKelvey, Maureen (eds) *Systems of Innovation: International Competitiveness*, reference collection. Cheltenham: Edward Elgar. (Explores the relative importance of national and sectoral influences on biotechnology development, placing them within an international perspective.)
* Bud, R. (1994) *The Uses of Life: A History of Biotechnology*, Cambridge: Cambridge University Press. (Presents a historian's overview of the modern developments in science which resulted in modern biotechnology.)
* Casper, S., Lehrer, M. and Soskice, D. (1999) 'Can high-technology industries prosper in Germany? Institutional frameworks and the evolution of the German software and biotechnology industries', *Industry and Innovation* 6(1): 5–24. (Argues that deep institutional structures within nations influence relative outcomes, including government policy and the creation of new firms.)
* Dibner, M.and Bulluck, J.A. (1992) 'US/European strategic alliances in biotechnology', *Biotechnology Forum Europe/International Journal of Biotechnology* 9 (10): 628–35. (Presents empirical material on alliances among different types of firms across nations, thereby indicating the complex and international nature of the collaboration phenomena.)
* Freeman, C. and Perez, C. (1988) 'Structural crises of adjustment: business cycles and investment behaviour' in G. Dosi, C. Freeman, R. Nelson, G. Silverbeg, and L. Soete (eds) (1988) *Technical Change and Economic Theory*, London: Pinter. (Argues that gaining economic benefits through shifts in technology depends on related changes in national institutional structures.)
* Hagedoorn, J. and Schakenraad J. (1992) 'Leading companies and networks of strategic alliances in information technology', *Research Policy* 21 (2): 163–91. (Presents empirical evidence of the importance of collaboration, through comparisons.)
* Hendersson, R., Orsenigo, L. and Pisano, G.P. (1999) 'The pharmaceutical industry and the revolution in molecular biology: exploring the interactions between scientific, institutional and organizational change' in Richard R.

Nelson (ed.) *Sources of Industrial Leadership: Studies of Seven Industries,* Cambridge University Press (Analyses the cognitive and institutional developments in biotechnology, in conjunction with the economic developments.)

* Jolly, D. and Ramani, S.V. (1996) 'Technology creation in the biotechnology sectors: the French connection', *International Journal of Technology Management* 12 (7–8): 830–48. (Explores the role for government policy and innovation within the French national context.)

* Lerner, J. and Merges, R.P. (1998) 'The control of technology alliances: an empirical analysis of the biotechnology industry', *The Journal of Industrial Economics* XLVI (2): 125–56. (Presents a more theoretical discussion of alliances and how control is related to benefits.)

* McKelvey, M. (1996) *Evolutionary Economics: The Business of Biotechnology*, Oxford: Oxford University Press. (Explores how and why early uses of genetic engineering in pharmaceuticals were developed.)

* McKelvey, M. (1997) 'Coevolution in commercial genetic engineering', *Industrial and Corporate Change* 6 (3): 503–32. (Examines the interactions among basic science, market forces, and new technologies in the commercialization of biotechnology.)

* Powell, W.W., Koput, K.W. and Smith-Doerr, L. (1996) 'Interorganizational collaboration and the locus of innovation: networks of learning in biotechnology', *Administrative Science Quarterly* 41: 116–45. (Provides a more sociological and organizational view on collaboration.)

* Rothaermel, F. (1999) 'Technological discontinuities and the nature of competition', Ph.D. thesis. Department of Management and Organisation. University of Washington, WA: USA. (Explores the role of competitive destruction and discontinuities in sectoral change, from an empirical and theoretical perspective.)

* Ryan, A., Freeman, J. and Hybels, R. (1995) 'Biotechnology firms', in G. Carroll and M.T. Hannan (eds) *Organizations in Industry: Strategy, Structure, and Selection*, Oxford: Oxford University Press, pp. 332–57. (Presents material about biotechnology institutional fields as part of a comparative project.)

* Saviotti, P.P. (1998) 'On the dynamics of appropriability, of tacit and of codified knowledge', *Research Policy* 26 (7-8): 843–56. (Explores the different types of knowledge involved in economic processes.)

* Senker, J. (ed.) (1998) *Biotechnology and the Competitive Advantage*, Cheltenham, UK: Edward Elgar. (Presents in-depth material about the development of biotechnology in Europe, including theoretical explanations of certain trends.)

* Sharp, M. (1990) 'Technological trajectories and corporate strategies in the diffusion of biotechnology' in E. Deiaco, E. Hörnell and G. Vickery (eds) *Technology and Investment: Crucial issues for the 1990s*, London: Pinter. (Explores the extent to which firm strategy differ to develop biotechnology, related to technological factors.)

* Swann, P., Prevenzer, M. and Stout, D. (eds) (1998) *The Dynamics of Industrial Clustering: International Comparisons in Computing and Biotechnology*, New York: Oxford University Press. (Focuses specifically on the clustering effect, including comparisons with IT.)

* Walsh, V. (1993) 'Stimulating demand: demand, public markets and innovation in biotechnology', *Science and Public Policy* 20 (3): 138–56. (Examines the role played by users, thereby uniting a focus on supply with demand.)

* Zucker, L., Darby, M. and Armstrong, J. (1995) 'Intellectual capital and the firm: the technology of geographically localized knowledge spillovers'. Working paper 4946. Cambridge, MA: National Bureau of Economic Research. (Argues that star scientists and locality are important ingredients in the market transactions to commercialize biotechnology.)

See also: INNOVATION

Steel industry

1 The world steel industry
2 From physical productivity to human resource management
3 Cyclical markets and capital shortages
4 New markets and products
5 Future directions in steelmaking
6 Conclusion: old economy – new economy

Overview

Steel is a basic industry undergoing a revolution from within and without. It is a pervasive economy in modern industrial economies. For this reason, the steel industry has long been seen as a strategic industry in national economic development. In the 1970s it was said that there were three key components to a developing country's economy: a flag; an airline; and a steel industry.

The steel industry commands the attention of managers and policy makers because of its historical linkage with industrial policies and the fact that, along with agriculture, it has been among the most litigious of industries in international trade disputes.

The steel mill along with the auto assembly plant were the two archetypes of the mass production industrial age. This proud past raises the question of the role of steel in the new economy of the Internet. Paradoxically the amount of steel that we consume in the modern economy is not going down in physical terms. Steel consumption is flat to slightly growing depending on the economic cycle. However the industry plays less of a role in terms of percentage of GNP (gross national product) and in employment.

Steel is no longer a discrete, let alone a hegemonic, industry. In the new economy, it is a subset of the advanced materials industry. In fact the steels now in use have had their information content increased so much that the average ton of flat rolled coil has 1500 data points captured during its production and processing. Steel's links to manufacturing and design are critical for its future in an information-based economy. For these reasons, understanding the steel industry is important for understanding the transitions between a mature 'smoke stack' industry and new industrial supply chains.

1 The world steel industry

Shifting capacity and trade

The world iron ore and steel trade is undergoing significant restructuring, with rapidly developing economies in regions such as China, India and South Korea emerging as key centres of growth in the sector (see GLOBALIZATION). Alternatively, the industrialized economies of the European Union, Japan and North America are gradually losing their dominant role. The developing Asian region will account for 67 per cent of the projected increase in annual steel consumption by 2010. Production in the region is projected to increase by 37.2 million tons (Hogan 1991; Labson 1997).

The decline of the British iron and steel industry since 1945 symbolizes the old story of the industry. However, the re-emergence of British Steel as an extremely competitive, aggressive, technology leader also represents the new story in steel (Blair 1997).

New steel players like Ispat International NV and its parent company, the LNM Group, grew from a single factory producing steel rod in Indonesia to the fourth largest steel producer in the world in less than a decade. Ispat's humble origins and rapid growth through a series of acquisitions of underperforming steel factories in Mexico, Canada, Trinidad, Germany, Ireland, Kazakhstan and the USA between 1992 and 1998 has amazed many observers. Founded by an Indian, incorporated in The Netherlands, headquartered in London and selling steel in eighty countries

Steel industry

Table 1 World steel production 1992 to 1998 (million metric tons)

Rank	Country	1998*	1997	1996	1995	1994	1993	1992	% change 1997–8
1	China	114.3	108.9	101.2	95.4	92.6	89.5	80.9	4.9
2	USA	97.7	98.5	95.5	95.2	91.2	88.8	84.3	−0.8
3	Japan	93.5	104.5	98.8	101.6	98.3	99.6	98.1	−10.5
4	Germany	44.7	45.0	39.8	42.1	40.8	37.6	39.7	−0.7
5	Russia	42.5	48.4	49.3	51.6	48.8	58.3	67.0	−12.2
6	Korea	40.0	42.6	38.9	36.8	33.7	33.0	28.1	−5.9
7	Italy	26.1	25.8	24.3	27.8	26.2	25.7	24.8	1.2
8	Brazil	25.8	26.2	25.2	25.1	25.7	25.2	23.9	−1.5
9	India	23.9	24.6	23.8	22.0	19.3	18.2	18.1	−2.9
10	Ukraine	23.5	25.6	22.3	22.3	24.1	32.6	41.8	−8.4
11	France	20.2	19.8	17.6	18.1	18.0	17.1	18.0	2.2
12	UK	17.3	18.5	18.0	17.6	17.3	16.6	16.2	−6.3
13	Taiwan	16.9	16.0	12.4	11.6	11.6	12.0	10.7	5.5
14	Canada	15.8	15.6	14.7	14.4	13.9	14.4	13.9	1.7
World		**775.3**	**799.0**	**750.5**	**752.4**	**725.2**	**727.5**	**719.7**	**−3.0**

around the world, Ispat is the first truly global steel company (Sull et al.1999).

Table 1 shows the position of world steel producers. China has moved past the traditional leaders from the USA and Japan in steelmaking capacity. Its capacity is more than double that of Germany or Russia.

The former leaders have not given up market share gracefully. Uneven capacity growth has been accompanied by chronic levels of international trade disputes. The steel industry, led by the USA, has been among the most litigious of any major manufacturing industry (Scott and Blecker 1997; Chung 1998; Mastel 1999). The steel industry has been a leading challenge for industrial policies (Ferner et al. 1997; Moore 1998; Dudley and Richardson 1999).

Competitiveness: the story of two steel industries

For twenty years, the integrated steel industry faced a major competitive challenge from minimill electric arc furnace (EAF) facilities. Using smaller scale, scrap-charged electric furnaces, the minimills had a substantial productivity and cost advantage at the hot metal end. They could produce molten steel more economically. With this advantage, they were able to increase market share, the share largely conceded at the commodity end of the business: wire rod, reinforcing bar, etc. The integrated mills kept the high end of the product and value added chain, i.e. flat products for auto body panels, appliance panels, etc.

By the 1990s the best of the integrated mills had caught up with the middle range of the minimills. The cost advantage up to the hot metal stage had been closed. Some of the integrateds incorporated the new minimill technologies either through subsidiaries or by directly building them into their existing integrated mill sites.

These trends are reflected in Table 2, which compares steel production costs in standard currency across the major producing countries. The proxy for the advanced minimills is the Thin Slab Mill (TSlb). Under *Process Costs* it can be seen that the traditional cost advantage for the minimills through the hot metal stage (*Liquid Steel*) had been eliminated.

In this competitive environment, the minimills did not stand still. Led by Nucor, new rolling capacity using thin slab casting made a direct challenge to the flat product lines. They did not necessarily penetrate the

Steel industry

Table 2 International steelmaking costs to produce cold-rolled coil (US$, March 1999)

Process costs (US$/ton CRC)	USA	Jap	Ger	UK	Can	Kor	Twn	Braz	Mex	CIS	Chn	TSlb
Coke ovens	97	86	99	86	100	77	81	92	88	52	66	–
Blast furnace	121	106	109	100	116	94	96	97	95	85	107	–
Liquid steel	170	150	150	137	165	135	140	133	137	110	144	173
Slab	205	175	178	162	190	153	163	150	153	126	173	200
HRC (P&O)	278	245	249	225	261	197	216	195	197	159	223	245
CRC	375	341	341	311	347	256	293	256	263	201	285	286
SG&A and taxes	402	382	379	339	374	282	320	279	281	215	314	300

most lucrative market for auto panels but they became a force in steel for auto parts and other fabricated applications. In response, some of the integrateds have now directly incorporated this latest minimill technology into their own operations. An example is the Direct Strip Production Complex just coming on line at Algoma Steel.

Integrated and EAF mills are significantly different in start-up costs and scale of operations. However, new technologies are bringing the two closer in line with each other. The initial capital investment required for an EAF mill is substantially less than that for an integrated mill. These mills can also operate efficiently on a smaller scale than integrated mills. These characteristics made it easier for new players to enter the market, and many did during the 1970s and 1980s. They also made it possible to locate in new areas, closer to end markets. New entrants brought with them new operating philosophies emphasizing high productivity, low fixed costs, new approaches to work organization and employee incentives, and rapid application of new technologies. They also had an advantage. In a cyclical industry the price of scrap tended to rise when demand for the final steel product was also high and to decline in steel slumps.

To meet this challenge, integrated mills have streamlined their organizations and changed their corporate cultures. Layers of management have been dramatically reduced, training expenditures for upgrading the skills of the workforce have tripled and focus has shifted to business unit efficiencies. They have also markedly improved their productivity through selective incremental capital investments.

Recently, technology has been drawing the two steelmaking processes closer. EAF mills are using more oxygen and gas and less electricity, whereas integrated mills are using greater amounts of electricity in the form of secondary steelmaking ladle furnaces. Some companies use both electric furnaces and the blast furnace-basic oxygen furnace process. For instance, Algoma Steel's new Direct Strip Production Facility combines thin slab casting and direct strip rolling with its traditional blast furnace steelmaking processes.

2 From physical productivity to human resource management

Traditionally the steel industry used physical productivity – man-hours per ton (MHPT) of steel produced – as its standard measure of productivity and competitiveness. In the 1980s when the leading integrated producers in Japan and the USA were at 4.5–5.0 MHPT, Nucor and the other minimill producers were at 1.0. By the late 1990s, the leading integrateds had improved their physical productivity dramatically so that they too were at about 1.0 MHPT in their best facilities. As Table 2 showed, the advantage of the minimills at the hot metal stage had been lost. The residual components of productivity advantage lay in organizational integration, skills and work organization. In this respect, steel was now confronted with the main issue facing other leading manufacturing industries (Lazonick 1998).

Ken Iverson led a revolution in steel industry management at Nucor. The secret to his success was *market-based management*, a relatively new set of management values and practices that aims to bring the power of a free market society inside companies. Market-based management attempts to replace the traditional command-and-control management approach with decentralized decision making that is designed to make full use of employees' specific knowledge. Employees' expanded decision-making authority is reinforced by a powerful incentive compensation system that rewards them handsomely for achieving corporate goals. The result is highly motivated employees who take ownership for their role in contributing to the success of the enterprise (Nobles and Redpath 1997; Ahlbrandt *et al.* 1997).

The productivity studies demonstrate that steel production lines using a set of innovative work practices, which include incentive pay, teams, flexible job assignments, employment security, and training, achieve substantially higher levels of productivity than do lines using the more traditional approach, which includes narrow job definitions, strict work rules and hourly pay with close supervision (Ichniowski and Shaw 1999; Berger 1999).

Japanese steel plants are significantly more productive than the US lines. However, US manufacturers that have adopted a full system of innovative human resource management (HRM) practices patterned after the Japanese system achieve levels of productivity and quality equal to the performance of the Japanese manufacturers (Ichniowski *et al.* 1997; Ichniowski and Shaw 1999).

Teamwork developments in the iron and steel industry potentially have far-reaching implications for steelworkers' occupational culture. The traditional seniority-based crew system has exerted considerable influence in shaping the occupational culture in steel. Labour–management relations in the industry have been dominated by attempts to move beyond Fordist command-and-control approaches that in the past have determined bargaining positions on both sides (Blyton and Bacon 1997; Bacon 1999; Frost 1997) (see INDUSTRIAL AND LABOUR RELATIONS).

3 Cyclical markets and capital shortages

The global steel industry has been hit with a dramatic fall in prices, particularly in North America, the major import market for offshore steel producers. This has set off a vicious economic circle for domestic producers. The impact of developments on the price side has been major declines in operating revenues, in turn bringing reductions in capital investment. The reallocation of steel industry investment is triggering an internal restructuring of operations.

The composite spot price for eight carbon steel products fell US$17/ton or 4.1 per cent in 1998. These annual averages, however, fail to capture the depth of the sudden price plunge that occurred in the summer of 1998. For instance, the domestic spot price for Hot Rolled (HR) sheet dropped 22.7 per cent and the import price tumbled 34.6 per cent.

Although it took longer than anticipated for the 'Asian flu' to spread to the North American steel industry, it has ultimately hit with a vengeance. The Asian flu and its aftermath have undermined the global steel supply and demand balance. North American integrated mills are suffering from a dearth of investment. From an average investment level (Capital Expenditure per Ton) of about US$55/ton, the industry expenditure has dropped to about US$33/ton.

The effect of this critical shortage of capital is to produce a disaggregation of the industry between 'hot-ends' (steelmaking furnace capacity) and rolling (processing and finishing mills). Integrated hot-ends are most in jeopardy given their high capital costs and the ready availability of high quality semi-finished capacity.

In the US integrated sector in particular, the deteriorating financial results are leading to a crisis in the 'hot ends' with scarce investment dollars being allocated to the rolling and finishing end of their facilities. Higher and higher levels of semi-finished slabs are being imported from offshore.

4 New markets and products

Steel, contrary to popular perceptions, has maintained its position relative to other materials within the material-content mix of cars in the 1990s. It has even increased in absolute amount in since 1995. The other major growth area for steel will be in residential construction. Steel studs and other galvanized applications are expected to make the construction market the second largest steel-consuming industry by 2010, to a level that rivals the auto industry.

The automotive industry is the largest, single end-user market for North American steel. While steel is shipped directly to parts manufacturers such as stamping plants or engine and transmission plants, increasingly the major automotive assemblers are purchasing steel centrally for their components suppliers.

In addition, the next generation of cars will be based on the Ultra Light Steel Auto Body, a holistic design of high strength, light weight steels that will substantially increase the strength of car frames, while decreasing weight significantly and increasing mileage consumption to 75 mpg. Production techniques for these steels will entail increased energy intensity at the processing and forming ends of the steelmaking process.

The automotive industry requires steel suppliers to qualify on the basis of demanding quality and reliability standards. Only qualified steel producers may compete in the continental bidding process. Steel is then shipped on a just-in-time basis under the conditions of a long-term – sometimes multi-year – contract. Steelmakers must also work with the auto companies years in advance of production to develop new steel grades and applications to meet the automakers' changing design specifications.

North American automotive producers have re-established their competitive position over the past few years, gaining market share over imports. However, they must:

- constantly reduce their costs to match international competition and keep their products affordable in the mass market;
- conform to increasingly strict environmental requirements; and
- achieve ever-increasing performance and quality standards.

Approximately 55 per cent of the weight of the average automobile consists of steel. A broad range of steel products are used, including sheet steel for the body, bars for springs, rods for drive trains and transmissions and wire for tyre cord. Different types of steel are also used, such as carbon, coated, alloy and stainless. However, the automotive industry's drive for corrosion resistance and lighter weight has led it to use plastics and aluminum for a number of applications.

Since the late 1980s, however, the development of lighter, stronger, more formable and more corrosion-resistant steels has enabled the steel industry to maintain its position and even recapture over a dozen applications. In each year from 1991 to 1996 the typical family vehicle had an increased steel content. Despite the huge quality improvements in automotive steel and its continued importance in the contemporary vehicle, steel represents only $1,000 of the cost of the average new car.

Steel has met the higher standards for corrosion resistance with new galvanizing and coating techniques. It retains an advantage over other automotive materials in terms of:

- crash resistance – due to its energy-absorbing properties, weldability and strength of welds, also a safety factor formability, which contributes to cost savings;
- reparability – which lowers costs;
- paintability – with less environmentally damaging processes than aluminium; and
- recyclability – easily, cheaply and an unlimited number of times (aluminum can be recycled a limited number of times and primary aluminum is five times as energy-intensive to produce as steel; many plastics are still difficult and costly to recycle).

US and other steelmakers are working together to achieve a quantum improvement in the energy efficiency of passenger cars. One example of this cooperation is the ULSAB Project, which is funded by an international consortium of steelmakers. In Phase 1, Porsche Engineering Services Inc., a North American unit of Porsche AG, concluded that using currently available, high-strength steels plus optimizing design and improving production methods would yield a total weight reduction of up to 35 per cent in the basic skeleton of a passenger car. In the second phase, completed in 1998, prototypes were built to demonstrate weight reductions and performance and cost improvements.

Construction markets for steel range from energy mega-projects through major pipeline projects and public infrastructure such as roads and bridges, to commercial building construction and residential construction. Canadian and US steelmakers are working together through the American Iron and Steel Institute and the Canadian Sheet Steel Building Institute to develop the market for steel framing for residential construction. With its strength, rigidity, consistency and recyclability, steel framing materials offer distinct advantages to house builders.

Since wood is the traditional material for this purpose, steelmakers are working with homebuilder associations as well as local and state and provincial governments to develop building codes for steel products and provide seminars on working with steel framing. Following a rapid market growth, more and more new homes today have steel framing. A growing attention to life-cycle costs is creating customer interest in new high-strength or even stainless grades for such traditional applications as concrete reinforcement and bridge construction. New coating techniques are adding to the attraction of steel cladding and roofing products.

5 Future directions in steelmaking

The steel industry is looking at several new production methods to increase throughput and yield, and to improve both product quality and environmental performance.

New sources of iron: Rising scrap prices in 1993 and 1994 caused steelmakers to realize that quality scrap may not be as readily available in the future as it once was and that alternative sources of iron units must be found. This led to the use of iron carbide, which is a reduced-iron feed (RIF), as a new feedstock for electric furnace mills. It is attractive because of its low residuals (such as copper, nickel, chrome, etc.) and its potentially high carbon content. Other alternatives for high-quality iron sources include the increased use of direct reduced iron by both types of steelmakers and the pre-treatment of scrap.

Substitutes for coke: The industry is starting to use alternatives to coke, for example, pulverized-coal injection (PCI). The use of PCI reduces the need for the cokemaking process. Stelco started up a PCI facility in June 1996. It is a joint venture with Mitsubishi, where both companies own and operate the plant.

Casting: In 1988, Nucor Corp. in South Carolina pioneered thin-slab casting, which involved pouring a 2" slab directly rather than pouring a 9" slab and then rolling it down to 2". Several companies have since followed suit. Others are moving to cast intermediate thicknesses. Several Canadian steel companies have experimented with thin-strip casting, the direct casting of an even thinner initial product. While these 'near net shape casting' processes have the potential to save on rolling costs and cycle time, they also pose challenges in controlling surface quality and, in the case of thin strip casting, in controlling the dimensions during the casting process.

Continuous process: The direction of change is towards making the whole steelmaking process a continuous flow. This has the potential to:

- increase yields through reduced wastage;
- reduce the overall cycle time and thus increase the output from given capital assets;
- reduce costs due to less production and handling steps. One movement in this direction was continuous casting, which decreased the amount of raw steel required for a given volume of finished steel product by 20 per cent. Another effort in creating a continuous flow is integrated casting and

hot rolling. Incremental changes throughout the process are moving in this direction.

Relentless cost pressure means that steel companies are constantly seeking to optimize the steelmaking process and downstream processing. The traditional steel mill operated as a complex sequence of discrete operations. Modern steel mills operate more like continous process chemical plants (Madhavan *et al.* 1998; Lixin *et al.* 2000).

Supply chain optimization does not stop at the steel plant gate. As part of the advanced materials industry, steel is vitally linked to downstream industries including material inputs management and product design, for instance in the auto parts industry (Gilbert and Ballou 1999; Sabourin 1999).

6 Conclusion: old economy – new economy

The steel industry's image is still that of an old, industrial commodity producer. The fact is that steel is every bit a part of the new information economy. Increasing the information content of the steel as it is being produced not only offers opportunities to optimize productivity, and minimize waste and energy consumption. It also directly impacts the design and manufacturing opportunities for steel-consuming industries.

A new stage for steel in the information economy has been heralded by the announcement by the big auto makers that they intend to place the whole $280 billion auto parts supply business on the Internet. Among the implications of this is a dramatic shift in pricing power. The large auto makers have been the price setters in hard bargaining with the steel companies. Auto parts manufacturers have historically been price takers from the steel companies. The big auto companies intend now to use their leverage to buy surplus steel and auction it off on the Internet to the suppliers. No doubt the steel industry will undergo another major shift in the early twenty-first century in integrating these new realities.

PETER WARRIAN
MUNK CENTRE FOR INTERNATIONAL STUDIES
UNIVERSITY OF TORONTO

Further reading

(References cited in the text marked *)

* Ahlbrandt, R., Fruehan, R. and Giarratani, F. (1997) 'The renaissance of American steel: lessons for managers in competitive industries', *International Journal of Human Resource Management* 8 (6): 857–73. (A managerial perspective on human resources and productivity.)
* Bacon, N. (1999) 'Union derecognition and the new human relations: a steel industry case study', *Work, Employment and Society* 13 (1): 1–17. (Charts the decline of unions in the steel industry and the rise of new employment relations.)
* Berger, P. (1999) 'The effects of high performance work practices on job satisfaction in the United States steel industry', *Relations-industrielles / Industrial-Relations* 54 (1): 111–35. (An analysis of new work practices.)
* Blair, A. (1997) 'The British iron and steel industry since 1945', *The Journal of European Economic History* 26, (3) (Winter): 571–81. (Summary of the British steel industry's trajectory of change from old open hearth mills to the newest technology and supply chains.)
* Blyton, P. and Bacon, N. (1997) 'Re-casting the occupational culture in steel: implications of changing from crews to teams in the UK steel industry', *The Sociological Review* 45 (1): 79–101. (Analysis of the culture of the steel workplace.)
* Chung, J.W. (1998) 'Effects of U.S. trade remedy law enforcement under uncertainty: the case of steel', *Southern Economic Journal* 65 (1): 151–9. (Reviews the impacts of US anti-dumping rules.)
  Degraeve, Z. and Roodhooft, F. (1998) 'Determining sourcing strategies: a decision model based on activity and cost driver information', *The Journal of the Operational Research Society* 49 (8): 781–9. (The challenges of e-commerce and diverse supply chain management.)
* Dudley, G. and Richardson, J. (1999) 'Competing advocacy coalitions and the process of "frame reflection": a longitudinal analysis of EU steel policy', *Journal of European Public Policy* 6 (2): 225–48. (Analysis of restructuring policies in the European steel industry.)
* Ferner, A., Keep, E. and Waddington, J. (1997) 'Industrial restructuring and EU-wide social measures: broader lessons of the ECSC experience', *Journal of European Public Policy* 4 (1): 56–72. (A discussion of European restructuring policies.)

* Frost, A. (1997) *The Role of Local Unions in Workplace Restructuring: Evidence from the North American Integrated Steel Industry*, Dissertation, Sloan School of Management, MIT, Boston, MA. (Analysis of the culture of the steel workplace.)
* Gilbert, S. and Ballou, R. (1999) 'Supply chain benefits from advanced customer commitments', *Journal of Operations Management* 18 (1): 61–73. (The challenges of e-commerce and diverse supply chain management.)
* Hogan, W. (1991) *Global Steel in the 1990s*, Lexington, MA: Lexington Books. (The best background overview of the world steel industry. Hogan discusses the traumatic 1980s and trends in the 1990s, particularly the twin thrusts of new technology and new capacity.)
* Ichniowski, C. and Shaw, K. (1999) 'The effects of human resource management systems on economic performance: an international comparison of US and Japanese plants', *Management Science* 45 (5): 704–21. (Results of groundbreaking study of the effects of comparative human resource management in productivity.)
* Ichniowski, C., Shaw, K. and Prennushi, G. (1997) 'The effects of human resource management practices on productivity: a study of steel finishing lines', *American Economic Review* 87 (3): 291–313. (Econometric analysis of the impact of human resources practices on steel industry productivity.)
* Labson, B.S. (1997) 'Changing patterns of trade in the world iron ore and steel market: an econometric analysis', *Journal of Policy Modeling* 19 (3): 237–51. (Useful technical analysis of trends in the 1980s and 1990s.)
* Lazonick, W. (1998) 'Organizational learning and international competition', in J. Michie and J.G. Smith (eds), *Globalization, Growth, and Governance*, Oxford: Oxford University Press. (Comparison of the organizational integration of different skill bases in US–Japanese competition in the 1970s and 1980s.)
* Lixin Tang, Liu Jiyin, Aiying Rong and Zihou Yang (2000) 'A mathematical programming model for scheduling steelmaking-continuous casting production', *European Journal of Operational Research* 20 (2): 423–35. (Techical analysis of continuous process flows in steelmaking and links to supply chains.)
* Madhavan, R., Koka, B.R. and Prescott, J.E. (1998) 'Networks in transition: how industry events (re)shape interfirm relationships', *Strategic Management Journal* 19 (5): 439–59. (Emergence of new supply chains in the steel industry.)
* Mastel, G. (1999) 'The U.S. steel industry and antidumping law', *Challenge* 42 (3): 84–94. (Reviews the contentious features of US antidumping rules.)
* Moore, M. (1998) 'European steel policies in the 1980s: hindering technological innovation and market structure change?' *Weltwirtschaftliches-Archiv* 134 (1): 42–68. (The impact of trade and industrial policies on technological innovation in the steel industry.)
* Nobles, W. and Redpath, J. (1997) 'Market based management – a key to Nucor's success', *The Bank of America Journal of Applied Corporate Finance*, 10 (3) (Fall): 104–16. (New management model in the steel industry based on thin-slab casting.)
* Reppelin-Hill, V. (1999) 'Trade and environment: an empirical analysis of the technology effect in the steel industry', *Journal of Environmental Economics and Management* 38 (3): 283–301. (Convergence of trade and technology-based changes in the world steel industry.)
* Sabourin, V. (1999) 'Technological revolutions and the formation of strategic groups', *Journal of Engineering and Technology Management* 16 (3/4): 271–93. (An interest-group analysis of policies affecting technological change in the steel industry.)
* Scott, R.E. and Blecker, R.A. (1997) 'Labour rents, adjustment costs and the cost of US steel trade restraints in the 1980s', *International Review of Applied Economics* 11 (3): 399–419. (A technical analysis of US trade policy in the steel industry.)
* Sull, D., Hayward, M. and Piramal, G. (1999) 'Spinning steel into gold: the case of Ispat International NV', *European Management Journal* 17 (4): 368–81. (A sample of the new players on the global steel trade stage.)

See also: COOPERATION AND COMPETITION; DEVELOPMENT AND DIFFUSION OF TECHNOLOGY; DYNAMIC CAPABILITIES; EMPLOYMENT RELATIONS; GLOBALIZATION; GROWTH OF THE FIRM AND NETWORKING; INDUSTRIAL DYNAMICS; INDUSTRIAL AND LABOUR RELATIONS

Electronics industry

1. Relevance
2. Historical perspective: the flagship model of industrial organization
3. Competition puzzles: empirical evidence
4. Possible explanations
5. Key questions for ongoing research

Overview

This article highlights fundamental changes in the electronics industry that have transformed its competitive dynamics and industrial organization: a high and growing knowledge intensity; the rapid pace of change in technologies and markets; and extensive globalization. That explosive mixture of forces has created two inter-related puzzles. The first puzzle is that a high degree of globalization may well go hand in hand with high and increasing concentration. This runs counter to the dominant view, based on the assumption of neo-classical trade theory, that globalization will increase competition and hence will act as a powerful equalizer both among nations and among firms. Multinational corporations, after all, may not be such effective 'spoilers of concentration', as claimed by Richard Caves (1982). The second related puzzle is that this industry fails to act like a stable global oligopoly, even when concentration is extremely high: market positions are highly volatile, new entry is possible and not even market leaders can count on a guaranteed survival.

Defining the *electronics industry* is tricky. Recent research (e.g. Afuah 1997) has shown that products are insufficient to define an industry when specialized suppliers exist; when there is complex market segmentation and abrupt change in demand patterns; when there is intense and unpredictable technical change; and when financial institutions accelerate the pace of industrial restructuring and increase uncertainty. All of these conditions prevail in the electronics industry – key sectors are in turmoil, with sectoral boundaries changing incessantly. For lack of a better alternative, however, we still have to use products and key technologies as a proxy definition.

Most studies have focused on the hardware side, i.e. electronics equipment and components. We include in addition software, information services and a variety of newly emerging markets that result from the convergence of digital information, audio and video, and communication technologies (e.g. Internet services). This broad definition reflects a fundamental shift in the centre of gravity of value generation (as defined in Lazonick 1991) away from hardware and component technology towards architectural design standards, software and knowledge-intensive services. These changes in technological and competitive dynamics have further increased the already high knowledge intensity and exposure to globalization, thus posing new challenges for industrial organization. The electronics industry thus is a good test case for studying competitive dynamics in a globalizing world.

We first explain why it matters to understand the economics of the electronics industry. Section 2 provides a historical perspective on how the structure of the electronics industry evolved, centred around a *symbiotic* relationship between computers and semiconductors. We briefly sketch the story of how IBM created the flagship model of industrial organization, by relying on global production networks (GPN) for manufacturing services, and by outsourcing the PC operating system (to Microsoft) and the microprocessor design (to Intel). Section 3 reviews empirical evidence on the electronics industry's competition puzzles. Some possible explanations are reviewed in section 4 of the entry: we distinguish sources of concentration and sources of market volatility. Finally, in section 5 we highlight key questions addressed in ongoing research that can further clarify this subject.

1 Relevance

Understanding what forces shape the competitive dynamics of the electronics industry is not just an issue for sector specialists. Addressing this question has broad ramifications for debates on possible new sources of economic growth.

There is a broad consensus that the electronics industry is of critical importance for enhancing productivity, competitiveness and long-term growth. This strategic industry argument is based on various propositions. One is that the industry has followed, for more than 25 years, 'Moore's Law', laid down by Gordon Moore, co-founder of Intel: every 18 months or so, the price of computing power has been halved. This change has provided a powerful incentive for a pervasive digitalization of economic transactions. A second proposition states that, provided appropriate organizational innovations are in place, the spread of computer-based information and communications technology (ICT) can drastically increase productivity across all stages of the value chain, and hence enhance a society's economic growth and welfare.

A third proposition emphasizes the potential of ICT to reduce the friction of time and space, a change that could fundamentally alter the nature of economic growth. Proponents of the 'New Economy', for instance, argue that ICT has accelerated the pace of change in economic structures and institutions, reducing the barriers to non-inflationary growth (OECD 2000). Strong expectations also exist with regard to the spatial impact: it has been argued for instance that IT enhances both the incentives and the possibilities to codify knowledge, which facilitates international knowledge diffusion, thus broadening the scope for globalization (e.g. David and Foray 1995). A fourth proposition finally highlights market failure: due to the massive externalities involved, investments are typically characterized by a gap between private and social rates of return (Arrow 1962). This requires corrective policy interventions that provide incentives, as well as the necessary infrastructure, support services and human resources.

These issues rank high on the priority lists of management and policy debates. Until the early 1990s, the automobile industry provided the role model with its shift from 'Fordist' to 'lean production'. This is no longer the case. Developments in the electronics industry are now the primary determinants of a 'New Industrial Organization' model (e.g. Chandler *et al.* 1998). Unrivalled in its degree of globalization and in its exposure to global competition, the electronics industry has become the most important breeding ground for changes in firm organization and industry structure.

Management debates for instance focus on new approaches to global supply chain management developed in the electronics industry, such as the BTO (built-to-order) production model of Dell Computer Corporation. The main concern is to reduce the high cost of coordination that results from extensive geographic dispersion, multiple sourcing, duplication of tasks and excess capacity. Equally important is that suppliers are now confronted with much more demanding performance, efficiency and time-to-market requirements. Effective time management is of the essence: Inventory turnovers have become a critical indicator of competitive success, in addition to profits and market capitalization (Fine 1998). Some observers claim that this constitutes a new 'American Model of Manufacturing' that is now being extended beyond electronics to a broad range of information-intensive and time-sensitive sectors that encompass food and garments as well as cars and aircraft (e.g. Florida and Sturgeon 1999; Kenney 2000).

Policy debates both in the USA and in the European Union (EU) highlight the role of ICT-based organizational innovations as major new sources of economic growth. The same is true for Asia's policy debates on post-crisis industrial upgrading. However, there is still substantial confusion. Most of the debates are centred on simple dichotomies that juxtapose for instance information (or knowledge, or network, or simply post-modern) society against industrial society; flexible specialization against mass production; and Wintelism against Fordism (e.g. Castells 1998; Borrus 2000). Such *reductionist* concepts are inadequate to explain the complex processes of organizational evolution in industry structure and firm behaviour that have transformed the electronics industry. A brief review of how the structure of the electronics industry evolved can help to clarify these issues.

2 Historical perspective: the flagship model of industrial organization

It was during the late 1940s, and due to the development of the mainframe computer and the invention of the transistor, that the USA established a firm worldwide leadership in the electronics industry. Despite important challenges, especially Japan's catching up in DRAM (dynamic random access memories), later followed by Korea, Taiwan and Singapore (e.g. Ernst and O'Connor 1992; Hobday 1995; Ernst 1994, 1997, 2000c; Mathews and Cho 2000), US leadership has remained remarkably stable.

Two explanations are offered in the literature (e.g. Langlois and Steinmueller 1999; Bresnahan and Malerba 1999). First, a rapid diffusion of basic technologies arguably has created a pool of independent specialized suppliers, the so-called semiconductor merchant firms that aggressively pursued international market-share expansion and technology development. A second related argument is that rapid technology diffusion in the USA reflects peculiar features of its competitive dynamics and industrial organization that were very different from those in Europe and Japan. Three features are normally highlighted: (1) a *symbiotic* relationship between computers and semiconductors; (2) government policy focuses on performance-orientated procurement; and (3) incentives that facilitate the entry of specialized supplier start-up companies.

These arguments have some plausibility. But they fail to tell the full story: the proliferation of specialized suppliers did not occur in isolation. While legally independent, these firms were closely interacting with large corporations (initially, AT&T and IBM, but later on including companies like Hewlett Packard and Intel) that acted as flagships of emerging production networks. Those networks emerged first within the USA, but were soon extended internationally. An early exposure to globalization is arguably one of the important distinguishing features of the US semiconductor industry that explains its early leadership (e.g. Tilton 1971; Ernst 1983). The same is true for its twin sister, the computer industry.

Computers

Let us briefly look at how IBM created the flagship model of industrial organization by relying on global production networks (GPN) for manufacturing services. Similar stories can be told for other major flagship companies (e.g. Ernst 1997; Borrus *et al.* 2000). IBM's move toward an integrated, worldwide operation dates back to 1949, when its World Trade Corporation was established. IBM's 'interchange plan' in Europe during the 1950s probably is one of the first systematic attempts to optimize its international operations by establishing a transatlantic production network. These efforts become much more systematic with the introduction of the IBM 360 during the early 1960s. Essential for its success was a concerted effort of IBM R&D laboratories and production facilities in the USA and Europe: the higher-end version 360/40, orientated toward scientific applications, was based on a design developed in IBM's Hursley laboratory in the UK, and the low-end 360/20 was developed in IBM's German labs in Boeblingen. By the mid-1960s, IBM had established a transatlantic production network where product development and manufacturing responsibilities were assigned to individual laboratories and production facilities: each development laboratory specialized in a particular technology and carried the development responsibility for a product or technology for the entire company. Each IBM plant, including the US facilities, was given a mandate to produce specific products both for the international and the local market (see GLOBALIZATION).

IBM thus was the first computer company to try a full-scale extension of its value chain across national boundaries, albeit still confined to the USA and Europe. This began to change during the 1960s: to reduce costs in manufacturing core memories for the 360 System, IBM began to shift the labour-intensive assembly of these components to low-cost 'offshore' locations in Asia. IBM's production network began to move beyond the transatlantic region: 'An organization was quickly established in Japan to find vendors to [wire core arrays by hand]. Soon the work expanded to Taiwan, where a few thousand people were employed wiring core frames by hand. It was slow, tedious, meticulous work, stringing wires in just the right manner through each of the thousands of tiny cores in each core plane. But the cost of labor there was so low that it was actually a few dollars [per unit] cheaper than with full automation in Kingston [New York]' (Pugh, 1984: 250–1).

IBM's move to Asia did not occur in isolation: it was soon followed by its competitors who also established core array wiring operations in Taiwan and Hong Kong. IBM thus gave rise to a new model of international production for American electronics firms: the redeployment of labour-intensive stages of final assembly to Asia. For quite some time, most of these activities were fairly mundane. Much of what was then called 'offshore sourcing' investment consisted of screwdriver assembly, with very limited local value added and almost no local linkages (Ernst 1983). This originally was an exclusive American affair. Two actors were the main carriers: producers and mass merchandisers of consumer devices, with GE and Sears & Roebuck being the most prominent examples; and medium-sized semiconductor 'merchant' firms that were then still struggling to establish themselves as independent vendors on the open market.

The flagship model in semiconductors

For semiconductors, the pioneer was Motorola which as early as 1967 established production lines in Hong Kong and South Korea. One year later, in 1968, it was followed by National Semiconductor and Texas Instruments which both chose to move first into Singapore. Four years later, both companies established their assembly lines for integrated circuits (IC) in Malaysia, and were joined in the same year by Intel. Originally, the expansion of American semiconductor firms into East Asia was primarily driven by two concerns: access to cheap assembly hands and the large tariff reductions they could reap by re-importing sub-assemblies from abroad. The over-riding goal was to improve return on investments (ROIs) through cost reductions that did not require the heavy capital outlays that would have been necessary for factory automation at home. American semiconductor firms insisted on equity control through the establishment of 100 per cent-owned affiliates, in order to minimize the risk of technology leakage. This practice is in accordance with the theory of foreign direct investment that argues that firms with strong proprietary advantages in technology have a preference for equity control.

Over time, this simple concern with short-term financial savings had to give way to more complex motivations. During the late 1970s, Japanese firms had succeeded in establishing a credible challenge by automating their domestic production facilities. In response, American semiconductor firms were forced to develop an international production strategy that would allow them to pre-empt possible attacks by Japanese firms through rapid cost reduction. It is during this period that companies like Intel, Motorola and National Semiconductor began to upgrade and automate their existing offshore chip assembly plants. In order to do so, they had to develop, albeit grudgingly, linkages with local suppliers and support industries. Equally important, they had to integrate these dispersed supply bases into integrated GPN.

When the US dollar appreciated during the early 1980s, cash-stripped American semiconductor firms moved one step further towards a full-blown flagship model by accepting forms of international production that did not necessarily involve equity control. This practice has given rise to the proliferation of a variety of international contract manufacturing arrangements, ranging from contract assembly to complete 'second sourcing' agreements. Together with the continuous upgrading of existing affiliates, these arrangements have conveyed substantial competitive advantages to American semiconductor firms.

Breakthrough: microprocessors and the PC

A breakthrough in the development of the flagship model came with the emergence of the microprocessor (MPU) that gave rise to a new kind of computer, the microcomputer (or PC). Both acted as disruptive technologies, as defined by Christensen (1997), reversing the established rules of competition. The MPU failed to have an impact on mainframes and minis because it did not initially offer the computing power and speed that these larger machines could get from multiple logic chips. Existing computer companies thus considered these machines as a small fringe market for hobbyists. The lower production costs of MPUs and their capacity to simplify motherboard design gave rise to an altogether new approach to the design of computer architectures, however, and soon created a thriving demand by new customers who did not need and could not afford the vast computing power of mainframes and minis.

An important turning point came with the Apple II, a relatively open and expandable machine that was designed for volume manufacturing. This compact and attractively designed machine created a highly profitable niche market that IBM, the dominant incumbent, could no longer ignore. On August 12, 1981, the entry of the IBM PC created a new dominant computing platform that has been instrumental in sustaining US leadership. Equally important, but less well known, are the implications for industrial organization. Both the Apple II and the IBM PC were designed around a limited number of standard components. They were designed also as an open box ready for expansion, reconfiguration and continuous upgrading. This architecture gave rise to extensive outsourcing and a rapid geographic dispersion of the value chain. For instance, for the IBM PC, floppy disk drives came from Singapore-based Tandon, power supply from Zenith, motherboards from SCI Systems and printers from Japan's Epson. For the Apple II outsourcing was even more extensive, and final assembly soon shifted to Singapore and Ireland.

Of critical importance however is that, in order to quickly achieve market dominance, IBM decided to outsource the PC operating system (to Microsoft) and the microprocessor design (to Intel). Langlois (1992: 1, 3) highlights one important aspect: the outsourcing of 'external capabilities' that 'reside within a network of interacting firms'. Of equal importance however is the impact on competitive dynamics and industrial organization. By outsourcing the operating system and the microprocessor, IBM enabled both Microsoft and Intel to capture de facto control over this new architectural standard.

The evolution of the microcomputer accelerated the spread of the emerging flagship model of industrial organization. Consider a stylized GPN (Ernst 1997): it combines a large, multidivisional multinational enterprise (the *flagship*), its subsidiaries, affiliates and joint ventures, its suppliers and subcontractors, its distribution channels and value-added resellers, as well as its R&D alliances and a variety of cooperative agreements, such as standards consortia. A network flagship like IBM or Intel breaks down the value chain into a variety of discrete functions and locates them wherever they can be carried out most effectively, where they improve the firm's access to resources and capabilities, and where they are needed to facilitate the penetration of important growth markets.

The flagship model raises a number of important issues that are highly contested in the literature. For instance, GPN do not necessarily give rise to less hierarchical forms of firm organization (as predicted for instance in Bartlett and Ghoshal, 1989). Network participants differ in their access to and in their position within, such networks, and hence face very different challenges. We use a *taxonomy* of network participants that distinguishes various hierarchical layers that range from flagship companies that dominate such networks, down to a variety of usually smaller, local network participants (Ernst 2001a). The flagship is at the heart of a network: it provides strategic and organizational leadership beyond the resources that, from an accounting perspective, lie directly under its management control.

The strategy of the flagship company thus directly affects the growth, the strategic direction and network position of lower-end participants, like specialized suppliers and subcontractors. The latter, in turn, 'have no reciprocal influence over the flagship strategy' (Rugman and D'Cruz, 2000: 84). The flagship derives its strength from its *control* over critical resources and capabilities, and from its capacity to *coordinate* transactions between the different network nodes. Both are the sources of its superior capacity for value generation. This taxonomy helps to distinguish the different capacities of these firms to reap potential network benefits, and the institutions and policies required to support weaker network participants.

Increasing vertical specialization is the fundamental driver of this flagship model of industrial organization. Flagships retain in-house activities in which they have a particular strategic advantage; they outsource those in which they do not (Teece 1986). It is important to emphasize the diversity of such outsourcing patterns. Some flagships focus on design, product development and marketing, outsourcing volume manufacturing and related support services (Ernst 2000a). Other flagships outsource as well a variety of high-end, knowledge-intensive support services. This includes for instance trial production (prototyping and ramping-up), tooling and equipment, benchmarking of productivity, testing, process adaptation, product customization and supply chain coordination. It may also include design and product development.

This outsourcing has given rise to a proliferation of specialized suppliers, segmenting the industry into separate, yet closely interacting horizontal layers (Grove 1996). The initial catalyst was the availability of standard components, which allowed for a change in computer design away from closed (IBM mainframe) to open, yet owned, architectural and interface standards for the PC and computer networks (especially the Internet). Tilton (1971) convincingly demonstrates that very early on, the ability to put a 'computer on a chip' opened up new possibilities of industry evolution, with American firms in control of not only the key technology but also the critical system integration capabilities. As a result, new options emerged for outsourcing, transforming an erstwhile vertically integrated industry into closely interacting, globally organized product-specific value chains (e.g. for microprocessors, memories, board assembly, PCs, operating systems, applications software and networking equipment). This process has been accelerated by the introduction of Internet-enabled virtual integration (Ernst 2001b). Each of these value chains consists of a variety of GPN that compete with each other, but that may also cooperate. The number of such networks and the intensity of competition varies across sectors, reflecting their different stage of development and their idiosyncratic industry structures (Ernst and Ravenhill 1999).

3 Competition puzzles: empirical evidence

The first puzzle: globalization and concentration

In important sectors of the electronics industry, globalization is accompanied by increasing concentration. We first look at peculiar features of globalization and then review data on concentration.

Peculiar features of globalization
Globalization in the electronics industry combines a massive, yet highly concentrated, international dispersion of the value chain, but one with an important organizational innovation – the spread of GPN (see GLOBALIZATION; MULTINATIONAL CORPORATIONS). These networks are a response to the flagship's increasingly pervasive outsourcing requirements and the demanding coordination requirements of geographic dispersion: they integrate the dispersed supply and customer bases of a global network flagship company (e.g. IBM, Cisco, Compaq, NEC, Acer or Samsung). The main purpose is to gain quick access to lower-cost foreign capabilities that are complementary to the flagship's own competencies. The creation of GPN reflects increasing pressures to exploit complementarities that result from the interactive nature of knowledge creation (Antonelli 1998).

Take the outsourcing of volume manufacturing and related support services that enables global brand-name companies to combine cost reduction, product differentiation and time-to-market. A peculiar feature of this new model of industrial organization is that manufacturing is de-coupled from product development, and is dispersed across firm and national boundaries. With an average annual growth of more than 25 per cent, the so-called *electronics manufacturing services* (EMS) market is one of the fastest growing electronics sectors, expanding twice as quickly as the total electronics industry. The role model for such changes is Solectron, the world's largest EMS provider, with revenues of US$ 8.4 billion during fiscal year 1999. With a compound annual growth rate of 43 per cent over the past five years, Solectron has now more than 46,000 employees in 41 locations worldwide, with more than 9 million square feet of capacity.

The network flagship outsources not only manufacturing, but also a variety of high-end, knowledge-intensive support services. Most research on the location of knowledge-intensive activities has focused on the role of R&D, but this may be too narrow a focus (for details, see Ernst 2000c). It is necessary to cast the net wider and to analyse the geographic dispersion of cross-functional, knowledge-intensive support services that are intrinsically linked with production. Even if these activities do not involve formal R&D, they may still give rise to considerable learning and innovation. The latter include for instance trial production (prototyping and ramping-up), tooling and equipment, benchmarking of productivity, testing, process adaptation, product customization and supply chain coordination.

The result is that an increasing share of the value-added becomes dispersed across the boundaries of the firm as well as across national borders. Let us look at some indicators. A good proxy of *geographic dispersion* are the growing methodological problems that one encounters when one tries to determine the importance of individual countries and regions in the world electronics market. The difficulties reflect the fact that final products, almost without exception, involve substantial inputs across the value chain that are produced in diverse locations across the globe.

Two measures exist: one is based on company *ownership*, the other on the *country of origin of exports*. Both market-share measures were largely similar, as long as trade was the most important vehicle for international market-share expansion. Both indicators however began to diverge once production dispersed across borders. Take semiconductors (Reed Electronics Research 1998): there is a huge gap between the US share of world exports (18 per cent) and its market share based on company ownership (32 per cent). This suggests that a very high share of US production is taking place overseas. The gap between ownership-based and export market shares is even higher for Asia (38 per cent by country of origin, versus 19 per cent by ownership), but is the inverse of the US relation, thus suggesting that Asia has attracted the bulk of investments not only from the USA but also from Japan and Europe.

Geographic dispersion however is heavily *concentrated* in a few *specialized local clusters*. For instance, the *supply chain* of a computer company typically spans different time zones and continents, and integrates a multitude of transactions and local clusters. The degree of dispersion differs across the value chain: it increases the closer one gets to the final product, while dispersion remains concentrated, especially for critical precision components. At one end of the spectrum is final PC assembly that is widely dispersed to major growth markets in the USA, Europe and Asia. Dispersion is still quite extended for standard, commodity-type components ('homogeneous products' in the parlance of industrial economists), but less so than for final assembly. For instance, keyboards, computer mouse devices and power switch supplies are sourced from many different locations, both in Asia, Mexico and the European periphery, with Taiwanese firms playing a major role as supply coordinators. The same is true for lower-end printed circuit boards.

Concentration of dispersion increases the more we move towards more complex, capital-intensive precision components: memory devices and displays are sourced primarily from Japan, Korea, Taiwan and Singapore; and hard disk drives from a Singapore-centred triangle of locations in Southeast Asia. Finally, dispersion becomes most concentrated for high-precision, design-intensive components that pose the most demanding requirements on the mix of capabilities that a firm and its cluster needs to master: microprocessors are sourced from a few globally dispersed affiliates of Intel, two secondary

American suppliers and one recent entrant from Taiwan, Via Technologies.

The *hard disk drive (HDD)* industry provides another example both for the breathtaking speed of geographic dispersion, as well as for its spatial concentration (Ernst 1997). Until the early 1980s, almost all HDD production was concentrated in the USA, with limited additional production facilities in Japan and Europe. Today, only 1 per cent of the final assembly of HDDs has remained in the USA, while Southeast Asia dominates with almost 70 per cent of world production, based on units shipped. Slightly less than half of the world's disk drives come from Singapore, with most of the rest of the region's production being concentrated in Malaysia, Thailand and the Philippines.

Let us take a closer look at firm-level developments. The GPN of Seagate, the current industry leader, provides a good example of *concentrated dispersion*. Today, Seagate operates 22 plants worldwide: 14 of these plants, i.e. 64 per cent of the total, are located in Asia. Asia's share in Seagate's worldwide production capacity, as expressed in square feet, has increased from roughly 35 per cent in 1990 to slightly more than 61 per cent in 1995 – an incredible speed of expansion. Concentrated dispersion is also reflected in the regional breakdown of Seagate's employment: Asia's share increased from around 70 per cent in 1990 to more than 85 per cent in 1995.

The fact that Asia's share in employment is substantially higher than its share in capacity, while the opposite is true for the USA, indicates a clear-cut division of labour: labour-intensive volume manufacturing has been shifted to Asia, while the USA retains the high-end, knowledge-intensive stages of the value chain. Asia has absorbed most of the high-volume assembly activities and the production of low- and mid-range components. Precision component manufacturing and R&D however remain firmly entrenched in a few highly specialized US regions like California and around Minneapolis. For instance, Seagate Magnetics, the affiliate that produces media, has concentrated all production in California. And wafer fabrication, a core process of head manufacturing, is concentrated in Minnesota, as is automatic slider fabrication for leading-edge magneto-resistant (MR) heads. This is in line with similar specialization patterns displayed by other leading HDD producers.

We need to add a further aspect: an extreme spatial concentration *within* East Asia, which now handles most of Seagate's volume manufacturing. Slightly more than 92 per cent of Seagate's capacity in Asia is concentrated in three locations: in Bangkok (almost 32 per cent), Penang (more than 30 per cent) and Singapore (a bit less than 30 per cent). And almost 50 per cent (26,000 out of 55,000) of Seagate's Asian employment is concentrated in its plant in the outskirts of Bangkok. These data indicate that Bangkok is the centre for low-labour cost volume manufacturing. Next comes Singapore with more than 27 per cent (15,000), substantially more than Malaysia's 16 per cent (9000 people). For both Singapore and Malaysia, the low ratio of employment relative to its share in Seagate's production capacity indicates that production facilities have been rapidly automated and include now higher-end manufacturing activities such as component manufacturing.

Over time, Seagate has developed a quite articulate regional division of labour in East Asia. Bottom-end work is done in Indonesia and China. Malaysian and Thai plants make components and specialize in partial assembly. Singapore is the centre of gravity of this regional production network: its focus is on higher-end products and some important coordination and support functions. It completes the regional production network by adding testing, which requires precision.

Concentration

Concentration in the electronics industry is high and often keeps rising, despite a heavy exposure to globalization. It is well known that, in terms of market shares, both computer operating systems and microprocessors are each overwhelmingly dominated by one company, Microsoft and Intel respectively. Concentration is also substantial for high precision key components that are critical for architectural design and performance features, such as DRAM, advanced displays and HDD. Let us look at relevant data for the latter industry.

Market share data indicate a very high degree of concentration: five companies account for roughly 85 per cent of worldwide non-captive HDD sales. Concentration ratios are also very high for key components. Take head assembly: the 10 largest head manufacturers account for 93 per cent of the market by volume, with the largest six firms alone controlling 78 per cent. One indicator of increasing concentration is the rapid decline in the number of worldwide drive manufacturers: the total shrank from 59 in 1990 to 24 in 1995, with most of the decline taking place after 1993. In 1995, nine companies went out of business, and only three companies entered the fray, all of them in niche markets. During the same year, Seagate, the current market leader, acquired Conner Peripherals, the company that, in 1992, was the world market leader. Furthermore, two heavyweights, Hewlett Packard and DEC, left the HDD industry altogether during 1996.

High and increasing concentration can also be found for other key components. Take DRAM, the largest segment of the semiconductor market. The DRAM market is now even more concentrated than the world oil industry was at the peak of the rule of the infamous *seven sisters*: six business groups control almost 88 per cent of the world market (up from 67.1 per cent in 1998). Of even more importance, the four top firms now control more than two-thirds of the DRAM market (up from 50.8 per cent in 1998).

We find increasing concentration even in the PC industry, an industry which only a decade ago was hailed by neo-liberals as a holy grail of free competition (Gilder 1988). The top four market players – Compaq, Dell, IBM and Hewlett Packard – have consistently expanded their combined global market share from less than 27 per cent in 1996 to 37.3 per cent in 1999. During this period, the four industry leaders have captured almost 70 per cent of PC unit growth worldwide. Concentration is substantially higher in the all-important US market, where the top four PC makers now hold about 68 per cent. Concentration is also very high and rapidly increasing for *notebooks*, an industry that used to be crowded with many competitors: the total market share of the ten largest firms was 64.2 per cent in 1995, rose to 68.3 per cent in 1996 and stands now around 75 per cent.

Similar trends can be observed in the electronics manufacturing services industry. While only a few years ago, many of these firms were of humble size, concentration is now increasing at a breathtaking pace, based on a wave of M&A (mergers and acquisitions). During 1999, more than 100 mergers occurred in this sector, up from 50 in 1997. If this trend continues, this industry will be soon dominated by handful of large, integrated manufacturing service providers, each with revenues of at least $10 billion. Solectron's recent purchase of Nortel's worldwide manufacturing operations documents the speed of these transformations. In one stroke, this acquisition expanded Solectron's global production capacity by 1.2m square feet, an increase of capacity of roughly 20 per cent.

Finally, concentration keeps rising rapidly even in newly emerging sectors such as Internet software and networking equipment, despite the fact that there are new entrants by the droves. In the market for ISPs (Internet service providers), huge global telecommunications companies, together with the market leader AOL, have aggressively increased their market share through a wave of M&A. Equally important is an increase in concentration in the rapidly growing ASP (application service providers) market. As that market becomes more profitable, large global players have become the dominant players. Included among these dominant ASPs are computer and software companies (Oracle, Sun Microsystems, IBM, Intel, and Hewlett Packard), telecommunications companies (AT&T and Qwest), consulting companies (KPMG) and financial firms (e.g. Merrill Lynch).

In the market for networking equipment, Cisco's original leadership position has been eroded by multiple attacks. Telecommunications equipment vendors, especially Nortel Networks and Lucent Technologies, have entered the fray. Cisco has responded in kind by entering the market for telecommunications equipment. In addition, computer companies, such as IBM, Compaq and Hewlett Packard are also now producing some networking equipment (e.g. switches, hubs and adaptor cards), although they are not yet as major players.

As a result, a small group of North American firms dominates networking equipment, with very limited competition from suppliers in Japan and Europe. Competition between the top firms (Nortel, Cisco, 3Com and Lucent) is very intense and has fuelled various rounds of mega-M&A, hence it is possible to talk about an unstable global oligopoly. As in other sectors of the electronics industry, increasing concentration goes hand in hand with substantial volatility of market positions. What sets the networking equipment industry apart, is the extremely rapid pace of technological change which is concentrated in two areas: increased network bandwidth, and transmission speed to alleviate congestion. The result is an industry in turmoil where incumbents as well as a handful of new entrants fiercely compete for market positions. Note however that the speed of change has slowed down since the beginning of the US recession in late 2000.

The second puzzle: concentration and volatility

This brings us to a second puzzle that is equally surprising: even when concentration is very high, the electronics industry fails to act like a stable global oligopoly (as predicted, for instance, by Borrus 1989 and Ferguson and Morris 1993). Take again the example of the HDD industry.

According to Blair (1972), oligopoly begins when the four largest firms hold more than 25 per cent of overall sales. Between 25 and 50 per cent, this oligopoly is loose and unstable, but above 50 per cent, it becomes firm and clearly established. With five companies holding roughly 85 per cent of the global market, we would have to conclude that the HDD industry is controlled by a very tight oligopoly. This conclusion however does not square well with the fact that the HDD industry is a continuous prey to cut-throat price wars and highly volatile market positions. Despite a number of major shake-outs, the industry remains highly unstable: market positions keep changing at short notice, and not even market leaders can count on a guaranteed survival.

For instance, Conner Peripherals was the market leader in 1992, with 24 per cent. Yet, one year later, Quantum had leapfrogged both Conner and Seagate to become No. 1. Conner Peripherals in turn fell back to the third position, and saw its market share erode to 16 per cent in 1994. In 1995, the industry experienced yet another round of swapping market leadership positions, with Seagate now recapturing the top position from Quantum.

Furthermore, successful entry did occur, albeit in an indirect manner. Probably the most interesting case is that of Matsushita Kotobuki (MKE), an affiliate of the powerful Matsushita group. Since 1984 Kotobuki had been content to remain an apparently humble contract manufacturer for Quantum, one of the leading American drive producers. Today, MKE produces Quantum's full product range, including the highly profitable high-end drives for mainframes and network servers. One wonders how long MKE will wait till it disconnects itself from Quantum and enters the market on its own. A second example of successful entry is the Korean Hyundai group which, in 1995, acquired 100 per cent ownership of Maxtor, one of the industry's pioneers. Since then, Maxtor has experienced a highly successful comeback, and is now considered to be one of the industry leaders in technology, quality and speed of response.

Major changes are currently again transforming this industry, with the result of a drastic repositioning of market shares and a redefinition of the rules of competition. The result is a pervasive profit squeeze and a fall in asset prices: HDD firms that are negatively affected by these developments are forced into a defensive chain reaction. The most prominent example is the erosion of Seagate's market leadership position since the fall of 1997. This decline in market share reflects an accelerated pace of market volatility. IBM, the sleeping giant, has finally woken up and is now aggressively competing for market share, based on its leadership in the technology of key components like MR heads. Japanese competitors (especially Fujitsu) have aggressively developed a highly productive low-cost production base in the Philippines. As Fujitsu is much larger than the current industry leader Seagate, it has the resources necessary for this aggressive frontal attack. Other new contenders include Toshiba, Hitachi, NEC and Samsung, all of whom have invested in an aggressive market share expansion strategy.

4 Possible explanations

The empirical evidence on the competitive dynamics of the electronics industry runs counter to much of the established literature. What are possible explanations?

Brief review of the literature

For quite some time, the *structure–conduct–performance (SCP)* paradigm dominated the debate on competition. In this view market structure, as captured by concentration of sellers, is the primary determinant of both conduct and performance. One of the classic sources (Bain 1958) argues that high levels of sellers' concentration, protected by high entry barriers, will induce firms to engage in price collusion, which inevitably will constrain static efficiency allocation as well as learning.

The SCP paradigm has lost much of its earlier grip on the debate. The theory of 'contested markets' argues that even highly concentrated industries will be forced to price competitively, provided they face the 'discipline of potential hit-and run entry' (Baumol *et al.* 1982). The crux of this analysis is the existence of 'sunk costs': the higher they are, the less likely is the market to be contestable. The electronics industry, with its high 'sunk costs' due to R&D, thus should be less contestable.

Globalization however implies that even markets that are characterized by substantial sunk costs may become contestable: foreign firms who have already incurred the necessary sunk cost in their home markets, may very well be able to enter overseas markets. This observation has provoked some counter-arguments that come to very different conclusions. As globalization leads to market expansion, sunk costs and scale economies increase apace, further increasing concentration. The latter may well square with intense price competition. Paradoxically enough, such price wars may cause higher concentration by forcing out marginal producers and by reducing margins for potential entrants (Sutton 1991).

Such, in fact, has been the case for the HDD industry: prices have been falling about 30 per cent per year for more than a decade, fostering increasing concentration. Note however, once concentration reaches a certain level, there may well be a reversal of pricing trends. For instance, the drastic increase in concentration in the PC industry reported earlier has led to some price increases during the first quarter of 2000, after a long period of dramatic price falls (Ernst 2000c).

An alternative approach

In short, the literature allows for conflicting explanations. A major weakness of the 'sunk costs' perspective is its failure to address the critical role of innovation. This is a general weakness of 'industrial organization' (IO) theory. According to Richard Lipsey, 'most I.O. theory is about competition in prices, quantities (short run) and capacity (long run) when in fact the competition that really matters, and that drives firms' successes and failures, is competition in technologies (very long run). ... (This) has led to increasingly fierce competition among oligopolistic firms even when there are only a few in any one industry' (letter to the author, October 10, 2000).

An alternative approach can be based on a recent paper by George B. Richardson (Richardson 1996) that argues that competition for *given* products is only the tip of the iceberg: 'We concentrate too much ... on monopoly revenue being obtained by the restriction of supply, and as threatened by entrants who might increase that supply' (Richardson 1996: 4). Yet, competition in reality centres on development and innovation. Such technological competition is especially true in the electronics industry. Christensen's excellent book on 'disruptive technologies' (1997) provides a second equally important source for an alternative explanation of the puzzling competitive dynamics of the electronics industry.

Competitive dynamics and innovation
Fundamental changes in the electronics industry have transformed its competitive dynamics: a high and growing knowledge intensity, combined with the rapid pace of change in technologies and markets has given

rise to an extensive globalization. Let us focus on the dual impact of ICT: it both increases the need for and creates new opportunities for globalization. This argument is based on two propositions. First, the cost and risk of developing ICT has been a primary cause for market globalization: international markets are required to amortize fully the enormous R&D expenses associated with rapidly evolving process and product technologies (Kobrin 1997:149). Of equal importance are the huge expenses for ICT-based organizational innovations (Ernst and O'Connor 1992: chap. 1). As the extent of a company's R&D effort is determined by the nature of its technology and competition rather than its size, this rapid growth of R&D spending requires a corresponding expansion of sales, if profitability is to be maintained. No national market, not even the US market, is large enough to amortize such huge expenses.

A second proposition explains why international production rather than exports have become the main vehicle for international market share expansion. Partly this change reflects the pace of liberalization: while originally international production was driven by the need to overcome protective barriers ('tariff-hopping'), over time liberalization has become a major pull factor. Of critical importance however has been the enabling role played by ICT: it has substantially increased the mobility, i.e. dispersion, of firm-specific resources and capabilities across national boundaries; it also provides greater scope for cross-border linkages, i.e. integration. Developments in ICT have substantially reduced the friction of time and space, both with regard to markets and production: a firm can now serve distant markets equally well as local producers; it can also now disperse its value chain across national borders, in order to select the most cost-effective location.

In addition, ICT and related organizational innovations provide effective mechanisms for the international diffusion of knowledge that is required to establish, operate and continuously upgrade spatially dispersed locations (Naughton 2000). It is now possible to construct an infrastructure that can link together and coordinate economic transactions at distant locations. This possibility has important implications for organizational choices and locational strategies of firms. In essence, ICT fosters the development of leaner, meaner and more agile production systems that cut across firm boundaries and national borders. The underlying vision is that of a network of firms that is able to respond quickly to changing circumstances, even if much of its value chain has been dispersed.

The growth of these networks has drastically changed the dynamics of competition. Again, we reduce the complexity of these changes and concentrate on the most important impact: the emergence of a 'winnertakes-all' competition model: ' ... the player with the largest share in a horizontal layer is the one who wins' (Grove 1996: 48). This outcome implies that economies of scale and scope are of critical importance for competitive success, especially for key components like microprocessors and operating systems. Equally important however is a capacity to control open-but-owned architectural and interface standards (Ernst and O'Connor 1992; Borrus *et al.* 2000).

A third important feature of the new competition model is found in the increasingly demanding requirements for time management and coordination. The rapid pace of change of ICT has drastically shortened the product lifecycle: only those companies thrive that succeed in bringing new products to the relevant markets ahead of their competitors. Of critical importance is that the firm can build *specialized* capabilities quicker and at less cost than its competitors (Kogut and Zander 1993). The increasing segmentation of the electronics industry furthermore requires a capacity to coordinate dense interactions between independent market segments that feed into the final system products.

Fourth, all of this reorganization needs to be combined with aggressive price cutting across the board. PC prices have fallen by 20 per cent or more over the last two years, giving rise to razor-thin profit margins – 1.5 per cent margins are the current average for standard PCs. Deflationary pricing pressures are driven by an apparently unstoppable move towards low-end products, such as cheap PCs and mobile devices, thus intensifying the industry's profit squeeze.

Finally, an important additional constraint is that pricing strategies at the level of systems brand-name companies (e.g. Compaq) or sub-assembly producers (e.g. Seagate) are determined by the frequently abrupt price changes implemented by the lead suppliers of key components (e.g. Intel). Even minor increases in the price of a microprocessor or a display can produce substantial losses. On the other hand, sudden price declines for such components can also have very negative consequences, if the company has overstocked these components. In 1999 for instance PC components declined in value at 1 per cent or more per month, giving rise to very high inventory costs.

Disruptive technologies

'Disruptive technologies' underperform relative to established products in mainstream markets today, but may be fully performance-competitive in the same market tomorrow. Disruptive technologies differ from 'sustaining technologies' which improve the performance of *established* products that mainstream customers in mainstream markets have traditionally valued. Disruptive technologies bring to a market very different products: they have features that, initially only a few fringe (and generally new) customers value. Products based on disruptive technologies are typically cheaper, simpler, smaller and, frequently, more convenient to use.

Disruptive technologies can help to explain why high concentration co-exists with high market volatility. The explanation derives from the puzzling fact that incumbents apparently face more severe barriers to invest in disruptive technologies than new entrants. This is so for four reasons: (1) these technologies are simpler and cheaper, and thus promise lower margins, not greater profits: 'It is very difficult for a company whose cost structure is tailored to compete in high-end markets to be profitable in low-end markets as well' (Christensen 1997: xx); (2) disruptive technologies are first commercialized in emerging and insignificant markets that large companies have great difficulties in addressing; (3) the incumbents' most profitable customers generally do not want, and initially cannot use, products based on disruptive technologies; and (4) a break of routine requires a different organizational design from sustaining technologies that can rely on customary routines.

In short, disruptive technologies provide a constant threat to the excessive product differentiation pursued by incumbents to reap the benefits of premium pricing. New entrants however face relatively low entry barriers for such technologies, compared to the entry barriers that characterize sustaining technologies.

Stylized model of competitive dynamics
That explosive mixture of conflicting requirements explains the co-existence of concentration and market volatility in the electronics industry. More specifically, we distinguish sources of concentration that may stabilize markets from sources of market volatility. Among the first, we highlight the role of 'scale economies' in manufacturing, and the heavy 'sunk cost' of rapid innovation and of developing complex capabilities. The latter are of increasing importance, reflecting a growing knowledge intensity.

As for the sources of market volatility, we consider: periodic spurts of rapid capacity expansion due to extremely short product cycles; a complex supply chain that leads to periodic shortages in key components; and disruptive changes in demand and technology. A sectoral approach is of the essence: we need to identify basic characteristics of an industry in order to understand what forces shape competitive dynamics. To illustrate this stylized model of competitive dynamics, we focus on data from the HDD industry.

Sources of concentration

Scale economies in manufacturing
Rising *minimum economies of scale* are an important driver of concentration in the HDD industry. In final assembly, scale economies are largely attributable to costly facility investments like the construction of 'clean room' environments and expensive test equipment. Huge investments are also required in precision tools, moulds and dies that are

required to make the various high-precision components and parts that go into the drive. For some of these components, like thin-film or MR recording heads, minimum economies of scale are as high as those required for integrated circuits.

Minimum economies of scale have grown very rapidly over time. For instance, in 1989 an annual production capacity of between 900,000 and 1 million units was regarded as economic scale (Ernst and O'Connor 1992: 194). Since then, a dramatic increase has occurred in minimum scale. Take the 1996 capacity figures reported by Maxtor-Hyundai, which is in line with other comparable projects. For its main plant in Singapore, Maxtor reports a capacity of 4 million drives, but this capacity is not per year, but just per quarter. In other words, annual capacity at this plant now is around 16 million units.

Sunk costs of innovation and capability development

A second important driver of concentration is the very high sunk costs of rapid innovation and of developing complex capabilities. The HDD industry is characterized by a breakneck speed of technical change: areal density, i.e. the amount of information that can be stored on a given area of magnetic disk surface is increasing at about 60 per cent a year. The speed of access to data is also rapidly increasing. In order to cope with both these requirements, HDD firms must be able to tap into scientific knowledge across a broad front, covering areas like magnetics, coding and electronics. They also need to master a variety of very demanding technological capabilities.

HDDs are high-precision machines that contain and rotate rigid disks on which data is magnetically recorded and that control the flow of information to and from those disks. This technology requires a variety of high-precision engineering capabilities, for instance for the production of miniature motors that need to work under extremely demanding tolerances. This industry also requires the mastery of incredibly complex process technologies that are used for coating disks with very thin films of magnetic materials (the so-called deposition technique) and for producing specialized integrated circuits. In addition to some of the most sophisticated component manufacturing technologies, the final assembly of these drives requires leading-edge automation techniques, such as surface-mount technology.

Yet, while manufacturing matters, it is only part of the story. Competitive success in this industry crucially depends on the capacity to develop innovative architectural designs that can provide cost-effective solutions to the manifold trade-offs that exist between size, storage capacity and access time of these drives. Finally, leading-edge software capabilities are an equally important prerequisite for developing a viable HDD industry. Both architectural design and software capabilities have been of crucial importance as instruments for product development and differentiation strategies. In short, generating a constant stream of new products and key components requires huge sunk costs. The latter deter potential new entrants; they also force incumbents to increase their market share.

Sources of market volatility

Extremely short product cycles

Competition in the HDD industry is driven by the speed of new product introduction, with the result that product life cycles become shorter and shorter. On average, a new product generation is introduced every nine months, and for some products the cycle can be as short as six months, almost as short as for fashion-intensive garments. These short cycles lead to a rapid depreciation of plants and equipment and of R&D. Like semiconductors, the HDD industry thus falls prey to a 'scissors effect' between rapidly increasing fixed capital costs and an accelerated depreciation of its assets (Ernst 1983). The result is that speedto-market is of critical importance – a firm must be able to ramp-up production quickly to competitive yields and quality.

Spurts of capacity expansion result from the importance of speed-to-market. Each time that a new product generation is introduced, HDD firms engage in a frantic race to become the first supplier. HDD producers thus have all become masters in ramping-up production at short notice. The result is a built-in tendency for an overshooting of investment relative to demand growth. This has a paradoxical consequence. As mismatches between demand and supply occur periodically, a capacity to exit rapidly becomes as important as a capacity for rapid capacity expansion. Fast ramping-up and ramping-down hang together and require very quick responses to changes in markets and technology.

Short product cycles thus are an important source of market volatility. Even with all the progress made in the flexibility of supply chain management, it is very difficult to avoid periodic mismatches between supply and demand. Each time the supply of HDDs overshoots demand, price wars break out. The result is that HDD producers must combine cost leadership with technology leadership and speed-to-market, a combination that can threaten even apparently unbeatable market leaders.

A complex supply chain

A complex supply chain can be a second important source of market volatility. Logistical requirements are very demanding in the HDD industry: a wide variety of high-precision components and sub-assemblies needs to be procured from a variety of suppliers that are spread over different time zones and continents. Such global supply chains are prone to frequent disruptions. Suppliers, for instance, can cause such disruptions through late delivery or through the delivery of defective materials. Of equal importance are periodic supply shortages for key components such as heads, media, integrated circuits and precision motors. Geographic distance often magnifies the impact of such disruptions. These supply shortages lead to another paradox. While HDD firms excel in the rapid ramp-up of the final assembly lines, disruptions in the supply chain can easily thwart this achievement: if everything else is in place, but one tiny component is missing, all the efforts to ramp-up production in time have been in vain.

That vulnerability keeps rising further with an increasing reliance on outsourcing. The case of Maxtor illustrates how deadly this vulnerability can be. Maxtor's main weakness has been a lack of strong in-house circuit design expertise, forcing the company to outsource key circuitry. In 1995, at the peak of a periodic shortage of DRAM and other chips, supply disruptions led to a dramatic fall in Maxtor's market share and its acquisition by Hyundai.

Disruptive changes in demand and technology

Finally, disruptive changes in demand due to competing technologies are powerful causes of market volatility. As suppliers of an intermediate input to the computer industry, HDD firms compete for design-ins by computer companies. The latter thus exert a considerable influence on the product mix, the product cycle and the pricing strategies of HDD vendors. Decisions on the product mix are shaped by the increasing storage requirements of computers and their applications. Annual increases in areal density and speed are fairly predictable, as long as there are no trajectory-disrupting innovations.

Two types of trajectory-disrupting innovations can be distinguished: a threat from competing technologies and breakthrough innovations in the drive design and in component technology that would drastically improve disk drive capacity, performance and cost. There are a number of competing technologies: optical storage offers higher capacity, tape drives lower cost, RAM chips far better speed and flash EEPROM more durability for portable applications. There is a widespread consensus that, so far, none of these competing technologies poses a serious threat to HDD.

Of critical importance however are breakthrough innovations in architectural design and in component technology that have periodically caused quite serious turmoil in the HDD industry. For instance, new optical data storage technologies are currently emerging that may have trajectory-disrupting effects. Such a technological change privileges newcomers to the HDD market like Sony and Philips which have strong positions in optical technologies; it creates a serious problem for the current market leader Seagate which is weak in these technologies.

No HDD company can afford to neglect such demand volatility. Much depends on the kind of customers to which the HDD company is linked. If these customers are established market leaders intent on sustaining the status quo, there is a danger that the HDD manufacturer may be locked into a trap of obsolete architectural designs. If however the HDD company succeeds in broadening its customer base to include computer companies that are content to develop new markets and applications, there are much stronger incentives to proceed with architectural paradigm shifts. A passive subordination to customer needs can be a trap: market leaders in the HDD industry often listened too attentively to their established customers and ignored new product architectures whose initial appeal was in seemingly marginal markets.

This dilemma implies that a firm's competitive position depends as much on the nature of demand as on the constraints resulting from available technologies (Christensen 1997). An exclusive focus on the development of key components may not be sufficient. Nor for that matter does a strength in architectural design alone guarantee competitive success. Both need to be combined with a capacity to identify and develop new markets for new applications. Take the example of IBM's storage division, the creator of the HDD industry. Although it was the first to develop most of the key components and although it was unrivalled in its accumulated capacity for architectural design, IBM was arguably the last firm in the industry to incorporate leading-edge components across the spectrum of its product line. Reflecting its high level of its organizational costs, IBM was eager to reap premium prices: it thus normally used sophisticated componentry only in high-end drives. This practice opened the door for new entrants like Seagate and others that were able to start with much lower organizational costs and hence could afford to develop new markets for smaller-size disk drives for desktop computers that generated much lower unit profits, but quickly grew into huge mass markets.

Strong product and market development capabilities thus are of critical importance for sustaining industrial leadership positions. The conclusion that matters for our purposes is that no HDD company can afford to neglect the possibility of trajectory-disrupting innovations. This fact of life obviously adds quite substantially to the complexity of the competitive challenges in this industry, broadening the scope for market volatility.

5 Key questions for ongoing research

This brief review of research on how competitive dynamics reshapes industrial organization in the electronics industry clearly indicates that we can no longer take for granted some of the earlier credos of competition theory. We need to take a fresh look at the determinants of market structure and firm behaviour. We need an analysis that takes into account the possibility of unexpected and radical transformation that is due to the extremely rapid change in technology and markets: 'The fact that we cannot, in the nature of things, predict changes that will radically transform the industry's landscape should not lead us to doubt that changes will come about; only ignorance of history, and poverty of imagination, would lead us to that conclusion' (Richardson 1997: 9).

Due to the rapid pace of change in ICT, radical transformations occur quite frequently in the electronics industry. The following quote from the director of the Rank Xerox Cambridge Laboratory illustrates the challenge:

> Both the pace and the acceleration of innovation are startling; nay terrifying. ... No-one can predict the ... range of skills which will need to be amassed to create and take advantage of the next revolution but one (and thinking about the next but one is what everyone is doing. The game is already over for the next).
> (Anderson 1997: 5)

This hectic pace of change arguably is the most important economic characteristic of the electronics industry.

First-mover advantages thus matter less, and leaders in a particular market are under constant threat of displacement:

[W]here the scope for innovation is particularly high, a fresh approach may often prove successful and past success and experience can trammel as well as support. Only myopia can lead one to believe that a commanding position is unassailably and continuously secure. ... The established firm, however mighty it may seem, can be brought down, or at least for a time eclipsed, by complacency, by arrogance, or simply by the fact that market opportunities or technical possibilities change in a way that favours others with different mind-sets, more relevant experience, more appropriate market connections, or simply greater luck.

(Richardson 1997: 7)

We still know very little about this important topic. Attempts to move a bit further ahead into this uncharted territory need to address, both theoretically and empirically, a number of important questions. For instance, to what degree can one generalize the above findings, i.e. how does the electronics industry differ from other knowledge-intensive manufacturing and service industries? Second, what conclusions can one draw from this analysis for the impact of globalization on market structure and competition in the great bulk of industries that are less knowledge-intensive and hence less prone to sunk costs, and that are also less time-sensitive and prone to disruptive changes in demand?

Third, to what degree have recent developments in ICT, and especially the Internet, further increased the already high knowledge-intensity and exposure to globalization, hence posing new competitive challenges for the electronics industry? Fourth, what changes have occurred in the locus of economies of scale and scope? And how has the increasing cost and risk of technology development affected entry barriers? Fifth, under what conditions can GPNs in these industries enhance the diffusion of knowledge *across* firm boundaries and national borders, and hence create new entry possibilities for smaller firms and economies? Sixth, how valid are claims that the electronics industry, and especially its incarnation in the USA, has given rise to a New Economy growth model that allows for higher rates of non-inflationary growth? What are its opportunity and welfare costs, and its impacts on a society's long-term innovation potential? What explains the global recession of the electronics industry since late 2000? And, finally, what are the normative implications for government policies and firm strategies that would facilitate attempts to increase market contestability?

In the final analysis, what really matters is the dynamics of change. We need an analysis that explicitly distinguishes different periods in the development of an industry. Such an evolutionary theory of industrial dynamics will show that the relationships between market structure, conduct and performance undergo considerable changes over time. The result is that, for each of these periods, different sets of strategies and policies are required in order to foster competitive success.

DIETER ERNST
EAST-WEST CENTER
HONOLULU, HAWAII
CENTRE FOR TECHNOLOGY & INNOVATION
(TIK)
UNIVERSITY OF OSLO

Further reading

(References cited in the text marked *)

* Afuah, A.N. (1997) 'Responding to structural industrial changes: a technological evolution perspective', *Industrial and Corporate Change* 6 (1): 183–202. (Explores how industry boundaries are changing in response to technological change.)
* Anderson, B., (1997) 'R&D knowledge creation as a bazaar economy', paper presented at workshop on Competition and Innovation in the Information Society, OECD, Paris, 19 March. (The director of the Rank Xerox Cambridge Laboratory identifies necessary changes in inter- and intra-firm knowledge management, in response to accelerated pace of innovation)
* Antonelli, C. (1998) *The Microdynamics of Technological Change*, London: Routledge. (Provides robust analytical framework for the new economics of knowledge creation, in response to the spread of information and communications technology.)
* Arrow, K.J. (1962) 'The economic implications of learning by doing', *Review of Economic Studies* June. (Classical micro-economic treatment of

externalities in innovation: analysis of the public good nature of technological knowledge is based on the assumption that knowledge and information coincide.)
* Bain, J.S. (1958) *Industrial Organization*, New York: John Wiley & Sons Inc. (Classical source on structure–conduct–performance (SCP) paradigm. Argues that high levels of sellers' concentration, protected by high entry barriers, will induce firms to engage in price collusion, which inevitably will constrain static efficiency allocation as well as learning.)
* Bartlett, C.A. and Ghoshal, S. (1989) *Managing Across Borders: The Transnational Solution*, London: Century Business. (A book that shaped generations of management debates. Argues that the transition to transnational production networks increases convergence among firm strategies toward less hierarchical forms of industrial organization.)
* Baumol, W.J., Panzer, J.C. and Willig, R.D. (1982) *Contestable Markets and the Theory of Industrial Structure*, New York: Harcourt Brace Jovanovich. (Standard text on 'contestable markets'.)
* Blair, J.M. (1972) *Economic Concentration*, New York: Harcourt Brace Jovanovich. (Provides taxonomy for assessing the stability of oligopolies.)
* Borrus, M. (1989) *Competing for Control. America's Stake in Microelectronics*, Cambridge, MA: Ballinger. (Argues that the defeat of the US semiconductor industry in computer memories is due to excessive internationalization and fragmented market structure.)
* Borrus, M. (2000) 'The resurgence of U.S. electronics: Asian production networks and the rise of Wintelism', in M. Borrus, D. Ernst and S. Haggard (eds) *International Production Networks in Asia: Rivalry or Riches?*, London: Routledge, pp. 57–79. (Argues that the resurgence of the US electronics industry is due to heavy reliance on global sourcing and the control of architectural standards by Microsoft and Intel.)
* Borrus, M., Ernst, D. and Haggard, S. (eds) (2000) *International Production Networks in Asia: Rivalry or Riches?*, London: Routledge. (Provides systematic theoretical and case study analysis of the spread of global production networks in Asia's electronics industry and their impact on competitive dynamics.)
  Bresnahan, T.F. (1999) 'New modes of competition: implications for the future structure of the computer industry', in J.A. Eisenach and T.M. Lenard (eds) *Competition, Innovation and the Microsoft Monopoly: Antitrust in the Digital Market Place*, Boston, MA: Kluwer Academic Publishers. (Argues that incumbents are vastly superior to newcomers due to network effects and accumulated capabilities; does not address the impact of the Internet.)
* Bresnahan, T.F. and Malerba, F. (1999) 'Industrial dynamics and the evolution of firms' and nations' competitive capabilities in the world computer industry', in D.C. Mowery and R.R. Nelson (eds) *Sources of Industrial Leadership. Studies in Seven Industries*, Cambridge: Cambridge University Press, pp. 79–132. (Explores the impact of technological change on competitive dynamics and evolution of the computer industry, without however addressing the impact of the Internet.)
* Castells, M. (1998) *The Information Age*, 3 vols, London: Blackwell. (A broad-brush, but highly influential manifesto of the New American Network Economy that has shaped much of the debate on the New Economy.)
* Caves, R.E. (1982) *Multinational Enterprise and Economic Analysis*, Cambridge: Cambridge University Press. (Thorough analysis of the forces that shape the behaviour of multinational enterprises, based on neo-classical trade theory and micro-economics.)
* Chandler, A.D., Hagstrøm, P. and Sølvell, Ø. (eds) (1998) *The Dynamic Firm. The Role of Technology, Strategy, Organization, and Regions*, Oxford: Oxford University Press. (Collection of innovative theoretical and applied contributions to the debate on how technology shapes location and the organization of firms and industrial districts.)
* Christensen, C.M. (1997) *The Innovator's Dilemma. When New Technologies Cause Great Firms to Fail*, Boston, MA: Harvard Business School Press. (Excellent theoretical and empirical treatment of complex inter-relations between demand, technology and firm behaviour. The concept of 'disruptive technologies' helps to explain why concentration may co-exist with high market volatility.)
* David, P. and Foray, D. (1995) 'Accessing and expanding the science and technology knowledge-base', *STI Review*, 16, OECD, Paris. (Argues that IT enhances both the incentives and the possibilities to codify knowledge, which facilitates international knowledge diffusion, but neglects the role of complementary tacit knowledge.)
* Ernst, D. (1983) *The Global Race in Microelectronics*, with a foreword by David Noble, Frankfurt and New York: MIT, Campus Publishers. (Analyses the drivers and impacts of early rounds of globalization in the semiconductor industry.)

* Ernst, D. (1994) *What are the Limits to the Korean Model? The Korean Electronics Industry Under Pressure*, a BRIE Research Monograph, Berkeley Roundtable on the International Economy, University of California at Berkeley. (Empirical and theoretical analysis of the achievements and limits of Korea's catching-up in the electronics industry.)
* Ernst, D. (1997) 'From partial to systemic globalization. International production networks in the electronics industry', report prepared for the Sloan Foundation project on the Globalization in the Data Storage Industry, *The Data Storage Industry Globalization Project Report 97-02*, Graduate School of International Relations and Pacific Studies, University of California at San Diego. (Combines historical and theoretical analysis of the emergence of global production networks in the electronics industry.)
* Ernst, D. (2000a) 'Inter-organizational knowledge outsourcing. What permits small Taiwanese firms to compete in the computer industry?', *Asia Pacific Journal of Management*, special issue on 'Knowledge Management in Asia', 17 (2) (August). (Explores how outsourcing by network flagships enables Taiwanese computer firms to build their capabilities.)
* Ernst, D. (2000b) 'Placing the networks on the web. Challenges and opportunities for managing in developing Asia', paper presented at the Second Asia Academy of Management Conference 'Managing in Asia: challenges and opportunities in the new millennium', December 15–18, 2000, Shangri-La Hotel, Singapore; forthcoming: *Industry & Innovation*, 2000, 9 (2), special issue on 'Global production networks, information technology and local capabilities'. (Analyses how the internet reshapes business organization and management in Asia's computer industry.)
* Ernst, D. (2000c) 'Moving beyond the commodity trap. Trade adjustment and industrial upgrading in East Asia's electronics industry', World Bank, Washington, DC; forthcoming: R.S. Newfarmer and C. Woods (eds) 'East Asia: from recovery to sustainable development', Discussion Paper Series, Washington, DC, World Bank. (Demonstrates that a narrow specialization on electronic commodities like computer memories produces periodic surplus capacity and price wars. Documents that post-crisis industrial upgrading has remained limited.)
* Ernst, D. (2001a) 'Global production networks and the changing geography of innovation systems. Implications for developing countries', special issue of *Journal of the Economics of Innovation and New Technologies*, on 'Integrating policy perspectives in research on technology and economic growth', ed. Anthony Bartzokas and Morris Teubal. (Analyses how globalization and information technology enhance knowledge exchange without co-location, and spells out policy implications.)
* Ernst, D. (2001b) 'Placing the networks on the Internet – a new divide in industrial organization', paper presented at the international Richard Nelson and Sidney Winter Conference, Aalborg, Denmark, June 12–15, 2001, organized by the Danish Research Unit on Industrial Dynamics (DRUID). (Explores key features of a new divide in industrial organization that results from the application of the Internet, and possible implications for the geography of innovation.)
* Ernst, D. and O'Connor, D. (1992) *Competing in the Electronics Industry. The Experience of Newly Industrialising Economies*, Paris: Development Centre Studies, OECD. (Combines historical and theoretical analysis of competitive dynamics in the electronics industry and its impact on late entry strategies.)
* Ernst, D. and Ravenhill, J. (1999) 'Globalization, convergence, and the transformation of international production networks in electronics in East Asia', *Business & Politics* (University of California at Berkeley.) I (1). (Demonstrates why partial convergence of business organization goes hand in hand with persistent diversity.)
* Ferguson, Charles H. and Morris, Charles R. (1993) *Computer Wars. How the West Can Win in a Post-IBM World*, New York: Times Books. (Tells the story of 'IBM's self-immolation', and argues that reintegrating innovation and manufacturing within global corporations, combined with aggressive technology policies, can re-establish US leadership in computers.)
* Fine, C. (1998) *Clockspeed: Winning Industry Control in the Age of Temporary Advantage*, Reading, MA: Perseus Books. (Documents the growing importance of time management in global and knowledge-intensive industries.)
Flamm, Kenneth (1988) *Creating the Computer. Government, Industry and High Technology*, Washington, DC: The Brookings Institution. (Classic study on the sources of US leadership in the computer industry, with a focus on the impact of innovation on competitive dynamics.)
Flamm, Kenneth (1999) 'Digital convergence? The set-top box and the network computer', in J.A. Eisenach and T.M. Lenard (eds) *Competition, Innovation and the Microsoft Monopoly: Antitrust in the Digital Market Place*, Boston,

MA: Kluwer Academic Publishers. (Provides evidence that telecommunications costs are finally beginning to decline at rates that resemble those found for semiconductors and computers, and explores the implications for competitive dynamics.)

* Florida, R. and Sturgeon, T. (1999) 'Final report to Sloan Foundation', manuscript, Cambridge, MA, MIT. (Argues that a new 'American Model of Manufacturing' based on global outsourcing is now being extended beyond electronics to the automobile industry.)

* Gilder, G. (1988) 'The revitalization of everything: the law of the microcosm', *Harvard Business Review* March–April. (Early proponent of the 'New Economy Doctrine': argues that the PC industry is immune to concentration, due to the rapid pace of innovation.)

* Grove, A.S. (1996) *Only the Paranoid Survive. How to Exploit the Crisis Points that Challenge Every Company and Career*, New York and London: Harper Collins Business. (The former Chairman & CEO of Intel provides a vivid account of how unexpected changes in markets and technology, combined with a drastic reduction in product life-cycles, constantly challenges leadership positions.)

Henderson, R. and Clark, K. (1990) 'Architectural innovation: the reconfiguration of existing technologies and the failure of established firms', *Administrative Sciences Quarterly*: 9–30. (Argues that sharp shifts in markets and technology are competence-destroying in their effects on incumbent firms and result in the displacement of market leaders.)

* Hobday, M. (1995) *Innovation in East Asia: The Challenge to Japan*, Aldershot: Edward Elgar. (Provides a sequential stages model of technology mastery for Asia's electronics industry that neglects the diversity of approaches and their non-linear evolutionary character.)

* Kenney, M. (ed.) (2000) *Anatomy of Silicon Valley: Understanding an Entrepreneurial Region*, Stanford, CA: Stanford University Press. (A collection of articles that argues that Silicon Valley represents the essence of America's New Entrepreneurial Economy.)

* Kobrin, S.J. (1997) 'The architecture of globalization: state sovereignty in a networked global economy', in J.H. Dunning (ed.) *Governments, Globalization and International Business*, Oxford: Oxford University Press. (Argues that scale economies in R&D act as the main driver of globalization in knowledge-intensive industries.)

* Kogut, B. and Zander, U. (1993) 'Knowledge of the firm and the evolutionary theory of the multinational corporation', *Journal of International Business Studies* 24 (4). (Argues that a firm's capacity to build specialized capabilities quicker and at less cost than its competitors is of critical importance for competitive success.)

* Langlois, R.N. (1992) 'External economies and economic progress: the case of the microcomputer industry', *Business History Review*, 66 (Spring): 1–50. (Argues that US leadership in the PC industry is due to the outsourcing of 'external capabilities' that reside within a network of interacting firms.)

* Langlois, R.N. and Steinmueller, W.E. (1999) 'The evolution of competitive advantage in the worldwide semiconductor industry, 1947–1996', in D.C. Mowery and R.R. Nelson (eds) *Sources of Industrial Leadership. Studies in Seven Industries*, Cambridge: Cambridge University Press, pp. 79–132. (Argues that the main sources of US leadership in the semiconductor industry are a rapid diffusion of basic technologies and peculiar features of its competitive dynamics and industrial organization.)

* Lazonick, W. (1991) *Business Organization and the Myth of the Market Economy*, Cambridge: Cambridge University Press. (By combining a historical and theoretical analysis of changes in industrial leadership positions, the book highlights the failure of economic analysis to come to grips with divergent organizational structures of business enterprises.)

Lipsey, R.G. 'Understanding technological change', East–West Center Working Papers, economics series, 13 (February). (An important alternative approach to the study of technology, markets and economic growth. Demonstrates the limits of neo-classical models that equate technological change with productivity growth.)

* Mathews, J. and Dong-Sung Cho (2000) *Tiger Technology: The Creation of the Semiconductor Industry in East Asia*, Cambridge: Cambridge University Press. (Traces the catching-up of East Asia in the semiconductor industry, based on processes of organizational learning.)

* Naughton, J. (2000) *A Brief History of the Future. The Origins of the Internet*, Weidenfeld & Nicolson: London. (Excellent history of the forces that have shaped the development of the Internet, and its impact on cross-border knowledge sharing, creation and utilization.)

* OECD (2000) *A New Economy? The Changing Role of Innovation and Information Technology in Growth*, Paris: OECD. (Concise overview of the role of innovation and information technology in economic growth.)

* Pugh, Emerson W. (1984) *Memories that Shaped an Industry. Decision Leading to IBM System/360*, Cambridge, MA: MIT Press. (An insider's account of how IBM established its leadership position in mainframe computers.)
* Reed Electronics Research (1998) *Yearbook of World Electronics Data*, vol. 2, *America, Japan & Asia Pacific*, Sutton, Surrey: Reed. (Standard source for trade and production data.)
* Richardson, G.B. (1996) 'Competition, innovation and increasing returns', DRUID Working Paper no. 96-10, July. (A masterful plea to place new product development and innovation at the centre of competition theory.)
* Richardson, G.B. (1997) 'Economic analysis, public policy and the software industry', DRUID Working Paper no. 96-4, April. (Explores why first-mover advantages matter less in the software industry.)
* Rugman, A.M. and D'Cruz, J.R. (2000) *Multinationals as Flagship Firms. Regional Business Networks*, Oxford and New York: Oxford University Press. (Emphasizes the hierarchical nature of networks. The focus is on localized networks within a region that include 'non-business infrastructure' as 'network partners'. The authors assume that a combination of TC and resource-based theory is sufficient to explain such forms of business organization.)
* Sutton, J. (1991) *Sunk Costs and Market Structure*, Cambridge, MA: MIT Press. (A methodologically brilliant treatment of sunk costs theory that however neglects the issue of innovation.)
* Teece, D. (1986) 'Profiting from technological innovation', *Research Policy* 15/6: 285–306. (Pioneering analysis of the systemic nature of innovation.)
* Tilton, J.E. (1971) *International Diffusion of Technology: The Case of Semiconductors*, Washington, DC: The Brookings Institution. (Essential reading for anyone interested in the historical sources of US leadership in the electronics industry. Many of its conclusions are still valid after almost 30 years!)

See also: COOPERATION AND COMPETITION; CORPORATE CONTROL; DEVELOPMENT AND DIFFUSION OF TECHNOLOGY; DYNAMIC CAPABILITIES; EAST ASIAN ECONOMIES; ECONOMIC GROWTH AND CONVERGENCE; ECONOMIC INTEGRATION, INTERNATIONAL; ECONOMY OF JAPAN; ELECTRONICS INDUSTRY; EVOLUTIONARY THEORIES OF THE FIRM; GLOBALIZATION; GROWTH OF THE FIRM AND NETWORKING; GROWTH THEORY; INDUSTRIAL DYNAMICS; MULTINATIONAL CORPORATIONS; SMALL AND MEDIUM SIZED ENTERPRISES; TELECOMMUNICATIONS INDUSTRY

Automobile industry

1 From craft production to mass production and lean production
2 Industry structure dynamics
3 Future projections

Overview

Peter Drucker christened the automobile industry 'the industry of industries' in 1946, and there are good enduring reasons for this label. In short, it has been at the forefront of thinking about how things are made and how we work.

Automobile manufacturing is the world's largest manufacturing activity, with just over 50 million new vehicles produced each year. One in every seven people is employed through the industry, either directly or indirectly. The indirect part is due to the need for a retail distribution network and the generation of demand for intermediate inputs (in the form of components and raw materials like steel and rubber). Governments have therefore looked to the industry as a major opportunity for national economic development, international trade and foreign direct investment.

The automobile is also the second largest expenditure item for households after housing. Many own a car, visit dealers, and are aware of the variety that exists in car models and options that reflect consumer preferences and lifestyles. The technological advances associated with the automobile transformed our idea about mobility, and will continue to do so with the advent of telematics and the Internet.

Throughout the twentieth century, the automobile industry has also been a significant source of innovative management thinking, transforming ideas about how best to make things. In the 1910s, Ford Motor Company's moving assembly line and standardized work replaced craft production. In the 1970s, Taiichi Ohno's Toyota Production System, and later, lean production techniques, were important managerial innovations with significance well beyond the automobile sector.

This article will start by tracking the fundamental changes in manufacturing methods that enabled the automobile industry to become a massive generator of economic wealth. It will then provide explanations of changes in industry structure over time. Lastly, the future shape of the industry will be discussed with reference to telematics, e-business and other technological developments.

1 From craft production to mass production and lean production

In the 1890s, in the USA and Europe, 'horseless carriages', as automobiles were better known then, were made one by one by craftsmen in metal and machine tool industries. Wealthy customers, employing chauffeurs and mechanics, placed orders to build a car to suit their precise desires. For them, customization was more important than economical cost or ease of maintenance. And this was no problem because each part was made one at a time, and craftsmen, who thoroughly understood mechanical design principles and the materials with which they worked, filed parts together until they fitted perfectly. Consequently, no two cars were, or needed to be, identical. The use of highly skilled workers and general-purpose machine tools resulted in a very low production volume. It is interesting to note that, particularly in England, a small number of craft-based firms have survived into the twenty-first century to serve small market niches populated with buyers willing to pay a lot and wait a long time for the privilege of dealing directly with the factory to order their unique vehicles.

Craft-based production was largely superseded by mass production techniques in the first two decades of the twentieth century. A popular image of mass production is Ford's Model T rolling out of a moving assembly line. In contrast to craft production, mass production was characterized by (1) complete inter-changeability of standardized parts and the simplicity of attaching them to each other; (2) a standardized product design that can be produced in large batches to achieve economies of scale, coupled with large buffers of inventory stock to prevent any interruptions in production; and (3) a centralized hierarchy that controls and coordinates specialized and narrowly defined tasks. Consequently, a Ford assembler's average task cycle – the amount of time he worked before repeating the same operations – declined from 514 minutes (i.e. 8.56 hours) in 1908 to 1.19 minutes with the introduction of the moving assembly line at the Highland Park plant in 1913. A reduction in human effort to build cars was associated with the reduction of skilled craftsmen and an increase in semi-skilled and unskilled assembly operators.

The enormous growth in labour productivity that was enabled by mass production led to a world car industry dominated by American producers. In the heyday of mass production in 1955, the Big Three (Ford, General Motors and Chrysler) accounted for 95 per cent of all American car sales, and North American production accounted for three-quarters of world motor vehicle production. But thereafter, the American market share declined, first with imports of European cars, then of Japanese and Korean cars, to the extent that by 1999, North American produced units were only 30 per cent of the global production level. In 1999, 56.3 million cars were produced, of which 17.6m were in North America, 16.5m in Europe and 16.6m in Asia-Pacific (Japanese producers accounting for 8m within the Asia-Pacific region).

The European car industry was more fragmented than that of the USA. Mass production principles were avidly studied by certain European manufacturers before the Second World War. But it was not until the 1950s that a return to civilian production enabled plants at Wolfsburg (Volkswagen), Flins (Renault) and Mirafiori (Fiat) to manufacture at a scale comparable to Detroit's major facilities. However, European manufacturers' competitive strength was never in production efficiency but lay in product differentiation and technical innovation. In particular, they made compact cars (e.g. VW Beetle), fun-to-drive sporty cars (e.g. MG), and later redefined the luxury car as a smaller vehicle with new technology. They introduced new product features such as front-wheel drive, fuel injection, unitized bodies and five-speed transmissions. The success of this product strategy is reflected in the European share in world car production being on a par with, or greater than, the US share during much of the 1960s and early 1970s.

The quadrupling of oil prices in 1973, and subsequent price increases in 1979, swung American consumers' demand away from the gas-guzzling American vehicles to energy-efficient import cars, especially from Japan. Competition from overseas led to a contraction of the US auto industry, and the workforce employed in vehicle assembly by the Big Three contracted. In the 1980s, Japanese manufacturers overcame the yen appreciation and the voluntary export restraints by setting up assembly plants – known as 'transplants' – within North America, and by designing bigger luxury cars. By 1999, imported car sales and sales from Japanese transplants in North America put together accounted for 40 per cent of total North American sales.

The visible 'flooding' of US and European markets by Japanese imports led to different interpretations of Japanese success. Smaller car sizes, cheap labour and a meticulous application of the American mass production principles were offered by some as explanations of their low costs. But more important than any of these factors was that Japanese manufacturers, and in particular Toyota, applied quite different principles of making things from mass production principles. The Toyota Production System, developed by Taiichi Ohno in the 1960s and 1970s, and lean production that was discovered in the 1980s, inverted some of the dimensions of mass production. In particular, standardized product design, interchangeability of parts and the moving assembly line were common features. But lean production relied on (1) more general resources (e.g. multi-skilled workers and general-purpose machines) for flexible production; (2) small buffers and lot sizes to facilitate a market strategy of responding quickly to demand fluctuations with a greater variety of product designs, and (3) more decentralized authority with greater lateral communication across functional boundaries, team work and operators' participation in quality circles and continuous improvement activities. The 'pull' system, rather than the 'push' system under mass production, led to greater production efficiency and quality improvements.

In 1989, according to an influential benchmarking study by the International Motor Vehicle Program (IMVP), North American and European assembly plants were found to be taking on average 50 per cent and 100 per cent longer respectively to assemble a car than their Japanese counterparts. Quality was also found to be considerably worse for American and European plants than in Japanese plants (Womack et al. 1990). The same study, repeated in 1993, shows a narrowing of performance gaps between plants in different regions, indicating the diffusion of lean production techniques throughout the world.

The superior efficiency of lean production over mass production is also reflected in product development performance. Clark and Fujimoto (1991) studied 29 product development projects during 1983–87 from auto manufacturers in Japan, the USA and Europe, and found that Japanese producers took 47 months worth of engineering time to design a new vehicle, compared with 60 months in the USA and Europe. A major reason for this difference lay in over-lapping product development phases and the effective use of suppliers as part of the development team.

To summarize, the world automobile industry faced at least two distinct transformations in the twentieth century, first from craft production to mass production originating in the USA, and second from mass production to lean production originating in Japan. These transformations have had an enormous impact on production efficiency and work organization. Benchmarking and learning between plants have led to similar production principles being adopted in different parts of the world. But the studies by an international research group, GERPISA, show that instead of a universal 'best practice', automotive companies continue to follow their own forms of work organization and production system that are shaped by different national environments and business histories.

2 Industry structure dynamics

In traditional economic analysis, economies of scale and barriers to entry explain industry structure. In the automobile industry, horizontal and vertical integration and de-integration may be explained by these factors, transaction cost economics and technology shifts.

In the 1890s approximately a hundred 'coach makers' emerged in the Detroit area of the USA, each involved in some aspect of manufacturing 'horseless carriages'. But by the middle of the twentieth century this horizontally fractured industry was consolidated into a few massive, vertically integrated corporations such as Ford and General Motors. To some extent, horizontal integration may be explained by the economies of scale introduced by mass production. But as White (1971) points out, the minimum efficient scale of an assembly plant was estimated to be 100,000–400,000 units per annum, and would have allowed theoretically for seven more independent manufacturers besides the Big Three in the 1960s USA. The high barriers to entry – especially large economies of scale in stamping, strong product differentiation and high capital requirements for new models – have prevented new entrants into the US industry. Oligopoly avoided price competition and relied on price leadership by General Motors.

Explanations of vertical integration were initially straightforward. The 1920s were a time for consolidating the assembly line techniques that had been developed by Ford a decade earlier. The Rouge complex in Detroit that opened in 1931 represented an extreme case of vertical integration with its own steel mill and forging factory. At this time, vertical integration took place mainly because Ford perfected mass production techniques before his suppliers had and could achieve substantial cost savings by doing everything himself. Also purchases in the open marketplace would not deliver the needed parts with close tolerances and regular delivery schedule.

Subsequent analysis using transaction cost economics focuses on the non-production cost advantage of vertical integration. In this framework, the integration of Fisher Body by General Motors is often cited as an example of automobile manufacturers' wish to pre-empt being 'held up' by opportunistic suppliers when the latter use tools and dies specific to a customer company (see TRANSACTION COST ECONOMICS). But a re-examination of primary historical sources suggests that the transaction cost focus on opportunism as a given predisposition is mistaken, and that more importantly the acquisition of independent proprietors, such as the Fisher Brothers, opened up careers for them within larger organizations. Vertical integration occurred, in this perspective, as part of a managerial revolution.

As an alternative to vertical integration, intermediate forms of organization, such as long-term supplier relationships based on trust, give the best of both market flexibility and organizational control. In Japan, 'relational contracting' between assemblers and suppliers is considered an essential complement to lean production, accounting for just-in-time delivery, low inter-firm buffer stocks, short product development lead-time, and joint problem solving for cost reduction and quality improvements.

In the 1980s, the global automobile industry has started to move back towards vertical disintegration. In the USA, Chrysler, the smallest of the Big Three, set an example by committing to long-term relationships for developing entire subsystems and to share the benefits of any cost-saving ideas with suppliers. Chrysler focused on designing, assembling and marketing vehicles while relying heavily on suppliers for component and technology development. By the late 1980s, the company emerged out of near bankruptcy to achieve the lowest cost structure and the highest average profit per vehicle amongst the Big Three. Ford and General Motors proceeded to compete by selling off their component divisions, Visteon and Delphi respectively. This vertical disintegration trend may be in part explained by an attempt to reverse the bureaucratic and organizational rigidities that possessed large established companies. But a technological factor is just as significant: the challenge of keeping ahead of competition across multiple technologies for the entire car has led major automobile manufacturers to focus on their core business, that is assembly, and to withdraw from component design and manufacturing.

But just as IBM lost its market power to Microsoft and Intel, the disintegration strategy of automobile manufacturers gives rise to potentially powerful independent suppliers of systems and modules, that in turn might lead manufacturers to vertically integrate at some future date. For the foreseeable future, however, large manufacturers of dashboards are forming alliances with electronics suppliers to become cockpit module suppliers. Similarly, large seat suppliers are acquiring smaller suppliers to increase their global presence, and to grow into interiors companies. There is talk of some interior suppliers taking one step further to assemble entire cars. If the outsourcing of entire automobile assembly happens not only for specialty cars but for mainline passenger cars, automobile manufacturers may find themselves withdrawing from assembly and focusing on design and marketing.

Globalization (in the sense of access to global markets) and excess capacity in the industry have led to a rapid horizontal concentration of automobile manufacturers. Many of the alliances are international. For instance, DaimlerChrysler, a German–US merger, with a link-up with Mitsubishi, cover the three continents. Ford's purchase of Jaguar, Volvo and Mazda, and Renault's equity stake in Nissan and Samsung, may be regarded in the same light.

To summarize, the global automobile industry consists of a handful of major international blocs of manufacturers. Suppliers are becoming increasingly concentrated with highly oligopolistic structures in the global markets for key parts such as seats. Globalization of markets and component sourcing has led to greater consolidation of both assembler and supplier segments of the industry.

3 Future projections

On one level, the global automobile industry may be characterized as mature, suffering from over-capacity and slow growth (see GLOBALIZATION). But it is also an industry with much future potential as the definition of the scope of the industry changes. The main forces behind the next stage of evolution of the automobile industry are the Internet, telematics and other technological developments.

The Internet is an enabler of a number of potentially fundamental changes in the way the automobile is designed, produced and sold. First, the Internet will enable consumers to configure the precise vehicle they want online, and receive delivery of such a 'built to order' car, just as in the case of Dell computers. Second, 'built-to-order' may promote the mixing and matching of physically independent 'modules' joined along a common interface in order to effect customization. Thus the product architecture of the automobile may shift from being integral to more modular. Third, a true 'build-to-order' production system differs from either mass production or lean production in introducing a high level of volatility in production scheduling that would require even more flexible working arrangements. Fourth, if automobile manufacturers outsource the production of modules, powerful suppliers would become the engine of new technological development for the automobile industry. In the extreme, the brand holders would emerge as 'consumer services' companies with little in-house final assembly that had been considered essential to a company's identity as an automobile manufacturer. Last, the Big Three are the first movers among major companies in announcing a full-scale business-to-business, industry-wide electronic market for components. This practice will certainly transform procurement practices and supplier relations, although it is unclear whether it will be used primarily for auctions to squeeze supplier margins or for information sharing to promote loyal business relationships.

Telematics is largely about bringing information technologies inside the vehicle. Specifically, in-car services range from personal communication (phone/fax, e-mail), convenience (travel and restaurant reservations, interactive shopping), safety (sensors to insure safe distances between cars), security (stolen vehicle tracking) to navigation (GPS locators with directions to destination). When the information-intensive vehicle is linked to a 'smart highway' or Intelligent Transportation System (ITS), even more services become possible, such as toll collection to congestion avoidance. Cars then become networked, that raises the question of whether and how the operating system of an online car will develop an industry standard. Other major technological changes on the horizon include alternative fuels to gasoline, such as fuel cells and electric cars; and new body materials such as aluminium and polymer composites that could be moulded in colours to eliminate painting. Any one of these developments has the potential to fundamentally alter the industry structure and the scope of what we continue to call 'the industry of industries'.

MARI SAKO
SAID BUSINESS SCHOOL, OXFORD UNIVERSITY

Further reading

(References cited in the text marked *)

Abernathy, W. (1978) *The Productivity Dilemma: Roadblock to Innovation in the Automobile Industry*, Baltimore: Johns Hopkins University Press. (A technological history of the automobile industry.)

Altshuler, A. et al. (1984) *The Future of the Automobile*, Cambridge, MA: MIT Press. (The first book of the research of the International Motor Vehicle Programme.)

Automotive News (2000) *Market Data Book*, May (www.automotivenews.com). (A useful source of data and news on the global auto industry with a US focus.)

Boyer, R., Charron, E., Jürgens, U. and Tolliday, S. (eds) (1998) *Between Imitation and Innovation: the Transfer and Hybridization of Productive Models in the International Automobile Industry*, Oxford: Oxford University Press. (A study by GERPISA researchers of the transfer and adaptation of productive models in the global automotive industry, resulting in 'hybridization', a complex interaction of productive models and national and societal effects.)

* Clark, K. And Fujimoto, T. (1991) *Product Development Performance: Strategy, Organization, and Management in the World Auto Industry*, Boston: Harvard Business School Press. (A systematic comparison of product development project organization and performance at US, European and Japanese car manufacturers.)

Cusumano, M. (1985) *The Japanese Automobile Industry*, Cambridge MA: Harvard University

Press. (A historical account of the development of the Japanese car industry from 1945, with a focus on Toyota and Nissan.)

Freyssenet, M., Mair, A., Shimizu, K. and Volpato, G. (eds) (1998) *One Best Way?* Oxford: Oxford University Press. (A study by GERPISA researchers of the evolution of 15 major Asian, North American and European car companies in terms of their technological, organizational, commercial and social 'trajectories', rejecting the notion of a universal one best way.)

Kochan, T.A., Lansbury, R.D. and MacDuffie, J.P. (1997) *After Lean Production: Evolving Employment Practices in the World Auto Industry*, Ithaca: Cornell University Press. (A compilation of how employment practices and industrial relations have been affected by the diffusion of lean production in 12 countries.)

Laux, J. (1992) *The European Automobile Industry*, Twayne. (A historical account of the origins and evolution of the car industry in Europe.)

Maxcy, G. and Silberston, A. (1959) *The Motor Industry*, Allen & Unwin. (An economic analysis of the British motor industry, focusing on the structure of costs and its implications for competition.)

Ohno, T. (1988) *Toyota Production System*, Cambridge MA: Productivity Press. (A description of the origins and the essence of the Toyota Production System by the pioneer and guru of the system.)

Rhys, D.G. (1972) *The Motor Industry: An Economic Survey*, Butterworths. (An economic analysis of the structure of demand and supply in the motor industry. Empirical evidence focuses on Britain with some international comparisons.)

Shiomi, H. and Wada, K. (eds) *Fordism Transformed: The Development of Production Methods in the Automobile Industry*, Oxford: Oxford University Press. (A collection of papers at a Fuji Business History conference on the application of Fordist production methods at various times in different parts of the world.)

* White, L.J. (1971) *The Automobile Industry since 1945*, Cambridge, MA: Harvard University Press. (An analysis of the US automobile industry, dated but useful for the application of economic theories to arrive at public policy prescriptions.)

* Womack, J.P., Jones, D.T. and Roos, D. (1990) *The Machine that Changed the World*, New York: Rawson Associates. (A best seller of the International Motor Vehicle Programme that first elaborated the Lean Production paradigm and benchmarked assembly plant performance across the world.)

See also: DYNAMIC CAPABILITIES; GLOBAL MACHINE TOOLS INDUSTRY; GLOBALIZATION; GROWTH OF THE FIRM AND NETWORKING

Service economy

1 A new service economy?
2 Some prospects for the service economy
3 Service economy redefined

Overview

The claim that contemporary society, in whatever period, is the genesis of a new society, a new economy, is so common that it almost appears to be a basic human attitude to coming to terms with social and economic development. The 1980s, cursed by the spectre of 'deindustrialization', bore sunrise industries in its womb, the 1970s straddled concerns for a humanizing, socially prioritizing society and incipient dehumanizing financial internationalization. We still remember the 'information society', the 'post-modern society', as well as the 'knowledge societies'. The argument of the dawn of a millennial New Economy is a member of a large family.

The ubiquity of such claims is a topic that is worthy of study in its own right. However, that is not our present purpose. Rather, this entry concerns the precursor and fountainhead of most of the labels used over the last five decades. First we will describe some broad aspects of recent development of the major advanced economies. This serves as a basis for outlining some issues related to the emergence of a service economy. The entry gives a brief annotated bibliography of selected works related to the proposal and further analysis and elaborations of the service economy thesis.

During the 1950s and 1960s the service economy – or society – thesis became the focus of a range of socio-economic studies and was widely held as a good epithet for the budding modern society. In a simple version the service economy thesis stated that contemporary industrial society – a society that developed during the nineteenth century in Europe and the US and replaced the previous agriculture based society – was on to be transformed. The industrial society had seen ever increasing levels of welfare and social organization, and would continue to do so for years ahead.

But this process also implied the demise of this industrial economy. We were on the brink of a new era – the era of the service society – with the service economy a direct and rightful descendant of the industrial economy. The service society – with all its positive affinities – was originally a modern idea of society. However, it soon became evident that the emergence of a service society could also imply an economy where the rapid welfare growth of the industrial society would come to a halt – the service society would seem to be a stagnant society. The subsequent transformations and elaborations of the service economy thesis may be seen as a reflection of a search for a new holy grail of economic growth in the place of the traditional engine of economic growth – manufacturing production.

Variant theses on the future of advanced economies may seem naïve and outmoded when viewed from a future vantage point. However, with their role in shaping contemporary policy and business responses, and in elucidating our understanding of ongoing change patterns, they are important. A core question then is whether these theses sufficiently incorporates our understanding of the underlying processes they purport to describe. At the core of these theses is the important insight that economic growth is a process that is intimately linked with structural change, and economic development is a process of incessant structural change. Whether we will be able to have informed anticipations of the long term challenges to business and social development, depends crucially on our ability to integrate available scientific and analytical insight of the core characteristics of this development.

1 A new service economy?

Soon after 1945 the claim was made that employment and production was shifting away from primary and secondary production, to an ever increasing dominance of *tertiary* production. A large and increasing share of employment was in service – or tertiary – sectors. This was first noted in the US, but data showed that the major European economies followed quickly. Over the next decades this raised two issues:

- What were the drivers of this process? Was the manufacturing 'engine of economic growth' carrying its own termination?
- What were the implications of a structural shift into a service economy in terms of welfare growth, structural composition, welfare creation and so on?

In the economic history of the industrialized countries, the industrial revolution stands out as a landmark event. The major European economies, starting from primarily agrarian based economies with related trade systems, had by the end of the nineteenth century turned into highly industrialized economies, with advanced manufacturing production systems. The productivity and income increase the new growth engine provided over two centuries has been exceptional. Agriculture and production of agro-based food stuffs today is hundredfolds its size just a century ago, with a marginal share of overall employment. With the growth and sophistication of manufacturing production, general living standards attained levels beyond the wildest speculations of the most imaginative individuals 150 years ago. The range of economic goods and opportunities available to us as consumers today bears almost no similarity to what was available to our grandparents. Besides its direct economic impact, industrialization and the growth of industrialized economies also had revolutionary and unforeseen repercussions on social organization, as well as on social life in general.

Should we see the transition to a service economy as a similar revolution with far-reaching consequences? Are we, as was Europe *c*. 1800, on the verge of a brave new world? If so, what will the characteristics of this 'new economy' be?

Before we consider this, we will have a brief look at what data records can tell us in gross terms about the shift to a service economy. The observation that guided the first attention given to the service economy thesis was the evolution in the structure of employment during the decades after 1950. Although employment grew in absolute terms in manufacturing as well as service production, the growth rate was larger in service sectors. So in relative terms the service share of employment grew, while primary and secondary sectors seemed to become less important. Though it was never really clear what sectors were 'service' sectors, the general apprehension was of an increasing share of immaterial, at the expense of material, production. This distinction between services goods, defined as immaterial goods, and material goods, is often used as a basis for discussing service economies in spite of its irrelevance as the basis of economic analysis. The British business weekly *The Economist*, famous for its often insightful quips, said 'services are anything you can sell but cannot drop on your foot'.

Nevertheless, something fundamental seemed afoot. An ever increasing share of employment was involved in activities that had a roundabout relation to the core of wealth, or value creation in distribution, in financial services, and in social and other community services. With such an employment indicator the US economy was already a service economy in 1947.

This structural pattern was also reflected in the composition of what was produced. Figure 1 gives the development of the share of services in overall gross product in the largest economies in the OECD-area over the a few decades up to the mid-1990s. Here, the service share is the combined share of trade, HORECA-services, transport and communication, FIRB-services, government, other community, social and personal services in overall GDP, measured in current prices. Since the 1970s generally more than 50 per cent of gross product has originated in what may reasonably be called service sectors. With a service economy defined as one in which more than 50 per cent of national employment or current value added, as measured in national accounts, is in these service sectors, all major OECD economies are today service economies. The US is the dominant service economy, with more than 70 per cent of the US GDP originating in service sectors. Over these decades, Germany has nearly

Service economy

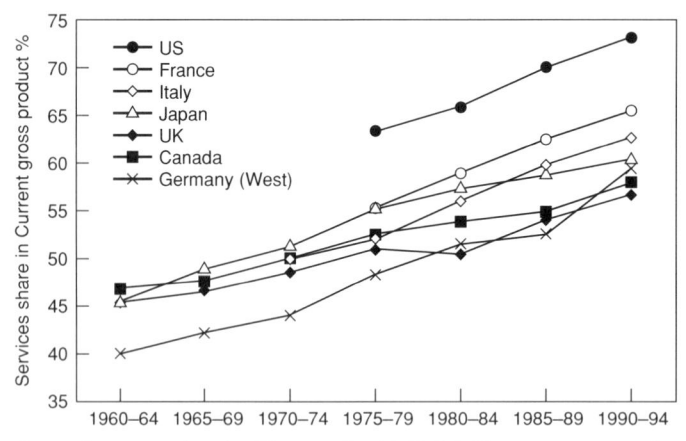

Figure 1 Service share of gross product in G7-countries 1960–94. Five-year averages based on sectoral decomposition of current GDP
Source: OECD National Accounts database.

closed its apparent 'service gap' to other major European economies.

Even during recent periods the service share has increased rapidly. As shown in Table 1, over the two decades 1975–94 the service share of GDP has increased significantly, on average around 10 percentage points or more in the G7-economies. The French economy had a service share of 67 per cent in 1994, more than 12 per cent higher than the service share in 1977. By the mid 1990s the share of GDP in market services excluding governmental services was at least 50 per cent in all but two G7-countries. Indeed, economic activities in service sectors dominate the picture in these countries, a dominance that has been rapidly increasing over several decades.

A similar picture to that sketched above may be obtained using employment instead of value added, or gross product, as structural indicator. Today, roughly two-thirds of employment in the OECD countries is in tertiary sectors. By 1990 aggregate OECD employment in trade, hotels and restaurants was larger than total employment in manufacturing industries. At the same time employment in financial and business services was larger than employment in manufacturing of machinery and metal products, including car and IT industries. The shift is a complex process; the variety of service sectors and their heterogeneity in social, functional and economic characteristics is substantial. The service society is not the usually depicted gloomy society of shoe shiners, hairdressers and hamburger flippers, if a service economy is 'a nation of hamburger stands, it is also […] a nation of management consultants, doctors, software designers, and international bankers' (Guile 1988).

From the start a service economy was conceptualized as an economy with a major share of its employment in service sectors. The rate and generality of this process suggested, however, that there were some generic drivers underlying this process, and that this shift boded for wide-reaching structural and social impacts. The traditional classification of production sectors into primary, secondary and tertiary modes of production suggested that economic and social development went through a series of major stage shifts. Up to the nineteenth century basically agricultural based production systems had dominated, while the development of manufacturing production and related technical change had led welfare and social development over the next 150 years. The service economy was conceived as an economy where tertiary production dominated in a more general sense – it was seen as a servicing economy. The many-faceted character of the process and the wide variety in terms of the service sectors involved suggests that there may be a complex web of drivers underlying this shift.

Table 1 Service share in current GDP G7-countries 1994 (%) (or latest available year). Increase per decade (%) 1975–94 (Or earliest available years)

		Market services	Governmental services	Total services	Increase per decade
Germany (West)	1975–94	48	10	59	5.2
France	1977–94	50	17	67	6.8
Italy	1975–94	51	12	63	5.9
UK	1975–94	50	10	60	4.0
Cananda	1975–92	42	16	58	3.1
US	1977–93	62	12	74	6.2
Japan	1975–94	54	8	61	3.6

Source: OECD National Accounts database

Economic developments over the last decades are seen to support these expectations. In spite of a lacking consensus of the detailed characteristics of the processes, the idea of a transition of the former industrialized countries into complex service- and knowledge-intensive economies is widely accepted today. The new economy of the twenty-first century is a variation of this theme.

2 Some prospects for the service economy

The dominant economic activity in a service economy is thus a wide range of service production, and opportunities for economic growth and further welfare enhancements would be shaped by these sectors. The question then is what, if any, are the commonalties behind these processes and what are possible outcomes of or challenges raised by these? A perusal of the answers given to the former question will be postponed to the next section. The prime purpose of this section is to outline some of the immediate prospects and challenges that the idea of a service economy raises, issues which still forms vibrant research agendas. But first we need to dispel with some of the myths of the service economy.

There is a strong, popular myth that service production is a kind of economic backwater, services are non-exportables, they do not accumulate, they are 'unproductive'. At best the core generator of economic growth in modern economic history, technical change, plays a marginal role in these sectors. The British Chancellor of the Exchequer Nigel Lawson claimed in 1988 that future employment growth, coming from services, implied that 'new jobs will be not so much low-tech, as no-tech'. According to this myth, an economically progressive service economy is a contradiction in terms.

These service myths are without any empirical and analytical foundations. They can be traced back to a two centuries old debate in the economics of that time, where the now obsolete distinction between productive and unproductive labour was made as a tool for analysing wealth accumulation. Through time the myth has survived by completely perverting the basis for the old debate, implying a message that is contrary to the emphasis of the original debate, and taken on an unintended normative dimension.

The characterization of services as no-tech almost completely misses the mark. The use of capital inputs, as in machinery and equipment, is in fact extensive in many service industries: some service industries are among the most capital intensive of all industries. In various forms of service production the role of technology may be different than in the standard picture of manufacturing production processes and product characteristics, but that does not imply that it is without importance.

In this respect service industries are depicted as importing various forms of technology from manufacturing technology

349

developing sectors; they are users with their technological development dominated by the development their supplying sectors achieves. This view of the technological capital inputs as generic with an 'off-the-shelf' availability for a range of user industries is misguided for two reasons.

- First, the use of technological inputs generally involves development of core specialized technologies, specialized towards functional and industrial characteristics of the user sector. Hence, technology supplying industries are generally highly specialized in terms of the user industry they serve. Along the scale from the development of large technological systems to more functionally specific core technologies, the general rule is more inclined towards the vital importance of specialization and close cooperation between supplier and user. Airline transport from 1930 onwards would have looked very different without the active role played in the early stages by major airline companies, towards aircraft and system development. Similarly, an important driver for development of the incipient IT industry in the 1950s and 1960s was the back office needs of banks and other financial service providers.
- Second, the intimate relation between producers and users of crucial technological capital inputs has its basis in a well known argument about economic change. The structural distinction as seen today may simply be the result of the process of evolving divisions of labour, reflecting past opportunities for specialization, market growth and productivity improvements.

One of the frequent characterizations of service products is that they are 'produced when they are consumed', service production is a bilateral relation between the service provider and the recipient. An implication of this idea is that such service transactions 'leave no traces' in the real world, interpreted as meaning that international trade in services is impossible other than in special circumstances.

However, there is one stylised fact that may have significant consequences for the further growth of our economies. The most striking fact about the industrialized economy has been its ability to keep up high rates of productivity growth and the industrialization processes that this record reflects over a period of almost two centuries. If we look to services for similar processes, there does not seem at present to be similar scope for sustained productivity growth.

Economic statistics indeed suggests that there is a 'productivity gap' between manufacturing and service sectors; rates of productivity growth has been larger in manufacturing than those of service industries. The consequences of this can be profound, and they may be illustrated with a very simple model economy. At first the model country is dominated by manufacturing production, the residual employment being in service industries. The society is dominated by manufacturing also in another sense; salary levels are generally set in manufacturing, manufacturing industries are the wage-leading sectors of the country. Productivity growth is larger in manufacturing than in services. Over time these productivity increases imply that:

- Employment will shift from manufacturing to services as a consequence of improved productivity in manufacturing;
- As market prices of service goods will rise indefinitely relative to manufactured goods, the cost share of services in (current) GDP will increase indefinitely; while
- The share of services in constant GDP may rise, be constant or decline dependent on the size of the productivity gap.

This is provided demand for services rises at least as fast as that of manufacturing with increased income levels. In the long run, service sectors will almost completely dominate both employment and the current value of production.

The simple assumptions of a productivity gap, systems of wage determination and relative income elasticities all find empirical support. If these characteristics are sustained in the long run, they have several implications for growth and development in the service era of our industrialized societies. Two of these are immediate:

- The transition will be accompanied by a productivity slowdown;
- Services will become increasingly expensive.

Economic growth rates will decline. In the initial phases overall economic growth rates will be dominated by productivity growth in manufacturing activities, while growth rates will be determined by productivity increases in service activities in later periods. The approach to a service economy will be a transition from 'progressive growth' to 'asymptotic stagnancy' (in the words of W. Baumol). It is also fairly easy to see that stagnancy will set in early in the process. The cost structure of any sector using inputs from 'asymptotic stagnant' sectors will be dominated by these inputs unless these inputs may be substituted away rapidly enough. The dominance of stagnant service inputs turns the user sector itself into an asymptotically stagnant sector. Could this explain the productivity slowdown; the fact that productivity growth since the early 1970s has been substantially lower than during the 1950s and 1960s? The US growth record affirms this; the productivity slowdown since 1972 is concentrated mainly in services (Gordon 1995).

Second, service products will become expensive. Their prices will increase without bounds relative to manufacturing products, with wage costs reflecting productivity levels in manufacturing rather than service sectors. In the simple model used here we have implicitly assumed away changes in the quality of the products over time. As the costs of producing service goods increase, their producers can either let this be reflected in their prices or lower these service products' quality by reducing labour inputs more rapidly than what is reflected in productivity growth. Over time we are thus lead to expect a reduction in the quality of the services provided to counteract effect of escalating production costs. We would expect this development to be more clearly pronounced in service markets where consumers' sensitivity to the price level of services is strongest. This 'cost disease' argument was first presented in Baumol (1967) as part of the contemporary debate on metropolitan development time. Provision of f.i. postal and sanitary services may provide several current examples of the cost disease argument at works.

Note that this implies that incomes will always increase. As long as the aggregate productivity is increasing, the main long term impact will be a reduction in the *growth rates* of aggregate income, not in income *levels*. But the process may have substantial structural impacts during the transition phase. As wages reflect manufacturing productivity levels, spiralling labour costs may have several consequences. Service producers are forced to utilize opportunities for reduced product quality. With increased relative costs, the opportunity costs of consumers' own production increase, and demand for new manufactured, i.e. high productivity growth, goods increase (this 'self-service' argument was introduced in Jonathan Gershuny [1978]), and reflects the rapid growth of production of for instance household appliances). If the resulting rise in labour costs cannot be fully reflected in prices, the income distribution within service sectors will be shifted away from capital income. As relative capital gains decline, owners will over time withdraw from these industries.

Finally, there will be an increasing pressure on the wage setting system of this economy; the relative decline of manufacturing employment will not be able to sustain the wage determining role of manufacturing. This process may have one of three outcomes. Either the role as economy-wide standard will be shifted from the high- to the low-productivity growth sectors; implying that the capital share of value added in the manufacturing sectors will start to increase. This will again widen the profitability gap of capital between the grand sectors, furthering the incentive for shifting entrepreneurial capital into manufacturing. Alternatively the two labour markets will disentangle, ultimately leading to a high income labour market for the sectors with high productivity growth and a low income market for the residual sectors. Third, the manufacturing based labour relations may be upheld by regulation beyond the model, either by the agents themselves or by some external authority. In this case the impact of the cost disease would be strong; relative to the other two cases relative costs of service production would be high.

The model thus suggests that the transition to a service economy may have substantial welfare impacts. Based on the assumption of a productivity growth gap between sectors with high productivity growth, conveniently called manufacturing and service sectors, the model suggests that in the long run the transition will lead to an income gap. The details of the process and who will turn out as respectively the haves and the have-nots are questions beyond those the model address. Evidently to address such questions require more specification of the model and the characteristics of the various factor, credit and product markets involved.

What essentially leads to this result in this model is the break down of the system of labour relations built up around manufacturing production. The transition process undermines the basically Fordist-based institutional set-up of the industrialized economies; with new forms of labour relations taking its place. Some indeterminate form of post-Fordist labour regulation systems emerges here as a direct reflection of the productivity gap and the inability to sustain the Fordist institutions. In spite of this, this simple model seems to capture well a complementarity between the substitution of Fordist labour regulation and a widening income gap that it is tempting to suggest this as a confirmation of a stylised fact of 'professionalized' economies.

This discussion is based on a rather simple distinction, that there are two sets of industrial sectors, one with high, the other with low productivity growth, with the productivity gap sustained over a long period. We also argued that this was in concord with empirical data. This immediately raises two questions, both of which may potentially undermine the validity of this assumption.

- First, the existence of a productivity gap is based on use of economic statistics, mostly national accounts. These statistics have well known limitations in their capture of service outputs and qualitative change. Is the productivity gap just a measurement error?

- Second, the conclusion is based on historical records. There is little systematic evidence, in spite of many conjectures, of productivity enhancing service related 'industrialization' processes similar to the industrialization processes that have revolutionised our economies over the last two centuries. May we envisage new forms of 'servicification' processes playing roles similar to industrialization towards manufacturing production since 1850?

Basically productivity of any industrial activity is a ratio of outputs of the production to the required inputs into it. Estimation of productivity levels thus basically requires independent estimates for outputs and inputs at any time. To have reliable estimates of productivity growth, these measures must in addition capture the impact of qualitative changes in both inputs and outputs. Still today, output of several sectors that are hard to measure are estimated by national statistical agencies in many countries on the basis of 'rules of thumb' or on inputs going into production. In particular this applies to several many service sectors. New statistical methodologies, new types of data and estimation methods are introduced on a large scale. However, though the size of the productivity growth gap is reduced, it does not close the gap: the productivity gap is not solely a measurement issue.

The latter possibility is perhaps the more interesting one. Are there any signs of new forms of 'industrialization' in service production that may initiate 'boot strapping' growth? Within certain services information technologies have played a substantial role in restructuring both production and potential scope of products. An immediate example is furnished by financial services over the last four decades, with a substantial automation of back office functions and rapid reshaping of front office functions. Large scale mass production of standardized service goods is well established in several services.

One of the core effects of the industrialization of the manufacturing enterprise, and the dramatic growth in productivity of the agricultural sectors, was the potential for specialized production of machinery and equipment as inputs into other sectors 'enabling' productivity enhancements. Are there potential service sectors that may play an 'enabling' role in the future? One of the dominant aspects of developments in the advanced economies over the last decade is the rapid growth of various forms of business services. More specifically it concerns the substantial growth of what may grossly be termed knowledge-intensive business services, professionalized services providing specialized service products to business customers. The growth of markets for knowledge products is perhaps the most telling indication of new developments.

3 Service economy redefined?

The thesis of an emergent service economy suggests a new 'industrial' revolution, a watershed between industrial society and a new service society. But since the activities called 'services' form an extremely heterogeneous bag, it is not immediate that the emerging economic structures deserve the label of 'service economy'. We will end this entry by asking if the service economy is appropriate as a characterization of ongoing structural change.

We noted the heterogeneity of the activities and functions we usually call services. By asking whether these service activities create leading structural characteristics of present day societies, we have implicitly asked if there are some common traits of the kind of activities that we call services that impart on the development of advanced economies in a coherent way. Given the negative, or residual, character of the identification of service or tertiary sectors, it is not surprising that it is difficult to identify such common characteristics – such as levels of employment – as indicators of structural changes. All this suggests that using the concept of a *service* economy based on employment or production shares to characterize long term determinants of structural processes is misplaced.

Since service sectors account for more than half the total employment in most OECD countries, they may be termed service societies in the traditional weak sense. The term is then describing what contemporary society is not; due to heterogeneities of the service sector, we cannot give a positive definition of the whole sector. If we use productivity developments as the characterising feature, a better term would be service-industrial society. One may even argue that as long as the productivity gap seems to be positive and real manufacturing GDP is substantial and growing, the concept of an industrial society is still the relevant one.

Nevertheless, what the statistics show is growing service *sectors,* and not necessarily growing service *functions*. The total service production may still be roughly constant, with the growth of services being a statistical artefact, caused by an increased 'outsourcing' of service functions. Such an argument would imply that we are far from any transition from an industrial to a service society. Even though such unbundling of service activities; that companies find it more efficient to outsource service functions, may be important, three qualitative phenomena show that this can only be a part of the story.

First, the enhanced inter-sectoral relations show links to the development of new information and communication technologies, which in itself gives the processes new aspects. Second, changes in employment in the 'grand sectors' embody a differential development in terms of what type of employment is shedded from the 'material' sectors. A high-skilled white collar labour force is not shed, on the contrary. So there is a structural change in terms of employment within these material sectors that is not consistent with a simple unbundling argument. These points leads to the conclusion that even though the 'outsourcing' argument may give important bits to the puzzle, it reveals only a part of the whole picture. Our conclusion is that the patterns of inter-industrial trade may support the use of terms like service societies to characterize these developments.

Even though we have rejected levels of employment as an argument in favour of the label, these levels point to some associated arguments. It is still unclear how the growth of service functions and occupations will affect work organization and social structures. Many approaches stress the emergence of 'post-Fordist' structures as a central characteristic of service or information economies, structures that will replace the 'Fordist' work organization and relations that complement manufacturing production.

The last argument may be extended to include the social and cultural environment of the population. As the activities called services engage the majority of the population in these countries, this majority will have its social framework shaped by participation in service-providing functions. To the extent that there are commonalities across different service functions in the shaping of social networks, work organization etc. these will shape contemporary society. Then contemporary society can be said to merit the label service society.

Two trends characterize ongoing structural changes of advanced economies as the emergence of a service economy, changes in the welfare state and wider governance issues and as a 'complexification' of economic activity. Both trends pose challenges to our understanding of present developments and raise the need for a better understanding of both overall economy-wide structural changes and changes at industry- and firm-level.

Overall service content, however measured, of the economy increases, with a shift towards higher skilled white collar employment in most industries, away from low- and un-skilled blue collar employment. This is accompanied by an increase in flexible, service-like production methods in several manufacturing industries; the evolution of 'post-Fordist' production. As the structure of labour markets and work relations have a strong Fordist heritage, there are strong contingencies between the dominant modes of production organization on the one hand and work organization and governance structures on the other. Increased flexibility of work arrangements and dissolving barriers between work and leisure, between education/training and knowledge and skill use suggest new forms of work relations in several functions. These processes could lead to increased externalization of service functions, and hence contribute to increased service employment.

Economic growth and the possible transition to a service economy is an highly endogenous and integral process. The role of services is highly contingent on the 'webs' or 'clusters' within which they participate. Furthermore, the dichotomy between manufacturing and service sectors is misguided. It mixes a distinction of characteristics of production processes with characteristics of economic products. There are symbiotic relationships within and between industries and sectors: the economic system is an evolving web of interlinked economic, technological and wider social interrelations.

Present OECD economies may deserve a label as service economies; drawing attention not to the service sectors themselves, but to the emergence of complex interrelations between new and altered services and other productive sectors in the economies, as well as to the altered social environments of these.

JOHAN HAUKNES
STEP GROUP, OSLO

Further reading

(References cited in the text marked *)

* Baumol, W.J. (1967) 'Macroeconomics of unbalanced growth: the anatomy of urban crisis', *American Economic Review* 57: 415–26. (Presents the original formulation of the cost disease argument.)
Baumol, W.J., Blackman, S.A.B. and Wolff, E.N. (1989) *Productivity and American Leadership: The Long View*, Cambridge: MIT Press. (Baumol's work is central for two reasons: first, it formulates the original productivity gap argument in a concise way that allowed a clear statement of the long run implications. Second, it is the only work in this period offering a theory of innovation in services, albeit a negative one.)
Boden, M. and Miles, I. (eds) (2000) *Services and the Knowledge-Based Economy*, London: Continuum. (A turn of the millennium reappraisal of the many concerns that have underpinned the service economy thesis during the last 50 years, reflecting debates in socioeconomic research on innovation-based economies in the late 1990s.)
Clark, C. (1957) *The Conditions of Economic Progress*, 3rd edn, London: Macmillan. (1st edn 1940) (Widely seen today as the locus classicus of the service economy thesis, with a service economy emerging through the combined effects of lower productivity growth in service sectors and higher demand elasticities for their products.)
Daniels, P.W. (1993) *Service Industries in the World Economy*, Oxford: Blackwell. (Today

about twenty per cent of world trade is in services. Daniels' book outlines and analyses several modes of trade in services up until *c.* 1990. Somewhat outdated in its statistics, but the discussion and analysis is still a valuable resource.)

Eiglier, P. and Langeard, E. (1987) *Servuction – le marketing des sèrvices*, Paris: Ediscience. (One of the most influential works coming out of a strong French tradition on service marketing. The integration of the customer in the service production process – the 'servuction' process – is a central concern. Their distinction between the base service, and several peripheral services affords a rich way of analysing service markets and strategies of service firms.)

Fisher, A.G.B. (1935) *The Clash of Progress and Security*, London: Macmillan. (Fisher developed the service economy thesis. The service economy is seen as result of a three-stage theory of economic development.)

Fuchs, V. (1968) *The Service Economy*, New York: NBER/Columbia University Press. (Classic work which was a significant precursor for much of the later literature. With Fuchs' work the modern agenda of research and analysis on service industries, based on four core drivers was established. Fuchs (1969) is a companion set of industry studies.)

Fuchs, V. (ed.) (1969) *Production and Productivity in the Service Industries*, New York: NBER/Columbia University Press.

* Gershuny, J. (1978) *After Industrial Society? – The Emerging Self-service Economy*, London: Macmillan. (A thorough criticism of the simplistic view of the service economy on the basis of service employment trends. Shows that the naïve interpretation of employment structures as the mode of analysing service societies was shown to be ill founded.)

* Gordon, R. (1995) *Problems in the measurement and performance of service-sector productivity in the United States*, in Productivity and Growth, Proceedings of a Conference, Economic Group, Reserve Bank of Australia. (Discusses the role of measurement problems in service statistics on the productivity paradox.)

Greenfield, H.C. (1966) *Manpower and the Growth of Producer Services*, New York: Colombia University Press. (The first author to call systematic attention to the rapid growth in supply of a wide range of producer services to businesses, with clients reaping economies of specialization in professional service firms offering in-house provision of these services.)

Grönroos, G. (2000) *Service Management and Marketing*, 2nd edn, New York: John Wiley & Sons. (Among the top-selling textbooks on service management with a view that strongly reflects a Nordic school of service management.)

* Guile, B.R. (1988) 'Introduction to services industries policy issues', *Technological Forecasting and Social Change* 34: 315–25. (Guile and Quinn ran several US research projects on technological development in service industries during the 1980s. This paper introduces a special issue of the journal TFSC based on these projects.)

Illeris, S. (1996) *The Service Economy – A Geographical Approach*, John Wiley (Provides a good overview, discussion and synthesis of this research, emphasizing in particular the role of new information and communication technologies in reducing the locational advantages of urban regions *vis-à-vis* business services.)

Kuznets, S. (1966) *Modern Economic Growth: Rate, Structure and Spread*, Yale University Press. (Seminal work on modern economic growth in industrialized economies where structural change is seen as an integral aspect of the growth process, reflecting exploitation of epochal innovations and concomitant changes in divisions of labour.)

Marshall, J.N. (1988) *Services and Uneven Development*, Oxford: Oxford University Press. (Provides a substantial review of analysis of producer services in economic geography, the geographical distribution and patterns of development in the UK. Its core concern is the uneven distribution of service production and the dynamics of service location.)

Normann, R. (2001) *Service Management – Strategy and Leadership in Service Business*, 3rd edn, Chichester: John Wiley & Sons. (Opened the debate on service management; the third edition is still highly readable for students and business managers.)

Petit, P. (1986) *Slow Growth and the Service Economy*, London: Frances Pinter. (Analyses the growth prospects of the service economy with a basis in the French Regulation School; placing employment analysis in a wide framework involving the overall structure and division of labour of all sectors.)

Porat, M.U. (1977) *The Information Economy*, 9 vols, OT Special Publication 77-12, Washington, DC: Office of Telecommunications, US Department of Commerce. (An extensive study of information production, dissemination and use: a tour-de-force of data and methodology use. Follows up and extends Machlup's 1962 study of knowledge production.)

Quinn, J.B. (1992) *Intelligent Enterprise*, New York: Free Press. (Quinn's argument is based on a service-based approach to corporate management which explicitly starts out from the service economy thesis. He argues that we are already in the service economy, and that corporate managers should focus on this.)

Singelmann, J. (1978) *From Agriculture to Services – The Transformation of Industrial Employment*, Beverly Hills: Sage Publications. (Impressive effort to analyse long term structural evolution of the major economies of the world in this classic study. Still regarded as analytically more tractable than the dominant standard classifications.)

Stanback Jr., T.M. and Knight, R.V. (1970) *The Metropolitan Economy*, New York: Columbia University Press.

Stanback, T.M. (1979) *Understanding the Service Economy – Employment, Productivity, Location*, Baltimore: John Hopkins University Press. (The study of metropolitan economies published in 1970 presented a typology of urban places distinguished by their underlying economic structure that still is a basis for current statistical classification schemes of regional economies in many countries. Urban centres with manufacturing bases were shown to be declining in importance relative to urban centres with large service components. This approach was later in the 1970s developed to include inter-regional trade, furthering the study of services as regionalized economic bases. See also Illeris [1996])

Stigler, G. (1956) *Trends in Employment in the Service Industries*, Princeton: NBER/Princeton University Press. (Less than ten years after the US became a service economy in the employment sense, George Stigler published the first substantial documentation and thorough analysis of these economy-wide employment trends.)

See also: BANKING SYSTEMS; DEVELOPMENT AND DIFFUSION OF TECHNOLOGY; ECONOMIC GROWTH; INNOVATION.

National economies and the international system

East Asian economies

1 Definition
2 Performance
3 Controversies
4 Recession and crisis
5 The question of transferability
6 Concluding remarks

Overview

The East Asian economies have been the most dynamic part of the world economy during the second half of the twentieth century. At the same time, their policies and institutions have often significantly diverged from what many people, including many East Asians themselves, regard as the best practice of the Anglo-American economies. As a result, the East Asian economies have been at the centre of numerous academic and policy controversies since the 1960s. In this entry, in an attempt to understand these rapidly changing and complex economies, we look at the evolution of major controversies surrounding the East Asian economies, followed by a brief discussion on the question of transferability of the East Asian model. Before we do that, however, we need to discuss some problems involved in the very definition of East Asian economies and also put their experiences into historical perspective.

1 Definition

Somewhat atypically for a geography-based category, the very definition of the East Asian economies can be contentious. The most widely-accepted definition, which is also adopted here, includes in this category Japan and the so-called first-tier newly industrializing countries (NICs) of South Korea (henceforth Korea), Taiwan, Hong Kong, and Singapore. The origin of this definition is rather obvious – between the 1960s and the mid-1980s, these were the fastest growing economies in the world.

However, since the early 1990s it has become increasingly common to include in this category the so-called second-tier NICs of Southeast Asia – such as Thailand, Malaysia, and Indonesia. Still others believe that China and Vietnam should also be included, as since the 1980s these economies moved away from Communist isolationism and have enjoyed rapid growth of the kind observed only in the above-mentioned countries.

This issue of definition is not just pedantic, but has an important policy implication. For, depending on one's definition of the East Asian economies, the lessons that we draw from their experiences can be quite different. For example, if we were to include only the original five of Japan and the first-tier NICs in this category, we would be likely to conclude that active state intervention is beneficial for economic development (Hong Kong being the exception that proves the rule) (see ECONOMY OF JAPAN). On the other hand, the inclusion of the Southeast Asian second-tier NICs, which developed on the basis of much less state activism than the original four (that is the original five minus Hong Kong), makes it possible to argue that a high degree of state activism is not necessary for rapid development.

In this entry, we define the East Asian economies as comprising only the original five for two reasons. First, it is only during the 1990s that people have started to define East Asia to include the second-tier NICs and the former Communist economies of China and Vietnam, and therefore most of the existing debates have been conducted with specific reference to the original five. Introducing the new countries therefore can blur the focus of many existing debates. Second, while the performances of the new wave of high-growth Asian economies are very impressive, there is a large gap between their performances and the performances of the original five, which grew faster and for longer than the new wave countries. Also, the new wave countries are yet to break into the rank of the advanced economies, while the original five all have done so already.

2 Performance

During the second half of the twentieth century, the East Asian economies as we define them (the original five) have grown at 5 to 6 per cent per year in per capita terms. Given that the per capita income growth rates of the European and the North American economies were typically not much above 1 per cent during the Industrial Revolution and just over 3 per cent even during the so-called 'Golden age of capitalism' (1945–75), this means that during this 50-year period the East Asian economies experienced literally the fastest economic growth in human history.

What is especially notable about the growth records of the East Asian economies is that their rapid growth is an entirely post-war phenomenon. Estimates of earlier performance are not totally reliable, but the highly respected study of the 32 largest economies of the world by Maddison (1989) puts the yearly per capita income growth figures of Japan, Taiwan, and Korea during 1900–1950 at one per cent, 0.4 per cent, and 0.1 per cent respectively. Not only are these very low by their own post-war standards, they are also quite low by international standards of the time.

During this period, the Japanese per capita income growth rate of 1 per cent was not only below average among the 17 major industrial countries (including the USSR) that were included in Maddison's study – Japan ranked the joint eleventh (with Germany and the Netherlands) among the 17 countries. Moreover, it was also lower than those of the six largest Latin American countries covered in the study (ranging from 1.8 per cent for Brazil and Chile to 1.2 per cent for Mexico and Peru). The Taiwanese and the Korean performances were even worse. Taiwan ranked twenty-fourth (jointly with the Philippines) and Korea twenty-sixth (jointly with Thailand) among the 32 countries included in the Maddison study – the last five places were taken up by Indonesia, India, Pakistan, Bangladesh (all of them at –0.1 per cent) and China (–0.3 per cent). The rapid post-war growth records of the East Asian economies were, therefore, completely unexpected from a historical point of view.

The post-war growth of the East Asian economies is also notable for having resulted in remarkable improvements in social indicators, something that has not happened in all experiences of rapid growth. The records of these economies in terms of improvements in infant mortality, life expectancy, educational achievement, and other indicators of human development have been very impressive. Of course, this is not to say that everything has been rosy. Political authoritarianism, human rights violation, corruption, union repression, gender discrimination, mistreatment of ethnic minorities, and so on, have all been problems in one degree or another in most of these economies. However, despite these blemishes, it would be fair to say that during the second half of the twentieth century the citizens of the East Asian economies have experienced improvements in income and general well-being that were unparalleled in human history.

3 Controversies

Given their spectacular performance records, it is only natural that there have been a number of heated controversies surrounding the East Asian economies – including, among others, industrial policy, corporate governance, democracy, institutions of employment, income inequality, education and culture.

Outside interest in East Asia obviously began with Japan. The initial debate on Japan was strongly influenced by the fact that, until the mid-1970s, it remained the only industrialized country of non-European extraction. Some participants in the famous debate among Marxist economic historians regarding the transition from feudalism to capitalism tried to attribute Japan's success to the uniquely European (that is, decentralized) nature of Japanese feudalism (the relevant essays can be found in Sweezy et al. 1976). In contrast, some others tried to explain its success in terms of the uniquely collectivist nature of the Japanese variety of Confucianism, which puts emphasis on group loyalty over personal edification that had been emphasized by the Chinese and the Korean varieties of Confucianism (Morishima 1982). The subsequent industrialization of other parts of Asia as well as the recent academic debates have revealed some problems with these early emphases on Japan's uniqueness, but the earlier debates were useful in bringing to our attention the role of social structure and moral values in economic development.

By the late 1970s, the spectacular success of the Japanese economy and the corresponding decline of many other industrialized countries generated a heated debate, especially in the USA, on the role of Japanese-style industrial policy (the debate is reviewed in greater detail in Thompson 1989; Chang 1994). Some argued that the centralized coordination of investment and technological upgrading (but not 'planning' in the conventional sense) helped the Japanese firms aggressively invest in 'sunrise' industries with large productivity growth potential and widespread externalities (Magaziner and Hout 1980, Johnson 1982 and Dore 1986 are classic examples). Others argued that Japanese industrial policy was not very extensive and not very effective even in those few areas where it existed. They also pointed out that the success of industrial policy in Japan depended very much on the unique bureaucratic structure and the collectivist nature of the country's culture and that it therefore cannot be emulated elsewhere.

Numerous studies that followed have revealed that the pro-industrial-policy authors had empirical facts on their side. Moreover, increasingly sophisticated theoretical arguments were provided to make sense of the Japanese-style industrial policy, which could not easily be comprehended through the dominant framework of neoclassical economics (Johnson et al. 1989; Chang 1994; Stiglitz 1996).

In the 1980s, growing attention was also being paid to the secrets of Japanese corporate success. Many argued that the structures of corporate governance, financing, and the organization of production that characterize the Japanese firms provide them with distinctive advantages over the western (or rather Anglo-American) firms (Dore 1987; Best 1990; Aoki and Dore 1994) (see ECONOMY OF JAPAN). The following characteristics were identified as important.

First, the Japanese firms were not run as properties of shareholders but as communities of the stakeholders, including the professional managers, workers, subcontractors, and local community, as well as the shareholders as the suppliers of capital (rather than as the owners, except in a purely legal sense). Second, through cross-shareholding among related enterprises and the legal ban on hostile takeover, the Japanese firms were protected from the short-termist pressures of the stock market and were thus able to pursue long-term strategies based on large investments in R&D and human resource development. Third, institutions like lifetime employment and the seniority wage system led Japanese workers to identify their interests more closely with those of their firms and thereby invest in firm-specific skills, which can be very important in certain industries, and to moderate wage demands. Fourth, the deliberate restriction of compartmentalization through horizontal information sharing and job rotation enabled the Japanese firms to minimize the wastes arising from lack of inter-departmental coordination and to encourage cross-fertilization of ideas. Last, the long-term subcontracting relationships supported by cross-shareholding, personnel exchange, and equity participation by the mother firm enabled the Japanese assemblers to cut down on inventory costs, to minimize the occurrence of defective parts, and to fully utilize the innovation capabilities of the subcontracting firms.

While no other country could and did import the Japanese institutions of corporate governance and production organization wholesale, the Japanese corporate success has led to a widespread emulation of certain aspects of Japanese production techniques and management skills since the 1980s all over the world.

Since the 1970s, the economic successes of first-tier NICs of East Asia have also attracted considerable attention and generated many important controversies. Until the mid-1980s, the focus of the debate concerning these countries was on trade policy.

Initially, many mainstream economists argued that the spectacular success of these economies derived mainly from their free trade policy and that it proved the folly of the import-substitution industrialization (ISI) strategy pursued by most of the other developing countries at the time. The World Bank and the IMF took this contention to their hearts and started imposing trade liberalization as a key condition for receiving their financial support during the 1980s, when many developing countries became dependent on such support following the second oil shock and the Debt Crisis (see INTERNATIONAL MONETARY FUND; WORLD BANK).

However, it soon became obvious that nothing like a free trade regime existed; widespread import protection remained in place in these countries. In response, some mainstream economists argued that import protection in these countries did not have ill effects, because their governments countered them with export subsidies, thus maintaining a virtual free trade regime where incentive neutrality between exports and production for the domestic market existed. Others, however, have shown that there was nothing neutral about trade regimes in these countries. They argued that the trade regimes that prevailed in these countries were a deliberate mixture of infant industry protection, relatively free trade in inputs, and export subsidies, rather than a simulation of free trade as the theory of virtual free trade would have us believe.

In the late 1980s, there was a full frontal attack by a group of heterodox economists and other social scientists on the then orthodoxy of free market, free trade East Asia (Amsden 1989; Wade 1990 are the best known early works along this line). They emphasized that all the first-tier NICs except Hong Kong practiced Japanese-style industrial policy, although Singapore was much more liberal than others in terms of foreign direct investment. They argued that these countries promoted industries with high growth potential and widespread externalities through an array of means, which included: infant industry protection; export subsidies; coordination of complementary investments; regulation of firm entry, exit, investments, and pricing intended to 'manage competition'; subsidies and restriction of competition intended to help technology upgrading. They also argued that these countries could successfully import and assimilate foreign technologies because they could: skilfully integrate their education and training policies with industrial policy; effectively initiate and subsidize private-sector R&D while also providing public-sector R&D in key areas; and deliberately regulate technology licensing and foreign direct investments in a way that maximizes technology spillover.

Many of those who emphasize the importance of industrial policy in the first-tier NICs draw our attention on the existence of the developmental state in these economies (the concept is due to Johnson 1982; further works in the tradition are compiled in Woo-Cumings 1999). The proponents of the developmental state thesis argue that what distinguishes the East Asian states from other states most clearly is not the policy tools that they used but their greater degree of autonomy from interest groups that enabled them to discipline the recipients of their supports when performance lagged. Evans (1995) advanced this argument further and developed the notion of embedded autonomy. He argued that the state autonomy possessed by the East Asian states was particularly beneficial because it was embedded in a dense policy network that linked them with the private sector, which provided a vital channel for information collection and interactive learning in the policy process.

The heterodox attack of the late 1980s prompted the World Bank, as the leading proponent of the orthodox interpretation of the East Asian experience emphasizing the role of market forces, to respond with the famous East Asian Miracle Report (henceforth EAM) in the early 1990s (World Bank 1993). The EAM acknowledged that there had been extensive state interventions in the East Asian economies and that some of these have been beneficial. However, it argued that industrial policy in these economies was largely unsuccessful, with the partial exception of Japan. It also put great emphasis on the fact that the second-tier NICs of Southeast Asia grew rapidly without such policy, thus suggesting that East Asian-style industrial policy is not necessary for successful economic development. It then questioned whether the East Asian-style industrial policy could be practised in other developing countries with under-developed bureaucracies and operating in an international environment much less tolerant of interventionist industrial and trade policies than in the 1960s or the 1970s.

The EAM has been subject to some severe criticisms, the details of which need not detain us. Many people were not impressed by its dilution tactic of including the Southeast Asian economies as an integral part of East Asia. The critics argued that this led to a blurring of the focus of the earlier debate that the EAM was supposed to be a part of, which after all was about the original five or even the big three (Japan, Korea, and Taiwan). A large number of commentators have also questioned the theoretical framework and the empirical methods underlying the study, especially those concerning the assessment of industrial policy (more detailed arguments can be found in the special section in the April 1994 issue of *World Development*).

One positive contribution of the EAM was to emphasize the issue of policy implementation. It especially drew our attention to the role of the institutions that link the government and the private sector (e.g. Japan's deliberation council) in helping countries implement policies effectively – an aspect that is succinctly captured in Evans' notion of embedded autonomy. Despite such contributions, many see the EAM on the whole as an unconvincing last ditch effort by the World Bank to deal with the rapidly accumulating evidence that conflicts with its earlier position – an attempt similar to the grafting of endless epicycles onto the earth's orbit by those geocentric astronomers faced with the evidence supporting heliocentric theories.

Shortly after the debate surrounding the EAM, there was a brief period when the so-called productivity debate was in the limelight. This debate was prompted by the celebrated article by the American economist Krugman (1994), who cited a number of growth accounting studies allegedly showing that the East Asian economies, once again with the exception of Japan, have grown almost exclusively on the basis of factor accumulation (greater investment and larger labour inputs) rather than productivity growth. He then argued that, as they will soon have exhausted the possibility of accumulation-based growth, these economies will grind to a halt in the near future – in a manner similar to what happened to the Eastern European accumulation-led economies in the 1970s. He asserted that this apparent parallel between the two groups of 'Eastern' economies shows the limitations of collectivist economies and the superiority of individualistic Western economies.

In response to Krugman, we should first of all point out that there are many growth accounting studies, for what they are worth, that contradict the studies that Krguman uses. We say 'for what they are worth', because growth accounting exercises are riddled with serious theoretical and statistical problems (for details, see Abramovitz 1989). More importantly, economic history shows that economies at the earlier stages of development are bound to rely more on factor accumulation than innovation and productivity growth but that they are able to make a transition to a productivity-driven growth regime – indeed, estimates show that in Japan, Korea and Singapore, productivity growth accelerated over time. Even more important is the fact that it is precisely with the help of the organizational and institutional capabilities that had been accumulated in the earlier stage of development that economies are later able (or not) to make a transition to a productivity-driven growth regime. It is because Krugman fails to understand the role of organizational and institutional factors in the process of economic development that he groups the East Asian economies together with the Eastern European socialist economies.

4 Recession and crisis

With the bursting of the asset bubble in the early 1990s, the Japanese economy entered a period of prolonged recession – in fact, the longest in its modern history. In the meantime, some East and Southeast Asian economies (Thailand, Malaysia, Indonesia, Korea, and Hong Kong) have experienced major financial crises, starting with the floating of Thai currency in July 1997.

These two events together, especially when set against the strong performance of the US economy during the last several years of the 1990s, have prompted many people to argue that Asian capitalism was in the end a house of cards. By the late 1990s, it was widely argued that the East Asian economies were in trouble because of the inefficiencies created by factors such as excessive state intervention, market-defying private-sector institutions (such as lifetime employment and pathological corporate governance institutions), corruption, and the lack of transparency in the management of government and corporations (Krugman 1998 was arguably the most influential advocate of this viewpoint; for criticisms, see Singh 1999 and Chang 2000).

In addressing this view, it should first all be emphasized that there never existed such thing as Asian capitalism. We can certainly discuss the East Asian model, practised by the big three, and to a lesser extent Singapore, but this model did not extend either to Hong Kong or the Southeast Asian economies. It is interesting, then, to note that it is mostly the more market-oriented economies of Hong Kong and Southeast Asia that are in crisis, rather than the countries that have practiced the East Asian model. The economies of Taiwan and Singapore were somewhat affected by the crises in the region but survived them more or less unscathed. Japan may have had a prolonged recession during most of the 1990s, but it is by no means in a crisis situation, except perhaps in terms of wounded national pride and the spreading sense of uncertainty about the future in the country. The obvious exception in this regard is Korea. However, given that the country had moved to a much more market-oriented model since the early 1990s, it is probably more accurate to attribute its crisis to the demise of the East Asian model in the country than to its perpetuation (Chang 1998).

Whether or not they assume a common Asian model, the fundamental problem with the arguments that tries to explain the Asian crisis in terms of the institutional deficiencies of the countries concerned is that these deficiencies are never clearly specified, but often summarized in the catch-all term of moral hazard (Chang 2000). Moreover, these arguments are not well supported by facts (Radelet and Sachs 1998; Chang 2000).

Although no one would deny certain economic and institutional weaknesses of the crisis economies of Asia, many people, across the ideological spectrum, see the origins of the crisis elsewhere. Many believe that the main causes of the Asian crisis lie in factors such as the deficiencies in the international financial architecture (e.g. unstable exchange rates, the absence of lenders of last resort); instability in the international capital markets due to increasing financial deregulation and globalization; premature capital market liberalization and opening in the absence of proper supervisory mechanism in the crisis countries. They argue that the crisis occurred because these factors have magnified the famous Kindlebergerian cycle of financial 'manias, panics, and crashes' that have been observed in virtually all financial crises since the seventeenth century (Kindleberger 2001).

Finally, whatever one's view on the Asian crisis is, the Japanese case needs to be discussed separately. Above all, it should be noted that, while poor by its own historical standards (Japan's per capita income grew at over 6 per cent up to the 1970s and at around 3.5 per cent even during the 1980s), the Japanese economic performance during the 1990s is by no means a disaster by international standards. For example, during the 1990s, a number of advanced economies have grown more slowly than Japan in per capita terms (Canada, Switzerland, Italy and Sweden). Once again in per capita terms, its performance during the 1990s was not much behind that of the US, which is supposed to have entered a new 'golden age' (however, note that, contrary to the popular myth, the US growth rate over the last decade is actually below its historical average). Between 1990 and 1999, the US grew at 2.6 per cent and Japan at 1.7 per cent in aggregate terms, but if we translate these into per capita terms their respective growth rates end up being 1.5 per cent and 1.4 per cent (respective population growth rates being 1.1 per cent and 0.3 per cent). At the time of writing (March 2000), it is becoming increasingly clear that the strong performance of the US economy over the last few years of the 1990s cannot be sustained much longer, given the Internet bubble and other structural weaknesses such as growing corporate and household debt, greater exposure of household income to stock market fluctuations, and growing employment insecurity.

What is even more notable about Japan is that, despite the economic and ideological pressures generated by the recession, most of the core characteristics of the Japanese model, such as lifetime employment and cross-shareholding, have been maintained, with some modifications on the margin. Moreover, the underlying core values such as the 'community model of firm' (the term is from Dore 1987), the emphasis on long-term innovation over short-term financial gains, and the emphasis on social cohesion through protective regulations (e.g. agriculture, retail trade) still seem to remain largely intact. Indeed, some commentators have argued that many of the recent modifications in the Japanese model, which are supposed to be pushing the country towards an Anglo-American road, are in many ways attempts to preserve, rather than undermine, these core values (Lazonick 1999; Dore 2000).

5 The question of transferability

Whatever lessons we may want to draw from the experiences of the East Asian economies, we will be always confronted by sceptics who ask whether the East Asian model, with so many unique institutions and cultural elements, is transferable to other countries.

In this context, it is interesting to note that many people who express scepticism about the transferability of the East Asian model are cavalier when it comes to the transferability of the market-dominated models of the Anglo-American economies. There may be an element of Anglo-centrism here, but the more important problem is the implicit assumption behind this argument that markets are easy to create and therefore can be transplanted anywhere, while institutions are difficult to transfer.

However, markets are *not* natural phenomena that develop spontaneously, and like other institutions, have to be deliberately constructed (Polanyi 1957, is a classic argument along this line). Thus seen, it is not tenable to argue that replicating the East Asian model requires institution building (and is therefore next to impossible) while replicating the Anglo-American model does not require it (and is therefore easy). They just require the building of different sets of institutions. Indeed, if the free market system is so natural and easy to replicate, the former socialist countries should not have had so much trouble establishing the market economy during the 1990s.

In other words, the argument that the East Asian model cannot be replicated elsewhere because of its unique institutions sees institutions as something fixed and underestimates the possibility of institutional transfer, adaptation, and innovation. In fact, if there is one lesson from the East Asian economies that is transferable everywhere, it is that the development of a late-developing country depends critically on how successfully it can engage in the importation, adaptation, assimilation, and innovation of not just technologies but more fundamentally institutions.

6 Concluding remarks

The East Asian economies have been the most dynamic economies in the world during the last few decades of the twentieth century, and indeed during the whole of human history. Their successes and failures have generated many heated debates that have significantly affected the way that we understand modern economy and society. While these economies have moved away from their traditional models to one degree or another (most dramatically in the Korean case), their importance in the world economy can only increase in the conceivable future. Therefore, a correct understanding of their past experience and current situation will remain valuable for the increasing number of policy-makers and business people who interact with the region, as well as for the scholars who are interested in the fields of economics, politics, sociology, and business studies.

HA-JOON CHANG
UNIVERSITY OF CAMBRIDGE

Further reading:

(References cited in the text marked *)

* Abramovitz, M. (1989) *Thinking about Growth*, Cambridge: Cambridge University Press. (A collection of classic essays on growth theory – with a dose of scepticism – by one of its founding fathers.)

* Amsden, A. (1989) *Asia's Next Giant*, New York: Oxford University Press. (An excellent history of Korea's development that was critical in shattering the free market orthodoxy on the East Asian NICs.)
* Aoki, M. and Dore, R. (eds) (1994) *The Japanese Firm*, Oxford: Oxford University Press. (A collection of state-of-the-art works on the Japanese firm.)
* Best, M. (1990) *New Competition*, Cambridge: Polity Press. (A comparative study of different modes of production organization that includes excellent chapters on Japanese production organization.)
* Chang, H-J. (1994) *The Political Economy of Industrial Policy*, London and Basingstoke: Macmillan. (Provides theoretical foundations for industrial policy with emphases on political economy and institutions.)
* Chang, H-J. (1998) 'Korea: the misunderstood crisis', *World Development* 26(8): 1555–61. (A narrative on the causes and the consequences of the 1997 financial crisis in Korea.)
* Chang, H-J. (2000) 'The hazard of moral hazard – untangling the Asian crisis', *World Development* 28(4): 775–88. (Criticizes the explanations of the Asian crisis emphasizing the institutional and political factors that created a moral hazard for investors.)
* Dore, R. (1986) *Flexible Rigidities: Industrial Policy and Structural Adjustment in the Japanese Economy 1970–80*, London: The Athlone Press. (A classic study of Japanese industrial policy in the 1970s, with an emphasis on the social bargaining process.)
* Dore, R. (1987) *Taking Japan Seriously*, London: The Athlone Press. (A collection of classic essays on various aspects of the Japanese economic system, with an emphasis on corporate governance.)
* Dore, R. (2000*) Stockmarket Capitalism vs. Welfare Capitalism – Japan and Germany versus the Anglo-Saxons*, Oxford: Oxford University Press. (A comparative study of different types of capitalism, with great emphasis on the Japanese economy in the 1990s.)
* Evans, P. (1995) *Embedded Autonomy – States and Industrial Transformation*, Princeton, NJ: Princeton University Press. (An excellent comparative study of state intervention in Korea, Taiwan, India, and Brazil, based on the notion of embedded autonomy.)
* Johnson, C. (1982) *MITI and the Japanese Miracle*, Stanford: Stanford University Press. (A classic study on the evolution of Japanese industrial policy from 1925–1975, with emphasis on the role of the bureaucracy.)
* Johnson, C., Tyson, L. and Zysman, J. (eds) (1989) *Politics and Productivity – How Japan's Development Strategy Works*, New York: Harper Business. (A collection of essays that provide theoretically sophisticated analysis of Japanese industrial policy up to the 1980s).
* Kindleberger, C. (2001) *Manias, Panics, and Crashes*, 4th edn, Palgrave: London and Basingstoke. (A classic work on the mechanics of financial crisis, with a wealth of historical information and profound theoretical insights.)
* Krugman, P. (1994) 'The myth of East Asian miracle', *Foreign Affairs* November/December 1994, 62–78. (The article that set off the 'productivity debate' by arguing that the East Asian economies cannot generate innovation.)
* Krugman, P. (1998) 'What Happened to Asia?', mimeo., Department of Economics, Massachusetts Institute of Technology. (Has been most influential in spreading the 'crony capitalism' explanation of the Asian crisis, despite never having been published.)
* Lazonick, W. (1999) 'The Japanese economy and corporate reform: what path to sustainable prosperity?', *Industrial and Corporate Change* 8 (4): 607–33. (An unconventional but highly original and profound analysis of the Japanese economy during the 1990s and its future.)
* Maddison, A. (1989) *The World Economy in the Twentieth Century*, Paris: OECD. (An authoritative study estimating the growth performance of the 32 largest economies in the world between 1900 and 1987.)
* Magaziner, I. and Hout, T. (1980) *Japanese Industrial Policy*, London: Policy Studies Institute. (A classic study of Japanese industrial policy during the 1960s and the 1970s, with excellent analyses of major industries.)
* Morishima, M. (1982) *Why Has Japan Succeeded?*, Cambridge: Cambridge University Press. (A famous, if highly controversial, book explaining the Japanese economic success in terms of its cultural values.)
* Polanyi, K. (1957) *The Great Transformation*, Boston, MA: Beacon Press. (A classic work emphasizing that the 'natural' order of free market needs to be deliberately constructed by the state.)
* Radelet, S. and Sachs, J. (1998) 'The East Asian financial crisis: diagnosis, remedies and prospects', *Brookings Paper on Economic Activity*, (1): 1–90. (An article criticizing the arguments that blame the Asian countries for the 1997 crisis and the IMF's role in it.)
* Singh, A. (1999) 'Asian "capitalism" and the financial crisis' in J. Michie and J. Grieve Smith (eds) *Global Instability – The Political Economy of*

World Economic Governance, London: Routledge. (A powerful critique of those arguments that see the 'end of Asian Capitalism' in the 1997 crisis.)
* Stiglitz, J. (1996) 'Some lessons from the East Asian miracle', *The World Bank Research Observer* 11 (2): 151–77. (An insightful synthesis of the theoretical and the policy lessons from the East Asian economic success.)
* Sweezy, P. *et al.* (1976) *The Transition from Feudalism to Capitalism*, London: New Left Books (A collection of major essays in the 1970s Marxist debate on the origins of capitalism in Western Europe and Japan.)
* Thompson, G. (1989) 'Introduction' in G. Thompson (ed.) *Industrial Policy – USA and UK Debates*, London: Routledge. (An insightful literature review of the USA and the UK debates on industrial policy during the 1980s.)
* Wade, R. (1990) *Governing the Market*, Princeton, NJ: Princeton University Press. (A major study of Taiwan's development that was very influential in shattering the 'free market' orthodoxy on the East Asian NICs.)
* Woo-Cumings, M. (ed.) (1999) *The Developmental State*, Ithaca, NY: Cornell University Press. (A collection of essays developing the tradition of developmental state theory of Chalmers Johnson in the 1990s context.)
* World Bank (1993) *The East Asian Miracle*, New York: Oxford University Press. (The controversial study of the East and the Southeast Asian economies from the World Bank responding to the heterodox critiques.)
* *World Development* (1994), The special section on the East Asian miracle: economic growth and public policy, ed. A. Amsden, 22 (4): 613–70. (A collection of essays debating the World Bank's East Asian Miracle Report – contains some key criticisms of the report.)

See also: ECONOMY OF JAPAN; INTERNATIONAL FINANCIAL STABILITY; INTERNATIONAL MONETARY FUND; MONEY AND CAPITAL MARKETS, INTERNATIONAL; WORLD TRADE ORGANIZATION.

Economies of central and eastern Europe, transition of

1 Understanding the transition process
2 Levels of attainment of transition
3 Micro-level transition

Overview

The economic transition of eastern and central Europe is a multi-phase process of abandoning communist economic institutions and mechanisms and replacing them with market structures and dynamics. This process takes place on both macro (national economy) and micro (firm) levels.

On the macro level, six phases of this process have been identified: the political phase, the early 'marketization' phase, the inflation control phase, the phase of building market institutions, the anti-recession economic policies phase and the growth policy phase. Within this context, the economies of central and eastern Europe are highly diversified; they include institutionally mature economies, economies which are still building institutions, monetarily unstable economies and politically unstable economies.

On the micro level, enterprises can be divided into five types: large, low-value-added state-owned enterprises in heavy industries; enterprises producing higher value-added marketable products; small businesses; large private enterprises; and enterprises with foreign capital participation (joint ventures). These different types of enterprise each face different transition problems in different economies.

1 Understanding the transition process

The transition of the post-communist economies which emerged in central and eastern Europe after the fall of the Berlin Wall in 1989 is understood here as a gradual movement away from a communist economy towards contemporary market mechanisms and institutions capable of sustaining economic growth. Communist economies (Kornai 1992), as a point of departure for the transition process, have the following as their most important characteristic features: (1) the political monopoly of the communist party guaranteed and enforced by totalitarian dictatorship; (2) the economic monopoly of the state, based on exclusive or absolutely dominating state ownership; (3) bureaucratic coordination of supply and demand (through central planning and administrative allocation of resources), excluding or distorting market mechanisms and the active role of such monetary categories as prices, wages, interest rates and exchange rates, which remain under strict government control; and (4) a communist welfare state providing (within the limits of production not needed for political or military objectives) for such needs as housing, health care, education and culture.

The communist economic system was created and forcefully imposed in order to provide an economic basis for the Marxian utopia of a class-free society. Communist rulers, who had ambitions to dominate the world politically and militarily, were always obsessed with equalling and surpassing the level of economic development and technological progress of the most advanced capitalist countries.

Communist economies collapsed not only because they were unable to fulfil promises of economic growth and prosperity, but because in the late 1980s they were also simply unable to continue functioning. Ambitious plan targets were never met (Zaleski 1980), and allocation of resources became chaotic and incidental. Low productivity levels (Sirc 1994), combined with exhaustion of extensive sources of growth (natural resources and foreign borrowing), put into jeopardy both political and military objectives and minimum standards of living of the populations

(Gregory and Stuart 1990). The system proved to be unable to maintain a minimum level of economic equilibrium and was increasingly characterized as 'economics of shortage' (Kornai 1980), defined as the lack of an adequate supply of consumer goods and production capacity under relatively stable and inadequately changing price levels (also known as 'repressed inflation'). Finally, as a result of unfulfilled promises and a shocking discrepancy between ideology and reality, the communist system completely lost legitimation, and massive political dissent (such as the Polish 'Solidarity' movement started in 1980) was impossible to stop (Staniszkis 1991).

In order to make an inventory of transition problems and to compare different countries, it is useful to visualize transition as a multiphase process. Kozminski (1992) proposes the following six stage model:

1 The political phase. This phase sees the elimination of the communist political monopoly and oppression apparatus, the resolution of ethnic conflicts and the formation of political parties and democratic institutions.
2 The early 'marketization' phase. This phase sees the liberation of prices from government controls, eliminating 'repressed inflation' and triggering a 'corrective inflation wave', internal convertibility of the currency (the legal right to buy and sell foreign currency), elimination of the legal barriers constraining private entrepreneurship and the 'privatization' of small businesses (see PRIVATIZATION AND REGULATION).
3 The inflation control phase. In this phase restrictive monetary policies are introduced, including the imposition of budget discipline through the curbing of subsidies and other forms of government spending (including social services).
4 The market institutions building phase. This phase sees the privatization of large state-owned enterprises, the implementation of a comprehensive mass privatization programme enabling large groups of people to acquire ownership (shares), the restructuring of government, banking system reform, tax reform, the creation of a capital market and partial 'marketization' of social and welfare services through the creation of institutions such as private retirement funds and medical plans.
5 The anti-recession economic policies phase. This phase sees the elimination of non-viable state-owned enterprises, the restructuring of viable industries, the development of a job creation and employment policy to compensate partially for the net job loss caused by restructuring, small business promotion, trade policies providing domestic business with temporary protection, stimulation of the formation of modern distribution channels and stimulation of foreign capital inflow.
6 The growth policy phase. This final phase sees the full convertibility of the currency, the formulation and implementation of a comprehensive industrial policy, the stimulation of international networking and business alliances and export-led growth.

The sequential character of the process implies that both 'premature' and 'delayed' policies bring complications and inhibit the transition process. Hungary's first stabilization plan, negotiated by the last communist government with the IMF and implemented in 1988, is a good example of a premature policy (see INTERNATIONAL MONETARY FUND). It lacked political support because the communists were still in power and the political phase of transition was just beginning. The institutions building phase in Poland, still not completed even in 2000 with consolidation of the banking industry, commercialization of social services and privatization of state-dominated industries still to be completed, provides an example of a delay in transition policies.

Successful completion of any one phase is conditioned by the implementation of measures included in earlier transition phases. Privatization cannot really gain momentum without banking reform and the establishment of a capital market. The capital market cannot function normally before inflation is under control. Foreign capital is not likely to come to economies affected by recession, or where market institutions and a legal system effectively protecting property rights are not yet in place.

Once one phase is completed, the next one has to be initiated without delay. Fixation on any one phase is due in most cases to only partially successful implementation; political distortions and a lack of professionalism can result in such policy mistakes as chaotic trade policies, for example a shift from unconditional opening of markets to protectionism. Delays and a lack of proper sequencing can easily lead to dangerous 'loops' in the transition process, meaning a return to earlier phases. Experiences of transition between 1989 and 2000 prove that both unsuccessful inflation control (Russia, Ukraine, Belorussia) and the lack of energetic and efficient anti-recession policy (Bulgaria, Lithuania, Latvia, Romania) can compromise political equilibrium and cause either a return to earlier phases or considerably delay the whole process of transformation.

The question of the possibility of return to the old communist economic system is seldom addressed. Such a question is not without relevance, however, in the light of electoral victories as early as in 1992 and in 1993 by post-communist parties in Lithuania, Poland, Hungary and several post-Soviet states. Fears of the return of the old communist system have so far proven to be unfounded, although some elements of socialism represented by certain mainstream political parties might be still viable in central and eastern European countries in transition. As Berliner (1992) points out, the 'socialist vision' was always twofold; its values included aversion to excessive social and economic inequality, and its institutions were organized under public ownership and with central economic planning. These public institutions are very unlikely to be rebuilt; their economic inefficiency is self-evident and they lack economic foundations and resources as well as political support. As far as values are concerned, Berliner again points out that 'paradoxically, liberal democratic capitalism offers a greater opportunity for the attainment of most socialist values than any socialism we have yet known' (Berliner 1992: 8). The return of communism in its old form is thus very unlikely, even in countries that are least advanced in the transition process.

2 Levels of attainment of transition

It is unlikely that any country could have a smooth journey through all the phases of transition. For example, some countries might be stuck for a long time in the earlier stages of the transition process. However, some countries will go through the transition process in a much more orderly way and in consequence at greater speed and at a lower cost than others. The winners will be the countries that do not experiment with 'big leaps' but rely on consistent, comprehensive, focused and well-timed policies, professionally implemented and well adjusted to local conditions. At time of writing in 2000, countries negotiating accession to the EU: the Czech Republic, Estonia, Hungary, Poland and Slovenia, appeared to be winners.

However, as noted above, the economies of central and eastern Europe are highly diverse, with the result that some have more difficulty than others in undertaking the transition process. Some countries are much more advanced than others; some are facing the danger of temporary setbacks; some have yet to resolve political problems conditioning the real start of the transition process. A multi-phase transition model enables the identification of four categories of post-communist countries:

1. Institutionally mature countries, which have completed the institution building phase and succeeded in developing political and economic links with the West. These countries are likely to have a business climate and infrastructure that are highly compatible with those of the West. These countries are capable of controlling inflation and are coming out of recession. In 2000, Hungary and Slovenia came closest to fitting this description.
2. Institution building countries are also capable of controlling inflation and have been successful at early 'marketization'. Some, such as Poland, have healthy and stable growth rates and have been successful in attracting foreign capital; others such as the Czech Republic are attractive locations for foreign investment in spite of temporary difficulties. Institution building

countries, however, have not yet completed the building of market institutions, in particular replacing the bankrupt communist welfare state, developing the legal framework of a market economy, law enforcement system and financial institutions.
3 Monetarily unstable countries are still in the early 'marketization' phase and are unable to control inflation or to control a 'corrective inflation' wave. Many former republics of the USSR, Bulgaria and Romania are among countries experiencing this problem, preventing them from taking further steps along the path to transition.
4 Politically unstable countries are still facing serious unresolved ethnic and political conflicts and consequently are unable to complete the political phase and begin transition. These countries have still to resolve all their accumulated transition problems: political, early marketization, inflation control, institution building and recession. First of all, however, they need political stability and firm establishment of democratic institutions. Russia is the most prominent country in this category.

Political instability can be easily identified as the most important single threat potentially inhibiting the transition process. Instability results from an inability to resolve conflicts by the means of negotiated compromises, to cooperate and to accept common platforms. This leads to political paralysis, anarchy, violence or even genocide, as in the former Yugoslavia or in Chechnya. Political instability is also fuelled by ill-conceived, poorly implemented and constantly changing government policies, corruption and bureaucratic red tape.

Addressing the problems of political instability requires the existence of a highly competent government which can solve the key problems of transition (Antal-Mokos 1998). However, governments capable of addressing and solving such problems in a competent and consistent way are still lacking in central and eastern Europe. The most advanced countries, those with the best prospects of successful transition, are also characterized by a relatively higher quality of civil service (Kaminski and Kurczewska 1995; Kornai 1990).

3 Micro-level transition

Transition on the macro level of national economic systems is highly dependent upon transition on the micro enterprise level of individual enterprises and the ability of managers and owners (including governments) to make these enterprises competitive. The identification of transition problems on the micro level calls for a typology of the postcommunist enterprises. Five types of postcommunist enterprises (excluding agriculture) can be identified:

1 large state-owned enterprises (SOEs) in the 'smokestack' industries and the military sector, also known as 'dinosaurs';
2 SOEs capable of turning out exportable products and maintaining the domestic market, but suffering from overemployment, lack of market access and marketing know how, and inadequate technology and equipment;
3 joint ventures (JVs) formed by SOEs or the government with foreign partners;
4 small private businesses;
5 large privately owned enterprises.

An analysis of thirty-six post-communist enterprises in Poland, Hungary, Czech Republic and Russia (Kozminski 1993) indicates that each type of enterprise has its own set of management problems and that at different stages of transition, different types of enterprises are of key importance. In institutionally mature and institution building countries, large private enterprises emerge. The problems faced by these enterprises are mainly strategic; often highly diversified, they have to define or redefine their mission, markets and clients, form adequate partnerships and alliances and – most important of all – find sources of capital enabling them to finance growth. The privatization process offers opportunities for acquisitions and mergers. Postcommunist enterprises, however, suffer from a lack of capital and must solve this problem first. Restrictive monetary policies and budget deficits that absorb all surplus capital make these problems even more pressing.

The 'dinosaurs'

Politically unstable and monetarily unstable economies are dominated by the fate of the 'dinosaurs', huge SOEs in heavy industries that drain scarce resources, aggravate financial crises and increase inflationary pressures. This problem is also important in institution building economies, but here it is less dramatic because new economic agents have already entered the game as result of successful early 'marketization'.

Restructuring of 'dinosaurs' requires an individualized approach, meticulous programming, adequate financing and prolonged, extensive negotiations with unions and other workers' organizations (including self-management), local governments, banks, clients and suppliers. The inherent weakness, instability, lack of consistent policy and lack of professionalism of post-communist governments suggest that the leading role in the restructuring of the 'dinosaurs' has to be played by their own management.

Not all 'dinosaurs' are hopeless cases. Some, especially but not exclusively those in the military sector, have relatively high technological levels, with modern equipment and highly trained engineers and workers. Such enterprises can develop partnerships with global market leaders or with local partners as suppliers. Polish shipbuilding industry provides examples of successfully restructured dinosaurs becoming world-class players on the global markets (Johnson and Loveman 1995). Some dinosaurs can be broken up and transformed into a number of smaller viable enterprises. Some, however, will need to be phased out of existence in an orderly manner.

Any restructuring effort requires from the beginning market analysis and identification of viable products which can compete and sustain the future existence and development of the company in an open economy. Projected sales of such products enable a determination of the viable size and structure of the company. Restructuring programmes based on such projected outcomes indicate an orderly way of both disposing of redundant resources, both human and material, and acquiring new resources that will enable the company to sell and compete. Such a programme also requires financial backing, with a package resulting from negotiations with banks and financial institutions, and often also requiring government guarantees. Access to markets, technology and financing can be also acquired through strategic business partnerships with domestic and foreign partners. Finally, such programmes can only be implemented if negotiated with workers' organizations and accepted by them. This can be particularly difficult given that the workforce employed by 'dinosaurs' is often highly politicized and difficult to deal with, and that post-communist managers have a strong preference for an authoritarian management style (Aleksandrowicz 1992; Pearce 1993).

Small businesses

Small businesses also play different roles at different stages of the transition process and in different types of post-communist economies. In politically unstable and monetarily unstable economies, small businesses make early 'marketization' happen and create a market environment, thus enabling the economy to reach a 'critical mass' of systemic transformation from planned to market economy relatively early. The examples of Poland and Hungary demonstrate that all private economic activities (even those which are unregistered or illegal) can play a positive role. In some cases, however, the massive involvement of organized crime in business (the 'mafiaization' of business) and links between criminal or shadow economy networks and politics have contributed to a parasitic image of private economic activity and the market economy. This is particularly true of Russia, Ukraine and other post-Soviet states.

In institution building economies, legalization of private small businesses and their full integration into the institutional framework of the market economy becomes a key issue. Banking systems, taxation and government industrial policy can help to promote private entrepreneurship in certain regions or sectors or by certain groups of people, enabling the integration process to proceed more quickly. In institutionally mature economies, small businesses create employment and 'cushion' large manufacturers from market fluctuations by providing a 'ring' or 'network' of small responsive suppliers, sub-contractors and providers of services.

Privatization

More advanced SOEs capable of producing marketable products, mainly in consumer goods and more technologically advanced industries, are the most likely targets of the first wave of large-scale privatization, based on public offerings of shares or the negotiated sale of large portfolios to foreign investors. A successfully implemented stabilization and anti-inflationary plan, which reduces aggregate domestic demand and exposes domestic firms to foreign competition, forces viable enterprises to revise their strategies and structures. Market analysis lays the foundations for adjustment and restructuring plans. Analysis of the main sources of competitive advantage and the main weaknesses of the firm enables the formulation of improvement programmes containing such elements as new production and quality management, product development programmes, inventory management, merchandise handling and customer service. Financing of the improvement programme is often linked to privatization. As Russian, Czech and to a lesser extent Polish experience shows, so called 'mass privatization' or 'voucher privatization' is less likely to trigger such improvement programmes. Massive distributions of equity, free of charge or at symbolic price, are usually not linked to changes in management that can turn around the enterprises.

Joint ventures

Joint ventures and foreign direct investment are likely to start playing a somewhat more important and more active role in institution building and institutionally mature economies. Foreign capital involvement is directly influenced by the country's ability to initiate and implement successful anti-recession policies. Foreign capital is mainly tempted by the size and the rate of growth of the market, but also requires political and monetary stability and a friendly business environment compatible at least to some extent with Western requirements.

An analysis of joint ventures with Western capital participation operating in post-communist countries (McDonald 1993) indicates that many of them fail because of short-term orientation, lack of serious commitment, the inability of partners to spell out clearly their objectives and to communicate these to each other, unstable legal and fiscal frameworks and incompetence and corruption on the part of the government administration.

The role of management

It is generally acknowledged that management skills are the most important single factor conditioning the success of transition on the micro level (Abell 1992; Shama 1993; Johnson and Loveman 1995). Different phases of enterprise restructuring (Kozminski 1997) call for different types of managerial skills:

- At the 'fight for survival' stage, when post-communist enterprises are first confonted with market forces and financial constraints, entrepreneurial and political skills play decisive role. Managers have to negotiate with the workers, the government and business partners. Products have to be repositioned and new distribution channels developed.
- At the 'functional restructuring' stage functional skills in such areas as marketing, finance, production management etc. play decisive roles. With respect to western management skills, enterprises have to be brought up to the minimum western performance levels.

Successful completion of the 'process restructuring' phase conditions the competitive advantage of central and east European enterprises when confronted on equal grounds with western companies. Customer and supplier relations and knowledge of the international markets have to be intensively developed.

The best of the post-communist enterprises aspire to market leadership and to enter the 'continuous improvement' phase of organization development. At this stage strategic and transformational leaderhip skills become the most important. Those economies where enterprises are capable of building up managerial skills in such a way are clearly the most successful transition economies.

ANDRZEJ K. KOZMINSKI
LEON KOZMINSKI ACADEMY OF
ENTREPRENEURSHIP AND MANAGEMENT

Further reading

(References cited in the text marked *)

* Abell, D. (1992) *Turnaround in Eastern Europe: In-Depth Studies*, New York: United Nations Development Programme. (Six case studies of enterprise restructuring in Poland, Slovenia and Croatia, with implications for management development.)
* Aleksandrowicz, P. (1992) 'Polscy menedzerowie najwyzszych szczebli' (Polish top executives), *Rzeczpospolita* 171–3. (Daily newspaper article in Polish presenting results of an opinion survey of a representative sample of top Polish managers.)
* Antal-Mokos Z. (1998) *Privatization, Politics and Economic Performance in Hungary*, Cambridge: Cambridge University Press (Macroanalysis of economic, social and political mechanisms of transition in Hungary with special attention paid to privatization of the state owned enterprises.)
* Berliner, J.S. (1992) 'Socialism in the twenty-first century', in M. Keren and G. Ofer (eds), *Trials of Transition: Economic Reform in the Former Communist Block*, Boulder, CO: Westview Press. (The author discusses the chances of survival and implementation of some of the elements of socialist ideology in contemporary market economies after the fall of the Soviet empire.)
Grancelli, B. (ed.) (1995) *Social Change and Modernization: Lessons from Eastern Europe*, Berlin: Walter de Gruyter. (Collection of papers presenting the latest state-of-the-art research on social, political and economic aspects of transition in central and eastern Europe.)
* Gregory, P.R. and Stuart, R.C. (1990) *Soviet Economic Structure and Performance*, New York: Harper & Row. (Academic textbook presenting history, mechanisms and results of the Soviet economic system from its to birth to the end.)
* Johnson S. and Loveman G.W. (1995) *Starting Over in Eastern Europe. Entrepreneurship and Economic Renewal*, Boston: Harvard Business School Press. (Case studies and analysis of entrepreneurship, enterprise restructuring and privatization in Poland).
* Kaminski, A.Z. and Kurczewska, J. (1995) 'Strategies of post-communist transformations: elites as institution builders', in B. Grancelli (ed.), *Social Change and Modernization: Lessons from Eastern Europe*, Berlin: Walter de Gruyter. (Essay analysing the role of elites in the process of transformation in central and eastern Europe.)
Kolodko, G. (2000) *From Shock to Therapy. The Political Economy of Post-Socialist Transformation*, New York and Oxford: Oxford University Press. (Comparative analysis of transformation of post-communist countries in the light of contemporary economic theory. Social and political aspects are present in the analysis).
* Kornai, J. (1980) *The Economics of Shortage*, Amsterdam: North Holland. (Macroeconomic theory explaining the cumulative mechanism of deficit in communist economies.)
* Kornai, J. (1990) *The Road to a Free Economy: Shifting From a Socialist System: The Example of Hungary*, New York: W.W. Norton. (This book presents a general survey of macroeconomic problems of transition and an original blueprint of a transition plan for Hungary. It is an example of a pragmatic approach to transition.)
* Kornai J. (1992) *The Socialist System: The Political Economy of Communism*, Princeton, NJ: Princeton University Press. (This book contains the most comprehensive analysis of the communist economic system. It describes its foundations, mechanisms and dynamics and provides useful insights into the legacy of communism.)
* Kozminski, A.K. (1992) 'Transition from planned to market economy: Hungary and Poland compared', *Studies in Comparative Communism* 24 (4): 315–32. (Article comparing macroeconomic policies adopted in Hungary and Poland during the first years of transition from plan to market.)
* Kozminski, A.K. (1993) *Catching Up? Organizational and Management Change in the Ex-Socialist Block*, Albany, NY: State University of New York Press. (The book describes organizational change on the enterprise level. Thirty-six cases of enterprises coping with transition in Poland, the Czech Republic, Hungary and Russia are presented and analysed.)
* Kozminski, A.K. (1997) 'Lessons from recession in Central and Eastern Europe: from survival to continuous improvement' in: Sarah S. King and Donald P. Cushman (eds) *Lessons From The Recession*, Albany, NY: State University of New York Press: pp. 151–77. (Empirically

grounded analytical model of enterprise restructuring in Central and Eastern Europe.)

Kozminski A.K. and Yip G.S. (2000) *Strategies for Central and Eastern Europe*, London: Macmillan Business. (Comparative analysis of strategies used by multinational companies in 11 countries of central and eastern Europe prepared by local experts using common analytical framework).

Lavigne M. 1995. *The Economics of Transition from Socialist Economy to Market Economy*, New York: St. Martin's Press. (Critical analysis of the first years of transition with detailed analysis of the communist system and its disintegration).

* McDonald K.R. (1993) 'Why privatization is not enough', *Harvard Business Review* 71 (May–June): 49–59. (This article presents empirical studies of several cases of privatization with foreign capital participation in Poland.)

* Pearce J.L. (1993) 'From socialism to capitalism: the effects on Hungarian human resources practices', *Academy of Management Executive* 5 (4): 75–88. (Empirical study presenting personnel management and human resource practices in Hungarian enterprises after the fall of communism.)

* Shama, A. (1993) 'Management under fire: the transformation of managers in the Soviet Union and Eastern Europe', *Academy of Management Executive* 7 (1): 22–35. (This article presents the results of empirical investigation, mainly interviews with managers, conducted in Russia and central Europe.)

* Sirc, L. (ed.) (1994) *Why the Communist Economies Failed*, London: Centre for Research into Communist Economies. (Collection of critical macroeconomic essays analyzing the mechanism and reasons of failure of communist economies.)

* Staniszkis, J. (1991) *The Dynamic of Breakthrough in Eastern Europe*, Berkeley, CA: California University Press. (Deep sociological analysis of the 'latent structures' of the fall of communism in central and eastern Europe.)

* Zaleski, E. (1980) *Stalinist Planning for Economic Growth: 1933–1952*, London: Macmillan. (Statistical macroeconomic and institutional analysis of the mechanism and results of Stalinist economic planning in Russia.)

See also: PRIVATIZATION AND REGULATION

Capitalism, varieties of

1 From managerial revolution to great depression
2 Depression, war, and divergent development
3 The 1960s: the heyday of managerial capitalism
4 The 1970s: surging inflation and corporatist responses
5 The 1980s and 1990s
6 Varieties of capitalism in the twenty-first century?

Overview

France, Italy, the Netherlands, China, Argentina – the history of their capitalist institutions over the last century all have their fascinating particularity. In this essay, though, we concentrate on Britain, the US, Germany and Japan, the four countries central to the 'Rhenish vs. Anglo-Saxon capitalism' debate which, for all its simplifications, involves central issues of both welfare and economic efficiency.

What pattern does a backward look over the last century of those countries' evolution suggest? Is it one of gradual convergence as the pressures of globalization relentlessly force abandonment of practices deeply rooted in national cultures? That is not the whole story, since the institutions of Japan and Germany were arguably more similar to those of the United States in the 1920s than they are today. Is it, then, the story of the rise and fall (at a differing pace in different countries) of a major twentieth-century heresy – the belief that state interference in the economy could have benign effects? (The 'mixed economy' notions of the 1960s being pale reflections of Soviet planning?) Hardly, since many of the distinctive features of the Japanese economy have nothing much to do with the state. So is it a story of the stubborn immutability of deep-rooted cultures? Hardly, since institutional evolution (and in Japan and Germany great institutional leaps) has been a feature of all four countries. Ebb and flow, then? Apparent convergence towards patterns of managerial capitalism in the 1960s, followed by renewed divergence in the 1980s as increasingly untrammelled market forces and the rising power of institutional investors have transformative effects, chiefly in the Anglo-Saxon countries. And then, again in the 1990s, renewed convergence as both the market forces and the investors become more global and increase their impact on Germany and Japan? A possible interpretation. By reviewing the detailed history of this ebb and flow, might one hope to arrive at a reasoned assessment of how far that convergence will go, which is, after all, a crucial determinant of the history of the next century? We certainly do not arrive at confident predictions. Perhaps the reader will.

1 From managerial revolution to great depression

Britain

The US and Germany were coming up fast, but, as the century began, Britain – the 'workshop of the world' – was still the global leader in GDP per capita and exports. Its manufacturing enterprises were still predominantly under family control, while ample supplies of locally concentrated and highly skilled craft workers enabled Britain to dominate the world economy without systematically educating and training technical specialists and administrative personnel to build managerial organizations (see Burgess 1975; Hobsbawm 1984; Harrison and Zeitlin, 1985; Lazonick 1990: chs 3–6). In industrial sectors that were characterized by the separation of share ownership from managerial control in other major capitalist economies, proprietary capitalism persisted in Britain through the first half of the twentieth century; top managers were often substantial shareholders by virtue of family connections (Hannah 1983; Chandler 1990:

pt 2; Church 1993). Even within science-based enterprises, technical specialists found little opportunity to become, over the course of their careers, generalist 'leaders of men', and, particularly in machine-based enterprises, control over work organization stayed in the hands of craft workers (Lazonick 1985; Lewchuk 1987).

If industry, located in the Midlands and the North, was the world's workshop, the City of London was the world's banker, and between workshop and bank, the difference in social status was clear. The skills of the Rothschilds and Barings were married to the social cachet of the landed gentry (only Queen Victoria stopped Gladstone from giving Rothschild a peerage in 1869), and successful middle-class manufacturers sent their sons to the same gentlemanly educational institutions – the 'aristocratic' public schools and Oxbridge – that supplied the future elite to City firms as well as to politics, law, colonial administration, and agriculture/estate management (Cassis 1985; Daunton 1992). And it was from those public schools, and from the arts, not science, departments of the elite universities, that growing business enterprises recruited their top managers when sons or sons-in-law were unavailable (Coleman 1973; Sanderson 1988). British engineers never acquired the social status that their counterparts enjoyed in the United States, Germany or Japan, even in chemical and electrical engineering, where companies had, perforce, to recruit university-educated engineers, much less in the machine-based industries (Lazonick 1985).

The power gap between top management who controlled the allocation of resources and the technical specialists upon whom businesses relied to improve process and product quality and reduce costs was also a social gap and a cultural gap. The consequent underdevelopment of modern managerial organization contributed to what the Liberal Industrial Inquiry of 1928 called 'remediable inefficiency' – a mixture of 'individualism instead of cooperation, secretiveness instead of publicity, neglect of marketing, indifference and often hostility to research' (Liberal Industrial Inquiry 1928, p.127).

The United States

It was in the United States that, by the 1920s, a much more powerful form of managerial capitalism evolved. Stock ownership came to be separated from managerial control. The Great Merger Movement at the turn of the century played a pivotal role in effecting this separation. Until then, a market in 'industrial' (as distinct from railroad or government) securities did not exist. Wall Street (led by J.P. Morgan) created the market in industrial securities by floating stocks and bonds to carry out mergers, using the money raised or the (now tradable) securities themselves to buy out, and typically retire, the owner-entrepreneurs (Navin and Sears 1955). Taking their places at the top were salaried managers who had worked their way up and around the increasingly formalized structures of the growing enterprises (Chandler 1977). As, during the first three decades of the twentieth century, the stocks of these dominant corporations came to be widely held by the public, the stock market became increasingly liquid while ever fewer stockholders had any interest in exercising their ownership rights to monitor corporate managers (Means 1930).

But the stock market played only a minor role in providing new capital. Retained earnings, not external sources of capital, became the financial foundation for investing in the further growth of the industrial enterprise. The managerial organizations which, as Berle and Means pointed out, thus became increasingly autonomous, melded and integrated both executive generalists and technical specialists (Berle and Means 1932). Their mass-production technologies vastly reduced the need for operator skills, thereby sharpening the line of division between manager and shop-floor worker.

As American industry made the transition from the machine-based first industrial revolution to the science-based second industrial revolution, higher education became central to supplying technical specialists to industrial corporations (Noble 1977; Servos 1980). Given the separation of ownership and control, these specialists could potentially over the course of their careers rise to generalist positions as upper-level managers within their enterprises. These university-educated managers took an ever more active interest in ensuring that, in terms of both teaching and research, the system of higher education served corporate needs. They began to create their own corporate research facilities and developed close links with the leading research universities.

New and more automated processes eliminated the need for many of the skilled craft workers. But, the high fixed costs of developing and installing new technology, and the cost of materials tied up in work-in-progress, meant that managers had to win the cooperation of production workers in maintaining the flow of work. In the 1920s 'welfare capitalism, company unions and corporate efficiency' went hand in hand (Jacoby 1997: 21). In what was called the 'non-union era', the promise of long-term employment, a greater recognition of seniority, employee welfare, and subordination of line management to personnel departments offered a softer approach to countering the threat of independent unions than the more directly repressive American Plan (Jacoby 1985; Lazonick 1990: chs. 7–8).

Germany

Of our two late developers, the German variety of capitalism is, like those of its British and US counterparts, more deeply rooted in history than the Japanese. Its educational preparation for industrialization was considerable, for instance. Whereas Japan's pre-Meiji education was, primarily, classical, moral and Confucian, in Germany state-building ambitions, particularly those of Prussia in the wake of its ignominious defeat by Napoleon, provided early incentives for the promotion of technical education. The diffusion of high-level scientific and technical education in the *technische hochschulen* from mid-century and the network of *ingenieurschulen* for more practical skills created in the 1890s gave German industry a competitive edge, particularly in chemicals, metals, electrical and heavy machinery (Gispen 1989; Konig 1993). The balance of German exports had already shifted from textiles and consumer goods to these technically based industries by the beginning of the century. Although there was still a greater predominance of family enterprise than in the US, the inheritors of those enterprises were much more likely to have a thorough technical training than in Britain. And in the enterprises that outgrew family control (even while, in the case of Siemens, Krupp, Thyssen, Wolff and many more, the family still held a majority share of the capital), the hierarchies of salaried managers allowed many of the technically trained to climb to the top (Kocka 1981; Brockstedt 1984; Pohl 1982; Feldenkirchen 1991).

The second distinguishing characteristic was the *venture-capital* role played by the leading banks, the *Grossbanken*, founded in the decades before and after unification. A typical sequence was as follows. The bank's own technical department or, later, their associated trustee (*Treuhand*) societies, would evaluate an entrepreneurial project and provided the loan capital to enable the new venture to become a going concern. This Hausbank would then arrange a public share flotation that enabled the enterprise to repay its bank loans, while leaving enterprise managers with control over retentions to finance future expansion. Even after the loans were repaid, the bank continued to hold seats on the supervisory boards (which controlled appointments to, and major financial commitments of, the management board) and, through the system of 'bearer shares', held extensive proxy voting rights. In the larger and stronger firms, links with other banks diluted dependence on the Hausbank, but the relation remained close (Barrett Whale 1930; Kocka 1980; Pohl 1984; Feldenkirchen 1991).

A third characteristic of German managerial capitalism was a greater mobilization, and further development of, the capacity for collective action. Compulsory membership in local chambers of the artisanal *handwerk* (an inheritance from Napoleon), and of the newer chambers of industry provided a basis for developing a widespread apprenticeship system in which firms were induced to train, not simply for their own needs but for their sector's collective needs. The direct continuity in many trades of traditional guild organizations made this easier – a factor wholly lacking in 'new country' United States, and largely destroyed by a century of slow pioneer industrialization in Britain (Sorge and Warner 1986). And the continuity was not merely a matter of 'cultural lag'. Bismarck consciously fostered these traditions by legally bolstering their licensing system as he sought to preserve socially stable artisanal production to counterbalance the dangerous proletarianization of the factory system.

The Bismarckian establishment sought other means of responding to the growing worker movement and deflecting the dangers of class-conflict observed in the early industrializers, notably the social insurance systems in which Germany was a pioneer (Streeck 1992: 112). Works councils to coopt the worker movement by giving it a legitimate but limited voice were also promoted in the 1890s but it was not until 1920 and the Weimar Republic, with a much stronger Social Democratic Party, that they became statutory – along with increased regulation of the employment contract and collective bargaining (Braunthal 1978; McKitrick 1994: ch. 6).

The expansion for war production, subsequent military defeat, the loss of international markets, and the victors' demands for reparations had a crippling effect on the German economy. The corporate sector responded to Germany's economic crisis by intensifying its capacity for collective action through the formation of industrial concerns (*Konzerne*) that created a dense web of interlocking shareholdings and directorates among companies. In the meantime the process of rationalization and concentration of industrial production during the Weimar years strengthened the power of industrialists and weakened that of workers and their unions. The *handwerk* sector suffered too, caught between the dynamic industrial enterprise on the one hand and the socialism of the working classes on the other. Its frustrations and fears helped in mobilizing the small business sector in what became the Nazi movement, against a ('red', Moscow-puppet, unGerman) labour movement (McKitrick 1994).

Japan

Japan was a later late-developer. In 1900, industrialization was barely a quarter century old. From the outset, the nation pursued a strategy of borrowing and improving upon Western technology. Critical to this development effort was the rapid creation of a high-quality system of higher education, supported by the state and pioneering industrialists (Yonekawa 1984). At the same time, Japan lacked the supplies of skilled craft labour in metalworking technologies that had accumulated in Britain, the United States and Germany over the course of the nineteenth century. Gradually, however, through education and training, Japan developed its critical metalworking sectors, and during the First World War was able to capture Asian export markets that the Europeans could no longer supply (Gordon 1985). Japan subsequently made great progress in the manufacture and export of cotton textiles and textile machinery, industries in which by the 1930s it had taken over world leadership from Britain (Mass and Lazonick 1990). While a relatively small number of cotton spinning companies integrated forward into weaving cotton textile manufacturing, they coexisted with large numbers of family enterprises that specialized in weaving. The widespread adoption of gas and electric engines increased the viability of these family enterprises in weaving, ceramics, export flatware, and engineering parts supply (Minami 1976).

In the late nineteenth century, state investments in armouries, shipbuilding, steel, mining, and railways (nationalized in 1906) fostered many of the early large-scale enterprises. But ownership and control over many of these state enterprises were handed to the *zaibatsu*, of which Mitsui, Mitsubishi, Sumitomo and Yasuda emerged as the most prominent. Meanwhile, groups of entrepreneurs launched successful joint-stock companies in a number of industrial sectors, including textiles, paper and engineering (mechanical, electrical and chemical) by investing in the training (often including long foreign sojourns) of key engineering personnel who could improve upon and adapt to local conditions technologies that were borrowed from abroad. During the first decades of the twentieth century, many of these joint-stock companies affiliated with the *zaibatsu*, which by the 1940s had become the biggest conglomerates in the world (Morikawa 1992).

Ownership of the *zaibatsu* was in the hands of powerful families who ran their empires by building substantial managerial organizations. From the late nineteenth century, they recruited engineers and administrators from the nation's new universities, and created promotion systems that enabled these managers to advance within the enterprise group over the course of their careers. The *zaibatsu* and their constituent enterprises were strategic in making long-term employment commitments to their personnel. As a general rule, they made these commitments only to highly trained technical and administrative employees within the managerial structure (Morikawa 1997). But, for lack of workers trained in industrial skills, in the decades between the wars, a small number of innovative enterprises began developing formal training and promotion schemes for key blue-collar workers as well (Gordon 1985). Yet, despite such incipient attempts to extend organizational integration to the shop floor, a distinguishing feature of the inter-war period was the emergence of class-conscious protest movements by those workers on low pay and in unstable employment. The intensified industrial unrest of the 1920s sparked off a brief policy debate between those who favoured the British legitimate conflict approach and those heirs of the Japanese transplant, Verein fur Sozialpolitik, who favoured the 'harmonize-suppress' approach. The latter won, and founded the influential Harmonization Society (*Kyochokai*) to mediate – often remarkably even-handedly – in industrial disputes.

American 'welfare capitalism' also had some influence on these developments. In fact, in 1930, one might have thought that managerial control and worker co-optation were the organizational pattern towards which the whole world was moving.

2 Depression, war, and divergent development

The depression changed all that. In the United States, intimations of welfare capitalism gave way to intensifying industrial conflict which became increasingly institutionalized. In contrast, in both Germany and Japan, a mixture of repression and patriotic mobilization put an end to the class conflict of the early 1930s, only to set up the two nations for a devastating defeat at the hands of the Allies. What emerged in Germany and Japan from the ashes of the Second World War were distinctive capitalist regimes characterized by substantial worker–manager cooperation and less worker–manager inequality of power and reward than in either of the Anglo-Saxon countries.

New Deal labour legislation in America made it possible to force powerful corporations to engage in collective bargaining, but their bargaining power in the recession was greatly limited. Despite a significant increase in government intervention into the economy under the New Deal, it would take US entry into the Second World War to pull the nation out of depression; in 1940 the unemployment rate was still 14.6 per cent. While industrial corporations failed to maintain steady employment for their 'hourly' workers during the 1930s, they made every effort to keep their organizations of salaried managers intact, and indeed, over the course of the 1930s expanded their R&D efforts (Mowery 1986: 191–2). During the Second World War, government spending vastly increased the research capabilities and production capacity of the major corporations.

The United States dominated the post-war world economy, with over 40 per cent of world GDP in 1950. This dominance was also reflected in the preponderant influence that America subsequently exercised and continues to exercise in post-war international institutions. Wartime expansion continued with the demand generated by European reconstruction, with the overseas spread of American corporations to Latin America and to Europe, and with the Cold War focus on high-technology military spending. Throughout this process, managerial control of enterprises was strengthened. Corporations and the state joined forces through the Taft-Hartley legislation of 1947 and the communist purges of 1949 to keep the growing power of the industrial unions in check. Meanwhile, the institutionalization of collective bargaining and seniority provisions of labour contracts improved the stability of employment and levels of pay for blue-collar workers (Brody 1980; Harris 1982; Lichtenstein 1985). Arms spending deepened technological relations among corporations, research universities, and the military, thus creating the post-war 'military-industrial complex' – a phrase coined by President Eisenhower as he departed from office and a structure described so incisively by John Kenneth Galbraith (1967) in *The New Industrial State*.

The legacy of the depression in Britain was the victory of the Labour Party in the 1945 election. When combined with the expansion of the welfare system and the commitment to full employment, nationalization of railways, steel and coal – industries that were all in dire need of modernization – greatly increased the role of the state. But the marginal infusions of new blood into the managerial cadres of the backward industries that were nationalized did little either to change the adversarial pattern of industrial relations or to rationalize management structures. In private industry, large firms increased their preponderance (the 100 biggest producing 30 per cent of manufacturing output in the early 1950s compared with 16 in 1909), and the takeover movement of the late 1950s finally reduced the scale of family ownership and family control. The salaried managers who now took control of companies still sought to emulate the aristocratic British elite, and thus segmented themselves from interaction with technical specialists while they remained reliant upon shop-floor workers to manage skill formation and work organization (Lazonick 1985). At the same time, financial interests in the City of London, which included equity-based pension funds, looked to the publicly traded industrial enterprises as sources of high returns. By the 1960s, a form of managerial capitalism had evolved in Britain, but it was one in which, compared with the managerial capitalisms that had emerged in the other advanced economies, British managers exercised little power over the 'stakeholders' within their enterprises (Wright 1962; Hannah 1986; Chandler 1990: ch. 9).

In Nazi Germany, the highly concentrated industrial sector provided ready foundations for its coordination by the Third Reich to mobilize the economy for war. Preparation for war and the actuality of war led to a strengthening of linkages among companies through the Nazi policy of enforced cartellization followed by their system of main committees and industrial rings. Especially during the early 1940s, the Nazis transformed the economy's traditional sectors by forcing many smaller enterprises to integrate their industrial operations with those of the larger combines. The authoritarian hand of the Nazi state also intervened to shape the skill formation system by integrating the apprenticeship training structures in the Handwerk sector with industrial needs, thus laying the foundation for the modern German system of apprenticeship (McKitrick 1994).

With Germany's defeat, the declared intention of the Allied Occupation forces, particularly the Americans, was to break the institutional support for Germany's distinctive variety of capitalism and to replace it with a system of so-called 'free enterprise'. But the onset of the Cold War, and the perceived importance of a strong West German economy as a bulwark against the power of the Soviets, led to a decline in the commitment to this path. What emerged from the war was a curious amalgam of old and new: ordo-liberal ideology, tough competition policy, compulsory Kammern membership, still strong and strongly hierarchical sectoral business associations, a reinforcement of a collectively-oriented training system (Shonfield 1965).

The final distinguishing characteristic of German capitalism crystallized fully in the post-war period when class conflict became contained on the one hand by the institutionalization of the zero-sum elements of the employment relationship in a highly organized wage bargaining system through industrial-sector union and employers' associations, and on the other by institutionalization of the positive sum elements in the system of co-determination. The West German movement for industrial democracy may have fallen short of its ambitions, but the post-war institution of codetermination, which ensures employee representation on the supervisory boards of corporate enterprises and on works councils that operate at the plant and enterprise levels, gave West Germany the most extensive formal system of employee representation in the world (Weidemann 1980).

Japanese wartime mobilization learned a lot from the German – notably in the imperative integration of small-firm supply networks which laid foundations for the modern system of long-term subcontracting. But the wartime changes had more profound consequences for what became established as the 'Japanese management system'. Some powerful strands in the Japanese version of 'fascism' (to accept the term loosely as covering the three Axis regimes) were as strongly anti-capitalist and more overtly socialist than German National Socialism. The Young Officer conspiracies (which paved the way for the army to take effective power out of the hands of all political parties) assassinated leading *zaibatsu* managers as well as bourgeois politicians. The managers were accused of being more interested in extracting revenues from their firms in the forms of dividends and directors' bonuses than committing these financial resources to the further development of the enterprises and hence of the nation.

Many younger bureaucrats shared these anti-capitalist sentiments, so that, when the war came, industrial mobilization was in the hands of men who believed passionately in organizational efficiency, but not in shareholders' rights. During the war, the stock exchange was closed, and the bureaucrats directed the allocation of bank loans to particular enterprises. Industry control associations run by experienced managers also rationalized trading relations of parts suppliers and controlled the allocation of raw materials. But the measure that had the most lasting effect on the post-war corporation was a decree that required Ministry approval of board appointments in major firms. Officials used that power to replace shareholder representatives with experienced and competent managers, mostly lifetime employees of their firms (Okazaki 1994). Until the arrival of foreign firms in the 1980s, Japan had practically no external labour market for executive talent.

The post-war dissolution of the *zaibatsu* under the Allied occupation served to consolidate this wartime shift in control over the allocation of corporate resources. The *zaibatsu* dissolution completely disenfranchised the *zaibatsu* owners and war-guilt purges forced large numbers of top managers to resign from their posts (Hadley 1970; Morikawa 1997). Managerial control was left in the hands of 'third-rank executives' – relatively young middle managers committed to catching up with the substantial development of technology in the West during the war, in close touch with the practical manufacturing problems, and with an acute sense of the need to commercialize technology if their firms were to survive. With the reopening of the stock market in 1949, these corporate managers refashioned in a much looser form the inter-firm and firm–bank relationships of the *zaibatsu* system by building a web of cross-shareholdings with other companies. This strategy of acquiring 'stable shareholders' (preferably shareholders one did business with) was greatly strengthened in the 1960s as defence against takeover by American companies that capital liberalization was making a real possibility (Hodder and Tschoegl 1993). The cross-shareholding system enabled an enterprise to maintain control over its revenues for the sake of developing its organizational and technological capabilities. This control over corporate revenues in turn created the financial foundations for both high levels of debt relative to equity through the 'main bank system' and the long-term employment of enterprise personnel.

The post-war labour compact was the final element in the system. The militant movement of the immediate post-war period was dominated by leaders bent on the replacement of capitalism by socialism (Moore 1983). But grass-roots unionism and the wartime workers' councils that replaced unions had always been enterprise-based; 'production control' – the union taking over the running of factories and shutting out managers – was a common form of strike in the late 1940s, and managers' attempts to cut back employment to match their reduced output was a major cause of strikes (Gordon 1985: pt 3). Out of the turbulence there emerged, by the mid-1950s, a settled compromise that recognized the negotiation and consultation rights of enterprise unions (which included white- as well as blue-collar workers and university graduates on management tracks for the first decade of their employment), and an implicit commitment of employers to provide 'lifetime employment' (Cusumano 1985; Hiwatari 1996).

Helping to transform that commitment into reality over the course of the 1950s were first the Korean War boom and then strong domestic consumer markets. Japanese household consumption grew on the basis of the ability of lifetime employees to share in the prosperity of their companies and the high level of income equality engendered by taxation and farm-subsidy policies as well as the conventions of the 'community firm'. Meanwhile, within companies, the development of multi-skilled production workers combined with organizational learning in which these workers interacted with engineers made possible the Japanese management practices – among them quality control, just-in-time, and continuous improvement (*kaizen*) – that were later to be adopted around the world.

3 The 1960s: the heyday of managerial capitalism

By the late 1960s, the final years of the Golden Age of post-war growth, managerial capitalism had become what seemed like a global norm. Everywhere, owners, now mainly public shareholders, had come to have less control than managers over the strategic direction as well as the day-to-day administration of the organizational empires they nominally owned (see MANAGERIAL THEORIES OF THE FIRM; MEANS, G.C.). The 'property system' on which theorists considered capitalism to be founded had been subtly modified. In Japan and Germany, juridical patterns of ownership meant in practice that the managers of industrial concerns were constrained only by ties of mutual dependence forged with the managers of banks and other enterprises whose world view, interests, and criteria of judgement coincided basically with their own. In the United States, as in Britain, 'there has been great reluctance to admit of a significant and enduring shift of power from the owners of capital', to quote Galbraith, but that is what had happened. As Galbraith (1967: 50) went on to say: 'A small proportion of the stock is represented at stockholders' meetings for a ceremony in which banality is varied chiefly by irrelevance. The rest is voted by proxy for the directors who have been selected by the management.'

Galbraith argued that the technological complexity of the activities in which major corporations were engaged demanded such an array of specialist knowledge that control over decision making had passed to the 'technostructure'. The *planning*, not just the implementation, of the operations of the company required the contribution and assessment of information not just by top management but a large group of subordinate employees that included, as Galbraith once told one of the authors, 'everyone who wears a tie'. Excluded from the 'technostructure' was the 'outer perimeter' of production and clerical workers who only had to do what they were told (Galbraith did not anticipate the Toyotism – or Saturnism – of the 1980s which brought even the shop-floor stratum in from the cold).

In the modern corporate enterprise, individual entrepreneurship and individual leadership had become more or less irrelevant (Galbraith 1967: 71). The planning habit was spreading: 'shortly after World War II ... many business corporations began formalizing a systematic means whereby a company seeks to become what it wants to be by the formulation of corporate-wide objectives and systematic performance controls ... for at least five years ahead' (US Bureau of the Budget, *Goal Setting and Comprehensive Planning*, 1963, quoted in Shonfield 1965). A McGraw-Hill survey found that by the early 1960s a survey of companies responsible for a half of total industrial investment could provide details of their investment plans three years ahead – compared with only 20 per cent in the late 1940s (Shonfield 1965).

The legitimacy of managerial control could be celebrated because, by and large, it was seen as delivering the goods. Growth rates were high (Table 1), unemployment was contained (Table 2), and in all four societies, the primary distribution of income was at least not becoming more unequal and the secondary distribution somewhat more equal, thanks to income taxes of a considerable, but at the time largely thought inevitable, degree of progressivity (Blinder 1980).

Table 1 GDP per capita: percent, average annual rates of growth by decades, 1950s–1980s

	Britain	United States	Germany	Japan
1950–59	2.6	4.0	8.5	8.6
1960–69	3.2	4.0	4.9	10.7
1970–79	2.4	2.8	3.1	5.3
1980–89	2.3	2.9	1.9	4.1

Source: Angus Maddison, *Dynamic Forces in Capitalist Development*, Oxford University Press, 1991: 216–19.

Table 2 Unemployment rates: annual average percentages by decades, 1950s–1980s

	Britain	United States	Germany	Japan
1950–59	2.5	4.4	5.0	2.0
1960–69	2.7	4.7	0.8	1.3
1970–79	4.4	6.1	2.2	1.7
1980–89	10.0	7.2	6.0	2.5

Source: Angus Maddison, *Dynamic Forces in Capitalist Development*, Oxford University Press, 1991: 262–5.

Largely as a result of the expansion of corporate employment and the strength of union bargaining, private pension plan coverage reached 41 per cent of the US work force in 1960, more than double the rate of coverage at the end of the war. Lyndon Johnson's Great Society project seemed to promise that the US, too, would use some of the proceeds of productivity growth to transform itself into a welfare state. With real hourly wages of US manufacturing workers rising on average by over two per cent per annum over these decades, and with blue-collar employees of major corporations becoming more consumption oriented and politically conservative, much was written about the 'end of ideology' and the 'bourgeoisification' of the working class.

Which is far from saying that the distributional conflict had been resolved. Germany and Japan had both settled down into relatively 'orderly' and predictable wage bargaining systems, but in Britain and the United States, conflict was endemic. Compared with Germany, days lost to strikes per employee between 1966 and 1970 were 38 times higher in Britain and 95 times higher in the United States (Flanagan *et al.* 1983: 225). In Britain, where plant-level shop stewards exercised considerable control over labour relations, the 'unauthorized' strike, or even the threat of one, was a most powerful bargaining weapon. It was this fragmentation of bargaining and the power of the shop stewards – itself reflecting a failure of British industrial managers to take control over shop-floor work organization – that made British manufacturing enterprises so vulnerable to worker actions and that reinforced Britain's lag in productivity growth (Bain 1983).

But the central topic of the 'whither capitalism' debates of the 1960s – the Cold War decade in which the communist and free market systems came closest to a nuclear exchange – revolved less around labour versus capital than around the state versus market theme. Although the dichotomy 'developmental state/regulatory state' did not enter into common discourse until the 1980s and the term 'industrial policy' only a little earlier, there was a widespread awareness that in Japan, growing faster in the 1960s than any large economy had ever grown before, the state had by no means abjured all its powers of direction and control that it had acquired during the war. Selective subsidies and tariff policies, preferential credits, five-year indicative plans to concentrate the thinking and direct the efforts of private business, investment cartels and recession cartels, were all seen as positive ingredients in Japan's growth recipe.

In Europe, Andrew Shonfield, in his *Modern Capitalism*, remarked that not even Schumpeter (1942) with his predictions that capitalism would eventually be socialized to eliminate the disruptions of economic crises had foreseen what had become obvious in Britain, France, Italy, Sweden, Austria; namely 'the vast importance of the authoritative calculations made by postwar governments, whose activities as entrepreneurs have become much the most important single force of the whole system' (Shonfield 1965). In Britain, for example, the creation in the 1960s of the tripartite National Economic Development Council and Organization and its multiple sector sub-committees was intended to inject a national planning element into the stimulation of investment and productivity improvement in the private sector.

Germany and the US stood out as having very low levels of public ownership and being dominated by a free market ideology that rejected state intervention in the economy. Yet, as Shonfield (1965) pointed out, the *ordo* part of the *ordo-liberalism* that Erhardt espoused, as well as the *soziale* part of the *soziale marktwirtschaft*, loomed large in the economy. It helped to make the tax take 34 per cent of German GNP in 1960, compared with only 28 per cent in Britain. At the *Land* level, public banks helped to foster and direct the growth of the *Mittelstand*, while the strength of hierarchically organized industry associations, albeit part of civil society rather than the state, played an important coordinating role.

And, as for the United States, given that Boeing and General Dynamics each sold some 65 per cent of their output to the state, Raytheon 70 per cent and Lockheed 80 per cent, given the post-Sputnik realization of the importance of the state's role in producing trained and educated manpower, given the industrial system's dependence on the state to regulate aggregate demand, given the close fusion of interests and concerns between corporate managers and state bureaucrats (and their frequent swapping of roles), who can doubt, argued Galbraith (1967), that the industrial system will 'evolve into a penumbra of the state', converging eventually with a Soviet Planning system evolving towards a greater concern with liberty and autonomy. That prediction was made, of course, well before the 'end of history' was in sight.

4 The 1970s: surging inflation and corporatist responses

The transition from the managerial capitalism of the 1960s to the neo-liberal free market system which became the dominant aspiration of the British and American governments in the 1980s was mediated by the traumas of the 1970s. The central problem, inflation, was common to all four economies. The resolution of the problem was primarily determined by the pattern of class conflict. Japan and Germany came through the crucible of the 1970s with their existing class compromise more or less intact, their form of capitalism reinforced. America, and to a much more overt degree Britain, came out of the decade with a decisive shift in the balance of power under way.

Most observers of post-war capitalism assumed that full employment would engender inflation, both through the labour market mechanisms embodied in the Phillips curve and because of an increasing bargaining power of unions combined with the power of corporations to administer prices. In the 1960s, however, Keynesian fine-tuning had kept inflation within acceptable – even benign – limits as long as growth fed both wages and profits. But the tendency, through the 1960s, for labour to gain a greater share of the proceeds of growth, was most marked in Britain where the profit squeeze was clearly affecting investment by the end of the decade (Glyn and Sutcliffe 1972: Appendix G).

The in-built factors producing inflation were vastly accentuated by the commodity price rise culminating in the great shift in oil prices brought about by OPEC. Both Japan and Britain had inflation rates of over 25 per cent in 1974–5. Yet Japan reduced inflation to single figures in one year, while Britain still had double-figure inflation – and much higher employment than Japan – at the end of the decade.

How did Japan do it? By a shift in the power balance within the framework of a stable, well-established pay bargaining system. Its 'spring offensive' (*shunto*) system was a single, decentralized but simultaneous, national bargaining round with clear wage leaders, and months of public pre-negotiation discussions which had the effect of setting 'expectations norms'. These discussions always had assumed some willingness of both employers and unions to think in terms of a common national interest in stable prices and increased productivity (an element conspicuously lacking in Britain). But unions – in part a carry-over from immediate post-war militancy – had, until the runaway inflation of 1975, considerable power to mobilize bargain-period strikes. And used it. But in that year the sense of national crisis and the combined jawboning of government and employer associations reduced the resolve of the unions to secure wage gains, and the initiative shifted – as it turned out permanently – to managers (Dore 1987).

Control of inflation was also made far easier by the fact that rapid increases in output (and thereby also of productivity) were possible through exports which contributed a great deal to the 24 per cent growth in real GDP, 1975–80. Japan had reached the optimal stage of development: world levels of technology and product quality plus wages still below those of its competitors.

A final important factor was the willingness (and, with a still highly controlled financial sector, the ability) of the government to sustain demand by deficit spending. Between 1975 and 1980 bond issues covered never less than 25 per cent and in 1979 as much as 35 per cent of government expenditure.

Germany, too, saw its already well-established, industry-by-industry wage bargaining system – with an institutionalized pattern of wage leadership by the Metal-Workers Union – reinforced and made more effective by what one might call 'arm's-length corporatism'. Employers and unions cooperated to deliver wage restraint, partly because of their shared knowledge of the independent Bundesbank's relentless determination to control inflation by monetary policy, whatever level of unemployment might result. 'Face-to-face corporatism' – the *Konzertiert Aktion* of 1967 to 1978 – also helped to create shared expectations between employers and unions, but a condition of the unions' participation was that there should be no attempt at norm-setting. Nor was the Bundesbank prepared to compromise its capacity for unilateral action (Streeck 1994: 121–2).

Germany had not been immune from the spill-over effects of France's May 1968 and Italy's 'hot autumn', and the mid-decade crisis was preceded by spells of wildcat strikes, which provided the background to formal legitimate strikes forcing double-digit wage rises in 1974. In agreeing to mildly reflationary measures at the end of the year, however, the Bundesbank made it clear that it expected restraint in the next round in return. And got it (Kloten *et al.* 1985). As a sweeetener, the unions got a major reinforcement of the system of enterprise codetermination in 1976.

It was the structure of social relations at the levels of the enterprise and the state that made Britain's plight worse than that of the others. The ability of craft unions, represented by their shop stewards, to control work organization and to reinforce their control through 'wildcat' strikes (i.e. strikes that ignored 'constitutional' procedures) reduced managers' power to restructure production processes, while the need to 'buy out' restrictive practices reduced their power to resist wage claims (McKersie *et al.* 1972). This labour–management conflict mapped, much more closely than in the other three countries, on to the political system – a major workers' party and a major bosses' party, both having enough electoral support to alternate in government as its inablity to solve basic conflicts discredited each government in turn.

So industrial and political antagonism multiplied each other by mutual feedback, and each successive UK government was more likely to tear down than build on the 'rationalizing' institutional innovations of the other. This vitiated both the attempts to 'constitutionalize' workplace industrial relations (the Industrial Relations Acts from 1971 onwards) and the attempts at incomes policy. Even during the periods when Labour was in power, 'face-to-face' or 'beer and sandwiches' corporatism was never very effective. Social contracts went little beyond horse-trading bargains; so much in social benefits and worker-protection legislation for so much wage restraint. The sense of a collective overriding interest in controlling inflation and raising productivity that served to modify the interest conflict in the smaller economies of Scandinavia, etc. seemed hard to generate (Crouch and Dore 1990). Central union negotiators could not deliver the restraint of their constituent unions, and the officials of those unions could not deliver the cooperation of their factory-level bargainers. And at the factory level the 'extra pay for extra productivity' loopholes in the wage increase norms were exploited by craft unions and complaisant management. Bargaining over the buying out of restrictive practices (which the system encouraged unions to invent for the purpose) became the norm. Despite a decline in real wages, from 1975 to 1977, thereafter – with unemployment also at high levels – wage gains once again began to outpace inflation and work stoppages were endemic. Talk of the country's 'ungovernability', a massive increase in strikes (from an average 3 million days lost in strikes in the 1960s to 29 million in 1979), particularly in the public services, prepared the way for Mrs Thatcher's electoral victory.

The 1970s were an equally unhappy decade for America, ending with the soon-to-be-ousted President Carter making speeches about the nation's 'crisis of confidence'. America's inflation sprang from the need to print money in the late 1960s to cover the cost of the ever more unpopular war in Vietnam. Nixon tried a wage and price freeze in 1971 and again in 1973, but its effects were overtaken by the impact of the oil crisis, and the experiment was not repeated (Gordon 1980: 141). Thereafter the government increasingly looked to monetary policy to control inflation and to financial deregulation to permit capital to maintain its rate of return. One of the seeds of later stock market developments was planted when the Employment Retirement Income Security Act (ERISA) of 1974, as amended in 1978, enabled pension funds, their real rates of returns decimated by inflation, to seek higher, even if riskier, returns through portfolio investments in corporate equities, high-yield (or 'junk') bonds, and venture-capital funds (Lazonick and O'Sullivan 2000).

There were concerns about labour problems – the bargaining strength of unions pushing wages ahead of productivity increases, worker alienation giving rise to absenteeism and low productivity (HEW 1972). But (the AFL-CIO/Democratic Party relation having nothing like the real class-sentiment base of the TUC/Labour Party alliance) it was not central to American politics, and it was not, as in Britain, the key issue triggering the following decades of neo-liberalism. That role was played, rather, by government regulation. The regulatory tide reached its peak in the Nixon years and it was the reactive growth of the anti-regulation, deregulation movement in the late 1970s (in which Chicago economists played a key role) which provided the leitmotif of the early Reagan years (Yergin and Stanislaw 1998).

5 The 1980s and 1990s

Nevertheless, a drastic reduction of the power of the unions was a crucial element of the new directions taken by the Anglo-Saxon economies. It was accomplished, in both countries, less by legislation (though the whittling down of employment protection and the ban on the closed shop in Britain, and the growth of 'right to work' state legislation in the US were important) than by recession – the great British manufacturing shake-out of 1980–81 and the concurrent American 'blue-collar' recession – and by spectacular government victories in marathon disputes with public sector unions – the air traffic controllers in the US, the steel workers, the railway workers and the coal miners in quick succession in Britain.

Top-end income and capital gains tax cuts, deregulation, particularly of the financial sector, tax provisions to stimulate equity investment, along with labour market 'flexibilization' policies were other supply-side policies which Reaganomics and Thatcherism had in common. Privatization – a clear assertion of belief in the importance of the profit motive which linked directly to 'shareholder value' doctrines – was more a British than an American concern because there was more to privatize. It was acknowledged that competition was an essential ingredient if the profit motive was to lead to efficiency, but, especially where it had to be artificially created in what had hitherto been monopolies (with great difficulty in the case of natural monopolies like railways and gas), privatization involved the creation of large-scale regulatory agencies.

Another more strikingly British than American phenomenon – because Britain's civil service and universities and health service still had nineteenth-century upper-middle-class traditions of public service suspected by the Thatcherites as hypocrisy – was the shift to individual bottom-lineism in reward structures. The managerial organizations of major firms like ICI, BP and Unilever had come to resemble the civil service in their career structures and incremental salary scales. They were transformed by performance pay and recruitment at market price. Notions of loyalty which once had precluded any 'lifelong' employee of one bank from moving to another became memories of a quaint outmoded past. Mobility via the market, rather than commitment to organizations, began increasingly to shape careers and ambitions. Market principles were brought into civil service employment, university teaching and to a lesser extent medicine.

It was mostly in the United States, however, that a central ingredient of the new Anglo-Saxon pattern was developed, namely the ideology of shareholder value, the dominant belief that the business enterprise was making its best social contribution, as well as serving its owners' purposes if it was run to maximize shareholder value – a concept in which, for quoted companies, the share price played a major role. Shareholder activism, responding to instances of managerial delinquency, the substitution of voice strategies for exit strategies forced on the larger funds with an index-linked portfolio, techniques of mobilizing large funds and the development of a junk-bond market for leveraged buy-outs, all contributed to the shift. The Garn-St. Germain Act of 1982 gave a great impetus to the last development by permitting savings and loans institutions (S&Ls) to engage in riskier lending activity. But the S&L fiasco did not diminish the pressures of institutional investors on corporate boardrooms.

Managers responded. Efficiency was pursued with relentless cost-cutting, particularly through downsizing, which permitted higher dividends and share buy-backs. (The latter became, by the 1990s, a major component of corporate distributions to shareholders, frequently financed by debt.) The managers were exceedingly well rewarded, thanks to increasing resort to devices to align managerial and shareholder interests, particularly the stock option. The 1980s and 1990s witnessed an explosion in top management income, much of it in the form of stock-based rewards (Lazonick and O'Sullivan 2000).

Britain was a faithful follower of these trends, which were further fuelled by the growth of pension funds (now over £800 bn and growing at £50 bn a year) with the whittling back of state pension systems, and by tax provisions that privileged those savings channelled into equity funds. Britain's explosion in managerial pay did not come until the 1990s when it was the 'fat cats' in the boardrooms of recently privatized former state enterprises which drew – and continues to draw – media attention (Plender 1997). As the figures for income distribution shifts during the 1980s became available (OECD 1993), it became obvious that this was only part of a widening income gap in Britain and the United States, not reproduced in the other two economies.

These institutional trends in the Anglo-Saxon economies were continuing trends throughout the 1980s and 1990s – confirmed in 1997 by the arrival of a Labour government in Britain which quite explicitly endorsed the neo-liberal policies it had once so vociferously denounced and sought to modify them only by marginally more caring welfare services and employee protection.

But the big difference in those economies between the 1980s and the 1990s was in economic performance: a change from stagnation to dynamism – in the United States even exuberant dynamism.

In the 1980s the main problem for American manufacturers of cars, machines and electronics products had been the emergence of formidable Japanese competitors who took larger shares of the US and world export markets in these products even as Japanese wages rose and the Japanese yen strengthened. America seemed to be losing ground, even in its bastions of high-technology strength. IBM started the decade (much aided by Cold War government research funding and procure-ment) with about 75 per cent of the world's computer market. It launched its personal computer business in response to a Silicon Valley start-up called Apple and in short order its PC became the industry standard, permitting IBM 'clones' such as Compaq in the 1980s and Dell in the 1990s to capture large shares of the PC market. The IBM strategy also created two new behemoths – Intel and Microsoft – the companies to which IBM had turned in 1980 to supply its personal computers with microprocessors and operating system software. But Japanese rivals seemed to be catching up fast, aided, to a degree which will for ever be disputed, by government-coordinated cooperative research programmes. Their success in capturing the semi-conductor manufacturing equipment market prompted a parallel American response – the lavishly funded Sematech scheme which began to bear fruit in the early 1990s. By that time the longest boom in American history – one which produced new jobs all across the skill spectrum and even halted the trend to income inequality – had begun. At its core were the high-tech industries. With its own native intellectual resources greatly supplemented by the brain-drain (via graduate schools) from Asia, Europe and Latin America, the American lead in electronics and biotechnology seemed, in selected fields at least, to increase (O'Sullivan 2000: ch. 6).

America, with its ballooning trade deficit, did not, overall, however, eclipse the export performance of Japan and Germany which continued to build on their long-standing strengths – organizational learning in firms whose institutions promoted cooperation across the authority hierarchy, the extension of close cooperation to suppliers, the willingness to make long-term investments (Lazonick 1990: ch. 10; see MULTINATIONAL CORPORATIONS). True, as a careful McKinsey study showed, they seemed to get lower returns on capital (McKinsey Global Institute, 1996). But that hardly affected competitiveness. And capital productivity was not, in any case, their first priority. Japan's problem in the 1990s, in fact, was an excess of capital: the backward-sloping supply curve for savings – more saving as interest rates fell – was a major source of the demand deficiency which not even massive Keynesian spending packages seemed able to cure.

Yet the ability to capture world markets – a source of great national self-confidence in both economies, especially in the bubbling Japan of the late 1980s – began to be eclipsed by other problems – persistent high unemployment in Germany, and post-bubble stagnation in Japan. Confidence ebbed badly, and pressures for convergence to the Anglo-Saxon (that is, the American) model began to receive a hearing.

Germany first. The export performance of the German economy grew stronger throughout the 1980s and the reunification process initially prompted a further upsurge in economic performance. However, unemployment, which, though rising substantially in the early 1980s, had remained at a lower level than in the United States and much, much lower than in most other European countries, through that decade, shot up to double figures in 1992–3 as the economy plunged into its worst recession since the Second World War. Talk of the strengths of German capitalism was replaced by anxious discussion of the viability of *Industriestandort Deutschland* (Germany as an industrial location). Employers became more vociferous in their claims that the high wages, short working hours, tight labour market regulations, and high taxes that prevail in Germany had undermined the competitive position of German enterprises. They warned that German companies would be forced to relocate production abroad if drastic reforms of corporate structures, and, indeed, the foundations of the social market economy, were not undertaken to ensure closer attention to the bottom line. Senior German managers seemed to be increasingly influenced by what was happening overseas, especially in the US corporate economy, and they displayed a growing propensity to adopt practices that until recently were regarded as anathema in German business circles. Companies such as Daimler-Benz and Deutsche Bank, previously seen as synonymous with the distinctive German post-war system of managerial capitalism, have emerged at the forefront of a shareholder value movement in Germany in the mid to late 1990s (O'Sullivan 2000: ch. 8).

However, corporate resource allocation processes are only beginning to be overhauled to accord with shareholder value logic. True believers, moreover, are sceptical that German managers know what they mean and mean what they say, when they speak of the merits of shareholder value for enhancing corporate performance. Their conversion may have more to do with their efforts to maintain control in the wave of mergers and acquisitions in which they are caught up than any serious commitment to the virtues of the Anglo-American management practices for generating superior performance.

It may be a mistake, however, to dismiss the rhetoric of German managers as grandstanding, faddish and self-serving. One of the most important lessons that can be drawn from the recent history of the American corporate economy is that 'organization men' can be induced to be ardent proponents of shareholder value, given appropriate incentives for self-enrichment.

On the other hand, the institutional defences of the German system are formidable. Codetermination within corporations, and the coordinated wage bargaining system, remain both legally and socially entrenched, and are both staunchly defended by unions which remain powerful in spite of all the structural changes which weaken unions everywhere. Moreover, as export performance picks up at the end of the decade, with little impact on employment figures, it is not obvious that a wave of downsizing in pursuit of shareholder value will make any contribution to what is recognized as the nation's most serious problem, and increasingly diagnosed – everywhere except in union circles – as an insider/ outsider problem, if not a straightforward real wages versus employment trade-off. The Alliance for Jobs which Kohl tried, and Schröder with difficulty succeeded in setting up, is having only limited success. The currency given to shareholder value rhetoric is one factor contributing to union intransigence.

Labour–management conflict is the least of the problems which seem likely to alter Japan's distinctive form of capitalism. The main factor is the devastating loss of national self-confidence, particularly after a premature burst of fiscal prudence halted the 1995–6 recovery from the post-bubble recession. Today, the dominant consensus, as reflected in the pronouncements of politicians, businessmen, bureaucrats and the mass media, is that the Japanese model was good for catch-up, but is too cumbersome and undynamic for the new global megacompetition among mature economies. Dynamism comes from competition, not from managerial planning: hence the need for wholesale deregulation, more auction markets less customer markets in trading between firms, active and flexible labour markets. Cross-shareholding distorts share prices and should be prevented. Personal morality needs to be overhauled: individuals should take responsibility for their own old age and illness; and for ensuring their employability in the labour market. Returns on equity should be the major measure of firm performance. Japanese society has been too preoccupied with equality of outcomes rather than equality of opportunity, etc., etc.

Much of this current 'philosophy' is being reflected, gradually, in legislation. Laws to permit holding companies, to facilitate share buy-backs, the unwinding of cross-shareholdings, the bringing of shareholder class-action suits against managers, and to legalize stock options as executive compensation, have all been passed in the 1990s (Dore 2000). Some leading firms like Sony (45 per cent of its shares held by foreigners) declare their total adherence to shareholder value objectives. But even in those firms, change in practice is another matter. Downsizing still means primarily protracted natural wastage. The cross-shareholding pattern is still dense. Wages and bonuses are sticky downwards and returns on equity remain low. Loyalties and obligations still count in subcontracting relations.

And in both Japan and Germany defenders of their systems seem lately to be speaking up more confidently. Toyota's Chairman tells an audience that includes Jack Welch that his firm is not going to abandon lifetime employment however much Standard and Poor's lowers their credit rating (*Nikkei*, 8 October 99). The Chairman of Altana tells *Der Spiegel* that 'Anglo-Saxon cold capitalism, which exclusively focuses on maximizing profits, will lead to a crisis in our system and to a decline of acceptance for the pillars of the social free market economy' (21 May 99).

Japan and Germany remain very different. Japan's economic institutions are deeply *socially* embedded in spite of a legal framework – company law, for instance – hardly different from that of Anglo-Saxon countries. By contrast, Germany's system derives its strength from its firm legal entrenchment. The crucial capital–labour relation is seen in Germany as a clear and conscious class compromise in a situation of structural antagonism. In Japan it is fragmented within community-like corporations, where managers identify more closely with their workers than with the providers of their capital. The systems differ, but they both produce economic behaviour and value priorities that continue to be very different from those of the Anglo-Saxon economies.

6 Varieties of capitalism in the twenty-first century?

Will they remain different? We can only give a bemused answer. Bemused, first, by the fact noted by Albert (1991) when he started the 'varieties of capitalism' debate, namely that it is not just product market competition and factor mobility that press for convergence. For all the social and economic-efficiency virtues of their systems, a lot of Germans and Japanese actually *admire* the American way of life, in spite of a widespread recognition that it involves bursting prisons and rapidly widening inequality. Bemused, secondly, by the phenomenon that recently reinforces that admiration – the sustained exuberance of the American economy and the hypnotic Greenspan's ability to persuade the world's fund managers that it has a new growth paradigm which will allow its price–earnings ratios, its outstanding margin loans, its consumer debt and its trade deficit to go on rising for ever without affecting the value of dollar assets (see GLOBALIZATION). Bemused, thirdly, by our memory of the days when the business schools now preaching shareholder value were abuzz with talk of planning, the technostructure and the social responsibility of capital, and of the more recent days when Japanese management (in general; not just production management) was supposed to be everybody's model.

And bemused, fourthly, by the impossibility, though we can see clearly some of the potential determinants of convergence or diversity, of assessing their effects. Is the search for a 'new financial architecture', after the Asian, Russian and Brazilian crises, going to slow down free capital flows? Will the shift in pension systems from publicly regulated fixed obligations to private risk-bearing financial assets proceed further in the Anglo-Saxon economies and become a serious trend in the others? How far will Chinese capitalism turn out to resemble the Japanese version as the weight of China in the world economy increases?

We leave readers to make their own predictions.

RONALD DORE
CENTRE FOR ECONOMIC PERFORMANCE,
LONDON SCHOOL OF ECONOMICS
AND
THE EUROPEAN INSTITUTE OF BUSINESS
ADMINISTRATION
(INSEAD)

WILLIAM LAZONICK
UNIVERSITY OF MASSACHUSETTS AT LOWELL
AND
THE EUROPEAN INSTITUTE OF BUSINESS
ADMINISTRATION
(INSEAD)

MARY O'SULLIVAN
THE EUROPEAN INSTITUTE OF BUSINESS
ADMINISTRATION
(INSEAD)

Note

Reproduced by permission from *Oxford Review of Economic Policy*, 15 (4), 1999: 102–20.

Further reading

(References cited in the text marked *)

* Albert, M. (1991) *Capitalisme contre capitalisme*, Paris: Seuil. (A widely read assessment of the pros and cons of 'Anglo-Saxon' versus

'Nippon-Rhenish' capitalism, with an emphasis on the virtues of patient capital.)

* Bain, G. (ed.) (1983) *Industrial Relations in Britain*, Oxford: Basil Blackwell. (The persistence and importance of shop steward control and 'custom and practice' in British industrial relations.)

* Barrett Whale, P. (1930) *Joint Stock Banking in Germany*, London: Macmillan. (A classic work on the role of the banks in Germany.)

* Berle, A. and G. Means (1932) *The Modern Corporation and Private Property*, New York: Macmillan. (The classic statement of the separation of asset ownership from managerial control in the US industrial corporation.)

* Blinder, A. (1980) 'The level and distribution of economic well-being', in M. Feldstein (ed.), *The American Economy in Transition*, Chicago: University of Chico Press. (The post-war tendency toward more equal distributions of income in the advanced economies into the 1970s.)

* Braunthal, G. (1978) *Socialist Labor and Politics in Weimar Germany: The General Federation of German Trade Unions*, Hamden, Connecticut: Archon Books. (The organization and impact of the workers' movement in Weimar Germany.)

* Brockstedt, J. (1984) 'Family enterprise and the rise of large-scale enterprise in Germany, 1871–1914', in A. Okochi and S Yasuoka (eds.), *Family Business in the Era of Industrial Growth: Its Ownership and Management*, Tokyo: University of Tokyo Press. (Changing balance between family firms and managerial hierarchies in German industry in the decades before the First World War.)

* Brody, D. (1980) *Workers in Industrial America*, New York: Oxford University Press. (Major assessment of the changing role of union organization in US mass production industries in the twentieth century.)

* Burgess, K. (1975) *The Origins of British Industrial Relations: The Nineteenth Century Experience*, London: Croom Helm. (Roots the British system of industrial relations in the key positions of skilled workers in the organization of work in the late nineteenth century.)

* Cassis, Y. (1985) 'Bankers in English society in the late nineteenth century', *Economic History Review*, 2nd ser: 38. (Social integration of a new financial elite with the old landed aristocracy.)

* Chandler, A. (1977) *The Visible Hand: The Managerial Revolution in American Business*, Cambridge, Mass: Harvard University Press. (Seminal work on the importance of managerial organization in the rise of 'big business' in the United States in the late nineteenth and early twentieth centuries.)

* Chandler, A. (1990) *Scale and Scope: The Dynamics of Industrial Capitalism*, Cambridge, Mass: Harvard University Press. (Major comparative analysis of the evolution of 'big business' in Britain, the United States and Germany in the twentieth century, with emphasis on investments in managerial, manufacturing, and distribution capabilities.)

* Church, R. (1993) 'The family firm in industrial capitalism: international perspectives on hypotheses and history, *Business History* 35. (Assesses the literature on the family firm, and its implications for the comparative analysis of capitalist development.)

* Coleman, D. (1973) 'Gentlemen and players', *Economic History Review*, 2nd ser. 26. (Important essay on the social segmentation between financial elites and industrial capitalists that emerged in late nineteenth-century Britain.)

* Crouch, C and Dore, R. (eds) (1990) *Corporatism and Accountability*, Oxford: Clarendon Press. (The relations among organized interests in the British political economy and their evolution from the corporatist 1970s to the neo-liberal 1980s.)

* Cusumano, M. (1985) *The Japanese Automobile Industry: Technology and Management at Nissan and Toyota*, Cambridge, MA: Harvard University Press. (Highly informative historical account of the evolution of the two companies that drove Japanese success in the automobile industry.)

* Daunton, M. (1992) 'Financial elites and British society, 1880–1950', in Y. Cassis (ed.), *Finance and Financiers in European History, 1880–1960*, Cambridge and New York: Cambridge University Press. (Contribution to the debate on the place of financial elites in the British social structure and the implications for their relation to industry.)

* Dore, R. (1987) *Taking Japan Seriously: A Confucian Perspective on Leading Economic Issues*, Stanford: Stanford University Press. (Some suggestions for institutional reform, feasible given British culture, which might be functionally equivalent to the institutions apparently responsible for Japan's industrial success.)

* Dore, R. (2000) *Stockmarket Capitalism, Welfare Capitalism: Japan, Germany and the Anglo-Saxons*, Oxford: OUP. (The reactions of the Japanese and Germans to the Anglo-Saxon 'shareholder value' movement.)

* Feldenkirchen, W. (1991) 'Banking and economic growth: banks and industry in Germany in the nineteenth century and their changing

relationship during industrialization', in W. Lee (ed.), *German Industry and German Industrialization*, London: Routledge. (The increasing autonomy of industrial corporations from bank control in German industrialization.)

* Flanagan, R., Soskice, D. and Ulman, L. (1983) *Unionism, Economic Stabilization and Incomes Policies*, Washington: Brookings Institution. (A comparative analysis of the role of industrial relations systems in adjusting to the inflationary conditions of the 1970s.)

* Galbraith, J. (1967) *The New Industrial State*, Boston: Houghton Mifflin. (Widely read argument of shift of power to the 'technostructure' in the modern industrial corporation.)

* Gispen, K. (1989) *New Profession, Old Order: Engineers and German Society, 1815–1914*, Cambridge: Cambridge University Press. (The development of engineering education and employment in Germany.)

* Glyn, A. and Sutcliffe, B. (1972) *British Capitalism, Workers and the Profit Squeeze*, London: Penguin. (Argument that in the 1960s British firms had been experiencing a profit squeeze that resulted in conflictual relations with workers.)

* Gordon, R. (1980) 'Postwar macroeconomics', in M. Feldstein (ed.), *The American Economy in Transition*, Chicago: University of Chicago Press. (The onset of stagflation in the US economy of the 1970s.)

* Gordon, A. (1985) *The Evolution of Labor Relations in Japan: Heavy Industry, 1853–1955*, Cambridge, MA: Harvard University Press. (Shows the origins of enterprise strategies to train and retain production workers in the era before enterprise unions and lifetime employment.)

* Hadley, E. (1970) *Antitrust in Japan*, Princeton: Princeton University Press. (Major account of the post-World War II dissolution of the Japanese zaibatsu by an American involved in the process.)

* Hannah, L. (1983) *The Rise of the Corporate Economy: The British Experience*, second edition, Baltimore: Johns Hopkins University Press. (Seminal research on the evolution of the managerial enterprise in the British economy.)

* Hannah, L. (1986) *Inventing Retirement: The Development of Occupational Pensions in Britain*, Cambridge: Cambridge University Press. (Pioneering research on the historical evolution of work-related pensions in Britain.)

* Harris, H. (1982) *The Right to Manage: Industrial Relations Policies of American Business in the 1940s*, Madison: University of Wisconsin Press. (Important account of the importance of the managerial ideology of the 'right to manage' in circumscribing the power of the new industrial unions in the United States in the 1940s.)

* Harrison, R., and Zeitlin, J. (eds) (1985) *Divisions of Labour: Skilled Workers and Technological Change in the Nineteenth Century*, Sussex: Harvester Press. (Important studies of the role of skilled production workers in shaping the evolution of technology in late nineteenth-century British industry.)

* HEW (1972) United States Department of Health. Education and Welfare, *Work in America*, MIT Press. (Documents the growing alienation of the US blue-collar labour force in the late 1960s and early 1970s and the constrained attempts to overcome it through job enrichment and enlargement.)

* Hiwatari, N. (1996) 'Japanese Corporate Governance Reexamined: The Origins and Institutional Foundations of Enterprise Unionism', paper prepared for the Conference on Employees and Corporate Governance, Columbia University Law School, November 22. (The transition from conflictual industrial relations to cooperative enterprise unionism in the 1950s.)

* Hobsbawm, E. (1984) *Workers: Worlds of Labor*, New York: Pantheon. (Seminal essays on the origins, organization, and influence of the British 'labour aristocracy' in the nineteenth century.)

* Hodder, J. and Tschoegl, A. (1993) 'Corporate finance in Japan', in S. Takagi (ed.), *Japanese Capital Markets: New Developments in Regulations and Institutions*, Oxford: Blackwell. (Account of the reduction of reliance on bank debt by Japanese corporations in the 1970s and 1980s.)

* Jacoby, S. (1985) *Employing Bureaucracy: Managers, Unions, and the Transformation of Work in America, 1900–1945*, New York: Columbia University Press. (The evolution of the internal relations between managers and workers within major US industrial corporations in the transition from the non-union era of the 1920s to mass unionization of the late 1930s and 1940s.)

* Jacoby, S. (1997) *Modern Manors*, Princeton: Princeton University Press. (US welfare capitalism since the New Deal.)

* Kocka, J. (1980) 'The rise of modern industrial enterprise in Germany', in A. Chandler and H. Daems (eds), *Managerial Hierarchies: Comparative Perspectives on the Rise of the Modern Industrial Enterprise*, Cambridge, MA: Harvard University Press. (Pioneering overview of the managerial revolution in Germany.)

* Kocka, J. (1981) 'The entrepreneur, the family, and capitalism: some examples from the early phase of industrialization in Germany', *German Yearbook of Business History*, Berlin: Springer Verlag. (The transition from proprietary to managerial capitalism in Germany's early industrial development.)
* Kloten, N., Ketterer, K-H. and Vollmer, R. (1985) 'West Germany's stabilization policy', in L. Lindberg and C. Maier (eds), *The Politics of Inflation and Economic Stagnation: Theoretical Approaches and International Case Studies*, Washington: Brookings Institution. (West Germany's adjustment to the inflationary conditions of the 1970s.)
* Konig, W. (1993) 'Technical education and industrial performance in Germany: a triumph of heterogeneity', in R. Fox and A Guagnini (eds), *Education, Technology and Industrial Performance in Europe, 1850–1939*, Cambridge: Cambridge University Press. (The importance of the early development of technical education in Germany's industrial development.)
* Lazonick, W. (1985) 'Strategy, structure, and management development in the United States and Britain', in K. Kobayashi and H. Morikawa (eds), *Development of Managerial Enterprise*, Tokyo: University of Tokyo Press. (Shows how differences in social structure affected the internal organization of US and British industrial corporations, with implications for the development and utilization of technology.)
* Lazonick, W. (1990) *Competitive Advantage on the Shop Floor*, Cambridge, MA: Harvard University Press. (Historical and comparative analysis of the relation between managerial organization and shop-floor skill and control in Britain, United States and Japan in the nineteenth and twentieth centuries.)
* Lazonick, W. and O'Sullivan, M. (2000) 'Maximising shareholder value: a new ideology for corporate governance', *Economy and Society*, 29: 1. (The roles of corporate growth, international competition, and financial restructuring in the rise of 'maximizing shareholder value' as a corporate ideology in the United States in the 1980s and 1990s.)
* Lewchuk, W. (1987) *American Technology and the British Vehicle Industry*, Cambridge: Cambridge University Press. (The role of British labour–management relations in shaping the use of US mass-production technology in the automobile industry from the 1920s.)
* Liberal Industrial Inquiry (1928) *Britain's Industrial Future* (Repr. London: Ernest Benn, 1976). (Attempt by a Liberal Party commission, that included Keynes, to understand the decline of British industrial power in the decade after the First World War.)
* Lichtenstein, N. (1985) 'UAW bargaining strategy and shop-floor conflict, 1947–1970', *Industrial Relations* 24, Fall. (The evolution of the seniority system for blue-collar workers in US industrial manufacturing.)
* Mass, W. and Lazonick, W. (1990) 'The British cotton industry and international competitive advantage: the state of the debates', *Business History* 32, October: 9–65. (The interaction of technology and organization in changes in international competitive advantage, with a focus on the rise of the Japanese in cotton textiles and machinery in the first decades of the twentieth century.)
* McKersie, R., Hunter, L. and Sengenberger, W. (1972) *Productivity Bargaining: The American and British Experience*, Washington: US Government Printing Office. (The role of US and British industrial relations systems in shaping bargaining between employers and unions over the relation between productivity and pay.)
* McKinsey Global Institute (1996) *Capital Productivity*, June. (Report on the changing sectoral importance of productivity growth across advanced economies.)
* McKitrick, F. (1994) 'The Stabilization of the Mittelstand: Artisans in Germany from National Socialism to the Federal Republic, 1939–1953', PhD dissertation, Columbia University. (Modernization of German handwerk in the Third Reich and its implications for the postwar apprenticeship system.)
* Means, G. (1930) 'The diffusion of stock ownership in the United States', *Quarterly Journal of Economics* 44. (Documents and explains the growing dispersion of holdings of corporate stock in the United States in the 1920s.)
* Minami, R. (1976) 'The introduction of electric power and its impact on the manufacturing industries', in H. Patrick (ed.), *Japanese industrialization and its social consequences*, Berkeley: University of California. (Role of small electric motors in the decentralization and productivity of labour-intensive industry in the early industrial development of Japan.)
* Moore, J. (1983) *Japanese Workers and the Struggle for Power, 1945–1947*, Madison: University of Wisconsin Press. (Detailed account of the militancy of the Japanese labour movement in the devastating aftermath of the Second World War.)
* Morikawa, H. (1992) *Zaibatsu: The Rise and Fall of Family Enterprise Groups in Japan*, Tokyo: University of Tokyo Press. (Major historical

work on the evolution of the Japanese zaibatsu from the Meiji Restoration to their dissolution after the Second World War.)
* Morikawa, H. (1997) 'Japan: increasing organizational capabilities of large industrial enterprises, 1880s–1980s', in A. Chandler, F. Amatori, and T. Hikino (eds), *Big Business and the Wealth of Nations*, Cambridge: Cambridge University Press. (Importance of managerial organization in the most successful zaibatsu and its legacy for the development of Japanese industrial enterprise in the 'era of high-speed growth'.)
* Mowery, D. (1986) 'Industrial research, 1900–1950', in B. Elbaum and W. Lazonick (eds), *The Decline of the British Economy*, Oxford: Oxford University Press. (Demonstrates the weakness of British industrial research in comparative perspective.)
* Navin, T. and Sears, M. (1955) 'Rise of a market in industrial securities, 1887–1902', *Business History Review* 29 (2): 105–38. (Classic article that, in combination with Chandler's later work, shows the relation between the growth of a liquid stock market in corporate equities and the managerial revolution in US business.)
* Noble, D. (1977) *America by Design: Science, Technology, and the Rise of Corporate Capitalism*, New York: Oxford University Press. (Shows how corporate interests transformed engineering education in the United States in the first decades of the twentieth century.)
* OECD (1993) *Employment Report*, Paris. (Data on comparative income distribution in the advanced economies.)
* Okazaki, T (1994) 'The Japanese firm under the wartime planned economy', in M. Aoki and R. Dore (eds), *The Japanese firm*, Oxford, OUP. (The importance of the Second World War in the transition to managerial control in Japan.)
* O'Sullivan, M. (2000) *Contests for Corporate Control: Corporate Governance and Economic Performance in the United States and Germany*, Oxford: Oxford University Press. (A critical account of the debates on corporate governance in the light of the comparative development of advanced economies.)
* Plender, J. (1997) *A Stake in the Future*, London: Nicholas Brearley. (Changes in British corporate governance in the 1990s.)
* Pohl, H. (1982) 'On the history of organization and management in large German enterprises since the nineteenth century', *German Yearbook of Business History*, Berlin: Springer Verlag. (The transition from family to managerial control on German business.)
* Pohl, H. (1984) 'Forms and phases of industry finance up to the Second World War', in *German Yearbook of Business History*, Berlin: Springer Verlag. (The role of banks and internal sources of funds in the development of German industry.)
* Sanderson, M. (1988) 'The English civic universities and the industrial spirit, 1870–1914', *Historical Research* 61. (The spread of technical education in the non-elite universities in the decades before the First World War reflecting the need for advanced training for industry.)
* Schumpeter, J. (1942) *Capitalism, Socialism, and Democracy*, New York: Harper & Row. (Classic argument by a leading economist for the need to understand the role of collective organization in driving innovation in the advanced economies.)
* Servos, J. (1980) 'The industrial relations of science: chemical engineering at MIT, 1900–1939', *ISIS* 71: 531–49. (Account of the tension between scientific pursuits and industrial relevance at the most important engineering university in the United States.)
* Shonfield, A. (1965) *Modern Capitalism: the Changing Balance of Public and Private Power*, Oxford: Oxford University Press. (A classic work on the 'mixed economy' in the post Second World War decades.)
* Sorge, A. and Warner, M. (1986) *Comparative Factory Organization: An Anglo-German Comparison of Management and Manpower in Manufacturing*, Brookfield, Vermont: Gower Publishing. (A pioneering comparative study of work organization.)
* Streeck, W. (1992) *Social Institutions and Economic Performance: Studies of Industrial Relations in Advanced Capitalist Economies*, London and Newbury Park, California: Sage. (German capitalism in comparative perspective.)
* Streeck, W. (1994) 'Pay restraint without incomes policy: institutionalised monetarism and industrial unionism in Germany', in R. Dore, R. Boyer and Z. Mars (eds), *The Return to Incomes Policy*, London: Pinter. (The role of German industrial relations in restraining inflation.)
* Weidemann, H. (1980) 'Codetermination by workers in German enterprises', *American Journal of Comparative Law* 28: 79–92. (West Germany's formal system of employee representation.)
* Wright, J. (1962) 'The capital market and the finance of industry', in G. Worswick and P. Ady (eds), *The British Economy in the Nineteen-Fifties*, Oxford: Oxford University Press. (The role of the stock market and stockholders in British corporations in the 1950s.)

* Yergin, D and Stanislaw, J. (1998) *The Commanding Heights*, New York: Simon and Schuster. (Account of the changing relations between governments and markets.)
* Yonekawa, S. (1984) 'University graduates in Japanese enterprises before the Second World War', *Business History* 26, July: 193–218. (Documents the importance of the Japanese university system in supplying personnel to managerial organizations during the first four decades of the twentieth century.)

See also: BANKING SYSTEMS; COMPARATIVE INCOME AND WEALTH DISTRIBUTION; CORPORATE CONTROL; EAST ASIAN ECONOMIES; ECONOMIC GROWTH AND CONVERGENCE; ECONOMIES OF CENTRAL AND EASTERN EUROPE, TRANSITION OF; ECONOMY OF JAPAN; EMPLOYMENT RELATIONS; GALBRAITH, J.K.; GLOBALIZATION; GROWTH OF THE FIRM AND NETWORKING; GROWTH THEORY; INDUSTRIAL AGGLOMERATION; INDUSTRIAL DYNAMICS; INNOVATION; INNOVATIVE ENTERPRISE, THEORY OF; INTERNATIONAL MONETARY FUND; KEYNES, J.M.; LABOUR MARKETS; MONEY AND CAPITAL MARKETS, INTERNATIONAL; MULTINATIONAL CORPORATIONS; PENSION SYSTEMS; PRIVATIZATION AND REGULATION; SCHUMPETER, J.; SKILL FORMATION SYSTEMS; VEBLEN, T.; WORLD BANK; WORLD TRADE ORGANIZATION

Banking systems

1 Universal banking
2 Banking systems from the 1930s to the first oil crisis
3 Banking after the demise of the Bretton Woods System
4 Coping with increased uncertainty
5 The Basel capital adequacy rules
6 Banking systems in the 1990s
7 The lender of last resort problem

Overview

In describing the nature and development of banking in the second half of the twentieth century, it is appropriate to speak of 'national banking systems'. Banking was in this period consciously organized as a series of national systems, as in most countries state authority played a decisive part in reforming the banking sector after the failures and rescues of the 1930s, transforming it into a highly regulated economic activity. State powers were also used, in more recent times, to lift some of the previously imposed regulation, and to reduce the market segmentation between different types of banks and between banks and other financial institutions. Moreover, in each country, the banking system was given a hierarchical structure. A government-owned or at least government-chartered central bank was formally placed at the centre of the banking system, surrounded by a few large commercial banks with which it entertained special relations that allowed it to conduct an effective monetary and credit policy. An outer layer of smaller banking institutions surrounded the inner core. The picture would be completed in some countries by special purpose long-term banks and in others by investment banks, to service the long-term investment needs of the economy.

For most of this period banking therefore retained a peculiar appearance, which differentiated it from unregulated sectors, and made it akin to public goods producing sectors. Until very recently, in fact, banks' balance sheets were considered as possessing peculiar features as far as both loans and deposits were concerned, having to do with the fact that a bank network, i.e. a set of interconnected banks, is capable of cumulative growth and shrinkage. The potential boom-bust features of banking networks, with the attendant consequences for the real economy, were noticed very early by state authorities and public opinions in most countries. The result was great regulatory activity *vis-à-vis* banking with the aim of preserving and enhancing the payments networks organized by banking systems and of maintaining a balanced flow of short and long-term credit to the real economy. Regulation reached its acme in the 1930s, after banking systems in many countries had collapsed. In the 1980s and 1990s, however, authorities in many countries seconded the tendency of banks towards despecialization of their functions, and integration of most money and credit markets. Sometimes, as in the United States, authorities even positively favoured the encroachment by other less regulated financial institutions on the traditional activities of banks.

1 Universal banking

The institutions contributing to forming what can be called a banking system have first and foremost the function of securing for a country a well-organized payments system. Perhaps the oldest function of banks, the payments system has remained the most important, especially after the largest part of the money supply of developed countries came to consist of bank deposits. A banking system is also supposed to provide the real sector of the economy with sufficient short- and long-term credit to permit stable economic growth.

Moreover, some banking systems have supplied the real sector with equity capital. Whether or not they have been allowed and even induced to do so by regulators, or indeed their proprietors and managers have been prepared to do so, has been a matter of historical expediency. Universal banking systems, as those where commercial banks are allowed to own equity capital are traditionally called, are said to have sprung up in countries where equity capital was scarcer because of insufficient national savings or more probably because national savings preferred less risky modes of investment such as the ownership of government bonds. In those countries banking was from an early stage segmented into two sub-sectors, one catering to the needs of small savers and thus investing their deposits in safe assets like government bonds, and the other consisting of banks started with the explicit purpose of financing the creation of large-scale industries in the capital-intensive sectors and subsequently catering for all their financial needs. This could be done by exploiting the deposit-creating capacity of banks, and the more rapidly and completely the deposits created by a bank came back to it after they had been loaned to an industrial or commercial client, the more safely the process of deposit creation would continue, and the wider it would become.

In well-functioning universal banking systems, the equity stake a bank took in a particular firm could either be later disposed of, in an orderly fashion, through a stock-exchange where the same bank would function as market-makers, or alternatively it could be kept as a sizable part of the bank's assets. This kind of universal bank did not try very hard to get the ordinary public's savings deposits. The part of the deposits they created which leaked out of their system they would try to get back as interbank deposits from savings banks. More frequently, however, they relied on having their cash needs catered for by borrowing from the central bank. A universal banking system of this kind would thus show a high or low degree of instability depending on the central bank's ability to view its role of lender of last resort as a normal rather than an exceptional one.

In some countries the role of universal banks in financing industry through direct equity stakes in its capital was taken by special credit institutions, almost always owned directly or indirectly by the state and thus equipped with a state guarantee. They collected savings directly from the public through the issue of guaranteed debentures and either made long-term loans to industry or bought equity with the proceeds.

Where private savings did not suffice to supply the long term capital needed by industry, the debentures issued by the special banks would be bought by other credit institutions, like savings or even commercial banks, which relied on the zero risk of those state-guaranteed debentures.

2 Banking systems from the 1930s to the first oil crisis

These variations on the theme of banking system organization were extended in number and size in the course of the forty years spanning the international financial crisis of the 1930s to the first oil crisis of the early 1970s. In that period national economic systems in most countries became closed and heavily regulated, with public ownership of economic institutions spreading, because of the crisis of the 1930s, to encompass both industry and banking. Foreign trade was much smaller with respect to GNP than it had been before and would become again in later decades. Price systems were thus largely national, and heavily influenced by the presence of national monopolies and oligopolies. Officially approved and even encouraged, cartels were the rule in most sectors, especially in banking. Price competition was discouraged as destructive. As a result, banks knew they were lending to, or taking equity in, firms which controlled their own prices and sold their products mostly on the domestic market, and were thus likely to be profitable enough to repay their loans and to involve a very low risk of failure. A high degree of financial leverage could therefore be reached and maintained for many years in many countries without endangering the stability of either the industrial system or the banking system. Under this regime, growth rates in most industrial countries were consistently higher than in previous or subsequent decades.

In the decades following the Second World War, however, national economic systems again showed a tendency to become more open, to allow a greater trade in not only visible goods but also services, and finally to abolish both short- and long-term capital controls. This openness tended to undermine the organizational mode of national economies that had prevailed since the 1930s. Greater trade integration reduced pricing power by national manufacturers, which in turn made loans to them or participation in their capital by banks considerably riskier. In addition, freedom of capital movement meant that domestic banks lost their control over national credit markets. Capital controls might even be maintained, but the possibility of exporting capital via the under- and over-invoicing of visible trade emptied them of most of their actual meaning.

Moreover, in most countries, laws and government policies had given savings banks and mutual banks favourable treatment over large commercial banks, enabling them to compete with large commercial banks in fields which had always been the latter's special preserves. What came to be known as banking despecialization pushed large commercial banks towards the few fields where they still had a traditional advantage, in particular towards foreign operations. The commercial banks tried to get back for themselves the business represented by large firms, by booking loans to and collecting deposits from these firms through wholly owned subsidiaries located in financial centres not subject to the mother country's national laws, where they could give their clients more favourable terms. An internationalization of banking thus emerged and was to become more marked after the international monetary crisis of August 1971, which ended with the scrapping of the Bretton Woods system – based on fixed exchange rates – and led to the first oil crisis of 1973.

3 Banking after the demise of the Bretton Woods system

Both events – the introduction of flexible exchange rates and the quadrupling of oil prices – greatly enhanced the transformation of banking systems all around the world that had been already taking place. Very large oil profits were concentrated in the hands of very few oil-exporting countries, most of them incapable of spending their larger revenues in the purchase of goods and services from oil-importing countries. These funds had thus to remain in liquid form, and be deposited, preferably at short-term, with the banks of the oil-importing countries. Countries which had large banks and which promptly scrapped all remaining capital controls were thus able to attract this money as deposits with their banks. Countries which did not have large banks and international currencies relied, instead, on visible exports to settle their international accounts. They tried to close their banking systems and even their industrial systems to foreign competition in order to regain control over their international accounts. But the roost came to be ruled by the countries which managed to open their banking systems to international capital flows and so to acquire the oil deposits which they were then able to transform into loans to less financially capable oil importers.

The second oil crisis of 1979 made the trend towards despecialization, internationalization and liberalization of banking even more stable and pronounced. Attempts by less financially able countries to protect their financial markets were largely unsuccessful, only managing to further reduce the competitiveness of their banking systems.

4 Coping with increased uncertainty

Since the 1970s, therefore, a very high degree of uncertainty has prevailed in the international economic system. Coping with uncertainty, under the forms of wildly fluctuating exchange rates and volatile short- and long-term interest rates and factor and product prices has profoundly transformed the banking systems of most countries. Fixed investment growth rates have declined and so have GDP growth rates, with respect to the previous three decades. Financial investment has become an important item on the balance sheets of industrial firms. Banking systems have had to learn how to cater to the new needs of their clients. A huge demand for hedging sprung up, with the resultant growth of all kinds of financial derivatives. Strong competition inside each country and across countries has involved most banking systems, and competitive pressures have led all banks to attempt to become more profitable by entering fields which they had previously shunned as too risky. Interest rate risk hedging and foreign exchange risk hedging have become imperative for most firms, and banks which have not been able to offer appropriate hedging instruments have lost market shares.

In addition, a wave of privatizations has swamped the banking sector in many countries where banks had fallen into public ownership after their failures in the 1930s or had been started as public institutions. Privatization has become an ideological battle-cry for many political parties, especially after the demise of the Soviet Bloc. But it has been positively encouraged in other countries by the government of the United States and by international financial institutions like the IMF and World Bank (see INTERNATIONAL MONETARY FUND; WORLD BANK).

5 The Basel capital adequacy rules

Increased uncertainty and larger fluctuations in exchange rates and interest rates, by adding to bigger balance of payments' financing problems for many countries, have led to increased financial instability. A succession of international financial crises has followed the much greater financial leverage of governments and firms. As a result, the countries that form the core of the international economic system have tried to impose controls on financial institutions, and especially on banks, in the form of capital adequacy rules. Banks have thus had to compete with non-banking firms for capital resources and have had to be able to show much greater profitability on their balance sheets. This competitive strategy has induced them to increase the level of riskiness of their assets, with the adverse selection threats attendant upon such a policy.

Liberalization and privatization of banking systems can be said to have induced the transformation of those systems back to the uncontrolled markets that were in place before the reforms prompted by the 1930s financial failures were enforced. Central banks have had to transform their supervisory activities into capital adequacy controls – mandated by the Bank for International Settlements in Basel, Switzerland – the only type of controls that are consistent with the status of independence from governments now required of them.

If we compare the present state of banking with the picture offered by banking systems in the late 1960s and early 1970s, we find that banks have changed almost beyond recognition. The quest for uncertainty reduction and profit maximization, two probably mutually inconsistent goals, has produced a type of retail banking where personal loans are more important than loans to small firms, and a type of corporate banking more and more skewed towards fee-earning activities and less and less towards straightforward lending. Such lending as does take place is couched in very complex securitized forms, to create financial instruments which can be re-sold in organized secondary markets, so that the credit-originating banks can reacquire liquidity. Because of capital adequacy rules banks tend to transform as many of their operations as they can into off-balance sheet items.

As a result banking systems are much less characterized by relationship-banking than they were before. The trend is towards the de-personalization of lending and its transformation into a commodity. As we have seen, every asset on the banks' balance sheet must now be potentially saleable on secondary markets that have developed even for the most blatantly personalized assets. Securitized debt is eagerly taken up by institutions that specialize in managing the savings of individuals and need to spread their assets between and fixed interest securities. Securitization's appeal is also explained by tax advantages. Low interest rates and the smaller relative needs of industry for external financial resources have reduced the availability of high-yielding assets. Moreover, securitized assets are packaged in a way that creates a feeling of risk reduction at all stages of the securitization and to all lenders taking part in it. This risk reduction may prove to be something of an illusion, borne out of the legal complexity of securitization agreements, which can remain untested only as long as insolvency does not hit the original debtors.

6 Banking systems in the 1990s

Thus all banks now look very much alike (see GLOBALIZATION). Specialized human capital is not needed any more, as it might reduce the banks' potential ability to address flexibility requirements. Markets have proliferated where assets which previously looked like the epitome of *intuitus personae* are restructured in order to appear standardized enough to be anonymously saleable. Lending to persons has replaced lending to companies to a remarkable extent, and is increasingly conducted as insurance companies write their car insurance policies, according to rules derived from probability theory rather than on individual credit-worthiness assessment. Because of the deep and continuous decrease of long-term interest rates which has gone on for many years, and reversed itself only in the second half of 1999, not only has securitization proceeded apace, to create enough high-yield bonds to replace government paper now earning very low yields, but the merger and acquisition movement in banking and finance has shown great dynamism, involving mostly institutions belonging to the same country, but also in some cases going across countries. Low interest rates are essential to all merger and acquisition operations, which usually end up with a higher level of leverage for the companies involved. This has been true for banks as well, and in most countries the degree of concentration has risen very considerably, with the creation of very few giant banks, and sometimes through the merging of banks and insurance companies to create financial supermarkets. Commercial banks have often also taken over investment and merchant banks.

Apart from the permissive factor represented by low interest rates, other variables influencing the merger and acquisition movement in banking have been the desire to create institutions 'too big to fail', as recent experience has confirmed the validity of this old belief and the readiness of authorities and public opinion to go to the rescue of illiquid or even insolvent large banks. Moreover, on the part of national authorities and ruling elites, there has been an attempt to create national champions which are big enough not to be swallowed up by foreign banks, now that national banking markets can no longer be defended by legal and institutional (especially regulatory) protectionism.

7 The lender of last resort problem

The resilience of the new international banking structure that is in the process of being created seems to depend on the preparedness of the United States Federal Reserve (FED) to play the part of lender of last resort every time events call for it. The totally liberalized world banking system has in fact turned out to be a highly leveraged one, as the pressure of competition prevents banks from keeping large reserves and induces them to run greater risks to improve their short-term profits. The Federal Reserve is the only important monetary authority, with the possible exception of the Bank of Japan, left without statutory requirements that strictly limit its capacity to freely create liquidity under the form of an internationally acceptable currency.

The European Central Bank, for instance, has no power to act as lender of last resort. Still, European banks are subject to strong competitive pressure from US banks, which try to increase their market share outside the US while at the same time being able to rely on the continuous flow of liquidity created by the FED on the US market.

A state of potential imbalance has thus been created. An internationally integrated banking system has evolved, but some of the giant banks that are its protagonists have their legal home in a country, the United States, and their balance sheets denominated in a currency, the US dollar, which can be freely created at the will of a politically accountable central bank, the Federal Reserve System; which is also able to supply its member banks with the reserves they may need.

Many other large banks, however, have their legal home in the countries of the European Union and their balance sheets are denominated in Euros, a currency created by the European Central Bank, an institution which is not endowed with supervisory functions and cannot act as lender of last resort whenever it feels that there may be a need for one, as its sole function, by Statute, is that of assuring price stability in the European Monetary Union. A banking crisis starting in Europe or at least involving European banks can thus become more stability-threatening than one involving banks legally situated in the US, as the ECB will be able neither to prevent the crisis nor to come to the rescue of European banks.

MARCELLO DE CECCO
UNIVERSITA' DI ROMA 'LA SAPIENZA'

Further reading

(References cited in the text marked *)

Carlin, W. and Mayer, C. (2000) 'How do financial systems affect economic performance?', in X. Vives (ed.) *Corporate Governance*, Cambridge: Cambridge University Press.

De Cecco, M. (ed.) (1986) *Changing Money*, Oxford: Basil Blackwell.

De Cecco, M. (1999) 'The lender of last resort' , in *Economic Notes*, 1,

Deeg, R. (1999) *Finance Capitalism Unveiled: Banks and the German Political Economy*, Ann Arbor: University of Michigan Press.

Edwards, J. and Fischer, K. (1994) *Banks, Finance and Investment in Germany*, Cambridge: Cambridge University Press.

Hellwig, M. (2000) 'On the economics and politics of corporate finance and corporate control', in X. Vives (ed.) *Corporate Governance*, Cambridge: Cambridge University Press.

Lazonick, W. and O'Sullivan, M. (1997) 'Finance and industrial development', (Parts I and II) *Financial History Review*.

Masahiko, A. and Patrick, H. (eds) (1995) *The Japanese Main Bank System: its Relevance for Developing and Transforming Economies*, New York: Oxford University Press.

Weinstein, D. and Yafeh, Y. (1998) 'On the costs of bank-centred financial systems: evidence from the changing main bank relation in Japan', *Journal of Finance* 53.

White, W. (1988) 'The coming transformation of continental European banking', *BIS Working Papers* Bank for International Settlements, Basel.

See also: GLOBALIZATION; INTERNATIONAL MONETARY FUND; MULTINATIONAL CORPORATIONS; WORLD BANK; WORLD TRADE ORGANIZATION

Economy of Japan

1. High economic growth, 1950–71
2. The oil shock and its aftermath, 1971–75
3. Stable economic growth, 1975–89
4. A bubble economy, 1985–90
5. The lost decade, 1991–2000
6. Industrial organization
7. Labour relations
8. Is Japan unique?

Overview

Since the end of the Second World War, the Japanese economy had sustained a high rate of economic growth, and by 1990 its per capita income surpassed that of the USA. Factors that contributed to the success of the Japanese economy – especially the role of the government, the role of business groups, and the relationship between management and labour – have been the focus of many articles and books. Some hailed the system as a Japanese model of economic development. The Japanese economic performance of the 1990s was quite a contrast to its past, and questions about the viability of the Japanese model in the new environment were raised. The most direct cause of the difficulty was the burst of the asset bubble – the sharp inflation of asset prices (1985–90) followed by the fall (1990–99) – that damaged the balance sheets of many financial institutions.

The period before the first oil crisis of 1973 is commonly known as the period of high-speed economic growth. During this period Japan maintained a high investment/gross domestic product ratio, while domestic saving levels were also sufficient for high investment to be made possible without the accumulation of foreign debts. Improvement in human capital, developed through a solid education and on-the-job training, was also an important factor for growth. Under the Bretton Woods regime, the yen was fixed at 360 yen/dollar until August 1971. The fixed exchange rate put the discipline on monetary policy, so that inflation was moderate and trade balances were maintained over a business cycle. Trade liberalization and tariff reduction proceeded gradually with GATT led trade rounds. The domestic financial system and external capital transactions remained regulated throughout the period.

After the fixed exchange rate of 360 yen/dollar was abandoned in 1971, the yen has experienced an appreciation trend, with large fluctuations. The appreciation was achieved with the background of relatively high economic growth and large current account surpluses. With a brief period of high inflation in 1971–74, partly due to the first oil crisis, stable growth (an annual rate around 4 per cent on average) with moderate inflation continued from 1975 to 1990. The industrial structure changed from textile and simple machinery goods in the 1950s and 1960s to heavy and electronics industries during the 1970s and 1980s.

The Japanese economy in the second half of the 1980s was known as the bubble period – characterized by sharp increases in asset prices, such as stock prices and land prices. In many places land prices tripled or quadrupled over the period of a few years. However, asset prices declined in the first half of the 1990s, and by 1995, price levels had returned to pre-bubble levels. This had various consequences, including the appearance of a large number of non-performing loans among the commercial banks.

The economic performance of Japan in the 1990s was low – an average annual growth rate being around 1 per cent from 1992 to 2000 – compared to its own past or other advanced countries in the same period. Moreover, many failures of financial institutions and corporate bankruptcies took place toward the end of the 1990s, and the 1990s became known as a 'lost decade' in Japan. Many factors contributed to this poor economic performance. The bubble – asset price inflation – of the second half of the 1980s deflated in the 1990s, which caused consumption to fall, investment to stagnate, and non-performing bank loans to mount. In 1997–98, three major banks failed and the economic growth rate in 1998 was minus 2.5 per cent, the worst record in the post-war period.

During the high-growth period, many policies looked unique. The industrial policy, in common terminology, is a wide-ranging combination of policies that influence the level and composition of industrial investment and production. It was generally interpreted as the nurturing of specific industries through subsidized (policy) loans from the development bank: for example, in the 1950s and 1960s, the coal, steel, shipbuilding and petrochemicals industries. Imports were strictly controlled until the early 1960s, and raw materials and intermediate goods, as opposed to consumption goods, were favoured.

In most of the post-war period, Japanese monetary and fiscal policy was prudent enough to produce high growth without excessive inflation (except in 1974–76). During the 1950s and 1960s, monetary policy was assigned to maintain a fixed exchange rate: Whenever the current account went into deficit due to a booming import demand, monetary policy was tightened, and when the current account was in surplus, monetary policy was relaxed. The relaxed monetary policy of 1972–73 combined with the oil price increases of 1973 produced very high inflation in 1974–76. In order to control inflation, a tight monetary policy was introduced in 1974. Inflation was quickly reduced, at the cost of a sharp decline in output. After 1975, monetary policy focused on keeping the inflation rate down.

Fiscal policy was fairly conservative in the 1950s and 1960s. The budget was fairly conservative in the 1950s and 1960s. The budget was essentially balanced every year until 1965, when government construction bonds (for infrastructure projects) were issued. Pure deficit-financing bonds have been issued as of 1975. Government deficits grew rapidly in the second half of the 1970s, but fiscal austerity during the 1980s reduced the issue of deficit-financing bonds to zero by 1990. However the slump in the first half of the 1990s, forced the government to issue new deficit-financing bonds after 1992. With the negative growth in 1998, the government increased deficit spending sharply from 1998 to 2000. The debt–GDP ratio soared to 130 per cent – the worst among the G7 countries – by the end of 2000.

Economic institutions and structural configuration are important in evaluating economic performance. Some critics argue that Japanese institutions and business practices are unique among the industrial countries, although close examination has revealed similarities with the USA and Europe. Various forms of loose relationships between corporations (*keiretsu*) have been of particular interest to researchers.

The yen has appreciated *vis-à-vis* the US dollar since 1971. In mid-1994, the yen reached ¥100:$1, and then in the spring of 1995, the value reached ¥80:$1. In less than a quarter of a century, the value of the yen against the dollar more than quadrupled (less than one quarter of ¥360 now purchases one dollar). Even with this appreciation of the yen, Japan has maintained large external surpluses throughout the 1980s and 1990s, except for brief periods immediately after the two oil crises.

Many of the unique features during the early stage of development are disappearing in the 1990s: the bank-centred *keiretsu* relationship is melting down in the wake of a banking crisis; and a lifetime employment commitment is being increasingly breached by distressed companies. The Japanese economy is becoming more akin to those of other large economies, such as the United States and withih the European Union.

I High economic growth, 1950–71

Economic growth

The Japanese economy experienced high economic growth from the beginning of the 1950s up to the first oil crisis in 1973, average economic growth rates exceeding 10 per cent. Before 1973, a reduction of growth to around a 3 per cent annual rate, a level which was considered to be reasonable in other industrial countries, was judged as a recession. Strong growth was mainly driven by a strong demand from investment and exports on the aggregate demand side, made possible by increasing productive capacity on the aggregate supply side. The ratio of investment to gross domestic product (GDP) had been fluctuating at around 20 per cent, a level considerably higher than other industrialized countries. The quality of the labour force was improved by increasing levels of education and by extensive on-the-job training. However, empirical studies tend to find that rapid growth in Japan can been mainly attributed to the rapid accumulation of capital and fast technological progress. About half the growth cannot be explained by labour or capital contribution and is thus attributable to technological progress and better usage of existing resources.

The Japanese household savings rate has been the highest among the OECD (Organization for Economic Cooperation and Development) countries. The savings rate increased from about 15 per cent in the mid-1950s to above 20 per cent in the beginning of the 1970s. The high savings rate during this period helped to keep investment high because capital had to be found domestically. Since then, the household saving rate in Japan has been declining, now standing at around 15 per cent. In the USA, in contrast, savings rates have been about 5 per cent, and those in Europe about 8 per cent in the UK and France, 12 per cent in Germany and 18 per cent in Italy.

Economic growth was so successful it became a 'motto' of economic policies in the 1960s. In 1960, the then Prime Minister Ikeda initiated a ten-year economic plan for 'income-doubling', a strong policy of support for high economic growth: for example, infrastructure investment in highways, bullet trains and industrial ports increased sharply. Although many critics were sceptical about the possibility of doubling national income in ten years (that is, an average of 7 per cent growth for ten years), the Japanese economy in fact achieved this goal even quicker.

Macroeconomic policy

During the period from 1949, when the value of the yen was fixed at ¥360:$1, to 1971, when the Bretton Woods regime collapsed, Japan tended to run trade deficits when an economic boom occurred. When trade deficits occur, the central bank must intervene to buy or sell foreign exchange at the fixed rate. With capital flow restricted in the 1950s and 1960s, trade surpluses meant an increase in foreign reserves and trade deficits a decrease. Hence, monetary restraint was applied whenever the trade account deficit persisted. Japanese macroeconomic policy was thus operating under the constraint of the fixed exchange rate system.

Japan was running chronic current account deficits in the 1950s and 1960s. Business booms during this period tended to rapidly increase imports, thus sending the trade balance into deficit and drawing down foreign reserves. In order to maintain the fixed exchange rate, the monetary authorities had to tighten policy to stop a boom. Towards the end of the 1960s, even during the boom, trade balances did not turn to deficits. Japanese trade surpluses and a refusal, along with Germany, to appreciate its currency within the Bretton Woods system, played a part in the demise of the system in 1971.

Although the decade of 'income-doubling' was regarded as a success, there was a brief period of trouble in the middle. The year 1965 was regarded as a severe recession. The growth rate suddenly dropped to 5 per cent from an average of 10 per cent growth for the decade. Financial troubles (a large securities firm came close to bankruptcy) magnified the trouble. This was the year in which the government decided to issue the so-called 'construction bonds' to supplement revenue, and continue spending on infrastructure. Prior to this, fiscal policy had been conservative, in the sense that the budget was balanced every year without issuing long-term government bonds.

Industrial policy

Some economists regard industrial policy, in addition to prudent macroeconomic policy, as responsible for Japan's success in economic growth and development. According to the conventional view, industrial policy encouraged 'sunrise' industries – industries that would flourish in the coming years. The theory is as follows. When an industry is in an 'infant' stage, it is better to nurture domestic firms through protection by limiting entry to the industry or by maintaining high tariffs: domestic firms thus capture domestic markets. The Ministry of International Trade and Industry (MITI) carefully monitor demand and supply projections and approve the expansion of capacity so that profit margins are guaranteed. New facilities are often helped by low interest-rate loans through the Development Bank. By taking advantage of scale economies and profits, the protected industries will quickly reach a stage that is internationally competitive in producing quality goods at cost efficient prices. Firms are then encouraged to export. Export subsidies, for example in the form of export insurance, are provided. By expanding markets to other countries, the firms continue to grow. How many industries fit this traditional mould is debatable. Steel and coal were designated as priority industries in the late 1940s. Later, in the 1950s and 1960s, shipbuilding, petrochemicals, oil-refining and aluminium were encouraged.

Steel and shipbuilding seem to be the success stories of such a policy, Japan becoming one of the leading countries in these industries in the 1980s. However, not all industries designated as important in industrial policy succeeded. The coal industry became a 'sunset' industry, soon after oil replaced coal for various uses and cheap coal became available on international markets. The aluminium industry was hampered from the beginning by the high electricity costs in Japan. More interesting cases are the motor and electronics industries, which succeeded without the benefit of an advantageous industrial policy. Although cars and televisions had been protected by relatively high tariffs in the 1950s, they did not receive any overt subsidies or particularly favourable entry restrictions. Indeed, when the MITI tried to merge some automobile companies in the early 1960s in order to achieve 'scale economies' by limiting competition, it was opposed by the motor industries. The MITI thus failed in its attempt to follow a traditional-style industrial policy. Now, a few decades later, most of the automobile companies (Toyota, Nissan, Honda, Subaru and Isuzu) have become winners in the world markets.

The Japanese electronics industry – from radio to black-and-white televisions, to colour televisions, to video recorders and finally to computers – is also one of the most important players in the world market. Sony, Matsushita (Panasonic) and Toshiba are household names in many countries. However, Sony and Matsushita each basically grew from a shop owned by a single individual to the status of a multinational company in a few decades, without the help of subsidized loans or entry restrictions. Hence, economists are divided in assessing the benefits and costs of industrial policy. Proponents cite industries with successful results; and sceptics cite examples of failure.

For better or worse, industrial policy was practised in the 1950s and 1960s. Since foreign exchange was scarce, import licences could work as a policy tool. Capital was scarce and a large pool of money in postal savings could be used as funds for policy (subsidized) loans. In the 1970s, however, the environment changed, with the scope for industrial policy becoming extremely limited in the 1980s.

2 The oil shock and its aftermath, 1971–75

The eventful five years from 1971 to 1975 brought many changes to Japan. The fixed exchange rate regime yielded to the floating exchange rate regime. This meant that the guide to monetary policy had to be changed. Oil prices quadrupled in a matter of several months from October 1973. Industrial policy, which had promoted heavy and chemical industries, needed a new direction. The Japanese economy, after high economic growth for twenty years, was at a crossroads.

On 15 August 1971, the dollar convertibility to gold was suspended and the dollar was unilaterally depreciated against major currencies, including the yen. This fundamental change in the foreign exchange regime was considered to be a surprise by many policy makers in Japan. In December, in an effort to return to the fixed exchange rate system, the Smithsonian agreement was struck, introducing a new parity (¥308:$1, an appreciation of 17 per cent from the Bretton Woods parity). In the spring of 1973, after the transition period, the yen and the European currencies became free floating.

In 1972, monetary policy was considerably relaxed, partly to prevent further yen appreciation (from the Smithsonian rate). Some policy makers thought even inflation should be tolerated in order to stop yen appreciation. Another reason for easy monetary policy was the initiative by Mr Tanaka (who became Prime Minister in July 1972) to 'reconstruct' Japan, which included large public works programmes to build bullet-train and highway networks. Inflation pressure built up in the first half of 1973. By the summer of 1973, the inflation rate crept up to more than 10 per cent.

The first oil crisis occurred in October 1973. The oil crisis brought severe inflation and recession, a combination called 'stagflation'. The oil embargo from OPEC (Organization of Petroleum Exporting Countries) in October 1973 and subsequent sharp increases in oil prices threw industrial economies into chaos. The Japanese economy was hardest hit. In 1974, inflation reached an annual rate of around 30 per cent and real GDP growth rate was negative. In order to fight inflation and inflationary expectation, monetary policy was dramatically tightened in 1974. Although growth was halted, inflation continued feeding itself through inflationary expectation. Inflation did not fall below 10 per cent until late 1975, or below 5 per cent until 1978.

3 Stable economic growth, 1975-89

In retrospect, a trend growth rate shifted sharply downwards at around the time of the oil crisis, 1973-74. The average growth rate from 1974 to 1990 was about 4 per cent, less than half that of the preceding fifteen years. A major reason for this reduction was the fact that the technological gap between the West and Japan narrowed, so that Japan could not simply import technology to produce competitive goods, but needed to spend more on research and development. As shipbuilding, steel and cars became the leading industries in output and exports, it became difficult to expand on the previous scale. Rapid industrialization also brought pollution in the 1960s. Social consciousness concerning the environment was raised as a result of several highly publicized pollution cases. Anti-pollution investment had to be increased throughout the 1970s.

A severe recession followed the first oil crisis, but only a mild recession followed the second oil crisis.

Monetary policy

After the economy shifted to a floating exchange rate system, a shortage of foreign reserves was no longer a concern for monetary policy. Monetary policy was freed from the obligation to preserve the fixed exchange rate. However, rapid yen appreciation became a major concern because of its adverse effect on export industries. The monetary authorities viewed the inflation experience of 1973-75 as a major policy failure. The Bank of Japan thus started to look for a better indicator, or intermediate target, for monetary policy. This was the monetary aggregate (M2), which has been emphasized since 1978, when its forecasts were first regularly announced.

In fact, the Bank of Japan successfully reduced the monetary growth rate gradually from the mid-1970s to 1987. As the rate was lowered, the inflation rate was also lowered. Whether this fact is proof of a successful implementation of monetarism is a matter of debate. Some researchers believe that monetary policy in the floating (post-1973) period reacted to the exchange rate: yen appreciation prompts intervention (selling yen, buying dollars) which, without sterilization, results in an expanding domestic money supply, which in turn lowers interest rates.

Fiscal policy

Deficit-financing bonds (that is, bonds to fill the fiscal deficits rather than for construction projects) were first issued in 1975, as an exception to the fiscal law, in order to combat the severe recession of 1974. The amount of deficit bonds increased quickly from 1975 to 1980. By 1980, the proportion of debt financing in Japan was one of the largest among the OECD countries. From 1980 to 1990, new issues of debt-financing bonds were gradually curtailed, finally reaching zero in 1990.

In general, budget sizes can be shown to have responded to business cycles; namely, recession prompted the government to form a bigger budget, even within the fiscal year, through supplementary budgets. In this sense, there is some evidence that fiscal policy was conducted to stabilize the economy.

The Japanese fiscal authority has more than just tax revenues with which to determine resource allocations. The Fiscal Investment and Loan Programme (FILP) is a Ministry of Finance administered programme, mainly funded by postal savings, which is loaned out to finance and subsidize public works and other government investment projects. It can be viewed as a capital budget. There are several special accounts which are financed by FILP, subsidized by general accounts (tax money) and/or funded by user fees.

Major national tax revenues were previously taken from personal income tax and corporate tax. Consumption tax, which is the name for a Japanese version of value added tax, was introduced in 1989. A uniform rate of 3 per cent is imposed on the value added at each stage of distribution. With the introduction of consumption tax, some selected excise taxes and transportation taxes were eliminated.

4 A bubble economy, 1985–90

Stock prices and land prices soared in the second half of the 1980s. Stock prices (measured in Nikkei 225) tripled in the four years from 1985 to 1989, while land prices (measured in residential land in six large cities) more than doubled in the four years from 1986 to 1990. However, consumer and wholesale price indices remained stable.

Several explanations have been offered for asset price increases in the second half of the 1980s. Economic growth rate became higher in the second half, that became the basis for optimistic forecast of the growth potential of the Japanese economy. Deregulation, in particular financial deregulation, invited foreign firms and institutions. Demands for office space in Tokyo increased in the mid-1980s. Monetary policy remained loose from 1986 to 1989. The official discount rate was lowered to the (then) record low of 2.5 per cent in 1987 and kept until the early 1989.

Although the initial increase was caused by optimistic views on the economy, the sharp asset price increase invited speculative activities. Corporations and individuals started to transact land and stocks for short-term gains. Self-fulfilling expectations started to play an important role toward the end of the decade. Price:earning ratios increased sharply, so that price increases were justified only by further price increases. The term for this in the finance literature is a 'bubble', so the economy in this period has been dubbed a 'bubble economy'. The lax monetary policy contributed to fuelling the bubble activities. Banks increased lending to real estate and construction companies (real estate developers). It was only a matter of time before the bubble would burst.

5 The lost decade, 1991–2000

Stock prices plummeted from a peak of 38,916 at the end of 1989 to about 15,000 in August 1992, while the stock market lost more than 60 per cent of its value in two and half years. Land prices also started to decline in 1991, and the downward trend has continued for the decade. Compared to the peak of 1991–92, the typical Tokyo land price in Tokyo fell to one-third of the peak in nine years.

One of the consequences of the bubble and its bursting was that many suffered substantial losses in their balance sheets. In particular, real estate companies and developers suffered from bad assets, for which they could not find buyers or use in development projects. Many failed to make interest payments to banks, with the result that banks' balance sheets deteriorated with non-performing loans. In 1993 and 1994, bank lending failed to grow. Several banks essentially failed and were absorbed by other banks.

Credit unions and smaller financial institutions started to experience difficulties on their balance sheets in 1992. Smaller banks started to fail in 1994–95. In 1995, one medium-size bank failed, and housing-loan companies collapsed. One of the twenty largest banks failed in 1997, followed by two large long-term credit banks in 1998. With many bank failures, the deposit insurance corporation exhausted the reserves, so that the insurance premiums were raised and the government strengthened the deposit insurance corporation. In 1998 and 1999, capital injection to commercial banks was implemented to restore capital that was damaged by massive loan losses.

Many factors contributed to the 'lost decade'. Economic growth rates were unusually low in the range of 0 to 1.5 per cent from 1992 to 1995. In 1996, economic growth rate exceeded 4 per cent and the long recession was considered to be finally over. The consumption tax (VAT) rate was hiked from 3 per cent to 5 per cent in April 1997, which dampened consumption and investment in the economy in the rest of the year. The Asian currency crisis, which started by the devaluation of the Thai baht in July 1997, worsened substantially in the autumn to winter of 1997. Exports to Asian countries from Japan dropped suddenly. Independently, a bank and two securities firms failed in Japan in November 1997. Both the Asian currency crisis and domestic financial crisis pushed the Japanese economy into a severe recession in 1998. The growth rate was lower than minus 2 per cent. The recovery in 1999–2000 was also very weak. Thus, the very low economic growth with worsening financial market conditions in the 1990s became known as a lost decade.

6 Industrial organization

Japanese industries are said to have a unique structure, the so-called *keiretsu* (company network), characterized by long-term business relationships, personal exchange, lending and borrowing on favourable terms and cross-share holdings. There are two kinds of *keiretsu*; horizontal (across different industries) and vertical (parts suppliers and a manufacturer, or a manufacturer and distributors). Both are characterized by long-term business relationships and cross-share holdings.

The Big Six enterprise group – Mitsubishi, Mitsui, Sumitomo, Ikkan (Dai-ichi-Kangyo), Fuyo and Sanwa – are the most prominent, traditional, horizontal *keiretsu* groups. Each group, with a large bank at the core, contains manufacturing firms in different industries and some service-sector firms. The firms are linked through informal financial and trading arrangements. For example, the Mitsubishi group is most often defined by participation in the 'Presidents' club of Mitsubishi. There are twenty-nine firms in the group (as of October 1993), including financial institutions (Mitsubishi Bank, Mitsubishi Trust, Meiji Life, Tokyo Marine and Fire), trading companies (Mitsubishi Corp.), shipbuilding and other heavy manufacturing companies (Mitsubishi Heavy Industries) and automobile companies (Mitsubishi Motors).

The Mitsubishi Bank holds about 4 to 5 per cent of the equities of most of the Mitsubishi group companies. In return, Mitsubishi group firms combined hold a quarter of Mitsubishi Bank's equities. Other pairs of Mitsubishi companies also hold each other's equity shares. Although only a few Mitsubishi companies are majority-owned by other Mitsubishi companies, about a quarter of total Mitsubishi firms' total equities are held by other firms in the group. In addition to cross-holding of equity shares, Mitsubishi manufacturing firms tend to borrow more from the Mitsubishi financial institutions than from other financial institutions.

Each group tries to extend and diversify its sectoral spans. Hence, all six groups end up having big banks, insurance companies, trading firms and major manufacturing corporations. Horizontal *keiretsu* rarely act in an oligopolistic manner, competing fiercely with each other.

There are several theories concerning the role of the horizontal *keiretsu*. One theory emphasizes the bank's role in monitoring management's effort. A bank can monitor management's effort through lending screening and by planting board members in the management team. Another theory limits the positive role of banks when a company becomes financially weak. Since a bank holds both equities and lending, it can act without conflict of interests as a source of (secured) loans and (unsecured) equities. Other researchers think that acrossindustry grouping is good for synergy – promoting externalities among different industries. Synergy produced by linking different firms is, however, difficult to quantify.

A typical vertical *keiretsu* group is formed by a manufacturer and its various parts suppliers. A vertical *keiretsu* can also be formed through a distribution channel, from a manufacturer to wholesale agents, to retailers. For example, Toyota has a group of parts suppliers – many small-scale family businesses and a few large stock-exchange-listed companies – with which Toyota cooperates in developing specifications in advance of mass production. Suppliers are chosen after product samples have been through various quality control tests.

Quality control is a major positive aspect of vertical *keiretsu*, and is made possible by the long-term relationship between the various organizations. Trust, reputation and long-term commitment play an important role. The 'lean production system', cutting down the level of inventory and asking the parts suppliers for just-in-time delivery, became a hallmark of Japanese production systems. The manufacturer values these efforts by parts suppliers, and rewards them with a implicit guarantee of continuing orders for many years.

Product distribution channels are sometimes controlled by manufacturers. A network of dedicated distributors may often be created to deal only with a particular brand. For example, Matsushita (Panasonic) stores deal exclusively with Matsushita products, and Sony stores likewise deal only with Sony products.

Since many banks became weak in the 1990s, the nexus of a horizontal *keiretsu* became weak. Many mergers, consolidation, and affiliation occurred across the *keiretsu* boundary. For example, Mitsui and Sumitomo banks announced a merger, and several manufacturing firms in the two *keiretsu* are planning a merger or affiliation.

Even in a horizontal *keiretsu*, changes are obvious. Exclusive part supplier, dealership or franchise relationships are weakening. Advances in information technology increasingly make it possible to outsource, look for least cost suppliers, and market to retail customers without dealership. Competition is now global, and strong domestic supplier and dealership is of less value to the multinational company. Industrial organization is changing, reflecting technological and other external changes.

7 Labour relations

It is striking that Japan has maintained a very low unemployment rate over the last thirty-five years. The unemployment rate was between 1 and 2 per cent in the 1950s and 1960s, and between 2 and 3 per cent since the mid-1970s. This performance is attributed to many institutional features in the labour market as well as a strong macroeconomic performance.

One such feature is the conventional stereotyped description of the Japanese labour market. Japanese workers, under the commitment of 'lifetime employment' at one company, accept any job assignments, and the seniority wage structure ensures that compensations are skewed towards the later stage of life. Unions cooperate with management. Stable employment and compensation make it possible to achieve high productivity increases and low unemployment.

However, this stereotyped view needs to be examined carefully. First, lifetime employment is limited to workers in large-size firms and comprises only about 30 per cent of the total number of male workers. The rest of the workers change jobs frequently, and go in and out of the labour market. Second, even for those who hold lifetime jobs, annual total compensation and working hours are quite flexible. Lifetime earnings vary across individuals of the same worker group, reflecting merit and overtime. Third, the relationship between labour unions and management became more cooperative only after the 1970s. In the 1950s and 1960s, some unions were quite confrontational, reflecting the political–ideological divide in Japan at the time.

During the 1990s, the unemployment rate steadily increased. By the end of the decade, the unemployment rate became nearly 5 per cent. The US unemployment rate showed a dramatic decline in the 1990s, and became lower than the Japanese unemployment for the first time in history. The crossing of the unemployment rates of the two countries was perceived in Japan as the symbol of malaise of the Japanese economy after the lost decade.

Despite publicity about involuntary unemployment at distressed companies, the abandonment of life employment is not widespread. Companies that are not (near) bankruptcy are still reluctant to layoff or fire regular employees. On the demand side, jobs are offered to temporary workers and contract workers. On the supply side, young workers are not taking up permanent jobs, but are content to be temporary workers. The lifetime employment system may be melting down at the entry level.

8 Is Japan unique?

Between the mid-1980s and mid-1990s, trade conflicts between the USA and Japan became increasingly bitter. The USA complained that the Japanese markets were not open to foreign goods (in particular US goods), and pressed for measures to guarantee 'market access'. Many officials in the US government, in particular United States Trade Representatives (USTR) have argued that the Japanese economy is unique in that, compared with other industrial countries, manufactured goods imports into Japan are low, as is direct investment. The USA demanded, with varying degrees of success, increased imports into Japan of semiconductors, supercomputers, satellites and cars. US proponents of the cause argued that the Japanese markets are structurally closed to foreign goods and capital, citing *keiretsu* and labour practices as examples. As Japan is regarded as unique, US critics argued, a unique approach to the problem, such as demanding 'measurable results' of market shares, can be justified. Thus, the semiconductor agreement had a foreign products' market share of 20 per cent in Japan as its target. The Japanese government became increasingly resistant to demands for numerical targets, as typified by the semiconductor agreement, partly because they were used as a basis for sanctions and partly because of the realization that Japanese 'uniqueness' is not necessarily a barrier to foreign goods and services but a sign of efficient business relationships.

Defenders of the Japanese argued that the current account position of one country is a reflection of saving and investment, and that the current account deficits of the USA were primarily a result of domestic economic performance, especially the low savings rate. A particularly bitter dispute over the access to the motor and auto parts markets in Japan, negotiated from July 1993 to June 1995, highlighted the nature of the conflict. Japan argued that the principal reason that US and other foreign car makers had not penetrated the market was that they did not produce cars fit for Japan's narrow roads and left-hand-drive system, nor for its consumer tastes, while the USA believed that there was a structural barrier.

The issue highlights the question of whether Japan's economy is in some way unique, in terms of both production and demand. As this entry has shown, Japan's economy developed under some unusual circumstances, and has also been strongly affected by the business culture and environment of Japan. The misunderstandings between Japan and its Western trading partners stem at least in part from the highly different economic circumstances which each of them face.

Many of the Japanese automakers, including Nissan, began to accept foreign capital participation and *de facto* managerial control. Many life insurance companies created joint ventures and entered into product development in cooperation with foreign firms. Some life insurance firms failed and have been taken over by foreign partners. The closedness of the Japanese economy to foreign capital is no longer at issue.

The uniqueness of the Japanese model is disappearing quickly at the end of the 1990s. This partly reflects an increasing integration of the Japanese economy to the rest of the world and partly a convergence of the Japanese economic structures to those of the United States.

TAKATOSHI ITO
HITOTSUBASHI UNIVERSITY

Further reading

(References cited in the text marked *)

Ito, T. (1992) *Japanese Economy*, Cambridge, MA: MIT Press. (General introduction to the

Japanese economy. Designed to be an undergraduate textbook, with full references to advanced studies. Easy to understand analyses of economic phenomena.)

Komiya, R., Okuno, M. and Suzumura, K. (1988) *The Industrial Policy of Japan*, San Diego, CA: Academic Press. (Comprehensive study on industrial policy, theory and practices.)

Kosai, Y. (1986) *The Era of High-Speed Growth*, Tokyo: University of Tokyo Press. (Focus on the Japanese economy up to the first oil crisis.)

Nakamura, T. (1995) *The Postwar Japanese Economy*, 2nd edn, Tokyo: University of Tokyo Press. (Good overview and description of the post-war macroeconomic situation.)

Yamamura, K. and Yasuba, Y. (eds) (1987) *The Political Economy of Japan*, vol. 1, Stanford, CT: Stanford University Press. (Collection of papers on selected topics. Knowledge of intermediate economics required.)

Economic growth and convergence

1. **Different perspectives**
2. **Growth accounting**
3. **The catch-up literature**
4. **'Barro' regressions**
5. **R&D, spillovers and growth**
6. **Theory and evidence**

Overview

Theoretical and applied work on economic growth is concerned with questions such as what the drivers of economic growth are, how these affect countries with different characteristics and what long-run economic outcomes should be expected. Is there a tendency towards convergence in the global economy so that GDP per capita in the long run will be the same everywhere? Or does the evidence suggest that the existing differences seem to persist or even increase over time (so-called divergence)? How may these different outcomes be explained?

The literature on growth is large and spans several centuries (see GROWTH THEORY). The literature on the formal modelling of economic growth is generally highly abstract and focuses on the level of the country or the global economy. Here we will put the main emphasis on the more recent developments, and on questions that have been central to applied research in this area. However, since both the focus and method of applied research depend heavily on theory, we start by briefly outlining some theoretical perspectives that have been influential on applied research on economic growth and convergence, and the issues that have been raised as a result.

1 Different perspectives

The idea that economic growth is associated with a tendency towards convergence dates back to the advent of the neo-classical growth theory in the 1950s (Robert Solow 1956; and others) (see NEO-CLASSICAL ECONOMICS). This theory, based on the familiar neo-classical assumption of so-called 'perfect competition', predicts that countries that differ in terms of initial productivity levels but not otherwise will in the long run converge towards the same level of productivity and the same rate of productivity growth. If countries differ also in other respects (population growth and savings propensities) convergence towards the same growth of productivity will still be achieved, but long-run productivity levels will differ (so-called 'conditional convergence'). The central mechanism behind growth and convergence in this perspective is 'mechanization', that is the substitution of capital for labour in production, which is assumed to occur at a faster rate in poor countries or regions than in the rich ones. However, because of decreasing returns to such substitution, this mechanism can only explain convergence, not long-run growth of productivity, which is assumed to be caused by exogenous technological progress. Hence, technology is in this approach regarded as an exogenous force, equally available to everyone everywhere free of charge (a so-called 'public good') that propels long-run growth.

Another approach to the study of growth and convergence/divergence is that associated with the works of economic historians such as Alexander Gerschenkron (1962) and Moses Abramovitz (1994) and economists applying Schumpeterian ideas to the operation of the global economy (see GLOBALIZATION). The central idea here is that some countries are at the technological frontier, while others lag behind. Although the technological gap between a frontier country and a laggard represents 'a great promise' for the latter (a potential for high growth through imitating frontier technologies), there are also various problems that may prevent backward countries from reaping the potential benefits of technology transfer to the full extent. Thus, catch-up is not something that can be expected to occur only through the working of market forces, but requires a lot of effort and institution-building on the part of a backward country. Hence, technology is here viewed rather differently from the traditional neo-classical approach. Abramovitz uses the concepts 'technological congruence' and 'social capability' to characterize the situation for latecomers. The first concept refers to the degree to which leader and follower country characteristics are congruent in areas such as market size, factor supply, etc. The second points to the various efforts and capabilities that backward countries have to develop in order to catch up (education etc.).

A third and more recent stream of thought (so-called 'new growth theory') combines aspects of the two approaches. The central contributor here is Paul Romer (1986, 1990). As in the other approaches growth is seen as driven by technological progress, which, however, is explained through the interplay of investments in new technology by private firms and positive spillovers from these investments to the society's collective knowledge-base. The effect of such positive spillovers is to continually raise the productivity of investments in new technology. Hence, due to spillovers, investments in new technology are not checked by decreasing returns as in the traditional neo-classical theory and growth of productivity may continue indefinitely. The presence of increasing returns also implies that there is no inherent tendency to convergence in the global economy (as suggested by the traditional approach) because without decreasing returns to new investments there is no reason to expect slower growth in rich areas (with a large knowledge base) than in poorer ones (with less accumulated knowledge).

2 Growth accounting

The advent of the traditional neo-classical growth theory led to a surge in empirical research on the sources of economic growth. Armed with this theoretical perspective economic practitioners started to analyse actual growth, weighting the growth of inputs with factor shares. For instance, the contribution of capital to economic growth was calculated as the growth of capital multiplied by the capitalists' share of national income. When the contributions from factor growth are added together in this way a residual may occur. This unexplained part of actual growth was dubbed 'total factor productivity growth', that is, the part of actual growth that cannot be attributed to any single factor. This methodology, so-called growth accounting, was first applied to historical data for the USA by Moses Abramovitz (1956) and later to selected OECD countries by Edward Denison (1967). Over the years this methodology has also been applied to many individual countries. For a good overview see Angus Maddison (1987).

The first exercises in this area showed that only a small part of actual growth could be attributed to growth of capital and labour. Up to 80 per cent remained unexplained and had to be classified as so-called total factor productivity growth. That the lion's share of actual growth had to be explained by exogenous technological progress and other unidentified sources was something many were not willing to accept. Various remedies were invented to improve on this result. The first was to adjust the factors themselves by taking into account the changes in quality and composition. For instance, new vintages of capital or labour were assumed to be more efficient than previous ones. To some extent this practice boiled down to no more than building the unexplained part of actual growth into the factors themselves. Second, it was suggested that additional factors such as economies of scale, investments in R&D, possible differences in productivity levels across countries and sectors and a host of other factors (crime, for instance) should be taken into account. As a result, the growth accountants were able to explain a much larger part of actual growth. There is one fundamental problem, however: The very existence of some of these additional factors actually contradicts the assumption of the theory on which the analysis was based. For instance, the theory explicitly assumes 'perfect competition', which implies no economies of scale.

This conflict between the underlying assumptions of the theory and the applied work to which it gave rise obviously raises a question on how the results should be interpreted. It was pointed out by Richard Nelson (1964) that growth accounting is not a tested theory of growth. Rather it is an analysis – or description – of a growth process based on certain assumptions which are taken as given (i.e. not tested). Hence, the validity of conclusions from such analyses will depend on whether these underlying assumptions are true or not. It is important to remember this need to validate the theory when assessing the lessons from applications of this methodology. For instance, in a relatively recent paper on the East Asian NICs it was claimed that accumulation of capital and labour explains everything there is to explain about the sources of economic growth (Young 1995) (see EAST ASIAN ECONOMIES). However, to assess such claims one has to find out whether the underlying assumptions, on which this conclusion is based, really hold. That means that one has to ask the following types of questions: Did perfect competition prevail? Were there no large firms with market power? No scale economics? Was technology freely available to everyone free of charge? Without answers to this these deeper questions growth accounting exercises cannot be used to draw conclusions about what drives growth.

3 The catch-up literature

Applied work on technology gaps and catch-up inspired by by Gerschenkron and others took several different routes. Gerschenkron and other authors provided illuminating case-studies based on material from specific countries. Quantitatively oriented economic historians such as Abramovitz and Maddison made detailed investigations into the changes in relative productivity across countries in the long run and various efforts that countries made to have an impact on this process. Applying an econometric technique, Cornwall (1976) regressed variables assumed to reflect the scope for catch-up, investment and (endogenous) technological progress on GDP growth for a sample of OECD countries. Later, in the 1980s, Pavitt and Soete (1982) and Fagerberg (1987) presented regression models that also included variables reflecting resources devoted to (or output from) innovation (patents/R&D). Inspired by the work by Abramovitz and others on technology gaps and growth William Baumol *et al.* (1989) applied regression models of the type just discussed to cross-country samples including up to 100 countries or more. Variables taken into account in that study included the scope for catch-up, measured, as in the other studies, by GDP per capita, investment, educational attainment and growth of population/labour force.

The results from these regression analyses led to a quite vivid debate about how the results should be interpreted (see Baumol 1986; DeLong 1988; Baumol *et al.* 1989). The conclusion of this debate was that while unconditional convergence could perhaps be established for the OECD countries in the post-war period, and probably occurred for some other countries as well, it does not hold for the world as a whole. However, when other variables were introduced, such as investment, education, etc., the scope for catch-up (approximated by the gap in productivity – or GDP per capita – between the country in question and the frontier) was found to be an important factor behind differences in growth in the world economy, but conditional on other variables (so-called 'conditional convergence'). Hence real world catch-up was found to be very far from the easy, quasi-automatic process envisaged by traditional theory in this area. These results should not be regarded as surprising except, perhaps, for some very firm believers in the traditional neo-classical theory. Writers in the traditions that developed out of the work of Joseph Schumpeter (1934, 1939, 1943) and Gerschenkron (1962) had never predicted global convergence (see SCHUMPETER, J.). On the contrary, these writers stressed that catch-up was possible but difficult, that countries wanting to succeed in catch-up processes had to undertake conscious efforts to succeed.

4 'Barro' regressions

These findings and the theoretical advances associated with them led to a surge of empirical work. What most applied researchers in this area have done is to follow the tradition from Cornwall, Baumol and others, applying single-equation regression models to cross-country data sets. For some reason this type of work is commonly referred to as 'Barro' regressions after an American economist, Robert Barro, who picked up this practice at a rather late stage (Barro 1991). Basically the models are identical to the ones suggested by Baumol *et al*. (1989), including variables such as the scope for catch-up, investment in physical capital, education, population growth and others, reflecting, for instance, differences in the policy stance. For overviews the reader is referred to Fagerberg (1994) and Temple (1999).

In an influential paper Levine and Renelt (1992) have argued that the various factors that have been emphasized in the empirical literature need to be tested in a systematic way in order to establish how sensitive the findings are to the inclusion of other possible explanatory variables. The method suggested by them consists of selecting a set of basic variables that are always included in the regression. These are basically the variables we have already mentioned (the scope for catch-up, investment, education and population growth). Other possible variables are included one by one and the sensitivity of the result is then tested by including up to three other variables drawn from a large pool of possible explanatory factors. If the result is always significant, it is termed 'robust'. If it is insignificant in at least one case it is considered as 'fragile'. This, it may be noted, is not a test of causality but of what can be established with some degree of certainty in the single-equation cross-country regression framework, given the available data. Important relationships may well be found to be fragile following this methodology. The principal finding of Levine and Renelt is that the most robust relationship is between growth and investment. Some support is also found for variables reflecting the scope for catch-up (proxied by GDP per capita gaps) and educational efforts. All other explanatory variables were found to be fragile, including a large number of policy variables, openness (defined in different ways) and political factors (such as democracy, stability, etc.). In a later study (King and Levine 1993), the level of financial development of the country was added to the list of robust relationships.

What new is there to be learned from this? Arguably not very much. That investment is correlated with growth should come as no surprise. Indeed, this is something that would be consistent with most theories in this area, including those that consider investment as endogenous to the growth process, as available evidence on time-series data seems to suggest (see Carroll and Weil 1993). It is also worth noting that the studies by Levine and others fail to include R&D and innovation, and thus throw little light on the mechanisms highlighted by the most recent versions of the new growth theories.

5 R&D, spillovers and growth

Another relevant strand of research attempts to measure private and social returns to R&D and innovation. This type of work has gone on for a long time, independently of the developments in growth theory, but attracts a growing interest due to the recent changes in formal theorizing. The literature has been surveyed by Griliches (1992) and Mohnen (1992). For a more recent overview see Verspagen (1995). Generally, these empirical exercises tend to find high private returns to investments in R&D, about twice as high as for other types of investment. This, of course, runs counter to traditional neo-classical perspectives on investment, according to which returns to different types of investments should be equalized. Hence, one of the central issues in this area, which we will not venture into here, has been how these high private returns can be explained. However, high as these private returns may be, social returns are commonly found to be even higher, indicating important positive spillovers from R&D, especially when conducted in private firms.

Recently, there have been some attempts to address these issues from a perspective that draws more explicitly on the advances in the growth literature. Central questions in this more recent literature are to what extent diffusion processes (or spillovers) are influenced by geographical (and other) boundaries, whether country size matters and what the most efficient carriers of technology diffusion are. The available evidence seems to indicate that diffusion of technology (spillovers) is hampered by distance and is generally easier and quicker within than across country borders (Jaffe 1986; Jaffe *et al.* 1993; Maurseth and Verspagen 1999). There is also some evidence suggesting that returns to R&D investment are higher in large countries (Coe and Helpman 1995; Gittleman and Wolff 1995), consistent with some of the suggestions from recent advances in growth theory. On the last question some recent exercises point to R&D embodied in imports of goods and services as a very efficient carrier of new technology (Coe and Helpman 1995; Coe *et al.* 1997). The conclusion, then, should be that foreign R&D embodied in imports is the primary source of growth in most countries, particularly the developing ones, and that openness to trade is what is required if a country is going to benefit from the global process of innovation and diffusion. However, others, using essentially the same type of indicator, fail to reproduce these results (Gittleman and Wolff 1995; Verspagen 1997) so that at present no strong conclusion can be drawn. Several recent contributions emphasize differences in 'absorptive capacity' (education, infrastructure, technological capabilities, etc.) as the most important factor explaining differences in growth and welfare across countries (Gittleman and Wolff 1995; Eaton and Kortum 1996; Eaton *et al.* 1998).

In general much of this work concurs with recent theorizing in this area (the 'new growth theory'). However, there have been few attempts to test the formal growth models to which these theories give rise in a more direct way. One exception is the work by Jones (1995a, 1995b). A fundamental property that all new growth models share is, as mentioned above, that large economies (with more 'knowledge') are more productive than smaller ones. However, this scale-effect also implies that as the economy grows larger, the rate of growth will also increase. Jones tested this and found little evidence in its support, raising doubts about the validity of such formal models and the predictions to which they give rise.

6 Theory and evidence

While traditional neo-classical theory treated technology as exogenous, and hence failed to explain growth, recent advances in formal theorizing have gone a long way in incorporating technology and innovation. This research has led to the creation of more complex models that in one sense may explain growth in a better way than before. These models are also more open in the sense that many different outcomes are possible, depending on what the key assumptions are. Many of these assumptions cannot be established on *a priori* grounds, at least not at the current state of formal theorizing, but need to verified through empirical research. Hence, empirical research in this area is not limited to testing the predictions of assumedly 'true' theoretical models, but also contributes actively to the formation of these predictions and influences the direction of further theoretical work. The empirical work on convergence–divergence in productivity and income across countries is in itself a good example of this interaction between theory and evidence.

That being said, formal growth theory is, as mentioned, a very abstract exercise, which at best yields predictions relevant for entire countries or the capitalist world as a whole. For a long time formal theory in this area ignored innovation completely, treating it as an exogenous (non-economic) event. More recently, with the advent of so-called 'new growth theory', innovation has been included in mainstream theory as an endogenous phenomenon. In this literature innovation is portrayed as any other activity, dependent on investments by profit-maximizing firms, but with positive spillovers (or externalities) at the national or global level which increase the productivity of future innovation and allow growth to occur. There is, however, no real understanding of what distinguishes an innovative firm from a non-innovating one. In fact, all firms are in a general sense assumed to be identical ('the representative firm') in this approach (although the concrete circumstances may differ), leaving no room for heterogeneity across firms, in contrast to what is suggested by so-called 'evolutionary' theories of economic development (Nelson and Winter 1982) (see EVOLUTIONARY THEORIES OF THE FIRM). Moreover, differences in institutional conditions across countries and the importance of these differences for innovation-processes (see, for instance, Lundvall 1995;

Nelson 1993; Edquist 1997) are normally disregarded or subsumed under very general headings such as 'absorptive capacity' and left unexplained. Hence, the existing theoretical literature on economic growth and the applied work it has stimulated does at best offer a partial view on the forces shaping economic growth and convergence–divergence, and needs to be supplemented by other approaches focusing on the interaction between (heterogeneous) firms and their institutional surroundings.

JAN FAGERBERG
UNIVERSITY OF OSLO

Further reading

(References cited in the text marked *)

* Abramovitz, M. (1956) 'Resources and Output Trends in the United States since 1870', *American Economic Review* 46: 5–23. (Analyses long-run US growth and shows that there is a lot traditional growth theory cannot explain.)
* Abramovitz, M. (1994) 'The origins of the postwar catch-up and convergence boom', in J. Fagerberg, B. Verspagen and N. von Tunzelman (eds) (1994) *The Dynamics of Technology, Trade and Growth*, Aldershot: Edward Elgar, pp. 21–52. (Analyses post-war growth with the help of concepts such as 'social capability' and 'technological congruence'.)
* Barro, R. (1991) 'Economic growth in a cross section of countries', *Quarterly Journal of Economics* 106: 407–43 (Uses regression analysis on data for a large number of countries in an attempt explore the issue of 'convergence'.)
* Baumol, W.J. (1986) 'Productivity growth, convergence and welfare: what the long run data show', *American Economic Review* 76: 1072–85 (Analyses long-run growth, started the controversy on 'convergence'.)
* Baumol, W.J., Batey Blackman, S.A. and Wolff, E.N. (1989) *Productivity and American Leadership: The Long View*, Cambridge, MA: MIT Press. (Uses regression analysis on data for a large number of countries in an attempt explore the issue of 'convergence'.)
* Carrol, C.D. and Weil, D.N. (1993) 'Saving and growth: a reinterpretation', *NBER Working Paper*, No. 4470, Cambridge (USA): National Bureau of Economic Research. (Analyses the relationship between saving and growth and presents evidence on the direction of causality.)
* Coe, D.T. and Helpman, E. (1995) 'International R&D spillovers', *European Economic Review* 39: 859–87. (Argues that international R&D spillovers are substantial and that open-ness to trade is important for benefitting from it.)
* Coe, D.T., Helpman, E. and Hoffmaister, A. (1997) 'NorthSouth R&D spillovers', *Economic Journal* 107: 134–49. (Argues that open-ness to trade is essential if developing countries are to benefit from international R&D spillovers.)
* Cornwall, J. (1976) 'Diffusion, convergence and Kaldor's Law', *Economic Journal* 86: 307–14. (An early and highly original contribution to the literature on 'convergence'.)
* De Long, J.B. (1988) 'Productivity growth, convergence and welfare', *American Economic Review* 78: 1138–54. (Questions the view that long-run growth is characterized by 'convergence' between countries.)
* Denison, E.F. (1967) *Why Growth Rates Differ: Post-War Experience in Nine Western Countries*, Washington, DC: Brookings Institution. (Applies growth accounting techniques to cross country growth evidence.)
* Eaton, J. and Kortum, S. (1996) 'Trade in ideas – patenting and productivity in the OECD', *Journal of International Economics* 40: 251–78. (Develops and estimates a model of the relationship between creation and diffusion of technology on the one hand and productivity on the other.)
* Eaton, J, Gutierrez, E. and Kortum, S. (1998) 'European technology policy', *Economic Policy* 27: 405–38. (Extends the previous analysis to discussions of technology policy.)
* Edquist, C. (ed.) (1997) *Systems of Innovation: Technologies, Institutions and Organizations*, London: Pinter. (A good introduction to the 'systems of innovation' literature and the role of institutions in long-run economic development.)
* Fagerberg, J. (1987) 'A technology gap approach to why growth rates differ', *Research Policy* 16: 87–99. (Explores the importance of R&D and innovation for catch-up processes.)
* Fagerberg, J. (1994) 'Technology and international differences in growth rates', *Journal of Economic Literature* 32: 1147–75. (Surveys theoretical and applied work on technology and growth.)
* Gerschenkron, A. (1962) *Economic Backwardness in Historical Perspective*, Cambridge (USA): The Belknap Press. (Discusses the conditions under which economically backward countries may catch up with the more advanced ones.)
* Gittleman, M. and Wolff, E.N. (1995) 'R&D activity and cross-country growth comparisons', *Cambridge Journal of Economics* 19: 189–207.

(Analyses empirical evidence on the importance of R&D for economic growth.)
* Griliches, Z. (1992) 'The search for R&D spillovers', *Scandinavian Journal of Economics* 94: S29–S47. (Surveys the theoretical and empirical literature on R&D spillovers.)
* Jaffe, A.B. (1986) 'Real effects of academic research', *American Economic Review* 79: 957–70. (Uses bibliographic techniques to analyse the impact of academic research.)
* Jaffe, A.B., Trajtenberg, M. and Henderson, R. (1993) 'Geographic localization of knowledge spillovers as evidenced by patent citations', *Quarterly Journal of Economics* 108: 55798. (Uses bibliographic techniques to explore the importance of distance and other factors for knowledge flows in the USA.)
* Jones, C.I. (1995a) 'Time series tests of endogenous growth models', *Quarterly Journal of Economics* 110: 429–525. (The first in a series of two papers questioning the validity of so called 'new growth theory'.)
* Jones, C.I. (1995b) 'R&D-based models of economic growth', *Journal of Political Economy* 103: 759–84. (The second in a series of two papers questioning the validity of so called 'new growth theory'.)
* King, R. and Levine, R. (1993) 'Finance and growth: Schumpeter might be right?' *Quarterly Journal of Economics* 108: 717–37. (Presents a so-called 'sensitivity analysis' of the importance of various factors (including finance) for economic growth.)
* Levine, R. and Renelt, D. (1992) 'A sensitivity analysis of cross-country growth regressions', *American Economic Review* 82: 942–63. (Presents a so-called 'sensitivity analysis' of the importance of various factors for economic growth.)
* Lundvall, B.Å. (ed.) (1995) *National Systems of Innovation: Towards a Theory of Innovation and Interactive Learning*, London: Continuum International Publishing Group/Pinter. (One of the first and most widely cited contributions to the literature on 'national systems of innovation'.)
* Maddison, A. (1987) 'Growth and slowdown in advanced capitalist economies: techniques of quantitative asessment', *Journal of Economic Literature* 25: 649–98. (An overview of long-run growth using descriptive statistics and growth-accounting techniques.)
* Maurseth, P. and Verspagen, B. (1999). 'Europe: One or several systems of innovation?' in J. Fagerberg, P. Guerrieri and B. Verspagen (eds) *The Economic Challenge for Europe: Adapting to Innovation-based Growth* , Aldershot: Edward Elgar, 149–74. (Uses bibliographic techniques to explore the importance of distance and other factors for knowledge flows in Europe.)
* Mohnen, P. (1992) 'The relationship between R&D and productivity growth in Canada and other major industrialized countries', Economic Council of Canada. (A contribution to and survey of the literature on the relationship between R&D and growth.)
* Nelson, R.R. (1964) 'Aggregate production functions and medium-range growth projections', *American Economic Review* 54: 575–606. (Discusses the limitations of empirical work based on traditional neo-classical growth theory/growth accounting.)
* Nelson, R.R. (ed.) (1993) *National Innovation Systems: A Comparative Analysis*, Oxford: Oxford University Press. (Presents a set of country studies emphasizing the role of R&D, innovation and supporting institutions/policies for long-run economic development.)
* Nelson, R.R, and Winter, S.G. (1982) *An Evolutionary Theory of Economic Change*, Cambridge: Harvard University Press. (Arguably the main contribution in the evolutionary literature on economic growth.)
* Pavitt, K. and Soete, L.G. (1982) 'International differences in economic growth and the international location of innovation', in H. Giersch (ed.) *Emerging Technologies: Consequences for Economic Growth, Structural Change, and Employment*, Tübingen: J.C.B.Mohr (Paul Siebeck). (Analyses differences in long-run growth and productvity using among other things data for R&D and patents.)
* Romer, P.M. (1986) 'Increasing returns and long-run growth', *Journal of Political Economy* 94: 1002–37. (Romer's first attempt to explain long-run growth by 'spillovers' to investments in 'technology'.)
* Romer, P.M. (1990) 'Endogenous technological change', *Journal of Political Economy* 98: S71–S102. (Introduces R&D and innovation in a more explicit way than before into the theory of 'endogenous growth'.)
* Schumpeter, J. (1934) *The Theory of Economic Development*, Cambridge, MA: Harvard University Press. (An English translation of Schumpeter's classic work in German from 1911 on the role of entrepreneurs and innovations for economic development.)
* Schumpeter, J. (1939) *Business Cycles I-II*, New York: McGraw-Hill. (A very extensive, but highly controversial, analysis of business cycles and long waves in long-run economic development.)

* Schumpeter, J. (1943) *Capitalism, Socialism and Democracy*, New York: Harper. (Presents Schumpeter's main ideas in a popular way and discusses the future of capitalism and capitalist institutions.)
* Solow, R. (1956) 'A contribution to the theory of economic growth', *Quarterly Journal of Economics* 70: 65–94. (Outlines the so-called neo-classical model of economic growth for which Solow was later awarded the Nobel prize.)
* Temple, J. (1999) 'The new growth evidence', *Journal of Economic Literature* 37: 112–56. (Contains a review of recent empirical work on economic growth.)
* Verspagen, B. (1995) 'R&D and productivity: a broad cross-section cross-country look', *Journal of Productivity Analysis* 9: 117–35. (A contribution to and survey of the literature on the relationship between R&D and productivity.)
* Verspagen, B. (1997) 'Estimating international technology spillovers using technology flow matrices', *Weltwirtschaftliches Archiv* 133: 226–48. (Uses input–output techniques to analyse technology flows.)
* Young, A. (1995) 'The tyranny of numbers: confronting the statistical realities of the East Asian growth experience', *Quarterly Journal of Economics* 110: 641–80. (Argues that so called 'conventional factors', i.e. capital accumulation and so forth, explain most of East Asian growth.)

See also: EVOLUTIONARY THEORIES OF THE FIRM; GROWTH THEORY; INTERNATIONAL MONETARY FUND; NEO-CLASSICAL ECONOMICS; WORLD BANK; WORLD TRADE ORGANIZATION

Exchange rate economics

1. The choice of exchange rate regime
2. Exchange rate determination
3. Spot and forward relationships
4. Exchange rate reform
5. Conclusion

Overview

The current exchange rate regime, subscribed to by the leading industrial countries, is one of quasi-flexible exchange rates and has existed since 1973. The present regime did not come into being as a result of a careful consideration of the supposed advantages of flexible rates, but rather as a result of dissatisfaction with the previous Bretton Woods regime of fixed but adjustable exchange rates, which, in turn, was a reaction to the experience of flexible exchange rates in the inter-war period. No sooner had the present regime been inaugurated than there was widespread discussion of the problems with the regime, particularly the relatively high volatility of exchange rates, and proposals for alternative regimes, based on greater fixity of exchange rates, have been widely canvassed. The evolution of exchange rate regimes would appear to be a classic example of history repeating itself.

In this article, three particular themes in the economics of exchange rates are examined. First, what criteria are relevant for a country or countries wishing to decide on the particular form of exchange rate regime best suited to their economic structure? Second, the determinants of exchange rates and the relationship between spot and forward rates are discussed. The final theme concerns the current proposals for the reform of the international monetary system. As will become evident, this theme is linked in a natural way to the material contained in the two other sections.

1 The choice of exchange rate regime

As noted above, the evolution of the exchange rate regime characterizing the international monetary system seems to be a classic example of history repeating itself. However, are there any clear guidelines for a country (or countries) wishing to decide on the optimal arrangements for the external value of its currency? One way of answering this question is to take the polar case in which a country wants to participate in a monetary union. This is a particularly relevant example given the continuing debate in Europe regarding the formation of such a union. The central advantage of participating in a wider monetary union is entirely analogous to the move from a barter economy to a money-using economy; the potential gains from such a move arise from the efficiency-enhancing effects on exchange (see ECONOMIC INTEGRATION, INTERNATIONAL).

For the purpose of illustration, we assume that the world comprises two countries, A and B. At the heart of any debate over whether A should rigidly lock its exchange rate to B is the issue of wage and price flexibility. For example, if wages and prices are perfectly flexible in A and B, there is no potential problem in both these countries' currencies participating in a currency union. Thus, if, after joining the monetary union, there is a shift in demand away from A-produced goods to B-produced goods (an asymmetric shock) all that would be required to maintain an efficient allocation of goods in A would be a change in the relative price of traded to non-traded goods. In the absence of such flexibility, the consequence of the demand change will be unemployed resources and the necessity of providing fiscal transfers. Changing the exchange rate is ruled out by definition. Given that wage and price stickiness is the rule rather than the exception, are there any other factors which would facilitate adjustment in the presence of both fixity of wages and prices and the exchange rate? This is where the optimal currency area (OCA) literature comes in (see KEYNES, J.M.). This literature focuses on the relationship between a country's labour, product and financial markets, and those of its trading partners.

Mundell (1961) argued that the size of an OCA would be constrained by the mobility of capital and labour between potential participants in the monetary union. Thus, in terms of the above example, the unemployment in A (and the implied over-employment in B) would be alleviated by a transfer of labour and capital from A to B. The relative openness of an economy has been emphasized by McKinnon (1963) as an important criterion in determining the extent of an OCA. Thus an economy that is relatively open (that is, a large proportion of its output is devoted to traded goods) will gain, in terms of maintaining price stability, by rigidly locking its exchange rate in the presence of asymmetric shocks. This is because with a relatively small non-traded goods sector a drop in demand for A's traded output would require a relatively large rise in the prices of its non-traded goods relative to traded goods in order to encourage an optimal resource allocation; hence any rise in internal prices would be relatively high for that country. The third key criterion is the degree of product diversification within a country. For example, Kenen (1969) has argued that countries with relatively diversified structures (that is, with a large range of traded goods) are better able to withstand an asymmetric shock to a particular component of their exports than a country with a rather limited range of exports. Such a country should be in a good position to relinquish its exchange rate instrument and fully participate in a monetary union.

The above criteria would seem to offer clear guidelines that could be followed by countries wishing to participate in a monetary union. However, it is likely that, taken together, the above rules will have limited practical usefulness; for any country, some of the criteria may point in one direction while for other countries they point in a different direction. What is needed, therefore, is some form of net cost–benefit analysis which gives a composite weighted criteria of the net benefits. The recent literature on assessing the merits of currency unions has in fact moved towards analysing the effects of different shocks on economies. The advantage of this approach is that a shock-absorption approach combines the net influence of several of the traditional criteria. This kind of work is still in its infancy (see Masson and Taylor (1993) for an overview) and much more research needs to be conducted before clear-cut prescriptions can be made.

2 Exchange rate determination

What then determines the external value of a country's currency? (Note that this article does not consider the determination of exchange rates within exchange rate bands or target zones and market intervention is abstracted from – see Hallwood and MacDonald (1994) for a further discussion of these topics.) What is usually taken to be the baseline view of exchange rate determination is purchasing power parity (PPP). This approach has been popular since at least the last century and asserts that a country's exchange rate is determined by the ratio of a domestic price level to an equivalent foreign price level. Conventionally, this relationship is assumed to hold because all of the goods entering the price series are tradeable and traded arbitrage between different trading centres is assumed to ensure that there are no profitable arbitrage opportunities. (Thus, if a UK-produced washing machine is cheaper than the equivalent US-produced machine – expressed in a common currency – it will be profitable to ship the good from the UK to the USA. In principle this process will raise prices in the UK and lower them in the USA, thereby restoring an equality.) Defining the exchange rate as the home currency price of a unit of foreign currency, this implies that an increase in home prices relative to foreign prices will produce a currency depreciation (and conversely for a rise in foreign prices). A further discussion can be found in MacDonald (1995).

It is now well documented that there are a number of important problems associated with PPP. There is the issue of which price series to use. Should it be an overall (that is, consumer/retail) price series, or a relatively narrow series (such as a wholesale price series)? The problem with the general measures is that they contain a substantial element of non-traded goods and it is therefore unlikely that goods arbitrage will be sufficient to force PPP. There is the further problem that for any particular price series the construction of the series will differ across countries, thereby complicating the calculation of PPP. The existence of the prices of non-traded goods in an overall price measure creates a further difficulty if productivity differences are present between countries – the so-called Balassa–Samuelson effect (see Officer 1976). The key question in any discussion of PPP is whether the concept should be interpreted as a short- or long-run concept; that is, is it expected to hold on a month-by-month basis or in some long-term period? It is clear from the writings of the leading proponent of PPP, namely Cassel, that PPP should be viewed as a long-run relationship; that is, one to which an exchange rate gravitates (Officer 1976). There is in fact a great deal of evidence supportive of the view that PPP is sustainable as a long-run concept (MacDonald 1995), but that it is less satisfactory as a short-run concept. How then do we explain the short-run behaviour of exchange rates?

An alternative approach to PPP, which brings in the capital account of the balance of payments, is the balance of payments view of the exchange rate (MacDonald 1988). This view asserts that the exchange rate moves to ensure the sum of the current and capital accounts of the balance of payments is zero or, alternatively, that the change in reserves is equal to zero. With no foreign exchange market intervention, this statement must be definitionally true. To understand why the exchange rate moves on any day, one has to analyse what particular kind(s) of foreign exchange transactions take place. This is not entirely satisfactory since it does not offer a general theory of the determinants of exchange rates. Further, because of the perceived excess volatility of exchange rates there has been considerable foreign exchange market intervention during the recent float as central banks attempt to attenuate exchange rate movements. The balance of payments view is not well suited to explaining exchange rate volatility. Therefore, a number of researchers have proposed using an asset market approach to exchange rate determination. This has two key advantages over the balance of payments view since it offers both a neat explanation for exchange rate volatility and also gives a general theory of exchange rate determination. The asset market approach to the exchange rate interprets the exchange rate as the relative price of two assets (that is, monies), instead of traded goods prices, as in PPP, or the price of foreign exchange that clears the balance of payments, as in the balance of payments view. The asset approach emphasizes the stock implications of exchange rate determination and, particularly, the forward-looking nature of the foreign exchange market. That is to say, in deciding whether to hold a particular currency an investor is interested not only in the implications of today's policy changes on the exchange rate, but also expected changes in the future (which are often signalled by today's changes). If future policy measures are likely to be unpredictable then this can impart considerable volatility into the current exchange rate.

The asset market model, particularly in its monetary guises, has for many years been the work-horse model of exchange rate determination, particularly from a pedagogic perspective. However, the empirical evidence on this class of model has been rather mixed, in the sense that its proponents are often unable to beat a random walk model of the exchange rate. That is, using today's exchange rate gives as good, or better, a forecast of the exchange rate in the future than a more sophisticated asset market model. This, however, is not a universal finding and there is now a good deal of evidence which suggests that these kinds of models do have explanatory power and can be used to successfully forecast currencies (MacDonald 1995). However, many think that the models have failed (see, for example, the survey by Frankel and Rose (1995)) and this has led to considerable interest in non-fundamental determinants of exchange rates, such as market microstructure and noise trading.

The market microstructure literature (see Flood (1991) and Frankel and Rose (1995) for excellent surveys of this fast-developing literature) takes as its starting point the fact that on an average trading day there is $1000 billion gross and $200 billion net of foreign exchange deals struck in the global foreign exchange market. How may this volume be explained? On the face of it, it would seem difficult to explain such volume in terms of new information about fundamentals which are observed on a normal trading day. Such a large trading volume would seem to undermine a central tenet of many fundamentals-based models, namely that agents form their expectations rationally. In such a world, the expected value held by any one agent must be the consensus, or average, value held by all agents – expectations are homogeneous. The market microstructure literature attempts to explain observable exchange rate patterns by combining the notion that foreign exchange traders hold heterogeneous expectations with an analysis of the environment within which traders operate. In addition to establishing that heterogeneity is an important characteristic of the operation of foreign exchange markets (Ito 1990; MacDonald 1992; MacDonald and Marsh 1996), current research has focused on trying to explain the large volume of foreign exchange transactions on a gross (between foreign exchange dealers) and a net (concerning non-financial companies) basis. It has also analysed why the majority of transactions are between dealers (around 90 per cent of foreign exchange trade is between dealers – inter-bank trade) and the way that information is transmitted to the market; the role of the bid–ask spread (that is, the spread between the prices at which a dealer buys and sells a currency) in this process has come under particular scrutiny.

Another view of exchange rate determination which has received a great deal of attention of late is that of noise trading or fads behaviour (see De Long *et al.* (1990) for a summary of this kind of model). From a modelling perspective, this view divides foreign exchange market participants into two categories: noise traders per se, who use non-fundamental methods such as chartist techniques to assess the value of a currency; and 'smart money', or rational agents, who trade on the basis of where an exchange rate is in relation to the fundamentals-based, or equilibrium, exchange rate. As their title suggests, the noise traders introduce noise or excess volatility into foreign exchange rates (and other asset prices), over-and-above that indicated by the relevant fundamentals. This is so for two reasons. First, noise trading activities are not random and do not cancel out across traders (their beliefs and sentiments are generally commonly held resulting in herd-like behaviour). Second, the fundamentalists are prevented from ensuring that the exchange rate continually tracks its equilibrium value because of the inherent riskiness of taking a contrary position to that developing in the market. For example, if the current exchange rate is becoming increasingly overvalued, relative to its equilibrium, the 'smart money' traders may not be able to quickly force the exchange rate back to equilibrium because of the uncertainty about what the price will do in the future. Thus if the exchange rate were to continue to appreciate, the rational agent who sold the currency before it peaked would make a capital loss, relative to a strategy of continuing to hold the currency. Researchers have reported some success in using this kind of model to explain the behaviour of the US dollar in the 1980s (Frankel and Froot 1990).

3 Spot and forward relationships

One of the key features of the recent experience with floating exchange rates has been, as noted, the fact that exchange rates have been highly volatile and hard to predict. Although this is not necessarily evidence against the efficient functioning of foreign exchange markets it, nevertheless, raises the question of the riskiness that it imparts into decisions made by companies, particularly multinationals, with respect to their investment, trade and movements of capital. The traditional response to exchange rate risk is to say that in an efficiently functioning market it can be hedged using a derivative market, such as the forward market. Is this in fact the case? To answer this question, it will be useful to examine what the academic literature has to say about the forward exchange market. (The operation of other derivative markets, such as the futures and options market, are not discussed here; these are not widely discussed in the literature).

A forward exchange rate is the price of foreign exchange agreed today (usually with a commercial bank) relating to some point in the future (the most widely traded contract is a three-month contract). If the forward rate is defined as $F^t_{t\vartheta k}$ (where 't' denotes the current period and '$t+k$' denotes the time the forward contract matures), then it is conventional to think of $F^t_{t\vartheta k}$ as being decomposed into a risk premium, λ_t, and the exchange rate expected to prevail at the time the contract matures, $S^e_{t\vartheta k}$, where 'e' denotes an expectation (that is, $F^{t\vartheta k}_t \therefore \rightarrow\vartheta\, S^e_{t\vartheta k}$). Much of the academic literature on the spotforward relationship has been concerned to determine the dominant factor driving F^{t+k}_t – is it risk or expectations of the future exchange rate? In trying to tie down the relative importance of these two terms a researcher is immediately confronted with the problem of how to measure the expected exchange rate, $S^e_{t\vartheta k}$. A common procedure in this regard is to assume that agents have rational expectations and therefore the actual exchange rate in period $t+k$ will equal the expected rate plus a purely random forecasting error (that is $S_{t\vartheta k} \therefore S^e_{t\vartheta k}\vartheta\, f_{t\vartheta k}$, , where '$f$' is a random forecast error). Conditional on this assumption, the forward rate should be an unbiased predictor of the future exchange rate. Regardless of the exchange rate or time period studied it has been demonstrated by many researchers that the forward rate is in fact an extremely biased predictor of the future exchange rate (the literature on this topic is voluminous – see Hodrick (1987), MacDonald (1988) and MacDonald and Taylor (1992) for surveys). This is usually interpreted as evidence of the existence of important risk premia in the foreign exchange market. However, such an interpretation is predicated on the assumption that agents are endowed with rational expectations. What if they are not?

To answer this last question it has recently become fashionable to use an independent measure of expectations. The existence of a variety of professional surveys of foreign exchange market forecasters' expectations greatly facilitates this process. Unfortunately, however, the use of such expectations does not settle the issue since they suggest that it is both risk and some form of expectation failure that is responsible for the rejection. The qualification 'some form' is important since it may not be irrationality per se that is the source of the rejection but rather a statistical issue such as the 'peso problem' or the existence of speculative bubbles (see Hallwood and MacDonald (1994) for a further discussion).

Given that risk does seem to be an important factor in foreign exchange markets, the question that arises is: 'Does it matter?' That is to say, does the existence of risk have an effect on foreign exchange transactions relating to trade and investment? This is essentially an empirical issue which has, in fact, been investigated by a number of researchers. A fair summary of this research effort would be to say that evidence of a statistically significant relationship between risk (usually modelled using some measure of exchange rate volatility) and trade and investment is ambiguous (MacDonald 2000).

However, one problem with trying to quantify the effects of risk on trade and investment is that, by definition, such studies cannot capture any trade and investment that does not take place because of the existence of risk and the cost of hedging this risk. Further, there is, in fact, only a rather limited range of forward contracts available (the most widely traded is the three-month contract) and although these may be ideally suited for companies wishing to hedge the risk from engaging in foreign exchange trade (that is, importers and exporters), they are less than ideal for a company wishing to make a long-term investment in a foreign country. The dramatic effect that the appreciation of the Japanese yen has had in wiping out a large proportion of Japanese overseas investments is an important example of this (see ECONOMY OF JAPAN). The deleterious implications of exchange rate volatility, and the costs (realized or potential) of foreign exchange risk, have led many to propose rethinking the nature of the exchange rate regime.

4 Exchange rate reform

As noted in section 2, the decision to choose a particular exchange rate regime depends on a number of factors and their interaction. Without doubt, most commentators have concluded from the recent floating experience that exchange rates, when left to float freely, are too volatile and they have therefore advocated some form of exchange rate fixity. The two most prominent reform proposals are due to Ronald McKinnon (1988) and John Williamson (1988).

The thrust of McKinnon's thesis is that the volatility of floating exchange rates is so great that it has a deleterious effect on trade in goods and capital; removal of this volatility should have a welfare-enhancing effect. In essence this plan involves the G3 countries – Germany, Japan and the USA – fixing the external values of their currencies; other countries may then choose to link their currencies on to one of the three key currencies depending on geographic location (thus there would be a Deutschmark zone in Europe, a yen zone for the Pacific rim and a US dollar zone for the Americas). It is argued that the exchange rates should be fixed in accordance with PPP (using wholesale or producer prices – the objective is to stabilize the prices of internationally traded goods). It is accepted that there may be some adjustment process allowed to get to these PPP values and this would be achieved with currency flexibility (in particular, exchange rates would be kept within narrow bands and monetary policy coordinated to move the currencies to their PPP levels). Once at these PPP values, however, the key currencies would be rigidly and irrevocably locked together and the behaviour of producer prices in each of the countries would be monitored to ensure that they do not stray too far from their PPP determined values. Any deviation from PPP should be corrected by the collective adjustment of monetary aggregates (that is, there would be complete policy coordination for monetary policy and, by implication, for fiscal policy as well) (see MONETARISM). Because of its advocacy of rigidly fixed exchange rates as the mode of exchange rate regime, the McKinnon plan is often interpreted as a form of 'gold standard without gold' (the classical gold standard required a country to rigidly fix the external value of its currency relative to gold).

The main criticism of the McKinnon plan is that in a bid to eliminate exchange rate volatility it eliminates all exchange rate flexibility. As indicated earlier, there are circumstances (for example, in the presence of asymmetric real shocks) in which some degree of exchange rate flexibility may be desirable. The McKinnon response to this would be to say that real exchange rate movements have little or no effect on the current account deficit, rather the deficit is determined by the government's fiscal deficit. Some support for this view may be adduced from Krugman's (1989) thesis that the pricing policies of multinational companies (so-called 'pricing to market') has resulted in current accounts being decoupled from exchange rates (see GLOBALIZATION; MULTINATIONAL CORPORATIONS).

An alternative proposal for the reform of the international monetary system has been offered by Williamson. His proposal, although sharing McKinnon's dislike for excessive exchange rate volatility, nevertheless argues that some exchange rate flexibility is desirable on the grounds of social efficiency. The nub of this proposal concerns the assignment of fiscal policy to the maintenance of internal balance (that is, a high level of employment/economic growth consistent with low inflation) and monetary policy, in particular, interest rate policy, for the maintenance of external balance (which may loosely be defined as exchange rate stability). The novelty of the Williamson proposal relates to the definition of external balance. In particular, the idea is to stabilize the actual exchange rate around the fundamental equilibrium exchange rate (FEER), where the latter is a form of equilibrium rate which ensures a 'sustainable' current account balance in the medium run (a period of about five years hence). Although the definition of internal balance is uncontroversial, the definition of external balance is not, since the concept of 'sustainability' is rather amorphous and open to debate.

The key advantages of the Williamson plan are its recognition that some exchange rate flexibility may be desirable and the provision of an alternative measure of the equilibrium exchange rate (to, say, PPP) in terms of the FEER. Thus, the approach recognizes that there may be real and nominal factors which keep an exchange rate away from its PPP defined level. Furthermore, in a world in which these factors are changing, the FEER provides a moving target rather than a static target. The plan, however, is not without its problems. There is, first, the actual computation of the FEER. Although this may appear a rather trivial practical problem, it has provided a very real barrier to the more widespread adoption of the approach. In particular, in order to define the FEER in five years a full-scale econometric model is required and this has prevented the approach being used more widely. A more fundamental problem with the approach is that it is not entirely clear what the link between the real exchange rate and the current account is in circumstances where there are important public and private sector imbalances (as exemplified most clearly in the twin deficit phenomenon, where a government fiscal deficit is reflected in a current account deficit; the US twin deficits in the 1980s are a classic example of this). There is also a question mark over the actual assignment of macroeconomic policy. Thus it could (and has) been argued that it may be better to use monetary policy for the maintenance of internal balance and fiscal policy for external balance (for example, Bryant et al. (1988) have demonstrated that monetary policy has relatively little impact on the current account even in the medium to long run).

5 Conclusion

The recent experience with flexible exchange rates has proven to be unsatisfactory to many because of the excessive volatility that exchange rates exhibit when they are market determined. It is currently fashionable, therefore, to propose alternative international monetary regimes based on greater exchange rate fixity. In this entry, some of these alternatives have been outlined, as have the criteria that are relevant for a country choosing to rigidly lock its exchange rate to its trading partners'. The kinds of factors that the exchange rate literature offers as the key determinants of exchange rates have also been discussed. This literature seems to be moving in the direction of non-fundamental factors, such as market microstructure and noise trading. However, there is now an accumulating body of positive empirical evidence to suggest that an exclusive reliance on non-fundamental explanations of exchange rate behaviour is premature.

RONALD MACDONALD
UNIVERSITY OF STRATHCLYDE

Further reading

(References cited in the text marked *)

* Bryant, R.D., Henderson, D., Holtham, G., Hooper, P. and Symansky, S. (1988) *Empirical Macroeconomics for Interdependent Economies*, Washington, DC: The Brookings Institution. (A comparative simulation exercise.)

Cassel, G. (1918) 'Abnormal deviations in international exchanges' *Economic Journal* 28: 413–15. (Non-technical study of purchasing power parity.)

* De Long, J.B., Schleifer, A., Summers, L.H. and Waldman, R.J. (1990) 'Noise trader risk in financial markets', *Journal of Political Economy* 98 (3): 703–38. (Relatively technical noise trader model.)

* Flood, M.D. (1991) 'Microstructure theory and the foreign exchange market', *Federal Reserve Bank of St Louis Review* 73 (6): 52–70. (A survey of the market microstructure literature.)

* Frankel, J. and Froot, K. (1990) 'Chartists and fundamentalists, and the demand for dollars', in A.S. Courakis and M.P. Taylor (eds), *Private Behaviour and Government Policy in Interdependent Economies*, Oxford: Oxford University Press. (Model of exchange rate determination with CHARTISS and fundamental behaviour; relatively technical.)

* Frankel, J.A. and Rose, A. (1995) 'An empirical characterisation of nominal exchange rates', in E. Grossman and K. Rogoff (eds), *Handbook of International Economics*, vol. 2, Amsterdam: North Holland. (A survey of work on nominal exchange rate modelling; relatively technical.)

* Hallwood, P. and MacDonald, R. (1994) *International Money and Finance*, Oxford: Blackwell. (Advanced textbook that provides an overview of the key themes in international money and finance.)

* Hodrick, R.J. (1987) *The Empirical Evidence on the Efficiency of Forward and Futures Markets*, London: Harwood Academic Publishers. (Survey on the efficiency of foreign exchange markets.)

* Ito, T. (1990) 'Foreign exchange expectations: micro survey data', *American Economic Review* 80 (3): 434–49. (Tests the efficiency of a Japanese survey database.)

* Kenen, P. (1969) 'The theory of optimum currency areas: an eclectic view' in R. Mundell and A. Swoboda (eds), *Monetary Problems in the International Economy*, Chicago, IL: Chicago University Press. (One of the key papers in the optimum currency area literature.)

* Krugman, P. (1989) *Exchange Rate Instability*, Cambridge, MA: MIT Press. (Advanced study of the causes and consequences of exchange rate volatility.)
* MacDonald, R. (1988) *Floating Exchange Rates: Theories and Evidence*, London: Unwin-Hyman. (Comprehensive survey of the literature on exchange rate economics.)

MacDonald, R. (1991) 'Exchange rate economics: an empirical perspective', in G. Bird (ed.), *Recent Developments in the International Monetary System*, London: Academic Press. (Selective survey of exchange rate economics.)

* MacDonald, R. (1992) 'Exchange rate survey data: a disaggregated G7 approach', *The Manchester School of Economic and Social Studies* 60: 147–62. (Tests the efficiency of a disaggregated G7 survey database.)
* MacDonald, R. (1995) 'Long-run exchange rate modelling: a survey of the recent evidence', *IMF Staff Papers* 42 (3): 437–89. (Relatively technical survey of recent purchasing power parity literature.)
* Macdonald, R. (2000) 'The role of the exchange rate in economic growth', Paper presented at the 250 year anniversary conference of the National Bank of Belgium (discussion paper).
* MacDonald, R. and Marsh, I.W. (1996) 'Are foreign exchange forecasters heterogeneous? Confirmation and consequences', *Journal of International Money and Finance*. (An examination of the heterogeneity of foreign exchange forecasts.)
* MacDonald, R. and Taylor, M.P. (1992) 'Exchange rate economics: a survey', *IMF Staff Papers* 39 (1): 1–57. (Selective survey of exchange rate economic literature.)
* McKinnon, R.I. (1963) 'Optimum currency areas', *American Economic Review* 53 (4): 717–25. (Emphasizes the relative openness of an economy as an important criterion in determining the extent of an OCA.)

McKinnon, R.I. (1976) 'Floating exchange rates 1973–74: the emperor's new clothes', *Carnegie Rochester Supplement to The Journal of Monetary Economics* 3. (Early study of the recent floating exchange rate experience.)

McKinnon, R.I. (1979) *Money in International Exchange: The Convertible Currency System*, New York: Oxford University Press. (Advanced textbook on international money and finance.)

* McKinnon, R.I. (1988) 'Monetary and exchange rate policies for international financial stability: a proposal', *Journal of Economic Perspectives* 2: 83–103. (A proposal for reform of the international monetary system.)
* Masson, P.R. and Taylor, M.P. (1993) *Policy Issues in the Operation of Currency Unions*, Cambridge: Cambridge University Press. (Survey of the theory and evidence on optimal currency areas.)
* Mundell, R. (1961) 'A theory of optimum currency areas', *American Economic Review* 51(3): 657–65. (One of the key references in the optimum currency area literature.)
* Officer, L.H. (1976) 'The purchasing power parity theory of exchange rates: a review article', *IMF Staff Papers* 23 (1): 1–60. (Early and comprehensive survey of purchasing power parity literature.)

Williamson, J. (1983) *The Exchange Rate System*, Washington, DC: Institute for International Economics. (Proposal for reform of the international monetary system.)

* Williamson, J. (1988) 'Comment on McKinnon's monetary rule', *Journal of Economic Perspectives* 2 (2): 113–19. (Proposal for reform of the international monetary system.)

See also: GLOBALIZATION; KEYNES, J.M.; MODELLING AND FORECASTING; MULTINATIONAL CORPORATIONS

Multinational corporations

1 Importance of multinationals in the world economy
2 Motivations and organizational forms
3 The theory of internationalization of firms
4 Patterns in multinational corporation activity
5 Future prospects

Overview

Multinational corporations (MNCs), alternatively known as multinational enterprises, international corporations or transnational corporations, are corporations owning and controlling production or other value-adding facilities in several countries. More generally, the term is used to refer to global chains of affiliated companies managed and controlled from a headquarters located in a specific country. The global expansion of an MNC is secured with foreign direct investment (FDI), which is defined as investment made abroad to secure a controlling interest in an enterprise. MNCs are important actors in the world economy, controlling large proportions of global output, international trade and the global pool of technology. Since the mid-1980s their importance in the world economy has risen dramatically with crossborder economic integration being pursued in different regions, due to the opening up of new opportunities and an improved investment climate in many host countries or regions.

1 Importance of multinationals in the world economy

Because of the large scale of their operations, multinational corporations (MNCs) account for a rather disproportionate share of the world's output and dominate a number of industries and services globally with a presence in most market economies. Companies such as Philips, Ford, Toyota, Unilever, GlaxoWellcome, Bosch, Sony, Nestlé, Singer, IBM, Coca-Cola and Holiday Inn, among many others, are household names in most countries. Multinational corporations account for nearly one-quarter of world output; between one-third and one-half of world trade takes place between affiliated companies or within MNCs. Since knowledge capital is central to the process of creation of MNCs, as will be shown later, their control over the global pool of technology is even more complete. About three-quarters of global patents are estimated to be under the control of multinational corporations.

Foreign direct investment (FDI) and other forms of MNC participation in the world economy are seen as channels of international transfer of productive resources such as capital, organizational and managerial skills, production and marketing technology, other intangible assets such as rights to use brand or trade names of parent, access to cheaper sources of raw materials and other inputs to the host country. Hence, MNCs are considered to be capable of fostering development and industrialization in their host countries. A large number of countries attempt to attract MNC investment through a variety of incentives and other policies (see GLOBALIZATION).

Although a number of MNCs came into being in the nineteenth century, FDI and other cross-border activities by corporations became an important phenomenon only in the post-Second World War period. In the 1960s and 1970s, however, excessive involvement of MNCs was resisted in many developing countries because of fears of neo-colonialism, as most MNCs originated in erstwhile colonial countries. The MNCs also wielded enormous economic and political influence due to their gigantic scale of operations and their market power. Hence, governments evolved policies to regulate MNCs and even nationalized their operations when it was deemed necessary. In the 1980s, however, the policy environment has become increasingly favourable to MNCs following liberalization of the foreign direct investment policies of a large number of countries.

2 Motivations and organizational forms

In terms of motivations, MNC operations abroad or FDI can be broadly classified into four types (Dunning 1993), depending on the nature of the investment being undertaken:

1 natural resource-seeking investments;
2 market-seeking investments;
3 efficiency-seeking investments;
4 strategic-asset seeking investments.

Natural resource-seeking investments are those made by MNCs abroad in order to seek privileged access to supplies of natural resources and raw materials or to exploit an abundance of certain raw materials in a particular country. Examples include plantation and mining investments in resource-rich developing countries, such as investments in tea and coffee plantations, iron ore and bauxite mining in India, rubber plantations in Liberia and Malaysia or copper mining in Chile and Zambia. However, investment in natural resources can also be made in industrialized countries such as Australia and Canada.

Market-seeking investments are defined as investments orientated towards developing or entering domestic markets in certain countries. These may include investments undertaken either to obviate host country tariff and non-tariff barriers, or investments aimed at precluding rivals or potential rivals from gaining new markets. These investments generally take the form of horizontal foreign direct investment and are by far the most common type of FDI.

Efficiency-seeking investments include investments made by MNCs to rationalize production globally according to factor costs in order to maintain their competitiveness. These investments result in a globally integrated production system where plants participating in rationalization across the world are integrated vertically. Finally, strategic asset-seeking investments include investments made abroad to acquire strategic assets such as brand or trade names, proprietary technology or market access. The acquisition of ICL in the UK by the Japanese firm Fujitsu, for example, aimed to improve Fujitsu's access to the European computer market.

The operations of multinational corporations abroad can take a variety of organizational forms. They can cover anything from a majority-owned subsidiary operation to taking a minority but controlling stake in an enterprise. Investment could also either be a greenfield investment or involve acquisition of an existing unit abroad. Finally, investment could take the form of a joint venture with a local enterprise, or be an independent or sole venture by the MNC.

3 The theory of internationalization of firms

The theory of the international operations of firms explains how a national firm evolves into a multinational enterprise. Hymer (1976) made the first attempt to understand the transition of a national firm into a multinational one. Previously, FDI flows were treated like any other international flows of resources, such as portfolio investments, and were thought to be driven by international factor price differentials. Hymer used the tenets of industrial organization approaches in his attempt to provide a theoretical basis for the overseas operations of national firms. Subsequently, this stream of theorizing has been enriched by the contributions of Kindleberger (1969), Caves (1982), Buckley and Casson (1976) and Dunning (1979), among others.

According to Hymer, a firm operating abroad must possess advantages that can more than offset the handicaps faced in an alien environment and cover the ensuing greater risks. These advantages are sometimes referred to as monopolistic advantages, and emanate from the ownership of proprietary assets possessed by firms such as brand goodwill, technology, managerial and marketing skills and access to cheaper sources of capital and raw materials. These advantages are first exploited abroad through exports from the country of origin. In later stages, local production is undertaken when locational factors begin to emerge that make production more profitable than exporting. The latter include factors such as tariffs and quantitative restrictions imposed on imports by host countries, communication and transport costs and inter-country differences in input/factor prices and productivity.

When undertaking local production, firms can choose further between foreign direct investment and 'arm's-length licensing' contracts under which production is undertaken by other, unrelated firms in the host country. In other words, a firm can exploit the revenue productivity of its intangible assets or ownership advantages, for example, knowledge, technology or brand names through FDI or internally within the firm, or it can choose to license these assets. The choice between FDI and licensing is usually determined by the transaction or governance costs involved in setting up licensing contracts. The higher the transaction costs, the higher the incentive to internalize the transaction and thus the greater the likelihood of FDI being chosen as a mode of foreign production. Transaction costs are generally high for market transactions of most intangible assets because of market failures arising from their nature as public goods, difficulty in making a convincing disclosure and buyer uncertainty, problems with the codification of knowledge and the risk of dissipation of brand goodwill. In practice, however, smaller firms lacking experience and resources in managing operations abroad may prefer to license their intangible assets. In summary, FDI takes place when ownership, locational and internalization (OLI) advantages are present. Dunning (1979) has woven these three preconditions for FDI to take place into a coherent framework referred to as the OLI or eclectic paradigm.

The ownership of firm-specific intangible assets or knowledge capital which may be in the form of technology, expertise, brand name goodwill and marketing skills is therefore a prerequisite for the foreign operations of a firm. MNCs are therefore important in sectors which are intensive in their use of knowledge capital. MNCs are generally characterized by: (1) high levels of expenditure on R&D; (2) a large proportion of professional and technical employees in their workforce; (3) new and technically more complex products; and (4) high levels of product differentiation or advertising. The importance of intangible assets for MNCs means that their market valuation greatly exceeds the value of their tangible assets such as plant and machinery.

4 Patterns in multinational corporation activity

The United Nations Conference on Trade and Development (UNCTAD) in Geneva estimated in the mid-1990s that there were about 44,000 MNCs in existence, controlling over 280,000 affiliates around the world. Over 80 per cent of these MNCs were based in the developed or industrialized countries. The largest few hundred MNCs accounted for the bulk of total assets, sales revenue and number of foreign affiliates; the largest 100 (excluding those in banking and finance) controlled US$4.2 trillion worth of global assets in 1995, of which about $1.7 trillion were held outside their home countries (UNCTAD 1997). Nearly all of these 100 largest MNCs were based in industrialized countries. The USA was the single most important country of origin, with 30 of the top 100 companies; 39 companies originated in the European Union (EU), Japan accounted for 18 and the remaining 13 originated in Switzerland, Sweden, Canada, Finland, Norway, Australia or New Zealand, and one each in South Korean and Venezuela. In terms of sectoral distribution of foreign assets of the top 100 MNCs, the automotive sector leads, with 21 per cent, followed by petroleum and mining (18 per cent), electonics (16 per cent), chemicals and pharmaceutical (13 per cent), and food and beverages (8 per cent). Details of the largest fifteen multinational corporations are shown in Table 1.

Trends in FDI flows reveal emerging patterns in the cross-border activities of MNCs. The scale of annual FDI flows rose dramatically in the second half of the 1980s. Compared to an annual average of US$55 billion, during the first half of the 1980s, global FDI flows averaged US$174 billion a year in the second half, peaking at US$209 billion in 1990. In the first two years of the 1990s the level of FDI declined, but then rose again in subsequent years. In 1996 the UN and International Monetary Fund estimated the flow of FDI at US$350 billion.

Among the factors that contributed to a rapid rise in FDI flows in the late 1980s was

Table 1 Top 15 largest MNEs (figures are for 1992 US$ billion)

MNE	Country	Industry	Total assets	Foreign assets	Total sales	Foreign sales
1 Royal Dutch Shell	UK/The Netherlands	Petroleum refining	100.8	69.4	96.6	45.5
2 Exxon	US	Petroleum refining	85.0	48.2	115.7	93.1
3 IBM	US	Computers	86.7	45.7	64.5	39.9
4 General Motors	US	Automobiles	191.0	41.8	132.4	42.3
5 Hitachi	Japan	Electronics	66.6	..	58.4	13.9
6 Matsushita Electric	Japan	Electronics	74.4	..	60.8	29.9
7 Nestlé	Switzerland	Food	31.3	28.7	38.4	37.7
8 Ford	US	Automobiles	180.5	28.0	100.1	33.2
9 Alcatel Alsthom	France	Electrical and electronics	44.4	..	30.7	18.0
10 General Electric	US	Electrical and electronics	129.9	24.2	57.1	8.4
11 Philips Electronics	The Netherlands	Electronics	28.6	22.9	33.3	31.0
12 Mobil	US	Petroleum	40.6	22.6	64.1	49.7
13 Asea Brown Boveri	Switzerland	Electrical and electronics	25.9	22.4	29.6	26.3
14 Elf Aquitaine	France	Petroleum	45.1	..	36.2	13.2
15 Volkswagen	Germany	Automobiles	46.6	..	54.7	29.4

Source: UNCTAD Division on Transnational Corporations and Development, *World Investment Report* (1994)

the cross-national economic integration among EU member states, which led to a sharp rise in FDI outflows from a few European countries towards other regional partners. The constant hardening of the yen following the Plaza Accord in 1985 eroded the competitiveness of Japanese corporations, prompting them to locate production abroad. Japanese corporations also located production in EU countries to overcome increasing protectionist barriers and to exploit the benefits of regional integration by becoming insiders. Developing countries around the world have liberalized their investment codes in an effort to attract greater volumes of FDI as part of their structural adjustment programmes, and economic reforms in central and eastern Europe opened up completely new markets for FDI. Finally, the newly industrializing countries of east Asia emerged as significant outward investors in the late 1980s.

The decline in the magnitude of FDI flows in the early 1990s can be explained in terms of completion of restructuring of EU businesses in anticipation of the Single European Market, and the recession in major industrial countries including Japan. The subsequent recovery from recession contributed in turn to a gradual recovery of global FDI flows (see ECONOMIC INTEGRATION, INTERNATIONAL).

The industrialized countries accounted for nearly 98 per cent of all FDI outflows in the early 1990s. Their share has declined slightly since, but still over 95 per cent of all FDI outflows originate in industrialized countries. The rest comes from a few newly industrialized countries largely in east Asia, such as South Korea, Taiwan, Hong Kong and Singapore. Several enterprises in these countries have accumulated the technological and managerial capability to expand overseas and become multinational in their own right. Here again, the impetus towards overseas production has come from rising wages, hardening of home country currencies and increasing protectionist tendencies in industrialized countries such as the EU Member States.

The industrialized countries also receive the bulk of FDI inflows. In the early 1980s, nearly three-quarters of all FDI inflows were received by industrialized countries. In the late 1980s, coinciding with the rapid rise in

FDI volume, the concentration of FDI among industrialized countries grew further, so that they received 85 per cent of global FDI inflows in 1990. Again, this was partly a result of heavy concentration of FDI inflows in the EU countries in the wake of the restructuring sparked off by the creation of the Single Market. The 1990s, however, have seen developing countries assume increasing importance in the distribution of FDI, with their share rising to 39 per cent in 1994. The inter-country distribution of FDI inflows has been highly uneven; just ten developing countries – China, Singapore, Argentina, Mexico, Malaysia, Indonesia, Thailand, Hong Kong, Taiwan and Nigeria – accounted for nearly 81 per cent of all developing country FDI inflows in 1994.

5 Future prospects

The current trends towards liberalization of restrictions on FDI, cross-national economic integration in different regions and liberalization of international trade in services suggest that MNCs will continue to grow in importance in the coming years. MNCs are, however, restructuring and constantly adapting themselves to the changing economic environment. The MNCs of the future may therefore be significantly different in terms of organizational structure from those of today.

Restructuring is changing the face of corporations on many fronts. For instance, the introduction of new organizational and manufacturing techniques such as lean manufacturing, just-in-time production and computer-integrated flexible manufacturing systems is shifting emphasis away from economies of scale and mass production. There is also a trend away from vertical integration towards concentration on core businesses and contracting out everything else in order to maintain competitiveness. Because of high tariffs and non-tariff barriers that insulated national markets in the past, MNC operations in different host countries had been organized as miniature replicas of themselves. With the increasing deregulation of trade worldwide and the formation of free trade areas in different regions, MNCs are now restructuring their national operations in a more productive manner than the 'multidomestic' style of the past. In the EU, for example, MNCs are rationalizing their operations on a pan-European basis. This restructuring takes the form of an international division of labour where one plant is responsible for the production of one or more items for the entire region. The other plants similarly concentrate on other items for the entire regional market.

Another important trend is the increasing formation of strategic alliances and joint ventures by MNCs to complement their intangible asset bundles with those of others. These alliances are becoming an increasingly important form of inter-MNC cooperation, especially in emerging core technology industries such as microelectronics, information technology and biotechnology.

NAGESH KUMAR
THE UNITED NATIONS UNIVERSITY INSTITUTE
FOR NEW TECHNOLOGIES

Further reading

(References cited in the text marked *)

* Buckley, P.J. and Casson, M. (1976) *The Future of Multinational Enterprise*, London: Macmillan. (This book was among the first to theorize the conditions for internalization of transactions of intangible assets within MNCs.)
* Caves, R.E. (1982) *Multinational Enterprise and Economic Analysis*, Cambridge: Cambridge University Press. (This book provides a useful survey of the theoretical and empirical literature on the subject.)
  Dicken, P. (1992) *Global Shift: The Internationalization of Economic Activity*, London: Paul Chapman Publishing. (This book usefully analyses trends in production, international trade and MNC activities globally and in select industries to understand the extent and patterns of internationalization of economic activity.)
* Dunning, J.H. (1979) 'Explaining changing patterns of international production', *Oxford Bulletin of Economics and Statistics* 41: 269–96. (Theoretical account of the preconditions for FDI.)
* Dunning, J.H. (1993) *Multinational Enterprises and the Global Economy*, Wokingham: Addison-Wesley. (This book provides a comprehensive and up-to-date perspective on the literature on different aspects of MNC activity in the global economy.)

The Economist (1995) 'Big is back: a survey of multinationals', 24 June: 1–23. (This survey examines emerging patterns in organizational styles and other trends in MNC activity.)

* Hymer, S.H. (1976) *The International Operations of National Firms: A Study of Direct Foreign Investment*, Cambridge, MA: MIT Press. (This Ph.D. dissertation made the first attempt to analyse the evolution of national firms into multinational corporations using an industrial organization theory approach.)

Julius, D. (1990) *Global Companies and Public Policy: The Growing Challenge of Foreign Direct Investment*, London: Royal Institute of International Affairs. (This book highlights the increasing importance of MNCs in the global economy and the challenge this puts before policy makers.)

* Kindleberger, C.P. (1969) *American Business Abroad: Six Lectures on Direct Investment*, New Haven, CT: Yale University Press. (A clear exposition of the subject.)

Kumar, N. (1994) *Multinational Enterprises and Industrial Organisation: The Case of India*, New Delhi: Sage Publications. (This book applies economic theory and statistical techniques to understand and evaluate the implications of MNC investments for a developing economy such as India.)

Kumar, N., with J. Dunning, R. Lipsey, J. Agarwal and S. Urata (1998) *Globalization, Foreign Direct Investment and Technology Transfers: Impacts on and Prospects for Developing Countries*, London and New York: Routledge. (Discusses emerging patterns in the overseas activity of MNCs originating from major industrialized and emerging source countries, and examines the implications of these trends for developing countries and for policy.)

* UNCTAD (1994) *World Investment Report 1994*, Geneva, United Nations. (Looks at transnational Corporations, employment and the workplace.)

* UNCTAD (1997) *World Investment Report 1997*, Geneva: United Nations. (This, one in a series of annual reports, is an important source of statistics and analyses of current trends in the activities of MNCs worldwide.)

See also: GLOBALIZATION; MULTINATIONAL CORPORATIONS; TRANSFER PRICING

Globalization

1 Historical prelude
2 Indicators of increasing integration
3 The surge in foreign direct investment
4 Global corporations and integration
5 The global organization of multinationals
6 The political economy of globalization
7 Conclusion

Overview

Globalization is the process of increasing integration of world civilization. The evolving definition of globalization reveals the extent to which the process itself has changed in the past decades. In the 1970s, globalization was viewed in terms of the increasing interdependence among states operating within well-defined borders. In today's economy, interdependence among nations is of less central interest, as powerful global actors (for example, multinational corporations and financial institutions) have created a world in which borders are less consequential. Globalization has come to signify integration among countries, occurring at deep levels of social, political and economic organization.

Commonly used measurements of globalization obscure this important transition in globalization processes. The extent of globalization can be captured through a number of descriptive indicators: parity in prices – prices and interest rates should converge with globalization; effect on behaviours – nation states, firms, and other actors consider their actions and others' actions in one state as influencing their interests in another; world culture – the sharing of cultural values across countries; ideological – the convergence in beliefs about what constitutes a desirable polity. Each of these indicators hides the distinction between *interdependence* and *integration*. Financial markets may converge to price parity, as long as investors can move money from one country to the other. They need not be integrated in the form of a world market for equities. Governments and firms may respond to the actions of their counterparts in other countries, and yet the political and economic significance of borders may be preserved. National cultures and ideologies can respond to foreign ideas in a reactionary way. Austrian churches are topped by onion-shaped cupolas and the French croissant is derived from the Islamic crescent. Yet both of these cultural artefacts are symbolic of the clash between competing and interdependent cultures, not their integration.

The period immediately after the Second World War saw the creation of international institutions to manage interdependence, under the tutelage of a few powerful countries. The success of these institutions in carrying out their original mandates of managing an increasingly interdependent world has varied, but those created in the economic sphere have unquestionably increased in membership and importance. The International Monetary Fund has grown from 44 to 178 members. The World Bank Group has expanded into project financing in developing countries. In the area of trade, the failed attempt to create an international institution in the 1940s has recently been resuscitated through the establishment of the World Trade Organization.

The transition from interdependence to integration is perhaps best seen in the many regional economic groupings that have been spawned over the last forty years. At the regional level, the process and impact of integration are the most obvious. The European Union is clearly the most prominent and far-reaching case of interdependent states seeking to resolve conflict and to enjoy the benefits of a wider market through economic, political and increasingly social integration. The example of the EU is reflected in the less ambitious efforts of other countries. The North American Free Trade Agreement (NAFTA) between the United States, Canada and

Mexico is a case of low-level integration in so far as it involves the elimination of tariffs and some limited harmonization of environmental and labour laws but does not involve complete harmonization of competition policies and free cross-border movements of people. Overall, the world trend is towards more integration, albeit at the regional level, with agreements in Latin America (for example, Mercosur) and in east Asia (for example, ASEAN), and increasing *de facto* integration in southern Africa occurring only in the past decade.

Interdependence and integration are not unilateral trends in world history. The post-Second World War experience suggested that there is a linear trend towards integration. At times, globalization was taken to imply a stronger theory of convergence, especially towards the dominant American model of capitalism and economic growth. Often labelled under 'modernization' theory, the belief that countries would have to converge to American institutions in order to grow fell to the sidelines, as European and Asian nations became wealthy despite very different institutions. In recognition of the multiple paths to wealth, there has been a growing interest in the varieties of national systems that support, in turn, distinctive comparative advantages. These systems include the relationships among labour and capital, the governance of top management, and the incentives to innovate (Nelson 1993; Kogut 1983).

The forces that sustain national differences even in the presence of strong pressures to globalize are not simply predicated on the economics of choosing the best system among a menu of systems. There are political and social factors that inhibit change, particularly those unleashed through the actions of threatened groups or governments. Because globalization influences relative power and social standing among established groups, it is a process that lies at the heart of social change and political policy in all countries. Extreme examples are the responses of countries (for example, Iran) undergoing rapid change which incur a reversal in their openness to the world economy. The debate is often not only cast in economic terms, but ideological and religious ones as well.

Furthermore, it is misleading to believe that globalization is deterministically driven by the development of new technologies in communication and transportation. These forces surely make globalization more possible and less costly. At the same time, improved communications technology means that new groups can emerge and organize more swiftly and effectively to contribute their voice to globalization debates at key policy fora. However, since groups and governments can influence the extent and pace of globalization, world integration and interdependence are not exogenous, self-propelling processes. They are the product of conscious decisions and strategies by powerful actors, and thus are both cause and effect of social and political change. Globalization means that governments and national firms are constrained in their capacity to carry out effective policies and strategies at the purely domestic level. But governments and firms are also powerful actors in their own right: as well as being influenced by the forces of globalization, they can influence the process themselves. Decisions to deregulate or to lower tariffs directly influence the degree of international commerce. In this regard, globalization is both an endogenous and exogenous factor determined in its pace and development by the actions of governments, firms, and other social actors, but influencing also in turn the behaviour of these same actors.

From the perspective of economic theory, integration appears inevitable because of the gains to eliminating institutional imperfections in the movement of goods, services and capital. These gains are both static (one-time increases in welfare) and dynamic, resulting from a powerful dynamic unleashed through positive feedbacks to integration. Larger markets should, in theory, lead to a more efficient allocation of world resources and increases in consumer welfare. Yet it is important to include in an assessment of the dynamic gains a recognition that the latter gains are sensitive to the process by which integration occurs (for example, by regions or by world agreement). The calculation of welfare gains should include costs that stem from the dislocation of workers and important social groups and institutions. Even if one were to show that integration improves world welfare in some global assessment of the costs and benefits, the distributional consequences are substantial, as are the effects on the relative power of nation-states.

Globalization, by the very definition of its expansiveness, covers a wide geographic and conceptual terrain. In the following entry, a short historical prelude and concise presentation of indicators of globalization are presented. The analysis of globalization as cause and effect in an historical process is illustrated through two applications. The first concerns the growth of the multinational corporation through foreign direct investment; the second summarizes some of the research on the political economy of globalization. By way of conclusion, the question as to whether globalization is in its current context an irreversible process is examined in detail.

1 Historical prelude

Interdependence and integration are forces that have marked world history. To a non-trivial extent, the massive migrations of early humans across long distances to reach new terrains are the emblematic example of globalization. The diffusion of myths and rituals through these migrations is evident in the common heritages of Indo-European civilizations and, more broadly, among civilizations that have enjoyed contact and communication.

This underscores the point that interdependence is not a characteristic that is unique to modern economies. Semitic traders – Syrians, Jews and Aramaeans – played an important role in the last centuries of the Roman Empire. Customs duties were low, with only 2 to 2.5 per cent of value levied at the borders of each province. Raw materials were sent back to the empire: gold and ivory from Africa, silk from China, spices from Arabia. But only high value to weight items could be transported, and there was a strong tendency for areas away from coastal areas and cities to resort to self-sufficiency. Since Rome had few luxury goods to offer in return, its trade with Asia was paid in gold and other specie, encouraging the debasing of its coinage. The breakup of Rome placed further taxes on the movement of goods, a situation that in many respects is only today being remedied.

Trade and commerce were also hampered by the absence of formalized international law and institutions, in addition to the costs of commerce and taxation. However, the lack of formalized rules and procedures was partly overcome by the development of informal cross-border networks established by traders. The role of particular ethnic groups, such as Armenians, Gujarati, Fijian Chinese, and Jews, in world trade has historically been of great importance not only for the transport and sales of goods, but also of ideas. These groups played the role of cross-cultural brokers, who succeeded in establishing cosmopolitan communities across long distances. Trade was possible because of strict rules of enforcement and the possibility of detection within these groups.

Establishing a date for the emergence of the world capitalist order is a perennially debated issue. Fernand Braudel (1979), whose studies are certainly the best-known statements on the origins of the world economy, places its emergence between the fifteenth and eighteenth centuries. No doubt there was still tremendous variation not only at the lowest levels of production, but also in the emergent markets for valuable goods and financial credit. Variations in prices for gold and silver caused large movements of the species in opposite directions. Europe generally placed a higher value on gold. With the importation of silver from the Americas, Europe was able to finance its deficit with Russia and Asia better than Rome. France demurred from the policy of hoarding gold, and silver fetched a higher price there. Nevertheless, prices among the major European states were already interdependent by the end of this period.

The period of rapid convergence in prices among regional and national markets was only realized in the 1800s with the fall in communication and transportation costs. News took about three weeks to travel from Venice to London in 1500; no improvement had been made by 1765. The famous story of the Rothschild family learning of the outcome of the battle of Waterloo through its own emissaries obscures the fact that the practice of owning private communications networks did

Table 1 Costs of air transportation, telephone calls and computers in 1990 dollars, 1930–90

Year	Average air transportation revenue per passenger mile	Cost of a three-minute call, New York to London	Department of Commerce computer price deflator (1990 = 1000)
1930	0.68	244.65	n.a.
1940	0.46	188.51	n.a.
1950	0.30	53.20	n.a.
1960	0.24	45.86	125,000
1970	0.16	31.58	19,474
1980	0.10	4.80	3,620
1990	0.11	3.32	1,000

Source: Herring and Litan (1995)

not originate with them and was hardly new. By the end of the century, with the creation of the telegraph, such practices were harder to put into effect. Transportation also was agonizingly slow. The slow pace of transport by road led to massive canal-building in the 1700s in England, France and elsewhere. By the end of the 1800s, low tariff rates and the massive outflow of capital – particularly from Great Britain and France – resulted in only minor differentials in traded goods and interest rates. Indeed, financial indices were more related across a few select industrial countries during the *belle époque* and the interwar years than since 1945.

In the course of history, the interlude from 1914 to 1989 may appear politically as a departure from a long-term trend towards the globalization of world markets and world culture. But the period prior to 1914 was primarily a period of interdependence among a small number of states. The aftermath of the Second World War has seen, instead, the creation of world institutions. The effects of these institutions, the secular growth in world trade and investment, and the rise of the multinational corporation as a powerful agent of globalization, have caused far-reaching changes in the world economy. Some of these changes are examined below.

2 Indicators of increasing integration

The recent pace of technological advance has allowed for a deeper integration of the classic factors of production of land, labour and capital. The globalization of the world economy, as we have stated, is not simply technologically determined, and the degree and pace of integration of these factors have been shaped by institutional and political influences. Table 1 illustrates how the costs of international integration, as represented by transportation, communication and information processing, have declined very sharply, particularly after the 1970s.

In the post-war period, falling tariffs and advances in air and freight transport allowed for a great expansion of world trade, leading to greater interdependence of national markets for goods. An expanded role for trade in national economies also brought with it greater interdependence at the level of macroeconomic and fiscal policies.

In recent years, the most far-reaching degree of integration has occurred in the area of capital. Both technological as well as political and economic developments have hastened the process of financial integration. Until very recently, financial markets remained relatively fragmented and national governments retained close control of domestic financial flows. Firms had little choice but to raise funds from domestic sources.

During the 1980s, a confluence of supply and demand factors made possible the rapid globalization and integration of financial market flows. On the supply side these included the deregulation of currency controls, innovations in financial instruments, and advances in communications and information technologies that allowed transactions to be executed rapidly across long distances. On the demand side were a wave of corporate restructurings that increased the need for new sources of financing, rapid growth in foreign investment and trade, and the adoption of free-market principles by a number of previously regulated economies.

Growth and internationalization have been particularly pronounced in equity, bond and foreign exchange markets, where capitalization exploded in the 1980s. Banks operate trading rooms that essentially represent globalized distribution systems for financial products such as equity, debt, foreign exchange and more exotic instruments such as derivatives. Global turnover in the world's foreign exchange markets reached $1 trillion per day in 1992. In 1981, about $200 billion worth of international bonds was issued; by 1992, the figure had reached nearly $1.8 trillion (Herring and Litan 1995). The market value of foreign equities traded on the London Stock Exchange grew from $738 billion in 1982 to $3.2 trillion in 1993. These figures illustrate how financial market integration over the 1980s made possible the instantaneous mobility of massive amounts of capital on a global basis.

While the markets themselves have become globalized, financial *systems* remain nationally bounded, highly interdependent but not integrated. Corporate debt–equity ratios remain highly differentiated among major Organization for Economic Cooperation and Development (OECD) countries, and national governments continue to pursue divergent macroeconomic strategies reflecting domestic pressures and historical policy trends. The bulk of national investment is sourced from domestic savings in the form of retained earnings – that is, funds that are not traded on any market. Another important cleavage among national systems lies in corporate governance: not only are there wide differences in how corporate governance and control is exercised, there has also been little internationalization of boards of directors, even as firms themselves become increasingly globalized in their operations. Finally, returns to capital have as yet failed to converge cross-nationally: this is an important measure of the degree to which the globalization of markets has engendered integration. Herring and Litan (1995) find that although rates have converged at the lowest levels of financial integration, real interest rates – the most important index of integration – have not reached parity across different financial markets.

Feldstein and Horioka (1980) found that despite large gross flows of capital between countries, net flows are low, and most national investments are financed out of national savings. This result has stood the test of many studies, with modest amendments. Sophisticated explanations suggest that an underlying cause may be that risk attitudes towards real interest rates are nationally determined. But the overall observation is that despite massive capital flows, national macroeconomic policies and domestic economic conditions still strongly influence investment despite the appearance of an open economy.

To add to the puzzle, the evidence also shows that price parity among goods is even more strongly affected by borders than prices of capital. In an interesting study, Engel and Rogers (1996) looked at price differences for the same goods on both sides of the border of Canada and the US, and price differences within Canada. Price differences increased gradually with increasing distances within Canada, but the increases changed by discrete amounts when compared across the border. Applying the metric of price differences per mile within Canada, Engle and Rogers concluded that the border between the US and Canada ought to be 2,300 miles wide! International trade has not created the expected parity in prices, the so-called law of one price, that it is supposed to engender.

To date, labour markets have remained far more fragmented than capital markets (see Ehrenberg 1994) (see LABOUR MARKETS). In the European Union, efforts to harmonize labour practices were resisted by unions in northern countries, particularly Germany, which hoped to protect the gains they had won domestically. In the UK, employers feared that they would lose managerial flexibility if they had to adopt the stringent rules governing treatment of employees prevalent in France and Germany. Trade unions in North America opposed the North American Free Trade Agreement (NAFTA), in anticipation of capital flight and loss of jobs. As barriers to trade and investment fall, multinational corporations are encouraged to rationalize production by configuring their activities efficiently across national borders; such moves may be perceived as 'social dumping' by labour organizations and other groups affected by the resulting reconfiguring of economic activities and payments.

Worldwide, workers from areas of political instability and economic hardship continue to emigrate to countries that offer them greater opportunities. From a long-term historical perspective, however, labour markets are now actually less integrated than they were before the First World War. Migration of workers accounts for only a small proportion of the global workforce, and is dwarfed by population growth. The number of immigrants to the USA over the 1980s was lower than it was in the first decade of the twentieth century. Unlike the period before the First World War, immigrant workers are now less likely to become integrated into the national labour force by becoming permanent residents, as labour laws become tighter in the face of slower economic growth (United Nations 1994). Unlike domestic markets for capital, labour has remained relatively segmented and immobile in this phase of international integration. In so far as national labour markets are integrated through the activities of multinational corporations, however, they have been affected by a surge in foreign investment in recent years. This phenomenon and its implications are explored below.

3 The surge in foreign direct investment

Neither the increased internationalization of economic activity nor the rapid improvement in cross-border communication and transport links is a new phenomenon. However, what sets the recent phase of internationalization apart from past waves is that it is primarily being driven by foreign direct investment (FDI) rather than by arm's-length trade. International capital flows have been quite large in the past, particularly in the last decades of the nineteenth century and prior to the First World War. Only the US stood out as unusual in having more outward flows of direct investment than portfolio flows (Wilkins 1974). Though a net debtor, the USA was the origin of many of the first multinational corporations, for example, Kodak, Singer and International Harvester. But the UK remained a vastly more important source of international capital overall, and dominated even direct investment flows until the Second World War.

The period after the Second World War showed a rapid increase in the US position overseas. Vaupel and Curhan (1973) found that in the period from 1939 to the mid-1970s, US multinationals accounted for about two-thirds of the increase in foreign direct stock and the growth in the number of overseas affiliates. In the 1960s, the largest 180 American multinational corporations were adding on average about six foreign subsidiaries per year to their growing overseas networks. This extraordinary dominance led to deep concerns in many countries over increasing economic dependence on the USA. Virtually all major OECD countries commissioned studies in the 1960s on the implications of direct investment, which for some countries, such as the UK, Canada and Belgium, had risen to remarkably high percentages of production in many industries. Important conflicts between nation-states occurred as a result; an example is the refusal of the French government to acknowledge that the American embargo against exports to China applied to the French subsidiaries of American multinational corporations. This concern over the impact of multinational corporations on domestic economies culminated in a series of non-binding policy statements by international institutions (for example, OECD guidelines on multinational corporations) and in the creation of new international agencies (such as the United Nations Centre on Transnational Corporations, which in the 1980s developed its own, ultimately unsuccessful, Code of Conduct for Transnational Corporations) (see MULTINATIONAL CORPORATIONS).

The concern over multinational corporations waned in many countries in recent years, a trend that is correlated with the diminished role of the USA in direct investment flows. With the gradual devaluation of the dollar – particularly after the collapse of the Bretton

Woods system in the early 1970s – the USA became a more attractive location for investment and by the late 1980s, inflows to the USA exceeded outflows by more than two times. European investment in particular increased. In the early 1980s, Japanese direct investment increased dramatically in the USA, rising to new highs in the mid- to late 1980s. Among developing countries, severe debt crises in the early and mid-1980s meant that a policy of imposing constraints upon inflows of hard-currency foreign investments to favour domestic producers was untenable.

The second half of the 1980s witnessed a sharp increase in foreign investment flows in the world overall. Between 1981 and 1985, yearly outflows of FDI averaged $48 billion; by 1986–90, world outflows more than quadrupled to reach an annual average of $168 billion (United Nations 1994). Worldwide outflows of foreign investment grew three times faster than both exports and gross domestic product, lending support to the claim that foreign investment had replaced trade as the engine of international economic integration.

The surge in FDI was overwhelmingly concentrated among developed countries, which accounted for about 95 per cent of the outflows and 84 per cent of the inflows of total flows in the latter part of the 1980s. Among the most notable changes over this period was the decline of the USA as a net investor and the corresponding rise of Japan as a home (source) country of FDI; the USA and Japan switched places as number one and number three respectively in terms of their shares of worldwide FDI outflows (the UK maintained its position in second place, but surpassed the US in terms of FDI outflows in 1999). Much of the new Japanese investment was motivated by perceptions of rising protectionism in the US market (see Kogut and Chang 1991), the rising value of the yen, which favoured local production over exports, and the desire on the part of Japanese multinationals to access technologies embedded in US firms. Similar forces were at work in Europe, where the European Community (EC) programme of unification threatened to cause substantial trade diversion, particularly from Japan.

Within Europe, the programme to eliminate non-tariff barriers to trade and open national markets to greater competition caused intra-European investment and merger and acquisition activity to rise rapidly in the late 1980s and early 1990s. The early phase of European integration, which began in the 1950s and eliminated regional tariff barriers to trade, expanded interdependence within Europe, particularly in terms of currency movements, but stopped short of political and economic integration. As of the mid-1980s, the EC remained a collection of relatively fragmented national markets, which was considered to be an important factor in the lagging productivity and technological performance of European firms. The 1992 programme, by proposing that economic, social and monetary policies be harmonized, implied a major restructuring of industry within the EC, potentially allowing a far greater division of labour across member countries. While efforts towards monetary integration fell short of expectations, significant progress was made at achieving greater economic integration, spurred both by harmonization of policies relating to business practices, as well as by a rapid increase in intra-EC FDI. Much of this investment was aimed at rationalizing production, both in anticipation of as much as in response to declining barriers to trade. Even as they were increasing investment in the EC, European multinationals increased their presence in the US market.

Perhaps the most spectacular rise in FDI came from Japan, particularly after 1985. Between 1988 and 1990, Japanese investment flows to the EC were 13 per cent higher than the total flows over the previous thirty-six years combined; flows to the USA, where Japanese firms already had a much larger stake, were 8 per cent higher in the same period than in the previous thirty-six years combined (United Nations 1991). In both locations, Japanese firms responded to diversification opportunities that were unique to those markets (Mason and Encarnation 1994). Japanese investment also grew rapidly in east Asia, as Japanese firms upgraded their domestic facilities and shifted more mature production to lower-cost locations. Whereas US multinationals had dominated east Asian countries as a home country for FDI in the 1970s, Japan became the dominant investor in the region by the 1980s (United Nations 1991). At the same time, foreign investment in Japan itself remained disproportionately low, even after controls on inward investment were relaxed. The persistence of low investment levels in Japan has been partly attributed to structural features of the Japanese economy, such as extensive cross-shareholding among business partners, that remain highly differentiated from its main economic partners. By the early 1990s, the phenomenal growth in FDI had waned, and indeed net flows were negative in 1991 and 1992, with the sharpest declines in outflows from Japan, the UK and Germany.

However, by the end of the 1990s FDI outflows resumed their rise, growing at an average rate of 30 per cent per year to reach $800 billion in 1999, more than three-fourths of which were to developed countries. The rise in outflows pushed FDI stocks to reach $4.8 trillion in 1999 and sales by foreign affiliates became more important than trade in delivering goods and services to foreign countries (UNCTAD 2000). Cross-border mergers and acquisitions have been an important driver of growth in FDI in the 1990s, indicating a wave of restructuring by multinational corporations on a global scale. Between 1987 and 1999 the value of cross-border acquisition grew sevenfold, reaching $720 billion in 1999 and involving 6,000 transactions: nearly two-thirds of this value was accounted for by only 109 'mega-deals' exceeding $1 billion, indicating a consolidation of private assets among a relatively small group of large corporations (UNCTAD 2000).

The impact of the surge of new investment changed the landscape of key industries among major recipient countries. In two consecutive studies of foreign investment in the US, Kogut and Gittelman (1994) found that 105 US-based affiliates of non-US multinationals qualified for inclusion in the 1994 *Fortune* 500 list of the largest US industrial corporations. Over the first half of the 1990s, the contribution of foreign affiliates to US manufacturing gross product – a measure of local value added –increased 40 per cent, reaching $339.5 billion by 1996; nearly 12 per cent of the American industrial workforce, or some 2.2 million persons, were employed by a foreign company, double the proportion from the 1980s. The presence of multinationals is particularly strong in technology-intensive, oligopolistic industries: about one-third of the top 125 foreign MNCs in the United States are clustered in three industrial sectors: chemicals and pharmaceuticals; electrical and electronic equipment, including computers; and transportation equipment. These industries are increasingly non-domestic in nature: in the US chemical/pharmaceutical industry, affiliates of foreign-owned companies account for about one-third of total US sales and assets and 40 per cent of industry employment. Petroleum, computers and the motion picture industry are other sectors where foreign investment now accounts for a significant share of sales, assets and employment.

4 Global corporations and integration

Until relatively recently, economic theory was by and large ill-equipped to explain the reasons for and implications of the expansion of the multinational corporation. The earlier literature focused on 'push' explanations for direct investment, namely those factors in the industry of the country of origin that motivated the outward investment. The dominant school of thought reflected the attention paid to the large portfolio flows prior to the Second World War and maintained that the multinational corporation resulted from the arbitrage of international differences in rates of return to capital. Hymer (1976) showed that this theory failed to explain why FDI was mainly concentrated among countries with similar rates of return and did not co-vary with other forms of capital flows, such as portfolio investment. His work developed an industrial organization foundation for the study of the multinational, which rested on the assumptions that: (1) multinational firms had to possess some advantage over host-country firms, such as superior marketing skills or technology, in order to justify the added costs of foreign production; and (2) that multinational firms had to be more efficient to internalize that advantage by controlling the foreign production rather than exporting or licensing. Hymer's explanation of multinational activity rested on the Bain structure–conduct–performance model, in which barriers to entry such as product differentiation and scale economies allowed firms to enjoy monopolistic advantages which could be profitably exploited in overseas markets. It is not surprising that many, including Hymer himself, came to be critical of multinational corporations because of their potential monopolistic abuse.

Hymer's work provided the basis for studies that hypothesized that the overseas activities of multinational corporations were aimed at extending oligopolistic rivalry from the home country to foreign locations. Indeed, most FDI has historically been, and continues to be, concentrated in industries characterized by high seller concentration, research and development (R&D) intensity and product differentiation – the hallmarks of oligopolistic industries (Caves 1982). The push factors isolated by Hymer have proven to be robust predictors of outward direct investment.

There has been, however, a gradual change in thinking about the multinational corporation, moving from intra-national interdependence to international interdependence to eventual recognition of the implications of integrated multinational networks. Intranational interdependence was the presumption in the early studies, which conceptualized outward investment as an extension of home-based activities. One of the most important studies on international investment was Vernon's (1966) analysis of FDI as an outcome of rivalry among oligopolists from one nation who extend their rivalry overseas only when their home market begins to mature. Firms invest abroad in order either to pre-empt or retaliate against the moves of domestic rivals. Indeed, analysis of the timing of foreign investments of US multinationals prior to 1970 reveals a pattern of bunching in oligopolistic industries, which supports the thesis of inter-firm rivalry as a determinant of overseas investment.

The recognition that oligopolistic reaction might occur at an international level was developed a decade after Vernon's early work. Graham (1978) demonstrated that oligopolistic interdependence was carried out across national borders. In an analysis of cross-investments by US and European multinational enterprises over the period 1950–70, he showed that European investments in the USA were associated with earlier incursions into Europe by US multinationals.

Oligopolistic models of multinational activity thus stressed the notion of national firms pushed abroad by the forces of international interdependence. As such, they carry a home-country bias, in which firms exploit advantages acquired in one country in the market of another. If models of oligopolistic interdependence and the advantages stemming from cross-border corporate networks can explain the factors pushing firms to become multinationals, what are the 'pull' factors that also account for the location of FDI? An obvious answer is that direct investment flows to locations where materials are found, or wages are relatively cheap. Certainly, investments of a vertical nature, that is for sourcing inputs, respond to differences in factor costs. But there was also a recognition of glaring anomalies, such as the very significant flows of direct investment concentrated among high-wage countries.

In a landmark study, Cantwell (1989) pointed out that the technological capabilities of the host country attract multinationals to invest in those locations. In this way, the multinational may acquire the knowledge and technologies that are embedded in particular locations. Here, Hymer's paradigm of the multinational being advantaged over host-country rivals is turned around, and it is the pull of location-specific country capabilities that attracts foreign investment. These localized advantages may be traced to national institutions that encourage and sustain specific forms of organizing local resources. In new science-based driven industries, opportunities for the emergence of start-up firms appear to be an important source of observed differences in the capacity of countries to innovate. These differences are linked to institutionalized incentives for individuals to commercialize their knowledge. Gittelman (2000) showed, for example, that biotechnology start-ups in France and the US are similarly innovative; the difference rests in the lower propensity of French scientists to join new companies. Thus, national systems can influence and sustain differences in innovation, even if the underlying science is developed and diffused internationally.

These works suggest that nations represent enduring islands of specialized but interdependent competences. The growing interdependence of the world in technology flows is deeply affected by the bridges built by multinational corporations between high-technology regions, in part to arbitrage differences in technological regulatory regimes. Although most R&D is still performed domestically, large multinational corporations perform a significant proportion of their research activities internationally. Kobrin (1991) finds that technological intensity in an industry is a significant determinant of cross-border integration of US multinationals. The 1980s have witnessed a proliferation of these strategic alliances in high-technology industries, such that the notion of 'national' technologies is losing meaning.

Push and pull theories fail to take account of the advantages of multinationality *per se*, in which the ability to coordinate a network of overseas affiliates provides opportunities that go beyond those in standard models of oligopolistic competition. Kogut (1983) noted that theories of direct investment were preoccupied with explaining the initial investment overseas and neglected to understand the implications of a multinational network. He proposes a model of foreign investment as a sequential process, in which the multinational network can be used to exploit international differences in institutional frameworks, provide learning and externalities and allow for joint economies of production on an international scale. That is, there are opportunities that can only be exploited by the multinational corporation; here, multinationality itself has become a source of advantage possessed by the firm.

The proposition that multinationality *per se* provides unique advantages raises the intriguing notion that the lack of integration in the public sector provides opportunities for private gains from integration. In a completely integrated market, prices would be equalized and the market conditions determining profitability would move together uniformly, such that there would be no advantage to having the option to shift operations from one part of the market to another. Where markets are less than completely integrated, however, it pays to buy the option to respond to changing relative conditions among locations. The option takes the form of a network of foreign affiliates that are jointly coordinated to maximize network-wide returns. In other words, it is the ability of multinationals to integrate their activities across markets that are not fully integrated that provides for profitable opportunities. Over time, it would be expected that the increased integration of multinational networks would drive increasing integration at the country level, as the process of deepening integrated corporate networks runs into political and institutional barriers.

The formation and growth of regional networks by multinationals has acted as a push factor in regional integration arrangements such as NAFTA and the European Union. It is instructive to note that in 1989, four years before NAFTA was put in place, US multinationals accounted for 27 per cent of Mexican exports to the USA and 42 per cent of Mexican imports from the USA; virtually all of which was in the form of intra-firm trade (United Nations 1992). The existence of intra-firm production networks spanning countries in a region shines a light on discrepancies between national regimes, putting pressure on governments to take actions that will shape the integration process in a mutually beneficial way. Arrangements at the policy level, in turn, can improve the profit performance of multinationals and encourage further integration by lowering some of the transaction costs associated with international arbitrage by, for instance, harmonizing product requirements and lowering barriers to trade. In such a scenario, integration at the firm level and integration at the policy level are self-reinforcing processes.

What is often hidden in these theories of push, pull, and the multinational network is the role of the multinational corporation in diffusing work practices. Many work practices are embodied in a complexity of organizational relationships; disentangling the grain from the chaff is difficult by observation only. As such, the multinational corporation can act to transfer best-practice knowledge and superior methods of organizing production to different locations in its overseas network. Wilkins (1974) has shown how these practices are often the basis of the initial investment overseas, but in turn, inspire competition. Indeed, the history by Chandler (1990), which compares large corporations in the USA, UK and Germany, has many examples of the initial success but eventual failure of overseas investment as foreign competitors learned how to do it better. The first Hymer condition, that a foreign firm must have an advantage to compete, can be satisfied initially but eradicated over time.

The early rise of American multinationals can be explained partly by their possession of the new organizing principles of standardization and mass production. Similarly, the wave of Japanese investments is a reflection, in part, of the transfer of organizing principles to new markets. There is evidence of the transfer of Japanese production *keiretsu* to US and European locations. These principles sometimes face important problems of adaptation, such as seen in the joint venture between Toyota and General Motors located in California.

No matter what the degree of adaptation, there is little doubt that speed of diffusion has been unalterably influenced by the existence of large multinational corporations. The slow speed of the diffusion of new technologies – agricultural innovations in the early industrial period diffused at the rate of one kilometre per year – belongs to a distant age. Not only does money move rapidly, but so do ideas and new organizing practices, because the world is now far more integrated through organizations that span across national borders.

5 The global organization of multinationals

The role of multinational corporations in the globalization of production, and the diffusion of ideas, is seen in the evolution of their international organization. In a seminal article, Perlmutter (1969) provided a basis for thinking about the relationship of structure to levels of international integration by setting out three orientations a multinational could adopt towards its foreign affiliates: ethnocentric, polycentric and geocentric, each progressively less culturally biased towards the home country. In the ethnocentric firm, affiliates are dependent upon the parent, which takes full responsibility for decision making and strategic activities such as research and development. The structure is highly centralized; overseas affiliates serve as little more than foreign points of entry for the outputs that emanate from the home-based parent. The polycentric organization introduces interdependence into the structure: although managed under a single umbrella, international affiliates are allowed to become somewhat independent of the parent in order to conform to the needs of their individual markets. Some decisions, such as marketing strategies, might be decentralized to the affiliate level, although overall resource allocation decisions remain with the parent. A geocentric organization is one which is highly decentralized, where responsibilities are delegated according to functional requirements rather than by home and host country distinctions.

Stopford and Wells (1972) traced the evolution of multinational structure as a function of multinational strategy. They found empirical support for the hypothesis that the more diversified a firm's international product mix and the greater the degree of internationalization, the more likely the firm was to move from an international division structure to a more rationalized international configuration. In the former case, overseas subsidiaries replicated the operations of the parent in the host country and operated relatively independently of the latter, resembling Perlmutter's polycentric organizations. To cope with rising complexity of product mix and growing internationalization, managers implemented structures that allowed for greater integration and coordination of activities. These included worldwide product divisions, which allowed for a high degree of integration and operating efficiency but weakened local responsiveness, area divisions, which carried the reverse properties, and matrix structures, which were intended to address the weaknesses of the first two but posed problems of managerial and co-ordination complexity.

Stopford and Wells' study demonstrated the evolution of structures to fit strategy, as US firms, which were competitive leaders in international markets, engaged in a learning process about the optimal mix between integration, responsiveness and complexity. Franko (1976) shows that late-moving European multinational enterprises skipped the international division phase and moved directly to global structures (area divisions, matrix and worldwide product). Moreover, whereas US firms tended to reorganize their structures in the home market first, European firms, which were far more internationalized and diversified, undertook domestic and foreign reorganization simultaneously, forgoing the learning, trial-and-error process of US firms. For US firms, domestic competitive strategy drove structural change, while for European firms it was primarily international competitive conditions that triggered a realignment of structure with strategy.

Recent additions to the structure literature have stressed the multinational as an integrated network of cooperative relationships, among affiliates as well as with firms outside the multinational corporation's organizational boundaries. Hedlund (1986) proposes a heterarchical model of the multinational firm. Such a firm employs a mix of organizing principles (ownership, joint ventures, subcontracting) to maximize flexibility in response to contingencies. Distinctions between headquarters and subsidiaries, home and host countries disappear: normative control replaces bureaucratic regulation and coercion and horizontal communication and coordination replace a hierarchical control structure. Others argue that multinational structures will evolve into differentiated organizations to reflect their external environments. Where barriers across countries and regions are high, intra-organizational coordination and integration will be relatively underdeveloped, while in regions of high integration, multinationals will evolve into dense network structures.

6 The political economy of globalization

The gradual emergence of multinational networks integrated by large organizations is the outcome of the co-evolution between the structure of international organizations and opportunities of the international environment. Governments have hardly faded away amid these changes, and attempts to regulate the entry and behaviour of multinational corporations have posed, and continue to pose, a threat of conflict between the firm and the host nation-state. But as the world has moved from interdependence to integration, the challenge to government policy has shifted from regulation of the firm to a more fundamental problem, as to whether broader political and social agendas can be realized in an environment of mobile capital and integrated world production.

An important line of work has concerned the influence of liberalization on the ability of governments to pursue domestic policies. This issue of independence from world markets has been at the heart of international monetary and trade economics for almost fifty years. Interest has focused on the tendency of trade to equalize prices of goods and factors among countries. The Stolper and Samuelson theorems (1941) clarified the implications for distributional costs within a country: nations may gain by trade, but the less abundant factor will be hurt.

The models by Fleming (1962) and Mundell (1962) extended these kinds of concerns to monetary policy. Their work posed the dilemma of a government trying to pursue two policies of internal and external stabilization with one control variable: the money supply. Under fixed exchange rates, monetary policy is rendered less effective by capital mobility; money seeks the haven with the highest risk-adjusted return. Flexible exchange rates obviate the effectiveness of fiscal policy, as interest rates and exchange rates counterbalance any stimulus.

These fundamental results, all formalized in the 1950s, did not percolate into the thinking on the political economy of government policies until the 1980s. Rogowski (1989) expanded the traditional literature on customs policy and distributional politics to consider how trade expansion and contraction influence domestic political alignments. His analysis proposes a counter-intuitive result: that expansion weakens the exposed group politically, but contraction strengthens it. The work of Rogowski, which can be taken as exemplifying a broader literature, is primarily a study of interdependence: how trade influences domestic political arrangements.

An important related issue concerns the effect of globalization on the ability of a government to pursue its national objectives. The constraint of the world economy would seem particularly severe for left-wing governments wishing to pursue social welfare policies. Budget deficits, high taxation depressing the return on capital, or financing by inflationary policies should, in theory, be constrained by international economic pressures in an environment in which capital is mobile.

The evidence has not shown this. Garrett (1995) found a fairly subtle relationship between leftist politics and globalization. At low levels, leftist governments pursued policies with few consequences for overall government spending and budget deficits but at higher rates of capital taxation. As internationalization increased, fiscal expansion increased for countries with leftist governments. Left-labour governments have pursued, in other words, a social welfare agenda despite increased internationalization.

All these studies point to a complex relationship between political policy and internationalization. The silver lining is that governments may be able to pursue activist policy agendas if markets perceive that the long-term productivity of the economy may be improved. If such a possibility is not to be admitted, then it becomes difficult to imagine how the success of a high tax, social welfare economy of a Germany can be explained.

However, in light of the currency crises of the early 1990s, there is strong evidence that bad macroeconomic policy leads to substantial penalties in conditions of high capital mobility. Eichengreen and Wyplosz (1991) have analysed the currency crisis in the efforts to achieve European monetary union. The shock to the system stemmed from the reunification of the two Germanies and the massive excess demand created by the collapse of the East German economy. Under a Mundell–Fleming model of adjustment under fixed exchange rates, such a crisis would be remedied by three alternatives: decreasing real wages, an inflationary policy to increase German prices and to satisfy demand through imports of relatively less expensive goods, or a revaluation of the currency to achieve the same effect as an inflationary policy. The policy of cutting real wages is constrained by the difficulties of coordinating and implementing such a policy. Inflationary policies are counter to the stated stance of the independent Bundesbank. Revaluing the Deutschmark – the preferred policy of the Bundesbank – was constrained by the public affirmations of political leaders in other European countries about maintaining the prevailing exchange rates. However, the strategy taken to maintain external stability was a resort to high real domestic interest rates. Financial markets did not find these policies credible given the high levels of unemployment. One by one, governments caved in to international pressures by devaluing their currency relative to the Deutschmark. But underneath these basic economic pressures was a dissatisfied Bundesbank that suggested publicly that exchange rates were out of alignment.

To some, the forces of globalization have effectively eradicated government control. Trade talks on liberalization are often stumped over such issues as how to tax the flow of information, when its origins cannot be determined. Currently, the absence of strong countervailing international agreements and institutions suggests that world integration has rendered national deviations, be it social or tax policy, more costly. But a more cautious estimate is that the very strength of these changes may be the cause for institutional responses.

In 1998, an international crisis devastated financial markets in Asia and the economies of Thailand, Philippines, Korea, Malaysia and Indonesia were plunged into chaos. Unlike crises in Latin America, the Asian crisis posed the puzzling question of why countries with strong growth and healthy balances of payments should suddenly be transformed from 'tiger' economies into sites of severe economic distress requiring the assistance of the

International Monetary Fund. Economists at the IMF laid the blame on weak internal governance systems. Weak governance allowed banks to lend to firms in a bubble environment, and often these banks stood in a circle of close ties linking government officials, their families and friends. Labelled 'crony' capitalism by the popular press, suddenly the tiger countries were viewed as earning their just reward that could only be solved by tight monetary policies, increased transparency, and further relaxing of national barriers to international capital flows.

Not everyone agreed with this assessment. The contrarian view is that there is a fundamental contradiction between the speed by which international capital moves and the institutional capability of developing nations to respond (Wade 2000). Financial markets in all countries are imperfect, and especially those in developing countries. At the same time, it is underlined, banks and firms from developed countries made massive loans and investments in the tiger countries, and presumably these western enterprises are appropriately governed and immune to charges of crony capitalism. The cause lies in a financial bubble episode, much like the one experienced in recent years in which capital markets vastly overvalued many new Internet companies. The source of the problem can be traced to an overflow of capital searching for quick returns on world markets. Unlike FDI, such flows of so-called 'hot money' are motivated by short-term investment horizons such that cross-border mobility is greatly increased. Thus, further international integration would be the wrong policy in this environment. Nations first must be given the chance to develop financial institutions that can sustain speculative cycles, presuming it is even possible to design such institutions. As is always the case with arguments that are often ideologically motivated – even when couched in sophisticated models – the evidence is ambiguous for choosing between the 'crony' and 'institutional' arguments. The IMF intervened in most of the Asian economies, severe recessions and hardship were experienced, and most returned to positive growth within a few years. However, countries that did not follow fully the IMF policies have also done well. Malaysia, in particular, angrily rejected IMF policies, attacked international speculators, and increased financial controls. It too returned to positive and sustained growth.

7 Conclusion

The force of economic globalization is not simply the domination of political action by world financial and real goods markets. Certainly, domestic policy freedom is more curtailed as interdependence increases. But there are three alternatives for achieving political ends that may fly in the face of short-term economic priorities. One is simply autarky; yet this policy path is ever exacting a higher opportunity cost due to the expansion and attractiveness of world trade and investment. Another is the pursuit of political and social objectives that lead to long-term growth in productivity. There is increasing evidence that nations that succeed in building institutions that support economic coordination and human capital formation can enjoy persisting high levels of productivity and income, despite the simultaneous pursuit of social policies that entail high levels of taxation and government-sponsored employment. Finally, there is the belief that countervailing measures may be enacted to regain political control. Eichengreen and Wyplosz (1991), for example, propose a Tobin-tax to throw sand in the gears of capital mobility in order to slow capital flight. But international coordination requires, still, the agreement of interdependent actors. In here lies the irony that the increasing integration of the world economy stands in sharp contrast to the uneasy division of the political landscape into independent, though interdependent, nation states.

BRUCE KOGUT

MICHELLE GITTELMAN
WHARTON SCHOOL AT THE UNIVERSITY OF
PENNSYLVANIA

Further reading

(References cited in the text marked *)

Bartlett, C.A., Doz, Y. and Hedlund, G. (eds) (1990) *Managing the Global Firm*, London: Routledge. (A collection of essays by noted researchers in international strategy, containing early statements exploring the multinational corporation as a network of subsidiaries.)

* Braudel, F. (1979) *The Structures of Everyday Life: The Limits of the Possible*, vols 1–3, New York: Harper & Row. (A vast work that details the history and evolution of modern social and economic life, from the Middle Ages to the Industrial Revolution.)

* Cantwell, J. (1989) *Technological Innovation and Multinational Corporations*, Oxford: Blackwell. (A landmark study on how knowledge accumulates in particular countries and provides competitive advantages to local firms and pulls direct investment from the outside.)

* Caves, R.E. (1982) *Multinational Enterprise and Economic Analysis*, Cambridge: Cambridge University Press. (This research textbook is the primary handbook on studies of foreign direct investment and includes a vast bibliography.)

* Chandler, A. (1990) *Scale and Scope*, New York: The Free Press. (Sweeping study of the varieties of capitalism and the role of big business that will remain an important and controversial work for some time.)

Dumez H. and Jeunemaître A. (2000) *Understanding and Regulating the Market at a Time of Globalization: The Case of the Cement Industry*, Basingstoke: Macmillan. (A detailed study of the globalization of an industry historically divided by national borders and the implications for regulatory policy.)

Dunning, J. (1993) *Multinational Enterprises and the Global Economy*, Addison-Wesley. (Comprehensive text covering research about the multinational corporation, from economics to cross-cultural studies.)

* Ehrenberg, R. (1994) *Labor Markets and Integrating National Economies*, Washington: The Brookings Institution. (One of a series of books published by US think-tank The Brookings Institution on the topic of world integration.)

* Eichengreen, B. and Wyplosz, C. (1991) 'The unstable EMS', *Brookings Papers on Economic Activity* 1: 51–124. (An exploration of the dynamics of the breakdown of the European monetary system in 1992 and 1993.)

* Engel, C. and Rogers, J. (1996) 'How wide is the border?', *American Economic Review* 86: 1112–25. (Stunning study of the significance of borders.)

* Feldstein, M. and Horioka, C. (1980) 'Domestic saving and international capital flows', *Economic Journal* 90: 314–29. (Now classic empirical study that shows financial markets are nationally segregated with implications for the continuing efficacy of national macroeconomic policies.)

* Fleming, J.M. (1962) 'Domestic financial policies under fixed and under floating exchange rates', *IMF Staff Papers* 9: 369–79. (The original contribution to the Mundell–Fleming model of the effects of monetary and fiscal policy.)

* Franko, L. (1976) *The European Multinationals*, New York: Harper. (An early study on the growth and organizational evolution of European multinationals.)

Froot, K. (1992) *Foreign Direct Investment*, Chicago, IL: University of Chicago Press. (Papers by leading scholars examining patterns of foreign direct investment in the 1980s and the history of multinational corporations' activities.)

* Garrett, G. (1995) 'Capital mobility, trade and the domestic politics of economic policy', *International Organization* 49 (4): 657–87. (Empirical investigation into the domestic political effects of increasing economic integration, showing that left-labour governments are not necessarily undermined by increased internationalization.)

* Gittelman, M. (2000) 'Mapping National Knowledge Networks: Scientists, Firms and Institutions in the United States and France'. Unpublished PhD thesis, University of Pennsylvania. (In-depth analysis of biotechnology patenting and scientists in France and the United States that shows directly how institutions matter to technological innovation.)

* Graham, E.M. (1978) 'Transatlantic investment by multinational firms: a rivalistic phenomenon', *Journal of Post-Keynesian Economics* 1: 82–99. (Shows that multinational investments are motivated by international oligopolistic competition.)

* Hedlund, G. (1986) 'The hypermodern MNC – heterarchy', *Human Resource Management* 25 (Spring): 9–35. (Sets out a view of the firm as a complex system tending towards multiple centres of competence as opposed to a hierarchical control structure.)

* Herring, R.J. and Litan, R.E. (1995) *Financial Regulation in the Global Economy*, Washington, DC: The Brookings Institution. (One of the Brookings series, a detailed analysis of international integration of financial markets.)

* Hymer, S. (1976) *International Operations of the National Firms: A Study of the Foreign Direct Investment*, Cambridge, MA: MIT Press. (The classic statement that moved the study of foreign direct investment out of the arena of international capital flows and into the arena of industry structure and competition and the transfer of technology.)

Keohane, R.O. and Nye, J.S. (1977) *Power and Interdependence: World Politics in Transition*, Boston, MA: Little, Brown. (A landmark study that moved international relations away from the study of the high politics of state strategy and into the realm of economics, resources and political will.)

* Kobrin, S.J. (1991) 'An empirical analysis of the determinants of global integration', *Strategic Management Journal* 12: 17–31. (Examines the relative importance of numerous factors, including technology and economies of scale, in determining the extent of overseas activities by US multinationals.)

* Kogut, B. (1983) 'Foreign direct investment as a sequential process', in C.P. Kindleberger and D. Audretsch (eds), *The Multinational Corporation in the 1980s*, Cambridge, MA: MIT Press. (Proposes a model of the multinational corporation which stresses the advantages of controlling an international network of affiliates.)

* Kogut, B., (ed.) (1993) *Country Competitiveness: Technology and the Organizing of Work*, New York: Oxford. (A collection of country comparisons arguing that national differences are sustained by systemic differences in the organization of technology and work, yet are altered by global diffusion of practices).

* Kogut, B. and Chang, S.J. (1991) 'Technological capabilities and Japanese direct investment in the United States', *Review of Economics and Statistics* 73: 401–13. (Gives empirical support to the hypothesis the US–Japanese technological rivalry is a determinant of Japanese foreign direct investment in the USA.)

* Kogut, B. and Gittelman, M. (1994) 'The largest foreign multinationals in the United States and their contribution to the American economy', Reginald Jones Center Working Paper, Philadelphia, PA: The Wharton School at the University of Pennsylvania. (Analyses the US-based operations of over 100 multinational corporations and compares the performance of foreign companies to domestic firms from the late 1970s to the present.)

* Mason, M. and Encarnation, D. (1994) *Does Ownership Matter: Japanese Investment in a Unifying Europe*, Oxford: Clarendon Press. (A collection of papers exploring various facets of one of the most prominent expressions of increasing integration, the expansion of Japanese multinationals into Europe.)

* Mundell, R.A. (1962) 'The appropriate use of monetary and fiscal policy for internal and external balance', *IMF Staff Papers* 9: 70–9. (The original contribution to the Mundell–Fleming model.)

* Nelson, R. (ed.) (1993) *National Innovation Systems*, Oxford University Press. (Collection of essays that describe different national systems for the organization of science and commercial research.)

* Perlmutter, H. (1969) 'The tortuous evolution of the multinational enterprise', *Columbia Journal of World Business* 4 (1): 9–18. (Classic essay linking the cultural orientation of a multinational corporation to its corporate strategy and the structure of its overseas network.)

* Rogowski, R. (1989) *Commerce and Coalitions: How Trade Affects Domestic Political Alignments*, Princeton, NJ: Princeton University Press. (Explores the domestic political consequences of the Stolper–Samuelson theorem that trade hurts those factors that are scarce and aids those that are abundant.)

* Stolper, W. and Samuelson, P. (1941) 'Protection and real wages', *Review of Economic Studies* 9: 58–73. (A classic analysis of the consequences of trade on factor price parity.)

* Stopford, J.M. and Wells, L.T. (1972) *Managing the Multinational Enterprise: Organization of the Firm and Ownership of the Subsidiaries*, New York: Basic Books. (Comprehensive study of the multinational corporation that documents the evolution of the organizational structures and strategies of international companies within the political context of host governments.)

* United Nations (1991; 1992; 1994; 2000) *World Investment Report*, Geneva: United Nations. (A series of annual reports that present comprehensive statistics on worldwide foreign direct investment trends and the activities of multinational corporations, as well as focusing on specific themes relating to multinational corporations in the world economy.)

* Vaupel, J.W. and Curhan, J.P. (1973) *The World's Largest Multinational Enterprises*, Cambridge, MA: Harvard University Press. (A sourcebook of tables showing detailed information on more than 25,000 overseas subsidiaries of US and non-US multinational corporations from 1900 to the mid-1970s.)

* Vernon, R. (1966) 'International investment and international trade in the product cycle', *Quarterly Journal of Economics* 80: 190–207. (Classic essay laying the theoretical groundwork for a life-cycle model of international business.)

* Wade, R. (2000) 'Wheels within wheels: rethinking the Asian crisis and the Asian model', *Annual Reviews Political Science*, 3: 85–115.

* Wilkins, M. (1974) *The Maturing of Multinational Enterprise: American Business Abroad from*

1914 to 1970, Cambridge, MA: Harvard University Press. (A well-documented study of the historical expansion of US firms overseas.)

Further resources

http://www.unctad.org

See also: CORPORATE CONTROL; DEVELOPMENT AND DIFFUSION OF TECHNOLOGY; ECONOMIC INTEGRATION, INTERNATIONAL; EXCHANGE RATE ECONOMICS; INTERNATIONAL FINANCIAL STABILITY; INTERNATIONAL MONETARY FUND; MONEY AND CAPITAL MARKETS, INTERNATIONAL; MULTINATIONAL CORPORATIONS; ORGANIZATION STRUCTURE; TRANSFER PRICING; WORLD BANK; WORLD TRADE ORGANIZATION

International financial stability

1 Economic theory
2 Can a crisis be detected?
3 Is there an alternative?
4 Conclusion

Overview

Judging from the flow of capital, the world is becoming more integrated at a rapid pace. In particular, more and more liquid capital is moving in and out of national markets in the pursuit of higher rates of return.

Multinational institutions and multilateral agreements foster greater capital mobility. The IMF has always included greater capital mobility as one of the cornerstones of its macroeconomic policies. In its *1999 World Economic Outlook* the IMF recommends that countries like India, which have lifted capital controls only gradually should implement greater financial openness. Similarly, with the passage of the General Agreement of Trades in Services (GATS) in December 1997, the WTO has introduced a wide-ranging multilateral agreement that could lead to greater capital mobility.

For most of the 1980s and the early 1990s, there has been a trend towards greater international capital mobility and towards more domestic financial deregulation. Both external and internal liberalization of financial markets are based on the same theoretical framework, and often go hand in hand. The standard economic development framework holds that greater capital mobility from outside the economy and within the economy is an integral part of successful development strategies. Allowing capital to move freely from one country to another as well as from one investment project to another would supposedly allow investors to seek out the most productive investments, which in turn should result in faster growth for the recipient economies than otherwise.

The benign view of financial liberalization (FL), though, has been called into question by the fact that, with deregulation, the frequency of financial crises has increased. In a comprehensive study of banking crises, the IMF found that during the period from 1980 to 1996, when FL became increasingly popular, two-thirds of its member countries had undergone significant banking sector problems. Over the course of the 1990s, a number of empirical studies have identified internal and external FL as a determining factor in fostering speculative bubbles and increased financial fragility.

Financial crises have repercussions for businesses both in the crisis countries and in trading partner countries. A financial crisis means a drop in demand in the respective economy and a sharp devaluation of the crisis country's currency. That is, domestic businesses see their local revenues plummet and import prices rise, which is partially offset by rising exports. For businesses in trading partner countries, a financial crisis elsewhere spells lower exports and more import competition. Between May 1998 and December 1999, US manufacturing lost more than 400,000 jobs, mainly as a result of the Asian financial crisis (Rothstein and Scott 1998). Thus, the challenge for policymakers is to ensure financial stability, while making sufficient funds available for productive investments.

The fact that FL has not fared as promised has forced economists to reconsider the rationale for external and internal liberalization, and to look at alternative approaches to develop financial markets. Of particular interest is the question of how international capital flows can be harnessed for the benefit of economic development without their potentially destructive side-effects.

1 Economic theory

The standard approach to financial market development, financial liberalization (FL) purports that deregulation improves an economy's efficiency (see ECONOMIC INTEGRATION, INTERNATIONAL). Thus, more international capital mobility and less domestic regulation should enhance the real economic performance of an economy. In contrast, some economists have argued that external liberalization, in particular, increases competitive pressures on domestic banks, and induces them to accept greater portfolio risks than they would in the absence of international competition (Demirgüç-Kunt and Detragiache 1998). Similarly, some critics of FL have argued that greater inside and outside liberalization increases the chance for financial crises as it entices investors to direct funds into short-term speculative projects (Grabel 1993; Weller 1999).

FL is generally understood as the deregulation both of external capital flows and of domestic financial markets. In particular, external liberalization includes full or partial capital account opening, leading to the potential for more short-term capital mobility and more foreign direct investment (FDI) flows in and out of an economy. Domestic policy recommendations that are intended to liberalize financial markets include the elimination of credit ceilings, of lending requirements or of entry restrictions, and the widening of the operational scope of financial market participants. Banks may be allowed to sell insurance, and investment bankers may be allowed to provide commercial loans.

The goal of FL is to eliminate financial constraints in order to provide sufficient funds for domestic producers for productive investments in plant and equipment. Thanks to deregulation, banks are expected to become more efficient, thus leading to more credit for business investments. For example, banks should find it easier to attract deposits after the elimination of interest rate ceilings and to borrow capital overseas once capital accounts have been liberalized. On the other hand, banks should be more inclined to lend without interest rate restrictions and with greater financial market competition. The liberalized allocation of financial resources directs funds towards their most efficient uses, thereby boosting investment, productivity and economic growth.

Experience suggests, however, that the theory of financial liberalization misses important dimensions of the way the world works. It has been recognized that the level of capitalization of banks can significantly influence their lending behaviour and their stability (Stiglitz 1994). Banks with low capital and lower than expected earnings may seek out high-risk, high return projects, thereby increasing financial instability. One of the most widely noticed example of this is the savings and loan (S&L) crisis in the USA in the late 1980s, when poorly capitalized banks undertook high-risk real estate ventures. In emerging economies, greater financial market competition, particularly from well-capitalized foreign banks, that may result from capital account liberalization may set this process in motion by lowering the profitability of domestic banks. In fact, 'an increase in the share of foreign banks leads to a lower profitability of domestic banks' (Claessens et al. 1998). Poorer profit expectations may even lower a bank's franchise value so as to leave it *de facto* bankrupt. Such banks stand to lose little or nothing from taking on larger portfolio risk and by engaging in speculative investments, mainly in the stock market or the real estate market.

More intensive competition is not the only factor that causes greater financial instability after FL. In addition to more financial market competition, financial firms may find more opportunities after FL, and they may find themselves driven to more speculative investments either through more intensive competition or in an atmosphere of 'deregulation euphoria'.

A crucial problem arises because opportunities to engage in more speculative financing are likely to increase after FL because of financial deregulation, which follows a period of real improvements, but which also gives rise to speculative bubbles. In particular, based on Minsky's (1986) 'financial instability hypothesis', some economists have argued that greater liberalization is likely to result in more speculative investments, and subsequently in more high-risk, high return investments, with potentially destabilizing consequences for the entire economy (Grabel 1993; Weller 1999).

According to this view, financial deregulation leads to short-term economic gains, and hence fuels optimistic expectations. After financial deregulation, liquidity improves and thus more funds are available for both productive and speculative purposes. The increase in investment opportunities is generally matched by a decline in governmental regulation in the financial market. An expanding real sector flush with capital, booming asset markets, increasing rates of return point towards an improving economy. With higher real interest rates and with expanding real and financial sectors, more funds are then attracted from overseas. More capital inflows, though, may lead to a real currency appreciation, hence attracting even more capital.

Unfortunately, changes in economic fundamentals after FL merely improve the economic situation in the short-run. A continued currency appreciation helps to attract capital, which follows the promise of short-term gains in deregulated financial markets. Both a continued overvaluation and the diversion of funds for speculative purposes, particularly into speculative uses in asset markets, such as the stock or the real estate market, generate the illusion of a sound and improving economy. Thus, otherwise well-capitalized, and sound banks are tempted to extend credit beyond prudent limits. While the real sector is hurt by a currency appreciation, by deteriorating terms of trade, and by the lack of credit (since it is going to other – more speculative – uses), financial markets still expand liquidity for speculative purposes in asset markets. The stock market and the real estate market are doing well, while simultaneously real output slows.

More financial speculation raises the chance of financial crises because banks face a larger downside risk. In particular, as the real sector slows down, debt-to-equity ratios are likely to rise, and the chance of bankruptcy increases. Similarly, asset market speculation means that at some point speculators' optimistic profitability expectations are not met, and they are unable to meet their own financial obligations. With rising defaults, international investors become more likely to withdraw their short-term funds, further weakening the economy. Rapid capital outflows translate into a lack of funds for ongoing projects, thus fuelling an economic downturn in all sectors of the economy. Capital outflows reverse the currency appreciation, thereby adding to the burden of those who owe loans denominated in foreign currency. With further increasing loan defaults, a downward spiral is set in motion that depresses financial and non-financial sectors alike.

It is important to understand that firms are in a precarious situation before a crisis occurs due to the emphasis on short-term returns that makes long-term financing harder to obtain. If investors can gain significant returns on speculative ventures in a short period, less funds will be allocated to more long-term productive investments, where investors have to be patient. Thus, firms will generally find it harder to secure long-term external financing after deregulation. Since smaller firms especially depend on external financing, the allocation of funds away from productive uses is likely to hurt small and medium-sized enterprises (SMEs) or start-ups more than large corporations. Consequently, productive investments may not be undertaken, and firms can lose their competitive advantages, thereby possibly increasing the default risk for banks, and fuelling the flames that ultimately lead to the firestorm of economic crises.

Adding to the vicious cycle is the fact that the government is caught in an unenviable situation. To avoid a financial crisis, governments often revert at least temporarily to raising interest rates to keep short-term capital from leaving. Thus, monetary authorities add to the growing burden for borrowers, raising in turn the default risk. Similarly, once a crisis is set in motion governments face increased demands on their budgets that have already been strained because of a slowdown in the real sector.

The empirical evidence on the connection between FL and financial crises has been mounting over the last few years. In a survey of banking sector problems the IMF found that two-thirds of its member countries have experienced banking sector problems between 1980 and 1996, that is the period when financial deregulation found widespread acceptance (Lindgren *et al.* 1996). Similarly, in a summary of recent studies on capital mobility, Blecker (1999) finds that at least for developing economies there is strong evidence that increased capital mobility raises the chance of crises. Further, Kaminsky and Reinhart (1999) find that FL often precedes a banking crisis. Similarly, Grabel (1998) shows that increased financial fragility has been a systematic occurrence after FL for the emerging economies that most recently experienced currency crises. In an econometric study of 26 emerging economies, Weller (1999) finds that countries are much more likely to experience banking and currency crises after FL than before.

Even though FL offers some advantages, most of them are short-lived in developing economies that have not developed the domestic institutions to control outflows of capital. For instance, liquidity constraints are likely to be reduced after liberalization. Since a non-trivial share of additional funds may find its way into speculative financing, though, not all businesses may benefit equally from the additional liquidity. Similarly, liberalization offers more access to new economies for multinational businesses. However, if a crisis occurs, demand in these economies may be depressed for lengthy periods. Finally, the liberalized environment may offer more business opportunities, but in a more volatile environment. That is, exchange rates, the availability of credit, and interest rates are likely to fluctuate significantly more after FL than before. With the ambiguities associated with FL in mind, the focus of the discussion has shifted back to optimal financial market development. If some form of liberalization is needed to arrive at more efficient financial systems, it has to be done under avoidance of the drawbacks.

2 Can a crisis be detected?

Aside from looking into alternatives to FL, policymakers could also consider institutional improvements that would allow for early detection of a looming crisis. Clearly, economic policies could then be adjusted on an as-need-be basis to avoid a crisis.

A number of empirical studies on financial crises have set out to identify predictors of currency and banking crises. In a seminal paper on currency crises Eichengreen et al. (1995) find that currency crises across a sample of 20 OECD countries over the period from 1959 to 1993 exhibit strong regularities. In particular, it is found that changes of monetary aggregates, budget deficits, foreign exchange reserves, of exports, of balance of payments deficits and of inflation have predictive power. A similar approach has been applied to five industrialized and 15 developing countries for the period between 1970 and 1995 by Kaminsky and Reinhart (1999) and Kaminsky et al. (1998). Here it is found that exports, the real exchange rate, the ratio of money supply to official reserves, and price indices have predictive power with respect to currency crises. Further, Corsetti et al. (1998) and Kaminsky and Reinhart (1999) find that banking crises often precedes currency crises. Corsetti et al. (1998) proxy the stability of the banking sector by the bad loan ratio, whereas Kaminsky and Reinhart (1999) rely on similar macroeconomic indicators for banking crises as for currency crises. Finally, Eichengreen et al. (1995) find evidence of contagion effects as the likelihood of a currency crisis occurring increases when a crisis has occurred elsewhere.

How valuable are the empirical studies in predicting crises? Berg and Pattillo (1998) analyse three studies, Kaminsky et al. (1998), Frankel and Rose (1996) and Sachs et al. (1996) assess their potential predictive power using the example of the Asian currency crisis. Frankel and Rose (1996) base their study on annual data from the IMF for more than 100 developing countries, which has the shortcomings that their crisis indicator cannot account for speculative attacks and that annual data are likely to miss short-term developments. Sachs et al. (1996) study macro-economic variables in 20 countries during the Mexican peso crisis. Since it is only based on one crisis and its global fall-out, albeit in a very detailed fashion, it may not be a suitable basis for predictions. Kaminsky et al. (1998) set out to find early warning signals for currency crises. Their research reviews 25 earlier studies on currency crises and identifies statistically significant indicators for crises. Consequently, 15 indicators (out of a possible 103) based on theoretical considerations and data availability are selected that are then used to find empirical regularities among 20 countries over the period from 1970 to 1995. Berg and Pattillo (1998) found that only the Kaminsky *et al.* (1998) approach could yield reasonable results.

There are two reasons why early warning signals are hard to find. First, empirical studies regarding financial crises appear to have limited success because adequate and timely data are not readily available, which is especially apparent in the studies on banking crises. Second, even if empirical research were successful in finding adequate indicators for looming crises, it is not clear whether policymakers could use this information to avoid a crisis. Early warning signals may simply inform policymakers of the unavoidable. If policymakers decide to use a particular early warning model, all market participants are likely to be aware of that. Hence, market participants are likely to act on the information early warning models provide, thereby leading to 'self-fulfilling prophecies'.

3 Is there an alternative?

The evidence of a link between greater deregulation and an increased frequency of financial crises suggests that more consideration should be given to possibilities of more financial market developments. In particular, domestic developments are favoured over the dependence on external capital flows in creating viable financial markets.

In fostering the local developments of stable financial systems, two issues are of importance. First, financial institutions need to receive priority over capital markets. Secondly, stable financial markets require public support, either in the form of prudent supervision and regulation or in the form of government subsidies.

Capital markets can provide some funds for investments, but their most important role lies in the transfer of ownership. The US equity market, arguably the world's most advanced capital market, has not been a net source of funds, but a net drain on funds since 1994 as the flow of funds statistics from the Board of Governors of the Federal Reserve system show. Obviously, smaller companies and start-ups have no or little access to capital markets and hence have to rely on financial intermediaries, such as banks, even more so than larger, more well-established firms.

Thus, most companies need to rely on banks and other external finance providers, such as venture capitalists, to a larger degree than on capital markets as a source of external funds. The example of the advanced economies suggests that in developing economies, the development of local finance providers needs to take priority over the development of deep and broad capital markets (UN 1999).

The development of stable financial institutions depends on public support. Particularly when financial markets are deregulated, regulatory and supervisory institutions need to be strengthened because of the increased possibilities for destabilizing, or even fraudulent, activities. Further, the development of alternative financial providers, such as credit unions, cooperative banks, savings banks or postal savings unions, can provide more funds without increasing financial fragility. Postal savings unions, for instance, played an important role in Japanese development by channelling the funds from large numbers of small deposits to large-scale development projects. These institutions, which can be restricted from engaging in speculative activities, can be used to stabilize the economy. However, because these institutions tend to serve a large number of small clients, their operations are costly. To be able to compete, especially if interest rates are deregulated, the higher costs of these institutions require public subsidies. Subsidies can come in the form of office space for postal savings unions, or in the form of tax credits. Credit unions in the USA, for instance, enjoy a tax-free status. Also, German savings banks are government guaranteed, which allows them to offer credit at below market rates.

The ability of a country to develop financial institutions and public policies to stabilize its financial markets is limited by a lack of capital controls and by entry into international agreements. For instance, in 1999, some aspects of the design of Germany's savings banking system were challenged under EU rules. Further, persistent government subsidies tend to be evaluated negatively by international capital markets. Hence, if a government decides to continue its subsidies, and if capital controls have been reduced, a country's sovereign bond ratings may be lower than otherwise, resulting in higher interest rates, and slower growth.

Financial market development consequently becomes a balancing act between the domestic development of financial institutions and the need to attract foreign capital. The public policy issue is then to determine which capital flows are desirable and which ones are not. The distinction between portfolio investment and foreign direct investment (FDI) is typically of considerable importance to such policy analysis.

Portfolio investment provides capital to the bond and stock markets from abroad. Whether portfolio investment increases the availability of new capital to firms depends on a number of factors. If, for example, foreign investors merely buy existing shares on the stock market, firms will not necessarily receive more funds. Further, if foreign investors purchase bonds there is not necessarily a control that prohibits firms from using these additional funds for their own speculative purposes. The fact that short-term portfolio investment, or 'hot money', has been found to be a significant determinant of financial crises suggests that these capital flows are unlikely to be allocated to productive uses. Hence, policies are required to slow down the flow of short-term portfolio investment and to encourage more long-term capital flows.

The Asian financial crisis during 1997 and 1998 refocused the attention of policy makers on capital controls. In particular, the unilateral imposition of strict capital controls by Malaysia in the fall of 1998 has served as a case study for the use of capital controls during currency crises (Ariyoshi et al. 2000) (see EAST ASIAN ECONOMIES). It is recognized that a country should have the right to control capital inflows and outflows if they are perceived as dangers to its economic stability.

Capital controls to slow short-term capital flows can take different forms. First, countries can impose so-called 'speed bumps' or minimum stay requirements. Under such requirements, international investors would be prohibited from withdrawing their funds prior to a pre-set time limit. Capital could only be withdrawn gradually, thereby ideally preventing a financial panic. Second, another approach is to adopt so-called 'Tobin taxes', or international capital transactions taxes, which would essentially levy a penalty on short-term capital withdrawal, while impacting longer-term capital mobility to a lesser degree. Chile's unremunerated reserve requirement (URR) that was in effect between June 1991 and September 1998 constituted an 'asymmetric Tobin tax' that was levied only on capital inflows. The URR was designed to make international loans with maturities of less than 90 days more expensive than loans with a greater maturity. Third, countries could also impose outright prohibitions of certain types of capital movements. For instance, countries can require that profits earned on foreign direct investments in a host economy are reinvested in that economy.

Comprehensive evaluations of the effectiveness of capital controls are rare. In a collection of 14 such country studies, Ariyoshi et al. (2000) provide a preliminary evaluation of the effectiveness of capital controls. They found that capital controls cannot substitute for sound macroeconomic policies; that no single measure can always be effective everywhere; that targeted controls leave sufficient room to be circumvented, and hence are likely to be less effective than comprehensive controls; and that the choice of controls is determined by the administrative capacity of a country. Further research on the applicability of these findings on a wider range of countries is needed.

Besides options to control short-term capital flows, policy makers have also focused their attention on attracting FDI. Some FDI includes the physical relocation of know-how and technology to the host economy. However, how much of the additional technology and transfer will benefit the local economy depends on national regulations of FDI. More specifically, wholly-owned subsidiaries are likely to guard their technological advantages very closely so as not to nurture competitors. In the case of joint ventures between foreign and local partners, such proprietary control is less likely to be the case. Public policies can encourage FDI that transfers technology to local producers. In some cases, foreign investors are required to partner with local businesses through limitations on the proportion of a local business that foreign residents can own, for example, no more than 49 per cent. Similarly, host economies can prohibit foreign residents from owning real estate.

4 Conclusion

Widespread internal and external deregulation of financial markets around the world has been linked to a rise in the frequency of financial crises. While financial liberalization often results in improved liquidity, a non-trivial share of the additional funds find their way into speculative projects rather than productive investments.

Greater volatility in global financial markets not only affects the respective economies if a crisis occurs, but also its trading partners. In particular, financial crises as signalled by rapidly devaluing currencies lead to a drop in domestic demand, to increasing import prices and to improving exports, thereby hurting businesses outside of export goods producing industries. Businesses in trading partner countries lose export markets and gain import competition, as exemplified by the widening of the US trade deficit to record levels in 1998 and 1999 in the wake of the Asian financial crisis.

Ensuring that financial deregulation does not increase the chance of financial crises requires better evaluation of economic trends and policies after liberalization. So far, economic research has had only very limited success in developing a set of 'early warning indicators' for currency crises. Further, research on banking crises, which have been found often to precede currency crises is even less developed, particularly because of the lack of adequate, timely and comprehensive data.

Alternatively, countries can consider different approaches to developing their financial systems. To be able to determine their own financial fates, countries need to recapture the leeway that is generally lost after external liberalization has come into effect. Countries can consider imposing capital controls and reshaping domestic financial institutions to insulate themselves from the drawbacks of liberalization.

CHRISTIAN WELLER
ECONOMIC POLICY INSTITUTE,
WASHINGTON, DC

Further reading

(References cited in the text marked *)

* Ariyoshi, A., K. Habermeier, B. Laurens, I. Otker-Robe, J.O. Canales-Kriljenko and A. Kirilenko (2000) *Country Experiences with the Use and Liberalization of Capital Controls*, forthcoming, Washington, DC: IMF. (A detailed study on the use of capital controls by fourteen emerging economies.)
* Berg, A. and C. Pattillo (1998) 'Are currency crises predictable? a test', IMF Working Paper #154/98. Washington, DC: IMF. (An evaluation of the usefulness of three previous studies in predicting the Asian financial crisis.)
* Blecker, R. (1999) *Taming Global Finance*, Washington, DC: Economic Policy Institute. (A critical assessment of the prevalent economic theories of the late 1990s as they apply to international finance, and as they are applied by the international financial institutions, such as the IMF and the World Bank.)
* Claessens, S., A. Demirgüç-Kunt and H. Huizinga (1998) 'How does foreign entry affect the domestic banking market?', Policy Research Working Paper #1918, Washington, DC: World Bank. (A comprehensive analysis of the performance of foreign and domestic banks after the entry of foreign banks based on company level data from the BankScope CD-ROM.)
* Corsetti, G., P. Pesenti and N. Roubini (1998) 'Fundamental determinants of the Asian crisis: a preliminary empirical assessment', mimeo, Yale University. (A detailed analysis of the determinants of the Asian financial crisis.)
* Demirgüç-Kunt, A. and E. Detragiache (1998) 'Financial liberalization and financial fragility', Policy Research Working Paper #1917, Washington, DC: World Bank. (An econometric analysis of the connection between liberalization and the frequency of crises, where the authors introduce a dummy for the time periods after liberalization. The liberalization dummy is a significant predictor of crises.)
* Eichengreen, B., A. Rose and C. Wyplosz (1995) 'Exchange market mayhem: the antecedents and aftermath of speculative attacks', *Economic Policy*, October: 251–312. (The seminal paper on the macroeconomic determinants of currency crises and speculative attacks. Using univariate and multivariate techniques, this study analyses the behaviour of real, financial and external variables during non-crises times, during times immediately before and right after a crisis.)

* Frankel, J. and A. Rose (1996) 'Currency crashes in emerging markets: an empirical treatment', *Journal of International Economics* 41: 351–66. (A preliminary analysis of the macroeconomic determinants of currency crises, similar to Eichengreen *et al.* (1995).)
* Grabel, I. (1993) 'Fast money, "noisy growth": a noise-led theory of development', *Review of Radical Political Economics* 25 (3): 1–8. (An application of Minsky's financial instability hypothesis to financial liberalization in developing economies. It is argued that greater liberalization results in more speculative investments and hence in more financial instability.)
  Grabel, I. (1998) '*Rejecting exceptionalism: reinterpreting the Asian financial crises*', in J. Michie and J. Grieve Smith (eds) *Global Instability and World Economic Governance*, London: Routledge. (Provides a detailed analysis of the structural macroeconomic causes of the crises in Mexico, South East Asia, and Latin America between 1995 and 1998.)
* Kaminsky, G., and C. Reinhart (1999) 'The twin crises: the causes of banking and balance-of-payments problems', *American Economic Review* 89 (3): 473–500. (The seminal paper on the macroeconomic determinants of currency and banking crises. The methodology used here is based on Eichengreen *et al.* (1995). The study's value lies in the comparison between currency and banking crises.)
* Kaminsky, G., S. Lizondo and C. Reinhart (1998) 'Leading indicators of currency crises', *IMF Staff Papers*, 45 (1). (A comprehensive survey of prior studies on indicators of currency crises.)
* Lindgren, C., G. Garcia and M. Saal (1996) *Bank Soundness and Macroeconomic Policy*, Washington, DC: International Monetary Fund. (A comprehensive study on banking sector problems in IMF member countries between 1980 and 1996. The study's value lies in its definition and identification of banking crises and banking sector problems.)
* Minsky, H. (1986) *Stabilizing an Unstable Economy, A Twentieth Century Fund Report*, New Haven and London: Yale University Press. (A detailed discussion of the application of Minsky's financial instability hypothesis to the US economy in the early 1980s.)
* Rothstein, J. and R. Scott (1998) 'American jobs and the Asian crisis', EPI Briefing Paper, January, Washington, DC: Economic Policy Institute. (This paper – written early in the Asian financial crisis – presents estimates of the possible impact of the crisis on US manufacturing jobs. Based on official statistics, increase in the trade deficit of $100 billion should result in a job loss of 750,000. The trade deficit rose by $182 billion and manufacturing jobs declined by 400,000 between March 1998 and March 1999.)
* Sachs, J., A. Tornell and A. Velasco (1996) 'Financial crises in emerging markets: the lessons from 1995', *Brookings Papers on Economic Activity* 1: 147–215. (A detailed analysis of the Mexican peso crisis and its global fall-out.)
* Stiglitz, J. (1994) 'The role of the state in financial markets', in M. Bruno and B. Pleskovic (eds) *Proceedings of the World Bank Annual Conference on Development Economics, 1993*, (Supplement to *The World Bank Economic Review* and *The World Bank Research Observer*.) Washington, DC: World Bank. (An application of asymmetric information theory to financial markets. This paper argues that there is a significant role for the state in financial markets due to information asymmetries inherent in financial markets.)
* UN (1999) *World Economic and Social Survey 1999*, New York: United Nations. (A comprehensive overview and evaluation of the financial market issues facing developing and transition economies.)
* Weller, C. (1999) 'Financial crises after financial liberalization: exceptional circumstances or structural weakness?', Center for European Integration Studies Working Paper B99-15, University of Bonn, Germany, September. (An econometric analysis of structural changes before and after financial liberalization and their impact on financial stability in emerging economies. This study uses the methodology introduced in Eichengreen *et al.* (1995), and applies it to both currency and banking crises and evaluates the possibility of structural differences before and after liberalization, rather than to rely on a dummy variable approach as Demirgüç-Kunt and Detragiache (1998) do.)

See also: EAST ASIAN ECONOMIES; ECONOMIC INTEGRATION, INTERNATIONAL; EXCHANGE RATE ECONOMICS; INTERNATIONAL MONETARY FUND; KEYNES, J.M.; MONEY AND CAPITAL MARKETS, INTERNATIONAL; WORLD BANK; WORLD TRADE ORGANIZATION)

Money and capital markets, international

1 Introduction
2 Efforts to open foreign markets to financial services trade: 1978–2000
3 *Tour d'horizon* of international capital markets
4 Conclusion

Overview

In the years following World War II, international capital mobility was limited, and much of the capital that did cross international boundaries was government-related or related to economic development loans or grants by international financial institutions such as the World Bank. Fifty years hence at the beginning of the new millennium, international capital mobility has grown to huge proportions and private flows dwarf official flows. In another reversal in this same period of time, international capital transactions today far exceed international trade in goods. Factors underlying these sweeping changes include: deregulation of exchange and capital controls at the national level; technological progress which has greatly increased the scope, product variety and speed of financial services trade; and the tremendous growth of emerging market economies which has extended markets and increased demand for international financing.

The economic effects on income, growth and efficient resource allocation resulting from this pronounced trend toward liberalization of financial services trade are distinctly positive, despite some financial crises during the 1990s that were disruptive for the countries involved.

This entry reviews the sustained and substantially successful efforts during the period 1978–2000 to open domestic financial markets to increased international activity on a nondiscriminatory or *national treatment* basis. During the 1960s–80s, growth in international capital activity was most pronounced in the banking sector. During the 1990s, growth in the securities sector moved ahead of banking, reflecting the particularly strong performance of international securities and derivatives transactions. The importance of the insurance sector has been greatest in industrial countries to date but international insurance activity is expected to show strong growth in middle-income countries as they become richer.

1 Introduction

This entry is divided into two main sections. First, it discusses the sustained US effort to open foreign financial markets to US financial institutions during the closing decades of the twentieth century at a time when the presence and importance of foreign financial institutions operating in US financial markets was growing rapidly. This US effort was carried out simultaneously at different levels: bilateral negotiations with a wide range of countries; regionally in such contexts as the North American Free Trade Agreement; and internationally in the General Agreement on Trade in Services.

The second part of the entry provides a brief *tour d'horizon* of selected financial markets around the world, both major markets in industrial countries, and the increasingly important, rapidly growing financial markets in emerging market economies. These financial market summaries include notable recent developments, the state of openness achieved, and key challenges to be faced in the future. The focus of both parts of the entry is primarily on international banking and securities markets.

2 Efforts to open foreign markets to financial services trade: 1978–2000

The modern-day origins of international trade in financial services lie in the 1960s and 1970s with the recognized phenomenon of increasing economic interdependence between economies and the increasingly rapid expansion of world trade relative to GDP growth. US banks had been significantly expanding their foreign operations and, with only slight delay, foreign banks were opening offices in the US or expanding already-established operations. The immediate rationale in both cases was to be available locally to serve home-country corporate clients who were expanding trade and services relationships in various parts of the globe.

International banking activity

As the foreign bank presence in the US increased, the competitive impact on the domestic banking industry became an issue because foreign banks were not accountable to the same regulatory and supervisory rules as domestic banks. That anomaly led Congress to enact legislation known as the *International Banking Act of 1978* (IBA). This law established a regulatory structure for foreign bank agencies and branches as part of a general *policy of national treatment*, the purpose of which was to promote competitive equality between domestic and foreign banking entities. (At the time of the IBA's enactment, there were approximately 120 foreign banks operating in the US with total assets of some $90 billion.)

The IBA provided six major changes in existing law and regulation. First, the IBA limited interstate deposit-taking activities of foreign banks in the same way domestic banks were constrained from engaging in such activity. Second, like domestic banks, foreign banks were offered the opportunity of seeking a federal licence or a state licence. Third, the Federal Reserve was empowered to impose reserve requirements on foreign banks in the US, just as it had been doing for domestic banks. Fourth, branches of foreign banks engaged in retail deposit taking were obliged to carry deposit insurance just as domestic banks had to do. Fifth, Edge Corporations engaging in banking were given broader powers to compete with foreign bank agencies and branches in the US, and foreign banks were allowed to own Edge Corporations. (Edge Corporations are federally and state-chartered corporations that are permitted to engage in a range of banking and investment activities outside the US, but whose US activities are limited to activities that are incidental to its international or foreign business.) Sixth, foreign banks in the US were obliged to follow the non-bank prohibitions of the Bank Holding Company Act just as domestic banks. Finally, Congress required the Administration to submit reports to Congress on a range of policy issues affecting domestic and foreign bank activity in the US and abroad.

The Reports that Congress mandated in the IBA provided timely, periodic reviews by the Administration and Congress over the next twenty years about the competitive problems and issues between US and foreign financial institutions in domestic and foreign financial markets. The first such Report in 1979 examined the extent to which US banks were granted or denied national treatment in conducting banking operations in 140 countries. The 1979 Report found that US banks had a substantial degree of access to most financial markets abroad of importance to them (both in terms of initial entry and powers they could exercise once entry had been accomplished), but that such treatment accorded to US and other foreign banks varied significantly from country to country. This treatment ranged from relatively free and open regulatory environments in most developed nations to quite restrictive conditions in some emerging market economies.

Japan was by far the most notable exception among developed countries. Its banks were the most aggressive of all foreign banks in terms of increasing their presence and market shares of banking activity in the US, while US banks encountered one difficulty after another in trying to enter and penetrate Japan's banking market. Soon after entering office in 1981, the Reagan Administration initiated bilateral talks with Japan aimed at remedying barriers to entry and participation in Japan's banking and financial markets. (Those talks, called *Yen–Dollar Talks*, continued to be held regularly through the Bush and Clinton Administra- tions.) Also of concern, however, were a number of emerging market economies in Latin America and Asia whose banking and financial markets were essentially closed to US and other foreign financial institutions.

The next Report to Congress in 1984 observed that foreign banks had more than doubled their presence in the US since the first report. At the same time, US banks had similarly extended their presence in overseas markets, and had expressed a desire to participate more actively in certain other countries whose international economic importance and financial sophistication had been growing rapidly. The report found that there had been improvement in the degree of national treatment received by US banks abroad during the five years since enactment of the IBA, but that substantial areas of discrimination against US firms continued to exist. Among developed countries, Japan was again the focal point of major concern, even though it had agreed to reduce or eliminate various barriers aimed at foreign financial institutions. (It was like peeling back a layer of an onion; other barriers were discovered to lie beneath the one that had just been resolved.) Other developed countries, notably Canada, Finland and Spain, had agreed to reduce some of their barriers to foreign bank activity, while more substantial improvements were realized by Norway and Portugal. The 1984 Report documented small improvements in opening banking sectors in India, Philippines, Taiwan and Thailand while noting that significant barriers to US bank entry in Brazil, Mexico and Venezuela remained unchanged.

Increasing international securities markets activity

The third Report to Congress appeared in 1986. Importantly, this report covered for the first time other segments of the financial services industry besides the banking sector, most notably securities markets and electronic funds transfer systems. While the report found evidence of further progress in opening foreign markets, there was also evidence of continued discriminatory treatment in several cases, including particularly in Japan.

In 1988, Congress mandated that the Administration provide a *National Treatment Study* every four years to both Houses of Congress regarding the foreign treatment of US financial institutions. The *1990 National Treatment Study* expanded its country coverage to include twenty-one banking and eighteen securities markets. Progress in opening various markets had occurred, but not to the extent desired by the Administration or Congress. With respect to Japan, ongoing bilateral negotiations produced some modest improvements in regulation. While Japan was found to provide *de jure* national treatment for foreign banks, the fact remained that foreign banks had been unable to gain more than a very minor share of traditional banking business — that is, *de facto* national treatment continued to be a problem. (On the other hand, foreign banks had been more successful in certain Japanese market niches, such as foreign exchange-related and fee-based activities.) With respect to securities markets, Japan had by this point become one of the world's largest. But as was the case in Japan's banking sector, foreign financial institutions confronted multiple barriers that kept their level of participation in Japanese securities markets far below participation levels they had already achieved in other foreign markets. Meanwhile, Japanese financial institutions (banks, securities firms and insurance companies) continued their rapid growth and penetration of US financial markets.

The 1990 National Treatment Study went on to note significant improvements in Canada and in many European countries. Progress in emerging market countries in Latin America and in Asia, however, continued to be very slow. The Administration, with Treasury in the lead, pledged to pursue vigorously its efforts to remove still-existing obstacles to national treatment for US financial firms operating abroad. These efforts were occurring bilaterally with several developed and emerging market economies, and multi-laterally in various forums, including the Organization for Economic Cooperation and Development, the World Bank and the International Monetary Fund.

By the time of the *1990 National Treatment Study*, the number of foreign banks in the US had climbed to 284 with total assets of $580 billion, or just under 20 per cent of all US banking assets. Foreign participation in the securities industry, including futures markets, and the insurance industry was reported to be expanding rapidly, as well.

Such continued growth in foreign banking presence in the US led to enactment in 1991 of the *Foreign Bank Supervision Enhancement Act*. The law was designed to fill certain gaps in the supervision and regulation of foreign banks by giving a stronger role to the Federal Reserve Board, and it sought to ensure that US banking policies would be implemented in a fair and consistent manner with respect to both domestic and foreign financial institutions. The Act required Federal Reserve approval for the establishment of both state-licensed and federally licensed branches and agencies. It limited the permissible activities of state-licensed branches and agencies to the activities permitted for federally licensed branches. It imposed new restrictions on deposit taking by foreign banks. Finally, the law mandated studies by the Treasury and the Fed to look into and compare capital standards applicable to foreign banks operating in the US and the risk-based capital requirements applicable to US banks.

Tensions between the US and Japan

At the beginning of the 1990s, frustration with Japan was running very high owing to its continued delay in providing foreign financial institutions with effective market access to its domestic financial markets. These feelings gave rise to a bipartisan legislative proposal known as the *Fair Trade in Financial Services Act* (FTFS) that would remain under active consideration in Congress through the end of 1994. The purpose of the legislation was to give the Treasury Secretary more leverage to negotiate financial market-opening agreements with other countries (starting first and foremost with Japan) which were found not to extend national treatment to US firms in their domestic markets. The specific leverage provided (after negotiations had first been tried) was to grant the Treasury Secretary authority to deny permission for any further expansion in US operations by foreign financial institutions of the offending country. Although there was a lot of support for the legislation, indeed at least at one point its enactment appeared imminent, opposition by the Federal Reserve Board and by the Bush and Clinton Administrations prevailed and it was never enacted.

In 1993, President Clinton asked Congress to hold off further consideration of FTFS while it pursued financial services negotiations under the Uruguay Round of trade negotiations. By the end of 1993, however, when it appeared that those negotiations would not yield a satisfactory agreement with regard to financial services (known as General Agreement on Trade in Services (GATS)), the Clinton Administration reversed its position and sent a signal to Congress to go ahead and reintroduce the FTFS legislation. The Administration believed it could use FTFS legislation as a 'club' to prod other countries to be more forthcoming on offers of commitments to market access than they had been in 1993, and that eventually a satisfactory GATS Agreement could be reached. Throughout 1994 expectations remained high that the legislation would finally pass Congress, but it was not to be. (Fed opposition, jurisdiction disputes between congressional committees, and disputes about details of the bill were the main causes.)

Although FTFS never became law, its serious consideration by Congress and the continued threat of enactment accomplished many of its intended objectives. In February 1995, the US Treasury and the Japanese Ministry of Finance signed a bilateral Financial Services Agreement under the US–Japan Framework for a New Economic Partnership as the latest step in a fifteen-year series of discussions on liberalization in financial services. This and other steps taken by Japanese authorities to deregulate financial markets and permit foreign financial firms to participate in domestic markets, when taken over a five- or ten-year period, were quite significant. (A further indication of Japan's intentions followed in late 1996 when the Japanese government announced its *Big Bang* financial liberalization initiative.) Partly because it moved slowly and grudgingly to open its financial markets, however, Japan received less credit than it deserved. It is also true that Japan's penetration of US financial markets reached its high water mark by the mid-1990s. The bursting of the country's 'asset bubble' in 1989 was followed by protracted economic and financial problems domestically that lingered for the entire decade of the 1990s. These woes forced Japanese financial institutions to retrench from markets around the world. Particularly in the latter half of the 1990s, Japanese retrenchment from US financial markets had become so apparent that US anxiety over Japan's domination of global economic and financial markets subsided and in fact it is no longer actively discussed.

The *National Treatment Study of 1994* was the acme in this twenty-year series of reports to Congress. Well over 700 pages in length, it reported on the banking sectors in 34 countries and the securities markets for 32 countries. It also reported in detail on the Uruguay Round of financial services negotiations and the 1994 North American Free Trade Agreement (NAFTA) which included the financial services sectors for the three member countries. Despite many improvements as a result of bilateral, regional and multilateral negotiations, the 1994 Report insisted that the lack of national treatment and lack of equality of competitive opportunity was still too prevalent in too many markets commercially important for US financial institutions. Foreign penetration and participation in the US banking market, however, was found to be levelling out, while foreign penetration and growth in the securities and insurance sectors was rising. As of mid-1994, 288 foreign banks from 60 countries were active in the US and accounted for $872 billion in assets or about one-fifth of the US total.

The *National Treatment Study of 1998* was more modest in length and country coverage compared to the 1994 Study. However, the 1998 Study struck a more positive tone than any previous Reports to Congress in terms of the observed ability of US financial firms to compete in offering financial services abroad. In particular, the report noted the successful conclusion of a financial services agreement under the *General Agreement on Trade in Services* (GATS) in December 1997. This was the first such agreement of its kind and it encompassed all financial services sectors (banking, securities, insurance, asset management, and advisory services). The final agreement involved a significantly broader range of countries and included substantially improved market access and national treatment commitments compared to those in the interim agreement of 1995. (The Uruguay Round of negotiations was originally due to end in 1993, but the GATS part of the negotiations was extended twice, finally ending in December 1997. The agreement was ratified in January 1999.) As of the end of 1999, there were 102 World Trade Organization (WTO) member countries with financial services commitments accounting for over 95 per cent of world trade in financial services as measured by revenues. (The WTO is the successor organization to the General Agreement on Tariffs and Trade, which was established after World War II to promote more liberal world trade.) The 1998 Report stated that much of the importance of the GATS accord lies in its making these national treatment commitments legally enforceable through the World Trade Organization's dispute settlement procedures. The 1997 GATS Agreement is the beginning of a multilateral process to liberalize global trade in services. Another round GATS negotiations began in 2000.

The *1998 National Treatment Study* reported that 271 foreign banks were operating in the US in that year and that their assets of $2.1 trillion were about 20 per cent of total US banking assets. Retrenchment by Japanese banks continued to be an important factor. Foreign participation in US securities and insurance markets continued to expand.

3 *Tour d'horizon* of international capital markets

Major markets

In the *European Union* (EU), creation of a single banking market among the fifteen member states continues to be a work in progress more than ten years after member country authorities first made that commitment. Any bank established in a member country has a 'passport' to provide banking services through local branches or across borders through the EU. (Foreign bank subsidiaries in any EU member state are accorded national treatment.) Each bank is regulated by the authorities of its home country and may provide financial products permitted by those home-country regulators throughout the EU. Differences in bank regulation and supervision and different national tax structures, however, have prevented the achievement of a single market. The decision to do away with national currencies by six EU member states and adopt the *euro* (implementation of which began in 1999 and is due to be completed by mid-2002), together with on-going efforts by the European Commission to bring greater harmony to financial services operations within the EU, should help the EU draw closer to its single banking market objective over time.

With regard to securities services, the EU is also attempting to create a single market, and to date there has been more progress in this area than in banking services. The impact of the euro has already proven to be quite significant, particularly in fixed income markets. Taking EU securities markets together, they are larger than Japan's but smaller than those of the US. The potential for future equity growth in European securities markets is considered to be excellent in view of several factors: the presence of large, unfunded pension liabilities, a steadily ageing population, low interest rates, growing national economies, and the fact that Europe's equity markets have considerable catching up to do before they reach a level comparable to markets in the US or Japan.

Japan's financial sector has been buffeted during the 1990s by the country's protracted economic stagnation, by a huge accumulation of non-performing loans, and by numerous scandals involving several domestic securities firms. Japan's large city banks have been forced to retrench from markets overseas. Although Japan provides *de jure* national treatment to foreign banks, foreign banks are marginal players in most segments of the domestic market. This results from a combination of the country's particular regulatory environment, its exclusionary business practices, and the fact that Japan is overbanked. Foreign acquisition of a Japanese bank is occurring for the first time in early 2000, thus marking a break in long-standing Japanese practice. In this case, the Japanese institution needed a bailout from government and also needed to be taken over by another, more healthy entity. The offer from the foreign financial bidder was apparently far stronger than bids from domestic financial institutions.

Japan's securities markets have traditionally been heavily regulated and compartmentalized; but a series of small changes are having cumulative effects that will become increasingly apparent in the future. For example, there have been a series of bilateral agreements with the US that have liberalized portions of the financial services sector, such as pension funds, and many restrictions on cross-border capital transactions have been removed. The *Big Bang* deregulation initiative of 1996 has brought about other important changes, but Japan's continued poor economic performance continues to cast a long shadow over financial markets. Finally, some significant consolidation among Japanese financial institutions will alter the size, composition and competitiveness of players in the industry.

United States financial markets are the largest, most open, most innovative in the world. Foreign participation has been extensive for years because of the international role of the US dollar and because foreign financial institutions wanted to be available locally to serve their home-country corporations which had established a US presence in order to serve the large and growing economy. US policy in financial services grants *national treatment* to foreign financial institutions. This means they are given *equal competitive opportunity* with domestic financial institutions. Foreign financial institutions wishing to establish a US bank operation may choose among a variety of options. The dual banking system provides opportunity for a federal or state licence; then there are several other options relating to the form of establishment, such as a branch or agency, a representative office, an Edge Corporation or an Agreement Corporation subsidiary. (An Agreement Corporation is similar to an Edge Corporation defined earlier.) Foreign bank operations in the US are large both in size (over $1 trillion in assets) and in market share (approximately 25 per cent of total assets of the commercial banking system). *The Interstate Banking Law of 1994* established a federal framework for interstate banking and branching for both domestic and foreign banks. The *Financial Modernization Act of 1999* permits commercial banks (including foreign banks) to affiliate with investment banks, insurance companies, and other kinds of financial services firms.

US securities laws provide national treatment to foreign brokers, dealers and investment advisers. Foreign issuers are generally subject to the same registration and reporting requirements as US issuers. The federal regulator, the Securities and Exchange Commission (SEC), has taken some steps in recent years to simplify access by foreign firms and issuers to US securities markets. Protection of US investors, however, remains a paramount objective of the SEC, and so disclosure requirements and accounting standards are rigorous. A dual securities system exists in the US. Besides the federal regulatory scheme, individual states have their own securities laws (referred to as 'blue sky' laws) and most require that broker-dealers and non-SEC registered investment advisers active in the state register with that state. Forms for state registration are generally the same as the forms for registration under federal securities laws. Foreign participation in US securities markets of all types is extensive and has grown considerably in recent years.

Emerging markets – Asia-Pacific

China's banking system is still heavily affected by the legacy of the old planned economy. State-owned banks account for a large share of the market; loans have traditionally been politically directed. Many state-owned banks face financial difficulty to one degree or another because of outstanding problem loans to unprofitable state-owned enterprises. China has begun to restructure its supervisory framework for financial institutions. Authorities are gradually opening the market to foreign banks but many restrictions continue to exist with respect to entry and the activities they are allowed to engage in. The agreement between the US and China on trade and services, reached at the start of 2000, is part of a plan to make China a member of the World Trade Organization, and it will lead to the relaxation of China's barriers to participation by foreign financial institutions over time. China's securities markets are in the very early stages of development. The regulatory structure is still taking shape and foreign participation at this juncture is very much restrained.

Hong Kong is now a Special Administrative Region of China but its monetary and financial regulatory structure remains autonomous. Hong Kong not only acts as a major gateway for China's trade and finance with the rest of the world, but it is also a regional financial centre second in size and significance only to Japan. Foreign banks regard Hong Kong as one of the most open, most transparent banking markets in the world. The Hong Kong Stock Exchange ranked among the ten largest exchanges in the world as the 1990s drew to a close. Operation and regulation of Hong Kong's securities markets meet high standards. Foreign participation has been active and extensive for years. While Hong Kong did suffer significantly from the Asian financial crisis, its financial markets survived intact and devaluation of its currency, which is pegged to the US dollar, was successfully resisted.

Korea was affected to a major extent by the Asian financial crisis in 1997–98. A reform programme with the International Monetary Fund and other international financial institutions was agreed to that required a number of broad-based financial reforms. Some of these reforms are still being implemented in 2000. Several domestic commercial banks were taken over by the government and other troubled banks were acquired by more healthy institutions. The government used large amounts of resources to help dispose of non-performing loans and to recapitalize weak financial institutions. Prudential regulation and supervision have been consolidated and strengthened; banks are now operating more openly and transparently than before. In 1999, the real economy recovered more rapidly than anticipated, and this may have taken away some of the urgency for swiftly completing Korea's financial reform commitments. Liberalization of foreign exchange and capital flows is taking place in stages and is due to be completed by the end of 2000. Foreign banks in Korea still face a variety of competitive barriers. As is the case in several emerging market countries, foreign bank funding and lending operations are tied to capital of the local branch rather than that of the parent company. Korea's securities markets are also changing in fundamental ways and specific changes are linked to the IMF programme. Government manipulation of equity markets has ended and supervisory authority for the securities industry now rests with a new, independent commission. Foreign participation in securities markets has been liberalized and is becoming more active.

Singapore's banking sector has traditionally been divided into two markets: a large, competitive offshore market with extensive foreign participation, and a domestic market that is over-banked and protected from foreign competition. The former has become quite active on a regional basis. In 1999, the Monetary Authority of Singapore began to implement a five-year plan designed to liberalize and open the domestic banking market to foreign competition. As a result, the dichotomy between these two markets will diminish over time. Singapore is actively pursuing the goal of making its debt and equity markets important to neighbouring countries in the Asia region. Steps are under way to encourage a deeper, more liquid government securities market. Domestic and foreign bond issuers are being courted with tax incentives to help develop the bond market. Other initiatives are being taken to modernize and expand the attractiveness of Singapore's equity and derivative markets. Singapore weathered the Asian financial crisis better than most countries, thanks in large part to its sound financial system.

Emerging markets – Europe

As the banking sector in the *Czech Republic* developed during the 1990s, the presence and activity of foreign banks grew rapidly and accounted for about one-quarter of all bank assets at the end of the decade. The government has continued to hold near majority interest in two large banks but a privatization process is under way. The government has also been moving toward stricter supervision of banks and simplified bankruptcy laws; these initiatives will help resolve non-performing loans and will help improve the banking sector's performance. Securities markets are still in the early stages of development. The short-term bond market and the derivatives market have been growing rapidly. The government is working to strengthen its laws and regulations pertaining to securities markets. The government does not restrict the establishment of foreign securities firms and foreign investors are allowed to purchase Czech equities. Foreign securities firms are present in the country and account for about one-third of the current membership in the Prague Stock Exchange. Other foreign financial firms have chosen to engage in various cross-border transactions rather than establish a physical presence in the Czech domestic stock market.

During the latter 1990s, *Poland* undertook a series of steps to reform and modernize its financial sector. Privately owned banks grew rapidly in size and market share, and foreign banks played an increasing role, especially by providing more competition through their better products and services. Supervision of banks has been much improved and a deposit insurance scheme has been implemented. Poland provides *national treatment* to foreign banks. Poland's securities markets have been rebuilt since communist rule ended. Among the various types of securities markets, the equities and Treasury bills markets are the most active. Poland grants *national treatment* to foreign firms wishing to engage in issuance and trading of securities.

Development and modernization of *Russia*'s financial sector has proceeded in fits and starts since communist rule ended in 1989. The collapse of the financial system in August 1998 amounted to a major setback in terms of progress that had been made up to that point. Although more than one year has passed since the crisis unfolded, banking and securities markets have not yet stabilized completely; it is uncertain how soon Russia will be able to resume efforts to liberalize its financial sector. Foreign banks and securities firms have engaged in a variety of activities in Russia, and some of them suffered very sizeable losses in the financial collapse of 1998.

Emerging markets – Latin America

Argentina's banking sector has experienced substantial change during the 1990s. Mergers and acquisitions, including several by foreign banks, privatization and liquidations have reduced the number of financial institutions by more than 50 per cent compared to 1990. Government-owned banks still exist and have a monopoly on public deposits. The securities market is relatively small compared to the banking sector because corporations tend to raise capital primarily through bank loans. The bond market is dominated by public sector issues. The mutual fund and private capital pension fund markets have been growing rapidly. There are no market access restrictions or capital controls in Argentina.

The *Brazilian* government permitted substantial foreign bank entry and expansion during the 1990s. Such government decisions, however, often entailed some form of toll on the foreign bank as the price of entry or expansion. The state banking system has been undergoing privatization and market activity by private sector banks has been increasing. Nevertheless, public sector banks continue to play an important role. The Sao Paulo Stock Exchange, the largest of Brazil's nine exchanges and also the largest in Latin America, has been growing rapidly in terms of volume and share appreciation. The government has been easing regulations to facilitate foreign portfolio investment, and net inflows, reflecting these changes, rose dramatically in the 1990s.

Mexico's financial sector has been strongly influenced by the NAFTA and by changes instituted in response to the country's 1994–95 financial crisis. Foreign financial affiliates have been allowed to engage in the full range of banking activities subject to some exceptions and market share restrictions which Mexico terminated as planned at the beginning of 2000. NAFTA opened the Mexican securities market to US and Canadian firms, and currently, foreign investment accounts for about 30 per cent of the market capitalization of Mexico's securities exchange, known as Bolsa. Mexico's financial crisis in the mid-1990s accelerated consolidation as a number of mergers and alliances occurred between domestic and foreign banks and there were several cases of direct government intervention to deal with the banking crisis. The tendency for Mexico's financial sector to liberalize and become more international in scope is continuing, as evidenced by a free trade agreement between Mexico and the EU in early 2000, which includes trade in financial services.

4 Conclusion

The growth of international money and capital markets during the closing decades of the twentieth century has been spectacular. Financial markets in industrial countries and in an ever-expanding number of emerging market economies are more open than ever before. The increasingly diverse financial activities offered in those markets contribute positively to growth in income and to growth in economic activity generally in all countries.

Despite important achievements in regard to the liberalization of international financial markets and to the provision of financial services across national borders, many problems remain to be addressed. One set of problems concerns emerging market economies that are lining up to join the World Trade Organization and want to participate more actively in the international economic community. How and at what pace should these countries open their financial markets to foreign competition? What ancillary steps are needed to minimize the risk of disruptions in their financial markets and economies as the liberalization process is realized? Another set of problems follows from recent financial crises during the latter 1990s in Asia, Latin America and Europe (mainly Russia). International discussions have been taking place in order to establish the origins of these crises and to identify steps and procedures nationally and internationally that can be taken to minimize their possible repetition. Stronger regulation and supervision of banks and other financial institutions, improved accounting standards and simplified bankruptcy laws are some of the main elements. Finally, the GATS 2000 negotiations will aim at further liberalization in financial services trade on a multilateral basis. The issues involved, like the nature of international financial activity today, are increasingly complex; they cut across national regulatory regimes and raise questions of prudential safeguards and potential systemic risk to the international system itself.

WILBUR MONROE
US TREASURY DEPARTMENT

Note

Mr Monroe is an International Economist at the US Department of Treasury. He is Deputy Director for the Office of International Banking and Securities Markets. The views and opinions in this article are solely those of the author and do not necessarily reflect those of the Treasury Department or any of its officials.

Further reading

Department of the Treasury (1990, 1994, 1998) 'National Treatment Study – Report to Congress on Foreign Treatment of US Financial Institutions', Washington, DC: US Government Printing Office. (Examines the degree of national treatment afforded US financial institutions in various banking and securities markets overseas, and the treatment of foreign financial institutions operating in the US.)

Dobson, W. and Jacquet, P. (1998) *Financial Services Liberalization in the WTO*, Washington, DC: Institute for International Economics. (Evaluates the 1997 WTO financial services agreement; includes case studies of financial systems in emerging market countries.)

Institute of International Bankers (various years, 1997, 1998, 1999) 'Global Survey – Regulatory and Market Developments: Banking, Securities, Insurance', New York: Institute of International Bankers. (An annual survey of economic and regulatory trends in financial markets around the world by a trade association of over 200 banking organizations that operate in the US and have their headquarters in 50 other countries.)

International Monetary Fund (Annual) 'International capital markets: Developments, prospects, and key policy issues', *World Economic and Financial Surveys*, Washington, DC. (Reviews developments and trends in a large number of the world's capital markets and banking systems.)

Key, S.J. (1997) 'Financial services in the Uruguay Round of the WTO', *Group of Thirty Occasional Papers*, 54, Washington, DC. (Discusses and analyses the significance and scope of the General Agreement on Trade in Services, which was negotiated in the Uruguay Round of Trade Negotiations.)

Key, S.J. (2000) 'GATS 2000: Issues for the financial services negotiations', *Series of Sectoral Studies on Trade in Services*, Washington, DC: American Enterprise Institute. (Analyses issues on the agenda for the GATS 2000 negotiations.)

Key, S.J. and Brundy, J.M. (1979) 'Implementation of the International Banking Act', *Federal Reserve Bulletin* October: 785–96. (Describes foreign bank activity in the US and analyses provisions of the International Banking Act.)

Kono, M. *et al.* (1997) 'Opening markets in financial services and the role of GATS', *World Trade Organization Special Studies*, Geneva. (Considers the role of GATS in financial services liberalization.)

Misback, A.E. (1993) 'The Foreign Bank Supervision Enhancement Act of 1991', *Federal Reserve Bulletin January*: 1–10. (Explains the purpose and provisions of the law.)

Organization for Economic Cooperation and Development (2000) 'Cross-border trade in financial services: economics and regulation', *Financial Market Trends*, Paris, France. (Examines the economic and regulatory aspects of cross-border trade in financial services, that is, the provision of financial services by a firm located in one country to a customer residing in another country.)

Economic integration, international

1 Introduction
2 Specific forms of international economic integration
3 Particular features of the integration process
4 The process of economic integration
5 Other aspects of integration

Overview

Regional economic integration can be viewed in terms of a hierarchy of arrangements which extend from the preferential tariff agreement to the free trade area, the customs union, the common market and, in the extreme case, the economic union. The latter is now frequently described as economic and monetary union.

Various economic benefits are said to arise from the removal of internal tariff and quota barriers to trade in goods between the partner economies, although some protection from import competition from third countries will remain. Further integration benefits arise from the removal of protective devices generally referred to as non-tariff barriers. Higher beneficial forms of integration would depend on the removal of internal obstacles to trade between the partners in services. A common market involves an attack on mainly government-inspired regulations which impede the free cross-frontier flow of services of production, that is, labour, professional persons, capital and business enterprise.

The highest form of economic integration is economic and monetary union. This does not just involve the removal of inter-state barriers to the free movement of goods and services, but also extends the integration process to monetary and fiscal matters. At a minimum such additional macroeconomic arrangements involve a system of fixed exchange rates between participating national currencies; at a maximum they imply the introduction of a single unified currency and national fiscal systems. Such an extension of integration carries with it additional economic benefits, as well as a further erosion of national economic sovereignty. The decision-making structures associated with the specific economic integration policies now in place in various parts of the world economy vary widely from highly centralized and administratively well-supported systems to those which exhibit considerable decentralization and minimal bureaucracy. Theorists of integration speculate that economic integration can spill over into political integration; the European Union is a classic case of the latter process at work.

1 Introduction

While international economic integration is not a new phenomenon, as witnessed by the German *Zollverein* in the nineteenth century, there is no evidence of the term being used in economic analysis prior to 1942. International economic integration denotes a state of affairs, or a process, involving the combination of previously separate national economies into larger economic arrangements. A distinction needs to be made between overall international economic integration via the General Agreement on Tariffs and Trade (GATT) and regional integration. It is the regional variety, with its attendant element of discrimination against third countries, which is the focus of this analysis.

One way of achieving the integration of previously separate national economies is to eliminate barriers to the flow of goods, services, factors of production (that is, labour, the professions, capital and business enterprise) and money between the constituent states. International economic integration goes beyond the conclusion of mere international cooperation agreements, although such acts of cooperation may be part of a larger scheme of economic unification.

2 Specific forms of international economic integration

The least demanding form of international economic integration is the preferential tariff agreement. In such an arrangement, the countries involved reduce but do not undertake to eliminate totally their import tariffs (customs duties) on the trade in goods flowing between them; meanwhile, they retain tariff protection on goods entering their economies from outside.

In a free-trade area arrangement the participants agree to remove totally their tariff (and quota) protection on the trade in goods flowing between them but remain free to determine the level of external tariff protection on goods entering their economies from third countries. Notably, in a free-trade area rules of origin have to be devised. These prevent what is called trade deflection. This is defined as the import of goods from third countries into the free-trade area by member state A, which has a lower external tariff than member state B, in order to re-export them to member state B.

In a customs union the member states agree to remove tariffs and quotas on intra-bloc trade but agree to introduce a common level of tariff protection on goods entering the union from third countries. This uniform protective arrangement is usually called the common external tariff (CET), although in the Rome Treaty which created the European Community (EC, part of the European Union, or EU – see Table 1; it is referred to as the common customs tariff (CCT). Arrangements of this kind are clearly discriminatory, since they represent free trade within the bloc but discrimination against the rest of the world. Postwar arrangements appear at first sight to have contravened GATT rules (see WORLD TRADE ORGANIZATION), since the latter called for non-discrimination in tariff arrangements. However, in practice, GATT rules provided an escape route. Provided the level of the CET was no higher than the average of the previous national tariffs, it satisfied GATT principles. Since the CCT of the EC was based on a straight arithmetical average of the previous national tariffs, it was deemed to be acceptable.

In a common market a customs union is supplemented by arrangements which permit the free flow of factors of production. Thus an individual can offer himself or herself for employment in any member state of the common market; capital can flow to where it can earn the highest remuneration; business executives can set up subsidiaries, branches, etc. in any of the participating states.

Finally, there is a concept of economic union or economic and monetary union. The 'economic' aspect of the union refers to the existence of a common market. The 'monetary' aspect relates to the associated monetary and fiscal arrangements, and may involve the introduction of a common currency together with highly unified fiscal arrangements. In effect, the member states become mere regions of the larger economic area. The variety of possible monetary and fiscal scenarios in such a union is detailed below.

3 Particular features of the integration process

It is important to emphasize that actual integration exercises may not fit neatly into any of the aforementioned scenarios. Thus, as we have seen, a customs union involves a CET combined with the total elimination of internal tariffs. However, the parties to an integration arrangement may reduce the internal barriers only partially, in which case the resulting arrangement is, in effect, a partial customs union.

It is equally essential to recognize that, while integration arrangements may be overall in character, they may also be only partial in coverage. For example, the European Coal and Steel Community (see Table 1) related purely to free trade between the partners in respect of iron, steel and coal. The European Free-Trade Association (EFTA – see Table 1) was essentially concerned with free trade in industrial goods and services – agricultural trade was largely excluded from the arrangement.

Integration exercises may also overlap. Thus when in 1973 the United Kingdom (UK) and Denmark deserted EFTA in favour of the EC the two trading blocs concluded a reciprocal free-trade arrangement. However, this

Economic integration, international

Table 1 Exercises in international economic integration

Integration exercise	Members	Nature of exercise
Association of South East Asian Nations	Brunei, Darussalam, Indonesia, Malaysia, Philippines, Singapore, Thailand	Preferential tariff agreement accompanied by programmes of economic cooperation over a wide field, including joint production projects
Caribbean Community	Antigua, Barbados, Guyana, Jamaica, Trinidad and Tobago, Grenada, St Lucia, St Vincent, Montserrat, St Kitts-Nevis-Anguilla, Belize	Customs union which envisages possibility of full economic union in due course
Central African Customs and Economic Union	Cameroon, Central African Republic, Chad, Congo, Equitorial Guinea, Gabon	Customs union
Central African Monetary Union	Same members as Central African Customs and Economic Union	Monetary union with common currency and union central bank
Central American Common Market	Costa Rica, El Salvador, Guatamala, Honduras, Nicaragua	Originally conceived as a free-trade area which would progressively develop into a customs union and then a common market
Council for Mutual Economic Cooperation	USSR, Bulgaria, Cuba, Czechoslovakia, East Germany, Hungary, Mongolia, Poland, Romania, Vietnam	Aim was not free trade but rather to plan production on a joint basis and to seek a bilateral trade balance between partners
Economic Community of West African States	Benin, Burkina Faso, Cape Verde, Cote d'Ivoire, Gambia, Ghana, Guinea, Guinea-Bissau, Liberia, Mali, Mauritania, Niger, Nigeria, Senegal, Sierra Leone, Togo	Customs union
European Coal and Steel Community	Same members as European Community – part of European Union	Originally a free-trade area agreement in respect of trade in coal, iron and steel products. A common external tariff for iron and steel introduced at a later stage
European Free-Trade Association	Norway, Sweden, Switzerland, Austria, Finland, Iceland, Liechtenstein, Portugal, UK	Free-trade area with reciprocal free-trade agreement (excluding agriculture) with European Union. Also closely tied in to European Community via European Economic Area agreement (but see below)
European Community	Germany, France, UK, Italy, Spain, Belgium, the Netherlands, Luxembourg, Portugal, Denmark, Irish Republic, Greece, Austria, Sweden, Finland	Originally called the European Economic Community and latterly the European Community. Initial aim was to create a common market. Maastricht Treaty on European Union envisages ultimate state of Economic and Monetary Union as part of the all-embracing European Union
North American Free-Trade Agreement	USA, Canada, Mexico	Free-trade area. Successor to US/Canada Free-Trade Agreement

applied only to the industrial and service sectors, since the EC had introduced extremely protective arrangements in relation to its farming sector, which would have been jeopardized by free trade in agricultural produce. Subsequently, most of the EFTA countries and the EC concluded the European Economic Area agreement, which integrated the majority of EFTA states into the EC single market. Most EFTA states are, however, now full members of the EC.

A distinction needs to be made between negative and positive integration. A good deal of the process of economic integration, certainly in the context of a free-enterprise economy, is indeed negative. It consists of removing barriers to the free and undistorted flow of goods, services, factors, etc. However, integration activity can also be positive – it can take the form of the development of common policies. An example would be the introduction of joint industrial development programmes. Thus a key feature of the activities of the Association of South-East Asian Nations (ASEAN – see Table 1) has been co-operation in industry. This has taken the form of joint production of basic industrial goods, the achievement of complementarity in national industrial development programmes and other joint industrial ventures. Joint industrial ventures have also been a key feature of the Central African Customs and Economic Union (CACEU – see Table 1). Specific projects have included joint industrial investments in the production of cotton textiles, insecticides, fertilizers, petrochemicals, pharmaceuticals and cement. Even the famous (or infamous) EC Common Agricultural Policy has had its positive aspect, since alongside the dismantling of barriers to internal trade in agricultural produce and the elimination of different national systems of agricultural price support there has been the positive aim of raising the level of farmers' incomes nearer to those of their industrial counterparts.

Mention must also be made of the concept of spill-over. Theorists of the economic integration process – referred to as neo-functionalists – have pointed to what has been called the expansive logic of integration. Functional spill-over emphasizes the idea that when a group of countries embarks on a scheme of limited economic integration spill-over effects are likely to arise which will drive them on to higher levels of integration. The following is an example of a spill-over effect. Assume that a group of countries has indeed embarked on a limited economic integration exercise which involves the free movement of goods, services and factors but excludes monetary matters. Because of the latter, exchange rates are free to rise and fall as market forces dictate. Subsequent experience may suggest that flexible exchange rates inhibit the flow of goods, services and factors. This tendency arises from the uncertainties associated with exchange-rate volatility. It may therefore be argued that flexible exchange rates should be replaced by fixed rates. Exchange rates, however, cannot remain fixed unless the monetary conditions in the member states are harmonized so as to give rise to uniform rates of inflation (or deflation). Such harmonization would require that national sovereignty over monetary matters would have to be given up in favour of centralized monetary coordination. It might indeed be concluded that stability would be better achieved by having a common currency. In short, although the member states may embark on a limited integration exercise, they may be driven remorselessly down the path to greater and greater economic integration. That at least was the expectation of the neo-functionalists.

The neo-functionalists also expected that economic integration would give rise to a political spill-over. Their theorizing was somewhat obscure, but the general proposition was very credible. In the first place, it was not unreasonable to expect that the process of economic integration could have a confidence-building effect. Successful efforts in the economic sphere could suggest the possibility of successful outcomes in policy areas that were not economic in character. Not only that, but pooled efforts could be expected to carry more weight than individual ones. Equally important was the point that the distinction between economic and non-economic issues is often difficult to draw.

In large measure, economic integration proceeds through the agency of free trade and competition. It has therefore assumed the existence of a substantial free-enterprise sector within the integrating partners. However, economic integration has also occurred in a state-enterprise context. This was so in the case of the Council for Mutual Economic Cooperation (CMEA or Comecon – see Table 1). The members of Comecon, which was founded in 1949, were those communist states which, until the reforms in eastern Europe, looked to the

Soviet Union for political leadership. The aim was not to trade freely – which was neither possible nor desired, given that trade was a state monopoly in each of the member countries – but rather to plan production on a joint basis and seek to ensure that the resulting trade flows balanced. However, the economic reforms in eastern Europe, together with the reunification of Germany, meant that this particular exercise in economic integration was doomed to extinction.

4 The process of economic integration

A distinction can be made between stage one and stage two of the integration process. Stage one covers the process up to and including the formation of a common market. It is therefore concerned with external protective arrangements coupled with the removal of barriers to the internal free movement of goods and services, and in the case of a common market this would extend to the establishment of conditions which enabled factors of production to move freely across frontiers. Stage two covers the further process of monetary integration, which would transform a common market into an economic union (economic and monetary union). It is therefore concerned with the unifying of policy in respect of the money supply, interest rates, exchange rates and fiscal matters.

The stage-one process

Preferential tariff arrangements and free-trade areas leave the participating states free in respect of their external trading relationships, and there is nothing that needs to be added, other than to recollect that rules of origin may be introduced (see discussion above and below). However, as has been noted, in a customs union (and a common market) a CET is established. In practice, a CET may be subject to exceptions – that is, not all countries may pay the tariff. For example, in the case of the EC the ex-colonial dependencies of the original members (and many of those of members who joined later) were allowed tariff-free access (for manufactured goods) to the EC internal market. Subsequently, the EC concluded a whole series of trade agreements that exempted individual countries and groups of countries from the CET. At a later stage the EC introduced the general system of preferences, which granted tariff-free quotas to developing countries in respect of their manufactured exports to the EC – that is, up to a specified quantitative level, imports into the EC were exempted from the CET (without reciprocity).

A CET may be accompanied by other protective devices. These include collectively negotiated import quotas (for example the multifibre arrangements concerning imports of textiles and clothing into the EC), collectively negotiated voluntary export restraints and collectively operated anti-dumping duties. In 1984 the EC adopted what has come to be called the new commercial policy instrument. It can be invoked against illicit practices that affect Community exports to the rest of the world, as well as Community imports. When such illicit practices are proved to exist, various retaliatory actions can be introduced by the Council of Ministers, including increasing the level of import duties and the application of quotas.

The removal of internal protection poses major problems. Quite clearly, it involves the abolition of tariffs on internal trade. Such liberalization may, however, be accompanied by rules concerning the degree of local content. For example, in the case of the North American Free Trade Agreement (NAFTA – see Table 1) textiles and apparel will be free of duty within NAFTA only if they are made from yarn or fibre also coming from within NAFTA, a provision likely to encourage firms using overseas supplies of yarn to switch to local suppliers. Another such rule is that cars require 62.5 per cent North American content to qualify for duty-free status within NAFTA, significantly higher than the 50 per cent provision in the existing pre-NAFTA agreement between Canada and the USA. Equally, tariff liberalization requires the removal of charges that are equivalent to tariffs. For example, in the case of the EC the Italian government was in the habit of applying what it called a 'statistical levy' to imports and exports. The EC Commission pointed out that this was the equivalent of a customs duty and should be eliminated. When the Italian government refused to comply, the matter was referred to the European Court of Justice, which upheld the Commission's action. Additionally, the removal of internal protection requires the abolition of quantitative restrictions on imports (and exports). Such quantitative restrictions can arise indirectly. A particularly good illustration is provided by the celebrated EC Cassis de Dijon case.

Cassis de Dijon is a French liqueur manufactured from blackcurrants. The German company Rewe-Zentral AG sought to import the French liqueur and requested an authorization from the West German Federal Monopoly Administration for Spirits. The latter body informed Rewe that West German law forbade the sale of liqueurs with less than 32 per cent alcohol content, although for liqueurs of the Cassis type a minimum of 25 per cent was allowed. This was no help to the Cassis importer as Cassis has an alcoholic content of only 15–20 per cent, and thus it was illegal to import it. Rewe contested the ban in the German courts and the matter was referred to the European Court of Justice for a preliminary ruling. The court declared that the German law in question was in these specific circumstances a measure equivalent to a quota and was therefore prohibited under Article 30 of the Rome Treaty. The minimum alcoholic content rule had in this particular case the effect of a zero import quota. Clearly, measures of this kind have to be rooted out if internal free trade is to be established in a free-trade area.

Tariff (and quota) barriers may be removed, but a host of non-tariff barriers (NTBs) remain to be dealt with. These are associated with public procurement, state subsidies, product standards, taxation arrangements, state monopolies, anti-competitive business practices and border formalities.

Public procurement poses a major NTB problem. In the EC government spending represents about 45 per cent of total spending. However, some of this is spending on wages and salaries, etc., whereas the problem from the point of view of internal trade liberalization is public spending on goods and services. This latter category amounts to approximately 15 per cent of total spending. Typically, such spending is carried out on a 'buy-national' basis, in which central, regional and local governments tend to support national champions rather than buying the best or the cheapest. Naturally, such behaviour negates the effectiveness of internal tariff disarmament. It therefore requires the institution of rules that require public authorities, at whatever level, to act in a non-discriminatory way. The EC approached this problem by requiring that public invitations to tender should be widely publicized within the Community, prescribing rules that favour open, as opposed to negotiated, tendering (the latter could involve only one firm being considered). Such measures require that decisions to purchase are based on the selection of the cheapest or the best and provide methods of redress where these principles are ignored. Interestingly, NAFTA included a modest agreement to open central government procurement to competition. Apparently, however, this provision need not bind lower layers of government.

State subsidies, too, can distort the competitive process, and can mean that domestic but inefficient sources of supply are able to survive while more efficient but unaided sources within the rest of the integrated area are put at a competitive disadvantage. Such subsidies may take the form of grants to bail out relatively inefficient and possibly loss-making domestic firms or industries (sectoral aids). Alternatively, subsidies may take the form of regional development grants (subsidies to capital or labour) – that is, regional aids. These may be justifiable as a means of compensating for some locational disadvantage, thus helping to raise depressed living standards, but the level of assistance may be excessive; in other words, the aid may more than compensate for locational disadvantages and become a disguised means of granting unfair competitive advantages. Aids may take the form of grants designed to cheapen the price of exports – that is, pure export aids. Since the late 1980s governments within the EC have tended to favour subsidies for research and less development (R&D) activity. Particularly difficult problems arise in connection with the public enterprise sector, since it is quite possible that in one state an industry may be in public ownership and in receipt of (possibly concealed) subsidies, whereas the same industry in another member state may be privately owned and be required to stand on its own. Individual states may also distort competition by advancing capital to their privately owned industries at less than commercial rates.

A system of surveillance, with powers to ban unfair and unjustified state subsidies, is essential if cross-frontier competition is to be fair. This approach has been adopted by the EC, with the enforcement task being devolved to the EC Commission. Distortion of competition can also arise as a result of differential fiscal concessions. This has been a major problem in the Caribbean Community (CARICOM – see Table 1) and led to the introduction of a scheme for the harmonization of fiscal assistance to industry. Distortions of competition and unfair competitive advantages may also arise if member states deliberately lower environmental, health and safety, minimum-wage and child-labour standards as a means of attracting footloose investment. NAFTA has led to the establishment of two commissions with powers to impose fines and remove trade privileges where such standards are lowered deliberately.

The role of product standards as an NTB has already been illustrated by the Cassis de Dijon case. Modern governments tend to intervene on a considerable scale in setting standards which cover the description, contents and design of goods, in order to prevent consumer deception. Standards also aim to protect consumers from injury, and can also lead to greater efficiency by providing for longer production runs and equipment compatibility. While such interventions in the marketplace are entirely legitimate, standards may differ between partner states and cross-frontier trade may therefore be prevented. This leads to a loss of beneficial competition and choice. Alternatively, goods may have to be modified to meet the standards of each member-state market, with a consequent loss of the economies of large-volume production. Two approaches to this problem are possible. One is mutual recognition of national standards – this is feasible where differences do not pose a threat to, for example, life and limb. However, where health, efficiency or compatibility issues are clearly involved, the only solution is to devise common or harmonized standards. Goods conforming to them will then be readily marketable throughout the integrated area. The EC has adopted both approaches – mutual recognition in some instances has been paralleled by action under Article 94 of the Rome Treaty, which provides for the adoption (by means of directives) of a legally based system of harmonized standards. These supersede national laws. CARICOM is also notable for the special attention it has given to this problem. A specially created Caribbean Common Market Council has been established to advise the Common Market Council of Ministers on this issue and to promote the development of uniform standards in the member states.

Taxation can also pose problems. Since the focus at this point is on the trade in goods and services, the taxation in question is indirect. The experience of the EC in this area is particularly instructive. Two issues arose, the preferred structure of indirect taxation and the rates to be imposed. The Community chose to adopt two main types of indirect tax – excise duties, together with some form of turnover tax. The major area of debate arose in connection with the actual form of turnover tax to be adopted. Two alternative models were on offer, the German cascade system and the French value-added tax (VAT). Ultimately VAT was chosen, since it did not bias industrial structures towards vertical integration, whereas (in order to minimize tax) the cascade system did.

VAT had another advantage, which is connected with the treatment of indirect taxes in international trade. Since tax rates are likely to differ from country to country, competitive distortions may arise because imports from countries with high tax rates can be undercut by domestic production in countries with low rates. In order to avoid this state of affairs the destination system has traditionally been employed in international trade. This means that goods for export are zero-rated and importing countries impose the same rate of indirect tax on imports as they apply to their own products. The perceived advantage of VAT was that it was relatively transparent – that is, it was easy for the EC Commission to verify that the tax remitted on exports was not excessive and did not give rise to a concealed export subsidy. However, one of the longer-term aims of the European single-market programme is to adopt the origin system, whereby goods are exported bearing VAT, but this will only be possible when national VAT rates have been approximated. In the meantime some distortions continue as shoppers cross borders to obtain goods in countries with lower VAT rates; this problem also arises in respect of unharmonized excise rates.

NTBs also arise in connection with monopoly. Here, two kinds need to be identified. On the one hand, there are state fiscal monopolies and, on the other, for the most part there is the problem of private market power. The former kind of NTB is a revenue-raising device – for example, an enterprise, probably state owned, is given a monopoly of the supply of some particular good. Alcohol and tobacco products are typical cases in Europe. Having a monopoly, the enterprise can restrict output, raise prices and earn monopoly profits. The profits can be claimed by the state as part of its tax revenues. To be effective, such monopolies have to be able to restrict and, if necessary, prohibit competing imports. Inevitably, therefore, an NTB arises and has to be addressed.

Market power – which is not exclusively private in origin, since state enterprises may be involved – can also arise through the agency of cartels, dominant (possibly monopoly) firms and mergers. All of these can give rise to NTBs that prevent or distort beneficial cross-frontier competition within the integrated area. Cartels may, for example, establish cross-frontier market-sharing agreements in which the producers in member state A agree not to sell in the market of member state B and vice versa. Dominant or monopoly firms may, by virtue of their control over the supply of a product in a particular domestic market, be able to induce dealers to deal with them exclusively, thus effectively sealing the market off from import competition. Mergers may also be a method by which the inconvenient competition of outside suppliers can be taken over and suppressed.

The EC has an outstanding record in dealing with NTBs arising through the agency of cartels, dominant firms and mergers. Article 81 of the Rome Treaty bans cartels that restrict competition, provided that there is an effect on inter-state trade. However, exemptions are possible where benefits arise and consumers share in them. In practice, naked price-fixing, output-restricting and market-sharing agreements, which offer no counterbalancing advantage, will be struck down automatically. The European Commission possesses impressive powers of enforcement and can impose severe fines. The abusive behaviour of dominant firms can also be attacked, providing there is evidence to show that the flow of trade between the member states is affected. Since 1989 large-scale mergers which create or strengthen a dominant market position and significantly impede competition can be banned. Public enterprises are also subject to these rules of competition.

The question of border formalities must also be mentioned briefly. These can significantly add to the cost of goods being traded in the integrated area and this detracts from the advantages deriving from economic integration.

Trade liberalization within an integrated area also requires that action should be taken to create free trade in services. The removal of internal tariffs is normally only relevant to trade in goods but not to trade in services. However, the elimination of NTBs is relevant to the liberalization of service trade. Apart from the kinds of NTBs discussed above, obstacles in this sector are often associated with governmental regulatory systems – as in insurance, banking and transport. These often restrict entry into particular sectors of economic activity.

When economic integration extends to the stage of a common market there is a need to create conditions in which factors of production are also free to move from state to state. To a large extent, integration requires the modification of various forms of state intervention. In the case of labour it requires liberalization of work-permit systems, transmission of information on job opportunities, making social security rights transferable, etc. In the field of professional services it involves in particular the harmonization of training requirements and the mutual recognition of diplomas, degrees, etc. In the case of capital it calls for the removal of exchange controls, the harmonization of corporation taxation (so that the allocation of capital is not distorted by differences in national rates etc.) and the conclusion of double-taxation agreements. The liberalization of business enterprise involves the harmonization of regulatory systems (in order that enterprises licensed in one member state can set up subsidiaries or branches in another member state) and the harmonization of national legal systems to facilitate cross-frontier business integration (mergers, joint ventures, etc.).

The advantages of the stage-one process
The advantages of the stage-one process are discussed most conveniently by focusing on the stage of integration immediately preceding the formation of a customs union. The advantages of liberalizing factor movements will be considered thereafter.

Although a customs union is an exercise in free trade, it is not a substitute for universal free trade, which economists have always regarded as beneficial. A customs union represents free trade within the bloc but discrimination against the rest of the world. For this reason, the effects may be beneficial or harmful. In other words, a customs union may give rise to trade creation or trade diversion and therefore is not unambiguously beneficial. In Table 2, in the case of good A, country I initially applies a non-discriminatory 50 per cent tariff in respect of imports from country II and country III. The most efficient producer of the good is country II, but it is excluded by the tariff. If country I and country II form a customs union but leave country III facing the tariff, there will then be a beneficial switch of production from the less efficient country I to the more efficient country II. This is *trade creation*. In the case of good B the most efficient supplier is country III, which supplies the good to country I prior to formation of the union. After the formation of the union, however, country II can undercut country III. There will be a switch of production from the more efficient country III to the less efficient country II that is not beneficial. This is *trade diversion*.

Whether a customs union is on balance beneficial depends partly on the relative magnitude of the types of conflicting effects outlined in the preceding paragraph. However, this static analysis does not take account of two further benefits, namely the possibility that the enlarged market will provide greater scope for economies of scale and that it is likely to give rise to a more intensely competitive environment. The latter could lead to a lowering of costs, and increased levels of investment and R&D spending. The customs union is also likely to confer greater bargaining power in international trade negotiations than would be enjoyed if the union states acted independently. A common market also involves the free movement of factors. Here, the major benefit is that factors are free to flow to the locations where they earn the highest return and produce the greatest economic welfare.

The stage-two process

The stage-two process consists of the transformation of a common market into an economic union, or economic and monetary union. This implies that the partners in the integration process embark on a programme of monetary integration. Monetary integration can itself be broken down into its monetary and fiscal components. These can be based, in turn, on either minimalist or maximalist models.

The monetary component
The monetary component of monetary integration may consist of an arrangement in which the participating states fix the rate of exchange between their separate national currencies. An arrangement of this kind can take the form of a fairly loose arrangement in which margins of fluctuation are allowed around fixed central exchange-rate parities, with the central parities being adjusted from time to time. This mode of operation was adopted in the Exchange Rate Mechanism (ERM) of the EC's European Monetary System (the latter was established in 1979). The monetary arrangement might, however, be stiffened by agreeing to fix exchange-rate parities irrevocably, with no margins of fluctuation. This measure could be combined with full convertibility of the member-state currencies. The term 'full convertibility' refers to a situation in which individuals or enterprises

Table 2 Trade creation and trade diversion

Good	Cost or cost plus duty per unit	Country III exporting to country I	Flow of trade	Goods produced by country I	Flow of trade	Country II exporting to country I	Results
A	Cost	14		17		12	Trade creation
	Cost plus duty prior to customs union	21	No trade: country I produces A	17	No trade: country I produces A	18	
	Cost plus duty after customs union	21	No trade	17		12	
B	Cost	12		20		14	Trade diversion
	Cost plus duty prior to customs union	18		20	No trade	21	
	Cost plus duty after customs union	18	No trade	20		14	

can change one member state currency into another in whatever quantity they wish whenever they wish. Such an arrangement is referred to as an exchange-rate union and is a minimalist monetary arrangement. However, such exchange rates would not be viable in the longer term unless national macroeconomic policies were coordinated so as to achieve a convergence of economic performance in matters such as national rates of inflation.

If a fixed quantity of one national currency can always be exchanged for a fixed quantity of another, in whatever quantity required, then one is, in effect, a substitute for the other. It could then be argued that, for convenience and economy, it would be logical to take the further but considerable step of replacing the separate national currencies with one union currency. This arrangement is referred to as a currency union and represents a maximalist monetary arrangement.

If the latter path is followed there is a need to establish a union central bank system to control the supply of the common currency and to determine the union interest-rate structure. An analysis of the ingredients of monetary union does not suggest that there is any unique formula governing the organization, political relationship and aims of such a central bank. It could be monolithic or it could be part of a federal arrangement in which the union central bank operated in conjunction with the pre-existing national central banks. The union central bank could be independent of political influence or, at the other extreme, it could take instructions from the political authorities. In practice, a dependent union central bank would be likely to be pulled in various directions by conflicting national interests. That being so, a significant degree of independence seems to be a more practical option. The objective set for a union central bank could be the achievement of price stability within the union, although some other overriding objective, such as the maintenance of a high level of employment or the achievement of more rapid economic development – or a combination of all of these – might be specified.

The union bank would be charged with managing the exchange rate of the union currency *vis-à-vis* outside currencies. To this end, it would be reasonable to assume that the member states would transfer their foreign-exchange reserves to the central bank. The union central bank might have total discretion with respect to the exchange rate. Alternatively, it might be allowed full control of day-to-day support operations but be subject to the general supervision of exchange-rate policy by the political authorities. The union central bank would take on the role of lender of last resort. It would presumably play some role in the prudential regulation of commercial banks.

The fiscal component

Monetary union, as already noted, also has a fiscal dimension. In short, member states could not be allowed to run budget deficits of unlimited size, since one way of financing them would be to borrow. Large-scale borrowing would tend to drive interest rates up, not only in the deficit state, but in the union as a whole, since national monetary systems would be fully unified, with one set of interest rates. A *minimalist* fiscal model therefore presumes that some central authority exists which can set limits to national budget deficits. Tax rates (and structures) might still be determined at national level, although if the model was similar to that envisaged by the EC, then while taxes would still be imposed and collected by each member state, their structure and rates would in the main be harmonized in line with the needs of the customs union and common market. A *maximalist* fiscal model would require that the imposition of taxes and the collection of revenues should be placed in the hands of some central authority. It might then pass some revenue back to the constituent states for local discretionary purposes. The central authority would also determine the appropriate level of the union budget deficit or surplus. In a democratic setting such a system would presumably be accompanied by a significant and parallel degree of political unification on the principle of no taxation without representation. The maximalist model outlined here, in respect of both its monetary and fiscal aspects, is that which was adopted by the USA.

A monetary union clearly involves the giving up of substantial amounts of economic sovereignty. For example, the powers to manipulate the supply of the currency, interest rates and exchange rates are surrendered. This prospect leaves individual members in a potentially vulnerable position. The possibility that they could suffer an asymmetric shock, and that income and employment levels could therefore fall, cannot be ruled out. In the absence of self-correcting mechanisms of wage–price flexibility or labour migration, considerable political tensions could build up. For this reason, a system of resource transfers to less prosperous states could be the price demanded by some states for agreeing to monetary unification. It is perhaps worth noting that significant resource transfers from richer to poorer constituent parts of the union are a feature of many federal arrangements.

While preferential tariff agreements, free-trade areas and customs unions are relatively common and a number of common markets or incipient common markets exist, exercises that have already advanced to the stage of monetary integration or propose advancing to it are relatively rare. One example is the Central African Customs and Economic Union (CACEU), to which has been added the Central African Monetary Union (see Table 1). It has a common currency, the Central African Financial Cooperation Franc, which is issued by the Bank of the Central African States. The EC, following the Maastricht Treaty on European Union, aims to turn its common market into an economic and monetary union with a common currency in the shape of the Euro. The supply of Euros would be in the hands of an independent European System of Central Banks. A high degree of fiscal integration would also exist; key features of the system would be harmonization of the structure and rates of indirect, and possibly direct, taxes, together with central control over national budget deficits. The Caribbean Community (CARICOM) also envisaged a move towards monetary integration.

The advantages of the stage-two process

A minimalist monetary arrangement, particularly with irrevocably fixed exchange rates, removes the uncertainty which floating exchange rates give rise to. This facilitates intra-union trade exchanges of both goods and services, and thus enables the integrating states to enjoy more fully the advantages of specialization according to comparative advantage, economies of scale, greater competition and wider choice. The removal of exchange-rate uncertainty also facilitates the intra-union flow of factors of production. Thus, for example, it enables further advantage to be taken of the ability of capital to flow to those locations where it will earn the highest return. If a maximalist arrangement is introduced in which a common currency emerges, two further advantages arise, namely the elimination of the transactions costs that arise when differing currencies have to be exchanged, and the greater transparency which arises when economic transactions can be evaluated in terms of one currency.

The pool of reserves that are required when a common currency emerges will be less than the sum of the national reserves held prior to union. The member states will therefore enjoy a temporary gain in that an external trade deficit can be financed by allowing reserves to fall to the lower required level. If the common currency becomes an international currency an element of seigniorage will arise. In other words, countries outside the union will be willing to hold the union currency as an asset; thus imports of goods and services into the union can be financed by increased outside holdings of the union currency rather than by exports. The seigniorage advantage can be exaggerated, since there will also be an outflow of interest payments. Finally, a common currency greatly increases the bargaining power of the participating states when engaging in international monetary negotiations. Individually, the members may carry little or no weight, but collectively they can exert an influence that reflects their regional interests.

5 Other aspects of integration

Economic integration exercises require a decision-making structure. Typically, this tends to take the form of a supreme body consisting of heads of state and government, who make key strategic decisions, and a council (or councils) of ministers, who meet more frequently to deal with specific policy issues. For example, in the case of the Economic Community of West African States (ECOWAS – see Table 1) the heads of state meet once a year and the council of ministers meets twice. They are supported by an executive presided over by an executive secretary. A similar arrangement exists in the EC, with the European Council at the top and the law-making EC Council of Ministers below. They are supported by an executive in the form of the European Commission.

Not all integration exercises incorporate a permanent central executive body. Thus CARICOM delegates the execution of policy to a series of committees consisting of the relevant ministers from each member state. Ministerial decision-making varies. The EC has moved increasingly to majority voting, whereas in ASEAN unanimity is the invariable rule. Integration exercises usually involve some arbitration body. ECOWAS has a community tribunal which interprets the founding treaty. The founding treaties of the EC delegate this task to the European Court of Justice.

Integration arrangements often give rise to a supporting development bank. Thus in the Central American Common Market (see Table 1) the Central American Bank for Economic Integration finances regional development projects. In the case of the EC, the European Investment Bank for many years channelled vast amounts of loan-based assistance into the backward regions of the union. In addition, the EC established a community budget which, apart from bearing the administrative cost of the union, also awards grants for such purposes as regional and social improvement.

DENNIS SWANN
LOUGHBOROUGH UNIVERSITY

Further reading

Bainbridge, T. and Teasdale, A. (1995) *The Penguin Companion Policy*, London: Penguin. (A glossary of European Community institutions, policies and definitions.)

Baldwin, R.E. (1994) *Towards an Integrated Europe*, London: CEPR. (A discussion of the consequences of enlarging the European Community to include eastern Europe.)

Gros, D. and Thygesen, N. (1992) *European Monetary Integration*, London: Longman. (An analysis of monetary integration in the EC context which includes a discussion of early attempts at monetary union.)

Healey, N.M. (ed.) (1995) *The Economics of the New Europe*, London: Routledge. (A survey of European Community economic policy.)

Henderson, R. (1993) *European Finance*, London: McGraw-Hill. (A survey of the financial and monetary aspects of the European Community.)

Jovanovic, M.N. (1992) *International Economic Integration*, London: Routledge. (An introduction to the various forms of economic integration which includes an account of COMECON [Council for Mutual Economic Assistance] and ASEAN.)

Montagnon, P. (ed.) (1990) *European Competition*, London: RIJA. (A survey of European Community competition policy.)

Nielsen, J., Heinrich, U. and Hansen, J.D. (1991) *An Economic Analysis of the EC*, London: McGraw-Hill. (A highly theoretical treatment of economic integration in the EC context, covering microeconomic and macroeconomic aspects of the process.)

Swann, D. (ed.) (1992) *The Single European Market and Beyond*, London: Routledge. (An account of the Single European Act of 1986, its emergence and its impact on the integration process.)

Swann, D. (1996) *European Economic Integration*, Cheltenham: Edward Elgar. (A review of the European Community economic policy following the Maastricht Treaty.)

Swann, D. (2000) *The Economics of Europe*, 8th edn, London: Penguin. (Presents an overall view of the European economic integration process, including the Single Market, the Maastricht Treaty and the Amsterdam Treaty.)

See also: MONETARISM; WORLD TRADE ORGANIZATION

World Bank

1 Structure and mission
2 A brief history: from bank to development agency
3 Criticism and response: projects, programmes and policies
4 New directions and further evolution

Overview

Created at the Bretton Woods Conference in 1944, the World Bank is the leading multilateral organization providing development assistance to developing countries and countries in transition. It is an important source of finance, raising funds in capital markets and providing loans to governments for about US$30 billion per year at below market rates. Originally focusing on large-scale infrastructures, Bank funding has diversified and ranges from projects in health and education, to state-wide reform programmes.

The World Bank is also the leading theorist and agenda-setter on development and poverty issues. Its own vision of development has evolved over the years, from capital intensive state-led development in the 1950s and 1960s, basic needs in the 1970s, macro economic stability and microeconomic efficiency in the 1980s to a comprehensive approach to poverty alleviation in the late 1990s.

Since the late 1960s, the evolutions of Bank strategies and of the international economy have been closely related. Among other things, Bank strategies respond to structural changes in the international economy and at the same time, given the Bank's influence, these strategies participate in shaping the evolution of national economies and the international system. By the late 1990s, the Bank was, with the International Monetary Fund (IMF) and the World Trade Organization (WTO) (see IMF and WTO); one of the three pillars of the system of global governance supporting the process of economic and financial globalization.

1 Structure and mission

The World Bank Group comprises five agencies:

- The International Bank for Reconstruction and Development (IBRD), commonly known as the World Bank, was established in 1945. As of 1999, it counted 181 members. Its sources of funds are paid-in capital, capital market borrowings, repayments on earlier loans, and retained earnings. It provides loans to middle-income countries and creditworthy poorer countries.
- The International Development Agency (IDA), established in 1960, is the Bank's concessional lending arm. It provides interest free loans to poor eligible countries. Sources of funds include contributions from government and transfers from IBRD profits.
- The International Financial Corporation (IFC) was established in 1956 to finance private sector investments and play a catalytic role with private investors by demonstrating the profitability of investments in poorer countries.
- The Multilateral Investment Guarantee Agency (MIGA), established in 1988, facilitates investment primarily by providing investment guarantees against non-commercial risks.
- The International Center for the Settlement of Investment Disputes (ICSID), created in 1966 to facilitate the settlement of investment disputes.

This entry focuses mainly on the IBRD and IDA.

The original mandate of the World Bank, as agreed in the Articles of Agreement of the Charter approved by Member States in the Bretton Woods Conference, is to: 'assist in the reconstruction and development of territories of members by facilitating the investment of capital for productive purposes' and to 'promote the long range balanced growth of international trade ... by encouraging international investment ... thereby assisting in raising productivity, the standard of living and conditions of labour'.

Importantly, Article IV stated that the Bank would make decisions on the sole basis of economic and financial justifications without making political considerations:

> The Bank and its officers shall not interfere in the political affairs of any member, nor shall they be influenced in their decisions by the political character of the member or members concerned. Only economic considerations shall be relevant to their decisions.

Project lending, a traditional Bank activity until recently, involves lending for projects for the extraction or use of natural resources, infrastructures such as dams, roads, powerplants. Sectorial lending is mostly aimed at the reform, restructuring and privatization of entire productive sectors, mainly the energy sector, one of the crucial components of every state's development and economic policy. A more recent instrument used by IDA and IBRD is the 'social safety net programme lending', the volume of which has substantially increased, together with the lending volume for structural adjustment programmes (SAPs) as a consequence of the financial crises that struck Asia and Latin America in the late 1990s. In the 1999 financial year, lending directly or indirectly connected to SAPs and Financial Rescue Packages accounted for 64 per cent of overall lending.

The private sector arms of the Bank, namely IFC and MIGA, lend not to governments but to companies. IFC participates in joint ventures to attract foreign capital and provide a seal of quality and reliability to the private investment. The surge of Foreign Direct Investment (FDI) on a global scale has been accompanied by a remarkable increase in volume of lending by IFC and MIGA, in line with the approach according to which the Bank's scarce resources should be used to 'catalyse' private sector flows, especially in countries out of the loop of FDI. MIGA in turn operates as an insurance agency to support private investments in countries with high political risk.

The International Center for the Settlement of Investment Disputes (ICSID) is an arbitration body to which companies can resort in case of violations of contractual agreements with governments and vice-versa. An institution almost unknown to the general public, ICSID was active in providing consultancy and know-how to OECD during the negotiations of the aborted Multilateral Agreement on Investments.

The World Bank governance structure is organized as follows: the Council of Governors gives general policy direction. It meets twice a year in spring and fall and is composed of the Ministers of Finance and Governors of Central Banks of member states. The implementation of the policy directions is the task of the Board of Directors, composed of 24 members. They represent either single member states (as is the case with the US, Japan, Canada, France, Germany, and the United Kingdom) or a constituency of states (Italy, for instance, represents a 'Mediterranean Constituency' with Italy, Portugal, Malta, Greece, Albania). The Head of the Board and President of the World Bank Group is always a US citizen, appointed by the US Administration. The current President, James Wolfensohn, is now serving his second five-year term.

2 A brief history: from bank to development agency

The International Bank for Reconstruction and Development (IBRD) was set up in 1944 at the Bretton Woods Conference, and opened its doors for business on 25 June 1946, in Washington DC. Under the impulse of the US Government, the Bank was created to provide loans for reconstruction and development to war-torn countries. Thirty-eight countries were members. Original capital subscriptions were small, and the Bank was dependent on private investors for funds, which underlined the importance of establishing its position on capital markets.

The Bank got off to a slow start. Demands for reconstruction loans quickly overstretched the capacity of the Bank to manage them properly, signalling that the needs for reconstruction funds had been largely underestimated. The Bank was a new and strange creature in the financial community and it took time to overcome Wall Street scepticism. The first years also witnessed a tense battle between the Bank management and the appointed governors. From 1948, the unfolding of the Cold War and the launch of US Marshall Plan Assistance (which dwarfed Bank efforts) entailed important changes in the external environment within which the Bank operated. Nevertheless, when Eugene Black took over the Presidency of the Bank in 1949, the foundations had been laid for its development.

The 1950s saw the Bank grow into a respected multilateral institution, the independence gained by its management protecting it from the Cold War frictions and the political strains induced by growing membership (67 members in 1958). The Bank also expanded organizationally, with the creation of its private-sector affiliate (IFC) in 1956 and of its soft-loan arm, the International Development Agency (IDA) in 1960. By the end of the decade, it had earned the stature of a triple A bond rating, and had become the fourth largest financier of international development projects. The Bank's recipe for success was conservative lending, a requirement for gaining the confidence of the international banking community. Loans went mainly for large infrastructure projects: power plants, railroad lines, highway networks and dams. These projects required investments that were too large and too uncertain, both politically and economically, to be attractive to private investors. World Bank historians suggest, however, that the availability of funds for these projects stimulated the philosophy that accorded a vital role to infrastructures in the development process, rather than the reverse.

The creation of the IDA manifested the recognition that development in former colonies was raising new challenges. Within the United Nations there was an ongoing struggle over the setting of a Special UN Fund for Economic Development (SUNFED) to provide support to newly independent countries that could not afford the loans at near to market rates that the Bank provided. At the same time the need for Bank operations in Europe and countries like Japan and Australia was diminishing. The IDA was a response to these international changes and organizational needs.

The Bank took further steps towards becoming a development agency in the 1960s. This was a time of development optimism and belief in state leadership. Although the bulk of its loans remained for large-scale infrastructure projects and agriculture (in 1968 66 per cent of loans went to basic infrastructure), the Bank also supported five-year plans, and invested more and more resources in Technical Assistance (TA). The purpose of TA was to support governments with weak capacities to identify needs and develop project proposals that could be acceptable to the Bank. Bank operations were geographically concentrated from 1945 to 1970, with five countries – Colombia, Brazil, Pakistan, India and Thailand – receiving around 35 per cent of all lending.

The Presidency of Robert McNamara (1968–80) marked a new phase in the Bank's history. During a period of increasing development pessimism and tensions in North–South relations (the oil shocks of 1973 and 1979; the Vietnam War; UN discussions on the New International Economic Order), World Bank lending increased fourfold in real terms, and shifted its orientation radically towards addressing poverty. McNamara became convinced that the Bank should transform itself into a development agency: 'we believe economic progress remains precarious and sterile without corresponding social improvement. Fully human development requires attention to both. We intend, in the Bank, to give attention to both' (address to the Board of Governors in Copenhagen in 1970). This view marked a departure from belief in the 'trickle down effect' – the view that poverty alleviation indirectly but automatically stems from economic growth – and called for projects that would reach the poor directly. Changes in the Bank's structure of lending were significant. In the late 1970s, the share of lending to rural areas and agriculture doubled to 28 per cent, while the share of loans for basic infrastructures fell to 35 per cent. New areas in which the Bank got engaged include population issues (health and education), unemployment and the environment. It is under McNamara that the 'pressure to lend' became one of the key features of the Bank's institutional culture.

During that period the Bank also became more prominently engaged in development theory as a way of defining what it considered to be appropriate development strategies (see WORLD TRADE ORGANIZATION). Following the realization that institutional and policy parameters influenced the success of development projects the Bank increasingly took up the role of policy adviser and developed its research capacity in this domain. It launched the World Development Report in 1978 which, with an average distribution of 120,000, is by far the most widely read document in development economics.

The lending spree and poverty orientation of the McNamara years came to a sudden halt in the early 1980s. The debt crisis that unfolded after Mexico's default in 1982 revealed the mistakes in previous development strategies and led to the development of the Bank's structural adjustment lending. The Bank also became a main proponent of the new pro-market ideology of the time, bringing to the forefront of development discussions key neoclassical economic tenets like 'getting the prices right'.

Structural adjustment programmes (SAPs) provide loans tied to state and institutional reforms in line with the so-called 'Washington consensus' on the best ways to organize an economy. Reforms consisted of trade liberalization, de-regulation, and privatization. The priority was on rolling back the state and inserting the national economies into the Northern-dominated global economy, while little attention was given to the complementarity between the private and public spheres of the national economy. SAPs thus led to a systematic undermining of the capacity of states to pursue independent and innovative development strategies. Countries in Latin America were the first to embrace this path of reform, followed by Eastern European countries after 1989, and then Africa and Asia in the 1990s.

3 Criticism and response: projects, programmes and policies

The World Bank is often the target of criticisms, in particular from citizen groups based in industrialized and developing countries. The international campaign '50 years is enough' culminated in 1994 calling for the closure of the Bank.

Criticisms against the Bank are as various as its operations. Critics have focused in particular on the economic, social, and ecological impacts of projects financed by the Bank; the social and political consequences of its structural adjustment programmes; and its development strategies in general (see INTERNATIONAL MONETARY FUND).

Projects

Until the late 1970s the Bank enjoyed a high reputation in terms of project management. But that reputation soured in the 1980s. The Wapenhans Report, a major study by the Operations and Evaluation Department released in 1992, revealed that projects throughout the 1980s had not performed according to expectations in one-third of the cases, mainly because of poor economic analysis. This under-performance was particularly the case for its core-business operations, lending for large infrastructures.

While the Bank's projects were increasingly failing according to its own narrow economic criteria, the criteria themselves came under intense criticism. In particular the Bank became a prime target for critics who drew attention to the ecological, cultural, and social costs of large infrastructures like dams and resource-extraction activities. In the early 1990s under pressure of citizen organizations, the Bank was forced to pull out from the Narmada Dam project in India. Major international mobilization also targeted its support to power-generating projects because of the potential impact on climatic change, and the Chad-Cameroon oil pipeline. While the share of the Bank's loans is relatively small in the overall financial package of these large projects, the Bank's involvement is crucial to bring in private investors.

The Bank responded in a number of ways to these criticisms. In the 1990s, it changed its operational policies and directives. The assessment of the environmental impacts of projects has become more stringent; an operational directive sets special procedures for projects that affect indigenous peoples; it reviewed its disclosure policy to increase the information made publicly available.

In 1993, as a consequence of the findings of the Morse Commission Report – the internal report on the Narmada valley development project – the Board of Executive Directors created the Inspection Panel, a three-member non-judicial body that provides an independent forum to private citizens who believe that their rights or interests have been or could be directly harmed by a project financed by the Bank due to a failure of the Bank to follow its policies and procedures. Affected people bring their concerns to the attention of the Panel by filing a Request for Inspection. The Panel makes a preliminary review of the request, considers a response from the Management, and recommends to the Board whether the claims should be investigated. If the Board approves a recommendation to investigate, the Panel proceeds with the investigation.

Another response of the Bank has been to broaden consultation processes with citizen organizations. For instance, with the World Conservation Union (IUCN) it takes part in the World Commission on Dams, which attempts to mediate a major global controversy democratically – the building and impact of large dams.

Programmes

Since their inception, the World Bank's structural adjustment programmes (SAPs) have been the target of major criticism for their economic, social, and political implications. While officially aiming to restore macroeconomic stability in the aftermath of the debt crisis, they imposed on people living in poverty and in vulnerability the costs of adjustment by decreasing state services, reducing public subsidies on basic goods like food, or introducing fees for health and education services and water. Riots and public demonstrations took place in many countries where the programmes have been implemented.

The Comprehensive Development Framework (CDF) introduced by World Bank President James Wolfensohn in 1998 is the most significant response to these criticisms, and echoes McNamara's reorientation of the Bank strategy in the late 1960s:

> Development is not just about adjustment. Development is not just about sound budgets and fiscal management. Development is not just about education and health. Development is not just about technocratic fixes ... Development is about getting the macroeconomics right – yes; but it is also about building the roads, empowering the people, writing the laws, recognizing the women, eliminating the corruption, educating the girls, building the banking systems, protecting the environment, inoculating the children ... Development is about putting *all* the component parts in place – together and in harmony.
>
> (Wolfensohn's address to the Board of Governors, 6 October 1998)

Another criticism of SAPs is the way they have been imposed on cash-starved countries by the Bank and the IMF, with far-reaching political implications in breach of Article IV of its Articles of Agreement. Bank (and IMF) conditionalities integral to structural adjustment lending contain strong policy prescriptions to the borrowing government including cutting unproductive expenditures, supporting privatization and deregulation to attract foreign capitals, increasing labour market flexibility and increasing prices of key consumption goods such as gasoline. The political implications of these measures often go much beyond good management of the economy.

In part as a response to that criticism, in late 1999, the Bank replaced its 'Country Assistance Strategy' by 'Poverty Reduction Strategy Papers' (PRSPs). The intention is to highlight that poverty reduction, not adjustment, is the paramount new objective of the Bank; but also that country ownership of a poverty reduction strategy is paramount. However, Bank management retains significant control over these strategies by expressing to the Board a judgement on whether the policies prepared by the countries are economically sound, independently of the legitimacy of the process of preparation of these documents.

Policies

Structural adjustment programmes come with conditionalities in terms of economic policies. The same package of policies referred to as the 'Washington consensus' have been pushed in all countries undertaking SAPs, irrespective of the particular economic, political, social or environmental context. The emphasis of the policies and the development strategy they entail is on microeconomic efficiency and integration into the global economy by promoting exports and attracting foreign investments.

The interpretation of the sustained growth of the East Asian economies up to 1997 has been a major battlefield for rival development theories. In 1993 the World Bank published the influential 'The East Asian Miracle' report that interpreted the success in East Asia in terms of the key principles of the Washington consensus. But critics were quick to point to a different story, in particular to the importance of price distortion ('getting prices wrong') in stimulating economic growth and to state-designed export strategies instead of straightforward trade liberalization (see ECONOMY OF JAPAN).

Importantly the report failed to foresee the financial crisis that hit these countries in 1997 and revealed some structural weaknesses in their development strategies. At the same time, the very disappointing performance of the Russian economy revealed the limits of the Washington consensus, while the success of China continued to show the existence of alternative successful development paths.

In 1999, Joseph Stiglitz, then chief economist of the World Bank, acknowledged publicly the limits of the Washington consensus in a series of speeches and academic articles. The main lesson he drew from Russia and the financial crisis in Asia was the key importance of adequate institutions to support the proper functioning of a market economy. The logical consequence of that point is the adoption of more gradualist approaches to adjustment to permit the required institutional development and change. This perspective led Stiglitz to voice strong criticisms against the conditionalities part of the IMF-led rescue packages offered to the Asian countries hit by the financial crisis and fully in line with the Washington consensus orthodoxy. While not following its chief economist entirely, the World Bank also distanced itself from the IMF on that occasion. Stiglitz's resignation from the World Bank in early 2000 has been attributed to his unorthodox position on the crises in Asia and Russia, and his departure leaves the future direction of World Bank development thinking uncertain.

4 New directions and further evolution

Since the late 1960s, the evolution of Bank strategies and of the international economy have been closely related. Bank strategies respond not only to internal organizational impulses and to the needs of its clients (national states) but also to structural changes in the international economy as a whole. Conversely, given the wide direct and indirect influence of the Bank, its strategies and policies participate in shaping the evolution of national and the international economies (see GLOBALIZATION).

Since the early 1980s the Bank has actively participated in promoting and shaping the process of economic globalization. In many developing countries, trade liberalization was not an outcome of negotiations within the frame of the General Agreement of Tariffs and Trade (GATT) but a result of reforms within the frame of SAPs. After the creation of the World Trade Organization in 1994, the Bank became, with the International Monetary Fund (IMF) and the WTO, one of the three pillars of the global economic governance system. Coordination between the three organizations is based on a shared belief in the benefits of trade and exchange liberalizations, complemented by various institutional mechanisms of consultation and co-ordination.

In this system, the role of the Bank is to provide funds, technical expertise, and political advice to compensate for the negative impacts of globalization on developing countries. The two new strategic directions introduced in the late 1990s – CDF and PRSPs – will take the Bank into a post-adjustment era. They are global responses to the increasing problems of social marginalization and the political risks it creates, which depart from the classic development view that these problems are best addressed as part of a strategy of nation building.

The challenges for the Bank will be numerous. It needs to convince its political masters that the strategy is sound at a time when many voices express criticism on the ever-increasing scale and scope of Bank operations and areas of responsibility. In the Metzler report released in the year 2000 a commission of the US Congress advocated a refocusing of the Bank mission. It will also need to retain the confidence of the financial markets from which it raises its resources at the same time as it increases lending in non-productive areas. It is more than likely that the Bank may be the victim of backlashes against globalization. Its current strategy to become a global safety net may eventually conflict with people's aspirations to regain democratic control over their destinies within the national space.

FRANCK AMALRIC
SOCIETY FOR INTERNATIONAL DEVELOPMENT, ROME

FRANCESCO MARTONE
CAMPAGNA PER LA RIFORMA DELLA BANCA MONDIALE, ROME

Further reading

(References cited in the text marked *)

Bello, W. (1994) *Dark Victory. The United States, the World Bank, and Global Poverty*, London: Polity Press. (A thorough analysis and criticism of structural adjustment programmes.)

Bergesen, H.O. and Lunde, L. (1999) *Dinosaurs or Dynamos? The United Nations and the World Bank at the Turn of the Century*, London: Earthscan. (Traces the history of the World Bank from a development bank to a development agency in comparison to changes within the UN system.)

Caufield, C. (1997) *Masters of Illusion. The World Bank and the Poverty of Nations*, New York: Henry Holt and Company. (An overall critical analysis of the World Bank's record in alleviating poverty.)

George, S. and Sabelli F. (1993) *Faith and Credit, The World Bank's Secular Empire*, Boulder, CO: Westview Press (An influential critical, sociological analysis of the World Bank.)

Kapur, D., Lewis J.P. and Webb, R. (eds) (1997) *The World Bank: Its First Half Century*, Washington, DC: Brookings Institution Press. (Comprehensive compilation of texts on the World Bank.)

Mason, E. and Asher, R. (1973) *The World Bank since Bretton Woods*, Washington, DC: Brookings Institution Press. (Official history of the first quarter-century of Bank operations.)

Rich, B. (1994) *Mortgaging the Earth, The World Bank, Environmental Impoverishment, and the Crisis of Development*, Boston, MA: Beacon Press. (A review of the Bank's environmental record.)

World Bank (various years) *World Development Report*, New York: Oxford University Press. (Main development policy documents produced by the World Bank.)

See also: EAST ASIAN ECONOMIES; ECONOMIC GROWTH AND CONVERGENCE; GROWTH THEORY; INTERNATIONAL FINANCIAL STABILITY; INTERNATIONAL MONETARY FUND; WORLD TRADE ORGANIZATION

European Central Bank

1 Towards European Economic and Monetary Union and a European Central Bank
2 Organization, statutes and independence of the European System of Central Banks
3 Operational policy
4 Emerging issues

Overview

The European System of Central Banks (ESCB) was conceived by the 1992 Maastricht Treaty to develop and implement monetary policy within the European Union (EU) single currency 'eurozone'. The ESCB came into effect in June 1998 and consists of the fifteen EU national central banks (NCBs) together with a core institution, the European Central Bank (ECB), whose Governing Council is the key decision-making body with regard to the overarching mandate to maintain price stability.

Traditionally central banks provide many facilities but four are core: the issue of the national currency; the conduct of monetary policy; acting as lender of last resort to the financial sector; and managing the exchange rate policy. Arguably a true ECB should manage these functions on an EU-wide basis, hence discussion of the ECB cannot be divorced from that of EMU with its common currency, unified monetary policy and irrevocably fixed exchange rates. However, these aspects imply both a high degree of independence from national governments and a transfer of powers from existing NCBs who now act as agents of the ECB. Such features have proved contentious issues with EU members in the run-up to the launch of the euro in January 1999. Moreover, other features are also proving controversial, notably the appropriate euro exchange rate, and the ECB's supervisory role in the 'eurozone'.

1 Towards European Economic and Monetary Union and a European Central Bank

Since the late 1950s Western European nations have followed a process of progressive regional integration. Initially the focus was removing trade restrictions (negative integration) by the creation of a *free-trade area* with the gradual elimination of tariffs, quotas and other trade barriers, followed later by a *customs union*, with a common external tariff. During the 1980s the emphasis switched towards policy harmonization (positive integration) via completion of the *single or common market* with factor mobility, and the parallel development of the European Monetary System (EMS), aimed at fostering closer monetary cooperation and stability. During this period integration was accompanied by a widening of the club from the original six European Economic Community (EEC) members (France, West Germany, Italy, Belgium, Luxembourg and the Netherlands) to nine (UK, Ireland and Denmark in 1973), to twelve (Greece in 1981, Spain and Portugal in 1986).

Monetary union and *economic and monetary union* represent higher levels of regional integration. In June 1988 the European Council confirmed the objective of the progressive realization of economic and monetary union and mandated Jacques Delors, then President of the European Commission, to propose concrete steps to attain this goal. The Delors Report defined *monetary union* as the total and irreversible convertibility of currencies; complete liberalization of capital transactions; full integration of banking and financial markets; the elimination of fluctuation margins; and the irrevocable locking of exchange rate parities. *Economic and monetary union (EMU)* was defined as: a single market with the free movement of goods, services, capital and labour; the strengthening of market mechanisms; and greater macroeconomic policy coordination (European Commission 1989).

The Delors Report proposed a three-phase approach to EMU, with the *first 'convergence' stage* from 1 July 1990, the aims of which were to consolidate the single market programme and encourage convergence of economic and monetary policies among member states. To realize later stages it was necessary to renegotiate the original 1957 Treaty of Rome, which established the EEC, so as to allow for new organizational structures, including a new central monetary institution. The resultant Treaty on European Union, signed in February 1992 ('Maastricht Treaty') incorporated, *inter alia*, the protocols on the Statute of the European System of Central Banks (ESCB), the European Central Bank (ECB), and the European Monetary Institute (EMI).

The establishment of the EMI on 1 January 1994 marked the start of the *second 'institutional' stage*. Located in Frankfurt, the EMI had its own legal personality and a senior decision-making council comprising a full-time President and the Governors of the member states' central banks. The latter endowed it with ECU 61.5 million and from the interest income generated by these financial resources it covered its running costs. Although often referred to as a pro-forma ECB, the EMI had no decision-making powers in the field of monetary policy. Indeed its transitory nature reflected the fact that in stage two, responsibility for monetary policy remained the preserve of national authorities in member states. In essence the two main tasks of the EMI were firstly, to strengthen central bank cooperation and monetary policy coordination, and secondly, to prepare for the establishment of the ESCB in stage three. Thus it provided a forum for consultation, advice and exchange of views on policy issues.

On 2 May 1998 the European Council decided that eleven member states (Belgium, Germany, Spain, France, Ireland, Italy, Luxembourg, the Netherlands, Austria, Portugal and Finland) met the criteria for participation in stage three. These nations then appointed the ECB Executive Board marking the formal establishment of the ECB on 1 June 1998. The EMI was liquidated, leaving the remainder of 1998 for testing systems in preparation for the single currency.

On 1 January 1999 the *third 'full EMU' stage* began with the irrevocable locking of exchange rates of the currencies of the eleven participating EU members and the introduction of a single monetary policy under the ECB's responsibility.

2 Organization, statutes and independence of the European System of Central Banks

The ESCB comprises the European Central Bank (ECB) and the national central banks (NCBs) of the EMU participants. Those NCBs of non-participants, for example the UK, are deemed members of the ESCB with special status: they conduct their respective national monetary policies but cannot participate in decision making regarding the single monetary policy for the 'eurozone'.

The 5,000 million euros subscribed capital of the ECB is provided by the NCBs with subscriptions based on respective shares of EU GDP and population. The paid-up capital comes from the eleven participating members who also provide foreign exchange reserve assets equivalent to 50,000 million euros, which the ECB holds and manages. The ESCB is governed by the decision-making bodies of the ECB: the Governing Council; Executive Board; and the General Council.

The *Governing Council* comprises all the ECB Executive Board and the Governors of the NCBs of the EMU participant member states. As the key decision-making body its main responsibilities are:

- to adopt guidelines and make decisions necessary to ensure the performance of tasks entrusted to the ESCB;
- to formulate the monetary policy of the EU, including, as appropriate, decisions relating to the intermediate monetary objectives, key interest rates and the supply of reserves in the ESCB, and to establish the necessary guidelines for their implementation.

The *Executive Board* consists of the President, Vice-President and four other members, all of recognized standing and professional experience in monetary or banking matters. They are appointed by the common accord of the member states' governments on a recommendation of the European Council, and following consultation with the European Parliament and the ECB Governing Council. The main responsibilities of the Executive Board are:

- to implement monetary policy in accordance with the guidelines and decisions laid down by the Governing Council of the ECB, and, in doing so, to give the necessary instructions to the NCBs; and
- to execute those powers delegated to it by the ECB Governing Council.

The *General Council* comprises the President, Vice-President and Governors of all the NCBs, including those without a derogation to participate in full EMU. The General Council performs those tasks taken over from the EMI that, owing to the derogation of some member states, still need to be performed in stage three. It also contributes to the ESCB's advisory, reporting and information-gathering functions.

In accordance with the Maastricht Treaty statutes the primary *objective* of the ESCB is to maintain price stability. It must also support the general economic policies of the EU, provided its inflation objective is not compromised, and act in accordance with the principles of an open-market economy. The main *tasks* of the ESCB are to:

- carry out monetary policy;
- conduct foreign exchange operations in accordance with the prevailing exchange rate regime of the EU;
- hold and manage the official foreign exchange reserves of the participating nations;
- ensure the smooth running of the payments systems; and
- participate as necessary in the formulation, coordination and execution of policies relating to prudential supervision and stability of the financial system.

This is a wide-ranging, demanding set of functions common to central banks, although not always conducted by them. Indeed, Mullineux (1985) suggests that some central banking functions might be operated more efficiently by other private and public sector bodies. He suggests the concentration of activities can create potential conflicts of interest. For example, if a central bank is responsible for the maintenance of financial stability in an economy, it may be forced to inject liquidity to forestall banking failures if there is a crisis of confidence in the banking system. In stimulating demand by expanding the money supply, or lowering interest rates, pressure may be reduced on the banking system. However, such actions may negate the objective of achieving price stability if the money supply growth rate exceeds that of output.

In designing the draft ESCB statutes the NCB governors were strongly influenced by the Deutsche Bundesbank both in terms of its historical success in maintaining the value of the D-Mark and in its organization. However, the ESCB's statutory objective to maintain price stability is narrower than the Bundesbank's mandate to promote also employment, balanced trade and growth.

The ESCB is supposed to be an independent system. The Maastricht Treaty is based on a belief that delegating monetary policy decisions to an independent institution with a clearly defined and specific mandate improves the quality of policy making, leads to more stable prices, and facilitates both sustainable real growth and improvements in living standards.

In examining ECB independence an important distinction is necessary between *political* (or goal) and *economic* (or instrument) independence (see Alesina and Grilli 1992 and Briault *et al.* 1996). *Political* independence may be defined as the ability of a central bank to set its own targets, without constraints or influence from government. To this end one important feature is the provision of long tenure for NCB governors and Executive Boards so as to overcome susceptibility to political pressures and volatility in the conduct of monetary policy. The ESCB statute makes the following provisions:

- a minimum renewable term of office for governors of five years;

- a minimum non-renewable term of office for members of the executive board of eight years;
- removal from office only in the event of incapacity or serious misconduct;
- the European Court of Justice empowered to settle any disputes.

A second feature is that in undertaking ESCB-related work neither the ECB nor any NCB, nor any member of the various decision-making bodies, may accept instructions from external bodies. Thus the ECB is autonomous and independent of national and EU authorities. This requirement has necessitated changes to legislation in some nations, such as the United Kingdom, in order to establish the independence of NCB governors. In any event in stage three member NCBs are effectively branch offices of the ECB without autonomous monetary powers.

Economic independence implies that the ECB may use, without restrictions, monetary policy instruments to pursue its monetary policy goals. In particular, the monetary financing by governments of budget deficits is prohibited, a significant constraint for nations with traditionally large public sector debts such as Belgium and Italy.

Healey and Levine (1992) suggest that monetary union affects national public finances in three ways. Firstly, the right to issue notes and coin is transferred to the ECB so that 'seignorage' profits are no longer available to national governments. Countries such as Portugal, Italy and Spain are particularly affected because their embryonic financial systems are often relatively dependent on cash and they have experienced traditionally high inflation rates. Accordingly, currency issues are an 'inflation tax' by which governments can fund current expenditure by issuing non-redeemable debt with a negative return equal to the inflation rate. In recent years the importance of this 'inflation tax' has reduced under the ERM/EMU convergence effect on EU interest rates and the completion of the single market fostering financial market integration. A second impact is that economic independence forbids the opening of ECB lines of credit for community or national public institutions, in contrast to pre-existing arrangements in countries such as France and Italy where central banks granted credit to their Finance Ministries for residual budget deficit financing. The ECB is banned from participating in the primary money market for national government bonds so monetarization of debt occurs only as a by-product of open-market operations consistent with the price stability objective. Thirdly, EMU prevents the use of 'surprise inflation' to amortize outstanding government debt by eroding its real value.

However, ECB independence has long been a contentious aspect of EMU (see, for example, Henderson 1993; Wood *et al.* 1993). At one level, no other part of the integration process has involved such a significant transfer of sovereignty from member states to the EU authorities. Mrs Thatcher, UK Prime Minister at the time of the Delors Report, objected to the 'centralization' in the operation of the ESCB; that control of core elements of national economic policy would be transferred from parliaments to an unelected and unaccountable European body. The concern lingers that a powerful central decision-making organization is created which lacks transparency and over which weaker members may have relatively little influence with regard to their domestic affairs. Hence there have been worries as to how the ECB can be made accountable yet remain independent. While statutes, strict reporting requirements, explicit objectives and plans may provide the accountability consistent with independence, they do not necessarily legitimize it, leaving the ECB open to political attack.

Moreover, even sensible central bank statutes are no guarantee of success; what matters more is the attitude and culture of those in charge. However, in an influential paper, Rogoff (1985) suggests that a welfare-improving point on the credibility-flexibility frontier could be secured by delegating monetary policy making to an authority with greater inflation-aversion than society as a whole – a *conservative* central banker. Under the model some loss of flexibility is traded for a gain in credibility, but Rogoff shows that provided that the degree of central bank conservatism (inflation-aversion) is not excessive, then society's overall welfare improves. The model implies that an independent central bank should lower average inflation but raise output variability.

Empirical tests of such models suggest that independent central banks out-perform more dependent ones (see Wood *et al.* 1993). Greater goal and instrument independence are associated with lower inflation. Moreover, most studies have failed to find a significant link between independence and the mean or variability of output growth or employment. At face value independence provides an inflation gain without the attendant costs of output or employment variability.

Making a central bank independent imposes a constraint on government interference in monetary policy; making the central bank accountable imposes a constraint on how it exercises this independence. In the context of the ECB its independence and primary objective are established in the Maastricht Treaty, which itself was subject to intense public scrutiny, debate and ratification, hence in turn affording some democratic legitimacy to ECB independence. Moreover, the Treaty imposes standards of accountability via regular quarterly reports, and an Annual Report to the European Parliament, Council and Commission. The European Parliament holds a general debate on the report received and its committees have the right to question the ECB President and Executive Board members. In addition, regular press conferences, statements on the economic situation, discussion and technical papers form part of a wider remit of intended accountability.

3 Operational policy

The ECB interprets the primary price stability objective as a 'year-on-year' increase in the Harmonized Index of Consumer Prices (HICP) for the 'eurozone' of less than 2 per cent. This definition signifies that the ECB is concerned about both inflation and deflation, as the term 'year-on-year increases' implies that prolonged decreases in the HICP would be inconsistent with price stability. Moreover, medium-term stability is sought, acknowledging that there may be short-term price volatility that cannot be controlled by monetary policy alone.

The operation of monetary policy in EMU raises two basic issues: the choice of variable(s) to serve as the *target(s)* for the price stability objective; and the *instrument(s)* used to attain the target(s). The Governing Council's own monetary strategy reflects the unique circumstances prevalent at the start of EMU. However, there is also a desire to inherit the success of member NCBs, hence there is some continuity with past strategies. The monetary policy rests on two pillars. The first and 'thicker' one is a broad monetary target, similar to that applied by the Deutsche Bundesbank, although for the ECB this is more a 'reference value' (initially an annual rate of 4.5 per cent) for the growth of a broad 'eurozone' money aggregate, M3. The second, 'thinner' pillar includes an assessment of a basket of economic indicators, including an inflation forecast, the exchange rate and estimates of output gaps. This twin-pillar policy does not fall neatly into the traditional classification of 'rule-based' or 'discretionary' monetary policies. The Bundesbank's monetary targeting, as per the ECB's first pillar, was deemed rule based, whereas the US Federal Reserve policy with its various instruments, is deemed discretionary. If anything, the ECB is more akin to the latter with the combination of a pliant monetary reference range, an unpublished inflation forecast and a mix of other indicators.

In order to implement monetary policy three types of instrument are available to the ESCB: open-market operations; standing facilities; and a minimum reserve system.

Open-market operations are important for steering interest rates, managing liquidity in the market and signalling the monetary policy stance. Five sets of tools are available, the most important of which are reverse transactions (applicable on the basis of repurchase agreements or collateralized loans). The ESCB may also use outright transactions, the issuance of debt certificates, foreign exchange swaps and the collection of fixed-term deposits. In initiating open-market operations the ECB decides on the instrument(s) to be used, and the terms and conditions for their execution. Four categories of operations exist:

- *Main Refinancing Operations (MROs)* are regular, liquidity-providing reverse repurchase transactions with a weekly frequency and fortnightly maturity executed by the NCBs on the basis of standard tenders.
- *Longer-Term Refinancing Operations (LTROs)* are liquidity-providing reverse transactions with a monthly frequency and three-month maturity.
- *Fine-Tuning Operations* are executed on an ad hoc basis in order to manage the liquidity situation in the market, and also to steer interest rates, notably to smooth the effects of unexpected liquidity fluctuations.
- *Structural Operations* occur via the issuance of debt certificates, reverse transactions, and outright transactions executed when the ECB wishes to adjust the structural position of the ESCB relative to the financial sector.

The ESCB operates two *Standing Facilities* to provide for, and absorb, overnight liquidity. These are administered by the respective NCBs. The *Marginal Lending Facility* provides counterparties with liquidity against collateral assets. The interest rate applied is the normal ceiling for overnight money market rates, while the *Deposit Facility* allows counterparties to deposit funds at an interest rate which represents the floor for overnight money market rates.

The ESCB also applies a *Minimum Reserve System* to credit institutions in the 'eurozone'. This has the twin objectives of monetary control, by stabilizing money market interest rates creating (or enlarging) a structural liquidity shortage, and money market management, by inducing (or enlarging) the banks' demand for reserves and the control of money expansion. Reserve requirements are calculated by applying a 2 per cent reserve ratio to deposits, debt securities and money market paper issued by credit institutions (except for maturities over two years). This requirement is met on an average over the reserve maintenance period, not on a daily basis. There is an allowance of 100,000 euros so that credit institutions with small reserve bases will not have to hold minimum reserves. However, the recent widespread trend to lower reserve requirements reflects increasing recognition of the implicit tax that unremunerated reserve requirements entail (Enoch and Quintyn 1996) (see SECURITIES AND EXCHANGE REGULATION).

During the first operational year of monetary policy in 1999, the main refinancing operation rate (MRO) was 3 per cent throughout the first quarter, 2.5 per cent from April, then 3 per cent from November. Very short-term rates, measured by the Euro Overnight Index Average (EONIA), remained close to the ECB main refinancing rate throughout the year. Most of the euro-system liquidity was provided to credit institutions through the weekly MROs (75 per cent) with much of the rest from LTROs and only a negligible amount from standing facilities. In principle all credit institutions in the 'eurozone' are potential counterparties (over 8000), although they must meet eligibility criteria set by both individual NCBs and the ECB. In practice only around 2500 are signed up, of which only 800 or so are active in the weekly MROs. It seems that many prefer to access liquidity from larger correspondent banks rather than the central bank.

4 Emerging issues

Various potential difficulties could arise between national governments and the ECB, linked to the traditional dual objectives of central banks: firstly, to stabilize prices and general economic activity via monetary and exchange rate policies; and, secondly, to maintain a stable financial and payments system.

With regard to the former, earlier reference was made to how the Maastricht Treaty forbids central bank financing of government deficits. In addition, under a Stability and Growth Pact EMU participating governments agreed penalties for running excessive deficits, for example a fine of 0.2 per cent of GDP for a deficit of 3 per cent of GDP, rising to 0.5 per cent for one of 6 per cent. However, the liberal interpretation of the EMU entry requirements raises doubts as to how binding such constraints might be. If excessive budget deficits arise, then ECB independence is compromised, yet if the ECB refuses to finance an excess, the result could be higher interest rates, 'crowding out' of domestic spending resulting in weak growth, and high unemployment with ensuing economic and political tensions.

The early history of EMU suggests, however, that the most likely area of dispute would be over the appropriate policy for the euro. The Maastricht Treaty (article 109.2) permits the European Council to 'formulate general orientations for exchange rate policy'. Thus the monetary independence of the ECB may be compromised as any exchange rate intervention will impact on the money stock. Either a central bank (via monetary policy) concentrates on restricting inflation *or* it maintains an exchange rate policy. This contrasts with the situation faced by the Deutsche Bundesbank whose mandate was safeguarding the currency and thus in active control of exchange rate policy. However, arguably the exchange rate mechanism (ERM) of the European Monetary System (EMS) worked well during the 1980s because of Bundesbank concern with inflation. If it had worried about avoiding ERM realignments it would not have forced dis-inflation and convergence on EU members. Although the Maastricht Treaty stipulates that exchange rate policy must be consistent with the price stability goal, there is still scope for members to debate how this is interpreted, especially the orientation and level of the exchange rate.

Indeed, just prior to the 1 January 1999 launch of the single currency, the feeling was that a strong, overvalued euro might harm EU competitiveness and the ECB would not permit benign neglect of the currency. However, by April 1999 Wim Duisenberg, President of the ECB, was expressing concern at the 10 per cent fall in the value of the euro against the US dollar. This decline revealed a paradox in that the weak euro had been one factor reducing the need for the ECB to cut interest rates. However, market sentiment suggested that a cut associated with efforts to spur growth might support the euro in contrast to conventional economic theory. In a low-inflation environment with growth at a premium, a cut in short-term rates may lead to expectations of higher long-term interest rates on the back of faster growth and these may cause the currency to rise. In the event the April 1999 ECB interest rate cut had little impact on the euro's prevailing downward spiral. In November 1999 a rise in the refinancing rate was explained as tightening monetary policy in the face of accelerating private credit and money supply growth, rising producer prices and wage expectations.

In one sense the euro is more of a psychological than economic issue. Within the EU the euro's external exchange rate matters less if 'eurozone' members trade mostly with each other. Indeed, if anything, the currency weakness in 1999 spurred EU exports yet did not raise the spectre of rising inflation as core inflation levels were low in most member states. However, in an international currency context, the economic size and potency of the 'eurozone' suggest that the euro should be a major future international intervention and invoicing currency. Much will depend on investor confidence in ECB monetary policy as well as the economic performance of the 'eurozone'.

Other areas of potential difficulty relate to the structure and supervision of the overall EU financial and payments system. The ECB is only one institution in the ECSB and, moreover, is a lean organization with a limited budget and staff. Sceptics might argue that it will not enjoy the same popularity that the Bundesbank had in Germany and faces political diversity in its dealings with the EC, EU Council of Finance Ministers (ECOFIN) and European Parliament.

The broader maintenance of a stable financial and payments system is not an explicit ECB objective. However, banking supervision is an important, if uncertain issue in Europe where the trend has been towards supervisory agencies that operate independently of their central banks, even though ultimately NCBs dominate through their 'lender of last resort' functions. Moreover, traditionally supervision has focused on a bank's balance sheet strength and compliance with capital adequacy and portfolio components requirements. This approach may be less relevant in increasingly liquid, securitized and integrated financial markets in which banks are active participants and crises can develop rapidly. As banks take on more market risks, they may depend on their central bank's willingness and ability to provide liquidity in times of need. While the ECB has some influence when levying minimum reserve requirements, it has no statutory regulatory respon- sibilities and in this sense is less likely to provide liquidity than conventional NCBs.

A related issue is thus whether EU banking supervision should be centralized. Apart from the provision of liquidity quickly at low credit risk, there are several arguments in favour of centralization. The advent of cross-border banking mergers, the growth of pan-European universal banks and a generally more competitive financial marketplace in Europe create coordination burdens for national supervisors. Furthermore, EMU requires a single clearing and payments system related to monetary policy and overseen by the ECB. At present the Trans-European Automated Gross Real-Time Settlement System (TARGET) is being developed for all NCBs. Indeed, if EU financial markets become more liquid with high-volume wholesale payments, then for effective monetary control the ECB may need to combine a defined 'lender of last resort' together with supervisory responsibilities. However, in so doing the ECB may be perceived as too powerful, especially in view of aforementioned concerns over its accountability. An independent regulatory agency, distinct from the ECB, may be more acceptable, however, there remains the issue of liquidity provision to the EU financial system in times of need.

ROGER HENDERSON
LEEDS BUSINESS SCHOOL

Further reading

(references cited in text marked *)

* Alesina, A. and Grilli, V. (1992) 'The European Central Bank: reshaping monetary policies in Europe', Ch. 3. in M.B. Canzoneri, V. Grilli and P.R. Masson (eds), *Establishing a Central Bank: Issues in Europe and lessons from the US*, Cambridge: Cambridge University Press. (A text which draws on US experience in setting out the design of an ESCB.)

Begg, I. and Green, D. (1996) 'Banking supervision in Europe and Economic and Monetary Union', *Journal of European Public Policy* 3 (3), September: 381–401. (Outlines approaches to future regulation and supervision of banking in EMU.)

* Briault, C., Haldane, A. and King, M. (1996) 'Central bank independence and accountability', *Bank of England Quarterly Bulletin*, February, 36 (1): 63–68. (Discusses the link between central bank accountability and independence.)

* Enoch, C. and Quintyn, M (1996) 'European Monetary Union: operating monetary policy', *Finance and Development*, September: 28–31. (Examines monetary policy targets and instruments under EMU.)

* European Commission (1989) *Report on Economic and Monetary Union in the European Community (Delors Report)*, Committee for the Study of Economic and Monetary Union, Luxembourg. (The proposal setting out the steps towards EMU.)

* European Commission (1992) 'Treaty on European Union' (Maastricht Treaty), Conf-up-uem 2002/92, Brussels: EC. (The Treaty setting out the protocols for the ESCB, ECB and EMI.)

* Healey, N.M. and Levine, P. (1992) 'Unpleasant monetarist arithmetic revisited: central bank independence, fiscal policy and European Monetary Union', *National Westminster Quarterly Review*, August: 23–37. (Examines conflicts in the roles of central banks in operating monetary policy.)

* Henderson, R. (1993) *European Finance*, Maidenhead: McGraw-Hill Europe. (Text covering various aspects of European banking and finance.)

* Mullineux, A.W. (1985) 'Do we need the Bank of England?', *Lloyds Bank Review* 157: 13–24. (Examines who should perform central bank functions.)

* Rogoff, K. (1985) 'The optimal degree of commitment to an intermediate monetary target', *Quarterly Journal of Economics*, November: 1169–90. (Argues that central bank independence can lower average inflation and raise welfare.)

Williams, D. and Read, R. (1998) 'The European Central Bank', Ch.10. in P. Templeton (ed.), *The Euro*, 2nd edn, Chichester: Wiley: 123–45. (Edited text on practical impacts of the euro.)

* Wood, G.E., Mills, T.C. and Capie, F.H. (1993) 'Central bank independence: What is it and what will it do for us?', Institute of Economic Affairs, Current Controversies No. 4, London: IEA. (Examines the concept of independence with reference to empirical data.)

Further resources

European Central Bank website with up-to-date publications, working papers, speeches, press releases, monthly bulletins and annual report: http://ecb.int

See also: SECURITIES AND EXCHANGE REGULATION

International Monetary Fund (IMF)

1 Origins
2 Changing role and structure
3 Recent developments and current debates

Overview

The International Monetary Fund (IMF), created at the Bretton Woods Conference in 1944, is a foremost international organization which has been intended to serve key functions related to the monitoring and management of the world monetary and financial system. These functions have evolved substantially over time but have included the provision of 'liquidity' to the world economy so as to permit the smooth and uninterrupted maintenance and growth of world trade and payments, 'surveillance' of national and world economies so as to provide timely information for use in policy decisions, and the provision of expert policy advice on macroeconomic and financial management so as to further national and international economic goals.

Originally conceived as the central institution supporting the maintenance of the fixed exchange rate system designed at Bretton Woods, the IMF came successively to be viewed as a potential 'world central bank', and as an agency with the dual tasks of supporting the management by countries of short-term economic crises and of longer term structural reform aiding their integration in the world economy. Along with the World Bank and the World Trade Organization (WTO), the IMF has become a pillar of the system of global governance supporting the process of economic and financial globalization. This enlarged role has occasioned substantial debate.

1 Origins

The IMF was born against the backdrop of war and the memory of a turbulent inter-war world trading and monetary system. The leading countries of the United Nations (the wartime alliance against the axis countries), and in particular the United States and the United Kingdom, sought to create a durable framework within which the inter-war problems of currency instability and competitive devaluation, defaults on international credit obligations, and the development of regional trading blocks tied to currency systems could be avoided, while furthering their own national interests. The solution to this problem, under the dominant intellectual influence of John Maynard Keynes of the United Kingdom and Harry Dexter White of the United States, was the 'gold exchange standard' or Bretton Woods system, in which countries other than the United States pegged their currencies at fixed exchange rates (or 'par values') to the United States dollar and the United States maintained a fixed rate of exchange between the US dollar and gold. Through this solution it was sought to establish a regime of substantial currency stability. However, countries with relatively low official reserves, net debtor positions and current account deficits (such as the United Kingdom) still risked the inability to maintain their declared par values. The primary goal of the IMF was to address this difficulty and thereby ensure the stability and durability of the Bretton Woods system.

The eventual shape of the IMF merged aspects of Keynes' plan for an international 'clearing union' (from which loans of a new international currency (the 'bancor') were to be made available up to a fixed quota to debtor countries, and to which creditor countries would be required to lend surpluses beyond a fixed level) with aspects of the White Plan in which a Stabilization Fund of national currencies available to be purchased by members would be created, and in which changes in exchange rates would be accepted only in the event of a 'fundamental disequilibrium' (see KEYNES, J.M.). In its final shape was embodied acceptance of the demand of the debtor countries (especially the UK) that surplus countries should in principle bear some of the 'burden of adjustment' and the demand of the surplus countries that debtor countries take appropriate responsibility for the maintenance of par values. The international currency envisioned by Keynes was not initially created.

Specifically, the Articles of Agreement of the IMF negotiated at Bretton Woods established a system of national 'quotas' based on negotiations and the assessment of a set of fundamental economic variables (such as the size of official reserves, national income, and the level of imports and exports). These quotas, although first established at Bretton Woods, have been repeatedly revised. A country's quota determines the amount of the subscription it must pay in to the fund, in the form of external reserve assets and its own currency. It also determines its voting strength (proportional to its quota beyond a common base level) and its access to IMF resources. In particular a portion of a country's quota (the 'gold tranche', later renamed the 'reserve tranche') could be drawn on with few (and later no) conditions. Borrowing from the Fund (essentially drawing on the resources provided to the IMF by other countries' subscriptions) beyond this amount would normally require the imposition of IMF 'conditionalities' (i.e. specific policy and performance requirements). The Fund's resources were to be extended to prevent countries having to depart from par values other than in conditions of 'fundamental disequilibrium'. Where it was deemed necessary by a country to depart widely from its par value, the IMF was authorized to judge whether a fundamental disequilibrium existed. The Articles of Agreement also required member countries to avoid imposing 'restrictions on the making of payments and transfers for current international transactions', other than for a transitional period, and to engage in periodic consultations with the Fund if they continued to do so. In this way the IMF's articles encapsulated its founders' vision of a conventionally liberal as well as stable world economic order. In accordance with its Articles of Agreement, the IMF headquarters was established in the territory of the member country with the largest quota, the United States.

2 Changing role and structure

In its first two decades, the IMF's role was largely within the framework of its original conception, although this conception was tested by and adapted to changing circumstances (see ECONOMIC INTEGRATION, INTERNATIONAL). In its very early years, the IMF's role was limited and overshadowed by bilateral agreements (such as the Marshall Plan) and other multilateral institutions (in particular the short-lived European Payments Union). However, by the early 1950s it had come into its own, playing a key role in maintaining the stability of a number of European currencies. In this period it developed a number of its critical operational doctrines and instruments. However, while the IMF's success in fostering exchange rate stability was high, its success in its second goal of fostering a regime of unrestricted current account convertibility was very limited.

Among the instruments first developed in this period was that of the 'Stand-by Arrangement', which subsequently became a standard aspect of IMF operational procedure. The first 'Stand-by Arrangement' was negotiated with Belgium in 1952. In effect, stand-by arrangements provide for a line of credit to be made available to a member country for a specified period and up to a specified value in return for its accepting specific economic 'conditionalities' relating to monetary and fiscal conduct. The widening role of the Fund and its capacity to impose conditionalities in return for its assistance also required it to develop specific doctrines regarding the approach to economic management best suited to the achievement of stability. Accordingly, in this period the Fund substantially strengthened its research capacity and developed a variety of specific operational methodologies. Foremost among these was the 'flow of funds' methodology known as 'financial programming', associated with Jacques Polak of the Fund, which continues to be its central tool for policy analysis. The financial programming approach involves 'a recognition of basic accounting identities supplemented with a small number of behavioural relationships and forecasts of key economic variables' (Mussa and Savastano 1999), which are said to permit determination of the requirements for attaining balance of payments equilibrium and low inflation. The specific content of favoured IMF conditionalities (and in particular the often 'contractionary' approach to the restoration of external and internal balance, through restrictive monetary and fiscal policy) was also developed in this period.

As the IMF's role increased toward the late 1950s it became apparent that its subscriptions by member countries might not be enough for it to deal with all possible contingencies. Accordingly, in 1962 the General Arrangements to Borrow through which the Fund arranged for a line of credit with which to borrow specified amounts from 11 industrial countries were created. The GAB has been activated periodically to help finance particularly large drawings from the Fund (in 1997 the GAB was supplemented by the New Arrangements to Borrow, which provide for an additional line of credit from 25 countries and institutions).

In its first two decades, although the IMF became an increasingly important institution, its success was overshadowed by the fraying of the Bretton Woods system caused by the weakening position of the US dollar associated with the shift of the United States balance of payments from a surplus to a deficit position and with the so-called 'Triffin dilemma'. The latter related to the tension (deriving from the pivotal role of the US dollar in the Bretton Woods system) between the need for an enlarged supply of dollars to provide liquidity for a growing global economy and the inability of the United States to provide this without the supply of dollars exceeding the quantity of US reserve assets to a degree that would jeopardize the convertibility of the dollar into gold, in turn undermining the value of the dollar as a source of liquidity (and therefore the basis of the system as a whole).

An early response to this unease, and indeed a growing sense of crisis, was the 'special drawing right' or SDR, which was born through the first amendment to the Articles of Agreement in 1969. The SDR was envisioned as a new source of liquidity and potential reserve asset that would be free from the structural weakness of the dollar. It was also in effect a new international currency in embryonic form, partially realizing Keynes' vision of the 'bancor'. The SDRs are monetary units (defined currently as a composite of national currencies), which do not have any actual reserve backing. They may be used for payments between official institutions, but generally not for private transactions. SDRs may be exchanged between holders in return for an ordinary reserve currency or other asset, and bear interest at market rates while maintained with the Fund. A fixed quantity of SDRs was initially (and in subsequent rounds) allocated to all member countries in proportion to their quota. The SDR was not able to play the role envisioned for it (in which the IMF would have become akin to a world central bank with the SDR its currency) effectively. Even today, total allocations of SDRs compose less than two per cent of non-gold official reserves. This small quantity of SDRs combined with their restricted role outside of official transactions has undermined its ability to become a new reserve asset. New allocations of SDRs, of special interest to debtor and less developed countries, have often been resisted by reserve currency countries on the ground that there is no requirement for increased global liquidity (and attendant danger that new allocations will undermine the value of existing reserves and generate inflationary pressures). Repeated negotiation on the development of a 'substitution account', through which existing reserves (particularly the US dollar) would be exchanged for new SDRs, has also been unsuccessful due to inability to agree on the sharing of the burden of the decreasing value of non-SDR official reserves such a procedure would entail.

The collapse of the Bretton Woods system between 1970 and 1973, due to the abandonment of the parity of the US dollar with gold, and the subsequent emergence of a flexible exchange rate system (or 'non-system'), created significant challenges for the IMF. The abandonment of fixed parities required the Fund to reform its role in fundamental ways. In particular a rising role for non-gold (i.e. currency) reserves, increased monetary instability, and a sharp rise in private international banking activity (related to heightened cross-border speculation, hedging, and real investment) increased the demand for the IMF's surveillance and balance of payments support activities. In the 1970s the IMF began to refine the economic doctrines that it would apply in a more comprehensive form in the subsequent decade. In particular, in 1975 it initiated the Extended Fund Facility (EFF) in order to enable the implementation of longer term conditionalities and programmes than were feasible under stand-by arrangements. Under the EFF a repayment horizon of up to eleven years was envisioned, during which fundamental reforms of trade and fiscal policy could be pursued. This innovation was born in part of a recognition that the IMF's concerns for currency stability required attention to underlying structural conditions, and in part of a renewed focus on the still unrealized Bretton Woods vision of the development of a conventionally conceived liberal international order.

By the late 1970s, the role of the IMF in relation to developing and middle income countries had taken on a heightened significance, as its role in relation to high income countries waned, due to the long-term improvement in the structural positions of many of them. Indeed, the Fund introduced specific facilities with which to address risks faced especially by developing countries (the Compensatory Financing Facility, introduced in 1963 to enable developing countries – especially producers of primary commodities – to cope with precipitate declines in export receipts, and the 'Oil Facility', established in 1974 to enable countries to manage sharp increases in oil prices). In the 1970s, calls from developing countries for a 'New International Economic Order' gave an added dimension to the ongoing debate over the international monetary system. In particular demands were made (all unrealized) for the IMF to create and finance stabilization and support funds for raw materials prices, and for the voting structure of the Fund to be reformed along more democratic lines.

The debate over the role of the IMF in the developing countries came to a head in the 1980s, with the onset of the debt crisis and the era of 'structural adjustment'. High levels of debt accumulated in the 1970s proved unsustainable for a large number of developing countries in the context of falling primary commodities prices and high world interest rates driven by conditions in industrial countries. The possibility of default on debt, especially by major borrowers such as Brazil, Mexico and Poland, threatened in turn the interests of creditors and the stability of the financial system in the industrial countries. This situation led to a heightened role for the IMF as a source of information, as a coordinator of public and private debt rescheduling efforts, and as a source of supplementary capital and policy advice. The IMF approach to stabilization and to the achievement of longer term viability of the balance of payments relied on its accustomed short-term instruments – devaluation and monetary and fiscal contraction – combined with longer term market-oriented reforms – increased openness to trade and, increasingly, internal deregulation and privatization. In this respect, IMF policy was increasingly influenced by the prevailing currents in the industrial world.

In 1986, the IMF created the Structural Adjustment Facility (SAF) followed in 1987 by the Enhanced Structural Adjustment Facility (ESAF). These new facilities marked the IMFs new focus on supporting medium and long-term market oriented policy reorientation. Sustained balance of payments crises in a variety of developing countries led to substantial reliance on these instruments and mounting criticism that the Fund's approach was both unsuccessful at attaining its economic goals and generated social costs of an unacceptable order (a trenchant example of such criticism is Cornia, Jolly and Stewart 1987).

The rejection of the centrally planned economic model which commenced in 1989 added another important dimension to the Fund's activities. The Fund was called upon to provide financial and policy support of a new kind, in many cases to new members. A new 'Systemic Transformation Facility' allowing large drawings from quotas was created to support the efforts of a number of these countries to develop private market economies. Over the course of the 1990s the Fund has however been extensively criticized for pursuing a policy approach and priorities argued to be inappropriate to the requirements of the 'transition' countries, and in particular for favouring fiscal retrenchment and a contractionary monetary approach to stabilization in a context in which fundamental microeconomic reorganization and the establishment of robust fiscal and political institutions required due consideration, as did the unusually dramatic distributional and social consequences linked by critics to the Fund approach.

3 Recent developments and current debates

In the 1990s, debate over the IMFs current and future role became more acute than ever. The immediate sources of this debate lay in the mixed record of the Fund in fostering prosperity and stability in the 'transition' countries, the continued controversial record of structural adjustment programmes in developing countries (and in particular the ongoing economic and social crisis in the highly indebted poor countries), and the perception that the Fund has limited and possibly inappropriate tools at its disposal to address the causes and consequences of recent high levels of instability in international financial markets. A growing popular awareness of the lack of direct democratic oversight over international markets and economic institutions has also influenced perceptions of the IMF.

As the IMF's approach to structural adjustment and reform has proved to be insufficiently effective, it has unprecedentedly and increasingly turned to conditionalities linked to institutional reform and 'governance'. These have been controversial as they have been perceived by some as an illegitimate challenge to national sovereignty (jealously guarded under the original interpretation of the Articles of Agreement). The Fund has also been accused of husbanding its resources excessively, especially in relation to debt relief in highly indebted poor countries (for which debt to the IMF itself has become an increasing burden) and meeting the requirements of a successful 'transition' from central planning. Finally it has been accused of promoting, at considerable economic and social cost, a lagging and inflexible economic paradigm.

In the context of countries in structural adjustment programmes, the focus of critics has been on their limited and slow success in fostering sustained and high growth and in safeguarding social achievements (as against the traditional Fund objectives of current account balance and low inflation). In the context of recent financial crises (especially those of East Asian and Latin American countries in 1997–8) the Fund has been accused of applying its traditional contractionary 'medicine' in a circumstance in which more focused microeconomic tools (such as financial sector restructuring) and alternative macroeconomic policies (such as short-term capital controls) may have been more effective. These criticisms have gained force in a global environment in which the sharply increased scale of the private flows of funds has arguably increased the likelihood of financial crises linked to self-fulfilling expectations, and to speculative attacks unlinked to 'fundamental' economic variables, and reduced the ability of official actors (including the IMF) to influence market behaviour. The ability of the IMF to significantly influence the level of global liquidity, or even to act as an effective 'lender of last resort' has accordingly come into question.

New issues regarding the appropriate role of the IMF have also arisen. In particular, whether the Fund generates 'moral hazard' (i.e. increased risk-taking behaviour) by providing finance that indirectly benefits private interests in the event of crisis, has been hotly discussed. As with other points of contention, some have called on the Fund accordingly to limit its role further (or indeed to be abolished) while others have called for it to expand its application of resources and ideas. Fundamental questions as to whether the IMF has – just past the mark of half a century – outlived its usefulness, at least in its current form, and whether its primary purpose has been, or ought to be, to enforce conformity in the rules and institutions which govern and link national economies, continue to give rise to vigorous debate.

SANJAY REDDY
COLUMBIA UNIVERSITY

Further reading

(References cited in the text marked *)

* Cornia, G., Jolly, R. and Stewart, F. (1987) *Adjustment with a Human Face*, Oxford: Oxford University Press. (A landmark in the critical response to structural adjustment policies.)
- Humphreys, N. (1999) *Historical Dictionary of the International Monetary Fund*, London: The Scarecrow Press. (A comprehensive dictionary of technical and historical terms linked to the IMF.)
- James, H. (1996) *International Monetary Cooperation Since Bretton Woods*, New York: Oxford University Press. (A magisterial survey of the politics and economics of the post-war monetary system.)
* Mussa, M. and Savastano, M. (1999) 'The IMF approach to economic stabilization', in *NBER Macroeconomics Annual 1999*, Cambridge, MA: National Bureau of Economic Research. (A systematic description of the IMF's methodology of policy analysis and design.)
- Solomon, R. (1982) *The International Monetary System, 1945–1981*, New York: Harper and Row. (An overview of the rise and decline of the Bretton Woods system.)

See also: EAST ASIAN ECONOMIES; ECONOMIC INTEGRATION, INTERNATIONAL; ECONOMIES OF CENTRAL AND EASTERN EUROPE; EUROPEAN CENTRAL BANK; GLOBALIZATION; INTERNATIONAL FINANCIAL STABILITY; KEYNES, J.M.; MONEY AND CAPITAL MARKETS, INTERNATIONAL; WORLD BANK; WORLD TRADE ORGANIZATION

World Trade Organization (WTO)

1 Introduction
2 Origin
3 Structure
4 Fundamental principles
5 Council for trade in goods
6 Council for trade in services
7 Council for trade-related aspects of intellectual property rights
8 Technical barriers
9 Plurilateral agreements
10 Trade policy review
11 Settlement of disputes
12 Controversial rulings
13 Controversies
14 Recent activities – plans for the future

Overview

The WTO is the international organization charged with enforcing a set of trade rules including the General Agreement on Tariffs and Trade (GATT), Trade Related Intellectual Property Measures (TRIPS), General Agreement on Trade in Services (GATS), among others. Its main functions are: administering WTO trade agreements, providing a forum for trade negotiations, handling trade disputes and monitoring national trade policies. WTO was established on 1 January 1995, as successor to GATT.

1 Introduction

The WTO is a powerful new global commerce agency, which transformed the GATT into an enforceable global commercial code. Prior to the Uruguay Round, GATT rules focused primarily on tariffs and quotas. Consensus of GATT members was required to enforce the rules. The Uruguay Round expanded GATT rules to cover services, property rights, and 'non-tariff barriers to trade'. These are food safety laws, product standards, rules on the use of tax dollars, investment policy and other domestic laws that impact trade. The WTO's rules limit what non-tariff policies countries can implement or maintain. The WTO administers a strengthened trade dispute resolution mechanism. Once a final WTO ruling is issued, losing countries have a set time to implement one of only three choices: change their law to conform to the WTO requirements, pay permanent compensation to the winning country or face non-negotiated trade sanctions.

2 Origin

From 1948 to 1994, the GATT provided the rules for much of world trade. Throughout those years, it remained a provisional agreement and organization. The original intention was to create an International Trade Organization (ITO) as the third specialized economic agency within the United Nations (UN) system next to the World Bank and the International Monetary Fund (IMF). The draft ITO Charter extended beyond world trade disciplines, to include rules on employment, commodity agreements, restrictive business practices, international investment and services. Although the ITO Charter was finally agreed at a UN Conference in Havana in 1948, the US government failed to convince the US Congress of the Charter's merits. Provisions on investment that allowed governments to treat foreign capital as they thought best caused major American business groups to withdraw their support for ITO. Even before the Havana conference, 23 of the 50 original participants of the ITO-project decided in 1946 under the leadership of the US government to go ahead with negotiations to reduce and bind customs tariffs. This first round of negotiations resulted in 45,000 tariff concessions affecting about one-fifth of the world's total trade. The 23 mostly advanced market economies also agreed on some trade rules. The combined package of trade rules and tariff concessions was named the GATT. It entered into force in January 1948. With the failure to ratify the ITO Charter, GATT became the principal framework for multilateral trade negotiations. Some eight negotiating rounds were successfully concluded. The last round, the Uruguay Round, involved more than 100 countries. The first six of these rounds, concluding in 1967 with the Kennedy Round, focused primarily on reciprocal negotiation of tariff concessions. These negotiations have led to the reduction of average world tariffs on manufactured goods from 40 per cent in 1947 to 5 per cent in the mid-1990s. The Tokyo Round that ended in 1979, directed, for the first time, substantial attention to non-tariff barriers to trade. Throughout this period, the developing countries have played a marginal role in GATT negotiations. Many developing countries criticized GATT for allowing the developed market economies to practise protectionism in areas where poor countries enjoyed a comparative advantage such as in agriculture and clothing manufacture. They, therefore, tried to bring issues of international trade into the UN system. They succeeded in forming the UN Commission on Trade and Development (UNCTAD) in 1964, but failed in their plan to make GATT that agency's committee on tariffs. Instead, thirty years later, after some developing countries had graduated to the status of 'newly industrialized countries' and many others had adopted market friendly developing strategies, the contracting parties of GATT were the ones which succeeded in having their newly formed organization, the WTO, accorded the privileges and immunities of specialized UN agencies, thereby pushing UNCTAD to the sidelines. However, the WTO addresses some of the original concerns of the developing countries by limiting the arbitrary power of the large trading countries through strengthening the dispute resolution mechanism and majority voting (see below). Therefore, the USA, having frequently engaged in unilateral action, had greater difficulty in accepting the establishment of the WTO.

3 Structure

The WTO has 136 countries as members (as of 11 April 2000). The European Union (EU) also has membership status in addition to each of its own members. The *Ministerial Conference* is the highest authority of the WTO. It is composed of representatives of all WTO members at ministerial level and may take decisions on all matters under any of the multilateral trade agreements. The Conference is required to convene at least every two years. The *General Council* acts on behalf of the Ministerial Conference on all WTO affairs. Furthermore, the Council convenes as the *Dispute Settlement Body*, to oversee the trade dispute settlement procedures, and as the *Trade Policy Review Body*, to analyse members' trade policies. The Council delegates responsibility to three other major Councils: for trade in goods (Goods Council), for trade in services (Services Council) and for trade-related aspects of intellectual property rights (TRIPS Council). These have subsidiary bodies. All councils and bodies consist of all WTO members. In these councils, the members are usually represented by different persons depending on seniority and expertise. In 1999, the WTO *Secretariat* had around 500 staff. It provides administrative and technical support for WTO delegate bodies, trade performance and trade policy analyses, and assistance in the resolution of trade disputes. Contributions to the WTO budget are calculated on the basis of each member's share of the total trade conducted by WTO members. The Secretariat is headed by its *Director-General* and four deputy Director-Generals. In 1999, WTO members selected Michael Moore from New Zealand and Supachai Panitchpakdi from Thailand to serve a split term as DirectorGeneral, with Moore serving first.

4 Fundamental principles

The WTO Agreement contains some 29 individual legal texts and more than 25 additional Ministerial declarations, decisions and understandings. All of these texts are based on a few fundamental principles. *Reciprocity* means that all trade concessions granted by one party must be matched by a concession of the equivalent value by another party or parties. *Non-discrimination*, or the 'most-favoured nation' (MFN) clause, states that any concessions granted to one WTO member must be granted to all other members. A number of exceptions apply, principally for customs unions, free-trade areas and for developing countries. The principle of '*national treatment*' requires goods, having entered a market, to be treated no less favourably than the equivalent domestically-produced goods. The tariff is the preferred form of protection because of its transparency and more precise measurability relative to non-tariff barriers. In order to achieve a stable and predictable trading environment, members '*bind*' their commitments to open their markets for goods or services. This process means that once a tariff level for a particular product has been agreed to (or in services, the degree of market access), it cannot be increased (or access limited) without compensation negotiations with the affected trading partners.

Exceptions apply concerning actions taken against dumping (selling at an unfair low prize), subsidies and special 'countervailing' duties to offset the subsidies, and emergency measures to limit imports temporarily, designed to 'safeguard' domestic industries. However, the right to make use of these exceptions is narrowly circumscribed. The WTO agreement contains detailed rules for calculating the amount of dumping, for conducting anti-dumping investigations, and on the implementation and duration (normally five years) of anti-dumping measures. It disciplines the use of subsidies, and it regulates the actions countries can take to counter the effects of subsidies. Finally, the WTO sets out criteria for assessing whether 'serious injury' has been caused by the surge in imports that would warrant the temporary restriction of imports ('safeguard' actions). It prohibits forms of circumvention of GATT rules such as voluntary export restraints. Members have to notify the WTO of all anti-dumping investigations and safeguard actions. Other exceptions to the fundamental principles apply when food supplies are threatened, or in cases of balance of payments problems.

5 Council for trade in goods

For trade in goods the original GATT agreement in its updated and amended form as the 'Marrakesh protocol to the GATT 1994'

applies. Developed countries agreed to cut their tariffs on industrial products from an average of 6.3 per cent to 3.8 per cent. They also increased the coverage of 'bound' tariffs from 78 per cent (developing countries, 21 per cent) of product lines to 99 per cent (73 per cent).

The original GATT allowed countries to use some non-tariff measures such as import quotas, and to subsidize domestic *agriculture*. The Final Act of the Uruguay Round stipulates the replacement of quantitative measures limiting market access by tariffs (i.e. a process of 'tariffication'). For products whose non-tariff restrictions have been converted to tariffs, governments are allowed to take special emergency actions ('safeguards') in order to prevent swiftly falling prices or surges in imports from hurting their farmers. Developed countries were committed to reduce tariffs, production subsidies (using calculations known as 'total aggregate measurement of support' or 'Total AMS'), and export subsidies by up to 36 per cent, in equal steps over six years. Developing countries were to reduce these measures by smaller amounts over ten years. Least developed countries were excepted. Measures with minimal impact on trade, such as research and disease control, can be used freely (called 'green box' measures). Also permitted are payments made directly to farmers that do not stimulate production ('blue box'). A separate agreement on food safety and animal and plant health standards (Sanitary and Phytosanitary Measures, SPS) allows countries to set their own standards as long as these are based on science (see section 12, the Beef Hormone case). Member countries are encouraged to use international standards, guidelines and recommendations such as the Codex Alimentarius. If an exporting country can demonstrate that the measures it applies on its exports achieve the same level of health protection as in the importing country, then the importing country is expected to accept the exporting country's standards.

From 1974 the Multi-Fibre Arrangement (MFA) provided the basis of international trade in *textiles and clothing*, enabling the major importers to establish quotas for protection against low-cost goods from developing countries. The MFA has come under the WTO's Agreement on Textiles and Clothing (ATC), which aims at integrating this sector into normal GATT rules over a ten-year period in four stages. The agreement allows for 'transitional safeguards' under the condition the importing country can show that its domestic industry is threatened with serious damage. They are subject to review by the Textiles Monitoring Body.

6 Council for trade in services

The General Agreement on Trade in Services (GATS), which was negotiated during the GATT Uruguay Round, is the first set of multilaterally-agreed and legally-enforceable rules and disciplines to cover international trade in services. It was a top priority for the developed countries. Because of the resistance of most developing countries it basically just spells out the conditions under which WTO members will negotiate in the future over liberalizing their markets for services. The main text contains the following basic obligations: total coverage of all forms of internationally-traded services ('cross-border supply', 'consumption abroad', 'commercial presence', 'presence of natural persons'), non-discrimination and transparency in regulations. The annexes deal with the rules for specific sectors. Each country lists specific commitments on service sectors and on activities within those sectors. The commitments guarantee access to the country's market in the listed sectors, and they spell out any limitations on market access and national treatment (plus on a separate list exceptions to the MFN principle of non-discrimination). Governments also agreed to continue negotiations in the following areas: basic telecommunications, maritime transport, movement of natural persons, and financial services. The Protocol to the GATS relating to movement of natural persons was concluded in July 1995. In May 1996, the US withdrew from negotiations to conclude an agreement on maritime transport services. On 1 March 1999, the Protocol on Maintenance or Expansion of Access to National Financial Markets went into effect. As of 30 September 1999, 61 members had accepted the Protocol. MFN principles cover more than 95 per cent of the world trade in banking, insurance, securities and financial information. Negotiations on trade in basic telecommunications ended in February 1997. The largest telecommunications markets (i.e. the USA, the EU and Japan) agreed to eliminate all remaining restrictions on domestic and foreign competition in the industry by 1 January 1998.

7 Council for trade-related aspects of intellectual property rights

The WTO Agreement on Trade-Related Aspects of Intellectual Property Rights (TRIPS) is an attempt to narrow the gaps in the way copyrights, patents and industrial designs are protected around the world, and to bring them under common international rules. Again the principles of non-discrimination apply. The standards for these intellectual property rights are largely based on the obligations of the World Intellectual Property Organization (WIPO) and the Paris and Berne Conventions. However, the agreement expands some of these standards: for example, computer programmes are to be protected as literary work for copyright purposes. The TRIPS describes in some detail how governments will have to ensure enforcement. A one-year period was granted for developed countries to bring their legislation and practices into conformity with the agreement. Developing countries were to do so in five years (or ten years if an area of technology did not already have patent protection) and least-developed countries in eleven years.

8 Technical barriers

A number of agreements aim at reducing non-tariff barriers by addressing technical, bureaucratic or legal issues such as technical regulations and standards, import licensing, rules for the valuation of goods at customs, the shipment inspection and rules of origin. The 'Agreement on Trade-Related Investment Measures' (TRIMS) extends the GATT principles to foreign direct investment issues. For example, measures that require particular levels of local procurement by an enterprise ('local content requirements') were declared inconsistent with GATT principles. Countries must inform the WTO of all investment measures that do not conform with the agreement. With the exception of the least developed countries, these measures had to be eliminated by 2000.

9 Plurilateral agreements

The majority of GATT agreements became multilateral obligations under the WTO; however, there remain two so-called plurilateral agreements which have a narrower group of signatories. The Agreement on Trade in Civil Aircraft (21 signatories in 1999) eliminates import duties on all aircraft and contains disciplines on government-directed procurement of civil aircraft. The Agreement on Government Procurement was revised in 1996 (27 signatories in 2000) to also cover local government entities and to reinforce rules guaranteeing fair and non-discriminatory conditions of international competition for government purchases. Two other plurilateral agreements, the International Dairy Agreement and the International Bovine Meat Agreement, were terminated in 1997.

10 Trade policy review

In order to increase compliance, governments have to inform the WTO of specific measures, policies and laws through regular 'notifications': especially any new anti-dumping or countervailing legislation, regulations affecting trade in services, and the loss of regulations concerning the intellectual property agreement. In addition, the WTO conducts regular reviews of member countries' trade policies. Reviews are conducted by the Trade Policy Review Body on the basis of a policy statement of the government under review and an independent report prepared by the WTO Secretariat. The world's four largest traders, the EU, the USA, Japan and Canada, are examined approximately once every two years. The next 16 largest trading countries are reviewed every four years. The remaining countries are reviewed every six years (exceptions are made for the least developed countries).

11 Settlement of disputes

WTO members are committed not to undertake unilateral action against perceived violations of the trade rules, but to seek recourse in the dispute settlement mechanism and abide by its findings. Settling disputes is the responsibility of the Dispute Settlement Body (DSB). The DSB has the sole authority to establish 'panels' of experts to consider the case, and to accept or reject the panels' findings or the results of an appeal. It monitors the implementation of the rulings and recommendations, and has the power to authorize retaliation when a country does not comply with a ruling. Panels are like tribunals. But unlike in a normal tribunal, the panelists are usually chosen in consultation with the countries in dispute. If the two sides cannot agree, the WTO Director-General will appoint them. This happens only rarely. Panels consist of three (occasionally five) experts from different countries who can be chosen from a permanent list of well-qualified candidates (usually trade lawyers), or from elsewhere. They serve in their individual capacities. The first stage requires bilateral consultations between the members concerned in an attempt to conclude a mutually acceptable solution to the issue (up to 60 days). If that fails, they can also ask the WTO Director-General to mediate. If consultations fail, the complaining country can ask in a second stage for a panel to be appointed. The accused country can block the creation of a panel once, but when the DSB meets for a second time, the appointment can no longer be blocked (up to 45 days). Each party to the dispute submits its arguments and then presents its case before the panel. The panel submits a full interim report of its findings to the parties. Officially, the panel is helping the DSB make rulings or recommendations. But because the panel's report can only be rejected by consensus in the DSB, its conclusions are difficult to overturn. The panel's final report should normally be given to the parties to the dispute within six months (exception: cases concerning perishable goods). The DSB has to adopt the final report within 60 days of issuance. Either side can appeal the decision. Appeal proceedings are limited to issues of law and legal interpretation covered by the panel report. Within the maximum period of 90 days three members of the Appellate body (of the seven permanent members with four-year terms) must issue a report, which the DSB has to accept or reject within thirty days. Rejection is only possible by consensus. If the country that is the target of the complaint loses, it must follow the recommendations of the panel report or the appeals report. If the recommendations are not implemented within a 'reasonable period' as determined by the DSB, the parties are obliged to negotiate mutually acceptable compensation, for instance, tariff reductions in areas of particular interest to the complaining side. If after twenty days, no satisfactory compensation is agreed, the DSB may authorize the complainant to 'suspend concessions or obligations' against the other party. The DSB monitors how adopted rulings are implemented.

12 Controversial rulings

By April 2000 some 190 trade disputes had been brought before the WTO. Thirty-four Appellate body and panel reports have been adopted since 1995. More than a third of the Completed Cases as of April 2000 were initiated by the USA. While most disputes received rather scant attention, five cases aroused much controversy. Three of them concerned the impact of US environmental regulations on the environmental practices of countries exporting to the USA. In the *Clean-Air* case, Venezuela challenged a US Clean Air Act regulation that required gas refiners to produce cleaner gas. The rule used the 1990 actual performance data of (mostly US) oil refineries which must be filed with Environmental Protection Agency (EPA) as the starting point for required improvements for refineries without reliable data (mostly foreign). The Appellate Body ruled against the US law. In 1997, the EPA changed the clean air rules to give foreign refiners the choice of using an individual (i.e. lower) starting point. In the *Tuna-Dolphin* cases, two panels held that even non-discriminatory measures, which conditioned the sale of both domestic and foreign tuna on the adoption of a particular, environmentally-friendly technology (using nets that do not harm dolphins), constituted violations of the GATT. However, the panels' reports were never adopted. In the *Shrimp-Turtles* case four Asian nations challenged provisions of the US Endangered Species Act forbidding the sale in the USA of shrimp caught in ways that kill endangered sea turtles. In 1998, the Appellate Body decided that 'requiring from exporting countries compliance with ... certain policies prescribed by the importing country' renders a measure not 'a priori' in violation of the GATT. However, it ruled that the specific way the US tried to save turtles ran foul of WTO rules. On 27 January 2000, the US stated that it had issued revised guidelines implementing its Shrimp-Turtle law which were intended to introduce greater flexibility in considering the comparability of foreign programmes and the US programme.

The *Beef Hormone* case concerned the right of countries to set their own sanitary standards under the Agreement on Sanitary and Phytosanitary Measures (SPS). The US challenged a EU ban on the sale of beef from cattle that have been raised with certain artificial growth hormones. The Appellate Body upheld an earlier Panel finding that the EU import prohibition was not based on scientific findings. On 26 July 1999, the DSB authorized the suspension of concessions to the EU by the USA and Canada in the respective amounts determined by the arbitrators as being equivalent to the level of 'nullification' (i.e. lost sales) suffered by them.

The *Caribbean Banana* case was the case which most deeply engaged some of the problems of the dispute settlement process regarding implementation. The US and some Central American governments argued that EU trade preferences for bananas from former European colonies in the Caribbean unfairly discriminate against bananas grown in Central America. In 1997, a WTO panel ruled in favour of the USA. By May 2000 the case was still not resolved.

13 Controversies

Power asymmetries

The WTO has been criticized for lack of democracy and transparency. Voting is based on the principal of 'one member-one vote', thus, in a formal sense, the WTO is more democratic than most other international economic organizations, where weighted voting is extensively used. Voting, however, has not yet taken place. Instead, decision making in the WTO follows GATT practice and is based on negotiation and consensus. The consensus practice enhances the negotiating leverage of smaller countries, providing them with *de facto* veto power. Nevertheless, the WTO is dominated by the large trading powers. The reasons are twofold. First, the markets of the large advanced industrial countries are considerably more attractive than those of small developing countries. Since the main currency in WTO bargaining is market access, large industrial countries are in a stronger position. A country's influence in the WTO system is therefore largely determined by its share of world trade, its trade dependence and the absolute size of its market. Second, smaller developing countries lack the resources to be present at all bargaining sites and to hire top trade lawyers for the complex details of international trade law. Furthermore, developed countries, especially the so-called QUAD countries (USA, Canada, Japan and the EU), have repeatedly made key decisions in closed meetings (called 'green room' process), excluding other WTO nations. The US implementing legislation contains a withdrawal clause. While withdrawal is an unlikely option, this review process puts a certain pressure on WTO panels not to stray too far from US interests.

Environmental concerns

The rulings of WTO panels on environmental laws (see above) have stirred much opposition. The distinction made by the Tuna-Dolphin panels between harmful products and harmful production processes, the latter not deserving exception from GATT principles, has been challenged and has been subsequently weakened. However, even the status of multilateral environmental agreements under trade rules has yet to be clarified.

Labour rights

The International Confederation of Free Trade Unions as well as a number of developed countries proposed a 'labour rights clause'. No internationally traded product shall enjoy WTO privileges which have been produced in violation of core labour rights such as the freedom of association, the right to collective bargaining, the prohibition of discrimination as well as of forced and child labour. Most trade representatives and some non-governmental organizations of developing countries as well as most economists and corporate leaders in developed countries have rejected this demand as protectionism in disguise. However, developing countries would benefit the most since fierce competition among themselves leads to the violation of those rights which are not only regarded as human rights but also as basic to development.

14 Recent activities – plans for the future

WTO member countries failed to meet their goal of launching a new round of multilateral trade negotiations ('Millennium Round') at their biennial ministerial conference held in November/December 1999, in Seattle, USA. The conference was suspended without initiating a new round or deciding if and when the conference might reconvene. In the aftermath, members agreed instead to begin negotiations limited to opening markets in agriculture and services according to the schedule set at the end of the Uruguay Round ('built-in agenda'). These negotiations, however, lack a deadline for completion.

The Secretariat works to blunt criticism concerning the lack of transparency and the neglect of developing countries by engaging in a dialogue with non-governmental organizations and by pushing an 'Integrated Framework for Least Developed Countries'.

The most immediate and important issue is the request by China to join ('accede to') the WTO. Although all WTO members must decide on the terms of accession, the outcome of the Chinese negotiations with the USA and the EU will be decisive.

CHRISTOPH SCHERRER
UNIVERSITY OF KASSEL

Further reading

Bhagwati, J. and Hudec, R.E. (eds) (1996) *Fair Trade and Harmonization*, 2 vols, Cambridge, MA: MIT Press. (Extensive discussion of new issues such as environment and labour from divergent perspectives.)

Croome, J. (1995) *Reshaping the World Trading System*, Geneva: World Trade Organization. (A well written history of the Uruguay Round by a high ranking GATT officer.)

Das, B.L. (1998) *The WTO Agreements: Deficiencies, Imbalances and Required Changes*, London, Penang: Zed Books and Third World Network. (Brief book listing concisely all the deficiencies of the WTO from the viewpoint of developing countries.)

Griesgraber, J.M. and Gunter, B.G. (eds) (1997) *World Trade. Toward Fair and Free Trade in the Twenty-first Century*, London: Pluto Press. (Level-headed critique of the WTO from a developmental perspective.)

Jackson, J.H. (1998) *The World Trade Organization. Constitution and Jurisprudence*, London: Royal Institute of International Affairs. (Concise description of dispute settlement process by an eminent authority.)

McDonald, B. (1998) *The World Trading System. The Uruguay Round and Beyond*, New York: St. Martin's Press. (An accessible, non-technical volume on GATT and WTO by an employee of the European Commission.)

Scholte, J., O'Brien, R. and Williams, M. (1999) 'The WTO and civil society', *Journal of World Trade* 33 (1): 107–23. (Discusses the efforts to increase transparency and participation at the WTO.)

Trebilcock, M.J. and Howse, R. (1999) *The Regulation of International Trade*, 2nd edn, London: Routledge. (Excellent textbook on international trade by two Canadian law professors.)

WTO: *http: www.wto.org*. The WTO website, in addition to current documents, contains two interactive guides, one explaining the functions and structure of the WTO in general, the other on the WTO and development.

WTO Address: Centre William Rappard, Rue de Lausanne 154, CH-1211 Geneva 21, Switzerland. phone: (22) 7395111; telex: 412324; fax: (22) 7395458.

See also: ECONOMIC GROWTH AND CONVERGENCE; ECONOMIC INTEGRATION, INTERNATIONAL; EXCHANGE RATE ECONOMICS; INTERNATIONAL MONETARY FUND; MULTINATIONAL CORPORATIONS; WORLD BANK

Theories and tools

Evolutionary theories of the firm

1 The genesis of modern evolutionary theories of the firm
2 The Nelson–Winter approach
3 Evolutionary and contractarian theories contrasted
4 Conclusion

Overview

This article explores the nature and genesis of evolutionary theories of the firm. Substantial attention is given to the seminal work by Richard Nelson and Sidney Winter, *An Evolutionary Theory of Economic Change* (1982). It is noted that Nelson and Winter use the metaphor of biological evolution to construct their theory. The underlying features in common with other 'evolutionary' and competence-based approaches to the theory of the firm are discussed. These are contrasted with contractarian and transaction cost approaches, such as that of Oliver Williamson (1985).

1 The genesis of modern evolutionary theories of the firm

Long ago, Alfred Marshall turned to biology for inspiration in his *Principles of Economics* (1890) and Thorstein Veblen suggested that the metaphor of Darwinian evolution could be applied to economics. However, the development of the evolutionary theory of the firm is largely a post-1945 phenomenon. It largely emanates from a famous controversy about the legitimacy of the assumption of profit maximization in economics.

Opposing the assumption, economists such as Richard Lester and Robert Gordon appealed to empirical studies of firm behaviour and argued that profit maximizing behaviour was neither typical nor feasible in the real world. In contrast, the neoclassical economist Fritz Machlup suggested that even if they are not fully conscious of them, business managers use complex, optimizing calculations, just as we try to choose the optimum speed and position when we try to overtake another vehicle with a car.

This debate about profit maximization has continued to this day, with several notable and important contributions. What is significant for the development of evolutionary economics is a contribution to this debate by Armen Alchian. In a famous article 'Uncertainty, evolution and economic theory' (1950), Alchian argued that Lester and Gordon were both wrong. Alchian contended that for the purposes of the debate it did not matter whether firms were trying to maximize or not. Market competition created an environment akin to natural selection where the more efficient would win out. Selective success, Alchian argued, depends on behaviour and results, not motivations. Furthermore, because agents operate in a world of uncertainty and may react in different ways to given stimuli, individual behaviour is not predictable. Nevertheless, even if firms never actually attempted to maximize profits, 'evolutionary' processes of selection and imitation would ensure the survival of the more profitable enterprises. Thus Alchian saw the idea of evolutionary selection less as a buttress and more as an alternative to the assumption that individual firms are actually attempting to maximize their profits. Although individual behaviour cannot be predicted, evolutionary processes ensure that patterns of development can be observed in the aggregate.

In response to Alchian, Edith Penrose (1952) argued that the biological analogy was misconceived, for at least two reasons. First, human agents are guided by purposes and intentions whereas Darwinian natural selection assumes that organisms are simply programmed by their genes. Second, the analogy was abused because there was no equivalent in the socioeconomic sphere to durable, heritable traits. Accordingly, there is nothing durable upon which socioeconomic 'natural selection' can operate.

Nevertheless, these important criticisms were largely ignored and the 'natural selection' idea was taken up by others, notably by Milton Friedman in a famous and frequently quoted essay published in 1953. Friedman performed a conjuring trick by turning the 'natural selection' idea back into a defence of the neoclassical assumption of profit maximization. Notably, in his 1950 essay, Alchian had no intention of laying the basis of an 'evolutionary' or alternative theory of the firm. What he did was to reintroduce an evolutionary and biological analogy back into economics which had been neglected after the deaths of Alfred Marshall and Thorstein Veblen in the 1920s.

This provided the grist for Sidney Winter's mill. During the 1960s, as a Ph.D. student at Yale University, he wrote an extensive critique of Friedman's 'natural selection' defence of the assumption of profit maximization. However, instead of rejecting the biological analogy he showed that rather special and restrictive conditions were required for market competition to produce the results that Friedman presumes. He demonstrated that under plausible conditions the 'natural selection' of profit maximizers would not work.

Winter pointed out that Friedman's 'natural selection' argument was imperfectly specified in that it did not show how maximizing behaviour was replicated through time. For selection to work there must be some sustaining feature that ensures that the maximizers or near-maximizers that are 'selected' through competition will continue for some time in that mode of behaviour. As Penrose had already observed, for natural selection to work there must be heritable variation in fitness. The heritable element was missing from Friedman's account. For selection to operate consistently in favour of some characteristics rather than others, behaviour cannot be purely accidental. There has to be some equivalent to the genetic constitution or genotype, such as the structural characteristics, routines or culture of the firm, which fixes, determines, moulds or constrains the phenotype in some way.

Winter suggested that routines in the firm have a relatively durable quality through time. They may help to retain skills and other forms of knowledge, and to some extent they have the capacity to replicate through imitation, personal mobility, takeovers and so on. Further, routines can change through managerial or other action when the firm's profits are below a satisfactory level. As he puts it in a later article: 'The assumption that firms have decision rules, and retain or replace them according to the satisficing principle, provides both genetic stability and an endogenous mutation mechanism' (Winter 1971: 247). (The 'satisficing principle' refers to Herbert Simon's idea that firms attempt to obtain satisfactory minima, rather than optimizing, in their behaviour.)

Hence Winter's work is a partial answer to Penrose as well as a direct attack on Friedman. Winter discovered in the routine an answer to Penrose's complaint that the heritable mechanisms were not clearly specified in earlier presentations of the evolutionary analogy in economics. He thus inadvertently returns to the ideas of Veblen and the 'old' institutionalists concerning the centrality of habit and routine in economic life, and the way in which habits and routines encapsulate working knowledge (see VEBLEN, T. B.).

2 The Nelson–Winter approach

An evolutionary theory of the firm was built on these theoretical foundations. Winter achieved this in collaboration with Richard Nelson. In 1982 they published their classic *An Evolutionary Theory of Economic Change*. To their joint venture, Nelson brought his rich theoretical and empirical knowledge of industrial economics, and Winter carried the important theoretical innovations that he had made to reinstate in economics the evolutionary analogy from biology.

The inspiration provided by this analogy was crucial and explicit. The term 'evolutionary' was adopted as 'above all a signal that we have borrowed basic ideas from biology, thus exercising an option to which economists are entitled in perpetuity by virtue of the stimulus our predecessor Malthus provided to Darwin's thinking' (Nelson and Winter 1982: 9).

As evidenced throughout their joint and individual works, both authors share a deep anxiety about the theoretical, empirical and practical limitations of neoclassical economics. This uneasiness is so profound that it leads to a rejection of the core assumptions of neoclassical economic theory. The 'reliance on equilibrium analysis, even in its more flexible forms, still leads the discipline blind to phenomena associated with historical change'. Furthermore, 'although it is not literally appropriate to stigmatize orthodoxy as concerned only with hypothetical situations of perfect information and static equilibrium, the prevalence of analogous restrictions in advanced work lends a metaphorical validity to the complaint.' Finally, they reject 'the assumption that economic actors are rational in the sense that they optimize' (Nelson and Winter 1982: 8).

Accordingly, Nelson and Winter developed an alternative theoretical framework to profit maximization for the analysis of the firm. Instead of such an optimizing procedure, they propose an evolutionary model in which selection operates on the firm's internal routines. Routines include 'characteristics of firms that range from well-specified technical routines for producing things, through procedures for hiring and firing, ordering new inventory, or stepping up production of items in high demand, to policies regarding investment, research and development (R&D), or advertising, and business strategies about product diversification and overseas investment.' In their analysis 'these routines play the role that genes play in biological evolutionary theory' (Nelson and Winter 1982: 14).

Routines are not simply widespread characteristics of much activity within organizations: they also have functional characteristics. Being concerned to show how technological skills are acquired and passed on within the economy, Nelson and Winter argue that habits and routines act as relatively durable repositories of knowledge and skills. In their words, routines are the 'organizational memory' (Nelson and Winter 1982: 99) of the firm. Furthermore, routines may have the capacity to replicate through imitation, personal mobility, and so on. Because of their relatively durable character and their capacity to replicate, routines act as the economic analogue of the gene in biology. They transmit information through time in a manner which is loosely analogous to the conservation and replication of information via the gene.

However, it is freely accepted that innovative activity is possible and much business behaviour is not essentially routine. Such irregular and unpredictable behaviour was accommodated in their evolutionary theory 'by recognizing that there are stochastic elements in the determination of decisions and decision outcomes' (Nelson and Winter 1982: 15). Here again there are clear parallels in the biological theory of evolution, where stochastic variation is important in many evolutionary models.

Just as the routine is the analogue of the gene, Nelson and Winter borrowed a second key concept directly from evolutionary biology. They develop the concept of 'search' to encompass changes in the routines of firms: 'Our concept of search obviously is the counterpart of that of mutation in biological evolutionary theory' (Nelson and Winter 1982: 18). This concept was illustrated by the evolutionary model in chapter 9 of their book. A threshold level of profitability is assumed. If firms are sufficiently profitable they attempt to maintain their existing routines and do no 'searching' at all. Here Nelson and Winter adopt Herbert Simon's important 'satisficing' idea: agents attempt to gain a given 'aspiration level' rather than to optimize (Simon 1957) (see SIMON, H.A.). However, if profitability falls below this level then 'firms are driven to consider alternatives ... under the pressure of adversity' (Nelson and Winter 1982: 211). They invest in R&D and attempt to discover new techniques so that profitability can be restored.

Third, there is a clear analogue to the idea of economic 'natural selection': 'Market environments provide a definition of success for business firms, and that definition is very closely related to their ability to survive and grow' (Nelson and Winter, 1982: 9). Clearly, this is the application of the analogy of market competition with the 'struggle for existence' in biology. In this third case, unlike the preceding two, there is much common ground with Alchian, Friedman and many others. However, unlike most of their predecessors, Nelson and Winter were careful not to endow market selection mechanisms or private ownership with the aura of a 'natural' order or the mantle of supreme efficiency.

The adoption of these three crucial analogues completes the link between the Nelson–Winter concept of economic evolution and the corresponding idea in biology. In biology, evolution requires three essential components. First, there must be sustained variation among the members of a species or population. Variations may be blind, random or purposive in character, but without them, as Darwin insisted, natural selection cannot operate. Second, there must be some principle of heredity or continuity through which offspring have to resemble their parents more than they resemble other members of their species. In other words, there has to be some mechanism through which individual characteristics are passed on through the generations. Third, natural selection itself operates either because better-adapted organisms leave increased numbers of offspring, or because the variations or gene combinations that are preserved are those bestowing advantage in struggling to survive. This is the principle of the struggle for existence. Nelson and Winter explicitly appropriate and amend these ideas from biology to build their evolutionary theory. This triad of ideas demarcates their 'evolutionary' approach from many different and contending uses of the term (Hodgson 1993, chapter 3).

However, whilst the theoretical approach of Nelson and Winter conforms to these three characteristics of evolutionary biology, they make it clear that it does not amount to an exact correspondence. We have already noted that whilst routines are relatively sturdy in socioeconomic terms they are nearly as durable as the gene in biology. In addition, when routines change their new characteristics can be imitated and directly inherited by imitators or subsidiary firms. For this reason, as several evolutionary theorists have pointed out, in the socioeconomic sphere the inheritance of acquired characteristics is possible and thereby socioeconomic evolution has 'Lamarckian' characteristics. Like the Lamarckian tradition in biology, there is also an emphasis on intention in behaviour (Hodgson 1993, chapter 14). This may be seen as a partial response to Penrose's 1952 objections to the use of the evolutionary analogy in economics.

The evolutionary metaphor provided the escape route from the rigidities of neoclassical orthodoxy. Despite many problems and dangers, modern biology is a rich source of ideas and approaches from which a revitalized economics may draw. In all, the application of an evolutionary approach to economics seems to involve a number of advantages and improvements over the orthodox and mechanistic paradigm. For instance, it enhances a concern with irreversible and ongoing processes in time, with long-run development rather than short-run marginal adjustments, with qualitative as well as quantitative change, with variation and diversity, with non-equilibrium as well as equilibrium situations, and with the possibility of persistent and systematic error-making and thereby non-optimizing behaviour.

3 Evolutionary and contractarian theories contrasted

Nicolai Foss (1993) argues convincingly that the primary bifurcation in theoretical analyses of the firm is between, on the one hand, contractarian and, on the other, evolutionary, resource-based or competence-based perspectives. This useful categorization places the work of Nelson and Winter in a broader and older tradition (Hodgson 1998a).

Consider the contractarian approach first. In the main this emanates from the work of Ronald Coase and emphasizes the cost of making and monitoring transactions. Important here is the 'transaction cost economics' of Oliver Williamson (1985), as well as 'nexus of contracts' and other related theories of the firm (see WILLIAMSON, O. E.). Despite their important differences, in these theories the informational and other difficulties in formulating, monitoring and policing contracts are the crucial explanatory elements.

In contrast, in the evolutionary or competence perspective the existence, structure and boundaries of the firm are explained by the associated existence of individual or team competences – such as skills and tacit knowledge – which are in some way fostered and maintained by that organization. Early precursors to this view include Adam Smith and Karl Marx, who saw the division and management of labour as crucial to the development of skills and providing a key rationale for the firm (see SMITH, A.; MARX, K.H.). But there is a variety of twentieth century exponents including Frank Knight (1921), Edith Penrose (1959) and Richard Nelson and Sidney Winter (1982). The central idea of competencies provides the basis for evolutionary and non-equilibrium theories of industrial competition and development as elaborated, for instance, by the latter two authors. Within this group there is also a diversity of views, particularly over the nature of (tacit) knowledge, the units and methodology of analysis, and the application of the evolutionary analogy. In some cases the biological analogy of 'natural selection' is not used. Nevertheless, and broadly, the competencies paradigm has attracted a wide and growing following and its ideas have made their way into the literature on corporate strategy.

One important difference between the two perspectives concerns the uses of static versus dynamic types of analysis. Williamson has repeatedly admitted that his approach is one of comparative statics. In contrast, evolutionary theories from Smith to Nelson and Winter tend to focus on processes of continuous change.

The relative neglect of learning, technological innovation and dynamic change is a most serious problem for a static or equilibrium-oriented approach. Innovation and learning are difficult to fit into equilibrium or comparative static analyses. Although Williamson emphasizes 'bounded' rather than global rationality he is uncomfortable with the concept of 'satisficing' and there is still a stress in his work on rational choice by agents with a finite set of known opportunities. In contrast, evolutionary theorists depart from the assumption of a given choice set and view human action as a process of reaction, adaptation and learning, with regard to changing information and circumstances. Indeed, the ability of the firm to foster human learning, technological innovation, and research and development may be a central reason for its existence.

Typically, neoclassical economics treats learning as the progressive discovery of pre-existing 'blueprint' information, or Bayesian updating of subjective probability estimates in the light of incoming data. As several critics have argued, this is a very limited way of conceiving of the role of learning, which in reality is much more than a process of blueprint discovery or statistical correction. Learning is not simply the acquisition of codifiable knowledge: there is also tacit knowledge. Problems do not themselves provide nor necessarily suggest solutions: much learning must involve intuition and creativity. If learning and creativity are ongoing then we cannot be in equilibrium.

Accordingly, evolutionary theories of the firm pay more attention to processes of learning and development within organizations. The agent is an explorer and creator rather than a strict maximizer. The firm is a changing organism, typified by both reactive and purposeful behaviours. The application of this broad theoretical approach to management is illustrated in Nelson (1991) and a number of other works.

4 Conclusion

In sum, some key features of evolutionary (or competence-based) approaches to the theory of the firm are as follows:

- The focus is on dynamism and development, rather than statics and equilibrium.
- Learning-by-doing is seen as a primary source of endogenous growth. This means that individuals themselves are in a process of development, in contrast to approaches that tend to take individuals as given.
- There is a recognition of the role of radical uncertainty and other chronic problems pertaining to information and knowledge in the firm.
- There is a recognition of tacit knowledge and the way in which it is not merely bound up with individuals but with relationships, routines and structures within the organization.
- The emphasis on learning and the tacit, idiosyncratic and context dependent nature of knowledge leads to the conclusion that not all activities within the firm are contractible.

In contrast to contractarian approaches, evolutionary and competence-based theories stress that the firm cannot be treated as if it were itself a market. Accordingly, the firm cannot be understood simply in terms of its revenues and costs. In contrast to the standard textbook theory, the firm is not understood principally through its cost and revenue curves. Instead, there is an emphasis on knowledge, learning, routines and other enhancible resources. In other words, evolutionary and competence-based perspectives understand the firm's competitive situation primarily in regard to the actual and potential comparative advantages bestowed by its resources, rather than by its market position. Accordingly, the task of management is to adjust and renew these resources and relationships, as their values are eroded or threatened by ongoing change.

GEOFFREY M. HODGSON
THE BUSINESS SCHOOL, UNIVERSITY OF HERTFORDSHIRE

Further Reading

(References cited in the text marked *)

* Alchian, A.A. (1950) 'Uncertainty, evolution and economic theory', *Journal of Political Economy*, 58, June: 211–22. (A classic article that started the intellectual development leading to evolutionary theories of the firm.)
* Foss, N.J. (1993) 'Theories of the firm: contractual and competence perspectives', *Journal of Evolutionary Economics*, 3 (2): 127–44. (A masterful analysis of the difference between evolutionary and contractarian approaches to the analysis of the firm. Highly recommended.)
  Foss, N.J. (ed.) (1997) *Resources, Firms, and Strategies: A Reader in the Resource-Based Perspective*, Oxford: Oxford University Press. (An excellent collection of readings on resource-based, competence based and evolutionary theories of the firm.)
  Foss, N.J. and Knudsen, C. (eds) (1996) *Towards a Competence Theory of the Firm*, London: Routledge. (A very useful collection of recent essays on resource-based, competence based and evolutionary theories of the firm.)
* Hodgson, G.M. (1993) *Economics and Evolution: Bringing Life Back into Economics*, Cambridge and Ann Arbor: Polity Press and University of Michigan Press. (A review of both institutionalist and non-institutionalist attempts to apply evolutionary and biological analogies to economics. An extensive bibliography is included.)
* Hodgson, G.M. (1998a) 'Evolutionary and competence-based theories of the firm', *Journal of Economic Studies*, 25 (1): 25–56. (A survey of the basis of, and literature on, evolutionary and competence-based theories.)
  Hodgson, G.M. (ed.) (1998b) *The Foundations of Evolutionary Economics: 1890–1973*, 2 vols, International Library of Critical Writings in Economics, Cheltenham: Edward Elgar. (An anthology of articles on the development of evolutionary approaches in economics.)
* Knight, F.H. (1921) *Risk, Uncertainty and Profit*, New York: Houghton Mifflin. (A classic work on the firm which emphasizes uncertainty and managerial competence.)
* Nelson, R.R. (1991) 'Why do firms differ, and how does it matter?', *Strategic Management Journal*, 12, Special Issue, Winter: 61–74. (An article illustrating the application of the evolutionary approach to strategic management.)
* Nelson, R.R. and Winter, S.G. (1982) *An Evolutionary Theory of Economic Change*, Cambridge, MA: Harvard University Press. (A now-seminal application of the evolutionary analogy to the theory of the firm.)
* Penrose, E.T. (1952) 'Biological analogies in the theory of the firm', *American Economic Review*, 42 (4): 804–19. (One of the most perceptive critiques of the use of the biological analogy in economics.)
* Penrose, E.T. (1959) *The Theory of the Growth of the Firm*, Oxford: Basil Blackwell. (Although its author had rejected biological analogies, this outstanding book really fits into the competence-based and thereby evolutionary approach to the analysis of the firm.)
* Simon, H.A. (1957) *Models of Man: Social and Rational. Mathematical Essays on Rational Human Behaviour in a Social Setting*, New York: Wiley. (The classic statement of behaviouralism, including explanations of such concepts as 'bounded rationality' and 'satisficing'.)
  Winter Jr, S.G. (1964) 'Economic "natural selection" and the theory of the firm', *Yale Economic Essays*, 4 (1): 225–72. (Winter's inspirational critique of Friedman's often quoted 'natural selection' argument for profit-maximizing behaviour.)
* Winter Jr, S.G. (1971) 'Satisficing, selection and the innovating remnant', *Quarterly Journal of Economics*, 85 (2): 237–61. (A sequel to Winter's 1964 article where the evolutionary approach is restated and further developed.)

* Williamson, O.E. (1985) *The Economic Institutions of Capitalism: Firms, Markets, Relational Contracting*, London: Macmillan. (In this work Williamson further develops the earlier insights of Coase and his transaction cost analysis into his theory of the firm, contrasting with competence-based and evolutionary approaches.)

See also: COASE, R.; GROWTH OF THE FIRM AND NETWORKING; INSTITUTIONAL ECONOMICS; MANAGERIAL THEORIES OF THE FIRM; MARSHALL, A.; MARX, K.H.; SMITH, A; WILLIAMSON, O.E.

Institutional economics

1 Introduction
2 The core assumptions of neo-classical economics
3 The 'new' institutional economics
4 The 'old' institutional economics
5 Conclusion: the 'old' institutionalism and the study of business and management

Overview

This essay compares three schools of thought in economics: first, the mainstream or 'neo-classical' school; second, the 'new' instittionalism of Douglass North, Andrew Schotter, Oliver Williamson and others; and third, the 'old' institutionalism founded in the United States by Thorstein Veblen, John Commons and Wesley Mitchell.

Neo-classical economics is defined as an approach to the analysis of socioeconomic phenomena that embodies the assumption of maximizing behaviour by economic agents, has a predilection for equilibrium analysis and excludes chronic information problems. Although many of the 'new' institutional economists adopt neo-classical assumptions, 'new' institutionalism is sometimes regarded as embracing a broader range of economic theorists. This raises the issue of the appropriate definition of the 'new' institutional economics. It is argued here that the 'new' institutionalists are united by their common acceptance of the individual as given, taking his or her preference function as fixed and exogenously determined.

The 'old' institutional economics involves a radical break from both neo-classical and 'new' institutional economics, although there are some concerns and themes that are common to the latter. The fundamental assumptions of the 'old' institutional economics, as examined here, are quite different. For instance, 'old' institutionalists do not start from the assumption of the given, atomistic individual. Equilibrium theorizing is typically replaced by evolutionary analogies. Accordingly, this 'institutional' economics is much more than the study of economic institutions: it is an alternative approach to the analysis of economic phenomena in general. It is further argued that, despite it being eclipsed in recent years by the rising 'new' institutionalism, the Veblen–Commons–Mitchell tradition has more to offer to business and management studies.

The literature of the 'old' and the 'new' economics is enormous and is growing rapidly. For reasons of brevity and clarity many bibliographic references are excluded here. More references to the literature and fuller bibliographies are provided in Hodgson (1988, 1998) and Hodgson *et al.* (1994).

1 Introduction

The relationship between modern mainstream economics and business studies is presently an uneasy one. Many economists pride themselves in the axiomatic rigour of their discipline, and often look upon much of the research work in business schools and management studies departments as unsystematic and anecdotal. Conversely, many management theorists have become critical of mainstream economics: for the alleged unrealism of its core assumptions, for its apparent failure to engage with real-world data, and for its apparently limited operational utility for business policy. Such developments are not only reflected in the widespread institutional divisions between economics departments and departments of business or management studies in the universities, but also by a wholesale rejection of 'economics' or the 'economic approach' in some quarters.

Whilst a critical attitude to mainstream economics might evoke some sympathy, a sweeping rejection of 'economics' by business analysts would rest upon a misunderstanding: one that is fostered by modern mainstream economics itself. The confusion arises because both advocates and critics jointly assume that the theoretical approach of modern mainstream economics is the only possible approach. Yet in the past, classical economists such as Adam Smith, David Ricardo and Thomas Robert Malthus adopted assumptions quite different from those that prevail in economics today (see SMITH, A.). Also there is currently a wide variety of schools of economic though which rival neo-classical orthodoxy: Marxian, Austrian, post-Keynesian, behaviouralist and 'old' institutionalist, to name a few. That is why it is important not to confuse modern mainstream economics with economics in general. Although it has a general – even overwhelming – influence, modern mainstream economics should be given a specific description. Hence we refer to 'neo-classical economics' here.

This article focuses on both the 'old' and the 'new' institutional economics and considers the former as the basis of an alternative general approach to economic analysis. Given this challenge at the foundation of the subject it is necessary to compare the characteristics of the 'old' institutionalism with those of neo-classical economics as well.

2 The core assumptions of neo-classical economics

The confusion over the nature and scope of economics results in part from the redefinition of the subject in the 1870s, as the 'marginal revolution' brought about a victory of the neo-classical theorists over their classical and Marxian rivals. The pioneering and influential neo-classical theorist William Stanley Jevons saw in his seminal work *The Theory of Political Economy* (1871) the 'great problem of economy' as being about the allocation of given goods and services in order to maximize the utility of individuals. Compared with his predecessors, this was a crucial shift of focus. Unlike Adam Smith in the *Wealth of Nations* and Karl Marx in *Capital*, attention was no longer primarily directed at the explanation of the workings of the economy in the real world, and how such an economy may grow and produce more goods and services (see MARX, K.; SMITH, A.). Instead, Jevons saw economics as being about the problem of allocating given resources through the mechanism of contractual exchange. The explanation of how such resources were produced was, in Jevons' view, 'a total inversion of the problem'. Jevons thus saw economics as mostly about the theoretical problem of economizing or optimizing, rather than the explanation of how real economies work and develop. The 'economic problem' became one of allocation via exchange rather than of production and growth.

Economics was thus less concerned with 'the wealth of nations' and gradually became 'the science of choice'. Accordingly, it became concerned with the application of a particular framework of analysis on general problems, rather than the analysis of a specific real-world object – the economy. This trend, started in the 1870s, was consolidated in the 1930s by Lionel Robbins in his famous *Essay on the Nature and Significance of Economic Science* (1935). Like Jevons, Robbins defined economics as the study of the proper method of allocating scarce physical and human means among competing ends. He explicitly abandoned the idea that economics was defined by the study of what could be described as economic phenomena. Since the publication of Robbins's essay the prevailing practice amongst economists has been to regard this subject as being defined by a single type of method or analysis, with an associated set of core assumptions.

In contrast, other sciences are defined as the study of a particular aspect of objective reality: physics is about the nature and properties of matter and energy, biology about living things, psychology about the psyche, and so on. The neo-classical definition of economics in terms of a single methodology and core theory – and not as the study of a real object, the economy – departs from the prevailing practice in other sciences. Notably, such a definition provides a convenient device for dealing with dissidents. Anyone who criticizes the assumptions of neo-classical economics may be simply described as a 'non-economist': even worse as a 'sociologist'. The questions of the realism, suitability, utility or appropriateness of those assumptions themselves are thus conveniently side-stepped.

More reasonably, anyone employing systematic and robust intellectual methods to the study of the real object that is widely described as 'the economy' should be described as an economist. It is important, therefore, not to treat economics as a single approach to analysis. Indeed, several prominent economists have become critical of the standard, neo-classical approach, both in general terms and in terms of its limited utility for managers. For instance, writing in the *American Economic Review* of 'the limits of neo-classical theory in management education' the well-known heterodox economists David Teece and Sidney Winter argued that most real-world management problems are dynamic, complex, messy and ill-structured. In these circumstances the neo-classical assumption of transparently rational decision making in a world of known outcomes or probabilities is of little use, at most: 'The economist's special brand of rationality has no special place in the repertoire of problem-solving approaches, whatever claims may be made for it as a universal logic of decision.' (Teece and Winter, 1984: 117).

How can neo-classical economics be characterized? (see NEO-CLASSICAL ECONOMICS). Although the possibility of defining neo-classical economics has been a matter of some debate and elaboration, its core assumptions may be taken to be as follows:

1. the assumption of rational, maximizing behaviour by agents with given and stable preference functions;
2. a focus on attained, or movements towards, equilibrium states;
3. the absence of chronic information problems (there is, at most, a focus on probabilistic risk: excluding severe ignorance, radical uncertainty, or divergent perceptions of a given reality).

Notably, these three attributes are interconnected. For instance, the attainment of a stable optimum under (1) suggests an equilibrium (2); and rationality under (1) connotes the absence of severe information problems alluded to in (3).

This particular definition of neo-classical economics clearly excludes members of the Austrian school of economics (Friedrich Hayek, Ludwig von Mises and others), particularly because of their explicit critique of attributes (2) and (3), and because of their rejection of typical conceptualizations of rationality under (1). There is also the pertinent question whether some recent developments in game theory can also be usefully described as 'neo-classical economics'. This question can only be answered by close inspection and refinement of the boundary conditions in the above definition.

It is also important to recognize that these core assumptions reflect the adoption of a mechanistic metaphor in economic theory. In a mechanistic world there are no information problems. Economic agents are seen as akin to particles subject to forces, interacting and often attaining an equilibrium outcome.

The current definition of economics elevates formalism and axiomatics to unwarranted heights. At the outset, the assumptions are taken as unquestionable and given. Agents must maximize because economists assume they do, and so on. For the theoretical economist the game becomes one of simply drawing logical conclusions from pre-ordained assumptions. Attempts to address the real world, or to evaluate basic assumptions on the basis of evidence, are downgraded. Arguably it is the rise and now overwhelming dominance of the neo-classical or 'rational choice' approach in modern economics that has caused many social scientists to become wary of 'economics' and the 'economic approach' as a whole.

The situation is dramatized by the current crop of textbooks in 'managerial economics'. These texts are above all concerned to apply the 'economic approach' to management problems. In this respect they amount to little more than the application of constrained optimization techniques. As a result a one-sided attempt is made to address the complexities of management decision making in the real world. It is assumed without question that constrained optimization by managers is generally possible: that the choice set is fully known and defined, and that the problem of optimization is not sufficiently complex to cause insurmountable problems of analysis and computation. Yet as Nobel Laureate Herbert Simon (1979) and others have repeatedly pointed out, typical decisions in the business sphere are characterized by radical uncertainty over the choice set and the costs and the benefits (see SIMON, H.A.). Furthermore, problems are generally sufficiently complex to pose severe analytical and computational difficulties even if the relevant parametric information is available.

Instead of assuming unquestioningly that optimization techniques are applicable, the 'managerial economists' should ask the following questions: Given typical business problems is it possible and desirable for managers to optimize? Given that decision making, analysis and calculation are themselves time and resource consuming, should managers try to optimize anyway? Should they try tirelessly to search for the optimum in the multi-dimensional decision-making space, or stop when they arrive at a decision that seems good enough? The mistaken definition of economics principally in terms of optimizing agents prevents the 'managerial economists' from asking these highly relevant questions.

Indeed, the concept of optimization is antithetical to innovation and entrepreneurship. It is in the very nature of creativity to risk the unknown. Innovation disturbs any equilibrium and creates knew and partially unforeseen opportunities. Optimization is essentially a static concept.

Having defined the theoretical core of neoclassical economics, we now move on to compare it with the 'new' institutional economics. It is notable that some of the 'new' institutionalists do apparently pay some heed to the concerns of Simon and others over the difficulties of global optimization.

3 The 'new' institutional economics

Since the mid-1970s there has been a remarkable growth in what was dubbed by Oliver Williamson as the 'new institutional economics'. Williamson took as a major inspiration the famous 1937 *Economica* article on 'The Nature of the Firm' by Ronald Coase (see COASE, R.). Other prominent 'new' institutionalist authors include Friedrich Hayek, Douglass North, Mancur Olson, Richard Posner and Andrew Schotter. Theorists working within or close to this field have gained some considerable recognition. Indeed, 'new' institutionalists Coase, North and Hayek have all been awarded the Nobel Prize in economics. Note, however, that outside economics the term 'new institutionalism' is sometimes used in different ways, particularly in organization studies.

The epithet 'new' was chosen precisely to distinguish the more recent approaches from the former and original school of institutionalists. Importantly, and in contrast to the writings of Veblen and his followers (see VEBLEN, T.B.), much of 'new institutionalism' has resulted from work within or close to the mainstream of economic theory. Accordingly, there are fundamental theoretical differences between the 'old' and the 'new' institutionalism. These will be elaborated later. The immediate task is to identify the key characteristics of the 'new' institutionalism.

Notably, not all 'new' institutionalists are neo-classical economists according to the above definition. Austrian writers such as Hayek, for example, are critical of neo-classical general equilibrium theory. In contrast, the analyses of other 'new' institutionalist theorists such as Williamson (1975, 1985) are more static in nature, and involve elements of the neo-classical approach (see NEO-CLASSICAL ECONOMICS; WILLIAMSON, O.E.). Furthermore, there are extensive differences of policy outlook in the 'new' institutionalist camp, with the almost unqualified pro-market stance of Hayek on the one hand, and the game-theoretic critique of free-market policies by Schotter (1981) on the other. As a result it would be erroneous to define the 'new' institutionalist economics in terms of a specific policy stance. However, even with the many important differences, and although there are non-neo-classical as well as neo-classical members of the set of 'new' institutionalist writers, it is argued below that all of these types of 'new' institutionalism share some common premises.

Taking individuals as given

In one sense the adjective is misleading, for all elements of the 'new' institutionalism are based upon some long-established assumptions concerning the human agent, derived from the influence of classic liberalism. Since its inception in the writings of John Locke and others, classic liberalism has overshadowed economics. A key common proposition of classic liberalism is the view that the individual can, in a sense, be 'taken for granted'. To put it another way, the individual, along with his or her assumed behavioural characteristics, is taken as the elemental building block in the theory of the social or economic system.

Strictly, it is not a question of whether a theorist is found to admit that individuals – or their wants and preferences – are changed by circumstances. Indeed, all intelligent economists, from Adam Smith to Friedrich Hayek inclusive, admit that individuals might so be changed. What is crucial is that the classic liberal economist may make such an admission but then go on to assume, *for the purposes of economic enquiry* that individuals and their preference functions should be taken as given. Thus the demarcating criterion is not the matter of individual malleability *per se*, but the willingness, or otherwise, to consider this issue as an important or legitimate matter for economic enquiry. The often-repeated statement by neo-classical economists that tastes and preferences are not matters to be explained by economics thus derives directly from the classic liberal tradition. It involves taking the individual 'for granted'. Likewise, the post-Robbins conception or definition of economics as 'the science of choice' generally takes the choosing individual and his or her preference functions as given. As a whole, the 'new' institutionalism has taken these same presuppositions on board.

Thereby the assumption of the abstract individual that is fundamental to classic liberalism is basic to the 'new' institutional economics as well. It is thus possible to distinguish the 'new' institutionalism from the 'old' by means of this criterion. This distinction holds despite important theoretical and policy differences within the 'new' institutionalist camp.

Methodological individualism

The assumption of rational, maximizing behaviour by agents with given and stable preference functions is generally associated with a view that it is desirable or possible to explain social or economic wholes in terms of the individuals constituting them. This view is known as methodological individualism and it is typically defined as the doctrine that all socioeconomic phenomena are in principle explicable only in terms of the individuals involved. Methodological individualists take the individual, along with his or her assumed behavioural characteristics, as the elemental building block in the theory of the social or economic system. Individuals are pictured abstractly as given, with given preferences and purposes. Clearly, assumptions of this type are typical of neo-classical economics, as well as of the 'new' institutionalism as a whole.

How should methodological individualism be evaluated? The obvious question to be raised is the legitimacy of stopping short at the individual in the process of explanation. If individuals are affected by their circumstances, then why not in turn attempt to explain the causes acting upon individual 'goals and beliefs'? Why should the process of scientific enquiry be arrested as soon as the individual is reached? If there are determinate influences on individuals and their goals, then these are worthy of explanation. In turn, the explanation of those may be in terms of other purposeful individuals. But where should the analysis stop? The purposes of an individual could be at least partly explained by the institutional and cultural context. These, in their turn, would be partly explained in terms of other individuals. But these individual purposes and actions could then be partly explained by cultural and institutional factors, and so on, indefinitely. We are here involved in an apparently infinite regress. Such an analysis never reaches an end. It is simply arbitrary to stop at one particular stage in the explanation and say 'it is all reducible to individuals' just as much as to say it is 'all social and institutional'. The key point is that in this infinite regress, neither individual nor social factors have legitimate explanatory primacy. The idea that all explanations have to be in terms of individuals is thus unfounded (Hodgson, 1988, 1998).

Methodological individualism implies a rigid and dogmatic compartmentalization of study. It may be legitimate in some limited types of analysis to take individuals as given and examine the consequences of the interactions of their activities. This particular type of analysis has a worthy place alongside other approaches in social science. But it does not legitimate methodological individualism because the latter involves the further statement that *all* social explanations should be of this or a similar type. In sum, because of its claimed universality methodological individualism is untenable.

The development of institutions

Having taken the individual 'for granted', the 'new' institutionalists then attempt to explain the emergence, existence, and performance of social institutions. Such explanations address the functioning of all kinds of social institutions in terms of the interactions between given individuals. Of course, the existence of institutions is seen to affect individual behaviour, but only in terms of the choices and constraints presented to the agents, not by the moulding of the preferences and indeed the very individuality of those agents themselves.

In other words, once institutions have emerged on the basis of individual behaviours, they are seen simply as providing external constraints, conventions or openings to individuals who are taken as given. It is assumed that individual actions lead to the formation of institutions, but institutions do not change individuals, other than by supplying information or constraints. The possibility that individuals themselves may be shaped in some fundamental manner by social institutions is not considered.

These common features of the 'new' institutionalism may be examined by way of Alexander Field's forceful critique of explanations of rules using rational-choice models. (See his two essays reprinted in Hodgson, 1993b.) Field points out that in attempting to explain the origin of social institutions the 'new' institutional economics has to presume given individuals acting in an already structured context. Along with the assumption of given individuals is the assumption of given rules of behaviour governing their interaction. What is forgotten is that in the original, hypothetical, 'state of nature' from which institutions are seen to have emerged, a number of weighty rules, institutions and cultural and social norms have already been presumed. Such initial institutional assumptions are unavoidable.

Take another important type of 'new' institutionalist theory. Game theorists such as Schotter (1981) also take the individual 'for granted', as an agent unambiguously maximizing his or her expected payoff. Further, in attempting to explain the origin of institutions through game theory, Field and others point out that certain norms and rules must inevitably be presumed at the start. There can be no games without rules, and thus game theory can never explain the elemental rules themselves. Even in a sequence of repeated games, or of games about other (nested) games, at least one game or meta-game, with a structure and payoffs, must be assumed at the outset. Any such attempt to deal with history using sequential or nested games is thus involved in a problem of infinite regress: even with games about games about games to the nth degree there is still one preceding game left to be explained.

On reflection, all theories must first build from elements that are taken as given. However, the particular problem of infinite regress that is identified here undermines any 'new institutionalist' claim that the explanation of the emergence of institutions can start from some kind of institution-free ensemble of individuals in which there is supposedly no rule or institution to be explained. Consequently, the 'new' institutionalist project to explain the emergence of institutions on the basis of given individuals has run into difficulties, particularly regarding the conceptualization of the initial state from which institutions are supposed to emerge. This is graphically illustrated in regard to the question of the market.

The conceptualization of the market

One of the striking features of neo-classical theory is that it does not normally conceive of the market in institutional terms. It typically presumes that the market is the ether within which the preferences and purposes of free-floating individuals are expressed. The market is not seen as an organized and functional entity but as an aggregation of mere individual traders and exchanges. The notion of the market as an institution, itself organized to structure – and even to some extent to constrain – economic activity is missing. In neoclassical theory the 'constraints' relate exclusively to market 'imperfections' of extra-market institutions.

Much 'new' institutionalist writing has this deficiency. In attempting to explain the emergence of specific institutions, it is assumed that the market has a prior existence, as an institution-free 'state of nature'. Thus, for instance, Williamson (1975: 20) writes that 'in the beginning there were markets' without noting the problem of examining the origin of market institutions. Likewise, in his discussion of economic growth, Olson (1982) first assumes a market and institution-free 'state of nature', associated with faster economic growth, which is subsequently retarded by the emergence of 'interest groups' and 'institutional sclerosis'. This wrongly suggests that markets themselves can be entirely free of institutional restrictions and coalitions of agents.

In contrast, a number of other writers have argued that the market is not a natural datum or ether, but it is itself a social institution, governed by sets of rules defining restrictions on some, and legitimating other, behaviours (Hodgson, 1988). For instance, the 'old' institutionalist Karl Polanyi argued at length that the market is necessarily tied up with other social institutions such as the state, and is promoted or even in some cases created by conscious design.

The theory of the firm

Superficially, Williamson's (1975, 1985) work on the theory of the firm seems to be a departure from much of neo-classical orthodoxy. For example, he claims to be influenced by Simon and the behaviouralist school, and if this influence were substantial it would suggest a break from the neo-classical axiom of maximizing behaviour based on individual rationality. However, on closer inspection it is evident that Williamson's break from neo-classical theory is partial and incomplete, and much of the core neo-classical apparatus is retained.

Following Coase's famous insight, Williamson argues that the existence of firms and their internal supersession of the market mechanism is due to the significant transaction costs involved in market trading. In Williamson's (e.g. 1985: 32) hands this Coasian idea is repeatedly linked with that of Simon: 'Economizing on transaction costs essentially reduces to economizing on bounded rationality'. Essentially, the problem is that Williamson has taken only part of Simon's argument on board and he is influenced too much by common but inaccurate interpretations of behaviouralism.

Simon's argument is that a complete or global rational calculation is ruled out, thus rationality is 'bounded'; agents do not maximize but attempt to attain acceptable minima instead. But it is important to note that this 'satisficing' behaviour does not simply arise because of inadequate information, but also because it would be too difficult to perform the calculations even if the relevant information were available.

Given this point, a prevailing interpretation of Simon's work can be faulted: the recognition of bounded rationality refers primarily to the matter of computational capacity and not to additional 'costs'. Accordingly, 'satisficing' does not amount to cost-minimizing behaviour. Clearly, the latter is just the dual of the standard assumption of maximization; if 'satisficing' were essentially a matter of minimizing costs then it would amount to maximizing behaviour of the neo-classical type. Contrary to some neo-classical interpretations, Simon's work does indeed involve a denial of maximizing behaviour. The term 'satisficing' was employed by Simon precisely to distance his conception from 'substantive' rationality and maximizing behaviour.

Symptomatically, Williamson uses the term 'bounded rationality' much more often than 'satisficing'. Basically, Williamson adopts the neo-classical, cost-minimizing interpretation of Simon and not the one that clearly prevails in Simon's own work. In Williamson's work 'economizing on transaction costs' is part of global, cost-minimizing behaviour, and this is inconsistent with Simon's own idea of bounded rationality. Whilst Williamson recognizes some of the informational problems, the fact that the cost-minimizing calculus remains supreme in his theory means that he has not broken entirely from the neo-classical assumption of maximization.

Consistent with the retention of the neo-classical model of optimizing behaviour, Williamson assumes that individual preference functions are unchanged by the economic environment and the institutions in which individuals are located. He also retains the neo-classical assumption of maximizing (or cost-minimizing) behaviour. Despite its apparent novelty, and its refreshing attempt to open up the 'black box' of the firm, Williamson's work lies close to the neo-classical pole of the 'new' institutionalist spectrum.

It seems that despite big differences in analytical methods and policy conclusions all varieties of 'new' institutionalism are united by their assumption that individual preferences and purposes are exogenous. In all cases the processes governing their determination and change are disregarded.

4 The 'old' institutional economics

Founded by Thorstein Veblen, John Commons and Wesley Mitchell in the United States in the first three decades of the twentieth century the 'old' tradition of institutional economics has a relatively small following today. Although the 'old' institutionalism has attracted a number of adherents of European origin, including K. William Kapp, Gunnar Myrdal and Karl Polanyi, it has never ever – at least until very recently – gained a significant hold in European universities. This is despite the fact that Gunnar Myrdal gained the Nobel Prize in economics in 1974 and his work influenced leading heterodox economists such as Nicholas Kaldor. However, two remarkable facts and features are worthy of note.

First, the 'old' institutional economics prospered in the United States in the 1920s to the extent that it largely dominated the American economics profession and even its prestigious journals such as the *American Economic Review*, the *Quarterly Journal of Economics* and the *Journal of Political Economy*. The spectacular decline of the 'old' institutional economics after World War II beside the juggernaut of neo-classical formalism is equally remarkable; it has allowed many leading American economists to forget what they find to be a primitive and embarrassing episode in their national professional past.

Second, in its dissent from at least two of the above core presuppositions of neo-classical economics, the 'old' institutionalism goes further than most other heterodoxies. Indeed, by finding its philosophical basis in the work of pragmatist philosophers such as Charles Sanders Peirce, the 'old' institutionalism expresses explicit nonconformity with the entire Cartesian and Newtonian framework of modern science. In particular, this involves a break from the conception of the isolated, contemplating, rational human agent. The idea of 'rational economic man' as encapsulated in neo-classical proposition (1) above is rejected by the 'old' institutionalists, to be replaced by the idea of the institutionalized agent, driven in the main by habit and routine.

Veblen (1919) clearly recognized the mechanistic foundations of neo-classical theory and proposed instead the adoption of an evolutionary metaphor taken from Darwinian biology (Hodgson, 1993a). Accordingly, 'old' institutionalists generally regard their economics as 'evolutionary' in character.

Images of the 'old' institutionalism

However, the task of identifying the theoretical core of the 'old' institutionalism should not be underestimated. The founders of this school were not entirely helpful in this regard. For instance, no adequate, systematic theory of industry, technology or the macro-economy appears in Veblen's work. Yet although Veblen failed to develop a systematic theory, he did look to the Darwinian theory of evolution for inspiration. He was also critical of others, such as the German Historical School, for allegedly shunning the task of theoretical analysis and development (Veblen, 1919: 58).

Commons made major contributions to the theory of institutions (Commons, 1934). In particular he applied some of Veblen's ideas on the 'natural selection' of institutions, but insisted that institutional evolution was more like artificial than natural selection. However, although sustained, his attempt to build a complete and systematic theory was also ultimately unsuccessful, and his legacy consists of a number of episodic insights and sometimes incompletely developed theoretical notions. Commons attempted to build a theoretical system, but again the result does not rank in stature with that of Marx, Walras or Marshall.

Turning to Mitchell, his role in the development of national income accounting was enormous and his influence over a generation of American applied economists was massive. His work provided an important foundation for the 'Keynesian revolution' in macroeconomics in the 1930s. Yet although he made major theoretical contributions, such as to monetary economics and to the theory of business cycles, his immersion in the processing of data left the task of theoretical development to others at a critical time.

In the inter-war period, the 'old' institutional economic theorists failed to build up and sustain the theoretical momentum built up by Veblen, Commons and Mitchell. In particular, little attention was given to the Veblenian research agenda of rebuilding economics by use of evolutionary concepts and metaphors taken from biology. In sum, the 'old' institutionalism established the importance of institutions and proclaimed the need for a genuinely evolutionary economics, but then proceeded in an increasingly descriptive direction, leaving many of the core theoretical questions unanswered. In the 1930s the perceived 'old' institutionalist preoccupation with measurement rather than theory gave many social scientists reason to reject the 'old' institutionalism.

Veblen's critique of rational economic man

It has been noted that the 'old' institutionalism offers the most fundamental critique of the core presuppositions of neo-classical economics. Regarding the idea of the rational, optimizing agent, Veblen (1919: 73) argued that neo-classical economics had a 'faulty conception of human nature' wrongly conceiving of the individual 'in hedonistic terms; that is to say, in terms of a passive and substantially inert and immutably given human nature'. It is important to note therefore, that Veblen's critique was directed not only at neo-classical economics, as defined above, but at all theories in which the individual is taken as given. This would include much work in the 'new' institutionalist camp.

The Veblenian theme of the endogeneity of preferences is persistent in the history of the 'old' institutionalism, up to the present day. For example, the account of the emergence of money, such as developed by Mitchell (1937) suggests that this event cannot be explained simply because it reduced costs or made life easier for traders. The penetration of money exchange into social life altered the very configurations of rationality, involving the particular conceptions of abstraction, measurement, quantification and calculative intent. It was thus a transformation of individuals and their preference functions rather than simply the emergence of institutions and rules. Similar themes are also found in the more recent writings of John Kenneth Galbraith with his continuing insistence that tastes are malleable and that the idea of 'consumer sovereignty' is a myth.

Accordingly, one of the reasons why any focus on the given individual is problematic is that it does not give sufficient emphasis to the role of institutions and culture in moulding and reconstituting individual preferences and beliefs.

Veblen's (1919: 73) critique of the economic agent as 'a lightning calculator of pleasures and pains' is justly famous, and even has a modern ring. The ironic 'lightning calculator' phrase suggests that the neo-classical theorists ignore the problems of global calculation of maximization of opportunities. This reminds the modern reader of Simon's idea of limited computational capacity and 'bounded rationality'. In describing economic man as having 'neither antecedent nor consequent' Veblen identified and criticized the uncreative and mechanistic picture of the utility-maximizing agent in neo-classical theory.

Veblen partially developed an alternative theory of human agency, in which 'instincts' such as 'workmanship', 'emulation', 'predatoriness' and 'idle curiosity' played a major role. The emphasis on habitual and 'instinctive' behaviour was intended to replace the utilitarian pleasure–pain principle, for example by rejecting the idea that work was an unambiguous 'disutility'.

One of Veblen's main arguments against the core assumptions of neo-classical theory was that they were inadequate for the theoretical purpose at hand. Like subsequent 'old' institutionalists, his intention was to analyse the processes of change and transformation in the modern economy. Neo-classical theory was defective in this respect because it indicated 'the conditions of survival to which any innovation is subject, supposing the innovation to have taken place, not the conditions of variational growth' (Veblen, 1919: 176–7). But the 'old' institutionalism seeks precisely a theory why such innovations take place, not a theory that dwells over equilibrium conditions with given technological possibilities. The question for Veblen was not how things stabilize themselves in a 'static state', but how they endlessly grow and change.

The 'old' institutionalists put stress both on the processes of economic evolution and technological transformation, and on the manner in which action is moulded by circumstances. Following Veblen, the individual's conduct is seen as being influenced by relations of an institutional nature: thus suggesting an alternative to neo-classical theory with its self-contained, rational individual, with autonomous preferences and beliefs, formed apart from the social and natural world: a 'globule of desire', to use Veblen's (1919: 73) famous and satiric phrase. There is a complete break from the atomistic, individualistic and utilitarian assumptions associated with neo-classical economics.

Clearly, this has implications for the economics of welfare. Instead of the neo-classical approach that sees problems of welfare in terms of the maximization of individual pleasure or utility, the 'old' institutionalists hold the view that it is possible to establish a meaningful discourse concerning objective human needs. In this regard there is again a profound break from utilitarianism and subjectivism.

The conception of the agent adopted by Veblen and later 'old' institutionalists is strongly influenced by the pragmatist philosophy of Peirce and others. Pragmatists reject the Cartesian notion of the supremely rational, calculating agent, to replace it by a conception of agency propelled in the main by habits and routinized behaviours. For Peirce, habit does not merely reinforce belief: the essence of belief is the establishment of habit. Accordingly, as Commons (1934: 150) put it, Peirce dissolved the antinomies of rationalism and empiricism at a stroke, making 'Habit and Custom, instead of intellect and sensations, the foundation of all science'. As a result, the 'old' institutionalism rejects the continuously calculating, marginally adjusting agent of neo-classical theory to emphasize inertia and habit instead.

Peirce's linking of habit and belief suggests a process by which habits of action connect with habits of thought and help to establish knowledge or skill. As Veblen argued, habits give the point of view from which facts and events are apprehended and reduced to a body of knowledge. Institutions create and reinforce habits of action and thought: 'The situation of today shapes the institutions of tomorrow through a selective, coercive process, by acting upon men's habitual view of things, and so altering or fortifying a point of view or a mental attitude handed down from the past' (Veblen, 1899: 190–1).

Such rigidities should not be regarded as a wholly negative impairment. Recent developments in modern anthropology and psychology also suggest that social and individual routines play an essential role in providing a cognitive framework for interpreting sense data and for transforming information into useful knowledge (Hodgson, 1988). Given that it is impossible to deal with and understand the entire amount of sense-data that reaches the brain, we rely on concepts and cognitive frames to select aspects of the data and to make sense of these stimuli. These habituated procedures of perception and cognition are learned, and acquired from our social surroundings. As cultural anthropologists argue, social institutions, culture and routines give rise to certain ways of selecting and understanding the world around us.

In addition, recognition of the pre-eminence of habit and routine does not exclude a notion of purposeful behaviour, particularly at the higher levels of mental activity (Veblen, 1919: 75; Hodgson 1988, 1993a). But there should be no false dichotomy between habit and purpose: even purposeful behaviour is guided and framed by habits of thought. This leaves open the question of the sources of creativity. It should not be assumed at the outset, however, that habit and novelty cannot be reconciled.

The nature of institutions

Both 'old' and 'new' institutional economists see institutions in broadly defined terms, not simply in the narrow sense of formal organizations. Institutions are durable systems of established and embedded social rules that structure social interactions. Language, money, systems of weights and measures, table manners, firms (and other organizations) are all institutions. We need to consider why institutions are durable, how they structure social interactions, and in what senses they are established and embedded. In part, the durability of institutions stems from the fact that they can usefully create stable expectations of the behaviour of others. Generally, institutions enable ordered thought, expectation and action, by imposing form and consistency on human activities. They depend upon the thoughts and activities of individuals but are not reducible to them. Institutions both constrain and enable behaviour.

In part, rules are embedded because people choose to follow them repeatedly. In addition, pragmatist philosophers and 'old' institutional economists argue that institutions work only because the rules involved are embedded in shared habits of thought and behaviour. Hence institutions are emergent social structures, based on commonly held habits of thought. Upon these structures, actual or potential patterns of social behaviour arise. Habits are the constitutive material of institutions, providing them with enhanced durability, power and normative authority. By reproducing shared habits of thought, institutions create strong mechanisms of conformism and normative agreement. However, Veblen and other 'old' institutionalists rebut the assumption that institutions must necessarily serve the functional needs of society. Instead, institutions are often regarded as 'archaic' or 'ceremonial'.

This definition of an institution suggests a place for the concept of power in economic analysis. A theoretical emphasis on power is indeed one of the hallmarks of the 'old' institutionalism, although the concept is itself complex and multi-dimensional. The definition of institutions also relates to the concept of culture. For the 'old' institutionalist, culture is much more than 'information': it is synonymous with the complex ensemble of social institutions that guide, mould and enable individual behaviour. Hence, the growth of social culture may be defined as 'a cumulative sequence of habituation' (Veblen, 1919: 241). Accordingly, the 'old' institutionalism sees individuals as situated in and moulded by an evolving social culture.

Processes similar to what Veblen (1899: 15–16) described as 'emulation' can be important in removing internal variation and stabilizing individual behaviour in social institutions. Indeed, recent studies from organizational sociology suggest that imitation plays a much larger role in the formation of social structures and organizations than previously supposed. For these and other reasons, institutions often take relatively stable and constrained paths of development.

Institutions may be regarded as relatively durable units of selection because of their cumulative and self-reinforcing characteristics. These can be understood in terms of a process of positive feedback. In this respect there is another contrast with neo-classical economics, where the formation of equilibrium relies upon negative feedback processes, such as diminishing returns to scale. Rather than equilibrium, positive feedback can engender lock-in, to use the modern term, where outcomes become frozen because of their self-reinforcing attributes. Such locked-in phenomena can thus be regarded as sufficiently stable units of selection in an evolutionary process.

In taking institutions as units and entities of analysis the 'old' institutionalism contrasts with neo-classical economics where the individual is taken as the irreducible unit of analysis. This does not mean, of course, that institutions are regarded as immutable. Institutions themselves may change. What is important is to stress the *relative* invariance and self-reinforcing character of institutions: to see socioeconomic development as periods of institutional continuity punctuated by periods of crisis and more rapid development.

Creativity, change and disequilibrium

It would be wrong to presume, however, that in its concerns with human behaviour the entire emphasis of the 'old' institutionalist is on the rigidity of habit and routine. Veblen devised the concept of 'idle curiosity' and this can serve as a genesis for diversity and variation. He suggested that the human tendency towards experimentation and creative innovation could generate novelty in an ongoing manner. This could lead to new and improved ways of thinking and doing, and consequently the generation of the greater variety. For Veblen, 'idle curiosity' is a major source of technological change.

We are led directly to a discussion of the second neo-classical core assumption of an equilibrating system. Mechanical equilibrium pertains to a closed system. By contrast, in an open system there is always the possibility of disturbance from the outside environment. Accordingly, the 'old' institutional economists 'have always considered the economy as an open system in continuous dynamic interaction with a more comprehensive social and political as well as physical system from which economic processes receive important organising (and disorganising) impulses and upon which they exert their own negative and positive influences' (Kapp, 1976: 213).

Instead of the notion of equilibrium borrowed from mechanics, Veblen and subsequent 'old' institutionalists turned to evolutionary biology for inspiration. Veblen saw instincts, habits and institutions in economic evolution as analogous to genes in biology, although they have nothing like the degree of permanence of the biotic gene and do not mutate in the same way. Nevertheless, such structures and routines have a stable and inert quality, and tend to sustain and thus 'pass on' their important characteristics through time.

The idea that routines within the firm act as 'genes' to pass on skills and information has been adopted more recently by Nelson and Winter (1982: 134–6) and forms a crucial part of their theoretical model of the firm. Accordingly, and despite making no reference to the earlier work of Veblen, their work is much closer to the 'old' institutionalism than to the 'new'.

Habits and routines are both relatively durable and present in a variety of forms in any complex economy. As in the case of Darwin's theory, this combination of variety with durability provides for Veblen a basis for evolutionary selection to work. Often unwittingly and without human design, certain institutions and patterns of behaviour become more effective in the given environmental context. Even without changes in the environment the evolutionary process can go on. But environmental changes can accelerate, hinder or disrupt the processes of selection, often in dramatic ways.

Veblen (1919: 74–5) wrote: 'The economic life history of the individual is a cumulative process of adaptation of means to ends that cumulatively change as the process goes on, both the agent and his environment being at any point the outcome of the last process.' This is a conception of evolution in which the set of constitutive elements may change in a process of cumulative causation. Furthermore, and strikingly, the individual and his or her preferences are not taken as fixed or given.

Veblen adopted a 'post-Darwinian' outlook that put an emphasis on 'the process of causation' rather than 'that consummation in which causal effect was once presumed to come to rest.' For Veblen, 'modern science is becoming substantially a theory of the process of consecutive change, realized to be self-continuing or self-propagating and to have no final term.' (Veblen, 1919: 37) Hence Veblen saw modern science as moving away from conceptualizations of equilibria and comparative statics. In arguing that economics should be an 'evolutionary science', Veblen (1899: 188) wrote: 'The life of man in society, just as the life of other species, is a struggle for existence, and therefore it is a process of selective adaptation. The evolution of social structure has been a process of natural selection of institutions.'

The 'selective, coercive process' of institutional replication is not, however, confined to a fixed pattern. Institutions change, and even gradual change can eventually put such a strain on a system that there can be outbreaks of conflict or crisis, leading to a change in actions and attitudes. Thus there is always the possibility of the breakdown of regularity: there will be moments of crisis or structural breaks when existing conventions or social practices are disrupted. In any social system there is an interplay between routinized behaviour and the variable or volatile decisions of other agents.

In Veblen's view the economic system is not a 'self-balancing mechanism' but a 'cumulatively unfolding process'. It is not well-known, but Veblen's idea of cumulative causation was an important precursor of other developments of the very same concept by Allyn Young, Gunnar Myrdal (1957), Nicholas Kaldor and K. William Kapp. Because of the momentum of technological and social change in modern industrial society, and the clashing new conceptions and traditions thrown up with each innovation in management and technique, the cumulative character of economic development can mean crisis on occasions rather than continuous change or advance.

Veblen's ideas are incomplete and often imprecise. In part, this stems from the limited development of evolutionary theory in biology at his time. However, despite its limitations, Veblen's writing stands out as the most successful attempt, at least until the 1970s, to incorporate evolutionary thinking into economics and social science. The principal component of this achievement is its embodiment of the idea of the cumulatively self-reinforcing institution as the socioeconomic analogue of the gene, to be subject to the forces of mutation and selection.

The characteristics of the 'old' institutionalism

The 'old' institutional economics, following the lead of Veblen, Commons and Mitchell, may be defined as an approach that has the following attributes:

1. the eschewal of atomism and reductionism in economic analysis, typically positing 'holistic' or organicist alternatives;

2. instead of the rational, calculating agent of neo-classical theory, the 'old' institutionalism sees human behaviour as normally driven by habit and routine, but occasionally punctuated by acts of creativity and novelty;

3. instead of an exclusive focus on individuals as units of analysis, the 'old' institutionalism regards self-reinforcing institutions as additional or even alternative analytical units;

4. the conception of the economy is of an evolving, open system in historical time, subject to processes of cumulative causation – instead of approaches to theorizing that focus exclusively on mechanical equilibria;

5. the 'old' institutionalism sees individuals as situated in and moulded by an evolving social culture, so that their preference functions are not given and fixed but are in a process of continuous adaptation and change;

6. likewise, technology is regarded as evolving, and as a primary motive force in socioeconomic development – in contrast to a theoretical framework that takes technology as fixed and exogenous;

7. there is a pervasive concern with the role and significance of power and of the conflict between both individuals and institutions in socioeconomic life;

8. instead of an utilitarian framework that evaluates human welfare in terms of individual utility or pleasure and separates considerations of means from those of ends, there is a focus on the identification of real human needs and on the design of institutions that can further assist their identification and clarification.

5 Conclusion: the 'old' institutionalism and the study of business and management

The historical connection between the 'old' institutionalism and management studies is not difficult to establish and is illustrated by a number of specific linkages. For example, the seminal 1938 work by Chester Barnard, *The Function of the Executive* bears traces of the influence of these economists. Not only were most social scientists in the United States influenced by the 'old' institutionalism at that time but also, like the 'old' institutionalists, Barnard was concerned to examine the actual processes of executive decision making rather than to proceed axiomatically from given assumptions about human behaviour. Barnard denied the neo-classical postulate of individual maximization and instead saw a 'zone of indifference' in managerial behaviour. In turn, after the Second World War, Simon refined and transformed Barnard's idea, turning it into his more general formulations of 'satisficing' and 'bounded rationality' in his 'behavioural' theory.

The enormous influence of Simon on management thinking does not need to be elaborated here. The repeated mention of Simon in the present essay will also have been noted by the reader. This is no accident. In fact, Simon (1979) has acknowledged that he has been influenced by the 'old' institutionalists, particularly Commons. Furthermore, Simon (1979: 499) goes on to say that 'the principal forerunner of a behavioural theory of the firm is usually called Institutionalism.' (In the context, the 'old' rather than the 'new' institutionalism is implied.) This is a remarkable and rarely quoted acknowledgement of the theoretical empathy between the 'old' institutional economics and Simon's behaviouralism.

Instead of maximizing behaviour, Simon and his followers argue that agents are disposed to use habits and 'rules of thumb' in decision making. This idea is strongly redolent of Peirce, Veblen and the 'old' institutional economics. There are plentiful examples in managerial science of similar assumptions being made about human behaviour, even if the influence of the 'old' institutionalists is unacknowledged.

For example, the increasing emphasis by management and business theorists on the role of culture within the business enterprise is a clear departure from the neo-classical approach that takes the individual as given. Culture, at least in the richer sense, does not simply involve the transfer of information but the moulding of individuals and their preferences. The distinctive type of collectivist culture found within the Japanese firm does not simply act as a constraint on individuals but affects them in such a way that some of their own ambitions are displaced by goals that can serve the prosperity of the enterprise. In tracing the feedback influences of such business institutions on individual preferences and purposes, such analyses are strongly redolent of the 'old' institutionalism. Arguably, in facing such phenomena as the rise of the Japanese firm, this approach is analytically superior to that of neo-classical economics and the 'new' institutionalism.

Given the practical and theoretical problems that continue to appear with the neo-classical assumption of maximizing behaviour, the 'old' institutionalism is now strategically well placed to make a comeback. This is precisely because the 'old' institutionalists regard assumptions about human behaviour to be generally subject to theoretical and empirical scrutiny rather than being the unchallengeable and constitutive axioms of economic science.

In economics there is an increasing amount of work being described as 'evolutionary' in character. This work emphasizes such core concepts as path-dependency, cumulative causation and lock-in, all of which have a strong 'old' institutionalist ring. It is argued that evolutionary analogies are far preferable to the mechanistic frame of thought that has dominated economics since Adam Smith. Like the 'old' institutionalism, emphasis is put on the analysis of technological change. If the biological analogy proves appropriate and fruitful, then the 'old' institutionalism is in a strong position to prosper from this development, particularly in the areas of institutional and technological change that are of crucial interest to managers.

GEOFFREY M. HODGSON
UNIVERSITY OF HERTFORDSHIRE

Further Reading

(References cited in the text marked *)

* Commons, John R. (1934) *Institutional Economics – Its Place in Political Economy*, New York: Macmillan. Reprinted 1990 with a new introduction by Malcolm Rutherford, New Brunswick: Transaction Publishers. (One of Commons's classic statements of his version of the 'old' institutional economics: a very

illuminating but at the most only partially successful attempt to systematize institutional economic theory.)

Eggertsson, Thrainn (1990) *Economic Behavior and Institutions*, Cambridge: Cambridge University Press. (A well-written, highly readable and very useful discussion of segments of the 'new' institutional economics but one that neglects vast tracts of the latter and ignores the 'old' institutional economics as a whole.)

Furubotn, Eirik G. and Richter, Rudolph (1997) *Institutions in Economic Theory: The Contribution of the New Institutional Economics*, Ann Arbor: University of Michigan Press. (A good introduction to the approach of the 'new' institutional economics.)

* Hodgson, Geoffrey M. (1988) *Economics and Institutions: A Manifesto for a Modern Institutional Economics*, Cambridge and Philadelphia: Polity Press and University of Pennsylvania Press. (A critique of neo-classical economics from a modern perspective but one that is inspired by the 'old' institutional economics. The latter part of the book is an attempt to develop the foundations of that approach. There is an extensive bibliography.)

* Hodgson, Geoffrey M. (1993a) *Economics and Evolution: Bringing Life Back into Economics*, Cambridge and Ann Arbor: Polity Press and University of Michigan Press. (A review of both institutionalist and non-institutionalist attempts to apply evolutionary and biological analogies to economics. An extensive bibliography is included.)

* Hodgson, Geoffrey M. (ed.) (1993b) *The Economics of Institutions*, Aldershot: Edward Elgar. (A collection of seminal articles, most of recent vintage, on both the 'old' and 'new' institutionalism.)

* Hodgson, Geoffrey M. (1998) 'The approach of institutional economics', *Journal of Economic Literature* 36 (1): 166–92. (An updated statement of the 'old' institutional economics.)

* Hodgson, Geoffrey M., Warren J. Samuels and Marc R. Tool (eds) (1994) *The Elgar Companion to Institutional and Evolutionary Economics*, Aldershot: Edward Elgar. (The first ever encyclopedic treatment of the 'old' and 'new' institutionalisms, as well as of related work on evolutionary economics. Contains 176 entries in two volumes.)

* Kapp, K. William (1976) 'The nature and significance of institutional economics', *Kyklos* 29, Fasc. 2, pp. 209–32. Reprinted in Samuels, Warren J. (ed.) (1988) *Institutional Economics*, vol. 1, Aldershot: Edward Elgar. (Perhaps the clearest and best short statement of the essence of the 'old' institutional economics by a postwar European institutional economist: essential reading.)

* Mitchell, Wesley C. (1937) *The Backward Art of Spending Money and Other Essays*, New York: McGraw-Hill. (A collection of highly readable essays by one of the fathers of the 'old' institutionalism. Some of the essays serve as ideal introductions to the field.)

* Myrdal, Gunnar (1957) *Economic Theory and Underdeveloped Regions*, London: Duckworth. (One of the classic statements of the 'cumulative causation' thesis by an 'old' European institutionalist.)

* Nelson, Richard R. and Winter, Sidney G. (1982) *An Evolutionary Theory of Economic Change*, Cambridge, MA: Harvard University Press. (A now-seminal application of the evolutionary analogy to the theory of the firm. Although inexplicit, aspects of this work are highly redolent of Veblenian institutionalism.)

North, Douglass C. (1990) *Institutions, Institutional Change and Economic Performance*, Cambridge: Cambridge University Press. (A recent statement of his views on institutional change by a leading 'new' institutionalist. It emphasizes transaction costs but differs from the work of Williamson by highlighting pathdependency.)

* Olson, Jr., Mancur (1982) *The Rise and Decline of Nations*, New Haven: Yale University Press. (A stimulating theory of economic development and decline by a 'new' institutionalist.)

Rutherford, M.C. (1994) *Institutions in Economics: The Old and the New Institutionalism*, Cambridge: Cambridge University Press. (An important and provocative overview of institutional thought.)

* Schotter, Andrew (1981) *The Economic Theory of Social Institutions*, Cambridge: Cambridge University Press. (This work applies game theory to the analysis of institutions. Although written in the genre of the 'new' institutionalism it contains important criticism of *laissez-faire* economic policies.)

* Simon, Herbert A. (1979) 'Rational decision making in business organizations', *American Economic Review*, 69: 493–513. (One of the many lucid statements by Simon of his behaviouralist theory, but one that mentions its institutionalist antecedents.)

Sugden, Robert (1986) *The Economics of Rights, Co-operation and Welfare*, Oxford: Basil Blackwell. (An important theoretical work by a 'new' institutional economist.)

* Teece, David J. and Winter, Sidney G. (1984) 'The limits of neo-classical theory in management

education', *American Economic Review (Papers and Proceedings)*, 74 (2): 116–21. (Argues convincingly that neo-classical economics is of limited use in management.)
* Veblen, Thorstein B. (1899) *The Theory of the Leisure Class: An Economic Study of Institutions*, New York: Macmillan. (Veblen's classic and highly influential analysis of the consumer behaviour of the rich. With this work the 'old' institutional school was founded.)
* Veblen, Thorstein B. (1919) *The Place of Science in Modern Civilisation and Other Essays*, New York: Huebsch. Reprinted 1990 with a new introduction by W.J. Samuels, New Brunswick: Transaction Books. (The most important collection of Veblen's essays. Veblen is often at his best in his essays and polemics and for this reason this work is invaluable both for the economic and the social theorist.)
* Williamson, Oliver E. (1975) *Markets and Hierarchies: Analysis and Anti-Trust Implications: A Study in the Economics of Internal Organization*, New York: Free Press. (In this work Williamson developed the earlier insights of Coase and his transaction cost analysis into his theory of the firm. It is a most important milestone in the development of the 'new' institutionalism.)
* Williamson, Oliver E. (1985) *The Economic Institutions of Capitalism: Firms, Markets, Relational Contracting*, London: Macmillan. (This is a further development of Williamson's analysis of markets and firms.)

See also: COASE, R.; EVOLUTIONARY THEORIES OF THE FIRM; GALBRAITH, J.K.; MEANS, G.C.; MILL, J.S.; NEO-CLASSICAL ECONOMICS; SIMON, H.A.; VEBLEN, T.B.; WILLIAMSON, O.E.

Neo-classical economics

1 Introduction
2 Theory of consumers' behaviour
3 The demand curve and its elasticity
4 Theory of production and costs
5 The price–output decision of the firm
6 Partial equilibrium analysis and perfect competition
7 Criticisms of neo-classical economics

Overview

Neo-classical economics is the approach to the subject which developed mainly in Europe (and particularly the UK) in the late nineteenth century. It is still regarded as the mainstream of economic thinking and has revived in recent years with the decline in emphasis on Marxist and Keynesian concepts.

Economists who led the 'neo-classical revolution' did not reject classical economics, with its emphasis on the efficiency of markets in allocating resources. Their contribution was to refine the analysis of markets by applying the logic of differential calculus – marginal analysis. The result is a model in which individuals maximize their own satisfaction and firms maximize profits. Provided that there is sufficient competition in all markets, the consequence of this pursuit of individual gain is optimum welfare for the community as a whole.

The logic of neo-classical economics underlies not only much of current political thinking but also much of the conceptual framework applied in 'practical' management disciplines – for example, finance, marketing and business strategy. This is because this logic is mainly deductive – once the assumption of maximization (of profit, sales, output or any other outcome) is adopted, the implications are theoretically irrefutable. Criticisms of neo-classical economics relate mainly to the excessive simplicity of the initial assumptions and/or to the impractical complexity of the derived implications for business decisions.

1 Introduction

Neo-classical economics comprises what most current students of economics would recognize as the mainstream of the subject. This is probably more true in the 1990s than it was forty years ago, when Keynesian economics was given more emphasis than now. Neo-classical economics was developed in the late nineteenth century and is associated with such names as Jevons, Walras and Marshall (see MARSHALL, A.). It used many of the concepts of the classical economists but refined them mathematically and (in the Walras general equilibrium) integrated them into a comprehensive theory of resource allocation through the mechanism of prices.

The key principle of neo-classical economics is that all decisions are motivated by a desire to maximize something: individuals seek to maximize utility from any given level of spending and firms seek to maximize production from any given level of inputs and also to maximize profits. Provided that markets are competitive, the result of all this individual maximization is an optimum for society as a whole – maximum welfare from existing resources.

The founders of neo-classical economics showed great awareness of and interest in the real world. Alfred Marshall's *Principles of Economics*, for example, contains many shrewd observations of fact which conflict with the simplified models represented diagrammatically in his explanatory footnotes or in the mathematical appendix. However, it is these models that students struggle to understand and, having conquered this difficulty of comprehension, tend to remember as 'Economics'. Stripped of real-world provisos, the theoretical content of neo-classical economics is straightforward deduction; it is hard to disagree with Boland's comment: 'Unfortunately, despite the many impressive displays of mathematical agility and prowess, not much has been accomplished beyond what can be learned from any elementary calculus textbook' (Boland 1985: 554).

In teaching elementary microeconomics to business school students, it is certainly true that the meaning of 'marginal' (as in marginal utility, marginal productivity, marginal cost and marginal revenue) is the most difficult notion to communicate. This concept, central to much neo-classical theory, is quite simply the first derivative of the variable concerned with respect to whatever independent variable is specified. Legend has it that Marshall wrote the mathematical appendix to *Principles of Economics* before he produced the text.

Neo-classical economists, like the classical writers before them, viewed economics as a science. Marshall wrote that 'the Laws of Economics are statements of tendencies expressed in the indicative mood and not ethical precepts in the imperative' (Marshall 1890: v), although he went on to state that economists had to take account of ethical influences on human decisions.

In terms of the three stages of scientific method defined by J.S. Mill – (i) inference or induction, (ii) deduction and (iii) validation – neo-classical economics tends to concentrate on the second and to venture cautiously into the third. In an excellent summary of Marshall's contribution to microeconomics, Ekelund and Hebert wrote of his version of economic science that it is 'but the working out of common sense refined by organized analysis and reason' (1983: 332). Many of the 'laws' of classical and neo-classical economics begin from presumptions based on 'common sense' – comparative advantage, diminishing marginal utility and diminishing returns are three well-known examples.

Because it contains a lot of abstract theory that can be viewed as a complex representation of (often misplaced) common sense in an unreal world of perfect information, rationality and rapid adjustment from one equilibrium to another, neo-classical economics is criticized from all sides. Before considering these criticisms, it will be useful to explore some of the economic theory that owes most to neo-classical origins: the theory of consumers' behaviour, the concept of elasticity of demand, partial equilibrium analysis, and the marginal product approach to factor markets, marginal analysis and the price–output decisions of the firm. In general, much of the theory is artificially precise and easy to criticize, but it can be of practical help in providing guidance for analysis of real business problems.

2 Theory of consumers' behaviour

It is difficult to understand why Adam Smith (see SMITH, A.) was troubled by the 'water–diamond' paradox – why was a diamond, which had limited usefulness, more expensive than water, which was essential for life? The answer lay in common sense – diamonds are scarce, water is abundant. This common sense was not introduced into formal economics until nearly a century after Adam Smith produced his *Wealth of Nations*, by William Stanley Jevons, professor of economics at Manchester University. In his *Theory of Political Economy* (1871), Jevons set out a theory of utility, in which the fundamental principle was the law of diminishing marginal utility (which he called 'the degree of utility'). Ekelund and Hebert define 'Jevons' Law' as follows: 'The degree of utility for a single commodity varies with the quantity possessed of that commodity and ultimately decreases as the quantity of that single commodity increases' (1983: 315). This can be represented graphically, as in Figures 1a and 1b. Algebraically, if the quantity consumed of commodity i is denoted by q^i, then $\partial U/\partial q_i^2$ is negative.

Note the formalization of common sense here: the notion that the more one consumes of a product the less value one places on a marginal unit is not based on statistical analysis but is acceptable because it is intuitively sensible. It does not apply to some addictive goods, such as alcoholic drinks, gambling or (for some people) 'morish' things like chocolates, grapes or listening to good music. Whenever it is used to justify redistribution of income from rich to poor, even ardent fans of neo-classical economics balk at it, on the dubious but incontrovertible grounds that interpersonal comparisons of utility are invalid. Note also the convenient but unrealistic assumption that consumption of every

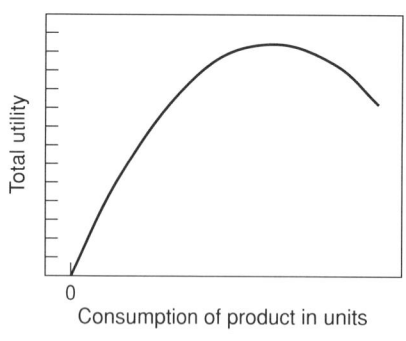

Figure 1a Total utility

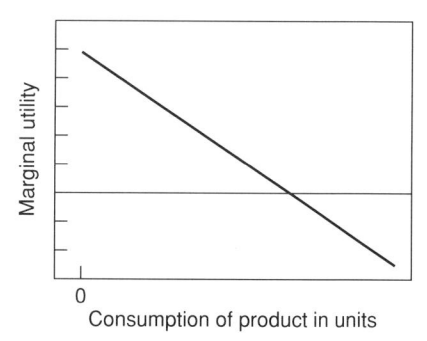

Figure 1b Marginal utility

commodity is a continuous variable: if I am deciding whether to buy a boat, a new car or a bigger house, what does $\partial U/\partial q$ or 'the increase in utility resulting from an infinitesimal increase in quantity consumed' mean?

Given diminishing marginal utility from all goods and services, an assumption that the quantity purchased of every product is infinitely divisible and, the only realistic assumption, that a consumer's income is finite, one can reproduce Jevons' equimarginal principle that the last penny spent on each of n products should yield the same utility:

$$\frac{\partial U}{\partial X_1} = \frac{\partial U}{\partial X_2} = \frac{\partial U}{\partial X_3} = \frac{\partial U}{\partial X_n} \quad (1)$$

Subsequent authors, such as Menger, Walras and Marshall (see MARSHALL, A.), developed this further by showing the relationship between marginal utility and price and therefore refining Jevons' theory of exchange:

$$\frac{\partial U}{\partial q_1}\frac{1}{P_1} = \frac{\partial U}{\partial q_2}\frac{1}{P_2} \ldots \text{etc.} \quad (2)$$

This states simply that the ratio between marginal utilities of products is inversely proportional to their prices. Marginal utility theory as presented here can be applied to the theory of demand, to explain how a change in price affects the quantity demanded of a product. First, there is a substitution effect: the equilibrium set out in equation (2) is disturbed. Second, a change in the price of any product consumed implies a change in real income, significant only when the product concerned accounts for a significant proportion of expenditure. This gives rise to changed expenditure allocated in accordance with equation (1).

Since about 1950, partly because of the influence of Hicks and Samuelson (see SAMUELSON, P.A.), the presentation of the neo-classical theory of consumers' behaviour has departed from the 'cardinal' utility approach presented above and adopted the 'ordinal' approach embodied in indifference curves. The nebulous and non-measurable concept of utility has been replaced by indifference curves, first devised by Edgeworth (in his 1881 work, *Mathematical Psychics*). These could be interpreted as contours of satisfaction (or utility), the advantage being that it is possible to describe one combination of consumption as preferable to another without assigning a cardinal value to utility of either combination.

In his later work (for example, *A Revision of Demand Theory*) Hicks abandoned the description 'indifference curve', preferring the term 'revealed preference', but this did not imply any shift towards empirical derivation. It was more an attempt to escape from the use of terms describing human thinking as opposed to behaviour. In essence, the presentation of the theory through indifference curves retains the fundamental assumptions of Jevons' utility theory. Diminishing marginal utility is reflected in the shape of the indifference curve, which is concave towards the origin (Figure 2).

The assumption that the consumer maximizes utility is implied by the tangency between the budget line (showing the combinations of any two products available to the consumer at existing prices) and the 'highest' contour of utility (indifference curve) that

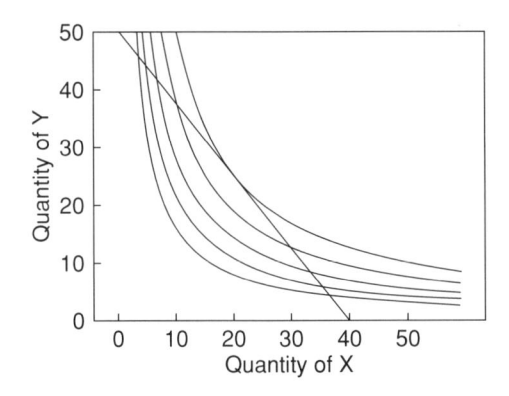

Figure 2 The indifference map

they can reach. The infinite divisibility of all products is, of course, still implicit in this presentation. The statement that the 'marginal rate of substitution' at the equilibrium point A is inversely proportional to the prices of the products:

$$\frac{dY}{dX} = \frac{Px}{Py} \qquad (3)$$

is hardly more comprehensible than equation (2) above; the only advantage is that the term 'utility' is avoided.

It is easy to ridicule the neo-classical theory of consumers' behaviour because by combining 'common sense' presumptions with unrealistic simplifications it takes the application of elementary calculus to an abstract extreme. It is also tautological, in the sense that altruism or masochism are accommodated as utility-enhancing. If I give my money to charity, I do so to get satisfaction (utility); work, as opposed to leisure, may bring disutility but this can be represented by a utility curve with a negative intercept and an accelerating negative slope.

However, utility theory can be useful in the analysis of practical business problems. For example, in examining the disincentive effects of direct taxation on employees' willingness to undertake overtime or extra responsibility, it is analytically useful to identify substitution and income effects – when income tax falls, the opportunity cost (price) of free time is higher but real income is also higher and the employee may feel able to afford more free time. Although the use of indifference curves or differential calculus would not be normal practice in the analysis of these problems, the basic logic can provide useful rigour.

3 The demand curve and its elasticity

The notion that a relationship can be specified between the quantity demanded (Q) and price (P) of a product, such that $Q = f(P)$, with all other influences upon Q held constant (*ceteris paribus*), was first proposed by the French economist A.A. Cournot in 1863. Ekelund and Hebert assert that Cournot 'discovered' this law of demand (*loi de débit*), but, like many of the other principles of neo-classical economics, it was not based on any empirical observation; 'conceived' might be a better word.

Most of the theory of demand included within an elementary microeconomics syllabus today was set out by Marshall in the *Principles of Economics*. Like Cournot, he recognized that the relationship $Q = f(P)$, the position and shape of the demand curve, would be determined by the factors held constant. He specified five of these:

- the time-period for adjustment;
- tastes, preferences and fashions;
- aggregate income or wealth;
- the purchasing power of money;
- the price and range of rival commodities.

Apart from the addition of complementary products and some reference to marketing expenditures, this is not unlike the list of 'demand conditions' presented in a modern text on demand theory.

Marshall went on to develop the concept of consumer surplus and to extend the demand curve concept to factor markets and therefore to production theory. In a short section on the difficulty of identifying a demand curve, mainly because of the effects of time lags and difficulties in establishing *ceteris paribus*, Marshall pinpointed statistical problems which continue to baffle econometricians today (1890: 92–7). It was also Marshall who

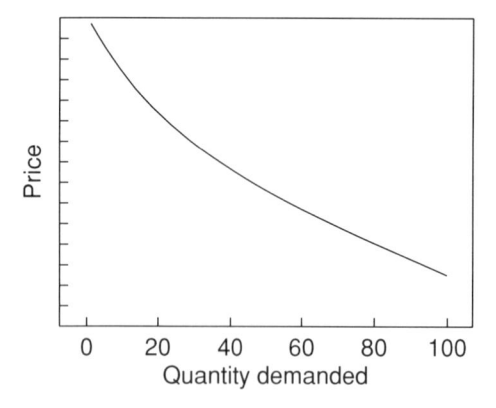

Figure 3a A demand curve

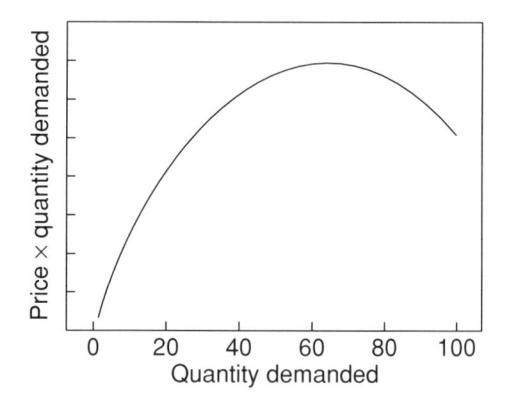

Figure 3b Corresponding total revenue

introduced the expression 'elasticity of demand' into economics and extended the concept to supply curves. Marshall did not define formally the difference between point- and arc-elasticity of demand.

General definition:

$$\frac{\Delta Q}{Q} \bigg/ \frac{\Delta P}{P} = \frac{\Delta Q}{\Delta P} \frac{P}{Q} \qquad (4)$$

Point-elasticity:

$$\frac{dQ}{dP} \frac{P}{Q} \qquad (5)$$

Arc-elasticity:

$$\frac{(Q_2 - Q_1)(P_2 + P_1)}{(P_2 - P_1)(Q_2 + Q_1)} \qquad (6)$$

However, he used a lengthy footnote and a complex note in the mathematical appendix to explain problems arising from changes in elasticity along the demand curve. Today, when students usually try to understand such things by manipulating figures on personal computers, it is important to introduce the arc-elasticity measure.

The term 'elasticity of demand' was originally used only with respect to price changes, but it has now been extended to other influences on demand. Some may wish that this jargon term had never been invented – Marshall's own alternative ('responsiveness') is more comprehensible, and 'sensitivity' corresponds exactly to the meaning of elasticity.

The statistical derivation of elasticities is often based on the assumption that these will be constant over small changes in the independent variable concerned. In this case, income- and price-elasticities may be derived as b and c respectively in the following equation:

$$Q = a\, Y^b\, P^c \qquad (7)$$

Here Y is real disposable income and P is the price adjusted for inflation. This approach is surrounded by dangerous pitfalls – autocorrelation, collinearity, heteroscedasticity and identification are all technical terms that one needs to understand before embarking on this kind of exercise. However, sometimes it works and can be quite satisfying.

The demand curve is normally drawn with P on the vertical axis and Q on the horizontal, whereas the explanation treats Q as the dependent variable. This is because the ultimate aim of demand analysis is to determine what revenues a firm (or entrepreneur) may derive by selling each of a range of outputs. Since total revenue = price × quantity, the relationship between revenue and quantity will depend on that between price and quantity:

Revenue $= PQ$

$\therefore Q \quad = f(P)$

$\therefore P \quad = \varphi(Q)$

$\therefore$ Revenue $= Q \times \varphi(Q) \qquad (8)$

Figure 3b shows how revenue would vary with quantity, given the demand curve in Figure 3a and the assumption that all units of the product are sold at the same price, indicated by the demand curve at each quantity.

The gradient of the revenue curve at any point is termed 'marginal revenue', a term first used (in French) by Cournot in 1838 but not rediscovered and used in English language economics until the 1920s (Blaug 1985: 318). The term is difficult to explain without using calculus. If the number of items sold (Q) is very large, it is sufficient to state that marginal revenue is price minus the loss of revenue resulting from the price change (ΔP) necessary to achieve the sale of the marginal item:

$$MR = P + Q(\Delta P) \qquad (9)$$

where ΔP is negative. More accurately:

$$MR = P + Q\left(\frac{dP}{dQ}\right) \qquad (10)$$

Demand theory, like other elements of neo-classical economics, appears to be a complex model based on simplifying assumptions. Quantity demanded refers to a homogeneous product, infinitely divisible, sold at the same price to all customers (although this last assumption can, of course, be modified). Consumers are assumed to be rational, consistent and informed. One might well conclude that demand theory is unrealistic and unusable.

However, the logic underlying demand theory can be useful in understanding or predicting the effects of price changes; an example is the notion that, in general, price-elasticity of demand rises in absolute terms as price rises. This logical principle was ignored by those who predicted dire consequences as a result of the oil price hikes of the mid-1970s, whose estimates of price-elasticity were based on observations at the low-price end of the demand curve. The emphasis placed by neo-classical economists on the dangers of the *ceteris paribus* assumption is also of great value in adding rigour to attempts to measure demand sensitivity in practice.

4 Theory of production and costs

The neo-classical theory of production is very similar in mathematical terms to the theory of consumers' behaviour. The principle of diminishing marginal utility is paralleled by

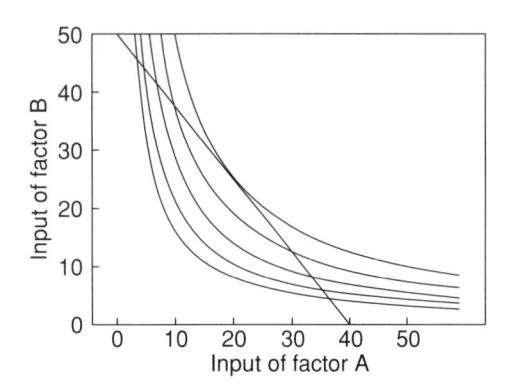

Figure 4 Isoquants (equal product curves)

the principle of diminishing marginal productivity – the notion that if additional inputs of one factor of production (productive resource) are applied in combination with fixed inputs of other factors, the product resulting from the marginal input will ultimately decrease. This more precise reformulation of the law of diminishing returns (a title used by Malthus and Ricardo) explains the relationship between output and costs in the short term (some inputs fixed).

In a similar vein is the principle that marginal utility is proportional to price: Equation (2) above is reproduced (under conditions of perfect competition) by inverse proportionality between marginal physical product and price of each factor:

$$\frac{\partial Q_1}{\partial n_1}\frac{1}{P_1} = \frac{\partial Q_2}{\partial n_2}\frac{1}{P_2} \text{ etc.} \qquad (11)$$

where n represents input of each factor. (Note that in the absence of perfect competition, this equation will not hold, first because the price of the product will vary with Q_i and second because the price of factor may vary with n_i.)

The 'isoquant' or equal product curve (see Figure 4) corresponds to the indifference curve of consumer behaviour theory, but the need for it is less because physical production is much more easily measured than utility. The unrealistic assumption inherent in all of this theory, that inputs and outputs are infinitely divisible, can be abandoned in the practical use of the isoquant approach, allowing the application of linear programming to production decisions (see Blaug 1985: 431–5).

Given the principle of diminishing marginal productivity and defining the short term as a period within which certain inputs are fixed, it follows that marginal cost must increase once output increases beyond a certain level and that this increase will accelerate. The relationship between total cost and quantity produced in the short term (some inputs fixed) is depicted in Figure 5a, while Figure 5b shows the corresponding values of average cost (C/Q) and marginal cost (dC/dQ).

Although the relationship between total cost and quantity (in the short term) is easy to explain and the concept of marginal cost is easier to understand than marginal revenue, it is questionable whether this form of cost curve should be used to model business behaviour. If most business decisions assume a linear total cost curve, with marginal cost constant up to a capacity level, then, even if this logic is faulty, should not economists incorporate into their models the way in which business decisions actually are taken, rather than how they ought to be?

Neo-classical economists cannot be held responsible for the treatment of the relationship between costs and quantity in the long run (Blaug 1985: 376). If the long run is defined as a period within which all inputs are variable, then the saucer-shaped long-run average cost (LRAC) curve (Figure 6) becomes difficult to explain. The downward portion of the curve to the left is usually explained by indivisibilities and specialization (which often amount to the same thing) combined with certain technical economies and the advantages of buyer power. The upward slope at the right-hand end is normally explained by management and co-ordination problems and possibly by monopsony – as the dominant buyer in a factor market, the firm has to pay an increasing price for a resource in limited supply.

It is convenient but confusing that these non-constant sections of the LRAC curve should be attributed to economies and ineconomies 'of scale'. It is precisely because factor inputs cannot be adjusted to scale with output that these changes arise.

The theory of production and costs has been developed far more than is presented in this short summary. The main point emphasized here is that, as in all neo-classical theory, this element is again based on the assumption of continuously variable outputs and inputs combined with the calculus of maximization and minimization.

5 The price–output decision of the firm

The firm's price–output decision was neatly set out algebraically by Cournot. If profit (Π) = revenue (R) – cost (C), and both R and C are related to Q (quantity produced and offered for sale), then the two conditions for profit maximization are:

(a) $$\frac{d\Pi}{dq} = 0$$

$\therefore$ $$\frac{dR}{dQ} - \frac{dC}{dQ} = 0$$

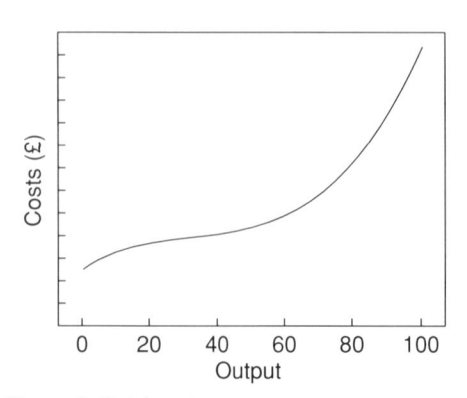

Figure 5a Total costs

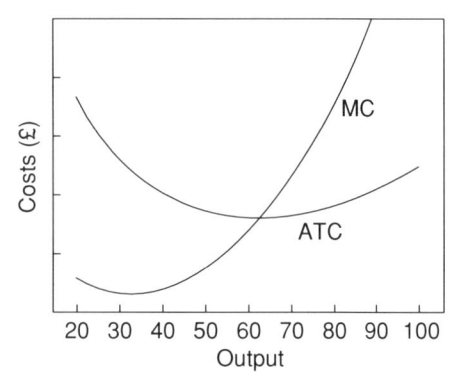

Figure 5b Marginal and average costs

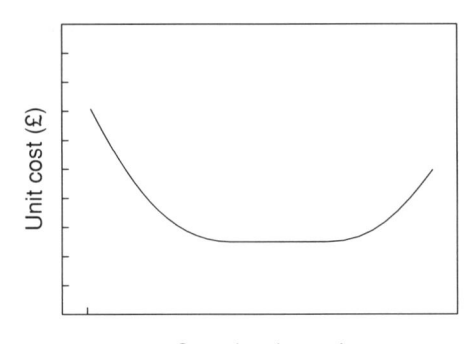

Neo-classical economics

Figure 6 Long-run average cost

$$\therefore \quad \frac{dR}{dQ} = \frac{dC}{dQ} \quad (12)$$

Marginal revenue = Marginal cost

(b) $\quad \dfrac{d^2\Pi}{dQ^2} < 0$

$\therefore \quad \dfrac{d^2R}{dQ^2} - \dfrac{d^2C}{dQ^2} < 0$

$\therefore \quad \dfrac{d^2R}{dQ^2} < \dfrac{d^2C}{dQ^2} \quad (13)$

Marginal revenue must be declining in relation to marginal cost. This profit-maximizing equilibrium is shown in Figures 7a and 7b.

Of all the elements of neo-classical economics, this is the one that could most easily be described as formalized common sense. It is much more convincing when presented in differential calculus to someone accustomed to such algebra than in a verbal or diagrammatic presentation. Because of a tradition that even mathematical theory should be presented verbally, Cournot's version (as summarized here) was not repeated by any of the Anglo-Saxon neo-classicists and, according to Blaug (1985), 'marginal revenue' did not appear in the English literature until the 1920s.

Some of the criticisms of this marginal analysis approach to profit maximization will be examined later in this entry, but in the meantime, there is one important implication that should be focused on: price decisions (which imply corresponding decisions on levels of output) are determined purely by marginal revenue and marginal cost.

$$\text{Marginal revenue} = \left(p + q \frac{dp}{dq} \right) \quad (14)$$

can be expressed in terms of p and price-elasticity of demand η:

$$\text{MR} = P\left(1 + \frac{1}{\eta}\right) \quad (15)$$

In ordinary English, the profit-maximizing (or loss-minimizing) price will be determined by marginal cost and what the market will bear. Fixed costs do not enter the calculation.

This conclusion has been dismissed as prescriptive rather than descriptive. In practice, it

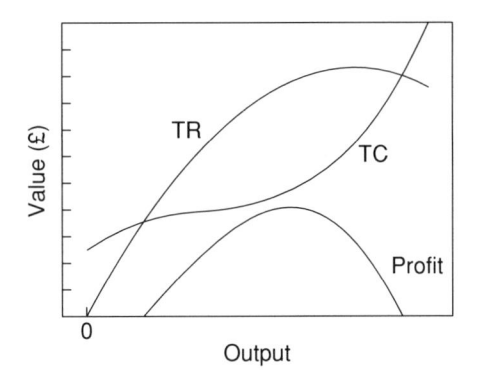

Figure 7a Total costs and revenue

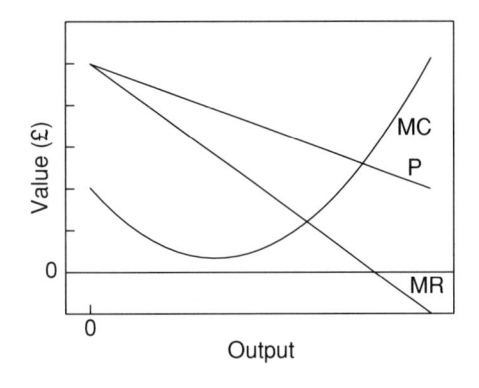

Figure 7b Marginal analysis (same data)

545

has been widely alleged, firms determine prices by adding a profit margin to unit cost at an expected level of sales (the standard cost principle). Summarizing several US and European studies, Scherer and Ross (1990) reported that a majority of companies used some kind of standard cost principle for price determination. However, these studies also showed:

1. contrary to the standard cost principle, most firms adjusted target profit margins to perceived price-elasticity of demand for each product or in each market segment;
2. when demand rose, most companies adjusted prices upwards;
3. when demand fell, very few companies implemented price increases, which the standard cost principle would imply (because fixed costs would be spread over a smaller volume).

It thus appears, as is true also of other elements of neo-classical economics, that the calculus of profit maximization cannot be dismissed as wrong in principle, but rather as spuriously precise. Managers do not know the demand curves for their products, output is not continuously variable, profits are not necessarily maximized within the short run; everything is less precise and less formal than the theory suggests. However, if the actual price–output decision is to be incorporated into a mathematical model, the profit-maximizing equilibrium of marginal analysis may be closer than critics imply. It is hard to model a vague approximation.

6 Partial-equilibrium analysis and perfect competition

It is still not widely understood that the principle that prices are determined by the interaction of independent demand and supply, as shown in the early chapters of most economics textbooks, depends upon the existence of perfect competition. The model of perfect competition is a theoretical abstraction. It assumes that the totality of goods and services can be parcelled into distinct 'industries' (Marshall's term) or markets within which there is a very high degree of product substitutability. The boundaries of these industries (or markets) are discontinuities ('gaps', in Robinson's (1969) words) in a continuum of substitution. When a market is 'perfect', prices will tend towards equality: 'The more nearly perfect a market is, the stronger is the tendency for the same price to be paid for the same thing at the same time in all parts of the market' (Marshall 1890: 270).

The mathematical reduction of this model is a market with many small firms all selling at the same price and producing at the output where this price is equal to (rising) marginal cost. If this price exceeds average cost, so that profits are being earned (in excess of the return on capital built into the average cost), then new competitors will enter the market, forcing prices down towards minimum average cost. Firms can increase profits temporarily only by reducing costs.

In the case of the firm, the quantity supplied at any given price is shown by the marginal cost curve (Figure 8a) and the short-run market (or industry) supply curve (Figure 8b) is derived by horizontal addition of the MC curves. If, to simplify the explanation, each of the n firms in the industry had identical MC curves and the quantity supplied at price P_1 were Q_1, then in the entire industry the quantity supplied would be nQ_1. In the short-run market, price and volume are determined by the intersection of the demand and short-run supply curves, but the entry of new firms and progressive reductions in cost mean that there is always a long-run supply curve moving steadily southeastwards in Figure 8b.

The impossibility of drawing a supply curve except under conditions of perfect competition becomes evident if it is assumed that a single enterprise acquires all the firms in the existing industry. Again for simplicity, it is assumed that marginal costs are unchanged, so that the former industry supply curve becomes the marginal cost curve of the monopoly. The profit-maximizing market price will now be P_2, because at the corresponding output Q_2, marginal cost is equal to marginal revenue. But marginal revenue is determined by the shape of the demand curve – in other words, the quantity supplied to the market at any given price is no longer independent of demand.

If perfect competition were universal, the market mechanism would lead to optimum

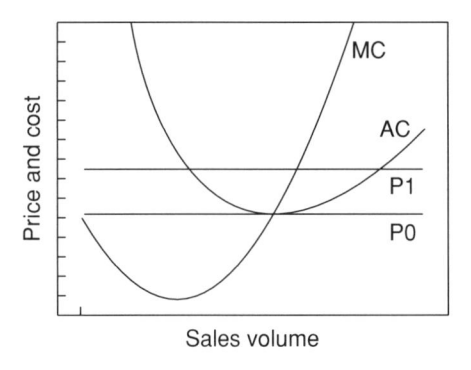

Figure 8a Perfect competition

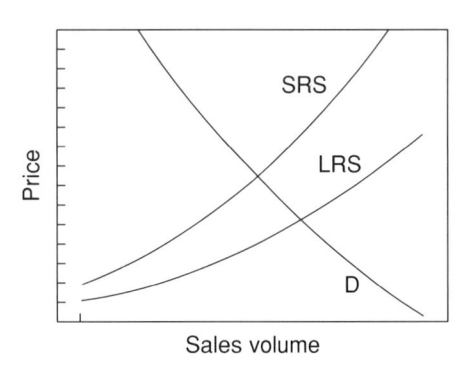

Figure 8b Perfect competition

economic welfare, provided that (as Marshall, in particular, recognized) allowance were made for compensation for external benefits and costs. However, perfect competition is rare and in the view of many critics of neo-classical economics is not desirable. Hayek has described perfect competition as 'the perfect absence of competition' (1945: 519). Competition requires a prize for the winner – some degree of market power or monopoly. If the prospect of this prize is taken away, why should firms compete?

Because perfect competition can be viewed as a welfare optimum, with price everywhere equal to marginal cost and with constant downward pressure on costs, it came to be regarded for many years as a zero point of monopoly power. In the view of some observers, this was erroneous. Glais and Laurent (1983) blame adherence to the partial equilibrium analysis of neo-classical economics for the preoccupation of European Community and French competition authorities with definition of relevant markets and computation of market share. The switch of emphasis in US antitrust policy towards market contestability follows a similar critique of the market share approach by Baumol (1982).

One of the main criticisms of partial-equilibrium analysis has long been proposed by adherents of the Austrian School. The neo-classical models moved instantaneously between equilibria; although time was taken into consideration, the *ceteris paribus* assumption was retained – nothing was allowed to interfere with movement to the new equilibrium and no attempt was made to analyse the inter-equilibria situation. This comparatively static approach can easily be criticized. It is disequilibrium that induces changes and these may prevent any restoration of equilibrium. Schumpeter's model of destructive capitalism, focusing on the stimulating effects of transitory monopoly power, exemplifies this criticism.

7 Criticisms of neo-classical economics

Neo-classical economics is based essentially on the application of differential calculus to common-sense generalities about the economic world: consumers maximize utility and producers maximize efficiency (under perfect competition) and profits. Objections to the theory take many forms.

1. *Bogus precision.* The claim is that neo-classical economics is spuriously precise in putting into mathematical form (algebra or geometry) notions that in reality can only be vague. This is true, but vague notions are difficult to treat logically. Provided that human beings are rational and consistent, the mathematical formulation of these notions may clarify their behavioural implications.
2. *The basic assumptions are wrong.* The seriousness of this criticism depends upon which assumptions are put into place instead of those of the neo-classical economists. For example, profit maximization may not be regarded as the sole goal of

the firm, particularly with the separation of ownership from management. If one composite goal is substituted for profit maximization, for example sales revenue maximization (Baumol 1967), managerial utility maximization (Williamson) or maximization of growth (Marris), then the calculus of the neo-classical model can be adapted to this alternative (see MANAGERIAL THEORIES OF THE FIRM; WILLIAMSON, O.E.). When maximization is replaced by satisfaction of multiple demands, as in the behavioural theories of Cyert and March, the integrated models of neo-classical economics no longer function.

Neo-classical economics emphasizes individuals – consumers and entrepreneurs. In the skeletal form in which it is usually presented, there is no discussion of the roles of institutions or governments. One of the unfortunate consequences of this is that perfect competition, the 'diffusion of economic power' is seen by some political economists as a goal in itself (see Jacquemin and de Jong 1977), even at the cost of inefficiency.

3 *It offers little macroeconomic analysis.* Like the classical economists, neo-classicists tended to rely on Say's Law, that supply creates its own demand, and supporters of the neo-classical school today emphasize growth of supply as the main driver of economic growth. Supply-side economics is entirely consistent with neo-classical theory in this respect. If there is unemployment, this is due mainly to obstacles to the downward flexibility of real wage rates – welfare benefits, employment protection and minimum wage legislation, trade unions exerting monopoly power, and tax systems that impose a poverty trap on low-income earners.

Keynes (see KEYNES, J.M.) cast considerable doubt on the notion that unemployment was due only to institutional impediments to the working of the market. He suggested the possibility of general unemployment resulting from a deficiency of aggregate demand when the overall economy was in equilibrium. This general unemployment would be eliminated in the long run by a fall in real wages, but it would only be eliminated completely if the wage-elasticity of demand for labour were at least unity in absolute terms. Formally, one can argue that, unless the elasticity of demand is exactly equal to minus 1, it is not possible to move along the demand curve without affecting aggregate demand and therefore shifting the curve. The methodology of microeconomics cannot be directly transferred to macroeconomics without consideration of the circular flow of income: the total of wages and gross profits in the economy is gross domestic product, which in a closed economy is the source of demand.

The neo-classical economists themselves accepted and discussed most of the criticisms lodged against them, but the founders of the school presented their arguments in the kind of closely-argued but complex prose that is now rare in English. It is easier to paraphrase their arguments into graphs, algebra and short statements. In the process, much of their less easily summarized material is ignored.

For example, Marshall (1890: 591) introduced the possibility that unemployment might occur through a deficiency of aggregate demand. Criticizing Say's Law, that supply creates its own demand, he pointed out that 'though men have the power to purchase they may not choose to use it.' He attributed general unemployment to lack of confidence to invest – not totally removed from the arguments in Keynes' *General Theory*, which appeared forty-six years later.

Neo-classical economics may be criticized for the spuriously precise mathematical logic that is used to deduce conclusions from hypotheses, and for assumptions based on preconceptions rather than scientific observation. The advantage of this approach is the rigour that it imposes on the logic. Newer schools of thought may introduce more realistic assumptions, but thanks largely to neo-classical economics, the logic whereby conclusions can be drawn from these assumptions must be internally sound. Neo-classical economists, more than any other group, have made it possible to separate positive from normative principles in economics; they have done much to make economics a science.

FRANCIS FISHWICK
CRANFIELD SCHOOL OF MANAGEMENT

Further reading

(References cited in the text marked *)

* Baumol, W.J. (1967) *Business Behaviour, Value and Growth*, New York: Harcourt Brace Jovanovich. (Contains the first formal exposition of the theory of sales revenue maximization.)
* Baumol, W.J. (1982) 'Contestable markets: an uprising in the theory of industry structure', *American Economic Review* 72. (Sets out for the first time the key arguments of contestable market theory.)
* Blaug, M. (1985) *Economic Theory in Retrospect*, 4th edn, Cambridge: Cambridge University Press. (Authoritative text covering history of mainstream economic thought; includes clear expositions of the work of all major neo-classical economists.)
* Boland, L.A. (1985) 'Neo-classical economics', in A. Kuper and J. Kuper (eds), *The Social Science Encyclopedia*, London: Routledge & Kegan Paul. (Short summary clearly defining key features of the neo-classical approach.)
* Cournot, A.A. (1863) *Principes de la théorie des richesses*, Paris: Hachette. (The succinct expositions given by Blaug, and by Ekelund and Hebert are far more accessible than the original.)
* Edgeworth, F.Y. (1881) *Mathematical Psychics*, New York: Kelley, 1953. (The succinct expositions given by Blaug, and by Ekelund and Hebert are far more accessible than the original.)
* Ekelund, R.B. and Hebert, R.F. (1983) *A History of Economic Theory and Method*, 2nd edn, New York: McGraw-Hill. (Similar work to Blaug but with more mathematics; particularly useful algebraic summary of Walras' contribution to economics.)
* Glais, M. and Laurent, P. (1983) *Traité d'Économie et de Droit de la Concurrence*, Paris: PUF (Presses Universitaires de France). (French text combining relevant economic theory with analysis of EU and French competition laws; clear exposition of limitations of neo-classical economics.)
* Hayek, F.A. (1945) 'The use of knowledge in society', *American Economic Review* 35. (Contains a critique of the model of perfect competition.)
* Hicks, J.R. (1956) *A Revision of Demand Theory*, Oxford: Blackwell. (A succinct exposition of this work is given by Blaug, and by Ekelund and Hebert.)
* Jacquemin, A.P. and de Jong, H.W. (1977) *European Industrial Organisation*, London: Macmillan. (Chapter 7, on competition policy, describes the application of neo-classical analysis to this important element of business–government relations.)
* Jevons, W.S. (1871) *Theory of Political Economy*, R.D.C. Black (ed.), New York: Kelley, 1970. (A paperback edition with commentary; Blaug, and Ekelund and Hebert offer useful accounts.)
* Keynes, J.M. (1936) *General Theory of Employment, Interest and Money*, London: Macmillan, 1970. (Discusses the origin of 'Say's Law'.)
* Marshall, A. (1890) *Principles of Economics*, 8th edn, London: Macmillan, 1920. (Often regarded as the Bible of neo-classical economics. Modern readers may find the verbal style ponderous and, if familiar with elementary calculus, will prefer the mathematical appendix. Marshall's work is clearly summarized by Blaug, and by Ekelund and Hebert.)
* Menger, C. (1871) *Principles of Economics*, trans. J. Dingwall and B.F. Hoselitz, Glencoe, IL: The Free Press, 1950. (The succinct expositions given by Blaug, and by Ekelund and Hebert are far more accessible than the original.)
* Robinson, J. (1969) *The Economics of Imperfect Competition*, London: Macmillan. (Useful accounts are given by Blaug, and by Ekelund and Hebert.)
* Samuelson, P.A. (1965) *Foundations of Economic Analysis*, New York: Atheneum. (Useful accounts are given by Blaug, and by Ekelund and Hebert.)
* Scherer, F.M. and Ross, D. (1990) *Industrial Market Structure and Economic Performance*, 3rd edn, Boston: Houghton Mifflin. (Comprehensive modern textbook of neo-classical economics, combining clear exposition of both theory and practical applications.)
* Schumpeter, J.A. (1947) *Capitalism, Socialism and Democracy*, London: Allen & Unwin. (Among the best known of Schumpeter's works, this includes his discussion of the ephemeral nature of monopoly.)
* Walras, L. (1874) *Elements of Pure Economics*, trans W. Jaffé, Homewood, IL: Irwin, 1954. (Modern English translation; Blaug, and Ekelund and Hebert offer more accessible accounts.)

See also: INSTITUTIONAL ECONOMICS; KEYNES, J.M.; MANAGERIAL THEORIES OF THE FIRM; MARSHALL, A.; SAMUELSON, P.A.; SMITH, A.; TRANSACTION COST ECONOMICS

Managerial theories of the firm

1 Background
2 The theories
3 Testing the theories
4 Results of the tests
5 A new owner-managed capitalism?
6 Conclusion

Overview

Managerial theories of the firm are economic theories of how the behaviour of modern management affects the working of the economic system, rather than the other way round. They have, however, been the subject of considerable research in business and management literature. This entry describes the theories on their own terms with particular reference to business research.

1 Background

The twentieth century has seen the emergence of business organizations – in the form of quoted public companies – that were on the one hand very large and on the other marked by a considerable degree of separation of ownership from management (see CORPORATE CONTROL). Shareholdings were often widely dispersed, reducing the potency of voting rights in most circumstances other than those of a takeover bid. Boards of directors came to be composed predominantly of full-time senior executives who nominated new members and initiated decisions concerning high management appointments and remuneration. High management became effectively responsible not only for operating the organization but also for strategic decisions concerning investment, finance, internal growth and diversification, profit retentions and acquisitions. Business corporations displayed a capacity for persistent, if irregular, long-term growth in size, and in consequence, in a typical advanced industrialized country, the share of the largest 100 corporations in total industrial value-added, which totalled less than 10 per cent in 1900, will, by the year 2000, range from 30–50 per cent. The value added by the largest US corporations exceeded the GNP (gross national product) of some small countries.

These concentrating phenomena are not inconsistent with co-existence of the 'other half' of the modern economy, where traditional capitalist modes (markets containing large numbers of small owner-managed businesses) effectively persist. In addition, towards the end of the century, technological developments, such as personal computers, which increased the comparative efficiency of small administrative units, and new institutional developments, such as corporate divestitures and management buyouts, may be reducing or reversing the previous concentrating tendencies.

The 'powers' of the managerial 'new class' are of course by no means unconstrained. On the one hand they are constrained by the stock market through the threat of 'involuntary' (meaning undesired by management, not shareholders) takeover, and by the debt market through threat of capital starvation; on the other hand they are constrained by the ever present force of competition in product markets. The world of 'managerial' capitalism is a jungle of competition among giants where no law prevents the invasion of one giant's territory by another. The problem for the science of economics was and is that this twentieth century industrial system, whatever its advantages and disadvantages to society, is extremely different from the model of the competitive economy that is not only universal in elementary economics textbooks but also underlies the prevalent research paradigm. In that paradigm, product markets are assumed to be supplied by large numbers of small, single-product, ownermanaged, price-taking firms with limited capacities for growth (see NEOCLASSICAL ECONOMICS).

2 The theories

Economists began responding to the problem in the mid-1950s, with first results being published in the following decade (strictly, from 1958 to 1972). The responses can be placed in three groups which may be called discretionary, growth-orientated and bureaucratic theories respectively. The original authors in the discretionary group were William Baumol and Oliver Williamson (Baumol 1959; Williamson 1964, 1970); in the growth-orientated group, Edith Penrose, Robin Marris and Dennis Mueller (Penrose 1958; Marris 1964; Mueller 1969, 1972) and finally, in the bureaucratic group, Joseph Monsen and Anthony Downs (Monsen and Downs 1965) (see WILLIAMSON, O.E.). Taken together the three groups have provoked a literature that is fifty to a hundred times larger than the further reading listed below.

The discretionary theories

These theories are based on the model of a firm with given assets, high management and an external market environment which is, in economist's language, monopolistic, oligopolistic or imperfectly competitive. The management does not have a significant stake in the ownership, and is also free of both operational and strategic supervision by owners. There exist well-defined demand curves for the firm's products. They can be shifted by means of marketing expenditure which may be internally financed and organized, externally contracted or both. Internally organized marketing expenditure is broadly defined to include any activity which might be considered to improve sales at a given price, including such activities as expanding the number of managerial subordinates with general functions. Simplifying somewhat, management is effectively responsible for three decisions, namely, price, marketing expenditure and their own remuneration. The question is, on what basis will these decisions be taken?

A convenient way to consider the answer is to combine marketing and management remuneration into a portmanteau item called 'expense'; then assume that as expense, thus defined, is increased, sales, at given prices, also increase but with diminishing effect. Define current profit as gross sales revenue less expense and all other current operating costs. The decision problem then resolves into choice of only two variables, price and expense level.

The problem is assumed to have a traditional maximum-profit solution. The discretionary theory assumes that the owners have neither sufficient power nor knowledge to impose on management the profit-maximizing policy; they do however have power in crisis, more specifically if reported profits become low. Managers know this, and base their decisions, whatever they may be, on a minimum reported profit constraint. (The level of this constraint is exogenous to the model, flowing from the general financial environment; consequently it appears that the discretionary models effectively relate to individual firms of this type operating in a sea of traditional firms. In an environment where the dominant type of firm was the discretionary type, it is not clear from where the minimum level of profit would come.)

Managers are endowed with an objective function which differs, in the direction of their own interests, from the profit-maximizing objective function. In Baumol's version (1959), subject to the constraint, the objective is gross sales value. One may envisage a graph with sales on the horizontal axis and profits on the vertical: profits are plotted against sales. Starting from the origin, as sales expand so do profits, but at a diminishing rate, so that in due course the profit–sales curve reaches a maximum and declines. The maximum indicates the profit-maximizing level of sales; the contrasting 'managerial' solution is found by drawing a horizontal line at the level of the minimum-profit constraint and finding the intersection with the expense–profit curve. Provided minimum profit is below maximum profit, the solution must involve 'excessive' sales relative to the profit-maximizing optimum. If for some exogenous reason the minimum profit level is increased (so the horizontal line shifts upward) the intersection moves to the left and the managerially optimal level of sales is reduced.

The excess of maximum profit level over minimum profit level is a quantitative measure of managerial discretion. The greater it is, the greater the predicted managerially selected sales level. When managerial discretion is zero (minimum profit equals maximum), managers must, according to prediction, choose the sales level that is optimal for owners.

In the Williamson version (1964) managers' motives and satisfactions were directly derived from expense as such; as well as managers' own emoluments, expense also contained benefits to high managers in hierarchical organizations from increasing the number of their own subordinates and also their perquisites of office. Thus managers displayed 'expense-preference'. (Williamson in fact kept emoluments and expense separate; their combination in this exposition is for simplification.) The resulting model is essentially similar to, but more complex than the Baumol model. At heart there is a similar diagram, but the horizontal axis now represents expense, with a resulting profits–expense curve yielding similar predictions (see WILLIAMSON, O.E.).

Williamson, however, brilliantly applied the analysis to the problem of testing the model. A typical commercial crisis for an individual firm would be represented in a sharp fall in demand, resulting, in effect, in a vertical decline in the profits–expense curve. It is possible to show that the predicted response involves a disproportionate reduction of expense as compared to other operating outlays. By careful case studies Williamson was able to confirm that firms in crisis did just this. By contrast the profit-maximizing model tends to predict that in crisis expense will be reduced more or less proportionately with other outlays. Consequently, the case studies confirmed the actual existence and practice of managerial expense-preference in the real-life economy.

In important later studies, which led in turn to his subsequent work in so-called transaction cost economics, Williamson (1970) argued that expense-preference was particularly likely in 'U-form' firms organized in functional divisions. The divisional outputs not being commensurable, the comparative performance of division chiefs could not be easily evaluated, making them prone to empire building. In the middle of this century, however, the U-form was being replaced by the 'M-form', where divisions were product-orientated, making for easier evaluation and freeing head office for strategic functions. The M-form is more 'efficient' than the U-form because the latter, in propagating expense in excess of profit-maximizing level, inflates the cost to owners of producing a given output. (Because marketing expenditure affects consumer tastes, and because expense-preference affects corporate employment and payroll, the total effect on society is less clear. Intuitively it seems likely that 'excess' resources absorbed by expense-preference would be better employed elsewhere, but no proof of this proposition has been published.)

The growth-orientated theories

The growth-orientated theories formally start from the same point as the discretionary theories – that management has power over a distinct objective function – but differ in being more complex, dynamic rather than static and more grandiose. By the last adjective is meant that the growth-orientated theorists (especially Marris and Mueller) see their model as pervasive among mature large corporations, setting the norms for high management behaviour in respect of internal growth, acquisition and own-remuneration decisions among the general population of such corporations. Marris first described the resulting economic system as one of 'managerial capitalism' (Marris 1964), a term which was subsequently adopted by other writers. The growth-orientated theories can therefore be said to be the most distinctively 'managerialist' of the managerial theories.

In the growth-orientated theories, the various possible candidates for inclusion in a managerial objective function are collapsed into the single motive of desire for sustainable long-run growth in the size (measured by assets, employment or real output) of the whole organization. This motive can be pursued by means of policies which, at a cost, open diverse new opportunities for sustainable expansion. As in the discretionary theories, pursuit of managerial desires is not unbridled but is subject to a degree of constraint arising from the existence of external owners, explicitly shareholders. Managers have the power to pursue a long-term growth rate faster than the one which would be optimal for shareholders, but the further they go, the more they are in danger of depressing the market value of the firm to the point where there is a serious risk of involuntary takeover, the latter being feared because it means loss of office.

Marris's version contains various distinctive features that combine together into a closed model quantitatively determining the planned long-run growth rate of the firm. Some of the elements come from outside Marris's own work (for example, Penrose 1958) and, in turn, some incomplete aspects of the model formed the basis of major further developments (for example, Mueller 1969, 1972). The starting point is in fact the highly original work of Edith Penrose. In that book the author characterizes the firm as an administrative organization capable of indefinite expansion. The *rate* of expansion is constrained by a limit on the rate at which new members of the management team can be effectively absorbed; new members require familiarization by the experience of working with old members; consequently the current absolute absorptive capacity for new management depends on the current absolute size of the existing team – a proposition which inevitably implies a constraint on the proportionate effective growth rate of the team through time. Marris generalized this 'Penrose theorem' to argue (without great influence) that the economics profession should turn away from attempting to base models on the concept of an optimum absolute size of the firm, but rather on the corresponding (proportionate) rate of change of size. The concept of 'diminishing returns to scale' should be replaced by a concept of diminishing returns to the growth rate, meaning that as the growth rate was accelerated past a certain point, for various reasons such as the Penrose theorem, *current* costs would tend to increase.

The full Marris model may be summarized as follows. First, sustainable long-run growth requires market growth; this can be achieved, at a cost, by search and research and development (R&D). In turn, new markets must be supported by new productive capacity. The combined costs of the Penrose effect, R&D and new capacity may be called the costs of growth. They require cash flow. Cash flow may be obtained from retained profits, new share issues and new debt. The amount of the last, in any given period, is constrained on the one hand by the unwillingness of lenders to offer unrestricted sums relative to the firm's existing scale, and on the other by managers' fears of the risks, to them, of excessive leverage. The financial effect of new issues is similar to that of retentions and for this reason (and also because it is in practice a small source of finance) may for simplicity be ignored. Hence for ease the problem may be posed as if the only source of finance for accelerating growth were retentions.

Suppose that the operating profit rate on existing assets from existing markets is given. By retaining cash (and thus lowering current dividends) in expectation of future growth of markets, profits and hence *future* dividends, management effectively throws the path of future dividends into the future; the accelerated path substitutes the prospect of higher future for lower current rewards for stockholders. Allowing for equivalence, before tax, of dividends and capital gains, such a change may, over a range, be welcomed by shareholders and tend to raise the market value of the firm on the stock market. Beyond a point, however, the effect must go the other way, as shareholders are increasingly 'stuffed' with more jam tomorrow, relatively to jam today, than they would desire.

It follows that the management can pursue a growth rate (implying specific costs of growth and profit retention ratio) that would maximize the firms's 'valuation ratio' (the name given by Marris to the ratio of market value to underlying assets, subsequently renamed q by economics Nobel laureate James Tobin). Alternatively the management may pursue a faster growth rate at the price of reducing the valuation ratio to below its maximum; this may be called an expression of 'growth-preference', paralleling Williamson's 'expense-preference'.

Marris then added two propositions: (1) management desires both growth and security from takeover; and (2) the risk of takeover will vary inversely with the valuation ratio. (A robust empirical relationship between low valuation ratio and statistically observed probability of takeover has in fact been found – see, for example, Bartley and Boardman 1986.) If managers have growth-preference, the model closes, with a unique management desired growth rate. Thus the factors which encourage 'managerial' behaviour encourage faster growth of firms, more expenditure on R&D and marketing and hence possibly faster growth for the economy. In the pursuit of the goal of growth managers have full incentive to make the firm's current operations as efficient as possible (operational inefficiency detracts from cash flow) and managerial behaviour is 'inefficient' only if it can be shown that the faster growth (as compared with that which would otherwise be the case) is in some way excessive from the point of view of society.

Mueller contributed major additions to these theories in two distinct ways. The first was a managerial theory of conglomerate merger seen from the point of view of the *acquiring* firm (Mueller 1969) and the second was a life cycle interpretation of firm growth (Mueller 1972). If managers desired growth but were limited by internal constraints, they could to some extent free themselves (again, not without constraint) by successive acquisitions of other going concerns. Thus, in the jungle, any firm may be a predator and any firm a victim. The typical potential predator to fear, from the point of view of the managerial firm, is another managerial firm. However, on account of the managerial firm's concern with their own security from takeover, acquirers would be unlikely to push their activity so far as to dilute the market value of their own shares sufficiently to create reverse risk of takeover of themselves. Hence the hypothesis implicitly predicts that over the broad range of mergers and takeovers, the net gains to acquiring firms' shareholders will be either slightly negative or not significantly different from zero.

Mueller's life cycle was a major qualification of Marris's linear characterization of the growth path of a firm. A firm is 'young' when it succeeds in finding or creating an unusually profitable group of new markets. The costs of growth at this time are low and, in consequence, the value-maximizing growth rate is comparatively high. Management can enjoy fast growth while also benefiting shareholders; their retained money is being better spent than they could invest it elsewhere. Eventually the new markets saturate and unless others similarly profitable are found, the firm becomes mature. The shareholders might well benefit if it were wound up, or at least, if significant profit retentions and attempted growth ceased. But now a Marris-like situation occurs. The management does not wish to cease growing and retains an increasing proportion of more modest profits to finance heavier growth costs. Growth slows, but does not cease, and remains faster than it would have been in the absence of effective managerial growth-preference. Mueller was able to re-interpret existing stock market studies to show they were convincingly consistent with this story.

The bureaucratic theories

Monsen and Downs (1965) started from the same general background, but developed a qualitatively different approach which especially contrasted with that of Marris. The main differences concerned were: (1) the definition of the managerial firm; (2) the authors' emphasis on the significance of internal organization; and (3) the nature of managerial motivation concerning growth.

Monsen and Downs defined a managerial firm as a firm with diffused shareholdings; a firm with concentrated shareholdings, whether or not actually owner-managed, was defined as 'owner-controlled'. Marris by contrast implicitly defined any firm not managed full-time by its controlling owners as managerial.

Regarding the significance of the internal organization, Monsen and Downs, antedating Williamson's later work on the same lines (Williamson 1970), pointed out that: (1) managerial firms were necessarily large and therefore necessarily organized in pyramidal hierarchies where the length of the chain of command (the height of the pyramid) increases with the size of the base – that is, with the number of people at the lowest level, a rough measure of the operating scale of the organization; and (2) because the salary and promotion prospects of subordinates depends on pleasing their superiors, information-transfer through the chain of command will be cumulatively biased. The two effects together mean that large firms, especially large non-concentrated ownership firms, are inherently inefficient; their high managers lose control of them. (Later Marris argued that because mathematically the height of the pyramid varies only as the log of the width of the base, the inefficiency effect of scale is weak and diminishing, and easily offset, he argued, by administrative scale economies and monitoring systems – an argument which is not generally accepted in the economics profession, especially in the USA.)

Finally, Monsen and Downs argued that managers of managerial firms would be more risk-averse than those of owner-controlled firms, because they expected to be blamed for failures but inadequately rewarded by the profits of success, which largely accrue to the shareholders. More specifically, these managers would tend to try to offer shareholders steady capital gains and earnings increases, in contrast to possibly more fluctuating but on average more lucrative possibilities. They would also tend to favour less risky types of R&D – an argument which has been interpreted for research purposes as a general aversion to R&D.

3 Testing the theories

It is desirable to distinguish between evidence which tests the broad hypothesis that managerial motivation in the modern corporation exists and is widely exercised, from results which attempt to discriminate between significantly different predictions of the three sub-groups of theories. Particularly significant are stark qualitative differences between the original Marris version of the growthorientated theory (Marris 1964) and the other two groups, differences which are clearest when Marris (1964) is compared with Monsen and Downs (1965), the former predicting that managerial firms will favour fast growth and comparatively high R&D, the latter virtually predicting precisely the opposite. The contrast is less clear-cut when the convincing Mueller life cycle argument (Mueller 1972) is accepted, because the evolution of managerial control in the sense of dispersed shareholdings is co-variant with the managerial phase of the cycle.

Testing may also be divided into direct and indirect. Direct testing looks for evidence of relations between ownership structure and relevant aspects of organizational behaviour, such as productivity, diversification, growth and R&D. Indirect testing looks for indirect evidence, such as merger and executive compensation behaviour, offering logical strong support for this or that main hypothesis. In the case of executive compensation, all the theories, discretionary, growth-orientated and bureaucratic, imply that in managerial firms compensation will be more closely related to firm size than executive performance. Growth-orientated theories also carry the implication that executive compensation will reward rate of change of size.

Hunt (1986) comprehensively surveys literature appropriate to direct testing of the bureaucratic theories and tabulates the relevant conclusions of some twenty previous quantitative studies. Hill and Snell (1989) use econometric path analysis to test a final model which, subject to the life cycle qualification (neither firm 'age' nor size being controlled for), appears to directly confront the bureaucratic models with Marris. Cubbin and Leach (1986) directly test Marris with a simultaneous equations econometric model specifically based on the detailed elements of the original (1964) model. (This work provides the only example, throughout the literature, of direct testing of a fully specified original model rather than a reduced-form model.) Mueller and Reardon (1993) directly test the growth-orientated theory prediction of comparatively low returns to retained profits.

Bartley and Boardman (1986) and Scherer (1988) indirectly test and/or survey tests of the growth-orientated theories (in effect in confrontation with the bureaucratic theories) by observations and surveys on merger/takeover data. Cubbin and Hall (1983) and Gomez-Mejia *et al.* (1987) do similarly with executive compensation.

4 Results of the tests

Hunt (1986) found that about half the studies he surveyed confirmed the proposition that overall economic performance of managerially controlled firms was inferior to that of shareholder-controlled ('control' being measured by share distribution). He also found some support for the idea that managerially controlled firms offer a more risk-averse time path of shareholder returns. Hill and Snell (1989) found that managerially controlled firms did more diversification, which supports Marris, but undertook less R&D, which does quite the opposite; they were also notably less productive as measured by value added per head. Unlike Hill and Snell, Cubbin and Leach (1986) control for firm age, and at the end of an analysis which cannot be fully described in a short space, conclude, 'These results are consistent with all managements being wealth maximizers or growth maximizers or a random combination of the two'. On the other side of the argument, Mueller and Reardon (1993) found that the returns to retained profits are indeed pervasively low, a result that in logic can only imply that retained profits are used to support faster growth rates than would be observed if firms were managed entirely in the interests of external shareholders.

With indirect testing, the results surveyed by Scherer (1988) give overwhelming support to the Mueller (1969) conglomerate merger hypothesis and thus support the growth-orientated theories generally. As it was to be ten years before the beginning of the spectacular takeover boom that provided the greatest confirmation, this is a remarkable example of successful theoretical prediction in the literal sense of the word. In the case of executive compensation, in what is again the most sophisticated theoretical-empirical analysis to be found in the relevant literature, Cubbin and Hall point to numerous logical traps in distinguishing traditional – that is, neo-classical – supporting results from results which support the managerial theories as a whole or discriminate between the three groups of them. At the end of a complex discussion they conclude that both the discretionary theories and the growth-orientated theories are well-supported, while the neo-classical alternative is not. In the data they studied (eighty UK quoted public companies, 1969–75), they also found that high management was especially strongly rewarded for achieving growth by acquisitions, thus further reinforcing support for the Mueller (1969) hypothesis. Gomez-Mejia *et al.* (1987) (who unfortunately missed seeing the Cubbin and Hall paper) reach comparable conclusions in support of the broad managerial hypothesis.

5 A new owner-managed capitalism?

In the twentieth century, the 'managerial' form of capitalism was a historically unique engine of economic growth. The case of Japan was particularly telling. Odagiri's thesis (1992) may be interpreted as suggesting that the Golden Age of very rapid industrial expansion, which lasted from the end of the Second World War to the late 1980s, was an example par excellence of 'successful' managerialism. He particularly stressed that institutional barriers to involuntary takeovers not only protected management but encouraged them to strive for internal growth, thus also fostering the growth of the economy at large. Odagiri was not the first to argue that managers of large Japanese industrial firms were typically motivated towards the welfare of the organisation as a collective entity. Aoki (1984a; 1984b) had already suggested a model in which the oligopolistic firms extracted profits from their customers which could be divided between owners and employees.

How will the twenty-first century compare? The question divides as between the old First World on the one hand, and the new emerging or transitional economies – such as those of Russia, China and India on the other. Towards the turn of the century old First World and especially US business developments displayed a number of distinctive characteristics mostly related in one way or another to the culmination of the IT revolution. While the cost of entry into new competition has been reduced the controllability of large organizations has been increased. Both small and large firms have flourished, and small firms have become large at spectacular rates. Payment of professional employees by means of stock options has increased as have also bond financing, management buy-outs, shareholder monitoring and takeover activity.

Does all this spell the end of First World managerialism? The case for the answer 'yes' is obviously strong. On the other hand the factors that led to the original managerial revolution are always with us. Are we really moving into a world where large organizations can be permanently owner-managed?

The answer may lie more in the sphere of political rather than traditional business studies. In the Anglo-Saxon countries (including the old British Dominions), but not in Continental Western Europe or Japan, the changing business climate has been accompanied by a substantial increase in income inequality both before and after tax. This has been ascribed in varying to degree to the technical effects of the IT revolution (by increasing the productivity and earning power of 'top' people whose effectiveness influences the productivity of many others; see e.g. Marris 1996) – combined with social acceptance of tighter links between personal productivity and reward (Atkinson 1999); to the shift of final demand away from the old oligopolistic and unionized industrial sector; and to the effects of changes in patterns of international trade, whereby the developed countries increasingly obtain their requirements of products containing comparatively low unskilled inputs from the developing countries (Wood 1994). Yet, although many of the same forces also occurred in Japan and continental Western Europe (a group which has more than half of the population of the whole First World), the change in distribution did not. As a result, in 2000, in Japan and Western Europe taken as a whole, the living standards of households in the bottom fifth of the income distribution were still absolutely higher to a significant extent, than in Anglo-Saxon countries taken as whole. By contrast, at the other end of the distribution, the situation was sharply reversed, not the least because in the ultimate, as compared with the penultimate decade of the century the two groups' relative performance as regards *average* GDP per head had also been reversed. Some observers see the Anglo-Saxon income-distribution changes as part and parcel of the 'new' capitalism, to be inevitably followed by the other countries; others see them as politically non-sustainable (Dore 2000). There is thus a possible connection between managerialism and income distribution which has never previously been discussed.

In Russia, as brilliantly described by Freeland (2000), a fervent attempt was made to convert an extreme type of command economy, almost overnight, into a full-blown owner-managed peoples' capitalism. The people were given vouchers which could be exchanged for shares in new firms created by auctioning previously state-owned concerns. It can be argued, however, that in the absence of any large amounts of legitimately privately owned capital, the subsequent debacle in which a large proportion of the nation's real assets was bought up at knock down prices by a tiny group of economic oligarchs, was probably inevitable. The current government is apparently attempting to rescue the situation (two 'oligarchs', now residing abroad have been arrested for extradition on various charges of fraud), it is difficult if not impossible to speculate on the typical form of business organization that might eventually emerge if and when the country recovers.

China and India between them hold nearly a half of the population of the Third World and hence many of the keys to the future of the planet's business. Although their economic histories in the second half of the twentieth century were very different, it is possible that might be less the case in the first half of the twenty-first. In the case of China, except in the comparatively short period of 'the great leap backward' in the 1960s the country under Communism made good economic progress. Almost from the death of Chairman Mao in 1976, economic policy began to creep towards pragmatism, marketization and various degrees of partial (and by no means transparent or democratic) privatization. A significant sector of the economy was turned over to large hybrid organizations called 'town and village enterprises' (Nolan 1998). In the south and eastern part of the country very fast economic growth, apparently without distributional effects, combined with extraordinarily rapid development of infrastructure, virtually to the end of the century. In 2000, although a large state owned heavily 'managerial' industrial sector remained both unprivatized and inefficient, the story was patently better than the Russian one. (Nolan 1995). Although a new middle class is displaying strong and energetic owner-capitalist instincts, it is possible that if, as many predict, by the year 2050 the Chinese economy will be one of the world's largest, its form of capitalism will not be traditional and could well be managerialist.

India presents a major enigma. For the first third of a century after national independence the economy was gravely held back by a form of failed democratic socialism, characterized by restrictive cultural traditionalism, massive protectionism and pervasive bureaucratic obstruction to all forms of enterprise: in the result both infrastructure and mass primary education were gravely neglected. Since the late 1980s, however, two factors have made for major change. The first is the emergence at the centres of power of an effective technocratic group of civil servants determined on economic liberalization. The second is an inherent intelligence among the educated elite which is particularly suited to the IT economy: Indian nationals who went to work in Silicon Valley are now beginning to return home to set up their own enterprises. GDP has strongly accelerated and population growth at last begun to decelerate. It is possible that an Indian economic miracle could be one of the surprises of the next half century. If so, it is also possible that India could bypass the managerial phase of organizational development, and move directly into the 'new' global capitalism, in such form as that may, eventually, prove to take.

6 Conclusion

The managerial theories, in opposition to positive neo-classical theories implying that management-managed firms not only ought to be, but effectively are, strategically directed largely in the sole interests of their shareholders, are theoretically convincing and very strongly empirically supported: in this respect they dominate empirical agency theory insofar as the latter tends to claim that the effects of separation of ownership from management are in practice negligible. In practice, managerial behaviour appears as a mixture of the behaviours associated with all three theoretical sub-groups, discretionary, growth-orientated and bureaucratic. A broad interpretation of the Mueller (1972) hypothesis – that the blend varies through the life cycle – is also well-supported.

Managerial firms do apparently tend to have both expense-preference and bureaucratic inefficiency. When these handicaps are present they imply loss of potential to grow. With given capacity to grow, however, managerial firms exercise growth-preference by attempting to, and to a degree succeeding in growing faster than the rate that would, in the given circumstances (including life cycle phase), be in the interests of their shareholders.

R.L. MARRIS
UNIVERSITY OF LONDON

Further reading

(References cited in the text marked *)

* Aoki, M. (1984a) *The Co-operative Game-Theory of the Firm*, Oxford: Oxford University Press. (A mathematical model where the division of the firm's total value added as between owners and employees is mediated by the management according to the principles of cooperative non-zero-sum game theory.)
* Aoki, M. (1984b) 'Aspects of the Japanese firm', in M. Aoki (ed.) *The Economic Analysis of the Japanese Firm*, Amsterdam, North Holland.
* Atkinson, A. (1999) Is Rising Inequality Inevitable? A Critique of the Transatlantic Consensus, *WIDER Annual Lectures 3*, Helsinki: UN University World Institute for Development Economics Research. (A brilliant critique of contemporary explanations of rising inequality supported by an original theory suggesting a sea change in social acceptance of links between personal productivities and rewards.)
* Bartley, J. and Boardman, C. (1986) 'Replacement-cost-adjusted valuation ratio as a discriminator among take over target and nontarget firms', *Journal of Economics and Business* 38: 41–55. (The definitive study of the hypothesis that the primary determinant of a firm's liability to take over is the ratio of stock market value to underlying assets.)
* Baumol, W. (1959) *Business Behavior, Value and Growth*, New York: Macmillan. (The first theoretical economic model of a managerial strategy which maximizes gross sales subject to earning adequate profit.)
* Cubbin, J. and Hall, G. (1983) 'Directors remuneration in the theory of the firm – specification and testing of the null hypothesis', *European*

Economic Review 20 (1–3): 333–48. (Outstanding theoretical and empirical analysis of executive compensation and managerial versus neo-classical theories of the firm; needs intermediate economics; uses calculus.)

* Cubbin, J. and Leach, D. (1986) 'Growth versus profit-maximization: a simultaneous-equations approach to testing the Marris model', *Managerial and Decision Economics* 7 (2): 123–31. (Impressive uses of advanced econometric technique to test the several elements of the theory.)

* Dore, R. (2000) *National Capitalisms in a Globalized World*, Oxford: Oxford University Press. (A lively thesis suggesting that the Japanese 'crisis' is part of a general 'Anglo-Saxonizing' of business and economic behaviour associated with rising inequality.)

* Freeland, C. (2000) *Sale of the Century*, New York: Little Brown. (A vivid and extremely well-informed account of the process whereby Russia, having set out with a plan of orderly and democratic privatization ended up with an economic oligarchy.)

* Gomez-Mejia, L., Tosi, H. and Hinkin, T. (1987) 'Managerial control, performance and executive compensation', *Academy of Management Journal* 30 (1) (March): 51–70. (The most comprehensive study in a large literature on the subject of executive compensation.)

* Hill, C. and Snell, S. (1989) 'Effects of ownership structure and control on corporate productivity', *Academy of Management Journal* 32 (1) (March): 25–46. (Definitive testing of managerial theories of the firm based on cross-sectional hierarchical regression analysis of over 100 out of 500 Fortune firms.)

* Hunt, H. (1986) 'The separation of ownership from control: theory, evidence and implications', *Journal of Accounting Literature* 5: 85–124. (Important survey of previous studies on the predictions of and results from managerial theories of the firm.)

* Marris, R. (1964) *The Economic Theory of 'Managerial' Capitalism*, London: Macmillan. (Core contribution to growth-orientated managerial theories; lively text peppered with equations.)

* Marris, R. (1996) *How to Save the Underclass*, London: Macmillan. (Surveys the various explanations of rising income inequality, with special reference to the least advantaged.)

Marris, R. (1998) *Managerial Capitalism in Retrospect*, London: Macmillan. (Contains an abridged version of the author's 1964 work, a survey of developments from 1964–94 and selected reprints of his essays and reviews.)

Marris, R. and Mueller, D. (1980) 'The corporation and competition', *Journal of Economic Literature* 18 (March): 32–63. (Essay-cum-survey on neo-classical and managerial theories of the firm and non-price competition in the twentieth century.)

* Monsen, R. and Downs, A. (1965) 'A theory of large managerial firms', *Journal of Political Economy* 73 (3) (June): 221–36. (Lucid, structured verbal argument, based on internal organization, that large corporations necessarily suffer bureaucratic inefficiency.)

* Mueller, D. (1969) 'A theory of conglomerate mergers', *Quarterly Journal of Economics* 83 (November): 643–60. (The first theory of merger and takeover from the point of view of acquiring firms.)

* Mueller, D. (1972) 'A life cycle theory of the firm', *Journal of Industrial Economics* 20 (3) (July): 199–219. (The original statement and first testing of the important life cycle hypothesis.)

* Mueller, D. and Reardon, E. (1993) *Rates of Return on Corporate Investment*, Washington, DC: Anti-Trust Division, Department of Justice. (Strong findings that internal returns are generally lower than returns that could have been earned if retained profits had been distributed.)

* Nolan, P. (1995) *China's Rise, Russia's Fall*, New York: St. Martin's Press. (Compares the different stories of economic reform and privatization in the two countries.)

* Nolan, P. (1998) *Indigenous Large Firms in the Chinese Economy*, London: London University School of Oriental Studies. (Describes large scale Chinese development of large business organizations whose structure is neither capitalist nor communist.)

* Odagiri, H. (1992) *Growth Through Competition and Competition Through Growth: Strategic Management and the Economy in Japan*, Oxford: Clarendon Press. (Explains the Japanese economic miracle with the aid of the managerial theory.)

* Penrose, E. (1958) *The Theory of the Growth of the Firm*, Oxford: Blackwell and New York: Wiley. (The foundation work on the idea of the persistently growing firm; highly original non-mathematical account of the internal administrative forces that encourage and restrain the growth rate.)

* Scherer, M. (1988) 'Corporate takeovers: the efficiency arguments', *Journal of Economic Perspectives* 2 (1) (Winter): 69–82. (Comprehensive and detached theoretical, empirical and historical survey of the apparent motives for, and efficiency effects of, takeovers.)

Managerial theories of the firm

* Williamson, O. (1964) *The Economics of Discretionary Behavior: Managerial Objectives in a Theory of the Firm*, Englewood Cliffs, NJ: Prentice Hall. (The author's prize-winning PhD dissertation; the classic exposition of his original model of managerial expense-preference with important empirical support.)
* Williamson, O. (1970) *Corporate Control and Business Behavior*, Englewood Cliffs, NJ: Prentice Hall. (Lucid discussion of how exigencies of internal organization affect actual behaviour of managerial firms.)
* Wood, A. (1994) *North-South Trade and Income Inequality*, Oxford: Oxford University Press. (Classic study of the effect on trade of raising then lowering the comparative earnings of unskilled workers in the First World while raising them in the developing world.)

See also: COASE, R.; CORPORATE CONTROL; GROWTH OF THE FIRM AND NETWORKING; MARSHALL, A.; NEO-CLASSICAL ECONOMICS; WILLIAMSON, O.E.

Enterprise ownership, types of

1 Proprietorships
2 Partnerships
3 Limited liability corporation
4 Joint stock corporation
5 Residual claimancy as a contractual role
6 Whither 'enterprise ownership'?
7 Is 'capitalism' a misnomer?
8 Dubious definitions in capital theory
9 The separation of ownership and control
10 From ownership to membership

Overview

The notion of the 'ownership' of an economic enterprise is surprisingly complex. This entry will sketch the major types of business enterprise from proprietorships to joint stock companies. The entry will challenge the usual implicit presumption that the current joint stock company is the 'End of History'. The challenge is launched by exploring the logical gap between the legal form of the corporation and the legal position of undertaking an economic enterprise as opposed to only supplying an input to the enterprise. We will see that the 'undertaking of the enterprise as a going concern' is a contractual role, a certain fact-pattern of contracts, and not a piece of property that can be bought, owned and sold. As relative prices and economic circumstances change, contracts are constantly being made and remade so the legal party undertaking an economic enterprise can change without there being any purchase and sale of the 'ownership of the firm'. Thus we will conclude that the notion of 'enterprise ownership' is in a certain sense a misnomer and, indeed, a misleading way to refer to the contractual fact-pattern of undertaking an enterprise.

With the undertaking of an enterprise conceptually distinguished from corporate ownership, I move on to explore the euthanasia of corporate ownership brought on by the mass stock market. That opens up new evolutionary pathways from the joint stock company to the corporation as a democratic work-community, an evolution that is already starting to take place – althought not without challenge – in some systems of corporate governance.

1 Proprietorships

A proprietorship is the simplest form of a one-person business. It is not incorporated so there is no separate legal person from the proprietor. The proprietorship would ordinarily have a separate bank account from the personal account of the proprietor, and it might operate under a certain DBA or 'Doing Business As' name. But the debts of the proprietorship are ultimately the personal debts of the proprietor so in the event of bankruptcy creditors can go after the assets of the proprietor. That is the unlimited liability aspect of this business form (see BUSINESS ECONOMICS).

Proprietorships are said to be 'bought' and 'sold' as if they were pieces of property, but closer scrutiny reveals a more complicated transaction. If we consider the proprietorship as having a separate balance sheet from that of the individual proprietor, then the assets on that business balance sheet are sold to the new proprietor (along with the right to use the DBA name) and the debts may be taken over by the new proprietor in partial payment for the assets. Beyond that the new proprietor replaces the old one in all the ongoing employment, supplier and customer contracts so that the contractual fact-pattern is transferred from the old to the new proprietor.

We immediately see a caveat to applying the notion of 'ownership' to a proprietorship. The reassignment of the contracts to the new proprietor is a matter of some delicacy as the other contractors – the employees, suppliers, or customers – might object and might withdraw from the contract. The old proprietor cannot 'sell' the future contractual compliance of the contractual partners even though that is part of the enterprise as a going concern. And that is true for all legal forms of enterprise in a market economy, not just for proprietorships.

2 Partnerships

A partnership is the contract-based multi-person generalization of the proprietorship. The partnership is formed by the contract (often using a standard form) assigning what each partner contributes and each partners' percentage of the profits and votes. The liabilities of the partnership are ultimately the debts of the partners in the sense that after exhausting the assets of the partnership, the creditors can go after the partners' personal assets proportional to their share. But should any partner go bankrupt, the remaining liability would shift to the other partners. Thus a partnership is not a separate legal person (in spite of separate bank accounts during normal operations) and the partners have unlimited liability for the debts of the partnership. Since the partnership contract needs to be redrafted whenever a partner changes, the partnership form is best suited to a stable set of partners. A 'limited partnership' is a hybrid form where there is one general partner with unlimited liability and a number of limited partners who only stand to lose their original investment.

3 Limited liability corporation

The limited liability corporation (LLC) is essentially a partnership repackaged as a separate legal person. Since an LLC is a separate legal person, a member only stands to lose the original investment in the event of bankruptcy. A creditor has no automatic recourse to the personal assets of the members unless they explicitly pledged personal assets as collateral. Each member has a certain percentage share so the percentages have to be recalculated whenever a member comes or goes. Like a partnership, the LLC is best suited to a stable set of members.

4 Joint stock corporation

This evolutionary track culminates in the joint stock company (JSC). It differs from the LLC in that a member or shareholder holds a certain number of shares so the percentage of ownership would have to be calculated as the ratio of owned shares over outstanding shares owned by all shareholders. In this manner, the percentages automatically adjust as new shares are sold or old shares are redeemed so the JSC is more suitable for private or public trading of shares. Ordinarily a company must satisfy stringent listing requirements before the shares can be offered for sale to any and all comers on a public stock market. An unlisted company is said to be 'closely held' and its shares can only change hands in private transactions between informed ('sophisticated') parties.

The origin of the expression 'joint stock' might be of interest. English corporations evolved out of the practice of merchants pooling together their resources to finance a ship voyage to sell commodities elsewhere and/or to purchase commodities elsewhere to resell them in England. The 'stock' was the inventory of goods aboard the ship. When pirates or natural disasters struck, the inventory or stock of some merchants might be damaged while the stock of others endured unscathed. How would the losses be apportioned? The system that emerged was to consider the inventories as 'joint stock' so each merchant would take a proportionate loss. This was consistent with the theory of the corporation as a separate artificial legal person – initially a person formed for the purpose of financing a voyage and dissolved thereafter.

As a separate legal person, a corporation owns assets that are not the assets of the shareholders and holds liabilities that are not the debts of the shareholders. A shareholder is no more liable for the corporation's debts than he or she would be for debts of any other person. By the same token, when two different legal persons each pay a tax, that would not ordinarily be considered 'double taxation' since each person is taxed just once. Unfortunately, the taxation of the corporation and of the shareholder as separate legal persons is often misleadingly referred to as 'double taxation'. This so-called 'double taxation' is just the flip-side of limited liability. Each legal person is taxed once.

5 Residual claimancy as a contractual role

We now must be careful about using words and concepts. It is useful at this point to introduce the economists' 'technical' description of an enterprise. Certain inputs (such as labour services, capital services and materials) are combined to produce an output. We will abstractly describe this by a production function $Q = f(X,Y)$ where X and Y are the quantities of the inputs (there could be any number of inputs but two will serve for exposition) and Q is the number of units of the outputs per time period (e.g., day week, or month). In a given enterprise in a market economy one legal party will undertake this process by buying the inputs X and Y at the respective unit prices P_x and P_y, and thereby claiming and selling the outputs Q for the unit price P. Since that party will have paid for the inputs and sold the outputs, it will net the profit or residual $PQ - P_x X - P_y Y$ so that party is called the 'residual claimant'.

How in a market economy does a legal party become the residual claimant? In our simplified example, the owner of X could buy Y, the owner of Y could buy X, or some third party entrepreneur could buy both X and Y. Then that party would bear the costs of those inputs used up in production and could lay claim to the produced outputs Q. The net value of the losses and gains is the residual. It all depends on who hires what or whom, i.e., on the pattern (direction) of the contracts. Thus, being the residual claimant is a contractual role, the contractual role of operating the technically defined enterprise $Q = f(X,Y)$ as a going concern. It is not a property right that one can buy and sell.

In particular, we have seen that this contractual role is not part of the ownership of any of the inputs X or Y. We have deliberately not identified X or Y with capital or labour to make this point. In a market economy with the employment relation, the owners of capital can hire labour, labour can hire capital, or a third party can hire both. Residual claimancy is determined by that pattern of contracts, not by who started off owning 'capital'. Note the ambiguity in expressions such as 'owner of a factory'. The owner of a factory building need not be the legal party undertaking production in the factory building, e.g., when the building is leased to another party. The residual claimant is the party who operates the factory as a going concern, and that is quite distinct from the ownership of the factory. Much conceptual confusion is created when the contractual role of operating a going concern is described as 'ownership of the firm'. Having a contractual role is not an 'ownership' type of thing.

6 Whither 'enterprise ownership'?

Now we can return to our original goal of elucidating the notion of 'enterprise ownership'. It all depends on what one means by 'enterprise'. A corporation is legally owned by the shareholders, but a corporation need not be the 'enterprise' in the sense of the going-concern operator. We can conceive of the inputs X and Y as each being owned by different corporations but we have no hint about the operator of the enterprise $Q = f(X,Y)$ until we know the pattern of contracts between the parties – until we know who hired what or whom. Thus the glib identification of 'corporate ownership' with 'enterprise ownership' (in the sense of the enterprise as a going concern) leaves something to be desired. Indeed, if by 'enterprise' we mean the contractual role of being the going concern operator, then there is no such thing as 'enterprise ownership'. In the jargon of economics, this means that there is no such thing as the 'ownership' of a production function or a production set. Having purchased all the inputs and borne those losses as the inputs are used up in production, one can claim and sell the outputs – all without any such thing as 'buying the production function'.

If an enterprise (in the going-concern sense) cannot be bought, owned or sold, what happens when we talk about someone 'buying a firm'. Ordinarily this will mean buying the shares in a company where the company currently is the residual claimant in a certain production process. But there is no 'ownership right' which forces the other contractual partners to maintain the same pattern of contracts in the future. Even prepaid contracts are of limited duration, so one cannot 'buy' the contractual role of being the residual claimant throughout the future. The employees, suppliers and customers are free to go elsewhere.

The present value of those future profits or residuals is usually called the 'goodwill' of the enterprise, and it is misleadingly said that one 'buys goodwill' when one pays more than the net value of the underlying assets and liabilities. But one buys no enforceable property rights when one 'buys goodwill'. After the expiration of the existing contracts, the contractual partners are free to make other arrangements, and one has no legal recourse to force them to continue the same contractual fact-pattern. Thus instead of the usual practice of accounting for purchased goodwill as an addition to assets, it would be more accurate to account for it as a subtraction from equity.

> The amount assigned to purchased goodwill represents a disbursement of existing resources, or of proceeds of stock issued to effect the business combination, in anticipation of future earnings. The expenditure should be accounted for as a reduction of stockholders' equity.
> (Catlett and Olson 1968: 106)

If and when the future earnings are made, then the equity can be accordingly replenished.

7 Is 'capitalism' a misnomer?

We are now in a position to arrive at a number of non-trivial results. For example, 'capitalism' was mis-named by Marx. We have seen that the 'enterprise' in the sense of a going concern is not owned at all, and particularly is not part of the ownership of one of the factors of production such as capital. Capital can be hired, rented, borrowed or leased in the capitalist system so the owner of capital is not necessarily the residual claimant. Marx thought otherwise by taking an inappropriate analogy with the role of land during feudal times. The landlord was then the Lord of the land in the sense that the rights to govern the people on the land were considered part and parcel of the land ownership. Marx thought the same idea carried over to capitalism with capital replacing land.

> It is not because he is a leader of industry that a man is a capitalist; on the contrary, he is a leader of industry because he is a capitalist. The leadership of industry is an attribute of capital, just as in feudal times the functions of general and judge were attributes of landed property.
> (Marx 1977: 450–1)

But we have seen that residual claimancy is a contractual role and is not part of the ownership of the means of production called 'capital'. Thus Marx mis-named the system as 'capitalism'.

8 Dubious definitions in capital theory

This analysis also implies that the usual definitions of 'asset value' in capital theory and the usual formulas of valuation in corporate finance theory are conceptually flawed. The usual definitions of the value of a capital asset assume that the owner of the asset is also the residual claimant throughout the lifetime of the asset (see CAPITALISM, VARIETIES OF).

> When a man buys an investment or capital-asset, he purchases the right to the series of prospective returns, which he expects to obtain from selling its output, after deducting the running expenses of obtaining that output, during the life of the asset.
> (Keynes 1936: 135)

But in fact the purchaser of a capital asset may or may not have that contractual role during the lifetime of the asset so one cannot treat the right to the future profits as part of the ownership of the capital asset. Corporate finance theory carries over the same valuation mistake to whole corporations by assuming that the corporation is always the residual claimant in the production processes using the capital assets of the corporation (as if corporations could not hire out capital instead of hiring in labour).

> There, in valuing any specific machine we discount at the market rate of interest the stream of cash receipts generated by the machine; plus any scrap or terminal value of the machine; and minus the stream of cash outlays for direct labor, materials, repairs, and capital additions. The same

approach, of course, can also be applied to the firm as a whole which may be thought of in this context as simply a large, composite machine.

(Miller and Modigliani 1961: 415)

The assumed contractual fact-patterns may or may not take place, but in any case the future residuals are not part of the present ownership of the machine or the corporation and thus they cannot be correctly capitalized into the value of the capital asset.

9 The separation of ownership and control

By analysing the notion of 'enterprise ownership' we have discovered a disconnection between capital and enterprise. A joint stock corporation is not necessarily the going-concern enterprise utilizing the capital assets of the corporation (e.g., factory building). As capital can be hired out, just as other factors can be hired in, the rights to the future profits are not part of the ownership of capital assets. Now we turn to another type of disconnection: the separation between ownership and control in the large publicly traded company.

While the general idea that the corporation would eventually outgrow the real possibility of shareholder control dates back to the nineteenth century (e.g., Marx and Marshall), the most definitive statement of the thesis of the separation of (shareholder) ownership and (managerial) control is in Adolf Berle and Gardner Means' *The Modern Corporation and Private Property* (1932) (see MARSHALL, A.; MARX, K.; MEANS, G.). As the mass stock market scattered the ownership of shares far and wide, the transaction costs of coordinated shareholder action escalated dramatically so that managers eventually learned how to effectively control the board of directors. Top corporate managers became in effect a self-perpetuating oligarchy. Indeed, there sometimes seems to be a good analogy between the relationship of Management to the Shareholders and the relationship between the Communist Party and the People. Management draws its nominal legitimacy from the Shareholders as does the Party from the People so the self-perpetuating oligarchy cannot be declared openly. Whenever clique A is overthrown by clique B in the internal elite power struggles, it is always presented as being in the interests of the Shareholders/People.

Another way to phrase this separation of ownership and control is to say that the ownership of the shares does not add up to the 'ownership of the company'. Each share has a distinct private owner with clear rights to buy, hold or sell the share, but the company as a whole does not have a private owner – so the control rights incident to ownership fall by default to the managers. This euthanasia of shareholder control throws open the normative question: 'Who should the managers represent?' If the shareholders have become like lottery ticketholders, then who should be running the lottery?

This is not a topic we can treat at any length here, but we can indicate some directions for the evolution of the concept 'enterprise ownership'. Indeed, in the course of analysis, the concept of 'ownership' of an enterprise has been weakened considerably. In particular, we have seen that residual claimancy or the enterprise as a going concern is not something that is owned at all but something that is undertaken by making an appropriate set of contracts.

One trend in the corporate governance literature is toward notions of 'stakeholder' governance, where stakeholders are variously defined as those who are affected by the company (which would include competitors) or the long-term partners in explicit or implicit contracts with the company. Stakeholder proposals have suffered from a lack of definiteness so that sometimes they end up as a kind of high-brow corporate socialism where Management is 'responsible' to all stakeholders (which means, in fact, accountable to none).

10 From ownership to membership

Another approach is to go back from the notion of 'enterprise ownership' to the notion of 'enterprise membership'. Is there a natural set of members in a company? Indeed, ordinary language usage has settled on a meaning of 'members of a company'. Pick up any book on business or management and look at the people whom the book refers to as the 'members' of the company. More than likely, it will be referring to the employees of the company. In a sense, corporations have evolved so that there are two companies. There is the 'company-in-law' whose members are the shareholders and who meet once a year in the ritualistic shareholder meeting, and there is the 'company-in-fact' consisting of the people working in the enterprise who meet every working day. These 'two companies' were observed long ago by Lord Eustace Percy.

> Here is the most urgent challenge to political invention ever offered to the jurist and the statesman. The human association which in fact produces and distributes wealth, the association of workmen, managers, technicians and directors, is not an association recognised by the law. The association which the law does recognise – the association of shareholder-creditors and directors – is incapable of production or distribution and is not expected by the law to perform these functions.
> (quoted in Goyder 1961: 57)

Answering this 'urgent challenge' would mean redefining the company-in-law in terms of the company-in-fact as a membership-based democratic organization. That would entail reinterpreting the common shareholders as non-voting preferred stockholders and it would mean reinterpreting the employment relation as a membership or workplace-citizenship relationship. Reinterpreting shareholders as a risk-sharing form of creditor would recognize their property rights in a proportionate part of the net asset value but it would not recognize any so-called property right to the future good will (discounted future pure profits). Indeed, we saw that this claim was only a bluff in the first place as there is no present property right to enforce future contractual fact-patterns.

These characteristics are starting to emerge in the major non-Anglo-American systems of corporate governance.

Against this pattern as it has developed in the West, the common stock shareholder of the Japanese company is more in the position of a preferred shareholder in a Western company. Having made an investment that is at risk, the shareholder is entitled to a return on that investment. Therefore dividends are paid, but not as a percent of earnings but as a percent of the par value of shares in the company.
(Abegglen and Stalk 1985: 184)

Correspondingly, the 'members' of the company are redefined from being the common stockholders to being the long-term employees.

> Although there is some danger of oversimplification in making such a statement, the most direct description of this situation is that Japanese corporations 'are controlled by, and exist for, their employees'. Japanese corporations are thus united bodies of corporate employees.
> (Matsumoto 1991: 27)

A similar trend has taken place in continental Europe with the spread of co-determination in Germany and the spread of various forms of works councils to other European Union countries on the continent.

DAVID ELLERMAN
WORLD BANK

Further reading

(References cited in the text marked *)

* Abegglen, J.C. and Stalk Jr, G. (1985) *Kaisha, The Japanese Corporation.* New York: HarperCollins. (A treatment by Western authors of how the large Japanese firm differs from the Anglo-American model corporation with shareholder primacy.)
Albert, Michel (1993) *Capitalism Vs. Capitalism*, trans. Paul Haviland, New York: Four Walls Eight Windows. (A semi-popular book by a French economist-businessman comparing the Anglo-American system to the German-Japanese system of capitalism.)
Beauchamp, Tom and Bowie, Norman (eds) (1993) *Ethical Theory and Business,* 4th edn, Englewood Cliffs, NJ: Prentice Hall. (See this anthology for writings, cases and references on stakeholder models of corporate governance.)
* Berle, A. and Means, G. (1932) *The Modern Corporation and Private Property*, New York: Macmillan. (The classic book showing the

'separation of ownership and control' that follows from dispersing shares on mass stock markets.)

Blair, Margaret M. (1995) *Ownership and Control: Rethinking Corporate Governance for the Twenty-First Century*, Washington, DC: The Brookings Institution. (One of the best recent treatments of these topics emphasizing the importance of firm-specific human capital and the inapplicability of 'ownership' concepts applied to the modern publicly traded corporation.)

* Catlett, G. and Olson, N. (1968) *ARS No. 10: Accounting for Goodwill*, New York: American Institute of Certified Public Accountants. (One of the few accounting publications to rethink the tricky notion of 'goodwill'.)

Dore, Ronald (1987) *Taking Japan Seriously*, Stanford, CA: Stanford University Press. (A most accessible comparison of the 'company-law' model and the 'community' model of a corporation which draws on the Japanese experience.)

Dore, Ronald (2000) *Stock Market Capitalism: Welfare Capitalism. Japan and Germany versus the Anglo-Saxons*, Oxford: Oxford University Press. (A most accessible comparison of the 'company-law' model and the 'community' model of a corporation which draws on the Japanese experience.)

Ellerman, David (1999) 'The democratic firm: an argument based on ordinary jurisprudence', *Journal of Business Ethics*, 21: 111–24. (An argument for the democratic concept of the corporation derived from first principles.)

* Goyder, G. (1961) *The Responsible Company*, Oxford: Basil Blackwell. (A classic in the literature on stakeholder governance where the members of the firm are the primary stakeholders.)

Handy, Charles (1996) *Beyond Certainty*, Boston, MA: Harvard Business School Press. (A leading organizational philosopher who argues for seeing a company as a community rather than a piece of property.)

Hansmann, Henry (1996) *The Ownership of Enterprise*, Cambridge, MA: Harvard University Press. (One of the few recent books to describe the full variety of corporate forms including various types of cooperatives and mutual companies.)

Kelly, Marjorie (ed.) *Business Ethics: Insider's Report on Corporate Responsibility*, Minneapolis, MN. (Feisty magazine on corporate responsibility and governance questions. Editor Kelly's editorials are well-worth it by themselves.)

* Keynes, J.M. (1936) *The General Theory of Employment, Interest, and Money*, New York: Harcourt, Brace & World. (The most influential economics book of the twentieth century.)

* Marx, Karl (1977). *Capital*, vol. I, trans. B. Fowkes. New York: Vintage Books. (Probably the most influential economics book of the nineteenth century.)

* Matsumoto, Koji (1991) *The Rise of the Japanese Corporate System: The Inside View of a MITI Official*, trans. Thomas I. Elliott, London: Kegan Paul International. (One of the best treatments of the Japanese corporate system by an insider with interesting comparisons to the Yugoslav socially owned firms.)

* Miller, M.H. and Modigliani, F. (1961) 'Dividend policy, growth, and the valuation of shares', *The Journal of Business* 34 (October): 411–33. (The definitive article on the standard theory of valuation applied to the corporation.)

Mitchell, Lawrence (ed.) (1995) *Progressive Corporate Law*, Boulder, CO: Westview Press. (An anthology of critiques of orthodox corporate law by progressive legal scholars.)

Sakakibara, E. (1993) *Beyond Capitalism: The Japanese Model of Market Economics*, Lanham, MD: University Press of America. (A statement by one of Japan's best-known international economists – 'Mr. Yen' – of how Japan is different.)

See also: BUSINESS ECONOMICS; CAPITALISM, VARIETIES OF; CORPORATE CONTROL; INDUSTRIAL AND LABOUR RELATIONS; INSTITUTIONAL ECONOMICS; INTELLECTUAL PROPERTY RIGHTS; MANAGERIAL THEORIES OF THE FIRM; MARSHALL, A.; MARX, K.H., MEANS, G.C.; MILL, J.S.

Rationality in economics

1 The rationality principle
2 Neo-classical rationality
3 Neo-classical rationality and the rationality principle
4 Rule-following and choice
5 Rule-following, skill and expertise
6 Decision making in economics and management

Overview

Rationality is a notion at the heart of both economics and business research. In their descriptive models, economists postulate that people behave rationally; and, in their normative models, many consultants and academics insist that business people ought to make rational decisions. But rationality is not an unambiguous concept, and it is certainly not uncontested as an economic postulate or a business goal. In this entry, a discussion of the meanings of rationality in economics is analysed in order to provide a framework for understanding the uses of – and limits to – the concept.

1 The rationality principle

As a point of orientation, a discussion of Karl Popper's well-known *rationality principle* should be raised (for an excellent discussion of Popper's principle and the debates surrounding it, see Caldwell (1994)). This will provide a framework and a language with which to discuss both rationality and the methodology of economics. According to Popper's principle, one should analyse social processes by assuming that agents act appropriately or reasonably in the situation in which they find themselves. This reflects a version of *situational analysis*, also known as *single-exit* modelling. Imagine attempting to predict which exit an agent will take from a sports stadium (Latsis 1976). An agent with free will could in principle choose any exit. But the structure of the situation postulated may will a typical and reasonable agent to use the exit nearest his or her seat.

Popper views situational analysis as an antidote to *psychologism*, the view that one can explain all social processes solely by reference to the psychological states of individuals (Popper 1966, 1967). Unlike psychology, economics and kindred social sciences are not about explaining the behaviour of individuals; rather, they are about how individual behaviour leads to larger social patterns and institutions – 'the unintended social repercussions of intentional human actions' (Popper 1966: 95) – an idea that goes back at least to Adam Smith and the Scottish Enlightenment (see SMITH, A.). Moreover, for Popper, one benefit of situational analysis is that knowledge of the agent's situation can compensate in large measure for detailed knowledge of the agent's psychology: the 'logic of the situation' may largely dictate behaviour, and the psychology – or even the 'rationality' – needed to make sense of the agent's actions (as one element in the explanation of unintended social phenomena) may be 'trivial' (Popper 1966: 97).

2 Neo-classical rationality

Popper contended (e.g. 1966: 97) that situational analysis is in fact the method of economics. I return to this claim below. What is indisputable, however, is that there has long been in economics a tendency to see rationality as a logical rather than a psychological principle. (It was probably Lionel Robbins's *An Essay on the Nature and Significance of Economic Science* (1932) that fully ensconced in the minds of economists the idea that their science is about the logic of means and ends rather than about the psychology of utility.) Given a framework of means and ends, the agent's behaviour reflects the solution to a logical problem of allocation. It was not a difficult leap to associate this logical problem with the mathematical problem of optimization, a leap that Walras and his followers had in fact already made. The English School, including Jevons and Edgeworth, also thought in terms of mathematical optimization, but their approach was underpinned by utilitarian psychology.

The neo-classical rationality assumptions are well-known, and it may seem unnecessary even to repeat them. I propose, however, to recast my description in a rather idiosyncratic way that will help highlight certain criticisms on which I want to focus below. The basic neo-classical model, I argue, combines the following four elements:

- self-interest;
- omniscience ('complete information');
- conscious deliberation (or an 'as if' equivalent);
- the representative agent.

The first two of these are much discussed; the third and fourth elements are less often noticed.

Self-interest

The assumption of self-interest has come under intense criticism, traditionally from outside economics, although increasingly from within as well. The main line of criticism tends to rest on a misidentification of self-interest with narrow selfishness. There is at least one other strand of criticism of the assumption of self-interest, one in which self-interested behaviour is contrasted with some kind of rule-following behaviour. For example, Sen (1976) uses language that suggests he is contrasting what is in the end rulefollowing behaviour with 'rational egoism'. But, as we will see in detail below, rulefollowing (or non-deliberative behaviour generally) is not opposed to self-interested behaviour but rather to case-by-case behaviour. One can follow rules that serve one's purposes or are even in one's narrow interest. Nor is it necessarily the case that following ostensibly altruistic rules leads to altruistic outcomes: as Douglas Heckathorn (1991) has shown, there exists an 'altruists' dilemma,' analogous to the more-famous prisoners' dilemma, in which following apparently other-regarding rules makes all parties worse off. In Smith's theory of the wealth of nations, individuals constantly strive to better their conditions. But those agents are not neoclassical optimizers, and indeed arguably follow a model of behaviour closer to the one I will advocate below. Although Smith insisted that 'it is not from the benevolence of the butcher, the brewer, or the baker that we expect our dinner, but from their regard to their own interest' (Smith 1976a, I.ii.2: 27), his was not a brief against unselfish motives. As the *Theory of Moral Sentiments* makes even more clear, Smith's agents even possess something very like a conscience. Smith's argument (in both works) is that, under the right institutional constraints, decentralized action leads to beneficial unintended social results – namely economic growth – *even when* such action is narrowly self-interested. In a complex world of dispersed and localized knowledge, it is difficult to anticipate the eventual effects of our behaviour on others, which means that other-regarding behaviour is far from sufficient to guarantee desirable outcomes, and may in some cases actually lead to undesirable outcomes.

Omniscience

Obviously, the issue of unintended consequences is related to the second assumption, namely omniscience. In neo-classical theory, this assumption usually goes by the title of 'perfect information', a term that ought to suggest that it is a limited conception: information can be perfect only against some standard. In the end, neo-classical agents are perfectly informed not in general but in respect of a particular structure set out for them by the analyst. The Arrow–Debreu general-equilibrium theory is the best known example of this, in which highly simplified agents are required to know all the utilities and production possibilities of all other agents. That's a lot to know – an impossible amount, as many have pointed out – but it is also a lot to know about very little. These same agents are not required to know, for example, which new production possibilities might be invented in the future, at least unless these possibilities are already known to the analyst and laid out as contingencies. In general, then, the perfection of the information agents must possess is relative to the situations in which those agents find themselves. As I have long argued (Langlois 1984), economics tends to forget that real people can be uncertain or ignorant not only about specific particular pieces of information within a known and given structure but also about the very nature of the problem situation they face. In neo-classical theory, agents are assumed to have perfect *structural knowledge*, that is, to know and be certain of the structure of the economic problem they face. When agents are ill-informed or uncertain in this theory, what they lack is *parametric knowledge* (or information), that is, they lack perfect information about the value of some parameter (like the true willingness to pay of a transacting partner).

Conscious deliberation

It is perhaps controversial to say that the agent in neo-classical theory is represented as consciously deliberating. As we saw, the method of situational analysis makes it possible to place most of the weight of explanation on the agent's situation, leaving little for deliberation. None the less, it is certainly the case that, in 'appreciative' theorizing (Nelson and Winter 1982: 46) and undergraduate instruction, economists depict agents as consciously considering their options and choosing among them. Moreover, as economics has moved beyond simple situational logic into the realms of mathematical optimization, the problems that agents are represented as solving are no longer trivial or their solutions obviously implied in the situation. How do agents solve these problems if they do not deliberate? And if they do deliberate, then psychology is on the table as a necessary part of economics, and we should work harder to understand how agents 'really' think.

The only alternative to is argue, with Milton Friedman (1953), that agents do not actually deliberate but none the less behave 'as if' they did (see FRIEDMAN, M.). Although embraced by practitioners as a justification of the *status quo*, Friedman's argument is typically scoffed at by students of economic methodology. And rightly so, perhaps. But the possibility of an 'as if' justification does suggest that we might in the end call upon the structure of the agent's situation, in some manner yet unspecified, to substitute for explicit deliberation. I will take up this strand again below.

Representative agent

Since Marshall, most economists have taken for granted that the agent of theory is a 'representative' one (see MARSHALL, A.). But there has been comparatively little discussion of the nature and status of this assumption, which is in fact at the crux of many recent evolutionary critiques of neo-classical theory (an exception is Kirman 1992). Because the object of our study is not agents for their own sakes but agents only as links in an explanatory chain, we need to abstract from real individuals to create artificial individuals who none the less retain some of the typical features of real individuals (Schütz 1943; Schütz and Luckmann 1973). But there are many ways to do this; and typification does not commit one to the assumption that all agents in the population are identical.

3 Neo-classical rationality and the rationality principle

Many writers (e.g. Latsis 1976; Caldwell 1994) have agreed with Popper that the method of situational analysis is the method of (neo-classical) economics. And there is no disputing that much of economics does in fact fit under this rubric. But it is also quite arguable that an equal or larger part of what goes on in economics is *not* situational analysis *à la* Popper.

As I have argued elsewhere (Langlois 1990; Langlois and Csontos 1993), the part of neo-classical economics that does *not* fit with situational analysis is that part of the canon to which most critics direct their attentions. An economic agent who is modelled as maximizing a foot-long Lagrangean is arguably not acting reasonably within the logic of the situation. Indeed, an agent who, faced with a complex situation, follows rules or heuristics of some kind is clearly acting far more reasonably and far more plausibly.

This is not to say that all conceptions of rule-following behaviour accord with situational analysis. Some approaches can indeed be seen as a version of what Popper called psychologism. This includes to some extent the original programme of behaviouralism put forward by Herbert Simon (1955, 1959) (see SIMON, H.A.). Like the neo-classicist, Simon implicitly sees it as an easy matter for the agent to understand the structure of the problem situation he or she faces; the hard part is to find the correct solution. Interpreting the neo-classical model as one of conscious deliberation, Simon points out that agents cannot in fact solve such problems: agents are 'boundedly rational'. (Actually, of course, it is not their rationality at all but their computational ability that is bounded.) In analogy with the functioning of digital computers, he proposes as an alternative seeing agents as following 'heuristics' or rules with which they are effectively programmed *ab ovo*. For example, agents may 'satisfice,' which means abiding by a programmed rule very like the one followed by the thermostat on your wall.

Again, however, some conceptions of rule-following are quite consistent with situational analysis, as are some 'maximizing' conceptions. These latter fall under the rubric of what we may call 'soft' rational-choice models. What I have in mind here is the kind of rough-and-ready price theory captured in, say, the late Paul Heyne's *The Economic Way of Thinking* (1999). This is the neo-classical economics of simple partial-equilibrium analysis: of scarcity, of opportunity cost, of supply and demand. It is the neo-classical economics that reminds us there is no free lunch. Soft rational choice is the baby that critics shouldn't throw out with the bathwater, even if there does remain a considerable amount of neo-classical bathwater worth draining.

4 Rule-following and choice

One significant development in economic theory that begins to address some of the concerns of critics is the New Institutional Economics (Langlois 1986b, 1992) (see INSTITUTIONAL ECONOMICS). Although this body of work does not obviously necessitate new behavioural foundations for economics, and in some minds is understood as a logical development of neo-classical theory (Eggertsson 1990), it none the less points to an important situational (and perhaps motivational) factor in economic explanation: the following of rules. At the most fundamental level, the notion of an institution itself refers to a rule-like regularity of behaviour (for example, to Schotter (1981: 11), a social institution 'specifies behaviour in specific recurrent situations, and is either self-policed or policed by some external authority'). Such institutions can be simple, like a convention or norm of conduct (drive on the right, be honest in dealings with trading partners), or they can be complex systems of rules of conduct, like a culture or perhaps even a business firm.

One aspect of such institutions is that the rules that comprise them must enter into the situations in which agents find themselves. In this guise, institutions can enter into rational-choice models as side constraints that delimit what is otherwise deliberative choice. But the interaction between rules and individual behaviour is actually a two-way street. Not only do rules constrain action, but economic action can in turn explain the origins of the rules: institutions emerge as the unintended results of individual action, and this is a process that we can explore theoretically. The most influential models in this area portray institutions like norms and conventions as emerging through a process of the repeated play of certain kinds of 'games', such as the coordination game or the prisoners' dilemma (Sugden 1986; Rowe 1989). Over time, the agents will hit upon strategies that are 'evolutionarily stable'; and these strategies, which are relatively simple bundles of rules, become institutionalized: 'institutionalization occurs whenever there is a reciprocal typification of habitualized actions by types of actors' (Berger and Luckmann 1966: 51). I habitually expect the typical driver coming toward me to stay on the right, and other drivers habitually expect the same of me.

This theory of the emergence of institutions raises two issues for the standard theory of rational choice – issues that have to do with the postulates of conscious deliberation and representativeness I have highlighted. Obviously, the evolutionary aspect of the story speaks to the issue of the representative agent. More interestingly for the moment, however, the idea that institutions are rules that somehow coalesced out of the strategies of agents brings to the fore the possibility that rules may not be (only) constraints but may actually be principles of action alternative to conscious deliberation. On the difference between rules as constraints and rules as principles of action, see Burrell (1967) and Pelikan (1992).

In some situations (like coordination games) there is no marginal incentive for agents to deviate from a convention. Thus one might argue that, once a convention is in place, agents consciously consider the convention as part of their problem situation and choose to follow it because it is, in each case, the best thing to do. The alternative interpretation, what Vanberg (1994: 13) calls *genuine rule-following*, is for the agent to abide by the convention independently of the considerations at hand in a particular case. Although it is clearly in my case-by-case interest to drive on the right-hand side in the USA, I just as clearly do not consciously deliberate the matter each time an oncoming car appears. Rather, the convention has become internalized for me: it has become a routine (Nelson and Winter 1982). Even when it is not in my case-by-case interest to follow the rule, as when I pull out of a parking lot onto a street in Melbourne, Australia, I may find myself driving on the right out of habit.

In other cases (like the prisoners' dilemma), agents may have a marginal incentive to deviate from a norm, and external sanctions are often necessary; but even in such cases, the very institutionalization of the strategy-as-rule arguably serves a kind of enforcement function. That is to say, the institutionalization of the norm serves as an enforcement function in 'routine' situations in which the pay-offs to violating the norm are not large. Sanctions thus do not *create* the norm; they exist to police unusual cases in which particular individuals may have a greater incentive to violate (Berger and Luckmann 1966: 52). If the sanctions do become the prime enforcement mechanism, then the norm itself may be out of line with relative scarcities and under pressure to change.

From one point of view, of course, the explanatory overlap is quite large between 'genuine' rule-following in this sense and a rational-choice view of rule-following. It is often hard to tell whether someone is behaving in a rule-like way because he or she is 'programmed' to do so or because, upon careful consideration, the agent always found the same course of action to be optimal. Moreover, one need only invoke information costs in order to explain why people might continue to follow rules even when it might strictly pay to violate them in particular cases. This is especially true if we consider rules in the sense of Herbert Simon, that is, as second-best procedures in the face of 'bounded rationality': satisficing really is optimal in a world of costly decision making.

None the less, I see two reasons to prefer the model of genuine rule following: plausibility and fruitfulness. Popper's principle of rationality makes the first point clear. If we want to represent the agent as acting reasonably within a situation, and if that situation is one of complexity and uncertainty, it may well be more plausible to see the agents as following some kinds of rules – at least in preference to seeing the agent as consciously maximizing. Moreover, whenever a fully compelling explanation would require a relatively rich description of behaviour, psychology is on the table. And a programme that stresses rule following might be desirable not so much from the point of view of an alternative model of behaviour as from the point of view of a research programme seeking more plausible accounts of human cognition and motivation. One such research programme moves in the direction of what we might call the *expertise* model of rationality (Langlois 1998), often understood in an explicitly evolutionary framework. Related examples of this approach include Choi (1993), Denzau and Douglass North (1994), Koppl and Langlois (1994), Lane *et al.* (1996) and Vanberg (1994). The reason why a rule-following programme is desirable is not because rule following is always more compelling than conscious deliberation but because approaches from rule-following (broadly construed) are blossoming nowadays in the literature of cognition, whereas the model of choice as conscious deliberation now appears to be a dead end rather than a starting point for further inquiry.

5 Rule-following, skill and expertise

The traditional Simonian programme of behaviouralism suffers from two problems. One of these I have already mentioned, namely the tendency to psychologism. Put differently, the model of action as rule-following behaviour programmed as in a computer can no more account for resourcefulness or creativity than can the model of the agent as a conscious optimizer over known and delimited variables. Indeed, the rule 'maximize the specified Langrangean' can well be interpreted as a behavioural heuristic, albeit not a particularly plausible one (Langlois 1990). It is the possibility of creativity and resourcefulness on the part of agents that permits the method of situational analysis to explain phenomena of unintended consequences.

The second (and perhaps related) problem with the simple behaviouralist programme, however, is that it is also arguably not even a very rich or fruitful account of rule-following behaviour. The reason has to do with the formative metaphor of the digital computer, which led to a picture of behaviour as programmed and mechanical. The alternative is to see rule-following as related to a more open-ended picture of cognition in which it is impossible (or at least not useful) to reduce behaviour to a set of rules with which the agent is programmed from the beginning. In this alternative, rule-following behaviour is more a matter of executing a skill than executing a programme. The distinction I have in mind has been well aired (albeit controversially) in the literature on the branch of computer science called artificial intelligence (Dreyfus 1979; Dreyfus and Dreyfus 1986). Set against an optimistic vision of computerized intelligence (typified, interestingly, by Herbert Simon), these critics assert that human cognitive processes are quite different from those of computers and, for many tasks at least, far superior. They do not deny that humans follow rules; but they do deny that, like computers, humans follow *explicit* rules. What makes human behaviour effective is the inexplicit or tacit character of human rule-following: people follow rules unconsciously, in a skilful or expert fashion; and people actually perform less well when they deliberately try to follow explicit rules (let alone when they try consciously to optimize).

Let me call this critical view the *expertise* model of behaviour. One way to see the difference between this model and simple behaviouralism is the following. In the behaviouralist account, abiding by rules is a second-best option in the face of 'bounded rationality'. Implicitly, then, one is always performing less than ideally well when satisficing or following a heuristic, where the ideal is set in terms of what could have been accomplished by explicit calculation or optimization given adequate resources. In the expertise account, (tacit) rule following can be inherently superior to deliberate action even in the ideal.

Recently, David Lane and his co-authors (1996) have mounted a major attack on rational-choice models from the perspective of expertise. What Lane et al. object to in their postulates of rational choice is the very notion of choice – or, rather, 'the primacy of choice over action itself' (1996: 45). Drawing on the literature of cognitive psychology, they argue that conceiving of situations as choices leads to an implausible model of behaviour, except perhaps in special situations. In most circumstances, action is governed by expertise, with conscious deliberation and planning entering as secondary considerations that are, however, themselves predicated on expertise.

Examples of expertise are familiar: catching a ball, flying a plane, or – to use Milton Friedman's famous example – playing billiards. These are activities we perform without conscious deliberation, and indeed paying attention to what one is doing often degrades performance: thinking consciously about one's performance is the mark of a novice. Skilled performers, moreover, cannot and need not translate what they are doing into explicit terms. All of this will be familiar to readers of Michael Polanyi (1958) on tacit knowledge. Lane and his co-authors direct the issue of expertise to the arena of decision making. If action based on expertise is more effective than conscious deliberation in most situations, then we ought to see *economic* action as a matter of skilled performance rather than deliberation.

Although Lane *et al.* are perhaps the most strident in pushing the expertise view of behaviour, they are by no means alone. Several other recent contributions have put forward models of behaviour that draw on many of the same sources and paint a strikingly similar picture (Choi 1993; Vanberg 1993, 1994; Denzau and North 1994; Koppl and Langlois 1994 – the work of Holland *et al.* (1986) seems to be a unifying thread here, as it is cited enthusiastically by Lane *et al.* 1996; Vanberg 1994; and Denzau and North 1994).

6 Decision making in economics and management

The conception of choice as skilled action would seem at first to leave little room for genuine decision making in economics and management. But this is so only if we understand genuine decision making in terms of a single general-purpose model of rational behaviour. The expertise view of action suggests that there are in fact multiple processes of decision making at work in human agents. This is very much in keeping with the perspective of evolutionary psychology, which sees the human mind not as a general-purpose thinking machine (like a digital computer) but rather as a congeries of special-purpose perceptual and cognitive engines that evolved in response to a variety of concrete problems of survival (Cosmides and Tooby 1994). In effect, the brain is a kind of distributed processing system that relies on the division of cognitive labour.

Under conditions of routine, rules substitute for conscious deliberation because case-by-case choice becomes unnecessary and inefficient. As in Smith's account of the division of labour, agents are made expert by repetitious action. With practice, they act with less and less deliberation, thereby narrowing their choices and freeing up conscious attention for other uses, including innovation (Berger and Luckmann 1966: 51). Alfred North Whitehead remarked that it is:

> a profoundly erroneous truism, repeated by all copy-books and by eminent people when they are making speeches, that we should cultivate the habit of thinking what we are doing. The precise opposite is the case. Civilization advances by extending the number of important operations which we can perform without thinking about them. Operations of thought are like cavalry charges in a battle – they are strictly limited in number, they require fresh horses, and must only be made at decisive moments.
>
> (Whitehead 1911: 61)

It is in this sense, as Lane *et al.* suggest, that rule-following behaviour is a *prerequisite* for economic calculation – a necessary condition for the economic way of thinking that soft rational choice posits. Economic choice as we normally think of it can happen only in a stable and predictable world in which most of the cognitive load is being carried by rules and routines. Joseph Schumpeter recognized this long ago. He assailed the idea that, because of habit and custom, economic behaviour is culturally relative, insisting that 'we can depend upon it that the peasant sells his calf just as cunningly and egotistically as the stock exchange member his portfolio of shares'. But, as Schumpeter is quick to add, 'this holds good only where precedents without number have formed conduct through decades and, in fundamentals, through hundreds and thousands of years' (Schumpeter 1934: 80).

Of course, Schumpeter was far more interested in situations of innovation and structural uncertainty. In such situations, following specific and well-adapted rules is not only ineffective but likely quite dangerous. Ronald Heiner (1983) has argued that rule-following is precisely the appropriate response to situations of unpredictable change. Because of limited competencies, agents become unreliable in using their full repertoire of actions, and sometimes take the wrong action. Agents will do better by limiting their repertoires in the face of uncertainty. And, since their actions will vary less than those of agents who attempt to wield a full repertoire and try to choose the best action on a case-by-case basis, these agents will appear to be rule-followers. Heiner's theory accords with the well-known findings of Robert Axelrod (1984), who discovered that, in a computerized round-robin tournament, those programs did better in surviving a repeated prisoners' dilemma situation that followed relatively simple solution rules rather than attempting to optimize or to behave in a complex way. Using a model based on Heiner's, I have tried to show (Langlois 1986a) that agents are likely to follow rules *both* in situations of uncertainty *and* in situations of routine. It will also be the case that the kinds of rules followed in routine situations will be different from those followed under uncertainty. In routine situations, the agent's actions will be highly specialized and concrete, whereas under uncertainty the rules will be more general and abstract in order to be more likely to be appropriate in a wide range of possible future states (Langlois 1986a).

One alternative to rule-following is conscious deliberation. But in truly novel situations, it is generally impossible to survey exhaustively all possible consequences of a decision.

> Here the success of everything depends on intuition, the capacity of seeing things in a way which afterwards proves to be true, even though it cannot be established at the moment, and of grasping the essential fact, discarding the unessential, even though one can give no account of the principles by which this is done.
>
> (Schumpeter 1934: 85)

This kind of intuition Schumpeter associated with the figure of the entrepreneur, as did Frank Knight, who spoke about the entrepreneur's faculty of judgement, by which he meant the ability to assess a person or a situation under conditions of genuine uncertainty (Langlois and Cosgel 1993).

If much of economic action thus consists in either the following of rules or the use of non-deliberative cognitive processes, are we left to believe that much of decision making is irrational – or at best arational? This is so only if our definition of rationality constrains us to see 'rational' as meaning the successful solution of a process of optimization. Rule following and entrepreneurial judgement are rational modes of decision making, even in Popper's sense. The sociologist James Coleman (1990) applied the term 'rational' to Max Weber's category of charismatic authority, a concept that underlies Schumpeter's theory of entrepreneurship (Langlois 1998). In a world in which all the rules are changing, following a charismatic figure is a way of solving an otherwise intractable problem of coordination. They are all ways of doing the best we can with what we have – and, indeed, of doing far better than we would if all we did was deliberate consciously.

RICHARD N. LANGLOIS
THE UNIVERSITY OF CONNECTICUT

Further reading

(References cited in the text marked *)

* Axelrod, R. (1984) *The Evolution of Cooperation*, New York: Basic Books. (A computer simulation shows how cooperation can emerge spontaneously.)
* Berger, P. and T. Luckmann. (1966) *The Social Construction of Reality*, New York: Doubleday. (Extends the sociology of Alfred Schütz; helped inspire the 'social constructivism' movement.)
* Burrell, D.B. (1967) 'Obeying rules and following instructions', in F.J. Crosson and K.M. Sayre (eds) *Philosophy and Cybernetics*, South Bend: University of Notre Dame Press. (Makes the distinction between rules as constraints and rules as causes of action.)
* Caldwell, B.J. (1994) 'Situational analysis', manuscript, University of North Carolina-Greensboro. To appear in J. Davis, D. Wade Hands and Uskali Mäki (eds) (1998) *Handbook of Economic Methodology*, Aldershot: Edward Elgar. (Excellent survey of situational analysis.)
* Choi, Y.B. (1993) *Paradigms and Conventions*, Ann Arbor: University of Michigan Press. (Proposes a novel theory of behaviour.)
* Coleman, J.S. (1990) 'Rational organization', *Rationality and Society* 2 (1): 94–105. (Argues for the rationality of what Max Weber called 'charismatic' authority.)
* Cosmides, L. and J. Tooby (1994) 'Better than rational: evolutionary psychology and the invisible hand', *American Economic Review* 84 (2): 327–32. (An exposition of evolutionary psychology aimed at economists.)
* Denzau, A.T. and C. Douglass North (1994) 'Shared mental models: ideologies and institutions', *Kyklos* 47 (1): 1–13. (An exploration of the role of ideas in institutions.)
* Dreyfus, H.L. (1979) *What Computers Can't Do: The Limits of Artificial Intelligence*, rev edn, New York: Harper Colophon. (A phenomenological critique of artificial intelligence scholarship.)

* Dreyfus, H.L., and S.L. Dreyfus (1986) *Mind over Machine: the Power of Human Intuition and Expertise in the Era of the Computer*, New York: Free Press. (A phenomenological critique of artificial intelligence scholarship.)
* Eggertsson, T. (1990) *Economic Behaviour and Institutions: Principles of Neoinstitutional Economics*, New York: Cambridge University Press. (The theory of institutions from a neoclassical perspective.)
* Friedman, M. (1953) 'The methodology of positive economics', in M. Friedman *Essays on Positive Economics*, Chicago: University of Chicago Press. (Friedman's famous methodological broadside: assumptions needn't be realistic.)
* Heckathorn, D.D. (1991) 'Extensions of the prisoner's dilemma paradigm: the altruist's dilemma and group solidarity', *Sociological Theory* 9: 34–52. (Shows that norms can generate 'too much' solidarity.)
* Heiner, R.A. (1983) 'The origin of predictable behaviour', *American Economic Review* 73 (4): 560–95. (Derives rule-following behaviour from the limited reliability of human action.)
* Heyne, P. (1999) *The Economic Way of Thinking*, 9th edn, Englewood Cliffs: Prentice-Hall. (Accessible introduction to economic reasoning.)
* Holland, J.H., K.J. Holyoak, R.E. Nisbett and P.R. Thagard (1986) *Induction: Processes of Inference, Learning and Discovery*, Cambridge: MIT Press. (Oft-cited account of cognition from a computer-science perspective.)
* Kirman, A.P. (1992) 'Whom or what does the representative individual represent?' *Journal of Economic Perspectives* 6 (2): 117–36. (Survey of the concept of representative agent.)
* Koppl, R.G. and R.N. Langlois (1994) 'When do ideas matter? A study in the natural selection of social games', *Advances in Austrian Economics* 1: 81–104. (An expertise model of human action.)
* Lane, D., F. Malerba, R. Maxfield and L. Orsenigo (1996) 'Choice and action', *Journal of Evolutionary Economics* 6: 43–76. (A manifesto for the expertise view of economic behaviour.)
* Langlois, R.N. (1984) 'Internal organization in a dynamic context: some theoretical considerations', in M. Jussawalla and H. Ebenfield (eds) *Communication and Information Economics: New Perspectives*, Amsterdam: North-Holland, pp. 23–49. (Proposes the distinction between structural and parametric uncertainty.)
* Langlois, R.N. (1986a) 'Coherence and flexibility: social institutions in a world of radical uncertainty', in Israel Kirzner (ed.) *Subjectivism, Intelligibility, and Economic Understanding: Essays in Honor of the Eightieth Birthday of Ludwig Lachmann*, New York: New York University Press, pp. 171–91. (An extension of Heiner's model (q. v.).)
* Langlois, R.N. (1986b) 'Rationality, institutions, and explanation', in R.N. Langlois (ed.) *Economics as a Process: Essays in the New Institutional Economics*, New York: Cambridge University Press, pp. 225–55. (Argues for an evolutionary account of institutions.)
* Langlois, R.N. (1990) 'Bounded rationality and behaviouralism: a clarification and critique', *Journal of Institutional and Theoretical Economics* 146 (4): 691–5. (A perspective on Simon's concept of bounded rationality.)
* Langlois, R.N. (1992) 'Orders and organizations: toward an Austrian theory of social institutions', in B. Caldwell and S. Böhm (eds) *Austrian Economics: Tensions and New Directions*, Dordrecht: Kluwer Academic Publishers. (A survey of the economics of institutions.)
* Langlois, R.N. (1998) 'Personal capitalism as charismatic authority: the organizational economics of a Weberian concept', *Industrial and Corporate Change* 7: 195–214. (Uses Max Weber to understand Schumpeter.)
* Langlois, R.N. and M.M. Cosgel. (1993) 'Frank Knight on risk, uncertainty, and the firm: a new interpretation', *Economic Inquiry* 31: 456–65. (An exposition and reinterpretation of Knight's views on uncertainty.)
* Langlois, R.N. and L. Csontos (1993) 'Optimization, rule following, and the methodology of situational analysis', in U. Mäki, B. Gustafsson and C. Knudsen (eds) *Rationality, Institutions, and Economic Methodology*, London: Routledge. (Argues for the compatibility of rule-following and situational analysis.)
* Latsis, S.J. (1976) 'A research programme in economics', in S.J. Latsis (ed.) *Method and Appraisal in Economics*, Cambridge: Cambridge University Press. (A critique of neo-classical economics from a methodological perspective.)
Loasby, B.J. (1976) *Choice, Complexity, and Ignorance*, Cambridge: Cambridge University Press. (Insightful and wide-ranging treatise on decision making.)
* Nelson, R.R., and S.G. Winter (1982) *An Evolutionary Theory of Economic Change*, Cambridge: The Belknap Press of Harvard University Press. (Classic reformulation of economics in evolutionary terms; introduces the concept of 'routines'.)
North, C. Douglass (1990) *Institutions, Institutional Change and Economic Performance*, New York: Cambridge University Press. (

Major contribution to the economics of institutions by a Nobel Laureate.)
* Pelikan, P. (1992) 'The dynamics of economic systems, or how to transform a failed socialist economy', *Journal of Evolutionary Economics* 2 (1): 39–63. (Makes the distinction between rules as constraints and rules as causes of action.)
* Polanyi, M. (1958) *Personal Knowledge*, Chicago: University of Chicago Press. (Articulates the concept of tacit knowledge.)
* Popper, K.R. (1966) *The Open Society and Its Enemies*, vol. II, 2nd edn, Princeton: Princeton University Press. (Popper's critique of Hegel and Marx.)
* Popper, K.R. (1967) 'La Rationalité et le Statut du Principe de Rationalité', in E.M. Claassen (ed.) *Les Fondements Philosophiques des Systèmes Economiques*, Paris: Payot. (Exposition of the rationality principle.)
* Robbins, L. (1932) *An Essay on the Nature and Significance of Economic Science*, London: Macmillan. (Classic reformulation of economics as a logical problem of allocation.)
* Rowe, N. (1989) *Rules and Institutions*, Ann Arbor: University of Michigan Press. (A game theory-based account of institutions.)
* Schotter, A. (1981) *The Economic Theory of Social Institutions*, New York: Cambridge University Press. (A game theory-based account of institutions.)
* Schumpeter, J.A. (1934) *The Theory of Economic Development*, Cambridge: Harvard University Press. (Schumpeter's classic account of the role of the entrepreneur in economic growth.)
* Schütz, A. (1943) 'The problem of rationality in the social world', *Economica* N.S. 10: 130–49. (An argument for means–ends rationality in 'pure' economic theory.)
* Schütz, A. and T. Luckmann (1973) *The Structures of the Life-World*, trans. R.M. Zaner and H.T. Engelhardt, Jr. Evanston, Ill.: Northwestern University Press. (An exposition of the Schützian sociology of institutions.)
* Sen, A.K. (1976) 'Rational fools: a critique of the behavioural foundations of economic theory', *Philosophy and Public Affairs* 6: 317–44. (Classic critique of neo-classical rationality from a Nobel Laureate.)
* Simon, H.A. (1955) 'A behavioural model of rational choice', *Quarterly Journal of Economics* 69: 99–118. (The 'satisficing' model of behaviour.)
* Simon, H.A. (1959) 'Theories of decision-making in economics and behavioural science', *American Economic Review* 49: 253–83. (Bounded rationality and its alternatives.)
* Smith, A. (1976a) *An Enquiry into the Nature and Causes of the Wealth of Nations*, Glasgow edn, Oxford: Clarendon Press. (A founding document of economics, it has lost no relevance over the years.)
  Smith, A. (1976b) *The Theory of Moral Sentiments*, Indianapolis: Liberty Classics. (Smith's treatise on moral philosophy.)
* Sugden, R. (1986) *The Economics of Rights, Cooperation, and Welfare*, Oxford, Basil Blackwell. (A game theory-based account of institutions.)
* Vanberg, V. (1993) 'Rational choice, rule-following, and institutions – an evolutionary perspective', in U. Mäki, B. Gustafsson and C. Knudsen (eds) *Rationality, Institutions, and Economic Methodology*, London: Routledge. (An argument in favour of the rule-following model.)
* Vanberg, V. (1994) *Rules and Choice in Economics*, London: Routledge. (An argument in favour of the rule-following model.)
* Whitehead, A.N. (1911) *An Introduction to Mathematics*, New York: Henry Holt and Company. (Insights on the human mind as well as on mathematics.)

See also: FRIEDMAN, M.; GROWTH OF THE FIRM AND NETWORKING; INSTITUTIONAL ECONOMICS; MARSHALL, A.; SIMON, H.A.; SMITH, A.

Trust

1 Notions of trust
2 Sources of trust
3 Measuring trust
4 Conclusions

Overview

The increasing interest in trust in the economics and business literature is part of a more general resurgence of interest in the social and institutional determinants of economic activity and performance. A basic theme in this literature is that trust plays an important role in promoting and sustaining economic exchange in situations characterized by some form of uncertainty. Arrow (1972), for example, has argued that trust is an element of any transaction conducted over time, such as when goods or services are provided in exchange for future payment. Within organizational research, it has been argued that trust lowers transactions costs and promotes risky investments in transaction-specific assets (Lorenz 1988; Nooteboom 1993). Fukuyama (1995) has identified trust as a key factor in national economic performance, and a growing empirical literature drawing on survey-based measures of trust has sought to confirm this hypothesis (Knack and Keefer 1997; La Porta et al. 1997).

Both individuals and institutions may be the object of one's trust. Trust is commonly defined as a belief concerning the likely behaviour of an individual, organization or institution that matters for the trustor's decision making. For example, one may have to decide whether to place a sum of money in a financial institution which runs the risk of going bankrupt. Or, you may have to decide whether to buy a used car which could turn out to be a lemon. Both of these situations are characterized by the fact that the trustee's behaviour matters for the actions of the trustor and that the trustor's actions have to be made prior to or independently of the possibility of monitoring the behaviour of the trustee (Gambetta 1988; Luhmann 1988).

As the above references to trust directed to either individuals or to society's institutions suggest, one finds multiple notions of trust in the literature. Corresponding to these different ideas about what trust amounts to, one finds different approaches to analysing the sources of trust. Different notions of trust in turn pose different problems of measurement in order to make trust an operational concept. These various issues are taken up in the sections below.

1 Notions of trust

One of the most common distinctions made in the literature is that between 'personal trust' and 'system trust'. This distinction is associated with the work of Luhmann (1979) and has been developed by Giddens (1990) in his work on modernity. The distinction concerns the object of trust rather than its sources, with personal trust referring to trust in a particular individual or group of individuals, while system trust designates trust in societal systems such as the legal system or the banking system. Personal trust entails a belief in the trustworthiness of an individual or group of individuals, while system trust implies no such belief. That is to say, one's trust in the banking system or the legal system transcends interpersonal experience or face-to-face relations. It does not necessarily imply that one trusts the individuals who constitute these systems. This raises the question of the foundations for such beliefs, a point returned to below.

In the organizational literature, there is a tendency to conflate inter-organizational trust with interpersonal trust. The quality of the relationship between a subcontractor and a client or between two firms engaged in a technological alliance is often discussed in the same terms as the quality of a relationship between an individual buyer and seller on the market. One can attempt to provide a microfoundation for this form of trust by drawing on

Livet and Reynaud's (1998) notion of 'organizational trust', which they define as a form of trust that depends on the members of a group involved in some collective endeavour holding the 'reasonable' belief that each is implicitly committed to it. Extended to inter-firm relations, this would imply, as Sako (1998) has suggested, that inter-organizational trust depends on multiple channels of communication being established between the two organizations at various functional levels. For extremely large organizations operating over large geographical spaces, however, it seems implausible that this condition could be respected. This suggests, much as Sydow (1998) has argued, that the notion of impersonal or system trust may provide a better starting point for understanding the forms of trust that link organizations.

A key issue raised in the literature on modernity is whether in technologically advanced societies there is a tendency for system trust to replace personal trust. This idea is often associated with Giddens (1990), who argues that impersonal forms of trust emerge in the presence of abstract systems where relations are 'disembedded' or lifted out from their local contexts and restructured across indefinite spans of time and space. It is also possible to read Luhmann's (1979) discussion of how system trust underwrites the development of personal trust as supporting this view concerning the evolution of trust in modern society.

The literature offers a number of useful distinctions concerning the properties of personal forms of trust (see Lazaric and Lorenz (1998) for a more complete review). One basic property is the distinction between 'intentions trust' and 'competence trust' (Sako 1992). The former refers to an individual's beliefs concerning the possible opportunism of another and more generally to questions of honesty and to whether explicit or implicit commitments will be respected. The latter form refers to trust in another person's ability to undertake a task or to fulfil a commitment, irrespective of that person's intentions. Intentions trust can be taken to signify that the trustor has formed a belief concerning the trustee's interests and the degree to which their relationship is marked by incentives alignment problems, while competence trust does not imply that any such judgement has been made.

Another key distinction is that between 'generalized trust' and 'person-specific trust'. The former notion of trust, developed especially in the literature on social capital, refers to the trust one holds for people in general about whom one has no specific knowledge. The latter form refers to the trust one may hold for an identified individual about whom one has knowledge, based either on one's past experience in dealing with that individual or on information provided by some trusted third party. An issue raised in the social capital literature is whether strong forms of inter-personal trust act to prevent the development of the more diffuse and impersonal forms of trust that support economic exchange in advanced economies. For example, Fukuyama (1995) in his book on trust and economic performance argues that strong family or group-based ties restrict the development of trust beyond the confines of the family or the group. Yamagishi (1988) and Yamagishi et al. (1998) draw on this distinction to account for the counterintuitive experimental finding that Japanese society, though characterized by the prevalence of strong social ties, produces less general trust than US society, where social and interpersonal ties are weaker.

2 Sources of trust

In accounting for trust or its absence, the literature focuses primarily on the question of personal forms of trust. One of the most common distinctions made is between trust based on values or norms and trust based on a calculation of one's self-interest. As regards norm-based trust, it is important to point out that the argument is not that norms directly produce trust, understood as a belief. Rather, norms are thought to produce trustworthiness understood as certain types of behaviour, such as behaving honestly in one's commercial dealings. The trust one may hold for another is then seen to be dependent on what one knows about that person's norms and values. Thus, it is quite possible for a trustworthy individual to distrust and to decide not to enter into a transaction with another because of what is known about his or her norms or values. Similarly, it is quite possible for an untrustworthy individual to trust and to seek to enter into relations of exchange with those who are thought to be trustworthy. On this account the amount of trust, and hence cooperative exchange, displayed by a community will depend on how widely diffused are norms prescribing trustworthy forms of behaviour.

The calculative view of trust, on the other hand, would argue that the trust one holds for another is based on what is known about the other person's interests, and in particular upon the evidence one has than the other person has an interest in behaving in a trustworthy manner. Pushed to an extreme, this argument reduces trust to rational choice in the form of maximizing one's expected utility. A popular tool used in developing this optimizing approach to trust is the theory of repeated games. Thus Kreps (1990), in his treatment of reputation effects, argues that trustworthy behaviour will be displayed in settings where the present discounted value of the future gains from acting in a way designed to maintain one's good reputation are greater than the one time gains achieved from reneging on one's commitments and thus losing one's good reputation. (Other authors adopting a rational choice approach to trust include: Axelrod 1984; Coleman 1990; Dasgupta 1988; Hardin 1998.)

The strongest methodological critique to this way of analysing trust has come from Williamson (1993), who argues that if trust simply amounts to calculation then it adds nothing important to the traditional analysis of decision making under risk (see WILLIAMSON, O.E.). Correspondingly, he argues that trust should be reserved for relations based on strong personal ties, such as ties of friendship, which on his account are of limited relevance to economic analysis. Regardless of what one thinks of Williamson's position on the importance of personal ties, there is clearly something valid in his critique. It is difficult to see, for example, that the notion of trust adds anything essential to Kreps' (1990) discussion of reputation effects in the context of the infinitely or finitely repeated prisoner's dilemma.

Arguably the strongest rebuttal to Williamson's stance is to argue that the notion of trust can usefully contribute to economic analysis in so far as one takes bounded rationality seriously and does not simply reduce it to subjective expected utility optimization in the face of risk, as Williamson (1993) implicitly does in arguing that individuals are farsighted and are able to anticipate changes in the environment. Bounded rationality, in the sense of truly unanticipated contingencies and limits on the possibility of calculating one's interests, creates a role for trust in an explanation for sustained cooperation in which a concern for one's self-interest is not absent (Lorenz 1993, 1999; Nooteboom 1993; Sabel 1992). Trust, on this account is a tentative judgement based on past experience and previous interactions, and it remains open to revision, based on what one discovers about another in an ongoing relationship.

Another set of distinctions that are often drawn upon in analysing the sources of trust are those proposed by Zucker (1986) between process-based, characteristic-based and institution-based trust. These distinctions focus on the mechanisms that produce trust rather than on the question of the rationality of trust. Process-based trust refers to trust derived from the knowledge one gains about another individual, either through repeated interactions or through information provided by trusted third parties. Characteristic-based trust refers to trust based on ascribed characteristics of an individual which cannot be produced at will, such as one's family ties, ethnicity or religious affiliation. Institution-based trust refers to the way formal institutions, such as systems of law, can promote trust between individuals independently of any personal knowledge based on direct interaction or otherwise.

Zucker's (1986) notion of institution-based trust, while focusing on the mechanisms which produce trust in interpersonal dealings, implicitly raises the question of system trust, or the trust one has in societal institutions, such as the legal system. For example, one's belief that an individual will live up to his or her contractual commitments may be shaped in part by how much confidence one has in the courts and the legal system. Moreover, in a manner that is complementary to Giddens (1990), Zucker (1986) argues that characteristic-based trust is in scarce supply in modern societies, which are characterized by an increasing reliance on institution-based trust, given that dealings go beyond the boundaries of the group or family connections.

3 Measuring trust

Most empirical efforts to measure trust concern 'generalized trust' or the trust an individual may hold for another about whom he or she has no knowledge based on past interactions or reputation. Within the economics discipline, much of the interest in this form of trust has been fuelled by the debate on social capital and by the possibility of drawing on survey-based indicators of trust which can be entered into macroeconomic growth regressions in much the same manner as measures of human capital; key contributions include: La Porta *et al*. 1997; Knack and Keefer 1997; Zak and Knack 1998. A second type of empirical research is based on laboratory experiments, where small groups of subjects are confronted with decision making in the context of social dilemmas which pose the issue of trust; see, for example, Berg *et al.* 1995; Glaeser *et al.* 1999; Robin and Ruffieux 1999; Yamagishi 1988.

Survey work

The two principal survey sources drawn on in the social capital literature in order to measure trust are the World Values Survey (WVS) for cross-national comparisons and the General Social Survey (GSS) for studies focusing on the USA. The WVS, which provides information on 29 market economies, is meant to be a random sample of between 500 and 3000 persons in each country, while the GSS has been administered 20 times in the USA since 1972 to a sample of between 1000 and 2000 persons (see Inglehart (1994) for a discussion of likely biases in the WVS sample frame). The question in the WVS and the GSS that is used to measure trust is: 'Generally speaking, would you say that most people can be trusted, or that you can't be too careful in dealing with people?' The standard trust indicator in empirical research is the percentage of the respondents replying that 'most people can be trusted'.

Based on this measure, there are significant variations in the level of measured trust across the countries surveyed in the WVS, ranging from a high of about 60 per cent in Norway to a low of about 7 per cent in Brazil. Amongst OECD countries, France, with a score of about 25 per cent, ranks lowest on the trust scale (Knack and Keefer 1997: 1285). The GSS survey indicates considerable variation across states in the USA, with high values of trust being concentrated in the north/northwest and the lowest values being found in the southeast (Alesina and Ferrara 2000: 33).

In addition to measuring the level of generalized trust, this literature seeks to assess its determinants, its consequences for economic performance and its relation to measures of confidence in societal institutions, such as the educational system or the legal system. There is not sufficient space here to systematically review this literature and only certain key results will be highlighted.

A number of studies find a positive and significant relationship between generalized trust and growth in per capita income using a Barro (1991) type specification controlling for education and the price of investment goods. (See, however, the study by Helliwell (1996) which shows that trust is significantly negatively related to productivity growth in a sample of 17 OECD countries.) Knack and Keefer (1997: 1260) find that the impact of trust on growth in per capita income is higher in poorer countries, which they interpret as supporting the view that trust is more essential for economic growth in countries where contract enforcement mechanisms are poorly developed and where access to formal sources of credit is limited. They also present regression results showing a positive and significant relation between trust and levels of output per worker and levels of physical and human capital per worker. They find no significant relation between trust and investment's share of GDP.

Knack and Keefer's (1997) results also show that there is a positive relationship between trust and a synthetic measure of confidence in society's institutions. The latter measure is based on responses in the WVS to how much confidence respondents have in their country's legal system, education system, police and civil service. If we take this synthetic measure as an indicator of respondents' levels of 'system trust', then the results suggest a positive link between the two types of trust.

As regards the determinants of generalized trust, the literature drawing on the GSS for the United States has been largely concerned with the relation between respondents' individual characteristics and trust, while the internationally comparative research has focused as well on the relationship between trust and certain structural characteristics of the nation under consideration. A key finding based on the GSS surveys is that measured trust is declining for later age cohorts. This supports Putnam's (1995) contention that social capital is declining in the USA. Other 'stylized facts' from this research are that generalized trust increases with income and education and is lower among racial minorities (Glaeser *et al.* 1999). Alesina and La Ferrara (2000) also report that women trust less in the USA. Studies based on the WVS show no significant relation between the age cohort and trust for most countries, while showing a more pervasive positive relationship between trust and schooling and between trust and income (Knack and Keefer 1997).

In terms of structural determinants, one of the key concerns of this literature is to explore the relation between generalized trust and measures of economic and religious polarization. Two of the more robust results are that trust is negatively correlated with a country's gini coefficient and that trust is lower in countries with a 'dominant hierarchical religion' as measured by the percentage of the population that is Catholic, Orthodox Christian or Moslem (La Porta *et al.* 1997). In a cross-state comparison of the USA, Alesina and La Ferrara (2000) similarly find a negative relation between trust and the gini coefficient. They find that the effect of religious affiliation on trust is insignificant and conclude 'that it is not the religious beliefs per se but the organized forms of religion in different parts of the world that may influence different social behavior'.

Experimental work

The most common design used in experimental research on trust is the 'investment game' associated with the work of Berg *et al.* (1995). The basic idea in this game is to divide subjects between two populations, senders and recipients. Each sender is allocated a sum of money and is asked to send some portion of it to an anonymous recipient. The experimenter then doubles or perhaps triples the amount sent and the recipient is asked to return some portion of the increased amount back to the anonymous sender. Sending money is interpreted as a show of trust on the part of the sender, while returning money is interpreted as an exhibition of trustworthiness or reciprocity on the part of the recipient.

One of the issues addressed in the experimental literature is whether observed behaviour conforms to the behaviour predicted by rational choice theory. Berg *et al.* (1995), in an experiment using a group of University of Minnesota undergraduates as subjects, reject the unique Nash equilibrium prediction for this game of sending zero money, since the large majority of their subjects send some. The authors conclude that trust is an economic primitive which should be included as part of the rational choice paradigm.

By relaxing the anonymity condition between sender and recipient, Glaeser *et al.* (1999) use a similar experimental design on a population of Harvard University undergraduates in order to assess how variations in social connections and certain ascribed characteristics influence trusting behaviour. Their results are partially asymmetric as regards trust and trustworthiness. The amount of trust (i.e. the amount of money sent) rises significantly with the amount of time the two individuals have known each other, while the effects of matching people with different nationalities or race, though negative, are not statistically significant. As regards trustworthiness, not only are the effects of the length of time the two subjects have known each other significant, but both racial and national effects are also sizeable and significant. Overall the authors conclude that racial or national heterogeneity may decrease trust in social groups. This result is consistent with a finding based on the GSS surveys that regions in the USA marked by greater racial heterogeneity are characterized by lower levels of generalized trust. This would appear to be contrary to the argument of Zucker (1986) that characteristic-based trust is of limited importance in modern societies.

4 Conclusions

Research over the past decade has considerably improved our understanding of trust and its relation to economic exchange and performance. Despite this, the literature remains marked by problems of conceptual clarity, while efforts to empirically measure trust are open to a number of criticisms. On the conceptual level, perhaps the most serious problem is the divide that exists between those, such as Zucker (1986) or Knack (2000), who argue that any factor serving to reduce uncertainty in economic exchange can be considered to be a source of trust, and those, such as Berg et al. (1995), who would argue that trust is what remains after eliminating the role of such factors as reputation in repeated interactions, contractual pre-commitments and possible threats of punishment in sustaining cooperation. Where the former would see trust at work, the latter would see behaviour motivated either by farsighted calculation or by the exercise of power.

In terms of accounting for trust, the sources of 'system trust', or the trust that individuals may place in such institutions as the public service or the legal system, remain poorly understood. While in the case of personal trust one may plausibly argue that one places one's trust in another because of what one knows about the other's interests or values, it should be obvious that this explanation cannot hold for complex systems, such as the legal system, or even for large and possibly geographically dispersed organizations. Societal institutions or large organizations are not unitary entities with well-defined interests or values, and their size and complexity preclude that any individual might have a clear understanding of the routines and operating procedures which determine their behaviour. One the other hand, as Hardin (1998) has argued, few would be satisfied with an account of trust in institutions that simply reduces it to a prediction of future behaviour based on induction from past behaviour. Gaining a better understanding of the nature and sources of system trust remains one of the key challenges facing those committed to the trust research agenda.

Survey-based empirical work, while making plausible the claim that trust is positively correlated to economic performance, has made little progress in identifying the mechanisms that underlie this relation. Moreover, this research is marred by the use of ambiguous indicators of trust. In the case of the WVS and GSS surveys, for example, it is not at all clear whether in responding positively to the question, 'would you say that most people can be trusted?' respondents are referring to most people they regularly transact with or to a wider population. Experimental work, by controlling what subjects know about each other, arguably provides superior measures of trust and trustworthiness. For the moment, however, this work has been confined to analysing the behaviour of a few unrepresentative populations of university students in controlled laboratory settings and its relevance to the everyday behaviour of people in general must remain in doubt.

In conclusion, while much progress has been made in analysing the determinants and consequences of trust, there is a need for greater conceptual clarity. In particular, there is a need for clarity on whether the use of legal sanctions or the exercise of power is compatible with a trusting relationship. Resolving such ambiguities is a necessary condition for defining appropriate measures for empirical research on trust. It is only through addressing such outstanding problems that the notion of trust will come to be generally recognized as having an important role to play in the analysis of economic exchange and business activity.

EDWARD LORENZ
CENTRE D'ETUDES DE L'EMPLOI,
NOISY-LE-GRAND, FRANCE

Further reading

(References cited in the text marked *)

* Alesina A. and E. La Ferrara (2000) 'The determinants of trust', NBER Working Paper No. 7621. (This text shows how individual and community characteristics influence how much people trust using data drawn from US localities.)
* Arrow, K. (1972) 'Gifts and exchange' *Philosophy and Public Affairs* 1: 343–62. (In this paper

Arrow introduces the notion of trust into his analysis of uncertainty.)

* Axelrod, R. (1984) *The Evolution of Cooperation*, New York: Basic Books. (A path-breaking attempt to use basic game theoretic concepts to explain the success and failure of cooperation.)

* Barro, R. (1991) 'Economic growth in a cross section of countries', *Quarterly Journal of Economics*, 106: 407–44. (Presents Barro's standard growth specification controlling for education and the price of investment goods.)

* Berg, J., J. Dickhaut and K. McCabe (1995) 'Trust, reciprocity, and social history', *Games and Economic Behavior* 10: 122–42. (The authors develop an experiment to study trust and reciprocity in an investment setting.)

* Coleman, J. (1990) *Foundations of Social Theory*, Cambridge MA: Harvard University Press. (Coleman is one of the major proponents of the rational choice approach to trust.)

* Dasgupta, P. (1988) 'Trust as a commodity', in D. Gambetta (ed.) *Trust: Making and Breaking Cooperative Relations*, Oxford: Basil Blackwell, 49–72. (Applies game theoretic concepts to the analysis of trust in economic exchange.)

* Fukuyama, F. (1995) *Trust: The Social Virtues and the Creation of Prosperity*, New York: Free Press. (This study links trust and networks to differences in national economic performance.)

* Gambetta, D. (1988) 'Can we trust trust?' in D. Gambetta (ed.) *Trust: Making and Breaking Cooperative Relations*, Oxford: Basil Blackwell, 213–38. (A multi-disciplinary volume which has done much to put trust on the research agenda in the social sciences.)

* Giddens, A. (1990) *The Consequences of Modernity*, Cambridge: Polity Press. (Links trust in systems to the 'disembedding' of social relations from local contexts in modern society.)

* Glaeser, E., D. Laibson, J. Sceinkman and C. Soutter (1999) 'What is social capital? the determinants of trust and trustworthiness', NBER Working Paper No. 7216. (Presents two experiments analysing trust and social capital using a sample of Harvard undergraduates.)

* Hardin, R. (1998) 'Trust in government', in V. Braithwaite and M. Levi (ed.) *Trust and Governance*, New York: Russel Sage Foundation, 927. (Considers the limits of a rational choice framework for explaining trust in societal institutions.)

* Helliwell, J. (1996) 'Economic growth and social capital in Asia', NBER Working Paper No. 5470. (This study purports to show that trust is negatively related to productivity growth in a sample of OECD countries.)

* Inglehart, R. (1994) *Codebook for World Values Surveys*, Ann Arbor, MI: Institute for Social Research. (Describes the likely biases in the World Value Survey sample frame.)

* Knack, S. (2000) 'Trust, associational life and economic performance', The World Bank, April. (Presents empirical evidence on trust and economic performance using a 25-nation OECD sample.)

* Knack, S. and P. Keefer (1997) 'Does social capital have an economic payoff? A cross-country investigation', *Quarterly Journal of Economics* 112: 1251–88. (Shows that trust and civic norms are stronger in nations with higher and more equal income and with better-educated and ethnically homogeneous populations.)

* Kreps, D. (1990) 'Corporate culture and economic theory', in J. Alt and K. Shepsle (eds) *Perspectives on Positive Political Economy*, New York: Cambridge University Press, 90–144. (Draws on the theory of repeated games to analyse the role of trust in organizations.)

* La Porta, R., F. Lopez-de-Salanes, A. Shleifer, and R. Vishny (1997) 'Trust in large organisations' *American Economic Review Papers and Proceedings* 87: 333–8. (Tests the proposition that trust promotes cooperation, especially in large organizations, using data from the World Value Survey.)

* Lazaric, N. and E. Lorenz (1998) 'The learning dynamics of trust, reputation and confidence', in N. Lazaric and E. Lorenz (eds) *Trust and Economic Learning*, Cheltenham: Edward Elgar Press, 1–22. (Provides a critical overview of recent work on trust and economic cooperation.)

* Livet, P. and B. Reynaud (1998) 'Organisational trust, learning and implicit commitments', in Lazaric, N. and E. Lorenz (eds) *Trust and Economic Learning*, Cheltenham: Edward Elgar Press, 266–84. (Provides a general definition of organizational trust based on the notion of 'reasonable' implicit commitments.)

* Lorenz, E. (1988) 'Neither friends nor strangers: informal networks of subcontracting in French industry', in D. Gambetta (ed.) *Trust: Making and Breaking Cooperative Relations*, Oxford: Basil Blackwell, 194–210. (Draws on case study material to analyse the role of trust in inter-firm relations.)

* Lorenz, E. (1993) 'Flexible production systems and the social construction of trust', *Politics and Society* 21 (3): 307–24. (Contrasts various approaches to explaining trust in economic relations.)

* Lorenz, E. (1999) 'Trust, contract and economic cooperation', *The Cambridge Journal of Economics* 3: 301–15. (Links trust to uncertainty

and presents a critique of the treatment of uncertainty in the incomplete contracts literature.)
* Luhmann, N. (1979) *Trust and Power*, Chichester: John Wiley. (This path-breaking work develops Luhmann's classic distinction between personal and system trust.)
* Luhmann, N. (1988) 'Familiarity, confidence, trust: problems and alternatives', in D. Gambetta (ed.) *Trust: Making and Breaking Cooperative Relations*, Oxford: Basil Blackwell, 94–107. (Distinguishes the concepts of familiarity, confidence and trust.)
* Nooteboom, B. (1993) 'Networks and transactions: do they connect?' in J. Groenewegen (ed.) *Dynamics of the Firm*, Aldershot: Edward Elgar Press, 9–26. (Argues that trust lowers transaction costs and promotes risky investments.)
* Putnam, R. (1995) 'Tuning in, tuning out: the strange disappearance of social capital in America', *PS: Political Science and Politics* 28 (4): 664–83. (Presents Putnam's view that social capital is declining in the USA.)
* Robin, S. and B. Ruffieux (1999) 'L'Economiste au Fond du Puits: L'Expérimentation de la Confiance', in C. Thuderoz, V. Mangematin and D. Harrison (eds) *La Confiance: Approches Economiques et Sociologiques*, Paris: Gaëtan Morin Editeur. (Presents the results of an experiment based on the investment game developed by Berg et al. (1995).)
* Sabel, C. (1992) 'Studied trust: building new forms of cooperation in a volatile economy', in F. Pyke and W. Sengenberger (eds) *Industrial Districts and Local Economic Regeneration*, Geneva: IILS, 215–50. (Argues for a link between social amnesia and trust in communities.)
* Sako, M. (1992) *Prices, Quality and Trust: Inter-firm Relations in Britain and Japan*, Cambridge: Cambridge University Press. (Compares the role of trust in inter-firm relations in Japan and the UK.)
* Sako, M. (1998) 'The information requirements of trust in supplier relations: evidence from Japan, Europe and the United States', in N. Lazaric and E. Lorenz (eds) *Trust and Economic Learning*, Cheltenham: Edward Elgar Press, 23–47. (Provides empirical evidence on the nature of trust in the US, UK and Japanese auto parts industries.)
* Sydow, J. (1998) 'Understanding the constitution of interorganizational trust', in C. Lane and R. Bachmann (eds) *Trust Within and Between Organizations*, Oxford: Oxford University Press, 31–63. (Examines the role of system trust in inter-firm relations.)
* Williamson, O.E. (1993) 'Calculativeness, Trust and economic organization', *Journal of Law and Economics* 36: 453–86. (Argues against the use of the concept of trust in economic analysis.)
* Yamagishi, T. (1988) 'The provision of a sanctioning system in the United States and Japan', *Social Psychology Quarterly* 51: 265–71. (Presents the results of a cross-societal experiment comparing cooperative tendencies in social dilemmas.)
* Yamagishi, T., K. Cook and M. Watabe (1998) 'Uncertainty, Trust and commitment formation in the United States and Japan', *American Journal of Sociology* 1: 165–94. (Develops the distinction between social commitment and trust based on experiments performed in the USA and Japan.)
* Zak, P. and S. Knack (1998) 'Trust and growth', IRIS Center Working Paper No. 219. (Presents empirical evidence showing that trust is positively associated with investment rates and growth in per capita income.)
* Zucker, L. (1986) 'Production of trust: institutional sources of economic structure, 1840–1920', *Research in Organizational Behavior* 8, 53–111. (Develops Zucker's classic distinctions between process-based, characteristic-based and institution-based trust.)

See also: EMPLOYMENT RELATIONS; EVOLUTIONARY THEORIES OF THE FIRM; GROWTH OF THE FIRM AND NETWORKING; INDUSTRIAL AND LABOUR RELATIONS

Monetarism

1. The development of monetarism
2. Historical monetarism
3. Modern monetarism
4. North American monetarism
5. British monetarism
6. International monetarism
7. New classical monetarism
8. The political economy of monetarism
9. Virtual monetarism

Overview

Monetarism is a school of thought in which its members share the view that fluctuations in economic activity are largely governed by fluctuations in the stock of money. While the school of thought is broad enough to accommodate disagreements within its ranks with regard to the extent of the influence money has on economic activity, or even the appropriate definition of money that best satisfies the main proposition, the common factor that binds all of them is the belief that ultimately inflation is caused by excess growth in the money supply. This latter view derives from the 'quantity theory of money'. In its simplest form, it is asserted that a relationship exists between the level of national income (measured in current prices) and the stock of money. Consequently the rate of growth of national income (GNP, GDP, etc.) will be strongly correlated with the rate of growth of the stock of money. If it is additionally asserted that in the long run the real value of national income (national income adjusted for the general price level) grows at a stable rate, then the rate of growth of money in excess of the rate of growth of real national income will result in inflation. In other words, an increase in the money supply will at first benefit economic activity by raising the level of income but over the longer period, as real income reverts to its historic rate of growth, the result is inflation. This view is encapsulated in the phrase 'inflation is caused by too much money chasing too few goods'.

Monetarism has gone through several incarnations. It has a long historical pedigree that strongly influenced pre-Keynesian economic thought. The influence of the monetarist school waned with the development of Keynesian economics. The label monetarism came even later – a term that was invented in the 1960s. It was Milton Friedman who in the 1950s restated the quantity theory as a theory of the demand for money. Monetarism became influential in the late 1960s and the decade of the 1970s, when inflation in the developed countries rose to double-digit figures. The British monetarist experiment of the 1980s was the closest that any economy has come to following a monetarist macroeconomic policy. Whether the experiment was a success or not is a topic for future historians. However, a key policy recommendation of monetarism is that low monetary growth is a necessary condition for low inflation. Monetary targets have been developed in many developed economies with this aim in mind. The history of monetary targeting has been mixed, but where it has been successful, as in Germany, the result has been a stable monetary environment and low inflation.

1 The development of monetarism

A formalization of the statement 'inflation is caused by too much money chasing too few goods' was set out by Professor Irving Fisher of Yale University in 1911. The total money value of transactions in an economy must by definition be the total money value of goods sold. This statement is decomposed into Fisher's 'Equation of Exchange'. If M measures the stock of money in circulation in a given period of time, V is the number of times it exchanges hands within the same time period, the product of these two terms must equal the current value of the number of transactions over the same period of time. The current value of transactions is the product of the total number of transactions, T, and the average price of each transaction, P. The equation of exchange is neatly expressed as:

$$MV = PT \qquad (1)$$

The term T represents every transaction that occurs in an economy and therefore the equation of exchange above simply states the truism that every transaction is matched by an exchange of money. The left-hand side of the equation is the stock of money times the number of times money changes hands. The central bank of a country usually produces a regular estimate of the stock of money, but T and P are special types of measures. The number of transactions does not take into account the differences between transactions of intermediate goods and transactions of final goods, or differences between capital transactions and transactions involving the use of capital goods (rents). However, the equation of exchange can also be expressed in terms of the familiar concept of national income, which represents the sum value of final goods (summing the value added at each stage of production).

An income version of the equation of exchange can be obtained by redefining velocity of circulation as the income velocity of exchange. Rather than the right hand side of the equation of exchange being written as PT it can be expressed as PY where Y is real national income/expenditure (real GDP). Thus the equation of exchange can be re-expressed in terms of an income version as:

$$MV' = PY \qquad (2)$$

An estimate of the general price index enables the demarcation of the total value of final national income/expenditure into its real component and price component. The total real value of income/expenditure over a given period of time will then be given by the current price value of income/expenditure (GDP) divided by the price level. This provides a measure of the real value of income/expenditure in terms of a base price level (GDP in constant prices). The income velocity of circulation V' is then defined as:

$$V' = \frac{PY}{M} \qquad (3)$$

Thus V' is not independently determined. The equation of exchange described as the quantity theory of money is not a theory in the real sense. It remains a truism. It is transformed into theory by introducing restrictions or behavioural propositions (an economic theory of how people and firms behave) that underpin each of the terms in the equation of exchange. In particular, the Classical economists of the nineteenth century and earlier periods assumed for simplicity that the level of real income is fixed at its full employment level or capacity level and that the income velocity of circulation is a constant. If these conditions hold, it follows that there is a one-for-one correspondence between changes in the money supply and changes in the price level.

The issue of causation implied in the statement that inflation is the result of 'too much money chasing too few goods' cannot be inferred even from the restricted version of the equation of exchange. The correspondence between prices and the money supply does not imply that the money supply causes inflation. The causation could just as easily run in the opposite direction.

The issue of behaviour and causation is clarified by examining the Cambridge cash-balance approach, which can be viewed as the British version of the quantity theory. The Cambridge version of the quantity theory developed as an oral tradition from the English economist Alfred Marshall (1842–1924) and was expressed by another Cambridge economist, A.C. Pigou in 1917. While Fisher's equation of exchange emphasized the transference of money between individuals in the process of exchange, the Cambridge version emphasized the holding of money by individuals.

The heart of the Cambridge theory is that people hold money for transaction purposes and that the principal determinant of the amount of money held is given by their income. From an economy-wide perspective this means that the aggregate demand for money is related to a nation's income. If the demand for money is denoted as M^d, then the economy-wide demand for money can be expressed as:

$$M^d = kPY \qquad (4)$$

where k represents some proportion. As a simplifying assumption the term k was taken to be a constant. However, at no time did the Cambridge economists believe that k was a constant in reality. Indeed Marshall expressed the view that it could vary with interest rates, and the size of the population. The constancy of k was purely an assumption of convenience. What was important about the formulation was that it represented a behavioural statement about individuals and firms demand for money. However, this formulation only represents one side of the market. The supply of money is also needed to move towards a theory of inflation that is consistent with monetarist thinking. In other words, the demand for money must be equated with the supply of money (M^s).

$$M^d = M^s \qquad (5)$$

The equilibrium condition above simply leaves the money supply to be determined. The Cambridge economists like many other classical economists were brought up on the 'gold standard', whereby the note issue by the Bank of England was backed by gold. This meant that the supply of money was largely determined by the amount of gold reserves and can therefore be taken as given or predetermined. Denoting the given stock of money as $\overline{M}$, the Cambridge version of the quantity theory of money can be expressed as:

$$\overline{M} = kPY$$

or more appropriately:

$$PY = \frac{1}{k}\overline{M} \qquad (6)$$

which indicates a clear direction of causation. If the stock of money is given by the stock of gold reserves an increase in gold reserves will increase the stock of money and national income will rise. If it is further assumed that the real value of national income is at the capacity level, then an increase in the money supply only increases the price level P. The link with the income version of the equation of exchange is also apparent. The income velocity of circulation V' in equation (2) is nothing but ($1/k$) in equation (6).

2 Historical monetarism

The connection between the debasement of the currency by governments, the finding of gold in the American continent and the violent movement of the general price level in the fifteenth, sixteenth and seventeenth centuries was made by many contemporary thinkers. However, it is generally accepted that Jean Bodin (1530–96) was the first to articulate the 'quantity theory of money'. It was published in his *Response* to the *Paradoxes sur le faict des Monnoyes* (1566) by M. de Malestroict and repeated in *Les six livres de la Republique* (1576). According to Bodin the universal rise in prices was largely the consequence of the increase in the supply of American gold and silver. Many thinkers developed the link between the circulation of currency (gold and silver) and prices throughout the sixteenth, seventeenth and eighteenth centuries. The concept of the velocity of circulation was developed by Sir William Petty (1623–87) and Richard Cantillon (1680–1734) who was the first to write of the *vitesse de la circulation*. John Locke (1632–1704) wrote on the practical necessity of holding cash and may be viewed as the founder of the cash-balance approach. However, monetarist writers especially point to the writings of the Scottish philosopher David Hume (1711–76) for the clearest exposition of the influence of money in the economy:

> though the high price of commodities be a necessary consequence of the encrease of gold and silver yet ... some time is required before the money circulates through the whole state ... it is only in this interval ... that the encreasing quantity that gold and silver is favourable to industry. When any quantity of money is imported into a nation, it is not at first disbursed into many hands, but is confined to the coffers of a few persons, who immediately seek to employ it to advantage ... they are thereby enabled to employ more workmen than formerly, who never dream of demanding higher wages, but are glad of employment from such good paymasters. If workmen become scarce, the manufacturer gives higher wages, but at first requires an encrease of labour; and this is willingly submitted to by the artisan, who can now eat and drink better, to compensate his additional toil and fatigue. He carries money

to market, where he finds every thing at the same price formerly, but returns with greater quantity and of better kinds, for the use of his family. The farmer and gardener, finding, that all their commodities are taken off, apply themselves with alacrity to the raising of more; and at the same time can afford to take better and more cloths from their tradesman, whose price is the same as formerly, and their industry only whetted by so much new gain. It is easy to trace the money in its progress through the whole commonwealth; where we shall find, that it must first quicken the diligence of every individual, before it encreases the price of labour.

David Hume, *Of Money*,
reprinted Chrystal (1990: 7–8)

What is especially noteworthy about this extract is the clear description of how money affects economic activity and the eventual inflationary outcome. The effect is through cash balances. The impact effect is on real output. The adjustment in prices comes only after a lag. The effect is only temporary until the costs of production, and thereby prices, adjust to the new money supply. The result of a temporary effect on real activity in response to a monetary expansion, with inflation to follow after is common to shades of monetarism.

3 Modern monetarism

Milton Friedman is generally considered to be the father of modern monetarism. From as far back as 1948, Friedman has been a consistent advocate of controlling the money supply as a means of stabilizing aggregate demand. In his emphasis on the importance of money he was following in the tradition of the Chicago school thought set out by Simons (1936) who had also advocated the control of the money supply to achieve a stable price level. Historical evidence supported the notion that changes in the money supply, over the long period, mainly influence the price level. Thus, control of the money supply is a prerequisite for a low and stable rate of inflation.

Two often-repeated statements attributed to Friedman are; 'inflation is always and everywhere a monetary phenomenon' and 'the lags are long and variable'. These two statements can be traced to the monumental empirical research Friedman conducted jointly with Anna Schwartz on US business cycles. The very first piece of solid empirical support for a monetarist interpretation of the business cycle was published by Friedman and Schwartz in 1963 (Friedman and Schwartz 1963a). They demonstrated that fluctuations in monetary growth had preceded the peaks and troughs of all the business cycles in the US since the Civil War. On average the lead in monetary growth to the peak of the cycle was about one half year, and one quarter year for the trough. But the lags varied considerably. In their *Monetary History of the United States, 1867–1960*, Friedman and Schwartz (1963b) showed that monetary changes took between one and two years to have an effect on prices and that the severe contraction of the great depression period 1929–33 was due to a sharp monetary contraction.

The basis of modern monetarism was Friedman's restatement of the quantity theory as a theory of the demand for money. In his famous article 'The Quantity theory of Money – A Restatement' (1956), Friedman attempted to restate the Chicago tradition of the quantity theory that had derived from Fisher's equation exchange as the same as the cash-balance approach of the Cambridge tradition. Friedman treated the demand for money as the demand for any other asset. The demand for money will depend on wealth, the yield on money relative to the yield on alternative assets, and the tastes and preferences of the asset holder. In essence Friedman was taking the cash-balance specification and stating that the fraction k was a stable function of a set of variables such as interest rates and wealth. What was novel about this approach was first, its generality and second, the proposition of its stability. By treating money as part of a portfolio of assets, Friedman recognized the important link between money and other types of assets and money as a necessary medium of exchange. Money is held ultimately for transactions, but while it is held it is a store value. Money is, as Friedman described it, 'a temporary abode of purchasing power'.

The step from the demand for money to the quantity theory comes by introducing various restrictions to the specification. Importantly the demand for money rises one-for-one with the price level (that is people will want to hold the same amount of money relative to the price level if nothing else changes), and the function k is predictable and inevitable. In mathematical terms the demand for money is specified as:

$$M^d = k(r_m, r_b, r_e, \ldots)PY \qquad (7)$$

The variables in the brackets are respectively the rate of interest earned on money balances, the rate of return on bonds and the real return on equity. Other variables that Friedman proposed were the expected rate of inflation, the level of permanent income (underlying long-term income) as a proxy for wealth, the ratio of human to non-human wealth (human capital, say education, relative to tangible capital) and a portmanteau variable to account for tastes and preferences.

Equation (7) is converted into the quantity theory by equating the demand for money with the supply and inverting the function k. Thus:

$$PY = v(r_m, r_b, r_e, \ldots)M^s \qquad (8)$$

where $v = 1/k$.

The prediction of the modern monetarist theory is that an expansionary monetary policy will disturb the portfolio relationship between money and other assets by altering the rate of interest. This will cause a substitution into other assets and goods as people attempt to divest themselves of the excess money. The act of attempting to pass the money around to others will bid up asset prices and goods prices. While asset prices rise relative to goods prices, economic activity will expand, but as inflation catches up, real economic activity will revert to its long-run trend and the excess money will be held because the price level has risen by an equivalent proportion to the original rise in the money supply. An important proposition that follows from the modern monetarist theory is that economic activity is more responsive to a monetary impulse than any other government-generated impulse on aggregate demand such as fiscal policy (government spending and tax policies). Furthermore, the effect of fiscal policy on real economic activity is in the long run negligible. The argument was made that an expansion in demand that arose out of an increase in government spending would eventually 'crowd out' private spending by an equivalent amount. The monetarist prediction is that although temporary, the multiplier effect of monetary policy is proportionately larger than that of fiscal policy. Additionally, the overall effect of fiscal policy on aggregate demand is negligible.

Empirical support for this proposition came from Friedman and Meiselman (1963) and the Federal Reserve Bank of St Louis (Andersen and Jordan 1968). But these results were fiercely contested by the Keynesian school. Empirical results for the UK were mixed. While Barrett and Walters (1966) found some support for the monetarist prediction, Artis and Nobay (1969) did not, Matthews and Ormerod (1978) found results for the UK similar to those of Andersen and Jordan (1968) for the USA. Although the debate on the effectiveness of monetary policy relative to fiscal policy remains unresolved, it is now generally accepted that monetary policy has important effects on aggregate demand.

The policy conclusion that comes out of the monetarist camp is that since the 'lags are long and variable', an active monetary policy would destabilize rather than stabilize economic activity. According to Friedman, the best monetary policy would be a constant rate of growth in the money supply. In contrast to the Keynesian school of thought that advocated active fiscal policy, Friedman also argued that governments should stick to a pre-arranged spending target, allowing revenues to rise and fall with the business cycle. Active fiscal policy would be impotent.

While the empirical debate raged in the academic journals theoretical support for monetarism was advancing in other quarters. Karl Brunner and Alan Meltzer were influential advocates of monetarism. They extended the basic monetarist model to include the banking sector. In fact the term 'monetarism' was first used by Brunner (1968). In the UK, strong support came from the Manchester University Inflation Workshop led by professors David

Laidler and Michael Parkin in the 1970s, and Professor Alan Walters (now Sir Alan) of the London School of Economics.

4 North American monetarism

Monetarism in the USA was based on two important propositions. First, the demand for money is stable and predictable and the supply of money is exogenous (determined outside the economic system) in the long run. The first proposition appeared to hold throughout the 1950s through to the early 1970s. However, financial innovations in the payments mechanism and the development of substitutes such as mutual funds alerted the governing parameters of the demand for money and raised questions about the appropriate definition of money. The empirical links between the money supply and national income began to break down. The gradual removal of ceilings on interest payments on bank deposits increased competition in the banking sector and hastened the de-linking of money and national income.

Empirical studies of causation between money and prices and money and national income tended to show a two-way causation between these variables. Thus while money influenced income and prices, it was also the case that money was influenced by these variables. The feedback from economic activity and inflation to money was explained by Brunner and Meltzer (1976) as the reaction of the banking system to inflation and the variables that influence the business cycle. The Federal Reserve has only a limited power to influence bank behaviour in the cycle and competition in the financial intermediation industry will continue to alter the proper definition of money. These factors led to the monetarist proposal of controlling the monetary base as a means of controlling the money supply.

The monetary base consists of the liabilities of the central bank. These are the notes and coins held by people, and the cash reserves of banks and depository institutions including the deposits of the commercial banks held by the central bank. The amount of cash reserves a commercial bank held was dictated by regulation or by prudential concerns. Cash had to be held in relation to the liabilities (mainly deposits) of the commercial banks because a regulatory reserve ratio requirement had to be satisfied or because banks had worked out the optimal amount of cash needed to be held in their vaults to meet customer withdrawals. The observed stability of the reserve ratio led the monetarists to argue that control of the monetary base was the best means of controlling the money supply. The argument was based on the manipulation of two accounting identities.

The stock of money, M, is made up of the stock of currency held by the general public, C, and the stock of bank deposits, D (or deposits that have cheque-writing facilities). The definition of base money, H (sometimes referred to as high powered money) is given by the sum of cash held by the general public and cash reserves, R, held by the banks and deposit-taking institutions. The two identities are shown in equations (9) and (10). By dividing (9) by (10) and dividing top and bottom by D, it is possible to arrive at a third expression shown in equation (11).

$$M = C + D \tag{9}$$

$$H = C + R \tag{10}$$

$$M = \left(\frac{\frac{C}{D} + 1}{\frac{C}{D} + \frac{R}{D}} \right) H \tag{11}$$

or

$$M = mH$$

where m is the money multiplier and $m = [\{(C/D) + 1\}/\{(C/D) + (R/D)\}]$. The money multiplier is made up of terms in the currency–deposit ratio and the reserve–deposit ratio. Assuming that the currency–deposit ratio is stable and predictable based on the portfolio behaviour of the private sector and the reserve–deposit ratio is determined by regulatory or prudential factors, the multiplier will be stable over the long period. Control of the money supply will be determined by control of monetary base.

Despite the pressure from the monetarist camp to adopt base money control methods, it is almost a universal fact that central banks around the world, including the Federal Reserve, have never operated on a pure base control method for any serious period of time. In general, central banks operate on the rate of interest at which they are willing to lend to commercial banks.

The critics of base money control argue that controlling base money will produce day-to-day shortages in the currency markets causing sharp fluctuations in short-term interest rates. The monetarists' counter argument is that interest rates would be determined by market forces and not by a government sensitive to political pressure. They also argue that banks will behave differently under a base money control than under an interest rate control system. Banks would hold a larger stock of reserves so as to minimize the costs of cash shortages and this action itself would reduce the volatility in short-term rates.

The notion that the money supply can be controlled by central banks controlling their own liabilities is basic to monetarist thinking. The view that the monetary base is exogenous has been expressed in most basic textbooks. In general no central bank behaves according to the base money system (see for example Goodhart 1989: ch. VI). Even if a central bank exploited its monopoly control over the access to cash it would typically be used to stabilize interest rates.

5 British monetarism

The contrast between the US monetarists' thinking on monetary control and the actual behaviour of central banks is seen more clearly in the case of monetary control in the UK. The debate on monetary base control was initiated in the UK with the government launching the Green Paper on Monetary Control in 1980. The Bank of England countered in the *Quarterly Bulletin*, making the familiar arguments about the function of central banks being to ensure that money markets have an orderly access to cash. The practice of supplying cash to the banking system at the bank base rate makes for the monetary base being determined by conditions of aggregate demand and not the other way round as the textbooks would have us believe. Monetary base is endogenous (determined within the economic system) and not exogenous. However, this does not mean that the Bank of England cannot exercise monetary control. Neither does it mean that monetarism is invalidated by the real world practices of the Bank of England and other European central banks.

The centrepiece of monetary control in the UK and that of many other central banks is the rate of interest at which they are willing to lend to the commercial banking system. This interest rate which is referred to as the bank base rate influences the money supply by altering the rate of interest at which commercial banks lend to the general public. The mechanics of how monetary control is exercised can be seen by an analysis of what is called the counterparts to the money supply. Like the monetary base analysis, the counterparts analysis manipulates the identities that define the monetary base and the money supply. It adds to the analysis by including the balance sheet of the banking system and the government budget constraint.

The government borrowing requirement (known as the public sector net cost requirement – PNSCR) can be funded by the sale of government bonds to the non-bank public and by printing base money. Let the symbol Δ represent the change in a variable so that Δx is the change in x over a defined period of time. Then

$$PSNCR = \Delta H + \Delta B \qquad (12)$$

where B is the stock government debt (bonds) outstanding and ΔB is the net sale of extra government debt.

A simplified balance sheet of the banking system would describe its assets as the stock of bank loans (L) and the stock of cash reserves (R). The banking sector's liabilities will be its deposits (D) and its non-deposit liabilities (shareholders equity – E). This is described by equation (13):

$$L + R = D + E \qquad (13)$$

Using the definition of money described by (9) we can eliminate D in (13) and we can also eliminate C in the expression by using (9) which produces:

$$L = M - H + E$$

Taking differences:

$$\Delta L = \Delta M - \Delta H + \Delta E \qquad (14)$$

Eliminating ΔH from (14) by substituting into (12) and re-arranging produces the final identity:

$$\Delta M = PSNCR + \Delta L - \Delta B - \Delta E \qquad (15)$$

Each item on the right hand side of equation (15) is a counterpart to the change in the money supply and can be analysed for its role in determining the money supply. In an open economy, equation (15) will be augmented by government funding from external sources and the banking system net operations in overseas lending and borrowing.

The PSNCR is the difference between government spending (including payment of interest on existing debt) and government revenues. Government borrowing can add to the money supply and ultimately has to be controlled if the money supply is to be controlled. The sale of government debt to the general public acts as a negative influence on the money supply. The funding policy of the government can have an influence on the money supply. The non-deposit liabilities of the banking system will also have a negative influence on the change in the money supply. The non-deposit liabilities are governed by the regulatory capital requirements that banks have to face and the provisions they build up to cover bad debts and non-performing loans. Finally, the largest item that influences the money supply is the increase in bank lending. Control of the money supply in the UK and in the European economies hinges around the control of bank credit.

The control mechanism flows from the interest rate to the banking system through to bank credit and then to the money supply. If money supply does not equal money demand, adjustments in the general price level and real income bring the demand for money into line with the supply of money. Thus a disequilibrium in the money market has the pervasive effect of altering aggregate demand and inflation.

A stable relationship existed between the rate of growth of M3 (currency plus current and deposit accounts of the banks) and inflation with a six to eight quarter lag throughout the late 1960s and the 1970s. The deregulation of the banking system in the early 1980s (abolition of exchange controls, lifting of regulations on deposit taking, abolition of HP controls and greater competition between the banks and building societies) led to the rapid expansion of M3. Inflation fell during the first half of the 1980s while M3 continued to accelerate unabated. The established links between the money supply and inflation had broken down.

The apparent breakdown in the links between money supply growth and inflation led to the splintering of the monetarist camp. One group, led by Professor Patrick Minford of Liverpool University and Sir Alan Walters, took the North American route and argued that monetary base (M0) provided the best indicator of inflation. Others, led by Tim Congdon, a leading City of London economist, argued that the broadest measure of money – extended to include building society deposits – is the best indicator of activity and inflation. An intermediate position was taken by a third group, led by Professors Roy Batchelor and Alec Chrystal of City University and Peter Spencer, another well-known City of London economist (now Professor at Birkbeck College, London University), which argued that the money supply should be weighted according to its 'moneyness' to provide the best indicator of inflationary conditions. According to the latter view, currency and non-interest bearing bank deposits will have the highest weight as they correspond to the use of money for transactions purposes alone. Interest-bearing bank and building society deposits will have a lower weight according to the rate of interest earned on the deposit relative to some reference rate of interest. The debate on which measure of money is the most appropriate is as yet a live issue and one that is hotly debated between the participants. What binds all of them together is that they all believe that the money supply has a strong but temporary effect on economic activity and inflation is ultimately a monetary phenomenon.

6 International monetarism

International monetarism can be viewed as an open economy version of the basic monetarist theory. Like monetarism it assumes that there is a stable and predictable demand for money, that in the long-run the quantity theory of money holds, so that inflation is driven by the rate of growth of the money supply and that in the long run the economy is at its capacity or full employment level. It adds two important elements to the conventional monetarist theory. First, it recognizes that in an open economy the money supply is given not just by domestic credit conditions but also the foreign exchange operations of the monetary authorities. The money supply is domestic credit plus foreign currency reserves. Second, it proposes that in the long run a country's exchange rate be given by 'purchasing power parity' or PPP for short.

The notion of PPP has roots that are as old as monetarism. Discussions on the virtue or otherwise of the PPP theory can be traced to academics writing in the sixteenth century at the University of Salamanca. The exchange rate is the price of one country's currency in terms of another. The theory of PPP states that in the long run the price of a good in one country will roughly equal the price in another, expressed in a common currency. If the exchange rate S is expressed as foreign currency per unit of domestic (say $s per £), then in the long run the sterling price of a good ($P_£$) expressed in US dollars will equal the dollar price of the good ($P_$$) in the USA.

$$P_£ S = P_$ \quad (16)$$

Equation (16) is an extreme version of PPP and is sometimes referred to as the 'law of one price'. Few economists today adhere to the extreme version of PPP for which the empirical evidence is at best mixed. However, for purposes of understanding the link with international monetarism the simple version will be used as an illustration.

International monetarism comes under the label of the 'monetary theory of the balance of payments'. In its simplest form it assumes that if a country is small relative to the world then it is a 'price taker' in the world market. Under fixed exchange rates (as for instance in the case of the gold standard), the domestic price level will be given by the world price level given the assumption of PPP. An increase in the domestic money supply will create an excess supply of money. The excess money cannot influence the price level since prices are pegged by the fixed exchange rate. Rather, the extra demand generated by the excess money creates a balance of trade deficit, which is paid for by the country's foreign currency reserves. As the reserves decline the money supply contracts thereby reducing demand. Equilibrium is restored when the money supply is restored to the original position where there has been a one-for-one displacement of reserves by domestic credit. The real value of money (real balances) is unchanged and output and the trade balance are restored to their original positions.

A floating exchange rate version of the theory states that an increase in the supply of money will lead to an equi-proportionate rise in prices – as predicted by the quantity theory of money. The PPP theory states that a rise in the price level lowers the competitiveness of the economy as domestic prices in foreign currency terms are now higher than world prices. Equilibrium is restored when the exchange rate is devalued equi-proportionately to the rise in the price level. In the long-run the real value of money is restored to its original position, output is at the long-run capacity or full employment level, purchasing power parity is restored and the exchange rate is devalued in strict proportion to the rise in the price level.

7 New classical monetarism

One of the most important subjects that have been associated with monetarism has been the temporary trade-off between inflation and unemployment. Friedman (1968) argued that the inverse relationship between inflation and unemployment was based on falsified expectations. The basis of Friedman's argument was related to the behaviour of the labour market in the macroeconomy. Workers bargain for money wages but their labour supply behaviour is based on real wages (money wages adjusted for the price level). Since workers bargain for money wages in discrete intervals, they do so on the basis of expected inflation. If inflation turns out to be higher than expected, then real wages turn out to be lower than expected. The demand for labour is inversely related to the real wage and therefore employment increases, output increases and unemployment falls. However, when workers realize that the money wage they bargained for does not fully compensate them for the actual rise in prices, they adjust their money wages in future bargaining rounds. When expectations catch up with reality, money wages will have adjusted to the point that real wages have been restored to their original position and employment, output and unemployment will have been restored to their original position. The inverse relationship between inflation and unemployment is only temporary. For example, an increase in the rate of growth of money increases inflation and reduces unemployment in the short run. In the long run, as inflation expectations catch up with reality, unemployment is restored to its 'natural rate' and there is no trade-off between inflation and unemployment.

The notion that the real part of the economy tends to some long run or 'natural' state is perfectly consonant with monetarist thinking. In the long run, the real part of the economy (real GDP, unemployment, investment) is determined by real factors such as productivity and thrift. Similarly, in the long run, inflation, money wages and other monetary measured variables are determined by the money supply.

A critique of this explanation of the inverse relationship has been made by the new classical school led by Sargent and Wallace (1975) and Lucas (1972). The concept of 'rational expectations' is based on the notion that people use all relevant information in the determination of expectations. An anticipated monetary expansion is included as part of the relevant information set and is discounted in expected inflation. This is an extreme form of monetarism. An expansion in the money supply will influence output only if its is unanticipated, otherwise its effect is felt only on the general price level. The result that an anticipated change in monetary conditions has no effect on the real economy is termed the 'policy invariance result' and has been the subject of considerable criticism. While the empirical evidence does not favour the policy invariance result, it is generally accepted that rational expectations theory has clarified the important distinction between the effects of anticipated against unanticipated policy.

One of the predictions of monetarism is that inflation is governed by current monetary conditions and that fiscal policy which is funded by the sales of government debt has no implications for inflation. The latter implication has been denied in a celebrated article by Sargent and Wallace (1981) called 'Some Unpleasant Monetarist Arithmetic'. Sargent and Wallace argue that bond financed government budget deficits represent deferred monetary expansion if the deficits are not to be matched by future budget surpluses. A tight monetary policy matched by a loose fiscal policy (bond financed budget deficit) will produce lower inflation now at the expense of higher inflation in the future. If markets anticipate the 'magnetization' of future budget deficits, expected inflation will increase and even current inflation may respond. According to Sargent and Wallace, tight monetary policy alone is insufficient to guarantee low inflation. Tight monetary policy has to be underpinned with a credible fiscal policy that leaves no room for monetary policy to be reversed in the future.

8 The political economy of monetarism

Milton Friedman may be the name that is usually associated with the doctrine of monetarism, but Margaret Thatcher is the name that immediately springs to mind in the application of monetarism as economic policy. The medium term financial strategy (MTFS) of the British government was unveiled in 1980 and made provision for the targeting of the rate of growth of money as a means of bringing inflation under control.

Monetary targets had been adopted in a number of countries in the developed world. West Germany and Italy adopted monetary targets in 1974, Canada, the USA and Switzerland in 1975 and Australia, France and the UK in 1976. However, it was the MTFS of Mrs Thatcher's government that first introduced pre-announced medium-term monetary targets.

Monetary targets in the UK were based on two strands of thinking. First, the monetarist notion that control of inflation necessitated the control of the rate of growth of money was met in the adherence to a monetary target. Second, medium-term monetary targets were set out to influence expectations of inflation and lay the foundations for a smooth transition to low inflation. The second strand of thinking reflected the influence of the rational expectations monetarists.

The UK experiment was marred by the behaviour of the favoured monetary aggregate (M3 – currency plus bank deposits) during the early period of the MTFS. The initiation of the MTFS coincided with the deregulation of the banking system, which led to the growth of the money supply accelerating at a time when inflation was falling. The monetary targets set in the MTFS were frequently breached. By 1987 the broad money target had been abandoned. The government maintained a target for the monetary base, M0. Monetarists began to squabble among themselves as to the appropriateness of the measure of money. By the end of the decade monetarists had lost favour in policy circles. The adoption of exchange rate targets and the entry of the UK into the Exchange Rate Mechanism signalled the demise of their influence in 1989. Although formal monetary targets had been abandoned, the UK government continued to publish monitoring ranges for M4 (M3 plus building society deposits) and M0 up until the adoption of inflation targets by the incoming Labour government in 1997.

Another experiment that produced mixed results was the policy of base money control, which was attempted by the Federal Reserve in 1979. The argument that any form of base control would lead to wider fluctuations in interest rates turned out to be correct. Although the trend in monetary growth was lowered, the fluctuations from month to month increased dramatically. By 1982, the policy was abandoned.

The difficulties associated with monetary targeting led country after country to formally or informally abandon such targets (Canada in 1982, Australia in 1985). It can be argued that had the policy been conducted in a different way the results may have turned out differently. This is an argument that cannot be varified or invalidated. The disenchantment with monetary targets in the UK and Europe developed into the case for joining the exchange rate mechanism (ERM) of the European Monetary System (EMS). But even after the collapse of the ERM in 1992, the countries of the European Union did not return to formal monetary targets. Many developed economies adopted inflation targets in the second half of the 1990s. Ironically, the birth of the euro and European Monetary Union (EMU) has provided a new lease of life for monetarism. The European Central Bank (ECB), while following an inflation target, monitors the rate of growth of eurozone M3 and has an informal target for the growth of the money supply. The success of the EMU and the ECB in meeting the inflation target set for it depends on the belief that it carries out and sticks to its monetary target.

9 Virtual monetarism

The potential for electronic money to replace cash transactions has raised questions about the implications for monetary policy. It has been suggested that if digital money comes to replace currency, this would undermine the central bank's ability to control the money supply, and meet monetary and thereby inflation targets. If there was a significant shift from currency into digital money, the demand for conventional money would decline, distorting the measure of the money supply, making it difficult for the monetary authorities (Federal Reserve, ECB, etc.) to conduct appropriate policy to meet specified inflation targets.

An electronic means of payment is not a new concept. Electronic Fund Transfer (EFT) for settling large value transactions has existed since the middle of the last century. Credit and debit cards are forms of electronic payments. But the technology of the payments system is in a continuous state of development. The electronic community is trying to develop a process that replaces paper and plastic with computer-driven technology. The challenge is to develop a technology that is secure, convenient, cost effective and most of all anonymous. However, the primary force behind the introduction of e-cash is cost. The estimated cost of maintaining the conventional cash-based payment system in the USA is $60 billion a year. Research conducted in the USA suggests that electronic payment ranges from between one-third to one-half of the costs associated with cheque payments.

The question for central banks is whether the development of e-cash undermines monetary control and therefore monetary policy. The effect on the total money supply depends on the extent to which currency is substituted for by e-cash and the amount of reserves banks are expected to hold against the e-cash issued relative to reserves held against conventional deposits. As Berentsen (1997) demonstrates, provided that less than 100 per cent reserves are held against e-cash, a decrease in currency caused by a substitution into e-cash will increase the total supply of money. The way this works is that a person deposits real currency to the bank and accepts e-cash in exchange. The increase in cash held by the bank represents an increase in reserves. Under a 100 per cent reserve system, the extra currency will have to be held against the equivalent increase in e-cash and there will be no increase in the total money supply. A unit of cash has fallen and an equivalent unit of e-cash has increased. Under a less than 100 per cent reserve system, a proportion of the extra reserves is used to expand loans in e-cash. These loans are held in the banking system in the form of e-cash deposits. Hence a unit decrease in cash will be more than matched by a larger than unit increase in e-cash. There is no reason to believe that central banks would impose 100 per cent reserves on e-cash in an attempt to control the money supply. To do so would be to inhibit the development of a cost-reducing technology. It follows that the development of digital money, e-cash, or cyber currency will be liquidity increasing. Would this mean that the development of e-cash would lead to difficulty in targeting and controlling the money supply?

Selgin (1996) asks the question whether e-cash is the friend or foe of monetarism. One of the arguments proposed by the North American monetarist school is that since financial innovation and deregulation will always chip away at the boundary between money and near-money, the simplest means of controlling the money supply is to control the monetary base (see also Minford and Walters above). Selgin (1996) argues that the development of e-cash strengthens the case for a strict money base control. The money base issue is outlined in equations (9)–(11) above. The development of e-cash would mean that the money supply would have to be measured as currency plus bank deposits plus e-cash supplied by the banks. In other words:

$$M = C + D + EM \tag{17}$$

where EM represents e-cash. Dividing equation (17) by equation (10) above we have:

$$\frac{M}{H} = \frac{C + D + EM}{C + R} \tag{18}$$

Dividing top and bottom by EM gives the following expression:

$$\frac{M}{H} = \frac{c + d + 1}{c + r} \tag{19}$$

where c, d and r are the ratios of currency to e-cash, deposits to e-cash and reserves to e-cash respectively. A long-standing argument against money base control is that the central bank would be unable to adjust the monetary base for unforeseen changes in the ratios of currency to e-cash and deposits to e-cash. However, if cash and bank deposits are replaced by e-cash, then the ratios c and d will go to zero and the money multiplier equation of (11) would look like:

$$M = \left(\frac{1}{r}\right) H \tag{20}$$

With two less variables to worry about, the central bank can control the total stock of money, which will comprise of e-cash by setting a reserve ratio and controlling base money, which will comprise of bank reserves. Since the cost of processing e-cash is expected to be considerably less than the cost of processing cash or cheques, there will be a strong economic impetus to get customers to switch to e-cash. The monetarist case for having a constant rate of growth of money becomes feasible because the central bank can set the reserve ratio r and control the supply of bank reserves. Selgin (1996) concludes that monetarists should be grateful to e-cash, for helping to bring a strict monetarist rule one step closer to perfection.

KENT MATTHEWS
CARDIFF BUSINESS SCHOOL
CARDIFF UNIVERSITY

Further reading

(References cited in the text marked *)

* Andersen, L.C. and Jordan, J.L. (1968) 'Monetary and fiscal actions: a test of their relative importance in economic stabilization', *Federal Reserve Bank of St Louis Review* 50 (11): 29–44. (This paper presents evidence to show that monetary policy in the USA has stronger effects on national income than fiscal policy. Using econometric methods, an empirical link is made between base money and national income.)
* Artis, M.J. and Nobay, A.R. (1969) 'Two aspects of the monetary debate', *National Institute Economic Review* 49: 33–51. (This paper attempts to replicate the findings of monetarists such as Andersen and Jordan (1968) for the UK. The basic finding is that monetary policy has a weak effect on national income and does not support the monetarist contention that money is the most important determinant.)
* Barrett, C.R. and Walters, A.A. (1966) 'The stability of Keynesian and monetary multipliers in the UK', *Review of Economics and Statistics* 48 (4): 395–405. (This paper tests for the length of lag between a monetary impulse and its effect on national income for the UK. The main finding is that a monetary shock takes as long as six months to filter through to economic activity and that both monetary and autonomous spending is important for the determination of national income. However there is considerable variation from decade to decade.)
* Berentsen, A. (1997) 'Digital money, liquidity and monetary policy', *First Monday*, http://www.firstmonday.dk
* Brunner, K. (1968) 'The role of money and monetary policy', *Federal Reserve Bank of St Louis Review* 50 (7): 9–24. (The monetary hypothesis is discussed in detail. The implications for economic policy and the operating procedures of monetary policy in the USA are examined and compared with competing theories.)
* Brunner, K. and Meltzer, A. (1976) 'An aggregative theory of a closed economy', in J. Stein (ed.), *Studies in Monetarism*, Amsterdam: North-Holland. (A theoretical model of the financial system is developed which supports the monetarist hypothesis. The model is advanced by the allowance for the interaction with the banking system and government funding policy.)
* Chrystal, K.A. (1990) (ed.) *Monetarism*, vols 1 and 2, Aldershot: Edward Elgar. (A collection of major readings on monetarism including several cited here. The levels of difficulty will vary from article to article.)
  Congdon, T. (1992) *Reflections on Monetarism*, Aldershot: Edward Elgar. (A very readable set of essays written by one of the leading City of London monetarist writers. Each essay is written by a lay audience and is largely re-prints of articles published by newspapers and popular journals. Each article has a strong policy message.)
* Fisher, I. (1911) *The Purchasing Power of Money*, New York: Macmillan. (The classical statement of the quantity theory of money as seen from a US perspective. The first to formally articulate the equation of exchange as recognized in macroeconomic textbooks.)
* Friedman, M. (1956) 'The quantity theory of money – a restatement' in M. Friedman (ed.), *Studies in the Quantity Theory of Money*, Chicago, IL: Chicago University Press. (Standard undergraduate reading on the modern statement of the quantity theory of money recast as the demand for money. This paper attempts to restate the Chicago monetarist tradition along the lines of the Cambridge oral tradition.)
* Friedman, M. (1968) 'The role of monetary policy', *American Economic Review* 58 (1): 1–15. (A full statement of the role of monetary policy. This paper examines the transmission mechanism of monetary policy. It discusses how money affects the economy, paying particular attention to the role of expectations. It also separates the transitional effects from the long-term effects.)
* Friedman, M. and Meiselman, D. (1963) 'The relative stability of monetary velocity and the investment multiplier in the United States, 1897–1958', in *Commission on Money and Credit, Stabilization Policies*, Englewood Cliffs, NJ: Prentice Hall. (This is one of the first papers that attempted to quantify the effects of monetary policy compared with autonomous spending. In doing so it attempts to test the monetarist hypothesis against the Keynesian hypothesis.)
* Friedman, M. and Schwartz, A.J. (1963a) 'Money and business cycles', *Review of Economics and Statistics* 45, supplement part B, February:

32–64. (An important precursor to Friedman and Schwartz (1982) and (1963b) offering a more detailed technical analysis of the role of money in determining economic activity.)

* Friedman, M. and Schwartz, A.J. (1963b) *A Monetary History of the United States 1867–1960*, Princeton, NJ: Princeton University Press for the National Bureau of Economic Research. (The seminal work by the two leading monetarist economists in the USA. This book examines the role of money in explaining the US business cycle over its history and including the period of the great depression.)

Friedman, M. and Schwartz, A.J. (1982) *Monetary Trends in the United States and the United Kingdom: Their Relation to Income Prices and Interest Rates, 1867–1975*, Chicago, IL: Chicago University Press. (An important study that looks at the long-run trends in money and economic activity in the two most important Anglo-Saxon economies. The empirical work cited in this book is the basis of much of modern monetarism.)

* Goodhart, C.A.E. (1989) *Money, Information and Uncertainty*, 2nd edn, Basingstoke: Macmillan. (A textbook used in modern final year honours and postgraduate courses in monetary economics. The book is distinguished by dealing with empirical issues of monetary policy as well as theoretical topics.)

* *Green Paper on Monetary Control* (1980), London: HMSO, Cmnd. 7858. (A consultation paper by the UK government.)

* Lucas, R. (1972) 'Expectations and the neutrality of money', *Journal of Economic Theory* 4 (2): 103–24. (Outlines in technical detail the implications of rational expectations for monetary policy. The main result is that in a market clearing economy, anticipated monetary policy has no effect on real economic activity. Only unanticipated monetary policy can have any influence on real economic activity.)

* Matthews, K.G.P. and Ormerod, P.A. (1978) 'St. Louis models of the UK economy', *National Institute Economic Review* 84 (2): 65–9. (This paper tests the monetarist hypothesis of Andersen and Jordan (1968) on UK data. It finds that the monetarist hypothesis can be supported and that monetary base has a powerful influence on economic activity while fiscal policy has no permanent effect.)

* Pigou, A.C. (1917) 'The value of money', *Quarterly Journal of Economics* 32: 38–65. (Provides a statement of the Cambridge version of the quantity theory. This statement is considerably more sophisticated than that of Fisher (1911) and the views associated with the Chicago school. It examines the influences on both the supply of money as well as the demand for money and presents the quantity theory as an equilibrium condition of demand equalling supply of money.)

* Sargent, T. and Wallace, N. (1975) 'Rational expectations, the optimal monetary instrument, and the optimal money supply rule', *Journal of Political Economy* 83 (2): 241–54. (Shows that different types of central bank monetary policy rules will always produce the same effect of not influencing real economic activity, if the monetary policy rules are anticipated.)

* Sargent, T. and Wallace, N. (1981) 'Some unpleasant monetarist arithmetic', *Federal Reserve Bank of Minneapolis Quarterly Review* 5 (3): 1–17, New York: Harper & Row. (This paper makes the argument that funding a govermnent budget deficit by issuing debt will only delay the inflationary implications of loose money. This is because the debt will eventually have to be monetized when the private sector reaches the maximum holdings of debt their portfolios will allow.)

* Selgin, G. (1996) 'E-money: friend or foe of monetarism?' The Future of Money in the Information Age', Cato Institute's 14th Annual Monetary Conference, May 23, *http://www.cato.org/moneyconf/*

* Simons, H. (1936) 'Rules versus authorities in monetary policy', *Journal of Political Economy* 44: 1–30. (The classical statement of rules versus discretion in monetary policy. The paper examines the arguments for simple rules against discretion according to the circumstances.)

Smith, D. (1987) *The Rise and Fall of Monetarism*, Harmondsworth: Penguin. (A very readable account of the monetarist experiment conducted during the Thatcher administration in the UK. The author is the economics correspondent for the *Sunday Times*.)

Vane, H. and Thompson, J.L. (1979) *Monetarism: Theory, Evidence and Policy*, Oxford: Martin Robertson. (An intermediate undergraduate textbook that covers the main issues of theory and empirical evidence on monetarism.)

See also: FRIEDMAN, M.; KEYNES, J.M.; MARSHALL, A.

Growth theory

1 **Introduction**
2 **Classical theories of growth**
3 **Contemporary growth theory**
4 **Conclusion**

Overview

Economic growth involves expansion of the total output produced by an economy. The purpose of growth theory is to analyse this process or, in other words, to explain how and why growth occurs. The focus of the enterprise is usually the long run. It is longer term, trend rates of growth, rather than the short-lived booms of the business cycle, that growth theory is typically concerned with, although some theories describe growth as an inherently cyclical process.

The analysis of growth is almost as old as the discipline of economics itself. This long history of development has witnessed the emergence of competing schools of growth theory, that differ in terms of what they identify as the 'engine' of growth. Neo-classical analysis emphasizes the development of factor inputs on the supply side, whereas in Keynesian theories, the demand for final output drives growth. Meanwhile, Marxian theories identify the social organization of the economy as critical, a concern that centres upon – but is by no means confined to – the struggle between workers and firms regarding the distribution of income. These competing interpretations of growth are the product of economists' differing conceptions of the essential properties of a capitalist economy – whether, for example, it is demand that reacts to supply or *vice versa*, or whether the economy is best thought of as a collection of impersonal, technical relations or a social and historically evolving construct. The fact that growth theorists disagree matters, because their theories offer different understandings of what causes growth and hence what might be done to promote it. Owing to the fundamental nature of these disagreements, however, it is likely that future developments in growth theory will only reinforce the current diversity of analyses.

1 Introduction

Growth theory, the means by which economists attempt to understand how and why economic growth occurs, derives its significance from the importance of growth itself. Since economic growth involves expansion of the total output produced by an economy, it plays a direct role in the improvement of material standards of living. It is safe to say that as long as increasing material standards of living remains a social objective, economic growth – and by extension, growth theory – will remain important topics. But it should also be recognized that, beyond its effects on material living standards, growth is associated with profound changes in the structure of societies. How things are produced, what is produced, how and where we live and the very constitution of civil society are all impacted by economic growth. Growth results in tremendous quantitative *and* qualitative changes, therefore, and it is as a result of this that attempts to understand the growth process are of such importance.

Capitalism has experienced a long history of economic growth. For approximately two centuries, the per capita output produced by advanced capitalist economies (such as the UK, the USA and more recently Japan) has expanded at the average annual rate of about 1.5 per cent per annum. Economics has an equally long history of trying to come to terms with the processes that have brought this about. The fruits of this endeavour make up not a single, unified body of thought, but a collection of competing perspectives. These perspectives mirror the major changes and developments that have taken place in economics itself over the past 200 years. As a result, it is possible to identify classical, neoclassical and Keynesian theories of growth, which differ according to what they identify as the principle forces responsible for causing growth. The remainder of this entry is devoted to discussing these different perspectives and their insights into the growth process. In the next section, classical theories of growth are discussed, with particular emphasis placed on the contributions of Marx. Section 3 discusses the Keynesian, neoclassical and neo-Marxian theories that fall under the rubric of contemporary growth theory. Finally, section 4 provides some conclusions and indications of the likely direction of future developments in the field.

2 Classical theories of growth

Many of the classical economists of the late eighteenth and early nineteenth centuries were pessimistic about the prospects for capitalist growth. Central to their concerns were natural resource constraints – more specifically, the limited availability of land. In the work of Thomas Malthus, for example, this constraint plays itself out in the drama of recurrent famines, as population growth periodically exceeds the expansion of the means of subsistence. David Ricardo's model, whilst being somewhat more sophisticated than Malthus', is no more encouraging. For Ricardo, increases in population must eventually result in increases in food prices, due to the limited availability of fertile land. This, in turn, places upward pressure on the subsistence wages that are assumed to be paid to workers, resulting in a profit squeeze in the industrial sector. Finally, as a result of this profit squeeze, industrialists are less inclined to accumulate capital, and the rate of growth slows down. Taken to the extreme, the outcome of this process is economic stagnation, a situation characterized by no (or extremely low) growth. The only beneficiaries of all this are landowners, towards whom income is continually redistributed. Workers never receive more than a subsistence wage, but as the rate of profit (and the rate of growth) decline, the return to land (rent) increases, thanks to rising food prices. Two important and enduring features of Ricardo's analysis are his recognition of social classes and the distribution of income between these classes as integral features of the growth process.

The pessimism of Malthus and Ricardo with regard to the prospects for capitalist growth has not been borne out by history. To a large extent, this is due to their neglect of the possibility of technical change liberating the economy from natural constraints and providing a basis for sustained growth in per capita output. But it is important to recognize that not all classical economists fall into this trap. One exception was Adam Smith, who analysed growth as a series of self-reinforcing increases in the division of labour and the extent of the market (see SMITH, A.). For Smith, increases in the division of labour (i.e. the development of ever more specialized roles in production for individual workers and firms) result in higher productivity, higher personal incomes, and hence increases in the extent of the market (i.e. the total demand for output). Meanwhile, increases in the extent of the market foster increases in the division of labour, by rendering feasible degrees of specialization in production that are only viable if output is sufficiently large (think of the absurdity of using an assembly line to produce just one car). This theory of self-sustaining growth has since been revisited by Nicholas Kaldor and his followers – on which, see the section entitled 'Keynesian growth theory: the demand side once more' below.

The second prominent 'optimist' amongst classical economists was Marx (see MARX, K.). This may seem an odd claim, given Marx's reputation as the *bête noire* of capitalists. But the truth is that Marx identified in the accumulation of capital (and attendant technical progress), and in the compulsion of capitalists to continually engage in accumulation, the unleashing of forces that would result in historically unprecedented expansions of output. For Marx, any constraints on capitalist growth lay not in the scarcity of natural resources nor difficulties in amassing capital, but in the *social organization* of capitalism. Capitalism is viewed as a society based on social classes and given to class conflict – most obviously, the conflict between workers and capitalists over the distribution of income between wages and profits. Marx regarded the existence of a 'reserve army' of unemployed workers as a prerequisite for capitalism, because it would disempower labour and, amongst other things, prevent profits from being eroded by wage gains. But fast growth will deplete the reserve army, creating a tendency for the bargaining power of workers and hence the wage share of income to rise. The resulting profit squeeze reduces the rates of accumulation and growth – only for this, in turn, to increase the reserve army, reduce the bargaining power of workers and the wage share of income, thus enhancing profitability and creating conditions for a new phase of faster accumulation and growth. Marx did not expect this cyclical growth process to continue indefinitely, however. His most famous prediction was that the tensions inherent in the social organization of capitalism would eventually result in its collapse, and the subsequent emergence of a classless, socialist society.

3 Contemporary growth theory

The late nineteenth and early twentieth centuries witnessed a hiatus in growth theory, as the marginalist revolution re-focused economists' attention on issues of resource allocation and price determination. But the debacle of the inter-war years provided renewed impetus for analysing growth, and thus emerged contemporary growth theory. The point of departure for contemporary theory is the work of Roy Harrod. This inspired responses from both neo-classical and Keynesian economists, which subsequently developed into research traditions in their own right, with respective emphases on the importance of supply and demand conditions in the determination of the growth rate. Finally, neo-Marxian models have emerged, which recall and extend Marx's insights into the social organization of capitalism and its impact on growth. These developments are surveyed in what follows.

The contemporary point of departure: Harrod's model

Although Harrod's initial contributions to economic dynamics precede the publication (in 1936) of Keynes' *General Theory*, they can be understood as having a distinctly Keynesian flavour. Central to Harrod's analysis is the dual role of investment, as both a source of additional productive capacity and a source of aggregate demand. According to Harrod, balancing the expansion of potential output (determined on the supply side) and actual output (determined by the expansion of total demand) is the ultimate goal of a growing economy, but is not easily achieved.

Harrod's model consists of three distinct growth rates: the natural, warranted and actual rates of growth. The natural rate of growth is that consistent with the full employment of the labour force. The warranted rate, meanwhile, is the equilibrium growth rate. If achieved, the warranted rate of growth ensures that a firm's expectations regarding the expansion of the economy, on which their investment plans are based, are realized. Finally, the actual rate of growth is, as its name suggests, the rate of growth that the economy actually achieves. The striking thing about these growth rates is that they are determined independently of one another, and in such a way that there is no obvious mechanism that will bring them into alignment. Only by chance will the natural, warranted and actual rates of growth be equal – but this is precisely what is required for the economy to achieve steady (i.e. constant proportional) growth with full employment. Moreover, the actual rate of growth tends to move further away from (rather than towards) the warranted rate of growth if the two are not equal to begin with. This is because of the perverse signals that these macroeconomic events send to firms, whose investment decisions are influenced by the proximity of the actual rate of capacity utilization to their preferred (target) rate. Clearly, this is not a world in which an 'invisible hand' can be relied upon to ensure harmonious economic outcomes. On the contrary, what Harrod showed was that when capitalist growth depends upon the independent investment decisions of many different firms, it is likely to be an uneven process in which firms are continually adapting to unanticipated outcomes and in which labour is unlikely to be fully employed.

Neo-classical growth theory: the supply-side response to Harrod

The emergence of neo-classical growth theory is most famously associated with the work of Robert Solow in the 1950s. Solow's model can be interpreted as an attempt to 'solve' the problems that Harrod identified as being intrinsic to growth, by showing that it is possible for steady growth with full employment to be the normal state of affairs. In order to do this, Solow assumes away the independent investment decisions of firms that are central to Harrod's model, and which make aggregate demand an important feature of growth analysis. Instead, he describes a world in which saving automatically creates investment. Attention then turns to the supply side of the economy, where the theory of production plays the dominant role in determining growth outcomes.

Two critical features of the theory of production employed by Solow are that capital and labour can be substituted for one another (so that different capital to labour ratios are possible) and that capital is subject to positive but diminishing marginal returns – i.e. increases in the amount of capital used by firms result in positive but successively smaller increases in the amount of output they produce. Now, suppose that firms are producing at a particular capital to labour ratio, and that this results in a particular level of output per worker. Because the labour force is assumed to be growing over time, firms must invest in new capital just to keep the capital to labour ratio (k) constant. But if the part of output per worker (y) that is saved and hence actually invested in new capital *exceeds* what is required to keep k constant, then k must increase. This will do two things. First, it will increase the amount of investment that is now required just to keep k constant. And second, it will increase output per worker (because of the positive marginal returns to capital) and hence, assuming that the saving rate is constant, saving and investment per worker. If the level of investment once again exceeds that necessary to keep k constant, then k will increase further. What brings this process to a halt is the fact that increases in output per worker (and hence saving and investment per worker) become successively smaller as k rises, because of the diminishing returns to capital. Eventually, a value of k will be reached at which the level of saving (investment) is only sufficient to keep the capital to labour ratio constant over time. At this point, y will also become constant. But because the labour force is growing over time, y (output per worker) can only remain constant if total output grows at the same rate as the labour force – i.e. if the actual rate of growth equals Harrod's natural rate of growth. In this way, by varying the capital to labour ratio, the economy automatically adjusts towards a steady rate of growth consistent with the full employment of the labour force.

The predictions of the Solow model about growth are diametrically opposed to those of Harrod's model. But a nagging problem remains. The economy's actual rate of growth is equal to the natural rate of growth, but the latter is taken as given – it is not determined within the model itself. In short, the Solow model does not explain the value of the precise rate of growth that the economy eventually achieves.

Since the mid 1980s, a 'second generation' of neo-classical growth theories has emerged that are designed to remedy this problem. The remedy arrives in the form of a re-consideration of the theory of production employed by Solow. Essentially, the assumption of diminishing returns to capital is dropped. In terms of the structure of the Solow model discussed earlier, this allows for perpetual increases in y based on increases in k. The precise rate of growth that the economy achieves is now determined by a process of accumulation, the rate of which is explicable in terms of economic theory (and need not, therefore, be taken as given).

Neo-classical endogenous growth (NEG) models, as they are called, are designed to explain the rate of accumulation that is now the proximate source of growth. Unlike the Solow model, which assumes perfect competition, imperfectly competitive firms play an important role in these models. The firm remains a curiously passive and asocial entity, however, maximizing profits subject to product market conditions and technical features of the production process that it takes as given.

A great variety of NEG models exists, partly because the theory allows anything that affects the propensity to save to influence the rate of growth. For example, the distribution of income, the rate of taxation, and households' preferences for thrift can all be connected to the growth rate. NEG models also differ in terms of *what* they describe firms as accumulating in order to grow. In some models, the focus is on fixed capital, but in others it is human capital (such as education and skills) or technological innovations. One problem with all this is that it encourages economic modelling for its own sake. As a result, in its current state of development, NEG theory represents a collection of different, theoretically plausible stories about growth, from which no real consensus emerges as to exactly what the determinants of the rate of growth are.

But whatever is being accumulated, and whatever is deemed to influence the rate of accumulation in NEG models, this second generation of neo-classical growth theories remains wedded to the supply-side vision of growth found in Solow. Growth results from increasing the quantity or efficiency of inputs into the production process. The *potential* output that these inputs are capable of producing is always what they *actually* produce: they are never under-utilized or forced to lie idle for want of final demand.

Keynesian growth theory: the demand side once more

This last point draws attention to the fact that neo-classical theories constitute only one perspective in contemporary growth analysis. Drawing on the insights of Harrod, Keynesian growth theories emerged in the 1950s which emphasize the independent role of investment and hence aggregate demand in the determination of growth outcomes. An excellent example of this tradition is the model developed by Joan Robinson, which draws on Michal Kalecki's insights into the two-sided relationship between investment and profits in a capitalist economy. On one hand, the expected rate of profit has a straightforward influence on the planned rate of investment, albeit one that is affected by firms' 'animal spirits' – that is their subjective propensities to act in an environment characterized by uncertainty about the future. On the other, the actual rate of investment plays a Keynesian role in generating the growth of income, and thus determines the realized rate of profit. Robinson showed that, given the state of firms' animal spirits, this two-sided relationship between investment and profits can be reconciled in an equilibrium at which the expected rate of profit motivates a planned rate of investment that, when implemented, generates a realized rate of profit equivalent to firms' initial expectations. Her model thus simultaneously determines both the rate of investment (and hence the rate of growth) and the rate of profit (and hence the distribution of income). The distributional results of Robinson's model were generalized by Luigi Pasinetti, who showed that Robinson's theory of the rate of profit along a full employment growth path does not depend on her special assumptions about the saving behaviour of workers. Nicholas Kaldor, meanwhile, showed that changes in the distribution of income were crucial to the achievement of steady growth with full employment (i.e. the reconciliation of Harrod's warranted and natural rates of growth), but that the scope for such changes was bounded by the minimum wage and profit rates acceptable to workers and firms respectively.

In general, however, the equilibrium rate of growth in Robinson's model is *not* consistent with full employment. The model also provides a long-run analogue of Keynes' 'paradox of thrift', according to which an increase in the propensity to save will, by depressing the level of income, leave the aggregate quantity of saving in the economy unchanged. In the Robinson model, an increase in the propensity to save depresses the rate of growth (and the rate of profit), offering a marked contrast to neo-classical growth theories, in which the rate of growth is either independent of the saving rate (as in Solow) or increased by a higher propensity to save (as in neo-classical endogenous growth theories).

Second generation analyses have explored the microfoundations of the Kalecki–Robinson model. Particular attention has been paid to firms' pricing practices, and the ability of firms to set mark-ups over prime costs that generate internal sources of funding for planned investment. Although the structure of product markets and labour relations is taken into account in these analyses, there remains a tendency to think of 'the firm' as a unified whole. The question remains as to how firm behaviour – and hence the rate of growth – might be affected by different corporate governance structures and the separation of ownership and control.

Second generation theories in the Kalecki–Robinson tradition have also explored the existence of a 'paradox of costs' in this model, according to which lower wages – despite reducing the cost of production for firms – result in a lower rate of growth. At first, this result seems counter-intuitive. Lower wages would appear to raise profitability, creating a stimulus for increased rates of accumulation and growth. Indeed, this 'exhilaration' result is quite possible. However, wages are not just a cost of production but also a source of income for workers, and hence a source of consumption demand. Because of the sensitivity of growth outcomes to demand conditions, a 'stagnation' result is also possible, arising from the depressing effect of lower wages on consumption expenditures, the utilization of existing industrial capacity and hence the rates of profit and accumulation.

A different type of second generation Keynesian growth analysis has been inspired by the later work of Nicholas Kaldor. Kaldor recalls the work of Adam Smith, emphasizing a growth schema in which productivity and demand influence each other in a self-reinforcing process of cumulative causation. He begins with Smith's central insight that the division of labour depends on the extent of the market. In Kaldorian models, demand-led expansions of output affect not only the degree of specialization within industries and firms, but also their willingness to invest in indivisible assets (and hence the capital-intensity of production) and the amount of learning by doing. Thanks to this demand-induced technological progress, the growth of productivity depends on the growth of demand and hence total output.

Kaldor then argues that by affecting the competitiveness of its goods, increasing productivity can enhance the demand for a region's exports, thus stimulating growth. Given the capacity for induced technological progress, this growth will, in turn, foster additional productivity gains, further enhancing competitiveness, and so on. The expansion of the economy in this fashion need not ensure full employment – indeed, the cumulative interaction between demand and productivity can result in self-sustaining virtuous or vicious circles of fast or slow growth, depending on whether an economy grows rapidly or slowly to begin with. The potential therefore arises for divergence in the per capita incomes of national economies. Unlike Kalecki–Robinson models, this approach takes explicit account of (endogenous) technical progress in the growth process, but does not discuss distributional issues. Neither approach connects the two by considering the impact of real wages on workers' willingness to cooperate with firms at the point of production, and hence the rate of growth.

An important branch of Kaldorian analysis is balance-of-payments-constrained growth theory. This introduces into Kaldor's growth schema the requirement that long-run growth be consistent with balance of payments current account equilibrium. The idea here is that running a perpetual balance of trade deficit involves a permanent net inflow of financial capital, and that this is neither desirable (because of the subsequent outflows of rent, interest and profit income that it involves) nor, given the mores of the international financial community, necessarily feasible in the long term. Introducing the balance of payments constraint produces the result that the rate of growth of exports and the income elasticity of demand for imports are the proximate determinants of an economy's rate of growth. Increasing the rate of growth involves relaxing the balance of payments constraint, by either increasing export competitiveness or encouraging import substitution.

Neo-Marxian models: the economy as a social construct

Not all contemporary growth theory can be traced back to the contributions of Harrod. The classical tradition remains vibrant, and since the late 1970s, has spawned two new (and closely related) research traditions. Reaching back to the contributions of Marx, the purpose of the Regulation and Social Structure of Accumulation (SSA) theories is to re-establish the central role of the social organization of the economy – and in particular, the social organization of the firm – in theories of capitalist growth. The emphasis of the

Regulation and SSA theories is overwhelmingly on the supply side of the economy – indeed, the precise role of demand-side factors remains ambiguous in these approaches. However, unlike neo-classical analysis, which treats the supply side in purely technical terms, neo-Marxian theories call attention to the social nature of capitalism, and its propensity to draw different interests into conflict with one another. Unlike Marx, however, their focus is not on the likely demise of capitalism as a result of these conflicting social forces, but rather on the way that social strife can be periodically ameliorated by social institutions, giving rise to sustained booms in capitalist accumulation and growth. For example, the welfare state, the commitment of policy makers to full employment, the granting of steady wage increases and the acceptance of managerial authority under the Fordist system of production are identified as social institutions which, by creating enduring and broadly consensual (and therefore conflict-resolving) 'rules of the game', promoted the long period of rapid capitalist growth from 1945–73. The rise and demise of stable constellations of social institutions – called modes of regulation or social structures of accumulation – are thus associated with the periodic acceleration/deceleration of the rate of accumulation in a model of cyclical growth. This model also describes the evolution of capitalism through qualitatively different epochs of growth, characterized by different social institutions governing production and distribution.

4 Conclusion

The central importance of its subject matter coupled with its long history of development have ensured that growth theory has always been – and remains – a matter of controversy. It is nevertheless possible to identify three broad traditions in growth analysis, distinguished according to what they identify as the principle forces that cause growth. Neoclassical theories focus on technical features of the production process, and in particular, increases in the quantity and efficiency of factor inputs as the explanation for growth. Keynesian theories emphasize the leading role of demand, suggesting that the expansion of demand affects not just the utilization of productive resources, but also – in the manner first discussed by Adam Smith – their very development over time. Classical theories rooted in the tradition of Marx identify production and distribution as innately social processes, and emphasize the importance of conflict between divergent interests – concerning the distribution of income, control over production, and so forth – in determining the rate of growth. Although these traditions are markedly different, it is inappropriate to conclude that they do not influence one another. For example, some neo-Marxian theories acknowledge an independent role for demand in determining growth outcomes, whilst some Keynesian theories accept that conflict between capital and labour shapes the growth process. However, it is highly unlikely that there will ever be a compelling synthesis of all three traditions, because of fundamental differences in the basic conceptions of capitalism that inform them. The future of growth analysis is likely to be characterized by continued diversity, then, rather than the emergence of a single, consensual, unified theory. This means that both the analysis of, and design of policies to promote growth will remain contentious issues.

MARK SETTERFIELD
TRINITY COLLEGE, CONNECTICUT

Further reading

Aghion, P. and P. Howitt (1998) *Endogenous Growth Theory*, Cambridge, MA: MIT Press. (An advanced but comprehensive discussion of second generation neo-classical (endogenous) growth theories.)

Asimakopulos, A. (1991) *Keynes's General Theory and Accumulation*, Cambridge: Cambridge University Press. (An introduction to Keynesian growth theory and its links to the short-period macroeconomics of Keynes.)

Bhaduri, A. and S. Marglin (1990) 'Unemployment and the real wage: the economic basis for contesting political ideologies,' *Cambridge Journal of Economics* 14 (4): 375–93. (An introduction to the central issues in second generation Kalecki–Robinson growth theory.)

Boyer, R. (1990) *The Regulation School: A Critical Introduction*, New York: Columbia University Press. (An introductory account of Regulation theory.)

Duménil, G. and D. Lévy (1994) *The Economics of the Profit Rate*, Aldershot: Edward Elgar. (A contemporary contribution to classical growth theory in the Marxian mode.)

Foley, D.K. and T.R. Michl (1999) *Growth and Distribution*, Cambridge, MA: Harvard University Press. (An advanced text that discusses classical, neo-classical and Keynesian growth theories.)

Gordon, D.M., R. Edwards and M. Reich (1982) *Segmented Workers, Divided Work*, Cambridge: Cambridge University Press. (A classic contribution in the social structure of accumulation tradition.)

Harcourt, G.C. (1972) *Some Cambridge Controversies in the Theory of Capital*, Cambridge: Cambridge University Press. (Comparative account of first generation Keynesian and neo-classical growth theories, with special emphasis on controversies surrounding their treatments of distribution.)

Jones, C.I. (1998) *Introduction to Economic Growth*, New York: W.W. Norton. (An introductory text that discusses first and second generation neo-classical growth theory.)

Jones, H.G. (1976) *An Introduction to Modern Theories of Economic Growth*, New York: McGraw Hill. (An introductory text that discusses first generation neo-classical and Keynesian growth theories.)

Marglin, S.A. (1984) *Growth, Distribution and Prices*, Cambridge, MA: Harvard University Press. (An advanced text that discusses classical, neo-classical and Keynesian growth theories.)

McCombie, J.S.L. and A.P. Thirlwall (1994) *Economic Growth and the Balance-of-Payments-Constraint*, London, Macmillan. (A comprehensive discussion of contemporary Kaldorian growth theory.)

Palley, T.I. (1996) 'Aggregate demand in a reconstruction of growth theory: the macro foundations of economic growth,' *Review of Political Economy* 8: 23–35. (A contemporary exposition of the Harrod model.)

Skott, P. (1989) *Conflict and Effective Demand in Economic Growth*, Cambridge: Cambridge University Press. (Explores the interface of Keynesian and classical growth theories.)

Solow, R.M. (2000) *Growth Theory: An Exposition*, 2nd edn, Oxford: Oxford University Press. (A comprehensive survey of first and second generation neo-classical growth theory.)

See also: ECONOMIC GROWTH AND CONVERGENCE; KEYNES, J.M.; MARSHALL, A.; MARX, K., MILL, J.S.

Modelling and forecasting

1. **Models as the basis for business forecasts**
2. **Reasons for building models**
3. **Models that promote understanding: measuring parameters**
4. **Using models to test theories**
5. **Using models to make predictions**
6. **The elements of model building**
7. **Non-stochastic model as explanatory basis**
8. **Problems with truly stochastic models**
9. **The history of econometric-based forecasting**
10. **Conclusion**

Overview

Econometric models by design attempt to capture or represent simultaneously the data of interest and the ideas about how the modelled economy functions as reflected in that data. Economists have been building such models for several decades. Their primary task is one of identifying a set of parameters or constants that can be seen to characterize the economy being modelled. Such models are thought to represent a cause-and-effect relationship between two types of observable quantities. The effects are the so-called endogenous variables being explained and the causes are the so-called exogenous or autonomous variables whose values are determined either by nature or by public policy. Exogenous variables are determined by events beyond anyone's control or by artificial constructs that by design are completely within the control of governmental policy makers (tax rates, subsidies, etc.). It is the fixed parameters that determine the effects of any changes in the causes. The hope has always been that econometric model builders could succeed in developing a model that would simulate accurately the workings of the economy. Such a model, if the values of all its fixed parameters could be measured, would provide an excellent and reliable tool for forming predictions and forecasts of the future state of the economy or of the effects of changes in government policies.

Forecasting researchers have for the most part been disappointed with the performance of econometrics-based forecasting models. The reason for the unsatisfactory performance has always been considered a puzzle, and few critics have ever thought that the puzzle could not be solved. Nevertheless, as long as econometrics is the basis for building forecasting models, it is very unlikely that the puzzle will be solved.

The obstacle that stands in the way of solving this puzzle is to be found at the very foundation of econometric methodology. It is the fundamental view that sees the task of econometric theory as one of developing techniques to measure the values of *fixed* parameters. While physics may be based on the notion that nature provides fixed parameters such as the gravitational constant, it is questionable whether society can truly be seen to be governed by a set of nature-given fixed parameters. To think that fixed parameters can be the basis for an explanation of all of society ultimately leads to the view that all individuals' actions are pre-determined by the nature-given fixed parameters.

This obstacle leads forecasters to a forced choice. On the one hand, if one recognizes that parameters can be fixed (if at all) only for short periods of time then only short-term forecasts are warranted and only when based on recently collected data. On the other hand, if one builds only short-term forecasting models, then the forecasts will be plagued by the noise inherent in short-term data such as daily records of prices. The noise is the result of unexpected, unusual events that can temporarily distort prices and other data from their usual seasonal or trend-related values. Many forecasting researchers seem to be resigned to the dilemma of either rejecting the possibility of making model-based forecasts or accepting the necessary level of inaccuracy that is inherent in econometrics-based forecasting. In this entry, the present state of model-based forecasting is examined and an attempt is made to determine whether there are ways to improve model-building methodology such that some or all of the limitations of econometric modelling can be overcome.

1 Models as the basis for business forecasts

Forecasting plays an essential role in almost every business enterprise. Forecasts range from simple short-term estimates of the delivery time of a firm's product to complex long-term estimates of future prices needed for investment decisions. There does not yet seem to be a reliable allpurpose forecasting technique and, as a result, different techniques have been developed for short- and long-term forecasting. While short-term techniques most frequently involve single-equation time-series extrapolations from available information and data, long-term techniques seem to require more elaborate multi-equation econometric modelling.

The popularity of personal computers has made forecasting an exercise almost all managers can do from their desks. But there are limitations on forecasting, the primary one being the informational basis that can be used. All quantitative forecasting is based on mountains of quantitative data. For example, one might need to collect figures for every month and every product over the last ten years for sales, production, output levels, inventories, material costs, wages paid, etc. The quality of such diverse information can have a profound impact on the quality of the forecast. It may also be costly to collect the needed data.

The primary means of organizing the data is to build a model. A model can be as simple as an equation which states that the sales volume will be proportional to the level of the national income. A model can also be much more complex, involving many more variables and many more equations. The development and maintenance of a complex model can be very expensive and so usually only very large firms are able to afford the development of such large forecasting models. If all that is needed is a forecast of the macroeconomic variables for the whole economy, there are numerous commercially available macroeconomic forecasts. Smaller companies usually find such services more cost-effective than developing their own model.

Effective use of forecasting models requires an appreciation of their limitations. The primary limitation of model-based forecasting is that the models and modelling techniques used are derived from the studies of econometric models. Econometric modelling techniques are, by design, suited to building and evaluating economic explanations rather than deriving economic predictions. For this reason simpler models usually perform as well or better than the more costly complex econometric models.

2 Reasons for building models

Model building is a common preoccupation of many business analysts and most economists today. For some, it is a matter of formalizing their ideas about how an economy or a business enterprise works. For others, it is a matter of being explicit when stating the assumptions made while making predictions or analysing data.

The benefits of being explicit are obvious and thus often taken for granted. Nevertheless, excessive formalization has been frequently called into question. The primary benefit of formalization is that it provides an easy access to ready-made mathematical proofs. Such proofs are thought necessary to assure the soundness of the logic of one's theory concerning how economies or business enterprises work.

The data available to model builders are rarely exact, as they are collected by people and people can make mistakes. Therefore, model builders must always contend with observation errors. Without such errors, building complex models would mainly be an exercise in applied algebra which involves solving a set of simultaneous equations given the observed values for the variables involved (the values of national income, the interest rate, etc.). For example, if the owners of a firm think that the sales level for its product is in fixed proportion to the level of the national income, they could try to calculate that proportion by observing both the national income level and the sales level at one point in time. Of course, if there are no observation errors, the owners could also test any theory that says the proportion is fixed by making observations at different points in time. But when it is recognized that observations can be inaccurate, it must also be recognized that, if the second observation implies a different proportion, it cannot be validly concluded that the true relationship between sales and national income is not a fixed proportion. Any apparent deviation from a fixed proportion may be due entirely to observation errors.

Formal models can vary in size and complexity. The simplest is the one-equation model which attempts to represent the relationship between time and a single observable variable of interest (monthly sales volume, for example). In such a model one might wish to identify a seasonal pattern or long-term trend. The most complex models will involve many equations and many variables. Macroeconomic models, which are used to describe an entire national economy, may have several thousand variables and equations. Such large models are designed according to accepted economic theories in order to somehow capture or organize all the available data about the economy in question. Such models can be used to test the accepted theories or just to represent a complex theory which purports to explain specific features of the economy.

3 Models that promote understanding: measuring parameters

From the beginning of the formal development of econometrics in the 1930s, the hope has been that econometrics would make it possible to marry economic theory with both mathematics and statistics. For some, this has been considered a question of measuring the constants that characterize an economy, much like parts of physics can be characterized by such things as the gravitational constant or the speed-of-light constant. For example, in economic theory it is often assumed that during any twelve-month period, aggregate expenditure on consumer goods (C) is a linear function of the aggregate national income (Y) for that period. Specifically, it is assumed that $C = \alpha + \beta Y$, where β is presumed to represent a psychologically-given 'marginal propensity to consume', that is, a nature-given constant (one published calculation of β concluded that the marginal propensity to consume is 0.74). In some versions of this theory of aggregate consumption, the coefficient α is considered a constant which reflects the minimum necessary expenditure for survival. There are other constants in economics such as the 'elasticity of demand' for specific goods (the numerical ratio of the percentage change in the quantity demanded of a product for a given percentage change in the price of that good). It is often felt that over a significant period of time the elasticities for some goods are relatively stable, and thus there have been many efforts to measure such elasticities.

The primary benefit from building econometric models is that they can deal simultaneously with many interrelated behavioural functions. For example, the consumption function given above ignores the fact that the level of aggregate consumption has an effect on the level of income. It also ignores the effect of changes in the level of aggregate business investment which in turn is affected by the level of the interest rate. Of course, the interest rate itself is not immune to changes in the level of business investment. Government activities such as tax collection and welfare expenditures can also affect the levels of aggregate income, consumption and investment. Econometric models can deal with all such interrelationships by including an equation for each represented relationship. In some cases, it is also possible to have different equations for different sectors of the economy (agricultural sector, industrial sector, etc.). Of course, attempting to represent all possible relationships, as well as recognize all possible differences between sectors, leads to very large models.

During the 1960s much effort was given to building large econometric models to represent an entire economy. The hope was that if the parameters of the assumed relationships which constitute the models could be measured, then government policies could be fashioned to yield desirable effects on the level of employment, inflation, etc.

4 Using models to test theories

The extent to which an econometric model attempts to represent a specific theory of how to interrelate all the observable variables (national income, aggregate investment, interest rates, etc.) determines how such a model can be seen as a useful tool to test that theory. Testing theories by building models of the theories is unavoidably a matter of judgement. The question posed is whether a particular model in some statistical sense 'fits' the available data.

There are two views of testing. One view says that a successful test is obtained when the model of an explanatory theory 'fits' the data according to acceptable statistical criteria. In short, a successful test is a confirmation. The other view says that a successful test is obtained when, by acceptable statistical criteria, the model fails to be confirmed. That is, the model does not 'fit' the data. Needless to say, whether a particular model is deemed to 'fit' or not depends on how strong or weak the criteria are – hence, the question of judgement.

Whether or not a model can be the basis for a test of an explanatory theory of the economy is a matter of logic. Specifically, since every model involves decisions on the part of the model builder (for example, is the relationship between consumption and income a linear relationship or a non-linear relationship?), any model which is deemed to be a 'bad fit' does not force us to give up our economic theory. Perhaps a different set of modelling decisions will lead to a model that does not yield a 'bad fit'.

Similarly, there are logical problems with any claim that our model represents a confirmation of our economic theory. Not only is there a judgemental question of the strength of our statistical criteria, there is always an open question as to whether a model of some other explanatory theory might also be confirmed with the available data. There is also a question of whether the inclusion of future data will still yield a confirming test.

5 Using models to make predictions

Assuming for the moment that we have a well confirmed econometric model, representing an explanatory theory which deals with many interrelated variables of the economy, how can such a model be used to make predictions about the future state of the economy? Since prediction about the future must somehow involve time, whether a model can be used for prediction depends on whether the explanatory theory represented actually includes at least one time-based relationship and how such a relationship has been represented in the model. From a theoretical point of view, there are many ways time can be recognized in a model. For example, even if humans do nothing, trees can grow, so a model might include an equation describing how the rate of growth varies with the size of a tree. Similarly, even though it may be true that aggregate consumption is a static relationship (such as the linear relationship discussed above) it is possible that over time there is variation in the distribution of that consumption between various goods. In this case, the model would have to disaggregate consumption so as to recognize changes in the distribution. If one is modelling the market for soft-wood lumber, not only must one recognize (and model) the dynamic aspects of growing lumber, one must also recognize changes in the demand for lumber such as that which is caused by changes in the interest rate. If there are reasons to think that the interest rate will fall next year, a model might be used to predict the price of soft-wood lumber next year, depending on one's conjecture as to the fall in the interest rate.

Whether a model can be used to make predictions (and thus forecasts) depends heavily on the extent to which that model adequately incorporates time-based relationships. The obvious time-based relationships are those dealing with investment. A decision today to invest depends heavily on what one thinks will happen at some date in the future. It may also depend on what has happened in the recent past.

There are two basic techniques to incorporate time in models. One technique is to recognize the recent past as 'time-lagged' variables.

For example, it is easy to see that some decisions today depend on what happened yesterday. Thus the relationship between aggregate investment and the level of aggregate income might be seen to be that today's aggregate investment is a linear function of both today's aggregate income and last year's aggregate investment. The other technique yields very complex models. Rather than simply recognizing two observed values for one variable of concern (this year's and last year's), all variables would be dated. By dating the variables it is possible in the year 1997 to treat the demand and supply for soft-wood lumber in the year 2001 as if it were for an entirely different product. That is, rather than modelling the same good at different points in time, a product available at two different points in time is recognized as two different products. While this view of time is commonplace in commodity markets, as a basis for building models it leads to very large and very complex models – if for no other reason than that it increases the number of variables that have to be modelled. While such large models might be appropriate for modelling an explanatory theory, given their complexity they are rather useless for making predictions. Thus, almost all models used to make predictions use the time-lagged variables approach.

Many decades ago, the hope was that we could model the business cycle. If we had such a model and it was confirmed, then we would have a basis to make predictions about where we are in such a cycle. Forecasting with such a model would be rather mechanical. There is, however, an obvious difficulty with this hopeful state of affairs. As noted above, all model building presumes that the parameters of a model are fixed or constant. In a Platonic sense, one cannot deal with change unless one first recognizes what is fixed – in short, change is apparent only relative to some fixed background. In other words, only after we have successfully estimated those fixed parameters can we have a basis to predict or understand how the variables we wish to predict are affected by the other variables that have an autonomous dynamic of their own.

6 The elements of model building

In recent years, economic theory has become synonymous with economic model building. There are some indications that theoretical business disciplines and the other social sciences are also moving in the direction of model building. While many models used are simple single-equation models representing time-series data, most methodological problems which involve model building arise from constructing complex models, that is, models consisting of multiple equations. However, one fundamental problem that *must* be addressed in any construction of a complex model is the formal problem related to the important philosophical idea that there cannot be a theory or model which explains everything, that is to say there must be some 'givens'. This problem is important both because it is logically prior to any attempt to use a model for statistical purposes and because it places constraints on the explanatory (or causal) significance of a model.

While it might seem desirable to build models for the purpose of predicting and forecasting, in econometrics all models are built to represent explanatory theories. Usually, econometric models represent explanations of variables such as the Gross Domestic Product (GDP), employment levels or the interest rates (see ECONOMIC GROWTH AND CONVERGENCE). And since all observations of such variables are subject to observation errors, most models are 'stochastic'. The term 'stochastic' is based on the idea of a target, and in particular on the pattern of hits around a target (the greater the distance a given unit or target area is from the centre of the target, the less frequent or dense will be the hits on that area). We might look at a model as a shot at the 'real world' target. There are many reasons why we might miss the target, but they fall into two broad categories: (1) ours was a bad shot (our model was invalid or false); or (2) the target moved (there is random *unexplained* variation in the objects we are attempting to explain or use in our explanation).

A stochastic model is one which allows for the movements of the target. In particular, stochastic models follow from a methodological decision *not* to attempt to explain anything *completely*. Every non-stochastic model does claim to offer a complete explanation and for this reason the logic in the underlying explanation must be non-stochastic (the only exceptions are those theories involving 'fuzzy logic' or 'chaos theory'). Fundamentally, it is the non-stochastic logic of the model that determines the model's usefulness. Only after the logic of an ideal explanatory model is worked out will the stochastic aspects, induced by the recognition that observation errors are unavoidable, be introduced.

7 Non-stochastic model as explanatory basis

The building of a non-stochastic model involves the following three methodological decisions regarding the form of the model: (1) to decide what variables are to be included; (2) to decide which of the included variables are to be considered as given (not to be explained); and (3) to decide what will be the form of the relationships between these variables – for example, whether it is to be linear, non-linear (quadratic, exponential, etc.), lexicographic, convex, continuous, increasing or decreasing. As will be explained, these three methodological decisions will result in the recognition of the three ingredients that characterize all models: endogenous variables, exogenous variables and parameters (which are sometimes called coefficients). Once the variables are specified, the form of the relations alone defines the parameters of the relationships. The three methodological decisions are not arbitrary, they are made such that the resulting model adequately represents a particular explanatory theory.

Obviously, which variables are givens and which are to be explained is dictated by the underlying theory. For example, the production of wheat might in some way be causally determined by annual rainfall, but annual rainfall in no way can be thought to be causally determined by the production of wheat. It might now be asked: 'What can the form of a model tell us about the theory which the model represents?'. Since almost every explanation involves a cause-and-effect relationship, the most important characteristic of a model's form is the 'causal statement' which it represents. The significance of this characteristic of models is addressed in relation to some of the uses to which models may be put. Two possible uses for models are considered: (1) an ontologico-theoretical use; and (2) an econometric use. The first is concerned more with the variables, the second more with the parameters.

First, consider the causal significance of models used for ontologico-theoretical purposes. The main idea that needs to be dealt with is the difference between the two types of variables (endogenous and exogenous). The main difference is that the model is designed to 'explain' the endogenous variables and does not attempt to 'explain' the exogenous variables. However, one thing which the exogenous and endogenous variables have in common is that they can be directly observable (whereas parameters are not).

As noted above, with respect to the variables of a model, the main characteristic of the form of a model is the causal statement it represents or posits. The causal statements are of the form: the values of such-and-such exogenous variables together 'cause' the values of such-and-such endogenous variables. This is not to suggest anything metaphysical by using the word 'cause'. The word is used because although the exogenous variables influence the endogenous variables, the endogenous variables *do not* influence or affect the exogenous variables. In other words, the model describes or represents a one-way-only relationship between exogenous and endogenous variables (such as the one between rainfall and wheat production). It is important to note that although the model as a whole posits a one-way relationship, the individual hypotheses or equations which together constitute the model need not represent one-way relationships – for example, they may be about the relationship between endogenous variables. In light of the philosophical idea mentioned earlier, namely that we cannot explain everything (there must be some 'givens'), we now ask: 'What if a theory, and hence the models representing it, does not involve or include any exogenous variables?'. If a model fails to recognize any exogenous variables, then that model runs the

Modelling and forecasting

serious risk of being trivial and of little use to anyone interested in policy matters (although the model may look rather impressive).

Note that it is possible for a model as a whole to have very few exogenous variables, but the model may be separated into independent sub-models for which the endogenous variables of one sub-model can be considered exogenous to the other sub-models. An example of this situation is the 'classical economic macro-model' where real output is an exogenous variable in the commodities market but is an endogenous variable in the production function.

For some economists and business analysts, an important aspect of any theoretical model may be its policy implications. The only variables which can be policy variables are the model's exogenous variables. When we consider changing some government or business policy we mean that we are changing one or more of the exogenous variables, and we depend on the model (or the underlying theory) to tell us what will happen – that is, on what will happen to the endogenous variables. What we think or expect will happen depends on the theory or model we have implicitly or explicitly in mind.

Apart from the exogenous and endogenous variables, the remaining ingredients of models are the parameters. Parameters play one specific role in an ontologico-theoretical model: they are used only to express the form of the model. For example, if we put forth the hypothesis that a country's aggregate consumption (C) is linearly related to that country's aggregate income (Y), we can represent this hypothesis by the linear equation $C = \alpha + \beta Y$. If instead we put forth the hypothesis that the relationship is quadratic, we might posit the non-linear equation $C = \alpha + \beta Y + \gamma Y^2$. Parameters α and β (and γ) appear solely as a result of the assumed form of the relationship. What is most important is to realize that we need not know the values of the parameters in order to appreciate the significance of the model in which they appear.

Note that sometimes we do need to specify a certain range of values to assure us that we have an equilibrium model (for example, whatever is the value of β, it must be true that $0 < \beta < 1$). But seldom does specifying the form require a *particular* value for any parameter. However, if one's hypothesis is that aggregate consumption, C, is proportional to aggregate income, Y, then one is claiming in effect that $\alpha = 0$. Unfortunately, in most cases it is impossible to 'measure' the parameters directly. If we could (implying they are observable), we might as well make them exogenous variables. In other words, the difference between exogenous variables and parameters is that we may directly observe the former but not the latter.

It should be noted that one of the implications of Karl Popper's view of science (1959) would seem to be that it is not necessary to know the values of the parameters in order to refute the model (and hence the theory it represents). The basic idea is that if, for instance, an hypothesis says the path of a planet around the sun is circular, then generally the hypothesis is compatible with any three positional observations. But it is not *necessarily* compatible with any four observations. Here the hypothetical form is expressed in general terms without specifying the particular values of the parameters (the hypothesis does not specify a *particular* circular path). It would only make it easier. However, to test the model it is absolutely necessary to know the values of endogenous variables since that is what a model or theory is attempting to explain. How much data on the endogenous variables is *necessary* is an epistemological problem which has been discussed elsewhere (Boland 1989). Although the exogenous variables need not be observable for Popper's falsifiability criterion, they must be directly or indirectly observable for testability.

To illustrate the ingredients and their causal significance, consider a simple model which purports to represent the market for some product such as wheat. That is, it represents the typical economics textbook's view of the determination of the market's price and quantity by representing the market's demand and supply curves as follows:

Model I

Let the demand curve be a linear relationship between Q, the total quantity purchased, and P, the price paid, with a negative slope ($-\beta$):

$$\alpha - \beta P - Q = 0 \qquad (1)$$

And let the supply curve be a linear relationship between the same Q and P but with a positive slope ($+\lambda$):

$$\gamma + \lambda P - Q = 0 \qquad (2)$$

In terms of a causal statement this model says that price and quantity are interdependent and are not dependent on (or caused by) anything else. But, since this model does not contain any exogenous variables, in effect it has no observable causes. That is, it must be admitted that in some sense the parameters are causes. But since they are neither variable (by construction) nor observable and since market prices and quantities vary from day to day, it begs the question as to why prices and quantities would ever vary.

To overcome such a problem, consider two observable exogenous variables such as the rainfall per year (R) and the size of the population (S), and the following model can be put forth:

Model 2

Let the demand curve now be:

$$\alpha - \beta P - Q + \mu S = 0 \qquad (1')$$

and the supply curve now be:

$$\gamma + \lambda P - Q + \omega R = 0 \qquad (2')$$

where R and S are the exogenous variables. This model then says that together R and S 'cause' the co-determination of P and Q. The important thing is that demand is 'caused' or affected by something different from what 'causes' or affects supply. And in each case the causes are observable.

Turning to the econometric use of these two algebraic market-equilibrium models, the econometrician is often interested in the values of the parameters of a model – which is by no means demeaning since, as has been noted above, the existence of parameters is used to indicate the form of a model. For various purposes it is sometimes desirable to know the values of a model's parameters. One obvious purpose is to use the model to form a market forecast or to conduct a what-if simulation by positing different values for the exogenous variables. In the case of Model 2, the only potential control variable (one which someone could cause to change) is the size and growth of population. Before an econometrician can attempt to 'measure' the parameters an important question must be considered: if we have a sufficient amount of data for the endogenous and exogenous variables, is it possible to deduce the values of the parameters? Particularly, can we deduce a unique set of values? This is often expressed by asking whether the model (when combined with sufficient observations) is capable of 'identifying' a unique set of values for the parameters.

Whether the values of the parameters of a model can be deduced from the observed values for the variables depends on the form of the model. The general requirement is that the hypothesis or equations used must 'look' different (they must assert different formal relationships between the variables). It turns out that what was necessary for the variables of a model (if it is to posit a causal or one-way relation between endogenous and exogenous variables) is also necessary for the parameters of a model. If it is to be possible to deduce the values of the parameters of a model, then it will be necessary that the form of a model be such that the model says something non-trivial or useful (the form of the model must assert a causal relation by saying something about exogenous and endogenous variables). The problem of specifying the form of a model so that the values of its parameters can be deduced from observations of the variables is called the 'identification problem'. We note that this problem is logically prior to the observation of the variables or any consideration of statistical data and hence logically prior to the estimation or measurement of the parameters. In other words, it is a problem for non-stochastic models as well as stochastic models.

Looking more closely at the identification property of a model, one finds the following concepts (as expressed in the language of early econometricians): a structure, a model and a property called identification. By a structure (of a non-stochastic model) we mean a specific set of structural equations such as would be obtained by giving specific numerical values to the parameters of a model. By a

Modelling and forecasting

(non-stochastic) model we mean only a specification of the form of the structural equations (for instance, their linearity and a designation of the variables occurring in each equation). More abstractly, a model can be defined as a set of structures. Identification refers to the property of a specific model which assures that, if the model is posited as being the hypothetical generator of the observed data, a unique structure can be deduced (or identified) from the observed data. The term 'hypothetical generator' means that whenever the true values of the parameters are given, if the observed values of the exogenous variables at one point of time are put into the model, the resulting values for the endogenous variables at that point of time are said to be 'generated' by the structure of the model.

There are two ways that a model may fail to possess the identification property. Either the model is such that no structure can be deduced or the model is such that more than one structure can be deduced from the same data. Attempting to avoid the possibility of either difficulty is called the problem of identification. To simply demonstrate the identification property and its similarity with the causal statements discussed above, consider again Model 1:

$$\alpha - \beta P - Q = 0 \qquad (1)$$

$$\gamma + \lambda P - Q = 0 \qquad (2)$$

Equation (2) looks like equation (1); both say that P and Q are linearly related and are not affected by any other consideration. The usual interpretation of the model of a market is to say the P and Q in the two equations are equilibrium values, that is, the price and quantity at which the market clears. To determine the values of these two endogenous variables, one usually treats the two equations as a set of simultaneous equations since they are claimed to be true simultaneously.

The algebraic solution for P and Q gives:

$$P = (\alpha - \gamma)/(\beta + \lambda) = p \qquad (3)$$

$$Q = (\beta\gamma + \alpha\lambda)/(\beta + \lambda) = q \qquad (4)$$

where p and q are the observed values for P and Q. It is very important to keep in mind that since by assumption and design, the values of the parameters (that is, the value for each of α, β, γ and λ) are fixed constants which means that no matter when the observations are made, the observed values of the P and Q will never change. That is, they cannot change unless the value of at least one of the parameters changes and this is exactly what has been ruled out by construction.

Now the question to consider here is whether we can use the observed values to calculate the values of the parameters. One way to attempt this is to multiply equation (3) by β and add to it equation (4):

$$\beta P + Q = \beta p + q.$$

Since the left-hand side of this equation is contained in equation (1), substituting the right-hand side into equation (1) gives:

$$\beta p + q = \alpha.$$

This is one equation in two unknowns (α and β). A similar exercise can be performed to use equation (2) and it, too, will produce one equation with two unknowns (γ and λ). Since in both cases this leaves us with more unknowns than we have equations, the observation of P and Q cannot be used to tell us anything about the fixed values of the parameters α, β, γ, and λ.

As an alternative, consider again Model 2:

$$\alpha - \beta P - Q + \mu S = 0 \qquad (1')$$

$$\gamma + \lambda P - Q + \omega R = 0 \qquad (2')$$

The solutions for P and Q are:

$$P = [(\alpha - \gamma)/(\beta + \lambda)] \\ + [\mu S/(\beta + \lambda)] - [\omega R/(\beta + \lambda)] \qquad (3')$$

$$Q = [(\alpha\lambda + \beta\gamma)/(\beta + \lambda)] \\ + [\lambda\mu S/(\beta + \lambda)] + [\beta\omega R/(\beta + \lambda)] \qquad (4')$$

The form of these two equations can be summarized as:

$$P = a_1 + a_2 S + a_3 R \qquad (3'')$$

$$Q = b_1 + b_2 S + b_3 R \qquad (4'')$$

These latter equations (using the shorthand coefficients, as and bs) can be estimated by simple linear regressions. That is, we can use merely three sets of observed values for P and Q for *different* observed values of R and S to calculate the as and bs (remembering that we are dealing with errorless observations). This is possible because, unlike Model 1 (where there is only one possible observed value for P and one possible observed value for Q), the observed values for P and Q can change whenever the observed values of R and S change.

Now if we multiply equation (3″) by β and add it to equation (4″), we get:

$$\beta P + Q = \beta a_1 + \beta a_2 S + \beta a_3 R + b_1 + b_2 S + b_3 R$$

or

$$\beta P + Q = (\beta a_1 + b_1) + (\beta a_2 + b_2)S + (\beta a_3 + b_3)R$$

which by rearranging and inserting into equation (1′) implies:

$$\beta a_1 + b_1 = \alpha$$
$$\beta a_2 + b_2 = \mu$$
$$\beta a_3 + b_3 = 0$$

which since we have already calculated the values of the as and bs we now have three equations and three unknowns that we can use to deduce α, β and μ. A similar exercise can be performed to deduce γ, λ and ω.

The crucial thing to note is what enabled us to use several observations of the variables to deduce the values of the parameters of our model. The ability was made possible by recognizing that we had to make the individual equations of the model look different. This was accomplished by adding just two exogenous variables to our model that had just two endogenous variables.

So what is needed to be sure we can calculate or 'measure' the values of the fixed parameters of a simple model of a market equilibrium is now evident. However, we have been assuming that all observations are without observation errors. Recognizing that errorless observations are virtually impossible, many more observations would be needed to calculate the values of the parameters. A crude way to think of this is as follows: in the above example, the observations needed to form a set of three simultaneous equations can be considered to be three random samples, where each sample consists of one observation for each of the variables. A common rule of thumb in statistical sampling is to say that the minimum number of observations for an adequate sample is thirty observations. Here, this would mean that we would need ninety observations just to calculate the values of the three parameters. Thus, the process of 'measuring' the parameters of even a simple model can demand a large quantity of data. But if we were trying to measure the parameters for a market over three or four months, ninety observations would not be very demanding.

8 Problems with truly stochastic models

Fifty years ago it was pointed out that statistically measuring parameters (as in the above illustration) can easily yield questionable results. The primary difficulty is that if we were merely to substitute the measured values of the parameters into the equations representing the demand and supply curves, we could not legitimately treat the P and Q as algebraic solutions to a set of simultaneous equations. The reason is that the rules of algebraic manipulation of any equation are based on the variables having exact values. But given the unavoidable observation errors, statistics would provide only averages with a probability of error over specified ranges. Said another way, consider again the assumption that aggregate consumption is linearly related to the level of aggregate income, that is, $C = \alpha + \beta Y$. Statistics might indicate a 90 per cent probability that the value of the marginal propensity to consume, β, is 0.74. And if the estimated value of the constant a is similarly accurate only with a 90 per cent probability, then the accuracy of the calculated level of aggregate consumption, C, may be off by as much as 20 per cent. In models with many more variables and parameters, the calculations could be off by very wide margins.

There are other more obvious problems with the process of making statistical estimates of the values of parameters. Almost all estimation of parameters is based on classical least-squares analysis whereby the estimates of the values of the parameters are those values which would minimize the errors between the calculated values and the observed values. All the rules of statistical inference using least-squares analysis are based on certain assumptions about the nature of the variables being observed. The rules of inference were devised for analysing data from controlled experiments. For example, in such situations one assumes that the independent variables (those usually on the right-hand side) are independent of each other. Since the entire point of building econometric models is that they allow us to recognize the interdependence of variables, the study of econometric theory is devoted to overcoming such deviations from the rules of classical statistical inference.

Modern econometric modelling addresses these and other methodological problems by explicitly recognizing that the equations representing relationships between observable variables may be inaccurate. To compensate for the inaccuracy, each equation of a model is adjusted by including a variable that accounts for the inaccuracy. For example, consider Model 2 above. This time the equations are rearranged to put the dependent variable, Q, on the left and the independent variables, P, S and R, on the right.

$$Q = \alpha - \beta P + \mu S \quad (1')$$

$$Q = \gamma + \lambda P + \omega R \quad (2')$$

The stochastic version of Model 2 is the following:

$$Q = \alpha - \beta P + \mu S + \varepsilon_1 \quad (1'')$$

$$Q = \gamma + \lambda P + \omega R + \varepsilon_2 \quad (2'')$$

where the εs correct for the inaccuracy, that is, they render into an equality what without them would be an inequality.

If observations are made at many points in time, the average error is zero by assumption. But there remain many problems that must be dealt with when estimating the values of the parameters with such a model, not the least of which is when the error variables are correlated either with each other or over time. The primary justification for the inclusion of error variables is the recognition that observations suffer from human errors. Thus, even if the underlying non-stochastic model accurately represented real-world relationships, the model would not likely represent an exact fit with the observed values of the variables. The assumption of a zero average error would be appropriate where the only reason for the inexactness is the common occurrence of observational errors. But there are other reasons for errors. The obvious one would be that the relationships are not linear. For example, the true supply relationship might be as follows:

$$Q = \gamma + \lambda_1 P + \omega_1 R + \lambda_2 P^2 + \omega_2 R^2 + \xi PR \quad (2''')$$

which means that unless $\lambda_2 P^2 + \omega_2 R^2 + \xi PR = 0$, the ε_2 in equation $(2'')$ exists partially to compensate for this so-called structural error. Similarly, it might be the case that the true supply relationship is instead:

$$Q = \gamma + \lambda P + \omega R + \xi W \quad (2''')$$

where W might represent the going average wage rate. In this so-called errors-in-variables case, the error variable ε_2 must compensate for the missing term ξW. Obviously in this case there would not seem to be a good reason for assuming a zero average error. In other words, the inclusion of error variables may not be enough to avoid inaccurate estimates and calculations.

9 The history of econometric-based forecasting

Earlier pre-1940s econometric studies were limited to correlation theory in the mould of classical statistical theory. The modern era of econometrics began in the early 1940s with the recognition that errors must be recognized within the models as noted above (Haavelmo 1944). Today it is safe to say that econometric theory has become a special branch of mathematical statistics, one with its focus being statistical analysis of non-experimental data.

The 1950s represented a consolidation of various approaches to econometric model building. In the 1960s, econometric modelling took centre stage in the economics profession. One reason for its domination was the worldwide popularity of Richard Lipsey's 1963 economics textbook, *Positive Economics*. Another factor was the expansion of government interventions in Western economies. Almost all of the government-sponsored econometric modelling in the 1960s was based on Keynesian economics (see KEYNES, J.M.). Many government policy makers were convinced that they could use large econometric models to 'fine tune' the economy. The 1970s saw a steady growth of econometric model building fostered mostly by the development and availability of large mainframe computers. An additional factor was the growth of available data banks. The 1980s continued the development with ever more sophisticated statistical estimation techniques and tools. By the end of the 1980s, anyone with a desktop personal computer could engage in sophisticated econometric model building with readily available and inexpensive computer software.

Until the end of the 1960s, almost all forecasting was limited to simple single-equation time series estimations. The only question ever at issue was whether one could identify trends or seasonality in the observed time-series. Forecasting in the 1970s benefited with the introduction of the so-called Box–Jenkins methodology (a sophisticated method of extrapolation) which provided a systematic approach to time-series analysis (Kennedy 1998, chapter 17). But the Box–Jenkins methodology was severely limited both by the need to assume that the time-series in question was sufficiently stable and by the need to have very large amounts of data available to be sure that the model of the time series could be identified.

In the 1970s, econometric models began to be used to make economic forecasts. The motivation behind this seems to have been a presumption that human judgement is inherently faulty. Somehow, computer-based forecasting was thought to be unbiased and able to handle data more efficiently than a human forecaster. The 1970s also saw a growth of literature devoted to evaluating the performance of econometric-based forecasts and in particular to comparisons with the performance of less complex time-series analysis. While econometric models could deal with many variables at the same time, as well as deal with complex interrelationships, such an ability came at the cost of requiring much more detailed data. Collecting such data is a costly process and so the question has always been whether the additional cost relative to simpler time-series analysis is warranted. Where the question of cost is involved there is always an opportunity for someone to set up a business to provide the data and even provide ready-made models and forecasts. Thus, beginning in the 1970s, we saw the creation of several commercially available econometric models and forecasts.

Several studies showed that econometric-based forecasting failed to live up to expectations (Dawes *et al.* 1994). Most experts in the field of econometric model building thought econometric forecasts should do well in the short run since the parameters could safely be assumed to be constant. Other people thought econometric forecasts might do well in the long run since econometric models were able to incorporate more variables and thus better capture the effects of long-term trends. Neither of these expectations has been upheld by documented performance. Some critics have even argued that minimizing errors during model fitting is not necessarily the best way to assure accurate forecasts.

10 Conclusion

The difficulty which faces all model-based forecasting involves a fundamental trade-off. The fundamental methodological problem facing every econometric model builder is that such models are based on the prior collection of data (for example, weekly prices for soft-wood lumber for the years 1955, 1956 ... 1994) and using these data to estimate the values of all nature-given parameters (in the spirit of physics). But there is no good reason why these parameters would remain constant over time. Specifically, if one's model is dealing with observations made over several years, it is highly unlikely that the parameters would be constant. One could try to overcome this problem of non-constant parameters by reducing the span of time over which the data are to be collected. There are two ways to do this but both have insurmountable problems.

Simply reducing the time span to where it is more likely that the parameters would remain constant is one method (for example, rather than collecting monthly average prices for the years 1955 to 1994, one could just collect the prices over the years 1985 to 1994). The difficulty is that, depending on the size of the model, there may not be sufficient observations to perform the estimation, that is, to identify the values of the parameters. The alternative is to collect weekly or daily data so that the reduced time span will still permit the assumption of constant parameters to be accepted without compromising the need for enough data. The difficulty with this alternative approach is that the data can be quite 'noisy'. That is, while monthly average prices can remain stable over an entire year, prices can vary widely day to day and week to week. Variability of daily or weekly prices is not per se a problem. The problem occurs when the variation is spurious. Perhaps during one week there was a power outage that limited supply, thus leading to a higher-than-normal price. Perhaps in another week there was an equally unusual drop in demand leading to a fall in the price. By using data averaged out over longer periods of time, many of the spurious variations will cancel out. A related difficulty with short-period data is that it is difficult to sort out whether or not the data are being affected by long-term trends or seasonal deviations.

With the above methodological considerations in mind, one can easily see why short-term forecasting is not very accurate. The reason is that the large data requirements needed to ensure that the model is identified means that more frequent data must be collected. Clearly, yearly data will not do since even ten years of data may not be enough for a forecast of next year's demand – and worse, such a long period of time calls into question any presumption of a stable set of fixed parameters. So it is more common to collect monthly, weekly or even daily data.

But as we have just seen, forecasts based on frequently collected data run the risk of being polluted by spurious noise that would not affect less frequently collected data. In longer-term forecasting, temporary positive events can be cancelled out by equally temporary negative events so that the yearly average is not affected. Obviously, monthly, weekly and daily data can give undue weight to either type of temporary event. And as we have just seen, long-term forecasts based on models require stable and constant parameters. But the longer the time period needed to collect sufficient data, the less likely it is that the parameters will remain constant. Unless the values of the parameters remain constant, the usual econometric methods used to measure those parameters will profoundly be called into question. And without unquestioned values for the parameters, model-based forecasts are virtually impossible. Thus we can see why in the minds of many critics of model-based forecasting, the trade-off between long-term and short-term forecasting is hopeless. Either way, the forecasts have not been accurate. This is most troubling for short-term forecasts since the inherent problem with all econometric modelling (viz, having to assume that the parameters are constant) would seem to be minimized. After all, it would seem reasonable to assume that the parameters for the entire economy are stable and constant over short periods of time.

Can these problems be overcome? There is little optimism expressed in the various survey articles that would indicate that these problems can be overcome. While some adventurous econometric theorists have proposed ways to deal with non-constant parameters, little of this work has been noticed by forecasting researchers. The reason remains the same. Specifically, forecast model builders must face the trade-off between avoidance of the questionable stability of a model's parameters when the time period for collecting data is reduced and the noise caused by increasing the number of observations in the reduced time period to accommodate the needs of identification. Of course, one can always ignore the trade-off and learn to accept and accommodate inherently inaccurate forecasting models.

LAWRENCE A. BOLAND
SIMON FRASER UNIVERSITY

Further reading

(References cited in the text marked *)

Armstrong, J.S. (1978a) 'Forecasting with econometric methods: folklore versus facts', *Journal of Business* 51 (4): 549–64. (This provocative essay argues that, contrary to evidence, some econometricians may think accurate short-term forecasts are provided by econometric models and that such forecasts are improved by making more complex models.)

Armstrong, J.S. (1978b) 'Econometric forecasting and the Science Court', *Journal of Business* 51

(4): 595–600. (Responds to the critics of his 'folklore versus facts' paper.)

* Boland, L. (1989) *The Methodology of Economic Model Building: Methodology after Samuelson*, London: Routledge. (Chapters 2 and 3 show that requiring economic models to be testable in Popper's sense means that models would have to be both small and simple.) Available free at *http://www.sfu.ca/~boland*

* Dawes, R., Fildes, R., Lawrence, M. and Ord, K. (1994) 'The past and the future of forecasting research', *International Journal of Forecasting* 10 (1): 151–9. (Four critical discussions of the state of forecasting research by leading researchers.)

* Haavelmo, T. (1944) 'The probability approach in econometrics', supplement to *Econometrica* 12. (This monograph forms the major part of the foundation of modern econometrics, arguing that the probability approach must be much more than the recognition of observational errors.)

Haavelmo, T. (1958) 'The role of the econometrician in the advancement of economic theory', *Econometrica* 26 (3): 351–7. (This presidential address reviews the first twenty-five volumes of *Econometrica*.)

* Kennedy, P. (1998) *A Guide to Econometrics*, Cambridge, MA: MIT Press. (A useful guide for the practical use of econometrics.)

Klein, L. (1957) 'The scope and limitations of econometrics', *Applied Statistics* 6 (1): 1–17. (A critical survey of the development of econometric theory by one of its most prominent practitioners.)

Klein, L. (1971) 'Whither econometrics?', *Journal of the American Statistical Society* 66 (334): 415–21. (A critical survey of the progress of econometrics since his 1957 article.)

* Lipsey, R. (1963) *An Introduction to Positive Economics*, London: Weidenfeld & Nicolson. (The textbook that first introduced systematic quantitative analysis to beginning economics students.)

Makridakis, S. (1986) 'The art and science of forecasting: an assessment and future directions', *International Journal of Forecasting* 2 (1): 15–39. (A critical survey of twenty-five years of forecasting research.)

Makridakis, S. (1991) 'Forecasting in the 21st century', *International Journal of Forecasting* 7 (2): 123–6. (An editorial discussing the dilemmas facing all builders of forecasting models.)

Makridakis, S. and Wheelwright, S. (1989) *Forecasting Methods for Management*, New York: Wiley. (A popular textbook that covers almost all forecasting methods.)

Miller, P. (1978) 'Forecasting with econometric methods: a comment', *Journal of Business* 51 (4): 579–84. (A comment on Armstrong (1978a) that adds an additional criticism which says that the main problem with econometric models is that they are seldom stable enough to form the basis for accurate forecasts.)

Morgan, M. (1990) *The History of Econometric Ideas*, New York: Cambridge University Press. (A popular history of econometrics covering both the early attempts to model business cycles and the pioneering work of Haavelmo.)

* Popper, K. (1959) *The Logic Of Scientific Discovery*, New York: Science Editions. (The English edition of his 1934 book that first argued that science is an enterprise of systematic criticism and hence that scientific theories need to be falsifiable and testable rather than verifiable.)

Zarnowitz, V. (1967) *An Appraisal of Short-term Economic Forecasts*, New York: Columbia University Press. (An early assessment of the performance of short-term forecasting.)

Zellner, A. (1978) 'Folklore versus facts in forecasting with econometric methods', *Journal of Business* 51 (4): 587–93. (A comment on Armstrong (1978a) that adds an argument for why forecasters should build simple models rather than complex ones.)

See also: BUSINESS ECONOMICS; ECONOMIC GROWTH AND CONVERGENCE; KEYNES, J.M.

Transaction cost economics

1 **The Coasean tradition**
2 **Critiques and alternatives**
3 **Policy implications and the future**
4 **Assessment**

Overview

The aim of this entry is to discuss the new avenues opened up to economic enquiry by the consideration of transaction costs. The origins of transaction cost economics (TCE) can be traced back to a classic article on the theory of the firm by Ronald Coase. In it, Coase tried to explain the existence of multiple person hierarchies (firms) in terms of market failures, which he claimed were due to the high costs of exchanging (transacting) in markets. Coase later extended his analysis to attribute the existence of Law and the State to market transaction costs.

After a long gestation period, Coase's ideas have been taken up, elaborated, extended and criticized by numerous economists. The emergent new perspective has found applications not only in explanations of economic phenomena, such as the market, the firm, the transnational corporation and the state, but also in sociology, economic history, development, organization studies and strategic management. It would appear that TCE has the potential to transform not only economics and social science, but also, perhaps, to provide the elements of a unified social sciences research programme. It comes as no surprise therefore that the originator of TCE, Ronald Coase, was awarded the 1991 Nobel Prize for economics. Moreover, the 1993 Prize went to a disciple of TCE, Douglass North. In his work, he has attempted to explain economic history by pursuing a brand of TCE theorizing that goes beyond conventional economic thinking. TCE is also currently finding applications in macroeconomics and is rapidly influencing both government policy on competition and industry, and the competitive and corporate strategies of firms.

Despite its widespread influence, TCE has been the focus of widespread criticism from various vantage points, such as economics, sociology and management studies, and a number of alternative perspectives have been proposed. This entry is intended to offer a bird's-eye view of these developments. Section 1 looks at the origin and development of the Coasean tradition and pays particular attention to the TCE explanation of the nature, and boundaries of the firm. Section 2 discusses some critiques and alternatives, while section 3 outlines the policy implications of TCE, anticipates future developments. Section 4 provides an assessment.

1 The Coasean tradition

Coase's main concern in the 1937 article was to explain the existence of firms (see COASE, R.). His starting point was that resource allocation in market economies is ordinarily regarded by theorists as taking place through the price mechanism. Yet he observed that economists often also employ the assumption that such allocation depends on the entrepreneur. These two assumptions, however, are incompatible. In Coase's view, the distinguishing mark of the firm is the supersession of the price mechanism. The question then arises as to how such alternative institutional forms of resource allocation come about.

Coase's answer is that the operation of the market is costly and that by forming an organization and allowing an entrepreneur to direct the resources (firm or hierarchy) certain 'marketing costs' are saved. 'Marketing costs' are the costs of using the price mechanism. Examples given by Coase include the cost of discovering the relevant prices and the cost of negotiating and concluding separate contracts for each transaction. Contracting costs in particular, he observed, are not eliminated but are greatly reduced if the entrepreneur (seen as one of the 'factors of production' within the firm) does not have to make a series of contracts with the other parties with whom he or she is cooperating (the other factors of production), but substitutes them for one contract; under the terms of this contract, the other factors agree to obey the directions of the entrepreneur within certain limits: 'It is the fact of direction which is the essence of the legal concept of "employer and employee"' (Coase 1937: 409).

Coase's argument was that, given the assumption that the market pre-exists or is a natural starting point, the very existence of firms implies that firms reduce costs associated with the price mechanism. This revolutionary insight was potentially damaging to the neoclassical tradition as it provided a reason why planning (including, perhaps, central planning) might be preferable to the market.

Although some insights resembling Coase's were developed in the 1960s and early 1970s, particularly by writers on the theory of the transnational corporation, it was not until Oliver Williamson's *Markets and Hierarchies* (1975) that an attempt to develop Coase's work into a full-blown research programme in economics was made (see COASE, R.; INSTITUTIONAL ECONOMICS; WILLIAMSON, O.E.).

Williamson on markets and hierarchies

Williamson's starting point was the same as Coase's, namely the assumption that 'in the beginning, there were markets' (Williamson 1975: 20). Given this, the core methodological elements of the perspective that Williamson outlined in *Markets and Hierarchies* are:

1 the transaction is the basic unit of analysis;
2 human agents are subject to bounded rationality and are characterized by self-interest and guile (opportunism);
3 the critical dimensions for describing transactions are frequency, uncertainty and transaction-specific investments, or asset specificity;
4 the attempt to keep transaction costs to a minimum is the principal factor that explains viable modes of contracting and should be the main concern of organizational design;
5 the assessment of transaction costs differences is a useful exercise in comparing institutions.

According to Williamson, a transaction occurs when a good or service is transferred across a technologically separable interface. Transaction costs are the costs of running the economic system, (Arrow 1970). Williamson thinks of these in contractual terms. Coase (1960) and North (1981) list search and information costs, measurement costs, bargaining and negotiation costs, and policing and enforcement costs as examples of transaction costs (see also Eggertsson 1990).

Williamson's concept of human agency has two important elements. First, there is 'bounded rationality', which refers to behaviour that is intended to be rational but is so only to a limited extent. Limits to rationality arise from limited knowledge, foresight, skill and time. Second, there is self-interest with guile; agents can be selective in information disclosure, can distort information or can try to deliberately mislead. Self-interest with guile is called 'opportunism' (also 'moral hazard' or 'agency'). The importance of these two behavioural assumptions, Williamson claims, is profound: given bounded rationality, all complex contracts are unavoidably incomplete and given opportunism, contracts unsupported by credible commitments cannot be regarded as promises. It follows that transactions should be organized so as to minimize these problems.

'Transaction-specific investments' (asset specificity) refers to the extent to which assets can be redeployed to alternative uses and to different users without loss of productive value. Forms of asset specificity include site specificity, human asset specificity, physical asset specificity and dedicated assets. Of the three critical dimensions for describing transactions, asset specificity is claimed to be more important and distinctive than uncertainty and frequency.

The co-existence of asset specificity, bounded rationality and opportunism creates a situation where market transaction costs can be so high that it is advantageous to supersede the market and organize resource allocation within a firm. This is due to a 'fundamental transformation'; from a potentially large numbers condition pre-contract, to a small numbers bilateral dependence, once a contract has been made. In the context of specific assets, opportunistic behaviour may lead to excessive market transaction costs, which render integration, seen as the internalization of the market, preferable. The 'internalization' of the market by the firm is due to the latter's ability to reduce transaction costs arising from the co-existence of all three factors. If any one of the three factors does not exist, markets can still allocate resources economically compared to firms. If rationality were not bounded, all potential problems could be settled from the outset and the problems of opportunism and asset specificity could be solved within the market. If there were no opportunism, the 'principle of stewardship' (whereby transactors can be relied upon to keep promises) could be used instead of a hierarchy of the sort found in a firm. Finally, if there were no asset specificity (and therefore no sunk costs), contestable markets – markets characterized by perfectly easy entry and costless exit – would exist.

Williamson considers the co-existence of all three factors as pervasive, implying the possibility of market supersession by hierarchies. The advantage of internal organization is that it facilitates adaptive, sequential decision making in circumstances where complex, contingent claim contracts are not feasible and sequential spot markets are hazardous. Problems from bounded rationality are thus reduced. Internal organization also attenuates opportunism, both because of the ability of authority to stop prolonged disputes and because members of a hierarchy are likely to feel that they are part of a whole. Convergent expectations are more likely to appear, which reduces uncertainty. Bargaining costs arising from asset specificity can similarly be reduced through the use of authority.

While hierarchical organization looks desirable for the reasons given above, Williamson points out that there are problems. These arise because the 'high-powered' incentives of markets can be blunted or lost by hierarchies. A related problem is the possibility of high transaction costs within firms or 'management costs' (Demsetz 1988). Thus there is a trade-off between high-powered incentives and bilateral adaptability. The combination of management costs and the loss of high-powered incentives can help to explain the boundaries between firms and the market (given the assumption of pre-existing markets). As Coase claimed, 'At the margin, the costs of organizing within the firm will be equal either to the costs of organizing in another firm or to the costs involved in leaving the transaction to be "organized" by the price mechanism' (1937: 404). The idea of leaving the transaction to be organized by the price mechanism is crucial here, as it implies that in the absence of internalization, markets (continue to) exist.

Transaction cost economics on the nature, integration and internal organisation of firms

Transaction cost economics (TCE) has been used by Williamson, to explain a number of important issues: the employment relation (between employer and employee), vertical integration, the evolution of multidivisional structures within firms, the conglomerate and transnational corporations (Williamson 1981) (see MULTINATIONAL CORPORATIONS). Of these, the employment relation was Coase's almost exclusive concern and it is arguably the most important (Malcolmson 1984; Kay 1992). This is because it seems that only the employment relation has the potential to explain the emergence of hierarchies from pre-existing markets. All the other issues listed above presuppose the existence of firms (Pitelis 1991). This idea is examined briefly below.

Vertical integration

Williamson explains vertical integration (VI; the extension of a firm's activities 'upstream', for example to raw materials, or 'downstream', for example to distribution) within his perspective on organizational failures. His approach is directly derived from Coase's observation that firms will tend to expand (integrate) up to the point at which it is equally costly not to. It follows that VI occurs for the same reason that makes firms come into existence. In Williamson's case, VI is due to post-contract hold-up problems in the context of asset specificity and opportunism, leading to high transaction costs.

With or without specific assets and/or opportunism, the TCE of VI is both powerful and widely regarded today as a most convincing explanation of VI (see, for example, Caves 1996 and Marris 1999). Empirical studies of vertical integration do provide evidence in favour of TCE-type factors (see Caves 1996) (although the interpretation of the econometric results can sometimes be doubtful).

Nevertheless, while arguments about opportunistic suppliers, specific assets and *ex post* bilateral dependencies may be legitimate explanatory factors of firms' decisions, the fact is that integration involves the internalization of more market transactions by an existing hierarchy; no explanation of new hierarchies from markets is offered.

Multidivisional (M-form) firms

Alfred Chandler (1962) analysed the emergence of firms with a multidivisional structure (M-form firms), which started to replace unitary firms (U-form firms) in the USA soon after the Second World War. The structure of the U-form firm involved a central office, which was responsible for both long-term strategic decisions and day-to-day operational decisions, and a number of divisions, such as production, marketing, finance, personnel, etc. The M-form firm, on the other hand, consists of a general office, which is responsible for strategic decisions alone, and a number of operating divisions, each one organized in the way the U-form firm was. The operational decisions are left with the divisional managers in this structure. Chandler's idea was that the adoption of the M-form was a response to firms' needs for diversification. By the early part of the twentieth century, a number of firms were already vertically integrated and realized that their know-how could be profitably applied in new product lines (Chandler 1977). The U-form created difficulties when the need arose to administer activities in different markets. The M-form was a way forward, as a firm would only have to add another division in a new product market to achieve its diversification plans. In this sense, Chandler's thesis was that strategy caused structure.

Williamson tells a different story. He claims that U-form firms were becoming so large that 'bounds on rationality were reached as the U-form structure labored under a communication overload, while the pursuit of subgoals by functional parts ... was partly a manifestation of opportunism' (Williamson 1981: 1555). This was because central offices were taking both strategic and operational decisions. The M-form firm, by creating 'semi-autonomous operating divisions (mainly profit centers) organized along product, brand or geographical lines' (*ibid.*: 1555), the operating affairs of which were managed separately, was able to reduce managerial opportunism, ease the confusion between strategic and operating goals and, importantly, reestablish the profit motive by reuniting ownership and control. In Williamson's view, the adoption of the M-form was due to its inherent control advantages, which reduced transaction costs. In this sense, it was size that led to the M-form firm: structure caused strategy.

In addition to these TC-related efficiencies, the M-form has also served to reduce transactions costs related to the external capital market. The M-form operates as an internal capital market, thus solving TC-related external capital market failures.

The debate on the M-form is big and ongoing. In this author's view (Pitelis 1991), moreover, there is little reason to see the two views as conflicting. Both Chandler-type and Williamson-type factors could be operative.

Worth noting, finally, are the problems of the M-form. Fransman (1994) observes that failure of the M-form to attenuate opportunism has led large firms, such as ATT and IBM, to introduce a more segmented form, the S-form, which allows much more authority to the various divisions than the M-form.

However, the merits of the two explanations of the M-form structure or of a synthesis is another case of the organizational form of an existing hierarchy.

Conglomerates and transnationals

In the case of the conglomerate firm, Williamson's argument is in terms of internalizing the external capital market because of failures in that market (Williamson 1975, 1981). Internalization increases the availability of information and the ability to control auditing, and facilitates performance assessment of the M-form-type divisionalized profit centres. Economies in transaction costs can be made by internalizing the production of separate goods. This is due to the possibility that firms will be better able to exploit the quasi-rents from the ownership of specialized resources, either physical capital or human know-how. In both cases, conglomeration, as compared to leasing or selling in the open market, can help reduce market transaction costs arising from opportunism, the problem of which is particularly acute in the case of organizational know-how because of its tacit and tangible nature. There is evidence in support of this analysis (Caves 1996); it is clear, however, that what is being explained is the behaviour of existing hierarchies. There is an explanation of why some market transactions are superseded, but not why hierarchies arise from markets (see CORPORATE CONTROL).

Williamson's treatment of the transnational corporation (TNC) is not extensive (see Williamson 1981). In essence, the TNC is once again attributed to hold-up problems due to asset specificity. There is a large debate on the role of transaction costs in the theory of the TNC, recently summarized in Pitelis and Sugden (2000). Williamson's version is one of at least three. Buckley and Casson's (1976) TC-based internalization theory of the TNC focused on appropriability problems of intangible assets, usually with a knowledge component, which are hard to sell in open markets due to the public good aspects of knowledge. Teece's (1986) assessment of the TC theory of the TNC suggests that TCE can help discriminate between transaction costs that need to be internalised or not. Hennart (2000) suggests that TNCs internalized inefficient labour markets abroad, given TNCs' superior ability to control foreign labour. Caves (1996) has a TC theory which, however, has elements of the resource-based theory (see below). He finds empirical support for this theory.

Criticisms of the TC explanation to the TNC involve its alleged failure to consider failures in the final product markets (see Hallwood 1994). It is also observed that in the case of the TNC both specific and non-specific assets are internalized (Kay 1992). Finally, it is argued that TNCs are not the result of market failure at all, but rather that firms are better than markets and other firms in transferring tacit knowledge (Kogut and Zander 1993). For our purposes, suffice it to note that the TNC too cannot explain why firms; TNCs, are already existing firms.

The employment relation
It seems that only the employment relation might have a legitimate claim to explain how new hierarchies arise from markets. Coase was aware of this and in his 1937 paper it is the employment relation that receives near exclusive attention (although more recently (Coase 1991) he has expressed regret for this and claimed that the firm involves more than the employment relation). In the Coasean tradition, it is 'failures' of pre-existing markets for labour which explain the emergence of hierarchies (the firm). TC explanations of vertical integration, M-form firms, conglomerates and transnational corporations simply explain the further internalization of markets by existing hierarchies. This raises the question of why labour markets 'fail' and what the exact nature of such failure is. It is useful to examine this in a historical context.

The capitalist firm, as embodied in the factory system, was the way of organizing work that succeeded the 'putting-out' system. In the putting-out system, a merchant-manufacturer 'put out' raw materials to dispersed cottage labourers to be worked up into finished or semi-finished products. In most cases, the labourers used their own equipment, such as looms or forges. Material was moved from home to home in batches under the direction of the merchant-manufacturer. In the factory system, on the other hand, labourers 'accepted' working under the employers' authority and doing as they were told, provided that the employer's behaviour fell within certain limits of acceptability. This agreement – the employment contract – replaced the market-type relationship that existed under the putting-out system.

What were the critical factors that led to the replacement of a market-type putting-out system by a factory system? In Williamson's story, the general reasons relate to TC economizing. Workers can possess 'idiosyncratic' job-related skills, which increase their bargaining power with employers. This and worker opportunism gave rise to the TC difficulties of such market-type employment relationships as the putting-out system: for example, protracted haggling. The long-term employment contract of the sort associated with Coasean firms can ameliorate, albeit not fully solve, the problem of asymmetric information between employers and employees. The employer can provide incentives to the employee to increase cooperation; for example, in the internal labour market the wage rate attaches to the job, not the worker (see LABOUR MARKETS). This can reduce individual bargaining and thus opportunism. Employees accept voluntarily the reduction in their freedom, but retain the right to cancel the authority relationship by leaving the employer. Although shirking by employees is not prevented, 'consummate' (as opposed to 'perfunctory') cooperation is encouraged. Employers' opportunism is reduced for reasons of reputation, a point going back to Coase (1937). Cheating firms become known quicker than cheating workers. This and the existence of unions, which monitor the firm's commitments, make cheating by firms less likely. Overall, according to this story, it is idiosyncratic transactions (ones that arise from a labourer having a particular skill) and opportunism which necessitate the emergence of the long-term employment relation.

There is substantial evidence to support the claim that the workers' ability to behave opportunistically under the putting-out system was high (Landes 1966). Accordingly, from the merchant manufacturers' point of view at least, there were good reasons why the market-based putting-out system should be replaced by the firm-like authority relation (similar considerations would apply in the case of 'purer' market-type employment contracts, for example of the spot contracting type). By making the ability to work (labour power) rather than a certain amount of product the subject of the contract, employers could increase their ability to control quality and monitor workers. The impetus for the factory system, according to North, was 'monitoring of the production process by a supervisor' (North 1981: 169). Williamson notes that this monitoring had obvious productivity advantages, such as the appropriation of the benefits of innovation and the checking of embezzlement and similar deceits.

There can be little doubt from the above that, from the merchant manufacturer's point of view, superseding the putting-out system by a more hierarchical organization had obvious advantages in terms of efficiency. This appears to be in line with Williamson's claim that such changes are driven by efficiency. However, this 'Williamsonian synthesis' is not uncontroversial.

2 Critiques, and alternatives

Markets first

As already suggested, the starting point of the Coase–Williamson framework is the idea that the market is the natural and/or original means of resource allocation and that non-market institutions need to be explained. However, there are problems with this idea. That markets predate firms is questionable, both conceptually and empirically: conceptually, because (single person) firms may be required for the production of exchanged products and thus for the market; and empirically, because, historically at least, it is not obvious that price-making markets predated (at least some) hierarchies, such as the state (North 1981) or the family. Williamson claims that the pre-existence of markets is a methodological assumption and one can get the same results by starting from hierarchies. This, however, is far from obvious. Starting from firms implies that markets are the making of firms too; at the very least, this questions the assumption of substitutability between markets and hierarchies.

Efficiency through economizing, strategizing, and power

The assumption that firms are the result of efficiency through 'economizing' (in transaction costs), and that this results in increasing efficiency, is questionable. First, it is possible that hierarchies result from, and in, efficiency of a non-TC economizing type (see below). In addition, one may question the process through which an efficient institution (the firm) comes to replace an inefficient one (the market). It is common among TC theorists to employ evolutionary arguments in order to explain the replacement process. North, for example, suggests that 'competition in the face of ubiquitous scarcity dictates that the more efficient institutions ... will survive and the inefficient ones perish' (1981: 7). While this possibility cannot be excluded, it is also possible that competition can lead to monopoly (Marx 1867); market inefficiencies need not necessarily lead to efficient firms. In addition, by way of counter-argument, one could suggest that many institutions tend to contain a self-sustaining pattern of actions; once a pattern is established, it may be maintained despite being socially sub-optimal (see, for example, Foss 1993).

A second line of criticism concerning the efficiency argument relates to the nature of efficiency and its beneficiaries, including the concept of Pareto efficiency. As suggested above, the move from putting-out to the factory system incorporated productivity gains through, in particular, the reduction of employee opportunism. But why should labourers have accepted the loss of their opportunity to be opportunist? It seems odd that independent craftsmen and women should have been willing to sacrifice their independence and obey employers' orders. It is plausible to expect that they would have been against such a change. If so, the firm was not efficient in the Pareto sense. Someone (the merchant) became better off, while someone else (the labourer) became worse off. A counter to this argument would be that from a purely pecuniary point of view both labourers and merchants might have become better off. Although this is a realistic possibility, the question arises as to whether the focus on pecuniary cost-benefits should not be extended to incorporate psychic cost-benefits. If it should be, the preference of putting-out labourers for independence (which Coase himself acknowledges) would appear to invalidate the claim that firms are Pareto-efficient in comparison to markets.

A related criticism is that the TC scenario ignores or downplays the role of power considerations. Such considerations can refer both to market power and to power in its more general sense, that of the ability of an agent to impose his or her will on others through coercion or even charisma. Regarding market power, it was noted above that competition can lead to monopoly, which is one of the major aspects of structural market failure according to conventional welfare economists. The ability of firms to give rise to, rather than solve, market failure has been extensively remarked. Particularly damaging, however, is the observation that market power and TC considerations may be inseparable, as it is often the case that firms attain monopoly power by reducing market transaction costs.

Williamson's response to the issue of power is two-fold. First, he re-interprets evidence on market or overall power in terms of efficiency. He then goes on to say that even if power considerations have merit, power issues have not been operationalized and are less operationalizable. This criticism, however, may be inaccurate (Pitelis 1998) and could well submit too much to the power argument (see Demsetz 1995).

Problems with methodology

Another problem with the TC approach concerns its ability to offer refutable hypotheses that differ from other perspectives. Methodologically, this is done by varying governance structures while holding the transaction constant. This, however, may be illegitimate, as changes in governance structures normally imply changes in the nature of the transaction costs involved; in other words 'a 'better' transaction may be a different transaction' (Dow 1987: 18).

The reliance of the TC perspective on methodological individualism – the reduction of institutions (see INSTITUTIONAL ECONOMICS) or other social phenomena to individual action alone could be questioned too. An alternative would be to explain individual behaviour in terms of institutions, or to at least recognize some sort of interaction between the two; the unit would then be not the individual but the social individual.

Another methodological problem is that the TC perspective is effectively a comparative static approach. A most important issue is how firms behave over time; arguably, the real issue is the 'innovative firm' (see Lazonick 1991). TCE assumes technology and innovation as constant. This is a most important problem. Arguably, the most important issue in economics is wealth creation through productivity enhancements through innovations. This is the agenda of Schumpeter (1942), Penrose (1959), Nelson and Winter (1982) and a host of important contributors in the field (see, for example, Lazonick 1991; Langlois 1992). Many such contributions acknowledge the importance of transaction costs, but see these as a dynamic, real time, historically informed phenomenon, usually blended with resource-knowledge-based and production costs-benefits (see Pitelis 1991).

Transaction costs' static nature also precludes it taking seriously into account the issue of knowledge as distinct from information (Fransman 1994), and the issue of knowledge creation (Penrose 1959) as opposed to its asymmetric distribution.

Other criticisms

Other criticisms of the TC perspective include its disregard of the macroeconomic structure as a potential factor in explaining the existence of various institutional functions (Pitelis 1991). Others have observed that the distinction between markets and firms is not as clear cut as the TC framework implies, so that firm-type behaviour in markets and inter-penetrations of markets and hierarchies can often be found. Cowling and Sugden (1998) have suggested that if one focuses on control rather than ownership, certain market-type relations, for example between TNCs and their sub-contractors, can be seen as intra-firm, rather than market, transactions. Other critiques refer to TCE's comparative neglect of institutional devices between markets and hierarchies, such as networks, strategic alliances, clans and other forms of relational contracting.

In his seminal 1972 contribution Richardson (1972) pointed to the extensive cooperation between firms, suggested that cooperation stands between market and hierarchy, and explained markets, hierarchies and cooperation in terms of the similarity and complementarity of activities, building on the work of Penrose (1959).

Concerning the particulars of Williamson's contribution, his emphasis and focus on bounded rationality, opportunism and asset specificity has been questioned by no less than Coase (1993) himself and Demsetz (1995). Coase (1993) has gone as far as to question the importance of anything that involves the term 'rationality' and questioned the importance of asset specificity. On 'opportunism', there is an ongoing debate (see Williamson 1993). This involves specific criticisms, for example, Williamson's exclusive focus on opportunistic suppliers or workers, but not employers. In contrast, Dow (1987) believes that authority is itself an inducement to opportunistic behaviour. Kay (1997) observed that in the case of the TNC both specific and non-specific assets are involved. He has also questioned whether transactions should always be viewed in contractual terms.

Concerning the links between Williamson's triad, and building on Coase (1993), it is not obvious how one can be (boundedly) 'rational' and opportunistic at the same time. Opportunism may well involve behaving in an apparently irrational way to achieve one's own long-term purpose, given recognition of rivalrous behaviour by others, if only one's self-interest is revealed. While such actions aim to be eventually rational, they are apparently irrational. How can one define rationality in this context, except by trying to define the other parties' 'real' interests? This, however, is clearly far too dangerous to be proposed by anyone. In its absence, rationality plus opportunism may not go together. Lastly, is bounded rationality also procedural as suggested by Simon (1991)? How does it link to collective rationality?

Demsetz (1995) has claimed that the Coase–Williamson treatment of uncertainty is too cavalier, and indeed Coase's critique of Knight's (1921) risk distribution theory of the firm inadequate. For Demsetz, one can generalize Knight's risk distribution theory of the division of tasks between employers (risk undertakers) and employees (who choose security for a stable wage) in terms of overall uncertainty reductions – one could say, transforming fundamental uncertainty (where probabilities cannot be assigned to events) with risk (where probabilities can be assigned). More generally, it could be suggested that TCE deals with risk, but not with fundamental uncertainty.

The ability of TCE to determine the boundaries of the firm has also been forcefully criticized by Marris (1999). Echoing earlier contributions by Penrose (1959; who noted that there are no obvious reasons why average administrative costs should increase as firms expand), Marris suggests that there is no reason to expect that average management costs increase over time, and that there is not necessarily an optimal point, where a declining average TC curve meets a rising administrative costs one.

Indeed the list of potential critiques is limitless, which, however, should not obscure the important contribution of both TCE and Williamson (see below).

The criticisms outlined above are indicative of the strong interest that TCE has aroused. Alternative perspectives have been proposed (although not necessarily as a direct response to TC ideas). Most notable among them are the pure neo-classical approach of Alchian and Demsetz (1972), the resource-based perspective and the radical perspective of Marglin (1974).

A neo-classical alternative

The starting point for Alchian and Demsetz's neo-classical approach is that there is no difference between the firm and the market, and that the firm is essentially a market: 'the firm can be considered as a privately owned market; if so, we could consider the firm and the ordinary market as competing types of markets' (Alchian and Demsetz 1972: 138). In a now famous quote, Alchian and Demsetz reject the idea that the firm has the power to settle issues by any authority superior to that available in ordinary markets: 'Telling an employee to type this letter rather than to file that document is like my telling a grocer to sell me this brand of tuna rather than that brand of bread' (*ibid.*: 120). Overall, the firm is a nexus of contracts and involves continuous renegotiation of the contracts between employers and employees in terms acceptable to both parties. Thus, there is a perfectly symmetrical relationship. The right to quit implies that firing can be bi-directional. The employer fires the employee and similarly the employee fires the employer by leaving.

Alchian and Demsetz suggest that the employer 'is the centralized contractual agent in a team production process – not some superior authoritarian directive or disciplinary power' (*ibid.*: 120). Team production, however, involves problems of metering performance, of rewarding good performance and punishing bad performance. To achieve this, a monitor is required to minimize shirking. To make sure that the monitor is monitoring him or herself, he or she should have the right to claim the residual profit. Thus, the employer is regarded as the coordinator or orchestrator of a private market (the firm). The right to claim residual profit ensures efficient production (compared to the ordinary market). Competition among potential coordinators, moreover, ensures that team members are not exploited.

The Alchian and Demsetz challenge has been criticized for pushing the ubiquitous presence of markets too far even by insiders of the TC tradition. More recently, both authors have independently accepted the existence and importance of direction in firms. Despite shortcomings, the Alchian and Demsetz scenario is valuable in that it re-emphasizes the well-known point that, from the point of view of exchange and in the purely legal sense, there is no essential difference between employers and employees, a point going back to Marx (1867). It is recognized that this equality may be constrained through the actions of one or the other party within the process of exchange (Putterman 1986), but not that agents can be unequal to start with, in their different roles in the production process, as employers and employees.

Important in Alchian and Demsetz moreover is the focus on the role of agency, ownership and teamwork. As observed below, the focus on teamwork (suitably re-interpreted) actually renders Alchian and Demsetz precursors of the resource-based perspective! In addition, the focus on shirking, monitoring, ownership and the role of a residual claimant has informed the huge literature on agency (see Jensen and Meckling 1976), property rights (see Barzel 1989) and the incomplete contracts theory of Grossman and Hart (1986) and Hart (1988) (see Foss 1993 and Holmstrom and Roberts 1998 for critical assessments and comparisons of these perspectives).

The resource/knowledge-based perspective

This perspective can be traced of the work of Adam Smith, Karl Marx and Joseph Schumpeter, among others, but arguably owes its recent motherhood to Edith Penrose's (1959) classic, *The Theory of the Growth of the Firm*. In brief, Penrose's view is that firms, seen as bundles of human and non-human resources under administrative coordination providing services, are better than markets in creating new knowledge, through teamwork and learning (learning by doing, learning by working with others, learning to learn, etc). New knowledge implies increased productivity and, *ceteris paribus*, excess resources, for use by profit-seeking entrepreneurs at zero marginal cost. This leads to endogenous growth and (through) endogenous innovations. Resources, knowledge and innovations thus generated also determine, up to a point, the direction of expansion. There is no limit to firms' size, but only to the rate of growth. This is mostly the result of management. Experienced management to plan and implement expansion is always required, but not available in the market. Therefore the availability and quality of management constrains at any point in time the rate of growth. Differential resources, thus services, knowledge, innovations and capabilities, and attempts to remove constraints to growth can help explain firm strategies; firms are better at doing some things than markets.

It is beyond the scope of this subsection to discuss these issues further. Suffice it to note that the resource-based theory is currently the main contender to TCE (for example, see Foss 1993 1997).

Worth noting are the following. First, contributions to TCE already mentioned, notably Caves (1996) and Teece (1986), invoke resource/knowledge-based arguments. Second, Demsetz (1995), building on Demsetz (1988), re-interprets the Alchian and Demsetz contribution in terms of intra-firm differential productivity benefits of teamwork. This brings him very close to the resource-based camp. Third, Williamson (1999) sees merit and promise in the resource-based view, but questions its record so far and its ability regarding operationalization.

It would appear that the future should involve elements of both TCE and resource/knowledge-based theorizing.

A radical perspective

Another alternative to the TC perspective is Marglin's account of the rise of the factory. In Marglin's 'What do bosses do?' (1974), the main claim was that, in contrast to neo-classical perspectives, the rise of the factory from the putting-out system had little or nothing to do with the technical superiority of large-scale machinery. The key to the success of the factory, as well as its aspiration, was the substitution of capitalists' for workers' control of the production process: 'discipline and supervision could and did reduce costs without being technologically superior' (Marglin 1974: 46). Marglin suggested that the reason for the factory system was the desire of capitalists to increase their control over labour. Given that workers had greater autonomy under the putting-out system, it cannot be presumed that they preferred the factory system. The factory system arose for reasons of control-distribution rather than efficiency. Marglin provided historical evidence to support his views. His perspective has been applied to a number of areas, including explanations for the M-form organization and the TNC (Pitelis 1991 provides a survey).

Williamson's response to Marglin's challenge is cautious and rather surprising. He accepts that there is merit in all explanations, including ones relating to power. He then re-interprets Marglin's analysis in a way consistent with his own views and suggests that Marglin's evidence is in line with the efficiency hypothesis (or a combined efficiency-power hypothesis). He goes on to suggest, however, that the main problem with power ideas is that they are even harder to operationalize than TC ideas.

Markets as hierarchies, agency and self-interest

Additional problems with TCE relate to the fact that the perspective downplays the production side (see, for example, Pitelis 1991; Demsetz 1995). Focus on the production side is important, as in capitalist economies the very existence of employers and employees (or principals and agents) implies an inequality whereby the one accepts the other's authority. Even if one agrees with the TCE view that this is a contractual process, the inequality still implies that every employment relationship is a hierarchical one, including the putting-out system. This would suggest that, seen from the point of view of capitalist production, markets too involve hierarchy. Accordingly, what Williamson and Marglin debate is not markets versus hierarchies but rather market versus non-market hierarchies. To take this point further, in hierarchically organized capitalist societies, where the production process is controlled by a minority of the stakeholders, hierarchy is inherent and what we observe is only the evolution of hierarchical forms (for example, from putting-out to the factory system). The evolution itself is due to the principals' (employers') aim of furthering their interests, by reducing worker opportunism (according to Williamson) or by increasing labour exploitation (according to Marglin) – which amount to the same thing anyway.

These observations have two other important implications for the TCE scenario. First, they expose the need for a discussion of agency: who drives the process of change? Coase and Williamson do not address this issue and it is implicit in their accounts that both principals and agents are behind the contractual process of change in their pursuit of mutual interest. However, this is conceptually suspect and historically uninformed. Conceptually, as Coase himself has observed, it is not obvious that someone will voluntarily relinquish autonomy to someone else, even given the possibility of material gain. For Coase, one's usual preference would seem to be for being one's own master (Coase 1937). This raises the possibility of imposition by one group over another, which is not only conceptually plausible, but is also supported by historical experience (see, for example, Heilbroner 1991). It is by basing his account on extensive historical analysis that North has taken the principals (in the outline of the decline of putting-out given above, these are the merchant manufacturers or emerging capitalist class) and their pursuit of their own interests to be the driving force behind institutional change.

The second important implication flowing from the idea that the driving force behind the evolution of hierarchies is the self-interest of principals is this: once we attribute to a particular actor (the principal in this case) the attribute of being the main orchestrator of institutional change, it follows that we cannot legitimately separate the actor's objectives and the reasons for the change, as it is the former that instigates the latter. Put this in the framework of the firm and it follows that one cannot first explain the existence of the firm (for example in terms of transaction costs) and then discuss its objectives. Existence and objectives are inseparable, as it is the principal's objectives that lead to the firm's existence. It follows that the objective of the analysis becomes the examination of the factors that motivate actors. It is this that will answer the question as to the objectives of firms.

It has been claimed elsewhere (Pitelis 1991, 1998) that conceptually and historically we can explain institutional change, including the emergence and evolution of the capitalist firm, in terms of principals' attempts to further their interests by seeking maximum benefits. This involves conflict with agents (labour) and rivalry with other principals (firms). In this framework, an important consideration faced by principals is the removal of constraints to growth, which is the means of achieving maximum long-term profits under conditions of uncertainty. Such constraints are found in the product market, labour market and capital market; they can also be managerial or technological. A number of important institutional changes can be explained within this framework, including the emergence of the capitalist state.

A theory of the state

Building on work by Coase (1960), Pitelis (1991) argues that it is possible to generalize the neo-classical perspective on the state (which is based on instances of market failures, like public goods, externalities and monopoly) in terms of TC reductions. In this framework, the state internalizes the private sector (market and firms) up to the point where additional transactions can be carried out equally inexpensively by the private sector. It follows that the observed institutional mix is optimal, that is, it reduces transaction costs. This, though, can be criticized for ignoring issues of agency (principals) and thus of predation and also the issue of production costs. Applying the framework referred to above, the state has also been explained in terms of principals' efforts to enhance their systemically determined interests. Transaction costs also feature in Douglass North's work (1981). In his 'neo-classical' theory of the state North assumes a ruler who tries to maximize rents and then, subject to this happening, to reduce transaction costs. Rulers face competition by rivals, which induces them to grant privileges to powerful groups, which generates the conditions for 'capture' of the state by special interests. This explains the emergence and persistence of inefficient property rights in economic history. North goes on to observe the need to include ideology in the analysis, thus moving his perspective well away from conventional and TC-type theorizing despite his own reference to 'neo-classical'. There is insufficient space to discuss North's contribution here. Worth noting in passing are the similarities between his perspective and alternative views, including the neo-liberal focus on self-interest seeking by state functionaries and state capture, as well as alternative views that focus on self-interest-seeking principals, capture and the ideology of legitimacy. North himself points to such similarities, which goes to show how exciting economics is now becoming. This, in part at least, is due to the TC perspective.

3 Policy implications and the future

The remarkable contribution of TC theorizing is not so much what some of its proponents believe it to have been, namely the explanation of the firm and the law, as the observation that economists' previous concern with minimizing costs of production assumed as constant the costs of exchange. Once it is recognized that exchange is not costless, a legion of possible new avenues for research appear. For example, potentially beneficial trades may not take place because of excessive transaction costs. Countries may fail to develop because their structure of property rights does not facilitate exchange and thus trade and growth. Institutions other than the firm and the state can be explained by similar theorizing. Macroeconomic (market and government) failures may be explained in terms of transaction costs (Pitelis 1991). The list is endless. Indeed, the TC perspective provides the possibility of an interdisciplinary economics and even a unified social science, although one should not disregard its considerable problems.

The TC perspective has substantial implications for both public strategy on industrial competition and for the competitive and corporate strategies of firms (see Williamson 1975; Teece 1986). The policy implication of conventional industrial economics and organization has traditionally been that oligopoly and monopoly are forms of market failure; government intervention is required to curb monopoly power and increase competition, for example through strong antitrust policies. TC analysis raises doubts about this prescription. If large firms result from TC-reducing conduct, efficiency will be the result and this has to be considered by public authorities.

The TC approach is also relevant to the competitive and corporate strategies of firms. It provides firms with an account of the conditions under which they should make or buy, integrate or dis-integrate, use U- or M-form organization, license or undertake foreign direct investment. It suggests what combination of market and hierarchy (for example, networks, strategic alliances, sub-contracting, etc.) might be appropriate. This is a most exciting potential development in strategic management. The revolutionary possibilities of the TC perspective are far from exhausted.

4 Assessment

In the view of this author, TCE has been one of the two major contributions to economics this century (the other being the resource- or knowledge-based perspective). Since the mid-1970s, it has changed the way we view virtually everything in economics: markets, firms, networks, history, economic development, the whole lot. The credit is due to Ronald Coase. Coase himself acknowledges that modern TC economics owes as much to Oliver Williamson. Despite Coase's own suspicion, and extensive critiques of the concepts of asset specificity, opportunism and (bounded) rationality, and despite extensive criticisms by others, Williamson's contribution to TCE and to economics more generally is hard to overestimate. Many fundamental ideas have emerged as criticisms of TCE. Valuable syntheses have emerged and are emerging. With all limitations and criticisms, it is very hard now to imagine E without TC.

CHRISTOS PITELIS
JUDGE INSTITUTE OF MANAGEMENT STUDIES
AND QUEENS' COLLEGE, UNIVERSITY OF
CAMBRIDGE

Further reading

(References cited in the text marked *)

* Alchian, A. and Demsetz, H. (1972) 'Production, information costs and economic organization', *American Economic Review* 62 (5). (The classic statement of the view that firms are internal markets, characterized by team work and requiring monitoring of shirking, including self-monitoring of the monitor through him or her being a residual claimant.)
* Arrow, K. (1970) 'The organization of economic activity: issues pertinent to the choice of market versus non-market allocation', in R.H. Haveman and J. Margolis (eds), *Public Expenditure and Policy Analysis*, Chicago, IL: Markham. (A TC-based explanation of the organization of economic activity that also deals with the government, and which precedes Williamson's 1975 book.)
* Barzel, Y. (1989) *Economic Analysis of Property Rights*, Cambridge: Cambridge University Press. (A property rights-based approach to economic analysis, which, among others, extends Alchian and Demsetz's analysis.)
* Buckley, P.J. and Casson, M.C. (1976) *The Future of Multinational Enterprise*, London: Macmillan. (A TC-based explanation of 'internalization' of markets by TNCs, which focuses on appropriability problems of intangible assets, which appeared almost simultaneously with Williamson's 1975 book.)
* Caves, R.E. (1996) *Multinational Enterprise and Economic Analysis*, 2nd edn, Cambridge: Cambridge University Press. (Updated classic by Caves. Among others, he proposes a TCE-based theory of the TNC, and discusses evidence in its favour. His version of TCE blends well with resource-based arguments.)
* Chandler, A.D. (1962) *Strategy and Structure: Chapters in the History of American Industrial Enterprise*, Cambridge, MA: MIT Press. (The evolution of the multidivisional structure, or M-form, in major US industrial corporations from the 1920s through the 1950s.)
* Chandler, A.D. (1977) *The Visible Hand: The Managerial Revolution in American Business*, Cambridge, MA: Harvard University Press. (The rise of the vertically integrated US managerial enterprise as the foundation for the further evolution of the multidivisional structure.)
* Coase, R.H. (1937) 'The nature of the firm', *Economica* 4 (16): 386–405. (The classic statement of the firm internalizing the market due to excessive market transaction costs.)
* Coase, R.H. (1960) 'The problem of social cost', *Journal of Law and Economics* 3: 1–44. (Coase's application of his 1937 thesis to the case of law, and the first statement of what was later termed 'Coase's theorem'.)
* Coase, R.H. (1991) 'The nature of the firm: meaning' and 'The nature of the firm: influence', in O.E. Williamson and S.G. Winter (eds) *The Nature of the Firm: Origins, Evolution and Development*, Oxford: Oxford University Press. (Coase's reflections on the history and influence of his 1937 article.)
* Coase, R.H. (1993) 'Coase on Posner on Coase', *Journal of Institutional and Theoretical Economics* 149 (1): 90–8. (Among others, why the master dislikes bounded rationality and even that he regards 'the concept of "rational utility maximization" as meaningless'.)
* Cowling, K. and Sugden, R. (1998) 'The essence of the modern corporation: markets, strategic decision-making and the theory of the firm', *The Manchester School* 66 (1) January: 59–86.

(Critical assessment of TC-based arguments on the firm that focuses on the role of strategic decision making and questions distinctions between markets and firms.)

* Demsetz, H. (1988) 'The theory of the firm revisited', in *Ownership, Control and the Firm: The Organization of Economic Activity*, vol. 1, Oxford: Blackwell. (A strong general critique of the TC perspective and extensions.)

* Demsetz, H. (1995) *The Economics of the Business Firm: Seven Critical Commentaries*, Cambridge: Cambridge University Press. (Vintage Demsetz. Excellent critical comments and developments on the state of the art of the theory of the firm. An absolute must.)

* Dow, G.K. (1987) 'The function of authority in transaction cost economics', *Journal of Economic Behavior and Organization* 8: 13–38. (A powerful critique of the TCE approach's neglect of the possible hazards of authority.)

* Eggertson, T. (1990) *Economic Behaviour and Institutions*, Cambridge: Cambridge University Press. (Excellent survey of developments in TCE, with a detailed account of new perspectives.)

* Foss, N.J. (1993) 'Theories of the firm: contractual and competence perspectives', *Journal of Evolutionary Economics* 3 (2): 127–44. (One of the best critical assessments of TCE and the resource-/knowledge-based perspective.)

* Foss, N.J. (ed.) (1997) *Resources, Firms and Strategies*, Oxford Management Readers, Oxford: Oxford University Press. (Very useful reader on the resource-based perspective.)

* Fransman, M. (1994) 'Information, knowledge, vision and theories of the firm', *Industrial and Corporate Change* 3 (3): 713–57. (Critique of treatment of knowledge in neo-classical and TC theorizing, and examination of alternative treatments, such as the Penrosean, resource-based one.)

* Grossman, S. and Hart, O. (1986) 'The costs and benefits of ownership: a theory of lateral and vertical integration', *Journal of Political Economy* 94: 691–719. (Important treatment of the role of ownership on integration, in an incomplete (nexus of) contracts framework.)

* Hallwood, C.P. (1994) 'An observation on the transaction cost theory of the (multinational) firm', *Journal of Institutional and Theoretical Economics* 150 (2): 351–61. (Critique of the of TCE approach to TNCs, in terms of its alleged failure to deal with imperfections in final markets.)

* Hart, O. (1988) 'Incomplete contracts and the theory of the firm', *Journal of Law, Economics and Organisation* 4 (1): 119–40. (Incomplete contracts-based approach to the firm that does not presuppose markets.)

* Heilbroner, R. (1991) *The Worldly Philosophers*, 6th edn, London: Penguin Books. (Classic treatment of the worldly philosophers with, among others, refreshing insight on real markets in history.)

* Hennart, J.-F. (2000) 'Transaction costs theory and the multinational enterprise', in C. Pitelis and R. Sugden (eds), *The Nature of the Transnational Firm*, 2nd edn, London: Routledge. (An employment contract-based theory of the TNC that builds on Coase, with elements of differential capabilities.)

* Holmstrom, B. and Roberts, J. (1998) 'The boundaries of the firm revisited', *Journal of Economic Perspectives* 12 (4) Fall: 73–94. (Critical observations and comparison of TC and incomplete contracts perspectives.)

Holmstrom, B. and Tirole, J. (1989) 'The theory of the firm', in R. Schmalensee and R.D. Willig (eds) *Handbook of Industrial Organisation*, vol. 3, Amsterdam: North-Holland. (Extensive critical survey of transaction costs and other theories of the firm.)

* Jensen, M.C. and Meckling, W. (1976) 'Theory of the firm: managerial behaviour, agency costs and ownership structure', *Journal of Financial Economics* 3: 304–60. (Classic treatment of agency, building on, and extending, Alchian and Demsetz.)

* Kay, N. (1992) 'Markets, false hierarchies and the evolution of the modern corporation', *Journal of Economic Behavior and Organization* 17: 315–33. (Criticisms of Williamson's reliance on asset specificity and of the new institutionalists' reliance on evolutionary process arguments, with particular emphasis on the U-form versus M-form debate.)

* Kay, N.M. (1997) *Pattern in Corporate Evolution*, Oxford: Oxford University Press. (Linkages-based theory of corporate evolution, with resource/knowledge-based focus and new insights.)

* Knight, F. (1921) *Risk, Uncertainty and Profit*, New York: Houghton Mills. (Knight's 1921 classic, on, among others, why firms exist, as well as his famous distinction between risk and uncertainty.)

* Kogut, B. and Zander, U. (1993) 'Knowledge of the firm and the evolutionary theory of the multinational corporation', *Journal of International Business Studies*, 4th quarter: 625–45. (Tacit knowledge-based theory of differential abilities by TNCs, critical to TCE and closely linked (albeit not referring) to Penrose's approach.)

* Landes, D.S. (ed.) (1966) *The Rise of Capitalism*, New York: Macmillan. (A very important source of historical insights on the rise of capitalism.)
* Langlois, N.R. (1992) 'Transaction costs economics in real time', *Industrial and Corporate Change* 1 (1): 99–127. (Critical assessment and extension of TC analysis, focusing on dynamic transaction costs, in real time.)
* Lazonick, W. (1991) *Business Organization and the Myth of the Market Economy*, Cambridge: Cambridge University Press. (Discussion of the 'innovative firm' and important critique of TC-based arguments.)
* Malcolmson, J. (1984) 'Efficient labour organisation: incentives, power and the transaction costs approach', in F. Stephen (ed.), *Firm Organizations and Labour*, London: Macmillan. (An expression of the powerful view that TC economizing could lead to increased market power.)
* Marglin, S. (1974) 'What do bosses do? The origins and functions of hierarchy in capitalist production', *Review of Radical Political Economics* 6: 60–112. (The classic statement of the view that the factory system served the interest of the capitalist by increasing control over labour.)
* Marris, R. (1999) 'Edith Penrose and economics', *Contributions to Political Economy* 18: 47–66. (Marris suggests that TCE fails to determine the size of the firm, while Penrose fails to determine the rate of growth. He suggests a way out.)
* Marx, K. (1867) *Capital*, vol. 1, London: Lawrence & Wishart, 1954. (Among others, distinguishes between firms and markets and presents the view that competition and monopoly are not polar opposites and that the one can lead to the other.)
* Nelson, R.R. and Winter, S.G. (1982) *An Evolutionary Theory of Economic Change*, Cambridge, MA: Harvard University Press. (Classic analysis of organizations in terms of evolutionary metaphors, including the introduction of the concept of 'routines'.)
* North, D.C. (1981) *Structure and Change in Economic History*, London and New York: W.W. Norton & Co. Inc. (North's classic application of his version of TCE to economic history.)
* Penrose, E.T. (1959) *The Theory of the Growth of the Firm*, Oxford: Oxford University Press; 3rd edn, 1995. (Penrose's classic resource/knowledge-based theory of the firm's endogenous growth, innovations, limits to growth, firms' evolution, monopoly and competition, and much more.)
* Pitelis, C.N. (1991) *Market and Non-market Hierarchies*, Oxford: Blackwell. (A critique and extension of the Coasean perspective to the theory of the state and macroeconomics.)
* Pitelis, C.N. (ed.) (1993) *Transaction Costs, Markets and Hierarchies*, Oxford: Blackwell. (A useful set of critical readings on the TC perspective.)
* Pitelis, C.N. (1998) 'Transaction cost economics and the historical evolution of the capitalist firm', *Journal of Economic Issues* XXXII (December): 999–1017. (Critique of TCE in terms of, among others, history-based considerations and links with resource-based perspectives.)
* Pitelis, C.N. and Sugden, R. (eds) (2000) *The Nature of the Transnational Firm*, 2nd edn, London: Routledge. (Useful set of readings on the theory of the TNC, with critical assessment and extensions of TC-based theories.)
* Putterman, L. (1986) *The Economic Nature of the Firm: A Reader*, Cambridge: Cambridge University Press. (A very useful selection of readings, including many classic pieces.)
* Richardson, G. (1972) 'The organisation of industry', *Economic Journal* 82: 883–96. (All-time classic on why and when market, hierarchy and, importantly, cooperation.)
* Schumpeter, J. (1942) *Capitalism, Socialism and Democracy*, London: Unwin Hyman; 5th edn, 1987. (Another all-time classic; competition is a dynamic process of creative destruction through innovations that lead to ephemeral monopoly; and much more.)
* Shelanski, H.A. and Klein, P.G. (1995) 'Empirical research in transaction cost economics: a review and assessment', *Journal of Law, Economics and Organisation* 11 (2) October: 335–61. (Extensive coverage of evidence on transaction costs, in support of the perspective.)
* Simon, H.A. (1991) 'Organizations and markets', *Journal of Economic Perspectives* 5 (2) Spring: 25–44. (On the prevalence and importance of organizations *vis-à-vis* markets, with a critical assessment of TCE.)
* Teece, D.J. (1986) 'Transaction costs economics and the multinational enterprise: an assessment', *Journal of Economic Behavior and Organization* 7: 21–45. (TC-based explanation of the TNC with some resource-based insights.)
* Williamson, O.E. (1975) *Markets and Hierarchies*, New York: The Free Press. (The original attempt to re-introduce the Coasean perspective, by one of its major proponents.)
* Williamson, O.E. (1981) 'The modern corporation: origins, evolution, attributes', *Journal of Economic Literature* 19 (4): 1537–68. (A very useful summary of Williamson's main ideas by himself.)

Williamson, O.E. (1986) *Economic Organisation: Firms, Markets and Policy Control*, Hemel Hempstead: Harvester Wheatsheaf. (A very useful selection of essays by Williamson on the topics mentioned in the title.)

* Williamson, O. E. (1993) 'Opportunism and its critics', *Managerial and Decision Economics* 14: 97–107. (Why opportunism matters for the (TC-based) theory of the firm, and critique to critics.)

* Williamson, O.E. (1999) 'strategy research: governance and competence perspectives', *Strategic Management Journal* 20: 1087–108. (Critical assessment of competence-based theory from a TC-based perspective; comparison and points for future developments.)

See also: BUSINESS ECONOMICS; COASE, R.; CORPORATE CONTROL; DYNAMIC CAPABILITIES; GROWTH OF THE FIRM AND NETWORKING; INSTITUTIONAL ECONOMICS; LABOUR MARKETS; MANAGERIAL THEORIES OF THE FIRM; MARSHALL, A.; MULTINATIONAL CORPORATIONS; NEO-CLASSICAL ECONOMICS; WILLIAMSON, O.E.

Innovative enterprise, theory of

1 Transforming the neoclassical theory of the firm
2 Transforming transaction-cost theory
3 Dynamic capabilities in a theory of innovative enterprise
4 Conclusion: industries, organizations and institutions

Overview

The purpose of this entry is to outline a theory of innovative enterprise that provides microeconomic foundations for understanding the evolving relation between industrial (technological, market and competitive) conditions that result in innovation and the institutional (financial, employment and regulatory) conditions that support an innovative economy. Critical to building this link is an understanding of the organizational conditions of the business enterprise, and the ways in which these organizational conditions interact with institutional conditions across industrial activities to create the 'social conditions of innovative enterprise' (see Figure 1) (Lazonick and O'Sullivan 1996, 2000). My own insights into the social conditions of innovative enterprise derive from comparative-historical analysis of advanced economic development brought up to the present (see Lazonick 2001).

First, I show how, by transforming the standard neoclassical theory of the optimizing firm, we can 1) expose the fundamental problem of the 'monopoly model' which, throughout the twentieth century and to the present, has underpinned the belief in the theory of the 'perfect market' economy as a system of resource allocation that yields superior economic performance, and 2) clarify the need for a theory of the organizational, as well as industrial, conditions for innovative enterprise. Second, I then perform a similar theoretical transformation on the transaction-cost theory of the firm, as developed by Oliver Williamson, in which organizational conditions are deemed to be central but which, like the standard neoclassical theory of the firm, lacks a theory of innovative enterprise (Lazonick 1991: chs 6 and 7). On the basis of these theoretical transformations, I argue that a theory of innovative enterprise must be able to comprehend the interaction of cognitive, behavioural

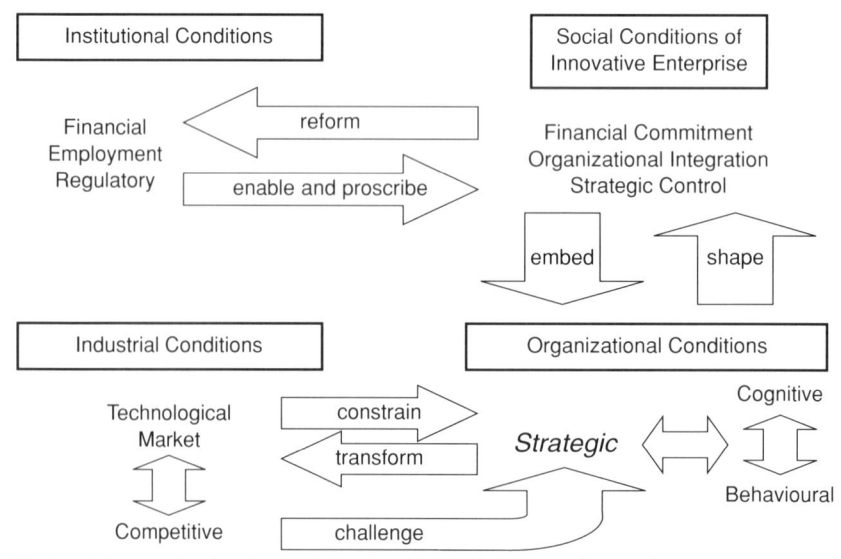

Figure 1 Industrial, organizational and institutional conditions in the innovation process

and strategic conditions – that is, organizational conditions – in the transformation of technological and market – or industrial – conditions. Third, I shall consider the relation of the theory of innovative enterprise thus outlined to the 'dynamic capabilities' perspective on the enterprise developed by US innovation economists during the 1990s. Having origins in the Williamsonian framework that stresses the importance of organizational conditions, dynamic capabilities theory has sought to combine findings from resource-based and evolutionary theories of the firm with empirical research, much of it industry-specific or enterprise-specific, in the fields of strategic management and the management of innovation. While I am in agreement with the emphasis of dynamic capabilities theory on the centrality of the organization of the innovation process, I argue that the dynamic capabilities approach has thus far ignored critical issues of strategic control within the innovative enterprise and the relation of strategic control to the organizational learning processes that are central to the development of an enterprise's core competences. Without an analysis of the integration of strategic control and organizational learning, a theory of the firm cannot address the central issues of the governance of innovative enterprise (O'Sullivan 2000a, 2000b).

I Transforming the neoclassical theory of the firm

The neoclassical theory of the optimizing firm avoids addressing the issue of innovative enterprise by assuming that, in its decisions to allocate resources, the firm takes technological and market conditions as given constraints. Neoclassical theory purports to be applicable to the real world of business, with implications for macroeconomic performance, by comparing such 'optimal' decision making – taking technological and market conditions as given constraints – under conditions of 'perfect competition' and 'monopoly'. Compared with perfectly competitive conditions, monopoly results in higher product prices and lower volumes of output. Elaborated within the Marshallian tradition of partial equilibrium in the 1920s and 1930s (see Lazonick 1991: ch. 5), this conventional perspective on industrial organization remains implanted within today's economics textbooks. Throughout the twentieth century, the comparison of conditions of perfect competition and monopoly provided the theoretical basis for the implementation of antitrust policies on the assumption that economic performance is enhanced when there are more rather than fewer competitors in an industry (see EVOLUTIONARY THEORIES OF THE FIRM).

The comparison of constrained optimization under conditions of perfect competition and monopoly contains, however, a fundamental flaw (see Figure 2). The problem is not with the logic of constrained optimization *per se* but with the logic of comparing the competitive model with the monopoly model within the constrained-optimization framework. If technological and market conditions make perfect competition a possibility, how can one firm (or even a small number of firms) come to dominate an industry? One would have to assume that the monopolist somehow differentiated itself from other competitors in the industry. But, the constrained-optimization comparison that yields the monopoly model argues that both the monopolist firm and perfectly competitive firms *optimize subject to the same cost structures* that derive from given technological and factor-market constraints. Indeed, except for the assumption that in one case the firm can make its profit-maximizing output decision as if it can sell all of its output at a constant price and that in the other case the firm is so large that it can only sell more output at a lower price, there is absolutely nothing in terms of the structure or operation of the firm that distinguishes the perfect competitor from the monopolist! So why would monopoly ever emerge under such conditions?

Of course, economists have argued that some industries, as exemplified by electric utilities, are characterized by natural monopoly. Relative to the size of the market to be served, the fixed costs of setting up an enterprise in an industry are so high that it is uneconomical to have more than one firm in the industry. But, if that is the case, then the comparison with the 'optimal' levels of product price and product output under competitive

Innovative enterprise, theory of

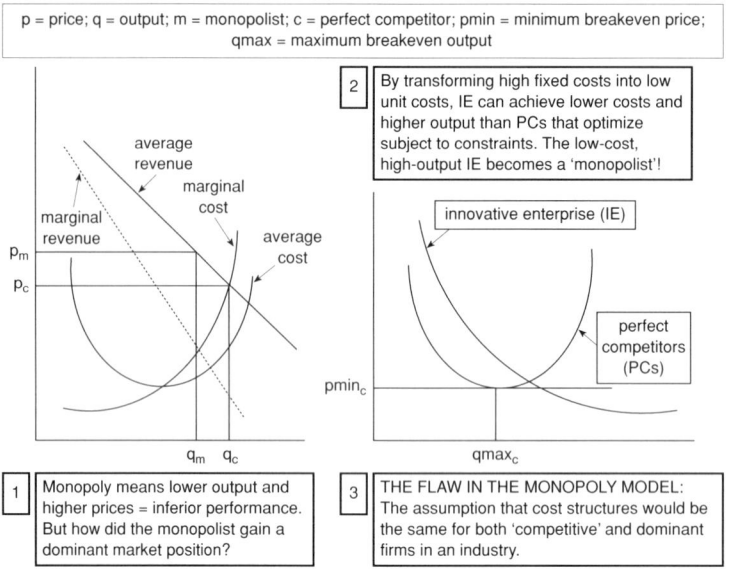

Figure 2 Competition and monopoly compared

conditions is irrelevant. If one opts for the 'natural monopoly' explanation for the concentrated structure of an industry, one cannot then logically invoke the 'perfectly competitive' comparison to demonstrate the inefficiency of monopoly. Recognizing the irrelevance of the competitive alternative, governments have long regulated utilities by (in principle at least) setting output prices that can balance the demands of consumers for reliable and affordable products with the financial requirements of utility companies for developing and utilizing the productive resources that enable the delivery of such products to consumers. In the presence of cumulative, collective and uncertain learning in the industry (see below), the analysis of the conditions for realizing such long-term projections concerning the evolving relation of demand for and supply of such products requires a theory of the innovative enterprise, not a theory of the optimizing firm.

To draw conclusions concerning the relative economic performance of the optimizing firm of neoclassical theory, its output and price should be compared with those that can be achieved by an innovative enterprise that transforms technological and/or market conditions (see Figure 3). To do so, the theory of innovative enterprise must have an analysis of the determinants of total fixed costs and the relation between average fixed costs and average variable costs during the innovation process. The task for a theory of innovative enterprise is to explain how, by changing its cost structure to generate output of a certain quality (or to generate output of a higher quality at a certain unit cost), a particular enterprise can emerge as dominant in its industry.

Unlike the optimizing firm, the innovative enterprise does not take as given the fixed costs of participating in an industry (see INNOVATION). Rather, given prevailing factor prices, the level of fixed costs that it incurs reflects its innovative strategy. This 'fixed-cost' strategy is not dictated by indivisible technology or the 'entrepreneur' as a fixed factor (typical ad hoc assumptions in the neoclassical theory of the optimizing firm), but by the innovative enterprise's assessment of the quality and quantity of productive resources in which it must invest to *develop* products that are higher quality and lower cost than those that it had previously been capable of producing and than those that (in its estimation) its competitors will be able to produce, given *their* investment strategies. It is this development of productive resources internal to the enterprise that creates the potential for an enterprise that pursues an innovative strategy p = price; q = output; m = monopolist; c = perfect competitor; pmin = minimum breakeven price; qmax = maximum breakeven output

- Technological and market conditions given by cost and revenue functions.
- The 'good manager' optimizes subject to technological and market constraints.
- The innovative enterprise transforms the technological and market conditions it faces to generate higher quality, lower cost products.
- There is no 'optimal' output. There is no 'optimal' price.

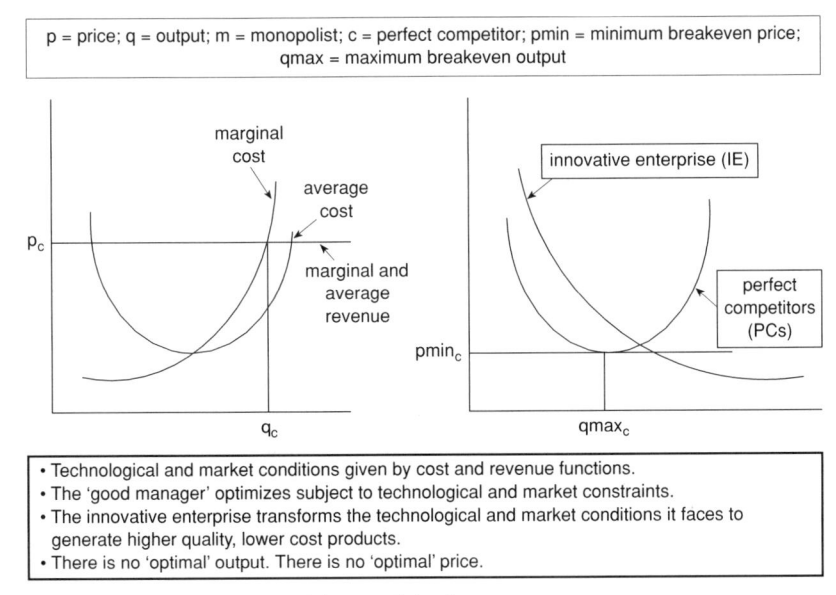

Figure 3 Transforming the conventional theory of the firm

to gain a sustained competitive advantage over its competitors and emerge as dominant in its industry.

Such development, when successful, becomes embodied in products, processes and people with superior productive capabilities than those that had previously existed. But the generation of superior productive capabilities will not result in sustained competitive advantage if the high fixed costs of the innovative strategy place the innovative enterprise at a cost disadvantage relative to less innovative, or even 'optimizing', competitors. An innovative strategy that enables the enterprise to generate superior productive capabilities may place that enterprise at a cost disadvantage because innovative strategies tend to entail higher fixed costs than the fixed costs incurred by rivals that optimize subject to given constraints.

For a given level of factor prices, these higher fixed costs derive from the *size* and *duration* of the innovative investment strategy. Innovative strategies tend to entail higher fixed costs than those incurred by the optimizing firm because the innovation process tends to require the *simultaneous development* of productive resources across a broader and deeper range of integrated activities than those undertaken by the optimizing firm (see references in Lazonick 1998; see also Patel and Pavitt 1997; Prencipe 2000). Hence, at a point in time, the innovative enterprise must generally make a broader range of investments in fixed plant and equipment and a deeper range of investments in administrative organization than would have to be undertaken by the optimizing firm. But in addition to, and generally independent of, the size of the innovative investment strategy at a point in time, high fixed costs will be incurred because of the duration of time required to develop productive resources until they result in products that are sufficiently high quality and low cost to generate returns. If the size of investments in physical capital tends to increase the fixed costs of an innovative strategy, so too does the duration of the investment in an organization of people who can engage in the collective and cumulative – or organizational – learning that is the central characteristic of the innovation process (O'Sullivan 2000a).

The high fixed costs of an innovative strategy create the need for the enterprise to attain a high level of *utilization* of the productive resources that it has developed. As in the neoclassical theory of the optimizing firm, given the productive capabilities that it has developed, the innovative enterprise may experience increasing costs because of the problem of maintaining the productivity of variable inputs as it employs larger quantities of these inputs in the production process. But rather than, as in the case of the optimizing firm, taking increasing costs as a given constraint, the innovative enterprise will attempt to transform its access to high-quality productive resources at high levels of output. To do so, it invests in the *development* of that productive resource, the *utilization* of which as a variable input has become a source of increasing costs (see Lazonick 1991: ch. 3).

The development of the productive resource adds to the fixed costs of the innovative strategy, whereas previously this productive resource was utilized as a variable factor that could be purchased at the going factor price incrementally on the market as extra units of the input were needed to expand output. Having added to its fixed costs in order to overcome the constraint on enterprise expansion posed by increasing variable costs, the innovative enterprise is then under even more pressure to expand its share of the market in order to transform high fixed costs into low unit costs. As, through the development and utilization of productive resources, the enterprise succeeds in this transformation, it in effect 'unbends' the U-shaped cost curve that the optimizing firm takes as given (see Figure 4). By shaping the cost curve in this way, the innovative enterprise creates the possibilities for gaining competitive advantage over its rivals (see Lazonick 1991: ch. 3, 1993).

Hence the innovative enterprise is not constrained by market demand to produce at the profit-maximizing output where marginal cost equals marginal revenue because, over the long run, it is not subject to increasing costs. The innovative enterprise may be subject to increasing costs in the short run, but, by continually confronting and transforming those technological and market conditions that result in increasing costs, the innovative enterprise can generate high-quality products, the unit costs of which decline as it reaps larger and larger market shares. The innovative enterprise thus not only has differentiated itself from its competitors but also has gained a sustained competitive advantage that is reinforced as it expands its level of output. In contrast to the neoclassical monopoly model that posits that an optimizing monopolist will choose to produce at a smaller volume of output and at higher prices than the aggregate of optimizing competitive firms in a particular industry, the innovative enterprise becomes dominant by transforming the industry cost structure and producing at a larger volume of output that it can sell at lower prices than the

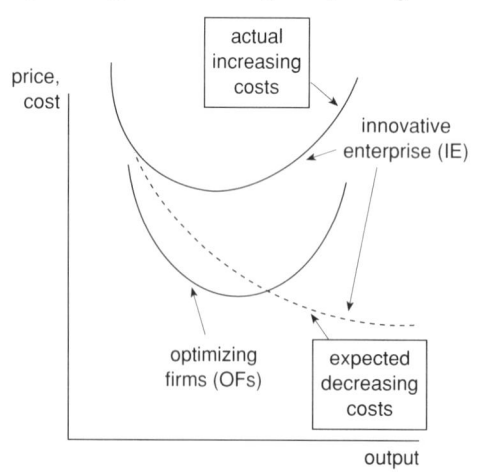

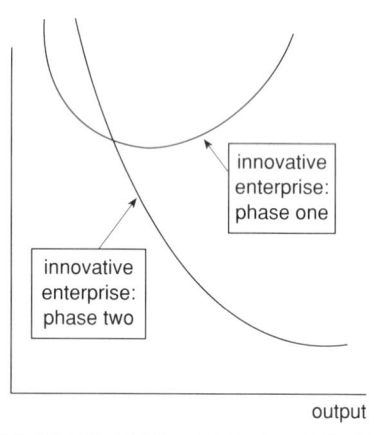

Figure 4 Industrial transformation: technology, markets and innovative enterprise

optimizing firms in the industry. By confronting and transforming technological conditions rather than accepting them as constraints on its activities, the innovative enterprise can outperform the 'optimizing' firm in terms of both output and cost.

The ability of the innovative enterprise to achieve decreasing costs even as it produces larger volumes of output relative to the size of the industry's market means that the neoclassical 'optimizing' rule of marginal cost equals marginal revenue is irrelevant to its output and pricing decisions. Constraining its level of output at a point in time is typically the presence in the industry of a small number of other innovative enterprises that compete among themselves for market share. Given the cost structure that it has put in place, the innovative enterprise can seek to increase its market share by offering buyers lower prices. But constraining such price reductions at a point in time is the need of the innovative enterprise to generate sufficient surplus revenues to invest in new technology, including the skills of workers and the building of an integrated organization to develop and utilize the new technology (such organizational integration may entail, for example, the remuneration of employees of the innovative enterprise at levels above and beyond those that their labour services would fetch on the open labour market) (Lazonick and O'Sullivan 2000). Such investments can enable the enterprise to maintain or extend its competitive advantage in a given market or transfer some of its productive capabilities to produce output for another market that can make use of these capabilities. In so far as the enterprise undertakes an innovative strategy in this diversification process, it will have to complement its existing capabilities with investments in, and the development of, new capabilities, thus adding to the fixed costs that it must utilize to achieve low unit costs.

The developmental impact of the innovative enterprise, therefore, manifests itself in a larger volume of output that it can, if is so chooses, make available to users at lower prices than the optimizing firm. By raising its output and lowering prices, the innovative enterprise grows to be larger than the optimizing firm. Neoclassical industrial organization takes the outcome – the enterprise's relatively large size – as its analytical starting point, thus avoiding the apparent need for a theory of the growth of the innovative enterprise. Neo-classical economists argue that, optimizing subject to given technological and market constraints, the 'monopolistic' firm will choose to raise prices and restrict output. Thus they avoid asking whether the large corporations that they observe are, and will remain, innovative enterprises or optimizing firms.

Unlike the optimizing firm that is the microeconomic foundation of the neoclassical analysis of industrial organization, the innovative enterprise has an interest in lowering prices as part of a strategy to increase the extent of the market available to it, which in turn lowers unit costs further as the enterprise reaps economies of scale. The economies of scale are not given to the industry but reflect the innovative enterprise's ability to transform the high-fixed costs of its innovative investment strategy, that in and of themselves place the enterprise at a competitive *disadvantage* relative to the optimizing firm, into the low unit costs that give it competitive *advantage*. Indeed, the innovative enterprise has the potential of not only outperforming the optimizing firm in terms of product quantity and price but also generating sufficient surplus revenues to pay higher wages to employees and higher returns to other stakeholders such as suppliers and stockholders. The innovation process, that is, can overcome the 'constrained-optimization' trade-offs between consumption and production in the allocation of resources and between capital and labour in the allocation of returns.

2 Transforming transaction-cost theory

Notwithstanding its entrenched position in the economics textbooks and in the system of belief of conventional economics, there have been powerful attacks on the 'monopoly model' as a foundation for evaluating the efficiency of the enterprise and welfare in the economy. In *Capitalism, Socialism, and Democracy*, Joseph Schumpeter (1950: 106) made his position clear:

What we have got to accept is that [the large-scale enterprise] has come to be the most powerful engine of [economic] progress and in particular of the long-run expansion of total output not only in spite of, but to a considerable extent through, this strategy that looks so restrictive when viewed in the individual case and from the individual point of time. In this respect perfect competition is not only impossible but inferior, and has no title to being set up as a model of ideal efficiency.

Richard Nelson and Sidney Winter (1982: 39) have credited 'the Schumpeterian view of capitalism as an engine of progressive change' with providing the fundamental inspiration for their evolutionary theory. But the most concerted attack on the 'monopoly model' has been made by Oliver Williamson (1975, 1985, 1996) as a basis for arguing against the American theory of antitrust that has the model as its foundation (see WILLIAMSON, O.E.). Building on Ronald Coase's (1937) famous article, 'The nature of the firm', Williamson has sought to explain why, in a 'market economy', hierarchies rather than markets might organize economic activity (see COASE, R.). Unlike Coase, however, Williamson locates 'transactions', and hence 'transaction costs', not only in market exchange but also within the firm. Therefore, to assess the relative performance of markets and hierarchies in allocating resources, one must compare the transaction costs of the two different modes of economic organization. It is Williamson's inclusion of behavioural and cognitive conditions as central to the theory of the firm that marks his contribution as an important advance over theories of the firm that ignore the role of organization in determining the performance of the enterprise.

What is the relation between Williamson's transaction-cost theory and a theory of the innovative enterprise that can explain the transformation of technological conditions, as illustrated in Figure 4? To answer this question requires a brief summary of the Williamsonian theory.

Williamson (1985: 8, 45) attributes 'transaction costs' to a behavioural condition that, following Kenneth Arrow, he calls 'opportunism' and a cognitive condition that, following Herbert Simon, he calls 'bounded rationality' (see SIMON, H.). Williamson defines 'opportunism' as a condition of 'self-interest seeking with guile.' 'Opportunism', says Williamson (1985: 47), 'refers to the incomplete or distorted disclosure of information, especially to calculated efforts to mislead, distort, disguise, obfuscate, or otherwise confuse'. In organizing transactions, markets and hierarchies possess different capabilities for 'attenuating opportunism', and hence for minimizing transaction costs. Market transactions provide a protection against opportunism because the market provides options for one party not to transact with another. In contrast, hierarchical transactions expose one party to the opportunism of another.

Yet such opportunism only becomes a problem in the presence of bounded rationality. In entering into transactions, economic actors have incomplete access to information and a limited ability to absorb that information to which they do have access. They make decisions that they intend to be rational – by which Williamson means to minimize costs – but they have a limited cognitive competence to do so. Bounded rationality is this condition of being 'intendedly rational but only limitedly so' (Williamson 1985: 45). With unbounded rationality, economic actors would not be reliant on others for information. Indeed, absent limits to their cognitive competence, decision-makers would know the opportunistic propensities of other actors and could simply avoid entering into transactions with those known to be prone to 'self-interest seeking with guile'.

The critical phenomenon that links the condition of bounded rationality with the condition of opportunism is uncertainty that is both cognitive and behavioural. The possibility of unforeseen 'disturbances' in the economic environment creates the need for 'adaptive, sequential decision making', and markets and hierarchies 'differ in their capacities to respond effectively to disturbances'. But for the condition of bounded rationality, the changing environment would not create cognitive uncertainty and pose problems of adaptation, because 'it would be feasible to develop a detailed strategy for crossing all possible bridges in advance' (Williamson 1985: 56–7).

The occurrence of these unforeseen disturbances creates opportunities for one party to a transaction to take advantage of the other. In the presence of parties to transactions who are looking for the opportunity to seek their own self-interest in deceitful, dishonest or guileful ways, cognitive uncertainty is transformed into behavioral uncertainty – that is 'uncertainty of a strategic kind ... attributable to opportunism'. As Williamson (1985: 58–9) goes on to argue: 'Behavioral uncertainty would not pose contractual problems if transactions were known to be free from exogenous disturbances, since then there would be no occasion to adapt and unilateral efforts to alter contracts could and presumably would be voided by the courts or other third party appeal.'

So what does the interaction of bounded rationality and opportunism tell us about the choice between markets and hierarchies, and hence about the activities in which a firm will engage? Given the behavioural condition of opportunism and the cognitive condition of bounded rationality, individuals who want to minimize transaction costs should choose to organize their transactions through markets rather than hierarchies. Markets permit those entering into a contract to attenuate opportunism by switching to other parties, and to operate within the constraint of bounded rationality by engaging in adaptive, sequential decision making.

Why then do firms exist and grow in a modern economy? The critical condition that, according to Williamson, favours hierarchies over markets is 'asset specificity'. Williamson introduced asset specificity as a *deus ex machina* into his argument when it became apparent that the assumptions of opportunism and bounded rationality provided an explanation for why *markets, not hierarchies*, would organize transactions (compare Williamson 1975 and 1985). The problem that Williamson wanted to explain, however, was why, given the possibility of organizing transactions by markets, hierarchies – that is, business organizations – exist. As Williamson (1985: 56) himself puts it: 'The absence of asset specificity [would] vitiate much of transaction cost economics'.

Asset specificity is inherent in 'transaction-specific durable assets', both human and physical, that cannot be deployed to alternative uses – that is, to other transactions – without incurring a financial loss. Williamson distinguishes between *physical* asset specificity and *human* asset specificity. Physical asset specificity can exist because of what he calls 'site specificity' – the physical immobility of invested resources that have been located in a particular place to be near a particular supplier or buyer – or because of 'dedicated assets' – the special-purpose nature of capital goods (even if they can be easily moved), especially when the investments have been made to service a limited extent of the market (in the extreme, a particular buyer). Human asset specificity can exist because of the need for continuity ('learning by doing') or collectivism ('team configurations) in the development of human resources (Williamson 1985: 34, 55–6, 95–6, 104).

Generally, what imbues assets involved in any specific transaction, therefore, with 'specificity' is the participation of particular parties, as investors, workers, suppliers, or buyers, in the transaction. 'Faceless contracting', characteristic of market transactions, is, according to Williamson (1985: 62, also 69, 195), 'supplanted by contracting in which the pairwise identity of the parties matters.' As a result, transaction-specific assets cannot be reallocated to another use without a loss.

Therefore, to generate revenues from these assets, the party that has invested in them requires *continuity* in its ability to utilize them. In effect, asset-specificity is a form of Marshallian fixed costs that requires that the asset be utilized for a high 'frequency' of transactions if these fixed costs are to be transformed into low unit costs (Williamson 1985: 52, 20, 72–3). But, in Williamson's framework, the *governance* of these transactions in the presence of asset specificity is critical to minimizing costs because, with bounded rationality, the participation of particular parties in transactions creates the possibility for opportunistic behaviour. Bounded rationality means that the economic actor cannot foresee future 'disturbances', while opportunism means that other parties to the transactions will deliberately take advantage of these disturbances to promote their own self-interests.

Non-market transaction relations exist, therefore, because of asset specificity, and, in the presence of bounded rationality and opportunism, the optimal governance of these relations must seek to minimize transaction costs. According to Williamson (1985: 387–8): 'Transactions, which differ in their attributes, are assigned to governance structures, which differ in their organizational costs and competencies, so as to effect a discriminating (mainly transaction cost economizing) match.' Specifically, he hypothesizes that 'market contracting gives way to bilateral contracting, which in turn is supplanted by unified contracting (internal organization) as asset specificity progressively deepens' (Williamson 1985: 78, see also 42).

But, when confronted with asset specificity, opportunism and bounded rationality, why does internal organization outperform market contracting? According to Williamson (1985: 60, see also 79, 151, 204), the economic virtues of internal organization lie in its relative ability to 'work things out':

> Whenever assets are specific in nontrivial degree, increasing the degree of uncertainty makes it more imperative that the parties devise a machinery to 'work things out' – since contractual gaps will be larger and the occasions for sequential adaptations will increase in number and importance as the degree of uncertainty increases.

These internal governance structures that 'work things out' add to the fixed costs of internal organization, and thus require that these costs be spread over larger numbers of transactions (that presumably result in more units of revenue-generating output) to obtain lower *unit* governance costs (Williamson 1985: 60, see also 72–3). As the frequency of transactions organized by a particular governance structure increases, economies of 'scale' and 'scope' appear. But these economies are not the result of spreading out the costs of indivisible technology and/or the fixed entrepreneurial factor as the post-Marshallian economists assumed. Rather, in the face of opportunism and bounded rationality Williamson contends that these economies of scale and scope are the result of economizing on the combined costs of asset-specific investments and the governance structures to 'work things out'.

The main virtue of Williamson's transaction-cost theory of the firm is that, in contrast to the conventional theory of the firm, he focuses on relationships among people who have specified cognitive and behavioural characteristics. The main problem with his theory is that he employs the constrained-optimization methodology to analyse the organizational and performance implications of bounded rationality, opportunism and asset specificity. That is, Williamson takes these cognitive, behavioural and technological conditions as given, and asks how those who control corporate resources optimize subject to these conditions as constraints. Hence Williamson's perspective contains no theory of innovative strategy – that is, a strategy for confronting and transforming these constraining conditions (see Lazonick 1991: chs 6 and 7). Indeed, Williamson specifically denies the importance of strategic corporate behaviour in the evolution of the US economy in the twentieth century (to which his transaction-cost analysis purportedly applies) – and in any case views corporate strategy as inherently predatory behaviour.[1]

Despite his invocation of 'asset specificity' as a central theoretical concept, Williamson's analysis does not address the issue of how productive resources are developed within an enterprise. As Williamson (1985: 143) recognizes explicitly:

> The introduction of innovation plainly complicates the earlier-described assignment of transactions to markets and hierarchies based entirely on an examination of their asset specificity qualities. Indeed, the study of economic organization in a regime of rapid innovation poses much more difficult issues than those addressed here.

So they do. By portraying corporate strategy as solely predatory behaviour and the organization of transactions by 'hierarchies' as a second-best solution to their organization by markets, Williamson's transaction-cost theory depicts the modern corporate enterprise as a 'market imperfection' that impedes the free flow of resources to alternative uses in the economy. The cause of this market imperfection is 'asset specificity' – a technological condition that is given to the firm. Also given to the firm in Williamson's transaction-cost theory are bounded rationality and opportunism. Opportunism is inherent in 'human nature as we know it' (Williamson 1985: 80), while bounded rationality is given by the limited capacity of individuals to absorb information. From the Williamsonian perspective, markets create 'high-powered' incentives for participants in the economy because the returns that participants can reap from the application of their efforts are not constrained by the need to share these returns with any other participants on a continuing basis (Williamson 1985: 132). The modern business corporation, in contrast, offers only 'low-powered incentives', as exemplified by the payment of salaries that segment remuneration from productive effort (Williamson 1985: 144–5). In the presence of asset specificity, and given the inherent limits on cognitive competence and the inherent human pursuit of self-interest with guile, for the Williamsonian firm 'to work things out' means to optimize subject to these technological, cognitive and behavioural constraints.

In sharp contrast, for a theory of the innovative enterprise, 'to work things out' is about how, through an investment strategy and an organizational structure, the enterprise transforms these technological, market, cognitive and behavioural conditions so that they support the generation of higher quality, lower cost products. From this perspective, the modern corporation can be viewed as an 'organizational success' rather than as a 'market imperfection' (Lazonick 1991: chs 2 and 6). Asset specificity results from an enterprise investment strategy to develop and utilize productive resources. The challenge for the innovative enterprise is then to transform these investments in physical and human resources into higher quality, lower cost products than had previously been available. Such an innovative transformation requires organizational learning.

The critical determinant of the success of the innovative strategy is what Mary O'Sullivan and I have called 'organizational integration' – a set of social relations that provides participants in a specialized division of labour with the incentives to cooperate in contributing their skills and efforts toward the achievement of common goals (Lazonick and O'Sullivan 1996, 1997a, 2000). Organizational integration can be strategic, functional and hierarchical, and the three types of organizational integration may interact dynamically

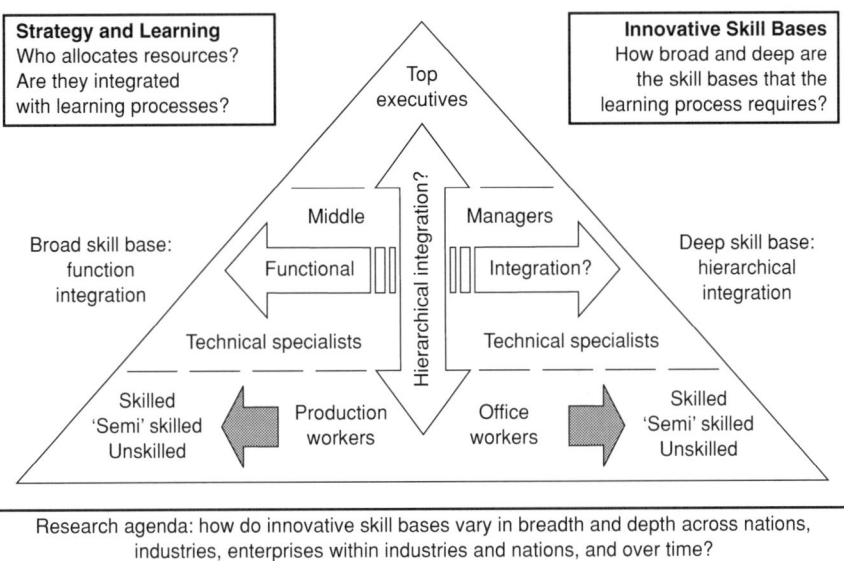

Figure 5 Organizational conditions: integration, learning and innovation

in the innovation process (see Figure 5) (see e.g. Lazonick 1998).

As such, organizational integration provides an essential social condition for an enterprise to engage in and make use of organizational learning – that is, learning that is *collective* and *cumulative* (O'Sullivan 2000a). Organizational learning is collective because it depends on the development of the skills and application of the efforts of an array of people in a specialized division of labour. Organizational learning is cumulative because the extent of the collective learning required for innovation makes it necessary to cumulate learning within an integrated organization. Moreover, as O'Sullivan (2000a, 2000b) argues, because the innovation process is not only cumulative and collective but also *uncertain*, the innovative enterprise must also be *strategic*, and hence for a theory of innovative enterprise the abilities and incentives of those who exercise *strategic control* are critical determinants of the types of specialized capabilities in which the enterprise invests to generate organizational learning and the incentives that are used to integrate the people bearing these specialized capabilities into the organizational learning process.

From the perspective of the innovative enterprise, the essence of organizational integration is that, by making possible organizational learning, it transforms 'bounded rationality' and 'opportunism' so that the cognitive and behavioural characteristics of participants in the enterprise contribute to the innovation process. Organizational integration can transform 'individual rationality' into 'collective rationality',[2] and thus unbounds the cognitive abilities available to the enterprise. Organizational integration can transform opportunism, and indeed transform 'human nature as [Oliver Williamson] know[s] it', by both generating and sharing the gains of the innovation process in ways that create 'high-powered' incentives – employment security, career opportunities, collective purpose – for the people on whom the enterprise relies to develop and utilize productive resources.[3]

The essence of the modern corporation as an innovative enterprise is that, through its investment strategy, it relies on 'asset specificity' as a developmental source of competitive advantage, and that, through its organizational structure, it unbounds 'rationality' and reduces 'opportunism' – or even transforms opportunists into cooperative members of a learning organization (see Figure 6). It is only when one has developed a viable explanation of the social foundations of innovative enterprise in the modern corporation that one can begin to analyse how, within an existing business enterprise, organizational success turns to organizational failure. From the perspective of the theory of innovative enterprise it can be posited that organizational integration dissolves into organizational segmentation as participants in the enterprise, and particularly, one might argue, those at the top, become prisoners of bounded rationality, act opportunistically, and seek to use accumulated assets as if they were general sources of revenues rather than the historical accumulations of organiza-

Transaction-Cost Theory		Theory of innovative enterprise
Given Constraints		*Innovative transformations*
Asset Specification (Industrial)	⇒	Enterprise investment strategy develops 'specific assets'
Bounded Rationality (Cognitive)	⇒	Organizational learning collectivizes 'rationality'
Opportunism (Behavioral)	⇒	Organizational incentives overcome 'opportunism'

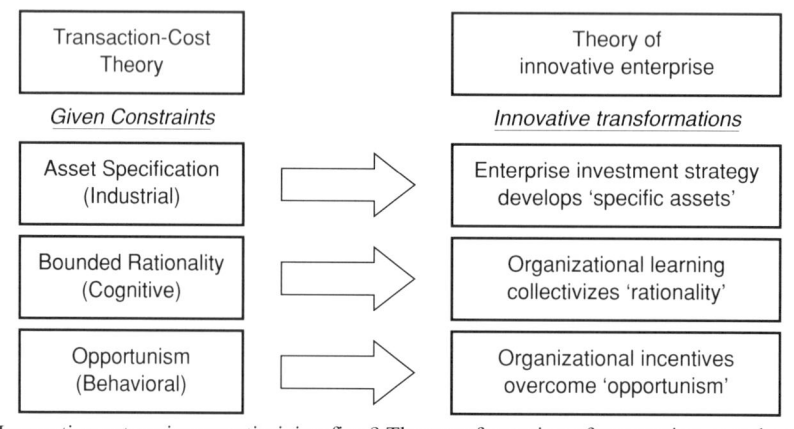

Figure 6 Innovative enterprise or optimizing firm? The transformation of transaction-cost theory

tional learning that provide the indispensable foundations for sustained competitive advantage.

3 Dynamic capabilities in a theory of innovative enterprise

Of the attempts that have been made to implant the analysis of innovation in transaction-cost theory, the most relevant for our purposes is that by Richard Langlois and Paul Robertson (1995) to construct what they call 'a dynamic theory of business institutions'. As Langlois and Robertson (1995: 1) put it at the beginning of their book, *Firms, Markets, and Economic Change*: 'One way to understand our project in this volume is to see it as an attempt to carry evolutionary economics more forcefully into the traditional bailiwicks of transaction-cost theory by presenting and applying an evolutionary theory of economic capabilities.' Focusing on the Coasian-Williamsonian question of why two or more distinct vertically related activities that could be performed by two or more distinct firms might be integrated into one firm, Langlois and Robertson invoke a process that they call 'systemic innovation'.

They argue that 'dynamic transaction costs' solves a coordination problem in the presence of the need for a systemic change. Systemic innovation requires the simultaneous change in a number of stages of production at once, and the individual actors who need to be involved in this change would not be able or willing to make the change without coordination. As Langlois and Robertson (1995: 4) state:

> The firm overcomes the 'dynamic' transaction costs of economic change. It is in this sense that we may say the firm solves a coordination problem: it enables complementary input-holders to agree on the basic nature of the system of production and distribution of the product. It provides the structure in a system of structured uncertainty.

More specifically, dynamic transaction costs are, according to Langlois and Robertson (1995: 35), 'the costs of persuading, negotiating, coordinating, and teaching outside suppliers'.

On the surface it may appear that Langlois and Robertson's 'dynamic transaction cost' theory is very similar to the theory of innovative enterprise that I have set out. In fact, they do not provide a theory of the relation between organizational strategy and organizational learning. Yet this relation is, I would argue, at the core of a theory of innovative enterprise. As a result, Langlois and Robertson put forth a dubious explanation of organizational integration – in this case, specifically vertical integration – as a relation among previously independent firms that exogenous technology imposes on participants in a specialized division of labour.

The first problem is that Langlois and Robertson introduce the notion of 'systemic innovation' in the same *deus ex machina* manner that, as I have already shown, Oliver Williamson uses the notion of 'asset specificity'. They provide no theoretical perspective of how, when and why systemic innovation appears. Unlike Williamson, however, Langlois and Robertson purport to be analysing the 'innovation process', thus rendering transaction-cost analysis 'dynamic'. Yet, for them, the appearance of a systemic innovation in a particular industry simply imposes an 'innovative strategy' on firms that these firms are compelled to adopt if they want to remain competitive participants in that industry.

The second problem is that, given the purported necessity for firms to adopt the systemic innovation, there is no learning in the Langlois–Robertson theory that goes beyond a core firm 'teaching' its outside suppliers that they can no longer remain independent firms but must join the vertically integrated firm. The assumption is that, given a choice, firms will want to remain independent of one another. As Langlois and Foss (1999: 210) have recently written, 'Langlois and Robertson (1995) build a broad theory of industrial dynamics around [the] idea' that

> much vertical integration occurs not when firms venture into new areas of similar capabilities but when firms are dragged, kicking and screaming, as it were, into complementary but dissimilar activities

because only in that way can they bring about a profitable reconfiguration of production or distribution.

The appearance of a systemic innovation leads a firm that plays the role of systems integrator to convince independent suppliers that they must give up their independence. The implicit assumption is that when such a change in vertical relations occurs, the presumed benefits of systemic innovation will be to some extent offset by the 'dynamic transaction costs' of overcoming the resistance of highly individualistic firms.

The desire to remain independent is a *possible* behavioural characteristic of the 'firm', but, in an age of mergers and acquisitions in which a firm's principals are often positioning themselves to be bought out (see Carpenter and Lazonick 2000), it is a characteristic that has to be demonstrated rather than assumed. Moreover, there are large literatures on supplier relations and strategic alliances that demonstrate that innovation can occur through cooperation across legally independent firms as well as within a firm as a distinct legal entity (see Figure 7) (see, e.g. Sako 1998 and Doz 1996). Indeed, for a theory of innovative enterprise, the biggest problem with the Langlois-Robertson perspective is that they treat the firm as if it were a unitary actor – that is, an individual – and hence do not put forth any framework or agenda for exploring the organization of individuals who occupy positions within the specialized divisions of labour within firms. The lack of such a perspective is problematic for an organization made up of only two people (think of a married couple), never mind a business enterprise with tens of thousands of employees. The willingness to see the firm as an individual reflects an individualistic bias in the analysis of 'industrial dynamics' that avoids such critical issues as a) the structure of strategic control within an enterprise and the process of strategic decision making, b) the transformation of individual learning into organizational learning in the innovation process, and c) the transformation of organizational learning into higher quality, lower cost products, thus transforming the high fixed costs of an innovative strategy into the basis for competitive advantage (see Figures 3 and 4) (Lazonick and O'Sullivan 2000). Indeed, I would argue that an understanding of how an innovative enterprise develops and utilizes productive resources across firms as distinct units of financial control will depend on the evolution of these capabilities within a dominant firm or

Evolution of industry structure

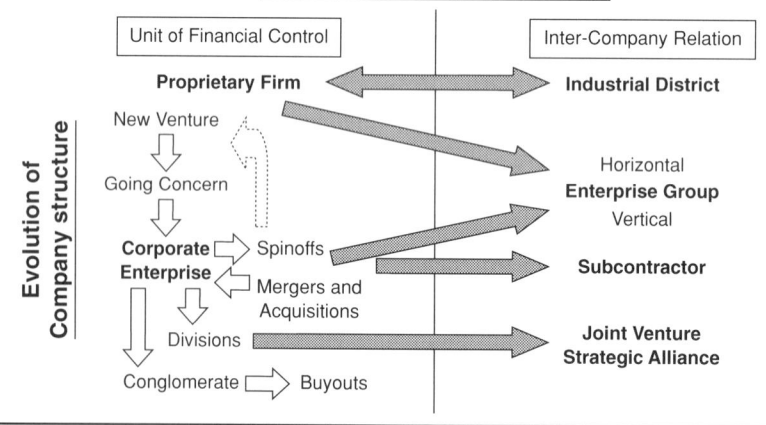

Figure 7 Organizational conditions: evolution of company and industry structures

firms within this network of relations (see Figure 7 for a schematic representation of such co-evolution).

Within the strategic management literature, there were during the 1980s and 1990s a number of contributions, many of them by people trained as economists, to the roles of strategy and learning in innovative enterprises.[4] The most developed statement of this perspective to date is that of David Teece, Gary Pisano and Amy Shuen (1997; see also Teece and Pisano 1994) (see DYNAMIC CAPABILITIES). Teece *et al*. (1997: 509) contrast the dynamic capabilities perspective with a dominant perspective in the management literature on 'strategizing' that entails 'engaging in business conduct that keeps competitors off balance, raises rival's costs, and excludes new entrants' and that conceives of 'rents' as 'flow[ing] from privileged product market positions'. Teece *et al*. (1997: 509–10) argue that

> the [dynamic capabilities] framework suggests that private wealth creation in regimes of rapid technological change depends in large measure on honing internal technological, organizational, and managerial processes inside the firm. In short, identifying new opportunities and organizing efficiently and effectively to embrace them are generally more fundamental to private wealth creation that is strategizing [against existing and potential rivals].

They see the distinctiveness of firms as opposed to markets as residing in the capabilities in 'organizing and getting things done' in ways that 'cannot be accomplished merely by using the price system to coordinate activity. The very essence of capabilities/competences is that they cannot be readily assembled through markets' (Teece *et al*. 1997: 517). Of the three elements of their framework – positions, processes, and paths – it is organizational processes that define their approach:

> We define dynamic capabilities as the firm's ability to integrate, build, and reconfigure internal and external competences to address rapidly changing environments. Dynamic capabilities thus reflect an organization's ability to achieve new and innovative forms of competitive advantage, *given path dependencies and market positions*.
>
> (Teece *et al*. 1997: 516, my emphasis)

Or, as Teece *et al*. (1997: 524) state later in the paper: 'The essence of a firm's competence and dynamic capabilities is presented here as being resident in the firm's organizational processes, that are in turn shaped by the firm's assets (positions) and its evolutionary path.' 'Organizational processes', they argue, 'often display high levels of coherence, and when they do, replication may be difficult because it requires systemic changes throughout the organization and also among inter-organizational linkages, which may be hard to effectuate' (Teece *et al*.: 1997: 519). They liken 'coherence' to Nelson and Winter's (1982: ch. 5) notion of 'routines', with the caveat that 'the routines concept is a little too amorphous to properly capture the congruence among processes and between processes and incentives that we have in mind' (Teece *et al*. 1997: 520). They stress the importance of learning processes that are 'intrinsically social and collective' and argue that the 'concept of dynamic capabilities as a coordinative management process opens the door to the potential for interorganizational learning' (Teece *et al*. 1997: 520).

Whereas *organizational processes* transform the capabilities of the firm over time, *asset positions* determine the firm's 'competitive advantage at any point in time' (Teece *et al*. 1997: 521). Teece *et al*. (1997: 521–2) describe asset positions under the separate headings of 'technological', 'complementary', 'financial', 'reputational', 'structural', 'institutional', 'market structure' and 'organizational' – that is, they include under the label 'asset positions' virtually any descriptive dimension of the firm as an organizational entity at any point in time. And while organizational processes can transform these characteristics of the firm, and hence its competitive capabilities over time, the firm's evolutionary path – its particular history – constrains the types of industrial activities in which a firm can be competitive. Teece *et al*. (1997: 523–4) stress that, although the firm's technological paths are constrained by its history, or 'path dependency', it nevertheless has the capacity to take advantage of technological opportunities created by 'new scientific breakthroughs'. The technological opportunities created by these breakthroughs, moreover, 'may not be completely exogenous to industry, not only because some firms have the capacity to engage in or at least support basic research, but also because technological opportunities are often fed by innovative activity itself' (Teece et al. 1997: 523).

Nevertheless, Teece et al. (1997: 524) argue, the firm's 'evolutionary path, despite managerial hubris that might suggest otherwise, is often rather narrow'. Strategic change is generally incremental, as new capabilities have to build cumulatively on the capabilities previously put in place. From the dynamic capabilities perspective, 'strategy involves choosing among and committing to long-term paths or trajectories of competence development' (Teece et al. 1997: 529). Teece, Pisano and Shuen say nothing specific about the locus of strategic control that ensures that the enterprise seeks to grow using the collective processes and along the cumulative paths that are the foundations of its distinctive competitive success. That is, they have nothing to say about who within the organization's hierarchical and functional division of labour should make strategic decisions to maintain the integration of strategy and learning and thereby sustain the innovation process. Nor do they have anything to say about how returns should be allocated to ensure the sustained finance – what O'Sullivan and I have called 'financial commitment' (Lazonick and O'Sullivan 1997b and 1997c) – to support the process of organizational learning. As a result, the dynamic capabilities approach has thus far provided no insights into the conditions under which strategic control might become segmented from the organizational learning processes that are central to the development of an enterprise's core competencies, or how, under such circumstances, the structure of strategic control can be transformed to effect the reintegration of strategy and learning.

Nor has the dynamic capabilities approach as of yet provided guidance for understanding how an enterprise can and should respond strategically when it is confronted by new competitors, supported by different institutional environments, whose dynamic capabilities render the enterprise's processes and paths, and hence asset positions, obsolete. But the 'dynamic capabilities' approach is an emergent perspective, and one that is, in its general orientation, consistent with the theory of innovative enterprise that I have proposed in this entry.

4 Conclusion: industries, organizations and institutions

At the conclusion of their paper, Teece, Pisano and Shuen (1997: 530) call for further theoretical and empirical work – an 'ambitious research agenda' – to help

> understand how firms get to be good, how they sometimes stay that way, why and how they improve, and why they sometimes decline. Researchers in the field of strategy need to join forces with researchers in the fields of innovation, manufacturing, and organizational behavior and business history if they are to unlock the riddles that lie behind corporate as well as national competitive advantage. There could hardly be a more ambitious research agenda in the social sciences today.

To undertake such a research agenda requires a theoretical perspective on the social process that enables business enterprises to transform industrial conditions in different times and places. If one accepts that business enterprises are social structures that are in turn embedded in broader (typically national) institutional environments, the theoretical perspective on innovative enterprise must put forth a model of the relations among *industrial conditions*, *organizational conditions* and *institutional conditions* in the process of transforming technologies and markets to generate products that are higher quality and/or lower cost than those that had previously existed (see Figure 1).

I shall conclude with a description of the basic structure of a theoretical perspective on the social conditions of innovative enterprise (referred to hereafter as the SCIE perspective). The SCIE perspective derives from syntheses of large bodies of existing comparative-historical research on the industrial, organizational and institutional foundations of economic development in the advanced economies over the course of the twentieth century (see Lazonick and O'Sullivan 1996, 1997a, 1997b, 1997c, 2000; Lazonick 1998; O'Sullivan 2000b).

Central to the SCIE perspective is the specification of the key characteristics of the industrial, organizational, and institutional conditions that can promote or constrain the innovation process. As illustrated in Figure 1, the key characteristics are:

- industrial conditions: *technological, market* and *competitive*;
- organizational conditions: *cognitive, behavioural* and *strategic*;
- institutional conditions: *employment, financial* and *regulatory*.

As a product of prior empirical research, the SCIE perspective provides a tool for further, generally more pointed and detailed, empirical research into the social conditions of innovative enterprise. As an iterative intellectual process for understanding complex and ever-changing economic systems, the empirical knowledge that we gain using the SCIE perspective as a theoretical framework enables the elaboration, amendment, and refinement of the perspective on an ongoing basis.

To understand how industrial, organizational, and institutional conditions, acting as elements of a social system, influence the innovation process, we must also specify the key characteristics of that process. Drawing on the literature on innovation, the innovation process can be characterized as *cumulative, collective* and *uncertain* (O'Sullivan 2000a). The innovation process is cumulative because the possibilities for transforming technological and market conditions today and tomorrow depend on the development of those conditions in the past. Hence, an innovative enterprise must engage in cumulative learning. The innovation process is collective because the transformation of technological and market conditions requires the integration of large numbers of people with specialized knowledge and skills so that they engage in cooperative interaction to develop and utilize productive resources. Hence, an innovative enterprise must engage in collective learning. The innovation process is uncertain because the cumulative and collective processes that can transform technological and market conditions to generate higher quality, lower cost products are unknown at the time at which commitments of resources to these processes are made. Hence, an innovative enterprise must be strategic in how it engages in cumulative and collective learning.

A theory of innovative enterprise must comprehend the implications of an innovation process that is cumulative, collective, and uncertain for the abilities and incentives of business enterprises to transform the technological and market, and hence competitive, conditions that characterize an industry at a point in time. The abilities and incentives of business enterprises to transform these industrial conditions to generate innovation in turn depend on the 'social conditions of innovative enterprise' as determined by the interaction of organizational and institutional conditions in the innovation process.

Industrial conditions

Technological conditions refer to the productive capabilities, embodied in both human and physical capital, that characterize an industry (or an enterprise within an industry, depending on the unit of analysis) at a point in time. Market conditions refer to the existing demand (in terms of quantity, quality, and price) for an industry's products and the existing supply of factors of production (in terms of quantity, quality, and price) in the economy. Competitive conditions refer to the differential ability (measured in terms of both productivity and cost) of enterprises in an industry (or the same industries in different institutional environments) to transform productive resources into revenue-generating products.

The technological and market conditions that characterize an enterprise at a point in time constrain the ability and incentive of that enterprise to develop and utilize productive resources over time. Innovation entails the transformation of existing technological and/or market conditions to generate higher quality and/or lower cost products. The success of an enterprise in transforming these technological and market conditions in turn transforms the competitive conditions facing other enterprises in the industry. These new competitive conditions may or may not induce an innovative response from these rivals. Challenged by an innovative enterprise, the competitive response of another enterprise may entail a strategy either to *adapt* on the basis of the pre-existing technological and market conditions or to *innovate* by itself seeking to transform these conditions to generate higher quality, lower cost products. The competitive viability of an adaptive response will itself be dependent on the relative success of the innovative competitor in transforming pre-existing technological and market conditions to generate higher quality, lower cost products (Lazonick 1991: ch. 3).

Organizational conditions

Cognitive conditions refer to the cumulated knowledge and available skill base on which at any point in time an enterprise can expect to develop and utilize its productive resources. Behavioural conditions refer to the set of incentives existing at any point in time that can motivate participants in the enterprise to use their knowledge and skill to develop and utilize productive resources. Strategic conditions refer to the structure of control within the enterprise at a point in time over the allocation of financial, physical, and human resources. Embodying these organizational conditions within the enterprise is a hierarchical and functional division of labour, which is itself influenced by the combination of industrial and institutional conditions in which the enterprise has evolved.

Strategic conditions determine whether an enterprise responds to changes in competitive conditions innovatively or adaptively. An enterprise's strategy is influenced by the cognitive conditions and behavioural conditions on the basis of which those who exercise strategic control in the enterprise can seek to transform technological and market conditions, often in response to changes in competitive conditions. The implementation of an innovative strategy to transform technological and market conditions entails strategic choices concerning a) whose knowledge and skill within the organization's hierarchical and functional division of labour will be developed and utilized, and b) what incentives will be offered to these different participants in the specialized division of labour to motivate them to cooperate in the pursuit of enterprise goals. Hence, the process of transforming industrial conditions generally entails the transformation of cognitive and behavioural conditions, with the types of organizational transformations that take place depending on the structure of strategic control within the enterprise. Cognitive, behavioural and strategic conditions do not evolve independently of one another, but rather as conditions within an organizational system that seeks to develop and utilize productive resources in particular industrial activities.

Institutional conditions

Financial conditions determine the ways in which a society allocates financial resources to states, enterprises and individuals for investment and consumption as well as the ways in which that society distributes financial returns to the holders of various forms of financial claims. Employment conditions determine how a society develops the capabilities of its present and future labour forces (and hence include education, research and training systems) as well as how it seeks to influence (for example, through government spending and union activity) the availability of employment and the conditions of work and remuneration. Regulatory conditions determine how a society assigns rights and responsibilities to different groups of people over the management of society's productive resources, including human resources, and how it imposes restrictions on the development and utilization of these resources. As in the case of organizational conditions, financial, employment and regulatory conditions do not evolve independently of one another but rather as conditions within an institutional system that seeks to develop and utilize an economy's productive resources.

Of particular importance for understanding the relation between a society's regulatory institutions and the performance of a modern economy dominated by corporate enterprises are the prevailing rights, responsibilities, and restrictions in the society over the management of *corporate* resources. A fundamental hypothesis that derives from the SCIE perspective is that institutional, organizational and industrial conditions interact historically to determine a unique set of rights, responsibilities and restrictions that characterize a particular economy and society in a particular era. This perspective hypothesizes that the historical emergence of institutional conditions related to finance, employment and regulation reflect the changing requirements of business enterprises (and especially corporate enterprises in a society in which they dominate business activity) for the development and utilization of productive resources.

Over time, these financial, employment and regulatory practices become institutionalized in laws and norms as well as the practices of related non-business organizations that play important roles in administering and undertaking the financial, employment, and regulatory functions. Insofar as they derive from the requirements of business organizations to develop and utilize productive resources, these institutions become 'embedded' in the financial, employment and regulatory practices of these business organizations themselves.[5] The SCIE perspective argues that, at a point in time, these social conditions determine the types of industrial transformations, and hence the type of industrial innovations, that can occur in the economy. Over time, however, the transformation of certain dimensions of these institutional and organizational conditions – in effect transformations of what may be called 'the political economy' – can open up new possibilities for innovative activity.

Social conditions of innovative enterprise

How then within this theoretical framework can we characterize the social conditions of innovative enterprise? From a characterization of the innovation process as cumulative, collective, and uncertain combined with a comparative-historical analysis of successful economic development in the twentieth century, we can identify three social conditions of innovative enterprise: *financial commitment, organizational integration, and strategic control*. The existence and forms of these social conditions of innovative enterprise reflect prevailing financial, employment and regulatory conditions that are embedded in prevailing cognitive, behavioural and strategic conditions.

Financial commitment is the social condition that allocates financial resources to sustain the process that develops and utilizes productive resources until the resultant products can generate financial returns. As a social condition for innovative enterprise, the need for financial commitment derives directly from the cumulative character of the innovation process – that is, from the need for learning. For an enterprise or economy that has accumulated capabilities, financial claims can take on an existence that, for a time at least, are independent of the need to reproduce or augment those capabilities. But, for innovation to occur within an enterprise or economy, a basic social condition is financial commitment from some source for a sufficient period of time to generate returns. A theory of innovative enterprise must show how, given the financial requirements of the transformation of technology and markets in particular industrial activities, institutions and organizations combine to provide the requisite financial commitment.

Organizational integration is the social condition that creates incentives for participants in the hierarchical and functional division of labour to apply their skills and efforts to engage in interactive learning in pursuit of organizational goals. As a social condition for innovative enterprise, the need for organizational integration derives directly from the collective character of the innovation process. Hence, a theory of innovative enterprise must show how, given the collective character of the transformation of technology and markets in particular industrial activities, institutions and organizations combine to create the necessary incentives for those who must engage in interactive learning.

Strategic control is the social condition that enables people within an enterprise who have access to financial commitment and who influence organizational integration to allocate resources in ways that can transform technologies and markets to generate innovation. As a social condition for innovative enterprise, the need for strategic control derives directly from the uncertain character of the innovation process. Hence, a theory of innovative enterprise must show how, given the uncertain character of the transformation of technology and markets in particular industrial activities, control over financial commitment and organizational integration rests with those people within the enterprise who, as strategic decision-makers, have a willingness and ability to use that control to attempt innovative transformations of technologies and markets.

The SCIE perspective posits a dynamic historical relation between organizations and institutions. One can in principle treat the business enterprise as an independent social entity in analysing the social conditions of innovative enterprise. Such an analysis entails an identification of the structure of strategic learning within the enterprise and its relations to the sources of financial commitment and the modes of organizational integration. In effect, the financial, employment, and regulatory arrangements that characterize the enterprise itself (rather than the wider society in which it is embedded) would constitute its 'institutional conditions', while, operating within these institutional conditions, the knowledge base, structure of incentives, and strategic orientations of the enterprise would constitute its 'organizational conditions'. To treat the enterprise as an independent social entity, however, would run the risk of ignoring how the institutional environment that extends beyond the enterprise proscribes and enables it to acquire and retain certain types of knowledge bases, to structure employment incentives for participants, and to consider strategic alternatives. That is, the evolution of the institutional environment in which an enterprise is embedded, as distinct from the 'institutional conditions' that have evolved historically within the enterprise itself, may have a significant impact on the social conditions of innovative enterprise as experienced by the enterprise. Moreover, insofar as innovative enterprises are able to reshape the conditions of strategic learning, financial commitment, and organizational integration in ways that are in conflict with prevailing institutional norms in the wider society, these new organizational conditions may over time encourage the reform of institutional conditions. Thus, the SCIE perspective seeks to understand the dynamic interaction between the organizational conditions of business enterprises and the institutional environments in which they operate, and the relation of these social conditions of innovative enterprise to the transformation of technological and market, and hence competitive, conditions in different industrial activities.

WILLIAM LAZONICK
UNIVERSITY OF MASSACHUSETTS AT LOWELL
AND
INSEAD

Notes

1 To quote Williamson (1985: 128): 'Suffice it to observe here that strategic behavior has relevance in dominant firm or tightly oligopolistic industries. Since most of the organizational change reported [here] occurred in nondominant firm industries, appeal to strategic considerations is obviously of limited assistance in explaining the reorganization of American industry over the past 150 years.' This despite numerous references by Williamson to the work of Alfred D. Chandler, Jr. (1962 and 1977). For Williamson (1985: 373, 376–80), strategic behaviour represents predatory attempts by corporations that already have dominant market power to bankrupt existing rivals and create barriers to entry against potential competitors. In Williamson's (1985: 128) words, 'Strategic behavior has reference to efforts by dominant firms to take up and maintain advance or preemptive positions and/or to respond punitively to rivals.' For a critique of Williamson's use of Chandler, see Lazonick 1991: ch. 7.

2 The seminal work on the role of the executive in integrating the individual into the organization is Barnard (1938), whose classic work basically focused on how

organizations can transform opportunism into cooperation.

3 For an elaboration of this critical point, see the discussion in Lazonick (1991: 226–7) that concludes the chapter entitled, 'The Innovative Business Organization and Transaction Cost Theory'. In a more recent article, Sumantra Ghoshal and Peter Moran (1996) have critiqued Williamson's notion of opportunism by arguing that, while markets foster self-aggrandizement, individualism and competition, organizations foster trust, collectivism and cooperation. They chastise scholars of strategy and organization who are 'increasingly embracing TCE – by proposing incremental modifications, like the inclusion of variables such as "trust"... , which their research reveals to be important – instead of challenging it on the grounds that such findings falsify its basic tenets' (Ghoshal and Moran 1996: 42). While Ghoshal and Moran make no reference to my extended critique of Williamson's theory contained in *Business Organization and the Myth of the Market Economy*, the final paragraph of their paper comes to conclusions that are very similar to mine concerning the significance of this integrative role of organization for the study of the economy: 'We believe that the time has come for these scholars to stop building on theories of organizations that persist with the myth of the market economy and to start afresh by developing an alternative theory that acknowledges the reality of the organizational economy' (Ghoshal and Moran 1996: 42).

4 See Lazonick and O'Sullivan (2000: Parts 5 and 6) for an extended review and evaluation of this literature from the perspective of the theory of innovative enterprise that is being proposed here.

5 The SCIE perspective has relevance for related work in economic sociology and institutional economics, the consideration of which is beyond the scope of this entry (see INSTITUTIONAL ECONOMICS). See Granovetter (1985) for the notion that the 'embeddedness' of social relations constrains self-interested behaviour and collective institutions; and North (1990) for a perspective on the relation between institutions and organizations that focuses on the creation of 'efficient markets' rather than, as we do here, 'innovative enterprises' as the foundation for superior economic performance.

Further reading

(References cited in the text marked *)

* Barnard, C. (1938) *The Function of the Executive*, Harvard University Press. (The classic work on the role of the business executive in eliciting cooperative effort from individual employees.)
* Carpenter, M. and Lazonick, W. (2000) The Optical Networking Industry (A), INSEAD case. (A study of the changing role of the stock market in the accumulation of corporate capabilities.)
* Chandler, A. (1962) *Strategy and Structure: Chapters in the History of the American Enterprise*, MIT Press. (The classic work on the historical evolution of the 'multidivisional structure' in the US economy.)
* Chandler, A. (1977) *The Visible Hand: The Managerial Revolution in American Business*, Harvard University Press. (A historical perspective on the development of the US economy in which managerial organization is central.)
* Coase, R. (1937) 'The nature of the firm', *Economica*, n.s. 4: 386–405. (The classic article, written from a neoclassical perspective, on why firms exist in a 'market economy'.)
* Doz, Y. (1996) 'The evolution of cooperation in strategic alliances: initial conditions or learning processes', *Strategic Management Journal* 17: 55–83. (Through comparative case-study analysis, assesses the relative importance of initial conditions and learning processes in determining the outcomes of strategic alliances.)
* Ghoshal, S. and Moran, P. (1996) 'Bad for practice: a critique of the transaction cost theory', *Academy of Management Review* 21: 13–47. (A critique of the Williamsonian notion of 'opportunism' from the perspective of the 'good' organizational practices in business enterprises.)
* Granovetter, M. (1985) 'Economic action and social structure: the problem of embeddedness', *American Journal of Sociology* 91: 481–510. (Classic article by a sociologist on why social relations exist in a market economy.)
* Langlois, R. and Foss, N. (1999), 'Capabilities and organization: the rebirth of production in the theory of economic organization', *Kyklos* 52: 201–18. (Argues that, by virtue of its neglect of production, the mainstream economics

literature on organization ignores the roles of routines and capabilities as coordinating devices.)

* Langlois, R. and Robertson, P. (1995) *Firms, Markets and Economic Change: A Dynamic Theory of Business Institutions*, Routledge. (The argument that 'systemic innovation' creates a dynamic role for firms in a market economy.)

* Lazonick, W. (1991) *Business Organization and the Myth of the Market Economy*, Cambridge University Press. (A critique of the theory of the market economy for its failure to recognize the role of business organization in the successful performance of the advanced economies.)

* Lazonick, W. (1993) 'Learning and the dynamics of international competitive advantage', in R. Thomson (ed.), *Learning and Technological Change*, Macmillan. (A framework for understanding how enterprises, industries, and economies transform cost structures through innovation rather than optimize subject to existing cost structures.)

* Lazonick, W. (1998) 'Organizational learning and international competition', in J. Michie and J. Smith (eds), *Globalization, Growth, and Governance*, Oxford University Press. (The interaction of hierarchical and functional integration in explaining the success of the Japanese manufacturing challenge of the post-World War II decades.)

* Lazonick, W. (2001) 'Understanding innovative enterprise: toward the integration of economic theory and business history', in F. Amatori and G. Jones (eds), *Business History Around the World*, Cambridge University Press. (The use of a 'historical-transformation' methodology to construct relevant economic theory and to use it to explore rather than ignore the realities of business organization.)

* Lazonick, W. and O'Sullivan. M. (1996) 'Organization, finance, and international competition', *Industrial and Corporate Change* 5: 1–49. (A comparative-historical analysis of organizational integration and financial commitment in the development of Britain, US, Germany, and Japan, with implications for international competition in terms of quality and cost.)

* Lazonick, W. and O'Sullivan, M. (1997a) 'Big business and skill formation in the wealthiest nations: the organizational revolution in the twentieth century', in A. Chandler, F. Amatori, and T. Hikino (eds), *Big Business and the Wealth of Nations*, Cambridge University Press. (A comparative-historical analysis of the organizations and institutions for skill formation in the US, Germany, and Japan in the twentieth century.)

* Lazonick, W. and O'Sullivan, M. (1997b) 'Finance and industrial development, Part 1: the United States and the United Kingdom', *Financial History Review* 4: 7–29. (A historical-comparative analysis of the roles of organizations and markets in committing finance to industrial development in the US and the UK in the twentieth century.)

* Lazonick, W. and O'Sullivan, M. (1997c) 'Finance and industrial development, Part 2: Germany and Japan', *Financial History Review* 4: 117–38. (A historical-comparative analysis of the roles of organizations and markets in committing finance to industrial development in Germany and Japan in the twentieth century.)

* Lazonick, W. and O'Sullivan, M. (2000) 'Perspectives on corporate governance, innovation, and economic performance', Report to the European Commission (DGXII) under the TSER Programme (see http://www.insead.edu/cgep). (The debates on corporate governance in terms of different perspectives on modes of resource allocation and economic performance, and the implications for understanding organizational learning and strategic management.)

* Nelson, R. and Winter, S. (1982), *An Evolutionary Theory of Economic Change*, Harvard University Press. (A pioneering effort to understand the persistence of business organizations, given the assumptions of neoclassical economic theory.)

* North, D. (1990) *Institutions, Institutional Change, and Economic Performance*, Cambridge University Press. (A theory of the role and evolution of institutions in a market economy.)

* O'Sullivan, M. (2000a) 'The innovative enterprise and corporate governance', *Cambridge Journal of Economics* 24: 393–416. (The characteristics of the innovation process and the implications for the current economic debates on corporate governance.)

* O'Sullivan, M. (2000b) *Contests for Corporate Control: Corporate Governance and Economic Performance in the United States and Germany*, Oxford University Press. (A critical account of the debates on corporate governance in the light of the comparative development of advanced economies.)

* Patel, P. and Pavitt, K. (1997) 'The technological competencies of the world's largest firms: complex and path-dependent, but not much variety', *Research Policy* 26: 141–56. (The need for large firms to have competencies in a wide variety of technological specializations to compete on global markets.)

* Prencipe, A. (2000) 'Breadth and depth of technological capabilities in CoPS: the case of the

aircraft engine control system', *Research Policy* 29: 895–911. (A case study that shows the importance of integration of capabilities both within a firm and across firms in complex product systems.)
* Sako, M. (1998) 'Supplier development at Honda, Nissan and Toyota: a historical case study of organizational capability enhancement', Said Business School, University of Oxford. (The importance of developing close and cooperative relations with suppliers for improving products and processes in the automobile industry.)
* Schumpeter, J. (1950) *Capitalism, Socialism, and Democracy*, third edition, Harper. (The classic work that argues that modern capitalism cannot be understood according to the principles of the market economy, and particularly if one adheres to the neoclassical monopoly model.)
* Teece, D. and Pisano, G. (1994) 'The dynamic capabilities of firms: an introduction', *Industrial and Corporate Change* 3: 537–56. (Introduction to a special issue devoted to analysing the ways in which enterprises develop innovative capabilities.)
* Teece, D., Pisano, G. and Shuen, A. (1997) 'Dynamic capabilities and strategic management', *Strategic Management Journal* 18: 509–33. (An initial effort to develop a theory of dynamic capabilities based on the relations among positions, paths, and processes.)
* Williamson, O. (1975) *Markets and Hierarchies: Analysis and Antitrust Implications*, Free Press. (An analysis of the relation between markets and hierarchies in an advanced economy as a critique of the neoclassical monopoly model.)
* Williamson, O. (1985) *The Economic Institutions of Capitalism*, Free Press. (The development of the transaction-cost critique of conventional economics that focuses on the roles of bounded rationality, opportunism, and asset specificity in determining the choices of organizational forms.)
* Williamson, O. (1996) *The Mechanisms of Governance*, Free Press. (A collection of essays that expands upon the transaction-cost theory developed in the author's previous work.)

See also: AEROSPACE INDUSTRY; AUTOMOBILE INDUSTRY; BIOTECHNOLOGY; CHEMICAL INDUSTRY; CLEANER PRODUCTION; COASE, R.; COOPERATION AND COMPETITION; CORPORATE CONTROL; DEVELOPMENT AND DIFFUSION OF TECHNOLOGY; DYNAMIC CAPABILITIES; EAST ASIAN ECONOMIES; ECONOMIC GROWTH AND CONVERGENCE; ELECTRONICS INDUSTRY; EMPLOYMENT RELATIONS; EVOLUTIONARY THEORIES OF THE FIRM; GLOBAL MACHINE TOOL INDUSTRY; GLOBALIZATION; GROWTH OF THE FIRM AND NETWORKING; GROWTH THEORY; INDUSTRIAL AGGLOMERATIONS; INDUSTRIAL DYNAMICS; INDUSTRIAL AND LABOUR RELATIONS; INNOVATION; INSTITUTIONAL ECONOMICS; INTELLECTUAL PROPERTY RIGHTS; MARSHALL, A.; MARX, K.; MULTINATIONAL CORPORATIONS; NEOCLASSICAL ECONOMICS; PENROSE, E.; SCHUMPETER, J.; SERVICE ECONOMY; SKILL FORMATION SYSTEMS; SMALL AND MEDIUM SIZE ENTERPRISES; SMITH, A.; STEEL INDUSTRY; TELECOMMUNICATIONS INDUSTRY; TRANSACTION COST ECONOMICS; WILLIAMSON, O.E.

Biographies

Smith, Adam (1723–90)

1 Introduction
2 Main contribution to economics
3 Conclusions

Personal background

- born before 5 June 1723 in Kirkcaldy, Fife, Scotland, the son of a customs official
- educated at University of Glasgow, 1737–40
- Snell Exhibitioner, Balliol College, Oxford, 1740–6
- professor at University of Glasgow, 1751–64
- tutor to the Duke of Buccleuch, 1764–6
- Commissioner of Customs, 1778
- died in Edinburgh on 17 July 1790 of stomach cancer

Major works

The Theory of Moral Sentiments (1759)
Lectures on Jurisprudence (1762–3; first published 1978)
The Wealth of Nations (1776)

Summary

Adam Smith (1723–90), the leading figure in the classical school of economics and prominent in the Scottish Enlightenment, is one of the few economists to be credited with founding economics. In his compendious work, *The Wealth of Nations*, he integrated the information and ideas provided by historical and contemporary authors to explain how an economy operates and how it can grow. He set out a system of natural liberty for an economy, justified free trade and inspired subsequent value and distribution theories. Both socialist and libertarian economists look to him as a precursor.

1 Introduction

Adam Smith was born into a prosperous Scottish family and baptised on 5 June 1723. His father, the Clerk of the Court Martial and Comptroller of Customs at Kirkcaldy, died before his only son was born. Smith was educated at the local burgh school then entered the University of Glasgow in 1737 to study Latin, Greek, Logic, Moral Philosophy, Mathematics and Natural Philosophy for an MA degree. In 1740, without graduating, he left Glasgow when he was awarded a Snell Exhibition at Balliol College, Oxford. This minor scholarship was intended to enable young men to train for the ministry in the Church of England. Disgusted by the poor quality of the teaching at the University of Oxford, Smith embarked on an extensive course of self-education. Smith returned to Scotland in 1746, resigning the exhibition in 1749.

He had no intention of entering the church's ministry so he looked for a career in the law or elsewhere. Encouraged by the Lord Advocate, he gave private lectures in Edinburgh for three winters on rhetoric, *belles-lettres* and philosophy. Anticipating his later views, Smith told his audience: 'Little else is required to carry a state to the highest degree of opulence from the lowest barbarism, but peace, easy taxes, and a tolerable administration of justice; all the rest being brought about by the natural course of things' (Smith 1983).

In 1751 he was appointed Professor of Logic at Glasgow; in 1752 he was translated to the Chair of Moral Philosophy. He interpreted his academic remit widely to lecture on rhetoric, ethics, jurisprudence and economics. From reconstructions of students' lecture notes, it is possible to see the breadth of Smith's erudition. He was an enthusiastic teacher, lecturing eight hours weekly and involved in university administration, being Dean of the Faculty 1760–2. The University of Glasgow conferred the LLD degree on him in 1762. Residence in Glasgow enabled Smith to gain a detailed knowledge of the views and methods of merchants, putting that knowledge to use in his later economic writings.

The publication of *The Theory of Moral Sentiments* in 1759 brought him considerable fame. Charles Townshend, Secretary of State and stepfather of the eighteen-year-old Duke of Buccleuch, was sufficiently impressed by the book to invite Smith to leave the University of Glasgow to accompany the duke on a grand tour of Europe. Smith was given a life pension of £300 per annum, the same amount as his previous academic earnings. From January 1764 to November 1766 Smith travelled with the duke and his younger brother to Paris, Toulouse and Geneva, meeting François Quesnay (1694–1774) and other leading physiocrats, as well as Voltaire. The death of the duke's younger brother in Paris ended Smith's only journey beyond Britain.

Smith spent the winter of 1766–7 in London working on a revision of *The Theory of Moral Sentiments*, as well as advising Townshend, then Chancellor of the Exchequer, on the sinking fund. For six years to 1773, Smith stayed at his mother's home in Kirkcaldy gathering information for and preparing drafts of *The Wealth of Nations*. From 1773 to 1777 he resided in London, with a nine-month break in Scotland in 1776 to visit his dying friend David Hume and his ageing mother. In 1773 he was elected to the Royal Society. In London his opinions were eagerly sought. However, his view that the problem of the American colonies should be solved by a union of the colonies with Britain, with American representatives in the House of Commons, was rejected; later it was used as a model for the union with Ireland in 1800. *The Wealth of Nations* was published on 9 March 1776 to the immediate acclaim of contemporary thinkers. He received a flat fee of about £500 from his publishers.

He was appointed Commissioner of Customs at a salary of £600 in 1778, diligently attending board meetings at the Royal Exchange (now the City Chambers) of Edinburgh and residing at Panmure House, Canongate. It was strange for the apostle of free trade to administer a protectionist trade policy but it had no effect on his revisions to *The Wealth of Nations*. In his last years he revised his major works and took an active part in the social life of the city, becoming famous for his Sunday night supper parties. He died of stomach cancer. His personal papers were burnt, on his orders, by his executors but his personal library substantially survives at Edinburgh University and in Tokyo. His grave in Canongate kirkyard, Edinburgh, has attracted respectful visitors from numerous countries.

2 Main contribution to economics

At the outset of his writing career, Smith wrote on moral philosophy. In *The Theory of Moral Sentiments* he set out to show that nature is a cosmic harmony and society is bound together by sympathy. Also, he introduced ideas which were to be central to *The Wealth of Nations*. He recognized that human behaviour is motivated by self-interest, but also by the contemplation of a grand and harmonious design for society. Nevertheless, there is an optimistic tone to the book. In his discussion of income distribution he states:

> The rich only select from the heap what is most precious and agreeable. They consume little more than the poor ... They are led by an invisible hand to make nearly the same distribution of the necessaries of life which would have been made, had the earth been divided into equal portions among all its inhabitants, and thus without intending it, without knowing it, advance the interest of the society and afford means to the multiplication.
>
> (Smith [1759] 1976: 184)

This passage is typical of the whole book. The underlying principles influencing society, including the idea of the 'invisible hand', are set out with economic mechanisms suggested but not discussed in detail.

As a professor of moral philosophy, he lectured on jurisprudence. Jurisprudence was regarded by Smith as including the study of trade, commerce, agriculture and manufactures as the police had the task of regulating markets. A copy of his lectures to the jurisprudence class for the winter of 1762–3 survives. It provides a clear insight into his early economic thinking. The influence of Francis

Hutcheson (1694–1746), who had taught Smith in the 1730s at Glasgow, is strong but there is also a preview of Smith's later theories. Already there is a critique of the mercantilist policies of prohibiting the export of bullion and maintaining a favourable balance of trade. He uses a four-stage theory of economic development with human history divided into the four ages of hunters, shepherds, agriculture and commerce. He sets out the important principle of the division of labour and distinguishes natural price from market price. But in his theory of value he uses a straightforward notion of scarcity to explain paradoxes such as water being necessary but cheap and jewels with an immense price but little usefulness: 'cheapness is a necessary consequence of plenty' (Smith [1762–3] 1978: 333).

Smith's visit to France enabled him to have discussions on economics with the Physiocrats, the French school of economics which believed that agriculture was the only productive sector of an economy and that government regulation of economic life should be minimal. Subsequently Smith diligently collected information from numerous sources to write a detailed survey of economics. The full title of Smith's magnum opus, *An Inquiry into the Nature and Causes of the Wealth of Nations of 1776* indicates clearly that he wanted to analyse the nature of economic growth. At the outset he stated that the welfare of a state is measured by the ratio of produce to population, similar to the modern measure of economic welfare, per capita gross domestic product. Smith attributes growth to the 'skill, dexterity and judgment with which its labour is generally applied' (Smith [1776] 1976: 10) and, less importantly, to the ratio of productive to unproductive labour.

The Wealth of Nations is divided into five books but has a continuous argument. Smith begins with determinants of productivity and income distribution then considers how capital is employed. He surveys the growth record of other nations, the diversity of economic systems and the activities of states in taxing and spending. The major themes are economic growth, value and distribution, the working of markets, international trade and the relationship between the state and the individual.

The human motive which starts an economy on a growth path is 'the desire of bettering our condition' (Smith [1776] 1976: 341) which prompts saving; the saving is invested to provide a capital fund which will make possible the employment of the labour force and the division of labour. Division of labour is a fundamental principle, the consequence of 'a certain propensity in human nature ... the propensity to truck, barter, and exchange one thing for another' (Smith [1776] 1976: 25). Using the example of pin-making, he explains that by dividing the tasks of human labour into its component parts, the dexterity of the worker increases, the time lost in one piece of work to another is saved and machinery can be invented as a consequence of analysing work into its sub-operations. However, Smith did appreciate that economic growth has its costs. The effect of the division of labour is to make a person who spends his life on a few simple operations 'as stupid and ignorant as it is possible for a human creature to become' (Smith [1776] 1976: 782).

Again, in this work Smith makes use of his 'four stages' theory to explain how value is determined and the national product is distributed among the landlord, the capitalist and the labourer. The determination of value changes as the economy has progressed from its earliest stage to a commercial society. It is only in the most primitive of human societies, the age of the hunters, that goods (beavers and deer) are exchanged according to the quantities of labour required to obtain the goods. Only then do labourers obtain the whole produce of their labour. With population growth and the accumulation of capital, land becomes private property and the landlord receives a share of the national produce as rent and the capitalist profits. Like Aristotle before him, Smith distinguishes 'value in use' from 'value in exchange'. He also contrasts market prices and natural prices. The proportion between supply and demand determines the market price but the natural price is 'the central price to which the prices of all commodities are continually gravitating' (Smith [1776] 1976: 75). This natural price is brought about by free competition and can be regarded as a long-run equilibrium price equal to the costs of production in the form of rent, profits and wages.

Smith's concept of the market mechanism is clear in his celebrated account of how in labour and capital markets (see LABOUR MARKETS) there will be equilibrating flows in response to differentials: 'The whole of the advantages and disadvantages of the different employments of labour and stock must, in the same neighbourhood, be either perfectly equal or continually tending to equality' (Smith [1776] 1976: 116). But he was aware, too, of market imperfections. In product markets, businesses are constantly trying to engage in collusive oligopoly: 'People of the same trade seldom meet together, even for merriment and diversion, but the conversation ends in a conspiracy against the public, or in some contrivance to raise prices' (Smith [1776] 1976: 145).

In the labour market there is, according to Smith, unequal bargaining. Smith states that the workmen desire to get as much, the masters to give as little as possible. The masters, being fewer in number, can combine much more easily. Moreover, the law authorizes, or at least does not prohibit, their combinations, while it prohibits those of the workmen (Smith [1776] 1976: 84-5)

After his discussion of the domestic economy, Smith turns his attention to different economic systems and to international trade. Having argued that the division of labour is the desirable course for the domestic economy, he justifies free trade in terms of the efficiency and productivity gains arising from a similar specialization internationally:

> The tailor does not attempt to make his own shoes ... All of them find it for their interest to employ their whole industry in a way in which they have some advantage over their neighbours and to purchase with a part of its produce ... whatever else they have occasion for ... What is prudence in the conduct of every private family, can scarce be folly in that of a great kingdom ... Would it be a reasonable law to prohibit the importation of all foreign wines, merely to encourage the making of claret and burgundy in Scotland?
>
> (Smith [1776] 1976: 456-8)

This trade theory based on 'absolute advantage' was part of Smith's attack on mercantilism. He also criticized the mercantilists for identifying wealth with gold and silver, not goods; also, for putting the interest of the producer above that of the consumer.

Smith disapproved of state intervention as subsidization of industry would divert economic activity away from its natural course. He saw the only justification for public institutions as being the benefits they conferred on society and the impossibility of the beneficiaries paying for them. Defence, law and order, the expenses of the sovereign and some public institutions were all that he recommended. As far as possible expenditure on the infrastructure was to be directly financed, for example, by tolls on roads and fees for education. Some taxation was necessary to finance this minimal state. The taxation should be according to ability to pay, certain, payable at the time of receipt of income and collected at minimum cost.

When faced with particular economic problems, Smith was willing to accept some departures from *laissez-faire*. Regulations on the issue of paper currency, support for the Navigation Acts which ruled that English trade be carried in English ships, and a maximum interest rate of five per cent are all advocated. But the individual was more important than the government in economic life. At the heart of his analysis Smith maintained the beneficial effects of the pursuit of self-interest:

> By directing that industry in such a manner as its produce may be of the greatest value, he intends only his own gain, and he is in this, as in many other cases, led by an invisible hand to promote an end which was no part of his intention.
>
> (Smith [1776] 1976: 456)

3 Conclusions

Schumpeter, in a celebrated criticism of Smith, noted that Smith's admirers praised *The Wealth of Nations* for the policies it advocated and for the fact that it contained 'no really novel ideas' but was a feat of coordination of previous economic writings. Also commended were Smith's accessible style and the fact that he 'was thoroughly in sympathy with the humours of his time' and 'advocated the things that were in the offing' (Schumpeter 1954: 185).

Gray, too, admitted that Smith was not a pioneer and could be confused, especially on value, but that he has the greatest name in the history of economics. He stated that 'before Adam Smith there had been much economic discussion; with him we reach the stage of discussing economics' (Gray 1980: 110). A more recent commentator on Smith, Hollander, sees in *The Wealth of Nations* 'not merely ... the extraordinary range of topics treated, but also ... Smith's demonstration of a high degree of interdependence between apparently unrelated variables culminating in his development of a more or less consistent 'model' of value and distribution' (Hollander 1973: 305).

Although Smith's method of economic exposition is literary, twentieth-century mathematical economists award him high marks. Samuelson (see SAMUELSON, P.A.) has written a strong defence of Smith and praises him for anticipating general equilibrium theory. The breadth of economic life discussed by Smith makes his work relevant to the discussion of modern business life: monetary economics, joint stock companies and entrepreneurship all commanded his attention (Laidler 1981; Anderson and Tollison 1982; Pesciarelli 1989). Smith's genius has been recognized throughout the world, with both ardent free marketers and socialists, even Lenin, acknowledging their debt to him (Mizuta and Sugiyama 1993).

DONALD RUTHERFORD
UNIVERSITY OF EDINBURGH

Further reading

(References cited in the text marked *)

* Anderson, G.M. and Tollison, R.D. (1982) 'Adam Smith's analysis of joint stock companies', *Journal of Political Economy* 90 (6): 1237–56. (An exposition of how corporations survive under competition through superior efficiency.)
  Campbell, R.H. and Skinner, A.S. (1982) *Adam Smith*, London: Croom Helm. (A precise biographical summary of his life, principal lecture courses and books.)
* Gray, A. (1931, 1980 with A.E. Thompson) *The Development of Economic Doctrine*, London: Longman. (A stimulating general survey of economics placing Smith in the context of other leading economists.)
* Hollander, S. (1973) *The Economics of Adam Smith*, Toronto: University of Toronto Press. (Smith's analysis of the price mechanism and economic development in its historical context.)
* Laidler, D. (1981) 'Adam Smith as a monetary economist', *Canadian Journal of Economics* 14 (2): 185–200. (An explanation of how Smith integrated his banking theory into his theory of economic development.)
* Mizuta, H. and Sugiyama, C. (eds) (1993) *Adam Smith: International Perspectives*, London: Macmillan. (International symposium papers which trace Smith's past and present influence.)
* Pesciarelli, E. (1989) 'Smith, Bentham and the development of contrasting ideas of entrepreneurship', *History of Political Economy* 21 (3): 521–36. (Smith's view of the entrepreneur as a risk taker, planner and organizer of productive forces.)
  Samuelson, P.A. (1977) 'A modern theorist's vindication of Adam Smith', *American Economic Review* 67: 42–9. (A mathematical proof that Smith's economic model survives the attacks of Ricardo and Marx.)
* Schumpeter, J.A. (1954) *History of Economic Analysis*, London: George Allen and Unwin. (A monumental study of how economic analysis developed from its earliest beginnings.)
  Skinner, A. and Wilson, T. (1975) *Essays on Adam Smith*, Oxford: Clarendon Press. (A collection of articles which demonstrate the relevance of Smith to modern economic discussions.)
* Smith, A. (1759) *The Theory of Moral Sentiments*, ed. D.D. Raphael and A.L. MacFie, Oxford: Oxford University Press, 1976. (Smith's first book which established his position as a leading thinker. This system of ethics is based on the principle of sympathy. He introduces the concept of the 'invisible hand' in his discussion of income distribution.)
* Smith, A. (1762–3) *Lectures on Jurisprudence*, ed. R.L. Meek, D.D. Raphael and P.G. Stein, Oxford: Oxford University Press, 1978. (A transcript of his lectures of 1762–3 and 1766. In the section on the police he provides his early thinking on the division of labour, price and monetary theories.)
* Smith, A. (1776) *An Inquiry into the Nature and Causes of the Wealth of Nations*, ed. R.H. Campbell and A.S. Skinner, Oxford: Oxford University Press, 1976. (His principles of economics which begins with an account of the role of the division of labour in economic growth

Smith, Adam (1723–90)

then presents theories of value, prices and distribution. Also he studies the relative opulence of nations, analyses mercantilism and physiocracy, argues for free trade, as well as discussing the role of the state and the nature of taxation.)

Smith, A. (1795) *Essays on Philosophical Subjects*, ed. I.S. Ross, Oxford: Oxford University Press, 1980. (Smith's views on astronomy, ancient logic and metaphysics, external senses, imitative arts, together with his contributions to the *Edinburgh Review* of 1755–6.)

Smith, A. (1977; 1987) *The Correspondence of Adam Smith*, ed. E.C. Mosner and I.S. Ross, Oxford: Oxford University Press. (Important letters with other leading philosophers of the day, including Hume and Bentham.)

* Smith, A. (1983) *Lectures on Rhetoric and Belles-Lettres*, ed. J.C. Bryce, Oxford: Oxford University Press. (Smith's first teaching in Glasgow 1762–3, which attempts to change the nature of rhetoric by introducing a Newtonian approach to the study of literature.)

See also: BUSINESS ECONOMICS; LABOUR MARKETS; SAMUELSON, P.A.

Mill, John Stuart (1806–73)

1. Introduction
2. Biographical data
3. Main contribution
4. Evaluation
5. Conclusions

Personal background

- born in London, 20 May 1806
- educated at home by his father, James Mill, and by Jeremy Bentham
- joined the East India Company as a clerk at the company's London offices, 1823
- arrested for distributing pamphlets in favour of birth control, 1823
- suffered nervous breakdown, 1826–7
- publication of his first major work, *A System of Logic*, 1843
- retired from East India Company, 1858
- MP for Westminster, 1865–8
- died 7 May 1873 at Avignon, France

Major works

A System of Logic (1843)
Principles of Political Economy (1848)
On Liberty (1859)
Utilitarianism (1862)
Auguste Comte and Positivism (1865)
Autobiography (1873)

Summary

John Stuart Mill was a leading political economist of the mid-nineteenth century. An intellectual descendant of the utilitarian school, he quickly evolved his own methodology and philosophy. While he did not reject utilitarian principles, he argued that people often behave in ways not associated with self-interest. Although his economics were mostly of an orthodox nature, his insistence that there were no universally valid laws and that economics was a subject requiring empirical study place him in an important position, linking the classical economists of the early nineteenth century with the neo-classicists of the twentieth century.

1 Introduction

Mill's economic theories are strongly influenced by his own beliefs about the nature of individuals and agencies. He had a strong personal dislike of conflict and debate, and seldom chose to attack other thinkers; instead, he examined their thought using a methodology he himself had developed and then incorporated it into his own work. A radical, he believed very strongly in subjects such as free will, liberty and the emancipation of women; in economic terms he was influenced by Adam Smith, Ricardo and Malthus as well as his own father (see SMITH, A.). For many thinkers both contemporary and modern Mill has remained something of an enigma, a fierce critic of both *laissez-faire* capitalism and socialism, a staunch defender of the free market and yet a believer in the role of government. His enduring contribution, however, was the establishment of economics as a discipline; he may be seen as both the last classical economist and the first modern economist.

2 Biographical data

It might almost be said that John Stuart Mill was destined from the moment of his birth to become a philosopher and political economist. His father, James Mill, was a noted thinker in his own right, a cobbler's son from a small village in Scotland who had risen to prominence as a writer and economist; among his circle of friends were Jeremy Bentham and David Ricardo. It was James Mill and Bentham who decided that, given the deficiencies of public education, they would educate Mill's son privately, and John Stuart Mill records in his *Autobiography* (Mill 1979) that he began studying Greek at the age of three, Latin at eight and chemistry at twelve.

After informally studying law he took a post as clerk with the East India Company (then charged with the civil administration of India, which was not technically part of the British Empire) in London, remaining with the Company for thirty-five years. A convinced utilitarian thanks to his education, he was close to Bentham and even served as the latter's secretary for several years. He helped found the London Debating Society in 1825; he also adopted a strong position in favour of the emancipation of women.

In 1826–7, however, Mill suffered a nervous breakdown. As he recovered, he began to change his views substantially on a number of issues. In particular he turned largely against the mechanical materialism of Bentham; more generally, he began searching for broader perspectives on logic, science and economics. He also developed a dislike of conflict and adversarial discussion, possibly as a result of the poor health which he suffered for much of his life; in the words of Halliday (1976: 31): 'He was bound to assert the truth whenever and wherever he could, but truth would neither be conceived nor quickened in conditions of conflict, nor would it be arrived at by means of narrow commitment'.

Mill rejected the notion that economic activity was governed by immutable laws. An admirer of Adam Smith, Mill believed that many of the political economists writing since Smith's time were wrong in their attempts to systematize Smith's views along rational lines. 'It became apparent to him ... that the key methodological issues with which all moral sciences had to contend was that their phenomena were of human origin' (Oakley 1994: x). This outlook pervades all Mill's writing, particularly *Principles of Political Economy* which first appeared in 1848.

The rejection of immutable laws in economics divided Mill from the utilitarians; at the same time his staunch defence of free will and civil liberty, along with his dislike of conflict, divided him from the socialists. He wrote articles defending the revolutionaries of 1848, but he abhorred the idea of revolution and he attacked the authoritarianism implicit in the socialism of Saint-Simon and Comte. The same dislike of authoritarianism led him to retire from the East India Company in 1858 when the British government took control of India from the Company in the aftermath of the Indian Mutiny (1857–8). In 1865 Mill was elected MP for Westminster; in parliament, his most notable achievement was to lead an attack on the Governor of Jamaica, who had used troops to quell civil unrest in the colony and caused the deaths of several hundred people. He failed to be re-elected in 1868. He died in Avignon, France, in 1873.

3 Main contribution

Mill's main contribution must be his insistence that there are no self-evident, universally applicable laws in economics and that empirical study is essential. He was one of the first writers to take this view, and his pragmatism and intellectual rigour make his work stand out even today among the many dogmatic, ideological tracts that have appeared both before and since.

In order to understand Mill's political economy, it is first necessary to understand his view that economic activity was governed by human nature. Further, human nature was not, as the utilitarians assumed, entirely governed by self-interest; people could and did behave in such a way as to benefit society as a whole. Mill did not reject the doctrine of necessity entirely, but he believed that free will and its expression were of fundamental importance in understanding economics. Because human behaviour did not always remain within the bounds associated with 'economic man', human economic behaviour was not always rational. In his *Autobiography* he wrote that while self-interest is often paramount, this is only because society makes it so; remove the pressures for survival and the common good will re-emerge as a motive. 'Education, habit and the cultivation of sentiments will make a common man dig or weave for his country as readily as fight for his country' (Mill 1979: 176).

In his writings on economic theory, Mill examined the thinking of conventional political economists since Adam Smith using the empirical standards he had laid down in his own work, *A System of Logic*. He found himself in broad agreement with most of them; the rational models they had worked out were valid.

A professed admirer of David Ricardo, Mill followed the latter's thinking on the determination of value and price; his views on economic cycles are similar to those of Malthus. Production is distributed through the means of exchange and distribution takes place to three classes – labourers, capitalists and landlords. The latter were separated from capitalists by the nature of property; while Mill believed that individuals had a right to private property which they had made or earned, they did not have an automatic right to land, which had not been made by human agency. In this, at least, Mill remained strongly influenced by the views of his father.

In some areas his thinking is entirely in line with that of Bentham and Ricardo. On labour, for example, he rejected state intervention and 'argued that the labourer must get what he can, though subject to the general interest' (Williams 1976: 9); utility should prevail. He also accepted that, although the poor should be encouraged to better themselves through education in order to achieve a better standard of living, assisting the poor through redistribution of wealth could be likened to slavery.

Mill's contribution did not so much reject the utilitarian view as modify it. Mill believed that 'under the rule of individual property, the division of the produce is the result of two determining agencies: competition and custom' (Mill 1994: 50). The non-rational (custom) and the rational (competition) co-exist in economics, depending on the behaviour of the individuals involved. In other words, the radical utilitarian views are valid, but they are not *solely* valid: non-rational influences must be taken into account as well.

It is thus Mill's philosophy which forms his economics. The existence of competition and custom requires that both individual and public agency have a role to play in society. Free will is essential, but so is social reform by agencies. Government, in Mill's view, came in two forms: authoritative, which controlled people through force and sanctions, and non-authoritative, which encouraged them to govern themselves through voluntary participation. He was strongly in favour of local government, being influenced in this respect by the views of democracy espoused by de Tocqueville.

These views come through in his writings on public utilities such as water and the railways, which Mill described as 'natural monopolies'. He did not believe that capitalists should be allowed to control these utilities as this was tantamount to allowing companies to levy a tax on the people, but neither did he believe that they should be controlled by government, with all its manifest inefficiencies:

> The inferiority of government agency, for example, in any of the common operations of industry or commerce, is proved by the fact, that it is hardly ever able to maintain itself in equal competition with individual agency, where the individuals possess the requisite degree of industrial enterprise, and can command the necessary assemblage of means.
>
> (Mill 1994: 331)

His argument was that utilities should as far as possible be decentralized and localized, with government maintaining what would today be called a strategic role but local enterprises providing day-to-day management of operations.

Mill was strongly critical of both capitalism and socialism. Capitalism, he argued, created inequalities; it was a selfish and egotistical doctrine, a source of class conflict and oppressive in that it did not allow wage labourers to develop and progress. Socialism offered the chance to redress these wrongs, but socialism had its own problems; among these Mill listed the disincentive to work, the loss of liberty, excessive stimulation of population growth and the disincentive to technological progress. Principally, however, Mill simply did not feel that any of the forms of socialism then being developed, including Marxian communism, were feasible. Socialism implied a static society, which Mill believed to be incompatible with human nature. Mill's answer to the problem drew from both doctrines; he argued for capitalism with worker involvement, including profit sharing and worker participation in management.

4 Evaluation

Reactions to Mill, in both his own lifetime and since, have been strongly mixed. Williams (1976: 9) comments that Mill has been seen variously as 'a brave noble spirit championing freedom in the face of a hostile environment, or as a mere representative thinker of mid-Victorian England, or as a crude individualist, or as a secret and intolerant dogmatist'.

More measured views see Mill as an important link in the chain of development of economic thought from Adam Smith through to the modern period. Riley, in his introduction to *Principles of Political Economy*, sums up Mill thus:

> Mill's philosophy is a superior version of utilitarian radicalism in which the basic tenets of the old school are retained yet integrated with a broader perspective on human nature, a perspective that goes well beyond self-interest (enlightened or otherwise) and takes account of the possibility that individuals might develop higher moral and aesthetic sentiments.
> (Riley in Mill 1994: xiv)

From an economic perspective, Mill was one of the first economists to argue the need 'to balance history and theory, induction and deduction' (Williams 1976: 25) and take a pragmatic view of economics and markets.

Mill died in 1873, by which time communism was becoming a powerful force and winning many converts. In the century of political and economic polarization which followed, Mill's 'radical' views do not at first sight seem to have had much of a following. Belief in liberty and free will pervaded his economic thinking, set him against the doctrinaire socialists, yet his insistence on the role of government, even in its non-authoritarian form, won him few friends on the political right. However, his influence has remained considerable. Ryan (1987) points out that the Fabian socialist movement in the UK followed Mill to some degree, and Hollander (1985) notes the continuities between Mill's classical economics and modern neo-classical theory (see NEO-CLASSICAL ECONOMICS). In practical terms, the experiments with a mixture of free markets and socialism during the 'New Deal' in the USA in the 1930s, and in the UK from the 1930s through to the 1970s reflect something of Mill's own search for a middle ground; though it is doubtful if Mill himself would have approved of any of these policies.

For modern businesses, the key point to take from Mill is probably his belief that humans do not always act according to the principles of economic self-interest. That most will do so most of the time is undoubted but, as Mill points out, once the pressures of daily survival are lifted, people sometimes show a tendency to consider the common good as well, and make decisions accordingly. Most marketing by charities and not-for-profit agencies is based on this very premise, but in many consumer goods and service sectors as well marketers must wrestle with the fact that consumers do not always act in their own best interests. Further, Mill's belief that workers can be motivated to work for their country as they might fight for it is an issue that could be usefully explored by human resource managers; it is likely that Mill would have approved, in theory at least, of post-war Japan where workers did indeed mobilize to work for both country and company, often quite against their own perceived self-interest.

5 Conclusions

Perhaps Mill's most important contribution lies in his insistence that economics needed to be treated as a discipline in its own right, requiring its own methodology and empirical study. In this he anticipated twentieth-century neo-classical economics. It can be argued that the study of economics has in some quarters gone too far down this road and is insufficiently related to factors such as politics and environment, and the human element that Mill stressed so strongly does not always receive the attention it deserves. Nevertheless, by separating economics from general political theory and giving it the beginnings of a methodology, Mill made a valuable contribution to modern economic science.

MORGEN WITZEL
LONDON BUSINESS SCHOOL

Further reading

(References cited in the text marked *)

Courtney, W. L. (1994) *The Life of J.S. Mill (1888)*, Bristol: Thoemmes Press. (A reprinting of Courtney's 1888 biography of the philosopher.)

Gray, J. and Smith, G.W. (1991) *J.S. Mill's On Liberty in Focus*, London: Routledge. (As well as providing authoritative commentary upon 'On Liberty', a selection of essays written by eminent scholars reflect a broader debate about the philosophical foundations of Mill's liberalism.)

* Halliday, R.J. (1976) *John Stuart Mill*, London: Allen & Unwin. (Examination of Mill and his work, emphasizing the change in Mill's thinking after 1826–7.)

* Hollander, S. (1985) *The Economics of John Stuart Mill*, 2 vols, Oxford: Blackwell. (A complete and authoritative examination of Mill's economics by one of the leading scholars in this field.)

Hollander, S. (2000) *John Stuart Mill on Economic Theory and Method: Collected Essays III*, London: Routledge. (This volume provides an accessible sourcebook on Mill's relationship with Ricardo, and the 'Classical School', as well as confirming his relevance for modern economics.)

Kurer, O. (1991) *John Stuart Mill: The Politics of Progress*, New York: Garland. (A good examination of Mill's political beliefs, including a clear account of his criticisms of capitalism and socialism.)

* Mill, J.S. (1973) *A System of Logic*, Buffalo, NY: University of Toronto Press. (The classic work which established Mill as a distinguished thinker and logician.)

* Mill, J.S. (1979) *Autobiography*, Harmondsworth: Penguin. (A popular edition of the final 1873 edition of Mill's autobiography.)

Mill, J.S. (1993) *Auguste Comte and Positivism*, Bristol: Thoemmes Press. (Reprint of the 1865 edition; an attack on Comte and positivist doctrines which influenced early socialist thinking.)

* Mill, J.S. (1994) *Principles of Political Economy and Chapters on Socialism*, J. Riley (ed.), Oxford: Oxford University Press. (Mill's major work on political economy, along with the chapters from his unfinished book on socialism.)

Mill, J.S. (1998a) *On Liberty and Other Essays*, J. Gray, (ed.), Oxford: Oxford University Press. (Modern volume contains four of Mill's best known essays, 'On Liberty', 'Utilitarianism', 'Considerations of Representative Government' and 'The Subjection of Women'.)

Mill, J.S. (1998b) *Utilitarianism*, R. Crisp, (ed.), Oxford: Oxford University Press. (This new edition of Mill's key text is supplemented by an extensive editorial introduction, an analysis of the text, substantial endnotes, suggestions for further reading and a full bibliography.)

* Oakley, A. (1994) *Classical Economic Man: Human Agency and Methodology in the Political Economy of Adam Smith and John Stuart Mill*, Aldershot: Edward Elgar. (A useful work which sets Mill in context with other political economists after Smith.)

* Ryan, A. (1987) *The Philosophy of John Stuart Mill*, 2nd edn, London: Macmillan. (A more general philosophical examination of Mill, including his work on logic and ethics.)

Schwartz, P. (1972) *The New Political Economy of J.S. Mill*, London: London School of Economics and Political Science. (Looks at Mill and Malthus together; an appendix reproduces some early nineteenth century pamphlets concerning birth control.)

* Williams, G.L. (ed.) (1976) *John Stuart Mill on Politics and Society*, London: Fontana. (A good introductory selection of Mill's writings, in paperback form.)

Wood, J.C. (1987) *J.S. Mill: Critical Assessments*, London: Routledge. (The articles in these reference volumes aim to provide a comprehensive account of Mill's life, thought and economics.)

See also: SMITH, A.

Marx, Karl Heinrich (1818–83)

1 Introduction
2 Method of analysis
3 Labour theory of value
4 Circuits of capital
5 Value and price
6 Schemes of reproduction
7 Endogenous technical change and crises
8 Conclusions

Personal background

- born 5 May 1818 in Trier into a respected middle-class Jewish family (which nevertheless had been forced to assimilate)
- attended university first at Bonn and then at Berlin, where he abandoned romanticism for Hegelianism
- became involved in liberal journalism, moving to Paris when the state authority closed down the paper for which he wrote
- became a communist and met Friedrich Engels for the first time
- 1843 married Jenny von Westphalen – a deeply devoted union which survived poverty, illness, the deaths of two of their five children and Marx's infidelity with their unpaid maid, Lenchen
- expelled from Paris, went to Brussels for three years and then to London in 1849, staying there for the rest of his life with his wife and family
- worked as a scholar, a journalist – and a political revolutionary (he and Engels published *The Communist Manifesto* in 1848)
- experienced poverty, insecurity and recurring bouts of bad health which eventually prevented him publishing all three volumes of *Capital* in his own lifetime
- died 14 March 1883

Major works

The Communist Manifesto, with F. Engels (1848)
A Contribution to the Critique of Political Economy (1858)
Capital, vol. I (1867)
Capital, vol. II (1885)
Capital, vol. III (1894)
Theories of Surplus Value (1905–10)

Summary

Since some of the tendencies which Marx identified (and his critics mistakenly interpreted as predictions) have not in fact occurred, he must rest content instead, as the late Ronald Meek told us, with being 'just another genius' (Meek 1967: 128). Marx was the most profound interpreter of the capitalism of his age, arguably of any age. He bequeathed to us a profound set of methods with which to approach issues of high theory, historical and philosophical analysis and policies embracing *Realpolitik* in the social sciences. This entry concentrates on these aspects of his contributions. His views on the operation of socialism and of its transformation to communism are on a different plane, often approaching in naivety those of Utopian Christian Socialists – hence the *non sequitur* involved in supposing that the overthrow of the USSR and Eastern European regimes discredits Marx's most enduring contributions, Baroness Thatcher notwithstanding.

1 Introduction

As Robert Heilbroner's excellent chapter on Marx in *The Worldly Philosophers* (Heilbroner 1991: 149–51) suggests, Marx was not an altogether admirable person. Possibly he was the victim of both his age and class – he would not allow his daughters to meet Engels' working-class mistresses and he did not think any of his sons-in-law were good enough for his daughters, for instance. Whether he was an anti-Semite as well is, at best, not proven (see Wheen 1999: 55–7, for a most balanced assessment). He could be crass, insensitive and grossly unfair to his critics and his predecessors. Yet all this is ultimately beside the point: the principle that he evolved, of soaking himself in historical facts and figures, and in the writings of those who came before him, initially criticizing them from within their own texts and then developing his own alternative theory and approach, incorporating and expanding, often changing profoundly what he had criticized and discarding what was misleading, incoherent or just plain wrong, is surely the right way to do original work in social science.

2 Method of analysis

Marx came to political economy from philosophy, trained especially in German philosophy and crucially influenced by the philosophical views of Hegel and the principle of dialectical change. The use of a dialectic led him always to look for internal contradictions both in systems of thought and in the working out of social processes. His organizing concept when he came to political economy was the notion of 'surplus' – how it was created, extracted, distributed and used in different societies. Marx looked at human history as succeeding epochs of different ways of surplus creation, etc.; he was determined to find by analysis of the power patterns of each, the seeds of both their achievements and their internal contradictions and eventual destruction and transformation as, through the endogenous processes thus discovered, one form gave way to the next. The jewel in his crown was his analysis of capitalism. Maurice Dobb (1946) gave a detailed historical analysis from a Marxist viewpoint of how feudalism gave way to capitalism. This entry concentrates on Marx's views on capitalism itself.

Marx's method of analysis may be likened to an onion. At the central core, which underlies the overlapping outer layers of skin, is the pure, most abstract yet fundamental model of the mode of production (Marx's phrase) being analysed. All fossils from the past, all embryos of what is to come, are abstracted from; the system is thus revealed in its purest form. Yet the aim is to show that the fundamental characteristics and relationships thus revealed are robust – that they survive intact the complications provided by adding back (in analysis) the inner and outer layers of skin of the onion, that they still remain the ultimate determinants of what is observed on the surface. This can be illustrated by the transition from volume I to volume III of *Capital* (the latter was written before volume I but only published after Marx's death, edited by Engels). Although there is little explicit mention in volume I of the (near) surface phenomenon of prices of production discussed in volume III, the links with the underlying labour values of volume I are always at the forefront of Marx's intention: not in the mainstream sense of providing a theory of relative prices (the neo-classicist interpretation of what the labour theory of value (LTV) is about) but in making explicit the link as a necessary part of the story of production, distribution and accumulation in capitalism.

3 Labour theory of value

Having mentioned the phrase, LTV, let us say what we understand by it. As discussed above, the principal task Marx set himself was to explain the creation of the surplus in capitalism. Naturally, he linked this in capitalism with an explanation of the origin of profits and the determination of the system-wide rate of profits in this mode of production. He identified in previous modes the role of classes in each, one dominant, one subservient, with reference to the creation of wealth and thus social and economic power, and the connection of their relationship to the creation of the surplus by a process of explicit exploitation of one class by another. For example, in feudalism the process was obvious: its institutions and laws ensured that the lords of the manor could physically extract from the serfs part of the annual product, either by making serfs work for a set period on the lords' lands or, because the serfs were tenants, by requiring them to 'hand over' part of the product of the land which their labour had brought forth.

When we get to pure competitive capitalism, such a process seems impossible. For one aspect of capitalism, purified in modern theory to become price-taking behaviour by all agents, with prices set by the impersonal forces of the market, in classical and Marx's times more robustly specified as a wide diffusion of power among individual capitalists and individual wage-earners, seems to make it impossible for individual capitalists to coerce free wage-earners into doing what they do not wish to do. They could always leave one and work for another, just as any one capitalist and his/her capitals could leave or enter any activity. Hence the tendency for rates of profit to be equalized in all activities and the need to explain what determined the origin and size of the systemic rate of profits to which their individual values tended. Moreover, each free wage-labourer was paid a definite money wage for all the hours he or she worked. Under these conditions how could exploitation occur or a surplus arise, and where did profits come from?

Marx answered this in terms of the distinction between necessary and surplus labour time associated with the class relations of capitalist society. Capitalists as a class (subset into industrial, commercial and finance capital) had a monopoly of the means of production and finance. Workers as a class, having only their labour power to sell, had to do as they were told in the workplace. As propertyless, landless but free wage-labourers, the proletariat whose creation was the by-product of feudalism giving way to capitalism, they had but one choice – either to work under the conditions established by the capitalist class or to withdraw from the system entirely – and starve. Therefore, the working day conceptually could be split into two parts: the hours needed with the existing stock of capital goods, methods and conditions of production to produce wage goods – necessary labour – and the rest – surplus labour – which was the source of surplus value in the sphere of production and of profits in the sphere of distribution and exchange. Marx adopted the classical idea, strictly Ricardo's, that all commodities had an embodied labour value, to explain how labour services, a commodity saleable just like any other in capitalism, would tend to sell at their values. But human labour had the unique property that it would create more value – produce more commodities – than was needed for its own reproduction and this was embodied in the commodities corresponding to this surplus labour time.

A subsidiary part of the story was that the actual operations of capitalism resulted in the waxing and waning of the reserve army of labour (RAL) – a much more suitable euphemism for the unemployed than the modern description of the same phenomenon as flexible labour markets – causing actual wages to tend towards (or fluctuate around?) their natural values (a purely classical story). But the main story was that while the surface phenomenon seemingly reflected fairness and efficiency – people being paid fully for what they did and all the hours they worked – this masked the underlying exploitation process arising from the situation of class monopoly. In the sphere of production there was a tendency towards equality in the length of the working day (week, year) and intensity of work too. In the sphere of distribution and exchange, abstracting from actual (market) prices, there was a tendency for the prices of production to be such that a uniform rate of profits was created (the first great empirical generalization of classical political economy) and for the profit components of the prices of production to be such as to constitute uniform rates of return on total capitals, similarly measured, in all activities.

4 Circuits of capital

The total capitals consisted of two parts: advances of wages to the wage-earners, variable capital (v) (variable because this component alone created more value than it started off with); and constant capital (c), 'dead' labour embodied in durable assets from previous rounds – circuits – of surplus labour, surplus value and profit creation and reinvestment. Marx famously pictured the capitalist process as the circuit of capitals:

$$M \to C \to C' \to M' \qquad (1)$$

where M and M' were money quantities with M' hopefully $> M$, and C and C' were commodities encompassing wage goods and services of constant capital which were transformed, again hopefully, through the production process into commodities (C') saleable at a profit – M'-M. On the way to creating *The General Theory* (1936), Keynes applauded Marx for this insight (see KEYNES, J.M.).

5 Value and price

Many have come to see the 'transformation problem' relating the underlying embodied labour values of commodities to their prices of production as a sterile exercise and debate. Yet viewed in this way it makes sense, both in explaining a fundamental characteristic of capitalism and in illustrating the power of Marx's method and approach. In order to show that anything classical political economy could do Marx could do as well and better, it was necessary to reconcile the pure theory of the origin of profits in the capitalist mode of production with the other major 'finding' of political economy – the tendency to a uniform rate of profit in all activities – and also to 'explain' what determined the size of the system-wide rate of profits. (Piero Sraffa, who had a deep knowledge of and admiration for Marx's work, always spoke of the rate of profits, indicating that it *was* the system-wide concept which needed to be explained within the classical and Marxist system). As Luigi Pasinetti said of his own modern variant of the theory of the rate of profits: 'It is macro-economic because it could not be otherwise' (Pasinetti 1974: 118).

The various conundrums arise because, while competition would ensure a uniform rate of exploitation (s/v, where s = surplus labour and v = necessary labour) in all industries because, as we have seen, free wage-labourers can always move from one occupation to another, there is nothing obvious or even not obvious in the forces of competition and their impact on technical progress to ensure that the corresponding organic compositions of capital (c/v) (with some licence, the capital–labour ratios) should also tend to equality. But since a well-known Marxist result is that: $r = s/v /(1 + c/v)$ when all variables are measured in terms of abstract socially necessary labour time, if the LTV meant that commodities were exchanged in proportion to their embodied labour amounts, there would not be a tendency, not even a long-run one, to equality of rates of profit (so measured) in all activities. Therefore, it became necessary to explain the deviations of the prices of production with their uniform profit components around the underlying labour values, at the same time requiring the explanation to embrace the magnitudes of surplus value, etc., in the sphere of production.

This step is what the various proposed 'solutions' of the transformation problem were meant to establish – Sraffa's is the most satisfying as Ronald Meek pointed out in his 1961 review article of *Production of Commodities by Means of Commodities* (Sraffa 1960). The fact that Marx's own solution was wrong and that Engels would not part with the promised prize to those who got it right (even when they did) is beside the point, Böhm-Bawerk and *Karl Marx and the Close of his System* (1889) notwithstanding. It also allows us to comment on another modern controversy arising from consideration of the transformation problem – Ian Steedman's argument (1975, 1977) that including joint-production techniques in a model of value, distribution and accumulation stopped the fundamental Marxist theorem (FMT) (as Michio Morishima dubbed it) going through. The FMT is the proposition that the necessary and sufficient condition to observe a positive rate of profits in the sphere of distribution and exchange is to have positive surplus labour (and value) in the sphere of production. Steedman argued that it was possible in a joint-production system to have *negative* surplus labour and value in the sphere of production associated with *positive* profits in the sphere of distribution and exchange.

But as a number of economists soon showed, for example, Morishima (1976), this is not so if Marx's sturdy intuition is specified appropriately in the model. Again, this is not just esoteric game-playing in order to fill out (or up) CVs, but an excellent example of making precise sense of a major insight which still has relevance today. For while the RAL no longer pushes *all* wage-earners' incomes down to subsistence levels, nevertheless recent macroeconomic policy has unwittingly been drawing on Marx's insights to create a potential surplus for greater profits and accumulation by creating cowed and acquiescent workforces whose necessary labour time has been much reduced. Of course, the policy makers have forgotten another Marxist insight that there are internal contradictions present in each mode of production. In modern capitalism, as in the capitalism of Marx's time, the policies used to create a potential surplus may simultaneously so dampen and depress the 'animal spirits' of the decision-making and accumulating class that the potential surplus may remain largely unrealized by actual accumulation and actual investment expenditure – the initial $C \to C'$ in the circuit above. Marx also recognized that industrial, commercial and finance capital must advance in tandem and that when they do not, crises occur. Hilferding (1910) was one of the first major writers on this theme. The dominance of industrial and commercial capital by financial capital has been a major cause of the instabilities in world capitalism of the past twenty years or more.

6 Schemes of reproduction

We now move on to lessons from volumes II and III, especially the role of the schemes of reproduction which played such an important part, often unrealized by the people employing them, in both the Keynesian/Kaleckian revolution and the immediate pre-war and post-war theories of growth. As Claudio Sardoni (1981) has made clear, to interpret the schemes of reproduction as precursors of steady state growth models is to misunderstand what Marx was doing. What Marx's three departmental schemata – wage goods, luxury goods, capital goods – were meant to make explicit were the consistency conditions needed to ensure, period by period, that total demands and total supplies, as well as their compositions, matched. Satisfying the conditions period by period did not imply steady growth over 'time' though it was, of course, a possibility. There is no suggestion in Marx, just as there was not in Joan Robinson's 'Golden Ages' (1956) (nor, to be fair, in Solow's (1956) original neo-classical growth model), that this was descriptive economics. Indeed, in the first two instances, the principal objective was to show just how very special the conditions of the various inter- and intradepartmental purchases and sales had to be, so as to make it a complete fluke if capitalism, left to itself with its myriad of decision makers doing their own thing, collectively brought such conditions about. Moreover, if they were not satisfied in fact, the authors went on to show how this could possibly precipitate a crisis and certainly serious malfunctioning. As Joan Robinson pointed out, Roy Harrod (her contemporary), in complete ignorance of a predecessor, discovered this all over again when he discussed the unstable nature of the warranted rate of growth. If the economy was on it, well and good, but if it was not, the system gave out signals which took the economy farther and farther away from it – and this, quite regardless of whether or not the warranted and natural rates growth were coinciding. In a not unrelated manner, Rosa Luxemberg (1913) argued that c/v would tend to increase to a point where the consumption of wage goods would be insufficient to absorb their production, that is, she raised the spectre of underconsumption, to be resolved initially by the courting of external markets through imperialism and sales of armaments.

7 Endogenous technical change and crises

Finally, in Marx's work, we have one of the first systematic attempts to provide a theory of endogenous technical progress. He attempted to show that the capitalist system would experience deeper and deeper crises, principally by changing methods of production in each cycle such that a tendency to a falling rate of profits was produced. (It was common to all economists up to and including Marx that there was such a tendency, it was over the explanation that they differed.) A falling rate of profits would, in the times when Marx was writing, stifle both the desire and the ability to accumulate (have things changed that much?). Because real wages tended to rise in the upswing and boom as the RAL shrank, labour-saving innovations would be induced and embodied in the stock of capital goods by current accumulation. It was sensible, indeed essential, for each individual capitalist to so respond, in order to try to survive in a fiercely competitive environment (just as it was sensible for them always to try to weaken the power of the wage-earners on the workshop floor); but the systemic result was to swell on trend the RAL and reduce the fund of living labour from which surplus labour and surplus value could be extracted for future accumulation. Thus falling realized profits would reduce both the desire and ability to accumulate – the fundamental contradiction of capitalism was to tend to induce just the sort of technical progress which ultimately would tend to destroy the system itself.

We know now that the details of the argument meant that this was only a possibility, not an inevitable result as Marx tended(!) to believe. The point is that looking at events in Marx's way leads us to concentrate on the appropriate variables and processes to be used and analysed respectively.

8 Conclusions

Marx's writings on economics generated a tradition of study combining economic history with classical political economy. Confrontation or class struggle had occurred in every mode of production both as an economic and a social/political confrontation. The development of successive forms and forces or modes of production is the process of historical materialism. Capitalism is that phase in this history at which labour power has become a commodity. Starting from the concept of embodied labour, Marx explained the exploitation in capitalism of the direct producers through both the relations of production and the appropriation of the surplus by the class which purchased their labour power. Struggle over the conditions of its sale and the production, distribution and use of the surplus it produced became part of the contradictory conditions which, through a dialectical process, resolved into new forms or, ultimately, new social relations or forces and so new modes of production. Marx saw final events as resolutions of already existing but conflicting features of the economic system. Value, therefore, is primarily a historically relative category, specific to capitalism. The measurement difficulty arising from reconciling labour-embodied values with prices of production can be regarded as no longer a problem if the labour theory of value is seen as a conceptual argument about the origins of the surplus and of expanded reproduction and change.

Marx recognized the drive for capital accumulation. He also recognized the contradictory tendencies present in this pursuit, demonstrating some possibilities in the circuits of capital. Therefore he was inconclusive about the exact nature of the collapse of capitalism.

G.C. HARCOURT
JESUS COLLEGE, CAMBRIDGE

P.M. KERR
FORMERLY UNIVERSITY OF LEICESTER

Note

We thank but in no way implicate Peter Nolan, Renée Prendergast, and Malcolm Warner for their comments on a draft of this entry.

Further reading

(References cited in the text marked *)

* Böhm-Bawerk, E. von (1889) *Karl Marx and the Close of his System*, trans. and ed. P. Sweezy, New York: Augustus M. Kelly, 1949. (Claimed to have found a fundamental inconsistency between the theory of value and distribution in volume I and that of volume III of *Capital*; includes a reply by R. Hilferding, *Böhm-Bawerk's Criticism of Karl Marx*.)

Dobb, M. (1937) *Political Economy and Capitalism: Some Essays in Economic Tradition*, London: Routledge and Sons, reprinted 1972, Westport, CT: Greenwood Press. (A modern statement of the strengths of Marxian analysis.)

* Dobb, M. (1946) *Studies in the Development of Capitalism*, London: Routledge and Kegan Paul. (Stimulated a tradition in Marx's method of historical materialism; Dobb saw the LTV not as a measure of relative prices but as a fundamental principle in explaining expanded reproduction and change.)

* Heilbroner, R. (1991) *The Worldly Philosophers*, 6th edn, Harmondsworth: Penguin, 1953. (Best introduction to the lives and contributions of the great economists ever written.)

* Hilferding, R. (1910) *Finance Capital*, trans. T. Bottomore, London: Routledge and Kegan Paul, 1981. (A treatise on the need for finance, commercial and industrial capitals to move in tandem to avoid crises.)

* Keynes, J.M. (1936) *The General Theory of Employment, Interest and Money*, The Collected Writings of John Maynard Keynes, vol. VII, London: Macmillan, 1973. (Compilation of Keynes' most important work.)

* Luxemberg, R. (1913) *The Accumulation of Capital*, trans. A. Schwarzschild, intro. by J. Robinson, London: Routledge and Kegan Paul, 1951.

(Argued that Marx had not foreseen the possibility that domestic market demand may fall short of supply: external markets and the development of imperialism were one solution.)
* Marx, K. (1858) *A Contribution to the Critique of Political Economy*, M. Dobb (ed.), trans. S. Ryazanshaya, London: Lawrence & Wishart, 1970. (Response by Marx to the works of earlier political economists, including Smith, Malthus and Mill.)
* Marx, K. (1867) *Capital*, vol. I, trans. from 3rd German edn by S. Moore and E. Aveling, Harmondsworth: Penguin, 1976. (First volume of Marx's classic text denouncing mid-Victorian capitalism and offering a new model of economics widely adopted by twentieth-century socialist governments.)
* Marx, K. (1885) *Capital*, vol. II, F. Engels (ed.) Harmondsworth: Penguin, 1978. (Second volume of Marx's classic work.)
* Marx, K. (1894) *Capital*, vol. III, F. Engels (ed.), Harmondsworth: Penguin, 1981. (Particularly useful on the phenomenom of production prices.)
* Marx, K. (1905–10) *Theories of Surplus Value*, K. Kautsky (ed.), Stuttgart: J.H.W. Dietz Nachf. (Outlines Marx's reasons for the existence of surplus in capitalism.)
* Marx, K. and Engels, F. (1848) *Manifesto of the Communist Party*, trans. H. Macfarlane, Harmondsworth: Penguin, 1978. (Very often cited tract, published coincidentally with the European revolutions of 1848, in which the authors called for the establishment of Socialism.)
* Meek, R.L. (1961), 'Mr Sraffa's rehabilitation of classical economics', *Scottish Journal of Political Economy* 8 (June): 119–36. (Brilliant review article, reprinted in Meek (1967), of Sraffa's classic, making explicit the relationship of Sraffa's analysis to classical and Marxist thought.)
* Meek, R.L. (1967) *Economics and Ideology and Other Essays: Studies in the Development of Economic Thought*, London: Chapman & Hall. (Measured and balanced essays on classical and Marxian political economy, past and present.)
* Morishima, M. (1976) 'Positive profits with negative surplus value – a comment', *Economic Journal* 86 (September): 599–603. (Refutation of Steedman's claim that joint-production systems could exhibit negative surplus labour and value with positive profits.)
* Pasinetti, L.L. (1974) *Growth and Income Distribution: Essays in Economic Theory*, London: Cambridge University Press. (A selection of Pasinetti's seminal essays on growth and distribution in the classical and Cambridge tradition.)

Popper, K. (1945) *The Open Society and its Enemies*, London: Routledge. (Two volumes, the second of which attacks Marx's claim for scientificity, arguing that it is impossible for a theory of dialectical materialism to be demonstrated as true or false.)
* Robinson, J. (1956) *The Accumulation of Capital*, London: Macmillan. (Joan Robinson's magnum opus, with classical and Marxian overtones, attempting 'to generalize *The General Theory* to the long period'.)
Rubin, I.I. (1928) *Essays on Marx's Theory of Value*, Detroit, MI: Black and Red, 1972. (Deeply insightful essays on the core of Marx's theoretical system.)
* Sardoni, C. (1981) 'Multi-sectoral models of balanced growth and the Marxian schemes of expanded reproduction', *Australian Economic Papers* 20 (December): 383–97. (Definitive interpretation of the purposes of the Marxian schemes of expanded reproduction.)
* Solow, R.M. (1956) 'A contribution to the theory of economic growth', *Quarterly Journal of Economics* LXX (February): 65–94. (The seminal paper on neo-classical growth theory, written independently but published at the same time as Trevor Swan's 1956 'Economic record' article on the same subject.)
* Sraffa, P. (1960) *Production of Commodities by Means of Commodities: Prelude to a Critique of Economic Theory*, Cambridge: Cambridge University Press. (Both a critique of the conceptual foundations of neo-classical theory and the provision of a formal structure of the classical surplus approach.)
* Steedman, I. (1975) 'Positive profits with negative surplus value', *Economic Journal* 85 (March): 114–23. (Attempts to show that in joint-production systems it is possible to have negative surplus labour and value associated with positive profits.)
* Steedman, I. (1977) *Marx after Sraffa*, London: NLB. (A systematic discussion of the implications of the analysis in Sraffa's 1960 book for the main propositions of Marx's system.)
Sweezy, P.M. (1942) *The Theory of Capitalist Development*, New York: Monthly Review Press. (Develops Marx's theory of crisis into the new forms of capitalism characterizing the twentieth century.)
* Wheen, F. (1999) *Karl Marx*, London: Fourth Estate. (A most readable and fair account of Marx's life and contributions.)

See also: KEYNES, J.M.

Marshall, Alfred (1842–1924)

1 Biographical data
2 Background to Marshall's economics
3 Early work and *Principles of Economics*
4 *Industry and Trade*
5 Beyond the academy

Personal background

- born 26 July 1842 in London
- educated at Merchant Taylors' School and entered St John's College, Cambridge University, in 1862 to prepare for the mathematical tripos
- 'Second Wrangler' in 1865 and elected fellow of his college
- appointed in 1868 as college lecturer in moral science at St John's
- by 1870 adopted economics as his life's work
- married Mary Paley (1850–1944) in 1877, forcing him to resign his fellowship
- moved to the new University College at Bristol and in 1883 moved to Balliol College, Oxford
- Professor of Political Economy at Cambridge University, 1885–1908
- *Principles of Economics* published in 1890
- voluntary retirement in 1908, bringing a last opportunity for sustained literary work
- died 13 July 1924 at Balliol Croft, his Cambridge home of many years

Major works

Economics of Industry (with M. Paley) (1879)
Principles of Economics (1890)
Industry and Trade (1919)
Money, Credit and Commerce (1923)

Summary

Alfred Marshall was the effective founder of the Cambridge School of Economics which rose to worldwide prominence in the inter-war years. His *Principles of Economics* (1890) exercised considerable influence on the development of economics, especially in English-speaking countries, and popularized tools still important in the working economist's toolbox. Marshall was an inspiring teacher, his most prominent students being John Maynard Keynes (1883–1946), the most famous economist of the twentieth century, and Arthur Cecil Pigou (1877–1959), pioneer of welfare economics, who was to succeed Marshall as professor at Cambridge. Among the leading economists of his era, Marshall was notable for his strong interest in industrial and labour questions and his persistent attempts to familiarize himself with the realities of business life and the concerns of labour. The new degree course in economics and related studies adopted at Cambridge in 1903 at Marshall's urging was an early attempt to provide for management education in conjunction with the training of economists. Marshall's *Industry and Trade* (1919) contains his most detailed and realistic discussion of business organization and management.

1 Biographical data

Marshall, whose father was an employee of the Bank of England, was born and spent his formative years in London. Educated at the venerable Merchant Taylors' School, he entered St John's College, Cambridge, in 1862 to prepare for Cambridge University's prestigious mathematical tripos. Emerging in the elevated position of 'Second Wrangler' in 1865, he was soon elected fellow of his college. Leaving mathematics and physical science behind, he embarked upon an intensive exploration of the moral and philosophical bases of human behaviour and society. Appointed in 1868 as college lecturer in moral science at St John's, he rapidly concentrated on economics which he had by 1870 adopted as his life's work. He soon established himself as Cambridge's leading teacher of the subject, but published little.

Marriage in 1877 to Mary Paley (1850–1944), an early student at what was to become Newnham College, forced Marshall to resign his fellowship. He left Cambridge for the new University College at Bristol, then in 1883 moved to Balliol College, Oxford. However, the unexpected death of the previous incumbent brought Marshall back to Cambridge at the beginning of 1885 as Professor of Political Economy. He held this chair until his voluntary retirement in 1908. The appearance of *Principles of Economics* in 1890 augmented notably his published output and cemented his international reputation and his standing as the UK's leading economist.

The years of professorship were onerous, with heavy teaching responsibilities, taken seriously, and substantial public service. Marshall struggled persistently, and not always diplomatically, to increase the provisions and resources for his subject within the university and to attract students capable of advancing economic science. The institution of the new economics tripos in 1903 secured growing room for his subject and planted the seed from which the Cambridge School was to develop, but resources and students continued to be scarce until after his retirement. Retirement brought a last opportunity for the sustained literary work that the busy years after 1890 had precluded, and Marshall's long labours were eventually, if incompletely, rewarded by the appearance of *Industry and Trade* in 1919 and *Money, Credit and Commerce* in 1923. He died in 1924 at Balliol Croft, his Cambridge home of many years.

2 Background to Marshall's economics

Economics in 1870 was settled into a rather quiescent state, still dominated in the UK by the ideas of the classical economists, especially John Stuart Mill (1806–73) (see MILL, J.S.). But stirrings of change were evident. The publication in 1871 of the *Theory of Political Economy* by William Stanley Jevons (1835–82) was a notable harbinger of the coming 'neo-classical revolution', an approach which was to emphasize demand, optimizing behaviour and mathematical formalization, while continuing the deductive tradition of the classical school (see NEO-CLASSICAL ECONOMICS). This tradition itself was under attack, especially in Germany, by an increasingly aggressive historical school, emphasizing induction and case studies. More generally, Darwinian ideas were challenging traditional certainties in fundamental ways and social concern with the plight of the poor was rising.

Marshall was strongly influenced by this intellectual milieu. Although prone later to exaggerate his subjective originality, it is clear that he did independently develop some key ideas of neo-classical economics. But he was always to remain critical of extended deduction based on extreme formalization, urging that deduction be guided by a close observation of history and context and make full allowance for non-quantitative aspects. He could follow the historical school only so far, emphasizing that observation without a guiding analytical framework could yield no knowledge of causes.

Influenced by Darwinian ideas, and especially the views of Herbert Spencer (1820–1903), Marshall placed considerable emphasis on the evolution of human character. Traits were seen as strongly dependent upon an individual's environment and upbringing. The improvement of humankind was to Marshall a more important aspect of economic growth than was humankind's increased command over nature, although the latter was to some extent a precondition for the former. Concern over those in poverty, over the enlightenment of the working classes, and over threats to the UK's continued economic progress from developments abroad and misguided policies at home, all underlay Marshall's strong desire to make economics relevant to practical concerns. While recognizing that economists as such had no special authority to speak on normative matters, he was not always careful to observe the positive–normative distinction. For him, economic issues and ethical concerns were intricately interrelated.

3 Early work and *Principles of Economics*

Marshall largely completed in the 1870s a book on foreign trade and protection but eventually chose not to publish it, although some of its theoretical appendices were printed for private circulation in 1879 as the *Pure Theory of Foreign Trade* and the *Pure Theory of Domestic Values*. These remarkable pieces, although not widely circulated, were sufficiently impressive to mark him as a major economic theorist. The year 1879 also saw the publication of *Economics of Industry* written by Marshall and his wife. Ostensibly an introductory textbook, this put forward a theory of factor pricing and income distribution along marginal-productivity lines which helps justify Marshall's claim to objective as well as subjective originality in the development of the marginalist neo-classical programme. This theory together with the 'Pure Theory of Domestic Values' was the core from which Marshall developed his *Principles of Economics*, composition of which began in 1881. The 1880s also saw a steady flow of occasional publications and his important monetary evidence to the Gold and Silver Commission, 1887–8.

Upon its appearance in 1890, *Principles* was widely acknowledged as an important addition to the literature of economics. Its impact came not so much from the theoretical advances it embodied, although there were some, as from its breadth and humanity of outlook and its weaving of the new ideas developed since 1870 into a larger tapestry, preserving what was best in the classical tradition (and in the process exaggerating somewhat the extent of continuity) while acknowledging to a degree the claims of historicism and evolutionism.

On a theoretical level, *Principles* is most noteworthy for its reliance on what has come to be termed a partial-equilibrium approach. This involves the analysis of interactions within a single market on the approximative assumption that surrounding circumstances are unaffected by what happens there. This approach sacrifices theoretical precision for ready applicability and remains prominent in applied economics. An extension of the partial-equilibrium approach is found in Marshall's period analysis, which analyses market equilibrium by ignoring those forces within the market that move slowly, or average out rapidly, compared to the length of the period whose ruling circumstances are to be explained. Associated with this period analysis is Marshall's concept of quasi-rent: the income of any productive factor in fixed supply for the length of period being considered can be regarded as a rent, determined by price rather than price determining. But this residual character of the factor return may not be preserved for longer periods. For sufficiently long periods, any payments necessary to maintain supply of the factor intact become price determining. Only if factor supply is truly exogenous (the Ricardian case) is the factor return always a pure rent.

Marshall's treatment of consumer demand for a commodity relied heavily on the assumption that the commodity was a negligible element in expenditure. His popularization and refinement of the consumer surplus concept relied on a similar condition. The powerful application of this concept to problems of welfare economics under both competition and monopoly was an important feature of his work.

In analysing supply conditions for a manufactured product, Marshall laid stress on scale economies and imperfect competition. The latter presumed that each firm must establish a particular clientele and supply network whose gradual acquisition is a form of investment, embodied in 'good will'. Rapid increase in sales would thus be difficult, necessitating large price reductions. Hence, rapid exploitation of internal economies of scale would be precluded, while over long periods a management life-cycle would diminish entrepreneurial drive and eventually terminate the business. This economics of the mid-Victorian family business could not accommodate satisfactorily the rise of the modern corporation. Although suggestive of later developments in imperfect competition theory, it has failed the survival test. On the other hand, the adjunct notion of external economies due to increased subdivision of function and osmosis of expertise as the *industry's* output increases has remained seminal, if elusive.

Principles closed with an extended discussion of income distribution among productive factors. Here a more aggregative approach was adopted. National income was viewed as the joint product of all factors, each of which received its marginal product. Marshall integrated a neo-classical marginal productivity approach to factor demand with a treatment of factor supply on classical lines. The economy-of-high-wages idea that increased wages might boost worker productivity and efficiency (partly through better diet and living conditions and eventually through broadened horizons and greater opportunities for self-improvement) was a prominent and complicating aspect of his presentation.

Marshall – always sensitive to criticism – spent much time and effort in revising the eight editions of *Principles* appearing in his lifetime, especially the first five. The substance of his views does not seem to have altered, however. He also worked for over a decade on a planned second volume to deal with money, foreign trade, industry, labour, government, and so on, a project eventually abandoned as unmanageable. In the sixth edition of 1910 the appellation 'Volume One' was replaced by 'An Introductory Volume'.

4 Industry and Trade

At the height of the tariff controversy in the UK in 1903 Marshall commenced a short book on the issue of the day. Its scope soon grew into a major study of national industries in relation to international trade, treating industrial, labour market and commercial developments and policies in the UK, France, Germany, the USA, etc. as the source of changes in international trade. When *Industry and Trade* at last appeared in 1919 it was an imperfect realization of this grandiose plan, while *Money, Credit and Commerce* of 1923 was less a continuation than an attempt to rescue early work that should have been developed in the abandoned second volume of *Principles*.

Despite a failure to apply to international trade the studies of national industry, and despite a selective consideration of individual industries, *Industry and Trade* remains a rich source of information and insight into managerial and commercial policies and possibilities for government guidance. The book's analytical focus is not on atomistic competition or entrenched monopoly (the cases dealt with in *Principles*) but on group action by trusts, pools, organized labour, etc. and on monopolies that are 'conditional' and subject to the ever-present threat of entry. The lack of a clear theoretical skeleton has caused the book to be slighted by economists, but it offers much of interest to students of management and business practice as well as to business historians.

5 Beyond the academy

Marshall strove persistently to glean first-hand knowledge of economic reality, visiting factories and working-class quarters. He spent the summer of 1876 in the USA studying the realities of protectionism. He was also an avid reader of factual economic literature and studies. He took every opportunity to question those from other walks of life who crossed his path or stayed with him in Cambridge. Despite this curiosity, he was hardly an extroverted man-of-the-world, and a lack of robustness served to narrow further the circle of his acquaintances and contacts outside Cambridge.

Before 1890 his outside contacts seem to have been mainly with trade unionists and social reformers. Service on the Royal Commission on Labour, 1891–4, together with the rise of militant 'new unionism', appears to have dampened his enthusiasm for labour movements. Increasingly, the enterprising and chivalrous captain of industry, fearlessly pioneering new paths and driven by the desire for constructive achievement rather than mere wealth, became the heroic figure in Marshall's world view – a figure threatened by the dragons of government control and the sirens of enervating protectionism. It is doubtful whether this figure was drawn fully from life. Marshall's acquaintance with leading businessmen seems to have been slight. Charles Booth (1840–1916), shipowner, is perhaps an exception, but the link here was Booth's pioneering studies of London poverty. Sir David Dale (1829–1906), ironmaster and a fellow member of the Labour Commission, was someone Marshall knew and admired, and the years in Bristol had acquainted him with a few local businessmen active in the affairs of the local college. But the letters secured from businessmen and other public figures to support Marshall's 1903 campaign for a new economics tripos in Cambridge suggest that the circle of his business acquaintances remained small. His views of the business world combined penetration and acuteness with an element of naivety.

The new economics tripos, although primarily designed to train economists, promised relevant alternatives for those intending to enter the higher ranks of business. Marshall's goal here was to provide a broad, flexible and knowledgeable outlook rather than a technical command of current business practice. His hopes in this direction were hardly met, but they did help garner outside support to counter Cambridge's curricular conservatism.

JOHN K. WHITAKER
UNIVERSITY OF VIRGINIA

Further reading

(References cited in the text marked *)

Groenewegen, P. (1995) *A Soaring Eagle: Alfred Marshall 1842–1924*, Aldershot: Elgar. (A full-scale biography.)

Groenewegen, P. (ed.) (1996) *Official Papers of Alfred Marshall: A Supplement*, Cambridge: Cambridge University Press. (Supplements Keynes 1926.)

Guillebaud, C.W. (ed.) (1961) *Alfred Marshall's Principles of Economics*, 9th (variorum) edn, 2 vols, London: Macmillan. (The first volume reprints the eighth edition of this book; the second provides variant passages from earlier editions and supporting documents.)

* Jevons, W.S. (1871) *The Theory of Political Economy*, London: Macmillan. (Pioneering work in neo-classical economics.)

Keynes, J.M. (ed.) (1926) *Official Papers of Alfred Marshall*, London: Macmillan. (Reproduces Marshall's important evidence to government enquiries.)

McWilliams Tullberg, R. (1990) *Alfred Marshall in Retrospect*, Aldershot: Edward Elgar. (Essays on Marshall's work and life by various authors, including 'Marshall on business' by J. Maloney.)

* Marshall, A. (1890) *Principles of Economics*, London: Macmillan. (First edition of his magnum opus, in which Marshall expounds his theories of value and distribution. Revised editions in 1891, 1895, 1898, 1907, 1910, 1916 and 1920.)

* Marshall, A. (1919) *Industry and Trade*, London: Macmillan. (A major treatment of applied economics and business history from a cosmopolitan perspective.)

* Marshall, A. (1923) *Money, Credit and Commerce*, London: Macmillan. (Expounds his theories of money and international trade.)

* Marshall, A. and Marshall, M.P. (1879) *Economics of Industry*, London: Macmillan. (First general statement of Marshall's theories of value and distribution, disguised as an elementary textbook.)

O'Brien, D.P. (1981) 'Alfred Marshall, 1842–1924' in D.P. O'Brien and J.R. Presley (eds), *Pioneers of Modern Economics in Britain*, London: Macmillan. (A scholarly survey of Marshall's work.)

Pigou, A.C. (ed.) (1925) *Memorials of Alfred Marshall*, London: Macmillan. (Reproduces many of Marshall's occasional writings and some correspondence; prefaced by J.M. Keynes' remarkable memoir.)

Whitaker, J.K. (ed.) (1975) *Early Economic Writings of Alfred Marshall, 1867–1890*, London: Macmillan. (Reproduces with commentary Marshall's early manuscripts, including the *Pure Theory* pieces.)

Whitaker, J.K. (1987) 'Alfred Marshall (1842–1924)', in J. Eatwell, M. Milgate and P. Newman (eds), *The New Palgrave: A Dictionary of Economics*, London: Macmillan. (An extended review and assessment with a comprehensive bibliography.)

Whitaker, J.K. (ed.) (1990) *Centenary Essays on Alfred Marshall*, Cambridge: Cambridge University Press. (Essays by different authors on various aspects of Marshall's work and life.)

Whitaker, J.K. (ed.) (1996) *The Correspondence of Alfred Marshall, Economist*, Cambridge: Cambridge University Press. (A comprehensive three volume edition of Marshall's correspondence and related documents.)

See also: KEYNES, J.M.; MILL, J.S.; NEO-CLASSICAL ECONOMICS

Veblen, Thorstein B. (1857–1929)

1 Biographical details
2 Veblen's critique of rational economic man
3 Technology and institutions
4 Foundations of evolutionary economics
5 Cumulative causation: against teleology

Overview

This entry discusses the work of the American institutional economist Thorstein Veblen (1857–1929). It is argued that he provides some of the most fundamental and radical criticisms of neoclassical economics. Veblen's analytical approach to both technology and institutions is discussed here, as well as his explicit application of the evolutionary analogy from Darwinian biology to economics and social science. Finally, mention is made of Veblen's concept of cumulative causation and its relevance to an understanding of the possible trajectories of capitalist development.

1 Biographical details

Thorstein Veblen was born in 1857. He was the fourth son and sixth child of Norwegian immigrants who settled in eastern Minnesota in the United States. Educated at Carleton College, Johns Hopkins University, Yale University and Cornell University, he took various university posts at Chicago, Stanford, Missouri and New York. As a student at John Hopkins University he came in contact with the brilliant philosopher and founder of pragmatism Charles Sanders Peirce. At Yale University he came under the influence of William Graham Sumner, the Social Darwinist. He read widely in biology, psychology and philosophy, as well as the social sciences. As well as Peirce and Sumner, the works of Charles Darwin, William James, Karl Marx, William McDougall and Herbert Spencer made an enduring mark.

Veblen's most important works date from the 1890s. In 1898 he published his classic article 'Why is economics not an evolutionary science?' in the *Quarterly Journal of Economics*. The following year saw the appearance of his first book *The Theory of the Leisure Class*. Although this is an original and sophisticated theoretical work, its satiric prose and mockery of the wasteful and idle practices of the rich turned it into a bestseller. Other academic articles followed in the *Quarterly Journal of Economics*, the *Journal of Political Economy* and elsewhere, the most important of which have been collected together in *The Place of Science in Modern Civilization and Other Essays* (1919a). Together these articles provide a devastating critique of neoclassical economics and the basis of a new approach to economics on 'evolutionary' lines. Neoclassical economics originated in the 1870s with the work of William Stanley Jevons, Alfred Marshal, Léon Walras and others, and is still the dominant school of thought in that subject. Veblen's critique was one of the first and most fundamental of this emergent paradigm.

In 1904 *The Theory of Business Enterprise* was published, followed by *The Instinct of Workmanship* in 1914, *Imperial Germany and the Industrial Revolution* in 1915, *An Inquiry Into the Nature of Peace and Terms of its Perpetuation* in 1917, *The Higher Learning in America* 1918, *The Vested Interests and the Common Man* in 1919, *The Engineers and the Price System* in 1921 and *Absentee Ownership and Business Enterprise in Recent Times* in 1923. Regrettably, the later works do not deliver the tacit promise of further theoretical development that is found in Veblen's writings from 1892 to 1915. He died in California in 1929.

Veblen was a radical and innovative thinker. He is remembered today as the founder of the school of 'institutional economics' which prospered in the United States between the First and Second World Wars. His writings sometimes bristle with biting and satiric phrases, critical of the institutions and practices of modern capitalism. Nevertheless, Veblen and his followers did not construct an integrated system of economic theory to follow that of Karl Marx, Alfred Marshall or Léon Walras (see MARSHALL, A.; MARX, K.). After the 1930s, the 'old' institutional economics lost ground to the rising generation of formal and mathematically inclined economists, led by Kenneth Arrow, Paul Samuelson, and others (see SAMUELSON, P.). By 1950 the institutional school was confined to a small minority of adherents. However, in recent years there has been a revival of the 'old' institutional economics in both Europe and America, and there is a renewed interest in Veblen's works. A large number of themes arise in Veblen's writings and a comprehensive review is not possible. Instead, a few topics of particular relevance for business and management are selected.

2 Veblen's critique of rational economic man

Veblen (1919a: 73) argues that neoclassical economics has a 'faulty conception of human nature' wrongly conceiving of the individual 'in hedonistic terms; that is to say, in terms of a passive and substantially inert and immutably given human nature'. Veblen's critique is directed at neoclassical economics and all theories in which the individual is taken as a given 'globule of desire', to use his satiric phrase. In *The Theory of the Leisure Class* and elsewhere, he argues that consumption is a 'conspicuous' and social rather than an individual process. Consumption is regarded as much more than the mechanical satisfaction of fixed individual needs; it is a cultural and communicative act by which humans signal status and social position, and thereby create further and future desires for others. Accordingly, tastes are malleable and the idea of unalloyed 'consumer sovereignty' is a myth. Indeed, Veblen's bestselling book is not only a major criticism of neoclassical economics but one of the founding texts in the modern science of marketing.

In one of his early essays, Veblen (1919a: 73) lambasts the neoclassical view of the economic agent as 'a lightning calculator of pleasures and pains'. He describes the economic man of the textbooks as having 'neither antecedent nor consequent'. Neoclassical economics gives no account of how human wants were formed and developed and instead portrays human agents as utility-maximizing machines. Veblen proposes an alternative theory of human agency, in which 'instincts' such as 'workmanship', 'emulation', 'predatoriness' and 'idle curiosity' play a major role. The emphasis on habitual and 'instinctive' behaviour replaces the utilitarian pleasure–pain principle.

Veblen's conception of the human agent is strongly influenced by the pragmatist philosophy of Peirce and James. Following them, he rejects the Cartesian notion of the supremely rational and calculating agent, instead seeing agents as propelled in the main by habits and routinized behaviours. Instead of the continuously calculating, marginally adjusting agent of neoclassical theory there is an emphasis on inertia and habit.

Veblen argues that habits give the point of view from which facts and events are apprehended and reduced to a body of knowledge. When they are shared and reinforced within a society or group, individual habits assume the form of socio-economic institutions. Institutions create and reinforce habits of action and thought: 'The situation of today shapes the institutions of tomorrow through a selective, coercive process, by acting upon men's habitual view of things, and so altering or fortifying a point of view or a mental attitude handed down from the past' (Veblen 1899: 190–1).

In contrast, in neoclassical economics the self-contained, rational individual has autonomous preferences, seemingly formed apart from the social and natural world. He or she is seemingly capable of optimizing behaviour when faced with a complex problem with enormous numbers of interdependent variables. Instead, Veblen sees the individual's conduct as being influenced by culture and institutions and guided by habit. There is a radical break from the atomistic, individualistic and utilitarian assumptions associated with neoclassical economics.

3 Technology and institutions

One of Veblen's most important arguments against 'economic man' and other core assumptions of neoclassical theory is that they are inadequate for the theoretical purpose at hand. Veblen's intention is to analyse the 'evolutionary' processes of change and transformation in a modern economy. Neoclassical theory is defective in this respect because it indicated 'the conditions of survival to which any innovation is subject, supposing the innovation to have taken place, not the conditions of variational growth' (Veblen 1919a: 176–7). But Veblen sees it as important to consider why such innovations take place, and not to confine ourselves to a theory that dwells over equilibrium conditions with given technological possibilities. The question for Veblen was not how things stabilize themselves in a 'static state', but how they endlessly grow and change.

Accordingly, along with the assumption of fixed preference functions, Veblen also criticizes the widespread assumption of a fixed set of technological possibilities in economic theory. One of his concerns is to examine the conditions for human creativity. With ironic phrases such as 'idle curiosity' he rejects the view that business interests and the potential for technological advance are always positively correlated.

Although Veblen does not see a conflict with technology as universal, he argues that technological change can often challenge established institutions and vested interests. In *The Theory of Business Enterprise* and elsewhere Veblen distinguishes between industry (making goods) and business (making money). This critical dichotomy parallels the earlier suggestion in *The Theory of the Leisure Class* that there is a distinction between serviceable consumption to satisfy human need and conspicuous consumption for status and display. Accordingly, Veblen is strongly critical of apologetic tendencies in social science which regard existing institutions as necessarily efficient or optimal. He rebuts the assumption that institutions must necessarily serve functional needs of society. Instead, he describes particularly regressive or disservicable institutions as 'archaic', 'ceremonial' or even 'imbecile'.

4 Foundations of evolutionary economics

Veblen sees the evolutionary metaphor as crucial to the understanding of the processes of technological development in a capitalist economy (see EVOLUTIONARY THEORIES OF THE FIRM). He is the first economist to apply the Darwinian evolutionary analogy from biology to economics. He argues that economics should become an 'evolutionary' and 'post-Darwinian' science. There is a current revival in 'evolutionary' approaches in economics but the Veblenian precedent for this type of approach is not always acknowledged.

Biological evolution is based on three essential features. First, there must be sustained variation among the members of a species or population. Variations may be blind, random or purposive in character, but without them, as Darwin insisted, natural selection cannot operate. Second, there must be some principle of heredity or continuity through which offspring have to resemble their parents more than they resemble other members of their species. In other words, there has to be some mechanism through which individual characteristics are passed on through the generations. Third, natural selection itself operates either because better-adapted organisms leave increased numbers of offspring, or because the variations or gene combinations that are preserved are those bestowing advantage in struggling to survive. This is the principle of the struggle for existence.

The same three principles can be found in Veblen's work. For instance, habits and institutions are regarded as relatively durable and the analogue of heritable traits. Veblen (1899: 190–1) writes: 'men's present habits of thought tend to persist indefinitely, except as circumstances enforce a change. These institutions which have so been handed down, these habits of thought, points of view, mental attitudes and aptitudes, or what not, are therefore themselves a conservative factor. This is the factor of social inertia, psychological inertia, conservatism'. Likewise, Veblen (1914: 86–9) recognizes the role of creativity and novelty with his concept of 'idle curiosity'. Veblen's recognition of the open-endedness of the evolutionary process is evidenced in his conception of 'change, realized to be self-continuing or self-propagating and to have no final term' (Veblen 1919a: 37). Finally, without drawing Panglossian or laissez-faire conclusions, Veblen (1899: 188) subscribes to a notion of evolutionary selection in the socio-economic sphere: 'The life of man in society, just as the life of other species, is a struggle for existence, and therefore it is a process of selective adaptation. The evolution of social structure has been a process of natural selection of institutions.'

In this respect Veblen is a more suited mentor for evolutionary economics than Joseph Schumpeter (see SCHUMPETER, J.), who eschews all natural and physical metaphors and states in his *History of Economic Analysis* (1954: 789) that in economics 'no appeal to biology would be of the slightest use'. Schumpeter's frequent use of the word 'evolution' should not mislead us into believing that his work was a precedent for the employment of a biological analogy. He does not define the term in biological terms and we do not find in his work the use of the three principles of evolutionary change (heritable traits, generation of variety, and selection) as outlined above. Richard Nelson and Sidney Winter describe their seminal work *An Evolutionary Theory of Economic Change* (1982) as 'Schumpeterian', yet they make explicit use of a metaphor from evolutionary biology. In this respect there are strong resemblances with some of Veblen's ideas. Accordingly, their work is better described as 'Veblenian', although they make no reference in that work to the earlier economist.

5 Cumulative causation: against teleology

During his lifetime, half-understood biological analogies were being widely applied to the social sciences, in attempts to justify all sorts of ideological positions from socialism to capitalist competition. Veblen is a clear exception and his understanding of biology is much more sophisticated. Contrary to many of his contemporaries, Veblen saw that the idea of Darwinian evolution meant that the future was unknown, unpredictable and indeterminate. In this respect he treated Darwin not only as a critic of apologetic defenders of capitalism but also as a rebuttal of Marx's teleological suggestions that history was leading inevitably to a single and communist future.

Veblen's answer to both the Marxian suggestion of the inevitability of communism and his rebuff to the neoclassical concept of equilibrium is his theory of cumulative causation. He sees both the circumstances and temperament of individuals as part of the cumulative processes of change: 'The economic life history of the individual is a cumulative process of adaptation of means to ends that cumulatively change as the process goes on, both the agent and his environment being at any point the outcome of the last process' (Veblen 1919a: 74–5). Directly or indirectly influenced by Veblen, the notion of cumulative causation has been developed by a number of economists, notably Nicholas Kaldor and the Nobel Laureate Gunnar Myrdal. The idea relates to the modern notion that technologies and economic systems can get 'locked in' – and sometimes as a result of initial accidents – to relatively constrained paths of development. Hence there is 'path dependence' rather than convergence to a given equilibrium or track of development. History matters.

Veblen's concept of cumulative causation is an antidote to both neoclassical and Marxian economic theory. Contrary to the equilibrium analysis of neoclassical economics, Veblen sees the economic system not as a 'self-balancing mechanism' but as a 'cumulatively unfolding process'. As Myrdal and Kaldor argue at length, the processes of cumulative causation suggest that regional and national development is generally divergent rather than convergent. This contradicts the typical emphasis within neoclassical economic theory on processes of compensating feedback and mutual adjustment via the price mechanism leading to greater uniformity and convergence.

Contrary to much Marxist and neoclassical thinking, Veblen argued that multiple futures were possible. Equilibrating forces do not always pull the economy back onto a single track. This exposes a severe weakness in

Marx's conception of history. Although Veblen has socialist leanings, he argues against the idea of finality or consummation in economic development. Variety and cumulative causation mean that history has 'no final term' (Veblen 1919a: 37). In Marxism the final term is communism or the classless society, but Veblen rejects the teleological concept of a final goal. This means a rejection of the ideas of the 'inevitability' of socialism and of a 'natural' or end-point in capitalist evolution. There is no natural path, or law, governing economic development. Accordingly, Veblen accepts the possibility of varieties of capitalism and different paths of capitalist development.

This standpoint is particularly relevant for recent debates about convergence versus divergence within global capitalism. Veblen's emphasis on the importance of institutions and culture, along with his notion of divergent and cumulative causation, suggests that multiple futures and multiple varieties of capitalism are possible. Despite the lack of an integrated and systematic theory in his writings, his analytical outlook makes him one of the most relevant economists and social theorists today.

GEOFFREY M. HODGSON
THE BUSINESS SCHOOL
UNIVERSITY OF HERTFORDSHIRE

Further reading

(References cited in the text marked *)

Dorfman, J. (1934) *Thorstein Veblen and His America*, New York: Viking Press. (The classic intellectual bibliography of Veblen.)

Hodgson, G.M. (1988) *Economics and Institutions: A Manifesto for a Modern Institutional Economics*, Cambridge and Philadelphia: Polity Press and University of Pennsylvania Press. (A critique of neoclassical economics from a perspective inspired by Veblen and other 'old' institutional economists. There is an extensive bibliography.)

Hodgson, G.M. (1993) *Economics and Evolution: Bringing Life Back Into Economics*, Cambridge, UK and Ann Arbor, MI: Polity Press and University of Michigan Press. (An extensive discussion and analysis of various approaches to evolutionary economics where the work of Veblen is prominent.)

Hodgson, G.M. (ed.) (1998) *The Foundations of Evolutionary Economics: 1890–1973*, 2 vols, International Library of Critical Writings in Economics, Cheltenham: Edward Elgar. (A collection of important essays on evolutionary economics by various authors, including several commentaries on the work of Veblen.)

* Nelson, R.R. and Winter, S.G. (1982) *An Evolutionary Theory of Economic Change*, Cambridge, MA: Harvard University Press. (A now-seminal application of the evolutionary analogy to the theory of the firm. Although the influence is unacknowledged, aspects of this work are highly redolent of Veblenian institutionalism.)

Rutherford, M.C. (1994) *Institutions in Economics: The Old and the New Institutionalism*, Cambridge: Cambridge University Press. (An erudite and thoughtful account of institutional thought with extensive attention to Veblen.)

Samuels, W.J. (ed.) (1988) *Institutional Economics*, 3 vols, Aldershot: Edward Elgar. (A useful anthology of essays on Veblen and other 'old' institutionalists.)

* Schumpeter, J.A. (1954) *History of Economic Analysis*, New York: Oxford University Press.

Seckler, D. (1975) *Thorstein Veblen and the Institutionalists: A Study in the Social Philosophy of Economics*, London: Macmillan. (Contains a sympathetic critique of Veblen. Sometimes misguided in its assessment, but contains extensive quotations and makes a number of useful points.)

Tilman, R. (1992) *Thorstein Veblen and His Critics, 1891–1963: Conservative, Liberal, and Radical*, Princeton: Princeton University Press. (A detailed and very interesting perspective on Veblen through the eyes of his critics.)

Tilman, R. (1996) *The Intellectual Legacy of Thorstein Veblen: Unresolved Issues*, Westport, CT: Greenwood Press. (An excellent overview of controversies surrounding Veblen's thinking.)

* Veblen, T.B. (1898) 'Why is economics not an evolutionay science?', *Quarterly Journal of Economics*, 12.

* Veblen, T.B. (1899) *The Theory of the Leisure Class: An Economic Study of Institutions*, New York: Macmillan. (Veblen's classic and highly influential analysis of the consumer behaviour of the rich. With this work the 'old' institutional school was founded.)

* Veblen, T.B. (1904) *The Theory of Business Enterprise*, New York: Charles Scribners, reprinted 1975 by Augustus Kelley. (A major and influential work on modern capitalist enterprise.)

* Veblen, T.B. (1914) *The Instinct of Workmanship, and the State of the Industrial Arts*, New York: Augustus Kelley, reprinted 1990 with a new

introduction by M.G. Murphey and a 1964 introductory note by J. Dorfman, New Brunswick: Transaction Books. (Regarded by Veblen as his most important book.)
* Veblen, T.B. (1915) *Imperial Germany and the Industrial Revolution*, New York: Macmillan, reprinted 1964 by Augustus Kelley. (A strikingly prescient and incisive work.)
* Veblen, T.B. (1917) *An Inquiry into the Nature of Peace and the Terms of its Perpetuation*, New York: Huebsch. (An attempt to lay bare the causes of war.)
* Veblen, T.B. (1918) *The Higher Learning in America: A Memorandum on the Conduct of Universities by Business Men*, New York: Huebsch. (A critique of business influence on universities.)
* Veblen, T.B. (1919a) *The Place of Science in Modern Civilization and Other Essays*, New York: Huebsch, reprinted 1990 with a new introduction by W. J. Samuels, New Brunswick: Transaction Books. (The most important collection of Veblen's essays. Veblen is often at his best in his essays and polemics and for this reason this work is invaluable both for the economic and the social theorist.)
* Veblen, T.B. (1919b) *The Vested Interests and the Common Man*, New York: Huebsch.
* Veblen, T.B. (1921) *The Engineers and the Price System*, New York: Harcourt Brace and World. (A work in which Veblen idiosyncratically sees the engineer as the agent of socialist revolution.)
* Veblen, T.B. (1923) *Absentee Ownership And Business Enterprise in Recent Times*, New York: Huebsch. (An early critique of the separation of ownership from both responsibility and control.)

See also: EVOLUTIONARY THEORIES OF THE FIRM; INSTITUTIONAL ECONOMICS; MARSHALL, A.; MARX, K.H.; SAMUELSON, P.; SCHUMPETER, J.

Weber, Max (1864–1920)

1 Introduction
2 Biographical data
3 Main contribution
4 Conclusions

Personal background

- born into a middle-class family in Erfurt, Germany, 21 April 1864
- took his Ph.D. and began his teaching career at the University of Berlin
- moved on to a position as Professor of Economics at the University of Heidelberg
- experienced a nervous breakdown in 1897 and was unable to do any serious work for several years
- began to re-emerge in 1904, coincident with a trip to the USA
- published his best-known work, *The Protestant Ethic and the Spirit of Capitalism*, in 1904–5
- most of his major works published in the next decade and a half, or posthumously
- died on 14 June 1920 while in the midst of his most important work, *Economy and Society*

Major works

The Protestant Ethic and the Spirit of Capitalism (1904–5)
Economy and Society (1921)
General Economic History (1927)

Summary

Max Weber (1864–1920) was a major social theorist whose ideas are of great relevance to business and management. Embedded in Weber's world historical studies is a general theory of the rationalization of society. Time has been kind to Weber's theory; society today is even more rationalized than it was in his day. His theoretical ideas are of particular relevance to the understanding of, among other things, modern formal organizations, the capitalist market, the professions and economies as a whole. Not only do Weber's ideas continue to be relevant today, but neo-Weberians are developing new ideas that have even greater applicability to modern society.

1 Introduction

After Karl Marx (see MARX, K.H.), Weber is the most important German social theorist. In fact, Weber had to grapple with, and distance himself from, Marxian theory. Weber, like Marx, had much to say about capitalism. However, to Weber capitalism was merely part of a much broader problem – modern rational society. Thus while Marx focused on alienation within the economic system, Weber saw alienation as a far larger problem occurring in many other social institutions. While Marx condemned the exploitation of the capitalist system, Weber was concerned with the increasing oppressiveness of the rationalized society. Marx was an optimist who felt that the problems of alienation and exploitation could be solved with the overthrow of the capitalist economy, but Weber was a pessimist who believed that the future held only increasing rationalization, especially if capitalism were overthrown. Weber was no revolutionary, but rather a careful and insightful analyst of modern society.

2 Biographical data

Max Weber was born into a middle-class family in which his parents had very different outlooks on life. His worldly father was a classic bureaucrat who ultimately rose to a position of some political importance in Germany; in contrast, Weber's mother was devoutly religious and even ascetic in her outlook. In a later biography, Weber's wife Marianne (Weber 1975) comments that Weber's parents confronted him with a difficult choice as a child, a choice that he agonized over for much of his life and one which had a profound effect on both his personal life and his scholarly work (Mitzman 1969).

Weber earned a doctorate from the University of Berlin in 1892 in his father's field (law) and began teaching at that university. However, his interests were already shifting towards his lifelong concerns – economics, history and sociology. His early work in these areas led to a position as Professor of Economics at the University of Heidelberg in 1896.

Not long after his appointment at Heidelberg, Weber had a violent argument with his father, who died shortly thereafter. Within a short period of time Weber suffered a nervous breakdown from which he was never to recover fully. However, by 1904–5 he had recuperated sufficiently to publish one of his best-known works, *The Protestant Ethic and the Spirit of Capitalism* (Weber 1904–5; Lehmann and Roth 1993). The subject-matter of this work, as reflected in the title, exhibited a concern for both his mother's religiosity (she was a Calvinist, the key Protestant sect in the rise of capitalism) and his father's worldly interests. It also demonstrated the ascendancy of his mother's orientation over his father's; an ascendancy that was to be manifest in a series of works focusing on the sociology of religion (Weber 1916, 1916–17, 1921), especially the impact of the major religions of the world on economic conduct.

In the last decade and a half of his life, Weber was able to publish his most important works. At the time of his death he was working on his most important book, *Economy and Society* (Weber 1921) which, although incomplete, was published posthumously, as was the also significant *General Economic History* (Weber 1927).

During his lifetime, Weber had a profound impact on scholars such as Georg Simmel, Robert Michels and Georg Lukács. His influence remains strong to this day with the continuing, and perhaps even accelerating, production of a wide array of neo-Weberian scholarship (Collins 1985).

3 Main contribution

In the area of business and management, Weber has been best known for his work on bureaucracy. However, that work is but a small part of his broader theory of the rationalization of Western society and many elements of that theory beyond his paradigm of a bureaucracy are relevant to scholars working in the area of business and management.

At the broadest level, the question that informs Weber's work is, why did the Occident develop a unique form of rationalization and why did the rest of the world fail to develop such a rational system? The paradigm case of the West's distinctive rationality is bureaucracy, but it is only one aspect, albeit a central one (along with capitalism), of a broad-based process of rationalization.

The rationalization concept in Weber's work is notoriously obscure, but the best definition of at least one key type – formal rationalization – is the process by which actors' choices of means to ends are increasingly constrained, if not determined, by universally applied rules, laws and regulations. The bureaucracy, a key domain of such rules, laws and regulations, is one of the defining products of this process of rationalization, but there are others such as the capitalistic market, systems of rational–legal authority, the factory and the assembly line. All have in common the fact that they are formally rational structures that constrain the individuals within them to act in a rational manner by pursuing ends through the choice of the most direct and efficient means. Furthermore, Weber saw more and more sectors of society coming under the domination of formal rationalization. Eventually, he envisioned a society in which people would be enslaved in an 'iron cage of rationality' made up of a near seamless web of these formally rational structures.

These structures, as well as the process of formal rationalization in general, can be seen as being defined by several dimensions (Eisen 1978). First, formally rational structures emphasize calculability, or those things that can be counted or quantified. The focus on quantity tends to lead to a de-emphasis on quality. Second, there is a focus on efficiency, or finding the best means available to an end. Third, there is great emphasis on predictability, or being sure that things operate in the same way from one time or place to another. Fourth, there is an emphasis on the control over, and ultimately replacement of, humans by non-human technologies. Finally, and reflective of Weber's profound ambivalence about the rationalization process, is the tendency of formally rational systems to have irrational consequences, in other words, the irrationality of rationality.

Rationality has many irrationalities, but the foremost among them is dehumanization. Modern formally rational systems tend, in Weber's view, to be inhuman places in which to function and this goes for the bureaucrat, the factory worker and the assembly-line worker, as well as the participant in the capitalist market. For Weber, there is a basic conflict between these formally rational structures devoid of values and individuals imbued with his notion of 'personality,' that is, those defined and dominated by such values (Brubaker 1984: 63).

The modern analyst of business and management is left with several concerns derived from Weber's work. At the most general level is the continuing relevance of Weber's general theory of increasing formal rationalization to the modern business world. The business world in particular, as well as society as a whole, would seem to be even more rationalized today than it was in Weber's day. Thus, the process remains relevant and, in fact, we need to be attuned to its spreading influence throughout the business world and the larger society.

Beyond the broad theory are more specific aspects of Weber's work, the most important of which for our purposes is the process of bureaucratization and the resulting bureaucratic structure. As one aspect of the rationalization process, the process of bureaucratization persists and bureaucratic structures continue to survive and even spread throughout the West, as well as the rest of the world. At the same time, Weber's 'ideal type' of a bureaucracy continues to be useful as a heuristic device for analysing organizational structures. The goal is to see how well these structures measure up to the elements of the ideal-typical bureaucracy. The ideal-typical bureaucracy remains a useful methodological tool even in this era of radically new, debureaucratized organizational forms. The ideal type is of utility in determining how far these new bureaucratic forms have strayed from the form as it was first described by Weber.

While the bureaucracy continues to be important, one may question whether it still is the 'paradigm case' of the rationalization process. It could be argued, for example, that the fast-food restaurant is today a better paradigm for the rationalization process than the bureaucracy (Ritzer 1993).

The bureaucracy is the organizational form characteristic of one of Weber's three types of authority – rational–legal authority which rests on the legality of enacted rules. There is also traditional authority which is based on the sanctity of immemorial traditions. Finally, charismatic authority rests on the belief of followers that a leader has extraordinary qualities. These authority types remain relevant to thinking about those who lead businesses and other types of organizations. Since the three types of authority are ideal types, any given leader may have their authority legitimized on the basis of some combination of all three types.

With the rout of communism throughout most of the world, Weber's thoughts on the capitalistic marketplace take on renewed importance. The capitalist market was both a key site of the rationalization process and a formally rational structure defined by all of the key elements outlined above. Further, it was crucial to the dissemination of the principles of formal rationality to many other sectors of society.

Weber envisioned a mortal struggle taking place in the modern world between formal rationality and a second type of rationality, substantive rationality. While in formal rationality choices of means to ends are determined by rules, laws and regulations, in substantive rationality those choices are guided by larger human values. The Protestant ethic is an example of substantive rationality, while the capitalist system, which was an 'unanticipated consequence' of that ethic, is, as we have seen, an example of formal rationality. That they are in conflict is reflected in the fact that capitalism became a system that was inhospitable not only to Protestantism, but to all religion. To put it another way, capitalism, and more generally all formally rational systems, reflect the increasing 'disenchantment of the world'.

In the modern world, one of the places in which this conflict is being played out is in the struggle between formally rational systems like bureaucracies and the substantively rational professions like medicine and law. The classic professions are being threatened by both formally rational bureaucracies like those associated with the government or private enterprise as well as by increases in formal rationality within the professions. As a result, the professions as we have known them are embattled and in the process of losing much of their power, prestige and distinguishing characteristics. In other words, they are undergoing a process of deprofessionalization. This is nowhere clearer than in the most powerful profession of all, the American medical profession (Ritzer and Walczak 1988).

We have mentioned two of the types of rationality employed by Weber (formal and substantive), but it should be pointed out that there are two others: practical (the day-to-day rationality whereby people accept given realities and attempt to deal with them as best they can) and theoretical (the effort to master reality cognitively through increasingly abstract concepts). It could be argued that the USA achieved much of its economic success by creating and refining a wide range of formally rational systems, for example, assembly lines, time-and-motion systems, organizational principles such as General Motors' divisional system, and innumerable others. It also could be argued that its more recent failures are traceable to relying too long and too exclusively on such formally rational systems. In contrast, it could be argued that the Japanese have succeeded by using formally rational systems often developed in the USA (as well as developing their own such as the just-in-time system) and supplementing them with substantive rationality (importance of the success of the collectivity), theoretical rationality (strong reliance on research and development, as well as engineering) and practical rationality (for example, quality circles). In other words, the Japanese have created a 'hyper-rational' system and this gives them an enormous advantage over American industry that continues to rely heavily on only one form of rationality (Ritzer and LeMoyne 1991).

4 Conclusions

Weber's most lasting contribution has been his theory of rationalization. That theory posits four types of rationality (formal, substantive, theoretical and practical) and argues that formal rationality was a distinctive product of the Occident and one that has come to dominate it. This theory has proved useful in analysing such traditional issues as the bureaucracy, the professions and the capitalist market, as well as a series of recent developments such as the rise of the fast-food restaurant, deprofessionalization and the recent ascendancy of Japanese industry and the parallel decline of American industry. Thus, Weber's ideas continue to be relevant to an understanding of a variety of recent developments in the business world and in the world economy. Theorists continue to clarify and amplify his ideas and researchers continue to apply Weber's ideas to a wide range of social settings.

GEORGE RITZER
UNIVERSITY OF MARYLAND
AT COLLEGE PARK

Further reading

(References cited in the text marked *)

Bendix, R. (1960) *Max Weber: An Intellectual Portrait*, Garden City, NY: Anchor Books. (Now classic overview of the life and work of Max Weber.)
* Brubaker, R. (1984) *The Limits of Rationality: An Essay on the Social and Moral Thought of Max Weber*, London: Routledge. (The best single source on Weber's thoughts about rationality.)
* Collins, R. (1985) *Weberian Sociological Theory*, Cambridge: Cambridge University Press. (Excellent example of neo-Weberian theory.)
* Eisen, A. (1978) 'The meanings and confusions of Weberian "rationality"', *British Journal of Sociology* 29: 57–70. (Useful discussion of the various dimensions of formal rationality.)
Kalberg, S. (1980) 'Max Weber's types of rationality: cornerstones for the analysis of rationalization processes in history', *American Journal of Sociology* 85: 1145–79. (Excellent discussion of Weber's rationalization theory and the

source for the four types of rationality employed in this biographical sketch.)
Lassman, P. (ed.) (1994) *Weber: Political Writings*, Cambridge: Cambridge University Press. (Essays dealing with another one of Weber's concerns – politics.)
* Lehmann, H. and Roth, G. (eds) (1993) *Weber's Protestant Ethic: Origins, Evidence and Contexts*, Cambridge: Cambridge University Press. (Collection of contemporary essays dealing with various aspects of Weber's classic work.)
* Mitzman, A. (1969) *The Iron Cage: An Historical Interpretation of Max Weber*, New York: Grosset & Dunlap. (A controversial psycho-biography of Weber which focuses on his often unsuccessful effort to work out the conflict between his mother and his father in his work and elsewhere.)
Parsons, T. (1937) *The Structure of Social Action*, New York: McGraw-Hill. (The work that introduced, many would say in a distorted manner, Weber's theory (and others) to an American audience and laid the basis for Parsonian theory and structural functionalism.)
* Ritzer, G. (1993) *The McDonaldization of Society*, Thousand Oaks, CA: Pine Forge Press. (The thesis of this book is that the fast-food restaurant is now a better paradigm of the rationalization process than the bureaucracy and that, if anything, that process is even more powerful today than it was in Weber's day.)
* Ritzer, G. and LeMoyne, T. (1991) 'Hyperrationality: an extension of Weberian and neo-Weberian theory', in G. Ritzer (ed.), *Metatheorizing in Sociology*, Lexington, MA: Lexington Books. (Creates the concept of hyperrationality to describe the co-existence of Weber's four types of rationality and uses that concept to explain Japan's economic successes and the recent failures of the USA.)
* Ritzer, G. and Walczak, D. (1988) 'Rationalization and the deprofessionalization of physicians', *Social Forces* 67: 1–22. (Argues that the medical profession is being swamped by formal rationalization and that this is leading to the deprofessionalization of medicine.)
Schluchter, W. (1981) *The Rise of Western Rationalism: Max Weber's Developmental History*, Berkeley, CA: University of California Press. (Important study of Weber's developmental history of rationalization.)

Sica, A. (1988) *Weber, Irrationality, and Social Order*, Berkeley, CA: University of California Press. (Unlike most other studies of Weber which focus on his work on rationality, this one deals with the issue of irrationality.)
Turner, S. (2000) *The Cambridge Companion to Weber*, Cambridge: Cambridge University Press. (A key work bringing together leading scholars on Weber and his work.)
* Weber, Marianne (1975) *Max Weber: A Biography*, trans. and ed. H. Zohn, New York: Wiley. (The definitive biography of Max Weber, by his wife.)
* Weber, M. ([1904–5] 1958) *The Protestant Ethic and the Spirit of Capitalism*, New York: Scribner's. (One of the classic works in sociology detailing the relationship between the ethos of Protestantism, especially Calvinism, and the rise of a spirit of capitalism in the West, a spirit that was ultimately connected to the development of capitalism and, more generally, formal rationality.)
* Weber, M. ([1916] 1964) *The Religion of China: Confucianism and Taoism*, New York: Macmillan. (Part of Weber's sociology of religion in which he discusses the barriers to the rise of capitalism and formal rationality within the major religions of China.)
* Weber, M. ([1916–17] 1958) *The Religion of India: The Sociology of Hinduism and Buddhism*, Glencoe, IL: Free Press. (Companion to *The Religion of China*. Here Weber shows how Hinduism and Buddhism served to impede the development of capitalism and formal rationality.)
* Weber, M. ([1921] 1963) *The Sociology of Religion*, Boston, MA: Beacon Press. (The most general statement of Weber's ideas on the sociology of religion.)
* Weber, M. ([1921] 1968) *Economy and Society*, Totowa, NJ: Bedminster Press. (Three volumes comprising the single best source for a sense of Weber's overall project and his general theoretical perspective.)
* Weber, M. ([1927] 1981) *General Economic History*, New Brunswick, NJ: Transaction Books. (Demonstrates that Weber saw the Protestant ethic as only one of many factors in the rise of Western capitalism and rationality.)

See also: MARX, K.H.

Keynes, John Maynard (1883–1946)

1 Beginnings
2 Emergent philosophy
3 Early economics
4 The gold standard debate
5 From *A Treatise on Money* to *The General Theory*
6 The Keynesian Revolution
7 The Second World War and after
8 Evaluation
9 Conclusion

Personal background

- born 5 June 1883, Cambridge, England
- educated at Eton and Cambridge
- combined careers of civil servant, financial speculator and academic with a strong appreciation of the arts
- chief representative of HM Treasury at the Paris peace conference, 1918
- married Lydia Lopokova of the Ballets Russes, 1925
- elevated to the peerage, 1942
- British representative at Bretton Woods conference, 1944
- died 21 April 1946

Major works

The Economic Consequences of the Peace (1919)
Treatise on Probability (1921)
A Tract on Monetary Reform (1923)
A Treatise on Money (1930)
The General Theory of Employment, Interest and Money (1936)

Summary

J.M. Keynes is not only the greatest economist of the twentieth century, he is also, still, the most controversial. He has been called the father of macroeconomics, but there had been others before him who had concerned themselves with analysis at the aggregate level. His achievement as a theorist was to appreciate the non-neutrality of monetary factors in the economy, fully integrating them into an explanation of how the economy works. Previous doctrines maintained that the role of money was to serve only as a convenient intermediary in exchanges of commodities: at best it had no effect, at worst it was responsible for fluctuations in prices which were expected to be temporary, and in the long run the economy would right itself and return to full employment.

Keynes' analysis explained for the first time why unemployment was not a mistake or due to a failure of entrepreneurial nerve but could result from rational choice. The costs incurred in achieving an expansion of employment, he pointed out, rise faster than the resulting sales of output; thus it becomes unprofitable to expand output and employment beyond a point which may be short of full employment. Since this situation will persist until some external force operates to change it, we have *unemployment equilibrium*, despite the fact that all agents are doing the best for themselves ('maximizing') within the constraints they face. Perhaps the most important point for the business person is that there are consequences of individual actions which cannot be foreseen: an investment may not pay the return which was expected, not because it was a bad idea but because it was implemented at the 'wrong' time – when, for example, others were not also investing and thereby boosting demand for the product as well as for their own.

1 Beginnings

John Maynard Keynes was born in Cambridge, England, the eldest of three children. His father, John Neville Keynes, was a Cambridge don (and later Registrar of the University) lecturing in logic and political economy. Political economy is the older name for economics and literally means the housekeeping of the state. It was perceived not as a technical discipline, but as a moral science, along with politics and philosophy. J.N. Keynes' work on the scope and method of political economy remains a classic. Maynard's mother, Florence Ada Keynes, was unusual for her time. Educated at Newnham College in the pioneering days of women's education at Cambridge, she was active in progressive social projects and became the first woman mayor of Cambridge. The family was Congregationalist.

Maynard's instruction in economics, along with the other essential subjects, began at home; his father supervised his studies and they worked together in the father's study. Maynard was perceived as exceptionally intelligent from an early age and was pushed rather hard, but where a lesser child might have found this onerous or have rebelled, he revelled in the work and excelled. He won a scholarship to Eton where he developed his knowledge of philosophy and began to cultivate an interest in and to collect rare books (he later collected Newton's alchemical papers). He went from there to King's College, Cambridge, where philosophy and ethics claimed his attention more than the subject he was reading, mathematics.

Keynes obtained a first class degree in 1905 and then, with Alfred Marshall's encouragement and supervision, stayed on in Cambridge to study for the economics examinations but elected to sit the Civil Service Examinations instead (see MARSHALL, A.). He came second and joined the India Office where he spent just two years. From 1908 to the outbreak of the First World War Keynes was back in Cambridge, lecturing in economics and revising his fellowship dissertation.

2 Emergent philosophy

Keynes and his Cambridge circle, especially the members of the exclusive group 'The Apostles', were much influenced by the philosophy of G.E. Moore. For Moore, the contemplation of beauty and the enjoyment of friendship were the true purposes of life, a view deeply subversive of Victorian values. His artistic interests spanned theatre, ballet, painting and rare books (he founded the Arts Council and the Arts Theatre at Cambridge). In Keynes these goals were balanced by the acceptance of a duty to contribute to public life, which he did in abundance. He was also keenly interested in the political philosophy of Edmund Burke. Keynes developed his Ideal, but was also prepared to develop the art of the possible (Fitzgibbons 1988; Helburn 1992; O'Donnell 1989; Skidelsky 1983).

While at the India Office, Keynes transformed an early critique of Moore into a pioneering work on the philosophy of probability, which he submitted to King's College as a fellowship dissertation in 1908. He was not elected until the following year (one of Keynes' few setbacks), after the thesis had been revised. It was not published until 1921, as *Treatise on Probability*.

The purpose of *Probability* is to derive principles of rational behaviour when there is true uncertainty. True uncertainty is to be distinguished from the type of uncertainty for which appropriate behaviour can be derived from classical probability. Classical probability pertains to experiments whose outcomes must be independent of time, both the time at which the experiment is conducted (context) and the sequence of the events within the experiment. The problem of decision making in the face of an uncertain future is qualitatively different from the controlled experiment – history does not repeat itself.

The rules of classical probability offer no insight into appropriate action under true uncertainty. Nevertheless, true uncertainty need not paralyse us or reduce us to pure guesswork. Clues exist to the probable relation between actions and their consequences in some cases. Repeated evidence from these clues, while not definitive, add to what Keynes called the 'degree of rational belief' in the probable connection between an action and the outcome. These probabilities provide a guide to rational action (Carabelli 1988; O'Donnell 1989). When, much later, Keynes wrote *The General Theory*, a central concept is behaviour under this kind of irreducible uncertainty.

3 Early economics

While at the India Office, Keynes closely examined India's monetary system and in 1913 published *Indian Currency and Finance*. Although the mode of analysis used is traditional, the book shows two features which characterize Keynes' work throughout his life and which would provoke the evolution of his thought: his thorough knowledge of economic institutions and his pragmatic approach to policy recommendations to improve those institutions (see INSTITUTIONAL ECONOMICS). He strongly supports the use of discretion over rule following in monetary matters and expresses a scepticism about the gold standard. When he came to oppose Britain's exchange rate policy after the 1914–18 war he had even more ammunition against the gold standard, but in this work his scepticism was based on his understanding that the success of the standard was not due to the standard itself but was contingent on the existence of a single, strong financial centre, which was London at that time. This understanding of the institutional and historical context was not at all part of the conventional wisdom of the day, which regarded the gold standard as self-evidently the source of monetary order.

Keynes entered the Treasury in January 1915 to work on wartime internal and external finance, and at the end of the war he was the Treasury's chief representative at the Paris peace conference. Keynes did not accept the implicit limitations of his brief but took the perspective of a highly placed statesman/politician. He bitterly opposed the settlement France was trying to impose on Germany, arguing that Germany could not pay what France was asking; the attempt would first bankrupt and then embitter her, and that was dangerous (and so it proved).

When his view did not prevail, Keynes resigned in protest and published his views as *The Economic Consequences of the Peace* (1919). The book was a sensation, both for the depth of its analysis of the economic causes of the war and the consequences of the proposed peace, but also for its vivid depiction of the way strong political forces were being played out at the conference and its devastating characterization of the chief participants. Keynes was now famous, not as an academic but in the world of affairs (he became a subject of David Low's cartoons). But in official circles the book was (understandably) considered deeply offensive. The Treasury sent Keynes into outer darkness – until they needed him again.

In the 1920s, Keynes returned to a life of lecturing at Cambridge (unpaid, in order to leave time for writing), journalism, financial dealings, academic writing and the fulfilment of Moore's goals of the enjoyment of friendship and of beauty. He spent part of each week at King's and at Gordon Square in London's Bloomsbury. Eventually he also took a lease on a house in Sussex. The academic was balanced by the man of affairs, the manager by the aesthete (Skidelsky 1992).

4 The gold standard debate

After the *Treatise on Probability* was revised for publication in 1921, Keynes the political economist employed his powers of persuasion in vigorous opposition to Britain's return to the gold standard. Keynes the academic put his ideas together as *A Tract on Monetary Reform* (1923). His position on the gold standard began where his *Indian Currency and Finance* had left off. The international context had changed. London's position as the world's sole, well-developed, strong financial centre could now be challenged by New York. Added to this was the fact that the debate entirely revolved around going back to the gold standard at the pre-war parity, despite the fact that prices in Britain had risen far higher than in the countries which constituted the competition – most notably America. Thus Britain would have to deflate, which she duly did. To those who understood monetary factors as creators of only temporary disruption this was perhaps not a daunting prospect, but to Keynes the personal tragedy and the social waste of the unemployment which would inevitably follow far outweighed the potential benefits of the standard.

Keynes was almost alone in his opposition, and it was an argument he lost. The gold standard was perceived as the only right arrangement, and the return to pre-war parity as the only honourable course, because to establish a lower parity would be to default in part to one's creditors. Britain had, of course, entered heavily into debt to fight the war, and a substantial portion of that debt was held abroad.

In the first two years after the war, Britain experienced one of the sharpest price fluctuations of her modern peacetime history. The retail price index rose 16 per cent in 1920, then fell by 28 per cent over the next two years. Still this fall was not enough to achieve parity and it had already had the effects Keynes feared: unemployment rose to 14 per cent in 1922 and continued to be high for the entire inter-war period, never falling below 10 per cent. The deflation in preparation for the return to gold was continued after the return (1925) to support the standard. Labour rebelled in 1926 with the General Strike, but it took the world recession provoked by the Wall Street crash and the collapse of world trade to make the gold standard finally untenable. Britain eventually came off in 1931.

In the face of all this upheaval, one can understand the impatience Keynes felt with the traditional methodology of the long run, disturbed by transitory monetary factors. In the *Tract on Monetary Reform* there is a famous statement, often taken out of context:

> But the *long run* is a misleading guide to current affairs. *In the long run* we are all dead. Economists set themselves too easy, too useless a task if in tempestuous seasons they can only tell us that when the storm is long past the ocean is flat again.
>
> (*CW* IV: 65)

In the tempestuous season associated with the return to gold, Keynes also displayed his distinct preference for avoiding unemployment, at the expense of profits if necessary (in *The General Theory* it was *rentier* income he was happier to see cut). In the *Tract* he argued for high interest rates to engineer a deflation of profits rather than a demand deflation which would cause incomes to fall and layoffs to rise. The contribution of that work to the Keynesian Revolution lies in its rejection of the long run as the foundation of economic analysis. This rejection was later to form the basis of the transition from *A Treatise on Money* to *The General Theory*.

5 From *A Treatise on Money* to *The General Theory*

Post-war events had emphasized the influence of banking and monetary policy on the economy (see FRIEDMAN, M.). Some economists, however, persisted in the misconception that money is neutral, affecting only 'nominal' variables. Keynes, who was always prepared to accept the evidence of his own eyes, could not sustain such a belief. He determined to write a treatise on money, consolidating his accumulated knowledge of the working of money markets and the role of money in the economy. What resulted is a scholarly work, somewhat ponderous in style, in two volumes following the traditional separation of the 'pure theory' of money from applied theory. The definitive treatise was not the medium for someone like Keynes, whose restless mind was constantly being stimulated by active participation in public affairs, who was learning all the time. Keynes' thinking developed in conjunction with his work for the Macmillan Committee on the Finance of Industry (Clarke 1988).

The *Treatise on Money* (1930) is an important work, both for the wealth of institutional and historical detail it contains and for its development of an approach towards the 'deviations' from the long run in which monetary and 'real' factors are integrated. It takes up the challenge of the *Tract* to discover what processes of adjustment are provoked by variations in demand, which result in unexpected ('windfall') profits and losses. Windfalls are defined as deviations from the 'flat sea' of a long-period equilibrium. This long-period equilibrium is completely traditional: just normal profits and normal real wages, with equilibrium prices determined by the quantity of money. Departures from long-period (full) employment are attributed to a lack of entrepreneurial nerve (if entrepreneurs would produce more they would discover they could sell it) and assumed to be temporary. Within the theory, wages must fall to cure unemployment.

These are thoroughly classical conclusions, but the *Treatise* contained an important step towards *The General Theory* in arguing that the rate of interest (the price of securities), instead of being determined by flows of saving and the demand for funds to finance investment, was set by the activities of optimistic and pessimistic speculators ('bulls' and 'bears'). These activities involved the deployment of the stock of financial wealth, not just flows. In modern terms, Keynes took a portfolio approach. The effect of concentrating on the activities of bulls and bears is to break the traditional link between the rate of interest and the rate of profit and thus the link to 'fundamentals'.

Speculators are not interested in fundamentals but in a quick profit on their financial dealings. (Keynes should know; he earned his living that way.)

When Keynes published the *Treatise* in 1930, the British economy had been depressed since 1922, and the slide to the bottom of the depression caused by the collapse first of American economic activity and then of world trade had begun. Could anyone really believe that eight years of unemployment of over 10 per cent (nine more years were to come) were due to 'transitory monetary factors'? There are those who, faced with a conflict between their theory and the evidence, will defend their theory, finding 'imperfections' in the world's performance. When Keynes perceived that the world and theory were out of line, he looked for a new theory.

In Cambridge, there emerged a group of brilliant younger colleagues (known as the 'Circus') who met to discuss the *Treatise*; they provided criticism, particularly of the inability of the work to explain variations in output except as random variation. Thus employment also was random. That was no explanation, and explanation was urgent. In mid-1931, with work for the Macmillan Committee out of the way, Keynes therefore began to revise his ideas to provide the needed explanation. In the course of doing so he produced his greatest work, which resulted in a radically altered structure for economic theory: *The General Theory of Employment, Interest and Money* (1936).

6 The Keynesian Revolution

The Keynesian Revolution is popularly understood to be the policy conclusion associated with *The General Theory*: governments should run deficits to counteract a slump. But others had advocated this policy long before Keynes. His complaint, indeed, was that this policy recommendation could not be supported by existing theory. The purpose of the work was to provide the theory which justifies that policy and outlines the circumstances in which it should be pursued. It is the theory, and even more, the method which underlies it, which is truly revolutionary.

The key concept of *The General Theory* is the 'principle of effective demand'. This principle states that employment is determined by aggregate demand, given prevailing wages and technical conditions of supply. Demand determines the level of output which it is profitable for firms to supply, as well as appropriate prices. This is true even for small firms, who in traditional theory are said to take prices as given. Keynes here made two obvious points: prices cannot be taken as given, for the market in which the goods are to be sold is in the (inherently uncertain) future; and prices facing an individual firm are conditional on the aggregate level of economic activity. Therefore there is no way that firms, even those too small to influence the market by their actions, can determine appropriate output and hiring policy without first taking a view ('forming an expectation') of aggregate demand. This is necessary because aggregate demand can vary, perhaps suddenly and unexpectedly but (in contrast to the 1930 work) not simply randomly. *The General Theory* explores the reasons for explicable, if not predictable, variation.

If demand is not adequate to justify full employment, there is 'involuntary unemployment' and there is no mechanism by which an adequate level of demand can be brought about by the actions of workers. If producers' expectations of demand are met at a level of production which does not absorb all the labour willing to work at the going wage, unemployment can continue indefinitely. Equilibrium will be a position of full employment only by accident, and equilibrium with unemployment is just as likely. It is not a mistake – expectations are fulfilled.

Where the 1930 work posits a long period with only one level of output (normal output) supplemented by random fluctuations, *The General Theory* explores the determination of output in the context where it actually takes place (when the capital stock is given and output can only be expanded by hiring more labour), hence the direct link between output and employment. Technically, this is known as the short period, but it can last a long or a short length of actual time depending on how quickly new capital comes on stream and begins to contribute to production. The classical sheet anchor of the long run has finally been abandoned and with it the 'classical dichotomy', whereby the quantity of money determined prices and 'real variables' were determined by 'real factors'. Aggregate demand is a monetary variable; there are no elements determined by purely 'real' forces. Monetary factors are neither neutral nor transitory (see MONETARISM).

The elements of aggregate demand are consumption and investment. Consumption is mainly determined by income and thus responds when aggregate income rises, but consumption cannot initiate such a rise. Investment, on the other hand, is free of current income, for two reasons: the purpose of investment is to expand the capacity to meet future, not current, demand; and at least some investment is not financed by current cash flow but by bank loans. Since banks can make loans which correspond to no prior saving, this source of lending makes possible an excess of investment over current saving, in contrast to the classical story where investment is constrained by the amount of saving. Saving is now adjusted to investment through increased income, not the other way round.

Both by reason of the potential volatility of entrepreneurs' expectations of future demand and the lack of any financial constraint other than bankers' evaluations, investment is the unpredictable element of demand. This is not all bad, for it is investment which can lift the economy out of recession in the short run and provide capacity and improved competitiveness in the longer term. Investment not only provides additional income equal to itself but also initiates further rounds of induced consumption expenditure such that the income generated will be a multiple of the original investment. This is the famous 'multiplier', an idea first mooted by Keynes and Hubert Henderson (*Can Lloyd George Do It?* 1929) and developed by Keynes' colleague Richard Kahn (1931).

The rate of interest is the price to be paid for borrowing to finance investment. The general level of the rate of interest, Keynes argued, is determined by the same forces as those described in the *Treatise*: the speculative expectations and activities of 'bulls' and 'bears'. If they, and bankers, share the same ups and downs of optimism as the investing producers, investment will be still more volatile.

It had been believed that if employers as a whole simply decided to produce more, they would find that they would sell the increased output, since employment and income would have risen (this is known as Say's Law – supply creates its own demand). An important part of Keynes' story is the 'fundamental psychological law' (as he called it) that less than the whole of a rise in income would be consumed (the marginal propensity to consume is less than one). Thus as income rises there is a gap to be filled if producers are to sell all their output. If investment is not forthcoming to fill that gap, there are two possibilities: give encouragement to investment or find some other way to fill the gap. Investment depends on expectations of the further future and the rate of interest. It is difficult to 'talk up' the future prospects of an economy to affect expectations (though some governments have tried this), and in time of recession it is extremely difficult to push interest rates down, because they are so low already. This is where the famous policy recommendation of government expenditure enters the picture – to fill a gap left by depressed investment in a time of high unemployment. The multiplier analysis shows that the resulting improvement in economic activity would go a long way towards financing the policy through lower unemployment benefit and higher tax yields.

The alternative 'cure' for unemployment proposed at the time (and by many others subsequently) was to lower wages. *The General Theory* shows that this proposition assumes that wages are only a cost, whereas they are both a cost and a source of demand (see LABOUR MARKETS). It is therefore impossible to argue that a cut in wages would leave demand unaffected. It is difficult to predict what would actually happen, but one certainly cannot assert that an unambiguous improvement would follow. Keynes was of the view that a cut in wages might actually damage employment.

7 The Second World War and after

The General Theory brought to fruition the long struggle to escape from established modes of thought which had begun in the dissatisfaction with long-period analysis expressed in the *Tract on Monetary Reform*. But Keynes was never solely a theorist. In the political context of the time the book's message was urgent. In the ten years between the General Strike and the 1936 work, the plight of the worker had worsened, and alternative systems were claiming to have the answer to unemployment and poverty, namely communism and fascism. But it was to be rearmament, not Keynes' ideas, which came to the rescue.

In 1937, Keynes suffered his first heart attack, with other complications. His activities were sharply reduced for the next two years, and when war broke out he planned to spend the duration in Cambridge, thus releasing those more fit for government or military service. But his urge to action and his expertise resulted in publications and speeches and quite soon a pamphlet on the pressing subject, *How to Pay for the War* (1940). Then he joined the Chancellor of the Exchequer's Consultative Council, and soon a room was found for him in the Treasury, where he concerned himself not only with the financing of the war but also with preparing to shape postwar trade and especially payments.

The *Treatise on Money* had ended with a plan for a supranational bank, an idea which Keynes had mooted even in his very first book. His proposal for an international clearing union, which became known as the Keynes Plan, formed the British starting point at the negotiations which culminated at Bretton Woods, where the framework for the international monetary system was agreed. The clearing union represented a complete break with any automaticity in international monetary mechanisms in favour of discretionary monetary management, albeit with a limited brief on this international scale. Keynes' concern was to prevent creditor countries from building up idle balances. This is a direct generalization to the international sphere of the concern in *The General Theory* that, especially in a recession, people would prefer liquidity, with the result that the rate of interest would remain high and exert a deflationary influence.

The Americans could not be persuaded to go as far as the Keynes Plan, not least because they knew that they were already a chief creditor and they feared a further outpouring of dollar loans. The resulting International Monetary Fund corresponded more closely to the less far-reaching plan of the American representative, Harry Dexter White. Keynes was in a weak bargaining position: he would soon have to negotiate an American loan to Britain. He dared not walk out, as he had done in Paris. The terms of the subsequent loan were quite onerous but the best Keynes could do. Despite his reservations, he argued passionately for its acceptance, most notably in a moving speech in the House of Lords, to which he had been elevated in 1942. The loan agreement was signed just in time for Parliament, which had been waiting for the outcome to ratify the Bretton Woods Articles of Agreement. Three months later, Keynes went to the inaugural meeting of the Bretton Woods institutions (the International Monetary Fund and World Bank) at Savannah, Georgia in March 1946. It was not, as Keynes expected, a pleasant party; there was an agenda of final details, but in these, all the old conflicts surfaced.

On the train back to New York, Keynes collapsed from exhaustion. A few weeks later, at his Sussex home on Easter Sunday, he suffered another heart attack. This time it was fatal.

8 Evaluation

Keynes' contribution can be evaluated on two levels: the contribution of his entire career as an economist and the contribution of the sourcebook of the Keynesian Revolution. This entry has stressed the continuous evolution of his thought and the application of his theoretical framework, as it evolved, to important social and political questions at the highest level.

Keynes' life as an economist was of a piece, even as his ideas evolved. This is something we are just beginning to realize as the result of extensive scholarship. It is often said that an economist must also be a philosopher, an historian, a politician. Keynes was all these and more, especially a polemicist and persuader, and he wielded a mighty pen. Skidelsky (1992) has argued that there was no centre to the man, that he was a follower of events. The view expressed here is that his ethics, political philosophy and mathematical philosophy all influenced the shape of his economic ideas until finally, in *The General Theory*, there was a unity between theory and policy which expressed his philosophical beliefs.

Keynes' economics was founded on his own observation both of institutions and psychology. This is not the usual way; economics has developed as a logical system based on what are asserted to be self-evident axioms – it is deductive. Keynes' economics was both deductive and inductive, the latter often the product of intuition and thus left implicit. There are examples in the above text: the evolution of the banking system to the point where credit requires no prior saving is the foundation of the shift from investment being determined by savings to its leading position in the determination of income; the psychology of consumption stops the economy from necessarily reaching full employment; the psychology of optimism and pessimism drives both investment and the securities markets.

Keynes' masterwork, *The General Theory of Employment, Interest and Money*, was perhaps too radical for its time, or even for today. It has only recently become appreciated how radical the work really is. Consider the psychological barriers to assimilating its message. It says that:

1. when there is widespread unemployment, workers have no ability to improve their employment prospects, as employment is determined by what employers expect demand to be, and the main element which alters demand from one period to the next is investment, which is also a decision of 'capital';
2. workers can bargain for a money wage, but the price level, and hence their real wage, is determined also by aggregate demand;
3. producers determine investment independently of saving, and households have no control over that element of aggregate demand through the provision of finance;
4. finance is in the hands of bankers, who can create credit with the stroke of a pen and who are as subject to waves of optimism and pessimism as the entrepreneurs;
5. the price of borrowing (the rate of interest) is determined in the market for securities, where speculators care little for the economic fundamentals (productivity or the profit of productive firms) but aim only to make money by outwitting each other and the central bank;
6. the lending which bankers do results in changes in the money supply, over which the public at large has no control, yet the willingness to lend determines employment, output and even future competitiveness.

All these things are true because production is organized along capitalist lines, where the ownership of the means of production is in the hands of a few (see CORPORATE CONTROL). These producers must commit themselves to hiring labour at contractual wages in order to produce for market sale in the future. By definition, the future, and thus the market, is uncertain. The producers therefore take the risk that their decisions will not be profitable – or not as profitable as they had expected. The workers, on the other hand, have uncertain employment and also have no bargaining power over their real wage: 'the market', in aggregate, determines prices and thus the real wage (see LABOUR MARKETS).

The monetary side of Keynes' story also pertains to a specific stage of institutional development. Unlike the classical theory of the rate of interest, which depends on flows of saving and investment, this theory recognizes the importance in advanced economies of markets for secondhand financial assets. This was a gradual but highly significant development. It allows the individual to hold a claim on the profits of business without the risks which are run by the entrepreneurs, who are 'locked in' to their investments and who must run them for profit and, if profits are disappointing, face the risk of bankruptcy. Financial claims are liquid to the individual, though of course they are not liquid for their holders collectively. The advantage to the individual is balanced by the divorce this market creates between long-term profits expected from running the business and the rate of return to the financial players.

The theory also recognizes, albeit implicitly, that bankers have the power to create money and thus to determine, at least in part, both the composition and the level of aggregate income. *The General Theory*, in other words, faces up to the world as it actually is, even if some of its power relations are unpleasant to acknowledge. It is not surprising that a theory which both goes against the established way of doing economics and recognizes some unpleasant facts should have a difficult passage. Almost as soon as the book was published the upholders of tradition began the process of bringing its message back into the fold. Eventually a system of simultaneous equations with past and future obliterated (and therefore uncertainty and expectations) came to represent Keynes' system: this was 'Keynesian economics', with its emphasis on government expenditure, even 'fine tuning', forgetting all of Keynes' caveats. The recovery of Keynes' economics can be said to begin in earnest with Leijonhufvud's 1968 work *On Keynesian Economics and the Economics of Keynes* – they are not at all the same.

9 Conclusion

Keynes demonstrated that in a modern monetary, capitalist economy, the economic system left to itself can produce long-standing unemployment. He concluded that the economic system needs some help if it is to produce the highest level of efficiency while preserving a liberal society. He favoured conscious monetary management, at both the national and the international levels, and some management also of investment, which tended to be short-sighted and capricious if left entirely in private hands. It has to be said that he was unduly optimistic about the selfless motivation of governments.

In the hands of his interpreters, 'Keynesianism' became formulaic. Keynes never relinquished the role of interpretation and judgement in economic affairs.

VICTORIA CHICK
UNIVERSITY COLLEGE LONDON

Further reading

(References cited in the text marked *)

Amadeo, E.J. (1989) *Keynes's Principle of Effective Demand*, Aldershot: Edward Elgar. (Exposition of the economics of *The General Theory* which pays special attention to the relation between that work and the *Treatise on Money*.)

Bryce, R.B. (1977) 'Keynes as seen by his students in the 1930s (i)', in D. Patinkin and J.C. Leith (eds), *Keynes, Cambridge and The General Theory*, London: Macmillan. (Best simple exposition of the basic ideas of *The General Theory*.)

* Carabelli, A.M. (1988) *On Keynes's Method*, London: Macmillan. (Traces the influence of the *Treatise on Probability* on Keynes' method, especially that of *The General Theory*.)

Chick, V. (1983) *Macroeconomics After Keynes: A Reconsideration of the General Theory*, Cambridge, MA: MIT Press. (A reconstruction of the economics of *The General Theory*. Technical but not mathematical.)

* Clarke, P. (1988) *The Keynesian Revolution in the Making*, Oxford: Clarendon Press. (Traces the interplay of Keynes' participation in the Macmillan Committee and the development of the *Treatise on Money*.)

* Fitzgibbons, A. (1988) *Keynes's Vision*, Oxford: Oxford University Press. (Explores Keynes' fundamental philosophy.)

Harcourt, G.C. and Riach, P. (eds) (1996) *Maynard Keynes' General Theory*, 2nd edn, London: Routledge. (Articles commissioned from many Keynes scholars; each has a chapter or topic of *The General Theory* to 'update'. Full bibliography of debates since *The General Theory* was published.)

Harrod, R.F. (1951) *The Life of John Maynard Keynes*, London: Macmillan. (Biography by a distinguished economist, a contemporary of Keynes.)

* Helburn, S.W. (1992) 'On Keynes's ethics', in P. Arestis and V. Chick (eds), *Recent Developments in Post-Keynesian Economics*, Aldershot: Edward Elgar. (Shows the relationship between Keynes' ethics, political philosophy and economics.)

* Kahn, R.F. (1931) 'The relation of home investment to unemployment', *Economic Journal* 41 (162): 173–98. (Original exposition of the multiplier.)

* Keynes, J.M. (1971–89) *The Collected Writings of J. M. Keynes*, 30 vols, eds. D.E. Moggridge and E.A.G. Robinson, London: Macmillan. (Works cited in this entry are contained in the volumes listed: *Indian Currency and Finance*, CW I; *The Economic Consequences of the Peace*, CW II; *A Tract on Monetary Reform*, CW IV; *A Treatise*

on Money, CW V; *The General Theory of Employment, Interest and Money*, CW VII; *Treatise on Probability*, CW VIII; *Can Lloyd George Do It?*, CW IX; *How to Pay for the War*, CW IX.)
* Leijonhufvud, A. (1968) *On Keynesian Economics and the Economics of Keynes*, Oxford: Oxford University Press. (Throws Keynesian economics and Leijonhufvud's interpretation of Keynes in sharp relief. Controversial interpretation.)
Moggridge, D.E. (1980) *Keynes*, 2nd edn, London: Macmillan. (Shorter biography and exposition of the development of Keynes' thought.)
Moggridge, D.E. (1992) *Maynard Keynes: An Economist's Biography*, London: Routledge. (Full, modern biography by the chief editor of Keynes' *Collected Writings*. Strongly based on original sources.)
* O'Donnell, R.M. (1989) *Keynes: Philosophy, Economics and Politics*, London: Macmillan. (Its basic proposition is that Keynes' thought can be perceived as a unity over these three fields of thought.)
Pasinetti, L.L. and Schefold, B. (eds) (1999) *The Impact of Keynes on Economics in the 20th Century*, Cheltenham: Edward Elgar Publishing. (Reconsiders the nature and significance of Keynes' theories and economic policies and contrasts interpretations of his thought, illustrating the diversity of Keynesianism in different European countries throughout the twentieth century.)
* Skidelsky, R. (1983, 1992) *John Maynard Keynes*, 3 vols, London: Macmillan. (Extensive, modern biography.)
Stewart, M. (1993) *Keynes in the 1990s*, London: Penguin Books. (A polemical sequel, of sorts, to the author's 'Keynes and after', looking at the economic policies of the last ten years in a Keynesian light and suggesting that the current recession bears all the hallmarks of the slump of the 1930s.)

See also: BUSINESS ECONOMICS; LABOUR MARKETS; MARSHALL, A.; SAMUELSON, P.A.

Schumpeter, Joseph (1883–1950)

1 Biographical data
2 Main contribution
3 Conclusions

Personal background

- born in Moravia, in what is now the Czech Republic, on 8 February 1883
- studied law at the University of Vienna
- entered economics as a lecturer at Czernowitz
- married three times, to Gladys Ricarde Seaver (1907), Annie Reisinger (1926) and Elizabeth Broody (1937)
- briefly entered politics in 1919 as the finance minister for the new Austrian Republic
- the majority of his career was spent lecturing in economics at Czernowitz, Graz, Bonn and Harvard
- made numerous contributions to the development of economics, including his famous business cycles theory
- died in his sleep on 8 January 1950

Major works

Wesen und Hauptinhalt der Theoretischen Nationalökonomie (1908)
Theorie der Wirtschaftlichen Entwicklung (1912)
The Theory of Economic Development: An Inquiry into Profits, Capital, Interest, and the Business Cycle (1934)
Business Cycles (1939)
Capitalism, Socialism and Democracy (1942)

Summary

In comparison to his contemporaries, Joseph Schumpeter's work is most distinct. His works, particularly his early works, were characterized by a passionate and optimistic style and he had a vision that permeated every piece he wrote. Multilingual, he had a keen interest in history, politics and society. While a sceptic of aggregates, he recognized the importance of the mathematical component of economics. Moreover, he had the ability to incorporate all facets of his broad knowledge of history, politics and mathematics into his writing.

Schumpeter often proposed economic theories that were rejected by his colleagues, namely Walras and Böhm-Bawerk. This was particularly true for his views on interest rates. For example, he believed that interest rates were institutionally and dynamically determined, a view which was in direct conflict with the views of Böhm-Bawerk, who believed interest rates were independent of institutions. Schumpeter argued that because interest rates were institutionally determined they could be zero in a stationary or centrally planned economy.

Schumpeter also proposed that capitalism would falter and be replaced by socialism, another view that was rejected by his colleagues. While some of his contradictory views appeared unfounded, one was brilliant and is undoubtedly Schumpeter's greatest contribution to the development of economics – his business cycle theory. Schumpeter disagreed with the classical economists and demonstrated that the economy was not in a permanent state of equilibrium but rather experienced periods of disequilibrium. Although the classical economists accepted that significant events such as wars were responsible for pushing the economy out of equilibrium, Schumpeter believed more powerful forces worked in the economy to produce these fluctuations.

1 Biographical data

Joseph Schumpeter was born on 8 February 1883 in the province of Moravia, then part of the Austro-Hungarian Empire and now in the Czech Republic. He was the only son of Alois

Schumpeter, Joseph (1883–1950)

Schumpeter, a cloth manufacturer who died when his son was young. His mother remarried to a member of the Austro-Hungarian army at Kalksburg in Vienna in 1893. Schumpeter graduated with high honours in 1901 from the Theresianum, where he acquired a taste for foreign languages and learnt to speak Greek and Latin fluently. His time there, coupled with his exposure to French, English and Italian at home, allowed him to speak a diverse range of languages fluently.

In 1901 Schumpeter enrolled at the University of Vienna as a law student. By 1906 he was a doctor of both Roman and Canon Law. The law degree encompassed units in economics and politics. He practised law for a short time, but realized that his passion was economics. In 1907 he married his first wife, Gladys Ricarde Seaver. In 1909 he was made a professor at Czernowitz, the capital of Bukowina, and later in 1911 accepted a position at the University of Graz where he was head of the economics faculty and offered courses in economic democracy and the problems of the social classes which featured heavily in his work.

Schumpeter's first book was published in 1908 and titled *Wesen und Hauptinhalt der Theoretischen Nationalökonomie*. This was followed in 1912 by *Theorie der Wirtschaftlichen Entwicklung*. These initial books played a vital role in establishing Schumpeter as an economic theorist. His first book introduced his theory of interest; the second book contained an expansion of this idea. In *Wesen und Hauptinhalt* he outlined that there was no direct relationship between the levels of income and savings. As the level of income rises it does not naturally follow that the level of savings will also rise.

One of Schumpeter's greatest contributions to economics was his business cycle theory, the early indicators of which were outlined in his third book, *The Theory of Economic Development: An Inquiry into Profits, Capital, Interest, and the Business Cycle* (1934) an expanded version of *Theorie der Wirtschaftlichen Entwicklung*. Schumpeter's initial publications exhibit characteristics evident in all of his work. While rarely utilizing the mathematical component of economics, he embraced it; however, he never underestimated the importance of historical knowledge in economics.

After his appointment at Graz, he entered politics, albeit briefly, being appointed the finance minister in the socialist cabinet for the new Austrian Republic in 1919. His political career was a learning experience as he had great difficulty in counteracting the excess inflation that plagued post-war Europe. He and the socialists had conflicting views on the direction which the Austrian economy should take and he left politics due to the differences which arose between his conservative economic policies and the socialists' radical economic and financial policies.

Following his foray into politics Schumpeter returned to academia where he remained until his death in 1950. During this time he served at both the University of Bonn in Germany and later at Harvard University. In 1926 he produced a paper that critically analysed the work of Schmoller, and held the position of Chair of Public Finance. The year 1926 was however one of great sorrow for Schumpeter as both his new wife, Annie Reisinger, and his mother died. These blows changed him from a lively optimist to a pessimist.

In 1932 he accepted a full-time position at Harvard, initially living with F.W. Taussig, and in 1937 he married his third wife Elizabeth Broody, who was a fellow economist. Schumpeter was one of the founders of the Econometric Society and its president from 1937 to 1941. A great honour was bestowed upon him in 1948 when he became the first foreign-born president of the American Economic Association. During his time at Harvard he had a full teaching load and wrote *Business Cycles* (1939) and *Capitalism Socialism and Democracy* (1942) before dying on 8 January 1950. His monumental *A History of Economic Analysis* was published after his death.

2 Main contribution

When Schumpeter became interested in economics the classical theory of employment dominated economic thought. The classical economists argued that unemployment never existed and that the economy permanently achieved full employment. Their theory promoted pure capitalism and argued that the economy functioned in the absence of government intervention. The classical economists believed that the economy had built-in stabilizers that ensured the economy always returned to equilibrium, and they emphasized that underspending never occurred due to Say's law, which implied that supply created its own demand.

A neo-classical economist who greatly influenced Schumpeter's work was Böhm-Bawerk, who believed that the accumulation of capital was a simple process which involved few fluctuations. Böhm-Bawerk argued that a proportion of household income that had been saved would be invested. This investment would result in the expansion of the capital base, resulting in increased output, employment and national income. He recognized that fluctuations would occur due to inconsistencies in monetary policy, time lags or vagaries of the multiplier; however, appropriate policies would return the economy to equilibrium.

Schumpeter, however, believed that such fluctuations were not of little significance but rather of great importance to the economy. He argued that the economy was not permanently in a state of equilibrium but rather that it experienced significant fluctuations in economic activity. Schumpeter recognized that periods of low economic activity occurred that were characterized by high unemployment, low profit levels, decreases in the consumption of goods, decreases in business confidence and increases in the level of savings. While agreeing that the multiplier and acceleration principles contributed to these economic fluctuations, more powerful forces acted upon the economy including technological and organizational innovations, entrepreneurial activity and the credit mechanism. One can deduce that Schumpeter's understanding of the forces responsible for change in the economy was greater than that of his neo-classical colleagues.

In his work Schumpeter often outlined the importance of economics in shaping a society, yet his analysis of society is often criticized. Like Karl Marx, he envisaged the destruction of the capitalist economic system (see MARX, K.H.). Schumpeter characterized capitalism by three features: the private ownership of the physical means of production; private profits and private responsibility for losses; and the creation of means of payments – bank notes and bank deposits – by private banks. He argued that the first two features suffice to define private enterprise. However, to Schumpeter no concept of capitalism could be satisfactory without including the set of typically capitalistic phenomena covered by the third.

Schumpeter believed that capitalism, despite its inability to achieve a greater equality in the distribution of income, was a very successful economic system and that it was responsible for greatly increasing the quality and quantity of goods and services consumed by society, leading to an increase in standards of living. However, he believed that capitalism would be destroyed because its success would result in a loss of its social structures. Despite being criticized for this belief, it illustrates the emphasis that Schumpeter placed upon the relationship between economics and society.

Schumpeter proposed a theory of interest rates that was in direct conflict with Böhm-Bawerk. He argued that a zero interest rate would exist in a static, semi-stationary or socialist economy. Moreover, to him, the rate of interest was institutionally and dynamically determined. This point conflicted with the view upheld by Böhm-Bawerk, who declared that the rate of interest was a basic economic category, independent of the concrete social and institutional arrangements. Schumpeter's interest theory is often criticized.

3 Conclusions

Joseph Schumpeter was a brilliant economist whose economic principles were revolutionary. While in academia he produced his great works, *The Theory of Economic Development, Capitalism, Socialism and Democracy* and *Business Cycles*. In these texts Schumpeter outlined his major contributions to economics, namely his theories on interest, capitalism and business cycles. His business cycle theory contradicted the accepted view that the economy was permanently in a state of equilibrium. Rather he argued that dynamic forces such as technological and organizational innovations, entrepreneurial activity and the credit mechanism are the primary causes of fluctuations in the economy.

JOHN CUNNINGHAM WOOD
EDITH COWAN UNIVERSITY
AUSTRALIA

Further reading

(References cited in the text marked *)

* Schumpeter, J. (1908) *Wesen und Hauptinhalt der Theoretischen Nationalökonomie*, Munich and Leipzig: Duncker and Humblot. (Contains Schumpeter's theory of interest and argues that there was no direct relationship between the level of income and savings.)
* Schumpeter, J. (1912) *Theorie der Wirtschaftlichen Entwicklung*, Leipzig: Duncker and Humblot. (Expands on his theory of interest rates and argues that as the level of income rises it does not naturally follow that the level of savings will also rise.)
* Schumpeter, J. (1934) *The Theory of Economic Development: An Inquiry into Profits, Capital, Interest, and the Business Cycle*, Cambridge, MA: Harvard University Press. (English language and revised edition of Schumpeter's 1912 book, containing his business cycle theory and his analysis of how economic growth occurs.)
* Schumpeter, J. (1939) *Business Cycles*, New York: McGraw-Hill. (Expands on his early ideas and highlights the critical role of entrepreneurs in the cyclical nature of economic development.)
* Schumpeter, J. (1942) *Capitalism, Socialism and Democracy*, New York: Harper and Brothers. (Integrates Schumpeter's political philosophy with his views on economics and provides an analysis of trends in capitalist and socialist political states.)
* Schumpeter, J. (1951) *A History of Economic Analysis*, New York: Oxford University Press. (Published after his death, this is an exhaustive survey of the development of economic ideas and analyses.)

Means, Gardiner Coit (1896–1988)

1 Introduction
2 Main contributions
3 Evaluation
4 Conclusions

Personal background

- born on 8 June 1896 in Windham, Connecticut, USA
- obtained a BA degree in chemistry and a PhD in economics from Harvard University in 1918 and 1933 respectively
- married Caroline F. Ware, 1927
- developed the doctrine of administered prices
- influenced the development of national economic planning
- formative influence on post-Keynesian economics
- died quietly at home on 15 February 1988

Major works

The Modern Corporation and Private Property (with Adolf A. Berle) (1933)
Industrial Prices and Their Relative Inflexibility (1935)
The Structure of the American Economy, part I: *Basic Characteristics* (1939)
Pricing Power and the Public Interest (1962)

Summary

Means developed the doctrine of administered prices as an alternative theory to orthodox economic theory. His primary contributions within the doctrine were administered prices, administrative inflation, the modern corporation and the necessity for government guidance of economic activity. He also contributed significantly to the development of indicative national economic planning.

1 Introduction

Means was born on 8 June 1896 in Windham, Connecticut. He entered Harvard at the age of eighteen, majoring in chemistry. With the outbreak of war in 1917, Means left Harvard to enlist in the Army and was eventually assigned to the Aviation Section of the Signals Corps where he spent his time learning how to fly aeroplanes. Upon his discharge in January 1919, he joined the Near East Relief, an organization dealing with Armenian refugees, and went off to Turkey. As part of his job in Turkey, Means had to obtain supplies from local markets which required him to engage in price and quantity bargaining with the merchants. Thus, he experienced at first hand a market situation in which prices were determined in the course of carrying out the transaction itself. Returning to the USA in 1920, Means entered Lowell Textile School to study wool manufacturing. After two years of study, he left and set up Means Weave Shop to make a high-quality (and high-priced) handwoven blanket of his own design. Through running the enterprise, Means became well acquainted with the Boston wool market and the textile machinery market; he quickly surmised that US industrial life was very different from what he had experienced in Turkey.

While still managing his textile enterprise, Means enrolled as a graduate student in Harvard's Department of Economics in 1924. His subsequent exposure to economic theory convinced him that it had little relevance to the modern corporatist economy of the USA in the twentieth century. After receiving his MA in 1927, Adolf Berle recruited him to work on his research project on the modern corporation. The outcome of the collaboration was *The Modern Corporation and Private Property* (1933) in which Means contributed the tripartite distinction between ownership, control and management and the economic arguments regarding the implications of:

1 the separation of ownership from control for the traditional theoretical roles of private property, wealth and the profit motive in directing economic activity and increasing social welfare;
2 enterprise size for costs;
3 enterprise size for the coordination of economic activities by the forces of supply and demand in the marketplace.

His work on the modern corporation also became the basis of his doctoral dissertation which he was awarded by Harvard in 1933.

Shortly after President Franklin D. Roosevelt took office in 1933, Means was recruited to a position of Economic Advisor on Finance to Henry Wallace, the Secretary of Agriculture. In taking the position, Means took it for granted that he would be trying to develop policies and instruments that would make the economy work more effectively. However, he found that his suggestions were not taken seriously by the policy makers. Therefore, he undertook an empirical study of wholesale prices and used the results to explain why Roosevelt's economic policies failed to produce economic recovery. The study was published in 1935 as *Industrial Prices and their Relative Inflexibility*. The impact of the study on the thinking of economists and policy makers was significant and Means used this fame to get transferred to the National Resources Committee, which had been set up to engage in indicative national economic planning. While at the committee he initiated a research project to develop a model of the US economy that could be used for economic planning. The fruits of the project were published in *The Structure of the American Economy*, part I: *Basic Characteristics* (1939). However, the rise in popularity of US Keynesianism resulted in the project being closed down before Means was able to fully develop the model (see KEYNES, J.M.).

After leaving the National Resources Committee, Means obtained the position of Associate Director of Research for the Committee for Economic Development, a business-sponsored, private research group originally concerned with government policies to ensure a full-employment transition to a peacetime economy. While at the Committee he instigated the collection of statistical series on money flows, now regularly published by the Federal Reserve Board in its flow of funds accounts. Means retired from the Committee in 1958 and spent his remaining years writing and lecturing on the modern corporate enterprise, its impact upon the economy and public welfare and its destructive implications for orthodox economic theory (Means 1962a; 1962b). He also testified before congressional committees on administered prices and administrative inflation. Means died quietly at home on 15 February 1988.

2 Main contributions

Means believed that the advent of the large modern corporation rendered many of the fundamental concepts of orthodox economics obsolete, with the result that new concepts had to be forged and a new picture of economic relationships created. In pursuing this agenda he developed the concepts of administered prices and administrative inflation and developed an alternative theory to orthodox economics, his doctrine of administered prices. The doctrine delineated the forces that affect the coordination of economic activity and determined the actual manner in which the modern corporate economy operated (see NEO-CLASSICAL ECONOMICS). In particular, instead of having all prices in the economy determined in their particular markets, Means had some determined in the market and the rest of the prices in the economy determined by corporate management and administered to the market. Consequently, when deficient demand shocks hit the economy, prices in the market sector would fall, thereby, in principle, maintaining output levels, whereas prices in the administered sector would remain relatively stable while output fell. Since the US corporate economy contained both sectors, Means argued that their interaction with regard to a deficient demand shock would produce a striking decline of prices in the market sector and a striking decline in production and hence unemployment in the administered sector. Thus, for Means, the stability of non-market-determined administered market prices was the primary reason for the breakdown in the coordination of economic activities which turned business fluctuations from being the dance-of-prices to a production and employment phenomenon.

Given the economic relationships embodied in the doctrine – such as administered prices, administrative inflation, target rate of return pricing, market power and non-market control of economic activity – Means emphasized their human and institutional nature and hence their amenability by social action. For example, given the existence of administered prices, Means argued that a serious deficiency of buying was unlikely to be corrected by any of the economic forces inherent in a modern economy in such a way as to bring about the full use of resources. Thus he concluded that the under-utilization of economic resources was a problem of social organization which could only be corrected through social or government industrial policy making.

The need for government involvement in guiding economic activity in order to avoid unemployment and thereby enhancing the quality of human life comes out clearly in Means' advocacy of indicative national economic planning. The call for economic planning was frequently heard during the interwar period, in part because of the apparent success of the five-year plans in the Soviet Union. Means also called for national economic planning, but with a democratic twist. Economic planning involved, he argued, the development of a range of different plans, each of which would bring about and maintain the full employment of the nation's economic resources; and the elected representatives would choose the plan which best fulfilled their political objectives. To back up his methodological approach to planning, Means endeavoured to develop a model of the US economy which could, for example, be used to determine the pattern of consumption, resource use and labour employment at different levels of national income. Although Means was unable to develop the model fully, he did develop the first multi-sector statistical model of the US economy, which also had the distinction of actually being used for planning purposes to determine the amount of capital equipment required by the iron and steel industry over the existing equipment at various levels of consumer income.

3 Evaluation

Orthodox economists' evaluations of Means' contributions to economics centre on administered prices, administrative inflation and the separation of ownership from control. Generally, orthodox economists question the empirical existence of administered prices and administrative inflation. The most noted attack on the former came from George Stigler and James Kindahl in their book *The Behavior of Industrial Prices* (1970). Upon examining the transaction price data which was collected especially for their study, Stigler and Kindahl claimed that it did not support the existence of administered prices. Means, Denis Carlton (1986) and others analysed the same price data and came to the opposite conclusion. As for the latter, various economists produced econometric studies which purported to show that price increases were weakly if at all correlated with industrial concentration and therefore claimed that administrative inflation did not exist. However, none of them realized that what they were testing was not Means' administrative inflation thesis, but something quite different.

For many years after Means had introduced the possibility that the separation of ownership from control might have an impact on the motivation of business leaders, it was commonly argued that where the separation did not exist, the owner attempted to maximize its profits, while for enterprises where it did exist the business leaders attempted to maximize growth, pursue satisfactory profit or engage in some other non-profit-maximizing behaviour. Means actually did not think that the separation of ownership from control had any impact upon the motivation of business leaders; so for him, whether business leaders attempted to maximize their profits or not depended more on empirical observation and the social and institutional nature of the corporate enterprise. Yet, since the 1970s orthodox economists have sought to refute Means' supposed claim, utilizing agency theory and thereby dismissing this contribution to economics. Thus, while orthodox economists grudgingly admit that Means had something interesting to say in a historical sense, they do not believe that he made any really important contributions to economics.

Non-orthodox economists such as post-Keynesians and institutionalists have a more positive evaluation of Means' contributions to economics. At a general level, they consider his analysis of the modern corporation as seminal and relevant as long as corporate capitalism exists; and accept the existence of administered prices and administrative inflation and Means' analysis of their impact on the coordination of economic activity. Moreover, they accept Means' dictum that the existence of the modern corporation requires a complete restructuring of economic theory and consider his doctrine of administered prices as contributing significantly to the reconstruction process. The post-Keynesians and institutionalists fully accept Means' economic arguments for the necessity of government involvement in guiding economic activity if full employment is to be achieved; they also fully accept his ethical position that opposing government involvement in the economy is immoral in that by doing so many members of society would be condemned to a life of misery (Samuels and Medema 1990).

At a more particular level, the institutionalists found Means' ideas on the corporation (specifically, concentration and size, the dispersion of stock ownership and the separation of control), the corporate system, the changing meaning of private property, the economy as a system of power and the corporation as private government very important and useful. His analysis of administered prices and the role of inflexible, administered prices in macroeconomic coordination failures, while somewhat in conflict with Keynes, has been readily accepted by post-Keynesians and institutionalists. However, recent work suggests that the empirical evidence used by Means does not support the proposition that administered prices contribute to macroeconomic coordination failure (Lee and Downward 1999).

4 Conclusions

Means developed the doctrine of administered prices as an alternative theory to orthodox economic theory. His primary contributions within the doctrine were administered prices, administrative inflation, the modern corporation and the necessity for government guidance of economic activity. He also contributed significantly to the development of indicative national economic planning.

While Means' contributions to economics have been depreciated by orthodox economists, they have, conversely, been well received by post-Keynesians and institutionalists. By reason of his iconoclastic personality, Means developed his doctrine without attempting to create a school of followers; yet his ideas have influenced and affected the theories and arguments of economists, orthodox or not, for over 60 years.

FREDERIC S. LEE
UNIVERSITY OF MISSOURI AT KANSAS CITY

Further reading

(References cited in the text marked *)

* Berle, A.A. and Means, G.C. (1933) *The Modern Corporation and Private Property*, New York: Macmillan. (Means' classical study of the modern corporation and its consequences for economic theory.)
* Carlton, D.W. (1986) 'The rigidity of prices', *American Economic Review* 76 (4): 637–58. (Re-examines the Stigler and Kindahl price data and concludes that administered prices exist.)

Lee, F.S. (1990) 'From multi-industry planning to Keynesian planning: Gardiner Means, the American Keynesians, and national economic planning at the National Resources Committee', *Journal of Policy History* 2 (2): 186–212. (Covers Means' work at the National Resources Committee and his model of the US economy.)

Lee, F.S. (1998) *Post Keynesian Price Theory*, Cambridge: Cambridge Univesity Press. (Covers Means's writing of *Industrial Prices* and delineates his doctrine of administered prices.)

Lee, F.S. (1999) 'Administered price hypothesis and the dominance of neoclassical price theory: the case of the *Industrial Prices* dispute', *Research in the History of Economic Thought and Methodology* 17: 23–42. (Examines the controversy surrounding Stigler's and Kindahl's claim that administered prices do not exist.)

* Lee, F.S. and Downward, P. (1999) 'Re-testing Gardiner Means' evidence on administered prices', *Journal of Economic Issues*, 33 (4). (Re-tests the empirical evidence used by Means

and finds that it supports the existence of administered prices but little else.)
* Means, G.C. (1935) *Industrial Prices and their Relative Inflexibility*, Washington, DC: GPO. (In this work Means first introduced the concept of administered prices; reprinted in *The Heterodox Economics of Gardiner C. Means: A Collection*.)
* Means, G.C. (1939) *The Structure of the American Economy*, part I: *Basic Characteristics*, Washington, DC: GPO. (Means' most articulate conception of the US economy.)
* Means, G.C. (1962a) *The Corporate Revolution in America*, New York: Crowell-Collier Press. (Contains mostly essays on administered prices, administrative inflation and economic policy.)
* Means, G.C. (1962b) *Pricing Power and the Public Interest*, New York: Harper & Brothers. (Means' best theoretical analysis of the corporate enterprise and its impact on the public interest.)
Means, G.C. (1991) *The Heterodox Economics of Gardiner C. Means: A Collection*, F.S. Lee and W.J. Samuels (eds), Armonk, NY: M.E. Sharpe. (A collection of Means' published and unpublished articles and papers.)
Means, G.C. (1994) *A Monetary Theory of Employment*, W.J. Samuels and F.S. Lee (eds), Armonk, NY: M.E. Sharpe. (An anti-Keynesian theory of employment written in 1947.)
* Samuels, W.J. and Medema, S.G. (1990) *Gardiner C. Means' Institutional and Post-Keynesian Economics: An Interpretation and Assessment*, Armonk, NY: M.E. Sharpe. (An interpretative survey of Means' contributions to economics.)
* Stigler, G.J. and Kindahl, J.K. (1970) *The Behavior of Industrial Prices*, New York: National Bureau of Economic Research. (A well-known empirical study, which concluded that administered prices do not exist.)

See also: GROWTH OF THE FIRM AND NETWORKING; INSTITUTIONAL ECONOMICS

Galbraith, John Kenneth (1908–)

1 Introduction
2 Main contribution to economics
3 Conclusions

Personal background

- born 15 October 1908 at Iona Station, Ontario, Canada, the son of a farmer and liberal politician
- educated in all branches of agriculture at Ontario Agricultural College, now the University of Guelph, 1926–31, graduating with distinction
- PhD student at Berkeley, University of California, 1931–4
- instructor at Harvard University, 1934–7
- acquires US citizenship and marries Kitty (Catherine Merriam) Atwater, 1937
- Social Science Council fellowship at University of Cambridge, 1937
- assistant professor at Princeton University, 1939–40
- head of economic research of the American Farm Bureau Federation, Chicago, 1940
- US price controller at the Office of Price Administration and Civilian Supply, 1941–3
- journalist then an editor of *Fortune* magazine, 1943 and 1946–8
- director of the US Strategic Bombing Survey, 1943–6
- Professor of Economics, Harvard University, 1948–75; Paul M. Warburg Professor of Economics, 1960–75
- US Ambassador to India, 1961–3
- President of the American Economic Association, 1972

Major works

A Theory of Price Control (1952)
American Capitalism: The Concept of Countervailing Power (1952)
The Affluent Society (1958)
Economic Development (1964)
The New Industrial State (1967)
Economics and the Public Purpose (1973)
A Life in Our Times (1981)
A History of Economics: The Past as the Present (1987)

Summary

John Kenneth Galbraith, who was born in 1908, is the most famous of twentieth-century American institutionalist economists. One of the first American converts to Keynesianism, he has consistently argued that governments should control the level of aggregate demand, using a mixture of fiscal policy and price and income controls. Much of his work, like that of an earlier institutionalist Thorstein Veblen (1857–1929) (see VEBLEN, T.B.), has attempted to explore the implications of the dominant role of corporations in modern economies. Surrounding the core of his work has been a study of economic development and the history of economic thought. The fluency of his pen has given him the status of a modern economic guru.

1 Introduction

Galbraith grew up in Ontario where his father, of Scottish descent, farmed, managed an insurance company and participated in the local Liberal Party. He was educated at the local Ontario Agricultural College (later Guelph University), studying a wide range of theoretical and practical agricultural subjects. It was there he discovered his major talent – writing – by contributing columns on agriculture to the local press.

His long career in economics took off when he became a PhD student at Berkeley, California, in 1931. He broadened his interests by researching into the structure of California's county government and by taking graduate courses in economics. In his first academic position, as an assistant to the Professor of

Agricultural Economics at Harvard in 1934, he again reached out into a wider study of economics, espousing the new macroeconomics of John Maynard Keynes (see KEYNES, J.M.). In 1937, he took up a Social Sciences Research Council fellowship at Cambridge where, unable to work with Keynes who was then recuperating from a heart attack, he gained from association with other leading macroeconomists there, including Michel Kalecki (1899–1970), Richard Kahn (1905–89) and Piero Sraffa (1898–1983). Much of his time in Cambridge Galbraith spent in private reading: 'I penetrated the thicket of the technical controversy surrounding Keynes's work and became one of the acknowledged oracles' (Galbraith 1981: 77). After Cambridge the Galbraiths travelled extensively in Europe and in 1939, he took up an assistant professorship at Princeton, soon to be interrupted by the demands of war work.

With the experience of price control work for the US National Defense Advisory Council in 1940, he was appointed to the powerful position of controller of prices in the USA at the Office of Production Management, occupying that key position from 1940 to 1943. His work on price control made possible his most theoretical work, *A Theory of Price Control* (1952) and led him thereafter to recommend prices and incomes policies. For the rest of the Second World War, he put to good use his growing literary talents, first as a journalist, then editor at *Fortune* magazine. His period in journalism was interrupted by his work in 1945 for the US Strategic Bombing Survey in Germany and Japan. He interviewed leading Germans, including Albert Speer, and concluded that bombing had been less successful than claimed in bringing the war to a conclusion.

He departed from *Fortune* in 1948. Back at Harvard, he resumed his academic career as an economics lecturer and Director of Agricultural and Marketing Research; after a year, he became a professor in economics, in 1960 he moved to the endowed Paul M. Warburg chair and retired in 1975. He has been a generous benefactor to Harvard giving the royalties of the second edition of *The Affluent Society* for the establishment of the Galbraith Teaching Prize and to the Fogg Art Museum a collection of miniatures. Although Harvard remained his base for decades, he developed his twin interests of Democratic Party politics and commentating on modern economies.

Before the Second World War he had campaigned for Franklin Roosevelt and had become a friend of the Kennedys through being tutor to Jack Kennedy at Harvard. Galbraith's talents as a speech writer were used in presidential campaigns by both Adlai Stevenson in 1952 and by John Kennedy in 1960. In 1961, Galbraith was appointed US Ambassador to India. This led to a new interest, economic development, which he explained to his Indian hosts and wrote about in many subsequent works. Opposed to growing involvement in the Vietnam War, Galbraith returned to Harvard in 1963. Subsequently he continued to work in presidential elections for the Democrats, even speaking for Clinton in 1992.

Galbraith's dissatisfaction with the working of market economies and his devotion to Keynesianism formed the basis for a series of highly successful books. At the core of his distinctive contribution to economics was his trilogy *The Affluent Society* (1958), *The New Industrial State* (1967) and *Economics and the Public Purpose* (1973). But his influence has not been limited to his writings. For decades he has been a popular lecturer throughout the world and the confidant of many leading politicians.

2 Main contribution to economics

Although he began his career as an agricultural economist, he quickly appreciated the significance of Keynesian macroeconomics. As early as 1939 in a discussion of farm income he emphasized the importance of the level of national income. His preference for fiscal policy over monetary policy and the efficacy of public works as a means of achieving full employment was stated as early as 1940.

His experience as a price controller in 1941–3 led to his reflections on the theoretical basis for price controls. In 1952 in *A Theory of Price Control*, Galbraith argued that price controls are needed to supplement the incentives and compulsions of an unplanned, disequilibrium economy. Not only is inflation checked, but unused resources are employed if direct price controls are used. However, Galbraith asserted that these controls must be used in conjunction with other macroeconomic policies.

In *American Capitalism* (1952) his controversial analysis of the modern corporation began (see CORPORATE CONTROL). He claimed that oligopoly had replaced the competitive environment true of the nineteenth century. With the growth of industrial concentration, the only check to corporations was the 'countervailing power' of trade unions and major purchasers of intermediate products, for example, car firms buying steel. This countervailing power, Galbraith claims, has given the economy the capacity for autonomous self-regulation. In such a decentralized economy the state is left with the roles of influencing the level of demand and restraining inflation through price controls. In *The New Industrial State* (1967) he claimed that the large corporations of the USA constitute the 'new industrial system'. The corporations are run by their managers, not their owners, who have created a 'technostructure' based on modern technology and planning. Through vertical integration, corporations are able to plan: this planning supersedes the market and eliminates uncertainty. Instead of seeking to maximize profits, modern corporations are concerned primarily with their survival and expansion. Consumer sovereignty is replaced by market control by corporations. To make the planning of corporations possible, the state has to control the level of aggregate demand through maintaining an adequate level of government expenditure. Galbraith modified this corporate view of the US economy in *Economics and the Public Purpose* (1973) by integrating small businesses into his analysis. Recognizing that smaller firms have little control over prices, Galbraith recommended exemption of the small business sector from anti-trust laws so that they could combine to stabilize prices and output.

His most famous work, *The Affluent Society* (1958), which long remained a best seller, argued that Keynesianism had wrongly developed into the philosophy of attempting to cure all social ills by the expansion of production. To maintain growth in production, firms have to create wants through advertising and marketing techniques; to maintain purchasing power, consumer debt has to rise, unchecked by monetary and fiscal policies. The promotion of private production is at the expense of the public sector, creating the social imbalance of private affluence and public squalor. In a vivid passage Galbraith describes the fate of a family taking their new automobile out for a picnic:

> They picnic on exquisitely packaged food from a portable icebox by a polluted stream and go on to spend the night at a park which is a menace to public health and morals. Just before dozing off on an air-mattress, beneath a nylon tent, amid the stench of decaying refuse, they may reflect vaguely on the curious unevenness of their blessings.
> (Galbraith 1958: 197)

The imbalance could be removed only by a change in the taxation system which keeps the growth in public revenues in line with the expansion of private incomes.

In *The Culture of Contentment* (1992), Galbraith returns to a broad social theme. He argues that the majority of the population consists of the economically and socially fortunate and it is under threat from the short-termism of economic policy, unpopular military action and the possibility of a revolt by the urban underclass. Only a return to strong Keynesian fiscal policy to keep recessions at bay and to improve cities can solve current problems.

Galbraith's experiences in India in the early 1960s gave him an interest in economic development. In *Economic Development in Perspective* (1962) and in its revised version *Economic Development* (1964) he argued for the formation of national plans which are appropriate to a particular stage of economic development with a balanced increase in the capital stock and technical development. A good plan has a strategy which combines the visible (capital plant), the invisible (sound management methods) and a theory of consumption (which determines the appropriate range of consumer goods to be available).

From the time of his postgraduate studies, Galbraith has maintained an interest in the history of economic thought, attempting to make sense of the Marshallian economics in which he was trained and of the Keynesian revolution through which he lived (see MARSHALL, A.). In his late work, *A History of Economics: The Past as the Present* (1987) Galbraith interweaves economic history and economic thought to demonstrate: 'Economic ideas, as Keynes averred, do guide policy. But the ideas are also the offspring of policy and of the interests which it serves' (Galbraith 1987: 299). To some extent in these words Galbraith is summarizing much of his own work.

3 Conclusions

The frequent generalizations and absence of modern analysis of data have inevitably exposed Galbraith to considerable criticism from both economists and business leaders. The air of authority which permeates Galbraith's work soon disperses when more detailed empirical works are considered alongside. The most authoritative critique of Galbraith is that by Friedman (1977). He aims blow after blow at the central ideas of the Galbraithian system. *The Affluent Society* is attacked for denigrating the tastes of ordinary people and ignoring the huge expansion of government expenditure. The propositions of *American Capitalism* are ruthlessly dissected: big business and unions are often allies rather than opponents generating countervailing power, as Galbraith claims; concentrations of power are in fact often unstable, as has happened with cartels. The empirical finding that the profits of large corporations are often more variable than the average for all quoted corporations is stated to refute much of *The New Industrial State*. The concept of 'countervailing power' has also been mercilessly dissected by other authors so that Galbraith has been forced to bow to his critics. Sharpe (1973), for example, argued that countervailing power is a feeble substitute for the market as it does not allocate property, regulate prices optimally, eliminate poverty or provide amenities and public services.

Allen (1967) uses his knowledge as an industrial economist to refute Galbraith's generalizations about the working of the US economy. In particular, he contradicts the ideas that large firms are more innovative than small and medium-sized firms, that large companies are immune from external pressures on their profits and that consumers are passive. Galbraith's view that corporate planning succeeds in prescribing the future volume of production, demand and prices of particular goods is without evidence.

Galbraith scores highly in the Social Science Citation Index but is not widely taught in graduate schools, perhaps because he has been too multidisciplinary in his approach to economics and at odds with the formal economic model building dominating modern economic theorizing. But despite being unanalytical and often careless in his judgements, he has within his great readership some academic followers, especially among institutionalist, radical and post-Keynesian economists – and even a hostile mainstream critic, Friedman, praises Galbraith for being the only person to write a theory of price control. Arthur M. Schlesinger, Jr., the US historian, sums up Galbraith as 'the great economist, social philosopher, politician, diplomat, satirist, novelist, wit, bon vivant, and generous-hearted friend at work and at play'.

DONALD RUTHERFORD
UNIVERSITY OF EDINBURGH

Further reading

(References cited in the text marked *)

* Allen, G.C. (1967) *Economic Fact and Fantasy*, occasional paper 14, London: Institute of Economic Affairs. (A detailed refutation of the assumptions Galbraith makes about business behaviour.)
Breit, W. (1984) 'Galbraith and Friedman: two versions of economic reality', *Journal of Post-Keynesian Economics* 7: 18–29. (The artistry of Galbraith is contrasted with Friedman's monetarist methodology.)
Colander, D. (1984) 'Galbraith and the theory of price control', *Journal of Post-Keynesian Economics* 7: 30–42. (Argues that Galbraith's theory is too classical and ignores the permanence of excess supply.)
* Friedman, M. (1977) *From Galbraith to Economic Freedom*, occasional paper 49, London: Institute of Economic Affairs. (Critical of the weak empiricism of Galbraith's works but appreciative of his price control analysis.)

* Galbraith, J.K. (1952a) *A Theory of Price Control*, Cambridge, MA: Harvard University Press. (Argues that price controls are needed to supplement the incentives and compulsions of an unplanned, disequilibrium economy.)
* Galbraith, J.K. (1952b) *American Capitalism: The Concept of Countervailing Power*, Boston, MA: Houghton Mifflin. (Controversial analysis of the modern corporation; claims that oligopoly had replaced the competitive environment true of the nineteenth century.)
* Galbraith, J.K. (1958) *The Affluent Society*, Boston, MA: Houghton Mifflin. (Argues that Keynesianism had wrongly developed into the philosophy of attempting to cure all social ills by the expansion of production.)
* Galbraith, J.K. (1962) *Economic Development in Perspective*, Cambridge, MA: Harvard University Press. (Argues for the formation of national plans which are appropriate to a particular stage of economic development with a balanced increase in the capital stock and technical development.)
* Galbraith, J.K. (1964) *Economic Development*, Cambridge, MA: Harvard University Press. (Revision of *Economic Development in Perspective*.)
* Galbraith, J.K. (1967) *The New Industrial State*, Boston, MA: Houghton Mifflin. (Claims that the large corporations of the USA constitute the 'new industrial system'.)
* Galbraith, J.K. (1973) *Economics and the Public Purpose*, Boston, MA: Houghton Mifflin. (Recommends the exemption of the small business sector from anti-trust laws so that they could combine to stabilize prices and output.)
* Galbraith, J.K. (1981) *A Life in Our Times*, Boston, MA: Houghton Mifflin. (A detailed autobiographical account of his education, writing and political career over seven decades.)
* Galbraith, J.K. (1987) *A History of Economics: The Past as the Present*, London: Hamish Hamilton. (Uses economic history and economic thought to demonstrate how economic ideas guide policy.)
* Galbraith, J.K. (1992) *The Culture of Contentment*, Boston, MA: Houghton Mifflin. (Describes the modern phenomenon of the contented wealthy: a large class of affluent people who have no short-term interest in using their resources to help the poorer classes.)
Galbraith, J.K. (1994) *The World Economy Since The Wars: A Personal View*, Boston, MA: Houghton Mifflin. (Traces the economic history of the twentieth century.)
Hession, C.H. (1972) *John Kenneth Galbraith and His Critics*, New York: W.W. Norton & Co. Inc. (A review of the principal criticisms of Galbraithian notions of countervailing power and competition.)
Lamson, P. (1991) *Speaking of Galbraith: A Personal Portrait*, New York: Ticknor & Fields. (A sympathetic account of his life, main books and their reception.)
McFadzean, Sir F. (1977) *The Economics of John Kenneth Galbraith: A Study in Fantasy*, London: Centre for Policy Studies. (An attack on the methodology of his analysis of the corporation.)
Reisman, D. (1980) *Galbraith and Market Capitalism*, London: Macmillan. (Demonstrates that Galbraith's contribution to economics is modest, apart from work on price control.)
Samuels, W.J. (1984) 'Galbraith on economics as a system of professional belief', *Journal of Post-Keynesian Economics* 7: 61–76. (Galbraithian economics is based on beliefs not empirical truths, as a shield for power.)
* Sharpe, M.E. (1973) *John Kenneth Galbraith and the Lower Economics*, London: Macmillan. (Emphasizes that Galbraith is influential as a social critic but erroneous in much of his economics.)

See also: CORPORATE CONTROL; KEYNES, J.M.; MARSHALL, A.

Coase, Ronald (1910–)

1 Introduction
2 Biographical data
3 Main contribution
4 Evaluation
5 Conclusion

Personal background

- Born 29 December 1910, Willesden, UK
- Studied at the London School of Economics
- Greatly influenced by Arnold Plant
- Applied economic analysis to the structure of business
- Worked in the USA after 1951
- Used economics to analyse legal institutions
- Joined the University of Chicago Law School in 1964
- Developed work on economic regulation
- Awarded the Nobel Prize for economics in 1991

Major works

'The nature of the firm' (1937)
'The problem of social cost' (1960)

Summary

Coase used economics to analyse the structure of institutions. He was the first economist explicitly to propose that the structure of business was determined by transactions costs. The organization of production within a firm saves on the costs of contracting with outsiders but it substitutes problems of internal control. This trade-off between external transactions costs and internal organization costs determines the size and scope of the enterprise. Coase also applied transactions cost analysis to problems of pollution and social costs more generally. He noted that systems of regulation or taxation which prevented people from coming to agreements with each other might be disadvantageous for society as a whole. From this insight flowed the modern economic analysis of tort law and of government regulation.

1 Introduction

The theme running through Coase's work is that institutional arrangements affect transactions costs and that these play an important part in determining economic results. Without transactions costs the structure of institutions would not matter. In practice, the way property rights are assigned and the costs of trading them matter a great deal.

2 Biographical data

Born in Willesden, North London, in 1910, Coase studied commerce at the London School of Economics (LSE), where he was influenced by Arnold Plant. He travelled to the USA in 1931 on a scholarship to study why the structure of firms varied across industries. The resulting paper was eventually published in 1937. Coase taught at the LSE until 1951 and worked at the offices of the War Cabinet (1941–6). Thereafter Coase left for the USA and worked at the State University of New York at Buffalo (1951–8), Stanford University (1958), the University of Virginia (1959) and finally the University of Chicago Law School (1964–81). In Chicago, Coase edited the *Journal of Law and Economics*. He was awarded the Nobel Prize for Economics in 1991.

3 Main contribution

In the early 1930s, there was no established theory to explain why some firms were highly vertically integrated – making their own components, distributing their own products and developing their own supplies of raw materials – while others were more specialized – using market contracts with other firms to obtain supplies and sell their output (see NEO-

CLASSICAL ECONOMICS). Similarly, no explanation existed for the fact that some firms produced a wide range of different goods while others were much more specialized. A descriptive taxonomy of firms existed – a set of boxes labelled 'vertically', 'horizontally' or 'laterally' integrated – but no explanation of the forces which might determine why firms adopt one form of organization rather than another (see MANAGERIAL THEORIES OF THE FIRM).

Coase's answer to this question, formulated on his trip to the USA and published in his 1937 paper 'The nature of the firm', was couched in very general terms and was ultimately to prove very fruitful. Activities were undertaken within firms rather than across markets when this was the less costly option. There is a cost of using the price mechanism which organization within the firm can avoid. Within the firm, resources are allocated by the conscious decision and authority of an entrepreneur or manager. People, when they join a firm, agree to be 'organized'. The use of market contracts requires the investment of time and resources in information gathering and contract negotiation and renegotiation, which can be cut down within the firm. Relations within the firm are characterized by durable contracts whose terms do not attempt to establish what is required of the parties in every detail. Coase sees the entrepreneur as the centre of a set of such contracts. Other people in the firm have contracts with the entrepreneur rather than with each other and this reduces the number of contractual links that have to be negotiated.

In his 1937 paper, Coase thus set out the modern 'nexus of contracts' view of the firm. In the process, he applied the most basic economic concepts of opportunity cost and substitution at the margin. The whole economy was not organized as a single firm because the costs of internal organization would rise with size and scope. The market and the firm were substitute mechanisms for achieving the coordination of resources (see GROWTH OF THE FIRM AND NETWORKING). Some activities would be much less costly to organize internally, while in the case of others the market might have clear advantages. With some activities, the decision would be finely judged and these marginal cases would be located at the boundary of the firm and the market.

There are close connections between Coase's early work on the firm and his later work on social costs. Indeed, the impact of the latter in 1960 encouraged a reappraisal of the former, which had been, until that point, admired but not used as the basis of further research. His 1960 paper, 'The problem of social cost', had a profound influence on the way economists thought about spill-over effects or 'externalities' (see MARSHALL, A.). The standard approach at the time was that the existence of some harmful effect associated with an activity – such as noise or air pollution – required the government to impose a tax on the offending activity equal at the margin to the value of the damage caused. This policy was linked to the economist A.C. Pigou.

Coase pointed out that this type of policy recommendation entirely ignored the possibility that people could come to voluntary agreements about such harmful activities. A person suffering from the noise of a neighbour might bribe the neighbour to reduce it, to confine it to certain times of the day or to erect sound-insulating barriers. These abatement activities would be carried to the point at which the marginal benefit of further peace and quiet to the purchaser was just equal to the extra cost of achieving it. Alternatively, the noisy person could purchase the consent of the sensitive neighbour to tolerate the noise. He or she might start by simply bribing the neighbour to accept small amounts of noise and then continue by erecting sound-insulating screens when these become cheaper than further bribes to the neighbour. Eventually, the benefit of making more noise will be less than the cost of compensating the neighbour (either by screens or money bribes) and the noisy activity will be pursued no further.

By formulating the problem in this way, Coase was able to clarify some major issues. First, Coase emphasized the reciprocal nature of external harm. The presence of a noise-sensitive neighbour might be as inhibiting and inconvenient to a noisy one as the other way round. Second, if there existed mutual advantages in coming to some agreement about noise, the parties would have an incentive to bargain to a point at which no further joint advantage was derivable. Third, this agreement would not depend upon the initial assignment of property rights (a point later disputed by theorists). Whether the noisy neighbour had to buy rights to make noise from the quiet one or the quiet neighbour had to buy rights to peace and quiet from the noisy one, the amount of noise that was eventually made or the size and effectiveness of the sound-insulating screens would be unaffected. Fourth, these results would only apply in a world in which transactions costs were negligible and property rights were clear. Where agreements were costly to negotiate and enforce it would not follow that the assignment of rights left the final allocation of resources unaffected or that people could always bargain to an efficient agreement. The structure of legal rules and institutions would therefore be important in determining how resources were allocated in areas where markets were missing.

4 Evaluation

The significance of Coase's analysis of the effect of transactions costs on economic organization was not immediately appreciated (see TRANSACTION COST ECONOMICS). By the late 1960s, however, researchers began to build on his foundations. Armen Alchian and Harold Demsetz (1972) and Oliver Williamson (1975, 1985) openly acknowledge Coase's influence on their work on the organization of firms (see WILLIAMSON, O.E.). These economists began to ask what factors determine the level of transactions costs. Williamson argues that firms form when transactions are frequent, where the environment is uncertain and where the transactors are vulnerable to 'opportunism'. Alchian and Demsetz emphasize the problems that arise where output comes from many team members and where the value of the individual contribution of each person cannot be observed.

Other economic theorists of the late 1970s and 1980s began to look more closely at the incentive properties of contracts. Instead of the stark choice between market and firm, this modern literature presents the world as a spectrum of contractual possibilities. The general problem is characterized as one of principal and agent, with the principal attempting to elicit effort from the agent in conditions of poor or non-existent information. This approach has been influential in the theory of the finance of the firm (for example, Jensen and Meckling 1976), where bond finance and equity finance are arranged to minimize agency costs, in the field of managerial incentive contracts (for example Jensen and Murphy 1990), where shareholders attempt to align managers' interests with their own, and in the analysis of the structure of the firm. Rubin (1978), for example, considers the franchise chain as a method of eliciting effort from the franchisee while giving the franchiser an incentive to maintain the value of the brand name.

Developments in the world of business have made the questions posed in Coase's paper ever more pertinent. The growth of multinational enterprise prompts the Coasian question of why activities located in many different countries should be coordinated in a single firm – a question investigated by Dunning (1973) and Buckley and Casson (1976) (see MULTINATIONAL CORPORATIONS). The use of joint ventures raises the issue of why such market-like agreements are sometimes preferred over a full merger. The observation that in some countries the same industries are more vertically integrated than in others, for example the motor industry in the USA compared with Japan, suggests that transactions costs must be lower in the less integrated environment. The reasons for this have been sought by economists and management theorists.

In the field of public policy, the 1980s and 1990s have forced Coasian analysis to the fore. Whether to privatize an industry in a vertically integrated form or to break it down into smaller components is a quintessentially Coasian question. To divide train companies from the owner of the track, or to insist on the division between the production of gas and its distribution, or the generation of electricity and its transmission is to insist on the use of market contracts at certain points in place of internal organization. Transactions costs and economic incentives are at the heart of these issues along with the idea that transactional inefficiencies may be worth incurring in order to achieve the benefits of greater competition.

Coase's 1937 paper forms the foundation stone of much of the modern economics and management literature on the structure of firms. Over time, however, modifications to his conception have become accepted. It is no longer assumed that the exercise of authority is the main characteristic which separates firm from market. Within the firm, people will often have a wide area of discretion and will act as agents rather than passive takers of instructions from the management. Similarly, recent thinking has tended to emphasize the generation of specialized capabilities within the firm – competitive advantages – which can only be exploited internally and cannot be traded directly using the market mechanism. The possibility of substitution between firm and market is thereby thrown into question in some circumstances. In the face of sudden and substantial innovation, for example, organization within the firm may be necessary to force through the necessary changes (Silver 1984).

Coase's work on social cost has been equally influential. His 1960 paper gave rise to much technical discussion about the so-called 'Coase theorem' and the precise circumstances in which it would hold. Economic theorists pointed out that even in a world of zero transactions costs the final allocation of resources would not be entirely independent of the initial assignment of property rights if a person's willingness to pay for a beneficial change or to avoid a harmful one varied with wealth. Although much of the subsequent discussion concerned the properties of Coase's system in conditions of zero transactions costs and a 'Coasian world' has come, paradoxically, to be understood in the economics profession as one without transactions costs, the long-term importance of Coase's contribution will be found in his insistence that transacting inevitably involves costs and that these affect economic behaviour and the efficiency of economic systems.

The growth of the study of law and economics, especially in the USA, was stimulated directly by Coase's work on social cost. Posner (1973) drew on it directly in his analysis of legal institutions. Where transactions are costly, the question of how rights should be allocated becomes a central one for economic students of the law. Posner advanced the proposition that if agreements are prevented by excessive transactions costs, rights should be assigned to the party that would value them most highly (and would hence purchase them), were transactions costs negligible. In other words, the law should mimic the market. More recently, free market environmentalists such as Anderson and Leal (1991) have emphasized the importance of establishing clear property rights in environmental resources so that a Coasian process of agreement can occur. In general, however, Coase's work cannot be used to assert the universal supremacy of market solutions over regulatory solutions to environmental and other problems. Sometimes transactions costs will be low enough to favour markets, whereas at other times some form of regulation may be preferred. The direct comparison of available institutions in realistic circumstances is ultimately the only way of adjudicating on these issues.

Although Coase's intellectual contribution is founded on two extremely influential scientific papers of a conceptual and theoretical nature, the corpus of his work more generally is based upon close observation of practical circumstances. It was, for example, his work on the allocation of radio frequencies by the Federal Communications Commission (Coase 1959) that led to the idea that a market in rights to frequencies would produce superior results. Similarly, his objections to marginal cost pricing in the public sector (Coase 1946) were based on very practical observations. If setting prices equal to marginal cost necessitated a subsidy, the costs of raising this revenue by increased taxation should be taken into consideration. Further, once subsidies are permitted, the incentive to maintain technical efficiency in the industry is undermined. Average cost pricing at least provides a rudimentary way of testing that total benefits exceed total costs. Coase's article on the lighthouse (1974) provides another example of this way of thinking. Students of economics would, from reading the textbooks, have reasonably assumed that no lighthouses could possibly have been provided before the state became involved. Coase shows this to be completely wrong historically and discusses the mechanisms by which lighthouse builders managed to overcome the transactions cost problem and gather lighthouse dues.

5 Conclusion

Transactions costs provide the leitmotif which runs through Coase's career. His influence has been profound within the economics profession, but it has also spread out more widely to management thinkers, who may be Coasians without knowing it. Although Coase has been honoured for theoretical work, his background in commerce has given him a commonsense approach to problems that has an appeal outside the economics profession narrowly construed.

MARTIN RICKETTS
UNIVERSITY OF BUCKINGHAM

Further reading

(References cited in the text marked *)

* Alchian, A. and Demsetz, H. (1972) 'Production, information costs and economic organization', *American Economic Review* 62 (5): 777–95. (Emphasizes information costs as the factor explaining organization within the firm.)
* Anderson, T.L. and Leal, D.R. (1991) *Free Market Environmentalism*, San Francisco, CA: Pacific Research Institute for Public Policy. (Recommends the greater use of property rights and legal remedies instead of regulation for environmental problems.)
* Buckley, P.J. and Casson, M. (1976) *The Future of Multinational Enterprise*, London: Macmillan. (Discusses the reasons for organizing multinational operations within a single firm instead of across markets.)
* Coase, R.H. (1937) 'The nature of the firm', *Economica* (new series) 4 (16): 386–405. (One of the two main papers mentioned in Coase's Nobel Prize citation.)
* Coase, R.H. (1946) 'The marginal cost controversy', *Economica* (new series) 13 (51): 169–82. (A paper which indicates Coase's distrust of 'theoretical' economics, that is, economics which ignores transactions costs.)
* Coase, R.H. (1959) 'The Federal Communications Commission', *Journal of Law and Economics* 2: 1–40. (Coase criticizes the Federal Communications Commission's method of allocating radio frequencies.)
* Coase, R.H. (1960) 'The problem of social cost', *Journal of Law and Economics* 3: 1–44. (An influential paper showing that the problem of social cost was a problem of transacting and property rights.)
* Coase, R.H. (1974) 'The lighthouse in economics', *Journal of Law and Economics* 17 (2): 357–76. (Coase shows how entrepreneurs can often think of ways to overcome transactions costs.)
* Dunning, J.H. (1973) 'The determinants of international production', *Oxford Economic Papers* 25 (3): 289. (Argues that multinational expansion occurs to make use of non-tradeable enterprise-specific advantages.)
* Jensen, M.C. and Meckling, W.H. (1976) 'Theory of the firm: managerial behaviour, agency costs and ownership structure', *Journal of Financial Economics* 3 (4): 305–60. (Established the 'agency cost' approach to corporate finance.)
* Jensen, M.C. and Murphy, K.J. (1990) 'Performance pay and top management incentives', *Journal of Political Economy* 98 (2): 225–64. (Discusses the compatibility of Chief Executive Officer incentive contracts with the theory of principal and agent.)
Medema, S.G. (1994) *Ronald H. Coase*, New York: St Martin's Press. (An overview of Coase's life and an assessment of his work.)
* Posner, R.A. (1973) *Economic Analysis of Law*, Boston, MA: Little, Brown. (The application of Coasian economic analysis to the study of law.)
* Rubin, P.H. (1978) 'The theory of the firm and the structure of the franchise contract', *Journal of Law and Economics* 21 (1): 223–33. (Rubin sees the franchise chain as an alternative to full integration – a very Coasian perspective.)
* Silver, M. (1984) *Enterprise and the Scope of the Firm*, Oxford: Martin Robertson. (Vertical integration is seen as a means used by entrepreneurs to force through change that market contracts could not handle.)
* Williamson, O.E. (1975) *Markets and Hierarchies: Analysis and Antitrust Implications*, New York: The Free Press. (The title clearly declares Coase's influence – hierarchies or firms as an alternative to markets.)
* Williamson, O.E. (1985) *The Economic Institutions of Capitalism: Firms, Markets, Relational Contracting*, New York: The Free Press. (A major work analysing the governance of transactional relations.)

See also: BUSINESS ECONOMICS; EVOLUTIONARY THEORIES OF THE FIRM; GROWTH OF THE FIRM AND NETWORKING; INSTITUTIONAL ECONOMICS; MARSHALL, A.; TRANSACTION COST ECONOMICS; WILLIAMSON, O.E.

Schumacher, Ernst Friedrich (1911–77)

1 Introduction
2 Biographical data
3 Main contribution
4 Evaluation
5 Conclusions

Personal background

- born Bonn, Germany, on 16 August 1911
- moved to the UK in 1930 as a Rhodes Scholar at Oxford
- went to Columbia University, New York, in 1932
- returned to Germany in 1934 and worked in commerce
- married Anna Maria Petersen, 1936 (died 1960)
- returned to the UK, 1937
- married Verena Rosenberger, 1962
- advisor to the National Coal Board, 1950–70
- awarded CBE, 1974
- died on 4 September 1977

Major works

Small is Beautiful, A Study of Economics as if People Mattered (1973)
A Guide for the Perplexed (1977)

Summary

E.F. Schumacher was best known as a vigorous advocate of small-scale economic activities. But he was also a pioneer of modern thinking on environmental issues and the economics of developing countries, the latter coupled with an interest in land issues. Although an economist by training, his contributions to economic thinking did not fit easily into mainstream economics, and his major influence was on thinking outside conventional economics. While much of his writing was influenced by orthodox and unorthodox religious thinking and philosophy (from Eastern religions as well as Christianity), his most influential work challenged the economic and political ideas of his time on their own ground.

1 Introduction

In his most famous work, *Small is Beautiful, A Study of Economics as if People Mattered* (1973), Schumacher offered a sustained argument for small-scale human activities, emphasizing environmental and green issues. He also proposed the introduction of a system of 'intermediate technology' to help the economies of developing countries, and the phrase has since been adopted by many other theorists.

Schumacher's writing is marked by its accessibility, which enabled him to reach a much wider audience than most academics. Indeed, his influence on other academics was limited. Yet, his arguments, particularly in *Small is Beautiful*, were rigorously argued, and challenged the more conventional academic views of his time. However, his other major book, *A Guide for the Perplexed* (1977), is something of an *ad hoc* mixture of religion and philosophy that many academics could dismiss as having little to do with their concerns.

Schumacher's theories and arguments now appear less remarkable, since many have become part of mainstream thinking on green issues, sustainable economics and the virtues of small size. On the other hand, his thinking remains unconventional in one sense because it runs counter to the free-market philosophies that have come to dominate politics in advanced industrial countries such as the UK and the USA, the former command economies of eastern Europe and many developing countries.

2 Biographical data

The son of a professor of economics, E.F. 'Fritz' Schumacher was born in Bonn, Germany, on 16 August 1911. In 1930, he moved to the UK to take up a Rhodes scholarship at Oxford University, and later went to the USA, where he was first a student and later a lecturer at Columbia University, New York.

Schumacher returned to Germany in 1934 but was unable to settle there. He moved back to the UK in 1937 and to Oxford in 1942. At the end of the Second World War, he became economic advisor to the British Control Commission in Germany. In 1950, he became economic advisor to the National Coal Board, the public corporation established to run the UK's coal industry. From 1963 to 1970, he was director of statistics for the Board. Schumacher had many other interests, including journalism, environmental issues and the economies of developing countries, particularly the rural aspects of such economies. In 1966, he founded the Intermediate Technology Group.

In 1973, Schumacher published *Small is Beautiful, A Study of Economics as if People Mattered*. Although the book (and especially its title) became very widely known, Schumacher never became a major media personality, unlike many other popular thinkers of the day. However, he inspired many who came into contact with him and his ideas have continued to be influential through a number of bodies with which he was associated or which were founded after his death. Among these are the Schumacher Society set up in 1977 in his memory, the Soil Association (of which he was president from 1970), the New Economics Foundation, the Schumacher College in Dartington, Devon, England and the E.F. Schumacher Society and Center located in Great Barrington, Massachusetts, USA. Schumacher died in 1977.

3 Main contribution

Virtually all of Schumacher's influential ideas are contained in *Small is Beautiful, A Study of Economics as if People Mattered*. These essays made an important contribution to thinking on organizational structures, environmental and green issues, forms of ownership, epistemology and the development of what were then termed 'Third World' countries.

The phrase 'small is beautiful' refers to Schumacher's strongly argued view that smallness in human affairs is to be preferred, whether in organizations or nation states. However, it was no simple matter of asserting that small was always better. Schumacher argued that, given the complexity of human social, political and economic arrangements, there is no single answer to the size question and we may need very different kinds of structures for different purposes. For all human activities, there is an appropriate scale. In Schumacher's time, however, large structures and systems were assumed to be either inevitable or the most efficient means of organizing society. Schumacher questioned these assumptions and claimed that almost all large-sized structures destroy human dignity, democracy, self-realization and standards of living. Where economic arguments were offered, based, for example, on economies of scale, these could also be challenged and shown to be wanting.

On environmental and green issues, Schumacher was an early critic of nuclear energy. He saw it as a health danger and raised the issues of nuclear waste and the decommissioning of nuclear power stations once their productive life was over. Other energy sources, and especially coal, he stressed, should not be treated as simple market commodities to be produced only as long as it was profitable to do so. What was crucial was the long-term supply of energy and the fact that the supply of all fossil fuels is finite, while under existing economic arrangements the demand for energy was increasing rapidly. The solution he proposed was a shift to a locally focused economy based on self-sufficiency and renewable energy sources and materials.

Schumacher's notion of 'intermediate technology' also deserves attention since, again, it has become a much used phrase. He proposed mixed technologies for any given project in order to achieve maximum local employment for modest inputs of capital. This might involve very sophisticated technology for some elements of production, but only where they were appropriate to the task. The object was not to be economically efficient simply in terms of capital output or labour productivity, but to involve as many local people as possible and to ensure self-sustaining local economic development. While modern knowledge can be applied in a great many ways, the capital-intensive technologies and economies of advanced industrial economies illustrate only a few possible applications.

Schumacher's epistemological arguments were unfashionable in his time but now receive more serious consideration. One example was his adoption of the distinction between *convergent* and *divergent* problems. Convergent problems are constructed problems, set by human beings and solved by logic and science. Once the solution has been written down it can be used by others. Divergent problems, on the other hand, cannot be solved by logic. They are common problems in politics, economics and social relations generally and involve attempts to overcome or reconcile opposites. For example, how can management reconcile the need for control over employees with increasing employee participation? In Schumacher's view, a divergent problem cannot be solved as if it were a convergent problem, although such solutions are attempted all the time.

Schumacher also attacked the epistemological assumptions underlying economic forecasting, particularly in the form of such measures as the five-year plan, which was popular in the economic management of command and developing economies of his time (see MODELLING AND FORECASTING). In Schumacher's view, the fallacy of forecasting was that human freedom was being left out of the argument. Some prediction is possible because human beings often do behave in habitual ways, but some humans do not and their actions result in both unpredictable events and departures from previous patterns. The longer the period covered by the forecast, the greater the extent of such departures. National plans, in particular, presuppose the power to ensure they will be carried out. In a free society, concentration of power in this sense is rare and, even in other kinds of societies, it often fails because of human resistance or evasion. Schumacher's argument was a variant of what is now called the anti-positivist position, a critique of attempts to explain human-centred activities and actions in terms of natural science models developed in the nineteenth century. Such models are considered inappropriate because they cannot incorporate the human attributes of freedom and purpose.

Schumacher also advocated 'feasibility studies', which differed fundamentally from forecasts or plans. Essentially, they consisted of explorations of the long-term effects of selected assumed tendencies. For instance, it could be assumed that some developing countries would attain living standards similar to those in advanced industrial societies by some year, y. A feasibility study might then be undertaken to work backwards from the assumed year in order to estimate the total energy, raw materials and capital required for such development. A study of this nature might well result in insights into what kind of developments were feasible, given assumptions about possible patterns of economic development. Feasibility studies were not forecasts or plans, therefore, but explorations of possible assumed trends.

Other themes in Schumacher's writing included organizations and ownership. He believed strongly in small organizations in which human beings do not feel alienated and in which they can realize their full potential. However, he accepted that large organizations were unavoidable in modern societies. The task, therefore, was to achieve smallness within the large organization. One principle he advocated was that of *subsidiarity*, that is, ensuring that decisions are made at the lowest level consistent with efficiency. Subsidiarity, he argued, enhanced human freedom and dignity and prevented the loss of self-worth that often results when people are involved in large-scale social structures.

Schumacher was a strong advocate of participation and cooperative ownership of enterprises. He was closely associated with the Scott Bader Cooperative, a plastic resin manufacturing company converted into a cooperative by its original owners. This became a much-cited example of a large-scale cooperative in the UK literature on cooperatives.

4 Evaluation

Schumacher's ideas – particularly on small-scale enterprise, environmental issues and epistemology – have now become part of wider arguments which have considerable influence. In some instances, the arguments have been amplified into major political and social messages, which have wide appeal in many countries, especially among young people.

Environmental groups have promoted the environmental message that Schumacher was among the first to articulate. In some countries, they have become the basis of new political parties often popularly called 'the Greens'. In other instances, existing political parties have adopted some of the ideas for their voter appeal. Some of Schumacher's other ideas have fared less well, however. For instance, dominant political parties in many advanced industrial societies still advocate the notion that economic growth is desirable as a solution to economic, social and political problems. The acceptance of green ideas of the kind advocated by Schumacher often sits uncomfortably alongside these older political ideas.

The promotion of the small-scale enterprise has become part of the ideologies of mainstream political parties in many countries. However, in this adaptation, the arguments have changed in ways that Schumacher would probably have found unacceptable. Governments in many advanced industrial societies actively support small businesses, but as the basis of a highly individualistic entrepreneurialism rather than as a vehicle for promoting human cooperation and dignity.

The anti-positivist epistemological stance of Schumacher has gained ground in many of the social sciences, although it is doubtful whether his writings have played a major role in bringing about such change. The change in interpretative and qualitative analyses in the social sciences has been particularly strong in sociology, for example. Even in Schumacher's own discipline, economics, there have been challenges to positivism and the associated emphasis on rational models of decision making and behaviour. In business and management studies, too, more attention is being given to qualitative issues, particularly in such areas as organizational behaviour.

Some of Schumacher's ideas have not made much headway. For example, his advocacy of new styles of ownership of economic organizations, particularly cooperatives, clashed with the rise of economic individualism and the restoration of management power in the 1980s and 1990s.

Of the many books that have influenced business thinking in the twentieth century, a great number offer solutions to what Schumacher called divergent problems, that is, problems for which there are by definition no logical solutions because of their very nature. Schumacher's ideas, particularly in *Small is Beautiful*, are different, since he carefully avoids simple solutions and hence his ideas have greater lasting significance. In several key areas, he was able to pick out themes which later assumed great influence and which, in several instances, are still working themselves out. What Schumacher does share with many other popular management and business writers is a highly accessible writing style that enabled him to reach and influence a wide audience. On the other hand, his writing has not promoted any considerable critique among academics and often is referred to simply in footnotes.

5 Conclusions

Schumacher believed that achieving an appropriate scale in all human activities, and especially in economic affairs, is crucial to human self-realization and dignity. The most appropriate scale, he argued, is usually small. The simple maximization of economic growth cannot produce and, indeed, is inimitable to, human happiness since it cannot deliver what it promised – prosperity and self-realization for all.

On the issue of economic and growth strategies adopted by developing countries, Schumacher argued that most could not achieve their aims since they neglected the rural basis of most of the populations' way of life and employed inappropriate technologies. Likewise, analytical strategies used by many economists and political decision makers were based on false epistemological premises which excluded the key characteristics of human participants.

To counter such problems, Schumacher advocated a return to seeing human beings as ends in themselves and argued for the construction of organizations, political arrangements and communities that ensure human participation and self-worth. If we are to avoid destroying the planet, he said, we must structure the economy in a way that is consistent with concern for the environment and the use of renewable sources of energy.

JAMES CURRAN
KINGSTON UNIVERSITY

Further reading

(References cited in the text marked *)

* Schumacher, E.F. (1973) *Small is Beautiful, A Study of Economics as if People Mattered*, London: Blond and Briggs. (Schumacher's seminal work, in which he sets out his most influential ideas.)

* Schumacher, E.F. (1977) *A Guide for the Perplexed*, London: Jonathan Cape. (Dismissed by many academics, this book brings religious and philosophical ideas into the debates on social, political and economic issues.)

Wood, B. (1984) *Alias Papa: A Life of Fritz Schumacher*, London: Jonathan Cape. (A very readable biography of Schumacher.)

Further resources

The E.F. Schumacher Center in Massachusetts, USA
http://www.schumachersociety.org (houses a 5,000 volume, computer-indexed library of books, etc. including Schumacher's personal library bequeathed to the Center by his widow).

See also: MODELLING AND FORECASTING

Friedman, Milton (1912–)

1 Introduction
2 Major contributions
3 Conclusion

Personal background

- born 31 July 1912, New York City
- educated at Rutgers and Chicago; Ph.D. from Columbia, 1946
- worked for the US National Resources Committee 1935–7
- worked for the division of tax research, US Treasury, 1941
- research staff with the National Bureau of Economic Research, 1937–81
- Associate Director at the division of war research, Columbia University, 1943–5
- awarded the Nobel Prize for Economics, 1976
- taught at the University of Chicago, 1948–77
- Paul Snowdon Russell Distinguished Service Professor of Economics, University of Chicago
- has lectured extensively at universities in Europe, Japan and Latin America; holds numerous degrees
- Fellow at the Hoover Institute, Stanford University since 1977

Major works

Essays in Positive Economics (1953)
A Theory of Consumption Function (1957)
A Monetary History of the United States, 1867–1960 (with Anna J. Schwartz) (1963)
Monetary Statistics of the United States (with Anna J. Schwartz) (1970)

Summary

Milton Friedman, the 1976 Nobel Prize winner for excellence in economics, is widely regarded as the leader of the Chicago School of Monetary Economics. This school stresses the importance of the Quantity Theory of Money as the key instrument of government policy. His contributions to the development of economics are extensive, ranging from economic methods to economic history to international economics.

1 Introduction

Throughout his long and distinguished career, Milton Friedman has made major contributions to economic analysis and the conduct of economic policy. This significant work encompasses economic methodology, money, economic history, micro- and macro-economics, economic policy and international economics.

Friedman was awarded the Nobel Prize in Economics in 1976 for his achievements in the fields of consumption analysis, monetary history and theory and for his demonstration of the complexity of stabilization policy.

As early as 1950 Friedman was a major critic of the dominance of Keynesian economics (see KEYNES, J.M.). He led the intellectual and public charge for a major re-evaluation of the role of the central bank in the conduct of monetary policy. However his contribution was not limited to the role of money in economic theory and policy and his challenging work in methodology, flexible exchange rates, the permanent income hypothesis and the issue of an inflation–unemployment trade-off were all significant contributions to knowledge.

Friedman's influence was not limited to the economic profession. His ideas with their forceful verbal and written presentation were known by political leaders in the USA and overseas, the press and to readers of his weekly column in *Newsweek*.

2 Major contributions

During his long and distinguished career Friedman has made major contributions in the key areas of economic analysis, including methodology, money, consumption, economic policy, inflation and unemployment, and debates over exchange rate policy.

In *Essays in Positive Economics*, Friedman made a powerful case for using implications rather than assumptions as a testing ground for economic theory. Indeed, his notion of the 'as if' hypothesis is crucial to understanding his extensive empirical works, especially in the fields of money. Friedman's first and major significant empirical work was undertaken with his associates in the Workshop in Money and Banking at the University of Chicago and in the National Bureau of Economic Research. This work culminated in three major publications: *A Monetary History of the United States, 1867–1960* co-authored with Anna J. Schwartz; an accompanying volume by Philip Cagan, *Determinants and Effects of Changes in the Stock of Money, 1875–1960*; and *Monetary Statistics of the United States*, co-authored again with Schwartz.

In these and subsequent works, Friedman led the charge of the Chicago School in its cry that 'money matters'. He attacked the way many economists had ignored the significance of money and monetary policy when analysing business cycles and inflation. Drawing upon his detailed historical analysis of money, Friedman re-formulated a new theory of the demand for money. His detailed empirical findings and analysis of the relationship between increases in money supply and the resulting changes in income and prices led him to argue that the demand for money is in fact very stable.

Friedman's pioneering work on money led him to a re-statement of the quantity theory of money in which the distinctive feature is a theory of the demand for real balances. He argued that while it was the case that monetary authorities controlled the nominal stock of money, what really mattered to the holders of money was the real quantity of money. He concluded that in a sense, the goal of monetary policy should be to ensure a long-term stable growth in the supply of money.

In his criticism of the approaches and support of Keynesians to economic policy, Friedman distinguished between three forms of lags which appeared in economic policy: the observation lag, the decision lag and the effect lag. He argued that these lags had major destabilizing effects and the challenge should be to simplify monetary policy to achieve stable growth in supply.

In the debates which raged in the economic profession, especially in the 1970s, it was Friedman who was the first to demonstrate that the assumption of a simple tradeoff between inflation and unemployment was only a temporary phenomenon. Moreover, he argued that in the long run, no such tradeoff existed.

Interrelated to Friedman's analysis of inflation and unemployment, was his pioneering work in international economics. In a 1950 essay, Friedman was an advocate for freely fluctuating exchange rates. His paper was written at a time when the Bretton Woods agreement, and the subsequent creation of the International Monetary Fund and the World Bank with its position of fixing exchange rates, was the prevailing wisdom. Friedman's analysis of how a movement to flexible exchange rates would improve the balance of payments adjustment was truly pioneering. He critically tore apart the arguments that flexible exchange rates would encourage destabilization and his position was vindicated some 20 years later when the world moved to a flexible exchange rate regime.

Friedman's work on consumption constitutes another example of his contribution to the development of economic analysis. He extended and refined the absolute income hypothesis to create a theory of consumption based on the hypothesis that permanent income, not annual income, is the *key* determinant factor when assessing total consumption expenditure. In his detailed work, *A Theory of the Consumption Function* (1957) he surveyed a large amount of empirical evidence with which the permanent income hypothesis is consistent and distinguished between temporary and permanent income – he concluded that a greater proportion of temporary income is saved than in the latter.

3 Conclusion

Friedman's contribution to the development and refinement of numerous areas of economic analysis has been significant, provocative, pathbreaking, public and challenging. His work on money, consumption, exchange rates and economic methodology have been major contributions. His work in economic history has led to a re-evaluation of the important linkages between money, monetary policy and growth in a nation's path of economic development. His role in the reinterpretation of the scope for discretionary action in monetary and fiscal policy in economic management have had significant impacts on how governments have conducted economic policy, especially since 1970.

JOHN CUNNINGHAM WOOD
EDITH COWAN UNIVERSITY AUSTRALIA

Further reading

(References cited in the text marked *)

Cagan, P. (1965) *Determinants and Effects of Changes in the Stock of Money, 1875-1960*, Ann Arbor, MI: University MicroFilms International. (Companion work to that of Friedman with the Workshop in Money and Banking.)

Friedman, M. (1953) *Essays in Positive Economics*, Chicago, IL: University of Chicago Press. (Provides a detailed account of Friedman's methodology and places an overriding stress on economics as a predictable science.)

* Friedman, M. (1957) *A Theory of the Consumption Function*, Princeton, NJ: Princeton University Press. (Re-assesses J.M. Keynes's consumption function analysis and argues that people adjust their consumption with respect to variations in their permanent income.)

Friedman, M. (1962) *Capitalism and Freedom*, Chicago, IL: University of Chicago Press. (A provocative work which embodies many of his liberal and political views.)

* Friedman, M. and Schwartz, A.J. (1963) *A Monetary History of the United States, 1867–1960*, Princeton, NJ: Princeton University Press. (An in-depth study of the topic, produced for the National Bureau of Economic Research.)

* Friedman, M. and Schwartz, A.J. (1970) *Monetary Statistics of the United States*, New York: Columbia University Press. (The result of the same period of empirical work as the 1963 publication, again produced for the National Bureau of Economic Research.)

See also: EXCHANGE RATE ECONOMICS; KEYNES, J.M.; MONETARISM

Penrose, Edith Tilton (1914–96)

1 Biographical background
2 Main contribution
3 A full life

Personal background

- born Los Angeles, 29 November 1914
- studied at the University of California at Berkeley and Johns Hopkins
- worked at the ILO in Geneva in 1939 with E.F. ('Pen') Penrose whom she married in 1945
- worked with Pen Penrose advising the US Ambassador in wartime London
- doctoral research into the international patent system supervised by Fritz Machlup, thesis published as *The Economics of the International Patent System* (1951)
- research fellowship in a College Business Exchange Program at Johns Hopkins involving case study of Hercules Powder Company
- peripatetic academic career alongside Pen Penrose in Australia, Iraq, Egypt and Lebanon
- 1959, published *The Theory of the Growth of the Firm*
- 1960, Pen and Edith moved back to London where Edith held a Readership at London University becoming Professor in 1964
- 1978, moved to chair at INSEAD
- 1984, retired and returned to England
- died Waterbeach, Cambridgeshire, 11 October 1996

Major works

The Economics of the International Patent System (1951)
The Theory of the Growth of the Firm (1959)
'The Growth of the Firm – A Case Study: The Hercules Powder Company', *Business History Review*, XXXIV: 1–23.

The Large International Firm in Developing Countries: The International Petroleum Industry (1968)

1 Biographical background

Edith Penrose's academic contributions and personal experiences are woven together. It is not possible to understand the range of her contributions, the shifts in her interests and the pace of her work without reference to the passages of her personal life. Obviously this inter-relationship is partially explained by Penrose's gender and by the constraints and limitations that she faced as a wife and mother. Penrose's varied contributions appear as creative responses to the situations in which she found herself. Her life was not smooth and predictable. But she created opportunities out of the twists and turns with which fate confronted her. In this sense there is an uncanny resonance between the way in which she lived her own life and her now famous theory of the growth of the firm. Penrose used her experiences and opportunities to build up a unique set of abilities and understandings, and then on the basis of these 'capabilities' responded to new opportunities, often turning personal setbacks, even tragedies, into fresh starts and novel ventures.

Born in 1914, Penrose spent her childhood in pioneering conditions. Her father was an engineer responsible for surveying highways under construction in California. She was brought up in road camps and attended small schools in out-of-the-way places. But she clearly seized the opportunity presented by the presence of a gifted English teacher at the high school in tiny San Luis Obispo to master an elegant prose style. Her first husband's death in a shooting accident left Penrose a very young widow with an infant son, circumstances that in the 1930s would have sunk most girls' ambitions. Penrose completed her BA at Berkeley. After a short interval as a social worker, opportunity knocked again in the form of a chance to go to work at the International Labour Office in Geneva with E.F. 'Pen' Penrose, who had been one of her teachers at Berkeley. Penrose's indomitable spirit is shown in her defiance of convention and willingness to expose herself to personal risk in seizing this opportunity. Leaving her infant son with her mother, she set off to a Europe over which war clouds were gathering. She and Pen worked first in Geneva and then as economic advisors to the US ambassador in wartime London where they married. As an older and more established academic, in these early years, E.F Penrose's patronage and tutelage undoubtedly helped Penrose. Subsequently their peripatetic academic life may not always have benefited her career. But their partnership was the bedrock of Edith Penrose's life and she accepted the shifts with all they involved, seizing new opportunities to work, often with Pen, on fresh topics as they occurred. This willingness to adapt her interests when faced with a new environment underpinned the range of her contributions.

Penrose returned with her husband to Johns Hopkins in 1950 where she resumed her studies and had three more children, one of whom tragically died in infancy. At Johns Hopkins, Penrose worked closely with Fritz Machlup. He supervised her Ph.D. thesis on the international patents system (subsequently published as a monograph) and they worked together on related articles. Machlup was also involved in Penrose's securing of the Fellowship, which led to her study of the Hercules Powder Company. Exposure to what she would subsequently call the 'insides' of a firm deeply influenced Penrose's subsequent work especially *The Theory of the Growth of the Firm* (hereafter *TGF*).

But once again Penrose's life was disrupted. Owen Lattimore, the eminent Mongolian scholar, was accused by McCarthy of being a communist spy. The Penroses took a prominent part in his defence. Loyalty to their friend and their principles meant that life at Johns Hopkins became unpleasant. The Penroses decided to take an extended sabbatical overseas working at universities first in Australia and then in Baghdad.

The publication of *TGF* in 1959 brought Edith Penrose instant recognition as a creative thinker. But its methodological and substantive parting of company with neo-classical economics branded its author as heterodox. Neither she, nor her work, was welcomed into the tight knit community of orthodox economists. The recent upsurge of interest in Penrose's theory of the growth of the firm has tended to originate in disciplines adjacent to economics, particularly management, where its importance has been increasingly recognized (see GROWTH OF THE FIRM AND NETWORKING; INSTITUTIONAL ECONOMICS). Nor did Penrose work through additional publications to woo orthodox economists to her side. She was too busy responding to the new opportunities of life in the Middle East. She became one of the first economists to study the oil industry. In 1968 she published a book on the international petroleum industry, following it with a collection of essays in 1971. On Pen's retirement in 1960, the Penroses came back to London, where Edith Penrose worked for much of the next too decades, first at London University (LSE and SOAS) but also at Templeton College, Oxford and at Bradford University. From 1978 to 1984 Edith Penrose held a position at INSEAD, acting as Dean of Research in her last two years. During her long and demanding academic career, Penrose also maintained a significant presence in public life, as Alec Cairncross's obituary in *The Independent* (19 October 1996) makes clear.

2 Main contribution

Edith Penrose provided many new ideas on management, patents and the petroleum industry, and was influential in public affairs in many countries, as a scholar, as a member of committees and as a teacher. But undoubtedly it is her book on the growth of the firm that has most (indeed growing) impact as reference to her entries in the *Social Science Citation Index* confirms. Her intellectual legacy is recognized through the eponym, 'the Penrosian Firm'. It might seem that Penrose is doubly honoured in that her name is associated with an institution, which appears central to economic life. But 'the firm' while clearly the hub of economic activity in the real world, until recently was a 'black box' as far as economic theory was concerned (see SMITH, A.; MARSHALL, A.; WILLIAMSON, O.E.). Penrose was a pioneer in terms of breaking open the firm and trying to understand how it worked. Today the Penrosian firm motivates an organizational perspective which is shared by a growing community of scholars from a range of disciplines. However, although *The Theory of the Growth of the Firm* is read and cited among economists, it has had more influence among emergent schools of management. Edith's distinctive way of studying the firm has not been to the taste of modern economists. Why?

First, Penrose's main research covered difficult terrain from the viewpoint of orthodox economics, located as it was within the problematic relationship between the firm and the market (Best and Garnsey 1999; Pitelis 1999). Second, Penrose developed a methodology to understand the growth of the firm which contrasts with the deductive logic preferred by modern theorists.

The firm, for Penrose, was a pool of resources organized in an administrative framework. To explain the growth of the firm, Penrose elaborated a *process* view of production and competition, which led her to distinguish between resources and productive services, and between productive services and productive opportunities. These distinctions enabled her to incorporate knowledge and technology into a dynamic theory of enterprise growth, which anticipated the 'resource-based' perspective in strategic management (Teece and Pisano 1994; Foss 1999).

Penrose argued that it was not the homogenous *resources* of conventional economic theory that were inputs into the production process but rather the *services* that these resources rendered (*TGF*: 25). The services which resources could render derived from the unique experience, teamwork and purposes of each enterprise; they were unique because of their individual evolution and this made the firm similarly unique. 'The services yielded by resources are a function of the way in which they are used – exactly the same resources when used for different purposes or in different ways and in combination with different types or amounts of other resources provides a different service or set of services, (*TGF*: 25). Experience involved making new productive services available to the firm in a knowledge-based process.

The process of production created new productive services as a by-product. But this meant a coordination problem: 'only by chance [will] the firm ... be able so to organize its resources that all of them will be fully used' (*TGF*: 32). These unused resources remain available to the firm. Managers attempt to use them in other activities which sets in motion the process whereby new knowledge is created, and with it unused resources with their further pressure on managers to find new activities (see MANAGERIAL THEORIES OF THE FIRM). The process is endless.

If the unintended creation of unused services was one dimension of the production dynamic, managers' ability to recognize possibilities for action was another. In an uncertain world, management had to be able to identify and respond to opportunities. In turn the pursuit of opportunities through new experience reverberated back to create new productive services (*TGF*: 53). 'From the Penrosian perspective, the firm strategically shapes the market rather than reacting to it, but within a moving, historically contingent environment' (Best and Garnsey 1999).

How did Penrose, who had after all experienced a conservative training in economics at Johns Hopkins under the tutelage of Machlup, escape from the confines of orthodox industrial organization to develop this dynamic vision of path-dependent growth? One crucial point here is that Penrose did not explicitly confront the orthodox paradigm, arguing instead that her interest was in a different topic. She eschewed the static concerns of mainstream theory to focus explicitly on the dynamic question of what determined the *growth* of the firm. It was a clever move to claim as her own this neglected territory where she was not forced by custom and practice to take a particular approach, or, alternatively, to defend a decision not to take that approach. Penrose avoided getting bogged down in the defence of an alternative approach in a discipline notorious for its methodological rigidity. To not use the standard methodology was after all to not really 'do economics'. In fact, Penrose's vision of the firm was heavily influenced by an atypical research experience. In 1954 Penrose, through Machlup's good offices, had obtained a fellowship which allowed her to spend six weeks studying the Hercules Powder Company 'with the full cooperation of all of its personnel' (Penrose 1960: 2). She produced the detailed case study of Hercules before she embarked on *TGF*. The study not only helps illustrate the arguments of the book but it almost certainly had an influence on the arguments of the book in the first place (Kay 1999).

Hercules Powder Company was formed as an anti-trust enforced de-merger of Du Pont. Penrose cites the importance of 'the creation of consumer demand as a consequence of entrepreneurial desire to find a use for available productive resources' (1960: 9). The impetus for new product development and moves to create new markets came from 'the extensive knowledge of cellulose chemistry possessed by Hercules [because it] provided a continuous inducement to the firm to search for new ways of using it'. This was the clue to the productive services and market opportunity dynamics: Hercules' technological base enabled it to enter new markets, which in turn led the company to refine its technological knowledge (Kay 1999).

The pivotal role of the case study in the genesis of Penrose's ideas has been hidden because the publisher deleted the chapter devoted to Hercules and consequently it was not published until 1960 when it appeared in *Business History Review*. The 'missing chapter' won the Newcomen Award for the best article published in the *Review* that year. *TGF* was thus not the product of deductive logic applied to a limited number of axioms and subsequently 'tested' with reference to the 'real world'. Penrose generalized from the case she knew in such detail and saw that her ideas about growth were consistent with other descriptive material. Her incisive summary of the Hercules Powder case study neatly captures the message of her book: 'Growth is governed by a creative and dynamic interaction between a firm's productive resources and its market opportunities. Available resources limit expansion; unused resources (including technological and entrepreneurial) stimulate and largely determine the direction of expansion. While product demand may exert a predominant short-term influence, over the long term any distinction between "supply" and "demand" determinants of growth becomes arbitrary' (Penrose 1960: 1).

Penrose's methodology is worth a closer look. For Penrose the world is inherently complex; we need theory to make sense of it and to act sensibly within it. Penrose's research method involved close observation and detailed documentation of individual firms (Garnsey 1998). But she used observation to refine her conceptual model, not to 'test' hypotheses. Brian Loasby suggests that Penrose developed 'connecting principles', as Adam Smith called them, invented patterns of knowledge that help us to understand what we observe and experience (Loasby 1991: 6; Penrose 1995: xiii–xiv). In this sense Penrose's method was interpretive. Her aim was not how to know 'the truth', but to endow experience with meaning. Her work denied the positivist dichotomies implicit in much economic research between theory and evidence, positive and normative, fact and value, theory and practice. For example, she argued against 'a distinction, far too commonly made, between a "real" world of history and a world of theory' (1989: 10). Theory and history are not in opposition; their relationship is 'one of genuine complementarity' (1989: 11). Without theory it is impossible to 'isolate from the seamless web the facts relevant to the questions we want to ask' (1989: 11). The 'facts' are not, however, freestanding but depend upon the questions being asked. 'But it is hard to ask questions without knowing why you ask them – that is to say without a theory' (1989: 12). Penrose likened theory to a camera: 'Our picture is a moving one and the camera must so select the facts it puts together as to depict the undepictable: the causal, unobservable, relationship between facts' (1989: 8). As we look closer the gulf between Penrose's methodology and the standard approach of mainstream economics widens.

3 A full life

Edith Penrose did not spend all her time in the calm pursuit of knowledge within university libraries or faculty clubs. Indeed during her time at Johns Hopkins, women were not admitted to the Faculty Club! She was caught up in, indeed part of, the economic and political turmoil of the twentieth century. She was married twice and the mother of four children. Her life had its tragedies as well as its triumphs and at times a less doughty spirit would have been defeated. Like the entrepreneurs of her own theory she made productive resources out of her own experience and then sought new opportunities in which to deploy them.

During her years of retirement outside Cambridge, the surge of interest in *TGF* took her by surprise. She enjoyed the satisfaction of seeing young scholars turning to her work with enthusiasm and appreciated the (albeit delayed) renown that her work so richly deserved. Perhaps Edith would have enjoyed more immediate success if her methodology had parted company with the mainstream of economic analysis less abruptly. It was strategic to depict her agenda as a complement to the mainstream, as a focus on the *growth* of the firm rather than its static equilibrium. But the downside of this self-presentation was to marginalize her contribution (Loasby 1999). Perhaps Edith would have enjoyed more recognition at a younger age if she had persisted with and consolidated the original product after 1959 instead of pursuing new projects. But here we have to think of the peripatetic academic life that Edith lived and the demands of the intellectual partnership she enjoyed with Pen. In the last analysis Edith Penrose sacrificed academic ambition for a more rounded intellectual and human existence.

MICHAEL BEST
UNIVERSITY OF MASSACHUSETTS AT LOWELL

JANE HUMPHRIES
ALL SOUL'S COLLEGE, OXFORD UNIVERSITY

Further reading

(References cited in the text marked *)

* Best, M. and Garnsey, E. (1999) 'Edith Penrose, 1914–1996', *Economic Journal* 109 (453): F187–F201. (Biography and intellectual appreciation.)
Early, J. (1960) 'Review of *The Theory of the Growth of the Firm*', *American Economic Review* L (5): 1111–12. (Contemporary review.)
* Foss, N.J. (1999) 'Edith Penrose, economics and strategic management', *Contributions to Political Economy* 18. (Links Penrose to the 'resource-based' perspective in strategic management.)
* Garnsey, E. (1998) 'A theory of the early growth of the firm', *Industrial and Corporate Change* 7 (3): 1–34. (Uses a Penrose-inspired model to explore the growth processes of the new enterprise.)
* Kay, N. (1999) 'Hercules and Penrose', *Contributions to Political Economy* 18. (Discusses the importance of the Hercules Powder study in the evolution of Penrose's theory.)
* Loasby, B.J. (1991) *Equilibrium and Evolution: An Exploration of Connecting Principles in Economics*, Manchester: Manchester University Press. (Locates Penrose in the history of economic thought.)
* Loasby, B.J. (1999) 'The significance of Penrose's theory for the development of economics', *Contributions to Political Economy* 18. (Locates Penrose in the history of economic thought.)
Machlup, F. and Penrose, E.T. (1950) 'The patent controversy in the nineteenth century', *Journal of Economic History* X (1): 1–29. (Early joint publication.)
Penrose, E.T. (1940) *Food Control in Great Britain*, Geneva: International Labor Office. (Wartime study.)
* Penrose, E.T. (1951) *The Economics of the International Patent System*, Baltimore, MD: Johns Hopkins Press. Spanish edition, 1974.
* Penrose, E.T. (1959) *The Theory of the Growth of the Firm*, 1st edn, Oxford: Basil Blackwell and New York: John Wiley & Sons; 2nd edn, 1980, Oxford: Basil Blackwell and New York: St. Martins; rev edn, 1995, Oxford: Oxford University Press. (Translated into Japanese, French, Spanish, Italian.)
* Penrose, E.T. (1960) 'The growth of the firm – a case study: the Hercules Powder Company', *Business History Review* XXXIV: 1–23.
Penrose, E.T. (1968) *The Large International Firm in Developing Countries: The International Petroleum Industry*, London: George Allen and Unwin.
Penrose, E.T. (1971) *The Growth of the Firm, Middle East Oil and Other Essays*, London: Cass.
Penrose, E.T. (1985) 'The Theory of the Growth of the Firm twenty-five years after', Uppsala: Acta Universitatis Upsaliensis, *Studia Oeconomiae Negotiorum* 20. (Retrospective assessment by the author herself.)
* Penrose, E.T. (1989) 'History, the social sciences and economic "theory", with special reference to multinational enterprise', in A. Teichova, M.

Levy-Leboyer and H. Nussbaum (eds) *Historical Studies in International Corporate Business*, Cambridge: Cambridge University Press; Paris: Maison des sciences de l'homme. (Discussion of some methodological issues raised by multinational enterprise.)

Penrose, E.T. and Penrose, E.F. (1978) *Iraq: International Relations and National Development*, London: Benn.

* Pitelis, C.N. (ed) (1999) 'Edith Penrose and *The Theory of the Growth of the Firm*', *Contributions to Political Economy* 18. (Collection of recent articles evaluating the contribution of *TGF* to several disciplines.)

* Teece, D. and Pisano, G. (1994) 'The dynamic capabilities of firms: an introduction', *Industrial and Corporate Change* (3): 537–56. Reprinted in G. Dosi, D. Teece and J. Chytry (eds) (1998) *Technology, Organization and Competitiveness*, Oxford: Oxford University Press. (Locates Penrose in modern managerial theories of the firm.)

See also: COASE, R.; GLOBALIZATION; GROWTH OF THE FIRM AND NETWORKING; INSTITUTIONAL ECONOMICS; MARSHALL, A.; MULTINATIONAL CORPORATIONS; SMITH, A.; WILLIAMSON, O.E.

Samuelson, Paul Anthony (1915–)

1 Biographical data
2 Main contribution
3 Assessment

Personal background

- born 15 May 1915, in Gary, Indiana
- 1932–5 undergraduate student at University of Chicago
- 1935–40 graduate student and then junior fellow at Harvard University
- 1940–7 Assistant and then Associate Professor of Economics, Massachusetts Institute of Technology
- from 1947, Professor and then Institute Professor of Economics, Massachusetts Institute of Technology
- 1970 Nobel Prize for Economics

Major works

Foundations of Economic Analysis (1947)
Economics: An Introductory Analysis (1948; 14th edn, with W.D. Nordhaus, 1992)
Linear Programming and Economic Analysis (with R. Dorfman and R.M. Solow) (1958; 1987)
The Collected Scientific Papers of Paul A. Samuelson (5 volumes, 1966–1986)

Summary

Samuelson has arguably been the dominant figure in post-war economics, his publications extending to virtually all branches of economic theory: the theory of the consumer, production theory, general equilibrium, international trade, welfare economics, the business cycle, Keynesian economics, inflation, economic growth, the theory of capital and optimal capital accumulation and many others. Kenneth Arrow has described him as 'omnipresent in American and even world economics' (Arrow 1967: 730). However, whereas some economists are remembered primarily because of certain key ideas with which they are associated, Samuelson's contribution has been primarily to change the way in which economists have approached their subject. His early work, in particular his doctoral dissertation (1947), argued the case for a mathematical approach to problems that had traditionally been tackled using non-mathematical methods. While economists such as Hicks used mathematics, they kept it in the background. In contrast, Samuelson gave mathematics a much more prominent role. He emphasized, in a way no one had done before, the formal derivation of qualitative predictions concerning variables that could, at least in principle, be observed.

1 Biographical data

Samuelson studied economics at Chicago, notably under Jacob Viner. In 1935, the conditions attached to a graduate scholarship forced him to leave Chicago, and he moved to Harvard to undertake his doctoral work. He has argued that, as a result of this move, he had the luck to be in the right place at the right time. Harvard had Edward Chamberlin, responsible for the monopolistic competition revolution, and Alvin Hansen, soon to become the most prominent American convert to Keynes (see KEYNES, J.M.). In addition, Harvard boasted J.A. Schumpeter and Leontief. It was here that Samuelson, before the age of twenty-five, wrote many of his most influential articles, and the doctoral dissertation that became *Foundations of Economic Analysis*. Samuelson's youth perhaps explains the fervour with which he argued the case for using mathematical analysis in economic theory. In 1940, he moved to MIT, as he put it, 'because he got a better offer', though the reasons why Harvard let him go are not clear. Since 1940, Samuelson has spent his entire career at MIT, leaving only for very short periods. Many of his colleagues testify to his vital role in turning his department at MIT into what many would regard as the world's leading economics department. The 'MIT' style of economics is one that many departments, in the USA and in the rest of the world, seek to emulate.

Apart from 1944–5, when he worked in the MIT Radiation Laboratory, Samuelson has been an academic economist throughout his career. He has, however, been involved in public life. His textbook, *Economics*, is probably the most successful economics textbook ever. For many years he was a regular columnist in *Newsweek*, and he was an advisor to US President Kennedy. Although his main reputation lies in economic theory, he has made important contributions to debates over macroeconomic policy, such as his advocacy of using demand management to create full employment in the 1960s, and his analysis of inflation policy in terms of a short-run tradeoff between inflation and unemployment.

2 Main contribution

Revealed preference

Since the so-called marginal revolution of the 1870s, economists had typically modelled consumer behaviour in terms of utility maximization, where utility (which depended on the quantities of various goods that were consumed) measured a consumer's level of welfare. One problem with this approach was that utility was unobservable. Using the language of logical positivism, it was a metaphysical concept. One response to this was the development by Hicks and Allen of indifference curve analysis, which enabled economists to dispense with the notion of measurable utility. Samuelson's approach was, at least at first sight, more radical. This was the theory of revealed preference.

The essential idea in revealed preference theory is very simple. The economist can observe prices, incomes and quantities purchased – nothing else. Suppose that a consumer has an income Y and is able to purchase two goods, 1 and 2, at prices P_1 and P_2. The budget constraint is that total expenditure is no greater than income: $P_1X_1 + P_2X_2 \leq Y$, where X_1 and X_2 are the quantities purchased. This can be represented by the budget line AB in Figure 1. Given this budget line, if the consumer chooses point C, we can conclude that the consumer prefers that combination of the two goods to all the other combinations that could have been chosen but were not: that C is revealed as preferred to all other points in the triangle OAB. Thus, if prices and/or income changes so that the budget line were to become A'B', we could conclude that the consumer would choose a point somewhere along the line CB' (assuming all income is spent). Points on A'C will not be chosen because the consumer could have chosen them when faced with AB, but did not do so.

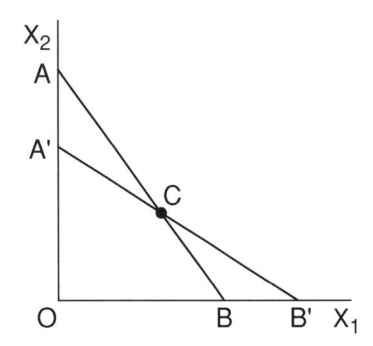

Figure 1

The significance of this approach is that Samuelson was able to derive (with a few exceptions) the same results as Hicks and Allen, notably the negative substitution effect, without referring to anything that could not be directly observed.

The business cycle

Samuelson's contribution here was to show how the business cycle might be analysed in terms of two simple relations: the multiplier and the accelerator. The multiplier is the relationship between investment and consumption (or income) that results from the process of income generation. Investment is spent, thereby generating income, which stimulates consumption. This gives rise to an equation of the form $C_t = cI_{t-1}$, where C_t is consumption in period t, c is the multiplier and I_{t-1} is investment in the previous period. A lag is assumed on the grounds that when investment (and hence consumers' income) rises, consumption does not rise immediately, but only with some delay. The accelerator is the relationship between investment and the *change* in consumption that arises from capital being required to produce consumption goods. This can be written as $K_t = vC_t$, where K_t is the capital stock at time t and v is the capital–output ratio. Ignoring depreciation, investment is the change in the capital stock, from which it follows that:

$$I_t = \Delta K_t = v(C_t - C_{t-1}). \qquad (1)$$

Putting these two equations together, we obtain an equation that determines the time path of consumption:

$$C_t = cv(C_{t-1} - C_{t-2}) \qquad (2)$$

Given appropriate values of c and v this equation will generate a cycle.

The significance of Samuelson's contribution (1938) was to show the importance of formal, mathematical analysis. For the model to generate cycles, the multiplier and accelerator coefficients must have specific values. Furthermore, Samuelson was able to show that unless cv is *exactly* equal to one, the cycles will either become larger and larger, or smaller and smaller, depending on whether cv is greater or less than one. This shows that additional assumptions need to be introduced to explain the business cycle, for in the real world the business cycle neither dies away nor explodes. This is something that would be very difficult to show without formal mathematical analysis.

Although use of the multiplier–accelerator model has declined since rational expectations have become fashionable in macroeconomics, for over three decades it became the standard framework in which to analyse the business cycle. What distinguished business cycle research after Samuelson from the earlier literature was the central role of this simplified, formal model: the business cycle came to be conceived in terms of a second-order difference equation, something that would, with some justification, have been unpalatable to leading writers before Samuelson, such as W.C. Mitchell.

The theory of international trade

Until the development of theories based on imperfect competition and game theory in the 1980s, the theory of international trade was, from the 1940s, dominated by what has come to be known as the Heckscher–Ohlin–Samuelson model. This treats international trade as an application of general equilibrium theory. Though some of the results can be generalized to larger models, the basic tool of analysis is a model with two countries, two factors of production (labour and capital) and two goods. In a particularly influential paper, published in 1941, Samuelson and Wolfgang Stolper showed that protection would raise the price of the relatively scarce factor. Thus if labour was the relatively scarce factor, protection would, under certain circumstances, raise wages by more than the price of the imported good. The 'orthodox' view that protection, through raising prices, would reduce living standards was not necessarily correct. Shortly afterwards, Samuelson derived conditions under which free trade in goods would result in equalization of factor prices, even if factors cannot move from one country to another.

As with so much of Samuelson's work, the significance of this work was not so much the specific conclusions reached, but the method. He tackled these problems using a simplified, but formal, general equilibrium model. It was general equilibrium effects, whereby changes in one market affected other markets and hence the overall equilibrium, that enabled him to derive surprising results (that seemed obvious once they were understood). For many years the $2 \times 2 \times 2$ (countries, factors, goods) model, the results of which could be illustrated if not proved graphically, became the standard fare of international trade theory. Samuelson's contribution was to make formal, general equilibrium modelling central to the theory of international trade.

The *Foundations of Economic Analysis*

Perhaps the most significant feature of this book was its unashamed advocacy of mathematical methods. Laborious verbal analysis of essentially simple mathematical ideas, Samuelson claimed, was a particularly depraved form of unrewarding mental gymnastics. This attitude was in stark contrast to that of Alfred Marshall, author of what was still the dominant economics textbook (see

MARSHALL, A.). This case was reinforced by Samuelson's argument that many economic problems were simply optimization problems. Consumers maximized utility subject to a budget constraint, and firms maximized profits subject to a production function. The theory of constrained optimization thus provided a unifying framework within which a range of diverse problems could be analysed. Equilibrium, in the sense of an optimum subject to constraints, was made central to economics.

The methodological principle underlying the *Foundations* was that economic theory should be concerned with the derivation of 'operationally meaningful' theorems. These were hypotheses about empirical data that might conceivably be refuted, if only under ideal conditions. This led Samuelson to emphasize the derivation of comparative static predictions: predictions about how various changes would affect equilibrium values of economic variables. For example, instead of being content to list the factors on which the price of a commodity might depend, Samuelson required economic theory to predict whether changes in these factors would cause the price to rise or fall. Many such results could be derived from the conditions for an optimum. Samuelson went further, however, with his 'correspondence principle' where he argued that further comparative statics results could be derived from the assumption that equilibrium was stable – that starting from any arbitrary price, the market price will move towards the equilibrium price. It turned out, however, that for technical reasons, the correspondence principle was much less useful than Samuelson had hoped. The idea that theory should be aimed at deriving comparative statics results, however, became firmly established.

Economics: An Introductory Analysis

Samuelson's *Economics: An Introductory Analysis*, the fourteenth edition of which was published in 1992 (by which time W.D. Nordhaus had entered as a co-author), was the book that finally displaced Alfred Marshall's *Principles of Economics* (1890) as the leading introductory textbook on economics (see MARSHALL, A.). Enormous numbers have been sold, of both the English and foreign-language translations, of which there have been many. It is an introductory textbook, yet it is vast in scope, including some material that newcomers find difficult. Though it presents economic ideas in a simplified form, its remarkable success owes much to the principle Samuelson adopted, that it should contain nothing that students would subsequently have to unlearn. The book has been regularly revised, its contents list serving as a barometer of the topics in which economists have taken an interest over the intervening four decades.

This book played a major role in the spread of Keynesian macroeconomics (see KEYNES, J.M.). Two aspects of this are particularly important. The first is what is usually called either the 45° line model of the 'Keynesian cross' (the analogy being with the 'Marshallian cross', the supply and demand diagram), shown in Figure 2. This diagram plots expenditure against national income. Consumption, C, increases with income, Y ($C = a + bY$, where a is autonomous consumption and b is the marginal propensity to consume), and aggregate expenditure is consumption plus investment (assumed independent of income), I. Equilibrium income, Y^e, is where expenditure, E, equals income. It is easy to use the diagram to show, for example, that a rise in investment will cause the expenditure line, $E = C + I$ to shift upwards, leading to a rise in the equilibrium level of income.

The second important feature of Samuelson's *Economics*, dating from the

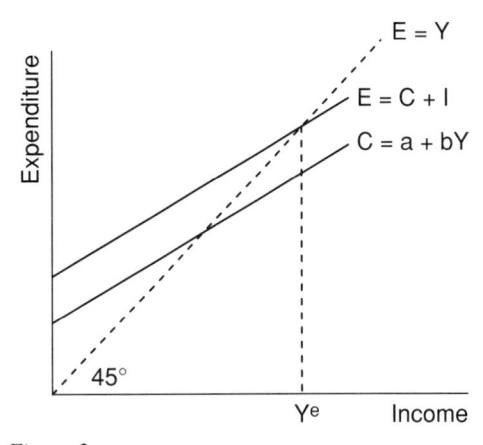

Figure 2

1950s, was what he termed the 'neo-classical synthesis'. At the level of economic theory this involved using neo-classical price theory (supply and demand, optimization – the economics of *Foundations*) for microeconomic and resource-allocation problems, and using Keynesian macroeconomics. At the level of policy it involved using monetary and fiscal policy to create full employment, varying the mix of the two types of policy to achieve the desired level of investment. Samuelson justified this approach, which is unacceptable to many economists because of its failure to provide a microeconomic underpinning for its macroeconomics, on the grounds that prices were, he believed, inflexible. He was thus prepared to take sticky prices as an assumption in doing macroeconomics. Samuelson is thus eclectic in his approach to economic theory in that he does not feel bound by a rigid set of assumptions.

3 Assessment

Samuelson's main contribution to economics has been to change the way in which economists have set about economic research. Perhaps more than any other economist, he represents the mathematical, model-building approach to economic theory (see MODELLING AND FORECASTING). His early work, notably *Foundations of Economic Analysis*, but also his work on the consumer, welfare economics, the business cycle and international trade, was all aimed at establishing the vital role of mathematics in economics. His subsequent work, even in areas such as the history of economic thought that traditionally have been less affected by the phenomenon, reinforces this, mathematics being used to analyse many new areas that would simply have been impossible to tackle without it. Outstanding examples are dynamics (how prices behave out of equilibrium, and the circumstances under which an economy will converge on an equilibrium) and optimal capital accumulation (given an initial and a desired terminal capital stock, what is the optimal time path for getting from one to the other?). Samuelson's emphasis on deriving comparative statics results concerning the effects of changes in policy or exogenous variables (assumed to be determined by non-economic factors) now pervades the whole of economics. Even where the economists are moving beyond the frameworks established by Samuelson (as in trade theory, where game theory is opening up new areas of research and new perspectives on old problems) the preference for formal methods and comparative static analysis has (for good or ill) remained.

ROGER E. BACKHOUSE
UNIVERSITY OF BIRMINGHAM

Further reading

(References cited in the text marked *)

* Arrow, K.J. (1967) 'Samuelson collected', *Journal of Political Economy* 75: 730–7. (The first two volumes of his collected papers surveyed, with a particularly interesting section on his views of the usefulness of neo-classical price theory.)
Brown, E.C. and Solow, R.M. (eds) (1983) *Paul Samuelson and Modern Economic Theory*, New York: McGraw-Hill. (Articles on Samuelson's contributions to various areas of economics, many written by colleagues or former students.)
Feiwei, G.R. (ed.) (1982) *Samuelson and NeoClassical Economics*, London: Kluwer. (Another collection of appraisals of Samuelson's contributions to economics.)
Fischer, S. (1987) 'Samuelson, Paul Anthony', in J. Eatwell, M. Milgate and P. Newman (eds), *The New Palgrave Dictionary of Economics*, London: Macmillan. (An excellent overview of Samuelson's contributions by a younger colleague at MIT.)
Lindbeck, A. (1970) 'Paul Anthony Samuelson's contributions to economics', *Swedish Journal of Economics* 72: 342–54. (The appraisal of Samuelson's work on the occasion of his being awarded the Nobel Prize in Economics.)
* Marshall, A. (1890) *Principles of Economics*, London: Macmillan. (First edition of Marshall's magnum opus, in which he expounds his theories of value and distribution. Revised editions in 1891, 1895, 1898, 1907, 1910, 1916 and 1920.)
McCloskey, D.N. (1986) *The Rhetoric of Economics*, Brighton: Harvester Wheatsheaf. (Chapter 5 contains a brief analysis of Samuelson's rhetoric, considering the literary devices he uses to establish the authority of mathematical argumentation.)
* Samuelson, P.A. (1947) *Foundations of Economic Analysis*, Cambridge, MA: Harvard University

Press. (Samuelson's doctoral dissertation which has had such a dramatic impact on modern economic theory.)

Samuelson, P.A. (1966–86) *The Collected Scientific Papers of Paul A. Samuelson*, 5 vols, London and Cambridge, MA: MIT Press. (Contains several hundred pieces covering all aspects of his work apart from popular writing. They give some idea of why Samuelson has made the impact on economics that he has.)

Samuelson, P.A. (1990) 'Paul A. Samuelson', in W. Breit and R.W. Spencer (eds), *Lives of the Laureates: Ten Nobel Economists*, 2nd edn, Cambridge, MA: MIT Press. (Samuelson's autobiographical reflections.)

Samuelson, P.A., Dorfman, R. and Solow, R.M. (1987) *Linear Programming and Economic Analysis*, New York: Dover Publications. (A look at modern methods of economic analysis.)

* Samuelson, P.A. and Nordhaus, W.D. (1992) *Economics*, London: McGraw-Hill. (The 14th edition of the textbook through which many students have been introduced to economics.)

Samuelson, P.A. and Stolper, W.F. (1941) 'Protection and real wages', *Review of Economic Studies* 9: 58–73. (Influential paper on international trade, in which the authors show that protection would raise the price of the relatively scarce factor.)

Wood, J.C. and Wood, R.N. (eds) (1989) *Paul Samuelson: Critical Assessments*, London: Routledge. (Four volumes of articles about Samuelson and his economics.)

See also: KEYNES, J.M.; MARSHALL, A.; NEOCLASSICAL ECONOMICS

Simon, Herbert Alexander (1916–2001)

1 Towards a science of administration
2 Towards a science of problem solving
3 A stream of ideas

Personal background

- born 15 June 1916 in Milwaukee, Wisconsin, the younger of two brothers
- father a German immigrant to USA, electrical engineer and inventor; mother an accomplished pianist
- BA in political science, University of Chicago, 1936
- married Dorothea Pye, 1937
- director of research group into municipal administration, University of California, Berkeley, 1939–42
- PhD in political science, University of Chicago, 1943, dissertation on decision making in organizations
- professor at Graduate School of Administration, Carnegie Institute of Technology, 1949
- Richard King Mellon Professor of Computer Science and Psychology, Carnegie Mellon University, 1966
- A.M. Turing Award for his work in computer science, 1975
- Nobel Prize in economics, 1978
- National Medal of Science, 1986
- American Psychological Association Award for Outstanding Lifetime Contributions to Psychology, 1993
- died 9 February 2001 aged 84

Major works

Administrative Behavior: A Study of Decision Making Processes in Administrative Organization (1947)
Organizations (with J.G. March) (1958)
The New Science of Management Decision (1960)
Human Problem Solving (with A. Newell) (1972)

Summary

In challenging classical economic theory, which ascribes business decision makers with near omniscience about options and with superhuman ability to compute the optimal choice, Herbert Simon has made a major impact upon our understanding of the processes of management. In place of a superrational economic model of man assumed by classical economics, he advocates an administrative model, a person of much more modest ability who is incompletely informed about available options and their outcomes and who therefore 'satisfices'. Satisficing is accepting a satisfactory outcome rather than striving to maximize utilities through ever more comprehensive search and involved computations. It is a process whereby decision makers take short cuts, use rules of thumb and a whole range of intuitive methods.

The associated psychological condition is 'bounded rationality', a condition whereby it is accepted that perfect knowledge about options can never be achieved in complex decision making. However, minimum performance standards can be set and once this minimum standard is reached an appropriate choice is made and search for further options stopped.

In broader terms, Simon therefore challenged prevailing economic theories of management and led a reaction against the Harvard case method of teaching which had become dominant in US business schools. It was for his ability to apply so many different perspectives, emanating from psychology, computer science, economic theory and political science that he was awarded the Nobel Prize for economics in 1978.

1 Towards a science of administration

If there is one passion that could be said to infuse the work of Herbert Simon, it would be the drive to develop a science of decision making. After taking a typically satisficing approach in his choice of career, which he described as being settled 'as much by drift as by choice', his home, peopled by intellectually active parents and stocked with books, prepared him for academic life. Following graduation from the University of Chicago in political science, an early research assistantship in the field of public administration led to the directorship of a public administration research group at the University of California, Berkeley.

His doctoral dissertation at the University of Chicago was based upon his administrative studies at Berkeley and was published with modifications as *Administrative Behavior: A Study of Decision Making Processes in Administrative Organization*. This book founded his reputation in the field of business administration and is now a classic, as witnessed by its progression to three editions. It acknowledges its debt to Chester Barnard, who provides a foreword and who had previously advocated the need to move thinking about management beyond an overconcern with formal structures to a concern with decision making and cooperation. The book gives an outline of the problems with administrative theory as it then existed. For instance, in trying to determine which basis of specialization an organization would use, the choice was usually presented as a choice between organization by purpose, process, clientele or place. These are not mutually exclusive criteria, however, and in order to think more clearly about the problem it is preferable to see an organization in terms of the 'facts' and the 'values' that guide decision making. Facts and values nest together in a hierarchy whereby the values of one level set the facts for a lower level. Value (or ethical) statements set the parameters within which decisions are made and by which outcomes are judged. Decision making takes place within a framework of 'givens' which an organization provides; in deciding upon a new machine, the management of a shoe factory does not question the need to make shoes or to make a profit but takes these as givens upon which more detailed search and extensive satisficing will ride. Rationality is therefore 'limited' or 'bounded'.

Administrative Behavior has the marks of a seminal work. It is not entirely coherent but is suggestive of the many avenues which Simon would later follow since engrained within this work are the three underlying concepts of bounded rationality, satisficing and search which are found throughout Simon's work.

This interest in the relationship between organizations and decision making was continued during his time at Carnegie Mellon through observation of decisions both in the field and in the laboratory. The second edition of *Administrative Behavior* further emphasized his belief that conventional economic assumptions about rationality were unrealistic and neglected the bounded rational nature of business decisions. These ideas were controversial and were attacked from a neo-classical viewpoint by economists such as Milton Friedman (see FRIEDMAN, M.). For the neo-classicists the assumption of economic man gave a sufficiently accurate account of human behaviour to allow predictions to be made in the aggregate. Later, in his Nobel Lecture, Simon reaffirms his belief in the need to adopt a more realistic view of human decision making and to make empirical observations of actual business decisions.

The book, *Organizations*, which Simon co-authored with J.G. March (with the collaboration of H. Guetzkow) develops the idea of satisficing and its associated condition of bounded rationality through a series of propositions, which are in principle scientifically testable. Bounded rationality is a psychological condition whereby decision makers realize they cannot obtain all the necessary information to fully evaluate options and hence they satisfice. One aspect of bounded rationality is limited attention focus; decision makers have to cope with many problems simultaneously. Some decisions are programmed and can be made by routines while for unprogrammed decisions organizations use extensive search routines.

Organizations also concerns itself with the motivation of individuals to participate in organizations and with the ability of people to resolve conflict. A major source of conflict in organizations derives from attention to subgoals. In a study with Newell (1972), Simon showed how managers from different functions interpreted the main issues in business decisions in different ways. These different interpretations are largely perceptions learned during professional training and subsequent experience.

Bounded rationality is a residual, a failure of omniscience whereby all options are not known, there is uncertainty about exogenous events and an inability to calculate consequences. This notion forms also the basis for a behaviourial theory of the firm which was developed further by Cyert and March (1963) in a book of that name. In this sense the firm, or more generally the organization, is a node of bounded rationality, search and satisficing.

The importance of search behaviour in the theory of bounded rationality was taken up by Stigler (1961) through an attempt to equate the cost of extra search with the marginal return to that search through improved outcomes. But as Simon points out, this requires decision makers to estimate marginal returns to extra search which, by the nature of the condition, cannot be done under bounded rationality. The theory of satisficing only requires that decision makers set a minimum aspiration as to the goodness required of those alternatives that come within their scope and choose the first that meets those aspirations.

2 Towards a science of problem solving

These ideas provided a base for a decade or so as a professor of administration at the newly founded Graduate School of Business Administration of the Carnegie Institute of Technology. After his concern with organizations, Simon's research in the mid-1950s turned increasingly to its psychological roots by examining the processes of human problem solving in greater depth and thereby contributing in a more general way to a behavioural theory of decision making.

An important aspect of Simon's thinking can be seen to have roots in Lewin's then fashionable field theory of psychology which points out that aspirations are not static but rise and fall with experience. With Newell, Simon came increasingly to explore these psychological roots by using computers as a central tool to simulate the way in which information is used in problem solving. Problem solving is seen to involve a highly selective search through a vast array of potentially available information. Selection of what is appropriate is based upon rules of thumb or heuristics in the manner of the previously developed idea of satisficing.

A central idea, whose origin can be seen in his earlier work on fact and value in decision making, is that problem solving is more effective if made within the structure of a hierarchy, what in one paper he described as the 'architecture of complexity'. Chess provided Simon with a major setting for testing propositions about these ideas. He has noted, through observation, that a chess grand master can solve chess problems more quickly than a novice because experience makes it possible to recognize patterns of standard moves that can be fitted together in a pattern. If pieces on a chess board are jumbled in a random way, thereby removing familiar learned patterns from the purview of the grand master, the difference between novice and grand master tends to disappear.

3 A stream of ideas

Through the breadth of his interests, teaching and writing and with fifteen books and over 500 articles to his name, Simon has been described as coming closest to the ideal Renaissance man. Although he has a reputation for being absent-minded ('part of the job description' as he said), it is impossible to ignore the influence that Simon has had when considering key sources of ideas about management and organization.

It is an influence that has also come about through a stream of ideas and an associated language finding a number of different niches also hewn by other scholars working on different problems across a range of disciplines. Sometimes the central ideas of the bounded rational model have been called the 'Carnegie School' of decision making due to Richard Cyert's as well as Simon's association with Carnegie Mellon University. James March later developed (in conjunction with Cohen) decision-making theory through a different, but not unrelated, set of ideas in the 'Garbage Can' model of decision making. Underlying these ideas is the contrast between economic and psychological views of decision making. Hence, Williamson (1975) places bounded rationality at the centre of an institutional economics in a theory attempting to understand the boundaries between market and hierarchical organizations in terms of a propensity to reduce transactions costs. A central problem of trying to conduct complex transactions in a market derives from bounded rationality in the sense that there can often be an asymmetry of knowledge between buyer and seller. Hierarchy is seen as a form of organization that allows greater flow of information than does a market and hence can ameliorate bounded rationality.

Although probably of greatest impact within North America, followed by other areas of the English-speaking world, the notions of bounded rationality, search and satisficing are likely to attract attention from scholars for years to come. Even if these ideas were to die today, Simon could be said to have been a major influence upon scholars of business and organization for over four decades.

RICHARD BUTLER
MANAGEMENT CENTRE
UNIVERSITY OF BRADFORD

Further reading

(References cited in the text marked *)

Barnard, C.I. (1938) *Functions of the Executive*, Cambridge, MA: Harvard University Press. (A foundation book for Simon, indicating the importance of decision making.)

* Cyert, R. and March, J.G. (1963) *The Behavioural Theory of the Firm*, Englewood Cliffs, NJ: Prentice Hall. (A pathbreaking book indicating the need to see the actions taken by firms in terms of bounded rationality.)

Klahr, D. and Kotovsky, K. (1989) *Complex Information Processing: The Impact of Herbert Simon*, NJ: Lawrence Erlbaum Associates, Inc. (Carnegie Mellon Symposia on Cognition.)

* March, J.G. and Simon, H.A. (1958) *Organizations*, New York: Wiley. (A classic book which builds a view of organizations from the microprocesses of decision making; a new edition appeared in 1993 which includes an introduction placing the material in its contemporary context.)

* Newell, A. and Simon, H.A. (1972) *Human Problem Solving*, Englewood Cliffs, NJ: Prentice Hall. (A good statement of Simon's approach to problem solving.)

* Simon, H.A. (1947) *Administrative Behavior: A Study of Decision Making Processes in Administrative Organization*, New York: The Free Press. (The book that launched Simon; the fourth edition appeared in 1997.)

* Simon, H.A. (1960) *The New Science of Management Decision*, New York: Harper Row. (Still a refreshing airing of the move against an overrationalistic view of decision making.)

Simon, H.A. (1962) 'The architecture of complexity', *Proceedings of the American Philosophical Society* 106: 467–82. (An early statement of Simon's approach to problem solving.)

Simon, H.A. (1979) *Models of Thought*, New Haven, CT: Yale University Press. (A later statement of Simon's approach to problem solving.)

Simon, H.A. (1996) *Models of My Life*, London: The MIT Press. (Autobiography looking at whether what he learned as a scientist explains other aspects of his life.)

* Stigler, C.J. (1961) 'The economics of information', *Journal of Political Economy* 69: 213–25. (Application of economic theory to the cost of information).

* Williamson, O.E. (1975) *Markets and Hierarchies*, New York: The Free Press. (Builds upon the notion of bounded rationality to develop a theory of how transaction costs can lead to market or hierarchical institutions.)

Williamson, Oliver E. (1932–)

1 Biographical data
2 Williamson and transaction costs
3 Williamson and behaviouralism
4 Institutions and efficiency
5 Conclusion

Personal background

- born 27 September 1932
- Professor of Economics at University of Pennsylvania, 1965–83
- Professor of Economics at Yale University, 1983–8
- applied and developed the transaction cost analysis of Coase
- Professor of Business, Economics and Law at University of California at Berkeley

Major works

Markets and Hierarchies: Analysis and Anti-Trust Implications: A Study in the Economics of Internal Organization (1975)
The Economic Institutions of Capitalism: Firms, Markets, Relational Contracting (1985)

Summary

This article discusses the work of the American new institutional economist Oliver Williamson. The key inspirations for Williamson have been the works of two Nobel Laureates, Ronald Coase and Herbert Simon. The article discusses how Williamson developed the earlier, transaction cost analysis of Coase to provide explanations of firm behaviour and structure. The relationships with the behavioural economics of Simon and Williamson's theory of organizational efficiency are both briefly evaluated.

1 Biographical data

Oliver Williamson (born 1932) is former Professor of Economics at Pennsylvania and Yale University and is currently Professor of Business, Economics and Law at the University of California at Berkeley. Williamson came to prominence in an article published in the *American Economic Review* in 1963 that argued that managers maximize their own utility, rather than, for example, profits or sales. However, it is for his application and development of the transaction cost analysis of Nobel Laureate Ronald Coase (born 1910) that he is most well-known (see COASE, R.). Williamson's first book in this genre was his *Markets and Hierarchies*, published in 1975. During the subsequent 25 years, Williamson has developed and extended this approach in a large number of books and articles, most notably his *Economic Institutions of Capitalism*, published in 1985 and his *Mechanisms of Governance*, published in 1996. His work is widely cited and has been inspirational for a large number of theoretical and applied researchers. His 1975 and 1985 books ranked as two of the three most highly cited books in economics in the Social Science Citations Index in 1990. His influence has not been confined to economics and it has extended significantly to both legal and business studies.

2 Williamson and transaction costs

A key work in the general development of the mainstream economic thinking about institutions was Williamson's *Markets and Hierarchies*, published in 1975. Williamson was the first to coin the phrase 'new institutionalism' and he used it to describe his approach (see INSTITUTIONAL ECONOMICS). With this phrase he simultaneously underlined his focus on the inner structures and workings of the firm and his distance from the 'old' institutionalism of Veblen, Mitchell and Commons (see VEBLEN, T.B.). In the next few years this term achieved a wide currency and the study of institutions has become commonplace for economists.

The main inspiration for Williamson was a much earlier and classic paper by Ronald Coase (1937). In this article Coase characterized the firm as an organization that supersedes the price mechanism and allocates resources by command rather than through price. As Coase (1937: 388) himself put it: 'Outside the firm, price movements direct production, which is co-ordinated through a series of exchange transactions on the market. Within a firm, these market transactions are eliminated and in place of the complicated market structure with exchange transactions is substituted the entrepreneur-co-ordinator, who directs production'. Coase explained this phenomenon by arguing that the firm arises because of the relatively greater 'cost of using the price mechanism' (1937: 390).

Following on from Coase, Williamson developed his central thesis that economic institutions such as the firm 'have the main purpose and effect of economizing on transaction costs' (Williamson 1985: 1). The approach of both Coase and Williamson can be characterized as contractarian, because institutions are seen as emerging from contracts between individuals. For example, firms with employment contracts emerge when the transaction costs of alternative market arrangements – such as using self-employed contractors – are too high.

However, the Coase–Williamson argument contrasts with other contractarian approaches that explain all firm and market phenomena solely in terms of contracts. Williamson recognizes a key polarity between 'markets' and 'hierarchies' and sees the latter as emerging because of specific, asset and information based efficiency considerations. However, a key difference between Coase and Williamson is that Williamson extends the transaction cost analysis from general comparisons of the firm and market to a comparison of different types of organization within the firm.

Much of Williamson's work is concerned with spelling out the implications of this approach. For example, he argues that if two firms trade with each other and rely on assets that are highly specific to that relationship and cannot readily or cheaply be traded elsewhere – an example is a steel mill relying on a local supply of iron ore – then the transaction costs of an enduring relationship are likely to be high and the firms are likely to have an incentive to vertically integrate in order to reduce those costs. Much of the empirical work on transaction costs looks at this issue of 'asset specificity'.

As another important example, Williamson compares two forms of hierarchical organization, the unitary ('U-form') and multidivisional ('M-form') structures. He argues that the M-form is often a more efficient way of administering particular types of transactions. It is argued that the M-form allows incentives to be aligned more closely to corporate goals and promotes the use of operational rather than functional criteria of managerial evaluation. On this basis it is claimed that the spread of the multidivisional firm in modern capitalism is explained.

A consequence of this widening of the scope of transaction cost analysis is that the cost of monitoring and enforcing all transactions, including employment contracts, are considered under the label of 'transaction costs'. This contrasts with Coase, who focused on 'marketing costs' and 'the cost of using the price mechanism'. Williamson's wider meaning of the term 'transaction cost' includes the internal cost of managing the workforce within the firm. The acknowledged danger in this approach is that the term 'transaction cost' becomes a 'catch-all phrase' including every possible cost under its head. Questions are then raised concerning the potential falsifiability of the theory.

3 Williamson and behaviouralism

In its close attention to non-market forms of organization, Williamson departs from much of mainstream economics. Furthermore, Herbert Simon and the behaviouralist school influenced Williamson; Simon is well known as a critic of mainstream assumptions of rationality (see SIMON, H.A.). However, on closer inspection it is evident that Williamson's break from neo-classical theory is partial and incomplete, and much of the core apparatus of neo-classical economics is retained. In fact, Williamson's claimed departure from orthodoxy sits uneasily alongside his repeated invocation that agents are marked by 'opportunism' (i.e. 'self-interest seeking with guile'). As conventionally presented, self-interested behaviour is a typical feature of 'economic man'.

Simon (1957) argued that complete or global rational calculation is ruled out, hence rationality is 'bounded'. Agents do not maximize but attempt to attain acceptable minima instead. It is important to note that this 'satisficing' behaviour does not simply arise because of inadequate information, but also because it would be too difficult to perform the calculations even if the relevant information were available. Contrary to a prevailing neo-classical interpretation of Simon's work, the recognition of bounded rationality refers primarily to the matter of computational capacity and not to additional 'costs'. Hence 'satisficing' does not amount to cost-minimizing behaviour. Clearly, the latter is just the dual of the standard assumption of maximization; if 'satisficing' were essentially a matter of minimizing costs then it would amount to maximizing behaviour of the neo-classical type.

Williamson (1989: 161) simply replicates this view when he accepts the term 'bounded rationality' rather than 'satisficing' because he regards the latter as 'a contentious and separate issue'. Clearly, Williamson adopts the neo-classical, cost-minimizing interpretation of Simon and not the one that clearly prevails in Simon's own work. In Williamson's work 'economizing on transaction costs' is part of global, cost-minimizing behaviour, and this is in fact inconsistent with Simon's idea of bounded rationality. The cost calculus remains supreme in his theory and there is no essential break with the neo-classical assumption of maximization.

4 Institutions and efficiency

According to Williamson, organizations with lower transaction costs are more likely to survive in a competitive world. In several passages Williamson (1975, 1985) asserts that because hierarchical firms exist, then they must be relatively efficient and more suited to survival. Thus, in his theoretical attempt to compare the efficiency of different types of firm structure, Williamson (1980: 35) concludes that 'it is no accident that hierarchy is ubiquitous within all organizations of any size ... In short, inveighing against hierarchy is rhetoric; both the logic of efficiency and the historical evidence disclose that non-hierarchical modes are mainly of ephemeral duration'.

However, this argument has been widely criticized, particularly for the neglect of path dependency. It also contrasts with the recent work of other 'new institutionalists' such as Douglass North, where path dependence is recognized. The explanation of emergence and survival in evolution is not the same thing as an explanation of efficiency, even if the latter may enhance the chances of survival in the future. Strictly, in order to explain the existence of a structure it is neither necessary nor sufficient to show that it is efficient. Inefficient structures do happen to exist and survive, and many possible efficient structures will never actually emerge or be selected.

Essentially, Williamson's transaction cost argument involves comparative statics (see TRANSACTION COST ECONOMICS). Typically, the incidence of transaction costs in equilibrium is compared in two or more governance structures, and the structure with the lowest costs is deemed to be more efficient. In fact Williamson (1985: 1434) admits that a shift from considerations of static to those of dynamic efficiency is not encompassed by his theory: 'the study of economic organisation in a regime of rapid innovation poses much more difficult issues than those addressed here ... Much more study of the relations between organisation and innovation is needed'. It is questionable whether the comparative statics approach can do justice to important dynamic developments such as technological change. Particularly on this point, 'evolutionary' (Richard Nelson and Sidney Winter) and 'competence-based' (Edith Penrose) theorists of the firm claim they have overcome the limitations of comparative statics.

Transaction cost analyses reduce the interaction between individuals to the calculus of costs. Individuals act as utility-maximizing automata on the basis of given preferences. Social institutions bear upon individuals simply via the costs they impose. Consistent with the retention of the basic neo-classical model of optimizing behaviour, Williamson assumes that individual preferences are unchanged by the economic environment and the institutions in which individuals are located.

Importantly, the assumption of given individuals and preferences is antagonistic to the notion that institutions transform individual preferences, purposes, conceptions and beliefs. Clearly there is an important contrast here with the 'old' institutionalism of Veblen, Commons, Mitchell, Galbraith and others. The contractarian emphasis in the new institutionalism means that non-contractual relations such as trust and loyalty are neglected. Just as seriously, the conception of the given individual cannot readily incorporate notions such as learning and personal development.

Williamson assumes that individual preferences are unchanged by the economic environment and the institutions in which individuals are located. However, it can be argued that an important difference between the market and the firm is that actors tend to behave in a different manner with differing goals. According to this alternative perspective, a key to understanding the nature of the firm is its ability to mould human preferences and actions so that a higher degree of loyalty and trust is engendered.

5 Conclusion

Whatever its limitations, Williamson's work is one of the most important developments in the analysis of economic institutions. It has been of enormous benefit in bringing questions of internal and intra-firm organization to the fore. Indeed, despite criticism, the Coase–Williamson argument for the existence of firms remains persuasive for many economists. Furthermore, recent work has gone a long way to bring empirical richness to the transaction cost story. Finally, transaction cost analyses have inspired key developments in corporate and competition policy.

GEOFFREY HODGSON
UNIVERSITY OF HERTFORDSHIRE

Further reading

(References cited in the text marked *)

* Coase, Ronald H. (1937) 'The nature of the firm', *Economica*, 4, November: 386–405. Reprinted in Williamson, Oliver E. and Winter, Sidney G. (eds) (1991) *The Nature of the Firm: Origins, Evolution, and Development*, Oxford and New York: Oxford University Press. (The classic article that established the transaction cost approach to the theory of the firm – later developed by Williamson.)

Pitelis, Christos (ed.) (1993) *Transaction Costs, Markets and Hierarchies*, Oxford: Basil Blackwell. (A set of critical essays on the transaction costs approach.)

* Simon, Herbert A. (1957) *Models of Man: Social and Rational. Mathematical Essays on Rational Human Behavior in a Social Setting*, New York: Wiley. (An early statement of the behaviouralism that inspired Williamson.)

* Williamson, Oliver E. (1975) *Markets and Hierarchies: Analysis and Anti-Trust Implications: A Study in the Economics of Internal Organization*, New York: Free Press. (Williamson's first major statement of the transaction costs approach.)

* Williamson, Oliver E. (1980) 'The organization of work: a comparative institutional assessment', *Journal of Economic Behavior and Organization*, 1 (1): 5–38. Reprinted and revised in Williamson (1985, chs. 9–10). (An notable attempt by Williamson to develop a theory of comparative organizational efficiency.)

* Williamson, Oliver E. (1985) *The Economic Institutions of Capitalism: Firms, Markets, Relational Contracting*, London: Macmillan. (A milestone development of Williamson's approach.)

* Williamson, Oliver E. (1989) 'Transaction cost economics', in Richard Schmalensee and Robert D. Willig (eds) *Handbook of Industrial Organization*, vol. 1, Amsterdam: North Holland, pp. 135–82. (A concise statement of Williamson's approach and analysis.)

Williamson, Oliver E. (1996) *The Mechanisms of Governance*, Oxford and New York: Oxford University Press. (The third volume in Williamson's trilogy on the firm.)

See also: COASE, R.; GALBRAITH, J.K.; GROWTH OF THE FIRM AND NETWORKING; INSTITUTIONAL ECONOMICS; MANAGERIAL THEORIES OF THE FIRM; MARSHALL, A.H.; NEO-CLASSICAL ECONOMICS; SIMON, H.A.; TRANSACTION COST ECONOMICS; VEBLEN, T.B.

Index

Abegglen, J.C., 566
Abernathy, W.J., 161
Abraham, K., 9
Abramovitz, M., 363, 413, 414
Ackerman, F., 24
Acquinas, T., 17
acquisitions *see* mergers and acquisitions (M&A), 327
action
   organizational, 165
activity-based costing (ABC)
   business economics, 178
Aderson, T.L., 724
aerospace industry, 269
   airplanes, 270
   analysis and evalution, 271
   background, 269
   civil transport, 270
   consolidation, 274
   cooperation and competition, 271
   economies of scale, 274
   general aviation, 271
   global division of labour, 275
      FSX Wars, 275
      offsets, 275
   helicopters, 270
   military sector, 271
   missile systems, 271
   origins and competitive context, 270
   rotorcraft, 271
   space vehicles, 271
   strategic trade and industrial policy, 273
      subsidies, 273
Aerospatiale Matra, 271, 274
Afuah, A.N., 319
agency
   transaction costs, 632
Agrawal, A., 132
Agryris, C., 164
Ahlbrandt, R., 314
Airbus Industrie, 270, 272, 274
Akerlof, G.A., 26, 176, 177
Alchian, A.A., 176, 515, 723
Aleksandrowicz, P., 372
Alesina, A., 492
America Online (AOL), 301

Anderson, B., 334
Anderson, G.M., 667
Ansoff, H.I., 176
Antal-Mokos, Z., 371
Antonelli, C., 324
Aoki, M., 159, 556
Apple Computer, 323
Argentina
   financial capital market, 468
Argyres, N., 161
Argyris, C., 164
Arianespace, 271
Ariyoshi, A.K., 457
Arora, A., 282, 283, 284, 308
Arrow, K.J., 92, 140, 157, 320, 644, 740
Asia Pacific
   employment, 326
Asian Crisis, 447
Asquith, P., 132
assets
   financial, 161
   reputational, 161
   specificity, 645
   structural, 161
   technological, 161
Association of South-East Asia Nations (ASEAN), 473
Atkins, W.S., 232
Atkinson, A.B., 62, 122, 123
automobile industry, 315, 317, 320, 340
   craft production, 340
   future prospects, 343
      build-to-order, 344
      telematics, 344
   globalization, 343
   industry structure, 342
   lean production, 341
   mass production, 340
   overview, 340
Azariadis, C., 25

Böhm-Bawerk, E., 141
Bacon, N., 314
Bain, G., 384
Bain, J.S., 329
Baker, G., 131

Index

Balassa-Samuelson effect, 423
Baldwin, C., 158
Ball, L., 12
Ballantine, B., 307
Ballou, R., 317
Bank of England, 592
banking
    systems, 397, 401
        1930s to first oil crisis, 398
        Basel capital adequacy rules, 400
        Bretton Woods, 399
        lender of last resort problem, 401
        overview, 397
        uncertainty, 399
        universal, 397
Banz, R., 135
Barbash, J., 24
Barney, J.B., 156, 157
Barrett Whale, P., 378
Barro, R., 415
Bartholomew, S., 309
Bartlett, C.A., 323
Bartley, J., 554, 555
Basalla, G., 90
Batchelor, R., 593
Baum, C.F., 137
Baumol, W.J., 174, 329, 351, 415, 551
Becker, G., 25, 144
behaviour, 752
Bercovitz, J.E.L., 162
Berg, A., 455
Berger, P., 314
Berle, A.A., 143, 377
Berliner, J.S., 370
Best, M., 146
Beveridge Curve, 28
Beveridge, W., 60
Bhagat, S., 132
Biddle, W., 269
biotechnology, 304
    background, 304
    influence, 306
    networks, clusters, alliances, 307
    new sector/new techniques, 305
    overview, 304
Black, B., 133
Blair, A., 311
Blair, J.M., 328
Blair, M., 5, 139, 144
Blau, F.D., 66, 69, 73
Blecker, R.A., 312, 454
Blinder, A., 383
Blyton, P., 314
Boardman, C., 554, 555
Bodin, J., 588
Boeing, 270, 274
Bombardier, 271
Bond, M.A., 68, 72
Borrie, G., 207
Borrus, M., 320, 321, 328, 330
bounded rationality, 528, 644, 748, 749, 752
Bower, J.L., 281
Bowles, S., 4
Braudel, F., 437
Braunthal, G., 379
Brazil
    financial capital market, 468
Breeden, D., 135
Bresnahan, T.F., 196, 321
Bretton Woods System, 499, 703
Briault, C., 492
British Aerospace (BAe), 271, 272, 274
British Gas, 206
British Steel, 311
Brockstedt, J., 378
Brody, D., 147
Bryant, R.D., 427
Buchele, R., 10, 11
Buckley, P.J., 200, 723
Bud, R., 308
Buechtemann, C., 8
built environment, 231
    analysis, 233
    background, 231
    context, 232
    evaluation, 235
    future prospects, 235
        construction output, 235
        costs and prices, 237
        education, training and skills, 237
        employment, 236
        government role, 237
        industrial structure, 237
        international competitiveness, 236
        management of project-based firms, 237
        production process, 235
        productivity, 236
        quality of products, 236
    governance, 234
    overview, 231
    patterns of demand, 233
    production, 232
    role of state, 234

Index

steel industry, 316
technological change, 234
use, 233
Bulluck, J.A., 305
bureaucracy, 693, 694
Burgess, K., 376
Bush, V., 99
business cycles, 742
business economics, 172
   activity-based costing, 178
   evolution, 172
      industry, 172
      prices, costs, markets, 173
   future, 178
   game theory, 177
   government regulation, 175
   information, 176
   overview, 172
   strategy, 176
   structure-conduct-performance, 174
   transaction costs, 177
buy-ins, 185

Cambridge School, 225, 587
Canada
   demographics, 107
Cantillon, R., 17, 588
capabilities
   dynamic, 649
capital
   circuits, 679
   definitions, 564
   global, 439
capital asset pricing model (CAPM), 132
capital markets
   international, 464
      emerging markets, 466
      major markets, 464
      overview, 460
capitalism, 391, 556, 564, 669, 707
   corporate response, 385
   current philosophy, 390
   depression and war, 380
   divergent development, 380
   Germany, 376, 378
   heyday, 383
   inflation, 385
   Japan, 379
   labour-management conflict, 386
   Marxian, 674
   overview, 376
   privatization, 387

   shareholder value, 387
   UK, 376, 386
   USA, 377
Carabelli, A.M., 698
Caribbean Community and Common Market (CARICOM), 476, 480
Carroll, C.D., 416
Casper, S., 309
Cassis, Y., 377
Casson, M., 200, 723
Castells, M., 320
Catlett, G., 564
Caves, R., 319
Central African Customs and Economic Union (CACEU), 473, 480
central and eastern Europe
   economic transition
      dinosaurs, 372
      joint ventures, 373
      levels of attainment, 370
      management, 373
      micro-level, 371
      overview, 368
      privatization, 373
      process, 368
      small businesses, 372
   privatization, 48
Chamberlain, E.H., 20, 173, 740
Chandler, A.D. Jr, 99, 147, 156, 279, 282, 320, 377, 381, 625, 656
Chang, H.-J., 361
change, 533
chemical industry, 278
   background, 278
   cartels, 282
   globalization, 284
   historical background, 279
   issues and themes, 282
   organic, 283
   overview, 278
   patents, 282
   petrochemicals, 283
   R&D, 282
   restructuring, 284
   university linkages, 282
   world exports, 281
Chicago School, 21, 23, 589, 731
Cho, D.-S., 321
Christensen, C.M., 323, 329, 331, 334
Christiansen, J., 10, 11
Chrysler, 343
Chrystal, A., 593

Index

Chung, J.W., 312
Ciccolo, J.H., 137
Claessens, S., 453
Clark, J.B., 20
Clark, K.B., 158, 159, 160, 342
Clarke, S., 94
cleaner production, 84
   concept, 84
   industrialization-sustainability link, 88
   overview, 84
   programmes, 86
      effects, 88
      Europe, 86
      government, 88
      United States, 87
Coase, R.H., 3, 157, 177, 216, 525, 622, 623, 644, 721, 723, 750
   biography, 721
   evaluation, 723
   major works, 721
   personal background, 721
   transaction costs, 721
Coe, D.T., 417
Cohen, W.M., 165
Colbert, J.B., 17
Coleman, D.C., 377
collective bargaining, 5, 23, 39
collusion, 196
Commission of the European Community (CEC), 208
Commission of the European Economic Community, 85
common customs tariff (CCT), 471
common external tariff (CET), 471, 474
Commons, J.R., 19, 34, 529
community
   skill formation, 57
competences
   competition/cooperation, 199
competition
   built environment, 236
   cooperation, 198
   perfect, 546
   steel industry, 312
   structure-conduct-performance (SCP) paradigm, 329
   technological phenomenon, 101
computers
   flagship model, 321
   microprocessors and the PC, 322, 327
Congdon, T., 593
conglomerates, 625

Conner Peripherals, 328
Construcciones Aeronauticas (CASA), 272
consumers
   behaviour, 543
consumption, 718
contractarian theories, 518
contracts
   implicit, 25
control, 711
   corporate, 148
      managerial theory, 147
      overview, 129
      shareholder theory, 130
      stakeholder theory, 143
   enterprise ownership, 565
Cool, K., 156
cooperation
   competence, 198
   competition, 198
   definition, 196
   inter-firm, 197
   knowledge, 198
   market power/failure, 196
   vertical/horizontal, 196
copyright, 75
Corbett, J., 137
core competences, 157
Cornwall, J., 415
corporate
   control, 148
corporate governance
   global, 439
   stakeholder, 150
corporatism, 42
Corsetti, G., 455
cost-of-living adjustments (COLAs), 23
costs
   built environment, 237
   theory, 543
   training, 145
Council for Mutual Economic Assistance (CMEA), 473
Cournot model, 177
creativity, 533
crony capitalism, 448
cross-border trade
   built environment, 236
   chemical industry, 281
Cubbin, J., 555
culture, organizational *see* organizational culture, 71
cumulative causation, 689

Cusumano, M., 383
Cutler, D., 136
Cyert, R.M., 174, 748
Czech Republic
    financial capital market, 467

D'Cruz, J.R., 323
Da Rin, M., 284
Daimler-Chrysler Aerospace (DASA), 271, 272
Daniel, K., 136, 137
Daunton, M., 377
David, P., 320
David, P.A., 95
Davidson, P., 135
Davies, S., 95
De Long, J.B., 415, 424
Debreu, G., 140
decision making, 746
    economics, 574
    garbage can model, 748
    price-output, 544
Deininger, K., 117, 120
Dell Computer Corporation, 320
demand
    aggregate, 701
    consumer, 683
Demirgüç-Kunt, A., 453
demographics
    crisis, 107
Demsetz, H., 176, 723
Denison, E.F., 414
Dertouzos, M.L., 213
Detragiache, E., 453
Dibner, M., 305, 307
Dierickx, I., 156
diffusion
    technology development, 90
Dispute Settlement Body (DSB), 509
diversity
    industrial relations systems, 37
Dodd, P., 132
Dodgson, M., 98
Doeringer, P., 24
Domhoff, G.W., 69
Donaldson, D., 145
Dore, R., 361, 387, 390, 557
Dosi, G., 98
Downs, A., 551, 554
Doz, Y., 164
Drucker, P.F., 165, 340
Dudley, G., 312

Dunlop, J.T., 24
Dunning, J.H., 723
dynamic capabilities
    implications, 165
    market, 157
    orchestration process, 164
        external sensing, 164
        organizational action, 165
    organizational/managerial, 159
    overview, 156
    path dependency, 162
        technological opportunites, 163
    positions
        financial assets, 161
        institutional assets, 162
        market assets, 162
        reputational assets, 161
        structural assets, 161
        technological assets, 161
    strategic, 161
    terminology
        core competencies, 157
        factors of production, 156
        organizational routines/competences, 157
        products, 157
        resources, 157
dynamics, industrial, 187
earnings
    residual, 139
East Asia
    economies
        controversies, 360
        definition, 359
        overview, 359
        performance, 360
        recession and crisis, 363
        transferability, 365
East Asian Miracle Report (EAM), 362
Eaton, B.C., 145
Eaton, J., 417
Eatwell, J., 24
Eckhaus, R.S., 145
Economic Community of West African States (ECOWAS), 481
economic growth
    accounting, 414
    catch-up literature, 415
    overview, 413
    perspectives, 413
    R&D, 416
    spillovers, 416

Index

theory/evidence, 417
'Barro'regressions, 415
economic integration
  international, 470
    features, 471
    fiscal component, 480
    market power, 477
    monetary component, 478
    overview, 470
    product standards, 476
    public procurement, 475
    specific, 471
    stage-one process, 474
    stage-two process, 478
    state subsidies, 475
    surveillance, 476
    tariffs, 470
    taxation, 476
    trade liberalization, 477
economic man, 687
economic performance, employment relations, 10
economics
  decision making, 574
  institutional, 522
  international financial stability, 452
  neo-classical, 709
economies of scale
  aerospace industry, 274
  electronics industry, 331
EDGAR database, 261
Edquist, C., 104, 418
education
  built environment, 237
efficiency, 752
  transaction costs, 627
efficiency wage models, 26
efficient market hypothesis (EMH), 134, 151
Eichengreen, B., 455
Electronic Communications Networks (ECNs), 262, 263
electronic data interchange (EDI), 208
electronics industry, 319
  built-to-order (BTO), 320
  competitive dynamics, 329
    disruptive technologies, 331
    innovation, 329
    market volatility, 332
    structure-conduct-performance (SCP), 329
    stylized model, 331
  concentration, 326
  capability development, 332
  scale economies, 331
  sources, 331
  sunk costs, 332
  volatility, 328
  defined, 319
  flagship model
    computers, 321
    microprocessors and the PC, 322
    outsourcing, 324
    semiconductors, 322
  globalization, 320, 324
  hard disk drive (HDD) industry, 326, 328, 332
    complex supply chain, 333
    disruptive demand and technology, 333
    short product cycles, 332
  historical perspective, 321
  mergers and acquisitions, 327
  New Industrial Organization model, 320
  ongoing research, 334
  overview, 319
  relevance, 320
electronics manufacturing services (EMS), 325
Ely, R.T., 19
Embraer, 271
Emilia-Romagna (Italy), 249
employment, 708
  affirmative action (AA), 67
  built environment, 236
  equal opportunities, 67
  harassment, 70
  hiring practices, 70
  managing diversity, 67
  organizational challenges, 72
  relations, 3
    economic performance, 10
    flexible, 7
    global, 7
    overview, 3
    strategies, 4
    training, 9
    worker representation, 5
  service economy, 348
  transaction costs, 626
Engels, F., 34
Enoch, C., 495
Enos, J., 279
enterprise
  innovative, 655

Index

ownership, 563
environment, pollution, 84
   cleaner production programmes, 88
environment, WTO rulings, 510
Environmental Protection Agency (EPA), 510
equal employment opportunity (EEO), 67, 72
Equal Employment Opportunity Commission (EEOC), 66
Equation of Exchange, 587
equilibrium, 19, 172, 522, 539, 707
Ernst, D., 321, 322, 323, 324, 325, 326, 329, 330, 332
Esping-Anderson, G., 25
ethnic divisions *see* gender and ethnic divisions, 66
EU Council of Finance Ministers (ECOFIN), 496
Europe
   employment relations, 11
   foreign direct investment, 441
European Aeronautic, Defense and Space Company (EADS), 273
European Association of Aerospace Industries, 270
European Central Bank (ECB), 490, 596
   European economic/monetary union, 490
   independence, 492
   issues, 495
   operational policy, 494
   organization, 491
   overview, 490
   statutes, 491
European Community (EC), 471, 480
European Free-Trade Association (EFTA), 471
European Monetary System (EMS), 490, 496, 596
European Monetary Union (EMU), 490, 496, 596
European System of Central Banks (ESCB), 490
European Union (EU), 439, 506
   financial capital market, 464
   regulatory agencies, 208
evolutionary economics, 688
evolutionary theories of the firm, 515
   evolutionary/contractarian contrast, 518
   Nelson-Winter approach, 516
   origins, 515
   overview, 515

understanding, 192
exchange rate, 421
   choice, 421
   determination, 422
   overview, 421
   reform, 425
   spot and forward relationship, 424
exchange rate mechanism (ERM), 496, 596
expertise, 573

Fabian Society, 672
Fagerberg, J., 415, 416
Fairchild Aerospace, 271, 274
Fama, E.F., 134, 135, 136, 158
Farrell, C., 150
feasibility studies, 728
Federal Reserve System, 591
Feldenkirchen, W., 378
Ferguson, C.H., 328
Fermer, A., 312
Financial Accounting Standards Board (FASB), 261
financial markets
   international, 460
Fine, C., 320
firms
   evolutionary theories, 515
   growth, 240
   managerial theories, 551
   theory, 528
fiscal policy, Japan, 404
Fisher, I., 140, 599
Fitzgibbons, A., 698
flagship model *see* electronics industry, 321
Flanagan, R., 384
flexibility
   employment relations, 7
      internal, 8
      labour market performance, 9
      numerical, 8
   industrial relations, 49
   labour market, 27
   network organization, 27
flexible
   firm, 27
Flood, M.D., 423
Florida, R., 320
Foden, D., 64
Fokker, 271, 274
Foray, D., 320
Ford Motor Company, 340, 342
forecasting, 728

761

Index

foreign direct investment (FDI), 440, 442
forward exchange rates, 424
Foss, N.J., 198
France
  demographics, 107
  income and wealth, 125
Frankel, J.A., 423, 455
Franks, J.R., 133
Fransman, M., 299
Freeland, C., 557
Freeman, C., 98, 138, 283, 307
Freeman, J., 219
Freeman, R.E., 5, 6, 12
French, K., 135
Freyssinet, J., 63
Friedman, M., 21, 22, 516, 570, 589, 731, 747
  economic analysis, 731
  major works, 731
  personal background, 731
Frost, A., 314
Fujimoto, T., 160, 342
Fujitsu, 328
Fullerton, H.N., 68
fundamental equilibrium exchange rate (FEER), 426

G8 countries, 30
Galbraith, J.K., 143, 174, 215, 221, 381, 383, 530, 716 - 720
  biography, 716
  consumption, 718
  corporate control, 718
  Keynesianism, 717
  major works, 716
  personal background, 716
  price controls, 717
Gambardella, A., 282, 283, 308
Gamble, A., 143
game theory, 177, 524, 742, 744
Gann, D.M., 232, 233, 234, 238
garbage can model, 748
Garvin, D., 160
gender and ethnic divisions, 66
  affirmative action (AA), 67, 72
  background, 66
  current position, 68
  equal opportunities, 67, 72
  historical context, 67
  interactional dynamics, 70
  organizational challenges, 72
  organizational culture, 71
  overview, 66
  representation in labour force, 68
General Agreement on Tariffs and Trade (GATT), 470, 471, 505, 507, 508
  Kennedy Round, 506
  Tokyo Round, 506
  Uruguay Round, 505, 507
General Agreement on Trade in Services (GATS), 508
General Motors, 342
Germany
  capitalism, 378, 386
  demographics, 107
  income and wealth, 117, 123, 125
  labour market, 29
  pensions, 107
  trade unions, 6
  training, 10
GERPISA, 342
Gerschenkron, A., 413, 415
Gershuny, J., 351
Ghoshal, S., 323
Giddens, A., 578
Gilbert, S., 317
Gilder, G., 327
Gintis, H., 4
Gispen, K., 378
Gittleman, M., 417
Glais, M., 200
Glickman, M., 135
globalization, 435
  automobile industry, 343
  chemical industry, 284
  electronics industry, 319, 320, 324, 329
    geographic dispersion, 325
  employment relations, 7
  firm expansion, 243
  foreign direct investment, 440
  history, 437
  integration
    corporation, 442
    indicators, 438
  multinationals, 445
  overview, 435
  political economy, 446
  private sector, 203
  semiconductor industry, 321
Glyn, A., 385
goals
  workfare, 64
Gomez-Casseres, B., 245
Gomez-Meija, L., 555

Index

Gordon, A., 380, 382, 387
Gordon, D., 25
Gordon, R., 351, 515
governance, 646
    skill formation, 52
government
    industrial relations, 42
    subsidies, 92
government *see* state, 237
Goyder, G., 566
Graaf, J.V. de, 175
Grabel, I., 453, 455
Grant, R.M., 178
Gray, A., 667
green issues, 726, 727
Gregory, P.R., 369
Griliches, Z., 94, 95, 216, 416
Grilli, V., 492
Grossman, S., 131
groups and teams
    steel industry, 314
Grove, A.S., 324, 330
growth
    firm, 240
        global expansion, 243
        knowledge-based theory, 241
        limits, 244
        networks, 244
        overview, 239
        resource-based theory, 241
        significance, 240
        transaction costs, 240
    theory
        background, 600
        classical, 601
        contemporary, 602
        Harrod's model, 602
        Keynesian, 604
        neo-classical, 602
        neo-Marxian, 605
        overview, 600
Guile, B.R., 348

Hadley, E., 382
Hagedoorn, J., 307
Hall, R.L., 173
Hallwood, P., 425
Hamel, G., 156
Hannah, L., 376, 381
Hannan, M.T., 219
Hansen, A., 21, 740
Harris, H., 147

Harrison, A.J., 123
Harrison, R., 376
Harrod, R., 21
Hart, O., 131
Hay, D., 196, 200
Hayek, F.A. von, 198, 524
Hayes, R.H., 156
Healey, N.M., 493
Heckscher-Ohlin-Samuelson model, 742
Heikkilä, M., 60
Heisler, J., 136
Helburn, S.W., 698
Heller, F.A., 143
Helpman, E., 417
Henderson, R.M., 156, 160, 309, 493
Herman, E., 133
Heyne, P., 571
Hicks, J.R., 740
Hill, C., 555, 556
Hirshleifer, J., 140
Hitch, C.J., 173
Hiwatari, N., 383
Hobday, M., 321
Hobsbawm, E., 376
Hodder, J., 382
Hodgson, G.M., 518
Hodrick, R.J., 425
Hogan, W., 311
Hollander, S., 279, 667
Hong Kong
    financial capital market, 466
Hounshell, D.A., 279
Houseman, S., 9
Howells, J., 104
Hudson, R., 256
Hughes, T.P., 94
human resource management (HRM)
    industrial relations, 35
    steel industry, 313
Hume, D., 588, 664
Hunt, H., 555
Hurst, J.W., 148
Hutcheson, F., 664
Hyundai, 328

Iansiti, M., 156, 159
IBM, 299, 321, 323, 328, 334
Ichniowski, C., 9, 314
income
    comparisons, 117, 119
    concept, 117
    overview, 117

Index

sampling under reporting biases, 118
unit of observation, 118
indifference curve, 540
individualism
   methodological, 526
industrial agglomeration
   clusters, 255
   core-periphery tendencies, 256
   definitions, 249
   districts, 253
   models, 256
   origins, 248
   overview, 248
   renewed interest, 252
   theory, 251
industrial conflict
   industrial relations, 43
industrial democracy
   industrial relations, 44
industrial dynamics, 187
   background, 187
   emergence, decline, rebirth, 188
   evolution, 192
   life cycle, 190
   overview, 187
   paradoxical stylized facts, 189
   research agenda, 193
industrial organization
   flagship model, 321
   weaknesses, 329
industrial relations, 33
   collective bargaining, 39
   comparative perspective, 36
   conflict, 43
   convergence, 37
   democracy, 44
   diversity, 37
   eastern Europe, 48
   economic rewards, 45
   flexibility, 49
   government, 42
   historical context, 34
   HRM strategies, 47
   international, 36
   internationalization, 48
   Japanization, 46
   labour, 39
   managers, 41
   new realism, 47
   new technology, 46
   overview, 33
   privatization, 48

role of state, 42
systematic analysis, 35
trade unions, 39
industry
   innovative, 649
inflation, 732
information and communications technology (ICT), 320, 330, 334
information society, 28
information technology (IT), 304, 320
   built environment production, 235
initial public offering (IPO), 137
innovation, 98
   overview, 98
   problems, 102
   process
      basic science model, 99
      firm-level model, 100
   research results, 102
      collaboration and interaction learning, 104
      complexity and variety in investment, 103
      importance of clusters, 104
      pervasive, 103
      science-technology interaction, 104
      systemic, 104
      uncertainty, 104
   technology development, 90
   theories, 98
innovative enterprise, 655
   dynamic capabilities, 649
   industrial conditions, 653
   institutional conditions, 654
   neoclassical theory, 639
   organizational conditions, 654
   overview, 638
   research agenda, 652
   social conditions, 655
   transaction-costs, 649
Insider Trading and Securities Fraud Enforcement Act (ITSFEA), 264
Insider Trading Sanctions Act (ITSA), 264
insider-outsider relationship, 26
institutional economics, 522
   background, 522
   neo-classical theory, 531
   overview, 522
   'new', 525
      development, 527
      individuals as given, 525
      market concept, 527

Index

methodological individualism, 526
   theory of the firm, 528
'old', 534
   business and management, 534
   change, 533
   characteristics, 534
   creativity, 533
   disequilibrium, 533
   images, 529
   nature of institutions, 532
   rational man, 529
institutions, 687, 750
   described, 523
   development, 527
   innovative, 652
integration
   economic, 470
Intel, 323, 326
intellectual property rights
   copyright, 75
   ICT challenge, 82
   institutions, 78
   national diversity, 78
   overview, 75
   patents, 75
      exclusion/diffusion of knowledge difference, 77
   privatization of knowledge, 80
   secrecy, 75
intellectual property, WTO agreement, 508
interest
   theory, 141
International Accounting Standards Committee (IASC), 261
International Bank for Reconstruction and Development (IBRD), 484
International Center for the Settlement of Investment Disputes (ICSID), 484
International Confederation of Free Trade Unions (ICFTU), 49, 511
International Development Agency (IDA), 483
international financial markets, 468
   overview, 460
   USA, 468
international financial stability
   alternatives, 456
   crisis detection, 455
   economic theory, 452
   overview, 452
International Monetary Fund (IMF), 30, 448, 499, 505, 703

developments/debates, 503
   origins, 499
   overview, 499
   role and structure, 500
International Motor Vehicle Program (IMVP), 342
international trade, 740
International Trade Organization (ITO), 505
internationalization
   industrial relations, 48
Internet, 299, 319
   automobile industry, 344
Internet Access Providers (IAPs), 299, 300
Internet Service Providers (ISPs), 299, 300
IS-LM analysis, 21, 23
Ispat International NV, 311
Italy
   demographics, 107
Iverson, K., 314

Jacoby, S., 378
Jacquemin, A., 196
Jaffe, A.B., 417
Japan
   capitalism, 379
   economy, 360, 365, 403
      bubble economy, 408
      fiscal policy, 407
      growth, 404, 407
      industrial organization, 409
      industrial policy, 405
      labour relations, 410
      lost decade, 408
      macroeconomic policy, 405
      monetary policy, 407
      oil shocks, 406
      overview, 403
      uniqueness, 411
   employment relations, 11
   financial capital market, 465
   foreign direct investment, 441
   trade unions, 6
   training, 10
Japanization, 46
Jenkinson, T., 137
Jensen, M.C., 130, 132, 137, 150, 723
Jevons, W.S., 19, 523, 539
joint stock corporation, 562
joint ventures
   central and eastern Europe, 373
Jolly, D., 309
Jones, C.I., 417

765

Index

Kahn, R.L., 20, 702
Kaldor, N., 529, 689
Kalecki, M., 20
Kaminsky, A.Z., 371
Kaminsky, G., 454, 455
Kaplan, S., 133
Kapp, K.W., 533, 534
Kaufman, A., 148
Kay, J.A., 178
keiretsu
    chemical industry, 280
Kelly, D., 143
Kelly, G., 143
Kenney, M., 320
Kerr, C., 24, 37
Keynes, J.M., 61, 548, 740
    General Theory, 19, 700
    Treatise on Money, 700
    biography, 697
    economic theory, 701
    effective demand, 701
    employment and income, 702
    evaluation, 703
    gold standard debate, 699
    IMF, 499
    major works, 697
    personal background, 697
    philosophy of probability, 698
Keynesianism, 21, 92, 93, 538, 586, 604, 705, 718, 743
Kindleberger, C., 364
Kirzner, I., 198
Kline, S., 98
Kloten, N., 386
Knight, F.H., 21, 519
knowledge
    competition/cooperation, 198
    firm, 241
    intellectual property rights, 77, 80
Kobrin, S.J., 330
Kochan, T.A., 4
Kocherlakota, N., 134
Kocka, J., 378
Kogut, B., 158, 330
Konig, W., 378
Kornai, J., 369, 371
Kortum, S., 417
Kozminski, A.K., 371, 373
Krugman, P.R., 363
    agglomerates, 249, 252
Kurczewska, J., 371

Kuznets, S., 117
Kyoto Agreement, 234
labour force
    gender and ethnic divisions *see* gender and ethnic divisions, 66
labour markets
    classical economics, 18
    de-regulation, 20
    dual, 24
    efficiency wage models, 26
    flexibility, 27
    globalization, 26
    implicit contracts, 25
    information society, 28
    insider-outsider relationship, 26
    internal, 24
    international, 29
    liberalization, 29
    macroeconomics, 20
    mercantilism, 17
    migrant worker, 29
    monetarism, 22
    neo-classicism, 19
    overview, 16
    rational expectations, 23
    scholasticism, 17
    segmented, 24
labour relations, 33
    Japan, 410
labour value theory, 677
Labson, B.S., 311
Laffont, J.J., 297
Laidler, D., 591, 667
Lampman, R., 122
Lane, D., 573
Langlois, R.N., 198, 321
Latin America
    financial capital market, 468
Layard, R., 11, 62, 63
Lazonick, W., 5, 99, 131, 137, 146, 147, 149, 150, 158, 199, 253, 254, 314, 319, 376, 379, 381, 387, 388, 389, 638, 639, 642, 643, 657
Leach, D., 555
Leal, D.R., 724
lean production
    automobile industry, 341
Leathers, C., 135
LeMoyne, T., 695
Leonard-Barton, D., 164
Lerner, J., 308
Lester, R.K., 213, 515

Lev, B., 158
Levine, D., 9
Levine, P., 493
Levine, R., 416
Levinthal, D.A., 164, 165
Levitt, B., 164
Levy, F., 12
Lewchuk, W., 377
Lewin, K., 748
Liebenstein, H., 175
life cycle model, 191
limited liability corporation (LLC), 562
Linbeck, A., 26
Lindgren, C., 454
Lintner, J., 135, 140
Lippman, S.A., 178
Lipsey, R., 329
Little, I.M.D., 175
Lixin, T., 317
Loasby, B.J., 199
Locke, J., 588
Lockheed-Martin, 270, 274
long-run average cost (LRAC), 544
Loveridge, R., 18, 24
Lowenstein, L., 133
Lucas, R., 23
Lundvall, B.A., 256, 417
Luxembourg Income Study, 117, 119
Lynch, L., 10

MacDonald, R., 422, 425
machine tool industry
    global
        data, 287
        developments, 288
        future, 291
        history, 286
        importance, 290
        innovation, 289
        overview, 286
Machlup, F., 515
macroeconomics
    Japan, 405
Maddison, A., 414
Madhavan, R., 317
Magenheim, E., 132
Magnus, A., 17
Magnusson, L., 64
Mahoney, J.T., 164
Malatesta, P., 132
Malerba, F., 93, 321
Malestroict, M. de, 588

Malkiel, B., 134, 135
Malone, T.W., 28
Malthus, T.R., 17, 523
management
    industrial relations, 41
    theory, 147
management by location
    central and eastern Europe, 370
managerial
    process, 159
managerial theories of the firm, 147, 550
    background, 550
    bureaucratic, 554
    capitalism, 556
    discretionary, 551
    growth-orientated, 552
    overview, 550
    testing, 555
        results, 555
Mansfield, E., 94
manufacturing processes
    cleaner, 85
March, J.G., 164, 174, 747, 748
marginal utility theory, 540
market
    concept, 527
    failure, 197
    power, 196
    skill formation, 53
markets
    dynamic capabilities, 158
    transaction costs, 632
Markowitz, H.M., 140
Marris, R., 174, 551, 552
Marsden, D., 5
Marsh, I.W., 424
Marsh, T., 137
Marshall, A., 19, 172, 515, 538, 539, 546,
    587, 681, 698, 742
    Industry and Trade, 684
    Principles of Economics, 682
    agglomerates, 249, 250, 251, 252
    biography, 681
    consumer demand, 683
    evolutionary theories, 683
    income distribution, 683
    major works, 681
    partial-equilibrium approach, 683
    personal background, 681
Martin, B., 105
Martin, R., 256
Marx, K., 98

Index

Marx, K.H., 18, 34, 523, 530, 628, 674
   circuits of capital, 676
   endogenous technical change and crises, 678
   labour theory of value, 675
   major works, 674
   personal background, 674
   political economy, 675
   schemes of reproduction, 678
   value and price, 677
Mason, E., 148
Mass, W., 379
Masson, P.R., 422
Mastel, G., 312
mathematics
   multiplier effect, 742
Mathews, J., 321
Matra, 271
Matsumoto, K., 566
Matsushita Kotobuki (MKE), 328
Maurseth, P., 417
Maxtor, 328
Mayer, C., 133
McDonald, K.R., 373
McDonnell-Douglas, 270, 274
McKelvey, M., 307, 308, 309
McKersie, R., 386
McKinnon, R., 426
McKitrick, F., 379
Meade, J., 20
Means, G.C., 143, 377, 711
   administered prices, 712
   economic planning, 714
   evaluation, 713
   major works, 711
   ownership and control, 713
   personal background, 711
measurement
   trust, 578
Meckling, W.H., 723
medium term financial strategy (MTFS), 595
Medoff, J., 5
Mehra, R., 134
mergers and acquisitions (M&A)
   electronics industry, 327
Merges, R.P., 308
Merton, R.K., 137
Mexico
   financial capital market, 468
Microsoft, 163, 323, 326
Miles, J., 237

Milgrom, P., 160
Mill, J.S., 18, 669
   biography, 669
   capitalism, 671
   evaluation, 671
   major works, 669
   personal background, 669
   political economy, 670
   public utilities, 671
   socialism, 671
Miller, M.H., 142, 565
Minami, R., 379
Minford, P., 597
Minnesota Innovation Research Programme, 102
Minsky, H., 453
Mitchell, W.C., 163, 530, 742
Mitsubishi Heavy Industries, 271
modelling and forecasting, 744
   building, 610
   econometric, 618
   measuring, 610
   non-stochastic, 613
      examples, 613
   overview, 608
   predictions, 611
   single-equation, 612
   stochastic, 617
      problems, 617
   testing theories, 611
modern portfolio theory (MPT)
   pensions, 112
Modigliani, F., 565
Mody, A., 164
Mohnen, P., 416
Mok, A.L., 24
Mok, R., 18
monetarism, 586
   behaviour and causation, 586
   British, 592
   historical, 588
   international, 594
   modern, 589
   new classical, 594
   North American, 591
   overview, 586
   political economy, 595
   virtual, 596
money, 732
   international markets, 468
   Japanese policy, 407
   Keynesian reform, 700, 703

Index

Monsen, J., 554, 555
Monteverde, K., 197
Montgomery, D., 147
Moore's Law, 320
Moore, G., 165, 320
Moore, G.E., 698
Moore, M., 312
Morck, R., 133
Morgan, K., 256
Morgenstern, O., 177
Morikawa, H., 380
Morris, C.R., 328
Mosley, H., 8
Mossin, J., 140
most-favoured nation (MFN), 506, 508
motivation
   multination corporations, 430
Motorola, 322
Mowery, D., 93, 165, 380
Mueller, D.C., 132, 551, 552, 554
Multi-fibre Arrangement (MFA), 507
multidivisional (M-form) structures, 625, 751
Multilateral Investment Guarantee Agency (MIGA), 483
multinational corporations (MNCs), 45, 319, 442, 449
   future prospects, 433
   importance, 429
   internationalization of firms, 430
   motivations, 430
   organizational form, 430
   overview, 429
   patterns of activity, 431
multiplier analysis, 702
Mun, T., 17
Mundell, R., 422
Murnane, R., 12
Murphy, K.J., 131, 723
Myrdal, G., 20, 529, 534, 689

NASDAQ over-the-counter market, 262
Nash equilibrium, 177
national central banks (NCBs), 490
National Health Service (NHS), 206, 207
National Market System (NMS), 263
National Science Foundation (NSF), 99, 299
National Semiconductor, 322
Naughton, J., 330
Navin, T., 377
Nelson, R., 689, 752
Nelson, R.E., 199, 644

Nelson, R.R., 92, 156, 160, 164, 417, 418, 515, 516, 519
neo-classical economics, 19, 570, 602, 643
   background, 538
   consumer behaviour, 539
   core assumptions, 523
   cost theory, 543
   criticisms, 547
   demand curve, 541
   partial equlibrium, 546
   perfect competition, 546
   price-output decisions, 544
   production theory, 543
   transaction costs, 630
neo-Marxian theory, 606
Netherlands
   pensions, 108
networks
   firm, 244
   organization
      flexible, 27
Neumann, J. von, 177
Neumann, M., 221
New Economy, 320
New York Stock Exchange (NYSE), 262
Newell, A., 747
newly industrializing countries (NICs), 359, 361
Nickell, S., 7, 11, 27
Nightingale, P., 105
Noble, D., 377
Nobles, W., 314
non-accelerating inflation rate of unemployment (NAIRU), 23
non-tariff barriers (NTBs), 475, 476
Nonaka, I., 93
North America
   monetarism, 591
North American Free Trade Agreement (NAFTA), 435, 444, 474, 475
North, D., 572, 574, 627, 633, 752
North, D.C., 522, 525

O' Donnell, R.M., 698
O' Sullivan, M., 5, 99, 129, 131, 137, 138, 147, 150, 199, 387, 388, 389, 390, 639, 647, 648, 650, 652, 653
O'Connor, D., 321, 330, 332
Odagiri, H., 556
Odonius, Geraldus, 17
Officer, L.H., 423
Ohlin, B., 20

Index

Ohno, T., 340, 341
oil shocks, 407
Okun, A., 25
oligopoly, 177
Olson, M., 525, 528
Olson, N., 564
optimal currency area (OCA), 421
organization
   action, 165
   innovative, 657
Organization for Economic Cooperation and Development (OECD), 231, 232, 234, 347, 354, 440
   pensions, 106
organizational
   process, 159
   routines, 157
   structure, 727
organizational culture
   gender and ethnic divisions, 71
over-the-counter market (NASDAQ), 262
ownership, 711, 728
   enterprise, 561
      capitalism, 564
      control, 565
      joint stock corporation, 562
      limited liability corporation, 562
      membership, 565
      notion, 565
      overview, 561
      partnerships, 562
      proprietorships, 561
      residual claimancy as contractual role, 563

Padavic, I., 69
Pandian, J.R., 164
Parker, M., 11
Parkin, M., 591
partial equilibrium, 546, 683
partnerships, 562
patents, 75
path dependencies, 162
Pattillo, C., 455
Pavitt, K., 415
pay-as-you-go (PAYG), 106
payment
   economic rewards, 45
Pearce, J.L., 372
Peck, J., 25
Peirce, C.S., 529

Penrose, E.T., 99, 146, 156, 199, 218, 515, 516, 518, 553, 734, 752
   biography, 734
   case studies, 737
   major works, 734
   personal background, 734
   processes, 736
   production, 736
   resources, 736
   theories of the firm, 735
pensions
   background, 106
   defined benefit, 107, 109
   defined contribution, 107, 109
   design, 109
   financial markets, 112
   investment management, 112
   management, 109
   overview, 106
   pillars of retirement income, 108
   structure, 110
   underperformance, 113
People's Republic of China (PRC)
   financial capital market, 466
Perez, C., 307
Pesciarelli, E., 667
petrochemicals, 283
Petty, W., 17, 588
Phelps-Brown, H., 22
Phillips Curve, 22, 24
Phillips, A., 22
Pigou, A.C., 587
Pigou, C., 20
Piore, M.J., 8, 24, 253, 256
planning
   economic, 713
Plender, J., 388
Pohl, H., 378
Poland
   financial capital market, 467
Polanyi, K., 365, 528
Polanyi, M., 573
political economy, global, 437
pollution, 84
Popper, K., 568
Porter, M.E., 149, 176
Posner, R.A., 176, 525, 724
Poterba, J., 136
Powell, W.W., 308
power
   international economic integration, 476
   transaction costs, 628

Index

Prahalad, C.K., 156
Prendergast, C., 145
Prescott, E., 134
price-output decisions, 544
prices
    built environment, 237
pricing
    control, 717
    global parity, 435
    transfer, 180
privatization, 203
    central and eastern Europe, 373
    eastern Europe, 48
    institutional aspects, 203
    international developments, 209
    overview, 203
    UK regulation, 205
production
    factors, 156
    theory, 543
products, 157
    life cycle assessments, 85
property rights, intellectual, 75
proprietorships, 561
public procurement, international economic integration, 475
Pugh, E.W., 322
purchasing power parity (PPP), 422, 426, 594
Pyle, J.L., 68, 72

QUAD countries (USA, Canada, Japan, EU), 511
Quah, D., 29
Quantum, 328
quasi-autonomous non-governmental organizations (quangos), 207
Quesnay, F., 17
Quintyn, M., 495

Radelet, S., 364
Raines, J.P., 135
Rainwater, L., 117
Ramani, S.V., 309
rational economic man, 530
rational expectations, 595
rationality, 695
    choice, 571
    expertise, 573
    neo-classical, 568
        conscious deliberation, 570
        omniscience, 569
    representative agent, 570
    self-interest, 569
    overview, 568
    principle, 570
    rule-following, 571
    skill, 573
    transaction costs, 623
Ravenhill, J., 324
Ravenscraft, D.J., 133
Raytheon, 270, 274
Redpath, J., 314
regulation, 205
    economic theory, 204
    international developments, 209
    international telecommunications market, 208
    private sector, 203
    regulators, 208
    research agenda, 207
    securities and exchange, 259
        background, 259
        broker-dealers, 262
        disclosure, 260
        ECN relationship, 262
        impact, 263
        investment advisors, 264
        investment companies, 264
        markets, 261
        overview, 259
        SEC-SRO relationship, 262
        transactions, 260
    UK privatization, 205
Reich, R.B., 28
Reinganum, M., 135
Reinhart, C., 454, 455
Renelt, D., 416
Republic of Ireland
    demographics, 107
research and development (R&D)
    biotechnology, 306, 308
    built environment, 234
    chemical industry, 278, 281, 282
    East Asia, 361, 362
    economic growth, 416
    joint, 196
    small and medium-sized enterprises, 217
Reskin, B.F., 69
resources
    firm, 242
Restow, W.W., 213
return on investment (ROI), 145
    semiconductor industry, 322

771

Index

revealed preference theory, 741
rewards
   distribution, 45
Ricardo, D., 17, 18, 523, 543, 669
Richardson, G.B., 199, 329, 334, 335
Richardson, J., 312
Ritzer, G., 694
Robbins, L., 523
Robert, J., 160
Roberts, K., 29
Robinson, A., 20
Robinson, J., 20, 173
Rogers, E.M., 94
Rogers, J., 5, 6
Rogoff, K., 493
Roll, R., 135
Romer, P.M., 414
Rose, A., 423, 455
Rosenberg, N., 93, 98, 104, 163
Rosewarne, S., 29
Rothaermel, F., 307
Rothstein, J., 452
Rothwell, R., 98
Rowley, R., 135
Ruback, R.S., 131, 132
Rubery, J., 25
Rubin, P.H., 723
Rugman, A.M., 323
rules
   rule-following, 573
Rumelt, R.P., 178
Russia
   financial capital market, 467
Ryan, A.M., 306, 307

Saab, 269, 271
Sabel, C.F., 8, 253
Sachs, J., 364, 455
Sachwald, F., 196, 200
Salop, S., 196
Salter, A., 234
Samuels, R.J., 270
Samuelson, P.A., 21, 667
   Foundations of Economic Analysis, 742
   biography, 740
   business cycles, 741
   evaluation, 744
   international trade, 742
   personal background, 740
   revealed preference theory, 741
satisficing, 748, 749
Saviotti, P.P., 308

Say's Law, 548, 702
Say, J.-B., 18, 92
Schön, D., 164
Schakenraad, J., 307
Scharfstein,, 131
Scherer, F.M., 133
Scherer, M., 556
Schleifer, A., 133
Schmookler, J., 92
Schotter, A., 522, 525
Schumacher, E.F., 726
   biography, 726
   convergent-divergent distinction, 728
   environment, 727
   evaluation, 728
   feasibility studies, 728
   forecasting, 728
   green issues, 727
   intermediate technology, 726
   major works, 726
   organizational structure, 727
   ownership, 728
   personal background, 726
   'small is beautiful', 727
Schumpeter, J.A., 98, 100, 101, 142, 156, 165, 220, 385, 415, 643, 666, 689, 740
   biography, 707
   capitalism, 709
   economics, 708
   employment, 708
   equilibrium, 709
   major works, 707
   personal backgroujd, 707
Schwartz, A., 589
Scott, R.E., 312, 452
Seagate, 326, 327, 328
Seager, H., 141, 142
Sears, M., 377
Securities and Exchange Commission (SEC)
   regulation issues, 259
securities and exchange, regulation, 259
securities markets
   regulation, 261
self-interest, 569
   transaction costs, 632
self-regulatory organizations (SROs), 262
semiconductors
   flagship model, 322
Senker, J., 305
service economy, 346
   concept, 348
   effects of industrialization, 352

Index

employment, 348
growth, 346
myths, 349
overview, 346
productivity growth, 350
prospects, 349
redefined, 353
transition, 351
wages, 351
welfare impacts, 352
Servos, J., 377
Shapiro, C., 29
shareholder theory, 130
control, 129
productive role, 137
residual earnings, 139
Sharp, M., 305
Sharpe, W.F., 135, 140
Shaw, K., 314
Shiller, R.I., 135
Shirai, T., 6
Shleifer, A., 132
Shonfield, A., 381, 383, 385
Shuen, A., 159, 164
Siebert, H., 27
Siegel, J., 134
Silver, M., 724
Simon, H.A., 174, 516, 517, 535, 571, 589, 644
bounded rationality, 746, 747
business administration, 748
decision making, 747, 748
major works, 746
motivation, 747
personal background, 746
problem solving, 748
satisficing, 746
Singapore
financial capital market, 467
Singh, A., 364
Sirc, L., 368
Skidelsky, R., 699, 703
skills, 573
association, 56
built environment, 237
community, 57
governance, 52
hierarchy, 54
market, 52
overview, 52
state, 55
Slade, M.E., 196

Slaughter, J., 11
small and medium-sized enterprises (SMEs), 248, 305
background, 213
dynamic view, 216
entry model, 221
evolutionary view, 223
exits, 220
overview, 213
public response model, 224
revolving door model, 223
start-ups, 220
static view, 214
survival, 222
technology, 216
Smeeding, T., 117
Smith, A., 17, 18, 93, 526, 631, 663, 669
economic systems, 666
four stages theory, 665
human motivation, 664, 665
income distribution, 665
jurisprudence, 664
labour market, 666
major works, 663
market mechanism, 666
personal background, 663
trade theory, 666
Smith, J.K., 279
Snell, S., 555
Snower, D., 26
social action, 36
socialism, 669
society
innovation, 655
Soete, L.G., 415
Solow, R.L., 213
Solow, R.M., 28, 60, 64, 413
Sorge, A., 379
Sougiannis, T., 158
South Korea
financial capital market, 466
privatization, 203
Soviet Union
small and medium-sized enterprises, 214
Spant, R., 123
Spencer, H., 682
Spencer, P., 593
spillover, economic growth, 416
spot exchange rates, 421
Spotton, B., 135
Squire, L., 117, 120
stakeholder theory, 143

Index

Stalk, G., 566
Stanislaw, J., 387
Staniszkis, J., 369
state
   cleaner production programmes, 88
   industrial relations, 42
   role in built environment, 234, 237
   skill formation, 55
   subsidies, international economic integration, 475
   transaction costs, 633
steel industry, 311
   capital shortages, 314
   competition, 312
   cyclical markets, 314
   future prospects, 316
   integrated and EAF mills, 312
   new economy, 317
   new markets and products, 315
   overview, 311
   shift from physical productivity to HRM, 313
   shifting capacity and trade, 311
   teamwork, 314
   trade disputes, 312
   world view, 311
Steinmuller, W.E., 321
Stewart, C., 123
Stigler, C.J., 748
Stigler, G., 24
Stiglitz, J.E., 25, 453
stochastic models, 614, 615
   non-stochastic, 613
Stokes, R.G., 283
Stolper, W., 742
strategic
   capabilities, 157
strategies
   employment relations, 4
Streeck, W., 6, 379, 386
Structural Adjustment Facility (SAF), 502
structural adjustment programmes (SAPs), 484
structure-conduct-performance paradigm, 172
Stuart, R.C., 369
Sturgeon, T., 320
Sull, D., 312
Summers, L., 12, 133, 135, 136
Sundbo, J., 98
supply chains
   computer industry, 325

Sutcliffe, B., 385
Sutton, J., 329
Swann, P., 308
Sweden
   income and wealth, 124, 125
   pensions, 109
Switzerland
   income and wealth, 123
   pensions, 108
systems
   theory, 35

Takeuchi, H., 93
tariffs
   international economic integration, 474
taxation
   estate, 122
   income and wealth, 122
   international
      economic integration, 476
   pensions, 109
   transfer pricing, 181, 183
Taylor, M.P., 422, 425
teams *see* groups and teams, 314
technological development, 90
   demand factors, 92
   described, 91
   diffusion process, 94
   government subsidy, 94
   innovation, 93
   learning, 93
   linear model, 91
   market failure, 92
   needs, 93
   overview, 90
technology, 46, 688
   concept, 101
   generic or specific, 101
   knowledge, organization, technique, 101
   machine tool industry, 291
   opportunities, 163
Teece, D.J., 162, 163, 165, 167, 178, 197, 218, 324, 524, 651
telecommunications
   international regulation, 208
telecommunications industry, 294
   downstream layers, 297
      new entrants, 297
      specialist technology suppliers, 298
   layer model, 294
      applications, 296
      customers, 297

Index

end-to-end connectivity, 296
equipment and software, 294
navigation and middle, 296
network, 295
overview, 294
TCP/IP, 296
upstream layers, 299
consolidation and specialization, 300
emergence of layer III, 299
future prospects, 301
web site, 294
Temple, J., 416
Texas Instruments, 322
Thaler, R., 134
Thomas, S., 307
Thurow, L., 213
Tilton, J.E., 94, 321, 324
Time Warner, 301
Tirole, J., 297
Tobin's q ratio, 553
Tollison, R.D., 667
Toyota Production System, 340, 341
trade
international, 742
economic integration, 477
Trade Related Intellectual Property Measures (TRIPS), 506, 508
trade unions, 5, 20, 34
USA, 439
Trade-Related Investment Measures (TRIMS), 508
training
built environment, 237
costs, 144
employee relations, 9
Trans-European Automated Gross Real-Time Settlement System (TARGET), 497
transaction cost economics (TCE), 622
agency, 632
assessment, 634
automobile industry, 342
boundaries, 630
bounded rationality, 629
Coasean tradition, 622
conglomerates, 625
cooperation, 629
criticisms, 629
efficiency, 627
employment relation, 626
future, 633
hierarchies, 623, 626
market-firm distinction, 629

markets, 623
markets first, 627
methodology, 628
multidivisional, 625
neo-classical alternative, 630
opportunism, 629
overview, 622
policy implications, 633
radical, 631
resource-knowledge-based, 631
self-interest, 632
state, 633
transnationals, 625
uncertainty, 629
vertical integration, 624
transaction costs, 177, 723, 750
firm, 241
market failure, 197
transformation, 644
transfer pricing, 180
concept, 180
emperical evidence, 182
overview, 180
solutions, 184
tax competition, 183
taxation
inbound investment, 182
international systems, 184
non-tax factors, 182
outbound investment, 180
Transmission Control Protocol/Internet Protocol (TCP/IP), 296, 299
transnational corporation (TNC), 26, 623
Triffin dilemma of dollar supply/demand, 501
trust, 578
characteristic, 580
institution, 580
inter-organizational, 578
measurement, 581
experimental, 582
survey, 578
notions, 578
overview, 578
personal, 578
process, 580
sources, 579
system, 583
Tschoegl, A., 382
Tushman, M.L., 161
Tyson, L., 9

Index

UN Commission on Trade and Development (UNCTAD), 506
uncertainty
   transaction costs, 629
unemployment, 700, 702, 731
   insurance benefits, 60
unitary (U-form) structures, 751
United Kingdom (UK)
   capitalism, 386
   demographics, 107
   income and wealth, 117, 124
   monetarism, 592
   pensions, 109
   privatization regulation, 205
United Nations (UN), 505
   cleaner production programmes, 87
   Conference on Environment and Development (1992), 88
United Nations Environment Programme (UNEP), 84
United States of America (USA)
   capitalism, 377, 380
   demographics, 107
   employment relations, 12
   financial capital market, 461
   foreign direct investment, 440
   income and wealth, 123, 125
   international finance
      banking activity, 461
      securities, 466
      US-Japan tensions, 463
   multinationals, 440
   pensions, 109
   trade unions, 5, 6
   training, 9

value-added tax (VAT), 476
Van der Ven, A., 103
Varian, H.R., 29
Veblen, T.B., 19, 143, 515, 525, 529, 686, 750
   biography, 686
   critique of rational economic man, 687
   cumulative causation, 689
   evolutionary economics, 688
   institutions, 688
   rational economic man, 530
   technology, 688
Verspagen, B., 416
vertical integration (VI)
   transaction costs, 624
Vickers, J., 200

virtual
   monetarism, 596
Vishny, R., 132

Walcxak, D., 695
Walras, L., 19
Walsh, V., 305, 306
Walters, A., 590, 591
Warner, M., 379
wealth
   comparisons, 124
   data sources
      estate tax, 122
      household surveys, 122
      income capitalization, 122
      wealth tax, 122
   definition, 121
   overview, 117
Webb, S. and B., 19, 34
Weber, M., 36
   agglomerates, 248, 249
   authority, 694
   biography, 692
   bureaucracy, 694
   major works, 692
   personal background, 692
   rationality, 693
Weidemann, H., 382
Weil, D.N., 416
Weller, C., 453, 455
Wernerfelt, B., 156
White, L.J., 342
Whitehead, A.N., 574
Whyte, W.F., 4
Wilkinson, F., 24
Williamson, J., 426
Williamson, O.E., 25, 157, 162, 177, 197, 215, 515, 518, 522, 525, 551, 552, 554, 644, 723, 748, 750
   behaviouralism, 751
   biography, 750
   efficiency, 752
   institutions, 752
   major works, 750
   markets and hierarchies, 623, 627
   personal background, 750
   rationality, 634
   theory of the firm, 528
   transaction costs, 750
   transaction theory, 644
   trust, 580
   uncertainty, 629

Index

Winter, S.G., 156, 160, 164, 199, 417, 516, 517, 524, 644, 689, 752
Wisconsi School, 34
Wolff, E.N., 124, 417
Womack, J.P., 160, 342
Wood, G.E., 494
worker representation, 5
workfare
  goals, 63
  history, 60
  neo-classical search theory, 62
  overview, 60
  policies, 61
    activating measures, 61
    social assistance, 61
    unemployment insurance benefits, 61
  problems, 64
works councils, 6
World Bank, 30, 119, 435, 483, 505
  criticism-response, 486
  history, 484
  mission, 483
  new directions, 488
  overview, 483
  pensions, 106
  policies, 488
  programmes, 487
  projects, 483
  structure, 483
World Confederation of Labour (WCL), 49
World Federation of Trade Unions (WFTU), 49
World Intellectual Property Organization (WIPO), 508
World Trade Organization (WTO), 276, 435, 505
  controversial rulings
    beef hormones, 510
    Caribbean bananas, 510
    clean-air, 510
    Shrimp-Turtles, 510
    Tuna-Dolphins, 510
  controversies
    environmental concerns, 511
    labour rights, 511
    power asymmetrics, 511
  Council for trade in goods, 507
  Council for trade in services, 508
  fundamental principles
    exceptions, 507
    national treatment, 507
    non-discrimination, 506
    reciprocity, 506
  origin, 505
  overview, 505
  plurilateral agreements, 509
    bovine meat, 509
    civil aircraft, 509
    dairy, 509
    government procurement, 509
  recent activities/future plans, 511
  settlement of disputes, 509
  structure
    Dispute Settlement Body, 506
    General Council, 506
    Ministerial Conference, 506
    Trade Policy Review Body, 506, 509
  technical barriers, 508
  World Trade Organization (WTO)
    aerospace subsidies, 273
World Wide Web (WWW), 300
WorldCom, 300
Wright, J., 381

Yellen, J.A., 26
Yergin, D., 387
Yonekawa, S., 379
Young, A., 534

Zaleski, E., 368
Zander, U., 158, 330
Zeitlin, J., 376
Zucker, L., 308
Zweigenhaft, R.L., 69